R. Gupta's®

CTET

Central Teacher Eligibility Test

Previous Years' Papers & Practice Test Papers

(Solved)

PAPER-I

FOR CLASS I-V TEACHERS

by

RPH Editorial Board

2027

EDITION

RAMESH PUBLISHING HOUSE, NEW DELHI

Published by
O.P. Gupta *for* Ramesh Publishing House

Admin. Office
12-H, New Daryaganj Road, Opp. Officers' Mess,
New Delhi-110002 ✆ 23275224, 23245124

E-mail: info@rameshpublishinghouse.com
For Online Shopping: www.rameshpublishinghouse.com

Showroom
• Balaji Market, Nai Sarak, Delhi-110006 ✆ 23282525 📱 9354373464
• 4457, Nai Sarak, Delhi-110006

Book Code: R-1596

ISBN: 978-93-5012-373-7

Price: ₹ 490

Printed at: Deepak Offset, Delhi

CONTENTS

PREVIOUS PAPERS (SOLVED)

PRACTICE TEST PAPERS (SOLVED)

R. Gupta's® USEFUL BOOKS FOR

CENTRAL TEACHER ELIGIBILITY TEST (CTET)

Book Code	Subjects	Price
R-2549	Guide to Social Science Pedagogy	180
R-2497	Guide to Science Pedagogy	140
R-2438	Guide to English Pedagogy	160
R-2354	CTET—22 Solved Papers (Dec '21–Jan '22) (Paper-I) (Class I-V) Primary Stage	340
R-2355	CTET—22 Solved Papers (Dec '21–Jan '22) (Paper-II) (Class VI-VIII) Math and Science	360
R-2356	CTET—22 Solved Papers (Dec '21–Jan '22) (Paper-II) (Class VI-VIII) Social Studies	340
R-1453	CTET—Paper-I Guide	520
R-1596	CTET—Practice & Previous Papers (Solved) Paper-I (Class I-V)	490
R-1455	CTET—Paper-II (Social Studies) Guide	560
R-1600	CTET—Previous & Practice Papers (Solved) Paper-II Social Std. Teachers (Class VI-VIII)	490
R-1457	CTET—Paper-II (Math. & Science) Guide	580
R-1598	CTET—Previous & Practice Papers (Sol.) Paper-II Maths & Sc. Teachers (Class VI-VIII)	440
R-1953	Handbook of Child Development & Pedagogy	90
R-2188	CTET & STETs—Child Develop. & Pedagogy	130
R-2805	CTET— 39 सॉल्वड पेपर्स (Dec'21–Dec'24) (Paper-I) (Class I-V)	620

Book Code	Subjects	Price
R-2648	CTET— 24 सॉल्वड पेपर्स (Dec'22–Jan'24) (Paper-II) सामाजिक अध्ययन शिक्षक	680
R-2294	CTET— 22 सॉल्वड पेपर्स (Dec'21–Jan'22) (Paper-I) (Class I-V)	340
R-2295	CTET— 22 सॉल्वड पेपर्स (Dec'21–Jan'22) (Paper-II) सामाजिक अध्ययन शिक्षक	360
R-2296	CTET— 22 सॉल्वड पेपर्स (Dec'21–Jan'22) (Paper-II) गणित एवं विज्ञान शिक्षक	360
R-1454	CTET—पेपर-I गाइड	520
R-1597	CTET—प्रैक्टिस एवं पिछले प्रश्नपत्र (हल सहित) पेपर-I (Class I-V)	490
R-1456	CTET—पेपर-II (सामाजिक अध्ययन) गाइड	580
R-1647	CTET—पिछले एवं प्रैक्टिस पेपर्स (हल सहित) पेपर-II सामाजिक विज्ञान (Class VI-VIII)	490
R-1458	CTET—पेपर-II (गणित एवं विज्ञान) गाइड	580
R-1599	CTET—पिछले एवं प्रैक्टिस पेपर्स (हल सहित) पेपर-II गणित एवं विज्ञान (Class VI-VIII)	430
R-1537	बाल विकास एवं शिक्षा शास्त्र	210
R-2352	CTET—बाल विकास एवं शिक्षाशास्त्र 50 प्रैक्टिस सेट्स (हल सहित)	190

R-1453

R-1454

R-1455

R-1456

R-1457

E-mail your order to: **order@rameshpublishinghouse.com** 2604

Ramesh Publishing House, 4457, Nai Sarak, Delhi-6

For Online Shopping: www.rameshpublishinghouse.com

Previous Years' Paper

Central Teacher Eligibility Test (CTET)

Paper-I (For Class I-V Teacher), February-2026

(Exam held on 08-02-2026)

PART-I : CHILD DEVELOPMENT AND PEDAGOGY

1. Extrinsic motivation comes from ______ while intrinsic motivation is based on ______.

1. personal satisfaction; rewards such as prizes
2. avoidance of punishment; rewards such as prizes
3. approval of others; personal satisfaction
4. personal satisfaction; approval of others

2. Which of the following are examples of authentic learning tasks for students in primary grades?

1. Copying answers from a friends' notebook.
2. Applying the concept of daily life.
3. Memorising a set of definitions.
4. Recalling factual information from textbook.

3. ______ refers to the time of development when an individual is most ready to acquire a new skill or ability and it is difficult to compensate for the loss of this later on in life.

1. Developmental Test
2. Sensitive Period
3. Zone of Proximal Development
4. Developmental Milestone

4. Talking aloud to oneself with no intent to communicate with other is ______ in childhood.

1. Uncommon and abnormal
2. Abnormal but not uncommon
3. Normal and common
4. Uncommon but normal

5. According to Piaget, which of the following is an example of assimilation?

1. A child realizes that a dog and a cat are both animals.
2. A child learns to ride a cycle with training wheels.
3. A child learns to tie their shoes for the first time.
4. A child learns a new word for a familiar object.

6. **Assertion (A):** Learning is always situated in a social context.

Reason (R): What is learned cannot be separated from how it is learned and used.

Choose the ***correct*** option:

1. Both (A) and (R) are true, but (R) is not the correct explanation of (A).
2. (A) is true, but (R) is false.
3. Both (A) and (R) are false.
4. Both (A) and (R) are true and (R) is the correct explanation of (A).

7. Which principle of development is illustrated in the following statement?

During infancy and early childhood, the limbs continue to grow faster than the hands and feet.

1. Cephalocaudal principle
2. Principle of centration
3. Principle of integration
4. Proximodistal principle

8. Which of the following are important to ensure meaningful learning?

(*i*) Provisioning of emotional support.
(*ii*) An atmosphere of competition and rivalry.
(*iii*) Opportunities for doing and experimenting.
(*iv*) Standardised curriculum.

1. (*ii*), (*iii*), (*iv*)
2. (*iii*), (*iv*)
3. (*i*), (*iii*)
4. (*i*), (*iii*), (*iv*)

9. Formative assessment assumes that:

1. only quantitative parameters give 'correct' feedback.
2. qualitative parameters are biased and subjective.
3. learners should also be involved in the process of assessment.
4. competition is essential for learning.

1. 3	**2.** 2	**3.** 2	**4.** 3	**5.** 4	**6.** 4	**7.** 4	**8.** 3	**9.** 3

10. Which of the following skill is not actively practiced in the process of 'reciprocal teaching'?

1. Memorizing 2. Predicting
3. Questioning 4. Clarifying

11. In response to the question, "Is it alright to steal the chocolate from the freezer in absence of your parents?" 4-year-old Meera replied, "It will be wrong because doing so can cause punishment from the parent." Meera's moral reasoning depicts which stage of Lawrence Kohlberg's theory of moral development?

1. Formal conventional 2. Post-conventional
3. Pre-conventional 4. Conventional

12. Assertion (A): An effective pedagogical strategy is to ask children to make linkages of new information with what they already know.

Reason (R): Identifying commonalities and differences can help children organize information which help them to think as well as remember better.

Choose the ***correct*** option:

1. Both (A) and (R) are true, but (R) is not the correct explanation of (A).
2. (A) is true, but (R) is false.
3. Both (A) and (R) are false.
4. Both (A) and (R) are true and (R) is the correct explanation of (A).

13. Which of the following is an effective way to reduce the influence of gender stereotypes amongst children prevalent is society?

1. Providing children with materials that are gender-specific.
2. Exposing children to diverse gender roles and encouraging them to pursue their interests.
3. Assuming that children will naturally incline towards gender-neutral activities and interests.
4. Encouraging children to conform to traditional gender roles.

14. Which of the following hinders the process of effective problem solving?

1. Concept mapping 2. Brainstorming
3. Analogical thinking 4. Response set

15. Which of the following is an effective strategy for teaching children with autism?

1. Avoiding use of any audio-visual aids.
2. Maintaining a predictable routine.
3. Using strict discipline and punishment.
4. Providing constant eye contact.

16. As per Jean Piaget's theory of development, children develop ______ by the end of sensorimotor stage.

1. Hypothetical logical reasoning
2. Object permanence
3. Symbolic thinking
4. Conservation

17. As per Lev Vygotsky, 'inner speech':

1. hinders the cognitive development of children.
2. is a sign of cognitive immaturity among children.
3. occurs from birth until the age of three.
4. helps in reasoning and organizing thoughts.

18. Principle of cephalocaudal development talks about ______ of development.

1. linear nature 2. multiple dimensions
3. orderly sequence 4. discontinuous nature

19. Assertion (A): Invented spellings, free explorations of writings provide teachers with opportunities of authentic assessment of learner levels.

Reason (R): Give the vast linguistic diversity in the classroom assessment in language should by dynamic.

Choose the ***correct*** option:

1. Both (A) and (R) are true, but (R) is not the correct explanation of (A).
2. (A) is true, but (R) is false.
3. Both (A) and (R) are false.
4. Both (A) and (R) are true and (R) is the correct explanation of (A).

20. Assertion (A): Creativity needs to be nurtured by p resenting practical problems and issues to children for contemplation and reflection.

Reason (R): Creative children have the ability to discover something that is novel and need intellectual stimulation.

Choose the ***correct*** option:

1. Both (A) and (R) are true, but (R) is not the correct explanation of (A).
2. (A) is true, but (R) is false.
3. Both (A) and (R) are false.
4. Both (A) and (R) are true and (R) is the correct explanation of (A).

21. Attention Deficit Hyperactivity Disorder is characterised by:

1. Ongoing patterns of impulsivity.
2. Restricted and repetitive behavioural patterns.
3. Delayed motor and language skills.
4. High levels of depression and mood swings.

10. 1	**11.** 3	**12.** 4	**13.** 2	**14.** 4	**15.** 2
16. 2	**17.** 4	**18.** 3	**19.** 4	**20.** 4	**21.** 1

22. In inclusive classroom the curriculum should be ______ and instruction should be ______.
1. standardized; uniform
2. flexible; uniform
3. standardized; differentiated
4. flexible; differentiated

23. According to Vygotsky's theory, the zone of proximal development refers to:
1. The level of skill or knowledge student is capable of mastering with help:
2. The level of skill of knowledge a students is unlikely to ever achieve.
3. The level of skill or knowledge a student must master to pass a test or receive a grade.
4. The level of skill or knowledge a student has already mastered.

24. Assertion (A): Teachers should provide a lot of scaffolding to children in the forms of prompts and cues.

Reason (R): Jean Piaget emphasized that more knowledgeable other play a significant role in advancing children's cognitive skills through social interaction.

Choose the ***correct*** option:
1. Both (A) and (R) are true, but (R) is the correct explanation of (A).
2. (A) is true, but (R) is false.
3. Both (A) and (R) are false.
4. Both (A) and (R) are true and (R) is the correct explanation of (A).

25. Students with mastery goal orientation set.
1. high goals to impress others.
2. low goals to avoid failure.
3. moderate goals motivated by fear and shame.
4. realistic learning goals.

26. Which of the following is an example of question that requires students to generate creative solutions?
1. How do you identify the subject of a sentence?
2. What are the various types of nouns?
3. How would you rewrite the given text from the perspective of an object rather than a person?
4. What is the definition of a noun?

27. Misconceptions among students should be ______ and intuitive guesses should be ______ among students in primary grades.
1. acknowledged; encouraged
2. dismissed; discouraged
3. acknowledged; discouraged
4. ignored; encouraged

28. The ability of hand-eye coordination, balance and manual dexterity is affected in:
1. Dyscalculia
2. Dysphasia
3. Dyspraxia
4. Dyslexia

29. Critical thinking in students can be promoted by:
1. Discouraging metacognition
2. Discouraging collaborations
3. Encouraging students to do rote rehearsal
4. Encouraging questions such as what, why, how

30. Development of children:
1. is a simple and unitary process.
2. unfolds in a random manner which does not have any pattern.
3. is multidimensional and multidirectional.
4. is synonymous with growth.

PART-II : MATHEMATICS

31. Ms. Rajlakshmi, a primary class mathematics teacher brings in a variety of concrete material in her classroom like bundles of match sticks, ice cream sticks, coloured buttons, base 10 blocks etc. to teach the concept of place value.

Which of the following principles of theory of Zoltan P. Dienes is being used by her?
1. Dynamic Principle
2. Iconic Mode
3. Perceptual Variability Principle
4. Mathematical Variability Principle

32. Main objective of teaching Pictographs in students is:
1. To utilize the free time of the students in the class
2. To engage students in the class activities
3. To represent data in an interesting way
4. To develop drawing skills in students

22. 4	**23.** 1	**24.** 2	**25.** 4	**26.** 3	**27.** 1
28. 3	**29.** 4	**30.** 3	**31.** 3	**32.** 3	

33. Which of the following is least appropriate in context of learning outcomes at foundational stage in mathematics?

1. Designing activities connected to real-life situations to strengthen the learning outcomes.
2. Children advance to the next level of learning outcomes only upon achieving certain level of proficiency at the current level.
3. Primarily summative assessment is used to assess the skills or concepts developed at each level.
4. Explicit and measurable learning outcomes are defined which are the pathways for competency acquisition.

34. Which among the following is an example of a real life situation which represents 'division as equal sharing'?

1. There are 60 toffees in a packet and Samir would like to distribute it to his friends. How many toffees each friend will get?
2. There are 30 students in a class. Teacher wants to form 5 groups of same size. How many students will be there in each group?
3. Divide 50 into 10 equal groups.
4. There are 10 biscuits in a packet. How many biscuits will be there in 5 such packets?

35. Which of the following statement is ***not*** correct?

1. One acute angle and one obtuse angle can be put together to make a straight angle.
2. Reflex angle is greater than 180° but less than 360°.
3. Two acute angles can be put together to make a reflex angle.
4. Two acute angles can be put together to make an obtuse angle.

36. One of the most important purposes of assessment in mathematics at primary school level is to:

1. find out important learning gaps and likewise make modification in the pedagogy
2. prepare learners for secondary and high school mathematics
3. find out mathematicians of the future
4. determine learner's intelligence levels

37. Which of the following is an example of a task based on creative thinking that can be given to students of grade 5?

1. Find the area of a rectangle using formula
2. Find the area of a rectangle whose length is half of its breadth
3. Write multiplication table of 7
4. Add 415 and 237 using column addition

38. Which of the following fractions are in descending order?

1. $\frac{3}{7}, \frac{5}{9}, \frac{8}{11}, \frac{4}{5}$ 2. $\frac{8}{11}, \frac{5}{9}, \frac{4}{5}, \frac{3}{7}$
3. $\frac{4}{5}, \frac{8}{11}, \frac{5}{9}, \frac{3}{7}$ 4. $\frac{3}{7}, \frac{4}{5}, \frac{5}{9}, \frac{8}{11}$

39. The numerical values of perimeter and area of a square are equal. The length of the side of the square is:

1. 2 units 2. 4 units
3. 8 units 4. 1 units

40. Which of the following letters has one line of symmetry?

1. O 2. X
3. S 4. V

41. Computational skills in mathematics can be enhanced by:

1. conducting hands-on-activities in class.
2. giving conceptual knowledge
3. clarifying concepts and procedures followed by a lot of practice
4. describing algorithms only

42. A triangular pyramid has:

1. 4 faces and 6 edges.
2. 3 faces and 6 edges.
3. 3 faces and 4 edges.
4. 4 faces and 4 edges.

43. If a six digit number $72x292$ is divisible by 36, then the value of $(3x + 2)$ is:

1. 16 2. 17
3. 20 4. 15

44. The difference between of the greatest and smallest five digit numbers that can be formed using the digits 8, 2, 7, 0 and 6 only once is:

1. 65942 2. 66942
3. 67942 4. 56942

45. According to National Curriculum Framework 2005, mathematics curriculum must incorporate mathematical processes which are:

1. Memorization and application of formulae and multiplication tables in problem solving
2. Problem solving using estimation, approximations and spatial reasoning
3. Doing quick mental calculations
4. Teaching and learning of procedures of problem solving

33. 3	**34.** 2	**35.** 3	**36.** 1	**37.** 2	**38.** 3	**39.** 2
40. 4	**41.** 3	**42.** 1	**43.** 2	**44.** 2	**45.** 2	

46. In a class, teacher prepared following table showing colours of eye of 40 students:

	Blue eye	Brown eye	Black eye
Boys	5	4	11
Girls	7	3	10

Teacher told four students to write one statement each about this table on black-board. They wrote:

(*a*) Number of boys and girls are equal.
(*b*) Mostly students have black eye.
(*c*) Total number of students having blue eyes is odd.
(*d*) Total number of students having brown eyes is odd.

Choose the ***correct*** option:

1. (*a*), (*b*) are true, but (*c*), (*d*) are false.
2. (*a*), (*b*) and (*d*) are true, but (*c*) is false.
3. (*a*) and (*c*) are true, but (*a*) and (*d*) are false.
4. (*a*), (*b*), (*c*) are true, but (*d*) is false.

47. According to NIPUN Bharat Mission, the states will ensure to achieve foundational numeracy till grade III by the end of the year:

1. 2027-28 2. 2024-25
3. 2029-30 4. 2026-27

48. Amita starts from the place A and reaches place B in 4 hours 44 minutes. From there, she returns to the starting place A in 3 hours 24 minutes. If she reaches back at 2.30 pm, then her starting time from place A was:

1. 6.00 am 2. 6.22 am
3. 6.24 am 4. 6.44 am

49. The missing number in the pattern 325, 259, 204, 160, 127, 105 ____ is:

1. 96 2. 98
3. 94 4. 90

50. Which of the following activities, most appropriately, represents the four stages involved in handling data i.e., collecting, organising, representing and interpreting data?

1. Asking the pupils to list their favourite food.
2. Asking the pupils to mark their birth dates on a calendar.
3. Asking the pupils to write the names of their favourite cartoons.
4. Collecting data about how pupils travel to school and then comparing the different modes of transport used by the pupils.

51. Radha bought 9 bags of rice each weighing 9 kg 995 g. Total weight of rice in the bags is:

1. 89.595 kg 2. 89.765 kg
3. 89.955 kg 4. 89.985 kg

52. While giving a rectangular page to Mohan, Mathematics teacher told him to make a square out of it. Mohan folded that paper from one side and made a square. At what level of Van Heile's theory of geometrical understanding Mohan is?

1. Level 2 (Relationship)
2. Level 1 (Analysis)
3. Level 0 (Visualisation)
4. Level 3 (Deduction)

53. Which of the following statements is least appropriate about mathematics curriculum for primary classes?

1. It should help in making connections in mathematics.
2. It should enhance relational understanding.
3. It must be dynamic and coherent in nature.
4. It should be joyful and rigid.

54. Problem solving method of teaching mathematics involves which of the following steps?

(*a*) Posing mathematical problems and instructing steps of solutions.
(*b*) Design a task based upon the current understanding of the students.
(*c*) Posing everyday problems and help learners make sense of the mathematics involved.
(*d*) Allowing the learners to actively take part in the finding solutions of the problems and justify the solutions.

Choose the ***correct*** option:

1. only (*a*) 2. only (*d*)
3. (*c*) and (*d*) 4. (*b*), (*c*) and (*d*)

55. Work of which Indian Mathematician can be associated with "Game Theory"?

1. Mahavira 2. Ramanujan
3. Brahmgupta 4. Aryabhatta

56. The perimeter of a rectangle is 410 m and its length is 123 m. The breadth of the rectangle (in m) is:

1. 82 2. 86
3. 88 4. 92

57. If HCF of two numbers is 18, then which of the following cannot be their LCM?

1. 128 2. 108
3. 72 4. 144

46. 2	**47.** 4	**48.** 2	**49.** 3	**50.** 4	**51.** 3
52. 3	**53.** 4	**54.** 4	**55.** 2	**56.** 1	**57.** 1

58. How many twin primes are there in the numbers from 1 to 50?

1. 6
2. 5
3. 4
4. 7

59. What is the difference of the place values of the two 8s in the number 2853847?

1. 799200
2. 792000
3. 799920
4. 7999200

60. Which of the following statement is least appropriate about the errors made by students in a mathematics classroom?

1. They can be determined by a diagnostic test.
2. They can be persistent if not identified.
3. They can be described but cannot be analysed.
4. They can be repeated.

PART-III : ENVIRONMENTAL STUDIES

61. At the elementary level, which one of the following topics would be most suitable for discussion and experience sharing in the EVS class?

1. Uses of water and concept of density.
2. Uses of water and soluble substances.
3. Dandi march and concept of evaporation.
4. Everyone does not get the facility of water equally.

62. A teacher of Environmental Studies should include the local context of the children in conducting his/her class activities. Which of the following should a teacher pay attention to in order to incorporate the local context?

1. The selection of local context should be in line with the discipline of the school.
2. The selection of the local context should be pedagogically imaginative and ethically correct.
3. Selection of local context should be from the textbooks of Environmental Studies.
4. Local context should be selected according to the convenience of a teacher.

63. An Environmental Studies teacher of class 4 made different groups of children in his class to do the task of making letter boxes on the theme Travel. During the work of making the model of the letter box, the teacher also assessed their work. Which of the following assessment tools would the teacher have used to assess children's activity?

1. Portfolio
2. Check List and Achievement test
3. Achievement test and Anecdotal records
4. Worksheet

64. Many lessons in the NCERT EVS textbook are based on real people and their real experiences. Why would the textbook development committee have included real people and their real experiences?

A. Children easily relate to real people.
B. During EVS, ideas can be discussed with the children by including their experiences.
C. It helps in reinforcing the idea that environmental studies can be done only in classrooms and through textbooks.
D. Real people and their experiences inspire children.

1. A, B and D
2. B, C and D
3. A, C and D
4. A, B and C

65. The territorial states of Karnataka are:

1. Maharashtra, Tamil Nadu, Gujarat
2. Odisha, Chhattisgarh, Kerala
3. Andhra Pradesh, Telangana, Odisha
4. Kerala, Andhra Pradesh, Telangana

66. They are many poems related to the environment in the textbooks of Environmental Studies. The teacher should also ask the children to create poems. Which one of the following process skills is mainly developed by writing poems?

1. Creative expression
2. Motor skills
3. Learning skills
4. Convergent skills

67. Ajay is a teacher of Environmental Studies and he wants to conduct a role play activity in his class. Which of the following topics would be most appropriate for a role play for the children?

1. Demonstration of solubility of various substances.
2. Evaporation of water.
3. Germination of seeds.
4. A family that gets only two buckets of water from a water tanker everyday.

68. On the map of a big city following scale is mentioned.

Scale : 1 cm = 845 m

If on this map the measured distance between two important locations of the city is 13.7 cm, the actual distance between he two locations is approximately:

1. 12.90 km
2. 11.57 km
3. 11.02 km
4. 12.50 km

58. 1	**59.** 1	**60.** 3	**61.** 4	**62.** 2	**63.** 1
64. 1	**65.** 4	**66.** 1	**67.** 4	**68.** 2	

69. Which one of the following tools is used to cut the dried leaves from the top of the onions in Karnataka?

1. Illige
2. Kurige
3. Knife
4. Khunti

70. The locations of Punjab and Kerala respectively with respect to Bihar are:

1. North-west; South-east
2. North-east; South-west
3. North-west; South-west
4. Due North; South-east

71. Which of the following is ***correct*** in the context of Environmental Studies?

A. The syllabus of Environmental Studies is title based in which the arrangement of titles is in a spiral and sequential manner.
B. The curriculum of Environmental Studies is theme based in which the arrangement of theme and sub-theme is in a spiral and sequential manner.
C. The curriculum of Environmental Studies is integrated.
D. Each lesson of the syllabus does not start with the main concept but starts with the main questions.

1. A, B and D
2. B, C and D
3. A, B and C
4. A, C and D

72. Consider the following Statement (A) and (B).

Statement (A): Sloth spends almost 20 hours a day sleeping.

Statement (B): Sloth lives for about 20 years and in that time they move around only 5 trees.

Select the ***correct*** code from the following:

1. (A) and (B) both are wrong
2. (A) is correct, but (B) is wrong
3. (A) is wrong, but (B) is correct
4. (A) and (B) both are correct

73. I am a tree of desert areas. I grow without much water. My wood is not affected by insects and bark is used for making medicine. Guess, who am I? Choose the ***correct*** answer from the following.

1. Desert Oak
2. Khejadi tree
3. Date Palm
4. Acacia

74. I am an Indian bird who lay eggs in between the stones. My nest is made of soft twigs, roots, wools, hair and cotton wool.

Who am I? Choose the ***correct*** answer from the following.

1. Crow
2. Woodpecker
3. Indian Robin
4. Indian Peafowl

75. As per the EVS curriculum, which one of the following topics related to "Family and Friends" should be most suitable for class 3 children?

1. Family Tree
2. Causes of the changing nature of the family
3. Changes in the family
4. Society as family

76. The distance between the capital of India (New Delhi) and the capital of Bihar (Patna) is 792 km. If an express bus covers this distance in 11 hours, the average speed of the bus in metre per second is:

1. 20 m/s
2. 36 m/s
3. 72 m/s
4. 15 m/s

77. Which of the following should **not** be the appropriate pedagogy to learn theme "food" of EVS?

1. The teacher should try to make the children express their own views.
2. Stimulate children's imagination to give them opportunities to construct knowledge.
3. Motivating the children to draw a labelled diagram of the digestive system.
4. Ask the children to draw their own picture and draw in their mind where the food goes from their mouth in the picture.

78. Choose the correctly matched pair(s).

Language	**Where it is spoken (State)**
(*a*) Malayalam	(*i*) Goa
(*b*) Konkani	(*ii*) Kerala
(*c*) Marathi	(*iii*) Jharkhand
(*d*) Gujarati	(*iv*) Karnataka
(*e*) Kannada	(*v*) Maharashtra
(*f*) Kuduk	(*vi*) Gujarat

1. (*a*)-(*ii*), (*b*)-(*i*), (*c*)-(*v*), (*d*)-(*vi*), (*e*)-(*iv*), (*f*)-(*iii*)
2. (*a*)-(*i*), (*b*)-(*ii*), (*c*)-(*iii*), (*d*)-(*iv*), (*e*)-(*vi*), (*f*)-(*v*)
3. (*a*)-(*i*), (*b*)-(*ii*), (*c*)-(*v*), (*d*)-(*iv*), (*e*)-(*vi*), (*f*)-(*iii*)
4. (*a*)-(*i*), (*b*)-(*ii*), (*c*)-(*iii*), (*d*)-(*iv*), (*e*)-(*v*), (*f*)-(*vi*)

79. Consider the following Statement (A) and (B).

Statement (A): Animals whose ears you can see have hair on their body. These animals give birth to young ones.

Statement (B): Animals, whose ears you cannot see and they donot have hair on their body, lay eggs.

Select the ***correct*** code from the following.

1. (A) and (B) both are wrong
2. (A) is correct, but (B) is wrong
3. (A) is wrong, but (B) is correct
4. (A) and (B) both are correct

69. 1	**70.** 3	**71.** 2	**72.** 1	**73.** 2	**74.** 3
75. 1	**76.** 1	**77.** 3	**78.** 1	**79.** 4	

80. What is the significance of Environmental Studies at the primary level? Choose the ***most appropriate*** option from the following.

A. It is child focused.

B. Its focus is to teach the environment to children.

C. Environmental Studies make children experience their environment.

D. Its objective is to develop positive attitude, problem solving skills and values.

1. B, C, and D
2. A and D
3. A, C and D
4. A, B and C

81. Fill in the blank:

(*i*) Urea : Inorganic fertilizer :: Cow Dung : _____

(*ii*) Gum : Natural adhesive :: _____ : Artificial adhesive.

Choose the ***correct*** options.

1. (*i*) Fertilizer, (*ii*) Fevicol
2. (*i*) Manure, (*ii*) Fevicol
3. (*i*) Organic fertilizer, (*ii*) Rubber
4. (*i*) Manure, (*ii*) Rubber

82. It is said that children learn a lot from their surroundings quite easily. Their experiences should be brought into the classroom, their questions answered and their curiosities satisfied. By doing so, the curriculum of EVS can be made more enriching and creative. In the context of the above, the curriculum of Environmental Studies is indicating which of the following principles?

1. Unknown to Known
2. Global to Local
3. Information to Understanding
4. Local to Global

83. A teacher demonstrates an experiment to his class how a mirror becomes hazy when we exhale air on it. Which general objective of teaching EVS is being achieved through this experiment?

1. Explain the concept of cold or hot air to children.
2. Explain the concept of inhalation and exhalation.
3. Demonstrating experiment to the children.
4. To engage children in exploratory and hands-on activities to acquire basic cognitive and motor skills through processes of observation, classification and inference.

84. Which of the following assessment criteria, at the district/state/national level, informs various stakeholders about a child's learning and also ensures quality of education?

1. Learning Objectives
2. Learning Outcomes
3. Learning Outcomes and Competencies
4. Specific Learning Objectives

85. In the following question. Assertion and Reason are followed. Read the statements carefully and choose the ***correct*** option from the following.

Assertion (A): The cultural resources of the communities are also very important for the learning of the child. Folk tales, folk songs, jokes, art etc. enrich the language and knowledge of the child.

Reason (R): The local environment of the child is not only physical or natural, but his socio-cultural environment is also local.

1. Both (A) and (R) are correct, but (R) is not the correct explanation of (A).
2. (A) is true, but (R) is false.
3. (A) is false, but (R) is true.
4. Both (A) and (R) are correct and (R) is the correct explanation of (A).

86. Read the following statement carefully and choose the correct option.

Assertion (A): A distinct centrally located spherical structure in a cell is called Nucleus.

Reason (R): Nucleus is surrounded by a jelly like structure called cytoplasm.

1. Both (A) and (R) are correct, but (R) is not the correct explanation of (A).
2. (A) is true, but (R) is false.
3. (A) is false, but (R) is true.
4. Both (A) and (R) are correct and (R) is the correct explanation of (A).

87. Read the Assertion (A) and Reason (R) carefully.

Assertion (A): The history of many places show us how many different cultural influences have helped to shape life and culture there.

Reason (R): Thus regions became very diverse because of their unique history for example Ladakh and Kerala.

Choose the ***correct*** option from the following.

1. Both (A) and (R) are true, but (R) does not explain (A).
2. (A) is true, but (R) is false.
3. (A) is false, but (R) is true.
4. Both (A) and (R) are true and (R) explains (A).

80. 3	**81.** 2	**82.** 4	**83.** 2	**84.** 3	**85.** 4	**86.** 1	**87.** 4

88. Read the following Assertion and its Reason and choose the ***correct*** answer.

Assertion (A): Without worker-bee, there would be neither beehive nor any nectar collections.

Reason (R): The male bees have very special role as workers.

1. Both (A) and (R) are true, but (R) is the correct explanation of (A).
2. (A) is true, but (R) is false.
3. (A) is false, but (R) is true.
4. Both (A) and (R) are true and (R) is the correct explanation of (A).

89. A person boarded Rajdhani train from New Delhi on 30 April, 2022 and reached Bhubaneshwar on 01 May, 2022. The train departed from New Delhi at 17:00 hours and reached Bhubaneshwar at 20:00 hrs. on 01 May, 2022. If the distance between New Delhi and Bhubaneshwar by train route is nearly 1701 km. The average speed of the train during this journey was:

1. 62.7 km/h
2. 63 km/h
3. 63.3 km/h
4. 60 km/h

90. In the following question. Assertion and Reason are followed. Read the statements carefully and choose the ***correct*** option from the following:

Assertion (A): The child's local objects are a natural source of learning which should be given primacy in the classroom.

Reason (R): When the living world in and around the school is available for contemplation, children will be aware of environmental issues and will be able to nurture their interest in them.

1. Both (A) and (R) are correct, but (R) is not the correct explanation of (A).
2. (A) is true, but (R) is false.
3. (A) is false, but (R) is true.
4. Both (A) and (R) are correct and (R) is the correct explanation of (A).

PART-IV : LANGUAGE-I — ENGLISH

Directions (Qs. No. 91-99): Read the *passage given below and answer the questions that follow:*

Soon some idea struck her and she went to the window and hollered, 'Roopa! Roopa!' After calling out for Roopa, she had a look at the things that she had brought for her. Roopa had to sit for her home science examination the next day and Tarawati had collected things like some kitchen items, a bucket, a mug and a stool that Roopa required for the practical examination.

While looking at the things that she had collected for Roopa, Tarawati recalled her husband who had died a few years ago. She remembered him berating her for not treating Roopa well. 'Roopa's mother! Do not think only sons deserve all love and care and not daughters'. I'm determined to give Roopa good education so that she leads a happy and meaningful life. You are not educated yourself. That's probably why you don't want her to be educated. This is not fair on your part. You must change your view and let her grow and flower into a happy, confident individual.

Thinking of her husband's admonition on this account, Tarawati felt emotional. The fact of the matter was that Roopa's parents differed on Roopa's upbringing and fought with each other on the issue. The fight continued for day together and often it was Roopa who intervened to broker peace between them. On his death-bed too, Roopa's father had cried and pleaded with her to treat Roopa in a nice manner. Hugging Roopa, he had told Tarawati, Take care of Roopa. Give her good education and let her decide the course of her life herself.' While recalling the interaction, tears rolled down Tarawati's eyes.

Meanwhile, the evening shadows were getting darker. Tarawati was exhausted and had a headache too. She looked at her dust-laden feet and then around the room. In order to bring some semblance of order, she forced herself to get up and get going. Then she called her daughter again, Roopa! Roopa!.

91. Why did Tarawati's husband 'berate' her?

1. For not treating their daughter well
2. For constantly quarrelling with him
3. For picking up fights with neighbours
4. For not doing the household work properly

92. Trawati's emotional state towards her daughter could be described as ______.

1. loving
2. indifferent
3. ambivalent
4. hostile

93. What social issue is highlighted in the passage?

1. caste
2. gender
3. communalism
4. poverty

94. Choose the word nearest in meaning to 'holler'.

1. shout
2. request
3. talk
4. quarrel

88. 2	**89.** 2	**90.** 4	**91.** 1	**92.** 3	**93.** 2	**94.** 1

95. 'Things were lying at sixes and sevens ...' means ____.

1. in proper order
2. in a disorderly state
3. being old and worn-out
4. being dirty and unwashed

96. Which of the following is opposite in meaning to 'admonition'?

1. flattery 2. praise
3. shriek 4. rebuke

97. The next day, Roopa had to appear in her examination in ____.

1. Home Science 2. Chemistry
3. Biology 4. English

98. Why was Tarawati not keen to get Roopa educated?

1. Because she did not know the value of good education
2. Because she did not want to spend money on Roopa's education
3. Because she did not want Roopa to go out
4. Because she did not love her

99. '... to broker peace between them.'
Identify the Part of Speech of the underlined expression.

1. Adjective 2. Preposition
3. Verb 4. Noun

Directions (Qs. No. 100-105): *Read the extract given below and answer the question that follow:*

Put away the road maps now.
To go there,
you do not need
helicopters any more;
wherever there is hunger,
there Kalahandi is.
The god of rain
turned away his face.
There was not one green leaf
left on the trees for supper.
The whole village a graveyard.
Cracked ground,
drab river sand.
All the plans failed;
the poverty line
receded further.

100. 'The god of rain/turned away his face'. Which figure of speech is used here?

1. alliteration 2. personification
3. oxymoron 4. transferred epithet

101. What does 'the poverty line/receded further' signify?

1. That poverty is of no consequence in the present-day world
2. That poverty is increasing
3. That poverty is a thing of the past
4. That poverty is going down

102. The village becoming a graveyard is a metaphor that:

1. people are migrating to other cities.
2. more graveyards are being planned.
3. people are living in graveyards.
4. people are dying in large numbers.

103. Kalahandi as described in the poem stands for:

1. prosperity 2. hunger
3. natural disasters 4. development

104. What natural calamity is the poet talking about?

1. drought 2. earthquake
3. landslide 4. floods

105. What is the dominant 'mood' of the poem?

1. sorrow 2. surprise
3. anger 4. relief

106. **Assertion (A):** Learning experiences in the classroom are deeply connected to children's lives and their contexts.

Reason (R): Learning experiences are designed to build on children's previous understanding.

Select the ***most appropriate*** answer from the options given below.

1. Both (A) and (R) are true, but (R) is not the correct explanation of (A).
2. (A) is true, but (R) is false.
3. (A) is false, but (R) is true.
4. Both (A) and (R) true and (R) is the correct explanation of (A).

107. Which of the following is NOT true of learning a language?

1. Language learning takes time.
2. Language learning is meaning making.
3. Grammar learning is essential for learning a language.
4. All learners can learn a language easily if sufficient engagement with language is given.

95. 2	**96.** 2	**97.** 1	**98.** 1	**99.** 3	**100.** 2	**101.** 2
102. 4	**103.** 2	**104.** 1	**105.** 1	**106.** 4	**107.** 3	

108. To assess whether students can use functional exponents for buying something in a shop, it would be appropriate for students to:

1. Write about their food preferences.
2. Read a short story between shopkeeper and customers.
3. Draw the scene between shopkeeper and customers.
4. Write short dialogue between shopkeeper and customers.

109. A teacher found some of the aspects of language learning e.g., reading with understanding a text on scientific concepts. She decided to pick students who find it difficult on the particular aspects. She took separate session for them to support them read and understand such text. What is this practice known as?

1. Higher Order Skills
2. Thinking Skills
3. Feedback Teaching
4. Remedial Teaching

110. Which one of the following is NOT a sub skill of reading?

1. Deducing the meaning and use of unfamiliar lexical items.
2. Scanning to locate specifically required information.
3. Knowing the spelling of each word.
4. Recognizing vocabulary, picking out key words.

111. Assertion (A): A student portfolio is purposeful collection of pieces of student work.

Reason (R): The Portfolio can encourage students to evaluate their own strengths and weaknesses.

Select the ***most appropriate*** answer from the option given below:

1. Both (A) and (R) are true, but (R) is not the correct explanation of (A).
2. (A) is true, but (R) is false.
3. (A) is false, but (R) is true.
4. Both (A) and (R) are true and (R) is the correct explanation of (A).

112. To help students to develop their vocabulary a teacher is using the material that contains language that has been made easier for students and is based on authentic material. This material is:

1. Role-cards
2. Bilingual dictionaries
3. Graded readers
4. Newspaper

113. A language teacher gives students a questionnaire in order to find out more about their learning styles and preferences. Here the teacher is in the role of a:

1. Planner
2. Provider of expert information
3. Diagnostician
4. Manager

114. A teacher of class I asks her learners to scribble, draw and write whatever children want on the walls. What does she encourage here?

1. joy and humour.
2. writing skill development.
3. initiation to writing the letters of alphabets.
4. emergent literacy development.

115. Which one of the following is ***incorrect*** about the pictures?

Pictures and illustration in books:

1. retain the interest of children.
2. to give them opportunity to draw such pictures.
3. help to present language in unfamiliar and memorable contexts.
4. support content.

116. Which of the following statement related to the young learners is **true**?

1. young learners find it hard to understand abstract concepts.
2. young learners partially understand the abstract concepts.
3. young learners get motivated by abstract concepts.
4. young learners understand the abstract concepts.

117. What steps would you take as a teacher to facilitate students' interaction in your class?

(*a*) Encourage the students to ask more questions.

(*b*) Conduct pair and group work and invite opinion from the students.

(*c*) Make them read the text loudly and respond individually so that individual learning takes place.

(*d*) Read the dialogues to each other to interact and ask question to each other.

1. (*b*), (*c*), (*d*) are correct
2. (*a*), (*b*), (*d*) are correct
3. (*a*), (*c*), (*d*) are correct
4. (*a*), (*b*), (*c*) are correct

108. 4	**109.** 4	**110.** 3	**111.** 4	**112.** 3	**113.** 3	**114.** 4	**115.** 2	**116.** 1	**117.** 2

118. Cognitive theory of language development, supports that language is:
1. learnt through reward and punishment.
2. learnt through interaction with in the society.
3. dependent on child's understanding of the concept before verbalizing it.
4. innate capacity of an individual.

119. Assertion (A): Language forms a critical aspect of cultural awareness and expression, which is considered among the major competencies to develop in children.

Reason (R): The competencies of cultural awareness and expression provide children with a sense of identity, belongingness, as well as an appreciation of other cultures and identities.

Select the ***most appropriate*** answer from the options given below:
1. Both (A) and (R) are true, but (R) is not the correct explanation of (A).
2. (A) is true, but (R) is false.
3. (A) is false, but (R) is true.
4. Both (A) and (R) are true and (R) is the correct explanation of (A).

120. Textbooks contains stories, poems, plays and other forms of writing by writers. We need to select such materials because they are ______.
1. written with the purpose to be used in textbooks
2. written by well known writers
3. they are in simple language
4. authentic and are in natural language

PART-V : भाषा-II — हिन्दी

निर्देशः (प्र.सं. 121-128 के लिए): *निम्नलिखित गद्यांश को पढ़कर पूछे गए प्रश्नों के उत्तर के लिए सबसे उपयुक्त विकल्प का चयन कीजिए।*

प्रत्येक व्यक्ति का जन्म राजा बनने के लिए हुआ है, इसे इस रूप में भी समझ सकते हैं कि हर व्यक्ति के पूरे जीवन का सतत संघर्ष एक सत्ता को पाना है। ऐसी सत्ता जिसकी प्रकृति, जिसकी सीमाएँ जिसके व्यवहार को वह व्यक्ति स्वयं निर्धारित करता है। इस संघर्ष के अलग-अलग रूप हम अपने आस-पास के तमाम रिश्तों में भी देख सकते हैं। परिवार के अंदर भी यह चीज दिखती है। उदाहरण के लिए एक परिवार में कोई एक व्यक्ति मुखिया बनकर अपनी भूमिका का विस्तार करता है और उस परिवार जैसी इकाई का राजा बनता है। कोई व्यक्ति अपनी कॉलोनी में लीडर बनता है तो कोई गली-मोहल्ले का राजा बनना चाहता है। कोई विधायक, सांसद, मुख्यमंत्री, प्रधानमंत्री बनकर अपनी सीमाओं का विस्तार करना और एक बड़े हिस्से का राजा बनना चाहता है।

जो इन सब चक्करों में नहीं है, अकेला व्यक्ति है, वह भी अपने शरीर का राजा बनना चाहता है। अपने शरीर पर अपना अधिकार भी बड़ी बात है।

121. गद्यांश के अनुसार ______ और ______ जीवन का सत्य हैं।
1. संघर्ष, मुख्यमंत्री होना
2. मुख्यमंत्री होना, सीमाएँ
3. सीमाएँ, परिवार
4. संघर्ष, नेतृत्व करना

122. गद्यांश के अनुसार ______ अपने शरीर का राजा बनना चाहता है।
1. लीडर
2. व्यक्ति
3. सांसद
4. मुखिया

123. गद्यांश के अनुसार मनुष्य–
1. पूरे विश्व पर आधिपत्य चाहता है।
2. अपनी भूमिका का विस्तार चाहता है।
3. अपने विचारों पर अधिकार चाहता है।
4. सतत संघर्षरत रहना चाहता है।

124. समूह से भिन्न शब्द है–
1. मुख्यमंत्री
2. सांसद
3. संघर्ष
4. राजा

125. 'इक' प्रत्यय का प्रयोग ______ शब्द में **नहीं** हो सकता?
1. व्यवहार
2. प्रकृति
3. जीवन
4. परिवार

126. गद्यांश के अनुसार एक व्यक्ति का जन्म ______ बनने के लिए हुआ है।
1. राजा
2. मुखिया
3. लीडर
4. परिवार

127. गद्यांश के अनुसार व्यक्ति ______ के लिए संघर्ष करता है।
1. सत्ता की सीमाएँ निर्धारित करने
2. बड़े साम्राज्य का राजा बनने
3. सत्ता प्राप्त करने
4. सत्ता को बढ़ाने

128. 'लीडर' शब्द है–
1. आगत
2. तत्सम
3. तद्भव
4. देशज

118. 3	**119.** 4	**120.** 4	**121.** 4	**122.** 2	**123.** 2
124. 3	**125.** 3	**126.** 1	**127.** 3	**128.** 1	

निर्देशः (प्र.सं. 129-135 के लिए): *निम्नलिखित गद्यांश को पढ़कर पूछे गए प्रश्नों के उत्तर के लिए सबसे उपयुक्त विकल्प का चयन कीजिए।*

इन दिनों फिर से हिंदी बनाम स्थानीय भाषाओं को लेकर शोर मचा है। इसमें कुछ चीजें समझने वाली हैं। सबसे पहले तो यही कि हिंदी हमारी मातृभाषा जरूर है, लेकिन कर्नाटक, तमिलनाडु, केरल समेत अन्य प्रांत में जन्म लेने वाले व्यक्ति के लिए यह मातृभाषा नहीं हो सकती। जितना प्रेम हमें हिंदी से है, उतना ही प्रेम पंजाब में जन्मे व्यक्ति को पंजाबी से होगा, कर्नाटक में जन्मे शख्स को कन्नड़ से होगा, तमिलनाडु में जन्मे व्यक्ति को तमिल से होगा। हिंदी राजभाषा है, उसका सम्मान सर्वोपरि है, मगर हमें यह भी ध्यान देना होगा कि हिंदी का सम्मान करने के अति उत्साह में कहीं हम अन्य भाषाओं का अपमान तो नहीं कर रहे? जैसे हमारी माता, वैसे ही सबकी माता। हिंदी हमारी मातृभाषा है, तो कन्नड़ तमिल, मलयालम, तेलुगु भी किसी न किसी की मातृभाषा है। हिन्दुस्तान हमारा राष्ट्र है, हिंदी इसकी एक प्रमुख भाषा, लेकिन तमिल, कन्नड़, पंजाबी, तेलगु, मलयालम आदि भी इसी राष्ट्र में बोली जाने वाली भाषाएँ हैं, जिनका बराबर सम्मान होना चाहिए। तभी हम गर्व से कह पाएँगे कि अनेकता में एकता हमारी सभ्यता है।

129. 'जैसी हमारी माता, वैसे ही सबकी माता।' वाक्य किस संदर्भ में कहा गया है?

1. भाषा के संदर्भ में
2. माता के संदर्भ में
3. राष्ट्र के संदर्भ में
4. राजनीति के संदर्भ में

130. 'हिंदी राजभाषा है, उसका सम्मान सर्वोपरि है।' से आशय है:

1. राजकीय कामकाज की भाषा होने के कारण हिंदी का सम्मान सबसे ऊपर है
2. राज्य विशेष की भाषा होने के कारण हिंदी का सम्मान सबसे ऊपर है
3. भारत की राष्ट्रभाषा होने के कारण हिंदी का सम्मान सबसे ऊपर है
4. राजाओं की भाषा होने के कारण हिंदी का सम्मान सबसे ऊपर है

131. 'अनेकता में एकता हमारी सभ्याता है।' वाक्य से आशय है:

1. विविधता ही किसी राष्ट्र की पहचान होती है
2. विविधता से ही समरसता आती है
3. विविधता होते हुए भी हम सब एक है
4. विविधता में एकता पुरानी बात हो गई है

132. 'स्थानीय' में प्रत्यय है–

1. नीय
2. ईय
3. इय
4. य

133. गद्यांश के अनुसार किस बात का शोर हो रहा है?

1. हिंदी बनाम क्षेत्रीय भाषाएँ
2. हिंदी बनाम आधुनिक भाषाएँ
3. हिंदी बनाम बोलियाँ
4. हिंदी बनाम तमिल

134. गद्यांश में निम्न में किस भाषा का जिक्र नहीं है?

1. पंजाबी
2. कन्नड़
3. तमिल
4. मैथिली

135. 'अनेकता' शब्द है–

1. विशेषण
2. क्रिया
3. प्रविशेषण
4. संज्ञा

136. एक अध्यापिका की एक वीडियो मिला। उसने महसूस किया कि यह वीडियो एक टॉपिक विशेष के लिए उपयुक्त है। अध्यापिका ने इस वीडियो को आधार बनाकर दो-दो के जोड़ों में कार्य करवाने की योजना बनाई। जोड़ों में कार्य करवाने की इस गतिविधि का उद्देश्य विद्यार्थियों को क्या करने के लिए प्रोत्साहित करना है?

1. साथ-साथ तेल गति से कार्य करने के लिए।
2. अध्यापिका के बिना स्वतंत्र होकर कार्य करने के लिए।
3. भाषा जागरूकता विकसित करने के लिए।
4. अपने कार्य का स्वयं आकलन करने के लिए।

137. भाषा अधिगम के लिए लघु कथाओं और वृतान्तों का संग्रह पूरक पठन सामग्री के रूप में निर्धारित किया जाता है। पूरक पठन सामग्री का मुख्य उद्देश्य क्या है?

1. गहन पठन (इन्टैंसिव पठन) को समुन्नत करना।
2. नैतिक मूल्य अधिगम को समुन्नत करना।
3. विस्तृत (एक्सटैंसिव) पठन को समुन्नत करना।
4. बहुभाषावाद को समुन्नत करना।

138. **अभिकथन (A):** उपचारात्मक शिक्षण, शिक्षण-अधिगम प्रक्रिया का महत्वपूर्ण भाग है।

कारण (R): उपचारात्मक शिक्षण का तात्पर्य है पुनः शिक्षण करना। यह आवश्यक नहीं कि यह शिक्षण इस दृष्टि से किया जाए कि पिछले शिक्षण द्वारा सही तरीके से नहीं सीखा गया है।

नीचे दिए गए विकल्पों में से **सर्वाधिक उपयुक्त** विकल्प का चयन करें:

1. (A) और (R) दोनों सही हैं लेकिन (R), (A) की सही व्याख्या नहीं है।
2. (A) सही है, लेकिन (R) गलत है।
3. (A) गलत है, लेकिन (R) सही है।
4. (A) और (R) दोनों सही हैं और (R), (A) की सही व्याख्या है।

139. पढ़ी गई कहानी को विद्यार्थी द्वारा अपने शब्दों में पुनः बताने के माध्यम से किसका आकलन किया जा सकता है?

1. प्रवाह
2. बोधगम्यता
3. स्मृति
4. सटीकता

129. 1	**130.** 1	**131.** 3	**132.** 2	**133.** 1	**134.** 4
135. 4	**136.** 2	**137.** 3	**138.** 4	**139.** 2	

140. भाषा शिक्षण के बारे में कौन-सी पूर्वधारणा गलत है?

1. अधिगम में शिक्षार्थी की प्रथम भाषा की मुख्य भूमिका होती है।
2. भाषा शिक्षण का मुख्य केन्द्र बिन्दु सम्प्रेषणात्मक गतिविधियों पर होना चाहिए।
3. भाषा शिक्षण में बोलने की अपेक्षा लिखने को अधिक महत्व देना चाहिए।
4. शिक्षार्थी जीवन की वास्तविक स्थितियों में प्रयोग करने की कोशिश द्वारा भाषा अर्जित करते हैं।

141. भाषा अध्यापक का मुख्य उत्तरदायित्व कौन-सा है?

1. शिक्षण के लिए विषयवस्तु का चयन करना।
2. विभिन्न कक्षाओं में शिक्षार्थियों का समूहीकरण।
3. शिक्षार्थियों को निर्देश देना।
4. शिक्षार्थियों की सम्प्रेषणात्मक आवश्यकताओं की पहचान करना।

142. बुनियादी चरण में बच्चे किसमें अधिक सुविधा मससूस करते है और बेहतर रूप से सीखते हैं?

1. कार्यपाली भाषा में 2. अपने घर की भाषा में
3. अंग्रेजी माध्यम में 4. निर्देश के माध्यम में

143. बच्चों को कहानी सुनाने के संदर्भ में कौन-सा कथन गलत है?

1. कहानियाँ बच्चों को वाक्य संरचना सीखने में मदद करती है।
2. कहानियाँ बच्चों में समस्या समाधान कौशलों का विकास करती है।
3. कहानियाँ बच्चों को जीवन में अनुसरण करने वाले नैतिक मूल्यों को सीखने में मदद करती हैं।
4. कहानियाँ बच्चों को नवीन शब्द सीखने और अपनी शब्द संपदा का विस्तार करने में मदद करती है।

144. भाषा की गतिविधि करवाते समय एक अध्यापक विद्यार्थियों का मिश्रित योग्यता वाला समूह बनाता है। इस प्रकार के मिश्रित योग्यता वाले समूह की रचना करने से ______।

1. प्रभुत्व दिखाने वाले विद्यार्थियों को मुक्त रूप से अभिव्यक्त करने के अवसर मिलेंगे।
2. विद्यार्थियों को एक-दूसरे की मदद करने के लिए प्रोत्साहित किया जा सकता है।
3. अध्यापक के कार्य-भार को कम किया जा सकता है क्योंकि अध्यापक सभी पर ध्यान नहीं दे सकता।
4. कमजोर विद्यार्थियों की पहचान की जा सकती है।

145. बच्चों को निम्नलिखित में से किसके अधिक से अधिक अवसर मिलने चाहिए?

1. प्रारंभिक आयु से ही दो लिखित भाषाओं के।
2. प्रारंभिक आयु से ही बहुविध मौखिक भाषाओं के।
3. प्रारंभिक आयु से ही बहुविध लिखित भाषाओं के।
4. प्रारंभिक आयु से ही दो मौखिक भाषाओं के।

146. **अभिकथन (A):** उद्गामी साक्षरता में चित्रकारी लेखक की शुरुआत के रूप में देखी जाती है।

कारण (R): चित्र एक प्रकार के संकेत हैं और इनमें अर्थ निहित होते हैं।

नीचे दिए गए विकल्पों में से **सर्वाधिक उपयुक्त** विकल्प का चयन करें:

1. (A) और (R) दोनों सही हैं लेकिन (R), (A) की सही व्याख्या नहीं है।
2. (A) सही है, लेकिन (R) गलत है।
3. (A) गलत है, लेकिन (R) सही है।
4. (A) और (R) दोनों सही हैं और (R), (A) की सही व्याख्या है।

147. छोटे-छोटे जोड़ों (मिनिमल पेयर) में ड्रिल करवाना। किसमें सुधार लाने की प्रभावशाली युक्ति है?

1. शब्दसंपदा 2. उच्चारण
3. बोध के साथ पठन 4. व्याकरण

148. निम्नलिखित में से कौन-सा भाषा अर्जन के व्यवहारवादी सिद्धांत से संबंधित **नहीं** है?

1. खाली बर्तन
2. प्रयास एवं त्रुटि (ट्रायल एंड एरर)
3. सामाजिक अन्तःक्रियाएँ
4. संक्रियात्मक अनुकूलन

149. कक्षा पाँच की अध्यापिका ने अपने विद्यार्थियों को एक कहानी लिखने का कार्य दिया। जिस समय विद्यार्थी कहानी लिख रहे थे, उस समय अध्यापिका कक्षा में निरीक्षण कर रही थी और जो विद्यार्थी गलत करता या नए शब्दों के बारे में पूछता, उनकी मदद भी कर रही थी। यहाँ अध्यापिका की भूमिका क्या है?

1. योजना निर्माणक 2. संसाधक
3. निदानशास्त्री 4. प्रबंधक

150. **अभिकथन (A):** पठन किसी शब्द को सही तरह से उच्चरित करने से कहीं बहुत अधिक है।

कारण (R): पठन डिकोड करना है।

नीचे दिए गए विकल्पों में से **सर्वाधिक उपयुक्त** विकल्प का चयन करें:

1. (A) और (R) दोनों सही हैं लेकिन (R), (A) की सही व्याख्या नहीं है।
2. (A) सही है, लेकिन (R) गलत है।
3. (A) गलत है, लेकिन (R) सही है।
4. (A) और (R) दोनों सही हैं और (R), (A) की सही व्याख्या है।

140. 3	**141.** 4	**142.** 2	**143.** 3	**144.** 2	**145.** 2
146. 4	**147.** 2	**148.** 3	**149.** 2	**150.** 1	

EXPLANATORY ANSWERS

1. Extrinsic motivation comes from external sources such as approval, rewards, or recognition from others. Intrinsic motivation arises from within the individual, where the activity itself gives satisfaction or enjoyment. Hence, approval of others represents extrinsic motivation, while personal satisfaction represents intrinsic motivation.
2. Authentic learning tasks are those in which children use what they learn in real-life situations. When students apply a concept in daily life, learning becomes meaningful, practical, and connected to experience. Copying, memorising, and only recalling textbook facts mainly test repetition, not authentic understanding.
3. Sensitive period is the stage of development when a child is especially ready to learn a particular skill or ability. During this period, learning happens more easily and naturally, and if the opportunity is missed, it becomes much harder to achieve the same level later. Therefore this term fits the statement exactly.
4. Talking aloud to oneself in childhood is a normal and common behaviour. It is often seen when children think through problems, guide their own actions, or regulate their behaviour. This kind of self-talk is a natural part of cognitive development and does not indicate abnormality.
5. According to Piaget, assimilation happens when a child takes new information into an already existing mental schema. Here, the object is already familiar, and the child is simply adding a new word to what is already known. The child is not creating a completely new schema, but fitting the new information into an existing one, so this is assimilation.
6. Learning is considered socially situated because it takes place through interaction with others, culture, and context. The reason states that learning cannot be separated from how it is learned and used, which directly supports this idea. Since learning methods and usage are embedded in social contexts, the reason correctly explains the assertion.
7. The proximodistal principle states that development proceeds from the center of the body outward to the extremities. In this case, limbs (closer to the body) grow faster than hands and feet (farther from the center), which clearly reflects outward growth from proximal to distal regions.
8. Meaningful learning requires emotional support to make learners feel secure and motivated, and opportunities for active engagement such as doing and experimenting to construct understanding. Competition and rigid standardised curriculum do not necessarily promote deep or meaningful learning, as they may limit creativity and personal connection.
9. Formative assessment focuses on continuous improvement and feedback. It emphasizes learner participation through self-assessment and reflection, helping students understand their own progress and areas for improvement rather than relying only on external evaluation.
10. Reciprocal teaching involves interactive strategies such as predicting, questioning, clarifying, and summarizing to enhance comprehension. It focuses on understanding and dialogue rather than rote memorization, so memorizing is not actively practiced in this process.
11. Meera's reasoning is based on avoiding punishment, which is a key feature of the pre-conventional level in Kohlberg's theory. At this stage, children judge actions as right or wrong based on their direct consequences rather than internalized moral values or social norms.
12. Linking new information with prior knowledge strengthens understanding by organizing ideas meaningfully. The reason correctly explains this by stating that identifying similarities and differences helps in structuring knowledge, improving both thinking and memory.
13. Reducing gender stereotypes requires providing children with varied experiences and role models. When children see both genders performing diverse roles, they are more likely to develop flexible thinking and choose activities based on interest rather than stereotypes.
14. Response set refers to a mental rigidity where a person continues to use a familiar strategy even when it is not effective. This inflexibility blocks creative thinking and prevents exploring alternative solutions, thereby hindering effective problem solving.
15. Children with autism benefit from structure and predictability, which reduces anxiety and helps them understand expectations. A consistent routine supports better learning, communication, and behavior management compared to unpredictable environments.

16. According to Piaget, by the end of the sensorimotor stage (around 2 years), children understand that objects continue to exist even when they are not visible. This ability, called object permanence, marks a major cognitive milestone and shows that children can form mental representations of objects.

17. Vygotsky considered inner speech as an internalized form of language that develops from social interaction. It plays a crucial role in self-regulation, planning, and thinking. Children use inner speech to guide their actions and organize their thoughts effectively.

18. The cephalocaudal principle states that development proceeds from head to toe in a systematic and predictable manner. This reflects an orderly sequence of development, where control over head movements develops before control over lower parts of the body.

19. Invented spellings and free writing allow children to express their understanding of language freely, giving teachers direct insight into their phonemic awareness, thinking patterns, and stage of language development, hence enabling authentic assessment. The reason is also valid because in linguistically diverse classrooms, fixed and rigid assessment methods fail to capture true learning levels. Therefore, assessment must be dynamic and flexible. This need for dynamic assessment directly explains why practices like invented spelling and free exploration are important, as they serve as effective tools suited to such diversity.

20. Creativity develops when children engage with real-life problems that stimulate thinking and reflection. The reason supports this by stating that creative children seek novelty and require intellectual stimulation, which is provided through such problem-based situations.

21. ADHD is primarily characterized by persistent patterns of inattention, hyperactivity, and impulsivity. Children often act without thinking, have difficulty waiting, and show impulsive behaviour consistently. Restricted repetitive behavior relates to autism, while depression or delays are not defining features of ADHD.

22. In an inclusive classroom, learners have diverse needs, abilities, and backgrounds. Therefore, the curriculum must be flexible to accommodate variations, and instruction must be differentiated so that each learner can access content according to their level and learning style.

23. Vygotsky's Zone of Proximal Development refers to the difference between what a learner can do independently and what they can achieve with guidance from a teacher or more knowledgeable person. It highlights the importance of support in learning.

24. Providing scaffolding through prompts and cues is an effective teaching strategy, so the assertion is correct. However, the reason is incorrect because the idea of "more knowledgeable other" and social interaction is given by Vygotsky, not Piaget. Hence the reason is false.

25. Students with mastery goal orientation focus on improving their competence and understanding. They set achievable and meaningful learning goals aimed at self-improvement rather than impressing others or avoiding failure, which reflects intrinsic motivation toward learning.

26. This question requires students to think imaginatively, shift perspective, and create a new version of the text. It involves higher-order thinking and originality, unlike the other options which test recall or basic understanding.

27. In primary education, misconceptions should be acknowledged so that teachers can address and correct them effectively. Intuitive guesses should be encouraged as they reflect children's thinking processes and help in developing conceptual understanding through exploration.

28. Dyspraxia is a developmental disorder that affects motor coordination and planning. It impacts skills like hand-eye coordination, balance, and fine motor abilities such as writing or handling objects, making these tasks difficult for affected individuals.

29. Critical thinking develops when students are encouraged to ask and explore questions. Questions like what, why, and how promote analysis, reasoning, and deeper understanding, unlike rote learning or discouraging reflection.

30. Child development involves multiple aspects such as physical, cognitive, emotional, and social growth. It also progresses in different directions, with some skills improving while others may stabilize or decline, making it a complex and dynamic process.

31. Dienes' perceptual variability principle states that a mathematical concept should be presented using different concrete materials and representations so that children focus on the underlying concept rather than specific objects. Using matchsticks, buttons, and base-10 blocks provides varied sensory experiences to understand place value.

32. Pictographs help students visually represent data using pictures or symbols. This makes data easy to understand, compare, and interpret, especially for young learners, rather than merely engaging them or developing drawing skills.

33. At the foundational stage, emphasis is on continuous and formative assessment rather than summative assessment. Learning outcomes are strengthened through ongoing observation and feedback, not just end-point testing.

34. This situation clearly represents division as equal sharing, where a total quantity is equally distributed into a given number of groups. The focus is on finding how much each group gets.

35. An acute angle is less than 90°, so the sum of two acute angles is always less than 180°, which cannot form a reflex angle (greater than 180°). Other statements are mathematically valid.

36. At the primary level, assessment is mainly diagnostic and formative. It helps teachers identify where students are facing difficulty and accordingly adjust teaching strategies to improve understanding rather than labeling or selecting students.

37. This task requires students to think beyond direct formula application and understand relationships between dimensions. It involves reasoning and interpretation, making it a creative thinking task compared to routine calculations.

38. Converting to decimals:

$$\frac{4}{5} = 0.8$$

$$\frac{8}{11} \approx 0.727$$

$$\frac{5}{9} \approx 0.556$$

$$\frac{3}{7} \approx 0.429$$

Arranging from highest to lowest gives $\frac{4}{5} > \frac{8}{11} > \frac{5}{9} > \frac{3}{7}$, so this is the correct descending order.

39. Perimeter of square $= 4s$

Area of square $= s^2$

Given $4s = s^2$

$s^2 - 4s = 0$

$s(s - 4) = 0$

$s = 4$ (valid length)

Hence side $= 4$ units.

40. Letter V has exactly one line of symmetry (vertical). O and X have multiple lines of symmetry, while S has no line of symmetry.

41. Computational skills become strong when children first understand the concept and the procedure behind an operation, and then practice it sufficiently. Only practice without understanding may create mechanical errors, while only explanation without practice does not build speed and accuracy. Therefore, a combination of conceptual clarity, procedural understanding, and repeated practice is the most effective way.

42. A triangular pyramid is also called a tetrahedron. It has one triangular base and three triangular side faces, so the total number of faces is 4. Its edges are the 3 edges of the base and 3 more edges joining the top vertex to the base vertices, making 6 edges in all.

43. For divisibility by 36, the number must be divisible by both 4 and 9.

Since the last two digits are 92, the number is divisible by 4.

Now sum of digits $= 7 + 2 + x + 2 + 9 + 2$

$= 22 + x$

For divisibility by 9, $22 + x$ must be divisible by 9. The required value is 27, so $x = 5$.

Now, $3x + 2 = 3(5) + 2 = 15 + 2 = 17$.

44. The greatest five-digit number using 8, 2, 7, 0 and 6 is 87620.

The smallest five-digit number using these digits is 20678, because 0 cannot be placed first.

Now, $87620 - 20678 = 66942$

Hence, the required difference is 66942.

45. According to NCF 2005, mathematics learning should move beyond rote memorization and mechanical procedure. It should develop mathematical thinking through problem solving, estimation, approximation, visualization, and spatial reasoning. These processes help children understand mathematics meaningfully and use it in practical situations.

46. Number of boys $= 5 + 4 + 11 = 20$

and number of girls $= 7 + 3 + 10 = 20$,

So (*a*) is true.

Total black eyes $= 11 + 10 = 21$,

which is the highest, so (*b*) is true.

Total blue eyes $= 5 + 7 = 12$,

which is even, so (*c*) is false.

Total brown eyes $= 4 + 3 = 7$,

which is odd, so (*d*) is true.

47. Under the NIPUN Bharat Mission, the target is to ensure that children achieve foundational numeracy by the end of Grade III by the end of the year 2026–27. This target is stated in the official NIPUN Bharat guidelines and reiterated in later government summaries.

48. Total time taken

$$= 4 \text{ hours } 44 \text{ minutes} + 3 \text{ hours } 24 \text{ minutes}$$
$$= 8 \text{ hours } 8 \text{ minutes}$$

She returned at 2:30 pm.

Starting time = 2:30 pm − 8 hours 8 minutes = 6:22 am

So, her starting time from place A was 6:22 am.

49. The pattern is:

$325 \rightarrow 259$, difference = 66
$259 \rightarrow 204$, difference = 55
$204 \rightarrow 160$, difference = 44
$160 \rightarrow 127$, difference = 33
$127 \rightarrow 105$, difference = 22

Next difference should be 11.

So, $105 - 11 = 94$

Hence, the missing number is 94.

50. This activity includes all four stages of data handling. First, data are collected about how students travel to school. Then the data can be organized into groups, represented in a table or graph, and interpreted by comparing which mode is used more or less. Therefore, it most completely represents the full process of handling data.

51. Each bag weighs 9 kg 995 g = 9.995 kg.

Total weight = 9×9.995 kg = 89.955 kg.

So, the total weight of 9 bags of rice is 89.955 kg.

52. At Van Hiele Level 0, a child recognizes and works with shapes by their overall appearance rather than by formally analyzing their properties. Mohan made a square by folding a rectangular page based on visual understanding of the shape. This reflects visualisation, not analysis of sides, angles, or formal relationships.

53. A good mathematics curriculum for primary classes should be flexible, meaningful, coherent, and connected. It should help children build relationships among ideas and develop understanding gradually. The word "joyful" is appropriate, but "rigid" is not, because rigidity goes against child-centered and activity-based mathematics learning.

54. Problem solving in mathematics requires designing tasks according to children's present understanding, connecting mathematics with real-life situations, and allowing learners to actively explore, solve, and justify their solutions. Simply posing a problem and instructing fixed steps does not truly develop problem-solving ability. Therefore, (*b*), (*c*), and (*d*) together represent the method correctly.

55. Among the given Indian mathematicians, Ramanujan is the one whose work is most commonly associated with ideas later connected with game theory. He is mainly known for number theory, infinite series, and deep mathematical insight, and in educational contexts his work is linked with developments related to game-theoretic thinking. Therefore, from the given options, Ramanujan is the best answer.

56. For a rectangle,

$$2(l + b) = 410$$

So,

$$l + b = \frac{410}{2} = 205$$

Given length $l = 123$

Therefore, $b = 205 - 123 = 82$

So, the breadth of the rectangle is 82 m.

57. If the HCF of two numbers is 18, then their LCM must be a multiple of 18. Among the given options, 108, 72, and 144 are all divisible by 18, but 128 is not divisible by 18. Therefore, 128 cannot be the LCM of two numbers whose HCF is 18.

58. Twin primes are pairs of prime numbers that differ by 2. From 1 to 50, the twin prime pairs are (3, 5), (5, 7), (11, 13), (17, 19), (29, 31), (41, 43). Thus, there are 6 twin prime pairs in this range.

59. In the number 2853847, the first 8 is in the hundred-thousands place, so its place value is 800000. The second 8 is in the hundreds place, so its place value is 800. Their difference is

$800000 - 800 = 799200$.

Hence, the required difference is 799200.

60. Errors made by students in mathematics can definitely be analysed. In fact, analysing errors helps the teacher understand misconceptions, learning gaps, and faulty procedures. Such errors may be diagnosed, may persist if ignored, and may also be repeated. Therefore, this statement is the least appropriate.

61. EVS at elementary level focuses on real-life issues, social awareness, and children's experiences. The issue of unequal access to water connects directly with children's surroundings and promotes discussion, empathy, and awareness, making it highly suitable for sharing experiences.

62. Incorporating local context requires thoughtful selection that enhances learning and respects cultural and social values. It should be meaningful, relevant, and sensitive, rather than based on convenience or limited to textbooks.

63. In an activity like making letter boxes on the theme "Travel," the focus is on continuous, process-based assessment rather than only final outcomes. A portfolio allows the teacher to collect and review children's work over time, including planning, creativity, participation, and progress during the activity. It captures a holistic picture of learning, unlike checklists or tests which assess limited aspects. Therefore, portfolio is the most appropriate tool for such activity-based assessment.

64. Real people and experiences help children connect learning with real life (A), allow inclusion of children's own experiences in discussions (B), and inspire them (D). Statement C is incorrect because EVS promotes learning beyond classrooms, not limited to textbooks.

65. Karnataka shares its boundaries with Kerala to the southwest, Andhra Pradesh and Telangana to the east and northeast respectively. Hence, this combination correctly represents its neighbouring states.

66. Writing poems allows children to express their thoughts, feelings, and ideas in imaginative and original ways. It encourages creativity, use of language, and personal interpretation of environmental themes, making creative expression the primary skill developed.

67. Role play is best suited for social and real-life situations where children can act out roles and understand perspectives. This situation involves human experiences, scarcity, and empathy, making it ideal for role play, unlike scientific processes.

68. Scale: $1 \text{ cm} = 845 \text{ m}$

Distance on map $= 13.7 \text{ cm}$

Actual distance $= 13.7 \times 845 \text{ m} = 11576.5 \text{ m}$

$= 11.5765 \text{ km} \approx 11.57 \text{ km}$

So, the approximate actual distance is 11.57 km.

69. In Karnataka, traditional agricultural tools vary regionally. The tool known as "Illige" is specifically used for cutting dried onion leaves from the top, especially in farming practices related to onions.

70. Bihar is located in eastern India. Punjab lies to the north-west of Bihar, while Kerala lies to the south-west of Bihar. Therefore, the correct directional relationship is north-west and south-west respectively.

71. EVS curriculum is theme-based, not title-based, and its themes and sub-themes are arranged in a spiral and sequential manner (B). It is integrated, combining concepts from science, social science, and environmental awareness (C). Lessons usually begin with questions to stimulate curiosity and inquiry rather than direct concepts (D). Statement A is incorrect.

72. In the EVS context based on standard Class 5 "Super Senses" content, a sloth is described as sleeping for about 17 hours a day, not 20 hours. It is also described as living for about 40 years and moving around only eight trees in that lifetime, not 20 years and five trees. Therefore, both the given statements are incorrect.

73. The Khejadi (*Prosopis cineraria*) is a desert tree that grows with very little water. Its wood is resistant to insects and its bark is used in traditional medicine, making it a well-known and important tree in arid regions like Rajasthan.

74. The Indian Robin builds its nest in sheltered places such as crevices between stones. The nest is made using soft materials like twigs, roots, wool, hair, and cotton, matching the description given.

75. For class 3 children, simple and relatable concepts are appropriate. A family tree helps children understand relationships within their family in a concrete and engaging way, whereas other options are more abstract and suitable for higher classes.

76. Distance $= 792 \text{ km} = 792000 \text{ m}$

Time $= 11 \text{ hours} = 11 \times 3600 = 39600 \text{ s}$

$$\text{Speed} = \frac{792000}{39600} = 20 \text{ m/s}$$

So, the average speed is 20 m/s.

77. EVS pedagogy emphasizes experiential, child-centered, and imaginative learning. Drawing a formal labelled diagram is more abstract and suited to higher classes. The other options promote imagination, expression, and conceptual understanding, which are appropriate at the primary level.

78. Malayalam → Kerala (*ii*)

Konkani → Goa (*i*)

Marathi → Maharashtra (*v*)

Gujarati → Gujarat (*vi*)

Kannada → Karnataka (*iv*)

Kuduk → Jharkhand (*iii*)

All pairs are correctly matched.

79. In EVS, animals with visible external ears are generally mammals; they have hair on their bodies and give birth to young ones. Animals without visible ears (like birds, reptiles) typically do not have hair and lay eggs. These are simplified classifications used at the primary level.

80. EVS at primary level is child-centered (A), helps children experience and explore their environment (C), and develops values, attitudes, and problem-solving skills (D). Statement B is limited because EVS is not just about teaching facts but about experiential learning.

81. Urea is an inorganic fertilizer. Cow dung is not an inorganic fertilizer; it is a natural source of nutrients and is used as manure. In the same way, gum is a natural adhesive, while Fevicol is a man-made or artificial adhesive. Therefore, both blanks are correctly filled by Manure and Fevicol.

82. The statement says that children learn easily from their surroundings, and their own experiences, questions, and curiosity should be brought into the classroom. This clearly means that learning should begin from the child's local and immediate environment and then gradually expand to wider understanding. Hence, the principle indicated here is Local to Global, not "Unknown to Known."

83. When the teacher shows that a mirror becomes hazy on exhaling, children are encouraged to observe carefully, think about what happened, and draw conclusions. This is not merely a verbal explanation of breathing. It mainly develops exploratory learning and basic scientific process skills like observation and inference, which is a major objective of EVS.

84. Learning outcomes tell clearly what a child is expected to know, understand, and be able to do after learning. At district, state, and national levels, they help teachers, parents, administrators, and policymakers understand children's progress and monitor the quality of education. Therefore, Learning Outcomes is the most appropriate assessment-related criterion here.

85. The assertion is correct because folk tales, songs, jokes, art, and other cultural resources enrich a child's language, imagination, and knowledge. The reason is also correct because a child's local environment includes not only the physical surroundings but also the social and cultural environment. Since these cultural resources come from that socio-cultural environment, the reason correctly explains why they are important for learning.

86. The assertion is correct because the nucleus is the distinct, generally spherical, centrally placed structure in a cell. The reason is also correct because the cytoplasm is the jelly-like substance surrounding the nucleus and other cell parts. However, this does not explain why that structure is called the nucleus. It only states its surrounding medium. Therefore, both are correct, but (R) is not the correct explanation of (A).

87. The assertion is correct because the history of a place often reflects the influence of migration, trade, geography, religion, and contact with different communities, which shape its culture and way of life. The reason is also correct. Regions such as Ladakh and Kerala became culturally diverse because of their own distinct historical experiences and interactions. Thus, the reason directly explains how different cultural influences shape regional life and culture.

88. The assertion is correct because worker bees collect nectar, build and maintain the hive, and perform most of the essential tasks of the colony. Without worker bees, the beehive cannot function properly and nectar collection would not take place. The reason is false because male bees, called drones, do not act as workers. Their role is mainly reproductive, not hive maintenance or nectar collection.

89. Time from 30 April 17:00 to 01 May 20:00

$$= 24 \text{ hours} + 3 \text{ hours} = 27 \text{ hours}$$

$$\text{Average speed} = \frac{1701}{27} = 63 \text{ km/h}$$

Hence, the correct option is 2 (63 km/h).

90. The assertion is correct because children learn most meaningfully from familiar local objects and experiences available in their immediate surroundings. The reason is also correct because when children observe and think about the living world around the school, they become more aware of environmental issues and develop interest in them. This clearly explains why local objects and surroundings should be given primacy in the classroom.

91. The passage clearly states that Tarawati's husband scolded her because she did not treat Roopa properly and did not value her as much as a son. He emphasized that daughters also deserve equal love, care, and education.

92. Tarawati shows mixed feelings toward Roopa. Initially, she was not supportive of her education, but later, recalling her husband's words, she becomes emotional and concerned. This reflects conflicting emotions, hence ambivalent.

93. The passage highlights discrimination between sons and daughters, especially in terms of education and care. It clearly focuses on gender bias within the family.

94. The word "holler" means to call out loudly or shout, which matches the context where Tarawati is loudly calling Rcopa.

95. The phrase "at sixes and sevens" means things are scattered or not organized properly, indicating disorder.

96. "Admonition" means a warning or scolding. The opposite of this is praise, which means expressing approval or admiration.

97. The passage explicitly mentions that Roopa had to sit for her home science examination the next day.

98. The husband says Tarawati is not educated herself and that is why she does not want Roopa to be educated. This indicates lack of awareness about the importance of education.

99. The phrase "to broker" is an infinitive form of a verb, where "broker" means to arrange or mediate peace. Hence, it functions as a verb.

100. The "god of rain" is described as turning away his face, which gives human qualities to a non-human entity. This is a clear example of personification.

101. The phrase "poverty line receded further" suggests that instead of improving, the condition of people is worsening. The line is moving away, indicating deeper poverty.

102. Comparing the village to a graveyard implies death and emptiness. It suggests that many people are dying due to severe conditions like hunger and drought.

103. The poem clearly states "wherever there is hunger, there Kalahandi is," indicating that Kalahandi symbolizes hunger and deprivation.

104. The absence of rain, dry land, no green leaves, and failed plans all point towards drought as the natural calamity being described.

105. The imagery of hunger, death, dryness, and suffering creates a deeply sad and tragic atmosphere, making sorrow the dominant mood.

106. Learning becomes meaningful when it is connected to children's real-life experiences and contexts. This is possible because teaching builds upon what children already know. Their previous understanding forms the base, making new learning relevant and relatable. Thus, the reason directly explains the assertion.

107. Language learning is a process of meaning-making and communication, and it develops gradually with exposure and use. While grammar supports accuracy, it is not essential in the initial stages of language acquisition. Children can learn language effectively through interaction even without formal grammar instruction.

108. To assess functional language use in real-life situations like buying goods, students should actively produce language. Writing a dialogue allows them to demonstrate practical communication skills such as asking, responding, and negotiating in a shop context.

109. When a teacher identifies specific learning difficulties and provides additional targeted support to help students overcome them, it is called remedial teaching. It focuses on addressing gaps and improving understanding in particular areas.

110. Reading involves skills like understanding meaning, identifying key words, and locating information. Spelling is related to writing rather than reading comprehension. Therefore, it is not considered a sub-skill of reading.

111. A portfolio is indeed a purposeful and organized collection of a student's work that reflects progress and learning. It is designed not just for storage but to help learners reflect on their performance. Since portfolios enable students to evaluate their strengths and weaknesses, the reason explains why such purposeful collection is important.

112. Graded readers are specially designed texts where language is simplified according to learners' levels while still being based on authentic contexts. They help students gradually build vocabulary and comprehension skills.

113. By giving a questionnaire to understand students' learning styles and preferences, the teacher is diagnosing their needs, strengths, and difficulties. This helps in planning suitable teaching strategies.

114. Allowing children to scribble, draw, and write freely helps them explore written expression naturally. It supports early stages of literacy where children begin to understand that writing conveys meaning, even before formal alphabet learning.

115. Pictures in books are mainly used to support understanding, maintain interest, and present content meaningfully. While drawing can be encouraged separately, providing pictures is not primarily meant to give students an opportunity to copy or draw them, making this statement incorrect.

116. Young children think mostly in concrete terms and learn better through direct experiences, objects, and real-life situations. Abstract ideas require higher cognitive development, which is still developing at early stages, so they find such concepts difficult to grasp.

117. Encouraging questions, group and pair work, and peer interaction through dialogues all promote meaningful classroom interaction. Option (c) focuses more on individual response rather than interaction, so it does not strongly support interactive learning.

118. Cognitive theory (Piaget) suggests that language development is closely linked with cognitive development. A child first develops understanding of concepts and then expresses them through language, meaning thought precedes language.

119. Language plays a key role in expressing culture and identity. The reason explains that cultural awareness helps children develop belongingness and appreciation of diversity, which directly shows why language is important in this process.

120. Textbooks should include authentic materials because they expose learners to real-life use of language. Natural language helps learners understand how language is actually used in meaningful contexts rather than artificially simplified forms.

121. गद्यांश में स्पष्ट कहा गया है कि प्रत्येक व्यक्ति का जीवन एक सतत संघर्ष है और वह किसी न किसी रूप में नेतृत्व या सत्ता प्राप्त करना चाहता है। इसलिए संघर्ष और नेतृत्व करना जीवन का सत्य बताया गया है।

122. गद्यांश में कहा गया है कि जो अकेला व्यक्ति है, वह भी अपने शरीर का राजा बनना चाहता है। इसलिए सही उत्तर 'व्यक्ति' है।

123. गद्यांश में बार-बार यह बताया गया है कि व्यक्ति अपनी सीमाओं और भूमिका का विस्तार करना चाहता है, चाहे वह परिवार में हो या समाज में।

124. मुख्यमंत्री, सांसद और राजा सभी पद या व्यक्ति को दर्शाते हैं, जबकि 'संघर्ष' एक क्रिया/अवस्था को दर्शाता है। इसलिए यह समूह से भिन्न है।

125. 'इक' प्रत्यय से बनने वाले शब्दों में सामान्यतः धातु या संज्ञा में ध्वनि-परिवर्तन होकर विशेषण बनता है, जैसे—प्रकृति → प्राकृतिक, परिवार → पारिवारिक, व्यवहार → व्यावहारिक। परंतु 'जीवन' में 'इक' प्रत्यय जोड़ने पर कोई मान्य और प्रचलित शब्द नहीं बनता (जैसे 'जीवनिक' मान्य नहीं है)। इसलिए सही उत्तर 'जीवन' है।

126. गद्यांश की पहली पंक्ति में ही कहा गया है कि प्रत्येक व्यक्ति का जन्म राजा बनने के लिए हुआ है।

127. पूरे गद्यांश में यह स्पष्ट है कि व्यक्ति का जीवन सत्ता प्राप्त करने के लिए संघर्ष है, चाहे वह किसी भी स्तर पर हो।

128. 'लीडर' शब्द अंग्रेजी भाषा से आया हुआ है, इसलिए यह आगत (विदेशी मूल का) शब्द है।

129. यह वाक्य भाषाओं के संदर्भ में कहा गया है, जहाँ लेखक यह बताना चाहता है कि जैसे हमें अपनी मातृभाषा (हिंदी) प्रिय है, वैसे ही अन्य लोगों को अपनी-अपनी मातृभाषाएँ प्रिय होती हैं।

130. हिंदी को राजभाषा कहा गया है, जिसका अर्थ है कि यह सरकारी कार्यों में प्रयुक्त होती है, इसलिए उसका सम्मान महत्वपूर्ण है।

131. यह वाक्य बताता है कि अलग-अलग भाषाएँ और संस्कृतियाँ होने के बावजूद हम एक राष्ट्र के रूप में जुड़े हुए हैं।

132. 'स्थानीय' शब्द की व्युत्पत्ति है—स्थान + ईय = स्थानीय। यहाँ 'ईय' प्रत्यय जुड़कर विशेषण बनाता है, जिसका अर्थ है 'स्थान से संबंधित'। इसलिए सही उत्तर 'ईय' है।

133. गद्यांश की शुरुआत में ही कहा गया है कि हिंदी बनाम स्थानीय/क्षेत्रीय भाषाओं को लेकर शोर मचा है।

134. गद्यांश में पंजाबी, कन्नड़, तमिल, मलयालम, तेलुगु आदि भाषाओं का उल्लेख है, लेकिन मैथिली का उल्लेख नहीं है।

135. 'अनेकता' एक भाववाचक संज्ञा है, जो विविधता या भिन्नता की स्थिति को दर्शाती है।

136. जोड़ों में कार्य (pair work) का मुख्य उद्देश्य विद्यार्थियों को सहयोगात्मक और स्वतंत्र रूप से सीखने के लिए प्रेरित करना होता है। इसमें वे शिक्षक पर निर्भर हुए बिना एक-दूसरे के साथ विचार साझा करते हुए कार्य करते हैं।

137. पूरक पठन सामग्री का उद्देश्य बच्चों में पढ़ने की रुचि विकसित करना और उन्हें अधिक से अधिक पढ़ने के अवसर देना है। यह विस्तृत पठन को बढ़ावा देता है, न कि केवल गहन अध्ययन को।

138. उपचारात्मक शिक्षण वास्तव में शिक्षण-अधिगम प्रक्रिया का महत्वपूर्ण भाग है, क्योंकि इसका उद्देश्य विद्यार्थियों की अधिगम-संबंधी कठिनाइयों, त्रुटियों और कमियों की पहचान करके उन्हें दूर करना होता है। इसलिए अभिकथन सही है। परन्तु कारण गलत है, क्योंकि उपचारात्मक शिक्षण केवल सामान्य पुनः शिक्षण नहीं है। यह विशेष रूप से इस दृष्टि से किया जाता है कि पिछले शिक्षण में जो सही ढंग से नहीं सीखा गया, उसे उपयुक्त विधि से सुधारा जाए। इसलिए सही उत्तर विकल्प 2 है।

139. जब विद्यार्थी कहानी को अपने शब्दों में दोबारा बताते हैं, तो यह उनकी समझ (comprehension) को दर्शाता है। यह बताता है कि उन्होंने कहानी का अर्थ कितना समझा है।

140. यह गलत धारणा है क्योंकि भाषा अधिगम में पहले सुनना और बोलना विकसित होता है, फिर पढ़ना और लिखना। संप्रेषणात्मक दृष्टिकोण में बोलने को प्राथमिकता दी जाती है, न कि केवल लिखने को।

141. भाषा अध्यापक का सबसे महत्वपूर्ण उत्तरदायित्व यह समझना है कि शिक्षार्थियों को भाषा किस प्रयोजन से चाहिए, वे किन परिस्थितियों में उसका प्रयोग करेंगे, और उन्हें किस प्रकार की भाषिक सहायता की आवश्यकता है। जब अध्यापक उनकी सम्प्रेषणात्मक आवश्यकताओं को पहचानता है, तभी वह उपयुक्त गतिविधियाँ, सामग्री और अवसर दे पाता है। अन्य कार्य भी महत्त्वपूर्ण हैं, पर भाषा-शिक्षण का मूल केन्द्र प्रभावी संप्रेषण ही है।

142. बुनियादी चरण में बच्चे अपनी घर की भाषा या परिचित भाषा में सबसे अधिक सहज महसूस करते हैं। इसी भाषा में वे अनुभव, भावनाएँ और विचार अधिक स्वाभाविक रूप से व्यक्त कर पाते हैं। इसलिए प्रारंभिक अधिगम घर की भाषा में अधिक प्रभावी, अर्थपूर्ण और बाल-केंद्रित होता है।

143. कहानी सुनाने का मुख्य उद्देश्य भाषा-विकास, कल्पनाशक्ति, शब्द-संपदा, वाक्य-संरचना और समझ का विकास करना है। यद्यपि कहानियों से कभी-कभी मूल्यबोध भी मिल सकता है, पर यह मान लेना कि उनका प्रमुख कार्य बच्चों को जीवन में अनुसरण करने योग्य नैतिक मूल्य सिखाना है, भाषा-शिक्षण के संदर्भ में उचित नहीं है। इसलिए यही कथन गलत है।

144. मिश्रित योग्यता वाले समूह में अलग-अलग स्तर के विद्यार्थी साथ काम करते हैं। इससे जो विद्यार्थी किसी कौशल में आगे हैं, वे दूसरों की सहायता कर सकते हैं, और जो अपेक्षाकृत कम सक्षम हैं, वे साथियों से सीख सकते हैं। इस प्रकार सहयोगात्मक अधिगम, सहभागिता और पारस्परिक समर्थन को बढ़ावा मिलता है।

145. छोटे बच्चों में भाषा ग्रहण करने की क्षमता बहुत अधिक होती है। प्रारंभिक आयु में उन्हें विभिन्न मौखिक भाषाओं को सुनने, समझने और बोलने के अवसर मिलें, तो उनकी भाषिक संवेदनशीलता, अभिव्यक्ति और बहुभाषिक क्षमता का विकास बेहतर होता है। लिखित भाषाओं की तुलना में मौखिक भाषा का अनुभव इस अवस्था में अधिक स्वाभाविक और उपयुक्त होता है।

146. उद्गामी साक्षरता में बच्चे प्रारंभ में चित्र बनाकर अपने विचार व्यक्त करते हैं, जिसे लेखन की शुरुआत माना जाता है। चित्र वास्तव में संकेतों का कार्य करते हैं जिनमें अर्थ निहित होता है। इसलिए कारण स्पष्ट रूप से बताता है कि चित्राकारी को लेखन की प्रारंभिक अवस्था क्यों माना जाता है।

147. मिनिमल पेयर (जैसे ship-sheep, bat-pat) के माध्यम से ड्रिल करवाने से ध्वनियों के सूक्ष्म अंतर को समझने और सही उच्चारण विकसित करने में सहायता मिलती है। इसलिए यह उच्चारण सुधारने की प्रभावी युक्ति है।

148. व्यवहारवादी सिद्धांत भाषा अधिगम को अनुकरण, पुनरावृत्ति, प्रयास-त्रुटि और प्रोत्साहन पर आधारित मानता है। "सामाजिक अन्तःक्रियाएँ" वाइगोत्स्की के सामाजिक-सांस्कृतिक दृष्टिकोण से संबंधित है, न कि व्यवहारवाद से।

149. अध्यापिका कक्षा में घूमकर विद्यार्थियों की सहायता कर रही है, उनके प्रश्नों का उत्तर दे रही है और नए शब्दों में मदद कर रही है। यहाँ वह एक सहायक या संसाधन व्यक्ति (facilitator/resource person) की भूमिका निभा रही है।

150. पठन केवल शब्दों का सही उच्चारण नहीं है, बल्कि अर्थ ग्रहण करना भी है, इसलिए (A) सही है। (R) भी आंशिक रूप से सही है कि पठन में डिकोडिंग शामिल है, लेकिन पठन केवल डिकोडिंग तक सीमित नहीं है, इसलिए (R), (A) की पूर्ण व्याख्या नहीं करता।

YOUR SPACE

Previous Years' Paper

Central Teacher Eligibility Test (CTET)

Paper-I (For Class I-V Teachers), December-2024

(Exam held on 14-12-2024)

PART-I : CHILD DEVELOPMENT AND PEDAGOGY

1. Mastery Oriented learners typically attribute success to ______ and failure to ______ .
A. ability and good luck; task difficulty
B. ability and effort; bad luck
C. ability and good luck; low ability
D. ability and effort; insufficient effort

2. Which of the following statement represents 'Proximodistal' principle of development?
A. Development is multidirectional and multidimensional.
B. Identical twins living in different cultures can develop at different rates.
C. Children develop ability to grasp the ball before putting beads in thread.
D. Children develop ability to sit up before standing.

3. According to Vygotsky children speak to themselves:
A. To aid thought and for self-regulation.
B. To provide self-reinforcement when adults are ignoring them.
C. Because they are egocentrc.
D. Because their thought is illogical.

4. Challenges in social communication are evident in:
A. Attention deficit hyperactivity disorder
B. Cerebral palsy
C. Austism Spectrum Disorder
D. Learning Disabilities

5. According to Vyogotsky's theory of learning and development, which of the following is an example of scaffolding?
A. Breaking a task down into smaller steps and providing support as needed.
B. Providing a student with a grade for their work as motivation.
C. Providing a student with a reading assignment and asking them to answer questions independently.
D. Demonstrating a skill to a student and then having them master it on their own.

6. Dysgraphia is characterised by:
A. Delayed motor skills
B. Difficulties in writing
C. Lack of reading fluency
D. Repetitive behavioural patterns

7. In order to help students to become good problem solvers, a teacher should emphasize on the practice of:
A. focusing on information that confirms existing beliefs and preconceptions.
B. approaching problems in a particular fixed fashion.
C. breaking large complex problems into smaller manageable problems.
D. centering only on one particular piece of information related to problem.

8. **Assertion (A):** Teachers should use multisensory materials to cater to needs of students in an inclusive classroom.
Reason (R): Inclusive classrooms should adopt standardization of curricular materials as well as assessment strategies.
Choose the **correct** option:
A. (A) is true, but (R) is false.
B. Both (A) and (R) are false.
C. Both (A) and (R) are true and (R) is the correct explanation of (A).
D. Both (A) and (R) are true, but (R) is not the correct explanation of (A).

9. In the constructivist view:
A. Individuals are passively influenced by enviornmental events.
B. Individuals are conditioned to learn new behaviours.
C. Learning is extending and transforming the current understanding.
D. Learning is simply writing associations on the blank slates of our brains.

1. D **2.** C **3.** A **4.** C **5.** A **6.** B **7.** C **8.** A **9.** C

10. **Assertion (A):** Effective teachers familiarize themselves with daily lives and socio-cultural backgrounds of learners.

Reason (R): Learning takes place in a social context.

Choose the **correct** option:

A. (A) is true, but (R) is false.
B. Both (A) and (R) are false.
C. Both (A) and (R) are true and (R) is the correct explanation of (A).
D. Both (A) and (R) are true, but (R) is not the correct explanation of (A).

11. Meaningful learning is primarily NOT about:

A. memorizing information
B. understanding the concept
C. constructing knowledge
D. developing skills

12. **Assertion (A):** Teacher should encourage boys of her class to participate in sports while assigning art decoration to girls.

Reason (R): Children acquire gender roles primarily because of the underlying biological differences.

Choose the **correct** option:

A. (A) is true, but (R) is false.
B. Both (A) and (R) are false.
C. Both (A) and (R) are true and (R) is the correct explanation of (A).
D. Both (A) and (R) are true, but (R) is not the correct explanation of (A).

13. Kinesthetic learners prefer to learn through ....

A. seeing B. touching
C. doing and moving D. listening

14. According to Howard Gardner while a scientist would exhibit high .... Intelligence, a sculptor would have high .... Intelligence.

A. Naturalistic; Spatial
B. Transductive; Spatial
C. Logical-mathematical; Bodily Kinesthetic
D. Spatial; Bodily Kinesthetic

15. Inclusion needs to be promoted through:

(*i*) Flexible curriculum
(*ii*) Cooperative learning
(*iii*) Segregation and labelling
(*iv*) Accessibility of building

A. (*ii*), (*iii*), (*iv*) B. (*i*), (*ii*), (*iii*), (*iv*)
C. (*i*), (*ii*), (*iii*) D. (*i*), (*ii*), (*iv*)

16. Children learn better if they experience:

A. Low level of alertness during activity
B. Moderate level of excitement to learn
C. High degree of anxiety to perform
D. Learned helplessness

17. **Assertion (A):** Children below the ages of 5-6 years should not be pressurized to write 'properly' and 'within the lines'.

Reason (R): Children gain a control of finer motor skills from 5-6 years onwards.

Choose the **correct** option:

A. (A) is true, but (R) is false.
B. Both (A) and (R) are false.
C. Both (A) and (R) are true and (R) is the correct explanation of (A).
D. Both (A) and (R) are true, but (R) is not the correct explanation of (A).

18. Children often come up with their own explanations of events around them. On being probed as to why does it rain Sia says, "God was tired of carrying the buckets of water on his shoulders". Such explanations:

A. Depict that children have an egocentric view and cannot consider other's viewpoint.
B. Illustrate that children are not capable of any reasoning.
C. Prove that children's thinking is much lesser than adults quantitively.
D. Indicate that children have naive understanding rooted in their cultural context with which they try to understand events.

19. Piaget described cognitive development as occuring in:

A. A continuous continuum
B. Four overlapping culture specific stages
C. Four qualitatively different stages
D. Three progressive levels

20. During play time at school, Rishab, a 7-year—old boy picked a doll to play with. Some of his peers made fun of him for his choice of toy. As a teacher who wants his students to grow up with gender role flexibility, which of the following would be the best response to the situation by the teacher?

A. Talk to Rishabh that dolls are suitable for girls and boys should not play with dolls.
B. Tell Rishabh that he should play with something else because his friends won't approve of him playing with doll.
C. Let Rishabh play with doll and tell other children that they can also choose any toy of their choice.
D. Quitely take away the doll and give a car toy to Rishabh without saying anything.

10. C **11.** A **12.** B **13.** C **14.** C **15.** D **16.** B **17.** C **18.** D **19.** C **20.** C

21. In developmental terms, a time frame where an individual upholds an amplified sensitivity to particular incentives for developing particular skills to function in an efficient manner is referred to as .... of development.

A. Incentive period
B. Stimulus period
C. Critical period
D. Encoding period

22. In order to cater to needs of students struggling with Attention Deficit Hyperactivity Disorder teachers should avoid:

A. Creating distractions and making noises
B. Flexibility in curricular materials and instructions
C. Breaking the task into small easily manageable parts
D. Using multi-sensory materials

23. Lawrence Kohlberg argued that:

A. moral development in children occurs in a continuous manner.
B. there are cultural differences in moral reasoning of children.
C. moral development occurs progressively in stages.
D. there are gender differences in moral reasoning of children.

24. At which level of Kohlberg's moral development does individual's ethical behaviour mainly depends on the mindset that "What do people think of me"?

A. Post-conventional
B. Non-conventional
C. Pre-conventional
D. Conventional

25. According to Jean Piaget a child who is unable to understand the logic behind simple mathematical reversals such as $4 + 5 = 9$ so $9 - 5 = 4$, it is because of:

A. animistic thinking
B. irreversibility
C. egocentrism
D. perceptual centration

26. **Assertion (A):** Teachers should distance themselves from students and place primary responsibility for learning on them only.

Reason (R): Learning takes place affectively in an authoritative rather than a democratic environment.

Choose the **correct** option:

A. (A) is true, but (R) is false.
B. Both (A) and (R) are false.
C. Both (A) and (R) are true and (R) is the correct explanation of (A).
D. Both (A) and (R) are true, but (R) is not the correct explanation of (A).

27. **Assertion (A):** Scaffolding provided by the teachers hinders the learning process of children.

Reason (R): Lev Vygotsky proposed that children learn independently by acting upon and manipulating the environment.

Choose the **correct** option:

A. (A) is true, but (R) is false.
B. Both (A) and (R) are false.
C. Both (A) and (R) are true and (R) is the correct explanation of (A).
D. Both (A) and (R) are true, but (R) is not the correct explanation of (A).

28. Which of the following correctly describes extrinsic motivation?

A. Motivation that comes from environmental consequences.
B. Motivation that comes from a sense of personal satisfaction.
C. Motivation that comes from personal enjoyment of the task.
D. Motivation that comes from internal factors.

29. Two important cognitive development milestones of sensorimotor stage of Piaget's theory of cognitive development are:

A. Animism and Transformation
B. Classification and seriation
C. Object permanence and deferred limitation
D. Reversibility of thought and hypothetic-deductive reasoning

30. Children:

A. Are born unruly and need to be socialized.
B. Come into this world with genetic codes that determine their destiny.
C. Are greatly influenced by the social cultural context they grow up in.
D. Come into this world as *tabula rasa* or blank slate.

21. C	**22.** A	**23.** C	**24.** D	**25.** B	**26.** B	**27.** B	**28.** A	**29.** C	**30.** C

PART-II : MATHEMATICS

31. What is the result when 7 kg 7 g is subtracted from 9 kg?
A. 1.93 kg B. 1.093 kg
C. 1.3 kg D. 1.993 kg

32. In class III, 150 children were asked to name their one favourite fruit and results for 5 favourite fruits were written in the form of the following table:

Name of the Fruit	Number of Children
Apple	28
Guava	26
Mangoes	44
Banana	14
Grapes	28

Choose the **correct** option:
A. Equal number of children have Apple and Guava as their favourite fruit.
B. The difference between the number of childrens who like grapes and those who like bananas is 16.
C. The number of children who like Mangoes and Banana is two times the number of children who like Guava.
D. Ten children do not like any fruit given in the table.

33. Which of the following is least appropriate about Formative Assessment in mathematics classrooms?
A. It helps to identify students' misconceptions
B. It provides cumulative evaluations that helps to rank children
C. To check the progress of students during instructional activities
D. To identify students' conceptual understanding

34. A person withdrew ₹ 4,560 from his bank account on 4th of a month and deposited ₹ 2,567 on 20th of the same month. If at the end of the month, balance is ₹ 3,125, then money (in ₹) at the start of the month in his account was:
A. 5,128 B. 5,118
C. 4,998 D. 5,213

35. A primary class mathematics teacher gave his students the following problem to solve:
"How many classes of 28 pupils would be needed for a school of 616 pupils?"
One of the student solved the problem in the following way:

1 Class = 28 Pupils
$10 \rightarrow 280$
$10 \rightarrow 280$
560
$2 \rightarrow 56 \rightarrow 10 + 10 + 2 = 22$ Classes
616

Which of the following is most appropriate for the algorithm used by the student?
A. The student has used both the distributive and associative laws of division to solve the problem.
B. The student has used an incorrect algorithm to solve the problem.
C. The student has used the associative law of division across addition to solve the problem.
D. The student has used the distributive law of division across addition to solve the problem.

36. A triangle having all sides of different lengths is called:
A. A scalene triangle
B. A right triangle
C. An equilateral triangle
D. An isosceles triangle

37. The sum of the prime numbers between 31 and 60 is:
A. 280 B. 311
C. 221 D. 227

38. The product of the predecessor of 201 and the successor of 4781 is:
A. 965560 B. 965650
C. 956200 D. 956400

39. What is the most appropriate cognitive skill that help students to recognize and group shapes according to their attributes and properties?
A. Conservation B. Decomposition
C. Classification D. Seriation

40. Students feel difficulty in solving division problems because:
A. Division problems have no utility in daily life.
B. There are no informal ways of solving division problems.
C. For solving division problems students need to know addition, subtraction and multiplication thoroughly.
D. Students do not like the sign of division.

31. D	32. D	33. B	34. B	35. D	36. A	37. A	38. D	39. C	40. C

41. Most II graders are able to add two quantities like four candies and three candies, but when asked to do 4 + 5 on a worksheet a large number of the same set of learners is unable to do so. What is the most appropriate explanation of this observation according to National Curriculum Framework 2005?

A. Learners are not interested in learning real-life mathematics
B. The learners are not ready for the use of abstract mathematical symbols
C. Learners are not taught addition properly
D. Some learners are poor in mathematical skills

42. A 3rd standard student, when asked to write one hundred and five in numeral form, s/he writes it as '1005'. This indicates that:

A. s/he needs more help in understanding the concept of place value
B. s/he is unfit to learn mathematics
C. The student is a slow learner
D. s/he is mischievous

43. Which of the following statements is NOT true with respect to the concept of Fractions?

A. It represents a part of a collection of same objects
B. The mathematical notation of a fraction can be represented as a ratio
C. It represents a part of a whole which is greater than 1
D. The mathematical notation of a fraction can be represented as a division problem

44. Radha walks 3 km 725 m per day on Monday, Wednesday and Friday, whereas she walks 2 km 9 m per day on Tuesday and Thursday. Total distance covered by her from Monday to Friday is:

A. 15.355 km B. 15.193 km
C. 16.975 km D. 16.202 km

45. Jasmine said, "A rectangle has two pairs of opposite sides parallel; a square also has two pairs of opposite sides parallel and so does a parallelogram. So, both rectangle and square are also parallelograms."

Jasmine is at .... stage of Van Hieles theory of geometric thinking.

A. Formal Deduction B. Visualization
C. Analysis D. Relationships

46. The sum of the greatest and smallest six digit numbers that can be formed from the digits 5, 9, 0, 2, 8 and 6 (without repetition) is:

A. 1192290 B. 1192209
C. 1292290 D. 1292209

47. The missing numbers in the pattern 12, 14, 17, 13, 8, 14, 21, ... are respectively:

A. 14, 5 B. 13, 4
C. 15, 7 D. 12, 3

48. The smallest four-digit number which is a multiple of 6, 7 and 4 is:

A. 1006 B. 1008
C. 1000 D. 1002

49. Which of the following has a definite length?

A. a ray B. a plane
C. a line D. a line segment

50. Which of the following is most appropriate for including open ended questions in mathematics class?

A. These questions develop critical thinking in students
B. Answers to these questions are not given in the book
C. These questions take more time to solve
D. These questions are not easy to copy from each other

51. Which of the following statements are true with respect to 'Data handling'?

A. A line graph is used to show comparison among categories of data.
B. A histogram is used to compare the parts of a whole.
C. A graphical representation of data is easier to understand when there is a trend or comparison to be shown.
D. A bar graph displays data that changes continuously over period of time.

52. How many planks of size 2 m × 35 cm × 8 cm can be made from a wooden block 8 m long, 70 cm wide and 40 cm thick?

A. 45 B. 40
C. 50 D. 48

53. A child solved a problem: $\frac{1}{2}+\frac{1}{3}=\frac{2}{5}$. What is the most appropriate inference drawn from the solution?

A. Child does not know how to represent fractions on number line
B. Child has extended the concept of addition of natural numbers to addition of fractions
C. Child does not know addition of numbers
D. Child does not know how to take L.C.M.

41. B	**42.** A	**43.** C	**44.** B	**45.** D	**46.** B	**47.** B
48. B	**49.** D	**50.** A	**51.** C	**52.** B	**53.** B	

54. According to National Education Policy 2020 Mathematics and Computational Thinking is to be given increased importance as:

A. It is foundational to evolving technologies like Artificial Intelligence (AI), machine learning and Data Science etc.

B. It can be a substitute for a teacher

C. It is the most difficult aspect of learning in school

D. It is foundational to human survival

55. According to National Curriculum Framework 2005 mathematics teachers need to shift towards:

(*a*) Promoting memorization and rigorous algorithms

(*b*) Mathematical reasoning and logic

(*c*) Becoming sole authority for right answers

Choose the **correct** options:

A. Only (*b*) B. (*b*) and (*c*)

C. Only (*a*) D. (*a*) and (*b*)

56. Which one of the following is the most effective way to introduce the concept of area to fourth graders?

A. Formula based method

B. Approximation and Estimation

C. Tessellations

D. Abacus

57. The value of $\frac{4}{7}+\frac{5}{14}-\frac{7}{8}$ is:

A. $\frac{3}{56}$ B. $\frac{5}{56}$

C. $\frac{3}{14}$ D. $\frac{5}{28}$

58. Which of the following letters has two lines of symmetry?

A. E B. U

C. H D. B

59. Which of the following is NOT related to Indian Mathematics?

A. Surya Siddhant

B. Baudhayan Sulba Sutra

C. Lilavati

D. Charak Samhita

60. The difference of the place values of 5 and 7 in the number 352876 is:

A. 49997

B. 50007

C. 49930

D. 49993

PART-III : ENVIRONMENTAL STUDIES

61. Read the Assertion and Reason properly.

Assertion: An elephant herd has only female and baby elephants.

Reason: Male elephants leave their herd after 14-15 years and move around alone.

Choose the **correct** answer from the following:

A. Assertion is true, but Reason is false

B. Assertion is false, but Reason is true

C. Both Assertion and Reason are true and Reason is the correct explanation of Assertion

D. Both Assertion and Reason are true, but Reason is not the correct explanation of Assertion.

62. Chapter 4 "Mangoes Round the Year" of NCERT Environmental Studies textbook has a story on making mango papad so that children not only understand the process and technique, but also appreciate the skills of cooking and preservation. As per NCF 2005, which general objective of teaching EVS is being achieved through this lesson?

A. To explain how much labour is neeed to make an object.

B. To discuss how various things can be made from the natural environment.

C. To develop understanding with the help of observation and examples related to our experiences in place of abstraction.

D. To develop an understanding of how Aam papad is made.

63. Mohan is a class V teacher of Environmental Studies. He writes the following activity on the blackboard in his class. "Find out about the availability of water at the time of your parents and grandparents and compare it with the current situation." For the above activity, which of the following strategies would be most appropriate?

A. Role Play

B. Project

C. Discussion

D. Interview

54. A **55.** A **56.** C **57.** A **58.** C **59.** D **60.** C **61.** C **62.** C **63.** B

64. Archana is a teacher of Environmental Studies teaching class IV. She forms two groups of children in her class and conducts a debate activity on the topic "Should the school have uniforms or not". Why did Archana organize a debate in her class? Which of the following may not be the most appropriate reason?
(*a*) Debate gives children an opportunity to think about and understand different aspects of a topic.
(*b*) Children are encouraged to express their views in the classroom.
(*c*) Children get an opportunity to share their experiences in the classroom.
(*d*) Children assess the knowledge of their peers through debate.
A. (*a*), (*c*) and (*d*) B. (*b*) and (*d*)
C. (*b*), (*c*) and (*d*) D. (*a*), (*b*) and (*c*)

65. Child describes different skilled work related to farming and their inheritance (from elders) in daily life.

The above statement is:
A. Learning indicator
B. Learning objective
C. Statement of competency
D. Learning outcome

66. The state/union territory having coast on the Bay of Bengal is:
A. Karnataka B. Kerala
C. Telangana D. Andhra Pradesh

67. Lesson 13 in NCERT's Class V Environmental Studies textbook describes the amazing journey of "Gaurav Jani". This lesson is a part of which of the following themes?
A. Interrelationship B. Work and Play
C. Family and Friends D. Shelter

68. In a constructivist EVS classroom, which of the following is NOT seen to be happening?
A. Children are just solving familiar problems.
B. Children are using their experiences to make new connections between concepts.
C. Children are learning by doing activities with concrete objects.
D. Children's experiences are being respected.

69. Siddhi is a teacher of class 4. She takes all the children of her class to the playground to play Kabaddi, while teaching them lesson 10 "Hu tu tu, hu tu tu" of the NCERT Environmental Studies textbook. Before playing the game, she also explains the rules of this game to all the children. Why does the teacher tell the children the rules before playing this game? Which of the following may be the most appropriate reason?
(*a*) She wants to draw the attention of the children that in life like in sports, we make rules.
(*b*) So that all the work is done properly.
(*c*) We are all bound by the rules in the same way in the society by which we settle differences and conflicts among ourselves.
(*d*) By making rules, the attention of all children is much more on the rules than on the game.
A. (*c*) and (*d*) B. (*a*) and (*d*)
C. (*a*), (*b*) and (*c*) D. (*a*) and (*b*)

70. Read the following statements and choose the **correct** option.

Assertion (A): Biomass and Fossil Fuels are the two main conventional sources of energy.

Reason (R): Conventional sources are those which are renewable in nature.
A. (A) is true, but (R) is false
B. (A) is false, but (R) is true
C. Both (A) and (R) are true
D. Both (A) and (R) are false

71. Consider the following statements A and B

Statement A: In 1969, Neil Armstrong was the first man to walk on the moon.

Statement B: In 2007, Kalpana Chawla set a new record for the longest space flight by a woman.

Select the **correct** code from the following:
A. A is correct, but B is wrong
B. A is wrong, but B is correct
C. A and B both are correct
D. A and B both are wrong

72. It has been observed that some mistakes are made while observing the learning and progress of children. These mistakes may be the result of our biases. Which of the following information should not be recorded as a bias?
A. Samples of the children's work in the portfolio.
B. Prior experiences regarding the ability and performance of the children.
C. Previous results related to the examination of any one subject and any area thereof.
D. Social background of the child.

64. *	**65.** D	**66.** D	**67.** D	**68.** A	**69.** C	**70.** A	**71.** A	**72.** A

73. Read the Assertion (A) and Reason (R) carefully.

Assertion (A): The goats from which the soft pashmina wool is collected are found on very high altitudes of 5000 meters in extreme cold.

Reason (R): A coat of warm hair grows on goats body which protects it from extreme cold.

Choose the **correct** option from the following:

A. (A) is true, but (R) is false.
B. (A) is false, but (R) is true.
C. Both (A) and (R) are true and (R) explains (A).
D. Both (A) and (R) are true, but (R) does not explain (A).

74. Read the statements I and II.

Statement I: Due to anaemia, children do not grow well, and their energy levels are low.

Statement II: Anaemia affects both, children's physical as well as mental health.

Choose the **correct** answer from the following:

A. I is true, but II is false
B. I is false, but II is true
C. Both I and II are true
D. Both I and II are false

75. Select the **correct** match from the following:

A. Lavani – Tamil Nadu
B. Bharatnatyam – Odhisa
C. Kathak – Karnataka
D. Bihu – Assam

76. Cows have Short front teeth and Large and flat side teeth for which one of the following?

A. Cutting grass and gnawing grass respectively
B. Gnawing grass and cutting grass respectively
C. Snipping grass and chewing grass respectively
D. Chewing grass and snipping grass respectively

77. What is the reason why tales and stories have been given an important place in the textbooks of Environmental Studies? Which of the following may be the most appropriate reason?

(*a*) At the primary level, the teachers of Environmental Studies narrate tales and stories with interest, that is why they have been given an important place.
(*b*) The use of stories has often been considered important in developing children's sensitivity to environmental issues.
(*c*) Because children easily relate themselves to the characters of the story, that is why they have been given an important place in the textbooks.
(*d*) Tales and stories are liked by the society, that is why they have been given an important place in the textbooks of the environment.

A. (*c*) and (*d*) B. (*a*) and (*b*)
C. (*a*) and (*d*) D. (*b*) and (*c*)

78. In the following question, Assertion and Reason are followed. Read the statements carefully and choose the **correct** option from the following:

Assertion: In the lessons of NCERT's Environmental Studies textbook, real incidents of common life, everyday problems and some burning problems related to today have been kept.

Reason: Children can debate openly on all these problems, be aware of the problems, be sensitive to them and make correct understanding.

A. Assertion is true, but Reason is false
B. Assertion is false, but Reason is true
C. Both Assertion and Reason are correct and Reason is the correct explanation of Assertion
D. Assertion and Reason are correct, but Reason is not the correct explanation of Assertion.

79. How much time 'boiled milk' takes for digestion in the stomach? Choose the **correct** answer from the following?

A. 4 hours B. 5 hours
C. 2 hours D. 3 hours

80. A person would not drown in the dead sea or a salty lake even if the person does not know how to swim. This is due to:

A. neither high nor low density of sea water
B volume of sea water
C. high density of sea water
D. low density of sea water

81. Which one of the following is a group consisting of elements only?

A. Steel, Iron, Zinc
B. Tin, Lithium, Sodium
C. Sodium, Brass, Potassium
D. Bronze, Copper, Aluminium

82. A teacher of Environmental Studies, while conducting an activity with some children, observes some important incidents and also makes a descriptive note of the same. Which of the following may be the tool of assessment?

A. Observation List B. Anecdotal Records
C. Rating Scale D. Portfolio

73. C **74.** C **75.** D **76.** C **77.** D **78.** C **79.** C **80.** C **81.** B **82.** B

83. Two Indian birds make nests which hang from the branches of trees or bushes. These two birds are:
A. Barbet and Sun-bird
B. Tailor bird and Indian Robin
C. Indian Robin and Weaver bird
D. Sun-bird and Tailor bird

84. Read the statements A and B carefully.

Statement A: During the cold season lizards go into a long and deep sleep.

Statement B: Some animals go into a long, deep sleep in certain seasons.

Choose the **correct** answer from the following:
A. 'A' is correct but 'B' is incorrect.
B. 'A' is incorrect but 'B' is correct.
C. Both 'A' and 'B' are correct and 'B' explains 'A'.
D. Both 'A' and 'B' are correct but 'B' does not explain 'A'.

85. A teacher in his environmental studies class, divides the children into groups and asks them to collect some objects present in the school. After that he sits with the children and asks them to distribute those objects into different groups. Children divide objects into different groups on the basis of their properties. What could be the most appropriate purpose for the teacher to conduct this activity?
A. Activity strengthens the cognitive domain to a greater extent than the other domains of learning in children.
B. The activity develops the child's understanding of all the concepts.
C. At the primary stage, children learn better by interacting with each other.
D. By doing the activity, children make very few mistakes in understanding the definition and facts.

86. Rakesh is a teacher of Environmental Studies of class V. He asks the children in his class to do an activity. In which, all children observe which "object floats in water and which sinks in water". After the activity some children ask the teacher why some objects sink in water and some objects float in water. What is the most appropriate thing a teacher should do in the following situation:
(*a*) The teacher should tell the children that this is happening because of the density.
(*b*) Give each child the freedom to observe, record their observations, and interpret those observations.
(*c*) Provide opportunity to each child to hypothesize, test and make activity based generalizations.
(*d*) Teacher should say that the main reason for this you will understand in your higher classes.
A. (*c*) and (*d*) B. (*a*) only
C. (*a*), (*b*) and (*c*) D. (*b*) and (*c*)

87. It is 10 A.M. now in India today, it is around noon of today in ....
A. Japan B. Singapore
C. London D. Karachi

88. In a child centered EVS classroom, which of the following activities would be LEAST likely to occur?
A. Children will also be seen sharing their experiences while discussing in the class.
B. Children will be seen in the classroom, listening to the teacher.
C. Children will be seen actively working in a variety of activities.
D. The seating arrangement will be seen to change according to the activity of the children.

89. A person boarded an express train on 30 January, 2023 at New Delhi for Bangalore. The train departed from New Delhi at 17:00 hours and reached Bangalore at 17:00 hours on 31st January 2023. If the distance between New Delhi and Bangalore by train route is nearly 1776 km. The average speed of the train during this Journey was:
A. 77.21 km/hr
B. 71.04 km/hr
C. 74 km/hr
D. 80.72 km/hr

90. In the following question, Assertion and Reason are followed. Read the statements carefully and choose the **correct** option from the following:

Assertion: The curriculum of Environmental Studies is theme-based and each theme is interrelated.

Reason: The main reason for keeping the syllabus of Environmental Studies theme-based is that it creates a deep understanding of each theme and each theme begins with questions.

Choose the **correct** answer from the following:
A. Assertion is true, but Reason is false
B. Assertion is false, but Reason is true
C. Both Assertion and Reason are correct and Reason is the correct explanation of Assertion
D. Both Assertion and Reason are correct, but Reason is not the correct explanation of Assertion.

83. D	**84.** C	**85.** C	**86.** D	**87.** B	**88.** B	**89.** C	**90.** C

PART-IV : LANGUAGE-I : ENGLISH

Directions (Qs. No. 91-99): *Read the passage given below and answer the questions that follow:*

Shreeram Lagoo was acting in a play staged at Ambernath's Gandhi School. We had managed to get the tickets for the play after much running around. We left the hosted quietly after eating dinner in the mess. The play started at 9.30 p.m. and it was already 9.15 p.m. Patil and I were rushing along the road to the station. Suddenly, we saw Upadhyayji coming from the opposite direction. He had seen us.

"Maharshi, where are you off to at this time?" he said reprovingly.

We looked at each other's face. Suddenly Patil spoke up, "Sir, I have a headache. We are going to the station to have some tea or coffee. We will be back right after drinking a cup."

"Why, don't you get tea and coffee in the mess"?

"We do, Sir, But today there wasn't any milk in the mess. That's why we are going to the station." Patil improvised.

Upadhyay said, "Come with me, I'll get you some coffee". He brought us to his home. The tickets for the play were squirrning in our pockets. We couldn't work out how to get him off our backs.

After seating us in the drawing room, he asked his wife to make the coffee and sat on the sofa across from us.

As soon as Mrs. Upadhyay entered the kitchen, I got up and said, "Ammaji, Warden Saheb is bothering you unnecessarily. I will make the coffee".

She was pleased to see me, "Maharshi, you go sit.... I will make it".

I went up to her and whispered, "Ammaji, both of us were going to the Gandhi School to see a play. Warden Saheb waylaid us and brought us here. See, here are the tickets, but he doesn't know anything".

Ammaji examined me from head to toe, "I see. Is it a good play?"

I said, "Ammaji, it is very good".

"Then why don't you go?" she said with a laugh.

"How can we go? Warden Saheb won't give us permission", I whispered.

She came into the drawing room. Listen, what kind of a warden are you? Why don't you let the children go and have some fun? Go, Maharshi, but don't be too late.

91. Mr. Upadhyay's professional role in the institution was that of ...
A. a teacher B. the hostel warden
C. an administrator D. the principal

92. 'We <u>had managed</u> ...' Identify the tense of the underlined expression.
A. Past Indefinite
B. Present Continuous
C. Present Perfect
D. Past Perfect

93. How did Mrs. Upadhyay receive the boys at home?
A. She received them coldly.
B. She was displeased with her husband for bringing them home.
C. She welcomed them.
D. She was unhappy to see them.

94. Which of the following statements is **True/False**?
(*a*) The boys had purchased the tickets in advance.
(*b*) Mrs. Upadhyay supported the boys in their endeavour.
A. (*a*) is True, but (*b*) is False.
B. (*b*) is True, but (*a*) is False.
C. Both (*a*) and (*b*) are True.
D. Both (*a*) and (*b*) are False.

95. Choose the expression similar in meaning to 'improvised' as used in the passage,
A. to make it up B. to declare
C. to tell the truth D. to shout

96. Why were the boys sneaking away from the hostel?
A. To have a stroll
B. To play football
C. To watch a movie
D. To see a play

97. Which of the following statements is **True/False**?
(*a*) Mr. Upadhyay met the boys inside the hostel.
(*b*) The boys were already getting late for the play.
A. (*a*) is True, but (*b*) is False.
B. (*b*) is True, but (*a*) is False.
C. Both (*a*) and (*b*) are False.
D. Both (*a*) and (*b*) are True.

91. B **92.** D **93.** C **94.** C **95.** A **96.** D **97.** B

98. What did Mr. Upadhyay do after hearing the boys?
A. He talked to them and walked away.
B. He took them home for coffee.
C. He did not react at all.
D. He allowed them to go.

99. 'The tickets for the play were squirming in our pockets.'
What literary device has been used in the underlined expression.
A. Personification
B. Simile
C. Alliteration
D. Oxymoron

Directions (Qs. No. 100-105): *Read the extract given below and answer the questions that follow:*

O what is that sound which so thrills the ear
Down in the valley drumming, drumming?
Only the scarlet soldiers, dear,
The soldiers coming.

O what is that light I see flashing so clear
Over the distance brightly, brightly?
Only the sun on their weapons, dear,
As they step lightly.

O what are they doing with all that gear,
What are they doing this morning, this morning?
Only the usual manoeuvres, dear,
Or perhaps a warning.

O why have they left the road down there,
Why are they suddenly wheeling, wheeling?
Perhaps a change in the orders, dear,
Why are you kneeling?

100. Where is the 'sound' coming from?
A. From a crowded street
B. From a group of commoners
C. From a contingent of soldiers
D. From a market place

101. The poem presents itself as a conversation ......
A. among three persons
B. in a crowd
C. among a group of people
D. between two persons

102. Which literary device has been used in the expression 'scarlet soldiers'?
A. simile
B. metonymy
C. alliteration
D. transferred epithet

103. The poem has been written in the form of ....
A. an elegy B. an epic
C. a ballad D. a lyric

104. Identify the rhyme scheme of these lines.
A. abcb B. abdc
C. baba D. abab

105. What emotional state does 'kneeling' reflect?
A. indifference B. anger
C. anxiety D. jubilation

106. Mother tongue based multilingualism advocates that ....
A. all children begin their schooling in English medium and in home language
B. all children study Hindi as their first language
C. all children begin their schooling in their mother tongue or home language
D. all children begin their schooling in the language of the State

107. Mark the INCORRECT statement among the following, regarding text-comprehension strategies:
A. Skimming is more apt for reviewing while scanning helps more with answering particular questions.
B. Both skimming and scanning involve rapid eye movement through the text.
C. Skimming involves going through the text rapidly while scanning involves looking for specific facts.
D. Skimming is more about in-depth reading while scanning is more of cursory reading.

108. When children start using language to ask about things, events and phenomenon around them, which of the following functions of language is used more than the others?
A. Informative B. Heuristic
C. Imaginative D. Regulatory

109. Which of the following features of human language enables humans to talk about things which are not present in immediate time and space?
A. Structure Dependence
B. Discreteness
C. Displacement
D. Arbitrariness

98. B **99.** A **100.** C **101.** D **102.** D **103.** C **104.** D **105.** C **106.** C **107.** D **108.** B **109.** C

110. Which of the following skills is NOT considered as a mark of reading with comprehension?
A. Organizing and assessing the sequence of events or ideas.
B. Mentally summarising the text read till now.
C. Focusing on individual letters/alphabets.
D. Anticipating the content ahead.

111. Which of the following is NOT a feature of the Grammar translation method of second language teaching?
A. Communicating directly in second language and then comparing the rules of grammar of the two languages.
B. Focusing more on the form than the function of language.
C. Comparing the grammatical rules of first and second language.
D. Learning and practicing the rules of grammar of the second language.

112. A teacher asks her students to reflect on how they have answered an experience-based question. She gave them and what and how they were thinking when they wrote that answer. This is an example of:
A. Metalingualism
B. Metasemiotics
C. Metacognition
D. Metaphor

113. Which of the following among Krashen's hypotheses is similar to Vygotsky's ZPD?
A. Natural order hypothesis
B. Affective filter hypothesis
C. Input hypothesis
D. Monitor hypothesis

114. According to Cummins' interdependence hypothesis, which of these are interdependent on each other?
A. Reading and writing in second language.
B. Basic interpersonal skills in first and second language.
C. Comprehension and production in second language.
D. Cognitive academic proficiency in first and second language.

115. Which of the following DOES NOT justify starting reading skills with words and short story text instead of letters and alphabets?
A. Words and texts are more interesting but letters are not.
B. Separate letters are more difficult to memorise than words.
C. Beginner readers can focus better on bigger units than smaller units.
D. Words and texts create meaningful associations which letters fail to do.

116. Which of the following is linguistically CORRECT about languages and dialects?
A. Languages have their own script but dialects do not have their own script.
B. There is no well-defined linguistic difference between a language and dialect.
C. Languages have written literature but dialects are only based on oral traditions.
D. Languages and dialects are linguistically different but geographically same.

117. Veera is a seven month old infant. She is now making vocalizations that combine consonants and vowels. She is communicating using which of the following?
A. Cooing
B. Linguistic speech
C. Phonemes
D. Babbling

118. What is productive vocabulary?
A. Words that we use in writing and speaking.
B. Words which are new to the reader.
C. Words which are recognized as we hear.
D. Words noticed when we read beyond the lines.

119. Which of the following is NOT explained by the concept of Language Acquisition Device (LAD)?
A. How children learn figurative language.
B. Why the linguistic output of children is more than the input they get.
C. How children learn their first language.
D. How children are able to learn language within a short span of 4-5 years.

120. In a speech community, it is observed that 's' is pronounced differently by two different socio-economic groups of speakers. This difference is an example of:
A. A socio-cultural variable
B. A socio-psychological variable
C. A socio-linguistic variable
D. A pragmatic variable

110. C **111.** A **112.** C **113.** C **114.** D **115.** C **116.** B **117.** D **118.** A **119.** A **120.** C

PART-V : LANGUAGE-II : हिन्दी

निर्देश (प्र.सं. 121 से 128 तक): *निम्नलिखित गद्यांश को पढ़कर पूछे गए प्रश्नों के उत्तर के लिए सबसे उपयुक्त विकल्प का चयन कीजिए।*

स्वातंत्र्योत्तर भारत की सबसे बड़ी ट्रेजेडी यह नहीं है कि शासक वर्ग ने औद्योगीकरण का मार्ग चुना, ट्रेजेडी यह रही है कि पश्चिम की देखा-देखी और नकल में योजनाएँ बनाते समय–प्रकृति, मनुष्य और संस्कृति के बीच का नाजुक संतुलन किस तरह नष्ट होने से बचाया जा सकता है–इस ओर हमारे पश्चिम शिक्षित सत्ताधारियों का ध्यान कभी नहीं गया। हम बिना पश्चिम को मॉडल बनाए, अपनी शर्तो और मर्यादाओं के आधार पर, औद्योगिक विकास का भारतीय स्वरूप निर्धारित कर सकते हैं, कभी इसका ख्याल भी हमारे शासकों को आया हो, ऐसा नहीं जान पड़ता।

121. हमें औद्योगिक विकास के लिए .... की आवश्यकता है।

A. अमेरिकी मॉडल B. यूरोपीय मॉडल
C. भारतीय मॉडल D. पश्चिमी मॉडल

122. 'शिक्षित' में मूल शब्द तथा प्रत्यय है :

A. शिक्षा + इत B. शिक्षा + ईत
C. शिक्षि + त D. शिक्षा + त

123. समूह से भिन्न शब्द है ....।

A. संस्कृति B. भारतीय
C. मर्यादा D. शर्त

124. योजनाएँ निर्धारित करते समय प्रमुख है ....।

A. प्रकृति की अपेक्षा मनुष्य की उन्नति का विशेष ध्यान रखना
B. प्राकृतिक सौंदर्य का विशेष ध्यान रखना
C. समय सीमा का ध्यान रखना
D. प्रकृति और मनुष्य के संतुलन को बनाए रखना

125. गद्यांश में किस बिंदु को अनुचित ठहराया है?

A. औद्योगिक विकास
B. पश्चिमी अंधानुकरण को
C. प्रकृति की उपेक्षा
D. प्रकृति को अधिक महत्व

126. स्वतंत्रता के बाद भारत की त्रासदी है ....।

A. पश्चिमी देशों का अंधानुकरण
B. भारतीय मॉडल
C. औद्योगीकरण
D. पंचवर्षीय योजनाएँ

127. गद्यांश में किसके संतुलन की बात की गई है?

A. प्रकृति, मानव और उद्योग
B. प्रकृति, मानव और मानवता
C. प्रकृति, मानवता और विकास
D. प्रकृति, मानव और संस्कृति

128. 'संतुलन' का विलोम शब्द है :

A. आसंतुलन B. असंतुलीत
C. असंतुलित D. असंतुलन

निर्देश (प्र.सं. 129 से 135 तक): *निम्नलिखित गद्यांश को पढ़कर पूछे गए प्रश्नों के उत्तर के लिए सबसे उपयुक्त विकल्प का चयन कीजिए।*

इस ब्रह्मांड में हम सभी की भूमिका महत्वपूर्ण है। कोई भी व्यक्ति किसी दूसरे से ज्यादा खास नहीं है क्योंकि परमात्मा की नजर में हम सब एक समान हैं। ध्यान-अभ्यास हमें सभी जीवों को एक समान देखने में मदद करता है। हम मानते हैं कि कोई भी व्यक्ति जो एक चौकीदार, क्लर्क या कैशियर है, वह उतना ही महत्वपूर्ण है जितना कि किसी कंपनी का कोई मालिक। हमें समझ आता है कि किसी कंपनी का मालिक कर्मचारियों के बिना काम नहीं कर सकता। चाहे वे अधिक वेतन पाने वाले हों या सबसे कम वेतन पाने वाले। सभी लोग अपनी-अपनी जगह महत्वपूर्ण हैं। भले ही हम बाहर से रंग, रूप, समाज, संस्कृति आदि के स्तर पर अलग दिखते हैं लेकिन पिता-परमेश्वर की संतान होने के नाते हम सभी एक समान हैं।

129. गद्यांश के अनुसार सभी व्यक्ति :

A. समान वेतन के अधिकारी हैं।
B. व्यवसाय में लगे हुए हैं।
C. एक समान हैं।
D. महत्वपूर्ण हैं।

130. गद्यांश के आधार पर कहा जा सकता है कि हम सभी समान हैं क्योंकि :

A. हम ईश्वर की संतान हैं।
B. हम कंपनी के कर्मचारी हैं।
C. हमारी जीवन-शैली समान है।
D. हमारा जीवन-लक्ष्य समान है।

131. सभी व्यक्तियों को समान दृष्टि से देखने में सहायक है :

A. व्यावहारिक होना
B. ध्यान का अभ्यास
C. समान दृष्टि का अभ्यास
D. आचरण का अभ्यास

121. C **122.** A **123.** B **124.** D **125.** B **126.** A **127.** D **128.** D **129.** C **130.** A **131.** B

132. किसी भी कार्य की सफलता में .... योगदान होता है।
A. सभी की सम दृष्टि का
B. पदाधिकारियों के श्रम का
C. सभी के परिश्रम का
D. सभी के धन का

133. समूह से भिन्न शब्द है :
A. संस्कृति B. ज्यादा
C. व्यक्ति D. महत्वपूर्ण

134. 'संस्कृति' शब्द में .... प्रत्यय का प्रयोग होगा।
A. इय B. ईय
C. इक D. इत

135. गद्यांश में सभी मनुष्यों को समान भाव से देखने एवं .... पर बल दिया गया है।
A. व्यवहार करने B. विशेष मानने
C. समान वेतन देने D. समान नौकरी देने

136. निम्नलिखित में से कौन-सा आकलन के बारे में सही **नहीं** है?
A. यह विद्यार्थियों की प्रगति की गति का मूल्यांकन करने में मदद करता है।
B. यह केवल अध्यापक द्वारा ही किया जा सकता है।
C. यह विद्यार्थी की प्रगति के बारे में समग्र दृष्टिकोण प्रदान करता है।
D. यह विद्यार्थियों की उपलब्धि के बारे में ठोस साक्ष्य प्रस्तुत करता है।

137. अधिगम में रह गई कमियों को देखने के संदर्भ में त्रुटि विश्लेषण महत्वपूर्ण है क्योंकि :
A. गलतियाँ शिक्षार्थियों की समझ में रह गई कमियों की ओर संकेत करती हैं।
B. गलतियाँ अवधारणा विकास और प्रेरणा को प्रदर्शित करती हैं।
C. अधिकतर त्रुटियाँ विद्यार्थियों के अनियत दृष्टिकोण के कारण होती हैं।
D. गलतियाँ शिक्षार्थी के मस्तिष्क और अधिगम की अवस्था को समझने में सहायक हैं।

138. निम्नलिखित में से कौन-सा स्टीफन क्रेशन द्वारा दी गई मॉनीटर परिकल्पना के संदर्भ में सही **नहीं** है?
A. 'क्या अर्जित किया गया है', 'सीखे' गए की मॉनीटरिंग करने में मदद करता है
B. शिक्षार्थी तभी मॉनीटर कर सकते हैं जब उन्हें नियमों की पर्याप्त जानकारी हो और पर्याप्त समय हो
C. यह द्वितीय भाषा अर्जन के संदर्भ में प्रयुक्त की जाती है
D. यह अर्जन और अधिगम के मध्य संबंध पर आधारित है

139. निम्नलिखित में से कौन-सा रचनात्मक आकलन का उदाहरण **नहीं** है?
A. समग्र लिखित परीक्षा और सत्र की विभिन्न अवधियों में दिए गए कुछ और कार्यों का मिश्रण
B. पूरे सत्र भर में लघु अवधि परीक्षा से लेकर सहपाठी समीक्षा जैसी होने वाली आकलन की युक्तियाँ
C. पूरे सत्र के दौरान मौखिक और लिखित कार्यों की शृंखला और रोल प्ले आदि
D. सत्र के अन्त में होने वाली सत्र परीक्षा

140. जब एक शुरूआती पाठक पाठ्यवस्तु की थीम, सांस्कृतिक पहलू आदि के बारे में अपने सामान्य ज्ञान का प्रयोग करता है, जिससे कि वह उस विशिष्ट पाठगत् सामग्री से अर्थ निकाल सके, तो यह क्या कहलाएगी?
A. तल-ऊर्ध्वगामी उपागम
B. तल-अधोगामी उपागम
C. ऊर्ध्व-अधोगामी उपागम
D. ऊर्ध्व-ऊर्ध्वगामी उपागम

141. निम्नलिखित में से कौन-सा पाठ्य सामग्री की बोधगम्यता और शब्दावली के विकास में मदद **नहीं** करेगा?
A. थीम मानचित्र B. चित्र शब्दकोश
C. शब्द मानचित्र D. वर्णमाला चार्ट

142. निम्नलिखित में से कौन-सा कथन आकलन के दो मुख्य प्रकारों के संदर्भ में सही है?
A. रचनात्मक आकलन अधिगम प्रक्रिया में सतत रूप से चलता है।
B. योगात्मक आकलन अधिगम प्रक्रिया से पहले और उसके दौरान किया जाता है।
C. रचनात्मक आकलन अधिगम के प्रकार्यों के स्थान पर नियमों पर अधिक ध्यान देता है।
D. योगात्मक आकलन वर्ष भर चलने वाले आकलन के प्रत्येक स्वरूप की समग्रता के बारे में है।

143. निम्नलिखित में से किसके द्वारा समावेशी कक्षा सृजित करने में मदद **नहीं** मिलेगी?
A. बहुभाषिक उपागम का अनुपालन करना
B. कक्षा में कुछ विद्यार्थियों को कक्षा प्रमुख (मॉनीटर) बना देना
C. सहपाठी समूह अन्तःक्रिया और पृष्ठ पोषण व्यवस्था
D. समूहों में कार्य करने के लिए देना

132. C **133.** B **134.** C **135.** A **136.** B **137.** D **138.** A **139.** D **140.** C **141.** D **142.** A **143.** B

144. 'प' को 'फ' की तरह लिखना या '6' को '9' की तरह लिखना किस तरह के बच्चों द्वारा यह सामान्य गलती की जाती है?

A. नामन विकार (एनोमिया)

B. पठन वैकल्य (डिस्लैक्सिया)

C. हकलाने वाले बच्चों द्वारा

D. वाचाघात (अफेजिया)

145. बुनियादी अन्तः वैयक्तिक सम्प्रेषणात्मक कौशलों को किस रूप में जाना जाता है?

A. दिन-प्रतिदिन के सम्प्रेषण के प्रयुक्त भाषा

B. अन्तरभाषा (इंटरलैंग्विज)

C. उच्च स्तरीय भाषा कौशल

D. अमूर्तता की भाषा

146. एक अध्यापक हिंदी भाषी विद्यार्थियों को द्वितीय भाषा के रूप में अंग्रेजी का अध्यापन करते समय उन्हें स्पष्ट रूप से नियम बताए बगैर अंग्रेजी में संक्षिप्त संवाद करने के संदर्भ और अवसर देता है और वह उनके वार्तालाप में प्रयुक्त उदाहरण उनके समक्ष प्रस्तुत करता है। धीरे-धीरे शिक्षार्थी अध्यापक की मदद से स्वतः ही नियम सीख लेते हैं। अध्यापक किस मॉडल/उपागम का अनुपालन कर रहा है?

A. सम्प्रेषणात्मक उपागम

B. प्रत्यक्ष (डायरेक्ट) विधि

C. व्याकरण अनुवाद विधि

D. श्रव्य-भाषिक विधि

147. निम्नलिखित में से कौन-सा सम्प्रेषणात्मक उपागम का गुणधर्म **नहीं** है?

A. स्पष्टता के साथ शिक्षण के स्थान पर व्याकरण के नियमों की खोज करना

B. सम्प्रेषणात्मक दक्षता का विकास करना

C. प्रकार्य की अपेक्षा नियमों पर अधिक ध्यान देना

D. भाषा का संदर्भगत प्रयोग

148. कथाओं की कौन-सी विधा बहुभाषावाद और बहु-संस्कृतिवाद को प्रतिपादित करने के लिए सर्वाधिक रूप से प्रासंगिक है?

A. विज्ञान कथा

B. अविश्वसनीय बात (लेन्दी टेल)

C. लोककथाएँ

D. आत्मकथाएँ

149. निम्नलिखित में से कौन-सा बाल साहित्य का अपेक्षित गुणधर्म **नहीं** है?

A. बड़ा फॉन्ट आकार और परिचित शब्द

B. आकर्षक चित्र

C. पशु पात्र

D. नैतिक मूल्यों का स्पष्टतः प्रदर्शन

150. निम्नलिखित में से कौन-सा अधिगम का मुख्य क्षेत्र (डोमेन) **नहीं** है?

A. भावात्मक

B. मनोगत्यात्मक

C. संज्ञानात्मक

D. सामाजिक सांस्कृतिक

EXPLANATORY ANSWERS

1. (D): Mastery-oriented learners believe success comes from their abilities and effort. When they face failure, they attribute it to insufficient effort rather than fixed or external factors, demonstrating their belief in their capacity to improve through persistence.

2. (C): The 'Proximodistal' principle refers to development progressing from the center of the body outward. This is evident as gross motor skills like grasping a ball develop before fine motor skills like threading beads.

The term 'Proximodistal' is derived from Latin words where 'proximo' means 'near' and 'distal' means 'far.' This principle explains that growth and development occur from the center of the body outward to the extremities. In other words, development progresses from areas close to the body's central axis (the spine) towards the outer parts of the body (arms, hands, fingers, legs, feet, and toes).

3. (A): Lev Vygotsky was a renowned Soviet psychologist whose theories have had a significant impact on how we understand child development, particularly in the realm of cognitive growth. One of his key contributions is the concept of 'private speech.'

Private speech is when children talk to themselves, either aloud or silently. This self-directed speech usually starts around the age of 2-3 years and continues until it eventually becomes internalized as silent, inner speech.

Purpose: Vygotsky believed that this kind of speech helps children:

- **Organize their thoughts:** It allows them to structure their thinking process, especially when they are confronted with new or challenging tasks,
- **Plan actions:** By talking through their actions, children can better understand what steps need to be taken.

144. B **145.** A **146.** A **147.** C **148.** C **149.** D **150.** D

- **Solve problems:** Self-directed speech helps in analyzing and breaking down problems into manageable parts.
- **Self-regulate:** It aids in managing their behaviour and emotions, providing them with cues to follow and enhancing their control over their actions.

4. (C): Social communication challenges, such as difficulties in understanding and responding to social cues, are a hallmark of Autism Spectrum Disorder (ASD). These challenges impact forming relationships and engaging in reciprocal communication.

Autism Spectrum Disorder (ASD): ASD is characterized by challenges in social interaction, communication, and repetitive behaviours. Individuals with ASD often have difficulty understanding social cues, maintaining eye contact, and engaging in typical social interactions. They may also have specific interests or engage in repetitive behaviours.

Attention Deficit Hyperactivity Disorder (ADHD): ADHD is primarily associated with issues of inattention, hyperactivity, and impulsivity. While social challenges can occur, they are not the primary characteristic.

Cerebral Palsy (CP): CP is a neurological disorder that affects movement, muscle tone, and posture. It is caused by damage to the developing brain, often before birth.

5. (A): Scaffolding, a concept in Vygotsky's theory, involves supporting learners by breaking tasks into manageable parts and gradually reducing assistance as they gain independence.

6. (B): Dysgraphia is a learning disability characterized by challenges in handwriting, spelling, and organizing written text, often making writing a frustrating and labour-intensive activity.

Types of Dysgraphia:

- **Motor Dysgraphia:** Problems with fine motor skills affecting the physical act of writing.
- **Dyslexic Dysgraphia:** Difficulties with spelling and converting phonetic sounds into written symbols.
- **Spatial Dysgraphia:** Problems with spatial awareness, affecting the organization and neatness of writing.

Diagnosis and Support:

- **Assessment:** Diagnosis is typically made by educational psychologists or specialists who assess the child's writing skills, motor abilities, and cognitive processing.
- **Interventions:** Support may include occupational therapy to improve fine motor skills, specialized tutoring, and the use of assistive technology such as speech-to-text software.
- **Accommodations:** Providing extra time for writing tasks, allowing oral presentations instead of written assignments, and using alternative methods for note-taking.

7. (C): Effective problem-solving requires analyzing and simplifying complex challenges. Teachers should encourage students to focus on manageable components to systematically address the larger problem.

8. (A): Multisensory materials cater to diverse needs in inclusive classrooms, promoting engagement and understanding. However, standardization of curricular materials does not align with the principle of inclusivity, as it fails to accommodate diverse learning needs.

9. (C): Constructivism emphasizes that learners actively build upon their prior knowledge, reshaping and extending their understanding through experience and reflection.

10. (C): Effective teachers integrate learners' daily lives and socio-cultural contexts into teaching. This aligns with the idea that learning is inherently social, as proposed in socio-cultural theories.

11. (A): Meaningful learning goes beyond rote memorization and focuses on understanding, applying, and connecting concepts to construct new knowledge. Memorizing information without understanding fails to create meaningful connections between prior knowledge and new ideas.

12. (B): Encouraging gender-stereotypical roles, such as assigning sports to boys and art to girls, perpetuates biases and restricts equal opportunities. Additionally, gender roles are not primarily determined by biological differences but are shaped by social, cultural, and environmental influences.

13. (C): Kinesthetic learners prefer engaging in activities that involve physical movement and hands-on experiences. They grasp concepts better by participating in actions and performing tasks rather than passively observing or listening.

Here are some key aspects of their learning style:

- **Active Participation:** They benefit from hands-on activities, experiments, and real-world applications.
- **Movement:** Incorporating movement into their learning process helps them retain information better. This can include activities like role-playing, building models, or performing physical tasks.

- **Touch and Manipulation:** Using tools, materials, and manipulatives to explore concepts.
- **Practical Examples:** They often find it easier to understand and remember information when they can physically interact with it.

14. (C): According to Howard Gardner's theory of multiple intelligences, a scientist would exhibit high Logical-Mathematical Intelligence, and a sculptor would exhibit high Bodily-Kinesthetic Intelligence. So, the correct answer is: C. Logical-mathematical; Bodily-Kinesthetic

Explanation:

- **Logical-Mathematical Intelligence:** This type of intelligence involves the ability to analyze problems logically, carry out mathematical operations, and investigate issues scientifically. It is typically associated with scientists, mathematicians, and logicians.
- **Bodily-Kinesthetic Intelligence:** This type of intelligence involves using one's physical body skillfully and handling objects adroitly. It is commonly found in athletes, dancers, surgeons, and, of course, sculptors, who work with their hands to create art.

Howard Gardner's theory suggests that individuals have different kinds of intelligences and strengths, and understanding these can help in educational and personal development.

15. (D): Inclusion in education refers to the practice of educating all students, regardless of their abilities or disabilities, in a supportive and participatory environment. The goal is to ensure that every student has the opportunity to succeed and feel valued.

- **Flexible Curriculum:** Adapting the curriculum to meet the diverse needs of all students ensures that everyone can access and engage with the learning material.
- **Cooperative Learning:** Encouraging collaborative activities helps build a sense of community and allows students to learn from each other's strengths and experiences.
- **Accessibility of Building:** Ensuring that the physical environment is accessible to all students, including those with disabilities, is crucial for inclusive education.

Therefore, the correct answer is (D) (*i*), (*ii*), (*iv*).

16. (B): Moderate levels of arousal optimize learning by keeping students engaged and motivated without inducing stress or anxiety. A balance helps maintain focus and encourages active participation in learning activities.

17. (C): Pressurizing young children to write "properly" before they develop fine motor control can lead to frustration. Motor skills required for precise writing typically develop around ages 5–6, supporting the need to focus on developmentally appropriate practices.

18. (D): Children's explanations of events, like rain, reflect their attempts to make sense of the world using their imaginative and cultural experiences. These responses showcase their developing reasoning rather than an inability to think logically.

19. (C): Piaget's theory describes cognitive development as occurring in four distinct stages: sensorimotor, preoperational, concrete operational, and formal operational.

- **Sensorimotor Stage (Birth to 2 years):** Infants learn through interacting with their environment using their senses and motor activities.
- **Preoperational Stage (2 to 7 years):** Children begin to use language and think symbolically but their thinking is still intuitive and egocentric.
- **Concrete Operational Stage (7 to 11 years):** Children develop logical thinking about concrete events. They gain a better understanding of the concept of conservation (quantity remains the same despite changes in shape or appearance).
- **Formal Operational Stage (12 years and up):** Adolescents develop abstract thinking and hypothetical reasoning. They can think about future possibilities and use systematic problem-solving.

20. (C): Promoting gender role flexibility involves encouraging children to explore activities freely, regardless of stereotypes. By normalizing Rishabh's choice and emphasizing that all toys are for everyone, the teacher fosters an inclusive and supportive environment.

21. (C): The critical period is a specific timeframe in development during which an individual is highly sensitive to environmental stimuli for acquiring certain skills. If these opportunities are missed, it may become challenging to develop these skills later in life.

The other options do not specifically refer to this sensitive developmental timeframe:

- **Incentive Period:** Not a standard term in developmental psychology.
- **Stimulus Period:** Vague and not specific to developmental sensitivity.
- **Encoding Period:** Generally refers to the process of encoding information into memory, not to a specific sensitive period in development.

22. **(A):** Teachers catering to students with ADHD should avoid creating distractions or noisy environments, as such stimuli can exacerbate attention difficulties. A calm and structured setting enhances focus and learning for such students.

23. **(C):** Kohlberg proposed that moral development occurs in six progressive stages within three levels (pre-conventional, conventional, and post-conventional).

Kohlberg's Stages of Moral Development:

1. **Pre-conventional Level:**
- **Stage 1: Obedience and Punishment Orientation:** Morality is based on avoiding punishment and obeying authority.
- **Stage 2: Individualism and Exchange:** Individuals recognize that others have different perspectives, and moral decisions are based on self-interest and reciprocity.

2. **Conventional Level:**
- **Stage 3: Good Interpersonal Relationships:** Morality is based on living up to social expectations and roles, and being "good" to gain approval from others.
- **Stage 4: Maintaining Social Order:** Morality is based on maintaining law and order, respecting authority, and fulfilling one's duties.

3. **Post-conventional Level:**
- **Stage 5: Social Contract and Individual Rights:** Morality is based on understanding that laws are social contracts that can be changed if they do not promote the general welfare. Individuals value rights and principles that may transcend the law.
- **Stage 6: Universal Principles:** Morality is based on abstract reasoning using universal ethical principles. Individuals follow internalized principles of justice, even if they conflict with laws and rules.

24. **(D):** At the Conventional level of Kohlberg's moral development, an individual's ethical behaviour mainly depends on the mindset of "What do people think of me?". So, the correct answer is: D. Conventional

The Conventional level of moral development is characterized by an emphasis on social relationships and conformity to societal norms and expectations. It includes two stages:

1. **Stage 3: Good Interpersonal Relationships (Interpersonal Concordance)**: At this stage, individuals make moral decisions based on the desire to maintain positive relationships and gain approval from others. They often ask themselves, "What do people think of me?" and strive to be seen as good and worthy by their peers and authority figures.
2. **Stage 4: Maintaining Social Order:** Individuals at this stage adhere to rules and laws to uphold social order. They prioritize fulfilling their duties and respecting authority to maintain societal stability.

In contrast, the Pre-conventional level focuses on self-interest and avoiding punishment, while the Post-conventional level is based on abstract reasoning and universal ethical principles.

25. **(B):** Irreversibility refers to the inability to mentally reverse an action or operation. In Piaget's preoperational stage, children struggle with logical reasoning, such as understanding the relationship between addition and subtraction.

26. **(B):** Teachers should foster a supportive and collaborative environment, taking shared responsibility for learning. Democratic classrooms encourage better engagement and learning, contrary to the authoritative approach mentioned.

27. **(B): Assertion (A):** "Scaffolding provided by the teachers hinders the learning process of children." This assertion is false. Scaffolding, a concept introduced by Vygotsky, refers to the support and guidance provided by teachers or more knowledgeable peers to help children learn new skills or concepts. Effective scaffolding actually facilitates learning by providing the necessary support until the child can perform the task independently.

Reason (R): "Lev Vygotsky proposed that children learn independently by acting upon and manipulating the environment." This reason is also false. While Vygotsky did emphasize the importance of children interacting with their environment, he also highlighted the crucial role of social interactions and guidance from more knowledgeable others in the learning process. Vygotsky's theory is centered around the idea that learning is a socially mediated process.

Both the assertion and the reason provided are false. So, the correct option is: B. Both (A) and (R) are false.

28. **(A):** Extrinsic motivation arises from external rewards or consequences, such as praise, grades, or tangible rewards. It contrasts with intrinsic motivation, which stems from internal satisfaction and enjoyment of the activity.

29. **(C):** During Piaget's sensorimotor stage, object permanence (understanding that objects continue to exist when out of sight) and deferred imitation (replicating actions observed earlier) are significant cognitive milestones.

30. (C): Children's development is shaped by the social and cultural environment, which influences their behaviour, beliefs, and values. Vygotsky's socio-cultural theory emphasizes the role of social interaction in cognitive development.

31. (D): 9 kg – 7 kg 7 g = 9000 g – 7000 g + 7 g

= 9000 g – 7007 g = 1993 g

$= \frac{1993}{1000}$ kg = 1.993 kg

∴ The required result = 1.993 kg.

32. (D): From given table:

(A) Number of children have Apple as their favourite fruit = 28 and Guava as their favourite fruit = 26.

(B) The difference between the number of children who like grapes and those who like banana = 28 – 14 = 14.

(C) The number of children who like Mangoes and Banana = 44 + 14 = 58

The number of children who like Guava = 26.

(D) Total Number of children

= 28 + 26 + 44 + 14 + 28 = 140

∵ 150 – 140 = 10

∴ Ten children do not like any fruit given in the table.

Hence, option (D) is the correct.

33. (B): Formative assessment is not intended for ranking or cumulative evaluations. Its primary purpose is to identify students' learning progress, misconceptions, and understanding during instruction, allowing teachers to adjust their teaching strategies to enhance learning outcomes.

34. (B): Let ₹ x was in his acount at the start of the month

Then, ₹ x + ₹ 2567 – ₹ 4560 = ₹ 3125

⇒ ₹ x + ₹ 2567 = ₹ 4560 + ₹ 3125

⇒ x + ₹ 2567 = ₹ 7685

⇒ ₹ x = 7685 – 2567

⇒ ₹ x = ₹ 5118.

35. (D): The student distributed the total number of pupils (616) into smaller, manageable parts (280, 280, and 56) and divided each part by the class size (28). This approach reflects the application of the distributive property of division over addition.

36. (A):

(A) A Scalene triangle – All sides are of different length

(B) A right triangle – One angle of triangle is 90°

(C) An equilateral triangle – All Sides are of equal length.

(D) An isoceles triangle – two sides are of equal length.

37. (A): The sum of the prime numbers between 31 and 60

= 37 + 41 + 43 + 47 + 53 + 59 = 280.

38. (D): The predecessor of 201 = 201 – 1 = 200 and the successor of 4781 = 4781 + 1 = 4782

∴ The required product = 200 × 4782 = 956400.

39. (C): Classification involves recognizing and grouping objects based on shared attributes or properties. This cognitive skill enables students to analyze shapes and categorize them according to features such as sides, angles, or symmetry.

40. (C): Division is a complex operation that requires a clear understanding of foundational concepts like addition, subtraction, and multiplication. Difficulties in division often arise when students lack proficiency in these basic skills.

41. (B): According to the National Curriculum Framework (2005), younger students may struggle with abstract concepts and symbols, such as 4 + 5 on a worksheet, because their understanding is rooted in concrete, real-life contexts like counting candies.

42. (A): Writing "1005" instead of 105 indicates a misunderstanding of place value. The student requires additional guidance to differentiate between hundreds, tens, and ones places and correctly represent numbers.

43. (C): Fractions represent a part of a whole or a collection, typically less than 1. A fraction greater than 1 is represented as a mixed number or improper fraction, but it does not describe the standard concept of fractions.

44. (B): The distance covered by Radha on Monday, Wednesday and Friday = 3 × 3 km 725 m

= 3 × 3725 m = 11175 m

And the distance covered by her on Tuesday and Thursday

= 2 × 2 km 9 m

= 2 × 2009 = 4018 m

∴ Total distance covered by her from Monday to Friday

= 11175 + 4018 = 15193 m

$= \frac{15193}{1000}$ km = 15.193 km.

45. (D): In Van Hiele's theory of geometric thinking, the "Relationships" stage involves recognizing relationships between geometric properties and logically connecting them. Jasmine identifies the shared properties of rectangles, squares, and parallelograms, placing her in this stage.

46. (B): Given digits = 5, 9, 0, 2, 8 and 6

$\therefore$ The greatest 6 digit number = 986520

and the smallest 6 digit number = 205689

$\therefore$ The sum of the greatest and smallest six digit numbers

= 986520 + 205689 = 1192209.

47. (B): 12 14 17 13 8 14 21 [13] [4]

+2 +3 −4 −5 +6 +7 −8 −9

Here, the missing number = ?? = 13, 4.

48. (B): LCM of 6, 7 and 4 = 84

$\because$ Smallest four-digit number = 1000

$\therefore$ 1000 = 84 × 12 − 8

$\Rightarrow$ 1000 + 8 = 84 × 12

$\Rightarrow$ 1008 = 84 × 12

$\therefore$ 1008 is a multiple of 6, 7 and 4.

49. (D): A line segment has a definite length because it is a part of a line bounded by two endpoints. Unlike a line or ray, it does not extend infinitely in any direction.

50. (A): Open-ended questions require students to think critically, explore multiple solutions, and justify their reasoning. They encourage creativity, deeper understanding, and application of mathematical concepts beyond memorized procedures.

51. (C): Graphical representations like line graphs, bar graphs, or pie charts help in visualizing data trends and comparisons effectively. They simplify complex numerical information, making it easier to interpret patterns and relationships in data.

52. (B): The number of planks of required size

$$= \frac{8 \text{ m} \times 70 \text{ cm} \times 40 \text{ cm}}{2 \text{ m} \times 35 \text{ cm} \times 8 \text{ cm}} = \frac{800 \text{ cm} \times 70 \text{ cm} \times 40 \text{ cm}}{200 \text{ cm} \times 35 \text{ cm} \times 8 \text{ cm}}$$

= 40.

53. (B): The child's incorrect solution shows they applied the rules for adding natural numbers directly to fractions without understanding that fractions require finding a common denominator. This indicates a misunderstanding of fraction operations.

54. (A): The National Education Policy 2020 emphasizes the importance of mathematics and computational thinking because they are essential for understanding and contributing to modern fields like AI, machine learning, and data science, which are integral to technological advancements.

55. (A): According to the National Curriculum Framework 2005, mathematics teaching should focus on promoting reasoning and logical thinking rather than rote memorization. Teachers are encouraged to create an interactive learning environment that fosters conceptual understanding.

56. (C): Tessellations, or tiling patterns, provide a hands-on way to introduce the concept of area to young learners. By covering surfaces with shapes without gaps or overlaps, students develop an intuitive understanding of how area measures the extent of a surface.

57. (A):

$$\frac{4}{7} + \frac{5}{14} - \frac{7}{8} = \frac{8+5}{14} - \frac{7}{8}$$

$$= \frac{13}{14} - \frac{7}{8} = \frac{52-49}{56} = \frac{3}{56}.$$

58. (C): The letter "H" has two lines of symmetry, one vertical and one horizontal, which divide it into identical halves. This makes it distinct from the other letters listed, which have either one or no lines of symmetry.

59. (D): While "Surya Siddhant," "Baudhayan Sulba Sutra," and "Lilavati" are related to Indian mathematics, "Charak Samhita" is a text focused on Ayurveda, the ancient Indian system of medicine, and is not connected to mathematics.

60. (C): The difference of the place value of 5 and 7 in the number 352876 = 50000 − 70 = 49930.

61. (C): Elephant herds typically consist of females and their offspring, as male elephants leave the herd upon reaching adolescence (14-15 years). They live solitary lives or form temporary bachelor groups, explaining the composition of elephant herds.

62. (C): The lesson uses the familiar context of making mango papad to help students connect learning to real-life experiences, fostering an understanding of processes and techniques through observation and relatable examples, as emphasized in NCF 2005.

63. (B): The activity encourages students to research, collect data, and analyze information about water availability across generations. This approach aligns with the project method, which promotes inquiry-based learning and fosters deeper understanding through exploration and investigation.

64. (*)

65. (D): A learning outcome describes what learners will achieve as a result of an activity or process. In this case, the description of skilled work related to farming and its inheritance reflects the knowledge and understanding students develop after engaging with the content.

66. (D): Andhra Pradesh is a state on the eastern coast of India, bordered by the Bay of Bengal. The other options, Karnataka, Kerala, and Telangana, either have a western coastline or are landlocked.

67. (D): Lesson 13 in the NCERT Class V EVS textbook revolves around "Gaurav Jani's" journey, focusing on themes of travel, discovery, and living in diverse shelters. This aligns with the "Shelter" theme, which emphasizes understanding different living conditions and lifestyles.

68. (A): In a constructivist EVS classroom, the focus is on exploring new ideas, making connections, and learning through experiences. Merely solving familiar problems does not promote the critical thinking and discovery central to constructivist learning.

69. (C): Siddhi explains the rules before playing Kabaddi to highlight the importance of rules in both games and societal interactions. Rules ensure fair play and help children understand how society resolves conflicts and maintains order. This approach connects life skills with the lesson.

70. (A): Biomass and fossil fuels are indeed conventional energy sources. However, conventional sources are generally non-renewable, such as coal and oil, while renewable sources like solar and wind energy fall under non-conventional categories. This makes the reason (R) incorrect.

71. (A): Neil Armstrong became the first man to walk on the moon in 1969, during NASA's Apollo 11 mission. However, Kalpana Chawla did not set a record for the longest spaceflight by a woman in 2007. She tragically passed away in the Columbia shuttle disaster in 2003.

72. (A): Recording samples of children's work in a portfolio provides an objective and unbiased view of their progress. Unlike prior experiences, examination results, or social background, which may reflect biases, this approach focuses on direct evidence of the child's learning.

73. (C): Pashmina wool comes from goats living at high altitudes, where extreme cold necessitates a thick coat of warm hair for insulation. This coat not only protects the goats but also serves as the source of the soft pashmina wool.

74. (C): Anaemia leads to poor physical growth, low energy levels, and overall weakness in children. It also affects mental health, including cognitive development, concentration, and learning ability, impacting overall well-being.

75. (D): Bihu is a traditional folk dance and festival associated with Assam. The other options are incorrectly matched with their states: Lavani is from Maharashtra, Bharatnatyam is from Tamil Nadu, and Kathak is prominent in North India.

76. (C): Cows have short front teeth suited for snipping grass and large, flat side teeth designed for chewing and grinding the grass. This dental structure supports their grazing and digestion processes.

77. (D): Tales and stories in Environmental Studies textbooks are included to develop sensitivity towards environmental issues and help children relate to the characters and situations. This makes the learning process engaging, relatable, and impactful.

78. (C): NCERT's Environmental Studies lessons include real-life incidents and problems to encourage students to debate, understand, and develop sensitivity towards social and environmental issues. The inclusion of relatable problems enhances critical thinking and awareness.

79. (C): Boiled milk is easier to digest due to the breakdown of proteins during the boiling process. It typically takes about 2 hours for the stomach to digest boiled milk.

80. (C): The high salt concentration in the Dead Sea increases the density of the water, making it easier for a person to float. The buoyant force exerted by the dense water prevents individuals from sinking, even if they cannot swim.

81. (B): This group contains only chemical elements, all of which are metals. Tin (Sn), Lithium (Li), and Sodium (Na) are pure elements, unlike other options that include alloys or compounds.

82. (B): Anecdotal records are descriptive notes made by a teacher while observing students during an activity. These records provide qualitative insights into students' behaviours, progress, and learning experiences.

83. (D): Both the sunbird and tailorbird create hanging nests. Sunbirds weave intricate nests, and tailorbirds use their beaks to "stitch" leaves together, creating secure, hanging structures.

84. (C): Lizards, along with other cold-blooded animals, go into a state of hibernation during cold seasons to conserve energy. This deep sleep is due to their inability to regulate body temperature in extreme cold conditions.

85. (C): The activity promotes peer interaction, enabling children to observe, discuss, and collaboratively categorize objects based on their properties. This interactive approach supports effective learning at the primary stage.

86. (D): The teacher should encourage students to observe, record, hypothesize, and test their ideas, helping them construct knowledge through exploration. This activity-based approach fosters critical thinking and a deeper understanding of concepts like density.

87. (B): India and Singapore are in neighbouring time zones, with Singapore being 2 hours 30 minutes ahead of India. When it is 10 A.M. in India, it is approximately noon in Singapore.

88. (B): In a child-centered EVS classroom, passive listening is least likely to occur. Instead, students engage in hands-on activities, discussions, and collaborative learning, with the teacher facilitating rather than dominating.

89. (C): The journey from New Delhi to Bangalore took 24 hours (17:00 on January 30 to 17:00 on January 31). Dividing the total distance (1776 km) by the time (24 hours) gives an average speed of 74 km/hr.

90. (C): The EVS curriculum is theme-based to create an interconnected understanding of concepts. Themes promote in-depth exploration and often begin with questions, encouraging inquiry-based learning. This structure makes the reason the correct explanation for the assertion.

91. (B): Mr. Upadhyay's professional role was that of the hostel warden, as evident from the boys' attempt to evade his attention while sneaking out of the hostel and his concern for their whereabouts.

92. (D): The phrase "We had managed" is in the past perfect tense, indicating an action that was completed before another past action.

93. (C): Mrs. Upadhyay received the boys warmly and even supported their desire to attend the play, showing her understanding and accommodating nature.

94. (C): The boys had purchased tickets for the play in advance, and Mrs. Upadhyay supported them by allowing them to leave for the play, despite her husband's initial objections.

95. (A): "Improvised" in this context means to create or come up with a solution on the spot, as Patil fabricated a reason for their outing when confronted by Mr. Upadhyay.

96. (D): The boys were sneaking out of the hostel to attend a play at Gandhi School, as indicated by the tickets in their pockets.

97. (B): Mr. Upadhyay met the boys outside the hostel, and the boys were already late for the play, which was set to start at 9:30 p.m.

98. (B): After hearing their excuse about needing tea or coffee, Mr. Upadhyay brought the boys to his home to offer them coffee instead.

99. (A): The phrase "tickets were squirming in our pockets" attributes human-like behaviour (squirming) to the tickets, which is an example of personification.

100. (C): The sound in the poem is described as "drumming," indicating the rhythmic marching or movements of soldiers.

101. (D): The poem is structured as a dialogue between two individuals, where one asks questions and the other responds.

102. (D): The phrase "scarlet soldiers" is an example of a transferred epithet. Here, the word "scarlet," which describes the color of the soldiers' uniforms, is transferred to the soldiers themselves. It emphasizes the vivid imagery of the scene rather than directly describing their physical characteristics.

103. (C): The poem follows the narrative style and rhythm of a ballad, telling a story in a structured and lyrical format.

104. (D): The rhyme scheme of the poem follows an abab pattern, where the first and third lines rhyme with each other, and the second and fourth lines rhyme with each other. This structure maintains a rhythmic flow and enhances the lyrical quality of the poem.

105. (C): The act of "kneeling" reflects fear or anxiety, as it suggests submission or a reaction to an imminent threat or distressing situation.

106. (C): Mother-tongue-based multilingualism emphasizes the importance of using a child's first language for initial education. This approach enhances comprehension, learning outcomes, and cognitive development as children grasp concepts better in their familiar language.

107. (D): Skimming involves quickly reading to grasp the overall idea of a text, while scanning focuses on locating specific information. Both are rapid reading strategies, but neither involves in-depth reading, making the given statement incorrect.

108. (B): When children use language to ask questions about the world around them, they are employing the heuristic function of language. This function is related to exploring and learning about the environment through inquiry and discovery.

109. (C): Displacement allows humans to use language to discuss things beyond the immediate time and space, such as past events, future possibilities, or abstract concepts, which is a unique feature of human language.

110. (C): Reading comprehension involves understanding the meaning of texts, summarizing, organizing events, and predicting content. Focusing solely on individual letters or alphabets does not contribute to comprehension and is unrelated to the broader context of the text.

111. (A): The Grammar Translation Method emphasizes grammatical rules, memorization, and translation rather than direct communication in the second language. This makes the given statement inconsistent with the method.

112. (C): Metacognition involves reflecting on one's own thought processes and strategies, as the teacher is encouraging students to analyze how they answered and what they were thinking, which aligns with metacognitive skills.

113. (C): Krashen's Input Hypothesis is similar to Vygotsky's Zone of Proximal Development (ZPD), as it emphasizes providing learners with comprehensible input slightly beyond their current level to facilitate learning.

114. (D): Cummins' interdependence hypothesis suggests that cognitive academic language proficiency (CALP) in the first and second languages is interdependent, meaning that skills and knowledge in one language can transfer to another.

115. (C): Starting with words and short texts instead of individual letters helps beginner readers as larger units like words are meaningful and provide context, making it easier to focus and understand compared to isolated letters.

116. (B): Linguistically, the distinction between a language and a dialect is often social, political, or cultural rather than structural. Dialects may have as complex structures as languages, and there is no clear-cut linguistic criterion separating them.

117. (D): At seven months, Veera is likely in the babbling stage, where infants produce repetitive consonant-vowel combinations (e.g., "ba-ba" or "da-da"). This stage is a precursor to actual language use and is an essential part of language development.

118. (A): Productive vocabulary refers to the set of words that a person can actively use in speaking and writing. It contrasts with receptive vocabulary, which includes words that one can recognize and understand but may not use actively.

119. (A): The Language Acquisition Device (LAD), proposed by Noam Chomsky, explains how children acquire the rules of their first language, including syntax and grammar. However, it does not account for learning figurative language, which depends on contextual understanding and social interaction.

120. (C): The variation in the pronunciation of "s" by different socio-economic groups is a socio-linguistic variable, reflecting how language use varies based on social factors like class, education, or region. These variations are studied in socio-linguistics to understand the relationship between language and society.

121. (C): गद्यांश में यह स्पष्ट कहा गया है कि हमें औद्योगिक विकास के लिए भारतीय परिस्थितियों, शर्तों और मर्यादाओं के आधार पर भारतीय मॉडल को अपनाने की आवश्यकता है, न कि पश्चिमी मॉडल की अंधानुकरण की।

122. (A): 'शिक्षित' शब्द में मूल शब्द 'शिक्षा' है और इसमें प्रत्यय 'इत' जोड़ा गया है, जिससे यह शब्द बना है।

123. (B): 'भारतीय' शब्द समूह में भिन्न है क्योंकि यह विशेषण है, जबकि अन्य शब्द जैसे 'संस्कृति,' 'मर्यादा,' और 'शर्त' संज्ञा शब्द हैं।

124. (D): गद्यांश का मुख्य बिंदु यह है कि योजनाएँ बनाते समय प्रकृति, मनुष्य और संस्कृति के बीच संतुलन बनाए रखने की आवश्यकता है, जो हमारे शासकों द्वारा उपेक्षित रहा।

125. (B): गद्यांश में पश्चिमी मॉडल की अंधानुकरण को अनुचित ठहराया गया है, क्योंकि इससे प्रकृति, मनुष्य और संस्कृति के बीच संतुलन को नुकसान पहुँचता है।

126. (A): स्वतंत्रता के बाद भारत की सबसे बड़ी त्रासदी के रूप में गद्यांश में पश्चिमी देशों के अंधानुकरण का उल्लेख किया गया है, जो कि एक अनुचित प्रक्रिया थी।

127. (D): गद्यांश में प्रकृति, मानव और संस्कृति के बीच संतुलन बनाए रखने की बात की गई है, जो योजनाओं के निर्माण में अनदेखा किया गया।

128. (D): 'संतुलन' का विलोम शब्द 'असंतुलन' है, जिसका अर्थ है संतुलन का अभाव। यह गद्यांश के संदर्भ में उपयुक्त है।

129. (C): गद्यांश में बताया गया है कि परमात्मा की दृष्टि में सभी मनुष्य एक समान हैं। चाहे उनका कार्य कोई भी हो, जैसे चौकीदार, क्लर्क या कंपनी का मालिक, सभी का महत्व बराबर है।

130. (A): गद्यांश में यह स्पष्ट किया गया है कि सभी मनुष्य समान हैं क्योंकि हम सभी परमेश्वर की संतान हैं। बाहरी भिन्नताओं के बावजूद, यह समानता हमें एक बनाती है।

131. (B): गद्यांश में ध्यान-अभ्यास को महत्वपूर्ण बताया गया है, क्योंकि यह हमें सभी जीवों को समान दृष्टि से देखने और उनके महत्व को समझने में मदद करता है।

132. (C): गद्यांश में यह बताया गया है कि किसी भी कार्य की सफलता में सभी व्यक्तियों का योगदान समान रूप से महत्वपूर्ण है, चाहे उनका पद या वेतन कुछ भी हो। यह सभी के परिश्रम से ही संभव है।

133. (B): 'ज्यादा' शब्द समूह से भिन्न है क्योंकि यह मात्रात्मक विशेषण है, जबकि अन्य शब्द संज्ञा या गुणवाचक विशेषण हैं।

134. (C): 'संस्कृति' शब्द में 'इक' प्रत्यय का प्रयोग होता है। 'संस्कृति' में यह प्रत्यय मूल शब्द 'संस्कृत' में जोड़ा गया है।

135. (A): गद्यांश में सभी मनुष्यों को समान भाव से देखने और समान व्यवहार करने पर बल दिया गया है। यह विचार कि हर व्यक्ति का महत्व समान है, समभाव और समानता को प्रोत्साहित करता है।

136. (B): आकलन केवल अध्यापक तक सीमित नहीं है। यह सहपाठियों, स्वयं विद्यार्थियों और अन्य स्रोतों के माध्यम से भी किया जा सकता है। यह शिक्षार्थियों की प्रगति और क्षमता को मापने का बहुआयामी उपकरण है।

137. (D): त्रुटि विश्लेषण से यह स्पष्ट होता है कि शिक्षार्थियों की अधिगम प्रक्रिया में कौन-सी कमियाँ रह गई हैं। यह शिक्षकों को विद्यार्थियों के अधिगम स्तर और मानसिक प्रक्रिया को समझने में मदद करता है।

138. (A): मॉनीटर परिकल्पना शिक्षण प्रक्रिया की निगरानी के लिए नहीं है। यह भाषा अर्जन और अधिगम के मध्य अंतर को समझने के लिए है। इसका मुख्य उद्देश्य अर्जन को सुधारना है, न कि केवल मॉनीटरिंग करना।

139. (D): रचनात्मक आकलन सतत और विभिन्न तरीकों से शिक्षार्थियों के प्रदर्शन को मापता है। सत्रांत परीक्षा, जो केवल एक बार होती है, रचनात्मक आकलन का हिस्सा नहीं है क्योंकि यह सतत प्रक्रिया का हिस्सा नहीं है।

140. (C): जब पाठक अपने सामान्य ज्ञान का उपयोग करता है और सामग्री से अर्थ निकालने का प्रयास करता है, तो इसे ऊर्ध्व-अधोगामी उपागम कहा जाता है। इसमें व्यक्ति पहले बड़े संदर्भ को समझने का प्रयास करता है और फिर इसे गहराई में समझता है।

141. (D): वर्णमाला चार्ट शब्दावली के विकास में मदद नहीं करता क्योंकि यह केवल अक्षरों का अभ्यास करने तक सीमित है। जबकि थीम मानचित्र, चित्र शब्दकोश और शब्द मानचित्र सामग्री को समझने और शब्दावली विकसित करने में मदद करते हैं।

142. (A): रचनात्मक आकलन सतत प्रक्रिया है, जो शिक्षण-अधिगम के दौरान निरंतर चलती रहती है। यह शिक्षार्थियों की प्रगति और समझ को सुधारने के लिए नियमित प्रतिक्रिया देता है।

143. (B): समावेशी कक्षाओं का उद्देश्य सभी शिक्षार्थियों को समान अवसर देना है। कुछ विद्यार्थियों को कक्षा प्रमुख बनाना असमानता का कारण बन सकता है और समावेशी वातावरण के विपरीत है।

144. (B): डिस्लैक्सिया वाले बच्चे अक्सर अक्षरों और अंकों को उल्टा लिखने या पहचानने में कठिनाई का सामना करते हैं। जैसे, वे 'प' को 'फ' और '6' को '9' के रूप में लिख सकते हैं। यह उनकी दृश्य-स्थानिक समझ में कमी और प्रतीकों की पहचान की समस्या से संबंधित है।

145. (A): बुनियादी अंतः वैयक्तिक सम्प्रेषणात्मक कौशल वह भाषा है जिसका उपयोग लोग दैनिक जीवन में करते हैं। यह सरल और व्यावहारिक होती है, जिसमें जटिलता या अमूर्तता कम होती है।

146. (A): प्रश्न में वर्णित विधि सम्प्रेषणात्मक उपागम पर आधारित है, जहाँ शिक्षक भाषा नियमों को सीधे नहीं सिखाता, बल्कि संवाद और संदर्भ आधारित उदाहरणों के माध्यम से सीखने के अवसर प्रदान करता है। इसका उद्देश्य छात्रों की सम्प्रेषणात्मक दक्षता को विकसित करना है।

147. (C): सम्प्रेषणात्मक उपागम का उद्देश्य भाषा का व्यावहारिक उपयोग और सम्प्रेषणीयता को बढ़ावा देना है। यह नियमों पर अधिक ध्यान देने के बजाय भाषा के संदर्भगत प्रयोग और दक्षता पर केंद्रित होता है।

148. (C): लोककथाएँ विभिन्न भाषाओं और संस्कृतियों का प्रतिनिधित्व करती हैं, इसलिए वे बहुभाषावाद और बहुसंस्कृतिवाद को प्रतिपादित करने के लिए सबसे उपयुक्त हैं। वे विविध सांस्कृतिक पृष्ठभूमियों और परंपराओं को समझने में मदद करती हैं।

149. (D): बाल साहित्य का उद्देश्य बच्चों की रुचि और समझ के अनुरूप होना चाहिए। नैतिक मूल्यों को स्पष्ट रूप से प्रदर्शित करने की आवश्यकता नहीं होती, बल्कि उन्हें कहानियों के माध्यम से परोक्ष रूप से प्रस्तुत करना अधिक प्रभावी होता है।

150. (D): अधिगम के तीन मुख्य क्षेत्र (डोमेन) हैं : संज्ञानात्मक, भावात्मक और मनोगत्यात्मक। 'सामाजिक-सांस्कृतिक' कोई अधिगम का मुख्य क्षेत्र नहीं है, बल्कि यह शिक्षा के अन्य पहलुओं से संबंधित है।

Previous Years' Paper

Central Teacher Eligibility Test (CTET)

Paper-I (For Class I-V Teachers), July-2024

(Exam held on 07-07-2024)

PART-I : CHILD DEVELOPMENT AND PEDAGOGY

1. Which of the following would support continuous and comprehensive evaluation?

A. Best works portfolio
B. Growth and learning progress portfolio
C. Standardized achievement test
D. Standardized intelligence test

2. **Assertion (A):** Teachers should constantly examine their own attitudes and biases while working with children.

Reason (R): The process of problem-solving is hindered by functional fixedness.

Choose the **correct** option.

A. Both (A) and (R) are true and (R) is the correct explanation of (A).
B. Both (A) and (R) are true but (R) is not the correct explanation of (A).
C. (A) is true but (R) is false.
D. Both (A) and (R) are false.

3. While talking about her poor marks in mathematics Avi says "I just don't have the sense for numbers" Avi is attributing his performance to:

A. Luck B. Task difficulty
C. Lack of effort D. Lack of ability

4. According to Lev Vygotsky's theory, which of the following is a recommended approach in order to optimize students' learning experience?

A. providing students with work that is completely unrelated to their current level of understanding.
B. providing students with work that is just beyond their current level of understanding, with appropriate support and guidance.
C. providing no support to students and leaving them to struggle on their own.
D. providing students with work that they can manage and complete individually.

5. Which of the following statement best describes the role of the teacher in progressive education?

A. The teacher is the primary source of knowledge.
B. The teacher serves as a facilitator.
C. The teacher implements the prescribed curriculum 'as it is'.
D. The teacher leaves the children on their own to work independently.

6. Howard Gardner's concept of Intelligence implicates that:

A. everyone processes and understands the world in the same way.
B. human beings differ in their abilities in different domains.
C. intelligence has only one dimension.
D. intelligence is only about 'practical' learning.

7. Which of the following sequence of representation of concept is in accordance with children's gradual development of cognitive abilities?

A. action-based, image-based, symbol-based
B. image-based, symbol-based, action-based
C. symbol-based, action-based, image-based
D. symbol-based, image-based, action-based

8. **Assertion (A):** Teachers should provide emotional support to children in the classrooms to ensure effective learning.

Reason (R): Emotions and cognition are related to each other in complex ways.

Choose the **correct** option.

A. Both (A) and (R) are true and (R) is the correct explanation of (A).
B. Both (A) and (R) are true but (R) is not the correct explanation of (A).
C. (A) is true but (R) is false.
D. Both (A) and (R) are false.

1. B	2. B	3. D	4. B	5. B	6. B	7. A	8. A

9. Which of the following statement about development is correct?

A. Development is a discontinuous process.
B. Development occurs in a spiral manner, not linear.
C. Development proceeds from specific to general.
D. Different aspects of development are independent to each other.

10. According to Lev Vygotsky, children regulate their own behaviour through the:

A. Processes of adaptation
B. Use of inner speech
C. Process of equilibration
D. Use of self-reinforcement

11. Which pedagogical approach would be adopted by teachers who firmly believe in constructivism to teach concepts of floating and sinking to class V children?

A. Lecture method
B. Showing videos
C. Showing power point presentation
D. Guided discovery

12. Which of the following is **not** an effective memory technique for meaningful learning?

A. Rote Rehearsal B. Mnemonics
C. Concept Mapping D. Elaborative Rehearsal

13. Which of the following is **not** a characteristic of a well-formulated critical thinking question?

A. It is open-ended and allows for multiple answers.
B. It is based primarily on factual information.
C. It requires analysis and evaluation of information.
D. It promotes higher-level thinking and problem-solving skills.

14. Assertion (A): Classroom pedagogy should be culturally responsive to meet the needs of students from diverse cultural backgrounds.

Reason (R): Equity in classroom can be ensured only through standardized curriculum and assessment.

Choose the **correct** option.

A. Both (A) and (R) are true and (R) is the correct explanation of (A).
B. Both (A) and (R) are true but (R) is not the correct explanation of (A).
C. (A) is true but (R) is false.
D. Both (A) and (R) are false.

15. Jagriti has learned that her dog, Rusty, is a Golden Retriever. When she sees another dog that looks similar to Rusty but is a different breed, she calls it a dog too. According to Jean Piaget's theory of cognitive development, which concept does this demonstrate?

A. Egocentrism B. Object permanence
C. Conservation D. Assimilation

16. Heredity totally determine an individual's:

(*i*) Sex (*ii*) Gender
(*iii*) Academic Success (*iv*) Learning Style

A. (*i*) B. (*ii*)
C. (*i*), (*iii*), (*iv*) D. (*ii*), (*iii*), (*iv*)

17. Assertion (A): Teachers should focus on asking questions in classroom and encouraging children also to ask questions rather than giving instructions.

Reason (R): Child-centred pedagogy means giving opportunities to children's voices and ensuring their participation.

Choose the **correct** option.

A. Both (A) and (R) are true and (R) is the correct explanation of (A).
B. Both (A) and (R) are true but (R) is not the correct explanation of (A).
C. (A) is true but (R) is false.
D. Both (A) and (R) are false.

18. Repetitive and ritualistic behaviour is an identifying characteristic of:

A. Autism Spectrum Disorder
B. Learning Disabilities
C. Attention Deficit Hyperactivity Disorder
D. Cerebral palsy

19. Learners feel engaged and actively involved in process of learning when:

A. activities are related to their context.
B. focus of learning is repetition and memorization.
C. socio-emotional needs of learners are ignored.
D. their prior knowledge is discarded and negated.

20. Children with 'learning difficulties' typically:

A. Have difficulties in reading due to their poor sight.
B. Have problems in regulating their emotions.
C. Have confusion with letter and alphabets that look alike.
D. Have very low IQ as diagnosed through standard intelligence tests.

9. B	**10.** B	**11.** D	**12.** A	**13.** B	**14.** C	**15.** D	**16.** A	**17.** A	**18.** A
19. A	**20.** C								

21. Feral children, those who experienced severe (human) social deprivation since very young age usually have delayed or hindered development and despite rehabilitation the improvement in certain domains of development is likely to be subordinate. This period wherein development is significantly influenced by environmental support is called _________.
A. deductive period
B. intuitive period
C. native period
D. sensitive period

22. Preconceived generalizations about behaviour of various gender are called:
A. Gender stereotypes
B. Gender discriminations
C. Gender identity
D. Gender typing

23. In an inclusive classroom:
A. 'Special children' always work on their own curriculum.
B. All children have access to and are included in classroom activities.
C. 'Special' children are looked upon as needy and dependent.
D. All children follow same curriculum and uniform pedagogy is adopted for all learners.

24. What is the primary purpose of asking critical thinking questions?
A. To enable students to develop procedural knowledge.
B. To assess students' knowledge and understanding skills.
C. To promote higher-level thinking and problem-solving skills.
D. To encourage students to memorize information.

25. Which of the following is correct about the process of learning, according to socio-constructivist theories?
A. Learning is an individualistic process that occurs in isolation.
B. Learning occurs only in a classroom or formal educational setting.
C. Learning is a passive process that occurs solely through observation.
D. Learning is a social process of meaning making.

26. **Assertion (A):** While some children start babbling and uttering two word sentences at 12 months, others don't do this till they are 20 months old.
Reason (R): Development milestones are only suggestive and development of individual children can be quite varied.
Choose the **correct** option.
A. Both (A) and (R) are true and (R) is the correct explanation of (A).
B. Both (A) and (R) are true but (R) is not the correct explanation of (A).
C. (A) is true but (R) is false.
D. Both (A) and (R) are false.

27. Growth in height and weight of children is an example of:
A. Quantitative change
B. Qualitative change
C. Change in affective domain
D. Change in cognitive domain

28. When presented with Heinz's dilemma, Arunima reasons: "The law wasn't set up for these circumstances. Taking the drug in this situation isn't really right, but it's justified."
Which stage of moral development is Arunima according to the theory of Lawrence Kohlberg?
A. Social concern and conscience
B. Morality of contrast, of individual rights and of democratically
C. Orientation towards punishment and obedience accepted law
D. Instrumental purpose and exchange

29. Which of the following is correct in context of gifted children?
A. Gifted children are free from risk of learning disability.
B. Gifted children certainly excel in all areas academic, social and emotional.
C. Gifted students are always happy, popular and well adjusted.
D. Gifted students learn at comparatively advanced pace than other students.

30. As per Jean Piaget, pre-operational stage is characterized by abilities to perform:
A. Classification and seriation
B. Conservation and abstract thinking
C. Imitation and reversibility
D. Symbolic play and animism

21. D	**22.** A	**23.** B	**24.** C	**25.** D	**26.** A	**27.** A	**28.** B	**29.** D	**30.** D

PART-II : MATHEMATICS

31. In order to identify individual differences of students in the mathematics class, which of the following assessment technique will not be appropriate?

A. Summative assessment
B. Formative assessment
C. Diagnostic assessment
D. Peer assessment

32. Which of the following resources is **best** suited to explain the concept of decimals?

(*a*) Number Chart (*b*) Dienes Blocks
(*c*) Taylor's Abacus (*d*) Graph Paper

Choose the **correct** option:

A. Only (*b*) B. (*b*) and (*d*)
C. (*a*) and (*c*) D. (*a*) and (*b*)

33. Students in a class are solving questions based on percentage discounts. One question requires the students to calculate the cost of two bikes, with a 8% discount on each bike. One of the groups calculates the total cost of the bikes and then deducts 16% from the total cost. The method used by this group is:

A. Correct and is the only way to calculate the discount and cost.
B. An alternate strategy to solve the question.
C. False, since they have deducted 16% discount from the total instead of 8%.
D. False, since they have deducted 16% from the total instead of 16% from the average of the total.

34. Arrangement of fractions $\frac{1}{9}, \frac{1}{21}, \frac{3}{7}, \frac{12}{63}$ in decreasing order is:

A. $\frac{3}{7}, \frac{1}{9}, \frac{12}{63}, \frac{1}{21}$ B. $\frac{3}{7}, \frac{12}{63}, \frac{1}{9}, \frac{1}{21}$

C. $\frac{12}{63}, \frac{3}{7}, \frac{1}{21}, \frac{1}{9}$ D. $\frac{1}{9}, \frac{12}{63}, \frac{3}{7}, \frac{1}{21}$

35. Which of the following learning experiences for children does not reflect the contribution of mathematics to everyday life and society?

A. Communication of mathematical ideas in writing using both formal and informal languages.
B. Meeting people from different areas of employment and exploring how they use mathematics in their work.
C. Collecting, organising, representing and interpreting data in day-to-day life.
D. Play small group games that draw on mathematical skills and concepts.

36. Which of the following represents the features of a mathematics laboratory?

(*a*) It is a place to enjoy mathematics through informal exploration.
(*b*) It provides opportunities to prove mathematical theorems through experiments.
(*c*) It provides opportunity to make conjectures, test them and to generalise observed patterns.
(*d*) It is used to assess students' knowledge of mathematics and grade them accordingly.

Choose the **correct** option.

A. (*a*) and (*d*) B. (*a*) and (*c*)
C. (*b*) and (*d*) D. (*b*) and (*c*)

37. One crore is:

A. ten million B. one million
C. one billion D. hundred million

38. In a certain week, the number of patients in a dental clinic was as follows:

Day	Number of patients
Monday	25
Tuesday	38
Wednesday	45
Thursday	18
Friday	36
Saturday	39

Based on above table, choose the **wrong** statement:

A. Range of the data is 27.
B. On most of the days, number of patients was more than 30.
C. Difference between the number of patients on Monday and Wednesday is 20.
D. Total number of patients was 200.

39. Which of the following Indian mathematicians are known as founders of 'numerical analysis'?

(*i*) Ramanujan (*ii*) Bhaskaracharya
(*iii*) Varahmihir (*iv*) Aryabhatta

Choose the **correct** option.

A. (*i*) and (*iii*) B. (*ii*) and (*iv*)
C. (*ii*) and (*iii*) D. (*i*) and (*iv*)

31. A **32.** B **33.** C **34.** B **35.** A,B,C,D **36.** B **37.** A **38.** D **39.** A

40. One egg has a mass of about 65 g, what is the mass of 2 dozen eggs?

A. 1.56 kg B. 1 kg 56 g
C. 1.304 kg D. 1 kg 544 g

41. Saumya joined her job on 13-01-1992 and she took retirement on 31-03-2023. Duration of her service was:

A. 30 years 10 months and 19 days
B. 30 years 9 months and 18 days
C. 31 years 2 months and 19 days
D. 31 years 2 months and 18 days

42. Two angles of a triangle are 50° and 30°. Then, the third angle of the triangle is:

A. 100° B. 40°
C. 60° D. 80°

43. National Curriculum Framework For Foundational Stage (NCFFS), 2022 highlighted the importance of the following components while teaching an abstract mathematical concept:

(*a*) Written Symbols (*b*) Experience
(*c*) Spoken Language (*d*) Picture

Which of the following is the appropriate sequence of these components while teaching an abstract mathematical concept?

A. (*c*) → (*a*) → (*d*) → (*b*)
B. (*b*) → (*c*) → (*a*) → (*d*)
C. (*c*) → (*d*) → (*a*) → (*b*)
D. (*b*) → (*c*) → (*d*) → (*a*)

44. Two columns are given as shown below:

Column-I	**Column-II**
(*a*) face of a black-board	(*i*) two end points
(*b*) a line has	(*ii*) one end point
(*c*) a ray has	(*iii*) represents a part of a plane
(*d*) a line segment has	(*iv*) no definite length

Column-I and **II** are matched as:

	(*a*)	(*b*)	(*c*)	(*d*)
A.	(*ii*)	(*iii*)	(*i*)	(*iv*)
B.	(*iii*)	(*ii*)	(*i*)	(*iv*)
C.	(*iii*)	(*iv*)	(*ii*)	(*i*)
D.	(*i*)	(*iii*)	(*iv*)	(*ii*)

45. 22 hm 8 dam is equal to:

A. 22800 m B. 2208 m
C. 2280 m D. 22080 m

46. If $x : y = p : q$, then which of the following is true?

(*a*) $x + y : y = p + q : q$
(*b*) $x - y : y = p - q : q$
(*c*) $x : p = y : q$
(*d*) $x + y : x - y = p - q : p + q$

A. (*a*) and (*b*) B. only (*c*)
C. (*a*) and (*d*) D. (*a*), (*b*) and (*c*)

47. 1233210 ÷ 5555 – 222 is equal to:

A. 1 B. 0
C. 2 D. 3

48. Which of the following statement(s) is/are true about numbers?

(*a*) All positive integers are whole numbers.
(*b*) All whole numbers are integers.
(*c*) All rational numbers are real numbers.
(*d*) All irrational numbers are real numbers.

Choose the **correct** option:

A. Only (*b*) B. Only (*c*)
C. (*a*), (*b*), (*c*) and (*d*) D. (*a*) and (*d*)

49. Which of the following are correct examples of the statement "mathematics is hierarchical in levels that are logically structured"?

(*a*) The concept of integers needs to be developed before the concept of multiplication and division of numbers.
(*b*) Multiplication follows and builds on the concept of addition.
(*c*) Number sense needs to be developed before the concepts of addition and subtraction.

Choose the **correct** option:

A. (*a*) and (*b*) B. (*b*) and (*c*)
C. (*a*) and (*c*) D. only (*b*)

50. 12 thousand + 13 hundred + 2 tens is equal to:

A. 12132 B. 130132
C. 13320 D. 121320

51. While teaching equations a teacher explains the concept of a linear equation having unique solution. She further asks, "If a solution is given then how many equations you can create"?

Choose the **correct** option:

A. One equation
B. No equation
C. Many equations
D. Two equations

40. A **41.** C **42.** A **43.** D **44.** C **45.** C **46.** D **47.** B **48.** C **49.** B
50. C **51.** C

52. Which among the following is/are true about the computation in basic operations for Grade-II learners?

(*a*) It involves child's ability to develop informal strategies.

(*b*) It involves child's ability to estimate.

(*c*) It involves child's ability to do calculations with large numbers.

Choose the **correct** option:

A. Only (*c*) B. (*b*) and (*c*)
C. (*a*) and (*c*) D. (*a*) and (*b*)

53. A mathematics teacher discusses the concept of open and closed curve in class. For better understanding of students she gave an example with four points. If the curve is open then nature of four points is:

A. All are collinear
B. Two of them must be collinear
C. Three of them must be collinear
D. Three of them must be non-collinear

54. The main approach suggested by National Curriculum Framework (NCF) 2005 in teaching learning of mathematics is:

A. Instructivism B. Pragmatism
C. Behaviourism D. Constructivism

55. The missing number (?) in the following: 43, 47, 53, 59, ?, 67, 71, 73 is:

A. 61 B. 60
C. 63 D. 65

56. In a mathematics class a teacher explains the concept of different angles. He/she realizes that scissors is a best example to explain ________.

(*a*) Vertically opposite angles
(*b*) Linear pair of angles
(*c*) Corresponding angles
(*d*) Alternate angles

Choose the **correct** option:

A. (*a*) and (*b*) B. (*a*) and (*c*)
C. (*c*) and (*d*) D. (*b*) and (*c*)

57. Raju has turpentine oil in 5 containers each of 20 L size. He fills them in 10 cans of 5 L, 10 cans of 2 L and rest in 1 L cans. Number of 1 L cans filled is:

A. 25 B. 30
C. 22 D. 28

58. Which of the following letters has no line of symmetry?

A. L B. A
C. M D. X

59. If (7 * 2) × (123) = 92496, then value of * is:

A. 2 B. 1
C. 4 D. 5

60. The difference between the greatest and smallest 6-digit numbers formed by using the digits 5, 1, 0, 3, 9 and 6 is:

A. 861741 B. 862731
C. 951741 D. 851731

PART-III : ENVIRONMENTAL STUDIES

61. EVS at primary level is recommended to be transacted in an integrated approach. The most appropriate reasons are:

(*a*) EVS draws issues from subjects like Science, Social Science and Environmental Education.

(*b*) It helps in developing holistic understanding.

(*c*) It helps to reduce burden of students and teachers.

(*d*) It is convenient to teach integrated EVS.

A. (*c*) and (*d*) B. (*b*) and (*c*)
C. (*a*) and (*b*) D. (*a*) and (*d*)

62. As an EVS teacher, you wish your students to be aware of their own safety around adults so that they (can take care of themselves and) do not fall prey to sexual harassment. Which step you think is most appropriate?

A. Teach them about POCSO Act, 2012
B. Teach them to avoid strangers
C. Hold workshops about 'Good Touch' and 'Bad Touch'
D. Hold self-defence workshops for girl students

63. Roshni, an EVS teacher displays a data chart for how many seeds out of 20 seeds each of mustard, green gram, Bengal gram and chilli seeds germinated. She asks students to explain why variation in the germination rates of different seeds occur. She wants to assess the skill of:

A. experiment
B. prediction
C. drawing inference
D. investigation

52. D **53.** A **54.** D **55.** A **56.** A **57.** B **58.** A **59.** D **60.** A **61.** C
62. C **63.** B, C

64. With respect to Telangana the respective locations of Gujarat and Bihar are:

A. North west; South east
B. South west; North east
C. North east; North west
D. North west; North east

65. Select maximum number of suitable tools of assessment to assess process skills in EVS.

(*a*) Teachers diary (*b*) Project work
(*c*) Drawing diagrams (*d*) Picture reading

A. (*a*), (*b*) and (*c*) B. (*b*), (*c*) and (*d*)
C. (*a*), (*c*) and (*d*) D. (*a*), (*b*) and (*d*)

66. On a Union Territory map on its one corner following scale is mentioned.

Scale, 1 cm = 155 m

If a person measures the distance between two cities as 19.7 cm, the actual distance between the two cities is approximately:

A. 3.10 km B. 31.00 km
C. 3.05 km D. 30.5 km

67. Mountaineers suffer nose bleeding at higher altitudes because:

A. The pressure in blood vessels exceeds outside pressure.
B. The pressure in blood vessels decreases than outside pressure.
C. The pressure in blood vessels equals the outside pressure.
D. Blood becomes thick at higher altitudes.

68. Select the group of poor conductors of heat from the following:

A. Wool, Wood, Iron
B. Air, Water, Copper
C. Air, Wool, Aluminium
D. Wool, Plastic, Wood

69. "Record how the seeds germinate into saplings from day 1 to day 10". Rita gave this task to her students before teaching the lesson on 'Germination'. She is trying to assess her students' ability to:

(*a*) draw and represent
(*b*) predict how germinating seeds would look like
(*c*) observe and record
(*d*) infer from the given activity

A. (*a*) and (*b*) B. (*b*) and (*c*)
C. (*b*), (*c*) an (*d*) D. (*a*), (*b*) and (*c*)

70. There is a species 'X' of plants that grow in a huge number but is found only in 'Y' part of India in the whole world. Which type of species is it?

A. Abundant B. Exotic
C. Endemic D. Endangered

71. Environment in EVS means:

(*a*) Man-made environment
(*b*) Natural environment
(*c*) Social environment
(*d*) Cultural environment

A. (*a*) and (*b*)
B. (*b*) and (*c*)
C. (*a*) and (*c*)
D. (*a*), (*b*), (*c*) and (*d*)

72. Select **incorrect** statement about elephant herds from the following:

A. Female elephants live in herds.
B. A herd has 20 to 25 female elephants and their young ones.
C. Male elephants live in the herd till they are 14 - 15 years old.
D. Male elephants of more than 15 years of age leave the herd and move around alone.

73. Map Reading activity in EVS classes develops certain abilities and skills in primary students. Those are:

(*a*) Understanding relative positions of places
(*b*) Understanding directions of places
(*c*) Understanding symbols and scale
(*d*) Drawing precisely according to the scale maps

A. (*a*), (*b*) and (*c*)
B. (*b*), (*c*) and (*d*)
C. (*a*), (*c*) and (*d*)
D. (*b*) and (*c*)

74. You are located at X and your school is located at Y. There is no straight path from your house to your school. So you first go to A which is about 125 m due north of X, then go to B which is 75 m due west of A, then go to C which is about 150 m due north of B and finally reach your school at Y which is 75 m due east of C. With respect to your school at Y, the correct direction of house at X is:

A. Due North
B. Due South
C. North west
D. South east

64. D	**65.** B	**66.** C	**67.** A	**68.** D	**69.** C	**70.** C	**71.** D	**72.** B	**73.** A	**74.** B

75. Saleem and Raju are young school goers. Saleem likes to eat lot of fried food and 'maida' products. Raju on the other hand eats home made healthy food but he never eats spinach and other green leafy vegetables. Which of the following disorders they are likely to suffer from, respectively?

A. Scurvy and Anaemia
B. Kwashiorkar and Anaemia
C. Obesity and Anaemia
D. Pellagra and Anaemia

76. Select from the following a group consisting of alloys only:

A. Brass, Bronze, Lithium
B. Magnesium, Aluminium, Steel
C. Steel, Brass, Tin
D. Steel, Brass, Bronze

77. Assertion: Stories and narratives have been used throughout the EVS textbooks.

Reason: Objective is to sensitise the child since he or she can empathise with characters in a story or narrative. Textbooks should sensitise the child to wide differences that exist within our society.

A. Both the Assertion and Reason are correct and Reason is the correct explanation of the Assertion.
B. Both the Assertion and Reason are correct but the Reason is not the correct explanation of the Assertion.
C. Assertion is true but the Reason is false.
D. The Assertion is false but Reason is true.

78. The volume of the earth consists of the following:

(*a*) 1% Crust
(*b*) 84% Mantle
(*c*) 15% Core

Choose the **correct** option from the following:

A. Only (*a*) and (*b*) are correct.
B. Only (*b*) and (*c*) are correct.
C. Only (*a*) and (*c*) are correct.
D. All (*a*), (*b*) and (*c*) are correct.

79. Read the Assertion (A) and Reason (R) below and choose the correct option.

Assertion (A): Travellers like Al-Biruni and Ibn Batuta travelled from India to different countries.

Reason (R): Travelling led to sharing of ideas between people.

A. Both (A) and (R) are true and (R) explains (A).
B. Both (A) and (R) are true but (R) does not explain (A).
C. (A) is true but (R) is false.
D. (A) is false but (R) is true.

80. An EVS teacher asks her students to imagine and answer, "What would have happened if all birds were killed at once from earth?" Such a question is:

A. Convergent question
B. Hypothetical question
C. Divergent question
D. Philosophical question

81. In NCERT textbook of class V there is a real story of Suryamani who lives in Jharkhand. The chapter depicts tribal life and role of Suryamani. Select the most important aspects addressed by the chapter relevant for students.

(*a*) Popular perceptions and biases about the tribal communities.
(*b*) Close relationship between forest dwellers (communities) and forests.
(*c*) Girls education how it changes their life.
(*d*) The forest products used by tribes.

A. (*a*), (*b*) and (*c*)
B. (*b*), (*c*) and (*d*)
C. (*a*), (*c*) and (*d*)
D. (*b*) and (*c*)

82. Which one/are of the following mountains is/are considered to be volcanic in origin?

(*a*) Mt. Kilimanjaro
(*b*) Fujiyama
(*c*) The Alps

Choose the **correct** option:

A. (*a*) and (*c*)
B. (*b*) and (*c*)
C. Only (*c*)
D. (*a*) and (*b*)

83. Consider the following statements (A) and (B).

Statement (A): Crows build nests on very low branches on a tree.

Statement (B): Weaver bird stitches two leaves to make its nest.

Select the **correct** code from the following:

A. (A) and (B) both are correct.
B. (A) and (B) both are wrong.
C. (A) is correct but (B) is wrong.
D. (A) is wrong but (B) is correct.

75. C **76.** D **77.** A **78.** D **79.** D **80.** C **81.** B **82.** D **83.** B

84. Read the following Assertion (A) and Reason (R) and choose the correct option.

Assertion (A): People can easily float on the surface of water of Dead Sea even if they do not know to swim.

Reason (R): Dead Sea has 300 gm of salt in one litre of water making it, the sea having highest salt concentration.

A. Both (A) and (R) are true and (R) explains (A).
B. Both (A) and (R) are true but (R) does not explain (A).
C. (A) is true but (R) is false.
D. (A) is false but (R) is true.

85. Samar asks his students to consult their family members to find out the names of different food items cooked by different methods like steaming, roasting, boiling, frying etc. The most appropriate reason for this activity is to:

A. encourage experimentation
B. improve social interaction
C. provide opportunities for children to work in groups
D. encourage home work

86. Which of the following best reflect experiential strategies in teaching EVS at primary level?

(*a*) Discussion
(*b*) Demonstration
(*c*) Field Trips
(*d*) Art integrated learning

A. (*a*), (*b*) and (*d*) B. (*b*), (*c*) and (*d*)
C. (*a*), (*c*) and (*d*) D. (*a*), (*b*) and (*c*)

87. Statement I: The EVS curriculum is framed within social constructivist perspective of learning.

Statement II: Piaget's ideas about children's learning with his in-depth study of children represent the social constructivist perspective.

A. Both the Statement I and Statement II are correct.
B. Both the Statement I and Statement II are false.
C. Statement I is true but Statement II is false.
D. Statement I is false but Statement II is true.

88. It is 7.30 P.M. in India today. It is 2 P.M. of the same day:

A. in London B. in Japan
C. in Dhaka D. in Karachi

89. Which of the following strategy promotes inquiry while teaching the theme 'Travel'?

A. Asking students to collect pictures of various means of transport.
B. Asking students to narrate their or their neighbours' experiences of travelling.
C. Asking students to make a digital presentation on vintage cars.
D. Showing pictures of various places of interest in nearby areas.

90. A teacher follows the following methods while teaching EVS: Think-Pair-Share, Reciprocal Peer Tutoring, Jigsaw Strategy and Peer Review. These are examples of:

A. Peer group learning
B. Constructivist approach
C. Didactic approach
D. Inductive approach

PART-IV : LANGUAGE-I—ENGLISH

Directions (Qs. No. 91-99): *Read the passage given below and answer the questions that follow:*

He must have seen us coming from some distance. By the time he loomed up in front of my headlights, the arms in the snow-caked overcoat were flailing desperately like windmills.

Pat gave a little gasp and I braked at once, though gently, or I might have followed his car into the ditch. But immediately I had second thoughts; there had been one or two nasty cases of hold-up in the papers recently. I wasn't going to take any chance with Pat, my sister, there. I changed down the gear and made to drive round him.

Pat was horrified. 'Aren't you stopping, Bill?' I shook my head. 'Too risky'.

It was then that I saw the car. It had skidded right across the road and was hanging nose down in the deep ditch. I braked again and brought the Mini-Moris gradually to a stop.

I slid back my window as he looked in and then I saw that he was bleeding from a cut in his cheek.

'Anybody else in the car?'

'No, on my own. If you could give me a lift'.

I nodded and he got into the back and slammed the door.

84. A **85.** B **86.** C **87.** C **88.** A **89.** B **90.** A, B

'Sorry about this, folks. I was beginning to think I was stuck there for the night. Not that you would call it a busy road, is it?'

'Not at twelve o'clock at night', Pat said, turning round to smile at him. 'We have been to a dance in Boling ford. Bill didn't want to go, but I was keen. He isn't a bad brother, really'.

91. Which of the following statements is/are right?

(*a*) The stranger did not seem to be badly hurt.

(*b*) Mini-Moris went past the stranger and then stopped.

A. (*a*) is right and (*b*) is wrong.
B. (*b*) is right and (*a*) is wrong.
C. Neither (*a*) nor (*b*) is right.
D. Both (*a*) and (*b*) are right.

92. Which of the following statements is/are correct?

A. There was snowfall, and a ditch along the road so Bill was driving very carefully.
B. Because of snow, he was driving very slowly.
C. It was night time, so there was no traffic on the road, so Bill was driving in a carefree manner.
D. It was the dead of night, so Bill was feeling drowsy while driving.

93. '... he loomed up in front of ...'

The underlined phrase means the same as:

A. fell down
B. appeared
C. drove up
D. looked up

94. '... brought the Mini-Moris gradually to a stop'.

The underlined is opposite in meaning to ________.

A. generally B. usually
C. suddenly D. mainly

95. Pat gave a little gasp and I braked at once.

The underlined is a/an ________.

A. Pronoun B. Preposition
C. Conjunction D. Interjection

96. It was then that I saw the car.

Identify the underlined clause.

A. Principal B. Noun
C. Adjective D. Adverb

97. Study the following statements:

(*a*) Pat is bold and compassionate.

(*b*) Bill is protective of Pat and not timid.

(*c*) A badly hit car was parked by the side walk.

A. (*a*) is right but (*b*) and (*c*) are wrong.
B. (*b*) is right but (*a*) and (*c*) are wrong.
C. (*a*) and (*b*) are right but (*c*) is wrong.
D. (*b*) and (*c*) are right but (*a*) is wrong.

98. Bill was travelling with:

A. his brother B. his sister
C. a friend D. a stranger

99. Which of the following statements is **not** correct?

After slowing down the car, Bill hesitated as:

A. it was a dark spot, so it might be a case of robbery.
B. only Pat, a woman was sitting beside him.
C. both (A) and (B)
D. in the cold, the car may not start again.

Directions (Qs. No. 100-105): *Read the extract given below and answer the questions that follow:*

'What dost thou do here?' the Bishop he said,
'I prithee now tell to me',
'I am a bold harper', quoth Robin Hood,
'And the best in the north countree'.

'O welcome, O welcome!' the Bishop he said,
'That music best pleaseth me.'
'You shall have no music', quoth Robin Hood,
'Till the bride and the bridegroom I see'.

With that came in a wealthy knight,
Which was both grave and old,
And after him a finikin lass,
Did shine like glistening gold.

'This is no fit match', quoth bold Robin Hood,
'That you do seem to make here;
'For since we are come into the church,
The bride she shall choose her own dear'.

100. Study the following statements:

(*a*) The Bishop asked Robin Hood the purpose of his visit.

(*b*) Robin Hood pretended to be a musician.

A. (*a*) is right and (*b*) is wrong.
B. (*b*) is right and (*a*) is wrong.
C. Both (*a*) and (*b*) are right.
D. Both (*a*) and (*b*) are wrong.

91. D	**92.** A	**93.** B	**94.** C	**95.** C	**96.** B	**97.** C	**98.** B	**99.** D	**100.** C

101. What was going to take place in the church?

A. a wedding B. a Sunday sermon
C. a baptism D. a funeral service

102. 'I prithee now ...'

The expression means:

A. I prevent you. B. I warn you.
C. I request you. D. I order you.

103. Robin Hood met the Bishop:

A. in the churchyard B. in the church
C. at his residence D. in the market

104. Which one of the following statements is **incorrect**?

A. The bridegroom was rich and handsome.
B. He was old and dull looking.
C. The bride was young and beautiful.
D. She was not eagerly waiting for the ceremony.

105. Which literary device has been used in the expression - 'Did shine like glistening gold'?

A. Simile B. Metaphor
C. Personification D. Hyperbole

106. A child does not write a paragraph on her own even after brainstorming the topic. However, she is able to write it under adult or peer guidance. This guidance is called __________.

A. Scaffolding B. Peer teaching
C. Peer counselling D. Team teaching

107. __________ is a type of learning in which a child has to use higher-order mental processes such as intelligence or reasoning.

A. Verbal learning
B. Concept learning
C. Motor skills learning
D. Structure learning

108. You as a teacher appreciate a child for her 'overall language use', though some of the words are misspelt by her. You are here using __________ approach in your class.

A. Whole language B. Communicative
C. Constructivist D. Structural

109. You are a Hindi speaking teacher, but you get posted in a primary school which is in the area of Punjab. Since you do not know the local language of that area, you should:

A. immediately apply for the transfer to a Hindi speaking area.
B. use the child's language as a resource and start teaching.
C. communicate in English.
D. motivate the community to learn Hindi.

110. __________ comprehension is the skill of reading a piece of text closely or intensely for the purpose of extracting specific information from the text.

A. Global B. Local
C. Inferential D. Evaluative

111. The purpose of diagnostic test in language learning is to:

A. Plan and prepare questions for summative assessment.
B. Inform the parents in the PTMs and ask them to pay attention.
C. Know the gaps in learner's understanding and take remedial steps.
D. Use the findings in the progress report of students.

112. Which one of the following is a correct statement about a textbook?

A. A textbook is the final thing for the teacher and the student.
B. It helps to achieve the objectives laid down in the curriculum.
C. It is a planning of educational activities for the session.
D. A textbook is irreplaceable.

113. Which of the following classroom practices helps a teacher to develop oral language among the students?

A. Chorus reading of the text with the teacher.
B. Chorus recitation of the poem after memorising it.
C. Participating in role-plays.
D. Practicing the correct pronunciation of new or unfamiliar words.

114. When we say 'Language is arbitrary', we mean to say that:

A. there is an inherent relation between the words of a language and their meaning.
B. the relation between words and their meaning is based on a valid reason and not on chance.
C. there is no inherent relation between the words of a language and their meaning.
D. Language follows prefixed principles.

101. A	**102.** C	**103.** B	**104.** A	**105.** A	**106.** A	**107.** B	**108.** A	**109.** B	**110.** B
111. C	**112.** B	**113.** C	**114.** C						

115. Deductive approach of teaching grammar advocates that, we should __________ first.

A. present examples
B. present rules
C. present genuine communication
D. provide practice through drills

116. __________ is a way of estimating or guessing beyond the facts.

A. Explanation B. Analysis
C. Inference D. Extrapolation

117. A language teacher must promote learners for free writing, as the key benefit of free writing is that:

A. it encourages learners to write fluently and creatively.
B. gives the freedom to write or not.
C. does not make them feel that they have to write much or be totally accurate.
D. can incorporate features of written language from their first language.

118. As a teacher of class V you ask the students to read the text thoroughly. Then you ask them to answer the questions with reference to the context (RTC). In this process, you are encouraging students for __________.

A. extensive reading
B. scanning
C. skimming
D. intensive reading

119. Language acquisition occurs only when the _______.

A. child is taught the rules of grammar
B. child is given practice in translation
C. child is given opportunity to read
D. child has exposure to the language

120. Excluding mother tongue in the classroom is the characteristic feature of the _________ method.

A. Natural
B. Bilingual
C. Audio-lingual
D. Direct

PART-V : LANGUAGE-II—हिन्दी

निर्देश (प्र.सं. 121 से 128 तक) : *निम्नलिखित गद्यांश को पढ़कर पूछे गए प्रश्नों के सही/सर्वाधिक उपयुक्त विकल्प का चयन कीजिए।*

एक दूसरा संकट ग्लेशियरों के तेजी से पिघलने और अचानक टूटने से खतरनाक बाढ़ और जलप्लावन का संकट है। पर्यावरण के इस संकट को लेकर देश के लोगों और सरकारों की चेतना का जो स्तर है, वह चिंता बढ़ाने वाला है। खेत खत्म हो रहे हैं, पेड़ काटे जा रहे हैं और जंगलों को लेकर सिर्फ आंकड़ों पर जोर है। उदारीकरण के बाद लोगों के रहन-सहन और जरूरतों में आया बदलाव अब मुसीबत बनने वाला है। हममें से हर की जिंदगी में गैर जरूरी सुविधाओं का भोग लगातार बढ़ा है। चालीस पार की उम्र वाले आसानी से अपने बचपन के दिनों को याद करके समझ सकते हैं कि संसाधनों का अंधाधुंध इस्तेमाल उनकी जिंदगी में किस कदर बढ़ चुका है। इसका असर मौसम, खेतों और फसलों पर पड़ रहा है। मार्च में खिलने वाले फूल अब फरवरी में नजर आते हैं। फरवरी में अचानक गरमी पड़ती है और गेहूं सूखने लगता है और जब तक फसल तैयार होती है अचानक बेमौसम की बारिश आकर उसे तबाह कर देती है। आम के बागवान शुरूआती बौरों को देखकर खुश तो होते हैं पर अचानक मार्च का आंधी-तूफान उनकी सारी खुशियों को निगल जाता है। पर्यावरण वैश्विक समस्या है पर उसका हल हमारी जरूरतों को कम करने में छिपा है।

121. पर्यावरण समस्या है ______ ।

A. भारत की
B. यूरोपीय देशों की
C. संसार भर की
D. एशिया की

122. गद्यांश के अनुसार संसाधनों के अंधाधुंध प्रयोग का प्रभाव ________ पड़ता है।

A. खेती एवं आँकड़ों पर
B. मौसम और आँकड़ों पर
C. मौसम एवं खेती पर
D. आँकड़ों और जल पर

123. 'बचपन' शब्द है ________ ।

A. भाववाचक संज्ञा B. व्यक्तिवाचक संज्ञा
C. जातिवाचक संज्ञा D. द्रव्यवाचक संज्ञा

124. गद्यांश के अनुसार चिंता का विषय है ______ ।

A. पर्यावरण के प्रति चेतना की कमी
B. उदारीकरण की नीति का होना
C. संसाधनों का उचित उपयोग
D. जंगलों से संबंधित आँकड़े

115. B **116.** D **117.** A **118.** D **119.** D **120.** D **121.** C **122.** C **123.** A **124.** A

125. 'ग्लेशियर' शब्द है ______ ।

A. आगत B. तत्सम
C. देशज D. तद्भव

126. गद्यांश के अनुसार पर्यावरण संरक्षण का सबसे उपयुक्त उपाय है ______ ।

A. आवश्यकताओं में कमी करना
B. वृक्षारोपण करना
C. भूमि अपरदन की रोकथाम करना
D. रहन-सहन के स्तर में वृद्धि करना

127. उदारीकरण के कारण :

A. अनावश्यक सुविधाओं के उपभोग में वृद्धि हुई है।
B. आवश्यक सुविधाओं के उपभोग में कमी आयी है।
C. अनावश्यक व्यय में वृद्धि हुई है।
D. आवश्यकताओं में वृद्धि हुई है।

128. 'वैश्विक' में मूल शब्द तथा प्रत्यय है ______ ।

A. वैश्वि + क B. विश्व + इक
C. विश्व + क D. वैश्व + इक

निर्देश (प्र.सं. 129 से 135 तक) : *निम्नलिखित गद्यांश को पढ़कर पूछे गए प्रश्नों के सही/सर्वाधिक उपयुक्त विकल्प का चयन कीजिए।*

जीवन में रौनक तब है, जब वह बड़े सहज और सरल तरीके से बिना किसी प्रपंच के जिया जाए। जीवन जैसा निश्छल, निष्कपट है, वैसा ही जिया जाए तो जीना वरदान बन जाता है। जीवन जैसा मिला है उसको हम वैसा ही जीते हैं, तो यह जीवन का सम्मान होता है। अधिकतर हमारा जैसा जीवन है, उसे छोड़ दिखावे का जीवन जीने लगते हैं। यह दिखावे का जीवन हमें बाहर तो अपने को कुछ बड़ा दिखाने में मदद करता है, लेकिन भीतर से खोखला भी करता चलता है। क्योंकि आडंबर से भरा जीवन अहंकार पर आधारित होता है और अहंकार हमारी जीवंतता को खा जाता है। अहंकार में हम केवल बाहर की तरफ देखकर जीते हैं जबकि जीवन कहीं भीतर बह रहा होता है।

129. निम्न में विशेषण है ______ ।

A. जीवंत B. सम्मान
C. वरदान D. जीवंतता

130. जीवन में खुशी आती है ______ ।

A. सरलता से B. भौतिक वस्तुओं से
C. कपटता से D. आडंबरता से

131. समूह से भिन्न शब्द है ______ ।

A. आडंबर B. अहंकार
C. असहज D. अधर्म

132. गद्यांश के अनुसार 'अहंकार में हम केवल बाहर की तरफ देखकर जीते हैं।' वाक्य का आशय है कि ______ ।

A. अहंकार हमें दूर तक देखने की शक्ति प्रदान करता है।
B. अहंकार हमें दिखावटी जीवन व्यतीत करने की ओर ले जाता है।
C. अहंकार हमें निश्छल जीवन व्यतीत करने की ओर ले जाता है।
D. अहंकार हमें सर्वस्व प्राप्त करने की ओर ले जाता है।

133. 'प्रपंच' से तात्पर्य है :

A. पाँच प्रकार B. आडंबर
C. पाँच पंच D. पाँच वायु

134. जीवन का सम्मान कैसे किया जा सकता है?

A. जीवन में सुविधाएँ जुटाकर
B. उच्च शिक्षा ग्रहण कर
C. जिस रूप में जीवन मिला है, उसे उसी रूप में जीकर
D. जीवन में मिली सब बाधाओं को समाप्त कर

135. 'आधारित' में प्रत्यय है ______ ।

A. त B. रित
C. धारित D. इत

136. भाषिक दक्षता शिक्षार्थियों को किसके समर्थ बनाती है?

A. व्याकरणिक रूप से सही और गलत वाक्यों में अन्तर करना।
B. भले ही व्याकरणिक रूप से सही न हो पर प्रवाह के साथ बोलने की दक्षता।
C. यह जानने की दक्षता कि कैसे और कहाँ भाषा का उचित रूप से प्रयोग करना है।
D. अधिक से अधिक अंग्रेजी का प्रयोग करना।

137. प्राथमिक स्तर पर एक अध्यापक अपने शिक्षार्थियों को रंग करने और चित्रकारी करने के लिए प्रोत्साहित करती है। यह किस तरह से मददगार है?

A. कक्षा में चुप्पी बनाए रखने में
B. सूक्ष्म गत्यात्मक कौशलों का विकास करने में
C. शिक्षार्थियों का मनोरंजन करने में
D. अध्यापक को अध्यापन से विश्राम देने में

138. बच्चे भाषा प्रभावशाली तरीके से तब सीखते हैं जब ______ ।

A. उन्हें भाषा में निपुण अध्यापक मिले
B. उन्हें अच्छी पाठ्यपुस्तक मिले
C. उन्हें रोका जाए
D. उन्हें प्रोत्साहन मिले

125. A **126.** A **127.** A **128.** B **129.** A **130.** A **131.** C **132.** B **133.** B **134.** C
135. D **136.** A, C **137.** B **138.** D

139. एक अध्यापिका अपनी कक्षा में समूह चर्चा और सहपाठियों में अन्तःक्रियाओं को महत्व देती है। वह विद्यार्थियों की सही वर्तनी या उच्चारण में गलतियों पर बहुत अधिक ध्यान नहीं देती है। वह कक्षा में किस उपागम का प्रयोग कर रही है?

A. पारम्परिक B. उदारवादी (एक्लैक्टिक)
C. संरचनात्मक D. रचनावादी

140. आपने महसूस किया कि पाठ में प्रयुक्त भाषा आपके शिक्षार्थियों के लिए बहुत ही कठिन है। आप भाषा को कुछ सरल करते हैं और अपने शिक्षार्थियों की आवश्यकतानुसार विषयवस्तु में भी कुछ परिवर्तन करते हैं। आपका यह कृत्य क्या कहलाएगा?

A. अंगीकार करना B. अनुकूलन करना
C. मूल्यांकन करना D. समीक्षा करना

141. आज राजू विद्यालय जा रहा है, इसलिए वह बहुत खुश है। अपने परिवार का वह पहला व्यक्ति है जो विद्यालय जा रहा है। उसके परिवार में इससे पहले कोई भी नहीं, यहाँ तक कि उसके अभिभावक कभी विद्यालय नहीं गए। राजू को किस शिक्षार्थी के रूप में जानेंगे?

A. प्रथम पीढ़ी B. द्वितीय पीढ़ी
C. हाशियाकृत D. अल्पसंख्यक

142. अध्यापन की दुनिया में प्रवेश करने के बाद आपने अनुभव किया कि पाठ्यपुस्तक की शुरुआत में शिशुगीत और चित्र कथाएँ होती हैं और अन्त में वर्णमाला होती है। भाषा शिक्षणशास्त्र में इस प्रकार की व्यवस्था किस उपागम के अन्तर्गत आएगी?

A. बॉटमअप उपागम (अधो शीर्षगामी)
B. टॉप डाउन उपागम (उर्ध्व अधोगामी)
C. इक्लैक्टिक उपागम (उदार वादी)
D. सौन्दर्यात्मक उपागम

143. जब भाषा स्वाभाविक रूप से सीखी जाती है, बिना किसी व्यवस्थित अभ्यास के, तब इसे क्या कहा जाता है?

A. विद्वत्ता B. अर्जन
C. स्वीकृति D. अधिगम

144. निम्नलिखित में से किसका एक महत्वपूर्ण गुणधर्म है, जिसमें शिक्षार्थी जोड़ों या समूह में एक-साथ मिलकर समस्या समाधान पर कार्य करते हैं?

A. सम्प्रेषणात्मक भाषा शिक्षण B. व्यवहारवादी उपागम
C. समग्र भाषा उपागम D. संरचनात्मक उपागम

145. 'प्रदूषण' टॉपिक पर पाठयोजना तैयार करते समय आपका पहला चरण क्या होगा?

A. प्रस्तावना संबंधी प्रश्न तैयार करना।
B. टॉपिक को बार-बार पढ़ना।
C. शिक्षण सामग्री का चयन करना।
D. उद्देश्य बनाना।

146. एक अध्यापक ने अपने शिक्षार्थियों को 'जल' पर एक अनुच्छेद लिखने के लिए कहा। शिक्षार्थियों ने विज्ञान और सामाजिक विज्ञान की कक्षाओं में जो पढ़ा था उसके आधार पर आपस में चर्चा आरम्भ की और उसके बाद अनुच्छेद लिखना शुरू किया। यह किस तरह का उदाहरण है?

A. प्रयोग में भाषा B. विज्ञान की भाषा
C. भाषा समूचे पाठ्यक्रम में D. सम्प्रेषणात्मक उपागम

147. आपका पालन-पोषण एक ऐसे गाँव में हुआ जहाँ सभी लोग हिंदी बोलते थे और आपने यह भाषा बिना विद्यालय गए ही सीख ली। बाद में जब आप विद्यालय गए तो आपने अंग्रेजी, संस्कृत, हिंदी और उर्दू सीखी। अब आप अंग्रेजी भाषा प्रवाह के साथ बोलते हैं। अब आपकी प्रथम भाषा कौन-सी है?

A. अंग्रेजी B. हिंदी
C. उर्दू D. संस्कृत

148. एक अध्यापक अपनी कक्षा में वास्तविक वस्तुएँ जैसे कि छतरी, बरसाती, पेचकस आदि लाती है। वह शिक्षार्थियों से कहती है कि प्रत्येक शब्द के बारे में दो या तीन वाक्य कहें। इस प्रकार की सामग्री को तकनीकी रूप से क्या कहा जाएगा?

A. भाषा निवेश B. शिक्षण उपकरण
C. उपकरण D. वास्तविक वस्तुएँ (रियलिया)

149. अपनी कक्षा में 'काल' का शिक्षण करते समय आप एक ही व्यक्ति के दो चित्र दिखाते हैं–

एक चित्र पन्द्रह वर्ष पहले का है और एक चित्र जो अभी-अभी खींचा गया है। आप इन चित्रों के आधार पर उस व्यक्ति के वर्तमान और भूत–वह कैसा दिखता है, उसकी आदतें–इन पर बात आरंभ करते हैं। आप किसका प्रयोग कर रहे हैं?

A. निर्देशात्मक व्याकरण (प्रैसक्रिप्टिव)
B. संरचनात्मक व्याकरण
C. शिक्षणशास्त्रीय व्याकरण
D. नियम आधारित व्याकरण

150. वे कथन जो किसी कक्षा विशेष या पाठ्यक्रम (कोर्स) के अन्त में विद्यार्थियों द्वारा अर्जित ज्ञान, कौशल और प्रवृत्ति का वर्णन करते हैं, वे क्या कहलाते हैं?

A. शिक्षण प्रतिफल B. अधिगम प्रतिफल
C. संख्यात्मक प्रतिफल D. बुनियादी साक्षरता प्रतिफल

139. D **140.** B **141.** A **142.** B **143.** B **144.** A **145.** D **146.** C **147.** B **148.** D
149. C **150.** B

EXPLANATORY ANSWERS

1. **(B):** Continuous and comprehensive evaluation (CCE) focuses on assessing a student's holistic development, covering both academic growth and other skill areas over time. A growth and learning progress portfolio is a tool that allows for the ongoing collection of various evidences of a student's learning and development, such as projects, assignments, and other activities. This method aligns with CCE as it provides a comprehensive view of student progress across different domains and over extended periods, allowing for modifications in teaching approaches based on individual needs.

2. **(B):** Assertion (A) emphasizes the importance of teachers being aware of their personal biases and attitudes to ensure they provide equitable and supportive environments for all students. Reason (R) discusses functional fixedness, a cognitive bias that limits a person to using an object only in the way it is traditionally used, which could hinder problem-solving. While both statements are true, (R) does not directly explain why teachers need to examine their biases as it pertains more to cognitive flexibility than to teaching practices.

3. **(D):** When Avi attributes his poor performance in mathematics to a lack of "sense for numbers," he is indicating a belief that he inherently lacks the ability in a specific area. This is an example of an internal, stable attribution, where the individual perceives the cause of their failure as something that is intrinsic to them and unlikely to change.

4. **(B):** Lev Vygotsky's theory emphasizes the Zone of Proximal Development (ZPD), which refers to the difference between what a learner can do without help and what they can do with guidance. Optimal learning occurs when students are given tasks slightly beyond their current capabilities but are supported through scaffolding—this promotes cognitive development by encouraging students to stretch their skills with the help of a more knowledgeable other.

5. **(B):** In progressive education, the teacher's role shifts from being the central source of knowledge to a facilitator who guides and supports students in their learning process. This educational philosophy advocates for student-centered learning environments where teachers encourage students to explore, ask questions, and engage in problem-solving, thereby fostering independent thinking and learning.

6. **(B):** Howard Gardner's theory of multiple intelligences proposes that intelligence is not a single general ability but a plurality of distinct abilities. His theory identifies several cognitive abilities, such as linguistic, logical-mathematical, spatial, musical, bodily-kinesthetic, interpersonal, intrapersonal, and naturalistic intelligences, suggesting that individuals vary in their strengths and combinations of these intelligences.

7. **(A):** This sequence reflects a developmental progression where children initially understand concepts through physical actions (action-based), then through mental images or visual representations (image-based), and finally through abstract symbols (symbol-based). This progression aligns with cognitive development theories, such as those by Piaget, which suggest that children move from concrete to more abstract forms of thinking as they mature.

8. **(A):** Assertion (A) states the importance of emotional support in classrooms, which is essential for creating a safe learning environment that promotes cognitive engagement and reduces anxiety. Reason (R) explains that emotions and cognition are interconnected, implying that a student's emotional state can significantly influence their cognitive processes and learning outcomes. The understanding of this connection substantiates the need for emotional support as a means to enhance cognitive functions.

9. **(B):** Developmental theories, such as those proposed by Lev Vygotsky, suggest that development does not occur in a straightforward, linear progression but rather in a spiral manner where abilities develop through cycles of advances and setbacks. This pattern reflects the complex interaction of various biological, cognitive, and socio-emotional factors that influence development over time.

10. **(B):** Vygotsky's concept of inner speech pertains to the internalization of language and its use for self-regulation and problem-solving. According to Vygotsky, children initially use language externally in social interactions but gradually learn to use it internally as a tool for guiding their thoughts and actions, particularly when faced with challenges or when planning their behaviour. This use of inner speech is crucial for cognitive development and self-regulation.

11. **(D):** In constructivist pedagogy, learning is seen as an active, constructive process where learners build new ideas or concepts based upon their current/past knowledge. The guided discovery method involves

the teacher facilitating the learning process by posing questions, problems, or scenarios rather than simply presenting facts. This method encourages students to explore and experiment, leading to a deeper understanding of concepts such as floating and sinking through hands-on activities and inquiry, which aligns with constructivist principles.

12. (A): Rote rehearsal involves repeatedly memorizing information through repetition, which is effective for short-term memory retention but not for meaningful learning that requires deep understanding and long-term retention. Meaningful learning techniques like mnemonics, concept mapping, and elaborative rehearsal are designed to create associations and enhance understanding by integrating new information with existing knowledge. In contrast, rote rehearsal does not facilitate this deeper level of processing and connection.

13. (B): Critical thinking questions are designed to stimulate higher-order thinking, requiring analysis, synthesis, and evaluation, rather than merely recalling facts. A well-formulated critical thinking question should challenge students to think deeply, reflect, and consider multiple perspectives, promoting open-ended discussions and problem-solving, rather than relying solely on factual recall.

14. (C): Culturally responsive pedagogy recognizes the importance of including students' cultural references in all aspects of learning, which can significantly enhance engagement and achievement by making learning more relevant and effective. However, standardized curricula and assessments often do not account for cultural diversity and may impose a one-size-fits-all approach that can actually hinder the goal of achieving equity in education.

15. (D): Jean Piaget's concept of assimilation involves incorporating new experiences into an existing framework without changing that framework. When Jagriti sees another dog that looks similar to her Golden Retriever, Rusty, and calls it a dog too, she is assimilating this new dog into her existing category of 'dog,' even though the breed might differ.

16. (A): Heredity determines an individual's sex based on the genetic makeup provided by the sex chromosomes (XX for females, XY for males). Gender, academic success, and learning styles, however, are influenced by a combination of genetic, environmental, and social factors and are not determined solely by heredity.

17. (A): Encouraging a question-driven classroom environment aligns with child-centered pedagogy, which emphasizes valuing children's perspectives and facilitating their active participation in learning. By focusing on inquiry rather than direct instruction, teachers promote a more engaging and responsive educational environment that fosters critical thinking and deeper understanding.

18. (A): Repetitive and ritualistic behaviours are hallmark signs of Autism Spectrum Disorder (ASD). These behaviours may include repetitive movements, routines, or speaking patterns, which are not typically seen in the other conditions listed.

19. (A): Learners are more engaged and involved in the learning process when the activities are contextually relevant, reflecting their backgrounds, interests, or real-world applications. This relevance helps students see the value in what they are learning and motivates them to engage more deeply with the material.

20. (C): Children with learning difficulties often exhibit specific challenges related to dyslexia, which includes confusion with visually similar letters and alphabets, impacting their reading and writing skills. This does not necessarily correlate with low IQ or poor sight, and emotional regulation issues are more characteristic of other developmental conditions.

21. (D): The concept of a sensitive period refers to a time frame in early development during which the presence of certain environmental stimuli is necessary for normal development of specific skills or behaviours. In cases of severe social deprivation, like with feral children, missed interactions during this critical period can lead to long-lasting developmental issues, as certain skills and behaviours don't develop optimally outside these sensitive periods.

22. (A): Gender stereotypes are over-generalized beliefs about the characteristics, attributes, and behaviours of males or females. These stereotypes can influence expectations and perceptions about gender roles in society, often shaping individual behaviours and opportunities from a young age.

23. (B): In an inclusive classroom, the emphasis is on providing all children, regardless of their abilities or disabilities, equal opportunities to participate in classroom activities. This approach fosters an environment of acceptance and belonging, aiming to educate all students together by accommodating individual needs within a unified framework.

24. (C): Critical thinking questions are designed to encourage students to think deeply, question assumptions, and evaluate information. These questions stimulate cognitive development by promoting analysis, synthesis, and evaluation, skills that are crucial for effective problem-solving and decision-making in complex situations.

25. (D): Socio-constructivist theories, such as those proposed by Vygotsky, emphasize that learning is inherently a social process where individuals construct meaning through interactions with others and the environment. This theory suggests that knowledge is co-constructed and that social interaction plays a fundamental role in the development of cognition.

26. (A): This assertion and reason pair accurately captures the essence of developmental variability among children. While there are typical age ranges for developmental milestones like babbling and forming sentences, individual differences are expected. The reason correctly explains that these developmental milestones are merely suggestive, not prescriptive, highlighting the natural variability in developmental timing among children.

27. (A): Growth in height and weight are examples of quantitative changes, which involve changes in amount or quantity that can be measured. These changes are observable and measurable aspects of a child's physical development and differ from qualitative changes, which relate to the development of new abilities or skills.

28. (B): Kohlberg's stages of moral development place Arunima's reasoning in this stage, where individuals recognize that while laws and rules generally serve the common good, there are times when they may conflict with fairness or human rights, justifying exceptions. Her reasoning reflects an advanced level of moral development focused on equity and justice.

29. (D): Gifted students are defined by their ability to perform at higher cognitive levels compared to peers of the same age. They often understand complex concepts quickly and can process information at a faster pace, leading to advanced academic performance in various domains.

30. (D): During the pre-operational stage, children engage in symbolic play, using objects to represent something else while giving life and intention to inanimate objects (animism). This stage is characterized by great strides in imagination and the ability to think symbolically, though thinking remains non-logical and non-reversible.

31. (A): Summative assessments are designed to evaluate student learning at the end of an instructional unit by comparing it against some standard or benchmark. These assessments are typically more formal, such as tests or exams, and are not as effective in identifying individual differences during the learning process because they do not provide ongoing feedback that can be used to adjust teaching strategies or understand specific student needs in real-time.

32. (B): Dienes blocks and graph paper are effective tools for explaining the concept of decimals. Dienes blocks can help students visualize and manipulate decimal values, illustrating parts of a whole and how these parts fit into the decimal system. Graph paper can be similarly useful by allowing students to draw models that represent decimal values, aiding in their understanding of place value and the spatial representation of decimals.

33. (C): When calculating a percentage discount on multiple items, the discount should be applied to each item individually, not to the total combined cost. The error made by the group in the question was that they calculated the discount by combining the percentages (16% total), which does not accurately represent an 8% discount on each individual item. Applying a single percentage to the total cost does not yield the same result as applying the percentage individually to each item and then summing the discounted prices.

34. (B): Here, LCM of 9, 21, 7 and 63 = 63

$\therefore$ Fractions are: $\frac{1}{9}\times 63, \frac{1}{21}\times 63, \frac{3}{7}\times 63, \frac{12}{63}\times 63$

$= 7, 3, 27, 12$

$\because$ Decreasing order : 27, 12, 7, 3

$= \frac{3}{7}, \frac{12}{63}, \frac{1}{9}, \frac{1}{21}$

$\therefore$ Arrangement of fractions in decreasing order is $\frac{3}{7}, \frac{12}{63}, \frac{1}{9}, \frac{1}{21}$.

35. (A, B, C, D): Each of the options provided reflects important aspects of how mathematics contributes to everyday life and society:

- **Communication of mathematical ideas in writing using both formal and informal languages:** This experience is crucial as it teaches children how to express mathematical concepts clearly and accurately, a skill that is essential in many professional and academic contexts. It helps in documenting and sharing mathematical ideas, promoting understanding and collaboration.
- **Meeting people from different areas of employment and exploring how they use**

mathematics in their work: This experience directly links mathematics to real-world applications, showing its relevance in various careers. It helps students understand the practical uses of mathematics and can inspire them to pursue STEM fields by demonstrating its value in everyday work environments.

- **Collecting, organising, representing and interpreting data in day-to-day life:** Data literacy is a fundamental aspect of modern life, influencing decisions in areas ranging from business to personal finance and health. This activity helps students develop critical skills in handling data, fostering analytical thinking and decision-making based on numerical information.
- **Play small group games that draw on mathematical skills and concepts:** Games are an engaging way to reinforce mathematical concepts and skills. They promote fun learning experiences and can improve problem-solving abilities, strategic thinking, and teamwork, all of which are important both in educational settings and in daily life.

Each of these activities enhances understanding and appreciation of mathematics by connecting it to practical, real-life situations and by fostering skills that are applicable in a broad range of contexts. Thus, all these options are appropriate and reflect the contributions of mathematics to life and society.

36. (B): A mathematics laboratory is a unique learning space that provides an opportunity for students to explore mathematical concepts through hands-on activities and experiments. It aims to make learning mathematics an engaging and enjoyable experience. The laboratory is not primarily used for assessments or grading, but rather for allowing students to experiment, make conjectures, and discover mathematical truths for themselves. Features (*a*) "It is a place to enjoy mathematics through informal exploration" and (*c*) "It provides opportunity to make conjectures, test them and to generalise observed patterns" describe this environment accurately.

37. (A): Ten million: In the Indian numbering system, one crore is equal to ten million. This is a basic numeric conversion widely used in countries that follow the Indian numbering system, such as India, Pakistan, Bangladesh, Nepal, and Sri Lanka.

38. (D): From given table:

(A) Range of the data

Maximum number of paitent – Minimum number of patient = (45 – 18) = 27 (Right)

(B) 4 days, number of paitents was more than 30 (Right)

(C) Difference between the number of patients on Monday and Wednesday

$= 45 - 25$

$= 20$ (Right)

(D) Total number of patient was 200 (Wrong)

$\because$ Total number of patient

$= 25 + 38 + 45 + 18 + 36 + 39$

$= 201$

$\therefore$ Option (D) is the wrong statement.

39. (A): Ramanujan and Varahmihir are recognized for their contributions to mathematical analysis and numerical techniques. Ramanujan's extensive work on infinite series and continued fractions significantly advanced the field of numerical analysis, while Varahmihir, though primarily an astronomer, applied mathematical concepts to his astronomical work, which often involved detailed calculations and numerical methods.

40. (A): Given, Mass of 1 egg = 65 g

$\therefore$ Mass of 2 dozen eggs $= 2 \times 12 \times 65$ g

$= 1560$ g

$= \frac{1560}{1000}$ kg

$= 1.56$ kg.

41. (C):

$$\begin{array}{r} 2023 - 03 - 31 \\ 1992 - 01 - 13 \\ \hline 31 - 02 - 18 \end{array}$$

$\because$ Retirement on 31-03-2023

$\therefore$ Duration of Service

$= 31$ years 02 months $(18 + 1)$ days

$= 31$ years 2 months and 19 days.

42. (A): The Third angle of the triangle

$= 180° - (50° + 30°)$

$= 180° - 80°$

$= 100°$.

43. (D): The National Curriculum Framework For Foundational Stage (NCFFS), 2022 suggests a progression from concrete to abstract when teaching mathematical concepts. Starting with direct experiences (b), using spoken language to describe these experiences (c), moving to visual representations like pictures (d), and finally formalizing with written symbols (a) aligns with how abstract concepts should be grounded in tangible, comprehensible experiences before transitioning to abstract symbols.

44. (C): Matching the characteristics:

- Face of a blackboard (*a*) represents a part of a plane (*iii*).
- A line (*b*) has no definite length (*iv*).
- A ray (*c*) has one end point (*ii*).
- A line segment (*d*) has two end points (*i*).

This matches descriptions accurately with their geometric properties.

45. (C): $\because$ 1 hm = 100 m, hm = hectometers and 1 dam = 10 m, dam = decameters

$\therefore$ 22 hm = 22 × 100 = 2200 m

and 8 dam = 8 × 10 = 80 m

$\therefore$ 22 hm 8 dam = 2200 m + 80 m

= 2280 m.

46. (D): $x : y = p : q$

$$\Rightarrow \quad \frac{x}{y} = \frac{p}{q}$$

By Componendo and Dividendo

(*d*) $$\frac{x+y}{x-y} = \frac{p+q}{p-q}$$

$\Rightarrow$ $x + y : x - y = p + q : p - d$ (Not true)

(*a*) $$\frac{x}{y}+1 = \frac{p}{q}+1$$

$$\frac{x+y}{y} = \frac{p+q}{q}$$

$\Rightarrow$ $x + y : y = p + q : q$ (True)

(*b*) $$\frac{x}{y}-1 = \frac{p}{q}-1$$

$$\Rightarrow \quad \frac{x-y}{y} = \frac{p-q}{q}$$

$\Rightarrow$ $x - y : y = p - q : q$ (True)

(*c*) $$\frac{x}{y} = \frac{p}{q}$$

$$\Rightarrow \quad \frac{x}{p} = \frac{y}{q}$$

$\Rightarrow$ $x : p = y : q$ (True)

Hence, (*a*), (*b*) and (*c*) are true.

47. (B): 1233210 ÷ 5555 – 222

= 222 – 222 = 0.

48. (C): Each of the statements in the options can be evaluated for correctness based on definitions within number theory:

(*a*) "All positive integers are whole numbers" is true because the set of whole numbers includes all positive integers starting from zero. Therefore, any positive integer is indeed a whole number.

(*b*) "All whole numbers are integers" is also true. The set of integers includes all whole numbers (0, 1, 2, ...) as well as their negative counterparts and zero.

(*c*) "All rational numbers are real numbers" is correct. Rational numbers, defined as the quotient of two integers where the denominator is not zero, are a subset of the real numbers, which include both rational and irrational numbers.

(*d*) "All irrational numbers are real numbers" is true. Irrational numbers, which cannot be expressed as a simple fraction, are part of the real number system, which encompasses all rational and irrational numbers.

Therefore, all statements (*a*), (*b*), (*c*) and (*d*) are correct. Each of these statements correctly represents relationships within different classes of numbers according to standard mathematical definitions.

49. (B): The statement "mathematics is hierarchical in levels that are logically structured" implies that foundational concepts in mathematics must be understood before more complex ones can be introduced.

(*b*) "Multiplication follows and builds on the concept of addition" is a prime example of this hierarchical structure. Multiplication can be viewed as repeated addition, which naturally extends the understanding of addition.

(*c*) "Number sense needs to be developed before the concepts of addition and subtraction" also fits this model perfectly, as having a basic understanding of numbers, their values, and relationships is crucial before beginning to operate on them with addition or subtraction.

Thus, options (*b*) and (*c*) accurately reflect the hierarchical and logical structure of mathematics learning.

50. (C): 12 thousand + 13 hundred + 2 tens

= 12000 + 1300 + 2 × 10

= 12000 + 1300 + 20

= 13320.

51. (C): Given a solution, numerous equations can be constructed to fit that solution. For instance, if the solution is a specific point on a graph, there are infinitely many lines (linear equations) that can pass through that point, depending on the slope. This shows the flexibility in constructing different equations from a single solution, making option C correct.

52. (D): For Grade-II learners, basic operations should involve:

(*a*) "It involves child's ability to develop informal strategies" is true as young learners often use intuitive methods like counting on fingers or using physical objects.

(*b*) "It involves child's ability to estimate" is also crucial, as estimation is a fundamental skill that supports numerical understanding and calculation checks.

(*c*) "It involves child's ability to do calculations with large numbers" is typically not appropriate for Grade-II learners due to their developmental stage, so options (*a*) and (*b*) are most relevant.

53. (A): In geometry, a curve is defined as open if it does not return to its starting point and does not enclose any area. If all four points used in an example of an open curve are collinear, they lie on a straight line, which is an example of an open curve. Thus, option A is correct.

54. (D): The National Curriculum Framework (NCF) 2005 strongly advocates for a constructivist approach in the teaching and learning of mathematics. This approach emphasizes learners constructing their own understanding and knowledge through experiences and reflecting on those experiences.
It encourages active engagement, problem-solving, and understanding concepts from within, aligning with option D.

55. (A): 43, 47, 53, 59, ?, 67, 71, 73
$\Rightarrow$ 43, 47, 53, 59, $\boxed{61}$, 67, 71, 73
This is the pattern of increasing prime number.
So, ? = the missing number = 61.

56. (A): Scissors are a practical example to demonstrate the concepts of vertically opposite angles and linear pair of angles:

- Vertically opposite angles are formed when two lines intersect, much like the blades of a pair of scissors intersect at the pivot point. The angles opposite each other at the intersection are equal, exemplifying vertically opposite angles.
- Linear pair of angles are adjacent angles whose non-common sides form a straight line. When scissors are partially opened, the angles formed at the pivot point by the blades with the handles form a linear pair, each summing up to 180 degrees. This makes option A correct as it accurately reflects the angles demonstrated by a pair of scissors.

57. (B): Total quantity of turpentine oil

$$= 5 \times 20 \text{ L}$$
$$= 100 \text{ L}$$
$$\therefore \quad 100 \text{ L} = 10 \times 5 \text{ L} + 10 \times 2 \text{ L} + x \times 1 \text{ L}$$
$$\therefore x \times 1 \text{ L} = 100 \text{ L} - 70 \text{ L}$$
$$\Rightarrow x \times 1 \text{ L} = 30 \text{ L}$$
$$\Rightarrow x \times 1 \text{ L} = 30 \times 1 \text{ L}$$
$$\Rightarrow \quad x = 30$$

Therefore, Number of 1 L cans filled is 30.

58. (A): A and M have vertical symmetry and X has both vertical and horizontal symmetry and L has no line of symmetry.

59. (D): Given, $(7 * 2) \times (123) = 92496$

$$\Rightarrow \quad (7 * 2) = \frac{92496}{123}$$
$$\Rightarrow \quad 7 * 2 = 752$$
$$\therefore \quad * = 5.$$

60. (A): Using the digits 5, 1, 0, 3, 9 and 6
$\therefore$ The difference between the greatest and smallest 6-digit numbers
= 965310 − 103569
= 861741.

61. (C): Environmental Studies (EVS) at the primary level is encouraged to be taught using an integrated approach for several reasons:

(*a*) "EVS draws issues from subjects like Science, Social Science, and Environmental Education" highlights the interdisciplinary nature of EVS, which covers a wide range of topics that benefit from being understood in a connected way, reflecting the integrated nature of the environment itself.

(*b*) "It helps in developing holistic understanding" emphasizes that an integrated approach in EVS helps students see the connections between different fields of knowledge and their application to real-world environmental issues, fostering a more comprehensive and practical understanding of the world.

These reasons support why EVS is most effectively taught through an integrated approach, making option C the correct choice.

62. (C): Hold workshops about 'Good Touch' and 'Bad Touch': As an EVS teacher wishing to address safety and awareness about sexual harassment, holding workshops that explain the concepts of 'Good Touch' and 'Bad Touch' is most appropriate because:

- This approach directly educates students on how to recognize inappropriate behaviour, which is crucial for personal safety.
- It empowers students by giving them the knowledge and confidence to identify and react to potentially harmful situations effectively.

Therefore, option C is the most suitable and direct method to address this important aspect of student safety.

63. (B, C): The question asks for the correct skill that Roshni is assessing by having students explain variations in germination rates of different seeds based on the displayed data:

- The correct skill in this context is drawing inference, which involves interpreting data and reaching conclusions about what the data shows regarding different conditions affecting seed germination. This skill is about understanding and explaining the 'why' behind observed data, which aligns closely with what Roshni is assessing.

64. (D): Regarding the respective locations of Gujarat and Bihar from Telangana:

- Gujarat is located to the northwest of Telangana.
- Bihar is located to the northeast of Telangana.

This geographical orientation correctly places Gujarat and Bihar relative to Telangana, making option D correct.

65. (B): Suitable tools of assessment to assess process skills in EVS might include:

(*b*) "Project work", which allows for practical application of learned concepts and skills in a real-world or simulated context.

(*c*) "Drawing diagrams", which helps in understanding and visualizing information or concepts clearly.

(*d*) "Picture reading", which aids in interpreting visual information and can be a tool for assessing observational skills and the ability to derive information from illustrations.

These tools are appropriate for evaluating different dimensions of process skills in EVS, making option B the best choice.

66. (C): To calculate the actual distance between two cities based on the map scale provided:

- Given scale: 1 cm = 155 m
- Measured distance on the map: 19.7 cm.

Actual distance calculation:

19.7 cm × 155 m/cm = 3053.5 m

This calculation shows that the actual distance between the two cities is approximately 3.05 km, confirming option C as correct.

67. (A): At higher altitudes, the atmospheric pressure decreases, but the blood pressure inside the body initially remains constant or could relatively increase due to lower oxygen levels stimulating certain physiological responses. This disparity between internal and external pressures can lead to nose bleeding as the pressure inside the blood vessels exceeds the reduced external atmospheric pressure, making option A correct.

68. (D): Conduction of heat is also called Thermal Conductivity. (Thermal meaning concerning heat). Among the metals some metals are very good, some are good and some are poor conductors of heat. In order of their thermal conductivity some of the common metals are arranged as: silver, copper, aluminium, iron, lead.

Metal mercury is a liquid and a good conductor of heat. It is the only liquid which is a good conductor of heat.

These materials are known poor conductors of heat. They do not easily allow heat to pass through them, making them effective insulators. Options including metals such as Iron or Aluminium are incorrect as these are good conductors of heat. Therefore, option D is correct.

69. (C): The task given by Rita involves several skills:

(*b*) "predict how germinating seeds would look like", as students imagine how seeds change day by day.

(*c*) "observe and record", crucial for tracking the daily changes in seed germination and development.

(*d*) "infer from the given activity", as students analyze and derive conclusions from their observations about germination.

This combination of skills being assessed makes option C the correct answer.

70. (C): A species 'X' that is abundant but only found in 'Y' part of India is described as endemic. This term is used for species that are native to a specific geographical location and not naturally found anywhere else. This specificity fits the description given, confirming option C as correct.

Endemic species are those that are found in just one region and nowhere else in the world. For example, kangaroos are originally endemic to Australia and are found nowhere else in the world. The cases where they have been spotted outside their natural habitat is due to humans introducing them when the animal was in captivity.

There are also other marsupials that are endemic only to Australia and its surrounding islands. The Tasmanian Tiger is one such animal that was endemic to Australia, Tasmania and New Guinea. But now, it is extinct.

As stated above, endemic species are those which are only found in a given region or location and nowhere else in the world. However, since endemic species are unique to a particular geographical region; they are more vulnerable to extinction. As a result, special efforts may be required to conserve them.

71. (D): In Environmental Studies (EVS), "environment" encompasses a broad spectrum of elements:

(*a*) "Man-made environment" refers to environments created or modified by humans, such as cities, roads, and infrastructure.

(*b*) "Natural environment" includes all naturally occurring ecosystems and geological formations.

(*c*) "Social environment" involves the conditions and cultures people live in and interact with, including social relationships and institutions.

(*d*) "Cultural environment" covers the shared beliefs, practices, artifacts, and values that characterize groups of people.

Together, these components make up the comprehensive view of the environment addressed in EVS, supporting a multidisciplinary approach to learning. Therefore, option D correctly includes all aspects.

72. (B): Incorrect statement about elephant herds: The correct answer is option B, which states that a herd has 20 to 25 female elephants and their young ones. Typically, elephant herds are indeed composed of female elephants and their young, but the size can vary more broadly than just 20 to 25 individuals. Herds can be smaller or significantly larger, depending on various factors including environmental conditions and social structure. Therefore, specifying only 20 to 25 females and their young as a typical herd size is not accurate.

73. (A): Map Reading activity in EVS classes develops certain abilities and skills in primary students:

(*a*) "Understanding relative positions of places" helps students grasp how different locations relate to one another spatially.

(*b*) "Understanding directions of places" aids in navigating and understanding the orientation of various geographic locations.

(*c*) "Understanding symbols and scale" is crucial for reading maps correctly, allowing students to interpret various symbols and scale measurements effectively.

These skills are fundamental to map reading, making option A the correct choice, as it includes all relevant skills except drawing precisely according to scale maps, which might not be emphasized as much in primary education.

74. (B): The correct direction from Y to X is South: Calculating the net movement and directions:

- Travel north from X to A: 125 m,
- West from A to B: 75 m,
- North from B to C: 150 m,
- East from C to Y: 75 m.

The net movement north (125 m + 150 m) and the fact there's no net east-west movement (75 m west then 75 m east cancel each other out) makes your house directly south of your school. Thus, B, "Due South," is correct.

75. (C): Assessing the potential health issues for Saleem and Raju:

- Saleem consumes high-fat and high-calorie foods, potentially leading to obesity.
- Raju avoids iron-rich green leafy vegetables, increasing his risk for anaemia.

Thus, option C, "Obesity and Anaemia," accurately describes their likely health disorders based on their diets.

76. (D): All mentioned materials are alloys:

- Steel is an alloy of iron and carbon.
- Brass is an alloy of copper and zinc.
- Bronze is an alloy of copper and usually tin.

Alloy: Alloy is a homogeneous mixture of one metal with one or more other metals or non-metals. An alloy is prepared by mixing metals in the molten state in a fixed proportion by weight but they may be homogeneous or heterogeneous in solid-state. Properties of Alloy- Various properties of metals like-malleability, ductility, strength, hardness, resistance to corrosion and appearance, etc are improved by alloying of metals.

Types of alloy: There are mainly three types of alloy in nature based on the composition of elements.

- **Binary alloy:** Alloys which made with two components are called a binary alloy. Example: Copper (Cu) + Zinc (Zn) = Brass (Alloy).

- **Ternary alloy:** Alloys which made with three components are called a ternary alloy. Example: Copper (Cu) + Zinc (Zn) + Nickel (Ni) = German Silver (Alloy).
- **Quaternary alloy:** Alloys which made with four components are called a quaternary alloy. Example: Ferrous (Fe) + Chromium (Cr) + Nickel (Ni) + Carbon (C) = Stainless steel (Alloy).

These materials are correctly identified as alloys, validating option D as the correct choice.

77. (A): Both the Assertion and Reason are correct, and the Reason is the correct explanation of the Assertion:

- **Assertion:** True, stories and narratives are used throughout the EVS textbooks to facilitate engagement and understanding.
- **Reason:** Also true, and it directly explains why stories are used—by helping children empathize with characters, they become more sensitive to social differences, effectively explaining the use of narratives in textbooks.

Option A is the correct choice as both the assertion and reason are correct and logically connected.

78. (D): The crust forms only 1 per cent of the volume of the earth, 84 per cent consists of the mantle and 15 per cent makes the core. The radius of the earth is 6371 km.

The uppermost layer over the earth's surface is called the crust. It is the thinnest of all the layers. It is about 35 km. on the continental masses and only 5 km. on the ocean floors.

The main mineral constituents of the continental mass are silica and alumina. It is thus called sial (si-silica and al-alumina). The oceanic crust mainly consists of silica and magnesium; it is therefore called sima (si-silica and ma-magnesium).

Just beneath the crust is the mantle which extends up to a depth of 2900 km. below the crust. The innermost layer is the core with a radius of about 3500 km. It is mainly made up of nickel and iron and is called nife (ni – nickel and fe – ferrous i.e. iron). The central core has very high temperature and pressure.

79. (D): The Assertion (A) states that travelers like Al-Biruni and Ibn Batuta traveled from India to different countries, which is incorrect. Both Al-Biruni and Ibn Batuta traveled to India from different countries; Al-Biruni from Uzbekistan and Ibn Batuta from Morocco. However, the Reason (R) stating that traveling led to sharing of ideas between people is true. Travelers like Al-Biruni and Ibn Batuta documented their journeys and interactions, which contributed significantly to the exchange of cultural, scientific, and geographical knowledge.

80. (C): The question posed by the EVS teacher about what would happen if all birds were suddenly removed from Earth encourages students to think about multiple outcomes and implications, engaging in divergent thinking: Divergent questions provoke a range of ideas and answers, suitable for developing critical thinking and creativity.

Convergent question: Convergent questions assist in problem-solving and are useful for basic processes such as measuring, communicating, comparing and contrasting. These questions are called close-ended questions as students are not expected to contribute to an original idea. They are supposed to find one single and fixed answer.

Hypothetical question: A hypothetical question is one based on supposition, not facts. They are typically used to elicit opinions and beliefs about imagined situations or conditions that don't exist.

81. (B): The chapter about Suryamani in the NCERT textbook for class V, depicting tribal life, primarily focuses on:

(*b*) "Close relationship between forest dwellers (communities) and forests" showcases the symbiotic relationship between tribal communities and their natural environment.

(*c*) "Girls education how it changes their life" reflects on the transformative power of education in the lives of tribal girls, exemplified by Suryamani's story.

(*d*) "The forest products used by tribes" provides insight into the practical and sustainable use of natural resources by tribal communities.

These aspects are vital for understanding the integrated lifestyle of tribal communities and the role of education in societal transformation, making option B the most relevant and correct choice.

82. (D): Mount Kilimanjaro is a dormant volcano in Tanzania. With three volcanic cones — Kibo, Mawenzi and Shira — it is the highest mountain in Africa and the highest single free-standing mountain above sea level in the world: 5,895 m above sea level and 4,900 m above its plateau base. It is also the highest volcano in the Eastern Hemisphere. Kilimanjaro is the fourth most topographically prominent peak on Earth. It is part of Kilimanjaro National Park and is a major hiking and climbing destination.

Mount Fuji is an active stratovolcano located on the Japanese island of Honshu, with a summit elevation of 3,776.24 m. It is the tallest mountain in Japan, the second-highest volcano located on an island in Asia (after Mount Kerinci on the Indonesian island of Sumatra), and seventh-highest peak of an island on Earth. Mount Fuji's exceptionally symmetrical cone, which is covered in snow for about five months of the year, is commonly used as a cultural icon of Japan and is frequently depicted in art and photography, as well as visited by sightseers, hikers and mountain climbers.

The Alps, however, are not volcanic but are formed by the uplift and folding of sedimentary rocks. This makes option D the correct choice, indicating that both Mt. Kilimanjaro and Fujiyama are volcanic.

83. **(B):** The correct evaluation of the statements regarding bird nesting behaviours is:

- **Statement (A):** Crows do not typically build nests on very low branches of a tree. They usually choose higher locations to avoid predators and disturbances, making this statement incorrect.
- **Statement (B):** Weaver birds do not stitch two leaves together to make their nests. Instead, they are known for their intricate nests woven from leaves and grass, which can involve weaving together multiple materials but not merely stitching two leaves.

Both statements A and B are factually incorrect regarding the specific nesting behaviours attributed to these birds, making option B the correct choice.

84. **(A):** Both (A) and (R) are true and (R) explains (A): The water of the Dead Sea is saltier than most of the other bodies of water on earth. The dead sea is as salty as 300 grams of salt in one litre of water. The extremely high concentration of dissolved mineral salts in the water causes the water to be denser than that of plain fresh water. Since our body weight is lighter (less dense) than the density of the water, our body is more buoyant in the Dead Sea, making it easy to float. For example, in freshwater our body doesn't float at all, it actually sinks. In the ocean, the human body starts feeling buoyancy and can float a bit. In the Dead Sea, the water is so dense that one can float easily even to the point that it's hard to stand on two feet. The dead sea is located in Israel. It is known as the most saline water body on the earth because of the large amount of salt present in the water, its density is very high. It is said that humans don't sink in the dead sea, they will keep floating. It is called the dead sea as no living organism can live in its highly saline water.

Option A is correct as both the assertion and the reason are accurate, and the reason logically explains the floating phenomenon in the Dead Sea.

85. **(B):** The activity designed by Samar to have students consult family members about various cooking methods:

- This task promotes engagement with family members, thereby improving social interactions and deepening students' understanding of cultural and familial practices around food. It serves as an excellent way to bridge school learning with real-world experiences and family involvement.

Option B is therefore the most appropriate reason for this activity, emphasizing the enhancement of social interactions through educational tasks.

86. **(C):** Environmental studies aid children in comprehending how things work and interact in their environment. At the primary level, it is an integrated subject area that incorporates knowledge from science, social science, and environmental education. Its aim is to help students acquire a holistic or integrated view of the environment in which they live.

Objectives of EVS at the primary level:

- To train children to locate and comprehend relationships between the natural, social and cultural environment.
- To create cognitive capacity and resourcefulness to make the child curious about social phenomena starting with family and moving on to wider spaces.
- To develop an awareness of environmental issues.
- To engage children in exploratory and hands-on activities to acquire basic cognitive and psychomotor skills through observation, classification, inference, etc.
- To be able to critically address gender concerns and issues of marginalization and cooperation with values of equality and justice and respect for human dignity and rights.

Experiential strategies in teaching EVS at the primary level should involve activities that provide hands-on, real-world experiences:

(*a*) "Discussion" allows students to share and reflect on their experiences.

(*c*) "Field Trips" offer direct engagement with the environment, enhancing learning through real-world exposure.

(*d*) "Art integrated learning" encourages creativity and expression connected to environmental studies.

These methods collectively foster a deep, experiential understanding of environmental concepts, making option C the most reflective of effective experiential teaching strategies.

87. (C): Statement I is true but Statement II is false:

- Statement I is correct as the EVS curriculum indeed adopts a social constructivist perspective, emphasizing learning through interaction, exploration, and reflection within a social context.
- Statement II is false because Piaget's theory, primarily focusing on stages of cognitive development, does not align directly with the social constructivist perspective, which is more closely associated with Vygotsky's theories that emphasize the importance of social interaction in learning.

Thus, option C accurately differentiates the correctness of these statements concerning educational theories.

88. (A): Given the time difference and typical time zone calculations:

- When it is 7:30 PM in India, it corresponds to early afternoon in London, considering India is typically 4.5 to 5.5 hours ahead of London depending on daylight saving times and specific time zone settings. Thus, 2 PM in London on the same day is a feasible and accurate reflection of this time difference.

Option A is therefore correct, with London being the city where it is 2 PM when it's 7:30 PM in India.

89. (B): Asking students to narrate their or their neighbors' experiences of travelling: This strategy:

- Encourages inquiry by prompting students to gather and share diverse, personal travel experiences, which can lead to discussions on various aspects of travel such as cultural encounters, logistical challenges, and personal insights.

Option B is correct as it actively promotes inquiry by engaging students in the collection and sharing of real-world experiences related to travel.

90. (A, B): The methods mentioned—Think-Pair-Share, Reciprocal Peer Tutoring, Jigsaw Strategy, and Peer Review—are indeed examples of both the Peer Group Approach and the Constructivist Approach.

(A) **Peer Group Approach:** Each of these methods involves significant peer interaction. Students are not just passive recipients of information; they actively engage with their peers in the learning process.

(B) **Constructivist Approach:** Constructivism emphasizes learning as an active, social process. These methods require students to engage with content in a way that builds on their prior knowledge and experiences, and they often learn by doing, discussing, and teaching, which are all key elements of constructivist pedagogy.

91. (D): The passage indicates that the stranger, though appearing with a cut on his cheek, did not seem severely injured as he was able to communicate clearly and did not request urgent medical help, supporting statement (*a*). The Mini-Moris initially drove past the stranger and then stopped after Bill saw the car in the ditch, confirming statement (*b*). Therefore, both statements are correct.

92. (A): The narrative highlights the presence of snow as the stranger's overcoat was snow-caked, and a ditch where a car was hanging nose down, suggesting challenging road conditions. Bill's cautious driving is evident from his controlled braking and gear changing, justifying the conclusion that he was driving carefully due to the road conditions.

93. (B): In the context, "loomed up" suggests the stranger suddenly became visible or emerged in front of the headlights, which aligns with the meaning of "appeared," indicating the stranger came into view.

94. (C): The phrase "gradually to a stop" indicates a slow, controlled stop. The opposite of gradually stopping would be stopping abruptly, which is captured by the term "suddenly."

95. (C): The word "and" in the sentence connects two independent clauses ("Pat gave a little gasp" and "I braked at once"), functioning as a conjunction to combine these parts of the sentence.

96. (B): The clause "that I saw the car" acts as a noun clause because it serves as the object of the verb "was" in the larger sentence structure, providing additional information about what Bill saw.

97. (C): The passage indicates that Pat, despite initial horror at not stopping, engages warmly with the stranger once he is in the car, suggesting a compassionate nature. Bill's protective instinct is evident as he initially chooses to drive past the stranger to ensure safety, affirming he is protective but not timid. The description of the car indicates it was in a ditch, not parked by a sidewalk, making statement (*c*) incorrect.

98. (B): The passage explicitly states that Pat is Bill's sister, as mentioned in the description of their interaction during the incident.

99. (D): The text does not provide any indication that Bill was concerned about the car not starting again due to the cold. His hesitations were solely based on the potential danger of the situation, addressing the concerns about safety at a dark spot and the presence of Pat, a woman, making options A and B plausible but not D.

100. (C): The Bishop's question "What dost thou do here?" directly asks Robin Hood about his purpose, confirming statement (*a*). Robin Hood's response that he is "a bold harper" implies he is presenting himself as a musician, although his intentions might be different, which supports statement (*b*) that he pretended to be a musician.

101. (A): The passage discusses the arrival of a bride and a bridegroom in the church, along with Robin Hood's comments related to the suitability of the match, indicating that a wedding ceremony was about to take place.

102. (C): The expression "I prithee" is an archaic way of saying "I pray thee," which translates to "I request you" in contemporary English, showing a polite or formal request.

103. (B): The setting of the encounter between the Bishop and Robin Hood is inside the church, as inferred from the dialogue and context of discussing a wedding and seeing the bride and bridegroom.

104. (A): The passage describes the bridegroom as "grave and old," which contradicts the statement that he was "rich and handsome." Therefore, option A is incorrect, making it the right choice as the statement that is incorrect.

105. (A): The use of "Did shine like glistening gold" to describe the bride employs a direct comparison using "like," which is characteristic of a simile.

106. (A): The term "scaffolding" in educational contexts refers to the guidance provided by an adult or more knowledgeable peer that supports a learner's development, helping them perform tasks they might not be able to complete independently.

107. (B): Concept learning involves understanding and categorizing based on features that define particular classes, requiring the use of higher-order mental processes such as intelligence and reasoning.

108. (A): The Whole Language approach to education emphasizes the use of language in its entirety, focusing on overall communicative effectiveness rather than specific linguistic correctness, such as spelling.

109. (B): As a teacher unfamiliar with the local language in a Punjabi area, using the child's language as a resource would involve leveraging the children's native language capabilities to facilitate teaching and learning, enhancing communication and understanding in the classroom. This approach aligns with modern educational strategies that emphasize inclusivity and cultural respect.

110. (B): Local comprehension involves focusing on specific details within a text rather than the general meaning or broader themes, which is essential for extracting particular pieces of information from the text.

111. (C): Diagnostic tests in language learning are designed to identify specific areas where learners may be struggling. The primary purpose of such assessments is to uncover these gaps in understanding so that teachers can take appropriate remedial actions to address these deficiencies.

112. (B): Textbooks are developed as resources to align teaching and learning activities with the curriculum objectives. They provide structured content and activities designed to meet specific educational goals.

113. (C): Role-playing allows students to practice speaking in different scenarios, helping them to develop their oral language skills. This method encourages active participation and simulates real-life interactions, making it a powerful tool for enhancing language proficiency.

114. (C): The statement that "Language is arbitrary" refers to the concept that words do not have any inherent connection to their meanings. This randomness in language means that the words used to represent objects or concepts are not logically connected to their meanings but are instead a result of linguistic convention.

115. (B): In the deductive approach to teaching grammar, the process begins with the presentation of grammatical rules, which is then followed by examples and practice. This approach emphasizes the understanding of rules first, which students can later apply in practical contexts.

116. (D): Extrapolation involves extending or projecting known information into an area not directly supported by existing data. This method is used to estimate or guess beyond the known facts, often by applying existing trends or patterns to new situations.

117. (A): Free writing promotes creativity and fluency by allowing students to express their thoughts without worrying about correctness or structure. This method helps build confidence and encourages a more natural writing style.

118. (D): When students read a text thoroughly and then answer questions that require referring back to the text, they are engaged in intensive reading. This form of reading focuses on detailed comprehension and understanding of the content, often involving analysis of language and structure.

119. (D): Language acquisition is significantly influenced by exposure to the language in various contexts. Providing children with a rich language environment where they can listen, speak, read, and write in the language facilitates natural learning and assimilation of the language.

120. (D): The Direct Method of language teaching focuses on the exclusive use of the target language in the classroom, excluding the mother tongue. This method emphasizes immersion in the language being learned, with all instructions and interactions conducted in that language.

121. (C): गद्यांश में उल्लेख है कि पर्यावरण के प्रति चिंता वैश्विक स्तर पर होनी चाहिए, क्योंकि यह समस्या सार्वभौमिक है और इसका प्रभाव सभी देशों और क्षेत्रों में महसूस किया जा रहा है।

122. (C): गद्यांश में वर्णन है कि अत्यधिक संसाधनों के उपयोग से मौसमी परिवर्तन और कृषि पर नकारात्मक प्रभाव पड़ रहा है, जैसे कि मौसम में अप्रत्याशित गर्मी और बेमौसम की बारिश।

123. (A): 'बचपन' एक ऐसा शब्द है जो किसी विशेष व्यक्ति, जाति या द्रव्य को नहीं दर्शाता बल्कि एक भावना या अवस्था को व्यक्त करता है, इसलिए इसे भाववाचक संज्ञा कहा जाता है।

124. (A): गद्यांश में यह स्पष्ट रूप से कहा गया है कि देश के लोगों और सरकारों की पर्यावरण के प्रति चेतना कम होने से खतरा बढ़ रहा है।

125. (A): 'ग्लेशियर' शब्द अंग्रेजी से आया है और इसे हिंदी में उपयोग किया जाता है, जिसे आगत शब्द कहा जाता है क्योंकि यह विदेशी मूल का है।

126. (A): गद्यांश के अनुसार, अनावश्यक सुविधाओं का उपयोग बढ़ने से पर्यावरणीय समस्याएँ बढ़ रही हैं, इसलिए इन आवश्यकताओं को कम करने से पर्यावरण संरक्षण में मदद मिलेगी।

127. (A): गद्यांश बताता है कि उदारीकरण के पश्चात, लोगों के जीवन शैली में परिवर्तन आया है जिससे गैर जरूरी सुविधाओं का उपभोग बढ़ा है।

128. (B): 'वैश्विक' में मूल शब्द तथा प्रत्यय है विश्व + इक : 'वैश्विक' शब्द का मूल 'विश्व' है जिसका अर्थ होता है संपूर्ण या सार्वभौमिक, और 'इक' एक प्रत्यय है जो इसे विशेषण बनाता है, इसका अर्थ होता है 'से संबंधित'।

129. (A): 'जीवंत' एक विशेषण है जो किसी व्यक्ति या वस्तु के जीवन से परिपूर्ण होने की गुणवत्ता को दर्शाता है। इसका उपयोग आमतौर पर किसी चीज की ऊर्जा और सक्रियता को व्यक्त करने के लिए किया जाता है।

130. (A): गद्यांश बताता है कि जब जीवन को सहज और सरल तरीके से जिया जाता है, बिना किसी प्रपंच के, तभी वह वरदान बन जाता है। यहाँ सरलता और सहजता को खुशी के स्रोत के रूप में माना गया है।

131. (C): आडंबर, अहंकार, और अधर्म शब्द जीवन और व्यवहार से संबंधित नकारात्मक गुणों को व्यक्त करते हैं, जबकि 'असहज' मुख्य रूप से एक भावनात्मक या शारीरिक स्थिति का वर्णन करता है जो असुविधा या अनारामदायकता को दर्शाता है।

132. (B): 'अहंकार में हम केवल बाहर की तरफ देखकर जीते हैं।' वाक्य का आशय है कि अहंकार हमें दिखावटी जीवन व्यतीत करने की ओर ले जाता है। गद्यांश बताता है कि अहंकार हमारी आंतरिक जीवंतता को कमजोर करता है और हमें केवल बाहरी दिखावे पर जीने के लिए प्रेरित करता है, जिससे भीतरी खोखलापन आता है।

133. (B): 'प्रपंच' शब्द का अर्थ होता है कपट या धोखा, जो आडंबर और दिखावटी व्यवहार से जुड़ा होता है। इसका प्रयोग उन स्थितियों के लिए किया जाता है जहाँ बाहरी दिखावा और वास्तविकता के बीच विरोधाभास हो।

134. (C): गद्यांश कहता है कि जीवन को जिस रूप में मिला है, उसे वैसे ही स्वीकार करना और जीना जीवन का सच्चा सम्मान है। यह हमें दिखावे से दूर रखता है और आत्म-स्वीकृति की ओर ले जाता है।

135. (D): 'आधारित' शब्द में 'आधार' मूल शब्द है और 'इत' एक प्रत्यय है, जो इसे एक विशेषण में परिवर्तित करता है, जिसका अर्थ होता है 'पर आधारित' या 'से संबंधित'।

136. (A, C): भाषिक दक्षता शिक्षार्थियों को व्याकरणिक रूप से सही और गलत वाक्यों में अंतर करना सिखाती है। साथ ही यह जानने की दक्षता प्रदान करती है कि भाषा का उचित रूप से कहाँ और कैसे प्रयोग करना है। इससे व्यक्ति स्वाभाविक और अधिक सहज तरीके से संवाद स्थापित कर पाता है।

137. (B): चित्रकारी और रंग भरने की क्रियाएं सूक्ष्म मोटर कौशलों के विकास के लिए महत्वपूर्ण हैं, जैसे कि हाथ और उंगलियों का संयोजन, जो बच्चों को लिखने और अन्य सूक्ष्म क्रियाओं के लिए तैयार करता है।

138. (D): प्रोत्साहन बच्चों को भाषा सीखने के लिए उत्साहित करता है और उनके सीखने की प्रक्रिया में सकारात्मक प्रभाव डालता है, जिससे वे अधिक गहराई से और सक्रिय रूप से भाषा सीखने में लगे रहते हैं।

139. (D): रचनावादी उपागम में सहपाठियों के साथ अन्तःक्रियाओं और समूह चर्चा को महत्व दिया जाता है, जहाँ छात्र सक्रिय रूप से ज्ञान का निर्माण करते हैं और गलतियाँ करने की स्वतंत्रता के साथ सीखते हैं।

140. (B): अनुकूलन यह सुनिश्चित करता है कि शिक्षार्थियों की विशेष जरूरतों को पूरा किया जाए, और यह शिक्षण सामग्री को उनकी समझ के स्तर और आवश्यकताओं के अनुसार बदलने की प्रक्रिया है।

141. (A): राजू के परिवार में पहली बार कोई विद्यालय जा रहा है, इसलिए वह 'प्रथम पीढ़ी' के छात्र के रूप में जाना जाता है, जिसका मतलब है कि उसके परिवार में उससे पहले किसी ने भी उच्च शिक्षा ग्रहण नहीं की है।

142. (B): टॉप डाउन उपागम में पाठ्यक्रम को सामान्य से विशेष तक आयोजित किया जाता है, जहाँ छात्रों को पहले सामान्य ज्ञान और संदर्भ प्रदान किया जाता है, फिर विशिष्ट विवरणों की ओर ले जाया जाता है।

143. (B): 'अर्जन' भाषा सीखने की उस प्रक्रिया को दर्शाता है जो बिना औपचारिक शिक्षण और विशेष अभ्यास के होती है, जैसे कि बच्चे अपनी मातृभाषा सीखते हैं। यह प्रक्रिया अधिक स्वाभाविक और नैसर्गिक होती है।

144. (A): सम्प्रेषणात्मक भाषा शिक्षण उपागम में शिक्षार्थी जोड़ों या समूह में मिलकर संवाद के माध्यम से समस्याओं का समाधान करते हैं। यह उपागम भाषा सीखने को व्यावहारिक संवाद के माध्यम से सजीव बनाता है, जिससे छात्र वास्तविक जीवन की स्थितियों में भाषा का प्रयोग करना सीखते हैं।

145. (D): पाठयोजना बनाने का पहला चरण उद्देश्यों को निर्धारित करना है। इससे शिक्षक यह तय कर सकते हैं कि विद्यार्थियों को क्या सिखाना है और किन परिणामों की अपेक्षा करनी है, जिससे शिक्षण सामग्री और विधियों का चयन अधिक प्रभावी तरीके से किया जा सकता है।

146. (C): जब शिक्षार्थियों ने विज्ञान और सामाजिक विज्ञान के अपने पूर्व ज्ञान का उपयोग करते हुए 'जल' पर अनुच्छेद लिखने के लिए चर्चा की, तो यह दर्शाता है कि वे अपनी विभिन्न विषयों की समझ को एकीकृत कर रहे थे। इस तरह की शिक्षण प्रक्रिया से छात्र विभिन्न विषयों के ज्ञान को समग्र रूप में समझने और लागू करने में सक्षम होते हैं।

147. (B): आपकी प्रथम भाषा हिंदी है क्योंकि आपने इसे अपने पालन-पोषण के दौरान बिना किसी विद्यालयी शिक्षा के प्राकृतिक रूप से सीखा। अंग्रेज़ी और अन्य भाषाओं का सीखना बाद में और अधिक संरचित और औपचारिक तरीके से हुआ, इसलिए वे आपकी द्वितीय या तृतीय भाषाएँ होंगी।

148. (D): जब अध्यापक कक्षा में छतरी, बरसाती, पेचकस जैसी वास्तविक वस्तुएँ लाते हैं, इसे तकनीकी रूप से 'रियलिया' कहा जाता है। रियलिया एक शिक्षण सहायक है जो शिक्षण प्रक्रिया को अधिक आकर्षक और यथार्थवादी बनाती है, जिससे छात्र वस्तुओं के वास्तविक उपयोग और महत्व को बेहतर ढंग से समझ पाते हैं।

149. (C): जब आप एक ही व्यक्ति के विभिन्न समय पर खींचे गए दो चित्रों का उपयोग करके 'काल' का शिक्षण करते हैं, तो यह शिक्षणशास्त्रीय व्याकरण का उपयोग है। यह दृष्टिकोण व्याकरणिक संरचनाओं को उनके उपयोग के सामाजिक और संदर्भगत महत्व के साथ प्रस्तुत करता है, जिससे छात्र व्याकरण के नियमों को जीवन से जुड़ी हुई स्थितियों में देख सकें और समझ सकें।

150. (B): जब किसी कक्षा विशेष या पाठ्यक्रम के अंत में विद्यार्थियों द्वारा अर्जित ज्ञान, कौशल और प्रवृत्ति का वर्णन करने वाले कथनों को 'अधिगम प्रतिफल' कहा जाता है। ये प्रतिफल शिक्षकों को यह समझने में मदद करते हैं कि छात्रों ने पाठ्यक्रम के दौरान क्या सीखा और किस हद तक सीखा, जिससे शिक्षण दृष्टिकोणों और सामग्री की समीक्षा और सुधार किया जा सके।

Previous Paper (Solved)

CTET—Paper-I, January 2024

(Exam held on 21-01-2024)

Part-I : Child Development and Pedagogy

1. Which of the following correctly describes intrinsic motivation?

A. Motivation that comes from personal enjoyment of the task
B. Motivation that comes from competition with others
C. Motivation that comes from a fear of punishment
D. Motivation that comes from external rewards

2. Assertion (A): In Lawrence Kohlberg's moral development theory children move from understanding consequences of acts to determine whether they are good or bad to understanding that rules and laws are flexible and can be changed.

Reason (R): Lawrence Kohlberg argues that moral development occurs progressively in stages.

Choose the correct option:

A. Both (A) and (R) are true, but (R) is not the correct explanation of (A)
B. (A) is true, but (R) is false
C. Both (A) and (R) are false
D. Both (A) and (R) are true and (R) is the correct explanation of (A)

3. Inclusion of students belonging to disadvantaged groups demands:

A. evidencing and encouraging identity-based stereotypes
B. isolation in the classroom on the basis of social affiliation
C. same-ability grouping of students in the classroom
D. awareness and sensitization towards diverse traditions

4. Assertion (A): Learners construct their own knowledge based on what they already know.

Reason (R): Finding patterns and making linkages with previous knowledge helps learners to process information meaningfully.

Choose the correct option:

A. Both (A) and (R) are true, but (R) is not the correct explanation of (A)
B. (A) is true, but (R) is false
C. Both (A) and (R) are false
D. Both (A) and (R) are true and (R) is the correct explanation of (A)

5. Reasoning, thinking and problem-solving are explained in which aspect of development?

A. Cognitive Development
B. Moral Development
C. Motor Development
D. Social Development

6. As per Howard Gardner's theory of multiple intelligence, which of the following set represents correct match of intelligence and associated characteristics?

A. Logical-Mathematical : skill of dance or athletic abilities
B. Musical : performance or composition skills
C. Spatial : skill of appreciating the natural world
D. Intrapersonal : skill in understanding and relating to others

7. Language development in primary classes is facilitated:

A. When teachers stress upon and enforce the use of formal language
B. When teachers ignore and dismiss the mother tongue of the children
C. When teachers begin from signs and symbols rather than concrete objects
D. When teachers use concrete examples to refer to abstract concepts

1. A	**2.** D	**3.** D	**4.** D	**5.** A	**6.** B	**7.** D

8. As per Jean Piaget's theory of cognitive development, which of the following ability distinguishes concrete operational thinking from Pre-operational thinking?
A. Decentering
B. Hypothetical reasoning
C. Object permanence
D. Coordination of senses

9. Which of the following statements about inclusive education is not correct?
A. Inclusive teaching means "adopting pedagogies that support needs of all learners".
B. An inclusive classroom "accommodates differences in language styles and promotes collaboration".
C. An inclusive classroom centres around "fixed curricula and standard assessment".
D. Inclusive teaching means "teaching in ways that do not exclude".

10. According to attribution theory of motivation which of the following is more likely to result in persistent effort and improved performance?
A. An external attribution for success and an internal attribution for failure
B. Internal attribution for failure as well as success
C. External attribution for failure as well as success
D. An internal attribution for success and an external attribution for failure

11. Which of the following statements is not correct about learning?
A. Learning implies reorganisation of prior conceptual schemes
B. Learning is facilitated by social action
C. Learning as a product rather than a process
D. Learning depends on learner's previous knowledge

12. While participating in a sports competition in class, Tanuj tells his friend that he will participate in the javelin throw and his sister can participate in jump rope because she is a girl and girls cannot throw javelin. This depicts:
A. Gender equality
B. Gender equity
C. Gender stereotyping
D. Gender constancy

13. In the course of development, children achieve gross motor skills before fine motor skills. This indicates that development is:
A. Cephalocaudal B. Linear
C. Proximodistal D. Anarchic

14. Which of the following is a typical characteristic of Dyslexia?
A. Difficulty in phonological processing
B. Difficulty in physical coordination
C. Difficulty in spatial awareness
D. Difficulty in creative problem solving

15. Which of the following would not be characterised as formative assessment?
A. An assessment given during the class to provide ongoing feedback to students and teachers
B. An assessment task that is helpful in comparing students as per a standard set of criteria
C. An assessment used to identify misconceptions in a student's learning
D. An assessment given at the beginning of a new concept to determine students' prior knowledge

16. Assertion (A): School curriculum should give reasonable space and value to learner's cultural knowledges.

Reason (R): Supporting students to uphold their cultural identities facilitates learning.

Choose the correct option:
A. Both (A) and (R) are true, but (R) is not the correct explanation of (A)
B. (A) is true, but (R) is false
C. Both (A) and (R) are false
D. Both (A) and (R) are true and (R) is the correct explanation of (A)

17. Which of the following types of questions can help assess a student's ability to evaluate information critically?
A. Questions that ask for the student's personal opinion
B. Questions that ask for examples that validate the text
C. Questions that ask for a summary of a text
D. Questions that ask for a simple definition of a term

18. According to Kohlberg's theory of moral development, at what stage are children self-centered and see their own benefit in doing something?
A. at the second stage in the first level
B. at the third stage in the second level
C. at the fifth stage in the third level
D. at the first stage in the first level

8. A	**9.** C	**10.** B	**11.** C	**12.** C	**13.** A	**14.** A	**15.** B	**16.** D	**17.** A	**18.** A

19. Impairment is a .... condition, while disability is a .... condition.
A. functional, biological
B. operative, physical
C. social, psychological
D. biological, functional

20. Which of the following aptly defines relationship between cognition and emotion?
A. Emotion and cognition are interdependent on each other
B. Cognition influences emotions but reverse is not true
C. Emotions influence cognition but reverse is not true
D. Cognition and emotion are two independent systems

21. Problem solving is fostered by:
A. Functional fixedness
B. Passive imitation
C. Response Set
D. Divergent thinking

22. Which of the following is a key principle of progressive education?
A. Students should be passive recipients of knowledge from their teachers
B. Learning should be based on authentic tasks
C. Curriculum should be predetermined and universal
D. Standardized testing is the best way to measure student learning

23. **Assertion (A):** Childhood is experienced differently by children across cultures.

Reason (R): Childrens' development is universal.

Choose the correct option:
A. Both (A) and (R) are true, but (R) is not the correct explanation of (A)
B. (A) is true, but (R) is false
C. Both (A) and (R) are false
D. Both (A) and (R) are true and (R) is the correct explanation of (A)

24. Socio-constructivist views of learning advocate that:
A. Learners actively construct knowledge
B. Effective learning is activated by lecturing and explaining
C. Effective learning takes place through the process of recall and rehearsal
D. Learners receive knowledge passively from others

25. Which of the following is a characteristic of effective feedback in the classroom?
A. It is broad and generic
B. It is only focused on the outcomes.
C. It is timely and specific
D. It is given only at the end of the task

26. Lev Vygotsky proposes that .... is important for self-regulation in children.
A. Inner speech B. Adaptation
C. Organization D. Disequilibrium

27. While divergent thinking .... convergent thinking ....
A. is fixed on one correct solution; encourages multiple answers
B. promotes mathematical abilities; promotes verbal abilities
C. promotes verbal abilities; promotes mathematical abilities
D. encourages multiple answers; is fixed on one correct solution

28. After getting 'out' in the game due to the rope getting stuck in her leg while jumping Aru says that the rope deliberately got her out. At what stage of Jean Piaget's theory of cognitive development do children reason like this?
A. Formal Operational stage
B. Sensory-motor stage
C. Pre-operation stage
D. Concrete Operational stage

29. Proximodistal principle states that in infancy:
A. development proceeds from head to toe.
B. development of language occurs rapidly as it is a sensitive period for development.
C. physical development occurs rapidly with the development of fine motor skills.
D. the limbs continue to grow faster than the hands and feet

30. Which of the following are examples of scaffolding?
(*a*) Think-aloud
(*b*) Prompts and cues
(*c*) Questions
(*d*) Half-solved example
(*e*) Rote Rehearsal
A. (*a*), (*b*), (*c*)
B. (*a*), (*b*), (*c*), (*d*)
C. (*a*), (*b*), (*c*), (*d*), (*e*)
D. (*a*), (*b*)

19. D	**20.** A	**21.** D	**22.** B	**23.** B	**24.** A	**25.** C	**26.** A	**27.** D	**28.** C	**29.** D	**30.** B

Part-II : Mathematics

31. See the number pattern given below:

1, 8, 27, 64, 125, ________, ________

What will be the next two terms?

A. 216 and 289 B. 256 and 343
C. 216 and 343 D. 256 and 289

32. What should be subtracted from the sum of 9909, 9099 and 9009 to obtain 25454?

A. 2365 B. 2536
C. 2563 D. 2356

33. Which of the following statement is most appropriate?

A. Charts are used in mathematics class as an effective teaching-learning material
B. Use of teaching-learning material in mathematics class consume students' time for practice
C. Students do not enjoy riddles in mathematics class
D. Mathematics lab is essential as it provides opportunities for hands on activities for students

34. Which of the following is true for word problems in school mathematics?

A. Word problems are not examples of mathematical modelling
B. Word problems are important in secondary classes only
C. Word problems focus more on procedural knowledge in mathematics
D. Word problems refer to exercises where the child formalises the situation into a form where a specific mathematical technique can be applied

35. According to National Education Policy (NEP) 2020, assessment of learners include:

A. Cognitive, affective and psychomotor domains
B. Cognitive, social and spiritual domains
C. Physical and psychological domains
D. Cognitive and physical domains

36. National Education Policy (NEP) - 2020 talks about "Knowledge of India". Which of the following are not included in it?

A. Tribal knowledge, indigenous and traditional ways of learning as part of various subjects like Mathematics, Astronomy, Medicine, Agriculture etc.
B. Field visits to different states as part of cultural exchange programmes.
C. Formal examination to assess the knowledge gained by the students.
D. Knowledge from ancient India and its contributions to modern India

37. According to National Curriculum Framework, 2005, which of the following processes are least relevant in a primary mathematics classroom?

A. Use of patterns
B. Visualization
C. Making connections and representations
D. Memorising formulae

38. Which of the following statements is/are most appropriate for the idea of cognitive conflict in teaching mathematics?

(*a*) Thoughtful efforts of a teacher to expose children to cognitive conflict can enhance their mathematical understanding.
(*b*) It is not useful for promoting mathematical understanding in children.
(*c*) Children get confused so cognitive conflict must be avoided.

Choose the correct option:

A. (*a*) and (*c*) B. Only (*a*)
C. Only (*c*) D. (*b*) and (*c*)

39. A number becomes double if it is increased by 8. What is the number?

A. 8 B. 12
C. 16 D. 6

40. The sum of all angles of a triangle is:

A. 90° B. 180°
C. 360° D. 60°

41. One millimetre is the same as:

A. 0.1 cm B. 0.01 m
C. 0.1 m D. 0.01 cm

42. Which of the following statements is correct?

A. 1 is a composite number
B. 1 is both, a prime and a composite number
C. 1 is neither prime nor a composite number
D. 1 is a prime number

31. C **32.** C **33.** D **34.** D **35.** A **36.** C **37.** D **38.** B **39.** A **40.** B **41.** A **42.** C

43. Brij had a wire of length 100 metres to cover the land of his choice. He wanted to take the biggest land. Which of the following measurements should he choose to take the biggest area?

A. 30 m × 20 m
B. 25 m × 25 m
C. 5 m × 45 m
D. 15 m × 35 m

44. A .... is always a regular polygon.

A. Square B. Pentagon
C. Circle D. Isosceles triangle

45. The parcel sending rates are given below :

Parcel weighing (50 grams or less) : ₹15.00; parcel weighing (for every additional 50 grams) : ₹7.00 Meena wants to send a parcel to her friend Charu in Delhi. The parcel weighs 350 g. Look at the charges and select the correct cost of sending the parcel:

A. ₹50 B. ₹55
C. ₹57 D. ₹42

46. Which of the following is/are related to early number concept formation?

(*a*) One to one correspondence
(*b*) Hierarchical inclusion
(*c*) Basic operations

Choose the correct option:

A. (*a*) and (*c*) B. (*a*) and (*b*)
C. (*b*) and (*c*) D. Only (*a*)

47. Which of the following is not true about 'multiplicity of approaches' in teaching mathematics?

A. It hampers the learning of child as it leads to confusion
B. Offering such a choice allows children to explore and use the approach that is most natural and easy for them
C. It is crucial for liberating school mathematics from the tyranny of the one correct answer
D. Very often, there are many ways of solving a problem

48. Yamina threw a die 10 times and got the following results:

5, 3, 6, 6, 1, 4, 5, 3, 3, 2

Which of the following numbers she got the maximum number of times?

A. 3 B. 1
C. 5 D. 6

49. A student of class III solved 26×5 as:

$$\begin{array}{r} 26 \\ \times\ 5 \\ \hline 1030 \\ \hline \end{array}$$

Revisiting which of the following will best remediate this misconception?

A. Concept of regrouping
B. Recalling multiplication tables
C. One to one correspondence
D. Multiplication of one digit by one digit

50. The value of 25.3 × 5 − 35 ÷ 5 − 3 × 18.5 is:

A. 64.0
B. 95.0
C. −26.5
D. 283.05

51. The number of degrees in $2\frac{2}{3}$ right angles is:

A. 285 B. 240
C. 330 D. 210

52. Which of the following is most appropriate to introduce 'Data Handling' at primary stage?

A. Within classroom, collecting statistics of students' height; favourite food; colour; cartoon etc. and asking questions related to data.
B. Showing population census of a city for five years and asking students to compare population growth.
C. Drawing a bar graph on the blackboard and asking students to read the data from it.
D. Asking the students to read time tables of bus and train timings

53. A frog jumps 3 steps and a rabbit jumps 7 steps at a time starting from a place O. At which of the following steps, they both will be jumping together?

A. 371 B. 378
C. 354 D. 343

54. How many packets of $\frac{1}{12}$ kg salt can be made from $7\frac{1}{2}$ kg of salt?

A. 60 B. 72
C. 90 D. 45

43. B	44. A	45. C	46. B	47. A	48. A	49. A	50. A	51. B	52. A	53. B	54. C

55. Which of the following should be the characteristics of mathematical language at primary level?

(*a*) It should be precise.

(*b*) It must be ambiguous as it can add openness in the subject.

(*c*) It should be reinforced through child's language used in everyday life.

(*d*) It must be highly technical as it will help students to communicate accurately in mathematics.

Choose the correct option:

A. (*a*), (*b*) and (*c*)

B. (*a*) and (*c*)

C. (*a*), (*c*) and (*d*)

D. (*a*) and (*d*)

56. While solving:

$$\begin{array}{r} 182 \\ -67 \\ \hline \ldots \end{array}$$

in class II, a teacher explained that we have to subtract 7 from 2 and 2 is smaller than 7. So we will borrow one from 8 and then we can subtract 7 from 12. One student told teacher : Mam! why we are borrowing from eight, as borrowing is not good. What a teacher should do in such a situation?

A. Teacher should change the word 'borrowing' to 'regrouping' and then show the process of regrouping

B. Teacher should tell the student to focus on learning the algorithm of subtraction

C. Teacher should ignore the student's question and continue with her work

D. Teacher should scold the student and make him sit.

57. Which of the following statement is least appropriate for encouraging mathematical learning?

A. Everyone can learn mathematics

B. Mathematics learning is not gender specific

C. Discourage intuition as it hampers the development of mathematical ideas

D. Failure does not imply that students cannot do mathematics

58. Which one of the following costs least?

A. 750 packets of ₹7.50 each

B. 7.5 dozen items of ₹750 each item

C. 75 dozen items of ₹7.50 each item

D. 75 packets of ₹750 each

59. Which of the following model is least appropriate to develop the conceptual understanding regarding the relationships of ones, tens and hundreds in early grade learners?

A. Money   B. Abacus

C. Place value chart   D. Dienes blocks

60. Which aspect of evaluation is used when a teacher ensures that test made by her fulfils the objectives and criteria of that test?

A. Practicality   B. Reliability

C. Consistency   D. Validity

Part-III : Environmental Studies

61. Which of the following best reflects child-centred strategies in teaching EVS at primary level?

(*a*) Discussion

(*b*) Demonstration

(*c*) Lecture

(*d*) Survey

A. (*b*) and (*c*)

B. (*c*) and (*d*)

C. (*a*) and (*d*)

D. (*a*) and (*b*)

62. Comprehensive evaluation means holistic way of evaluating a student. The ways in which an EVS teacher can assess her students for comprehensive evaluation in EVS are:

A. half yearly and annual exams

B. rating scale during assessment of activities

C. portfolio

D. teachers' observation

63. You wish that students learn by peer-learning strategies. Which strategy will you adopt to form groups?

A. Make a homogeneous group of students according to their scores in examination

B. Make a heterogeneous group based on participation and cooperation

C. Form a group of 5 students of same gender and socio-economic background

D. Make a roll number-wise groups of 4/5 students

55. B	**56.** A	**57.** C	**58.** A	**59.** C	**60.** D	**61.** C	**62.** *	**63.** B

64. Read the following Statement (A) and Statement (B) below and choose the correct option :

(A) : About 4700 years ago, some of the earliest cities flourished on the banks of river Indus and its tributaries.

(B) : About 1500 years ago, cities developed on the banks of the Ganga and its tributaries.

A. Both (A) and (B) are not true
B. (A) is true, but (B) is false
C. (A) is false, but (B) is true
D. Both (A) and (B) are true

65. Assertion : The theme 'Family and Friends' is a major theme in EVS and 'Plants and Animals' are presented as a subtheme of 'Family and Friends'.

Reason : The interdependence of human beings and other forms of life is highlighted through themes.

A. The assertion and the reason are correct, but the Reason is not the correct explanation of the Assertion
B. Assertion is true, but the reason is false
C. The statement of the assertion is false, but the reason is true
D. Both the assertion and reason are correct and the Reason is the correct explanation of the Assertion

66. Which of the following strategies promotes inquiry while teaching the theme 'Food'?

A. Demonstrating fireless cooking of sandwiches, shikanji (lemon water) etc.
B. Asking students to find out food preferences of their family members.
C. Showing pictures of various preserved food items used in different regions of India.
D. Asking students to collect pictures of various food items.

67. Which of the following sets depicts the themes of EVS at primary level?

A. Food, Material, Shelter
B. Family and Friends, Travel, Natural resources
C. Shelter, Travel, Things we make and do
D. Weather, Water, Travel

68. Read statements (A) and (R) properly and then answer the following questions.

(A) : Silkworm can find his female worm from many kilometers away by her smell.

(R) : Some female insects release 'Pheromones' which can be recognised by their males by smell.

Choose the correct answer:

A. Both (A) and (R) are correct, but (R) does not explains (A)
B. (A) is correct, but (R) is incorrect
C. (A) is incorrect, but (R) is correct
D. Both (A) and (R) are correct and (R) explains (A)

69. Seema, an EVS teacher organised a field trip to zoo for her students. Which of the following are the most appropriate objectives of the trip to the zoo?

(*a*) Recall names of animals in the zoo
(*b*) To relate concepts related to animals
(*c*) To promote process skills
(*d*) Assessment of students' learning at the zoo

A. (*b*), (*c*) and (*d*)
B. (*a*), (*c*) and (*d*)
C. (*a*) and (*b*)
D. (*a*), (*b*) and (*c*)

70. What is the mass of an object with a density of 12 g/ml and a volume of 3 ml?

A. 24 g
B. 36 g
C. 4 g
D. 15 g

71. The territorial states of Haryana are:

A. Uttar Pradesh, Uttarakhand, Madhya Pradesh
B. Himachal Pradesh, Punjab, Bihar
C. Bihar, Punjab, Uttar Pradesh
D. Himachal Pradesh, Rajasthan, Uttar Pradesh

72. Read the given statements carefully and choose the correct option.

Assertion (A): We can cook food easily at sea level as compared to higher altitudes.

Reason (R): At high altitudes, boiling point of water increases.

A. Both (A) and (R) are true, but (R) is not the correct explanation of (A)
B. (A) is true, but (R) is false
C. (A) is false, but (R) is true
D. Both (A) and (R) are true and (R) is the correct explanation of (A)

64. B	**65.** D	**66.** B	**67.** C	**68.** D	**69.** A	**70.** B	**71.** D	**72.** B

73. Doctors prescribed blood test for patients to confirm malaria. Blood test is done to:
A. check iron in blood
B. check for eggs of female anopheles mosquitoes in blood
C. check for microbes in blood
D. check for haemoglobin in blood

74. It has been observed by bird watchers that there is a peculiar species of birds. The male bird make their own nests and the female bird looks at all the nests and selects the one she likes the best and decides in which nest to lay her eggs. The name of the bird is:
A. Weaver bird
B. Indian Robin
C. Sun bird
D. Tailor bird

75. Students conduct a survey in their homes and neighbourhood to find out the number of members and approximate amount of water used in each family. What skills and processes are developed through this activity?
A. questioning, inferring, expression
B. hypothesising, inferring, expression
C. prediction, experimentation, observing
D. questioning, experimentation, sensitivity towards environment

76. A chapter in EVS textbook of NCERT describes Wahida Prism and her experience in the Navy as a doctor. What are the reasons for including this chapter?
(*a*) Her experience challenges gender stereotypes
(*b*) Her story gives a peep into the life of a medical officer in the armed forces
(*c*) Understanding that prism reflects 7 colours
(*d*) Understanding the difficulties faced by her and her ways of tackling them
A. (*b*), (*c*) and (*d*)
B. (*c*) and (*d*)
C. (*b*), (*d*) and (*a*)
D. (*a*), (*b*) and (*c*)

77. Consider the following statements (A) and (B).

Statement (A): Bora is a common variety of rice used in Assam.

Statement (B): Paddy grows well in clayey soil and requires a lot of water.

Select the correct code from the following.
A. (A) and (B) both are wrong
B. (A) is correct, but (B) is wrong
C. (A) is wrong, but (B) is correct
D. (A) and (B) both are correct

78. "Pochampalli" is famous district for its beautifully designed bright coloured sarees and for the special kind of weave which is also called Pochampalli. It is a part of:
A. Karnataka
B. Maharashtra
C. Telangana
D. Tamil Nadu

79. An EVS teacher asks her students to think and answer "Why do we feel comfortable in woollens clothes during winter". This question is a:
A. analytical question
B. hypothetical question
C. factual question
D. convergent question

80. Read the following statements carefully:

Statement (I): EVS syllabus is divided into 6 themes Water, Relationships, Food, Transport, Shelter, and How things work.

Statements (II): The themes of EVS are close to children's life.
A. Both Statements (I) and (II) are false
B. Statement (I) is true and Statement (II) is false
C. Statement (I) is false and Statement (II) is true
D. Both Statements (I) and (II) are true

81. Textbooks of EVS should reflect the recommendation of NCF 2005 of linking students' life at school to their life outside. This implies:
A. Textbook is the only source of knowledge
B. Textbook supports students to construct knowledge through all the given activities
C. Teachers need to use textbooks as one of the teaching learning resource
D. Students are compelled to memorise few important concepts of EVS

73. B	**74.** A	**75.** A	**76.** C	**77.** D	**78.** C	**79.** A	**80.** C	**81.** B

82. Read the following statements carefully and choose the correct options:

Statement (A): Xylem transports water and minerals from roots to rest of the plant.

Statement (B): Phloem translocates food from leaves to various parts of the plant.

A. Both (A) and (B) are false
B. (A) is true, but (B) is false
C. (A) is false, but (B) is true
D. Both (A) and (B) are true

83. Alex, an EVS teacher of class 3 while introducing the theme 'Work We Do' helps his students to cut colourful strips of paper and weave the strips to make a mat. The edges are glued together to make a beautiful mat. Which of the following objectives should Alex help his students focus?

(*a*) learning about colours, patterns and developing an aesthetic sense.
(*b*) relating the activity to weaving done by weavers.
(*c*) memorising the steps of making mat.
(*d*) choosing papers of attractive colours and learning cutting of strips perfectly.

A. (*b*), (*c*) and (*d*)
B. (*a*), (*c*) and (*d*)
C. (*a*) and (*c*)
D. (*a*), (*b*) and (*d*)

84. Nina, an EVS teacher of class 5 gives a group assignment to her students that they have to visit nearby agricultural farms and find out information about the implements used by farmers during agriculture and the type of crops they grow. They also have to collect photographs and prepare a report. What process skills and learning indicators are involved here?

A. Questioning, experimentation, sensitivity towards environment
B. Hypothesising, inferring, expression
C. Prediction, experimentation, observing
D. Questioning, expression, inferring

85. Which one of the following regarding Johad is correct? Choose the correct option.

A. It filters impurities from water
B. It pumps groundwater into nearby wells
C. Stores water from rivers
D. It is a community based rain water harvesting system

86. An EVS teacher taught about animals to her students and ask them to do the following task:

(*a*) Write names of various animals around them
(*b*) Observe activities of different animals
(*c*) Classify animals into categories based on observations
(*d*) Define the term 'Animal'

Which of the above is NOT appropriate for students of primary level as per the nature of EVS at primary level?

A. (*b*) and (*c*)
B. Only (*c*)
C. Only (*d*)
D. (*a*) and (*c*)

87. Ravi took some water in a glass. He puts a lemon in it. Then, he keeps adding a lot of salt into the water, half a spoon at a time. After some time, he notices that:

A. Lemon floats in water
B. Lemon splits in water
C. Lemon remains mid-way in glass of water
D. Lemon sinks in water

88. Which one of the following statements regarding Al-Biruni is NOT true ? Choose the correct answer.

A. More than a thousand years ago, he came to India
B. He did not write anything about ponds in India
C. He has praised the making of ponds in India
D. The place that Al-Biruni came from is now called Uzbekistan

89. Which one of the following statements regarding Ghadsisar Lake is NOT true?

A. It was built around 650 years ago
B. It was connected with nine lakes
C. It is in use till today
D. King Ghadsi of Jaisalmer got it made

90. Consider the following statements about beehives:

(*a*) Honey bees live in beehives. Every beehive has one queen Bee that lays eggs.
(*b*) There are only a few males bees in the hive which have special roles as workers.
(*c*) Most of the female bees in the hive are worker bees who work all the day in making the hive and also looking after the baby bees.
(*d*) The worker bees fly around Litchi flowers in search of nectar for honey.

The correct statements are:

A. (*c*) and (*d*)
B. (*a*) and (*c*)
C. (*a*) and (*d*)
D. (*a*) and (*b*)

82. D	83. D	84. D	85. D	86. C	87. A	88. B	89. C	90. C

Part-IV : Language-I—English

Directions (Qs. No. 91-99): *Read the passage given below and answer the questions that follow.*

Yet as soon as she saw him, she did not look as Alfred thought she would look : she smiled, her blue eyes never wavered, and with a calmness and dignity that made them forget that her clothes seemed to have been thrown on her, she put out her hand to Mr. Carr and said politely, "I'm Mrs. Higgins. I'm Alfred's mother."

Mr. Carr was a bit embarrassed by her lack of terror and her simplicity and he hardly knew what to say to her, so she asked, "Is Alfred in trouble ?"

"He is. He's been taking things from the store. I caught him red-handed. Little things like compacts and toothpaste and lipsticks. Stuff he can sell easily," the proprietor said.

Mrs. Higgins put out her hand and touched Sam Carr's arm with an understanding gentleness, and speaking as though afraid of disturbing him, she said, "If you would only listen to me before doing anything". Her simple earnestness made her shy; her humility made her falter and look away, but in a moment she was smiling gravely again and she said with a kind of patient dignity, "What do you intend to do, Mr. Carr ?"

"I am going to get a cop. That's what I ought to do."

"Yes, I suppose so. It's not for me to say, because he's my son. Yet I sometimes think a little good advice is the best thing for a boy when he is at a certain period in his life," she said.

Alfred couldn't understand his mother's quiet composure, for if they had been at home and someone had suggested that he was going to be arrested, he knew she would be in a rage and would cry out against him.

91. '... her humility made her falter....'

Choose the word opposite in meaning to the underlined one.

A. frankness B. intrigue
C. hitch D. pride

92. Which of the following statements is not correct?

A. Outside, her conduct was like that of a caring mother.
B. When she introduced herself, Mr. Carr felt stupefied
C. He felt that he would have to forgive Alfred
D. At home, Mrs. Higgins would have been enraged

93. Which of the following statements is not correct?

A. He stole cream, compact and lipstick from the store
B. At Mr. Carr's accusation, Alfred's mother felt intimidated
C. Yet, she was very gentle in responding to him
D. Alfred was a petty thief

94. Having looked at his mother, Alfred was:

A. scared B. pleased
C. surprised D. shocked

95. '..... he hardly knew what to say to her.'

The underlined is a/an .... clause.

A. Noun B. Adjective
C. Adverb D. Principal

96. Study the following statements:

(*a*) When she entered the drug store, Mrs. Higgins was not properly dressed.
(*b*) She looked like the mother of a guilty person.
(*c*) Mr. Carr did not expect her to be calm and dignified.

A. (*b*) and (*c*) are right, but (*a*) is wrong
B. (*a*) and (*c*) are right, but (*b*) is wrong
C. (*a*) and (*b*) are wrong, but (*c*) is right
D. (*a*) and (*b*) are right, but (*c*) is wrong

97. '.... made them forget that her clothes seemed...'

The underlined word is a/an ....

A. Pronoun
B. Preposition
C. Conjunction
D. Noun

98. '.... her blue eyes never wavered'.

Choose the word nearest in meaning to the underlined one.

A. hesitated
B. waved
C. snickered
D. advanced

91. D	**92.** C	**93.** C	**94.** C	**95.** A	**96.** B	**97.** C	**98.** A

99. Study the following statements:
(a) Mr. Carr intended to get Alfred arrested.
(b) Mrs. Higgins wanted him to be given a chance to reform himself.
A. (*b*) is right and (*a*) is wrong
B. Both (*a*) and (*b*) are right
C. Both (*a*) and (*b*) are wrong
D. (*a*) is right and (*b*) is wrong

Directions (Qs. No. 100-105): *Read the extract given below and answer the questions that follow.*

All the world is a stage,
And all the men and women merely players;
They have their exits and their entrances;
And one man in his time plays many parts,
His acts being seven ages. At first the infant,
Mewling and puking in the nurse's arms;
Then the whining school-boy, with his satchel
And shining morning face, creeping like snail
Unwilling to school. And then the lover,
Sighing like a furnace, with a woeful ballad
Made to his mistress' eyebrow. Then a soldier,
Full of strange oaths, and bearded like a pard,
Jealous in honour, sudden and quick in quarrel,
Seeking the bubble-reputation
Even in the cannon's mouth.

100. What do all men and women do?
A. indulge in indoor games like chess, cards, etc.
B. play outdoor games like football, cricket, etc.
C. fight wars
D. perform various roles in life

101. '..... their exits and entrances.....'

The figure of speech used here is:
A. Metaphor
B. Personification
C. Hyperbole
D. Simile

102. Why is the lover's sign compared to a furnace?
A. He feels emotionally charged
B. He offers warmth to his beloved
C. He is writing a ballad
D. He gets angry very soon

103. Identify the figure of speech used in the first line.
A. Metaphor B. Personification
C. Hyperbole D. Simile

104. A school-boy:
A. looks beautiful in the morning
B. likes his teachers
C. both (D) and (A)
D. is reluctant to go to school

105. A soldier is jealous about his honour as:
A. he is very sensitive about his honour
B. he is ferocious like a leopard
C. he wants to win at any cost
D. he is jealous of his enemy

106. Which one of the following statements is NOT correct with respect to the given sentence?

Sentence : Rhymes, songs and chants are ways for children to:
A. memorize words and sentence structure
B. practise pronunciation
C. enhance expression and the rhythm of sentences
D. extend vocabulary

107. Which approach/method doesn't encourage learners to use their native language in a language class?
A. Communicative approach
B. Direct method
C. Audio-lingual method
D. Natural approach

108. Which one of the following is NOT true about using the library at the primary level?

The library should not just be seen as a storage space for books, rather
A. as an active environment for engagement with books.
B. teachers and other adults can also model reading behaviour in the libraries
C. a read-aloud of the textbook can be best done in a library
D. learners can be exposed to a variety of genres of children's literature

109. Literacy teaching approach that emphasise the relationship between letters and sounds is:
A. grammar translation
B. situational approach
C. phonics instruction
D. whole language approach

99. B	**100.** D	**101.** A	**102.** A	**103.** A	**104.** C	**105.** A	**106.** C	**107.** B	**108.** C	**109.** C

110. A student of class V says, "I give my work a final check for accuracy before submitting it to the teacher." The student is working at the writing stage of:

A. Re-drafting B. Proof reading
C. Peer-evaluation D. Drafting

111. A third-grade teacher wishes to establish a reading corner in her class. In making the judgements for selecting a children's book, which one of the following questions would be most important to be considered *first*?

A. Are the books written for the independent reading level of most students in the class?
B. Will the books help address the goals of the third-grade reading curriculum?
C. Will these books be appropriate for use in more than one instructional context?
D. Are the authors of these books well-known and respected authors of children's literature?

112. Which approach/method is geared towards the learner's main goal of using language in a real-life context?

A. Communicative approach
B. Direct method
C. Audio-lingual method
D. Natural approach

113. A teacher in class III asked her learners to ask their partners five questions about their abilities using the word 'can', e.g can you swim ? This type of activity enhances:

A. Controlled oral practice
B. Free speaking
C. Passive listening
D. Oral fluency practice

114. Which one of the following is NOT correct about teaching grammar effectively?

A. Elicit relevant rules of grammar
B. Provide practice in communication
C. Learn grammar by memorizing its rules
D. Promote genuine communication

115. A teacher is planning to collect a variety of Teaching Learning Materials (TLM) for his class II students. Which one of the following is NOT a correct criterion for choosing TLMs?

A. The material chosen should provide adequate opportunities for the children to explore and experiment with curiosity
B. The material chosen should be preferably locally made or locally available, as this would allow for easy replacement
C. The material chosen should be made by the children only and have some roughness to avoid slipperiness
D. The material chosen should be attractive and safe for children of this age group to use

116. A teacher asked the learners to exchange workbooks and check their partners work. The objective of this task is to:

A. give practice in using new vocabulary
B. give controlled practice of structures
C. develop the skill of peer correction
D. give practice in extensive reading

117. Children in the foundational stage are more engaged in learning when:

A. they use multiple senses and actively use their hands
B. they trace or write letters repeatedly in their notebooks
C. they focus only on developing fine motor skills
D. they sing rhymes after the teacher

118. Which one of the following is NOT the principle for textbook design at the foundational stage?

A. Presentation Principle
B. Concrete Principle
C. Technology Principle
D. Curriculum Principle

119. To create an inclusive, welcoming and joyful environment that supports every child's participation in achieving the competencies outlined in the National Curriculum Framework (NCF) can be best done by:

A. majorly focusing on the learners good health and well being.
B. displaying children's work from different domains of development.
C. decorating the classroom for a colourful environment.
D. conducting indoor activities and avoiding them from outdoor activities in scorching heat

120. Which one of the following should be mastered to be literate?

A. Sight vocabulary and pattern recognition
B. Decoding and language comprehension
C. Accuracy and phonological comprehension
D. Phonological awareness and fluency

110. B	**111.** D	**112.** A	**113.** D	**114.** C	**115.** C	**116.** C	**117.** A	**118.** B	**119.** B	**120.** B

Part-V : Language-II—हिन्दी

निर्देश (प्र.सं. 121 से 128): *निम्नलिखित गद्यांश को पढ़कर पूछे गए प्रश्नों के सही/सर्वाधिक उपयुक्त विकल्प का चयन कीजिए।*

इस बार मौसम विज्ञानियों ने घोषणा की हुई है कि अल नीनो प्रभाव के कारण मानसून कमजोर रह सकता है। चैत के महीने में बारिश होने के हालात पर घाघ ने भी यही कहा है। चैत यानी मार्च-अप्रैल के दिनों में अगर बारिश होती है तो सावन सूखा जा सकता है। बात सिर्फ इस बार के मानसून की नहीं है। अमेरिका में हाल ही में ताजे पानी के हालात पर हुए एक सम्मेलन में संयुक्त राष्ट्र संघ के महासचिव एंटोनियो गुतेरेज ने एक रिपोर्ट जारी की है। इसमें कहा गया है कि 2050 तक पानी का सबसे बड़ा संकट भारत में आने वाला है। भारत पर संकट इसलिए है क्योंकि गंगा, यमुना, ब्रह्मपुत्र और सिंधु जैसी नदियों का पानी धीरे-धीरे कम होता जाएगा। सिर्फ गंगा की बात करें तो 2500 किलोमीटर लम्बी यह नदी उत्तराखंड से बंगाल के बीच कई राज्यों से गुजरती है। इसके किनारों पर बसे महानगरों, कस्बों और गाँवों की करीब चालीस करोड़ की आबादी की पानी से जुड़ी जरूरतों को यह पूरा करती है। इसके पानी का स्रोत गंगोत्री ग्लेशियर है। पर्यावरण विज्ञानियों का दावा है कि पिछले 87 साल में तीस किलोमीटर लम्बे इस ग्लेशियर का पौने दो किलोमीटर हिस्सा पिघलकर गायब हो चुका है। अभी जलवायु परिवर्तन का जो हाल है, वह पूरे हिमालय क्षेत्र के लिए खतरनाक माना जा रहा है। भारत के हिस्से वाले हिमालय में 9775 ग्लेशियर बताए जाते हैं। इनमें अकेले उत्तराखंड में 968 हैं। अब अगर इनके पिघलने की रफ्तार तेज होती जाती है तो क्या होगा?

121. गद्यांश में किस संकट की बात की गई है?
A. रोजगार संकट B. जल संकट
C. पर्यावरण संकट D. खाद्य संकट

122. गंगा के किनारे बसे लोगों की आबादी लगभग है:
A. 30 करोड़ B. 40 करोड़
C. 96 करोड़ D. 87 करोड़

123. गद्यांश के अनुसार 2050 तक पानी का सबसे बड़ा संकट आनेवाला है :
A. भारत में B. संयुक्त अरब अमीरात में
C. पाकिस्तान में D. अमेरिका में

124. अल नीनो का प्रभाव पड़ता है :
A. जल स्रोतों पर B. मानसून पर
C. मानव पर D. जलवायु पर

125. 'इस ग्लेशियर का <u>पौने दो किलोमीटर</u> हिस्सा पिघलकर गायब हो चुका है।' वाक्य में रेखांकित पद है :
A. परिमाणवाचक विशेषण B. गुणवाचक विशेषण
C. सार्वनामिक विशेषण D. संख्यावाचक विशेषण

126. भारत की नदियों में जल कम होता जा रहा है। इसका कारण है :
A. ग्लेशियरों का तेजी से पिघलना
B. ग्लेशियरों के क्षेत्रफल में कमी आना
C. ग्लेशियरों के क्षेत्रफल में वृद्धि होना
D. ग्लेशियरों का न पिघलना

127. नदियों का पानी <u>धीरे-धीरे</u> कम होता जाएगा। वाक्य में रेखांकित पद हैं :
A. क्रिया B. क्रिया विशेषण
C. प्रविशेषण D. विशेषण

128. 'पर्यावरण' में उपसर्ग और मूल शब्द हैं :
A. परि + अवरण B. परि + आवरण
C. पर + आवरण D. पर्या + आवरण

निर्देश (प्र.सं. 129 से 135): *निम्नलिखित गद्यांश को पढ़कर पूछे गए प्रश्नों के सही/सर्वाधिक उपयुक्त विकल्प का चयन कीजिए।*

इस संसार में सब कुछ अस्थायी है। पाप और पुण्य दोनों इस संसार से संबंधित हैं, इसलिए पाप और पुण्य भी अस्थायी हैं। पुण्य सुख देकर और पाप दुख देकर अंत को प्राप्त होता है। लेकिन पाप और पुण्य में थोड़ा अंतर यह है कि पुण्य का फल यदि हम नहीं चाहते तो उस फल को अस्वीकार करने के लिए स्वतंत्र हैं। पाप लोहे की जंजीर है तो पुण्य सोने की। बंधन दोनों में है। लोहे की जंजीर से छूटने का आदमी का मन भी करता है लेकिन सोने की जंजीर से जो बंधा हुआ हो उसको वह बंधन प्यारा लगने लगता है। उसमें उसको धन नजर आता है उससे छूटने का मन नहीं करता।

129. 'स्वतंत्र' का विलोम है :
A. परतंत्र B. दासता
C. परतंत्रता D. गुलाम

130. पाप और पुण्य दोनों की तुलना क्रमशः .... और .... की जंजीर से की गई है।
A. लोहे, पीतल B. लोहे, स्वर्ण
C. पीतल, लोहे D. स्वर्ण, लोहे

121. B **122.** B **123.** A **124.** B **125.** A **126.** A **127.** B **128.** B **129.** A **130.** B

131. समूह से भिन्न शब्द है :

A. स्वतंत्र B. अस्थायी
C. प्यारा D. फल

132. पुण्य में उसके फल को :

A. हम स्वीकार करने के लिए बाध्य हैं
B. किसी दूसरे के लिए उपयोग में ला सकते हैं
C. प्राप्त करना बहुत श्रमसाध्य है
D. हम स्वीकार नहीं भी कर सकते

133. इस संसार में कुछ भी .... नहीं है।

A. पूर्ण B. स्थायी
C. अस्थायी D. अपूर्ण

134. पाप और पुण्य दोनों .... हैं।

A. अस्थायी B. स्वाभाविक
C. हानिकारक D. स्थायी

135. गद्यांश के अनुसार पाप और पुण्य :

A. दोनों में फल की इच्छा रहती है
B. दोनों से मुक्ति अनिवार्य है
C. दोनों में बंधन है
D. दोनों में स्वतंत्रता है

136. कोई भी व्यक्ति किसके द्वारा सर्वाधिक उपयुक्त तरीके से द्वितीय भाषा सीख सकता है?

A. अपने समाज में सहजात वाचकों (मूलभाषा बोलने वालों) के सतत सम्पर्क के माध्यम से
B. श्रव्य भाषिक विधि के अनुसार संवादों को दोहराना और अभ्यास करना
C. लक्ष्य भाषा के किसी वाचन पाठ्यक्रम में दाखिला लेकर
D. ऐसी कक्षा जहाँ आप व्याकरण पर ध्यान केन्द्रित करते हैं और अध्यापक से सहायता प्राप्त करते हैं

137. पठन सीखने में सबसे बड़ी चुनौती प्रेरणा और अच्छा बालसाहित्य पाने की है। इस चुनौती को दूर करने के लिए :

A. अभिभावकों को अपने घर में एक छोटा सा पुस्तकालय बनाने के लिए प्रोत्साहित करना चाहिए
B. बाल साहित्य की सरलता से उपलब्धता जिससे पठन के लिए प्रोत्साहन और रुचि पैदा हो
C. विद्यालय के अधिकारियों को चाहिए कि वे बच्चों को पुस्तक मेले ले जाया करें जिससे कि वे पुस्तकें पढ़ने के लिए प्रोत्साहित हों और रुचि पैदा हो
D. अध्यापकों को गृहकार्य के रूप में प्रतिदिन एक पुस्तक पढ़ने के लिए अभिप्रेरित करना चाहिए

138. एक अध्यापक ने कक्षा पाँच के विद्यार्थियों को शीघ्रता से एक कहानी पढ़ने और उसके बाद चार चित्रों को क्रम में लगाने के लिए कहा। इस गतिविधि का क्या उद्देश्य है?

A. सारांशीकरण के लिए पठन का अभ्यास करवाना
B. विशिष्ट सूचना जानने के लिए पठन का अभ्यास करवाना
C. कहानी में आए नए और कठिन शब्दों की पुनरावृत्ति
D. चित्र कार्डों को क्रम से लगाना

139. प्राथमिक स्तर पर भाषा कौशल का आकलन करने के लिए भाषा अध्यापक को मुख्यतः किस पर ध्यान केन्द्रित करना चाहिए?

A. विराम चिह्नों का प्रयोग
B. उचित गति के साथ पठन
C. समझ के साथ पठन
D. वर्णमाला के अक्षरों की पहचान करना

140. एक अच्छी वाचन (बोलना) गतिविधि वह है जिसमें :

A. शिक्षार्थी अधिक सुनते हैं
B. शिक्षार्थी अधिक बातचीत करते हैं
C. अधिकांशतः मुखरित विद्यार्थियों की ही सहभागिता रहती है
D. अध्यापक अधिक व्याख्या करते हैं

141. बुनियादी चरण में आकलन के उपकरण और प्रक्रियाओं की अभिकल्पना इस तरह होनी चाहिए :

A. जो बच्चे के अधिगम अनुभव का सहज विस्तार बन सकें
B. शिक्षार्थी की प्रगति का उसके समग्र कक्षा प्रदर्शन के संदर्भ में वर्णन और विश्लेषण किया जाना चाहिए
C. अध्यापक सभी शिक्षार्थियों की उपलब्धि का आकलन करने के लिए एक ही विधि का प्रयोग कर सकते हैं
D. जिससे जाँचपत्र व परीक्षाएँ शिक्षार्थियों के लिए स्पष्ट व उचित हो सके

142. कक्षा में छोटे बच्चों के लिए मुद्रित पुस्तकों के साथ-साथ श्रव्य पुस्तकें और छोटे बच्चों की स्पर्शग्राही योग्यताओं का इस्तेमाल करने वाली पुस्तकें होनी चाहिए क्योंकि :

A. यह अध्यापकों को आकलन के लिए विभिन्न पुस्तकों का प्रयोग करने की स्वायत्तता देती है
B. विविधता वाले शिक्षार्थियों तक पुस्तकें अधिक सुलभ बनाती है
C. अध्यापक पर अधिक बोझ नहीं डालती हैं
D. कक्षा में विविधता आती है और बच्चों को विविधता बहुत पसंद है

131. D **132.** D **133.** B **134.** A **135.** C **136.** A **137.** B **138.** A **139.** C **140.** B **141.** A **142.** B

143. "भाषा अधिगम एक गहन प्रक्रिया है जो जन्म के समय से शुरू होती है और जीवन पर्यन्त चलती है।" क्या आप इस कथन से सहमत या असहमत हैं?

A. मैं इस कथन से असहमत हूँ
B. मैं इस कथन से आंशिक रूप से सहमत हूँ
C. मैं इस कथन से आंशिक रूप से असहमत हूँ
D. मैं इस कथन से सहमत हूँ

144. शिक्षार्थी व्याकरण के नियम और शब्द संपदा को कंठस्थ कर रहे हैं, अधिकांश कार्य मातृभाषा में हो रहा है। भाषा अध्यापक द्वारा अपनी कक्षा में किस विधि का प्रयोग करना चाहिए?

A. प्राकृतिक उपागम
B. सम्प्रेषणात्मक शिक्षण
C. व्याकरण अनुवाद
D. प्रत्यक्ष (डायरेक्ट) विधि

145. बच्चों का संज्ञानात्मक विकास और भाषा :

A. मनुष्य का सहजात उपकरण है जिसके द्वारा वह भाषा में निपुणता प्राप्त करता है
B. विकास में कोई संबंध नहीं है
C. उस संस्कृति और समुदायों से घनिष्ठ रूप से संबंधित है जिसमें बच्चे रहते हैं
D. उद्दीपक प्रतिक्रिया संबंध के सिद्धांत और अनुकरण की प्रक्रिया से संबंधित है

146. समग्र भाषा उपागम क्या है?

A. कौशल आधारित
B. ध्वनियों का मिश्रण
C. ध्वनि-संकेत संबंध में निष्कर्ष निकालना
D. अर्थ आधारित

147. यदि बच्चे अपने परिवेश में दो भाषाओं का बोलना सुनते हैं, दो भाषाओं को सुनने के ये अवसर :

A. बच्चों को लाभ पहुँचाते हैं
B. कोई प्रभाव नहीं डालते हैं
C. समझ में भ्रमित करते हैं
D. बच्चों को नुकसान पहुँचाते हैं

148. इस प्रकार के पठन के कुछ अधिगम उद्देश्य और कार्य हैं। शिक्षार्थियों से अपेक्षा रहती है कि वे विषयवस्तु को विस्तार से ध्यानपूर्वक और सावधानीपूर्वक पढ़ें, यह है :

A. गहन पठन (इटैंसिव)
B. निर्देशित पठन
C. आनन्द के लिए पठन
D. विस्तृत पठन

149. पाठ के आरंभ में एक अध्यापक ने अपनी कक्षा के शिक्षार्थियों को समूहों में बाँटा और कहा कि अभी हाल ही में पढ़े गए समाचार पत्र के रुचिकर आलेख के बारे में बात करें। बोलने (वाचन) की यह गतिविधि किसलिए है?

A. नियंत्रित मौखिक अभ्यास
B. निर्देशित मौखिक अभ्यास
C. सक्रिय श्रवण
D. मौखिक प्रवाह अभ्यास

150. विद्यार्थी अध्यापक द्वारा दिये गए आदर्श वाक्यों को दोहराकर भाषा के प्रतिमान (पैटर्न) सीखते हैं। वे वाक्यों को कंठस्थ कर लेते हैं और सही तरीके से ड्रिल करने पर अपने अध्यापक द्वारा सकारात्मक पुनर्बलन प्राप्त करते हैं। अध्यापक द्वारा क्या किया जा रहा है?

A. सम्प्रेषणात्मक उपागम
B. कुल भौतिक प्रतिक्रिया
C. संरचनात्मक उपागम
D. श्रव्य भाषिक विधि

EXPLANATORY ANSWERS

1. (A): Intrinsic motivation refers to the drive that propels individuals to engage in activities for the sheer enjoyment and satisfaction derived from the activities themselves, rather than for some external reward or pressure. This form of motivation is characterized by a personal interest or pleasure in the task, making it self-sustaining. Unlike extrinsic motivation, which is fueled by external factors such as rewards, competition, or the avoidance of punishment, intrinsic motivation is fueled by internal desires. For instance, a person who plays a musical instrument because they genuinely enjoy the process and the challenge it presents, rather than for the sake of winning a competition or pleasing others, is intrinsically motivated. This concept is fundamental in various fields, including education, where fostering intrinsic motivation can lead to a deeper and more enduring form of engagement with learning materials.

143. A	**144.** C	**145.** C	**146.** D	**147.** A	**148.** A	**149.** D	**150.** D

2. **(D):** Lawrence Kohlberg's theory of moral development indeed suggests that moral reasoning, which is the basis for ethical behaviour, evolves through a series of stages. In the early stages, children base their understanding of right and wrong on direct consequences to themselves, such as punishment or reward. As they grow older and advance in their moral reasoning, they begin to see beyond immediate consequences and start to understand societal rules and laws. Importantly, they recognize that these rules and laws serve a societal good but are not inflexible; they can be questioned and changed if they do not serve justice. This progression towards a more principled understanding of morality, where ethical decisions are made based on abstract reasoning about justice, rights, and the common good, aligns with Kohlberg's assertion that moral development occurs progressively in stages. The reason (R) accurately explains the assertion (A) as it highlights the developmental, progressive nature of moral reasoning as conceptualized by Kohlberg.

3. **(D):** Inclusion of students from disadvantaged groups in the educational setting is fundamentally about recognizing and valuing diversity, promoting equality, and ensuring that all students feel respected and valued. This involves awareness and sensitization towards diverse traditions, cultures, and experiences to create an inclusive environment where differences are celebrated rather than marginalized. Such awareness and sensitization help to break down prejudices, stereotypes, and barriers to participation and achievement. By understanding and respecting diversity, educators can foster a sense of belonging and community among students from various backgrounds. This approach stands in contrast to strategies that might isolate students or reinforce identity-based stereotypes, which can exacerbate feelings of exclusion and hinder the educational progress of disadvantaged groups.

4. **(D):** The assertion that learners construct their own knowledge based on what they already know is a central tenet of constructivist theories of learning, which posit that learning is an active process of constructing rather than acquiring knowledge. Learners build new understandings and knowledge by connecting new information to existing cognitive structures, experiences, and prior knowledge. The reason provided, that finding patterns and making linkages with previous knowledge helps learners to process information meaningfully, directly supports this assertion by explaining how the process of making connections between new and existing knowledge facilitates meaningful learning. This approach emphasizes the importance of the learner's active role in their own learning process, suggesting that effective learning occurs when individuals are able to integrate new information with what they already understand, thereby constructing new understanding in a meaningful context.

5. **(A):** Cognitive development encompasses the progression of learning and thinking skills, including reasoning, problem-solving, and understanding the world around us. This aspect of development is concerned with how we perceive, think, understand, and interact with our environment, through processes such as memory, language, thinking, and reasoning skills. Cognitive development theory, most famously proposed by Jean Piaget, outlines how children's cognitive abilities evolve in stages, enabling increasingly complex understanding and problem-solving abilities. This developmental aspect is distinct from moral, motor, and social development, which focus on understanding right from wrong, physical abilities, and interpersonal skills, respectively. Cognitive development is foundational to academic learning and problem-solving in everyday life, highlighting its importance in understanding how individuals grow and interact with the world.

6. **(B):** Howard Gardner's theory of multiple intelligences proposes that individuals have various distinct types of intelligences, each with its own set of skills and ways of learning. Among the intelligences he identifies, musical intelligence is characterized by skills in performance, music appreciation, and composition. Individuals with strong musical intelligence have a keen ability to recognize musical patterns, tones, and rhythms, and are often skilled at creating and performing music. This intelligence is not just about the ability to play an instrument or sing, but also includes a deep understanding of music's structure, form, and the emotional conveyance through musical expression. Gardner's theory challenges traditional notions of intelligence being solely based on linguistic and mathematical abilities, suggesting that talents in areas like music are equally indicative of one's intelligence.

7. **(D):** In the context of language development in primary classes, using concrete examples to explain abstract concepts is a highly effective strategy. This approach is based on the understanding that young learners grasp concepts more readily when they can relate them to tangible, real-world examples. By linking new vocabulary and language structures to objects, actions, and experiences familiar to the students, teachers can facilitate deeper understanding

and retention. This method also helps in making learning more engaging and relevant to the students' everyday lives. Contrary to approaches that might emphasize formal language use or disregard the importance of the mother tongue, this strategy acknowledges the critical role of context and experiential learning in language acquisition.

8. **(A):** Decentering is a cognitive ability that emerges during the concrete operational stage of Jean Piaget's theory of cognitive development, distinguishing it from the preoperational stage. Decentering allows a child to consider multiple aspects of a situation simultaneously, rather than focusing on a single aspect. This development marks a significant shift from preoperational thought, which is characterized by egocentrism and a focus on one dimension at a time. Decentering enables children to understand concepts such as conservation—the understanding that quantity remains the same despite changes in shape or appearance. This ability significantly impacts how children interact with and understand their world, allowing for more complex logical thinking and problem-solving.

9. **(C):** An inclusive classroom is designed to be welcoming and accommodating to all students, regardless of their abilities, backgrounds, or needs. The statement that an inclusive classroom centers around "fixed curricula and standard assessment" contradicts the fundamental principles of inclusive education. Inclusion emphasizes flexibility in teaching methods, curricula, and assessments to cater to the diverse learning styles and requirements of all students. This approach aims to ensure that education is accessible and meaningful for everyone, adapting to the needs of students rather than expecting all students to fit a standard mold. Fixed curricula and standardized assessments often fail to recognize or accommodate the unique strengths and challenges of individual learners, making this statement incorrect in the context of inclusive education principles.

10. **(B):** According to attribution theory, which focuses on how individuals attribute causes to successes and failures, attributing outcomes to internal factors (such as effort or ability) can have significant motivational implications. When individuals attribute their success to internal factors, such as their own efforts or abilities, they are more likely to feel competent and in control, which fosters motivation and persistence. Similarly, attributing failures to internal, potentially controllable factors, like lack of effort, can motivate individuals to work harder and improve their performance. This dual internal attribution promotes a growth mindset, encouraging the belief that abilities can be developed through dedication and hard work, leading to persistent effort and improved performance over time.

11. **(C):** The statement that learning is a product rather than a process is not correct about learning. Learning is widely recognized as a dynamic and continuous process that involves the acquisition, modification, and reinforcement of knowledge, skills, behaviors, and values. This process perspective emphasizes the ongoing nature of learning, where individuals build upon and reorganize their prior knowledge and experiences over time. Viewing learning merely as a product overlooks the essential aspects of how learning occurs and evolves. The process of learning is facilitated by various factors, including social interaction, the learner's previous knowledge, and the active engagement with new information, making it a complex and multifaceted phenomenon rather than a finite outcome.

12. **(C):** The scenario described, where Tanuj believes his sister should not participate in javelin throw because she is a girl and implies that girls cannot throw javelin, is an example of gender stereotyping. Gender stereotypes are oversimplified and widely held beliefs about the characteristics, attributes, and behaviors of individuals based on their gender. These stereotypes can limit the opportunities and experiences available to individuals by suggesting that certain activities, roles, or behaviors are inherently suited to one gender over another. By suggesting that his sister cannot participate in javelin throw because of her gender, Tanuj is reflecting a gender stereotype that associates physical strength and certain sports with males, disregarding individual abilities and interests.

13. **(A):** The statement that children achieve gross motor skills before fine motor skills indicates that development follows a cephalocaudal trend. The cephalocaudal principle of development states that growth and development proceed from the head down. This means that children typically develop control and coordination of their head and upper body before their lower body and legs. Gross motor skills, which involve large muscle activities such as crawling, walking, and jumping, generally develop before fine motor skills, which involve more precise movements of the hands and fingers, like writing and manipulating small objects. This pattern supports the cephalocaudal direction of physical development, highlighting a predictable sequence in which children gain motor skills.

14. (A): A typical characteristic of dyslexia is difficulty in phonological processing. Dyslexia is a learning disorder characterized by difficulties with accurate and/or fluent word recognition and by poor spelling and decoding abilities. These difficulties are often the result of a deficit in the phonological component of language that is unexpected in relation to other cognitive abilities and the provision of effective classroom instruction. Phonological processing refers to the ability to discern and manipulate sounds in words, a critical skill for reading and spelling. Individuals with dyslexia may struggle with tasks such as recognizing the sound structure of language, which can affect their ability to decode words, spell, and read fluently.

15. (B): An assessment task that is helpful in comparing students as per a standard set of criteria would not be characterized as formative assessment. Formative assessment is designed to provide feedback to both students and teachers about the learning process. It is intended to identify learning gaps and misconceptions, monitor progress, and adjust teaching strategies accordingly to support student learning. Formative assessments are typically conducted during the learning process and are not primarily used for grading or ranking students. Instead, their main purpose is to inform and improve the ongoing teaching and learning process. Comparing students against a standard set of criteria aligns more closely with summative assessment, which aims to evaluate student learning at the end of an instructional period by comparing it against some standard or benchmark.

16. (D): Both the assertion (A) that the school curriculum should give reasonable space and value to learners' cultural knowledges, and the reason (R) that supporting students to uphold their cultural identities facilitates learning, are true, and (R) is indeed the correct explanation for (A). Recognizing and incorporating learners' cultural backgrounds and knowledges within the curriculum is essential for creating an inclusive and respectful learning environment. This approach acknowledges the diverse experiences and perspectives that students bring to their education, making learning more relevant and engaging for them. By valuing and integrating cultural identities in education, schools can enhance students' sense of belonging and self-esteem, which are critical for their cognitive and social development. Supporting students' cultural identities does not only promote respect and understanding among diverse student populations but also enriches the learning experience for all, fostering a more comprehensive understanding of the world.

17. (A): Questions that ask for the student's personal opinion can help assess a student's ability to evaluate information critically. Critical evaluation involves analyzing, synthesizing, and assessing information to form a judgment or opinion. When students are asked to provide their personal opinion on a topic, especially if they are encouraged to support their viewpoint with evidence or to consider multiple perspectives, they engage in higher-order thinking. This process requires them to critically analyze the information, weigh different arguments, and articulate their reasoning, showcasing their ability to engage with the material at a deep level. Such questions move beyond mere recall or understanding of facts, pushing students to apply, analyze, and evaluate information, which are key components of critical thinking.

18. (A): According to Kohlberg's theory of moral development, children are self-centered and see their own benefit in doing something at the second stage in the first level. This stage, known as the "Individualism and Exchange" stage, is where children start to recognize that there is not just one right view that is handed down by the authorities. They see that different individuals have different viewpoints, but their moral reasoning is based on individual needs and interests. At this stage, the perspective is still very much self-focused, with actions often motivated by the rewards or benefits to themselves, rather than by loyalty, gratitude, or a sense of justice.

19. (D): Impairment is a biological condition, while disability is a functional condition. This distinction highlights that impairment refers to any loss or abnormality of psychological, physiological, or anatomical structure or function. In contrast, disability refers to the restrictions or lack of ability to perform an activity in the manner or within the range considered normal for a human being, which results from an impairment. This differentiation is important in understanding that while impairment may be a condition of the body, disability arises from the interaction between individuals with an impairment and their environmental and attitudinal barriers that hinder their full and effective participation in society on an equal basis with others.

20. (A): The relationship between cognition and emotion is best defined as interdependent on each other. Research in the fields of psychology and neuroscience has increasingly shown that cognitive processes (such as thinking, reasoning, and decision-making) and emotional processes influence each other in significant ways. Emotions can affect how we think and make decisions, while our cognitive processes can influence how we experience and regulate our emotions. This interdependence suggests that emotions and cognition are deeply intertwined, with each continually affecting and modifying the other. Understanding this relationship is crucial for grasping the complexity of human behavior and mental processes, as it challenges the traditional view of emotions and cognition as separate systems.

21. (D): Problem solving is fostered by divergent thinking. Divergent thinking is a thought process or method used to generate creative ideas by exploring many possible solutions. It involves breaking away from traditional patterns to look at things in different ways. Unlike functional fixedness, passive imitation, and response set, which can limit the ability to see beyond established uses or solutions, divergent thinking encourages flexibility, imagination, and innovation. This type of thinking is essential for effective problem solving because it enables individuals to come up with novel solutions to problems, consider a wide range of alternatives, and approach issues from multiple perspectives.

22. (B): A key principle of progressive education is that learning should be based on authentic tasks. Progressive education emphasizes the importance of learning experiences that are relevant. to students' lives and interests, and that prepare them for active participation in a democratic society. Authentic tasks are activities that are grounded in real-life situations and challenges, allowing students to apply their knowledge and skills in contexts that mirror the complexity and ambiguity of the real world. This approach contrasts with traditional education models that may rely more on rote memorization and passive learning, advocating instead for active engagement, critical thinking, and problem-solving skills.

23. (B): (A) is true but (R) is false. Childhood experiences vary greatly across different cultures due to varying cultural norms and practices (A is true). However, claiming that children's development is universal oversimplifies the impact of cultural differences on developmental processes. While some developmental milestones are biologically driven, how these milestones are reached and valued can differ widely across cultures (R is false). Therefore, while certain aspects of development may be biologically universal, the experience and context of development are heavily influenced by culture.

24. (A): Socio-constructivist views of learning advocate that learners actively construct knowledge. This perspective holds that learning occurs as individuals engage with their environment, including the social and cultural contexts in which they live. Knowledge construction is seen as an active process where learners make sense of their experiences through interaction with others and the world around them. This view contrasts with traditional views of learning as a passive receipt of information, emphasizing instead the importance of social interaction, collaboration, and the active role of the learner in constructing understanding.

25. (C): A characteristic of effective feedback in the classroom is that it is timely and specific. Effective feedback provides learners with detailed, constructive information about their performance and how they can improve. Timeliness ensures that the feedback is relevant and actionable, allowing students to make adjustments while the learning is still in progress. Specificity helps to clarify expectations and provides clear direction on how to enhance future work. Feedback that is broad, generic, or focused only on outcomes without addressing the process can be less helpful to learners. Additionally, while feedback at the end of a task can be beneficial, ongoing feedback throughout the learning process is critical for supporting student growth and development.

26. (A): Lev Vygotsky proposes that inner speech is important for self-regulation in children. Vygotsky's theory emphasizes the crucial role of language in cognitive development, particularly how internal dialogue or inner speech enables individuals to plan, guide, and monitor their behavior. According to Vygotsky, inner speech develops through the internalization of external language interactions, starting from early social communications with parents and caregivers. As children grow, they begin to use language not only for communication with others but also as a tool for thinking and problem-solving independently, which is a fundamental aspect of self-regulation.

27. (D): While divergent thinking encourages multiple answers, convergent thinking is fixed on one correct solution. Divergent thinking is a cognitive process used to generate creative ideas by exploring many possible solutions. It values flexibility and is open-ended, often leading to unique and unconventional answers. In contrast, convergent thinking involves narrowing down the multiple possibilities to find a single, correct answer to a problem. It is typically associated with logical reasoning, decision-making, and problem-solving where a specific solution is required.

28. (C): Children reason that inanimate objects have intentions or purposes (such as a rope deliberately causing someone to get out in a game) during the pre-operational stage of Jean Piaget's theory of cognitive development. This stage, occurring approximately between the ages of 2 and 7, is characterized by symbolic thinking, egocentrism, and animistic thinking, where children believe that non-living objects have feelings, thoughts, and intentions. This stage showcases the beginning of logical or operational thought, although thinking at this stage is still intuitive and egocentric.

29. (D): The proximodistal principle states that development proceeds from the center of the body outward, meaning that the limbs develop before the hands and feet. This principle of development suggests that infants gain control over their shoulders and arms before their hands and fingers. The proximodistal trend describes the direction of growth and development, which occurs from the most central parts of the body (proximal areas like the torso) out towards the more distant parts (distal areas like the hands and feet).

30. (B): Examples of scaffolding include think-alouds, prompts and cues, questions, and half-solved examples. Scaffolding is a teaching method that involves providing support to students as they learn new concepts or skills. The support is gradually removed as students become more competent and confident, enabling them to perform independently. Think-alouds allow students to observe the cognitive processes used in problem-solving. Prompts and cues guide students' thinking or action in the right direction. Questions stimulate thinking and reflection. Half-solved examples give students a framework to complete tasks. Rote rehearsal, which involves memorizing through repetition, is not typically considered a form of scaffolding, as it does not necessarily help students understand underlying concepts or apply knowledge in new situations.

31. (C): The given number pattern (1, 8, 27, 64, 125) represents the cubes of natural numbers starting from 1.

$$\begin{array}{ccccccc} 1 & 8 & 27 & 64 & 125 & \boxed{216} & \boxed{343} \\ \downarrow & \downarrow & \downarrow & \downarrow & \downarrow & \downarrow & \downarrow \\ 1^3 & 2^3 & 3^3 & 4^3 & 5^3 & 6^3 & 7^3 \end{array}$$

Therefore, the next two terms are 216 and 343.

32. (C): Let the required number which is subtracted be x

According to the question,

$9909 + 9099 + 9009 - x = 25454$

$\Rightarrow 28017 - x = 25454$

$\Rightarrow x = 28017 - 25454$

$\Rightarrow x = 2563$

Hence, the required number will be 2563.

33. (D): The statement that "Mathematics lab is essential as it provides opportunities for hands-on activities for students" is most appropriate. Mathematics labs create an environment where students can explore mathematical concepts through practical activities, experiments, and manipulatives. This hands-on approach helps to demystify abstract concepts, making mathematics more engaging and accessible to students. It allows for experiential learning, where students can directly observe and participate in the learning process, enhancing their understanding and retention of mathematical ideas.

34. (D): Word problems refer to exercises where the child formalizes the situation into a form where a specific mathematical technique can be applied. This statement is true as word problems in school mathematics involve taking real-life scenarios or abstract situations and translating them into a mathematical format that can be solved using known mathematical principles or operations. Word problems are essential for developing problem-solving skills, as they require students to apply their mathematical knowledge in context, integrating both procedural and conceptual understanding.

35. (A): According to National Education Policy (NEP) 2020, the assessment of learners includes cognitive, affective, and psychomotor domains. This comprehensive approach to assessment is designed to evaluate not only the intellectual abilities of students (cognitive domain) but also their emotional and attitudinal development (affective domain) and their physical skills and coordination (psychomotor domain). This holistic view of assessment reflects the policy's aim to foster an education system that supports the all-around development of students, preparing them for the various challenges of life and ensuring their growth as well-rounded individuals.

36. (C): "Formal examination to assess the knowledge gained by the students" is not included in the National Education Policy (NEP) - 2020 under the topic of "Knowledge of India". NEP 2020 emphasizes the integration of India's rich cultural heritage, including tribal knowledge, traditional ways of learning, and contributions from ancient India to various subjects. However, it aims to move away from high-stakes testing to more holistic, formative, and adaptive methods of assessment to foster learning and development. The focus on formal examinations as a primary means of assessment does not align with the policy's broader educational goals, which include experiential learning, critical thinking, and a deep understanding of Indian culture and knowledge systems.

37. (D): According to the National Curriculum Framework, 2005, "Memorizing formulae" is least relevant in a primary mathematics classroom. The NCF 2005 advocates for understanding mathematical concepts through exploration, reasoning, and problem-solving rather than through rote memorization. It emphasizes the importance of using patterns, visualization, and making connections and representations to develop a deeper understanding of mathematical ideas. This approach aligns with the framework's goal of making mathematics more meaningful and enjoyable for students, encouraging them to see mathematics as a part of their daily lives rather than a set of abstract rules to be memorized.

38. (B): The statement that "Thoughtful efforts of a teacher to expose children to cognitive conflict can enhance their mathematical understanding" is most appropriate for the idea of cognitive conflict in teaching mathematics. Cognitive conflict is a pedagogical strategy that involves presenting students with information or problems that challenge their existing preconceptions, leading them to question and revise their understanding. This process can be highly effective in deepening mathematical understanding, as it encourages active engagement with concepts and promotes higher-order thinking skills. The idea that cognitive conflict is not useful or that it should be avoided due to potential confusion misunderstands the role of challenge and inquiry in learning. When carefully managed, cognitive conflict stimulates learning and conceptual change.

39. (A): Increasing 8 by 8 = 8 + 8 = 16

Double of 8 = 8 × 2 = 16

Therefore, the number will be 8.

40. (B): The sum of all angles of a triangle is 180°. This is a fundamental property of triangles in Euclidean geometry, applicable to all triangles regardless of their type (scalene, isosceles, or equilateral).

41. (A): One millimeter is the same as 0.1 cm. The conversion between millimeters and centimeters is based on the fact that there are 10 millimeters in one centimeter. Therefore, 1 mm equals 0.1 cm.

42. (C): 1 is neither prime nor a composite number. By definition, a prime number is a number greater than 1 that has no positive divisors other than 1 and itself. A composite number is a positive integer that has at least one positive divisor other than 1 and itself. Since 1 does not meet the criteria for being a prime number and it also cannot be classified as a composite number, the correct statement is that 1 is neither prime nor a composite number.

43. (B): To cover the biggest land area with a wire of length 100 meters, Brij should choose the dimensions that maximize the area enclosed by the wire. The perimeter of the land must be 100 meters to use the entire length of the wire. Among the given options, a square with sides of 25 m each (option B) would use the entire wire and maximize the area, since a square has the maximum area for a given perimeter among rectangles. The area would be 25 m × 25 m = 625 m^2.

44. (A): A square is always a regular polygon. A regular polygon is defined as a polygon that is equiangular (all angles are equal in measure) and equilateral (all sides have the same length). A square meets both of these criteria, making it a regular polygon.

45. (C): To calculate the cost of sending a 350 g parcel, consider the initial rate for the first 50 g is ₹15.00, and for every additional 50 g, the rate is ₹7.00. Since the parcel weighs 350 g, it exceeds the first 50 g by 300 g. The correct cost of sending the parcel weighing 350 g is ₹15 + ₹42 = ₹57.

46. (B): Early number concept formation is related to (a) one-to-one correspondence and (b) hierarchical inclusion. One-to-one correspondence is a fundamental mathematical concept where each object in one set is matched with exactly one object in another set, and vice versa, which is crucial for understanding counting and quantity. Hierarchical inclusion is the understanding that a number includes all the numbers before it, an essential concept for grasping the relationship between numbers and for the development of number sense. Basic operations, such as addition, subtraction, multiplication, and division, are built upon these foundational concepts but are considered a more advanced aspect of number understanding.

47. (A): The statement that "It hampers the learning of child as it leads to confusion" is not true about the 'multiplicity of approaches' in teaching mathematics. Offering multiple approaches to solving problems in mathematics is actually beneficial as it acknowledges the diverse ways in which students understand and engage with mathematical concepts. This approach allows students to explore and find methods that work best for them, enhancing their understanding and fostering a more inclusive and adaptable learning environment. It encourages critical thinking and problem-solving skills by showing that there can be various valid ways to arrive at a solution.

48. (A): Yamina got the number 3 the maximum number of times when she threw a die 10 times. The results given were 5, 3, 6, 6, 1, 4, 5, 3, 3, 2, and among these numbers, 3 appears three times, which is more than any other number in the list.

49. (A): Revisiting the concept of regrouping will best remediate the misconception demonstrated by the student's solution of 26×5 as "1030". The student seems to misunderstand how to handle the multiplication process, especially when it involves carrying over or regrouping numbers. Understanding regrouping—or carrying over as it applies to multiplication—is essential for correctly solving multi-digit multiplication problems and ensuring that each digit is accurately accounted for in the calculation.

50. (A): Given,

$25.3 \times 5 - 35 \div 5 - 3 \times 18.5$

$= 25.3 \times 5 - 7 - 3 \times 18.5$

$= 126.5 - 7 - 55.5$

$= 126.5 - 62.5$

$= 64$

51. (B): A right angle is 90 degrees. To find the number of degrees in $2\frac{2}{3}$ right angles, we multiply the fraction by 90 degrees, we get

$= 2\frac{2}{3} \times 90°$

$= \frac{8}{3} \times 90°$

$= 240°$.

52. (A): Introducing 'Data Handling' at the primary stage is most appropriately done through activities that are relatable and engaging for young learners. Collecting simple statistics within the classroom environment, such as students' heights, favorite foods, colors, cartoons, etc., and then asking questions related to this data, makes the concept tangible and relevant to their everyday experiences. This approach allows students to actively participate in the collection, analysis, and discussion of data, fostering their understanding of basic data handling concepts in a meaningful context.

54. (C): No. of packets $= \frac{\text{Total amount of salt}}{\text{Weight of one packet}}$

$= \frac{7.5 \text{ kg}}{\frac{1}{12} \text{kg}}$

$= \frac{7.5 \times 12}{1}$

$= 90$ packets.

55. (B): The characteristics of mathematical language at the primary level should include that it is precise and should be reinforced through the child's language used in everyday life. Mathematical language should be clear and accurate to help students understand concepts without confusion, but it should also connect with their everyday experiences and expressions to make the learning relevant and accessible. Ambiguity and highly technical language are not suitable for primary-level learners as these can hinder understanding and engagement with the subject.

56. (A): In such a situation, the teacher should consider changing the word 'borrowing' to 'regrouping' and then show the process of regrouping. This approach addresses the student's concern in a constructive way and provides an opportunity to clarify the concept by using terminology that accurately reflects the mathematical process involved. Regrouping is a more precise term that can help students understand the operation without attaching potentially negative connotations to the learning process.

57. (C): The statement least appropriate for encouraging mathematical learning is to discourage intuition as it hampers the development of mathematical ideas. Intuition is a valuable component of mathematical thinking and learning; it helps students form connections, explore concepts, and develop deeper understandings. Encouraging intuition, alongside systematic learning and problem-solving strategies, can enrich students' mathematical experiences and foster a more comprehensive understanding of the subject.

58. **(A):** To determine which of the following costs the least, we'll calculate the total cost for each option:

(A) 750 packets of ₹7.50 each = ₹5625.00

(B) 7.5 dozen items (90 items) of ₹750 each item = ₹67500.00

(C) 75 dozen items (900 items) of ₹7.50 each item = ₹6750.00

(D) 75 packets of ₹750 each = ₹56250.00

On comparing we see that least cost is ₹5625.00 which is of 750 packets of ₹7.50 each.

59. **(C):** The least appropriate model to develop the conceptual understanding regarding the relationships of ones, tens, and hundreds in early grade learners is a place value chart. While a place value chart is a useful tool for visualizing and understanding place value, it might be less interactive or tangible compared to other options like money, an abacus, or Dienes blocks. These other models provide hands-on experiences that can help solidify understanding of place value in a more concrete and engaging way for young learners.

60. **(D):** When a teacher ensures that a test made by her fulfills the objectives and criteria of that test, she is concerned with the validity of the evaluation. Validity refers to the extent to which a test measures what it is supposed to measure. In this context, ensuring that the test aligns with the learning objectives and accurately assesses the intended knowledge and skills demonstrates a focus on the test's validity. This aspect of evaluation is crucial for providing meaningful and useful assessments that accurately reflect students' understanding and abilities.

61. **(C):** Child-centered strategies in teaching Environmental Studies (EVS) at the primary level prioritize active learning, where students are encouraged to explore, ask questions, and engage with the material in a meaningful way. Discussion and survey are two methods that align well with this approach. Through discussion, students are given a platform to express their thoughts, share their experiences, and learn from one another, fostering a collaborative learning environment. Surveys, on the other hand, involve students in gathering information, either through observations, interviews, or research, which not only aids in learning about the topic at hand but also develops their investigative skills. These strategies support the constructivist theory of learning, which posits that learners construct knowledge through their experiences and interactions with the world around them, making them active participants in their learning process.

63. **(B):** Forming heterogeneous groups based on participation and cooperation for peer-learning strategies is an effective approach to enhance learning outcomes. This method ensures that groups are diverse, with students bringing different strengths, abilities, and perspectives to the table. Heterogeneous grouping encourages students to learn from each other, promotes social skills, and fosters a more inclusive learning environment. It allows for peer tutoring, where students can help each other understand concepts or skills that they may find challenging, leveraging the varying levels of knowledge, skills, and competencies within the group. This approach also helps to break down barriers between students of different academic abilities, encouraging collaboration and mutual respect. By valuing participation and cooperation, the teacher emphasizes the importance of process and effort in learning, rather than solely focusing on outcomes.

64. **(B):** The statement that about 4700 years ago, some of the earliest cities flourished on the banks of the river Indus and its tributaries is true and reflects the period of the Indus Valley Civilization, one of the world's oldest urban cultures. This civilization is known for its advanced urban planning, architecture, and social organization. On the other hand, the statement about cities developing on the banks of the Ganga and its tributaries about 1500 years ago might be seen as misleading or partially incorrect. Urban centers along the Ganga did become prominent, but this development can be traced back further and continued over a broad period. The growth of urban centers in the Gangetic plains is a significant part of India's historical narrative, involving complex social, cultural, and political dynamics over centuries. Thus, while both statements hold elements of truth regarding the historical development of urban centers in India, the specificity of the timelines and the implications might require more nuanced understanding and context.

65. (D): Both the assertion and reason are correct, and the reason is the correct explanation of the assertion. The theme 'Family and Friends' in EVS education serves as a foundational concept to explore the interconnectedness of human beings with the natural world, including plants and animals. Presenting 'Plants and Animals' as a subtheme of 'Family and Friends' effectively emphasizes the interdependence of all forms of life. This pedagogical approach is designed to foster empathy and understanding among students towards the environment and its various inhabitants. By integrating these themes, EVS education aims to cultivate a sense of responsibility and stewardship in students towards maintaining a balanced and healthy ecosystem. The reason underlines the educational philosophy behind this approach, which seeks to highlight the integral relationships and mutual dependencies between humans and the environment, supporting the assertion's validity.

66. (B): Asking students to find out the food preferences of their family members promotes inquiry while teaching the theme 'Food'. This strategy encourages students to engage actively with their learning by conducting research within their own families. It facilitates the development of inquiry skills such as questioning, investigating, analyzing data, and communicating findings. Students not only learn about diverse food preferences and dietary habits but also appreciate cultural and individual differences. This approach makes learning more relevant and meaningful by connecting classroom knowledge with real-life contexts, fostering curiosity and a deeper understanding of the theme.

67. (C): The themes of EVS at the primary level, as depicted in option C, "Shelter, Travel, Things we make and do," are reflective of the curriculum's focus on connecting children with their immediate environment as well as the wider world. These themes are designed to engage students in exploring and understanding their surroundings, the diverse ways people live and work, and the various means through which we interact with and modify our environment. By studying these themes, students develop an awareness of different aspects of human life, natural resources, and the interdependence of humans and the environment. These themes also encourage the development of skills such as observation, inquiry, and critical thinking, which are crucial for understanding environmental studies.

68. (D): Both statements (A) and (R) are correct, and (R) explains (A). Silkworms, like many other insects, rely on chemical signals for communication. The assertion that a silkworm can find his female worm from many kilometers away by her smell is supported by the reason that some female insects release pheromones, which are chemical substances that can be recognized by their males by smell. Pheromones play a critical role in mating behaviors, allowing males to locate females over considerable distances. This chemical communication is crucial for the survival and reproduction of many insect species, including silkworms. The explanation provided by (R) about the release and detection of pheromones elucidates the mechanism behind the ability of silkworms to find mates, making it the correct explanation for (A).

70. (B): The mass of an object can be calculated by multiplying its density by its volume. Given a density of 12 g/ml and a volume of 3 ml, the mass of the object is calculated as

$$\text{Volume} = 12\text{g/ml} \times 3 \text{ ml} = 36\text{g}$$

This formula is based on the principle that density is defined as mass per unit volume, making it a straightforward calculation for determining the mass of an object when its density and volume are known.

71. (D): The territorial states bordering Haryana are Himachal Pradesh, Rajasthan, and Uttar Pradesh. Haryana is located in the northern part of India and shares its borders with these states, each of which contributes to the geographical and cultural diversity of the region. This proximity to multiple states influences Haryana's climate, agriculture, economy, and culture, making it a state with rich and varied interactions with its neighbors.

72. (B): The assertion (A) that we can cook food more easily at sea level as compared to higher altitudes is true because the atmospheric pressure is higher at sea level, which keeps the boiling point of water at its normal temperature of 100°C (212°F). The reason (R) provided, however, is false; at high altitudes, the boiling point of water decreases due to the lower atmospheric pressure. This decrease in the boiling point means that water boils at a lower temperature, which can make cooking certain foods more time-consuming or difficult because the lower temperature may not be sufficient to cook the food properly. Therefore, while cooking is indeed more challenging at higher altitudes, the explanation regarding the boiling point of water is inaccurately stated in the reason.

73. (C): Blood tests for malaria are done to check for the presence of microbes, specifically the Plasmodium parasites that cause the disease, in the blood. Malaria is transmitted to humans through the bites of infected female Anopheles mosquitoes. Once in the bloodstream, the parasites multiply in the liver before infecting and destroying red blood cells. The detection of these parasites during a blood examination is crucial for diagnosing malaria and determining the appropriate treatment. Blood tests for malaria do not focus on checking for iron levels, mosquito eggs (as mosquitoes do not lay eggs in blood), or solely for hemoglobin levels, but rather on identifying the causative pathogens.

74. (A): The weaver bird is known for its unique nesting behavior, where the male weaves intricate and elaborate nests from grass and other plant materials to attract females. The female weaver bird inspects the nests built by multiple males and selects the one she prefers for laying her eggs. This behavior is a fascinating example of mating rituals in the animal kingdom, where the construction skills and effort of the male play a crucial role in mate selection. The intricate nests, often suspended from tree branches, are not only remarkable for their construction but also serve as a demonstration of the male's fitness and ability to provide a safe environment for the offspring.

75. (A): Conducting a survey in homes and the neighborhood to find out the number of members and the approximate amount of water used in each family develops several key skills and processes, including questioning, inferring, and expression. Through this activity, students learn to formulate relevant questions to gather data, apply critical thinking skills to analyze and infer information from the collected data, and express their findings in a coherent manner. This hands-on approach encourages active learning and engagement with real-world issues, such as water usage and conservation. It fosters an understanding of the importance of sustainable practices and raises awareness of environmental concerns, contributing to the development of responsible and informed citizens.

76. (C): The inclusion of Wahida Prism's experience in the Navy as a doctor in an EVS textbook serves multiple educational purposes, including (a) challenging gender stereotypes, (b) providing insight into the life of a medical officer in the armed forces, and (d) highlighting the difficulties faced by her and her ways of tackling them. This chapter is significant because it showcases the contributions of women in traditionally male-dominated fields, breaking down gender barriers and inspiring students to think broadly about career possibilities and gender roles in society. By learning about her experiences, students gain a realistic view of the challenges and rewards of serving in the armed forces, and the resilience and problem-solving required to overcome obstacles. The reference to a prism reflecting 7 colors (c) does not relate to the context of Wahida Prism's story and her achievements.

77. (D): Both statements (A) and (B) are correct. Statement (A) indicates that Bora is a common variety of rice used in Assam, which reflects the regional agricultural practices and the types of rice cultivated in this area. Statement (B) accurately describes the cultivation requirements of paddy, which is the rice plant. Paddy indeed grows well in clayey soil, which can retain water more effectively than other types of soil, and it requires a significant amount of water for cultivation, reflecting the agricultural needs of this crop. These statements together provide insight into agricultural practices and the specific conditions required for growing certain crops, such as rice in Assam.

78. (C): "Pochampalli" is a famous district known for its beautifully designed bright-colored sarees and for the special kind of weave which is also called Pochampalli. It is located in the state of Telangana, India. Pochampalli sarees are renowned for their traditional geometric patterns in Ikat style of dyeing. The unique weaving techniques and vibrant colors make these sarees distinctive and highly valued in the textile industry and among saree connoisseurs. This craft is not just a cultural heritage but also an important aspect of the local economy, supporting the artisans and weavers of the region.

79. (A): Asking students to think and answer "Why do we feel comfortable in woolen clothes during winter" is an analytical question. This type of question requires students to analyze information, apply their understanding of scientific principles, and think critically about the properties of materials (in this case, wool) and how they interact with the human body and the environment. Analytical questions encourage students to explore the underlying reasons for observed phenomena, fostering deeper learning and comprehension. In this instance, students would need to consider the insulating properties of wool, how it traps air to retain body heat, and how this contributes to comfort in cold conditions.

80. (C): Statement (I) is false as the EVS syllabus is not specifically divided into just the six themes mentioned. The EVS curriculum encompasses a wide range of themes designed to connect children with their environment, though the themes listed are indeed part of the broader curriculum. Statement (II) is true; the themes of the EVS curriculum are intentionally chosen to be close to children's life experiences. This approach is adopted to make learning relevant and meaningful, ensuring that students can relate their educational experiences to the world around them. By integrating themes that reflect students' real-life experiences, the curriculum aims to foster curiosity, critical thinking, and a deeper understanding of environmental and social issues.

81. (B): Reflecting the recommendations of NCF 2005, textbooks in Environmental Studies (EVS) should link students' life at school with their life outside, implying that textbooks support students to construct knowledge through all the given activities. This approach emphasizes active learning, where students engage with the content through exploration, inquiry, and hands-on activities. By connecting the curriculum with students' real-life experiences, textbooks become a tool for constructing knowledge rather than merely transmitting information. This pedagogical strategy encourages critical thinking, problem-solving, and a deeper understanding of environmental and social issues, fostering a more meaningful and integrated learning experience.

82. (D): Both statements (A) and (B) are true. Xylem is responsible for transporting water and minerals from the roots to the rest of the plant, playing a crucial role in the plant's vascular system. This process is essential for the plant's growth and development, as it provides the necessary nutrients and water to various parts. Phloem, on the other hand, translocates food produced in the leaves through photosynthesis to various parts of the plant, including the roots. This distribution of nutrients supports the plant's overall energy needs and contributes to growth and development. These two systems work together to ensure that plants receive the water, minerals, and nutrients needed to thrive.

83. (D): In the activity described, Alex is helping his students focus on (a) learning about colors, patterns, and developing an aesthetic sense, (b) relating the activity to weaving done by weavers, and (d) choosing papers of attractive colors and learning cutting of strips perfectly. These objectives are aligned with the theme 'Work We Do' by connecting a simple, hands-on activity with broader concepts of art, craft, and traditional livelihoods. The activity not only fosters creativity and fine motor skills but also introduces students to the concept of weaving as a profession, thereby providing a tangible connection to the types of work people do. It encourages appreciation for cultural arts and crafts and the skills involved in creating everyday objects.

84. (D): The group assignment described involves several process skills and learning indicators, including questioning, expression, and inferring. Students are required to question as they investigate the types of crops grown and the implements used in agriculture. Expression is involved as they prepare a report and possibly present their findings, requiring them to organize and communicate their observations effectively. Inferring is also a key skill as students draw conclusions from their observations and the information gathered during their visits to agricultural farms. This assignment promotes active learning and engagement with the environment, enhancing students' understanding of agricultural practices and their importance to the community.

85. (D): Johad is correctly described as a community-based rainwater harvesting system. Johads are traditional water storage structures that are used to collect and store rainwater for agricultural and domestic purposes. They are an important part of water conservation practices in several parts of India, particularly in arid and semi-arid regions. By capturing runoff during the monsoon season, johads help recharge groundwater levels, provide water for irrigation, and mitigate the effects of drought. This system reflects an indigenous knowledge and sustainable approach to water management that is community-oriented, promoting the wise use and conservation of water resources.

86. (C): Asking students to define the term 'Animal' may not be the most appropriate task for students of primary level as per the nature of EVS at the primary level. Environmental Studies (EVS) at the primary level is designed to engage students in exploring and understanding their environment through observation, inquiry, and hands-on activities rather than through formal definitions or rote memorization. The emphasis is on building connections with the natural world, fostering curiosity, and encouraging students to learn through their experiences and interactions. Tasks such as writing names of various animals, observing activities of different animals, and classifying animals based on observations are more aligned with the experiential and inquiry-based approach recommended for EVS education at this stage.

87. (A): When Ravi adds a lot of salt to the water, the density of the water increases. An object's buoyancy, or its ability to float, is affected by the density of the fluid it is submerged in. As the salt concentration in the water increases, it becomes denser than the lemon, making the lemon float. This experiment illustrates principles of density and buoyancy, showing how changes in the composition of a fluid can affect the floating or sinking behavior of objects in that fluid.

88. (B): The statement that Al-Biruni did not write anything about ponds in India is NOT true. Al-Biruni, a scholar from the region that is now Uzbekistan, came to India more than a thousand years ago. He extensively documented Indian society, culture, sciences, and geography, including observations on the construction and significance of water storage systems like ponds in India. His writings provide valuable insights into the historical and cultural landscape of India during his time. Al-Biruni's accounts praise various aspects of Indian civilization, including its scientific knowledge and engineering practices.

89. (C): The statement that Ghadsisar Lake is in use till today is NOT true. Ghadsisar Lake, also known as Gadsisar Lake, is a historic water conservation tank located in Jaisalmer, Rajasthan, India. It was built around 650 years ago and was indeed connected with other lakes. However, the assertion that it is in use till today might not accurately reflect its current status primarily as a tourist attraction rather than a functional water resource. While it remains a significant historical and architectural site, its primary function today may not be as a water source for the city.

90. (C): The correct statements about beehives are (a) Honey bees live in beehives. Every beehive has one queen bee that lays eggs, and (d) The worker bees fly around Litchi flowers in search of nectar for honey. In a beehive, the queen bee's primary role is to lay eggs, while the worker bees, which are female, are responsible for various tasks including foraging for nectar and pollen, making honey, building the hive, and caring for the young. The male bees, known as drones, have the primary role of mating with the queen. They do not work like the worker bees. This distinction clarifies the roles within the hive and highlights the worker bees' significant contribution to the hive's maintenance and the production of honey.

91. (D): The word opposite in meaning to "humility" is "pride". Humility refers to a modest or low view of one's own importance, while pride involves a higher opinion of oneself, sometimes to the point of arrogance.

92. (C): The statement that is not correct is "He felt that he would have to forgive Alfred". The passage does not indicate Mr. Carr felt compelled to forgive Alfred; rather, he expressed his intention to get a police officer involved due to Alfred's thefts.

94. (C): Having looked at his mother, Alfred was surprised. The passage describes Alfred's inability to understand his mother's quiet composure, indicating his surprise at her demeanor in contrast to how he expected she would react under such circumstances.

95. (A): The underlined phrase "he hardly knew what to say to her" functions as a noun clause. It describes Mr. Carr's state of uncertainty or confusion regarding how to communicate with Mrs. Higgins, serving as the object of the sentence.

96. (B): The correct statements are (a) "When she entered the drug store, Mrs. Higgins was not properly dressed", and (c) "Mr. Carr did not expect her to be calm and dignified". These statements are supported by the passage, which describes Mrs. Higgins's unexpected composure and the initial description of her appearance. Statement (b) is incorrect because there is no indication that she looked like the mother of a guilty person; rather, her demeanor was described positively.

97. (C): The underlined word "that" is a conjunction. It is used to introduce a subordinate clause "her clothes seemed to have been thrown on her," which provides additional information about the reason for their forgetting.

98. (A): The word nearest in meaning to "wavered" is "hesitated". To waver means to show indecision or to fluctuate in opinion, intention, or direction. In the context of the passage, "her blue eyes never wavered" suggests that Mrs. Higgins maintained steady eye contact without showing hesitation or uncertainty.

99. (B): Both statements (a) "Mr. Carr intended to get Alfred arrested" and (b) "Mrs. Higgins wanted him to be given a chance to reform himself" are correct. The passage explicitly mentions Mr. Carr's intention to involve the police and Mrs. Higgins's suggestion that a little good advice might be more beneficial for Alfred at this point in his life, reflecting her hope for his chance to reform.

100. (D): All men and women perform various roles in life. This metaphorical statement illustrates the concept that life is like a stage play, where individuals take on different roles throughout their lives, contributing to the drama and narrative of human existence.

101. (A): The figure of speech used in "their exits and entrances" is a metaphor. It compares life to a stage play without using words like "as" or "like", where "exits" and "entrances" represent the birth and death of individuals, highlighting the transient nature of human life.

102. (A): The lover's sigh is compared to a furnace because he feels emotionally charged. The metaphor suggests the intensity and passion of the lover's feelings, burning with desire or love, similar to the heat generated by a furnace.

103. (A): The figure of speech used in the first line, "All the world is a stage," is a metaphor. It directly compares the world to a stage, implying that life is a performance and that people are actors playing various roles throughout their lives, without explicitly using words like "as" or "like".

104. (C): A school-boy is reluctant to go to school as he was creeping like snail but at the same time his face was also shining.

105. (A): A soldier is jealous about his honor because he is very sensitive about his honor. The text highlights the soldier's concern for reputation and valor, often to the point of engaging in quick and sudden quarrels to defend or uphold his honor, indicative of a high sense of pride and sensitivity to how he is perceived by others.

107. (B): The Direct Method does not encourage learners to use their native language in a language class. This method emphasizes immersion in the target language as the medium of instruction. The principle behind the Direct Method is that students will develop a better understanding and fluency in the new language by being exposed to it directly, without the intermediary of translation from their native language. It focuses on everyday vocabulary and sentences, encourages spontaneous use of the language, and prioritizes oral skills over reading or writing at the initial stages. The method assumes that learning a second language should mimic the way we naturally acquire our first language, with a strong emphasis on listening and speaking. This contrasts with approaches that might blend the use of the native language for explanations or clarifications, underlining the Direct Method's unique position in language learning methodologies.

108. (C): Stating that "a read-aloud of the textbook can be best done in a library" is NOT true about using the library at the primary level. Libraries serve as vibrant, interactive spaces that encourage exploration, discovery, and love for reading among children. They should be seen as environments where students can engage actively with a wide range of books, not just as places for reading textbooks aloud. The primary role of the library is to expose learners to diverse genres, authors, and subjects that extend beyond their textbooks, fostering a culture of reading for pleasure and curiosity. While libraries can host read-aloud sessions, these are more effectively used for storytelling, sharing picture books, or introducing children to literature that they might not encounter in their regular classroom activities. This approach helps to build a broader appreciation for reading and literature, making the library a cornerstone of a child's literary journey rather than a mere extension of the classroom.

109. (C): Phonics instruction emphasizes the relationship between letters and sounds, making it a literacy teaching approach that focuses on teaching the alphabetic principle—the understanding that there are systematic and predictable relationships between written letters and spoken sounds. Through phonics, children learn to decode words by sounds, which aids in their ability to read and spell. Phonics instruction involves teaching children to recognize the sounds that individual letters and groups of letters make, how to blend these sounds together to form words, and how to segment words into their constituent sounds. This method is crucial in early literacy development because it equips children with the foundational skills needed to decode new words, enhancing their reading fluency and comprehension. Unlike the grammar-translation or whole language approaches, which may focus more on meaning and use of language in context, or the situational approach, which relies on teaching language through situations that are relevant to the learners, phonics instruction provides a systematic way of understanding how language is constructed, offering a building block approach to reading and writing.

110. (B): The student who says, "I give my work a final check for accuracy before submitting it to the teacher," is working at the writing stage of proofreading. Proofreading involves reviewing a piece of writing to correct grammatical errors, typos, spelling mistakes, and to ensure accuracy in the text before it is considered complete and ready for submission. This stage is distinct from re-drafting, which involves revising the content and structure of the writing, and from peer evaluation, where feedback is sought from classmates. Drafting is the process of creating the initial version of the writing, so the correct answer is proofreading, which is the final review to catch and correct minor errors and ensure the work is polished.

111. (D): Are the authors of these books well-known and respected authors of children's literature? In a hypothetical scenario where this is considered the most important criterion, the rationale could be that books by well-known and respected authors of children's literature are likely to offer high-quality content that is engaging, developmentally appropriate, and potentially aligned with broader educational goals. These authors have a track record of writing books that not only captivate children's interests but also often incorporate themes and language that support literacy development. However, this perspective might overlook the immediate curriculum alignment and the specific reading levels of the students, focusing instead on the broader value of introducing students to acclaimed literature.

112. (A): The communicative approach is geared towards the learner's main goal of using language in real-life contexts. This approach focuses on enabling students to communicate effectively and fluently in the target language. It emphasizes the importance of interaction, meaningful communication, and the use of language for real-life purposes over the rote learning of grammatical structures. The communicative approach involves various activities that simulate real-life situations, encouraging students to use the language in a way that is practical and relevant to their daily lives and interactions.

113. (D): Oral fluency practice. In this hypothetical scenario, asking and answering questions using "can" to discuss abilities is seen as a practice aimed primarily at enhancing oral fluency. This interpretation would suggest that the activity's main goal is to improve the students' ability to communicate thoughts and questions smoothly and naturally in a conversational context. The focus would be on the flow of speech rather than the accuracy of the grammatical structure, encouraging students to think and respond quickly in English, thus building their confidence and fluency in the language. This view emphasizes the fluid use of language in real-life communication over the controlled practice of specific grammatical forms.

114. (C): The statement that is NOT correct about teaching grammar effectively is "Learn grammar by memorizing its rules." Effective grammar teaching involves more than just memorization of rules; it incorporates eliciting grammar rules through examples and context, providing opportunities for practice in meaningful communication, and promoting genuine communication where grammar is used in context. Memorizing rules without understanding their application or practicing them in context can lead to rote learning without a real grasp of how to use the grammar in actual communication.

115. (C): The criterion that is NOT correct for choosing Teaching Learning Materials (TLMs) for class II students is "The material chosen should be made by the children only and have some roughness to avoid slipperiness." While involving children in the creation of learning materials can be beneficial for engagement and learning, it is not practical or necessary for all materials to be made by the children only. Additionally, the emphasis on roughness to avoid slipperiness does not adequately address the primary concerns for TLMs, which should be attractiveness, safety, educational value, and appropriateness for the children's age and developmental level. TLMs should be chosen based on their ability to enhance learning, their safety for use by children, and their relevance and accessibility to the learning context.

116. (C): The objective of asking learners to exchange workbooks and check their partner's work is to develop the skill of peer correction. This teaching strategy encourages students to engage in active learning by evaluating and providing feedback on each other's work. Peer correction fosters a collaborative learning environment, enhances critical thinking skills, and allows students to learn from one another's mistakes and successes. This method can also help students become more aware of common errors and improve their understanding of the subject matter.

117. (A): Children in the foundational stage are more engaged in learning when they use multiple senses and actively use their hands. Engaging multiple senses in learning activities, such as touching, seeing, hearing, and moving, helps young children to better process and retain information. Hands-on activities encourage exploration, experimentation, and interaction with materials, which are critical for the cognitive development and understanding of concepts in young learners. This approach contrasts with more passive forms of learning, making learning more meaningful and enjoyable for children at this stage.

118. (B): Concrete Principle, as not a principle for textbook design at the foundational stage, this would be a misunderstanding. In educational contexts, the Concrete Principle is actually essential, particularly at the foundational stage. It emphasizes the importance of using tangible, real-world examples to help young learners grasp abstract concepts. This principle supports the idea that learning is most effective when students can relate new information to their own experiences and the world around them. Therefore, the Concrete Principle is not only relevant but crucial for designing textbooks for early education, as it aids in making learning material accessible and engaging for young minds.

119. (B): To create an inclusive, welcoming, and joyful environment that supports every child's participation in achieving the competencies outlined in the National Curriculum Framework (NCF), displaying children's work from different domains of development can be best done. This approach recognizes and celebrates the unique contributions of each child, fostering a sense of belonging and pride in their achievements. Displaying children's work not only makes the learning environment more personal and engaging but also encourages peer recognition and appreciation of diversity. It supports inclusivity by valuing all students' efforts and learning outcomes, thereby contributing to a positive and motivating classroom atmosphere.

120. (B): To be considered literate, mastering decoding and language comprehension is essential. Literacy involves not only the ability to read written words (decoding) but also the ability to understand, interpret, and critically analyze texts (language comprehension). These skills are foundational to effective reading and are crucial for academic success and lifelong learning. Decoding allows readers to recognize words, while comprehension enables them to extract meaning from the text, connect ideas, and apply knowledge in various contexts. Together, these competencies constitute the core of literacy, enabling individuals to engage fully with written materials.

121. (B): गद्यांश में जल संकट की बात की गई है। इसमें अल नीनो के प्रभाव के कारण मानसून के कमजोर पड़ने, संयुक्त राष्ट्र संघ के महासचिव द्वारा जारी रिपोर्ट में 2050 तक भारत में पानी के सबसे बड़े संकट की चेतावनी, और हिमालयी ग्लेशियरों के पिघलने के खतरे के बारे में चर्चा की गई है। यह सभी तथ्य जल संकट की स्थिति को दर्शाते हैं।

122. (B): गद्यांश के अनुसार, गंगा के किनारों पर बसे महानगरों, कस्बों, और गाँवों की आबादी लगभग 40 करोड़ है। इस आंकड़े से गंगा नदी की महत्वपूर्णता और इस पर निर्भर जनसंख्या के विशाल आकार का पता चलता है, जो पानी की आवश्यकताओं के लिए इस नदी पर निर्भर करती है।

123. (A): गद्यांश में बताया गया है कि 2050 तक पानी का सबसे बड़ा संकट भारत में आने वाला है। संयुक्त राष्ट्र संघ के महासचिव द्वारा जारी रिपोर्ट में यह चेतावनी दी गई है, जिससे भारत में जल संसाधनों की स्थिति पर गंभीर चिंता व्यक्त की गई है।

124. (B): गद्यांश में अल नीनो के प्रभाव को मानसून पर पड़ने वाले असर के संदर्भ में उल्लेखित किया गया है। अल नीनो एक जलवायु परिघटना है जो समुद्र के तापमान में परिवर्तन के कारण होती है और इसका सीधा प्रभाव मानसूनी वर्षा पर पड़ता है, जिससे कमजोर मानसून या वर्षा में कमी आ सकती है।

125. (A): ''पौने दो किलोमीटर'' परिमाणवाचक विशेषण है क्योंकि यह ग्लेशियर के पिघलने के कारण गायब हो चुके हिस्से की मात्रा या लंबाई को व्यक्त करता है। यह विशेषण ग्लेशियर के खोए हुए हिस्से की ठोस मात्रा का संकेत देता है, जो पर्यावरणीय परिवर्तनों के प्रति चिंताजनक संकेत है।

126. (A): गद्यांश के अनुसार, भारत की नदियों में जल कम होता जा रहा है का मुख्य कारण ग्लेशियरों का तेजी से पिघलना है। हिमालयी ग्लेशियरों का पिघलना नदियों के पानी के स्तर में कमी लाता है, जिससे जल संकट की स्थिति और भी गंभीर हो जाती है।

127. (B): ''धीरे-धीरे'' क्रिया विशेषण है क्योंकि यह नदियों के पानी के कम होने की प्रक्रिया की गति या तरीके को व्यक्त करता है। यह बताता है कि पानी का स्तर किस प्रकार से कम हो रहा है, जो कि एक धीमी और सतत प्रक्रिया है।

128. (B): ''पर्यावरण'' शब्द में ''परि'' उपसर्ग है और ''आवरण'' मूल शब्द है। ''परि'' का अर्थ है चारों ओर या आसपास, और ''आवरण'' का अर्थ है ढकने वाला या आच्छादन। इसलिए, ''पर्यावरण'' शब्द का अर्थ है वह आच्छादन या वातावरण जो हमें चारों ओर से घेरे रखता है।

129. (A): ''स्वतंत्र'' का विलोम ''परतंत्र'' है। ''स्वतंत्र'' का अर्थ होता है स्वयं के द्वारा निर्णय लेने की स्थिति या आजादी, जबकि ''परतंत्र'' इसका विपरीत है, जिसका अर्थ है किसी दूसरे के अधीन रहने की स्थिति या आजादी का अभाव। यहाँ गद्यांश में व्यक्त ''स्वतंत्र'' शब्द के विलोम के लिए ''परतंत्र'' शब्द सटीक बैठता है।

130. (B): पाप और पुण्य की तुलना क्रमशः लोहे और स्वर्ण की जंजीर से की गई है। यह उपमा बताती है कि पाप एक प्रकार का बंधन है जिससे मुक्त होने की इच्छा होती है, जैसे लोहे की जंजीर; वहीं पुण्य भी एक बंधन है लेकिन इसे लोग अधिक स्वीकार्य और आकर्षक मानते हैं, जैसे सोने की जंजीर।

131. (D): ''फल'' शब्द इस समूह से भिन्न है क्योंकि ''स्वतंत्र'', ''अस्थायी'', और ''प्यारा'' शब्द भावनाओं, स्थितियों या गुणों को व्यक्त करते हैं, जबकि ''फल'' एक वस्तु या किसी कार्य के परिणाम को दर्शाता है।

132. (D): पुण्य में उसके फल को हम स्वीकार नहीं भी कर सकते हैं। गद्यांश में यह विचार व्यक्त किया गया है कि जबकि पुण्य का फल सुखद होता है, व्यक्ति को इसे स्वीकार करने या नहीं करने की स्वतंत्रता होती है।

133. (B): इस संसार में कुछ भी ''स्थायी'' नहीं है। गद्यांश की प्रारंभिक पंक्तियाँ स्पष्ट करती हैं कि संसार में सब कुछ अस्थायी है, जिसमें पाप और पुण्य भी शामिल हैं।

134. (A): पाप और पुण्य दोनों ''अस्थायी'' हैं। गद्यांश के अनुसार, दोनों ही संसार से संबंधित हैं और अंततः समाप्त हो जाते हैं, इसलिए वे अस्थायी हैं।

135. (C): गद्यांश के अनुसार पाप और पुण्य दोनों में ''बंधन'' है। इसके माध्यम से यह दर्शाया गया है कि चाहे पाप हो या पुण्य, दोनों ही किसी न किसी रूप में बंधन का कारण बनते हैं, जिससे मुक्त होने की चाह या आकर्षण हो सकता है।

136. (A): कोई भी व्यक्ति द्वितीय भाषा सर्वाधिक उपयुक्त तरीके से अपने समाज में सहजात वाचकों (मूलभाषा बोलने वालों) के सतत सम्पर्क के माध्यम से सीख सकता है। इस प्रक्रिया में, व्यक्ति न केवल भाषा की ध्वनियों और व्याकरणिक संरचनाओं को समझने में सक्षम होता है, बल्कि वह भाषा के प्रयोग के संदर्भों और वास्तविक जीवन की स्थितियों में इसके प्रयोग को भी बेहतर ढंग से समझ पाता है। इससे भाषा की स्वाभाविकता और प्रासंगिकता का अनुभव होता है, जो भाषा सीखने की प्रक्रिया को और अधिक प्रभावी और दीर्घकालिक बनाता है।

137. (B): पठन सीखने में प्रेरणा और अच्छा बालसाहित्य पाने की चुनौती को दूर करने के लिए बाल साहित्य की सरलता से उपलब्धता जिससे पठन के लिए प्रोत्साहन और रुचि पैदा हो, सबसे प्रभावी उपाय है। जब बाल साहित्य आसानी से उपलब्ध होता है, तो बच्चे नई किताबों और कहानियों के साथ खुद को जोड़ पाते हैं, जिससे उनकी पठन की रुचि बढ़ती है और वे नियमित रूप से पढ़ने के लिए प्रेरित होते हैं।

138. (A): एक अध्यापक द्वारा कक्षा पाँच के विद्यार्थियों को शीघ्रता से एक कहानी पढ़ने और उसके बाद चार चित्रों को क्रम में लगाने के लिए कहने का उद्देश्य सारांशीकरण के लिए पठन का अभ्यास करवाना है। इस गतिविधि के माध्यम से, विद्यार्थियों को कहानी की मुख्य घटनाओं को समझने और उन्हें उचित क्रम में व्यवस्थित करने का अवसर मिलता है, जो कि सारांशीकरण की मूलभूत क्षमता को विकसित करता है। यह गतिविधि पठन समझ और विश्लेषणात्मक कौशल को बढ़ावा देती है।

139. (C): प्राथमिक स्तर पर भाषा कौशल का आकलन करने के लिए भाषा अध्यापक को मुख्यतः समझ के साथ पठन पर ध्यान केन्द्रित करना चाहिए। इस स्तर पर, यह महत्वपूर्ण है कि शिक्षार्थी न केवल पाठ को पढ़ सकें बल्कि उसे समझ भी सकें। इससे उनकी भाषा समझ और व्याख्यात्मक क्षमता में विकास होता है। विराम चिह्नों का प्रयोग, उचित गति के साथ पठन, और वर्णमाला के अक्षरों की पहचान भी महत्वपूर्ण हैं, लेकिन समझ के साथ पठन बच्चों के भाषा सीखने की प्रक्रिया में गहराई और संदर्भ जोड़ता है।

140. (B): एक अच्छी वाचन (बोलना) गतिविधि वह है जिसमें शिक्षार्थी अधिक बातचीत करते हैं। ऐसी गतिविधियाँ छात्रों को अपने विचारों को व्यक्त करने, संवाद करने की क्षमता को विकसित करने, और साथी छात्रों के साथ ज्ञान का आदान-प्रदान करने का अवसर प्रदान करती हैं। इस प्रकार की गतिविधियाँ संचार कौशल को मजबूत करती हैं और भाषा सीखने में गहराई जोड़ती हैं।

141. (A): बुनियादी चरण में आकलन के उपकरण और प्रक्रियाओं की अभिकल्पना इस तरह होनी चाहिए कि जो बच्चे के अधिगम अनुभव का सहज विस्तार बन सकें। इस प्रकार के आकलन से शिक्षार्थियों को अपनी सीखने की यात्रा में प्रगति करने का अवसर मिलता है, जिससे वे नई जानकारियों को अधिक प्रभावी ढंग से अवशोषित और समझ सकते हैं। इस तरह के आकलन शिक्षार्थियों को अपने सीखने की प्रक्रिया में सक्रिय भागीदार बनाते हैं।

142. (B): कक्षा में छोटे बच्चों के लिए मुद्रित पुस्तकों के साथ-साथ श्रव्य पुस्तकें और छोटे बच्चों की स्पर्शग्राही योग्यताओं का इस्तेमाल करने वाली पुस्तकें होनी चाहिए क्योंकि यह विविधता वाले शिक्षार्थियों तक पुस्तकें अधिक सुलभ बनाती है। इससे विभिन्न शैक्षणिक जरूरतों और सीखने की शैलियों वाले बच्चों को भी शिक्षा की प्रक्रिया में समान रूप से भाग लेने का अवसर मिलता है। इस प्रकार की पुस्तकें शैक्षणिक सामग्री को अधिक समावेशी और इंटरैक्टिव बनाती हैं, जिससे बच्चों के लिए सीखने का अनुभव और भी रोचक और प्रभावी होता है।

145. (C): बच्चों का संज्ञानात्मक विकास और भाषा उस संस्कृति और समुदायों से घनिष्ठ रूप से संबंधित है जिसमें बच्चे रहते हैं। सामाजिक-सांस्कृतिक सिद्धांतों के अनुसार, भाषा सीखने और संज्ञानात्मक विकास की प्रक्रियाएँ सामाजिक इंटरैक्शन और सांस्कृतिक प्रथाओं के माध्यम से आकार लेती हैं। इस दृष्टिकोण में, भाषा विकास को बच्चों के अनुभवों और उनके सामाजिक वातावरण के साथ उनके इंटरैक्शन के संदर्भ में समझा जाता है, जिससे उन्हें अपने समुदाय की भाषा और संस्कृति को समझने और उसमें भाग लेने की क्षमता विकसित होती है।

146. (D): समग्र भाषा उपागम एक अर्थ आधारित दृष्टिकोण है। यह उपागम भाषा सीखने के लिए व्यक्तिगत कौशलों जैसे कि वाचन, लेखन, बोलना, और सुनना पर अलग से ध्यान केंद्रित करने के बजाय, इन कौशलों को एक एकीकृत प्रक्रिया के रूप में देखता है, जो संचार और अर्थ के सृजन पर आधारित होती है। इस दृष्टिकोण में, भाषा अधिगम को वास्तविक जीवन के संदर्भों और उपयोगों के माध्यम से समर्थन दिया जाता है, जिससे शिक्षार्थियों को भाषा का अधिक प्राकृतिक और सार्थक उपयोग करने में सक्षम बनाया जा सके।

147. (A): यदि बच्चे अपने परिवेश में दो भाषाओं का बोलना सुनते हैं, तो दो भाषाओं को सुनने के ये अवसर बच्चों को लाभ पहुँचाते हैं। द्विभाषी वातावरण बच्चों को संज्ञानात्मक लचीलापन, बेहतर ध्यान नियंत्रण, और भाषाओं के बीच स्विच करने की क्षमता जैसे कई संज्ञानात्मक लाभ प्रदान करता है। यह उन्हें विभिन्न सांस्कृतिक परिप्रेक्ष्यों को समझने और उनके साथ संवाद करने की क्षमता भी विकसित करता है, जिससे उनके सामाजिक और शैक्षिक विकास में मदद मिलती है।

148. (A): जब शिक्षार्थियों से अपेक्षा रहती है कि वे विषयवस्तु को विस्तार से ध्यानपूर्वक और सावधानीपूर्वक पढ़ें, तो यह गहन पठन (इंटैंसिव) का उदाहरण है। गहन पठन में, लक्ष्य विशेष भाषा तत्वों, वाक्य संरचना, शब्दावली, और विषयवस्तु की गहराई से समझ को विकसित करना होता है। इस प्रकार के पठन में, शिक्षार्थियों को विशेष रूप से चुने गए पाठ के छोटे अंशों पर केंद्रित किया जाता है ताकि वे भाषा की जटिलताओं को समझ सकें और उनका विश्लेषण कर सकें।

149. (D): पाठ के आरंभ में एक अध्यापक द्वारा अपनी कक्षा के शिक्षार्थियों को समूहों में बाँटकर हाल ही में पढ़े गए समाचार पत्र के रुचिकर आलेख के बारे में बात करने के लिए कहना मौखिक प्रवाह अभ्यास के लिए है। इस तरह की गतिविधि में, शिक्षार्थियों को अपने विचारों को स्वतंत्र रूप से व्यक्त करने और संवादात्मक बोलने के कौशल को विकसित करने का अवसर मिलता है। यह उन्हें अधिक सहजता से और तरलता के साथ बोलने में सक्षम बनाता है, जिससे उनके मौखिक संचार कौशल में सुधार होता है।

150. (D): विद्यार्थी अध्यापक द्वारा दिए गए आदर्श वाक्यों को दोहराकर भाषा के प्रतिमान सीखते हैं, वाक्यों को कंठस्थ कर लेते हैं और सही तरीके से ड्रिल करने पर अपने अध्यापक द्वारा सकारात्मक पुनर्बलन प्राप्त करते हैं, इससे यह संकेत मिलता है कि अध्यापक द्वारा श्रव्य भाषिक विधि (Audio-lingual method) का प्रयोग किया जा रहा है। इस विधि में, भाषा सीखने के लिए मुख्य रूप से श्रवण और वाक्यांशों के दोहराव पर जोर दिया जाता है। यह विधि भाषा के ध्वनियों और संरचनाओं को ड्रिल्स और अभ्यास के माध्यम से अध्यापन करने पर केंद्रित है, जिसमें विद्यार्थियों को लगातार प्रतिक्रिया और सुधार प्रदान किए जाते हैं।

Previous Paper (Solved)

CTET—Paper-I, August 2023

(Exam held on 20-08-2023)

Part-I : Child Development and Pedagogy

1. Dysgraphia is a:

A. Speech disorder characterized by stuttering and errors in articulation.
B. Locomotor disorder characterized by gross motor impairment.
C. Neurological disorder characterized by trouble in forming letters and shapes.
D. Psychological disorder characterized by lack of attention and impulsive behaviour.

2. The approach to educating gifted children which moves them through curriculum at an unusually rapid pace is known as:

A. Differentiated instruction
B. Enrichment
C. Acceleration
D. Immersion

3. Teachers who are working towards inclusive classrooms:

(*i*) Create curriculum adaptations
(*ii*) Incorporate diverse perspectives
(*iii*) Examine their own implicit bias
(*iv*) See diversity as an obstacle

Which of the above are correct?

A. (*i*), (*ii*), (*iii*), (*iv*) B. (*i*), (*ii*), (*iii*)
C. (*i*), (*iii*), (*iv*) D. (*ii*), (*iii*), (*iv*)

4. While __________ agencies of socialisation are predominantly important in infancy, __________ agencies of socialization also become important in early childhood.

A. tertiary; secondary B. primary; secondary
C. secondary; primary D. secondary; tertiary

5. According to Lev Vygotsky:

A. Social factors influence language development, but not cognitive development.
B. Cognitive development facilitates language development.
C. Language development and cognitive development advance independent from each other.
D. Language development facilitates cognitive development.

6. At which level of Lawrence Kohlberg's moral reasoning, do children typically believe that people should live up to the expectations of the society and behave in "good" ways?

A. Post-operational level
B. Pre-conventional level
C. Conventional level
D. Pre-operational level

7. Read the following statements and choose the correct option:

Assertion (A): Interaction with more knowledgeable others, such as teachers and peers, can provide the necessary support and guidance to help learners develop their understanding and skills.

Reason (R): Social interaction is a key component of learning and development.

A. Both (A) and (R) are false.
B. Both (A) and (R) are true and (R) is the correct explanation of (A).
C. Both (A) and (R) are true, but (R) is not the correct explanation of (A).
D. (A) is true, but (R) is false.

8. What is the main goal of 'assessment for learning'?

A. To identify students who can be categorised as 'slow learners'
B. To evaluate student performance and assign grades
C. To provide feedback to students that can be used to improve their learning
D. To compare student performance to a standard or benchmark

1. C **2.** C **3.** B **4.** B **5.** D **6.** C **7.** B **8.** C

9. At which age can children engage in word play and like jokes and riddles that involve a play on words?
A. Twelve years B. One year
C. Three years D. Seven years

10. Carol Gilligan has critiqued Kohlberg's theory of moral development:
A. From a social cognitive perspective.
B. From a feminist perspective.
C. For not giving adequate importance to genetic factors.
D. For using case study as the research method.

11. One of the main characteristics of pre-operational thought according to Jean Piaget is ________ which refers to the tendency to focus on one aspect of a situation and neglect others.
A. Causation B. Centration
C. Decentration D. Transduction

12. In early childhood, growth ____ and thinking is ________, while in middle childhood, growth ________ and thinking is ________.
A. slows, somewhat egocentric; is steady, logical
B. is steady, somewhat egocentric; slows, logical
C. is steady, logical; slows, egocentric
D. slows, logical; is steady, egocentric

13. Which of the following is a gross motor skill?
A. Knitting
B. Swimming
C. Cutting along the outline of a circle on a paper
D. Cutting along the outline of a big rectangle on a paper

14. Physical growth and development follow the ______ and ________ principles of development.
A. integration (simple to complex); differentiation (complex to simple)
B. cephalocaudal (top-down); proximodistal (inner to outer)
C. proximodistal (top-down); cephalocaudal (inner to outer)
D. differentiation (simple to complex); integration (complex to simple)

15. According to Howard Gardner, a philosopher has ________ type of intelligence and a sculptor has more ________ type of intelligence.
A. linguistic; interpersonal
B. spatial; intrapersonal
C. intrapersonal; spatial
D. interpersonal; linguistic

16. Experiential learning stresses on:
A. Control of teacher on the learning of children.
B. The role of reinforcement in learning.
C. Importance of critical reflection.
D. Learning as a product rather than a process.

17. Which of the following is an effective method to enhance problem-solving skills in children?
A. Discouraging independent thinking and focusing on declarative knowledge
B. Encouraging them to avoid difficult problems
C. Providing them with readymade solutions to problems
D. Giving them opportunities to brainstorm and make intuitive guesses

18. Read the following statements and choose the correct option:
Assertion (A): Teachers should create a meaningful environment which seeks active participation and engagement of all children.
Reason (R): All children are intrinsically motivated to learn and are capable of learning.
A. Both (A) and (R) are false.
B. Both (A) and (R) are true and (R) is the correct explanation of (A).
C. Both (A) and (R) are true, but (R) is not the correct explanation of (A).
D. (A) is true, but (R) is false.

19. Which of the following process does ***not*** contribute to the course of learning?
A. Organization B. Categorization
C. Conceptualization D. Decontextualization

20. Which of the following is an example of a question that requires students to reflect on their own thinking?
A. What is the relationship between nouns and verbs in a sentence?
B. What is the definition of a verb?
C. How do you change a verb to the present tense?
D. How has your thinking about the use of verbs changed since the beginning of the class?

21. Which of the following is an example of an internal attribution for failure?
A. I received a low grade because the teacher is a tough grader.
B. I failed the test because I didn't study enough.
C. I didn't get good marks because the teacher was biased.
D. I failed the test because my friends were distracting me.

9. D	**10.** B	**11.** B	**12.** B	**13.** B	**14.** B	**15.** C	**16.** C	**17.** D	**18.** B
19. D	**20.** D	**21.** B							

22. Read the following statements and choose the correct option:

Assertion (A): At a very early age, girls in most cultures across the world choose dolls as toys while boys prefer to play with cars.

Reason (R): Children organize information about what is considered appropriate for a boy or a girl on the basis of what a particular culture expects and behave accordingly.

A. Both (A) and (R) are false.
B. Both (A) and (R) are true and (R) is the correct explanation of (A).
C. Both (A) and (R) are true, but (R) is not the correct explanation of (A).
D. (A) is true, but (R) is false.

23. As per Lev Vygotsky, ____________ plays a significant role in the development of conceptual abilities among children.

A. Tangible rewards
B. Peer collaboration
C. Social isolation
D. Standardized curriculum

24. According to Lev Vygotsky's theory, inner speech:

A. is a way for children to communicate with an imaginary friend.
B. is a sign of cognitive immaturity.
C. is a sign of developmental delay.
D. is a way for children to regulate their own thinking.

25. Four-year-old Aparna says that a button is alive because it helps tie her shirt together. According to Jean Piaget, her thinking is characterized by:

A. Transductive reasoning
B. Animistic thinking
C. Centration
D. Hypothetical-deductive thinking

26. Which of the following is a typical characterstic of students having autism?

A. Superior ability of differentiating fiction from fact
B. Advanced socio-emotional reciprocity
C. Frequent repetitive and recurring behaviour
D. Higher level of communication skills

27. Read the following statements and choose the correct option:

Assertion (A): To facilitate critical thinking among learners, teachers should expose them to diverse situations and differing perspectives.

Reason (R): Students learn and enrich their abilities to think critically and creatively as they engage in conversations across differences.

A. Both (A) and (R) are false.
B. Both (A) and (R) are true and (R) is the correct explanation of (A).
C. Both (A) and (R) are true, but (R) is not the correct explanation of (A).
D. (A) is true, but (R) is false.

28. The primary goal of learning should be:

A. Memorization of facts.
B. Becoming excellent at rote rehearsal.
C. Competing with peers.
D. Development of critical thinking.

29. Children learn more effectively if a concept proceeds from:

A. Generic to Specific. B. Abstract to Concrete.
C. Complex to Simple. D. Rational to Empirical.

30. Variability in learning styles of students:

A. Should be valued and seen as a reflection of human diversity.
B. Should be ignored and attempts should be made to bring uniformity in learning styles.
C. Should not be taken into consideration during teaching-learning process.
D. Should be seen as a barrier and hindrance to teaching-learning process.

Part-II : Mathematics

31. Which of the following statements about nature of mathematics are most appropriate?

(*a*) It helps the child to be creative.
(*b*) It helps in nurturing the child's imagination.
(*c*) It is based on deductive reasoning.
(*d*) It is always convergent.

Choose the correct option:

A. (*a*), (*b*) and (*c*) B. (*b*) and (*c*)
C. (*a*) and (*c*) D. (*a*) and (*b*)

22. B	23. B	24. D	25. B	26. C	27. B	28. D	29. A	30. A	31. A

32. To develop appreciation for mathematics among children, a teacher performs the following activities in the class. Choose the one which is ***not*** effective to achieve her objective.

A. She always praises the student who achieves highest marks in the class in the term-end examination.
B. She shows to children the videos on Indian mathematicians and their contributions.
C. She gives mathematical puzzles and magic squares to be solved in the class.
D. She establishes a mathematics corner in her class where students can perform various mathematical activities.

33. Which of the following statements is ***not*** correct?

A. Errors of the students give information about their thought process.
B. Errors in mathematics are part of learning.
C. Errors in mathematics help teachers in planning their lessons.
D. Errors of the students should be overlooked as pointing errors will demotivate them.

34. Which of the following statements is ***not*** correct about assessment?

A. Norm-referenced assessment is useful in diagnostic testing and remedial teaching.
B. Criterion-referenced assessment is to evaluate the mastery learning of the students.
C. Criterion-referenced assessment is useful in diagnostic testing and remedial teaching.
D. Norm-referenced assessment tells us where a student stands as compared to other students in his/her performance.

35. Mathematical learning material:

(*a*) Helps teachers in demonstrating the formulae.
(*b*) Helps students in self-learning.
(*c*) Helps teachers in providing instructions.
(*d*) Develops learning environment in the class.

Choose the correct option:

A. (*c*) and (*d*) B. (*a*) and (*b*)
C. (*b*) and (*d*) D. (*b*) and (*c*)

36. According to the National Education Policy (NEP) 2020, olympiads and competitions in various subjects will be __________ across the country.

A. made easier B. strengthened
C. discouraged D. reduced

37. Concepts like more-less, long-short, far-near, big-small, etc. are:

A. Vague terms for comparison.
B. Antonyms, not necessary for learning mathematics.
C. Simply English language adjectives.
D. Important pre-number concepts.

38. According to the National Curriculum Framework, 2005, classroom researches have indicated a fairly systematic devaluation of girls as incapable of mastering mathematics even when they perform well in mathematics. What is the most appropriate reason for this?

A. Poor performance of girls in mathematics is due to the fear of mathematics prevalent in them.
B. Mathematics, by its nature, is a male-dominated subject.
C. Gendered constructs of society have led to the belief that boys use more innovative strategies for problem-solving and thus have better conceptual understanding.
D. The mathematical abilities in boys are innate.

39. Classroom researches have shown that most of the students find mathematics more difficult than the other subjects they study in the same class. Which of the following aspects of the nature of mathematics adds to this fear?

A. The vast knowledge base of mathematics
B. The scope of multiple answers to a given question in mathematics
C. The scope of a number of different methods to solve a problem in mathematics
D. The abstract nature of primary concepts in mathematics

40. Who among the following has worked in the field of mathematical astronomy?

A. Aryabhatta B. Bhaskara I
C. Ramanujan D. Mahavira

41. A vegetable seller was selling spinach for ₹ 60 per kg. Sonu purchased 350 g of spinach for which the vegetable seller took ₹ 21 (₹ 6 + ₹ 6 + ₹ 6 + ₹ 3) from Sonu. Which of the following statements is/are true regarding the mathematical skills used by the vegetable seller?

(*a*) This mathematical skill is ambiguous.
(*b*) This skill is not useful to solve mathematical problems in class.
(*c*) Such skills help in developing alternate strategies for solving mathematical problems.

Choose the correct option:

A. (*a*) and (*b*) B. Only (*a*)
C. Only (*b*) D. Only (*c*)

32. A	33. D	34. A	35. C	36. B	37. D	38. C	39. D	40. B	41. D

42. Which of the following depicts a situation where children are constructing knowledge on their own?

A. The best student in the class reads aloud the multiplication tables and rest of the students repeat after him/her.

B. Children are reciting multiplication tables in a chorus.

C. Children are given manipulatives like number grids, tokens arranged in rectangular arrays and they are exploring multiplication patterns using them.

D. Teacher has written incomplete multiplication tables on blackboard and children are completing the tables by writing them on blackboard.

43. Which of the following is the most appropriate way to help a primary school learner visualize the equivalence between the fractions $\frac{2}{3}$ and $\frac{4}{6}$?

A. Using Division method

B. Using LCM (Least Common Multiple) method

C. Using Fraction Discs

D. Using Calculators

44. A teacher uses role play method in mathematics class. Her aim is:

A. Keeping children busy.

B. Projecting ideas.

C. Entertaining children.

D. Maintaining discipline.

45. Subitizing plays an important role in developing the number sense. Which of the following is an example of a student demonstrating the skill of subitizing?

A. Student recognizes the number 6 as 1 added to 5.

B. Student rolls a die and is able to say it is four without actually counting the dots.

C. Student recognizes the number 4 as the number with 1 taken away from 5.

D. Student recognizes the number 5 as the successor of 4.

46. Priyadarshini mixed 4.8 kg of almonds, 2500 g of raisin and 3.5 kg of cashews and packed the mixture equally into three dozen packets. What is the weight of each packet?

A. 650 g B. 250 g

C. 300 g D. 500 g

47. The side of a square is 5 cm. How many times will the new area become, if the side of the square is doubled?

A. 8 times B. 2 times

C. 3 times D. 4 times

48. Which one of the following groups have all 3-dimensional shapes?

A. Cube, Cuboid, Semi-circle, Cone

B. Cube, Cuboid, Circle, Cone

C. Cube, Cuboid, Circle, Triangle

D. Cube, Cuboid, Sphere, Cylinder

49. Sangeeta wants to buy a soap that costs ₹ 10. She has a five-rupee coin, 2 one-rupee coins and 5 fifty-paise coins. How much more money does she need to buy the soap?

A. ₹ 2.50

B. ₹ 0.50

C. ₹ 1.50

D. ₹ 2.00

50. Select the group of fractions in an ascending order:

A. $\frac{1}{4} < \frac{1}{3} < \frac{1}{2}$ B. $\frac{1}{2} < \frac{1}{4} < \frac{1}{3}$

C. $\frac{1}{2} < \frac{1}{3} < \frac{1}{4}$ D. $\frac{1}{3} < \frac{1}{4} < \frac{1}{2}$

51. What is the missing number in the pattern given below?

1, 6, 15, ____, 45, 66, 91

A. 36 B. 28

C. 32 D. 25

52. Read the following table:

Blood Group	Number of Students
A	9
B	6
O	12
AB	3
Total	30

What is the ratio of the most common and rarest blood groups?

A. 1 : 4 B. 1 : 3

C. 4 : 1 D. 3 : 1

53. Which of the following statements is ***not*** true?

A. A kite becomes a rectangle if its opposite angles are equal.

B. A rectangle becomes a square if all its sides are equal.

C. A rhombus becomes a square if all its angles are equal.

D. A parallelogram becomes a rectangle if all its angles are equal.

42. C	**43.** C	**44.** B	**45.** B	**46.** C	**47.** D	**48.** D	**49.** B	**50.** A	**51.** B	**52.** C	**53.** A

54. Ammini is arranging 36 identical squares in the form of different rectangles. How many different types of rectangles can she make with these squares?
A. Eight
B. Four
C. Five
D. Six

55. Rubina started her journey by car at 16:50 hours and finished at 21:15 hours on the same day. The time taken in completing the journey is:
A. 4 hours 35 minutes B. 3 hours 25 minutes
C. 4 hours 25 minutes D. 3 hours 35 minutes

56. A whole number is added to 100 and the same number is subtracted from 100. The sum of the two resulting numbers so obtained is:
A. 200 B. 0
C. 50 D. 100

57. 'One hundred lakh' is also known as:
A. One billion B. Ten crore
C. One crore D. One million

58. Which of the following arrangements represents a descending order of numbers?
A. 10.5, 1.50, 1.055, 1.05, 1.005, 0.155
B. 1.05, 1.005, 1.50, 1.055, 10.5, 0.155
C. 10.5, 1.05, 1.055, 1.50, 1.005, 0.155
D. 10.5, 1.50, 1.05, 1.055, 1.005, 0.155

59. Which of the following is ***not*** a factor of 3630?
A. 11 B. 3
C. 5 D. 9

60. The sum of 5 – 5 + 5 – 5 + 5 – 5 ......, to odd number of terms is:
A. 15 B. 0
C. –5 D. 5

Part-III : Environmental Studies

61. A teacher wants to select synchronous communication with her students for teaching EVS. Which of the following will she choose?
A. Phone calls, pre-recorded videos, tele-conferencing
B. E-mail, social media posts, phone calls
C. Instant messaging, blogs, tele-conferencing
D. Video conferencing, online chat sessions, phone calls

62. If theme Travel: Railway Station depicts utilisation of a community resource in EVS, which of the following will complete – theme Food : ________?
A. Agricultural farm B. Forest
C. Shopkeeper D. Farmer

63. While teaching EVS, a teacher's statement/question, which encourages students to elaborate on an answer either on their own or from the response of their peers, is:
A. Probing B. Conditioning
C. Chaining D. Trial and error

64. Anita prepares a unit plan to teach the theme Family. Which of the following will be the title of her unit plan?
A. Families : Migrating families
B. Types of Family : Nuclear and Joint
C. Family : Relationships within a Family
D. Family : Relationships, Gender Roles, Occupations, as socio-cultural entity in changing times

65. Ms. Sheetal likes to use stories and poems in primary classes to explain various concepts of EVS. The most appropriate logic for her using stories and poems is to:
(*a*) Complete the EVS syllabus as well as students have heard them before coming to school.
(*b*) Encourage the students to write their own poems and stories.
(*c*) Make the students aware of diversity in language and culture.
(*d*) Make the lessons more interactive, enjoyable and interesting.

Choose the correct option:
A. (*b*) and (*c*)
B. (*a*) and (*b*)
C. (*b*), (*c*) and (*d*)
D. (*a*), (*c*) and (*d*)

66. Which of the following options is a major objective of teaching EVS from classes I to V?
A. Acquiring skills to carry out hands-on activities independently
B. Preparing students for studying science at the middle level
C. Developing in-depth understanding of the basic concepts of the subject
D. Helping learners link classroom learning to life outside the school

54. C	**55.** C	**56.** A	**57.** C	**58.** A	**59.** D	**60.** D	**61.** D	**62.** A	**63.** A
64. D	**65.** C	**66.** D							

67. An EVS teacher demonstrates an experiment in class in which an egg sinks in a tumbler with water, but floats upon adding salt to the water. Which of the following is the most appropriate explanation she can give to students' enquiry?

A. Allow each student to conclude on their own by adding different items in water.
B. The egg floats due to density of water.
C. You will learn the correct reason in higher classes.
D. Conduct and observe the experiment with different amounts of salt.

68. Read the following statements and choose the correct option:

Assertion (A): Learning of EVS needs to be oriented to process skills relating to observation, identification, classification, etc.

Reason (R): Through acquiring various process skills, the learning outcomes of EVS learning are expected to be achieved.

A. (A) is false, but (R) is true.
B. Both (A) and (R) are true and (R) is the correct explanation of (A).
C. Both (A) and (R) are true, but (R) is not the correct explanation of (A).
D. (A) is true, but (R) is false.

69. An EVS teacher should lay emphasis on ________ while preparing question paper for summative assessment

A. Length and objectives of the question paper
B. Content coverage and objectives of the question paper
C. Total marks and content coverage of the question paper
D. Length and total marks of the question paper

70. Which of the following is ***not*** a learning outcome in EVS for students of Class III?

A. Voices opinion on good and bad touch
B. Voices opinion on issues observed/experienced and relates to social practices such as discrimination in ownership of resources
C. Observes rules in few local, indoor, outdoor games
D. Identifies directions of classroom

71. You have to select EVS textbooks for your students of classes III to V. Which of the following criteria is most appropriate for this purpose?

A. Pictures in the book should be big and colourful.
B. The language should be simple and according to the mental level of students.
C. The textbook should be illustrated and appealing to students.
D. The textbook should be child-oriented and devoid of any stereotypes or derogatory attitudes based on gender, caste, class and religion.

72. Read the following statements and choose the correct option:

Assertion (A): At the primary level EVS has themes instead of topics.

Reason (R): Theme-based EVS learning is easy for teachers and students as compared to topics.

A. (A) is false, but (R) is true.
B. Both (A) and (R) are true and (R) is the correct explanation of (A).
C. Both (A) and (R) are true, but (R) is not the correct explanation of (A).
D. (A) is true, but (R) is false.

73. You want to encourage hands-on activities for students of EVS. Which of the following is the most appropriate activity?

A. Map reading from a globe
B. Collecting coins of different countries
C. Developing an EVS kit from available material
D. Drawing parts of different plants on a chart

74. Formative assessment of EVS is ________.

(*a*) Assessment for learning
(*b*) Assessment of learning
(*c*) Assessment as learning
(*d*) Assessment about learning

Choose the correct option:

A. (*c*) and (*d*)
B. (*a*) and (*b*)
C. (*a*) and (*c*)
D. (*b*) and (*c*)

75. Read the following statements and choose the correct option:

Assertion (A): Field trips are an effective pedagogical strategy in EVS.

Reason (R): Field trips promote memorisation of objects, events and places.

A. (A) is false, but (R) is true.
B. Both (A) and (R) are true and (R) is the correct explanation of (A).
C. Both (A) and (R) are true, but (R) is not the correct explanation of (A).
D. (A) is true, but (R) is false.

67. D	**68.** B	**69.** B	**70.** B	**71.** D	**72.** C	**73.** C	**74.** C	**75.** D

76. With respect to Gujarat, the locations of Uttar Pradesh and Andhra Pradesh, respectively, are:
A. North-West; South-West
B. North-East; South-West
C. North-East; South-East
D. North-West; South-East

77. Rama plays cricket with his friends every evening. Which energy does he use to play cricket?
A. Light energy B. Chemical energy
C. Muscular energy D. Sound energy

78. When we burn fuels we get:
A. Only light energy
B. Heat and light energy
C. Mechanical and light energy
D. Light and sound energy

79. Which one of the following is 'sticky rice' and is a common variety of rice in Assam?
A. Bora rice B. Arborio rice
C. Bomba rice D. Ponni rice

80. Select from the following the best period of the year for the people of Bihar to start a bee-keeping programme:
A. October to December
B. February to April
C. April to June
D. August to October

81. Match Column-I and Column-II:

Column-I	Column-II
(*a*) Cumin	I. Appears like a nail
(*b*) Saffron	II. Originated in South America
(*c*) Chillies	III. Yellow in colour
(*d*) Clove	IV. Small but fragrant

	(*a*)	(*b*)	(*c*)	(*d*)
A.	I	III	II	IV
B.	IV	III	II	I
C.	III	IV	I	II
D.	IV	I	III	II

82. The coastal State/Union Territory of Bay of Bengal is:
A. Odisha B. Karnataka
C. Kerala D. Telangana

83. Consider the following statements about forests:
(*a*) 'Torang' means forest in Kuduk language.
(*b*) The Village Council (Panchayat) in Jharkhand decides which family will get how much land for farming, by lottery.
(*c*) The Right to Forest Act, 2007 gives the rights to people who have been living in the forest for at least 15 years.
(*d*) About three-fourth people in Mizoram are linked to the forests.

The correct statements are:
A. (*b*) and (*c*) B. (*a*) and (*c*)
C. (*a*) and (*b*) D. (*a*) and (*d*)

84. What is the mass of an object with a density of 24 g/mL and a volume of 6 mL?
A. 146 g B. 142 g
C. 143 g D. 144 g

85. Consider the following statements about snakes and identify the ***incorrect*** one from the following:
A. They swallow their food whole.
B. Snakes have sharp teeth.
C. Poisonous snakes have fangs.
D. They chew up their prey.

86. Bronze is an alloy made by melting the following:
A. Tin and copper
B. Copper and zinc
C. Aluminium and zinc
D. Zinc and tin

87. Select the correct statements about elephants from the following:
(*a*) A three-month-old baby elephant generally weighs about 100 kg.
(*b*) An adult elephant can eat more than 200 kg of leaves and twigs in one day.
(*c*) Elephants do not rest very much; they sleep for only two to four hours in a day.
(*d*) Elephants like to play with mud and water.
A. (*b*) and (*d*) B. (*a*) and (*b*)
C. (*a*) and (*c*) D. (*c*) and (*d*)

88. Consider the following statements (*a*) and (*b*):

Statement (*a*): In Manali, houses are constructed with wood, slanting roofs and elevated on strong bamboo pillars.

Statement (*b*): Manali receives a lot of rain and snowfall.

Choose the correct option:
A. (*a*) is incorrect, but (*b*) is correct
B. Both (*a*) and (*b*) are correct
C. Both (*a*) and (*b*) are incorrect
D. (*a*) is correct, but (*b*) is incorrect

76. C **77.** C **78.** B **79.** A **80.** A **81.** B **82.** A **83.** D **84.** D **85.** D
86. A **87.** D **88.** A

89. Read the following statements and choose the correct option:

Assertion (A): On applying pressure, gas can be compressed easily.

Reason (R): When we apply pressure to a gas, the intermolecular space between gaseous particles decreases and it gets compressed.

A. (A) is false, but (R) is true.
B. Both (A) and (R) are true and (R) is the correct explanation of (A).
C. Both (A) and (R) are true, but (R) is not the correct explanation of (A).
D. (A) is true, but (R) is false.

90. Consider the following main functions of plants:
(*a*) To produce and store food
(*b*) To give strength and support to the plant
(*c*) To transport water and minerals from roots to other parts of plant

The main function(s) of the stem is/are:

A. Only (*b*) and (*c*) B. Only (*b*)
C. Only (*a*) and (*b*) D. (*a*), (*b*) and (*c*)

Part-IV : Language-I—English

91. Choose the strategy that matches the example.

'I focus on the language I use to make sure it is correct.'

A. Translanguaging B. Memorising
C. Revising D. Self-monitoring

92. Students in Class II sing a song, 'Head and shoulders, knees and toes'. They touch the correct part of their body as they sing the song. Which method is the teacher using to teach them?

A. Eclectic
B. Audio-lingual
C. Communicative Language Teaching
D. Total Physical Response

93. Students work in groups to answer five questions about vocabulary from the previous unit. Then, they exchange questions with another group and try to answer the questions. This is an example of:

A. Peer assessment
B. Self-assessment
C. Feedback
D. Reading assessment

94. I like it when the teacher gives me a card with a word or phrase on it and I have to act it out for the rest of the class so that they guess the word.

Find the learners' comments with the learners' preferences listed below:

A. I remember language well when I am kinesthetically involved.
B. I remember language well when I see it.
C. I remember language well when I hear it.
D. I remember language well when I memorise the phrase from the card.

95. Read the following statements and choose the correct option:

Assertion (A): All children who enter school are competent language users according to their age.

Reason (R): Due to language and cultural diversity, they are unable to demonstrate their abilities.

A. (A) is false, but (R) is true.
B. Both (A) and (R) are true and (R) is the correct explanation of (A).
C. Both (A) and (R) are true, but (R) is not the correct explanation of (A).
D. (A) is true, but (R) is false.

96. Manjeet of Class V speaks in different ways to his teacher, to his friends and also to a two-year-old child. It means Manjeet knows how to use language in social situations. What is this attribute of a language known as?

A. Act of speech B. Naturalist
C. Semantics D. Pragmatics

97. A mother notices that her child sometimes says things that she has never heard adults or her siblings say. She is confused, as she believes that the child learns language by imitating people in her family and immediate surroundings. Her belief resonates with:

A. Multilingualism B. Nativism
C. Behaviourism D. Constructivism

98. The set of skills that develop before children begin formal reading instruction and which provide the foundation for later academic skills is:

A. Emergent literacy
B. Emergent solution
C. Emergent curriculum
D. Emergent properties

89. B	**90.** A	**91.** D	**92.** D	**93.** A	**94.** A	**95.** D	**96.** D	**97.** C	**98.** A

99. A grandmother loves to read out stories from books to young children at home and, in this way, exposes them to books and new ideas, and the children are actively engaged in this process. This technique is known as:
A. Aloud reading
B. Model reading
C. Shared reading
D. Dialogic reading

100. An approach to teaching reading that starts with basic elements like letters and phonemes and teaches children that phonemes can be combined into words before moving on to reading as a whole is:
A. Structural approach
B. Top-down approach
C. Bottom-up approach
D. Whole language approach

101. Read the following statements and choose the correct option:

Assertion (A): Use of phonetic spelling slows down the ability to learn to spell correctly.

Reason (R): When young children use spellings that they 'invented' rather than conventional spellings, it does not slow down their ability to learn to spell correctly.
A. (A) is false, but (R) is true.
B. Both (A) and (R) are true and (R) is the correct explanation of (A).
C. Both (A) and (R) are true, but (R) is not the correct explanation of (A).
D. (A) is true, but (R) is false.

102. In learning a new language, many students often lack confidence when speaking due to the language's unique pronunciation rules. One way to overcome this problem is by:
A. Correcting errors whenever they happen.
B. Letting children read aloud in class.
C. Using game-like activities that require verbal interaction in the classroom.
D. Conducting special speech therapy with a counsellor and practice through drills.

103. A teacher of Class III is presenting new vocabulary to the learners. Which one of the following is an effective way to present the new vocabulary?
A. The teacher should write its meaning on the blackboard and ask learners to learn it by heart.
B. The teacher should tell them the antonyms of words and give the meaning in their language.
C. The teacher should give them a concise definition of words.
D. The teacher should try to explain a word's meaning in the situation in which it occurs.

104. Learning a language is a matter of __________.
A. skill B. acquisition
C. process D. product

105. Match the ways of reading with what readers do:

Ways of reading	*What readers do*
(*a*) Predicting	I. They determine how writers feel based on how they write.
(*b*) Inferring attitude	II. They use parts of the text to help them understand unfamiliar lexis.
(*c*) Deducing meaning from context	III. They look at how the information is structured, by noticing headings or introductory phrases.
(*d*) Intensive reading	IV. They focus on how language is used in a piece of text.
(*e*) Identifying text organisation	V. They use titles and pictures to give themselves ideas about what the text is about.

	(*a*)	(*b*)	(*c*)	(*d*)	(*e*)
A.	IV	III	II	I	V
B.	V	I	II	IV	III
C.	I	IV	V	II	III
D.	II	I	III	IV	V

Directions (Qs. No. 106-114): *Read the passage given below and answer the questions that follow by selecting the correct/ most appropriate option.*

In the middle of her solo trip to Mizoram last month, Geeta Garud, 69, was walking on a narrow ledge, "making my way behind a waterfall, trying out something I wouldn't have in my younger years. And I realised how travelling solo was such a liberating experience."

Before going on her week-long holiday, she was hesitant about travelling by herself. Garud had asked friends and family but found no takers. Yet there she was, alone, relishing a challenging trek. "Why was I being dependent on others? Being alone gives you a sense of freedom."

She ended up having many firsts. She danced impromptu at a festival in Reiek, waded into a river, and went horse-riding. "I had opportunities to try horse-riding when I was younger, but could not work up the courage. This time, I thought, if not now, I may not get another chance," says Garud, who was an athlete in her youth and had played cricket.

99. D	100. C	101. A	102. C	103. D	104. A	105. B

She was at her farm in Koregaon during the lockdown and had felt the lack of social connections. It motivated her to travel as soon as things eased.

"Travel is also about meeting people; I felt that sense of joy and freedom when I finally did it." She is planning to travel to Europe next and has decided not to take a friend or relative along. She intends to revisit the joy of travelling alone and relishing a sense of freedom all over again.

106. Which of the following statements is ***incorrect***?

Travelling alone in distant Mizoram at the age of 69:

A. was very enjoyable but very tiring.
B. was a novel experience for Garud.
C. she was taking a big risk.
D. she was breathing an air of freedom.

107. Garud travelled alone as:

A. a companion would have offered her unasked for advice.
B. it was less expensive.
C. no one agreed to accompany her.
D. she did not like company.

108. Which of the following statements is true/false?

(*a*) Initially, she did not like to go alone.
(*b*) She wanted only a friend to go with her.

Choose the correct option:

A. Both (*a*) and (*b*) are false.
B. (*a*) is true and (*b*) is false.
C. (*b*) is true and (*a*) is false.
D. Both (*a*) and (*b*) are true.

109. Study the following statements:

(*a*) She practised only for a day before dancing in a festival.
(*b*) Horse-riding is a courageous skill.
(*c*) Her experience as an athlete helped her in trying horse-riding.

Choose the correct option:

A. (*a*) and (*b*) are false, but (*c*) is true.
B. (*a*) and (*b*) are true, but (*c*) is false.
C. (*b*) and (*c*) are true, but (*a*) is false.
D. (*a*) and (*c*) are true, but (*b*) is false.

110. Which one of the following statements is ***not*** true?

A. Garud's family owned a farm at Koregaon.
B. During lockdown, Garud felt isolated and lonely.
C. A friend might not have let her wade into a river.
D. Walking on a narrow ledge is an easy task.

111. "And I realised how travelling solo was ..... ."

The underlined expression is a/an _______ clause.

A. Adverb B. Principal
C. Noun D. Adjective

112. 'Garud had asked friends and family but found no takers.'

The underlined word is a/an ___________ .

A. Interjection B. Noun
C. Pronoun D. Conjunction

113. 'She was hesitant ..... .'

Choose the word nearest in meaning to the underlined one.

A. willing B. keen
C. disinclined D. harmless

114. '..... relishing a challenging trek.'

Choose the word opposite in meaning to the underlined one.

A. realising B. disliking
C. revealing D. denying

Directions (Qs. No. 115-120): *Read the poem given below and answer the questions that follow by selecting the correct/most appropriate option.*

Gather ye rosebuds while ye may,
Old Time is still a-flying;
And this same flower that smiles today
Tomorrow will be dying.

The glorious lamp of heaven, the sun,
The higher he's a-getting,
The sooner will his race be run,
And nearer he's to setting.

That age is best which is the first,
When youth and blood are warmer;
But being spent, the worse, and worst
Times still succeed the former.

Then be not coy, but use your time,
And while ye may, go marry;
For having lost but once your prime,
You may forever tarry.

115. The poem is addressed to a/an _________.

A. old unmarried woman
B. gardener
C. young woman
D. old friend

106. D **107.** C **108.** B **109.** C **110.** D **111.** B **112.** D **113.** C **114.** B **115.** C

116. The example of the sun is given to:
A. describe the glory of his light.
B. describe the fast passage of time.
C. show his warmth.
D. warn of his setting.

117. What does the poet tell us about young age?
A. Time will soon pass and it is a time to find one's love.
B. It is a time to work hard.
C. Time will soon pass.
D. It is a time to find one's love.

118. Which of the following statements is true/false?
(*a*) Gathering rosebuds is the same as enjoying one's life.
(*b*) The sun can't keep on shining forever.
Choose the correct option:
A. Both A and B are false.
B. A is true and B is false.
C. B is true and A is false.
D. Both A and B are true.

119. 'And this same flower that smiles today.'
Identify the figure of speech used in this line.
A. Hyperbole B. Simile
C. Metaphor D. Personification

120. Identify the figure of speech used in: 'The glorious lamp of heaven, the sun'.
A. Hyperbole
B. Simile
C. Metaphor
D. Personification

Part-V : Language-II—हिन्दी

निर्देश (प्र.सं. 121 से 127 तक): *निम्नलिखित गद्यांश को पढ़कर पूछे गए प्रश्नों में सही/सबसे उपयुक्त उत्तर वाले विकल्प को चुनिए।*

जीवन में कभी अभाव का दुख, कभी स्वभाव का और कभी दुर्भाव का और इससे भी ऊपर सदैव तनाव का दुख घेरे रहता है। इन्हीं दुखों के वशीभूत हम टकराव की जिंदगी जीते हुए बिखराव का दुख भोगते हैं। दुखों से सभी डरते हैं, क्योंकि दुख अप्रिय हैं। दुखों से दूर रहने और सुख पाने की चाह में हम नए-नए पापों में प्रवेश करने लगते हैं। यही हमारी सबसे बड़ी भूल होती है। पाप का फल सुख रोकता है। सुख चाहिए तो पापों से मुक्त होने की चाह जागृत करनी होगी। दुखों से छुटकारा और सुख प्राप्ति का एकमात्र मार्ग है धर्म को आत्मसात करना। जहाँ धर्म है, वहाँ पाप नहीं है और जब पाप नहीं तो वहाँ दुख नहीं। जहाँ दुख नहीं वहाँ सुख को अनंत होने का पूरा अवसर प्राप्त होता है। दुख हमारी भूल और मानवीय स्तर से गिरकर घिनौने कर्मों का फल है।

121. गद्यांश के अनुसार सबसे बड़ा दुख है :
A. अभाव का B. स्वभाव का
C. पीड़ा का D. तनाव का

122. सबसे बड़ी भूल है :
A. सुख पाने के लिए गलत काम करना।
B. सुख पाने के लिए साधना करना।
C. दुख से छुटकारे के लिए संन्यास लेना।
D. दुख से दूर भागना और एकांतवास।

123. सुख कहाँ होता है?
A. जहाँ मानवता नहीं होती।
B. जहाँ धन-संपदा हो।
C. जहाँ धर्म होता हे
D. जहाँ सुखी लोग रहते हैं

124. गद्यांश के मूल विषय में शामिल नहीं है :
A. दंड B. सुख
C. दुख D. धर्म

125. गलत कार्य करने से ________ की हानि होती है।
A. पाप B. सुख
C. दुख D. सम्मान

126. किस शब्द में 'इक' प्रत्यय का प्रयोग संभव है?
A. धर्म B. सुख
C. दुख D. पाप

127. समूह से भिन्न शब्द है :
A. धर्म B. सुख
C. दुख D. पापी

निर्देश (प्र.सं. 128 से 135 तक): *निम्नलिखित गद्यांश को पढ़कर पूछे गए प्रश्नों में सही/सबसे उपयुक्त उत्तर वाले विकल्प को चुनिए।*

भारत में पर्व, उत्सव और मेलों की सदियों पुरानी परंपरा है। इनके जरिए ना सिर्फ संस्कृति समृद्ध होती है, बल्कि स्थानीय अर्थव्यवस्था को भी बहुत ताकत मिलती है। मणिपुर में 'संगाई महोत्सव' आयोजित किया गया। मणिपुर इतने प्राकृतिक सौंदर्य, सांस्कृतिक समृद्धि से भरा ऐसा राज्य है कि हर कोई यहाँ एक बार जरूर आना चाहता है। 'संगाई महोत्सव'

116. B **117.** A **118.** D **119.** D **120.** C **121.** D **122.** A **123.** C **124.** A **125.** B **126.** A **127.** D

जैसे आयोजन निवेशकों और इंडस्ट्री को भी आकर्षित करते हैं। इस बार का आयोजन पहले से और भी ज्यादा भव्य स्वरूप में सामने आया है जो मणिपुर के लोगों की भावना और उनके जज्बे को दिखाता है। यह महोत्सव पहले इम्फाल तक ही सीमित रहता था, लेकिन इस बार पूरे राज्य में इसका आयोजन किया गया है। जब ऐसे आयोजनों को ज्यादा से ज्यादा लोगों के साथ जोड़ा जाता है, तभी इसकी पूरी क्षमता सामने आ पाती है।

128. 'संगाई महोत्सव' का आयोजन _______ में किया गया।

A. उत्तर-पूर्वी राज्यों　　B. सभी राज्यों
C. मणिपुर　　D. शंघाई

129. भारत की परंपरा में निम्नलिखित में से कौन-सा शामिल **नहीं** है?

A. संघर्ष　　B. त्योहार
C. उत्सव　　D. मेले

130. मणिपुर ________ के लिए प्रसिद्ध है।

A. कला और कारीगरी　　B. स्थानीय उद्योग
C. प्राकृतिक सौंदर्य　　D. उत्सव-महोत्सव

131. संगाई महोत्सव के आयोजन से _______ को भी लाभ मिलता है।

A. अर्थव्यवस्था　　B. सांस्कृतिक उत्सव
C. विदेशी पर्यटन　　D. प्राकृतिक सौंदर्य

132. पहले और अब के महोत्सव के आयोजन में मूल अंतर क्या है?

A. पहले मणिपुर में, अब दक्षिण भारत में
B. पहले इम्फाल में, अब पूरे उत्तर-पूर्व में
C. पहले केवल इम्फाल में, अब पूरे राज्य में
D. पहले मणिपुर में, अब उत्तर भारत में

133. 'महोत्सव' का संधि-विच्छेद है :

A. मह + उत्सव　　B. महो + त्सव
C. महा + उत्सव　　D. महान + उत्सव

134. 'इत' प्रत्यय का उदाहरण है :

A. प्रकृति　　B. सांस्कृतिक
C. संस्कृति　　D. आकर्षित

135. गद्यांश में किसकी क्षमता के सामने आने की बात की गई है?

A. स्थानीय कलाओं की　　B. महोत्सव की
C. मणिपुर की　　D. सांस्कृतिक समृद्धि की

निर्देश (प्र.सं. 136 से 150 तक): *नीचे दिए गए प्रश्नों के लिए सही/सबसे उपयुक्त विकल्प चुनिए।*

136. छोटे बच्चों के लिए पाठ योजना बनाते समय अध्यापिका ने समग्र भौतिक प्रतिक्रिया (TPR) विधि पर ध्यान केन्द्रित करने का निर्णय लिया। पाठ में समग्र भौतिक प्रतिक्रिया (TPR) शामिल करने के लिए अध्यापिका को निम्नलिखित में से क्या करना चाहिए?

A. गतिविधि न करवा कर प्रश्न पूछे जाएँ और उत्तर देने के लिए प्रोत्साहित किया जाए।
B. कक्षा में कुछ शारीरिक गतिविधियाँ करनी चाहिए।
C. ऐसी गतिविधियाँ करवाएँ जो अपनी-अपनी सीट पर बैठे-बैठे हो सकें और जोड़ों या समूह में काम करने के मौके दें।
D. कक्षा में कुछ श्रवण संबंधी गतिविधियाँ करवायी जाएँ।

137. व्याकरण सिखाने का कौन-सा उपागम इस मत को प्रोत्साहित करता है कि भाषा अधिगम नियमों को सीखने से संबंधित है?

A. व्याकरण अनुवाद　　B. निगमनात्मक
C. आगमनात्मक　　D. सम्प्रेषणात्मक

138. एक अध्यापक कक्षा V के शिक्षार्थियों को मुक्त लेखन कार्य देने की योजना बना रहा है। अधिकांश अध्यापकों द्वारा निम्नलिखित में से किस बात पर ध्यान केन्द्रित करना चाहिए?

A. शिक्षार्थियों की लिखावट
B. विषय-वस्तु की सटीकता
C. विषय-वस्तु में प्रवाहता
D. प्रवाह और सटीकता दोनों पर ही ध्यान देना चाहिए

139. 'टॉप-डाउन' से आशय है—'समग्र अर्थ पर ध्यान देना'।

'अधोमुखी (बॉटम-अप)' से क्या आशय है?

A. लघु-उत्तरीय प्रश्न पूछने पर ध्यान देना
B. पाठ्य-वस्तु और अमूर्त विचारों के सार पर ध्यान देना
C. पठन-पूर्व पर ध्यान देना
D. पाठ्य-वस्तु के शब्दों और वाक्यों पर ध्यान देना

140. भाषा अध्यापक का प्राथमिक दायित्व क्या होना चाहिए?

A. शिक्षार्थियों को निर्देश देना
B. शिक्षार्थी की सम्प्रेषणात्मक आवश्यकताओं की पहचान करना
C. शिक्षण के लिए उपयुक्त विषय-वस्तु का चयन करना
D. शिक्षार्थियों के विभिन्न वर्ग समूह बनाना

141. एक छोटी बच्ची कोई एक पुस्तक उठाती है, उसे सीधी तरफ से पकड़ती है, और उसके पृष्ठ पलटती है। इन सबमें क्या सम्मिलित है?

A. उद्गामी समाधान कौशल
B. उद्गामी (इमरजेन्ट) साक्षरता कौशल
C. उद्गामी पाठ्यचर्या
D. उद्गामी गुणधर्म

128. C	**129.** A	**130.** C	**131.** A	**132.** C	**133.** C	**134.** D	**135.** B	**136.** B	**137.** B
138. C	**139.** D	**140.** B	**141.** B						

142. निम्नलिखित कथनों को पढ़िए तथा सही विकल्प का चयन कीजिए :

अभिकथन (A): शिक्षार्थी भाषा अर्जित करते हैं क्योंकि वे ऐसा करने के लिए आनुवंशिक रूप से पूर्वानुकूलित होते हैं और ऐसे में परिवेश की कोई भूमिका नहीं होती है।

तर्क (R): भाषा अर्जन में शिक्षार्थी-केन्द्रित कक्षायी परिवेश का बहुत गहरा प्रभाव पड़ता है।

A. (A) गलत है, परन्तु (R) सही है।
B. (A) और (R) दोनों सही हैं तथा (R), (A) की सही व्याख्या है।
C. (A) और (R) दोनों सही हैं, परन्तु (R), (A) की सही व्याख्या नहीं है।
D. (A) सही है, परन्तु (R) गलत है।

143. पठन सिखाने के उस तरीके को क्या कहा जाता है जिसमें शब्दों के अर्थ को प्रयुक्त संदर्भों के अनुसार समझने पर बल दिया जाता है?

A. संरचनात्मक उपागम
B. सम्प्रेषणात्मक उपागम
C. अधोमुखी (बॉटम-अप) उपागम
D. समग्र भाषा उपागम

144. भाषा के बारे में चिन्तन करने और बात करने की योग्यता को क्या कहेंगे?

A. अधिभाषिक (विचार-विमर्श) योग्यता
B. ध्वन्यात्मक जागरूकता
C. निपुण वक्ता
D. उद्गामी साक्षरता

145. एक माँ ने कक्षा II की अध्यापिका से पूछा कि मैंने इस बात पर ध्यान दिया है कि मेरी बच्ची कभी-कभी ऐसे शब्द बोल जाती है जो उसने कभी अपने वयस्कों या भाई-बहनों से नहीं सुने हैं। यह कैसे संभव है?

इस प्रश्न का निम्नलिखित में से सबसे उपयुक्त उत्तर क्या है?

A. रचनावादी उपागम के अनुसार, बच्चे नई भाषाएँ आविष्कृत करते हैं।
B. बच्चे भाषा केवल अपने वयस्कों के अनुकरण से ही सीखते हैं।
C. मनुष्य का मस्तिष्क भाषा सीखने के लिए सहज रूप से अनुकूलित है।
D. बच्चे भाषा तभी सीखते हैं जब हम बच्चे के भाषायी विकास पर पुनर्बलन देते हैं।

146. प्रारंभिक साक्षरता को सुसाध्य बनाने की एक युक्ति है, जिसमें एक वयस्क और एक बालिका दोनों साथ-साथ एक पुस्तक देख रहे हैं, वयस्क प्रश्न पूछता है और आपसी संवाद को प्रोत्साहित करता है। फिर दोनों की भूमिका बदलती है, बालिका वयस्क से प्रश्न पूछती है। यह युक्ति क्या कहलाती है?

A. कथा वाचन
B. मॉडल पठन
C. साझा पठन
D. संभाषिक पठन

147. एक अध्यापक शिक्षार्थियों के भाषा के श्रवण कौशलों का विकास कैसे कर सकता है?

A. शिक्षार्थियों को वह सब सुनने के लिए कहना जिसे वे निष्क्रिय होकर सुनते हैं।
B. शिक्षार्थियों से कक्षा में और कक्षा के बाहर सतत रूप से बात करके।
C. अन्य भाषिक कौशलों को सम्बद्ध किए बिना केवल श्रवण कौशलों पर ध्यान केन्द्रित करना।
D. शिक्षार्थियों के लिए ऐसे अवसर सृजित करना जिनमें वे तरह-तरह के भाषा स्रोतों और लोगों से सुन सकें और अन्य श्रवण संबंधी गतिविधियों में संलग्न हो सकें।

148. निम्नलिखित कथनों को पढ़िए तथा सही विकल्प का चयन कीजिए :

अभिकथन (A): प्राथमिक स्तर पर भाषा में सटीकता बहुत ही महत्वपूर्ण है।

तर्क (R): व्याकरण प्राथमिक स्तर की पाठ्यचर्या का अभिन्न अंग है।

A. (A) गलत है, परन्तु (R) सही है।
B. (A) और (R) दोनों सही हैं तथा (R), (A) की सही व्याख्या है।
C. (A) और (R) दोनों सही हैं, परन्तु (R), (A) की सही व्याख्या नहीं है।
D. (A) सही है, परन्तु (R) गलत है।

149. भाषा, भाषा अधिगम की प्रकृति और शिक्षण-शास्त्रीय व्यवस्थाओं में दोनों की अनुप्रयोगिता के बारे में सैद्धान्तिक स्थितियों एवं मतों को क्या कह सकते हैं?

A. युक्ति (तकनीक)
B. पाठ्यक्रम
C. विषय-वस्तु
D. उपागम

150. रचनात्मक मूल्यांकन क्या है?

A. परिवर्तन से संबंधित नहीं है।
B. शिक्षण-अधिगम प्रक्रिया में क्या हो रहा है।
C. अधिगम में हो रहे विकास और सुधार से संबंधित है।
D. कोर्स में एक पूर्वनिर्धारित या विशेष चरण में किया जाता है।

142. A **143.** D **144.** A **145.** C **146.** D **147.** D **148.** A **149.** D **150.** C

EXPLANATORY ANSWERS

1. **(C):** Dysgraphia is a neurological disorder characterized by difficulties with handwriting, and sometimes by troubles with other motor tasks. People with dysgraphia often struggle to form letters or write within a defined space. Their handwriting might appear twisted or inconsistent, and they might have difficulty with tasks like tying shoes or buttoning shirts, although these motor issues are not universal for all with the disorder. Dysgraphia is not a reflection of a person's intelligence. It is rooted in issues of brain function that make these specific tasks more challenging. Early intervention can be very beneficial, and strategies often include occupational therapy to enhance motor skills and teaching different techniques for writing or using tools like computers to assist with written tasks.

2. **(C):** Acceleration refers to the educational strategy of moving gifted children through the curriculum at a pace that matches their learning capabilities. This approach understands that some gifted students master topics quicker than their age peers, so it aims to challenge them appropriately. Methods of acceleration can include early admission to kindergarten or first grade, grade-skipping, and early graduation from high school or college. It's different from differentiation (which modifies content, process, or product based on student readiness, interest, or learning profile) or enrichment (which provides depth and complexity to regular content). Immersion is more about intense exposure to a particular subject or environment (e.g., language immersion programs). Acceleration has been shown to be one of the most effective strategies for meeting the needs of gifted learners, though it's essential to ensure the student's social and emotional readiness before implementing this strategy.

3. **(B):** Inclusive classrooms aim to provide equitable learning opportunities for all students, regardless of their abilities, backgrounds, or needs.
   (*i*) Curriculum adaptations are essential to meet the diverse needs of students. These adaptations can include changes in content, process, or product based on student readiness, interest, or learning profile.
   (*ii*) Incorporating diverse perspectives ensures that all students see themselves reflected in the curriculum and that they learn about others' experiences and viewpoints. It promotes mutual respect and understanding.
   (*iii*) Examining one's implicit bias is crucial because every teacher brings their own set of beliefs, experiences, and biases to the classroom. Being aware of these biases helps teachers ensure that their actions and decisions are fair and equitable.

4. **(B):** Primary agencies of socialisation are those immediate environments and relationships that first influence a person, such as family, which is predominant during infancy. These are the initial contacts a child has and thus play a crucial role in laying the foundation for social behavior, values, and identity. As the child grows and starts venturing out of the immediate familial environment, secondary agencies of socialization, like schools, peer groups, and media, become essential. These play a significant role in early childhood as the child begins to interact with a broader world, learn societal norms, values, and develops interpersonal skills.

5. **(D):** Lev Vygotsky, a renowned developmental psychologist, posited that language and thought are inherently interlinked and that language development facilitates cognitive development. He introduced the concept of the Zone of Proximal Development (ZPD), which is the difference between what a child can do independently and what they can do with assistance. Vygotsky believed that social interaction, especially dialogues with more knowledgeable others (like adults or peers), is vital for cognitive development. Through these interactions and the use of language, children can internalize knowledge and learn new cognitive strategies. Essentially, for Vygotsky, language is a primary tool of cognitive development, and the two are deeply intertwined.

6. **(C):** Lawrence Kohlberg's theory of moral development consists of three main levels: Pre-conventional, Conventional, and Post-conventional. Within the Conventional level, individuals seek to meet the standards of others, such as parents, peers, or society at large. They believe that maintaining social order is essential and often view "good" behavior as behavior that pleases or helps others and is approved by them. In this level, moral reasoning is based on conforming to social norms and the expectations of authority figures or the broader society. It is during this level that children typically believe that people should live up to societal expectations and behave in "good" ways.

7. **(B):** Both statements are rooted in Vygotsky's socio-cultural theory of cognitive development. Assertion (A) aligns with Vygotsky's concept of the Zone of Proximal Development (ZPD), which is the difference between what learners can do without help and what

they can achieve with guidance from someone more knowledgeable. This "more knowledgeable other" can be a teacher, peer, or even a parent. They provide the scaffolding, or structured support, needed for the learner to acquire new skills or understanding. Reason (R) asserts that social interaction is fundamental to learning and development, which is a cornerstone of Vygotsky's theory. He believed that cognitive development is deeply rooted in social interactions and that these interactions lead to internalization, or the process of embedding external knowledge and making it a part of one's internal cognitive structure. Therefore, both (A) and (R) are true, and (R) provides a correct explanation for (A).

8. **(C):** 'Assessment for learning', often referred to as formative assessment, is primarily used to provide feedback to students to enhance their learning. The primary objective isn't to assign grades or rank students, but to understand where the students are in their learning journey and provide guidance on how they can improve. This feedback can be immediate or can take place over a period of time. By offering insights into their strengths and areas of improvement, 'assessment for learning' helps students to become more reflective and self-regulating in their learning processes.

9. **(D):** By around seven years of age, many children begin to appreciate and engage in word play, including jokes and riddles that involve a play on words. Their linguistic skills have developed to a point where they can understand puns, double meanings, and other linguistic intricacies. This phase of enjoying word-based humor aligns with Piaget's concrete operational stage of cognitive development, where children begin to think more logically about concrete events. They become less egocentric and can see things from multiple perspectives, making them more receptive to the twists and turns of word play.

10. **(B):** Carol Gilligan critiqued Lawrence Kohlberg's theory of moral development from a feminist perspective. Gilligan believed that Kohlberg's stages were more applicable to males and were based on a male standard of moral reasoning. She argued that women often approach moral dilemmas differently, emphasizing relationships and care for others. In her work "In a Different Voice," Gilligan proposed that women tend to think in terms of care and responsibility in relationships (an "ethic of care"), whereas men tend to think in terms of rights and rules (an "ethic of justice"). While not all researchers agree with the gender distinction Gilligan proposed, her critique highlighted the importance of understanding diverse perspectives in moral reasoning.

11. **(B):** In Jean Piaget's theory of cognitive development, one of the primary characteristics of the pre-operational stage (which typically spans ages 2 to 7) is "centration." Centration refers to a child's tendency to focus on one salient aspect of a situation while neglecting other possible aspects. This can be seen in tasks like conservation experiments, where a child may focus on the height of water in a glass, for instance, and ignore its width, leading them to believe that the amount of water has changed when it's simply been poured into a differently shaped container.

12. **(B):** In early childhood, growth is steady, and thinking is somewhat egocentric, while in middle childhood, growth slows, and thinking becomes more logical. During early childhood, children are in Piaget's pre-operational stage, where their thinking is characterized by egocentrism, meaning they find it challenging to see situations from another's perspective. By the time they reach middle childhood, many have entered Piaget's concrete operational stage, where they can think more logically and understand concepts like conservation. Physiologically, growth is often steady in early childhood and then slows down as children approach puberty, which usually begins after middle childhood.

13. **(B):** Swimming is considered a gross motor skill. Gross motor skills involve the larger muscles of the body and are responsible for activities like walking, jumping, running, and swimming. These skills usually develop before fine motor skills, which involve smaller muscle movements. In contrast, tasks like knitting or cutting along the outline of a shape on paper are fine motor skills because they require precision and coordination of small muscles, particularly those in the hands.

14. **(B):** Physical growth and development follow the cephalocaudal (top-down) and proximodistal (inner to outer) principles. The cephalocaudal principle suggests that development progresses from the head (top) downward. This means that children typically gain control over the upper parts of their bodies before the lower parts. For instance, infants can hold their heads up before they can walk. The proximodistal principle indicates that development starts from the center of the body and moves outward. This means children gain control over their torso before refining the movements of their extremities. For example, babies can move their arms in a sweeping motion before they can dexterously manipulate objects with their fingers.

15. **(C):** According to Howard Gardner's theory of multiple intelligences, a philosopher typically exhibits intrapersonal intelligence. Intrapersonal intelligence

is the capacity to understand oneself, one's feelings, fears, motivations, and strengths. It's a kind of self-awareness. On the other hand, a sculptor would predominantly exhibit spatial intelligence. Spatial intelligence refers to the ability to visualize with the mind's eye and comprehend spatial relationships between objects. This form of intelligence is crucial for activities that involve a keen understanding of space, shape, and form, such as sculpture, architecture, and certain visual arts.

16. (C): Experiential learning emphasizes the importance of critical reflection. Developed by David Kolb, experiential learning is a process where knowledge is gained through a cycle of doing and then reflecting on the experiences. The Experiential Learning Cycle suggests that we learn by having experiences, reflecting on those experiences, drawing abstract conclusions from our reflections, and then testing these conclusions in new situations. Critical reflection is a central aspect of this model, as it allows learners to deepen their understanding, relate their experiences to prior knowledge, and adjust their actions based on insights.

17. (D): Giving children opportunities to brainstorm and make intuitive guesses is an effective way to enhance their problem-solving skills. Encouraging independent thinking, exploration, and the willingness to try different solutions fosters creativity and resilience. When children brainstorm and make guesses, they actively engage with the problem, consider various perspectives, and learn through trial and error. These processes develop critical thinking, adaptability, and confidence in their ability to tackle challenges.

18. (B): Both Assertion (A) and Reason (R) are grounded in contemporary educational philosophies that prioritize student-centered learning environments. (A) is valid as creating a meaningful environment that encourages active participation and engagement benefits all children. It caters to diverse learners and ensures they are involved in the learning process, thereby making learning more impactful. (R) aligns with the belief that all children have an intrinsic motivation to learn and are capable of learning, given the right environment and opportunities. If educators believe that all children can learn and are motivated to do so, they will create environments that promote participation and engagement. Thus, (R) is the correct explanation of (A).

19. (D): Decontextualization does not contribute to the course of learning in the same manner as the other options. While organization, categorization, and conceptualization are processes that help learners structure information, make sense of it, and relate it to existing knowledge, decontextualization refers to removing something from its original context. In many learning scenarios, understanding the context is crucial for comprehension. However, in some advanced learning situations, decontextualization can be useful to understand abstract concepts by removing them from distracting or irrelevant contexts. Still, among the given options, it is the least directly associated with facilitating the learning process.

20. (D): The question "How has your thinking about the use of verbs changed since the beginning of the class?" requires students to reflect on their own thinking. This is a metacognitive question, as it prompts students to think about their thought processes, how they have evolved, and what they have learned. Metacognitive questions encourage learners to be aware of their learning journey and adjustments they might have made along the way.

21. (B): "I failed the test because I didn't study enough." is an example of an internal attribution for failure. Attributions are reasons that individuals give for their successes or failures. An internal attribution assigns the cause of an event to personal factors, implying that the individual had control over the outcome. In contrast, external attributions assign the cause to outside forces or situations. In the given example, the person attributes their failure to their own lack of preparation, which is an internal factor.

22. (B): Assertion (A) notes a general observation that, in many cultures, girls often choose dolls as toys while boys might gravitate towards cars. Reason (R) indicates that children organize and act upon information based on cultural expectations of gender-appropriate behavior. Both statements are generally true. The toy preferences of boys and girls are influenced by societal and cultural norms, as well as marketing strategies, parental choices, and peer behaviors. Over time, children absorb these norms and develop a sense of what's "appropriate" for their gender. As a result, many internalize and express these learned preferences in their play, even if there's no inherent reason for dolls to be considered "girls' toys" or cars to be "boys' toys". Thus, (R) is the correct explanation for (A).

23. (B): According to Lev Vygotsky, peer collaboration plays a significant role in the development of conceptual abilities among children. Vygotsky believed in the importance of social interactions in cognitive development. He introduced the idea of the Zone of Proximal Development (ZPD), which refers to the difference between what a child can do on their own and what they can do with help. Interactions, especially with peers, provide opportunities for children to work within their ZPD, thus promoting cognitive growth.

24. **(D):** According to Lev Vygotsky's theory, inner speech is a way for children to regulate their own thinking. Vygotsky believed that as children grow, their external dialogues (speech with others) become internal dialogues (speech with themselves). This inner speech is not merely silent speech but is a critical tool for thought. It helps children to plan, strategize, and guide their actions. Over time, as they mature, this inner speech becomes more abbreviated and symbolic, reflecting the child's evolving cognitive processes.

25. **(B):** Four-year-old Aparna's belief that a button is alive because it helps tie her shirt together is an example of animistic thinking. According to Jean Piaget's theory of cognitive development, children in the preoperational stage (typically aged 2 to 7) often attribute life-like qualities to inanimate objects. This is termed animism. Animistic thinking arises because young children are not yet able to fully differentiate between animate and inanimate entities based on intrinsic properties, so they might attribute life-like qualities based on the function or utility of objects.

26. **(C):** Frequent repetitive and recurring behavior is a typical characteristic of students with autism. Autism spectrum disorder (ASD) is characterized by challenges with social interaction, communication, and repetitive behaviors. Individuals with autism might engage in repetitive motions or "stimming," like rocking or hand-flapping, and may show intense interest in particular topics or objects. The other options listed are generally not typical characteristics of autism.

27. **(B):** Assertion (A) posits that to cultivate critical thinking in students, teachers should immerse them in diverse situations and contrasting viewpoints. Reason (R) suggests that students enrich their critical and creative thinking abilities as they engage in conversations across differing views and situations. Both statements are valid. Exposing students to diverse perspectives not only broadens their knowledge base but also encourages them to think critically, evaluate multiple viewpoints, and construct informed opinions. Engaging in conversations across differences allows them to challenge their assumptions, recognize biases, and develop a more rounded understanding of topics. Hence, (R) correctly explains (A).

28. **(D):** The primary goal of learning should be the development of critical thinking. While memorization of facts and rote rehearsal might be useful tools in some contexts, they do not necessarily foster a deep understanding or the ability to apply knowledge in novel situations. Critical thinking, on the other hand, involves analyzing, evaluating, and synthesizing information, allowing learners to make informed decisions, solve problems, and understand the world around them. Cultivating critical thinking skills prepares students to navigate an ever-changing world and equips them with the tools to be lifelong learners.

29. **(A):** Children learn more effectively if a concept proceeds from Generic to Specific. Starting with a broad, overarching idea or concept allows children to grasp the fundamental essence of a topic. Once this foundation is established, delving into specific details or examples can help consolidate and deepen their understanding. This approach also helps in drawing connections between related concepts, facilitating a more integrated learning experience.

30. **(A):** Variability in learning styles of students should be valued and seen as a reflection of human diversity. Recognizing and accommodating different learning styles can lead to more inclusive and effective teaching. Every student is unique, and what works for one might not work for another. By valuing this diversity, educators can tailor their instruction to meet the diverse needs of their students, ensuring that all learners have an equal opportunity to succeed. Ignoring or trying to suppress these differences can hinder the learning process and deprive students of the chance to engage with the material in a way that's most meaningful to them.

31. **(A):** Mathematics does indeed foster creativity in children. While many view math as a rigid and structured subject, it often requires creative problem-solving, especially when dealing with complex problems or novel situations. Mathematics also nurtures a child's imagination. For instance, when learning about geometric shapes or algebraic patterns, a child often visualizes and imagines scenarios, patterns, and solutions. Deductive reasoning is a foundational aspect of mathematics, where conclusions are reached based on previously known facts or premises. Therefore, statements (*a*), (*b*), and (*c*) are the most appropriate descriptions of the nature of mathematics.

32. **(A):** Praising only the student who achieves the highest marks in the term-end examination is not effective in fostering an appreciation for mathematics among all children. Such an approach can demotivate others who may not score the highest but are still making significant progress or showing a genuine interest in the subject. It could create an environment of competition rather than appreciation and exploration. The other options encourage exploration, understanding, and appreciation of mathematics in a broader and more inclusive sense.

33. **(D):** Errors in students' work provide valuable insights into their thought processes and can help teachers understand where students might be struggling. They are indeed part of the learning process, and they can assist teachers in planning their lessons more effectively. However, the statement that errors should be overlooked because pointing them out will demotivate students is not correct. Addressing errors in a constructive manner is essential for learning. It's not about criticizing the student but about helping them understand and learn from their mistakes. Proper feedback, when delivered empathetically, can be instrumental in a student's learning journey.

34. **(A):** The statement "Norm-referenced assessment is useful in diagnostic testing and remedial teaching." is not correct. Norm-referenced assessments are designed to compare and rank test takers in relation to one another, usually giving a "percentile" sort of ranking. Such assessments do not specifically highlight areas of individual strength or weakness, but rather how one student performed relative to others. On the other hand, criterion-referenced assessments evaluate a student's performance based on a predetermined criterion or a set standard. These are more useful for diagnostic testing and remedial teaching as they can pinpoint specific areas a student might be struggling with.

35. **(C):** Mathematical learning material helps students in self-learning as they can interact with the material, explore, and understand concepts at their own pace. It also develops a learning environment in the class as it encourages exploration, inquiry, and hands-on learning. When students actively engage with learning materials, the classroom environment becomes more dynamic and conducive to understanding complex mathematical concepts.

36. **(B):** According to the National Education Policy (NEP) 2020, olympiads and competitions in various subjects will be strengthened across the country. The policy emphasizes excellence in learning and understanding, aiming to foster creativity and critical thinking. Strengthening olympiads and competitions can motivate students to achieve higher standards and engage more deeply with the subject matter.

37. **(D):** Concepts like more-less, long-short, far-near, big-small, etc. are important pre-number concepts. Before diving into specific number operations and more complex mathematical concepts, young learners often begin by understanding these basic comparative ideas. They form the foundation for spatial reasoning, measurement, and other vital mathematical understandings. These pre-number concepts are crucial in developing a child's intuitive sense of quantities, dimensions, and relations, which will later be essential when engaging with more advanced mathematical concepts.

38. **(C):** According to the National Curriculum Framework, 2005, classroom researches indicate gendered constructs of society have led to the belief that boys use more innovative strategies for problem-solving and thus have better conceptual understanding. Despite their performance, girls often face biases rooted in societal gender norms and expectations. This has perpetuated the stereotype that boys are inherently better at subjects like mathematics, even when empirical evidence from classroom performance does not support this notion.

39. **(D):** The abstract nature of primary concepts in mathematics often contributes to the fear or difficulty students face. Mathematics deals with concepts that are sometimes intangible and require a level of abstract reasoning. For instance, understanding the concept of numbers, variables, or certain geometric properties demands a shift from concrete thinking to abstract reasoning. For many students, making this shift can be challenging, leading to the perception that mathematics is more difficult compared to other subjects that might be more grounded in tangible or real-world examples.

40. **(B) :** Bhaskar I, also known as Bhaskaracharya, was an Indian mathematician and astronomer. He was a major contributor to both mathematics and astronomy in the sixth century AD. He is particularly famous for his works on mathematics, including Lilavati and Algebra. In these texts he presented many mathematical formulas and methods. In astronomy, Bhaskar I had calculated the movements of the planets, the events of solar and lunar eclipses and their timings accurately. Because of his contributions he is considered a major personality in Indian astrology and astronomy. Bhaskar I made major contributions to mathematical astronomy and was one of the notable people working in this field.

41. **(D):** The mathematical skill demonstrated by the vegetable seller is one of breaking down the price for different amounts of spinach to arrive at the total cost for 350 g. This skill involves division and multiplication concepts. Statement (*c*) "Such skills help in developing alternate strategies for solving mathematical problems" is true. These real-world skills demonstrate that mathematics isn't just about rote memorization but about understanding concepts and applying them in practical scenarios. Often, such alternate strategies are more intuitive for individuals and showcase the flexibility of mathematical operations.

42. (C): In the option "Children are given manipulatives like number grids, tokens arranged in rectangular arrays and they are exploring multiplication patterns using them," children are actively engaged in the learning process, manipulating objects, and discovering mathematical patterns on their own. This approach aligns with constructivist learning theories where learners actively construct knowledge through experiences. In contrast, the other options involve more passive forms of learning where knowledge is delivered to students rather than being actively constructed by them.

43. (C): Using Fraction Discs is the most appropriate way to help a primary school learner visualize the equivalence between the fractions 2/3 and 4/6. Fraction discs or other manipulatives provide a tangible representation of fractions, allowing students to visually see and compare fractions. When students manipulate these discs, they can directly observe that two parts out of three (2/3) cover the same area as four parts out of six (4/6), reinforcing the concept of equivalent fractions.

44. (B): When a teacher uses the role play method in a mathematics class, her primary aim is projecting ideas. Role-playing in mathematics can help illustrate mathematical concepts, theories, or problems in a more interactive and relatable way. For instance, students could role-play scenarios involving buying and selling to understand subtraction and addition or act out story problems to understand the relationships between numbers. This method helps in making abstract mathematical ideas more concrete and comprehensible for students.

45. (B): Subitizing is the ability to instantly recognize the number of objects in a small group without counting them. In the option "Student rolls a die and is able to say it is four without actually counting the dots," the student is demonstrating the skill of subitizing. They are instantly recognizing the number of dots on the die without having to count each dot individually. This ability forms the foundation for more advanced number sense and mathematical operations.

46. (C): Weight of almonds = 4.8 kg = 4800 g

Raisin weight = 2500 g

Cashews weight = 3.5 kg = 3500 g

Total weight = 10800 g

$$\text{Weight of each packet} = \frac{10800}{36} = 300 \text{ g.}$$

47. (D): Side of square = 5 cm

Area of square = $(5)^2 = 25 \text{ cm}^2$

Now, Side of square = 10 cm

Area of square = $(10)^2 = 100 \text{ cm}^2$

$$\text{Required area} = \frac{100}{25} = 4 \text{ times.}$$

48. (D): Cube, Cuboid, Sphere, Cylinder have all 3-dimensional shapes.

49. (B): Cost of a soap = ₹ 10

She has total money = ₹ 5 + ₹ 2 + ₹ 2.5 = ₹ 9.5

₹ 10 – ₹ 9.5 = ₹ 0.50

∴ Required money = ₹ 0.50.

50. (A): LCM of 2, 3, 4 = 12

$$\frac{1}{4} = \frac{1\times3}{4\times3} = \frac{3}{12}$$

$$\frac{1}{3} = \frac{1\times4}{3\times4} = \frac{4}{12}$$

$$\frac{1}{2} = \frac{1\times6}{2\times6} = \frac{6}{12}$$

∴ 3, 4, 6 are in ascending order.

Hence, $\frac{1}{4} < \frac{1}{3} < \frac{1}{2}$ are in ascending order.

51. (B):

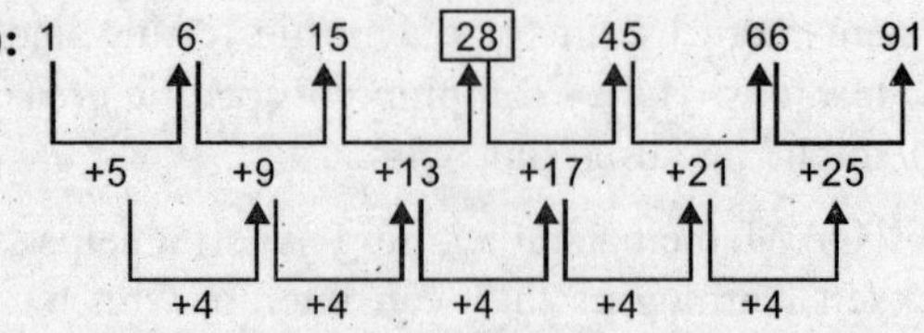

Hence, 28 will come at the place of question mark.

52. (C): Required ratio = $\frac{12}{3} = \frac{4}{1} = 4 : 1.$

53. (A): A kite becomes a rectangle if its opposite angles are equal. This statement is not true.

55. (C): Journey started by car at 16:50 hours

Finishing time = 21:15 hours

Time taken in completing the journey

= 21:15 hours – 16:50 hours = 4:25 hours

= 4 hours 25 minutes.

56. (A): A whole number is added to 100 and subtracted from 100

100 + 0 = 100

100 – 0 = 100

Sum of 100 + 100 = 200

100 + 1 = 101

100 – 1 = 99

Sum of 101 + 99 = 200

....

....

100 + 20 = 120

$100 - 20 = 80$

Sum of $120 + 80 = 200$

Hence, the sum of resulting numbers = 200.

57. **(C):** One hundred lakh = 10000000

∴ One hundred lakh is also known as one crore.

58. **(A):** $\frac{105}{10}, \frac{150}{100}, \frac{1055}{1000}, \frac{105}{100}, \frac{1005}{1000}, \frac{155}{1000}$

$= \frac{10500, 1500, 1055, 1050, 1005, 155}{1000}$

Clearly, 10.5, 1.50, 1.055, 1.05, 1.005, 0.155 represent a descending order of number.

59. **(D):**

$3630 = 11 \times 330$

$3630 = 3 \times 1210$

$3630 = 5 \times 726$

$3630 = 3 + 6 + 3 + 0 = 12$

which is not divisible by 9.

Hence, 9 is not a factor of 3630.

60. **(D):** The sum of 5 – 5 + 5 – 5 + 5 – 5, ... to odd number of term = 5

First term = 5

Sum of first, 2nd and 3rd term = 5 – 5 + 5 = 5

Sum of first to 5th term = 5 – 5 + 5 – 5 + 5 = 5

Hence, the sum of 5 – 5 + 5 – 5 + 5 – 5, ... to odd number of terms = 5.

61. **(D):** Synchronous communication refers to real-time interactions where participants communicate at the same time. The option "Video conferencing, online chat sessions, phone calls" aligns best with this definition. Video conferencing allows for real-time discussions with visual aids, online chat sessions enable instant messaging and feedback, and phone calls provide direct voice communication.

62. **(A):** If the theme "Travel: Railway Station" depicts the utilization of a community resource in EVS (Environmental Studies), then the theme "Food: Agricultural farm" would be the analogous depiction. Just as a railway station is a community resource for travel, an agricultural farm is a community resource for food production.

63. **(A):** Probing is the technique wherein a teacher encourages students to elaborate on an answer, either on their own or building upon the responses from their peers. Through probing questions, educators can delve deeper into a topic, encourage critical thinking, and ensure a comprehensive understanding of the subject matter. The other options listed do not specifically involve the act of seeking an elaborative or in-depth response from students.

64. **(D):** The title "Family: Relationships, Gender Roles, Occupations, as socio-cultural entity in changing times" provides a comprehensive perspective on the theme of "Family." It not only addresses relationships within a family but also incorporates gender roles, occupations, and the socio-cultural context. This holistic approach can help students understand the diverse aspects of family structures and their roles in society, especially in the context of evolving times.

65. **(C):** Using stories and poems in primary classes to explain various concepts in EVS can make lessons more interactive, enjoyable, and interesting. Additionally, this approach can make students aware of diversity in language and culture. Encouraging students to write their own poems and stories can also be an effective way to engage them further and foster creativity. While completing the syllabus is important, it's unlikely the primary motivation for using stories and poems is just because students have heard them before coming to school.

66. **(D):** The primary objective of teaching EVS (Environmental Studies) from classes I to V is "Helping learners link classroom learning to life outside the school." Environmental Studies is interdisciplinary and encompasses various aspects of the environment, social issues, and human interactions. By linking classroom learning to real-life scenarios, students can better understand their surroundings, the importance of sustainable practices, and their roles in society. This holistic approach prepares them for future studies and responsible citizenship.

67. **(D):** The most appropriate response to students' enquiry in this context would be "Conduct and observe the experiment with different amounts of salt." By encouraging students to conduct and observe variations of the same experiment, they can better understand the effect of salt concentration on the buoyancy of the egg. It promotes hands-on learning, critical thinking, and reinforces the concept of density and its relationship with buoyancy.

68. **(B):** The Assertion (A) states that "Learning of EVS needs to be oriented to process skills relating to observation, identification, classification, etc." This is true as the nature of Environmental Studies demands a practical approach where students engage with the environment and its various components through observation, identification, and other process skills. The Reason (R) states "Through acquiring various process skills, the learning outcomes of EVS learning are expected to be achieved." This is also true, and it directly supports the assertion because by acquiring these process skills, students are better equipped to understand and engage with the subject matter, hence achieving the intended learning outcomes. Therefore, both (A) and (R) are true, and (R) is the correct explanation of (A).

69. **(B):** When preparing a question paper for summative assessment in EVS, the emphasis should be on "Content coverage and objectives of the question paper." The primary goal of summative assessment is to evaluate students' understanding and knowledge of the content covered during a specific period or course. Ensuring that the content is comprehensively covered in the assessment, while aligning with the learning objectives, ensures that students are evaluated on all relevant aspects of the subject.

70. **(B):** Voicing an opinion on issues observed/experienced and relating to social practices such as discrimination in ownership of resources is a rather advanced learning outcome and is typically expected from older students who are more capable of critical thinking and reflection on societal issues. The other listed outcomes, such as voicing opinion on good and bad touch or observing rules in local games, are more age-appropriate for Class III students.

71. **(D):** While simplicity of language, appealing illustrations, and child orientation are all essential criteria for selecting textbooks, it's paramount that the textbook should be devoid of any stereotypes or derogatory attitudes based on gender, caste, class, and religion. This ensures that students receive an unbiased, inclusive, and respectful education, fostering values of equality and tolerance from a young age.

72. **(C):** Assertion (A): 'There are themes rather than subjects in EVS at primary level' is correct. Teaching EVs in a theme-based manner is more relevant and engaging than teaching them in a topic-based manner at the primary level.

Reason (R): 'It is easier for teachers and students to learn theme-based EVS than subjects' is correct. Theme-based learning provides teachers with greater freedom and flexibility to engage in an engaging process with students. However, saying that theme-based EVS is 'easy' to learn actually limits the importance and usefulness of theme-based learning.

73. **(C):** Developing an EVS kit from available material is the most appropriate hands-on activity. While all the given options are interactive in nature, creating an EVS kit requires students to engage directly with multiple components of the environment. They can incorporate natural items, create models, or use tools that allow them to investigate and experiment with different environmental, social, and scientific concepts. This hands-on approach not only fosters understanding but also encourages creativity and problem-solving.

74. **(C):** Formative assessment in EVS is primarily "Assessment for learning" and "Assessment as learning". Formative assessment is used to monitor student learning and provide ongoing feedback that can be used by teachers to improve their teaching and by students to improve their learning. "Assessment for learning" helps educators recognize where students are struggling and address problems immediately, while "Assessment as learning" involves students in the assessment process where they monitor their own learning, ask questions, and use assessment feedback.

75. **(D):** Assertion (A) is true: Field trips are indeed an effective pedagogical strategy in EVS as they offer real-world experiences and a more holistic understanding of environmental, social, and scientific concepts. Reason (R) is, however, false: The primary purpose of field trips is not to promote memorization of objects, events, or places. Instead, they are intended to provide experiential learning, foster curiosity, and enable a deeper understanding of the topics at hand. Thus, while the assertion is true, the given reason is not the correct explanation for it.

76. **(C):** If we observe the geographical map of India, Gujarat is situated on the western part of the country. To its north-east lies the state of Uttar Pradesh. Moving further southeast from Gujarat, we reach the coastal state of Andhra Pradesh.

77. **(C):** Muscular energy is derived from the conversion of chemical energy stored in the food we eat. When Rama is playing cricket, his body's muscles contract and relax to enable movement, hitting the ball, running, and other activities associated with the game. This repeated contraction and relaxation of muscles requires energy. In the human body, adenosine triphosphate (ATP) is the primary molecule responsible for storing and transferring energy. When muscles contract, ATP is broken down, releasing energy that powers muscle cells. It's worth noting that the food we eat, after digestion, is broken down into glucose, and through various metabolic processes, is used to produce ATP. So, while Rama is directly using muscular energy, it is the chemical energy stored in his food that gets transformed into muscular energy, allowing him to play.

78. **(B):** Fuels, be it wood, coal, gasoline, or any other type, store potential chemical energy. When burned (or combusted), this chemical energy is released in the form of heat and light. This is a fundamental principle behind most of our energy production methods. For instance, in thermal power plants, coal is burned to produce heat which then converts water into steam. This steam powers turbines which generate electricity. The release of heat and light energy from

fuels is due to the exothermic nature of the combustion reaction.

79. **(A):** Bora rice, or glutinous rice, is a type of short-grained Asian rice that becomes particularly sticky when cooked. It's prevalent in Assam and other North-Eastern states of India. This rice has a unique texture and flavor and is often used in local delicacies, especially in festive treats. It plays a crucial role in Assamese cuisine and culture, particularly during Bihu, the state's most celebrated festival. Traditional Assamese dishes like 'Pitha' and 'Laru' made during Bihu use Bora rice as their primary ingredient. The stickiness of the rice comes from its high amylopectin content, which is a type of starch.

80. **(A):** Beekeeping, also known as apiculture, requires careful consideration of the local climate and the flowering seasons of plants. From October to December, many plants bloom in Bihar, providing bees with ample nectar and pollen sources. This period marks the post-monsoon season where the weather is neither too cold nor too hot, making it conducive for bee activity. Furthermore, initiating beekeeping during this time ensures that by the time spring arrives, the bee colonies are well-established and can take advantage of the major blooming season that spring brings.

82. **(A):** Among the given options, Odisha is the only state that has a coastline along the Bay of Bengal. Karnataka and Kerala are coastal states, but they are situated along the Arabian Sea, while Telangana is a landlocked state. Odisha's coastline stretches for about 485 kilometers along the northeastern part of the Bay of Bengal, making it an essential coastal state in the eastern region of India.

83. **(D):** The Kuduk language, spoken by the Paharia tribe in Jharkhand, uses the word 'Torang' for forest.

- Mizoram, located in the northeastern part of India, has a significant forest cover, and a large proportion of its population is associated with the forest in one way or another.
- The statement about the Village Council (Panchayat) in Jharkhand deciding land allocation by lottery is not accurate.
- The correct name of the Act is the "Forest Rights Act, 2006" (not 2007). The Act recognizes the rights of the forest-dwelling communities, but the specifics about the duration of residence might be interpreted differently.

84. **(D):** Density is defined as mass per unit volume.
Using the formula: Density = Mass/Volume
Given, Density = 24 g/mL and Volume = 6 mL
Mass = Density × Volume Mass
= 24 g/mL × 6 mL = 144 g.

85. **(D):** Snakes do not have the capability to chew their food. Instead, they swallow their prey whole. Their jaws are specially designed to expand and swallow prey that is much larger than their head. While snakes do have teeth, they don't use them for chewing but rather for holding onto their prey and guiding it into their throat.

86. **(A):** Bronze is an alloy primarily made of copper, with tin added. Historically, it was the first alloy to be used extensively by humans, marking the beginning of the Bronze Age. The addition of tin to copper improves the metal's hardness and durability. This alloy has been used for various applications, from weapons and tools to sculptures and bells, because of its favorable properties.

87. **(D):** Elephants, being the largest land mammals, have unique behaviors and habits. They don't sleep much, usually only two to four hours a day. This limited sleep pattern is still a subject of research. Elephants also love to play in mud and water. Mud baths serve multiple purposes for elephants: they act as sunscreen, protect against insect bites, and help cool the elephant. Water plays a crucial role in an elephant's life, not only for drinking but also for bathing and playing. It's a common sight to see elephants enjoying water sprays and mud baths in their natural habitat or even in captivity.

89. **(B):** Gases have molecules that are widely spaced apart, and there's a lot of empty space between them. When pressure is applied to a gas, the space between its molecules reduces, causing them to come closer together. This leads to the compression of the gas. This principle is utilized in various everyday applications, including the operation of gas cylinders.

90. **(A):** The stem plays a vital role in providing support to the plant, helping it stand upright, which is function. It also acts as a channel for the transportation of water, minerals, and nutrients from the roots to the leaves and other parts of the plant, which is function. While the stem does play a role in storing food in some plants, it's not its primary function across all plants. The main site for the production of food (through photosynthesis) is the leaves, not the stem. However, certain plants like potato store food in their stems.

91. **(D):** Self-monitoring refers to the process of being aware of, and attentive to, one's own performance or output. When a person focuses on ensuring that the language they use is correct, they are consciously overseeing their own linguistic output to make sure it adheres to proper norms and standards. This kind of introspective awareness is crucial for learners, especially when mastering a new language, as it aids in catching and rectifying mistakes in real-time, promoting better learning outcomes.

92. **(D):** Total Physical Response (TPR) is a method of teaching language that incorporates physical movement to react to verbal input. The aim is to associate physical movement with the linguistic terms, fostering a more immersive learning experience. When students sing "Head and shoulders, knees and toes" and simultaneously touch the corresponding body part, they are physically responding to the verbal input. TPR is especially effective in the early stages of language learning and with young learners, as it engages multiple senses, making learning more memorable and enjoyable.

93. **(A):** Peer assessment refers to students assessing the performance or work of their classmates. In the scenario described, after working in groups to answer vocabulary questions, students exchange their questions with another group. The act of one group assessing or evaluating the responses of another group is an example of peer assessment. This method of evaluation not only helps students understand assessment criteria but also fosters collaboration, critical thinking, and the ability to give and receive constructive feedback. Peer assessment can be a powerful tool in the educational process, promoting self-awareness and an understanding of the subject matter from different perspectives.

94. **(A):** The activity described involves acting out a word or phrase, which is a kinesthetic learning style. Kinesthetic learners absorb information best when they can use physical activities as part of the learning process. By acting out the word or phrase, the learner is physically engaged, making it easier for them to remember and understand the language. This type of learning taps into the motor memory of the learner, which can be especially effective in recalling and understanding information.

95. **(D):** It's true that all children who enter school are competent language users according to their age. This is based on the premise that children, by the time they enter school, have already acquired a significant amount of their native language and can communicate effectively within their age group. However, the statement that they cannot demonstrate their abilities due to language and cultural diversity is incorrect. While cultural and language differences can sometimes present challenges in traditional classroom settings, they don't render children incapable of demonstrating their linguistic abilities. It's important for educators to recognize and value the linguistic backgrounds of all students and to provide learning environments that support and celebrate diversity.

96. **(D):** Pragmatics refers to the study of how context influences the way language is interpreted. It deals with the way speakers use language in different social situations and the various factors that influence our interpretation of language, such as the relationship between the speakers, the setting of the conversation, and the shared knowledge of the participants. When Manjeet adjusts his speech based on who he is speaking to, he is demonstrating an understanding of the social rules and contexts that dictate appropriate language use. This ability to adjust one's language based on social cues and situations is a key component of pragmatics.

97. **(C):** Behaviourism, particularly in the context of B.F. Skinner's theory, posits that language is learned through imitation, reinforcement, and other forms of conditioning. According to this theory, children learn language by mimicking the speech they hear and then receiving feedback (either positive or negative) on their attempts. The mother's belief that her child learns language by imitating people aligns with this theory. However, the fact that the child sometimes says things she hasn't heard from adults or siblings challenges strict behaviorist views and suggests that there's more to language acquisition than mere imitation.

98. **(A):** Emergent literacy refers to the early skills and knowledge about reading and writing that precede traditional literacy instruction. These foundational skills include understanding the directionality of text, recognizing that print carries meaning, developing a sense of story structure, recognizing letters and some letter-sound correspondences, and scribbling as a precursor to writing. These skills develop through exposure to books, shared reading experiences, and other literacy-rich activities, long before formal reading instruction begins in school.

99. **(D):** Dialogic reading is a shared reading activity where the adult and the child have a dialogue or conversation around the content of the book. Instead of passively listening, the child becomes an active participant. The adult uses prompts to encourage the child to talk about the book and expands on what the child says, guiding their understanding and engagement. This technique goes beyond just reading aloud; it turns the reading session into an interactive experience, fostering deeper comprehension and engagement. The grandmother's technique of reading stories and actively engaging the children in a conversation about the content embodies the principles of dialogic reading.

100. **(C):** The bottom-up approach to reading instruction begins with the smallest units of language, such as letters and phonemes, and builds up to larger units like words, sentences, and complete texts.

This approach is grounded in the idea that reading comprehension is a process of constructing meaning by decoding the letters and words on a page. Thus, understanding the basic elements of language and their relationships is key. Only after mastering these basic elements do learners move on to more complex reading tasks.

101. **(A):** Phonetic or "invented" spelling is a normal part of children's development as they learn to write. It represents children's attempts to use their developing knowledge of phonics (the relationship between letters and sounds) to spell words the way they sound. The statement in Assertion (A) claims that using phonetic spelling slows down the ability to learn to spell correctly, which is not supported by evidence. Many educators believe that children's use of invented spelling does not hinder their eventual acquisition of conventional spelling, as indicated in Reason (R). Over time, with exposure to correct spelling through reading and explicit instruction, children typically transition from invented to conventional spelling.

102. **(C):** Engaging students in game-like activities that require verbal interaction is an effective way to build their confidence in speaking a new language. Such activities make language practice fun, interactive, and less intimidating. They allow students to practice pronunciation, vocabulary, and conversational skills in a low-pressure environment. Unlike error correction, which can make students self-conscious, or reading aloud, which might not address pronunciation issues, game-like activities promote spontaneous language use. These activities encourage students to think quickly, respond in real-time, and interact with peers, all of which boost their speaking confidence.

103. **(D):** Contextual learning is a crucial component of vocabulary acquisition. Introducing new vocabulary words within a context helps learners to create mental associations and aids in comprehension and recall. When a teacher explains a word's meaning in the situation in which it occurs, they provide a framework for learners to understand and remember the word more effectively. This is much more meaningful than simply providing a definition or translation. The context in which a word is used provides clues about its meaning, which can be more engaging and memorable for learners than a standalone definition.

104. **(A):** Learning a language is a matter of skill. Language learning involves the acquisition of a set of skills: listening, speaking, reading, and writing. Like other skills, these develop and improve through regular practice, exposure, and use. While there is an element of acquiring knowledge (like vocabulary and grammar rules) in language learning, the real proficiency comes from the ability to use the language effectively in real-life situations, which is a skill. This differentiates it from mere knowledge-based subjects.

105. **(B):**

- **Predicting:** Readers often use clues such as titles, subtitles, images, and introductory sentences to predict what a text might be about. This helps set the context and prepares them for what they are about to read.
- **Inferring attitude:** This involves understanding the writer's feelings or attitudes based on how he/she express themselves in the text. It's more about reading between the lines and understanding the nuances in the choice of words and tone.
- **Deducing meaning from context:** When readers come across unfamiliar words, they often look for clues within the surrounding text to understand the meaning. They might consider the sentences before and after the unfamiliar word to deduce its meaning.
- **Intensive reading:** This type of reading is focused and detailed, aiming to gain a deep understanding of the text. Here, readers focus on the language, structure, and the intricate details of the text.
- **Identifying text organization:** This involves recognizing the structure and layout of a text. By noticing headings, subheadings, bullet points, or introductory phrases, readers can get a sense of how the information is organized and presented.

106. **(D):** The passage mentions that Geeta Garud found traveling solo to be a "liberating experience." This indicates that she felt a sense of freedom while traveling alone. The passage does not provide any information that suggests the journey was tiring for her. Thus, the statement that resonates with her experience as mentioned in the text is that she was breathing an air of freedom.

107. **(C):** In the passage, it is mentioned that "Before going on her week-long holiday, she was hesitant about travelling by herself. Garud had asked friends and family but found no takers." This indicates that she had sought companionship for her trip but did not find anyone willing to accompany her.

108. **(B):** The passage mentions that Geeta Garud was initially hesitant about traveling by herself, which validates statement as true. However, the passage does not mention that she wanted only a friend to go with her. She had asked both friends and family, making statement false.

109. **(C):** There's no mention in the passage that she practiced for a day before dancing, making statement (*a*) false. The passage does mention her taking up horse-riding, which can be seen as a courageous skill, validating statement (*b*) as true. Furthermore, the fact that she was an athlete in her youth might have given her the confidence to try horse-riding, making statement (*c*) true.

110. **(D):** The passage describes Geeta Garud walking on a narrow ledge behind a waterfall as something she wouldn't have tried in her younger years, suggesting that it was a challenging activity. Thus, the statement that walking on a narrow ledge is an easy task is not true based on the context provided.

112. **(D):** The word "but" is used to introduce a contrast or exception to the previous statement. In this context, it contrasts the fact that she had asked friends and family with the fact that she found no takers. This function makes "but" a conjunction.

113. **(C):** The word "hesitant" refers to being unsure or reluctant about doing something. "Disinclined" is a word that also means being unwilling or averse to do something, making it the closest in meaning to "hesitant."

114. **(B):** The word "relishing" means to enjoy or take pleasure in something. The opposite of enjoying or taking pleasure in something would be "disliking" or not enjoying it. Thus, "disliking" is the antonym for "relishing."

115. **(C):** The poem emphasizes the fleeting nature of youth and beauty, urging the addressee to make the most of their time while they are young. With references to "Gather ye rosebuds while ye may" and "while ye may, go marry," it's clear that the poem is addressing a young woman, encouraging her to seize the moment and make the most of her youth.

116. **(B):** The sun in the poem represents the passage of time. As mentioned, "The glorious lamp of heaven, the sun, The higher he's a-getting, The sooner will his race be run," it indicates that as the sun rises and reaches its zenith, it's also approaching its setting. This metaphorically highlights the idea that even at the peak of one's youth, aging and the eventual decline is inevitable.

117. **(A):** Throughout the poem, the poet emphasizes the transitory nature of youth and the importance of seizing the moment. In lines like "Then be not coy, but use your time, And while ye may, go marry," the poet explicitly suggests that young age is not only fleeting but also the ideal time to find one's love and get married.

118. **(D):** The line "Gather ye rosebuds while ye may" metaphorically suggests that one should enjoy and make the most of their life when they are young and vibrant, which validates statement (*a*) as true. The description of the sun, "The glorious lamp of heaven, the sun, The higher he's a-getting, The sooner will his race be run," implies that just as the sun cannot shine forever, youth and beauty are temporary, making statement (*b*) true as well.

119. **(D):** In the line "And this same flower that smiles today," the flower is attributed with the human quality of smiling. Giving human traits to an inanimate object is a literary device known as personification.

120. **(C):** The line "The glorious lamp of heaven, the sun" equates the sun with a lamp, without using words like "as" or "like." This direct comparison between two unlike things, suggesting they are the same, is a literary device known as metaphor. The sun is metaphorically referred to as a lamp that lights up the heaven.

121. **(D):** प्रस्तुत गद्यांश में स्पष्ट कहा गया है कि 'जीवन में कभी अभाव का दुख, कभी स्वभाव का दुख और कभी दुर्भाव का दुख और इससे भी ऊपर सदैव तनाव का दुख घेरे रहता है।' इससे स्पष्ट है कि सबसे बड़ा दुख तनाव को माना गया है।

122. **(A):** चूँकि दुखों के वशीभूत हम टकराव की जिंदगी जीते हुए बिखराव का दुख भोगते हैं। दुखों से सभी डरते हैं, क्योंकि दुख अप्रिय है। दुखों से दूर रहने और सुख पाने की चाह में हम नए-नए पापों में प्रवेश करने लगते हैं। यही हमारी सबसे बड़ी भूल है। अतः प्रश्नानुसार सुख पाने के लिए गलत काम करने को ही सबसे बड़ी भूल माना गया है।

123. **(C):** सुख की कामना में मनुष्य नित्य नए-नए पाप कर्म को करता जा रहा है। यही पाप का फल सुख के आस्वादन को रोकता है। सुख की इच्छा रखने के लिए आवश्यक है कि सर्वप्रथम पाप कर्मों से मुक्त होने की चाह रहे। यही पाप कर्मों से मुक्ति सुख की तरफ ले जाता है। अतः दुख से छुटकारा प्राप्त करना है तो उसका एकमात्र रास्ता है—धर्म को आत्मसात करना। क्योंकि जहाँ धर्म है वहाँ पाप नहीं, जहाँ पाप नहीं वहाँ सुख है।

124. **(A):** दिया गया गद्यांश पाप कर्म, पाप का फल, दुख, सुख प्राप्ति के मार्ग को विषय बनाकर लिखा गया है। दुख के कारणों के बारे में बताया गया है कि यह हमारी भूल और हमारे मानवीय स्तर से गिरकर घिनौने कर्मों का फल है। पूरे गद्यांश में दंड की चर्चा नहीं है।

125. **(B):** गलत कार्य करने से सुख की हानि होती है। क्योंकि दुखों से दूर रहने और सुख की इच्छा में हम नए-नए पाप करते रहते हैं। यही पाप कर्म हमारी सबसे बड़ी भूल है जो हमें सुख प्राप्त करने से रोकता है।

126. **(A):** प्रत्यय शब्दों के अंत में लगकर शब्दों की विशेषता में परिवर्तन ला देते हैं। 'इक' प्रत्यय से निर्मित शब्द—सामाजिक, धार्मिक, आर्थिक, दैनिक, नैतिक, ऐतिहासिक, सांसारिक, प्रायोगिक, साप्ताहिक, जैविक, शैक्षिक, प्रामाणिक, प्राथमिक आदि।

127. **(D):** सुख, दुख और धर्म भाववाचक संज्ञा है जबकि पापी का संबंध पाप करने वाले व्यक्ति से है, यह विशेषण है।

128. **(C):** संगाई महोत्सव का आयोजन मणिपुर में किया गया। इसके माध्यम से मणिपुर के लोगों की भावना और जज्बे को दिखाया गया। यह महोत्सव निवेशकों और औद्योगिकीकरण में भी महत्व रखता है।

129. **(A):** भारत में पर्व, उत्सव और मेलों की सदियों पुरानी परम्परा है। यह हमारी जीवंत संस्कृति का उदाहरण है। भारत की परम्परा में संघर्ष का कोई जिक्र नहीं है। गद्यांश का विषय भारतीय परम्परा और मणिपुर में आयोजित 'संगाई महोत्सव' है।

130. **(C):** गद्यांश में कहा गया है कि मणिपुर प्राकृतिक सौन्दर्य, सांस्कृतिक, समृद्धि से भरा ऐसा राज्य है कि हर कोई यहाँ एक बार जरूर आना चाहता है। यहाँ मणिपुर की विशेषता उसके प्राकृतिक सौन्दर्य और संस्कृति से है।

131. **(A):** 'संगाई महोत्सव' जैसे आयोजन निवेशकों और इंडस्ट्री को आकर्षित करते हैं। इस प्रकार के उत्सव से ना सिर्फ संस्कृति समृद्ध होती है, बल्कि स्थानीय अर्थव्यवस्था को भी बहुत ताकत मिलती है।

132. **(C):** 'संगाई महोत्सव' पहले इम्फाल तक ही सीमित रहता था। अब इसे ज्यादा से ज्यादा लोगों को साथ जोड़ने के लिए पूरे राज्य में आयोजित किया जाता है।

133. **(C):** दो वर्णों (स्वर या व्यंजन) के मेल से होने वाले विकार को संधि कहते हैं। इसमें दो-दो शब्दों के मेल से तीसरे शब्द की रचना होती है। संधि के तीन प्रकार हैं–1. स्वर, 2. व्यंजन और 3. विसर्ग।

महोत्सव में गुण संधि है। महा + उत्सव = महोत्सव।

134. **(D):** 'आकर्षित' में मूल शब्द आकर्षण एक संज्ञा विशेषण है जिसमें तद्धित प्रत्यय (गुणवाचक तद्धित प्रत्यय) 'इत' जुड़ने से बना शब्द 'आकर्षित' गुणवाचक विशेषण कहा जाएगा। वैसे शब्दांश जो संज्ञा, सर्वनाम और विशेषण इत्यादि में लगकर नवीन शब्द की रचना करते हैं, उसे तद्धित प्रत्यय कहते हैं।

135. **(B):** गद्यांश में कहा गया है कि 'संगाई महोत्सव' जैसे आयोजन निवेशकों और इंडस्ट्री को भी आकर्षित करते हैं। ऐसे आयोजनों को ज्यादा से ज्यादा लोगों के साथ जोड़ा जाता है तभी इसकी पूरी क्षमता सामने आ पाती है। इससे स्पष्ट है कि पूरे गद्यांश में महोत्सव की क्षमता की बात कही गई है न कि स्थानीय कला, मणिपुर और सांस्कृतिक समृद्धि की।

136. **(B):** पाठ पढ़ाना, विशेष रूप से छोटे बच्चों के लिए, आनंददायक, रोचक, दोहरावदार और समझने योग्य होना चाहिए। कक्षा में लागू की जा सकने वाली वैकल्पिक विधियों में से एक तथाकथित सम्पूर्ण भौतिक प्रतिक्रिया है। समग्र भौतिक प्रतिक्रिया (TPR) पद्धति एक निर्देशात्मक दृष्टिकोण है जिनमें भाषा सीखने को सुदृढ़ करने के लिए शारीरिक गति और क्रियाओं का उपयोग करना शामिल है। यह युवा शिक्षार्थियों के लिए विशेष रूप से प्रभावी है। TPR में, छात्र शारीरिक क्रियाओं के माध्यम से बोली जाने वाली भाषा के आदेशों का जवाब देते हैं और यह सक्रिय जुड़ाव शब्दावली और भाषा रचना को आंतरिक बनाने में मदद करती है।

137. **(B):** व्याकरण शिक्षण के निगमनात्मक दृष्टिकोण में व्याकरण के नियमों को प्रस्तुत करना और फिर उन नियमों का अभ्यास करने के लिए उदाहरण और अभ्यास प्रदान करना शामिल है। यह इस विश्वास को प्रोत्साहित करता है कि भाषा सीखना नियमों को सीखने और उन्हें लागू करने का मामला है, जो आगमनात्मक दृष्टिकोण के विपरीत है जो एक्सपोजर और उपयोग के माध्यम से व्याकरण नियमों की खोज पर जोर देता है।

138. **(C):** विशेष रूप से युवा शिक्षार्थियों को निःशुल्क लेखन कार्य देते समय सटीकता के बजाय प्रवाह पर ध्यान देना महत्वपूर्ण है। लक्ष्य छात्रों को स्वयं को अभिव्यक्त करने और अपने विचारों को स्वतंत्र रूप से संप्रेषित करने के लिए प्रोत्साहित करना है। लिखावट और सटीकता को बाद के चरणों में अलग से संबोधित किया जा सकता है।

139. **(D):** पढ़ने की समझ में, 'नीचे से ऊपर' दृष्टिकोण में पाठ के अर्थ को समझने के लिए उसके शब्दों और वाक्यांशों पर ध्यान केंद्रित करना शामिल है। यह दृष्टिकोण समझ बनाने के लिए व्यक्तिगत शब्दों और वाक्यों का विश्लेषण और डिकोडिंग पर जोर देता है, जबकि 'ऊपर से नीचे' समग्र अर्थ और संदर्भ पर ध्यान केंद्रित करता है।

140. **(B):** भाषा अध्यापक से अपेक्षाएँ की जाती हैं कि–विद्यालयी दुनिया बच्चों की दुनिया से कुछ अलग होती है, जिसके कारण उनमें संकोच, झिझक आदि भाव प्रायः देखने को मिलता है। ये भाव बच्चों के शिक्षा ग्रहण करने के मार्ग में बाधक होते हैं। ऐसे में शिक्षक के समक्ष शिक्षा देने के साथ ही उनमें निहित इन भावों को दूर करने की भी चुनौती होती है। इस चुनौती में सबसे पहला पड़ाव बच्चों से जुड़ाव का होता है। इसके लिए अध्यापक को जरूरी है बच्चों की सम्प्रेषणात्मक आवश्यकताओं की पहचान करे तथा वार्तालाप के लिए सहज वातावरण का निर्माण करे।

141. **(B):** उद्गामी (इमरजेन्ट) साक्षरता कौशल का तात्पर्य प्रारम्भिक मूलभूत कौशल और व्यवहार से है जो बच्चों में तब विकसित होता है जब वे लिखित भाषा और उसके घटकों से परिचित हो जाते हैं। परिदृश्य में क्रियाएँ बच्चों की किताबों के प्रति बढ़ती जागरूकता, उनके अभिविन्यास और सामग्री तक पहुँचने के लिए पन्ने पलटने की अवधारणा को दर्शाती है जो सभी उभरते साक्षरता विकास के संकेत हैं।

142. **(A):** **भाषा अर्जन :** इस प्रक्रिया में बालक सुनकर, बोलकर भाषा ग्रहण करता है तथा निरंतर परिमार्जन करता रहता है। भाषा सीखने की प्रक्रिया में भाषा अर्जन की प्रक्रिया महत्वपूर्ण होती है। सीखी हुई भाषा को समझने की क्षमता अर्पित करना तथा उसे दैनिक जीवन में प्रयोग में लाने को भाषा अर्जन कहते हैं। प्रसिद्ध भाषा वैज्ञानिक नोआम चॉमस्की का मानना है कि बच्चों में भाषा अंतर्निहित एवं जन्मजात होती है। चॉमस्की का दृढ़ विश्वास है कि

शिक्षार्थी भाषा अर्जित करने की क्षमता के कारण ही भाषा सीखते हैं। उनमें भाषायी विकास एक काल्पनिक भाषा उपकरण (Language Acquisition Device) द्वारा होता है। उन पर परिवेश का गहरा प्रभाव पड़ता है।

143. **(D):** समग्र भाषा उपागम बच्चों के भाषायी विकास की स्पष्ट समझ पर बल देती है।

- भाषा को समग्रता की दृष्टि से देखने पर ही भाषा प्रयोग में अर्थ निर्माण की प्रक्रिया बन पाती है। भाषा को टुकड़े में पढ़ने पर वाक्य का अर्थ गुम हो जाता है।
- समग्रतावादी दृष्टिकोण रखने वाला शिक्षार्थी भाषा को पूर्ण व अर्थपूर्ण वाक्य के रूप में सीखना प्रारम्भ करता है।

144. **(A):** भाषा मुख से उच्चरित होने वाली वह ध्वनि है जिसका प्रयोग मनुष्य अपने मन के विचारों का आदान-प्रदान करने के लिए करता है। भाषा एक औजार है जिसका उपयोग मनुष्य जिंदगी से जुड़ने के लिए तथा जिंदगी के अनुभवों को साझा करने के लिए करता है।

- चिंतन मानसिक क्रिया का ज्ञानात्मक पहलू है। यह मन की बातों से सम्बन्धित मानसिक क्रिया है। चिंतन इच्छा संबंधी क्रिया है जो किसी असंतोष के कारण आरम्भ होती है और प्रयास के आधार पर चलती हुई उस स्थिति पर पहुँच जाती है जो इच्छा को सन्तुष्ट करती है।
- भाषा के प्रत्येक क्षेत्र में चिंतन शामिल होता है। भाषा के बारे में चिंतन करने की योग्यता को अधिभाषिक योग्यता कहा जाता है। हम अपनी विचाराभिव्यक्ति में जब कोई चिंतन करते हैं तो वह भाषा का ही कोई न कोई रूप होता है। भाषा ध्वनि प्रतीकों की वह व्यवस्था है जिसके द्वारा कोई मनुष्य बोलकर या लिखकर स्पष्टता के साथ अपने विचारों को दूसरे व्यक्ति तक पहुँचा सकता है और दूसरों की बात समझ सकता है।

145. **(C):** बच्चों में भाषा को तेजी से और रचनात्मक ढंग से सीखने की अद्भुत क्षमता होती है। हालाँकि वे वयस्कों और अपने आस-पास के वातावरण की नकल करके सीखते हैं, वे भाषायी रचनात्मकता और नवीनता का भी प्रदर्शन करते हैं। ऐसा इसलिए संभव है क्योंकि मानव मस्तिष्क स्वाभाविक रूप से भाषा प्राप्त करने के लिए पूर्व निर्धारित है। बच्चे मात्र निष्क्रिय नकल करने वाले नहीं हैं, वे प्राप्त भाषा इनपुट को सक्रिय रूप से संसाधित करते हैं और इसका उपयोग अपनी भाषायी संरचनाओं के निर्माण के लिए करते हैं। इस घटना को अक्सर 'उत्तेजना की गरीबी' के रूप में जाना जाता है, जहाँ बच्चे व्याकरणिक रूप से सही वाक्य उत्पन्न करने में सक्षम होते हैं जिन्हें उन्होंने पहले कभी सीधे नहीं सुना है।

146. **(D):** संभाषिक पठन एक ऐसी तकनीक है जिसका उपयोग प्रारम्भिक साक्षरता को सुविधाजनक बनाने के लिए किया जाता है जहाँ एक वयस्क और एक बच्चा एक किताब के बारे में बातचीत में संलग्न होते हैं। वयस्क बच्चे से प्रश्न पूछकर, कहानी पर चर्चा करके और भविष्यवाणियाँ करके सक्रिय रूप से भाग लेने के लिए प्रोत्साहित करता है। फिर भूमिकाएँ बदल जाती हैं और बच्चा प्रश्न पूछने वाला और पुस्तक के बारे में वयस्कों के साथ बातचीत में शामिल होने वाला बन जाता है। यह संवादात्मक दृष्टिकोण भाषा के विकास, समझ और पढ़ने के प्रति प्रेम को बढ़ावा देने में मदद करता है।

147. **(D):** श्रवण कौशल का अर्थ होता है सुनने की कला विकसित करना। श्रवण कौशल ग्रहित कौशल (जिसे ग्रहण किया जा सके) होता है जिसमें छात्र के मस्तिष्क की एकाग्रता व संयम जरूरी होता है। सुनते समय ध्वनियाँ उसके मन-मस्तिष्क पर अंकित हो जाती हैं, यह अंकित ध्वनियाँ ही छात्र की भाषा ज्ञान का आधार बनती है। अच्छी प्रकार से सुनने के कारण ही छात्र ध्वनियों के सूक्ष्म अंतर को समझ पाता है। श्रवण कौशल ही अन्य भाषा कौशल को विकसित करने का आधार बनता है। इसमें ध्वनियों के सूक्ष्म अंतर को पहचानने की क्षमता विकसित होती है। यदि छात्र के श्रवण इंद्रियों में दोष है तो ना ही छात्र भाषा सीख सकता है और ना ही अपने मनोभावों को व्यक्त कर सकता है। अतः इसका भाषा ज्ञान शून्य के बराबर ही रहेगा। अतः एक अध्यापक अपने छात्रों को श्रवण के उपयुक्त तत्वों को जुटाकर ही श्रवण कौशल को विकसित कर सकता है।

148. **(A):** प्राथमिक स्तर पर भाषा में सटीकता नहीं अपितु भाषा के प्रति बच्चों में आकर्षण तथा व्याकरण को पाठ्यचर्या का हिस्सा होना आवश्यक है। अतः अभिकथन गलत है जबकि तर्क सही है।

149. **(D):** शिक्षण की प्रणाली को ही उपागम कहते हैं, उपागम को अंग्रेजी में Approach कहते हैं। शिक्षण विधियाँ शिक्षण उपागम पर ही आधारित होती हैं। किसी भी भाषा शिक्षण उपागम को समझना एक सैद्धांतिक दृष्टिकोण है, कि भाषा क्या है? इसे कैसे सीखा जा सकता है? जैसे किसी भी पाठ को पढ़ने के लिए एक पाठ योजना बनाते हैं और इस पाठ योजना में छात्रों को पाठ समझाने के दृष्टिकोण से अधिक शिक्षण विधियों का प्रयोग करते हैं तो यहाँ पाठ योजना एक उपागम है एवं जिन तरीकों से शिक्षण करवाया जाता है, वह शिक्षण विधियाँ हैं। भाषा, ध्वनि शब्द और वाक्य के क्रियात्मक व प्रयोगात्मक शिक्षण के प्रमुख उपागम हैं।

150. **(C):** रचनात्मक मूल्यांकन छात्रों के प्रदर्शन का आकलन करता है। उसका मुख्य उद्देश्य शिक्षक और छात्र दोनों के लिए निरंतर प्रतिक्रिया प्रदान करना है जो शिक्षण प्रक्रिया में सफलताओं और असफलताओं से संबंधित है। इसका उपयोग निर्देश देते समय छात्रों को सीखने की प्रगति की निगरानी के लिए किया जाता है। छात्रों की प्रतिक्रिया सफल अधिगम को पुष्ट करती है और विशिष्ट लक्षण त्रुटियों की पहचान करती है जिनमें सुधार की आवश्यकता होती है। एक शिक्षक के लिए, रचनात्मक मूल्यांकन निर्देशों और उपायों को अधिक प्रभावी बनाने के लिए जानकारी प्रदान करता है।

Previous Paper (Solved)

CTET—Paper-I, January/February 2023

(Exam held on 07-02-2023)

PART- I

Child Development and Pedagogy

1. The progression of development of children in primary years is from:
A. simple to complex B. abstract to concrete
C. global to local D. specific to general

2. Which of the following is a 'sensitive period' for language development?
A. Early childhood B. Middle childhood
C. Adolescence D. Pre-natal

3. The process by which children learn their societal role is referred to as ________.
A. socialisation B. assimilation
C. accomodation D. adaptation

4. At which stage of cognitive development do children begin imitation and achieve object permanence?
A. Sensorimotor B. Preoperational
C. Concrete operational D. Formal operational

5. In Jean Piaget's theory a child who perceives the sun as being alive because it gives out light is demonstrating:
A. animistic thinking B. centration
C. irreversibility D. object permanence

6. Which of the following concepts is **not** proposed by Lev Vygotsky?
A. Zone of Proximal Development
B. Schema
C. Scaffolding
D. Social Interaction

7. Which of the following statements is a correct pedagogical implication of Lev Vygotsky's theory:
A. Encouraging competition among students rather than collaboration
B. Encouraging desired behaviour through rewards and reducing undesired behaviour through punishment
C. Scaffolding the students by providing appropriate prompts and cues
D. Promoting association between stimulus and response

8. According to Kohlberg the first stage of moral development is characterised by:
A. Seeing rules as fixed and absolute
B. Maintaining affection and approval of others
C. A duty to uphold laws and rules for their own sake
D. Abstract universal principles that are valid for all humanity

9. In a progressive classroom:
A. children are forced to learn according to the prescribed syllabus.
B. children engage in activities that realise their potential.
C. children are labelled and segregated based on their abilities.
D. children work to get rewards and avoid punishments.

10. Which of the following type of intelligence was described by Howard Gardner ?
A. Generic Intelligence B. Linguistic Intelligence
C. Physical Intelligence D. Specific Intelligence

11. In a primary classroom the teachers should ________ 'private speech' – self talk that guides thinking and action.
A. encourage B. discourage
C. ignore D. punish children for

12. Seeing the role of boys at home and in the society, Mohan refused to play the role of a girl in a program organized in the school, saying that because he is a boy, he will not wear a girl's dress. It shows:
A. Gender role flexibility
B. Gender equality
C. Gender mobility
D. Gender typing

13. The process of teaching and learning for students of differing abilities in the same class is referred to as:
A. differentiated instruction
B. standardized instruction
C. stimulation
D. conditioning

14. In socio-constructivist classroom what is the primary mode of assessment?
A. Recall-based objective type tests
B. Collaborative projects
C. Standardized tests
D. Norm-referenced tests

15. The most important objective of the assessment of learners is:
A. To reflect on the effectiveness of the pedagogy and modify it to enhance learning.
B. To complete one of the tasks assigned to teachers.
C. To complete records and registers.
D. To create same ability grouping in class.

16. Providing choice and options to students from a range of activities and experiences based on their interests, needs and diversity of learner's background, follows the principle of:
A. inclusion
B. labelling and segregation
C. competition
D. exclusion

17. Which of the following does **not** promote cultural sensitivity in class?
A. Organising activities related to different cultures
B. Encouraging sharing of experiences by students about their culture
C. Celebrating festivals of dominant cultures only
D. Accepting and respecting diverse backgrounds of each student

18. Challenges in reading texts and comprehending long passages is a challenge for students with:
A. dyscalculia B. dyslexia
C. hearing impairment D. dysgraphia

19. Which of the learning materials is **not** suitable for children with hearing impairment?
A. Audiobooks
B. Printed books
C. Videos with subtitles
D. Three-dimensional charts and maps

20. What type of questions should a teacher ask in order to identify creative children in her class?
A. Fill in the blanks
B. Multiple choice questions
C. Questions with right and wrong options
D. Open-ended questions

21. It is important to________ experiences that a child brings to school.
A. ignore B. dismiss
C. build on D. disregard

22. How do children learn?
(*i*) Making and Doing things
(*ii*) Reading and Writing
(*iii*) Talking and Listening
(*iv*) Thinking and Reflecting
A. (*i*), (*iv*) B. (*iii*), (*iv*)
C. (*i*), (*iii*), (*iv*) D. (*i*), (*ii*), (*iii*), (*iv*)

23. In which of the following class are students likely to learn well?
A. Teacher emphasizes passive reception of knowledge.
B. Teacher believes only children with high IQ can do well in academics.
C. Teacher allows children to follow their own pace of learning.
D. Teacher follows standard curriculum for all children.

24. When teachers include experiences of children and give examples from their socio-cultural context, it fosters a sense of __________ in children.
A. belonging B. inferiority
C. anger D. alienation

25. The processes of problem-solving is promoted through:
A. analogical thinking
B. passive imitation
C. response set
D. functional fixedness

26. Children's misconceptions and errors:
A. are extremely detrimental to teaching-learning process
B. show their irrational ways of thinking
C. serve as significant inroads to childrens' thoughts
D. confirm their inferiority to adults

27. ________ is a sign that the learning activities have become mechanically repetitive for the child and are not of interest.
A. Joy B. Curiosity
C. Excitement D. Boredom

28. **Assertion (A):** Learning should be facilitated by inducing fear of punishment in children.

Reason (R): Rewards and punishment are highly effective in ensuring meaningful learning.

Choose the correct option:
A. Both (A) and (R) are true and (R) is the correct explanation of (A)
B. Both (A) and (R) are true, but (R) is not the correct explanation of (A)
C. (A) is true, but (R) is false
D. Both (A) and (R) are false

29. Which of the following factors affect learning?
(*i*) Interest of the students
(*ii*) Perceived relevance of the concept
(*iii*) Development level of the students
(*iv*) Strategies of teaching-learning
A. (*i*), (*iii*) B. (*i*), (*iv*)
C. (*ii*), (*iii*) D. (*i*), (*ii*), (*iii*), (*iv*)

30. Which of the following statements is correct about the interaction of person, environment and behaviour in learning settings?

A. Personal factors have no effect on the elements of environment.

B. All three forces – personal, environmental and behavioural are influenced by each other.

C. Behaviours seldom affect social environment.

D. Feedback from the environment cannot affect self-esteem of the individual.

PART- II

Mathematics

31. I am a four-digit number less than 2000. My first digit is one-fourth of the third digit (from left) and last digit is 8 times that of first. If the sum of first three-digits is 7, identify me.

A. 2481 B. 1842
C. 1428 D. 1248

32. There were 15 families in a flood relief camp. 300 kg of rice has to be distributed among the families. If it was distributed equally among all families, how much rice will each family get?

A. 20 kg B. 15 kg
C. 35 kg D. 30 kg

33. Two numbers which are in the ratio 11 : 17 have LCM 4675. These numbers are respectively:

A. 55 and 85 B. 275 and 425
C. 165 and 255 D. 330 and 510

34. A ten-digit number 774958 N_1 96 N_2 is divisible by 8 and 9. Then, the values of N_1 and N_2 can be respectively:

A. 7, 8 B. 0, 8
C. 5, 8 D. 6, 4

35. What is the sum of the place values of digit 4 in the number 5432413?

A. 400004 B. 400400
C. 404000 D. 400040

36. The sum of the smallest five-digit number and the largest four-digit number is:

A. 19099 B. 29999
C. 10999 D. 19999

37. Which direction will you face, if you start facing East and make $1\frac{1}{2}$ of a revolution clockwise?

A. North B. South
C. East D. West

38. Value of $\left(5\frac{1}{3}-2\frac{2}{3}\right)$ right-angles is equal to:

A. 210° B. 240°
C. 270° D. 300°

39. The number of lines of symmetry in a kite is/are:

A. 0 B. 1
C. 2 D. 4

40. Priya went to a shop with a ₹ 500 note. She purchased one soap, one toothpaste, one hair oil, one shampoo and one comb for ₹ 36, ₹ 85, ₹ 110, ₹ 160 and ₹ 13 respectively. She gave to the shopkeeper ₹ 500 note and he returned her ₹ 95. She checked and found that:

A. Shopkeeper has returned ₹ 1 less.
B. Shopkeeper has returned ₹ 1 more.
C. Returned amount is correct.
D. Returned amount is ₹ 9 less.

41. Mr. Hari made a will in which he gave his two children Arya and Bharati plots of sizes 20 m × 90 m and 30 m × 60 m respectively. But the children were not happy. The correct reason can be:

A. Arya was unhappy as he felt that area of Bharati's plot is more.
B. Bharati was unhappy as she felt that perimeter of Arya's plot is more.
C. They thought that areas of their plots are not equal.
D. Arya was unhappy as he felt perimeter of Bharati's plot is more.

42. Water is filled in a tank, using a pipe such that after each 1 minute water level rises by 2 cm. Keerthi started measuring the height at 9:45 am. At 9:47 am, height of water was 23 cm. What was the height of water level at 9:40 am?

A. 9 cm B. 10 cm
C. 11 cm D. 16 cm

43. The blood groups of 25 students of a certain class of a school are as follows:

A, O, A, B, AB, O, A, O, A, B, O, B, A, AB, AB, A, B, A, B, O, B, AB, A, O, B

What is the difference of the number of students having blood groups A and AB?

A. 1 B. 2
C. 3 D. 4

44. What is the difference between the average and range of the observations 32, 41, 54, 35, 26, 23, 28, 33, 38 and 40 ?

A. 3 B. 4
C. 6 D. 8

45. Observe the following pattern :

$5^2 = 12 + 13$

$7^2 = 24 + 25$

$11^2 = 60 + 61$

and so on,

Now what should be the missing numbers in the equality

17^2 = ____ + ____ ?

A. 84, 85 B. 104, 105
C. 134, 135 D. 144, 145

46. Faiza says that $\frac{1}{8}$ is a greater fraction than $\frac{1}{2}$.

Which of the following is most appropriate for the error made by Faiza? It is a ______.

A. Procedural error B. Conceptual error
C. Careless error D. Language error

47. According to National Curriculum Framework, 2005, the mathematics curriculum should be:

A. Coherent and Static
B. Ambitious and Static
C. Static and activity-oriented
D. Ambitious and Coherent

48. Which of the following can be considered as a base to develop "algebraic thinking" among primary grade learners?

A. Starting with simple patterns of repeating shapes and then moving to complex patterns involving numbers.
B. Using graphical method to introduce algebraic equations.
C. Introducing algebraic identities to solve the problems.
D. Emphasizing the use of algebra in daily life.

49. When asked to multiply 25 by 7, a student adds 25 seven times. Which of the following statements is correct with respect to the given context?

A. The use of formal algorithm needs to be emphasized over informal strategies.
B. The strategy used by the student can not be assessed by the teacher.
C. The student has creatively extended the knowledge of addition to multiplication.
D. The student has no conceptual understanding of both addition and subtraction.

50. Children's mathematical reasoning abilities at primary level can most appropriately be inferred by:

A. step-by-step completion of questions given as home task
B. achievement in regular MCQ-based tests
C. analysing their errors
D. memorising of formal algorithms

51. Which of the following is/are responsible for fear and failure in mathematics according to National Curriculum Framework, 2005?

(*a*) Predominance of symbolic language
(*b*) Cumulative nature of mathematics
(*c*) Gender-Specific abilities
(*d*) Formative assessment techniques

Choose the correct option:

A. Only (*d*) B. (*a*) and (*b*)
C. (*b*) and (*c*) D. (*a*) and (*c*)

52. While deducing the area of a parallelogram from a rectangle, the most common transformation that a teacher does to relate the formula of area of these two shapes is:

A. Flip
B. Rotation
C. The transformation is not possible
D. Translation

53. Which of the following statements is true for teaching of Data Handling in primary classes?

A. It should not be introduced as students of primary classes won't be able to handle the data.
B. It doesn't relate to mathematical concepts in arithmetic and geometry.
C. It can be introduced informally in primary classes as students of primary classes can relate it to their daily life experiences.
D. It demands higher cognitive skills which are not possessed by students of primary classes.

54. Which of the following is **not** true for the use of manipulative aids in mathematics at upper-primary level?

A. They help in understanding complex concepts in mathematics.
B. They are used to utilize leisure time in a mathematics classroom.
C. They act as a pedagogical resource for assessment.
D. They help in concrete representation of abstract concepts in mathematics.

55. 'An elastic band of 10 cm length is stretched by 5 cm. What is the new length of the elastic band ?'

Hemlata presents the above word problem to the students in her class. The underlying concept that she is referring to is:

A. Addition B. Ratio
C. Multiplication D. Proportion

56. Following is the conversation between two students about their mathematics class:

A : Lots of questions were going round in my head but I was too scared to ask them.

B : I feel scared of asking questions in mathematics as I would look stupid if I got it wrong.

The situation depicts:

(*a*) A teacher-centered classroom

(*b*) Lack of fearless environment in the mathematics class

(c) Excuses made by most of the students in a mathematics classroom

(*d*) Lack of conceptual understanding of the teacher

Choose the correct option:

A. (*a*) and (*c*)
B. (*b*) and (*d*)
C. Only (*c*)
D. (*a*) and (*b*)

57. According to the National Education Policy (NEP), 2020, the important principle for imparting quality education and making children self-learners is

A. Learning what to learn
B. Learning where to learn from
C. Learning how to learn
D. Learning whom to learn from

58. Which of the following is important for a teacher while teaching "Estimation"?

A. Teacher must explain that there is one best way to estimate.
B. Teacher should neglect the answers of students whose answers are farthest off from the estimated answer.
C. Teacher should motivate the students with the closest estimate.
D. Teacher should give space for a range of reasonable answers followed by a discussion.

59. The primary objective of a diagnostic test in mathematics is

A. To emphasize parents to keep home tuitions for the child
B. To prepare report-cards of the children
C. To understand the child's learning gaps in mathematics
D. To distribute children in different sections of a class

60. A student in a mathematics class says that a square is both a parallelogram and a rectangle. He further says all rectangles are also parallelograms. According to Van Hiele's theory of geometric thinking, the student is at which level of geometric thinking ?

A. Relationships
B. Analysis
C. Visualization
D. Axiomatic

PART- III

Environmental Studies

61. The Edible part of tapioca plant is A and this is grown abundantly in B . A and B respectively are:

A. Leaf, Meghalaya
B. Stem, Kashmir
C. Root, Kerala
D. Flower, Tamil Nadu

62. Deficiency of A causes anaemia. B and C are rich sources of A. A, B and C respectively are:

A. Calcium, Milk, Eggs
B. Iron, Milk, Eggs
C. Iron, Spinach, Dates
D. Calcium, Spinach, Dates

63. Anjali travels from New Delhi to Thiruvananthapuram in a train. Which of the following rivers will she be crossing during her train journey?

A. Narmada, Godavari, Ganga
B. Yamuna, Damodar, Krishna
C. Narmada, Krishna, Godavari
D. Yamuna, Mahanadi, Godavari

64. Crows make nests on a tree using pieces of wood but X which does not make its own nest lays eggs in the crow's nest. X is:

A. Indian Robin
B. Weaver Bird
C. Koel
D. Sparrow

65. In X district of Y , Itr, rosewater and kewra water are prepared on large scale. X and Y are:

A. Madhubani, Bihar
B. Kannauj, Uttar Pradesh
C. Worli, Maharashtra
D. Solan, Himachal Pradesh

66. Assertion (A): A boiled egg put in a mug of water sinks whereas it floats when put in salt water.

Reason (R): The density of egg increases on boiling.

Choose the correct option:

A. Both (A) and (R) are correct and (R) is correct explanation of (A)
B. Both (A) and (R) are correct, but (R) is not correct explanation of (A)
C. (A) is correct and (R) is incorrect
D. Both (A) and (R) are incorrect

67. Nowadays we see many wells which are completely dried up. What could be the main reason for this?

(*a*) People have started installing boring pumps in the nearby areas of the wells.

(*b*) The soil in the nearby areas of the wells are concretised.

(*c*) Water from wells in not used as it is contaminated.

A. (*a*) and (*b*)
B. (*a*) and (*c*)
C. Only (*b*)
D. Only (*c*)

68. One of the common methods to prevent mosquitoes breeding in rainy season is to put kerosene on stagnant water. The reason for this is:
A. Kerosene cuts off oxygen supply to mosquitoes
B. Mosquitoes are trapped in kerosene
C. Kerosene contains substance which kills mosquitoes
D. The smell of kerosene repels the mosquitoes

69. Which of the following States/Union Territories have coastline on Bay of Bengal?
A. Karnataka, Maharashtra, Kerala
B. Odisha, Tamil Nadu, Andhra Pradesh
C. Puducherry, Karnataka, Goa
D. Daman, Puducherry, Telangana

70. In a village in India, houses are made up of thick walls and are plastered with mud. The roofs of the houses are made of thorny bushes. This village is likely to be in a:
A. desert region
B. snowy region
C. high rainfall region
D. forest region in the plains

71. Assertion (A): Sweet Potato is a root.

Reason (R): It stores food.

Choose the correct option:
A. Both (A) and (R) are correct and (R) is correct explanation of (A)
B. Both (A) and (R) are correct, but (R) is not correct explanation of (A)
C. (A) is correct and (R) is incorrect
D. Both (A) and (R) are incorrect

72. Assertion (A): In Jhoom farming, weeds are cut and burnt instead of pulling out.

Reason (R): Ash mixes with soil which increases soil fertility.
A. Both (A) and (R) are correct and (R) is correct explanation of (A)
B. Both (A) and (R) are correct, but (R) is not correct explanation of (A)
C. (A) is correct and (R) is incorrect
D. Both (A) and (R) are incorrect

73. Assertion (A): Earthworm is referred to as a farmer's best friend.

Reason (R): Earthworms destroy the weeds.

Choose the correct option:
A. Both (A) and (R) are true and (R) is correct explanation of (A)
B. Both (A) and (R) are true, but (R) is not correct explanation of (A)
C. (A) is true, but (R) is false
D. Both (A) and (R) are false

74. Rajiv wants to make compost in his home. Which of the following type of waste should be put in the compost pit?
A. Aluminium foil, Vegetable peels, Egg shells
B. Vegetable peels, Filtered tea leaves, Paper
C. Vegetable peels, Polythene, Paper
D. Aluminium foil, Milk packets, Newspaper

75. A seed is
A. living as it is product of plant
B. non-living as we can cook it
C. living as it can grow into plant
D. non-living as it does not respire

76. Which of the following should be done by EVS teacher while assessing students?
(*a*) Write qualitative statements about students.
(*b*) Focus only on a few aspects of students.
(*c*) Make record of information with focus on learning potential of students.
(*d*) Compare previous record of students

Choose the correct option:
A. (*a*), (*b*), (*c*)
B. (*a*), (*b*), (*d*)
C. (*a*), (*c*), (*d*)
D. (*b*), (*c*), (*d*)

77. Which of the following is an important feature in school field trip in EVS teaching?
A. Awakens students' interest to learn and get new learning information.
B. Both teacher and students get a break from regular teaching-learning practice.
C. The funds for teaching-learning are properly utilized.
D. Parents feel happy to see their children going on picnic.

78. EVS curriculum has followed a theme-based approach to:
A. cover wide range of concepts in one go.
B. save resources.
C. help in assessing knowledge of children holistically.
D. enable students to be concerned about society and nature both.

79. In the context of EVS teaching, NCF 2005 does **not** propose
A. Hands-on-activities
B. Thematic approach
C. Linking students' experience and context
D. Knowing technical terms

80. In the teaching-learning of EVS, poems and stories are effective because they can
(*a*) nurture curiosity in children.
(*b*) nurture aesthetic sense in children.
(*c*) provide contextual learning environment.
(*d*) explain various abstract environment.

Choose the correct option:
A. (*a*), (*b*) and (*d*) B. (*b*), (*c*) and (*d*)
C. (*a*), (*b*) and (*c*) D. (*a*) and (*b*)

81. Environmental studies education for primary students intends that:
A. Students become less inquisitive.
B. Students become more inquisitive.
C. Students make fewer mistakes.
D. Students develop good drawing and writing skills.

82. EVS pedagogy advocates the following practices *except*:
A. Capacitating students for critical thinking and problem solving.
B. Acknowledging textbooks are superior over actual life experiences.
C. Promoting collaboration amongst students.
D. Nurturing the creativity and curiosity of students.

83. What do we call the folder in which students put their worksheets, observation reports and other materials collected during a term?
A. Portfolios B. Anecdotal records
C. Project D. File

84. Why is 'Community' important for teaching-learning in EVS at primary level?
A. It is an easily available resource.
B. It comprises wise and elderly people.
C. It provides learning opportunities in a real setting.
D. It does not need any funds for expenditure.

85. Which of the following represents characteristics of an EVS textbook?
(*a*) It caters to the needs of students from diverse backgrounds.
(*b*) It contains true stories and incidents.
(*c*) It presents natural and socio-cultural content in an integrated manner.
(*d*) It focusses on explanation of abstract concepts.
Choose the correct option:
A. (*a*), (*b*) and (*c*) B. (*a*) only
C. (*b*), (*c*) and (*d*) D. (*a*), (*c*) and (*d*)

86. 'Do this and find out' in different topics of EVS book aims at:
A. keeping students engaged.
B. providing hands-on experience to students.
C. learning scientific terms.
D. attaining learning outcomes through good performance in examination.

87. Which of the following are objectives of studying EVS?
(*a*) Enabling students to learn and recall key terms and distinctions.
(*b*) Enabling students to do questioning.
(*c*) Enabling students to reject each other's culture.
(*d*) Enabling students to grow into responsible citizens.
Choose the correct option:
A. (*a*), (*b*) and (*c*) B. (*b*) and (*d*)
C. (*a*), (*b*) and (*d*) D. (*a*), (*c*) and (*d*)

88. In NCERT textbook of EVS, priority and space has been given to:
A. Provide opportunities to learners for contemplation and wondering.
B. Explain basic concepts of the subject.
C. Explain definition of key terms.
D. Include large number of practice sheets.

89. NCF 2005 has not recommended any textbook for EVS for classes I and II. The most appropriate reason/reasons is/are
(*a*) to provide contextual learning environment.
(*b*) as students of class I and II are very young to learn EVS.
(*c*) EVS is suitable for class III onwards.
(*d*) to reduce load of curriculum on primary grade children.
A. (*a*) and (*d*) B. (*a*) and (*c*)
C. (*b*) and (*d*) D. (*b*) and (*c*)

90. A competent EVS teacher uses pedagogical processes which are:
A. True to child's life.
B. True to subject.
C. True to school.
D. True to child's life and subject.

PART- IV

Language : English

Directions (Qs. No. 91-98) : *Read the passage given below and answer the questions that follow:*

1. If you have time on your hands, a trip to Paithan, a few kilometers from Aurangabad, is recommended before calling it a day. It is famous for the Jaikwadi Dam and even more popular for the exquisitely woven and brightly colored Paithani silk sarees with rich silver or gold borders. Before taking the bus back to Mumbai you must remember to pick one up!

2. The Ajanta caves were our final destination. Located about 104 kilometers away, it is a two-and-a-half-hour drive from Aurangabad. Consisting of 29 rock-cut cave

monuments, the Ajanta caves were an outstanding display of craftsmanship, testimony to the perseverance of the artists.

3. Dating back to the 2nd century BC, the caves house some of the best paintings and sculptures of this age, considered to be masterpieces of Buddhist religious art. The frescoes on the walls of the caves are breathtakingly beautiful. Stripped of much of its grandeur with the passage of time and due to neglect, the remnants of colour on the frescoes on ceilings and walls live on as a silent witness of its heyday. The Tiger Hill close by, easily reached by car, offers an impressive panoramic view of the horse-shoe-shaped Ajanta caves and the surrounding area.

4. As a student of history, with a special love for historical architecture, the fact that I would be left spellbound by Aurangabad is no wonder. But today when I look back, I realize that it is much more than just history that captured my heart. It is the peaceful co-existence of the past and the present and the simplicity that the city exudes that left an indelible imprint on my mind. Being closely intertwined with history and spared from the excessive ravages of the modern world, Aurangabad and its vicinity has a distinct charming character of its own.

91. By 'calling it a day' the writer means
A. ending/concluding something.
B. beginning something.
C. deciding to meet someone.
D. going off to see someone.

92. Paithan is not famous for
A. its silk sarees.
B. its gold and silver jewellery.
C. the Jaikwadi Dam.
D. its beautiful, colourful weaves.

93. The writer was most impressed with his visit to Aurangabad because of
A. its exquisite architecture.
B. the large number of monuments that can be visited here.
C. its proximity to the Ajanta and Ellora caves.
D. the peaceful co-existence of the past and present here.

94. The word underlined in the phrase 'excessive ravages of modern life' is an example of
A. Adjective B. Noun
C. Adverb D. Verb

95. Ajanta is a popular tourist spot because
A. of its Tiger Hill.
B. of its frescoes and paintings.
C. of its view of the Ajanta caves.
D. of its closeness to the historical town of Aurangabad.

96. Which of the following words is closest in meaning to the word 'exquisitely'? (para 1)
A. intricately B. delightfully
C. joyfully D. deliberately

97. Which of the following words is opposite in meaning to the word 'perseverance'?
A. Determination B. Doggedness
C. Procrastination D. Grit

98. From the text it is evident that the writer is most interested in
A. politics B. religion
C. history D. architecture

Directions (Qs. No. 99-105): *Read the passage given below and answer the questions that follow:*

1. "I think we might have something to eat first," said the grandfather, "what do you think?"

2. Heidi in the excitement of bed-making had forgotten everything else; but now when she began to think about food she felt terribly hungry, for she had had nothing to eat since the piece of bread and little cup of thin coffee that had been her breakfast early that morning before starting on her long, hot journey. So she answered without hesitation, "Yes, I think so too."

3. "Let us go down then, as we both think alike," said the old man, and he followed the child down the ladder. Then he went up to the hearth, pushed the big kettle aside, and drew forward the little one that was hanging on the chain, and seating himself on the round-topped, three-legged stool before the fire, blew it up into a clear bright flame. The kettle soon began to boil, and meanwhile, the old man held a large piece of cheese on a long iron fork over the fire, turning it round and round till it was toasted a nice golden yellow color on each side. Heidi watched all that was going on with eager curiosity. Suddenly some new idea seemed to come into her head, for she turned and ran to the cupboard, and then began going busily backwards and forwards. Presently the grandfather got up and came to the table with a jug and the cheese, and there he saw it already tidily laid with the round loaf and two plates and two knives each in its right place; for Heidi had taken exact note that morning of all that there was in the cupboard, and she knew which things would be wanted for their meal.

4. "Ah, that's right," said the grandfather, "I am glad to see that you have some ideas of your own," and as he spoke he laid the toasted cheese on a layer of bread, "but there is still something missing."

5. Heidi looked at the jug that was steaming away invitingly, and ran quickly back to the cupboard. At first she could only see a small bowl left on the shelf, but she was not long in perplexity, for a moment later

she caught sight of two glasses further back, and without an instant's loss of time she returned with these and the bowl and put them down on the table.

99. Heidi had forgotten about her hunger because she had been:
A. busy looking around her grandfather's house.
B. looking at the beautiful mountain scenery.
C. busy talking to her grandfather.
D. busy making her bed.

100. Grandfather toasted the cheese by:
A. putting it directly on the fire.
B. putting it on the hearth.
C. putting it on a fork.
D. putting it inside a kettle.

101. The fact that Heidi was used to housework can be seen from the fact that she had:
A. helped her grandfather clean his room.
B. laid the table perfectly.
C. lit the fire in the hearth.
D. helped her grandfather cook breakfast.

102. The word 'perplexity' (para 5) used in this text means:
A. certainty B. confusion
C. annoyance D. irritation

103. 'Without an instant's loss of time', means:
A. urgently
B. immediately
C. seriously
D. sincerely

104. The relationship of the grandfather and the granddaughter as depicted here appears to be one of:
A. surprise and excitement.
B. surprise and appreciation.
C. appreciation and respect.
D. admiration and generosity.

105. Heidi watched all that was going on with eager curiosity. The underlined word is an example of a/an:
A. Noun B. Adjective
C. Adverb D. Pronoun

106. 'Children start out as clean slates and language learning is printing of linguistic habits on these clean slates.'
This idea is supported by:
A. Piaget B. Vygotsky
C. Chomsky D. Skinner

107. Which one of the parameters is **not** important for assessing paragraph writing?
A. Topic sentence
B. Supporting details
C. Good Handwriting
D. Coherence

108. For dealing with difficult words in the text, a language teacher first converts the words into mother tongue and then asks the students to memorise it. She is using:
A. Grammar translation method
B. Direct method
C. Structural approach
D. Communicative approach

109. The three stages of phonological awareness are
A. syllables, words, sentences
B. sounds, pitch, tone
C. syllables, rhymes, phonemes
D. depth, speed, rhythm

110. A teacher gave a worksheet to the students based on the summary of the chapter read and dropped every fifth word from it. She asked them to fill the missing words. What is this test known as?
A. A cloze test
B. Fill in the blanks
C. Complete the summary
D. Writing test

111. Which of the following statements is **not** true for reading?
A. Reading is sounding out words and decoding
B. Reading is constructive
C. Reading is the ability to read, process and understand the text
D. Reading is the ability to understand the meaning the author is trying to convey

112. A language teacher gives a task to identify adjectives used for the main character in the story to her 5th Graders. This reading activity is:
A. Intensive reading
B. Extensive reading
C. Skimming
D. Collaborative reading

113. Which of the following statements is true for enhancing pronunciation skills in children?
A. Students should practice pronunciation so that they sound exactly like native speakers.
B. Students should be made to repeat words many times in a day.
C. Students should be helped to have intelligible pronunciation.
D. Teacher should conduct pronunciation drills to make them pronounce like native speakers.

114. In a language class students are asked to write "How they celebrated their birthday". Then they are asked to exchange their writings with their partner and give feedback. This type of assessment is ______.
A. Summative Assessment
B. Group Assessment
C. Peer Assessment
D. Self-Assessment

115. Which of the following is true for 'Dialect' and 'Accent'?
A. Accent relates to the actual language used and dialect refers to the way that language is spoken.
B. Accent refers to colloquial words and phrases that often reflect identity and dialect refers to the way the language is spoken.
C. Dialect relates to the actual language used and accent refers to the way that language is spoken.
D. Dialect refers to colloquial words and phrases that often reflect identity and Accent refers to the technical vocabulary to help people articulate experiences, events and concepts in specialized contexts.

116. A teacher can make her students effective speakers by:
A. Asking them to narrate the stories which they have memorised.
B. Making them learn few sentences they need to use during social interaction.
C. Providing opportunities to express themselves in class.
D. Making them learn and speak the paragraphs they need to reproduce during term-end exams.

117. In preparing a fourth class to take a standardized reading test, the teacher is best advised to:
A. tell the children the test is very important and they should do the best they can.
B. coach the below grade level readers, as the rest of the class will do well anyway.
C. give the learners practice in answering questions similar to the type that will appear on the test.
D. ditto key questions from a previous test and allow the learners to answer them.

118. In a class students are asked to compile portfolios of their written work for summative assessment e.g. choosing their best six pieces of writing. This type of assessment is:
A. of no use
B. student friendly
C. teacher-centered
D. not an assessment

119. Given below are two statements about language learning. Read the statements and choose the correct option.
(*a*) An individual can learn a language at any age but it is easier to do so at a younger age.
(*b*) Language can be learnt through exposure.
A. Both (*a*) and (*b*) are true
B. (*a*) is true, but (*b*) is false
C. (*b*) is true, but (*a*) is false
D. Both (*a*) and (*b*) are false

120. During a writing activity in class, teacher asks students to brainstorm on the theme of writing given to them. This is a strategy for ______ stage of the writing process.
A. Prewriting B. Reviewing
C. Drafting D. Publishing

PART- V

Language : Hindi

निर्देश (प्र.सं. 121 से 129): *निम्नलिखित गद्यांश को पढ़कर पूछे गए प्रश्नों के सही/सबसे उपयुक्त उत्तर वाले विकल्प को चुनिए।*

आजकल बड़े-बड़े कल-कारखानें, उद्योगशालाएँ अपनी धुआँ उगलती चिमनियों से वायुमंडल में प्राणघातक जहरीली हवाएँ प्रसारित कर रही हैं। इन उद्योगशालाओं और कारखानों में प्रयुक्त होने वाला पानी अनेक प्रकार के जहरीले रसायनों से युक्त अवशेष के रूप में नदियों में बेहिचक उँड़ेला जा रहा है जो नदियों के प्राकृतिक जल को अपेय बना रहा है। इसके अलावा सड़कों पर दौड़ते वाहन, उनका धुआँ और जहरीली गैसें भी इस प्रदूषण में अपना अंशदान कर रही हैं। इस चौतरफा आक्रमण से मानव सभ्यता का बच पाना एक कठिन कार्य लग रहा है क्योंकि प्राणवायु के अभाव में जीवन के संभव रहने की कल्पना भी नहीं की जा सकती।

121. वायुमंडल में प्राणों को संकट में डालने वाली विषैली हवाएँ कौन फैला रहा है?
A. कारखानों की चिमनियाँ
B. कारखानों की नालियाँ
C. बड़े-बड़े कल कारखानें
D. कारखानें और प्रयोगशालाएँ

122. गद्यांश के आधार पर नदियों के जल को प्रदूषित कर रहा है:
A. कारखानों से निकलने वाली जहरीली वायु
B. कारखानों से निकलने वाला धुआँ
C. घरों से निकलने वाले अपशिष्ट पदार्थ
D. कारखानों से निकलने वाला रसायन युक्त पानी

123. इनमें से कौन-सा वायु प्रदूषण का कारक **नहीं** है?
A. वाहन B. उद्योग
C. कारखाने D. विद्यालय

124. 'प्राणवायु के <u>अभाव</u> में जीवन के संभव रहने की कल्पना भी नहीं की जा सकती।' वाक्य में रेखांकित पद के स्थान पर प्रयुक्त किया जा सकता है:

A. अभावपूर्ण B. अनुपस्थिति
C. अतिशयता D. अभावग्रस्त

125. गद्यांश के आधार पर 'चौतरफा आक्रमण से मानव सभ्यता का बचना असंभव है।' वाक्य से तात्पर्य है:
A. शत्रुओं द्वारा किए जा रहे आक्रमणों से मानव का अस्तित्व संकट में है।
B. वायुमंडल के प्रदूषित होने से मानव का अस्तित्व संकट में है।
C. पड़ोसी देशों द्वारा किए जा रहे आक्रमणों से मानव सभ्यता संकट में है।
D. अनेक रोगों के कारण मानव सभ्यता पर संकट छाया हुआ है।

126. 'बड़े-बड़े' शब्द युग्म है:
A. पुनरुक्त शब्द
B. विलोम शब्द
C. पर्यायवाची शब्द
D. सार्थक-निरर्थक शब्द

127. 'चौतरफा' में समास का भेद है:
A. द्वंद्व समास
B. द्विगु समास
C. तत्पुरुष समास
D. बहुव्रीहि समास

128. 'बेहिचक' शब्द है:
A. तत्सम B. तद्भव
C. आगत D. देशज

129. 'प्रसारित' शब्द में प्रत्यय है:
A. प्र B. रित
C. इत D. त

निर्देश (प्र.सं. 130 से 135): *निम्नलिखित कविता को पढ़कर पूछे गए प्रश्नों के सही/सबसे उपयुक्त उत्तर वाले विकल्प को चुनिए।*

कोई व्यक्ति विशेष नहीं तेरा अपना है,
जो यह समझे हाय! देखता वह सपना है।
तुझको सारे जीव एक से ही प्यारे हैं
कर्मों के फल मात्र यहाँ न्यारे-न्यारे हैं
हे मातृभूमि! तेरे निकट सबका सम संबंध है,
जो भेद मानता वह अहो! लोचनयुक्त भी अन्ध है।

130. कविता में किसे संबोधित किया गया है?
A. समस्त जीवों को
B. मातृभूमि को
C. लोगों को
D. न्यारों को

131. कवि ने किस नासमझी पर दुख व्यक्त किया है?
A. मातृभूमि द्वारा लोगों में भेद करने को मानना
B. मातृभूमि द्वारा लोगों में भेद करने को
C. मातृभूमि द्वारा सभी से नजदीकी रिश्ता बनाना
D. मातृभूमि द्वारा अलग-अलग फल देना

132. मातृभूमि की किस विशेषता की ओर संकेत किया गया है?
A. सभी को अपना न मानना
B. सभी को समान फल देना
C. सभी पर समान उपकार करना
D. सारे जीवों को स्वप्न दिखाना

133. सभी प्राणियों को उनके कार्यों के अनुसार
A. भेदभाव पूर्ण व्यवहार मिलता है
B. भेदभाव मिलता है
C. अलग-अलग जीव मिलते हैं
D. अलग-अलग परिणाम मिलते हैं

134. 'लोचनयुक्त' से तात्पर्य है:
A. जो लालच करते हैं B. जो देख सकते हैं
C. जो साहसी हैं D. जो शक्तिशाली हैं

135. विशेषण शब्द **नहीं** है:
A. प्यारे B. सम
C. न्यारे D. संबंध

136. भारत में विद्यालयी शिक्षा के संदर्भ में बहुभाषावाद के लिए कौन-सा कथन सही है?
A. बहुभाषावाद का प्रयोग भाषाओं और विषयों के शिक्षण-अधिगम के लिए एक संसाधन के रूप में होना चाहिए।
B. बहुभाषिक कक्षाओं का यह उद्देश्य है कि सभी विद्यार्थी जहाँ तक संभव हो अधिक से अधिक भाषाएँ सीख सकें।
C. बहुभाषिक कक्षा में प्रत्येक विद्यार्थी को अंग्रेजी सीखनी चाहिए और अंग्रेजी माध्यम के विद्यालय में पढ़ना चाहिए।
D. बहुभाषिक कक्षा में प्रत्येक बच्चे को मातृभाषा से शुरू करते हुए हिन्दी, फिर अंग्रेजी इस तरह से तीन भाषाएँ सीखनी चाहिए।

137. भाषा शिक्षण के किस उपागम में समूची पाठ्य सामग्री के अर्थ पर ध्यान दिया जाता है बजाय कि एक-एक शब्द के अर्थ पर?
A. विभिन्न दर्शनग्राही उपागम
B. समग्र भाषा उपागम
C. संरचनात्मक उपागम
D. सम्प्रेषणात्मक उपागम

138. 'वाक् समुदाय' लोगों का वह समूह है जो:
A. विशिष्ट उद्देश्यों के लिए भाषा के विशिष्ट प्रकार में बात करते हैं
B. भाषा के प्रयोग के संदर्भ में एकसमान मानकों का प्रयोग करते हैं
C. जिनके एकसमान वाक् विकार हैं
D. एकसमान भाषा का शिक्षण करते हैं

139. कक्षा पाँच की अध्यापिका अपने विद्यार्थियों को कहानी सुनाते समय रचनावादी उपागम का प्रयोग करती है। उसे अपनी कक्षा में किस युक्ति का अनुसरण **नहीं** करना चाहिए?

A. कहानी की थीम से सम्बन्धित शिक्षार्थियों के पूर्व ज्ञान का सहारा लेना चाहिए
B. कहानी के अन्त का अनुमान लगाने के अवसर देने चाहिए
C. कहानी को कंठस्थ करके कक्षा में वर्णन करना चाहिए
D. कहानी के पात्रों पर विमर्श करने के मौके देने चाहिए

140. निम्नलिखित में से कौन-सा भाषा अर्जन के दौरान आरंभिक शब्द त्रुटि का अतिशय रूप से विस्तार का उदाहरण है?

A. बच्चे उड़ती हुई सभी चिड़ियों को गौरेया कहते हैं
B. बच्चे प्रवाह के साथ नहीं बोल पाते हैं
C. बच्चे किसी बात को अभिव्यक्त करने के लिए केवल मुख्य शब्द का सहारा लेते हैं, जैसे "माँ सेब खाती" है
D. बच्चे अपनी बोली गई बातों को दोहराते हैं

141. भाषा शिक्षण के किस उपागम में अर्थ के प्रति समझ बनाने की जगह वाक्यों के प्रतिरूपों को याद करने पर बल दिया जाता है?

A. व्याकरण अनुवाद विधि
B. सम्प्रेषणात्मक उपागम
C. प्रत्यक्ष विधि
D. संरचनात्मक उपागम

142. गहन पठन क्या है?

A. सरसरी तौर पर पठन
B. गंभीर पठन
C. पठन से पूर्व
D. सामूहिक पठन

143. निम्नलिखित में से कौन-सा डिसर्थ्रिया का लक्षण है?

A. लेखन में कठिनाई
B. ध्वनि, वर्ण या शब्दों का दोहराव या लंबी तान में बोलना
C. माँसपेशियों की कमजोरी के कारण ध्वनि निकालने में जीभ और होंठ के समन्वयन में कठिनाई
D. जिन शब्दों को बच्चे सुनते व पढ़ते हैं, उन्हें समझने में कठिनाई

144. निम्नलिखित में से कौन-सा पठन का उपकौशल **नहीं** है?

A. सम्बद्धता स्थापित करना
B. अनुमान लगाना
C. अन्तःक्रिया करना
D. विश्लेषण करना

145. पठन के बारे में निम्नलिखित कथन पढ़कर सही विकल्प का चयन करें:

(*a*) पठन एक ऐसी प्रक्रिया है जिसमें पाठ्य सामग्री से सूचनाएँ और ज्ञान अर्थ निर्माण के साथ-साथ ग्रहण किया जाता है।
(*b*) डिकोडिंग लिखे हुए शब्दों को सही तरह से उच्चारित करने के लिए अक्षरों के नमूनों के ज्ञान के साथ-साथ अक्षर-ध्वनि संबंध के ज्ञान का इस्तेमाल करने की क्षमता है।

A. (*a*) और (*b*) दोनों सही हैं
B. (*a*) सही है लेकिन (*b*) गलत है
C. (*b*) सही है लेकिन (*a*) गलत है
D. (*a*) और (*b*) दोनों गलत हैं

146. कक्षा दो की अध्यापिका अपनी कक्षा में मुद्रित समृद्ध परिवेश का सृजन करना चाहती है। वह निम्नलिखित में से कौन-सा कार्य करवा सकती है?

A. दीवार पर उपयुक्त ऊँचाई पर कहानी और पोस्टर लगाना
B. बच्चों को कहानियाँ सुनाना
C. कक्षा की दीवार को सजाने के लिए दीवार पर फूल और पशुओं के चित्र चिपकाना
D. मुद्रित लिपि के अनुसार बच्चों को लिखने के लिए कहना

147. नीचे भाषा कौशलों के विकास के लिए कुछ गतिविधियाँ दी गई हैं। निम्नलिखित में से कौन-सी श्रवण कौशल के विकास के लिए प्रयुक्त की जा सकती है?

A. अध्यापक कहानी में आए पात्रों की भौतिक आकृतियों का वर्णन करने और उनका चित्र बनाने के लिए कह सकती है
B. बच्चों को कहानी पढ़ने के लिए कहा जाए
C. बच्चों को याद रखने योग्य घटना सुनाने के लिए कहा जाए
D. बच्चों को अपने से पढ़ी गई कहानी प्रस्तुत करने के लिए कहा जाए

148. मनुष्य भाषा उसी प्रकार से सीखते हैं जिस तरह से वयस्कों के अनुकरण व पुनर्बलन के माध्यम से अन्य दूसरे कौशल व क्षमताएँ। भाषा अर्जन का यह विचार किससे सम्बन्धित है?

A. संज्ञानात्मक उपागम
B. प्राकृत उपागम
C. व्यवहारवादी उपागम
D. सामाजिक-सांस्कृतिक उपागम

149. नॉम चॉमस्की ने यह विचार दिया था कि मनुष्य सहजात भाषिक क्षमता के साथ पैदा होते हैं। इस क्षमता को किसकी उपस्थिति में परिवेश से जुड़े मौखिक निवेश से समर्थित होने की जरूरत है?

A. भाषा अर्जन उपकरण
B. भाषा अधिगम उपकरण
C. व्याकरण अर्जन उपकरण
D. अधिगम भाषा उपकरण

150. बच्चों को अवकाश गृहकार्य के रूप में अपनी रुचि की कोई दस कहानियाँ पढ़ने के लिए कहा जाता है। इस तरह से उन्हें क्या करने के लिए प्रोत्साहित किया जा रहा है?

A. गहन पठन
B. विस्तृत पठन
C. सरसरी तौर पर पठन
D. बारीकी से पठन

ANSWERS

1	2	3	4	5	6	7	8	9	10
A	A	A	A	A	B	C	A	B	B
11	**12**	**13**	**14**	**15**	**16**	**17**	**18**	**19**	**20**
A	D	A	B	A	A	C	B	A	D
21	**22**	**23**	**24**	**25**	**26**	**27**	**28**	**29**	**30**
C	D	C	A	A	C	D	D	D	B
31	**32**	**33**	**34**	**35**	**36**	**37**	**38**	**39**	**40**
D	A	B	B	B	D	D	B	B	A
41	**42**	**43**	**44**	**45**	**46**	**47**	**48**	**49**	**50**
B	A	D	B	D	B	D	A	C	C
51	**52**	**53**	**54**	**55**	**56**	**57**	**58**	**59**	**60**
B	A	C	B	A	D	C	D	C	A
61	**62**	**63**	**64**	**65**	**66**	**67**	**68**	**69**	**70**
C	C	C	C	B	B	A	A	B	A
71	**72**	**73**	**74**	**75**	**76**	**77**	**78**	**79**	**80**
B	A	C	B	C	C	A	C	D	C
81	**82**	**83**	**84**	**85**	**86**	**87**	**88**	**89**	**90**
B	B	A	C	A	B	B	A	A	D
91	**92**	**93**	**94**	**95**	**96**	**97**	**98**	**99**	**100**
A	B	D	B	B	A	C	C	D	C
101	**102**	**103**	**104**	**105**	**106**	**107**	**108**	**109**	**110**
B	B	B	B	A	D	C	A	C	A
111	**112**	**113**	**114**	**115**	**116**	**117**	**118**	**119**	**120**
A	A	C	C	C	C	C	B	A	A
121	**122**	**123**	**124**	**125**	**126**	**127**	**128**	**129**	**130**
A	D	D	B	B	A	B	C	C	B
131	**132**	**133**	**134**	**135**	**136**	**137**	**138**	**139**	**140**
A	C	D	B	D	A	B	B	C	A
141	**142**	**143**	**144**	**145**	**146**	**147**	**148**	**149**	**150**
D	B	C	C	B	A	A	C	A	B

EXPLANATORY ANSWERS

1. During the primary years, children develop cognitively, emotionally, and socially. Their development progresses from simple to complex as they build upon previous knowledge and experiences. Initially, children start with simple tasks and concepts and gradually move towards understanding and performing more complex tasks and ideas. As they develop, their thinking evolves from concrete to abstract, and their understanding becomes more sophisticated.

2. A sensitive period for language development is early childhood. Early childhood is the critical period for language development, during which children are most receptive to acquiring language skills. This period usually ranges from birth to around 5 or 6 years of age.

3. The process by which children learn their societal role is referred to as socialisation. Socialisation is the process through which children learn the norms, values, behaviors, and roles expected of them in their society, helping them become functional members of their social groups.

4. The sensorimotor stage (birth to approximately 2 years) is when children begin to imitate others and develop object permanence, understanding that objects continue to exist even when they are not in sight.

5. In Jean Piaget's theory, a child who perceives the sun as being alive because it gives out light is demonstrating animistic thinking. Animistic thinking is a type of preoperational thought where children attribute life-like qualities to inanimate objects, such as believing that the sun is alive because it provides light.

6. Schema is a concept proposed by Jean Piaget, referring to mental structures that help individuals organize and interpret information. Lev Vygotsky's theories focused on the Zone of Proximal Development, Scaffolding, and Social Interaction as key elements in cognitive development.

7. Vygotsky's theory emphasizes the importance of social interaction and support in learning. Scaffolding refers to the guidance and support provided by a more knowledgeable person, which helps students to learn and accomplish tasks they could not achieve independently.

8. According to Kohlberg, the first stage of moral development is characterized by Seeing rules as fixed and absolute. The first stage in Kohlberg's theory of moral development, called the Pre-conventional level, involves obedience and punishment orientation, where individuals see rules as fixed and absolute, and they obey to avoid punishment.

9. In a progressive classroom children engage in activities that realize their potential. A progressive classroom focuses on the individual needs and interests of each student, allowing them to engage in activities that help them develop their skills and reach their full potential.

10. Howard Gardner proposed the theory of Multiple Intelligences, which includes Linguistic Intelligence as one of the types. This refers to the ability to use language effectively, both in spoken and written forms.

11. In a primary classroom, teachers should encourage 'private speech' – self-talk that guides thinking and action. Private speech, as described by Vygotsky, is an essential part of cognitive development, as it helps children to internalize language and think through problems. Teachers should encourage this behavior, as it aids in learning and self-regulation.

12. Gender typing refers to the process through which children acquire and internalize gender roles and expectations. In this case, Mohan has internalized the traditional gender roles and expectations for boys, which leads him to refuse to wear a girl's dress.

13. The process of teaching and learning for students of differing abilities in the same class is referred to as differentiated instruction. Differentiated instruction is an approach where teachers adapt their teaching methods, materials, and assessments to meet the diverse needs, interests, and abilities of students within a single classroom.

14. Socio-constructivist classrooms emphasize collaboration, social interaction, and active learning. Collaborative projects allow students to work together, share ideas, and construct knowledge collectively, making it the primary mode of assessment in this approach.

15. The most important objective of the assessment of learners is to reflect on the effectiveness of the pedagogy and modify it to enhance learning. Assessment should primarily serve to inform teachers about their students' progress, the effectiveness of their teaching methods, and any necessary modifications to improve learning outcomes.

16. Providing choice and options to students from a range of activities and experiences based on their interests, needs, and diversity of learners' backgrounds, follows the principle of inclusion. Inclusion is the practice of ensuring that all students, regardless of their abilities, backgrounds, or needs, have equal access to educational opportunities and can participate fully in the learning process.

17. Promoting cultural sensitivity involves acknowledging and respecting the diversity of cultural backgrounds and experiences among students. Celebrating only dominant cultures can marginalize students from other cultural backgrounds, limiting inclusivity and understanding.

18. Challenges in reading texts and comprehending long passages are challenges for students with dyslexia. Dyslexia is a learning disorder that affects reading, spelling, and comprehension, making it difficult for individuals to decode and process written language.

19. Audiobooks rely on auditory input, making them unsuitable for students with hearing impairments. Alternative materials, such as printed books, videos with subtitles, and three-dimensional charts and maps, can be more accessible for these students.

20. Open-ended questions allow students to think critically, creatively, and express their unique perspectives. By asking open-ended questions, teachers can identify students who demonstrate original thinking, problem-solving skills, and creativity.

21. Building on the experiences that children bring to school helps make learning more meaningful and relevant to their lives. It also acknowledges and values their prior knowledge and experiences, fostering a sense of belonging and engagement in the classroom.

22. Children learn through a variety of approaches, including: (*i*) Making and doing things (hands-on experiences), (*ii*) Reading and writing (literacy skills), (*iii*) Talking and listening (communication and social interaction), (*iv*) Thinking and reflecting (cognitive processes and critical thinking).

23. When teachers allow students to follow their own pace of learning, they accommodate individual differences, learning styles, and interests. This approach fosters engagement, motivation, and a better understanding of the content.

24. When teachers include experiences of children and give examples from their socio-cultural context, it fosters a sense of belonging in children. Incorporating students' experiences and socio-cultural contexts in the learning process helps create a sense of belonging, as it acknowledges and values their backgrounds and perspectives, making learning more meaningful and relatable.

25. The process of problem-solving is promoted through analogical thinking. Analogical thinking involves identifying similarities between different situations or concepts and applying knowledge from one context to another. This type of thinking is crucial for problem-solving, as it allows individuals to recognize patterns, transfer knowledge, and find creative solutions to new problems.

26. Children's misconceptions and errors serve as significant inroads to children's thoughts. Children's misconceptions and errors provide valuable insights into their thought processes, understanding, and development. Teachers can use these as opportunities to address misunderstandings and facilitate learning, rather than viewing them as detrimental or irrational.

27. Boredom is a sign that the learning activities have become mechanically repetitive for the child and are not of interest. Boredom often indicates that learning activities have become repetitive, uninteresting, or disconnected from the child's interests and needs. It's essential for educators to recognize boredom and adjust their teaching strategies to re-engage students in the learning process.

28. Fear of punishment can negatively impact learning, as it creates a hostile learning environment and may discourage risk-taking and exploration. Additionally, while rewards and punishment can be effective in modifying behavior, they do not necessarily promote meaningful learning or intrinsic motivation.

29. All of the factors listed can affect learning: (*i*) Interest of the students, (*ii*) Perceived relevance of the concept, (*iii*) Development level of the students, (*iv*) Strategies of teaching-learning.

30. In learning settings, personal factors, environmental factors, and behavioral factors are interrelated and influence one another. Understanding this complex interaction can help educators create more effective and supportive learning environments for their students.

31. Required no. = 1248

1248 is less than 2000

$1 + 2 + 4 = 7$

Last digit is 8 times first = $1 \times 8 = 8$

$$\text{First digit} = \frac{1}{4} \text{ of the third digit}$$

$$= \frac{1}{4} \times 4 = 1.$$

32. Each family Rice will get $= \frac{300}{15} = 20$ kg.

33. Let numbers are $11x$ and $17x$

$$11x \times 17 = 4675$$

$$\Rightarrow \quad x = \frac{4675}{187} = 25$$

LCM = 4675

$\therefore$ Numbers are $11 \times 25 = 275$

and $17 \times 25 = 425$.

34. $\because$ 774958 N_1 96 N_2 is divisible by 8 and 9

Put $N_2 = 8$

To divide by 8 last three digit must be divisible by 8

$\therefore$ 968 is divisible by 8

$7 + 7 + 4 + 9 + 5 + 8 + N_1 + 9 + 6 + 8 = N_1 + 63$

if $N_1 = 0$ then 63 is divisible by 9

Hence, the value of N_1 and N_2 = 0 and 8

$\therefore$ 7749580968 is divisible by 8 and 9.

35. Given number = 5432413

Place value of digit 4 in 413 = 400

Place value of digit 4 in 432413 = 400000

Sum of place values of digit 4 in 5432413

$= 400000 + 400$

$= 400400$

36. The smallest five digit number = 10000

The largest four digit number = 9999

Sum of the smallest five digit no. and the smallest four digit no.

$= 10000 + 9999 = 19999.$

37.

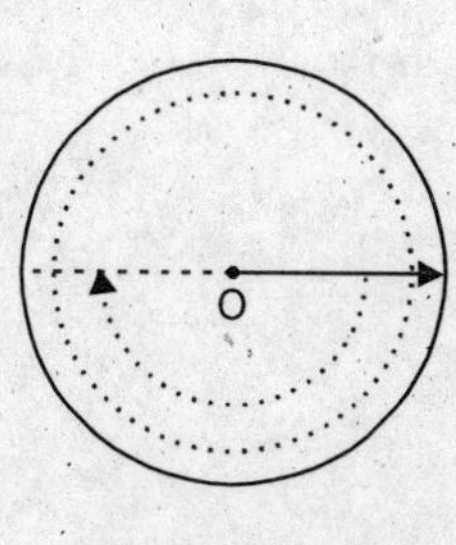

$\because$ Face is in East direction. After $1\frac{1}{2}$ revolution clockwise face will be in west direction.

38. Value of $\left(5\frac{1}{3}-2\frac{2}{3}\right)\times 90°$

$$= \left(\frac{16}{3}-\frac{8}{3}\right)\times 90°$$

$$= \frac{8}{3}\times 90°$$

$$= 8 \times 30° = 240°$$

39. The number of lines of symmetry in a kite is one.

40. Total cost = ₹ 36 + ₹ 85 + ₹ 110 + ₹ 160 + ₹ 13
= ₹ 404

₹ 500 – ₹ 404 = ₹ 96

The shopkeeper returned ₹ 95

Clearly, Shopkeeper has returned ₹ 1 less.

41. Arya

20 m × 90 m

Area of plot = 20 × 90
= 1800 m^2

Perimeter = 2 (90 + 20)
= 2 × 110 = 220 m

Bharati

30 m × 60 m

Area of plot = 30 × 60
= 1800 m^2

Perimeter = 2(60 + 30)
= 2 × 90 = 180 m

The correct reason can be the perimeter of Arya's plot is greater than perimeter of Bharati's plot .

Hence, Bharati was unhappy as she felt that perimeter of Arya's plot is more.

42. The height of water level at 9 : 40 am was 9 cm.

∵ Height of water at 9 : 47 = 23 cm

Height of water at 9 : 45 = 23 – 4 = 19 cm

Height of water at 9 : 40 = 19 – 10 = 9 cm.

43. No. of students having blood group A = 8

No. of students having blood group AB = 4

Difference of the number of students having blood groups A and AB = 8 – 4 = 4.

44. Average $= \frac{32+41+54+35+26+23+28+33+38+40}{10}$

$$= \frac{350}{10} = 35$$

Range = Maximum – Minimum
= 54 – 23 = 31

Required difference = 35 – 31 = 4.

45. $5^2 = 12 + 13$

$7^2 = 24 + 25$

$11^2 = 60 + 61$

$17^2 = 144 + 145$

∴ $17^2 = 289 = 144 + 145$

Hence, the missing numbers are 144, 145.

46. Faiza says that $\frac{1}{8}$ is greater fraction than $\frac{1}{2}$

Clearly, $\frac{1}{2}$ fraction is greater than $\frac{1}{8}$.

The most appropriate for the error made by Faiza is a conceptual error.

Previous Paper (Solved)

CTET—PAPER-I, JANUARY 2022

(Exam held on 04-01-2022)

PART- I

Child Development and Pedagogy

1. Which of the following is an example of use of gross motor skills?
A. Balancing on one foot
B. Squeezing a pea
C. Turning pages of a book
D. Holding a pencil

2. Development changes are a result of:
A. Unique combination of genetic and environmental circumstances.
B. Only genetic makeup of an individual.
C. Only socio-cultural factors.
D. Neither hereditary nor environmental factors.

3. The period from 2 years to 6 years is referred to as:
A. Infancy B. Early childhood
C. Middle childhood D. Adolescence

4. **Assertion (A):** A lot of children's play in the cities is based on reality T.V. shows that they see.

Reason (R): Apart from family and peers these days media is becoming an important agency of socialization of children.

Choose the correct options.
A. Both (A) and (R) are true and (R) is the correct explanation of (A)
B. Both (A) and (R) are true, but (R) is not the correct explanation of (A)
C. (A) is true, but (R) is false
D. Both (A) and (R) are false

5. Which of the following factors are considered important by Piaget to facilitate learning?
(*i*) Mobility of the teacher
(*ii*) Provisioning of diverse materials
(*iii*) Providing moderately novel experiences
(*iv*) Ensuring positive and negative reinforcement
A. (*ii*), (*iv*) B. (*i*), (*ii*), (*iii*)
C. (*ii*), (*iii*), (*iv*) D. (*i*), (*ii*), (*iii*), (*iv*)

6. At which stage do children have an animistic view of the larger world and believe that the trees and plants as well as moving clouds and rolling stones can have motives and intentions?
A. Sensori-motor stage
B. Pre-operational stage
C. Concrete operational stage
D. Formal operational stage

7. Language plays an important role in the cognitive development of children in the theory of:
A. Lev Vygotsky
B. Jean Piaget
C. Howard Gardner
D. Lawrence Kohlberg

8. According to Vygotsky, children learn by:
A. having competitions
B. interaction with peers
C. striving for rewards and avoiding punishments
D. making stimulus-response connections

9. In a child-centered classroom children:
A. are looked at as passive imitators.
B. are actively engaged in construction of knowledge.
C. are eager to copy answer from blackboard as it is.
D. have to be passive listeners only.

10. Which of the following is a correctly matched pair?

A. Punishment and Obedience orientation	–	Laws are not fixed but can be changed for the good of the society.
B. Good-Boy – Good-girl orientation	–	One earns approval by being nice.
C. Law and Order orientation	–	Ethical principles are self-chosen than on the basis of the value of human rights.
D. Social Contract orientation	–	Physical consequences of an action determine whether it is good/bad.

11. In Howard Gardner's theory person high on .... intelligence can recognize and are aware of the beauty of different species of flora and fauna.
A. spatial B. naturalistic
C. musical D. inter-personal

12. National Education Policy 2020 recommends:
A. Multilingualism
B. Monolingualism
C. Standardization of curriculum
D. Standardization of assessment

13. A teacher holds the perception that boys are more intelligent and risk taking and girls are obedient and sincere and treats them accordingly. This is an example of:
A. gender bias B. gender constancy
C. gender equity D. gender equality

14. Assertion (A): Teachers should use a wide variety of assessment tools and technique to assess children.

Reason (R): No single assessment tool is capable of providing information about a child's progress and learning in different areas of development.

Choose the correct option.
A. Both (A) and (R) are true and (R) is the correct explanation of (A)
B. Both (A) and (R) are true, but (R) is not the correct explanation of (A)
C. (A) is true, but (R) is false
D. Both (A) and (R) are false

15. Which of the following situation does NOT illustrate assessment for learning?
A. Students actively think about where they are, where they are going and how to get there.
B. Teachers give constructive qualitative feedback to facilitate learning.
C. Constant comparisons are made between the students to enhance performance.
D. Several methods of formative assessment such as peer and self-assessment are used.

16. Inclusive Education requires:
A. Flexible pedagogies
B. Inaccessible building
C. Rigid mindsets
D. Standardized curriculum

17. Which of the following disability causes challenges in 'social communication'?
A. Autism B. Dyscalculia
C. Dysgraphia D. Locomotor disability

18. Which of the following helps in inclusion of learners from disadvantaged and deprived groups?
A. Consideration of diversity
B. Decontextualized curriculum
C. Pedagogy centered towards dominant group
D. Standardized testing

19. Provision of multiple modes of representation of content will help in inclusion of:
(*i*) students with hearing impairment
(*ii*) students with visual impairment
(*iii*) students facing learning difficulties
(*iv*) students facing locomotor difficulties
A. (*i*) B. (*ii*), (*iii*)
C. (*i*), (*ii*), (*iv*) D. (*i*), (*ii*), (*iii*), (*iv*)

20. Which of the following is a correctly matched pair of appropriate accommodation strategy for inclusion of students which specified disability?
A. Dyscalculia : Provision of calculator
B. Dyslexia : Assigning lengthy written assignments
C. Hearing Impairment : Giving audio tapes
D. Visual Impairment : Providing picture books

21. In early grades, which of the following approaches is preferable for teaching-learning process?
A. Imitation without understanding
B. Learning by doing
C. Passive listening
D. Rote-memorisation

22. Assertion (A): Participation in the social life of the school is significant for learning to occur.

Reason (R): Learning is primarily a social activity.

Choose the correct option.
A. Both (A) and (R) are true and (R) is the correct explanation of (A)
B. Both (A) and (R) are true, but (R) is not the correct explanation of (A)
C. (A) is true, but (R) is false
D. Both (A) and (R) are false

23. Teachers can make classroom activities meaningful by:
A. dividing them in disconnected chunks
B. giving ambiguous instructions about them
C. presenting them in decontextualized manner
D. situating them in the authentic context

24. Which of the following pedagogical practices does NOT contribute positively in teaching-learning process?
A. Curriculum adaptation as per needs
B. Experiential learning for students
C. Innovation in curricular planning
D. Rigid exam-centered teaching strategies

25. Assertion (A): A teacher should connect content to be taught with students' daily life experiences.

Reason (R): Children come to school with valuable life experiences that teachers need to pay attention to.

Choose the correct option.
A. Both (A) and (R) are true and (R) is the correct explanation of (A)
B. Both (A) and (R) are true, but (R) is not the correct explanation of (A)
C. (A) is true, but (R) is false
D. Both (A) and (R) are false

26. Which of the following helps learners evaluate their own learning and check their understanding?
A. Forgetting
B. Imitation
C. Metacognition
D. Rote-memorization

27. Misconception among children are:
A. Abnormal
B. Atypical
C. Natural
D. Rare

28. A student experiencing 'learned helplessness' is likely to:
A. show enthusiasm in learning
B. focus on mastery-oriented goals
C. focus on performance-oriented approach goals
D. withdraw from learning activities

29. Which of the following is an example of intrinsic motivation?
A. learning a new language out of interest
B. drawing a picture to win a cash prize
C. participating in a sport to win an award
D. studying to get praise of parents

30. Which of the following is an environmental factor which impact learning?
A. Attitude
B. Motivation
C. Personality traits
D. School

PART- II

Mathematics

31. A square has a bounding of 16 cm. From each of the four corners of this square, a small square of side 1 cm is cut off. What will be the length of the boundary of the remaining figure?
A. 12 cm
B. 14 cm
C. 16 cm
D. 18 cm

32. What will come in the blank?
2 thirds + ... = 11 twelfths
A. 9 thirds
B. 1 third
C. 3 twelfths
D. 13 twelfths

33. On her birthday Merlin's mother gave her a packet of toffees to share with her friends. Merlin gave $\frac{2}{7}$th of toffees to Aditi, $\frac{1}{6}$th to Amol, $\frac{2}{5}$th to Farhan, and $\frac{1}{7}$th to Jery. If she is left with only 2 toffees, then how many toffees were there in the packet.
A. 105
B. 210
C. 315
D. 420

34. A shopkeeper has some eggs. He wants to put them in trays which can have exactly 12 eggs. He filled 9 trays with eggs and left with 5 eggs. How many more number of eggs does he need so that no egg is left out after completing the 10th tray?
A. 5
B. 6
C. 7
D. 8

35. Savita went to ATM to withdraw some money. She got five notes of ₹ 2000, four notes of ₹ 500 and nine notes of ₹ 100. On counting she found that 1 note of ₹ 2000 and 1 note of ₹ 100 are less in the whole amount. How much amount did she enter for withdrawal?
A. 14000
B. 14500
C. 15000
D. 16500

36. Anu brought 2 kg 500 g Laddu, 3 kg 250 g Jalebi and 4 kg Rasgullas from a sweet shop. The shopkeeper packed everything together in boxes with a maximum capacity of 750 g. How many boxes required to pack all the items?
A. 15
B. 13
C. 14
D. 12

37. The four traffic lights of a cross road change after 30s, 45s, 1 minute and 75s respectively. If these lights changed simultaneously at 1:35 pm, then they will change simultaneously again at.
A. 2:05 pm
B. 1:50 pm
C. 2:10 pm
D. 1:55 pm

38. Rae and Reena have arranged the bricks horizontally one above the other. If the length, width and height of each bricks are 6 inches, 3 inches and 3 inches, respectively then how many rows of the bricks will be required to create a 3.5 meter wall?
A. 46
B. 58
C. 42
D. 64

39. Rama reads the following details on a packet before throwing it on 3rd July 2021.
Date of packing: 10th Jan 2021
Best before 180 days from the date of packing
Which of the following statement, is correct?
A. She should throw the packet as the date of expiry has been already crossed
B. She can still use the packet for almost one more week
C. She can wait for another six months as it will get expired after 180 days
D. The packet got expired on 10th June 2021 so she should throw it.

40. Teacher gave some objects to children that include a matchbox, a ball, a book, a steel glass and a rope. She asked them to identify the objects which have the most numbers of corners. Which of the following statements is correct for the above situation?
A. Rope should be selected as it is the longest among all the given objects
B. Book should be selected as it has more number of corners than the matchbox
C. Matchbox and book should be related as both of them can be classified in the same category of objects having edge, faces and corners
D. Ball should be selected as it has infinite corners

41. A closed shape made up of three or more than three line segments is called:
A. Triangle B. Quadrilateral
C. Polygon D. Polyhedrons

42. The temperature of a city is 23.5°C at 9 pm. If the temperature drops by 0.7°C every hour after that, then at what time the temperature will be 17.2°C?
A. 2:00 am B. 3:00 am
C. 5:00 am D. 6:00 am

43. Which of the following statements is true for the mean and median of the scores

15, 8, 13, 1, 23, 15, 20, 1
A. Mean is greater than the median
B. Median is greater than the mean
C. Both mean and median are equal
D. Median cannot be determined as there are even number of scores

44. The angles of rotations (rotational symmetry) of an equilateral triangle are:
A. 90°, 180°, 270°, 360°
B. 60°, 120°, 180°
C. 120°, 240°, 360°
D. 60°, 120°, 180°, 240°, 300°, 360°

45. Identify the next term of the given pattern

1ZA, 4YB, 9XC, 16WD, ...
A. 81VE B. 25VE
C. 25EV D. 81EV

46. Which of the following is NOT a stage/level of Van Hiele theory of geometrical reasoning?
A. Visualization B. Concrete operation
C. Analysis D. Axiomatic

47. "Continuous and comprehensive" evaluation in mathematics would include:
(*a*) Detailed feedback on the students conceptual understanding
(*b*) Only the collective progress of the class in terms of percentage of students failed or passed
(*c*) Progress of the students throughout the year
(*d*) Minimum levels of learning in mathematics

Choose the correct options:
A. (*b*) and (*d*) B. (*a*), (*b*) and (*d*)
C. (*a*) and (*c*) D. only (*b*)

48. Which of the following statements is NOT true about mapping in mathematics?
A. Mapping forms the basis for many topics in higher mathematics
B. Mapping strengthens spatial thinking
C. Mapping promotes proportional thinking
D. Mapping only includes drawing of a map of one's surroundings

49. Which of the following is a closed ended question?
A. List five-3-digit numbers that have digit 5 at the tens place
B. Draw a shape where the sum of all sides is 36 cm
C. Write five whole numbers between 178 and 184
D. List two sets of five numbers that have a sum of 50

50. Which of the following is NOT a type and utility of numbers?
A. Cardinal numbers B. Ordinal Numbers
C. Aesthetic Numbers D. Nominal Numbers

51. While teaching about measurement of length, a teacher asked the students to measure their table using hand spans and paper clips instead of measuring directly by a scale. What is the most appropriate reason for during this activity?
A. She wants to engage the children in hands-on activity because it is interesting for students
B. She wants her students to learn how to measure length correctly using paper clips
C. She wants her students to practise old ways of measurements using objects
D. She wants the students to understand the need for standard units for measurement

52. A primary school mathematics teacher asked the students to take out 'Ruler' as she was going to teach the topic on length measurement. Students got confused how can they take out a king or queen. Such words are called Homonyms. How can teachers address this challenge in classroom?
A. By asking the English language teacher to teach the word meanings of such words in English class
B. Teacher should draw the attentions of students to the specific meaning being used in mathematical context whenever such words appear in teaching
C. Teacher should prepare a list of such words with their meanings and ask students to memorise them
D. Teacher should ignore this as students eventually would learn many such words when they would practice more question

53. A class III teacher reads out the following problem to her students

"If I subtract '2 ones' from '2 tens' what will be the answer"

One students responded the answer is zero.

Which of the following statement is correct for the above context?

A. The answer given by the student is correct
B. Teacher should use concrete materials to strengthen the concept of place value in student
C. Teacher should give 10 similar problems to practice
D. Teacher should ignore the response of the student and should herself give the right answer and move to next problem to solve

54. While planning a lesson on the concept of addition of fractions a teacher is using the activity of rectangular strip folding. The above activity is a:

A. Content activity
B. Post content activity
C. Pre content activity
D. Wastage of time

55. Which one of the following is the most important characteristic of a good mathematics text book at primary level?

A. Concepts should be introduced through contexts
B. It should only contain numerous questions for practice
C. It should be attractive and colourful
D. Concepts should be introduced through formal algorithms

56. The National curriculum framework (2005) considers that mathematics involves 'a certain way of thinking and reasoning'. The vision can be realized by:

A. Giving special coaching to students
B. Adopting exploratory approach, use of manipulatives connecting concepts to real life, involving students in discussions
C. Rewriting all the text book of mathematics
D. Emphasizing on solving problems given in text book

57. As a mathematics educator what advice will you give to prospective teachers to improve children's performance in mathematics.

A. Get children as many books as possible for practice work
B. Advice parents for tutoring children at home
C. Help children make connections between conceptual and procedural knowledge
D. Plan remedial classes for children at the end of the year

58. The statement 'Teacher acts as a Facilitator, helps students to discover relationships and seek pattern for themselves' is most suited with:

A. Role play
B. Inductive method
C. Analytical method
D. Demonstration

59. A primary class teacher asks his students to collect data on number of boys and girls studying in class V in their neighbourhood (including at least five households). Which of the following most appropriately describes the purpose of this activity?

A. To make students aware of gender differences in their neighbourhood
B. To introduce the topic of data handling
C. To make children familiar with their community
D. To give holiday home work to students

60. Which of the following is NOT one of the steps of problem solving given by Polya.

A. Understanding the problem
B. Devise a Plan
C. Recreate the plan
D. Carry out the plan

PART- III

Environmental Studies

61. Crocodiles are mainly killed by poachers

A. for horns
B. for skin
C. for teeth
D. for scent

62. Bora is a common variety of 'glutinous' rice. It is mainly found in:

A. in Assam
B. in Bihar
C. in Odisha
D. in Tamil Nadu

63. In winters, grandmothers often use a solution of the following to protect the kin from dryness:

A. Rose water and distilled water
B. Rose water, glycerine and lemon juice
C. Lemon juice and milk
D. Rose water and vinegar

64. A bird that makes a nest hanging from the branch of a small tree or shrub is:

A. Sun bird
B. Crow
C. Barbet
D. Indian Robin

65. PNR on train ticket shows:

A. Passenger number record
B. Passenger name record

C. Personal name record
D. Personal number record

66. In Malayalam mother's elder sister is called as:
A. Valliamma B. Ammumma
C. Themma D. Didu

67. Which one of the following places is in Kerala?
A. Valsad B. Kozhikode
C. Udupi D. Malakheda

68. The village got its name from the many khejri trees growing there. The people of this village take great care of the plants, trees and animals. In India this village is:
A. in Uttarakhand B. in Uttar Pradesh
C. in Rajasthan D. in Maharashtra

69. The head of a herd of elephants is:
A. smallest female elephant
B. oldest female elephant
C. largest male elephant
D. smallest male elephant

70. Pottery is made strong:
A. by baking B. by smelting
C. by roasting D. by burning

71. The part of the plant that can be used for the treatment of toothache?
A. Fennel B. Clove
C. Fenugreek D. Poppy seeds

72. Identify the correct sequence of making 'Chapati' from wheat flour.
A. kneading flour into a dough, making small balls of the dough, rolling out the balls and then cooking it on fire.
B. making small balls of the dough, kneading flour into a dough, rolling out the balls and then cooking it on fire.
C. making small balls of the dough, rolling out the balls, kneading flour into a dough and cooking it on fire.
D. kneading flour into a dough , rolling out the balls and making small balls of the dough and cooking it on fire.

73. In dance the main poses and expressions demonstrates:
A. dance performance
B. feelings
C. confidence
D. hand and face movements

74. Children who cannot speak and hear, they learn?
A. through sign language
B. through native language
C. through their local language
D. through braille

75. Which of the following is different from others?
River, mountain, lake, pond, spring
A. river B. mountain
C. lake D. spring

76. Which of the following indicates the child centred nature of Environmental Studies at primary level?
(*a*) children's life at school must be linked to their life outside the school
(*b*) discourage rote learning
(*c*) departure from bookish learning
(*d*) having sharp boundaries among school, home and the community for the learning
A. (*a*) and (*b*) only B. (*a*) and (*c*) only
C. (*a*), (*b*) and (*c*) only D. (*b*) and (*d*) only

77. Which of the following can be the objective of Environmental Studies at primary level?
(*a*) encouraging children to reflect on their own learning
(*b*) engaging children by giving space, time and freedom to generate new knowledge.
(*c*) treating children as participants in learning, not as receivers of a fixed body of knowledge.
(*d*) treating the prescribed textbook as the sole basis of resources for learning.
A. (*a*), (*b*) and (*c*) only B. (*a*), (*c*) and (*d*) only
C. (*b*), (*c*) and (*d*) only D. (*c*) and (*d*) only

78. Which of the following statements is true in relation to Environmental Studies at primary level?
A. Environmental Studies (EVS) in Classes III to V as a subject integrates the concepts and issues of science, social science and environment education.
B. This subject is there in classes I and II and issues and concerns related to it are given through Language and Mathematics.
C. The language used in the EVS textbooks are formal.
D. It is based on a single subject approach

79. Which one of the following should be minimized in the EVS classroom?
A. Free debates B. Picture reading
C. Narratives D. Descriptions

80. Real challenge for EVS learning at primary level is:
A. Definitions and information
B. Rote learning
C. Descriptions of concepts
D. Opportunities for childrens to express themselves

81. Which of the following themes consists of subthemes in the syllabus of EVS at primary level?
A. Family and friends B. Water
C. Work and play D. Food

82. Authentic and meaningful learning of EVS can be given through:

(*a*) Narratives
(*b*) Real dialogues
(*c*) Process of experimentations
(*d*) Assessment of answer given by students as right and wrong

A. (*a*), (*b*) and (*d*) only B. (*c*) and (*d*) only
C. (*b*), (*c*) and (*d*) only D. (*a*), (*b*) and (*c*) only

83. Issues of theme "travel" can only be meaningful for the students:

A. if debates are conducted around the issues
B. if audio-visuals are shown to students
C. if demonstrations are given by teachers
D. theme based worksheets are given to students

84. Besides EVS textbooks, which one of the following may be a good resource for EVS learning?

A. Field visits B. Radio
C. Wikipedia D. Encyclopaedia

85. Socio-cultural issues related to Water Theme can be effectively learnt through:

(*a*) Role-play
(*b*) Real dialogue among students
(*c*) Field trip
(*d*) Demonstration and home work

A. (*a*), (*b*) and (*c*) only B. (*c*) and (*d*) only
C. (*d*) only D. (*c*) only

86. EVS textbook contain real stores, narratives and real events for the learning of EVS because:

(*a*) they are rich source of information and learning.
(*b*) they inspire students, teachers and the community.
(*c*) they can provide us an opportunity to revisit experiences we are familiar with.
(*d*) they make the pedagogy of EVS easy for the teachers

A. (*d*) only B. (*b*) only
C. (*c*) only D. (*a*), (*b*) and (*c*) only

87. For consolidating the learning of EVS, focus of assessment should be on:

A. for learning B. of learning
C. as learning D. informal learning

88. Raja, an EVS teacher uses an assessment tool that clearly indicates achievement criteria across all the components of students' work from written to oral to visual. Teacher is using:

A. Rubrics B. Check list
C. Anecdotal record D. Observation sheet

89. Self-assessment in EVS is:

(*a*) assessment as learning
(*b*) learning about learning
(*c*) judgements about achievements and the outcome of learning.
(*d*) assessment of learning.

A. (*a*), (*b*) and (*c*) only B. (*c*) only
C. (*a*) and (*c*) only D. (*a*), (*c*) and (*d*) only

90. Learning of EVS is based on the principle of:

A. simple to complex B. complex to simple
C. global to local D. abstract to concrete

PART- IV

Language-I : English

Directions (Qs. No. 91-99) : *Read the passage given below and answer the questions that follow by choosing the correct/most appropriate options.*

The Ganga is the lifeblood of hundreds of millions of people in India and Bangladesh. Every day, they depend on its water for drinking, cooking and washing. Farmers rely on the river for water for their crops. Hindus worship the Ganges as a Goddess named Ganga. Yet this river is threatened by pollution and by the increasing water demands of industries, cities and a growing population.

The Ganga begins in the Himalayas, the highest mountain range in the world. The river flows southeast across the plains of Northern India. It enters Bangladesh and is joined by the Brahmaputra river and the Meghana river. There the river's name changes to the Padma river. It forms a delta 220 miles (350 km) wide, which is shared by India and Bangladesh. Finally, the river empties into the Bay of Bengal.

In comparison with many other major world rivers, the Ganga is short, with a length of about 1,560 miles (2,150 km) for most of its course, the river is wide and its waters are slow-moving.

The main sources of the Ganga are Bhagirathi and the Alaknanda. The water in these rivers comes from glaciers high in the Himalayas. Melting glacial ice sustains the Ganga and its tributaries.

Monsoon plays a major role in the life of the Ganga river and in the lives of the people who live along its banks. The monsoon can cause terrible floods in the Ganga delta region. From its mountain source to its wide delta, the Ganga flows through a variety of ecosystems.

91. Which of the following statements is ***not true*** in the light of the passage above?
A. The Ganga runs wide for most of its course
B. It supports diverse eco-systems
C. Glaciers melt directly into the Ganga
D. The Ganga water depends much on the monsoon rains

92. Which of the following words is similar in meaning to the word, 'rely' as used in the passage? (para 1)
A. expect B. depend
C. submit D. promote

93. Which part of the speech is the underlined word in the sentence given below?
"It <u>then</u> enters Bangladesh and is joined by the Brahmaputra and the Meghana river".
A. Adjective B. Conjunction
C. Adverb D. Preposition

94. The greatest human challenge to the Ganga is:
A. growing population, industries and pollution
B. erratic monsoon
C. uncontrolled tributaries
D. agricultural dependence

95. The Ganga river is described as the "lifeblood" of people because:
A. people depend on the river for sustainance and survival
B. it is a holy river
C. it springs from the Himalayas
D. it is one of the oldest rivers of the country

96. The Ganga can be called a "Shared river" because:
A. it connects countries and weaves different civilizations together
B. it flows into the ocean and mingles with other waters
C. it is more beneficial to Bangladesh than India
D. it emerges out of the mountain ranges of the great Himalayas

97. The name of the Ganges changes to Padma river when it:
A. enters the Bay of Bengal
B. enters Bangladesh and is joined by the Brahmputra River and the Meghana river
C. flows through the plains Northern India
D. finally merges into the unknown seas

98. Which of the following is opposite in meaning to the word 'major' as used in the passage? (para 5)
A. unimportant B. insignificant
C. minor D. medicine

99. Which part of the following sentence contains an error?
(*a*) The car/(*b*) is in/(*c*) remarkably good condition/(*d*) of its age
A. (*b*) B. (*c*)
C. (*d*) D. (*a*)

Directions (Qs. No. 100-105) : *Read the poem given below and answer the questions that follow by choosing the correct/most appropriate options.*

The crucified planet Earth
Should it find a voice
and a sense of irony,
might now well say
of our abuse of it,

"Forgive them Father,
They know not what they do"
The irony would be that we know what
we are doing.
When the last living thing
has died on account of us,
how poetical it would be
If Earth could say,
in a voice floating up
perhaps
from the floor
of the Grand Canyon
"It is done"
People did not like it here.

100. Who is the speaker of the line, "Forgive them, Father, they know not what they do" in the above poem?
A. The Earth B. People
C. The heavens D. The planets

101. Identify and name the figure of speech used in 'Crucified Earth'?
A. Personification B. Conceit
C. Allegory D. Paradox

102. A sense of destructive fear pervades the poem. What prompts the poet to signal this note on apocalypse?
A. People did not like being on Earth
B. Earth itself no longer welcomes humans
C. God did not grant them forgiveness
D. Man has recklessly ruined and exploited nature

103. Which of the following is ***not true*** according to the extract?
A. We do not know what we are doing
B. We are destroying what sustains us
C. We are waiting for a saviour
D. We are too naive to understand the implications of our actions

104. "People did not like it here" is an example of:
A. hyperbole B. sarcasm
C. paradox D. metonymy

105. According to the poet, if the Earth is given a chance for any utterance, what would it say to God?
A. Stop the extinction of mankind
B. Forgive the wrongful deeds of men

C. Fix responsibility for the mindless destruction of the Earth
D. Give people the strength to resist temptation

106. Which one of the following is the highest level of writing skill?
A. Correct spelling
B. Digraph writing
C. Articles writing
D. Using difficult words in Sentences

107. Being a language teacher, you would like to adopt which form of the content?
A. Concrete descriptive and analytical
B. Abstract descriptive and analytical
C. Concrete descriptive and Conceptual
D. Abstract Conceptual and Conceptual

108. According to the Piaget, the process of language acquisition is:
A. associative B. matching
C. strategic D. social

109. A student whose home language and School language are different, how can you, as a teacher, help as a resource?
A. By giving him extra attention in class
B. Using multilingualism as resource in the classroom
C. By giving him flexibility in homework related work
D. By teaching in the class in his mother tongue

110. Consider the Statement (*a*) and (*b*) regarding Translanguaging.
(*a*) Translanguaging is a flexible form of multilingualism.
(*b*) Translanguaging is switching between the languages one known in order to maximise communicative potential.
A. (*a*) is true, (*b*) is false
B. (*a*) is false, (*b*) is true
C. Both (*a*) and (*b*) are true
D. Both (*a*) and (*b*) are false

111. What is used as a tool for learning language in whole language approach?
A. Actions B. Literature
C. Nursery rhymes D. Toys

112. The central role in total physical response is of:
A. teacher B. parents
C. family D. student

113. What is meant by 'reading skills' on the basis of National Curriculum Framework (NCF) 2005?
A. Correct pronunciation
B. Reading Syllables
C. Reading with understanding
D. Reading difficult sentences

114. What is the educational aspect of a language textbook?
A. Spelling of Book
B. Place of picture in Book
C. Selection of Content
D. Beautiful content with picture typography

115. Consider the activities assigned to the students. Which of the following activities should you try out to develop communication skills?
(*i*) He .... (is/are) on actor.
(*ii*) On the weekend, I'm going to .... in the morning and will return by 5 pm in evening.
(*iii*) Ask your friend where he/she likes to visit on weekend and why.
(*iv*) Ask your classmate two points which she/he considers while group discussion.
A. (*i*), (*ii*), (*iii*) B. (*ii*), (*iii*)
C. (*i*), (*ii*) D. (*iii*), (*iv*)

116. According to Krashen, ... is a subconscious process.
A. learning B. acquisition
C. listening D. communication

117. According to Vygotsky, children who make extensive use of .... learn complex tasks more effectively than the other children.
A. inner speech
B. individual speech
C. private speech
D. silent speech

118. According to Jean Piaget, a language develops from .... to .... speech.
A. private to individualized
B. private to socialized
C. egocentric to socialized
D. socialized to egocentric

119. During classroom discussion, a class VI student is presenting his/her own perspective over 'causes of corruption'. Neither he/she is convinced with other's ideas nor is he/she trying to look from other's perspective. Hence, according to Piaget, in which type of speech is he/she involved in?
A. ego-centric speech
B. social speech
C. individual speech
D. private speech

120. In order to make the students understand the grammatical structures, a language teacher should;
A. provide rich written material and let the students discover different structures.
B. provide extensive grammatical exercises to the students.
C. ask students to memorise structures from the book.
D. give an assignment to the students over different structures.

PART- V

Language-II : Hindi

निर्देश (प्र.सं. 121 से 128): *दिए गए गद्यांश को पढ़कर पूछे गए प्रश्न के लिए सबसे उपयुक्त विकल्प का चयन कीजिए।*

एक आदमी ने घृणा से एक तरफ थूकते हुए कहा, "क्या जमाना है! जवान लड़के को मरे पूरा दिन नहीं बीता और बूढ़ी औरत दुकान लगा के बैठी है।" दूसरे साहब अपनी दाढ़ी खुजाते हुए कह रहे थे, "अरे जैसी नीयत होती है अल्ला भी वैसी ही बरकत देता है"।

सामने के फुटपाथ पर खड़े एक आदमी ने दियासलाई की तीली से कान खुजाते हुए कहा, "अरे इन लोगों का क्या है? ये लोग रोटी के टुकड़े पर जान देते हैं।" परचून की दुकान पर बैठे लाला जी ने कहा, "अरे भाई, उनके लिए मरे-जिए का कोई मतलब न हो, पर दूसरे के धर्म ईमान का तो ख्याल करना चाहिए। जवान बेटे के मरने पर तेरह दिन का सूतक होता है और वह यहाँ सड़क पर बाजार में आकर खरबूजे बेचने बैठ गई है। हजार आदमी आते-जाते हैं। कोई क्या जानता है कि इसके घर में सूतक है। कोई इसके खरबूजे खा ले, तो उसका ईमान-धर्म कैसे रहेगा? क्या अँधेर है!"

पास-पड़ोस की दुकानों से पूछने पर पता लगा उसका तेईस बरस का जवान लड़का था, घर में उसकी बहू और पोता-पाती हैं। लड़का शहर के पास डेढ़ बीघा भर जमीन में कछियारी करके परिवार निर्वाह करता था। खरबूजों की डलिया बाजार में पहुँचाकर कभी लड़का स्वयं सौदे के पास बैठ जाता, कभी माँ बैठ जाती।

लड़का परसों सुबह मुँह अँधेरे बेलों में से पके खरबूजे चुन रहा था। गीली मेंड़ की तरावट में विश्राम करते हुए एक साँप पर लड़के का पैर पड़ गया। साँप ने लड़के को डस लिया।

लड़के की बुढ़िया माँ बावली होकर ओझा को बुला आई। झाड़ना-फूँकना हुआ। नागदेव की पूजा हुई।

121. परचून की दुकान का आशय है:
A. दवाइयों की दुकान
B. आटा-दाल आदि की दुकान
C. खिलौनों की दुकान
D. कपड़ों की दुकान

122. लोगों ने बुढ़िया के दुकान लगाने पर कटाक्ष क्यों किया?
A. बेटे की मृत्यु के उपरांत भी दुकान लगाई
B. बेटे की मृत्यु पर शोक सभा नहीं बुलाई
C. बेटे की मृत्यु पर घर में चूल्हा जलाया
D. बेटे की मृत्यु पर भोज का आयोजन नहीं किया

123. बुढ़िया के बेटे की मृत्यु का कारण था:
A. गीली मेंड़ पर फिसलना
B. गिरकर बेहोश हो जाना
C. साँप का डसना
D. खेत में करंट का लगना

124. बुढ़िया ने ओझा को क्यों बुलाया?
A. साँप को खोजकर मारने के लिए
B. साँप की पूजा-अर्चना करने के लिए
C. साँप के जहर की दवाई देने के लिए
D. साँप का जहर उतारने के लिए

125. स्त्रीलिंग शब्द नहीं है:
A. तरावट
B. पानी
C. सड़क
D. घृणा

126. शहर में खरबूजे बेचने का काम कौन करता था?
A. केवल बेटा
B. केवल माँ
C. बेटा और माँ दोनों
D. बेटा और बहू

127. 'क्या अँधेर है!' वाक्य में रेखांकित शब्द से तात्पर्य है:
A. सही बात
B. झूठी बात
C. गलत बात
D. कड़वी बात

128. बाजार से जुड़ा शब्द नहीं है:
A. दुकान
B. सौदा
C. तरावट
D. बरकत

निर्देश (प्र.सं. 129 से 135): *दिए गए गद्यांश को पढ़कर पूछे गए प्रश्नों के लिए सबसे उपयुक्त विकल्प का चयन कीजिए।*

जुलाई से अक्टूबर, घनघोर बारिश के महीने! यानी लोगों के पास बहुत सारा खाली वक्त या कहो आसपास के जंगलों से बाँस इकट्ठा करने का सही वक्त। आमतौर पर वे एक से तीन साल की उम्र वाले बाँस काटते हैं। बूढ़े बाँस सख्त होते हैं और टूट भी तो जाते हैं। बाँस से शाखाएँ और पत्तियाँ अलग कर दी जाती हैं। इसके बाद ऐसे बाँसों को चुना जाता है जिसमें गाँठें दूर-दूर होती हैं। दाओ यानी चौड़े, चाँद जैसे फाल वाले चाकू से इन्हें छीलकर खपच्चियाँ तैयार की जाती हैं। खपच्चियों की लम्बाई पहले से ही तय कर ली जाती है। मसलन, आसन जैसी चीजें बनाने के लिए बाँस को हरेक गठान से काटा जाता है लेकिन टोकरी बनाने के लिए हो सकता है कि दो या तीन या चार गठानों वाली लम्बी खपच्चियाँ काटी जाएँ। यानी कहाँ से काटा जाएगा यह टोकरी की लम्बाई पर निर्भर करता है।

आमतौर पर खपच्चियों की चौड़ाई एक इंच से ज्यादा नहीं होती है। चौड़ी खपच्चियाँ किसी काम की नहीं होतीं। इन्हें चीर कर पतली खपच्चियाँ बनाई जाती हैं। पतली खपच्चियाँ लचीली होती हैं। खपच्चियाँ चीरना उस्तादी का काम है। हाथों की कलाकारी के बिना खपच्चियों की मोटाई बराबर बनाए रखना आसान नहीं। इस हुनर को पाने में काफी समय लगता है।

टोकरी बनाने से पहले खपच्चियों को चिकना बनाना बहुत जरूरी है। यहाँ फिर दाओ काम आता है। खपच्ची बाएँ हाथ में होती है और दाओ दाएँ हाथ में।

129. गद्यांश में मुख्य रूप से वर्णन है :

A. बाँस से बनने वाली चीजों का
B. बाँस को भिन्न तरह से काटने का
C. खपच्चियों की लम्बाई का
D. खपच्ची काटने में होने वाले खतरे का

130. 'दाओ' है :

A. एक प्रकार का बाँस B. एक प्रकार का चाकू
C. एक प्रकार के लोग D. एक प्रकार की खपच्ची

131. 'पतली खपच्चियाँ लचीली होती हैं' में 'पतली' में विशेषण है :

A. संख्या बोधक विशेषण B. गुण बोधक विशेषण
C. परिणाम बोधक विशेषण D. सार्वनामिक विशेषण

132. गद्यांश में खपच्चियों को चिकना बनाने में प्रयोग किया जाता है :

A. दाओ B. मसलन
C. आसन D. उस्तादी

133. 'खपच्चियाँ चीरना उस्तादी का काम है' वाक्य में .... भाव निहित है।

A. तकनीक और कला का
B. कला और सौंदर्य का
C. तकनीक और खतरे का
D. खतरे और सावधानी का

134. 'चाँद' का पर्यायवाची नहीं है :

A. मयंक B. राशि
C. विज्ञ D. राकेश

135. बाँस का सामान बनाने के लिए .... खपच्चियों का प्रयोग किया जाता है।

A. मोटी B. पतली
C. चौड़ी D. पुरानी

136. किसी भाषा की उपभाषिक विशेषताओं के संबंध में कथन (अ) और (ब) पर विचार करें।

(*a*) ध्वनि की प्रबलता सिर्फ वह नहीं है जो आप कहते हैं, बल्कि वह है कि आप कैसे कहते हैं।
(*b*) स्वरशैली का अर्थ है आवाज या भाषण में विभिन्नता।

A. (*a*) सही, (*b*) गलत है
B. (*a*) गलत, (*b*) सही है
C. (*a*) और (*b*) दोनों सही हैं
D. (*a*) और (*b*) दोनों गलत हैं

137. किसी एक बच्चे द्वारा परिवार के सदस्यों की सहायता से सबसे पहले अर्जित की जाने वाली भाषा क्या कहलाती है?

A. प्रथम भाषा B. द्वितीय भाषा
C. क्षेत्रीय भाषा D. विदेशी भाषा

138. यदि किसी कक्षा के विद्यार्थी संप्रेषण के दौरान सीमित शब्दावली का प्रयोग करते हैं, तो उनकी शब्दावली को बढ़ाने का सबसे अच्छा तरीका क्या होगा?

A. विद्यार्थियों से संप्रेषण के दौरान प्रयोग करने योग्य शब्दों के पर्यायवाची और विलोम शब्दों की सूची बनाने के लिए कहें।
B. विद्यार्थियों को अधिक से अधिक किताबें पढ़ने और उनमें से शब्दों को लिखने के लिए कहें।
C. विद्यार्थियों को दिन में दो या तीन बार पाठ को सस्वर पढ़ने के लिए कहें।
D. विद्यार्थियों को समूह में संवाद करने के लिए कहें व उन्हें संप्रेषण में प्रयुक्त शब्दों को नए शब्दों से बदलने की अनुमति दें।

139. अपनी जटिल प्रकृति के बावजूद भाषा सहजात व्याकरणिक ज्ञान की मदद से अर्जित की जाती है। यह विचार किसके द्वारा प्रतिपादित सिद्धांत से संबंधित है?

A. स्टीफेन क्रेशन B. नॉम चॉमस्की
C. लेव वायगोत्स्की D. जीन पियाजे

140. जब बच्चे या तो खुद से बात करते हैं या किसी ऐसे व्यक्ति की खुशी के लिए जो उस समय चल रही गतिविधि में शामिल है। वह किस तरह के भाषण में शामिल है?

A. सामाजिक भाषण में B. निजी भाषण में
C. आत्मकेंद्रित भाषण में D. व्यक्तिगत भाषण में

141. कथन (*a*) और (*b*) पर विचार करें।

(*a*) भाषा चिंतन प्रक्रिया से जुड़ी हुई है।
(*b*) भाषा संभाषण की संरचना और संभाषण कार्यों का अभ्यास करने में मदद करती है।

A. (*a*) सही है, (*b*) गलत है
B. (*a*) गलत है, (*b*) सही है
C. (*a*) और (*b*) दोनों सही हैं
D. (*a*) और (*b*) दोनों गलत हैं

142. वायगोत्स्की के अनुसार, बच्चों में भाषा का विकास कब होता है?

A. जब वे दूसरों के साथ बातचीत करते हैं
B. जब वे भौतिक वस्तुओं के साथ बातचीत करते हैं
C. जब वे स्वयं से बातचीत करते हैं
D. जब वे चुप रहते हैं

143. निम्न में से कौन-सा कथन नॉम चॉमस्की के द्वारा प्रस्तावित भाषा अर्जन के सिद्धांत पर लागू नहीं होता?

A. भाषा की गहन संरचना
B. रचनान्तरण व्याकरण
C. अर्जन उपकरण
D. बच्चे के वातावरण की मुख्य भूमिका

144. निम्नलिखित का मिलान करें

कॉलम A	कॉलम B
(*a*) निवेश परिकल्पना	(*i*) जेम्स अहर
(*b*) कुल भौतिक प्रतिक्रिया	(*ii*) प्रभु
(*c*) कार्य आधारित भाषा शिक्षण	(*iii*) स्टीफन क्रेशन
(*d*) भाषा और मस्तिष्क	(*iv*) नॉम चॉमस्की

	(*a*)	(*b*)	(*c*)	(*d*)
A.	(*ii*)	(*iv*)	(*iii*)	(*i*)
B.	(*iii*)	(*ii*)	(*i*)	(*iv*)
C.	(*iv*)	(*iii*)	(*ii*)	(*i*)
D.	(*iii*)	(*i*)	(*ii*)	(*iv*)

145. निम्नलिखित में से कौन-सा कथन पियाजे के अनुसार सही है?

A. विचार भाषा से पहले है।

B. भाषा विचार से पहले है।

C. भाषा और विचार दो स्वतंत्र अवधारणाएँ हैं।

D. भाषा और भाषण तीन वर्ष की अवस्था के आस-पास एक साथ सम्मिलित हो जाते हैं।

146. एक शिक्षक एक लेख पढ़ने के दौरान विद्यार्थियों को इन चरणों का पालन करने का निर्देश देता है/देती है। प्रत्येक अनुच्छेद या खंड के लिए एक शीर्षक वाक्य खोजें या लिखें; कई विशिष्ट बिन्दुओं को समाहित करने वाले मुख्य विचारों की पहचान करें; प्रत्येक मुख्य विचार के लिए कुछ सहायक जानकारी प्राप्त करें; अनावश्यक जानकारी या विवरण को हटा दें। शिक्षक यहाँ किस रणनीति का उपयोग कर रहा है/रही है?

A. पहचानना
B. सारांशित करना
C. अनुमान लगाना
D. स्पष्ट करना

147. एक शिक्षक भाषा का अभ्यास कराने के लिए लक्ष्य भाषा में गहन मौखिक बातचीत का प्रयोग कर रहा/रही है। इस विधि को किस रूप में जाना जाता है?

A. प्राकृतिक विधि
B. शास्त्रीय विधि
C. द्विभाषीय विधि
D. श्रव्य भाषिक विधि

148. भाषा के अन्तःक्रियात्मक मॉडल के बारे में विषम कथन का चयन करें।

A. पारस्परिक संबंधों के प्रति समझ बनाने के रूप में भाषा।

B. व्यक्तियों के बीच परस्पर सामाजिक लेन-देन करने के साधन के रूप में भाषा।

C. प्रामाणिक सन्देश देने और प्राप्त करने के साधन के रूप में भाषा।

D. व्याकरण और शब्दावली के परस्पर संबंध को स्थापित करने के साधन के रूप में भाषा।

149. रोहिणी कक्षा पाँच के विद्यार्थियों के सामने एक विषय-सामग्री प्रस्तुत करना चाहती है, उसे निम्नलिखित में से किस बिंदु पर विचार करना चाहिए?

(*i*) शिक्षण गतिविधियों का उपयोग (संवाद और सूचना में रिक्तता)।

(*ii*) लक्ष्य भाषा के औपचारिक, संवादात्मक और अन्य पहलुओं को प्रदर्शित करना।

(*iii*) जहाँ आवश्यक हो वहाँ उचित सहायता प्रदान करना।

(*iv*) ड्रिलिंग की आदत विकसित करने का प्रयास।

A. (*i*), (*ii*), (*iii*)
B. (*i*), (*ii*), (*iv*)
C. (*i*), (*iii*)
D. (*ii*), (*iv*)

150. एक भाषा शिक्षक एक समूह परियोजना पर विद्यार्थियों के प्रदर्शन का आकलन करना चाहता है, यहाँ व्यक्तिगत प्रदर्शन के मूल्यांकन के मापदंड के क्या आधार होंगे?

A. समान आयु के साथियों के प्रदर्शन के आधार।

B. प्रत्येक विद्यार्थी का स्वयं का पिछला स्तर।

C. समूह प्रदर्शन का स्तर।

D. सभी के लिए एक समान मानदंड।

Answers

1	2	3	4	5	6	7	8	9	10
A	A	B	A	B	B	A	B	B	B
11	**12**	**13**	**14**	**15**	**16**	**17**	**18**	**19**	**20**
B	A	A	A	C	A	A	A	D	A
21	**22**	**23**	**24**	**25**	**26**	**27**	**28**	**29**	**30**
B	A	D	D	A	C	C	D	A	D
31	**32**	**33**	**34**	**35**	**36**	**37**	**38**	**39**	**40**
C	C	D	C	C	B	B	A	B	C
41	**42**	**43**	**44**	**45**	**46**	**47**	**48**	**49**	**50**
C	D	B	C	B	B	C	D	C	C
51	**52**	**53**	**54**	**55**	**56**	**57**	**58**	**59**	**60**
D	B	B	C	A	B	C	B	B	C
61	**62**	**63**	**64**	**65**	**66**	**67**	**68**	**69**	**70**
B	A	B	A	A	A	B	C	B	A
71	**72**	**73**	**74**	**75**	**76**	**77**	**78**	**79**	**80**
B	A	B	A	B	C	A	A	D	D

81	82	83	84	85	86	87	88	89	90
A	D	A	A	A	D	A	A	A	A
91	92	93	94	95	96	97	98	99	100
C	B	C	A	A	A	B	C	C	A
101	102	103	104	105	106	107	108	109	110
A	D	C	B	B	C	A	C	B	C
111	112	113	114	115	116	117	118	119	120
B	A	C	C	D	B	C	C	A	A
121	122	123	124	125	126	127	128	129	130
B	A	C	D	B	C	C	C	B	B
131	132	133	134	135	136	137	138	139	140
B	A	C	C	B	C	A	D	B	B
141	142	143	144	145	146	147	148	149	150
C	A	D	D	A	B	A	D	A	B

Explanatory Answers

1. **Gross Motor Skills Development:** As children develop their gross motor skills (*e.g.*, crawling, standing, balancing on one foot and walking), they become more coordinated in their body movements, more sophisticated in the activities in which they engage, and more advanced in physical skills that provide a foundation for academics—for example, eye-hand coordination and balance. Many gross motor skills are enhanced through creative arts activities such as movement and drama. Specifically, the Head Start Framework identifies the following gross motor skills as ones that preschoolers should be encouraged to develop:

   - **Movement:** Coordination of body alone and when using objects.

     Example: Children sitting on a chair with shoes and socks off, picking up small objects with toes and depositing them in a nearby bucket.

   - **Navigation:** Movement of body through space and use of directionality.

     Example: Placing a hard-cooked egg on a spoon and having children walk from Point A to Point B. Having them on their hands and knees and pushing an egg with their nose from Point A to Point B.

   - **Balance:** Control of body during physical movements.

     Example: Arranging several hula hoops of different colours on the floor, and having children jump from one colour to another, and then hop to the closest hula hoop.

3. An **infant** is the more formal or specialised synonym for the common term baby, meaning the very young offspring of human beings. The term may also be used to refer to juveniles of other organisms. A newborn is, in colloquial use, an infant who is only hours, days, or up to one month old.

   Early childhood is a stage in human development. It generally includes toddlerhood and some time afterwards. Play age is an unspecific designation approximately within the scope of early childhood. In this phase there is significant synaptic growth and myelination of neural fibers in the brain, especially within the frontal lobes.

   Middle Childhood: The period extends from age 6 to age 11 years. During this time, the growth rate is slow but steady. Physical development during middle childhood is less dramatic than in early childhood or adolescence. Growth is slow and steady until the onset of puberty when individuals begin to develop at a much quicker pace.

   Adolescence is a transitional stage of physical and psychological development that generally occurs during the period from puberty to adulthood. Adolescence is usually associated with the teenage years, but its physical, psychological or cultural expressions may begin earlier and end later. Puberty now typically begins during preadolescence, particularly in females. Physical growth (particularly in males) and cognitive development can extend into the early 20s. Age provides only a rough marker of adolescence, and scholars have not agreed upon a precise definition. Traditionally, it includes ages 10 to 19, but an expansive definition includes ages 10 to 24 to account for a more comprehensive understanding of this phase of life.

6. Famous cognitive psychologist, Jean Piaget proposed an important theory of cognitive development. This perspective focuses on how children construct their

understanding of the world as they pass through four stages of cognitive development through assimilation (responding according to existing schemas) and accommodation (modifying a schema to fit new information). Each of these age-related stages consists of different ways of thinking. Each stage represents a fundamental change in how children understand and organize their environment. In Piaget's words, it is said that 'Children think differently from adults'.

Piaget's Stages of Cognitive Development

Stage	Approximate Age	Features
Sensori-motor stage	Birth to 2 years	Infants gain knowledge of the world through their senses and motor skills.
Pre-operational stage	2 to 7 years	Children begin to use words and numbers to represent aspects of the world through her or his perspective.
Concrete operational stage	7 to 11 years	Children begin to think logically about concrete things but have difficulty in understanding abstract concepts.
Formal Operational stage	11 years and beyond	Adolescents think about abstract and theoretical concepts; use logic to find creative solutions to problems.

7. Lev Vygotsky proposed another major theory of cognitive development. Vygotsky's view emphasizes that cognitive skills need to be interpreted developmentally, are mediated by language, and have their origins in social relations and culture. Zone of proximal development (ZPD) is Vygotsky's term for the range of tasks that are too difficult for children to master alone but that can be learned with the guidance and assistance of adults and more-skilled children. Scaffolding is an important concept in Vygotsky's theory. He also argued that language plays a key role in guiding cognition. Applications of Vygotsky's ideas to education include using the child's zone of proximal development and scaffolding, using more-skilled peers as teachers, monitoring and encouraging children's use of private speech, and accurately assessing the zone of proximal development. These practices can transform the classroom and establish a meaningful context for instruction. Like Piaget, Vygotsky emphasized that children actively construct their understanding of the world. Unlike Piaget, he did not propose stages of cognitive development, and he emphasized that children construct knowledge through social interaction. In Vygotsky's theory, children depend on tools provided by the culture, which determines which skills they will develop. Some critics say that Vygotsky overemphasized the role of language in thinking.

8. Vygotsky believes that young children are curious and actively involved in their own learning and the discovery and development of new understandings/ schema. However, Vygotsky placed more emphasis on social contributions to the process of development, whereas Piaget emphasized self-initiated discovery.

According to Vygotsky (1978), much important learning by the child occurs through social interaction with a skillful tutor. The tutor may model behaviors and/or provide verbal instructions for the child. Vygotsky refers to this as cooperative or collaborative dialogue. The child seeks to understand the actions or instructions provided by the tutor (often the parent or teacher) then internalizes the information, using it to guide or regulate their own performance.

12. The New National Education Policy was approved by the Union Cabinet on 29 July, 2020 to bring about transformational reforms in school and higher education systems in the country. The first education policy of the 21st century replaces the 34-year-old National Policy on Education (NPE), 1986. Also, the Ministry of Human Resources and Development was renamed the Ministry of Education.

Some important recommendation:

- Through the open schooling system, the NEP 2020 will bring 2 crores out of school children back into the mainstream.
- The current 10+2 system in the school will be replaced by a new 5+3+3+4 curricular structure corresponding to ages 3-8, 8-11, 11-14, and 14-18 years respectively.
- In higher education, Gross Enrolment Ration to be raised to 50% by 2035 and 3.5 crore seats to be added in higher education.
- Higher Education curriculum to possess Flexibility of Subjects.
- NEP 2020 will also emphasise in setting up of the Gender Inclusion Fund, Special Education Zones for disadvantaged regions, and groups.
- To increase the public investment in the education sector to reach 6% of GDP at the earliest and for this, both the Centre and the States will work together.
- In both schools and higher education, NEP will promote Multilingualism. Therefore, the National Institute for Pali, Persian, and Prakrit, Indian Institute of Translation and Interpretation to be set up.
- So these are some important points about India's New National Education Policy (NEP), 2020. Hoping that this policy will boost employment in the country and will radically transform our educational ecosystem.

16. Inclusive Education requires flexible pedagogies. Inclusion in education is based on the belief that every child can learn and realise her full potential if provided equal opportunities to participate in school, supported with resources required as per her condition and taught in a manner appropriate to her needs.

Ideally, a child must receive education in an environment that is the least restrictive and is most conducive to his/her needs. This means that general education is the placement of first choice for all wherein a child with disabilities is with her/his peers without disabilities to the maximum degree possible. Such an education is called Inclusive Education. It is the most effective and equitable of the various models of education for the overall growth and development of all children in both curricular and co-curricular domains. Children studying in an Inclusive school develop confidence and imbibe values of sharing and participation. Thus, inclusion is a basic human right and not a privilege.

The term inclusive education appeared in literature in the late 1980s as an alternative to special education, to give access to children with special needs coming from diverse background.

17. Autism is a PDD (Pervasive Development Disorder). These disorders are considered to be the result of some structural differences in the brain that are usually evident at birth or become apparent as the child begins to develop. Autism is a development disorder which involves wide range of problematic behaviour. This includes defect in language, perception, motor development not related to reality and social situations. Sometime intellectual ability is also hindered as there is impairment on memory as well.

Causes of Autism Spectrum Disorder: Scientists are not certain about what causes ASD, but it is likely that both genetics and environment play a role.

The counselor can provide following method of counseling:

- Help the client in mastering the fundamentals of social behaviour
- Development of some language skills
- Behavioural counseling
- Parental counseling
- Training children to do their own work
- Engaging the child in various activities
- Behaviour modification techniques etc.

20. Dyscalculia sometimes called dysarithmia, is a disability resulting in difficulty learning or comprehending arithmetic, such as difficulty in understanding numbers, learning how to manipulate numbers, performing mathematical calculations and learning facts in mathematics. It is sometimes informally known as "math dyslexia", though this can be misleading as dyslexia is a different condition from dyscalculia.

Dyscalculia is associated with dysfunction in the region around the intraparietal sulcus and potentially also the frontal lobe. Dyscalculia does not reflect a general deficit in cognitive abilities or difficulties with time, measurement, and spatial reasoning. Estimates of the prevalence of dyscalculia range between 3 and 6% of the population. In 2015, it was established that 11% of children with dyscalculia also have ADHD. Dyscalculia has also been associated with Turner syndrome and people who have spina bifida.

26. Metacognition helps learners evaluate their own learning and check their understanding. Metacognition is an awareness of one's own thought processes and an understanding of the patterns behind them. The term comes from the root word meta, meaning "beyond", or "on top of". Metacognition can take many forms, such as reflecting on one's own ways of thinking and knowing when and how to use particular strategies for problem-solving. There are generally two components of metacognition: (1) knowledge about cognition and (2) regulation of cognition.

Metamemory, defined as knowing about memory and mnemonic strategies, is an especially important form of metacognition. Academic research on metacognitive processing across cultures is in the early stages, but there are indications that further work may provide better outcomes in cross-cultural learning between teachers and students.

30. The learning environment dramatically affects the learning outcomes of students. Schools' open space and noise, inappropriate temperature, insufficient light, overcrowded classes, misplaced boards and inappropriate classroom layout all make up factors that could be confounding variables distracting students in class.

31. Given, perimeter of a square = 16 cm

$\Rightarrow \quad 4 \times \text{side} = 16$ cm

$\Rightarrow \quad \text{side} = 4$ cm

$\because$ A small square of side 1 cm is cut off from each corner

$\therefore$ The length of the boundary of the remaining figure

$= 16 - 4(2) + 4(2)$

$= 16 - 8 + 8$

$= 16$ cm.

32. 2 third + x = 11 twelfth

$$\Rightarrow \quad \frac{2}{3} + x = \frac{11}{12}$$

$$\Rightarrow \quad x = \frac{11}{12} - \frac{2}{3}$$

$$= \frac{11-8}{12}$$

$$= \frac{3}{12}$$

$$\Rightarrow x = \frac{3}{12} = 3 \text{ twelfth.}$$

33. Let the number of toffees $= x$

Then, $x - \left[\frac{2x}{7} + \frac{x}{6} + \frac{2}{5}x + \frac{1}{7}x\right] = 2$

$$\Rightarrow x - \left[\frac{60x + 35x + 84x + 30x}{210}\right] = 2$$

$$\Rightarrow x - \frac{209}{210}x = 2$$

$\Rightarrow 210x - 209x = 420$

$\Rightarrow x = 420$

Hence, there were 420 toffees in the pocket.

34. Here, the total number of eggs = 12 × 10 = 120

∴ The number of eggs needed

= 120 – [12 × 9 + 5]

= 120 – [108 + 5]

= 120 – 113

= 7.

35. Let amount enter for withdrawal = ₹ x

Then, ₹ x – [₹ 2000 + ₹ 100]

= ₹ [5 × 2000 + 4 × 500 + 9 × 100]

⇒ ₹ x – ₹ 2100 = 10000 + 2000 + 900

⇒ ₹ x = ₹ 2100 + ₹ 12900

⇒ ₹ x = ₹ 15000.

36. The total weight of sweets (items)

= 2 kg 500 gm + 3 kg 250 gm + 4 kg

= 9 kg 750 gm = 9750 gm

Capacity of box = 750 gm

∴ The number of boxes required to pack all the items

$$= \frac{9750}{750} = 13.$$

37. LCM of 30, 45, 60, 75 = 900

∵ 900 seconds = 60 seconds × 15

= 15 minutes

Hence, they will change simultaneously again at 1:35 pm + 15 minutes

= 1:50 pm.

42. Total temperature drop = 23.5°C – 17.2°C = 6.3°C

$$\therefore \quad \text{Time} = \frac{6.3°C}{0.7°C} = 9 \text{ hours}$$

[given, the temperature drop by 0.7°C every hour]

Hence, temperature will be 17.2°C at 9 pm + 9 hr

= 6 am.

43. Scores in ascending order:

1, 1, 8, 13, 15, 15, 20, 23

Here, $n = 8$ (even number)

$$\therefore \quad \text{Median} = \frac{1}{2}\left[\frac{n}{2}\text{th term} + \left(\frac{n}{2}+1\right)\text{th term}\right]$$

$$= \frac{1}{2}[4\text{th term} + 5\text{th term}]$$

$$= \frac{1}{2}[13 + 15]$$

$$= \frac{1}{2}[28]$$

$$= 14$$

$$\text{and Mean} = \frac{1+1+8+13+15+15+20+23}{8} = 12$$

Hence, Median is greater than the mean

⇒ Median (14) > Mean (12).

45.

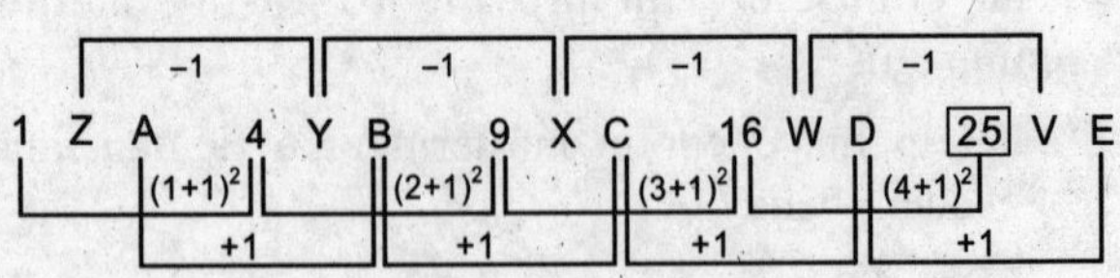

Hence, the next term = 25VE.

Previous Paper (Solved)

CTET—PAPER-I, JANUARY 2021*

PART- I

Child Development and Pedagogy

Directions (Qs. No. 1 to 30): *Answer the following questions by selecting the* ***correct/most appropriate*** *options.*

1. In order to address learners from diverse backgrounds, a teacher should:
A. use standardized assessment for all.
B. use statements that strengthen negative stereotypes.
C. avoid talking about aspects related to diversity.
D. draw examples from diverse settings.

2. Problem-solving abilities can be facilitated by:
A. encouraging use of analogies.
B. generating fear among students.
C. focusing on drill and practice.
D. encouraging fixed process of solving the problems.

3. In order to address the needs of students who are facing learning difficulties, a teacher should NOT:
A. do individualized educational planning.
B. practice rigid structures for pedagogy and assessment.
C. use multiple audio-visual aids.
D. use constructive pedagogical approaches.

4. _______ is the primary Identifying feature of creativity.
A. Hyperactivity B. Inattentiveness
C. Low comprehension D. Divergent thinking

5. Which of the following is most effective mode of teaching-learning?
A. Observation without analysis
B. Imitation and repetition
C. Rote memorization of content
D. Exploration of relationships between concepts

6. A teacher should analyse the various errors made by students on a given task because:
A. she can segregate those who made more errors in comparison to others.
B. learning is solely based on correction of errors.
C. she can decide degree of punishment accordingly.
D. understanding of errors are meaningful in the teaching-learning process.

7. Motivation to learn can be sustained by:
A. giving very easy tasks to children.
B. focusing on rote-memorisation.
C. punishing the child.
D. focusing on mastery-oriented goals.

8. Shame _______
A. is very effective to motivate the children to learn.
B. should be generated frequently in teaching-learning process.
C. has no relation to cognition.
D. can have negative impact on cognition.

9. Constructivist view of learning suggests that children ________ construction of their own knowledge.
A. play an active role in
B. are solely dependent on textbooks in
C. have no role to play in
D. are solely dependent on adults for

10. Which of the following belief is good for learning?
A. Efforts don't make any difference.
B. Failure is uncontrollable.
C. Ability is improvable.
D. Ability is fixed.

11. Conceptual understanding among students is likely to improve in the settings which emphasise on:
A. frequent examinations.
B. inquiry and dialogue.
C. competitions.
D. textbook-centric pedagogy.

12. It is difficult for children to learn when:
A. learning is socially contextualized.
B. content is represented through multiple ways.
C. information is presented in disconnected chunks.
D. they are intrinsically motivated.

13. Best state of learning is:
A. moderate arousal, no fear.
B. no arousal, no fear.
C. high arousal, high fear.
D. low arousal, high fear.

14. Individual differences in development of children can be attributed to:
A. neither heredity nor environment.
B. interplay of heredity and environment.
C. heredity only.
D. environment only.

15. During a task, Saina is talking to herself about ways she can proceed on the task. According to Lev Vygotsky's ideas on language and thought; this kind of 'private speech' is a sign of:

**Exam was held on 31-01-2021.*

A. Ego-centricism. B. Psychological disorder.
C. Cognitive immaturity. D. Self-regulation.

16. Evaluation practices should aim at:
A. identifying students' needs and requirements.
B. identification of high-achievers for prize distribution.
C. labelling of students.
D. segregation of students for ability-based groups.

17. After observing that students are struggling to proceed further on an ongoing activity, a teacher decides to provide cues and hints in form of what, why, how. According to Lev Vygotsky's theory, this strategy of teacher will:
A. cause withdrawal tendency among students.
B. be meaningless in process of learning.
C. demotivate the children to learn.
D. act as a scaffold for learning.

18. After getting hurt during a play activity, Rohan started crying. Seeing this, his father responded, "Don't behave like girls, boys don't cry". This statement by the father:
A. reduces gender bias.
B. promotes gender equality.
C. reflects gender stereotype.
D. challenges gender stereotype.

19. In a progressive classroom:
A. ample opportunities should be provided for construction of knowledge.
B. students should be labelled on the basis of their academic scores.
C. a teacher should follow fixed curriculum.
D. the emphasis should be on competition among students.

20. According to Lawrence Kohlberg's theory, "Performing an act and doing something because others approves it", represents ________ stage of morality.
A. Post-conventional B. Formal conventional
C. Pre-conventional D. Conventional

21. Which of the following is correct in the context of socialization of children?
A. Peers are primary socialization agents and family is a secondary socialization agent.
B. Family and mass-media both are secondary socialization agents.
C. School is a secondary socialization agent and family is a primary socialization agent.
D. School is a primary socialization agent and peers are secondary socialization agents.

22. Theory of multiple intelligence emphasizes that:
A. There are several forms of intelligences.
B. There are no individual differences in intelligence.
C. Intelligence Quotient (IQ) can be measured only by objective tests.
D. Intelligence in one domain ensures intelligence in all other domains.

23. Pre-operational stage in Jean Piaget's theory of cognitive development characterizes _______ .
A. Hypothetico deductive thinking
B. Ability to conserve and seriate objects.
C. Development of abstract thinking
D. Centration in thought

24. Which of the following statement is correct in context of development?
A. Development occurs only during the period of childhood.
B. Development is multi-dimensional.
C. Development has the same rate of growth across cultures for everyone.
D. Development occurs only through learning that takes place in school.

25. Lev Vygotsky's social-cultural perspective of learning emphasizes importance of _____ in the learning process.
A. Motivation B. Equilibration
C. Cultural tools D. Attribution

26. In his theory of cognitive development, Jean Piaget explains cognitive structures in terms of ________.
A. Zone of proximal development
B. Schemas
C. Psychological tools
D. Stimulus-response association

27. In on Inclusive classroom emphasis should be on:
A. segregation of students based on their social identity.
B. providing opportunities aiming at maximizing potential of individual children.
C. performance oriented goals.
D. undifferentiated instructions

28. According to Right of Persons with Disabilities Act (2016), which of the following term is appropriate to use?
A. Student with physical disability
B. Student with crippled body
C. Retarded student
D. Handicapped student

29. Sequence of development among children from birth to adolescence is:
A. concrete, abstract, sensory.
B. abstract, concrete, sensory.
C. sensory, concrete, abstract.
D. abstract, sensory, concrete.

30. Individual differences in a progressive classroom should be treated as:
A. criteria for making ability-based groups.
B. important for planning of teaching-learning process.
C. a hindrance to the process of learning.
D. a failure on the part of teacher.

PART- II

Mathematics

Directions: *Answer the following questions by selecting the* ***correct/most appropriate*** *options.*

31. Which of the following is least likely to impact teaching-learning in mathematics?
A. Knowing ways in which assessment affected the confidence of learners
B. Providing complete solutions to students' wrong answers
C. Enhanced quality of feedback
D. Using results of assessment to modify teaching

32. Rohit realises that square is both a rhombus and a rectangle. He is at what stage of Van Hiele's visual thinking?
A. Level 2 (Relationships)
B. Level 3 (Deduction)
C. Level 0 (Recognition)
D. Level 1 (Analysis)

33. "The sum of any two whole numbers is a whole number."

This property of whole numbers is referred to as:
A. associative property
B. distributive property
C. closure property
D. commutative property

34. Which of the following statements regarding mathematics teaching-learning is **incorrect**?
A. Mathematical knowledge can be created in primary class students through observation of pattern and generalisations.
B. Argumentation and negotiation play an important role in creating mathematical knowledge.
C. Mathematical learning is a social process involving dialogue.
D. Culture and context has no role in constructing mathematical knowledge.

35. Which of the following statements is/are true regarding teaching 'Numbers' at primary level?
(*a*) Intuitive understanding of numbers should be encouraged.
(*b*) Writing numbers should be taught in sequence.
(*c*) Writing of numbers as Numerals should preceed counting.
(*d*) Order irrelevance of numbers should be encouraged.
A. (*a*) and (*d*) B. (*c*) and (*d*)
C. (*a*) and (*b*) D. (*b*) and (*c*)

36. Which of the following is the most important aspect of teaching of mathematics at primary level?
A. Preparing for higher education and employment.
B. Promoting and preparing for technology.
C. Making mathematics part of children's life experiences.
D. Developing rigour in calculations.

37. Which of the following statements is **NOT correct** with regard to nature of mathematics?
A. Primary level mathematics is concrete and does not require abstraction.
B. Mathematics uses special vocabulary to communicate ideas precisely.
C. Argumentation skill is important in construction of mathematical knowledge.
D. Mathematical concepts are hierarchical in nature.

38. Which of the following activities is **most likely** to develop spatial reasoning among students?
A. Identifying tessellating figures
B. Drawing bar graphs to represent data
C. Identifying patterns in a number-chart
D. Solving Sudoku puzzles

39. Which of the following is most suitable for teaching children the concept of fractions?
A. Number charts B. Cuisenaire rods
C. Abacus D. Geoboards

40. In which of the following statements, number 'three' is used in ordinal sense?
A. All groups have three team members.
B. This box contains many sets of three pencils.
C. I live on the third floor of this building.
D. This house has three rooms.

41. Identify the correct statement.
A. The units of perimeter and area are same.
B. The shape of figure determines the perimeter.
C. If two figures have same area, their perimeters are equal.
D. If two figures have same perimeter, their areas are equal.

42. Identify the correct statement with respect to the mathematics curriculum.
A. The concept of negative numbers should be introduced at primary level for better understanding.
B. The concept of area-measurement should be introduced only at upper primary level.
C. The foundation of algebraic thinking can be laid at primary level.
D. The concept of fractions should be introduced only at upper primary level.

43. Identify the correct statement with regard to introducing the concept of triangles at primary level.
A. Children should be exposed to triangles of all types but exposure to other figures should be avoided.
B. Children should be exposed to triangles of all types and also to other figures.
C. Definition of a triangle should be provided first.
D. Children should only be exposed to equilateral triangles to avoid confusion.

44. In a division sum, the divisor is 5 times the quotient and twice the remainder. If the remainder is 5, what is the number?
A. 25 B. 48
C. 52 D. 15

45. The sum of five consecutive numbers is 20. What is the sum of first three consecutive numbers?
A. 11 B. 12
C. 5 D. 9

46. A wire in the form of a square encloses an area of 144 cm^2. How much area is enclosed if the same wire is bent in the form of a rectangle of length 16 cm?
A. 128 cm^2 B. 96 cm^2
C. 124 cm^2 D. 48 cm^2

47. Amongst the following fractions, the largest and second largest fractions, respectively are

$$\frac{5}{6}, \frac{3}{4}, \frac{1}{2}, \frac{2}{3}, \frac{3}{5}$$

A. $\frac{3}{5}$ and $\frac{2}{3}$ B. $\frac{3}{4}$ and $\frac{1}{2}$
C. $\frac{5}{6}$ and $\frac{3}{4}$ D. $\frac{5}{6}$ and $\frac{3}{5}$

48. Asmita reaches school for a meeting 15 minutes before 8.30 am. She reached half an hour earlier than her colleague who is 40 minutes late for meeting. What is the scheduled time of the meeting?
A. 8.45 am B. 8.05 am
C. 8.15 am D. 9.10 am

49. In how many ways, 48 small squares of 1 cm × 1 cm can be arranged so that the resulting area is 48 cm^2?
A. 5 B. 2
C. 6 D. 4

50. In school assembly, students of a class are standing in a line. Ruhi is 19th from both ends. How many students are present in that class?
A. 36 B. 40
C. 38 D. 37

51. A number is larger than half of 100. It is more than 6 tens and less than 8 tens. The sum of its digits is 9. The tens digit is the double of the ones digit. What is the number ?
A. 54 B. 81
C. 72 D. 63

52. The rates of various stationery items are given below:

A packet of crayons	–	₹ 15.50
A packet of pencils	–	₹ 14.00
A packet of sketch pens	–	₹ 22.50
One scissors	–	₹ 17.00
One eraser	–	₹ 2.00
One sheet of glazed paper	–	₹ 2.50
A pack of decorative stickers	–	₹ 5.00

Sohail buys one packet of crayons, two packets of pencils, one packet of sketch pens, one scissors, 5 sheets of glazed papers and one pack of decorative stickers. How much would he be required to pay?
A. ₹ 100.50 B. ₹ 102.00
C. ₹ 98.00 D. ₹ 86.50

53. A train starts from Patna on 30th May, 2010 at 23:40 hours and reaches Mumbai on 1st June, 2020 at 5:15 hours. What is the total travel time of train?
A. 29 hours 15 minutes B. 28 hours 25 minutes
C. 28 hours 20 minutes D. 29 hours 35 minutes

54. In a five digit number, the digit at the hundreds place is three-fourth of the digit at ten thousands place and the digit at tens place is two-third of the digit at hundreds place. The digit at tens place is square of the smallest prime number and the digit at thousands place is the largest single digit prime number. If the digit at unit place is the largest single digit odd number, then the number is:
A. 83419 B. 42937
C. 87649 D. 49327

55. What should be subtracted from the sum of 8008, 8088 and 8808 to obtain 17863?
A. 7041 B. 7141
C. 6121 D. 6131

56. A bucket of 16 litres capacity is filled to the brim with water. Water from this bucket is to be transferred into smaller utensils. A mug filled to capacity has to be dipped 50 times to completely transfer the water in the bucket into the utensils. What is the capacity of the mug?
A. 275 mL B. 320 mL
C. 225 mL D. 250 mL

57. A taxi meter shows charges of ₹ 50 for the first two kilometres of journey and ₹ 16 for every subsequent kilometre travelled. Manju pays ₹ 258 as fare to travel from her house to the railway station. How far is the railway station from her home?
A. 15 km B. 18 km
C. 12 km D. 13 km

58. The following table shows marks obtained out of 100 by Maria and Shehnaz in five subjects:

	Maria	Shehnaz
English	74	81
Maths	88	78
Social Science	65	77
Hindi	73	72
Science	90	82

Based on the table above identify the correct statement from among the following:

A. Shehnaz's aggregate marks in Maths and Science are more than Maria's aggregate marks in these subjects.
B. The aggregate marks of Maria and Shehnaz are equal.
C. Maria has scored more marks than Shehnaz in all the subjects except the languages.
D. Maria has scored more marks than Shehnaz in only two subjects.

59. Which of the following is a desirable teaching-learning practice in the context of Mathematics?

A. Open book tests should be avoided.
B. Students should be told to follow the prescribed steps of solving problems.
C. Open ended questions should be avoided to prevent confusion.
D. Intuitive understanding of concepts should be encouraged.

60. Following are some questions posed by the teacher in the mathematics classroom:

(*a*) What is the area of the rectangle whose one side is 5 cm and perimeter is 30 cm?
(*b*) Find a set of numbers whose median is 4.
(*c*) List all prime numbers between 0–8.
(*d*) Tell me anything mathematical information you know about rectangles.

A. (*a*) is closed ended and (*b*), (*c*) & (*d*) are open ended questions.
B. (*a*) & (*c*) are closed ended and (*b*) & (*d*) are open ended questions.
C. (*a*) & (*b*) are closed ended questions and (*c*) & (*d*) are open ended questions.
D. (*a*), (*b*) & (*c*) are closed ended and (*d*) is open ended question.

PART- III

Environmental Studies

Directions : Answer the following questions by selecting the correct/most appropriate options.

61. Mapping skills in EVS help develop

A. recording skill
B. understanding of relative position of places
C. the skill of drawing landscapes
D. the skill of predicting and calculating

62. Smayan of class V usually does not do his given class work. The best measure to address the situation could be to

A. talk to parents and counsel them.
B. give him alternative and simpler home work.
C. talk to him to find his difficulty and adjust class work accordingly.
D. make another child help complete his class work.

63. Muskan organized a debate on the topic 'Use of diesel vehicles in transportation should be prohibited'. What is the purpose of organizing this debate by Muskan in classroom?

A. She wants to sensitise students on advantages of using modern vehicles.
B. It helps students in appreciating multiple perspectives on this issue.
C. She wants to sensitize students on the need to ban diesel vehicles completely in transportation.
D. It would help in knowing student's views and correcting them.

64. There is a paragraph in class V EVS textbook based on Al-Biruni's observation of construction of ponds in India some thousand years ago. What would be the purpose of including this paragraph?

(*a*) It helps learners to identify sources of history.
(*b*) It helps learners to improve their recording of observations.
(*c*) It helps learners to appreciate technology present in India some 1000 years back.
(*d*) It helps learners to appreciate the role of evidence in history.

A. only (*a*) & (*d*)
B. only (*a*) & (*c*)
C. (*a*), (*b*), (*c*)
D. (*a*), (*c*), (*d*)

65. The integrated nature of EVS helps to:

A. follow child-centered approach and introduce larger number of concepts.
B. learn from information and description provided.
C. reduce the curriculum load and introduce specific topics.
D. reduce curriculum load and help children to learn meaningfully.

66. Which of the following is NOT a broad indicator of EVS assessment?
A. Concern for equality B. Concept mapping
C. Co-operation D. Concern for justice

67. Questioning as a strategy in teaching-learning of EVS is used for:
A. Promoting adherence to rules
B. Arousing curiosity in classroom
C. Maintaining discipline
D. Drawing attention

68. With over fifty students in her class, Vani wants to engage them in an activity which involves maximum number of senses to enhance learning. Which of the following activities will be suitable for this purpose?
A. using smart classroom for relevant a-v material.
B. organizing field trip to a nearby place.
C. inviting resource persons from community to demonstrate their skills.
D. encouraging group discussion.

69. Why does Iqra encourage her learners to read newspaper and magazines in EVS?
A. These help learners to become independent.
B. These help learners become competitive.
C. These are entertaining resources available.
D. These help learners to engage with the real world.

70. In which one of the following states the meaning of "Torang" is jungle?
A. Mizoram B. Jharkhand
C. Assam D. Odisha

71. Your house is located at X and your school is located at Y. Although your school is just opposite but you cannot go straight because of the busy highway in between. So, you first go 125 m due south, then cross a 100 m long subway which is due east and finally reach your school at Y which is 125 m due north. With respect to school at Y your house at X is:
A. 100 m due west B. 125 m due north
C. 125 m due south D. 100 m due east

72. Today we cannot think of food without chillies. These were brought to our country by traders coming from:
A. South America B. South Africa
C. Afghanistan D. England

73. A boy boarded a train on 4th June, 2020 at Nagarcoil for Madgaon. The train departed at 22:30 hours from Nagarcoil and reached Madgaon at 04:30 hours on 6th June, 2020. If the distance covered by the train during this time interval is 1145 km, the average speed of the train was nearly:
A. 40.5 km/h B. 42.5 km/h
C. 36.5 km/h D. 38.5 km/h

74. Which one of the following statements is **NOT** true for the honeybees and beehives?
A. Most of the bees in the hive are worker bees.
B. There are only a few males in the hive.
C. Every beehive has one queen bee that lays eggs.
D. Male bees are very important for the hives.

75. The Constitution of our country was prepared under the leadership of:
A. Dr. Bhim Rao Baba Saheb Ambedkar
B. Sarvapalli Dr. Radha Krishnan
C. Mohandas Karamchand Gandhi
D. Sardar Vallabh Bhai Patel

76. Consider the following functions for plants:
(*a*) To give support to the plant
(*b*) To provide humus
(*c*) To store food
(*d*) To absorb water and minerals
The functions of roots are:
A. (*b*), (*c*) and (*d*) B. (*a*), (*c*) and (*d*)
C. (*a*) and (*b*) only D. (*c*) and (*d*) only

77. Which one of the following is **NOT** a Union Territory of India?
A. Manipur B. Chandigarh
C. Laddakh D. Jammu & Kashmir

78. Which among the following produce crude oil (Petroleum)?
A. Gujarat and Tamil Nadu
B. Bihar and Bombay High
C. Bombay High and West Bengal
D. Assam and Odisha

79. Select from the following a group of birds each member of which is able to see distinctly the object four times as far as we can see.
A. Crows, Kites, Nightingales
B. Eagles, Kites, Vultures
C. Doves, Crows, Peacocks
D. Eagles, Pigeons, Parrots

80. Pochampalli is a town of Southern State of India which is famous for its beautifully designed bright-coloured Pochampalli sarees and for the special kind of weave which is also called Pochampalli. This town is now a part of:
A. Telangana B. Tamil Nadu
C. Karnataka D. Kerala

81. Select from the following a group of eatables each member of which is rich in iron.
A. Amla, Cabbage, Tomato
B. Cabbage, Amla, Spinach
C. Jaggery, Amla, Tomato
D. Amla, Spinach, Jaggery

82. Which one of the following did experiments with pea plants and found that pea plant has some traits which come in pairs - such as rough or smooth, tall or short, yellow or green etc.?

A. George Mestral
B. Charles Darwin
C. Dr. M.S. Swaminathan
D. Gregor Johann Mendel

83. In which one of the following states most villagers construct their wooden houses 3 to 3.5 m above the ground on strong bamboo pillars with sloping roofs?
A. Assam B. Odisha
C. Rajasthan D. Laddakh

84. With respect to the location of Delhi on the map of India the directions of the locations of Gandhinagar (Capital of Gujarat) and Patna (Capital of Bihar) respective are:
A. north-east and south-west
B. south-west and north-east
C. south-east and south-west
D. south-west and south-east

85. How will you plan for an integrated EVS classroom?
A. Arrange separate teachers for science and social science.
B. Arrange separate teacher specializing in environmental science
C. Combine two or more subject areas into one lesson.
D. Separate all the subjects into a different plans.

86. Which of the following is one of the six themes suggested in the EVS syllabus as per NCF 2005?
A. Things we make and do
B. How things work
C. Material
D. Natural Resources

87. What should be avoided in anecdotal records?
(*a*) Identifying mainly problematic situations
(*b*) Making statements of judgement
(*c*) Identifying strengths and weaknesses
(*d*) Identifying child's areas of interests and relationships, etc.
A. (*a*), (*b*) and (*c*) B. (*a*), (*c*) and (*d*)
C. (*a*) and (*b*) D. (*c*) and (*d*)

88. Smita wanted to sensitize her learners about gender disparity and stereotypes related to work. What should Smita choose to do in her class from the following suggestions?
A. Ask only boys to sweep the classroom daily.
B. Invite a student's mother to class who is an auto driver.
C. Present students with stereotypical models.
D. Show flashcards of different kinds of work.

89. Puneet gave his class V learners an outline of human body and asked them to draw the digestive system before teaching chapter on food. Puneet wanted to:
A. identify learners with good drawing skills.
B. evaluate learners on the process of digestion.
C. test if learners could make labelled diagrams.
D. elicit learners' ideas about digestion.

90. Which of the following is **not correct** with respect to formative assessment?
A. It is to monitor student's progress.
B. Any information on learning of child can help in formative assessment.
C. It is to be reported in every quarter of report card.
D. It helps the teacher in taking timely action for enhancing learning.

PART- IV

Language-I : English

Directions (Qs. No. 91-99) : *Read the passage given below and answer the questions that follow by selecting the **correct/most appropriate** options:*

1. Each drop represents a little bit of creation and of life itself. When the monsoon brings to northern India the first rains of summer, the parched earth opens its pores and quenches its thirst with a hiss of ecstasy. After baking in the sun for the last few months, the land looks cracked, dusty and tired. Now, almost overnight, new grass springs up, there is renewal everywhere, and the damp earth releases a fragrance sweeter than any devised by man.

2. Water brings joy to earth, grass, leaf bud, blossom, insect, bird, animal, and the pounding heart of man. Small children run out of their homes to romp naked in the rain. Buffaloes, which have spent the summer listlessly around lakes gone dry, now plunge into heaven of muddy water. Soon the lakes and rivers will overflow with the monsoon's generosity. Trekking in the Himalayan foothills, I recently walked for kilometers without encountering habitation. I was just scolding myself for not having brought along a water bottle when I came across a patch of green on a rock face. I parted a curtain of tender maiden hair fern and discovered a tiny spring issuing from the rock-nectar for the thirsty traveler.

3. I stayed there for hours, watching the water descend, drop by drop, into a tiny casement in the rocks. Each drop reflected creation. That same spring, I later discovered, joined other springs to form a swift, tumbling stream, which went cascading down the hill into other streams until, in the plains, it became part of a river. And that river flowed into another mightier river that kilometers later emptied into the ocean. Be

like water, taught Laotzu, philosopher, and founder of Taoism. Soft and limpid, it finds its way through, over or under any obstacle. It does not quarrel; it simply moves on.

91. Which one of the following words is most opposite in meaning to the word 'descend' (para 3) as used in the passage?
A. hover B. zoom
C. flow D. ascend

92. Which part of speech is the underlined word in the following sentence?

Almost overnight new grass spring up.
A. Adjective B. Adverb
C. Preposition D. Pronoun

93. Which part of the following sentence contains an error?

He knew / (*a*) that he will / (*b*) go back / (*c*) on his promise / (*d*)
A. (*c*) B. (*d*)
C. (*a*) D. (*b*)

94. Which of the following statements is not true?
A. The sweltering heat comes to an end.
B. The damp earth releases a sweet fragrance.
C. There is renewal everywhere.
D. New grasses spring up.

95. The earth does not look ______ before the onset of the monsoon.
A. dusty B. tired
C. cracked D. brown

96. Children respond to the first rains of summer by:
A. running and playing in the rain.
B. singing songs
C. giving shouts of joy.
D. floating paper boats in the water.

97. The tiny spring issuing from the rock is hidden by
A. bushes and creepers.
B. tall grass.
C. thick moss.
D. maiden hair fern.

98. To become part of a river, a tiny drop has to:
A. suffer a lot.
B. merge its identity.
C. have a lot of strength.
D. depend on external forces.

99. Which of the following words is most similar in meaning to the word 'pounding' as used in para 2 of the passage?
A. palpitating B. sinking
C. shaking D. benumbing

Directions (Qs. No. 100-105): *Read the extract given below and answer the questions that follow by selecting the* ***correct/most appropriate*** *options:*

I think that I shall never see
A poem lovely as a tree.

A tree whose hungry mouth is prest
Against the earth's sweet flowing breast;

A tree that looks at God all day,
And lifts her leafy arms to pray;

A tree that may in Summer wear
A nest of robins in her hair;

Upon whose bosom snow has lain;
Who intimately lives with rain.

Poems are made by fools like me,
But only God can make a tree.

100. Name the figure of speech used in lines 3 and 4.
A. Metonymy B. Alliteration
C. Simile D. Personification

101. Identify and name the figure of speech used in "Poems are made by fools like me'.
A. Simile B. Hyperbole
C. Metaphor D. Personification

102. The word, 'mouth' in line 3 refers to the ______ of the tree.
A. trunk B. roots
C. crown D. branches

103. The tree presses its mouth against the sweet earth's flowing breast to:
A. draw inspiration from it.
B. express its love for it.
C. express its gratitude to it.
D. draw sustenance from it.

104. The tree prays to God by:
A. producing fruit and flowers.
B. providing shade to travellers.
C. swinging its branches.
D. lifting her arms

105. Which of the following statement is **not** true in the context of the poem?
A. The tree allows birds to build their nests in it.
B. It lives closely with rain.
C. The tree welcomes the snow on its bosom.
D. The tree symbolizes strength and stability.

Directions: *Answer the following questions by selecting the* ***most appropriate*** *options.*

106. A student of class IV is having some problem in writing. She may have
A. dysphasia B. dyscalculia
C. dyslexia D. dysgraphia

107. It specifies the rules which govern the arrangement of words into phrases, clauses and sentences.

A. Syntax B. Cohesion
C. Discourse D. Semantics

108. A teacher of class VI has labelled the classroom objects such as blackboard, door, window, fan, table, chair ete, in different languages (Hindi, English, Urdu, Sanskrit etc). Here the classroom as a whole:
A. is focusing on three language formula.
B. is a rich resource for promoting multilingualism.
C. is learning through the grammar-translation method.
D. is creating a language confusion in students.

109. The assessment process not only assesses students' learning but also assesses teacher's teaching process. This statement is:
A. partially right B. baseless
C. fully wrong D. fully right

110. The language which is learnt from environment without any explicit teaching is:
A. Third language B. School language
C. First language D. Second language

111. A teacher is facing the problem of students' poor spelling. She listed probable causes for it and then decided to frame some steps to overcome it. This whole process is:
A. Action research
B. Applied research
C. Problem solving
D. Improving spelling

112. Reading picture book means:
A. to help learners to draw neat and colorful pictures
B. that children love pictures and it will be a fun-loving class.
C. exposing learners to different styles of drawing.
D. to help learners to understand and analyze the pictures.

113. Before starting a new chapter from a textbook, a teacher should at first focus on ________.
A. relating the story with the previous experiences of learners.
B. the grammatical structures in the chapter and difficult words.
C. the background setting of story, its history etc.
D. the work profile of the poet/writer.

114. Teacher asks learners to read aloud in the English class. This way of reading will:
A. enable a learner to be a fast reader.
B. help the teacher to complete the syllabus within the stipulated time.
C. enable learners to develop reading skill with understanding.
D. enable learners to read with correct pronunciation using the punctuation marks.

115. A language teacher firstly, asks students to introduce themselves to each other in the class. Then she asks them to introduce their friend to each other. This activity will help them to increase:
A. PPPP B. ELT
C. BICS D. CALP

116. Literature should be included in language classroom because:
A. it develops moral values among the learners.
B. it exposes them to different genres, culture, and social issues.
C. it helps learners to be budding writers.
D. it gives exposure to different grammatical forms and structures.

117. A teacher makes her learners respond to her actions and speech only by bodily movements. What is this known as?
A. Communicative Approach
B. Play-way method
C. Total Physical Response
D. Task Based Language Teaching

118. In a language class students are memorizing the dialogues through drill and practice and the teacher is correcting their pronunciation, mistakes immediately. They are practicing the dialogues in chorus. The teacher is following the:
A. Audiolingual method
B. CLT method
C. Direct method
D. Natural method

119. The oral errors of the students can be best corrected if the teacher:
A. ignores the error as it may hamper their learning
B. asks other students to help him as peer tutoring is must in schools.
C. corrects an error directly after the student has made the error.
D. points out the error in general and lets the student try to correct himself first.

120. As a pair activity, the teacher gives her learners almost the same pictures and asks them to find the difference between the two students, ask each other questions to discover how the two pictures are different. This can be a:
A. cloze based activity
B. crosswords activity
C. grammar activity
D. speaking activity

PART- V

Language-II : Hindi

निर्देश (प्र.सं. 121 से 128): *दिए गए अनुच्छेद को पढ़कर पूछे गए प्रश्नों प्रश्नों के* ***सही/सबसे उपयुक्त*** *उत्तर वाले विकल्प चुनिएः*

किताब का विषय और सामग्री उस आयु वर्ग के हिसाब से हो जिसके लिए आप पुस्तक चुन रहे हैं। छोटे बच्चों के लिए रोजमर्रा की समस्याएँ और घटनाएँ पुस्तक का विषय हो सकती हैं। उदाहरण के लिए, स्कूल से घर लौटते समय रास्ते में मिलने वाले कुत्ते से डर लगना। इस वर्ग के बच्चों की कहानियों की एक विशेषता होती है– शब्दों, वाक्यों और घटनाओं की पुनरावृत्ति। बच्चों को मजेदार शब्द और वाक्य दोहराना अच्छा लगता है। आप किसी बच्चे को खेलते देखिए, आपको इस बात का सबूत मिल जाएगा। इसके अतिरिक्त पुनरावृत्ति से उन बच्चों को पढ़ने में प्रवीणता हासिल करने में मदद मिलती है जो अभी सीखने की प्रक्रिया में हैं।

इस स्तर की कहानियाँ बहुत अधिक लंबी या जटिल नहीं होनी चाहिए। उनमें बहुत ज्यादा घटनाएँ या पात्र नहीं हों तो बेहतर है।

121. 'छोटे बच्चे' में छोटे' .... विशेषण है।

A. परिमाणवाचक B. संख्यावाचक
C. गुणवाचक D. सार्वनामिक

122. 'पुनरावृत्ति' का संधि-विच्छेद है–

A. पुनः + अवृत्ति B. पुनरा + वृत्ति
C. पुनः + रावृत्ति D. पुनः + आवृत्ति

123. निम्न में कौन-सा शब्द कारक चिह्न नहीं है?

A. से B. और
C. के लिए D. की

124. पुस्तक का चयन .... के आधार पर करना चाहिए।

A. उपलब्धता B. कीमत
C. आयु वर्ग D. नैतिक शिक्षा

125. छोटे बच्चे की पुस्तक का विषय मुख्य रूप से होना चाहिए–

A. दैनिक जीवन B. वीर पुरुष
C. राजा–रानी D. नैतिक मूल्य

126. बच्चों को कैसे शब्द दोहराना अच्छा लगता है?

A. लंबे B. मजेदार
C. सरल D. जटिल

127. सीखने की प्रक्रिया में पुनरावृत्ति का महत्त्व है, क्योंकि–

A. पढ़ने में कुशलता प्राप्त होती है।
B. लिखने में कुशलता प्राप्त होती है।
C. बच्चे को कहानी याद हो जाती है।
D. घटनाएँ याद हो जाती हैं।

128. पुस्तक चुनते समय कम महत्त्वपूर्ण है–

A. आयु वर्ग B. कीमत
C. विषय D. सामग्री

निर्देश (प्र.सं. 129 से 135): *दिए गए अनुच्छेद को पढ़कर पूछे गए प्रश्नों के* ***सही/सबसे उपयुक्त*** *उत्तर वाले विकल्प चुनिएः*

चिनार वृक्ष सामान्यतया मध्यम आकार के, मध्यम से अधिक ऊँचे आकार के होते हैं। इनकी ऊँचाई 50 मीटर अथवा इससे भी अधिक हो सकती है। इसकी लकड़ी का घनत्व बहुत अधिक होता है तथा यह मजबूत और कठोर होती है । चिनार की लकड़ी सफेद होती है तथा इसके किनारे पीले अथवा लाल रंग के होते हैं। इसकी लकड़ी पर सरलता से पॉलिश की जा सकती है तथा रंग भी किया जा सकता है। इसकी लकड़ी न तो आसानी से कटती है और न आसानी से टूटती है। किंतु यह टिकाऊ भी नहीं होती है, अतः कीमती फर्नीचर आदि इससे नहीं बनाए जाते।

चिनार वृक्ष का तना सुंदर और आकर्षक होता है एवं इस पर काँटे नहीं होते, किंतु छूने पर यह खुरदुरा लगता है। चिनार वृक्ष के तने की छाल अविकसित सी होती है तथा यह पहाड़ी बनकर झरती रहती है। इससे इसका तना शल्क वाला दिखाई देने लगता है। इसके पुराने वृक्षों की छाल झरती नहीं है, किंतु इसमें लंबी-लंबी दरारें पड़ जाती हैं। चिनार वृक्ष की छाल का रंग धूसर, हरापन लिए धूसर अथवा सफेदी लिए हुए धूसर रंग का होता है, शरद ऋतु में चिनार का वृक्ष अपनी छाल का रंग बदलता है और नारंगी अथवा नारंगीपन लिए सुनहरे रंग का हो जाता है। चिनार वृक्ष की शाखाएँ कत्थई रंग की होती हैं तथा आसानी से नहीं टूटतीं किंतु वृक्ष के बढ़ने के साथ ही ये नीचे झुकने लगती हैं और कभी-कभी वृक्ष के नीचे से गुजरने वालों से टकराने लगती हैं।

129. चिनार की लकड़ी होती है–

A. सफेद B. काली
C. पीली D. लाल

130. 'अतः कीमती फर्नीचर आदि इससे नहीं बनाए जाते।' वाक्य में विशेषण शब्द है–

A. इससे B. बनाए
C. कीमती D. फर्नीचर

131. समूह से भिन्न शब्द है–

A. पतली–दुबली B. लाल–लाल
C. कभी–कभी D. लंबी–लंबी

132. इनमें से चिनार की लकड़ी का कौन-सा गुण नहीं है?

A. आसानी से नहीं टूटती है।
B. आसानी से पॉलिश हो जाती है।
C. आसानी से कट जाती है।
D. आसानी से नहीं कटती है।

133. चिनार का तना होता है–

A. भुरभुरा B. कँटीला
C. चिकना D. खुरदुरा

134. चिनार वृक्ष अपनी छाल का रंग कब बदलता है?

A. बसंत में
B. सर्दी में
C. गर्मी में
D. बरसात में

135. इनमें से कौन-सा शब्द समूह से भिन्न है?

A. धूसर छाल
B. चिनार वृक्ष
C. लंबी दरारें
D. पुराने वृक्ष

निर्देशः *नीचे दिए गए प्रश्नों के लिए सबसे उचित विकल्प का चयन कीजिएः*

136. प्राथमिक स्तर पर भाषा-शिक्षण के संदर्भ में कौन-सा कथन सर्वाधिक उचित है?

A. सभी बच्चों की प्रगति समान रूप से ही होनी चाहिए।
B. बच्चों को विभिन्न प्रकार का बाल साहित्य पढ़ने के अवसर दें।
C. बच्चों को क्रम से भाषा कौशल सिखाए जाने चाहिए।
D. बच्चों को केवल भाषा की पाठ्य-पुस्तक ही दी जाए।

137. बच्चों के भाषा-विकास के लिए जरूरी है, बच्चों को–

A. व्याकरण सीखने के लिए प्रोत्साहित करना।
B. साहित्य पढ़ने के लिए पुरस्कृत करना।
C. अनुकरण के लिए प्रोत्साहित करना।
D. भाषा-प्रयोग के अवसर देना।

138. माया अकसर शब्दों को लिखते समय अक्षरों को छोटा-बड़ा लिखती है या उनके बीच समान दूरी नहीं रख पाती। माया संभवतः .... के कारण ऐसा करती है।

A. डिस्ग्राफिया
B. अरुचि
C. लापरवाही
D. अज्ञानता

139. 'भाषा अर्जन क्षमता' सिद्धांत .... से संबंधित है।

A. स्किनर
B. वाइगोत्स्की
C. चॉम्स्की
D. पियाजे

140. बच्चों की लेखन क्षमता का आकलन करने की दृष्टि से कौन-सा प्रश्न सर्वाधिक बेहतर है?

A. 'बहादुर बित्तो' में संज्ञा शब्दों को चिह्नित कीजिए।
B. बहादुर बित्तो' कहानी को शीर्षक दीजिए।
C. 'बहादुर बित्तो' शीर्षक कहानी लिखिए।
D. 'बहादुर बित्तो' कहानी का अंत बदलकर लिखिए।

141. 'पोर्टफोलियो' .... में मदद करता है।

A. समस्त क्षमताओं की जानकारी देने
B. क्रमिक प्रगति का आकलन करने
C. कार्य को संचित करने
D. बच्चों को भययुक्त वातावरण देने

142. भाषा का मनुष्य की .... और मनुष्य के .... के साथ गहरा संबंध होता है।

A. अस्मिता, विचार
B. वैचारिकता, व्यापार
C. अस्मिता, व्यापार
D. व्यावहारिकता, व्यवहार

143. ज्यादातर बच्चे, स्कूल की शिक्षा की शुरुआत से पहले ही भाषा की .... और .... को आत्मसात कर पूर्ण भाषिक क्षमता रखते हैं।

A. चुनौतियों, प्रचलनों
B. जटिलताओं, नियमों
C. चुनौतियों, अवसरों
D. जटिलताओं, मानकों

144. प्राथमिक स्तर पर पढ़ाने वाली सुनीता अपनी कक्षा के बच्चों को प्रतिदिन एक कहानी पढ़कर सुनाती हैं और उस पर चर्चा करती हैं। आप इस कक्षा के बारे में क्या कहेंगे?

A. पढ़ने और मौखिक अभिव्यक्ति का विकास हो रहा है।
B. सुनीता अपने शिक्षक-प्रशिक्षण की रीतियों को निभा रही है।
C. कहानी सुनाने से समय नष्ट हो रहा है।
D. कहानी पर चर्चा भाषा-विकास को अवरुद्ध करती है।

145. पढ़ने की कुशलता में सर्वाधिक महत्त्वपूर्ण है–

A. तीव्र गति
B. उच्चारणगत शुद्धता
C. शब्द पढ़ना
D. अर्थ-निर्माण

146. संयुक्त परिवारों में बच्चों का भाषा-विकास अपेक्षाकृत बेहतर होता है। इसका आधार है–

A. परस्पर अंतःक्रिया
B. परस्पर प्रश्नोत्तर
C. बड़ों की परिपक्व भाषा
D. बच्चों द्वारा बड़ों का अनुकरण

147. भाषा के माध्यम से बच्चों का ज्ञान-क्षेत्र भी विस्तृत होता है। जिसमें सर्वाधिक योगदान है–

A. विभिन्न प्रकार की कविताओं का
B. विभिन्न प्रकार की सांस्कृतिक गतिविधियों का
C. राष्ट्रीय समाचार-पत्रों/पत्रिकाओं का
D. बाल साहित्य की पुस्तकों का

148. प्राथमिक स्तर पर भाषा सीखने-सिखाने की सबसे पहली शर्त है–

A. बाल साहित्यकारों का साहित्य
B. चार्ट, पोस्टर से सुसज्जित कक्षा
C. सरल पाठ्य-पुस्तक
D. निवेश-समृद्ध संप्रेषण का वातावरण

149. पहली–दूसरी कक्षा में अनेक बच्चे हिंदी भाषा सीखते समय अपनी मातृभाषा का प्रयोग करते हैं। यह–

A. वैध नहीं है।
B. बहुत गलत है।
C. स्वीकार्य है।
D. अस्वीकार्य है।

150. रूपा चौथी कक्षा को पढ़ाती हैं। उन्होंने गुजराती लोक कथा 'मुफ्त ही मुफ्त' पढ़ाने के बाद बच्चों से पूछा कि उनकी भाषा में आदर के लिए किन शब्दों का प्रयोग किया जाता है, जैसे गुजराती भाषा में 'भाई' 'बेन' का प्रयोग किया जाता है। रूपा का उद्देश्य है–

A. बहुभाषिकता को संबोधित करना
B. अभ्यास प्रश्न को करवाना
C. अन्य भाषाओं को जानना
D. सभी बच्चों को अवसर देना

Answers

1	2	3	4	5	6	7	8	9	10
D	A	B	D	D	D	D	D	A	C
11	**12**	**13**	**14**	**15**	**16**	**17**	**18**	**19**	**20**
B	C	A	B	D	A	D	C	A	D
21	**22**	**23**	**24**	**25**	**26**	**27**	**28**	**29**	**30**
C	A	D	B	C	B	B	A	C	B
31	**32**	**33**	**34**	**35**	**36**	**37**	**38**	**39**	**40**
B	A	C	D	A	C	A	A	B	C
41	**42**	**43**	**44**	**45**	**46**	**47**	**48**	**49**	**50**
B	C	B	A	D	A	C	B	A	D
51	**52**	**53**	**54**	**55**	**56**	**57**	**58**	**59**	**60**
D	A	D	C	A	B	A	B	D	B
61	**62**	**63**	**64**	**65**	**66**	**67**	**68**	**69**	**70**
B	C	B	D	D	B	B	B	D	B
71	**72**	**73**	**74**	**75**	**76**	**77**	**78**	**79**	**80**
A	A	D	D	A	B	A	A	B	A
81	**82**	**83**	**84**	**85**	**86**	**87**	**88**	**89**	**90**
D	D	A	D	C	A	C	B	D	C
91	**92**	**93**	**94**	**95**	**96**	**97**	**98**	**99**	**100**
D	B	D	A	D	A	D	B	A	D
101	**102**	**103**	**104**	**105**	**106**	**107**	**108**	**109**	**110**
A	B	D	D	D	D	A	B	D	C
111	**112**	**113**	**114**	**115**	**116**	**117**	**118**	**119**	**120**
A	D	A	D	C	B	C	A	D	D
121	**122**	**123**	**124**	**125**	**126**	**127**	**128**	**129**	**130**
C	D	B	C	A	B	A	B	A	C
131	**132**	**133**	**134**	**135**	**136**	**137**	**138**	**139**	**140**
A	C	D	B	B	B	D	A	C	D
141	**142**	**143**	**144**	**145**	**146**	**147**	**148**	**149**	**150**
B	A	B	A	D	A	C	D	C	A

Explanatory Answers

2. Principles for teaching problem solving:
    - **Model a useful problem-solving method:** Problem solving can be difficult and sometimes tedious. Show students by your example how to be patient and persistent and how to follow a structured method, such as Woods' model described here. Articulate your method as you use it so students see the connections.
    - **Teach within a specific context:** Teach problem-solving skills in the context in which they will be used (e.g., mole fraction calculations in a chemistry course). Use real-life problems in explanations, examples, and exams. Do not teach problem solving as an independent, abstract skill.
    - **Help students understand the problem:** In order to solve problems, students need to define the end goal. This step is crucial to successful learning of problem-solving skills. If you succeed at helping students answer the questions "what?" and "why?", finding the answer to "how?" will be easier.
    - **Take enough time:** When planning a lecture/tutorial, budget enough time for: understanding the problem and defining the goal, both individually and as a class; dealing with questions from you and your students; making, finding, and fixing mistakes; and solving entire problems in a single session.
    - **Ask questions and make suggestions:** Ask students to predict "what would happen if ..." or explain why

something happened. This will help them to develop analytical and deductive thinking skills. Also, ask questions and make suggestions about strategies to encourage students to reflect on the problem-solving strategies that they use.

- **Link errors to misconceptions:** Use errors as evidence of misconceptions, not carelessness or random guessing. Make an effort to isolate the misconception and correct it, then teach students to do this by themselves. We can all learn from mistakes.

Thus, Problem-solving abilities can be facilitated by encouraging use of analogies.

4. Divergent thinking is a thought process or method used to generate creative ideas by exploring many possible solutions. It typically occurs in a spontaneous, free-flowing, "non-linear" manner, such that many ideas are generated in an emergent cognitive fashion. Many possible solutions are explored in a short amount of time, and unexpected connections are drawn. Following divergent thinking, ideas and information are organized and structured using convergent thinking, which follows a particular set of logical steps to arrive at one solution, which in some cases is a "correct" solution. The psychologist J.P. Guilford first coined the terms convergent thinking and divergent thinking in 1956.

5. The 6 E's and S (Engage, Explore, Explain, Elaborate, Evaluate, Extend, and Standards) lesson plan format was developed by teachers in consultation with faculty from schools of education and is based on a constructivist model of teaching. The lesson plans are based on constructivist instructional models with activities and sections of the plan designed to have the students continually add (or construct) new knowledge on top of existing knowledge. So most effective mode of teaching–learning is exploration of relationship between concepts.

7. Differentiating tasks so they are appropriately challenging allows students to maintain optimal engagement. When students are working just within their current ability, they are drawn in by their curiosity to find the answer and spurred by the belief that they can find the answer. Teachers can also encourage students to set authentic learning goals rather than performance goals. Students can practise using mastery-orientation language when writing weekly, monthly, or long-term goals. Goals that begin 'to learn...', 'to understand...', or 'to master... [a particular skill]' support this orientation, while goals such as 'to get... grade', 'to earn more points than last quiz' or 'to meet my parent's goal of...' all express performance goals. Teachers can reinforce mastery-orientation by modeling it in their own goal setting.

8. A "sense of shame" is the feeling known as guilt but "consciousness" or awareness of "shame as a state" or condition defines core/toxic shame (Lewis and Tangney). The person experiencing shame might not be able to, or perhaps simply will not, identify their emotional state as shame, and there is an intrinsic connection between shame and the mechanism of denial." The key emotion in all forms of shame is contempt (Miller and Tomkins). Two realms in which shame is expressed are the *consciousness of self as bad* and *self as inadequate.* People employ negative coping responses to counter deep rooted, associated sense of "shame worthiness". The shame cognition may occur as a result of the experience of shame affect or, more generally, in any situation of embarrassment, dishonour, disgrace, inadequacy, humiliation, or chagrin.

9. **Constructivist curriculum** based on the constructivist theories of Piaget and Vygotsky where learning involves active interaction between the child and the environment with the teacher acting as a facilitator, mentor, coach and partner in problem-solving.

Katz (1999) suggests that a constructivist approach is both active and interactive as it encourages the child to actively construct his or her own knowledge. Katz (1999:1) states: 'On the constructivist side, it is assumed that child-initiated exploration, well "scaffolded" by adults, is the developmentally appropriate way to support children's learning".

Examples of a constructivist curriculum can be seen in most early childhood services in Australia where children are provided with a range of play-based experiences that allow for choice as well as experiences that are adult directed. Practitioners facilitate and influence children's play and exploration by carefully constructing the learning environment. For example, the practitioner might set up a dramatic play experience such as a shoe shop with an emphasis on problem-solving, negotiating and exploration of number and measurement.

12. Learning is the process which is done or completed or can be achieved only when all the relevant informations are given in proper or sequential manner. If any information is provided in disconnected manner, it would be difficult for learner to acquire any sound knowledge.

13. The Yerkes–Dodson law is an empirical relationship between pressure and performance, originally developed by psychologists Robert M. Yerkes and John Dillingham Dodson in 1908.

Levels of arousal: Researchers have found that different tasks require different levels of arousal for optimal performance. For example, difficult or intellectually demanding tasks may require a lower level of arousal (to facilitate concentration), whereas tasks demanding stamina or persistence may be performed better with higher levels of arousal (to increase motivation).

Because of task differences, the shape of the curve can be highly variable. For simple or well-learned tasks, the relationship is monotonic, and performance improves as arousal increases. For complex, unfamiliar, or difficult tasks, the relationship between arousal and performance reverses after a point, and performance thereafter declines as arousal increases.

The effect of task difficulty led to the hypothesis that the Yerkes–Dodson Law can be decomposed into two distinct factors as in a bathtub curve. The upward part of the inverted U can be thought of as the energizing effect of arousal. The downward part is caused by negative effects of arousal (or stress) on cognitive processes like attention (e.g., "tunnel vision"), memory, and problem-solving.

15. Private speech is typically observed in children from about two to seven years old. Private speech or "self-talk" is observed speech spoken to oneself for communication, self-guidance, and self-regulation of behaviour. Private speech is often thought to enhance the developing early literacy skills and help to increase a child's task performance, success, and achievement. Numerous sources trace the first theories of private speech back to two early well-known developmental psychologists, Vygotsky and Piaget. Both of these psychologists mainly studied private speech in young children, yet they had different views and terms.

In *Thought and Language*, Vygotsky argued that egocentric speech was a part of normal development of communication, self-guidance, self-regulation of behaviour, planning, pacing, and monitoring skills. Vygotsky explains that private speech stems from a child's social interactions as a toddler, then reaches a peak during preschool or kindergarten when children talk aloud to themselves. Private speech serves as "the social/cultural tool or symbol system of language, first used for interpersonal communication is used by the child overtly not for communication with others, but for intrapersonal communication and self-guidance." Private speech slows down in late elementary school years and children stop talking aloud, and instead start to use inner speech.

17. Vygotsky believed that when a student is in the zone of proximal development for a particular task, providing the appropriate assistance will give the student enough of a "boost" to achieve the task.

To assist a person to move through the zone of proximal development, educators are encouraged to focus on three important components which aid the learning process:

- The presence of someone with knowledge and skills beyond that of the learner (a more knowledgeable other).
- Social interactions with a skillful tutor that allow the learner to observe and practice their skills.
- Scaffolding, or supportive activities provided by the educator, or more competent peer, to support the student as he or she is led through the ZPD.

18. A gender stereotype is a generalised view or preconception about attributes or characteristics, or the roles that are or ought to be possessed by, or performed by women and men. A gender stereotype is harmful when it limits women's and men's capacity to develop their personal abilities, pursue their professional careers and make choices about their lives. For example: After getting hurt during a play activity, Rohan started crying. Seeing this, his father responded, "Don't behave like girls, boys don't cry". This statement by the father reflects gender stereotype.

20. Lawrence Kohlberg sought to refine and extend the ideas of Piaget and the pioneering work of James M. Baldwin (1894) by creating a comprehensive three-stage theory.

(*i*) Preconventional Level	Stage-1 Punishment-obedience orientation
	Stage-2 Instrumental-exchange orientation
(*ii*) Conventional Level	Stage-3 Good-boy-nice-girl orientation
	Stage-4 System-maintaining orientagion
(*iii*) Postconventional Level	Stage-5 Social-contract situation
	Stage-6 Universal-ethical-principles orientation

According to Kohlberg (1969, 1976) this shift in focus is characteristic of conventional level of moral reasoning. Concern with law and order is an important aspect of conventional reasoning. Rule breaking is considered to be inherently immoral because it creates chaos in a stable social system. Reasoning at this level fits what many societies consider to be acceptable moral rules.

Thus, Lawrence Kohlberg's theory, "Performing an act and doing something because others approves it", represents conventional stage of morality.

21. All types of socialization may be classified into two broad groups, viz. primary socialization and secondary socialization. This division is based on the primary and secondary needs of individuals. The basic physical needs such as thirst, hunger etc. are called primary needs while secondary needs are those which emerge to meet primary needs e.g. the need for learning skills to earn livelihood. Family satisfies the basic needs of human beings, therefore, it is called primary institution where as a school is a secondary social institution because it meets the derived needs of the children. The parents are primary socializing agents of the child whereas the school teachers are the secondary socializing agents. Inculcation of norms and values within the family is called primary socialization while the process of imbibing norms, values and behavioural patterns of school may be called secondary socialization. Primary socialization takes place in infancy and childhood. This is the most crucial stage of socialization as the child learns basic behaviour pattern at this stage. Generally secondary socialization starts from the later stage of childhood and goes up to maturity. However the process of socialization never stops in life. The school, peer groups and other institutions in which I a person is placed in life play the role of socializing agents.

22. Howard Gardner (1983), an American Psychologist, proposed the theory of multiple intelligences. In his book 'Frames of Mind', he pointed out that he did not believe there was "one form of cognition which cut across all human thinking. There are multiple intelligences with autonomous intelligence capacities." So, intelligence cannot be viewed as a single entity. There are different types of intelligences which are independent of each other. Further, people may have varied combinations of these intelligences.

According to Gardner (1999), intelligence is much more than IQ as high IQ in the absence of productivity does not equate to intelligence. Gardner initially proposed eight types of intelligence which later on he increased to nine. Thus Gardner views each individual as a unique combination of various intelligences, hence we cannot say that one is more intelligent and another is less intelligent. Each one of us is talented in unique ways. The utility and value of each type of intelligence is culturally determined in the sense that individual's intelligent performance is determined according to the high desirability, usefulness and demands of society for particular types of intelligence. For instance, one type of intelligence highly valued in a particular society may be of little significance in another.

Theory of multiple intelligence emphasizes that there are several forms of intelligences.

25. Sociocultural theory grew from the work of seminal psychologist Lev Vygotsky, who believed that parents, caregivers, peers, and the culture at large were responsible for developing higher-order functions. According to Vygotsky, learning has its basis in interacting with other people. Once this has occurred, the information is then integrated on the individual level.

According to Vygotsky, children are born with basic biological constraints on their minds. Each culture, however, provides "tools of intellectual adaptation." These tools allow children to use their abilities in a way that is adaptive to the culture in which they live. For example, while one culture might emphasize memory strategies such as note-taking, another might use tools like reminders or rote memorization.

26. Psychologist Jean Piaget (1896-1980), was the most well known and influential theorist for cognitive development. Piaget was interested in how children reacted to their environments. He proposed a more active role for them as suggested by learning theory. He envisioned a child's knowledge as composed of schemas, basic unit of knowledge used to organise past experiences and serve as a basis for understanding new ones.

Piaget's theory of cognitive development is a comprehensive theory about the nature and development of human intelligence first developed by Jean Piaget. It is primarily known as a developmental stage theory, but in fact, it deals with the nature of knowledge itself and how humans come gradually to acquire it, construct it, and use it. Moreover, Piaget claims the idea that cognitive development is at the centre of human organism and language is contingent on cognitive development.

27. An **inclusive classroom** is a term used within American pedagogy to describe a classroom in which all students, irrespective of their abilities or skills, are welcomed holistically. It is built on the notion that being in a non-segregated classroom will better prepare special-needs students for later life. In the United States, the Rehabilitation Act of 1973 guaranteed civil rights to disabled people, though inclusion of disabled students progressed slowly until the No Child Left Behind Act of 2001, after which almost half of US students with disabilities were soon in general classrooms.

This has placed a considerable burden on teachers and school boards, who are often unprepared and suffer from stress and frustration, affecting the success of programs. An advocated solution is co-teaching, doubling teaching staff to support an inclusive classroom.

44. Let the quotient $= x$

then, the divisor $= 5x$

and, the reminder $= \frac{5x}{2}$

Given, the remainder = 5

$\therefore \quad \frac{5x}{2} = 5$

$\therefore \quad x = 2$

$\because$ The number = the dividend

= divisor × quotient + reminder

$= 5x \times x + \frac{5x}{2}$

$= 5 \times 2 \times 2 + 5$

$= 20 + 5 = 25.$

45. Let the five consecutive numbers are x, $x + 1$, $x + 2$, $x + 3$ and $x + 4$

Then, $x + x + 1 + x + 2 + x + 3 + x + 4 = 20$

$\Rightarrow 5x + 10 = 20 \Rightarrow 5x = 20 - 10 = 10$

$\Rightarrow x = \frac{10}{5} = 2$

The sum of first 3 consecutive numbers

$= x + x + 1 + x + 2$

$= 3x + 3 = 3 \times 2 + 3 = 6 + 3 = 9$

46. $\because$ A wire in the form of a square encloses area

$= 144 \text{ cm}^2$

$\Rightarrow \quad (\text{Side})^2 = (12)^2 \text{ cm}^2$

$\Rightarrow \quad \text{Side} = 12 \text{ cm}$

$\therefore \quad \text{Perimeter} = 4 \times \text{side} = 4 \times 12 = 48 \text{ cm}$

Again, Same wire is bent in the form of a rectangle, length = 16 cm

Perimeter of square = Perimeter of rectangle

$\Rightarrow \quad 48 = 2(l + b)$

$\Rightarrow \quad 48 = 2(16 + b)$

$\Rightarrow \quad 16 + b = 24 \Rightarrow b = 24 - 16 = 8 \text{ cm}$

$\therefore$ Area of rectangle $= l \times b = 16 \times 8 = 128 \text{ cm}^2$

Hence, area enclosed in the form of a rectangle $= 128 \text{ cm}^2$.

47. Here, LCM of 6, 4, 2, 3 and 5 = 60

$\frac{5}{6} = \frac{5}{6} \times 60 = 50,$

$\frac{3}{4} = \frac{3}{4} \times 60 = 45, \quad \frac{1}{2} = \frac{1}{2} \times 60 = 30,$

$\frac{2}{3} = \frac{2}{3} \times 60 = 40, \quad \frac{3}{5} = \frac{3}{5} \times 60 = 36,$

The largest and second largest fraction

$= \frac{5}{6}$ and $\frac{3}{4} \left[\frac{5}{6} = 50, \ \frac{3}{4} = 45\right].$

48. Asmita reaches school for a meeting

= 8.30 am – 15 minutes = 8.15 am

Her colleague reaches = 8.15 am + 30 minute = 8.45 am

Now, Scheduled time of the meeting

= 8.45 am – 40 minutes = 8.05 am

50. The number of students present in that class are

= 19 + 18 = 37.

52. The sum required to pay

$= 15.50 + 2 \times 14 + 22.50 + 17 + 5 \times 2.50 + 5$

= ₹ 100.50.

53. The total travel time of train

= From 30th May, 2020 at 23 : 40 to 31th May, 2020 at 23 : 40 + from 31st May, 2020 at 23.40 to 5.15 am 1st June, 2020

= 24 hour + 5 hours 15 minutes + 20 minutes

= 24 hours + 5 hours 35 minutes

= 29 hours 35 minutes.

54. The Given that

The digit at tens place = (Smallest prime number)^2

$= 2^2 = 4$

and the digit at thousands place = largest single prime number = 7

and the digit at unit place = the largest single digit odd number = 9

$\because$ The digit at tens place

$= \frac{2}{3}$ of the digit at hundreds place

$4 = \frac{2}{3} \times$ (digit at hundreds place)

$\therefore$ The digit at hundreds place $= \frac{4 \times 3}{2} = 6$

and the digit at hundreds place

$= \frac{3}{4}$ of digit at ten thousands place

$\Rightarrow \quad 6 = \frac{3}{4} \times$ (digit at ten thousands place)

$\Rightarrow$ The digit at ten thousands place $\frac{6 \times 4}{3} = 8$

Hence, the number = 87649.

55. Required number

= 8008 + 8088 + 8808 – 17863

= 24904 – 17863 = 7041.

56. The capacity of the mug $= \frac{16 \text{ litres}}{50}$

$= \frac{16 \times 1000 \text{ mL}}{50} = 16 \times 20 \text{ mL} = 320 \text{ mL}.$

57. Fair for the first 2 kilometres = ₹ 50

Remaining amount = 258 – 50 = 208

$\therefore$ Distance of the railway station from her home

$= 2 \text{ km} + \frac{208}{16} \text{ km} = 2 \text{ km} + 13 \text{ km} = 15 \text{ km}.$

58. The aggregate marks of Maria

= 74 + 88 + 65 + 73 + 90 = 390

And the aggregate marks of Shehnaz

= 81 + 78 + 77 + 72 + 82 = 390

Here, the aggregate marks of Maria and Shehnaz are equal.

Previous Paper (Solved)

CTET—PAPER-I, DECEMBER 2019*

PART- I

Child Development and Pedagogy

Directions: *Answer the following questions by selecting the* ***correct/most appropriate*** *options.*

1. The most critical period of acquisition and development of language is:
A. pre-natal period B. early childhood
C. middle childhood D. adolescence

2. Which of the following is a stage of moral development proposed by Lawrence Kohlberg?
A. Latency Stage
B. The social contract orientation
C. Concrete operational stage
D. Industry vs. Inferiority stage

3. During classroom discussions, a teacher often pays more attention to boys than girls. This is an example of:
A. Gender bias B. Gender identity
C. Gender relevance D. Gender constancy

4. Which of the following is an effective strategy to reduce children's gender stereotyping and gender-role conformity?
A. Discussion about gender bias
B. Emphasizing gender-specific roles
C. Gender-segregated play groups
D. Gender-segregated seating arrangement

5. Which of the following theorists while viewing children as active seekers of knowledge emphasized the influence of social and cultural contents on their thinking?
A. John B. Watson B. Lev Vygotsky
C. Jean Piaget D. Lawrence Kohlberg

6. While working on a jig-saw puzzle, 5 years old Najma says to herself, "Where is the blue piece? No, not this one, darker one that would go here and make this shoe".

This kind of talk is referred to by Vygotsky as:
A. private speech B. talk aloud
C. scaffolding D. egocentric speech

7. Giving cues to children and offering support as and when needed is an example of:
A. reinforcement B. conditioning
C. modelling D. scaffolding

8. Which of the following behaviours characterize the 'concrete operational stage' as proposed by Jean Piaget?
A. Hypothetico-deduction reasoning; propositional thought
B. Conservation; class inclusion
C. Deferred imitation; object permanence
D. Make-believe play; irreversibility of thought

9. Which of the following is a Piagetian construct in the context of cognitive development of children?
A. Schemas B. Observational learning
C. Conditioning D. Reinforcement

10. Primary objective of Assessment should be:
A. assigning rank to students.
B. understanding children's clarity and confusions about related concepts.
C. labelling students as per their score.
D. marking pass or fail in the report cards.

11. Which of the following statements about intelligence is correct?
A. Intelligence is a fixed ability determined at the time of birth only.
B. Intelligence can be accurately measured and determined by using standardized tests.
C. Intelligence is a unitary factor and a single trait.
D. Intelligence is multi-dimensional and a set of complex abilities.

12. Ruhi always thinks of multiple solutions to a problem many of which are original solutions. Ruhi is displaying characteristics of a/an:
A. creative thinker B. convergent thinker
C. rigid thinker D. egocentric thinker

13. In a situation of less participation of students belonging to a deprived group in teaching-learning process, a teacher should:
A. ask the children to withdraw from school.
B. accept this situation as it is.
C. lower her expectations from such students.
D. reflect on her own teaching and find ways to improve student's involvement.

14. In an inclusive classroom, a teacher ________ Individualized Education Plans.
A. should not prepare
B. should occasionally prepare

**Exam was held on 08-12-2019.*

C. should actively prepare
D. should discourage the preparation of

15. The primary characteristic of children with 'dyslexia' includes:
A. attention deficit disorders
B. divergent thinking; fluency in reading
C. inability to read fluently
D. engaging in repetitive locomotor actions

16. The concept of 'Inclusive Education' as advocated in the Right to Education Act, 2009 is based on:
A. the behaviouristic principles
B. a sympathetic attitude towards disabled
C. a rights-based humanistic perspective
D. mainstreaming of the disabled by offering them primarily vocational education

17. In the constructivist framework, learning is primarily:
A. based on rote-memorization.
B. centered around reinforcement.
C. acquired through conditioning.
D. focused on the process of meaning-making.

18. 'Naive theories' that children construct about various phenomenon:
A. should be ignored by the teacher.
B. should be punished by the teacher.
C. should be 'replaced' by correct one through repetitive memorization.
D. should be challenged by presenting counter evidence and examples.

19. Child-centered pedagogy promotes:
A. exclusive reliance on text books.
B. giving primacy to children's experiences.
C. rote memorisation.
D. labelling and categorization of students base on ability.

20. Emotions and cognition are _______ each other.
A. completely separate from
B. independent of
C. inter-woven with
D. not related to

21. Which of the following statements about learning is correct from a constructivist perspective?
A. Learning is the process of reproduction and recall.
B. Learning is the process of rote memorization.
C. Learning is conditioning of behaviours by repetitive association.
D. Learning is the process of construction of knowledge by active engagement.

22. Presenting students with clear examples and non-examples:
A. is an effective way to encourage conceptual change.
B. leads to confusion in the minds of students.
C. causes gaps in their understanding of concepts.
D. focuses on procedural knowledge rather than conceptual understanding.

23. Repeatedly asking children to engage in learning activities either to avoid punishment or to gain a reward:
A. decreases extrinsic motivation.
B. increases intrinsic motivation.
C. would encourage children to focus on mastery rather than performance goals.
D. decreases children's natural interest and curiosity involved in learning.

24. Which of the following practices promote meaningful learning?
(*i*) Corporal punishment
(*ii*) Co-operative learning environment
(*iii*) Continuous and comprehensive evaluation
(*iv*) Constant comparative evaluation
A. (*i*), (*ii*) B. (*ii*), (*iii*)
C. (*i*), (*ii*), (*iii*) D. (*ii*), (*iii*), (*iv*)

25. How can teachers facilitate understanding of complex concepts in children?
A. By delivering a lecture
B. By organizing competitive events
C. By repetitive mechanical drill
D. By providing opportunities for exploration and discussion

26. A primary school teacher can encourage children to become effective problem solvers by:
A. offering materialistic rewards for every small tasks.
B. emphasizing only on procedural knowledge.
C. dismissing and penalizing 'incorrect answers'.
D. encouraging children to make intuitive guesses and then brainstorming on the same.

27. In which of the following periods does physical growth and development occur at a rapid pace?
A. Infancy and early childhood
B. Early childhood and middle childhood
C. Middle childhood and adolescence
D. Adolescence and adulthood

28. Which of the following is NOT a principle of development?
A. Development is lifelong.
B. Development is modifiable.
C. Development is influenced by both heredity and environment.
D. Development is universal and cultural contents do not influence it.

29. The primary cause of individual variations is:
A. the genetic code received by the individuals from birth parents
B. the inborn characteristics
C. the environmental influences
D. the complex interplay between the heredity and the environment

30. Which of the following are examples of secondary socializing agency?
A. Family and neighbourhood
B. Family and media
C. School and media
D. Media and neighbourhood

PART- II

Mathematics

Directions: *Answer the following questions by selecting the **correct/most appropriate** options.*

31. Three brands of pens A, B and C are available in packets of 10, 12 and 24 respectively. If a shopkeeper wants to buy equal number of pens of each brand, what is the minimum number of packets of each brand, he should buy?

A. A = 10, B = 12, C = 5
B. A = 5, B = 12, C = 10
C. A = 10, B = 5, C = 12
D. A = 12, B = 10, C = 5

32. The side of a square is 4 cm. It is cut into 4 equal squares. What is the area of each small square?

A. 4 cm^2 B. 1 cm^2
C. 16 cm^2 D. 8 cm^2

33. Which of the following statements is not correct?

A. All prime numbers are odd numbers.
B. There are infinitely many prime numbers.
C. A prime number has only two factors.
D. There are only four single digit prime numbers.

34. A number that is divisible by all the numbers from 1 to 10 (both inclusive) is:

A. 10 B. 100
C. 604 D. 2520

35. Ayesha has only ₹ 5 and ₹ 10 coins with her. If the total number of coins she has 25 and the amount of money with her is ₹ 160, then the number of ₹ 5 and ₹ 10 coins with her are:

A. 18 and 7 respectively
B. 10 and 15 respectively
C. 15 and 10 respectively
D. 20 and 5 respectively

36. Evaluate: $17.5 \times 3 - 21 \div 7 - 3 \times 12.5$

A. 52.5 B. 12
C. 120 D. 50

37. One-sixth of the trees in a garden are neem trees. Half of the trees are Ashoka trees and the remaining are eucalyptus trees. If the number of neem trees is five, how many eucalyptus trees are there in the garden?

A. 5 B. 10
C. 15 D. 20

38. A train leaves Delhi on 29th August, 2019 at 16 : 30 hours and reaches its destination on 31st August at 08 : 45 hours. The total travel time of the journey is:

A. 36 hours 15 minutes B. 38 hours 45 minutes
C. 39 hours 45 minutes D. 40 hours 15 minutes

39. In which of the following, lengths have been arranged in decreasing order?

A. 8500 mm, 800 cm 8 mm, 80 dm 8 cm, 8 m
B. 80 dm 8 cm, 8500 mm, 8 m, 800 cm 8 mm
C. 8 m, 80 dm 8 cm, 8500 mm, 800 cm 8 mm
D. 8500 mm, 80 dm 8 cm, 800 cm 8 mm, 8 m

40. A 180 cm long wire is formed into a rectangle. If the width of this rectangle is 30 cm, what is its length?

A. 45 cm B. 60 cm
C. 90 cm D. 120 cm

41. When asked to write 44, some students of grade II wrote it as 404. As a teacher, how will you address this?

A. correct their answer in their copies
B. explain principle of exchange using concrete material
C. group them with those who have done it correctly
D. tell them to find out correct answer

42. The main purpose of introducing 'mapping' in the primary Mathematics curriculum is/are:

(*a*) to promote spatial thinking.
(*b*) to promote proportional reasoning.
(*c*) to make subject easy and interesting.
(*d*) to break the monotony of numbers.

A. (*a*) & (*c*) B. (*a*) & (*d*)
C. (*a*) & (*b*) D. (*b*) & (*c*)

43. Which of the following topics are not part of primary school Mathematics curriculum as per NCF 2005?

A. Tessellation B. Symmetry
C. Patterns D. Ratio

44. Which of the following resources/TLM can be used by the teacher to show that two rectangles of different dimensions can have same area without using formula?

(*a*) Scale (*b*) Graph paper
(*c*) Thread (*d*) Tiles

A. Only (*b*) B. (*b*) & (*d*)
C. Only (*c*) D. (*a*) & (*d*)

45. Which of the following could be contributing factor to under-achievement in mathematics?

A. Gender
B. Socio-cultural background
C. Nature of Mathematics
D. Innate ability of person

46. Which of the following is the most appropriate strategy to explain that $\frac{1}{4}$ is less than $\frac{1}{3}$?

A. using LCM method B. using paper strips
C. using Dienes blocks D. using number chart

47. Which of the following is the most important aspect of making lesson plan while teaching Mathematics to primary school children?
A. following the sequence of text-book.
B. presenting mathematical concepts in structured manner.
C. providing opportunities to students to allow construction of concepts.
D. writing activities and questions for reference.

48. Which of the following can NOT be considered a feature of a constructivist Mathematics classroom?
A. The role of language and dialogue in learning Mathematics is given due attention.
B. The teacher acknowledges that students may construct multiple understandings from a given interaction.
C. Objective type test items are used as the primary means of assessment.
D. Connections between Mathematics and other curricular areas are highlighted.

49. Which of the following statements is in agreement with the constructionist view of Mathematics?
A. Mathematics is about learning facts.
B. Mathematicians are required to discover the 'truths'.
C. Mathematics is entirely objective.
D. Visualisation is an important aspect of Mathematics.

50. Which of the following activities is best suited for the development of spatial understanding among children?
A. Drawing the top view of a bottle
B. Locating cities on a map
C. Noting the time of moon rise
D. Representing numbers on a number line

51. Which of the following is NOT true with respect to the learning of Mathematics?
A. Ability to perform and excel in Mathematics is innate.
B. Teachers' beliefs about learners have powerful impact on learning outcomes.
C. Students' socio-economic background impacts their performance in Mathematics.
D. School's language of instruction can impact a child's performance in Mathematics.

52. Identify the type of the following word problem:
"I have 6 pencils. Manish has two more than me. How many pencils does Manish have?"
A. Comparison addition B. Comparison subtraction
C. Takeaway addition D. Takeaway subtraction

53. Which of the following is NOT true of the Hindu-Arabic system of numeration?
A. The position of a digit in a number dictates its value.
B. It is additive in nature.
C. It follows the base 2 system.
D. It is multiplicative in nature.

54. Identify a desirable practice for teaching Geometry at primary level?
A. Geometry at primary level should be limited to recognition of simple basic shapes.
B. The teacher should begin by giving clear definitions of simple shapes and showing examples.
C. Children should be given ample opportunities to develop an intuitive understanding of space.
D. Developing extensive geometric vocabulary need not be an objective at primary level.

55. Which of the following is an indicator of mathematical reasoning?
A. Ability to provide definitions of mathematical concepts.
B. Ability to provide a justification for a mathematical procedure.
C. Ability to calculate efficiently.
D. Ability to recall the correct formulae in different situations.

56. The price list of vegetables in a super market is given as follows:

Item	Quantity	Price (₹)
Tomato	1 kg	40
Potato	2 kg	25
Carrot	250 g	20
Bottlegourd	1 kg	10
Chillies	100 g	10
Lemon	4 pieces	10

Sanjay buys $\frac{1}{2}$ kg tomatoes, 1 kg potatoes, $\frac{1}{2}$ kg carrot, 250 g chillies and 6 lemons. He gives a note of ₹ 200 to the bill clerk at the counter. How much money will he get back?
A. ₹ 112.50 B. ₹ 87.50
C. ₹ 86.50 D. ₹ 97.50

57.
- I am a 2 digit number.
- The digit in tens place and the digit in units place are consecutive prime numbers.
- The sum of digits is multiple of 3 and 4.

The number is:
A. 57 B. 23
C. 35 D. 13

58. The parking rates of car in a railway station parking are depicted as follows:
(*a*) Upto 2 hours – ₹ 50
(*b*) More than 2 hours and upto 5 hours – ₹ 75
(*c*) After 5 hours – ₹ 10 per extra hour upto 8 hrs.
(*d*) More than 8 hours and upto 12 hours – ₹ 150
(*e*) More than 12 hours and upto 24 hrs – ₹ 250

Rajeev parks his car at 7.00 a.m. and comes back to pick it up at 4.30 p.m. on the same day. How much money does he have to pay?

A. ₹ 135 B. ₹ 150
C. ₹ 130 D. ₹ 100

59. Which of the following is at third place when the numbers are arranged in ascending order?
7.07, 7.70, 7.707, 7.007, 0.77

A. 7.70 B. 7.007
C. 7.07 D. 7.707

60. In a five digit number, the digit at ten's place is 8, digit at units place is one-fourth of the digit at ten's place, the digit at thousands place is 0, digit at hundreds place is twice that of units place and the digit at ten thousands place is thrice the digit at unit's place. What is the number?

A. 64082
B. 64028
C. 46028
D. 60482

PART- III

Environmental Studies

***Directions : Answer the following questions by selecting the correct/most appropriate** options.*

61. A person boarded an express train on 29th November, 2019 at Surat (Gujarat) for Nagarcoil (Kerala). The train departed from Surat at 19:45 hours and reached Nagarcoil at 11:45 hours on 1st December, 2019. If the distance between Surat and Nagarcoil by train route is nearly 2120 km, the average speed of the train during this journey was:

A. 132.5 km/h B. 60 km/h
C. 53 km/h D. 45 km/h

62. Which one of the following is a weight lifter of international fame?

A. Sunita Williams B. Bachhendri Pal
C. Suryamani D. Karnam Malleshwari

63. Which one of the following is a group of roots?

A. Beetroot, Potato, Ginger
B. Carrot, Turmeric, Ginger
C. Sweet Potato, Radish, Turmeric
D. Carrot, Beetroot, Radish

64. Desert Oak is a tree which is found in:

A. Abu Dhabi B. Australia
C. desert of Rajasthan D. the desert of UAE

65. Consider the following statements about Nepenthese, a plant which hunts.

(*a*) This plant is found in Australia, Indonesia and Meghalaya in India.
(*b*) It has a pitcher-like shape and the mouth is covered by a leaf.
(*c*) It can trap and eat only small insects.
(*d*) It emits a pleasant sound to attract small insects which get trapped and cannot get out.

The correct statements are:

A. (*a*) and (*b*) only B. (*a*) and (*c*) only
C. (*b*) and (*d*) only D. (*a*), (*b*) and (*c*)

66. In which one of the following states of India is Dandi seashore located where Mahatma Gandhi did his famous march before independence?

A. Andhra Pradesh B. Karnataka
C. Maharashtra D. Gujarat

67. High fever with shiver which can be treated with the bark of Cinchona tree is:

A. typhoid B. malaria
C. chikungunya D. dengue

68. A doctor is located at X and his hospital is located at Y. There is no straight lane from the doctor's house to the hospital. So, the doctor first goes to A which is 600 m due east of X, then goes to B which is 450 m due south of A, then to C which is 120 m due west of B and finally reaches the hospital at Y which is 90 m due north of C. With respect to the hospital the correct direction of the doctors house is:

A. north-east B. north-west
C. south-east D. south-west

69. "Cheraw" is the dance form of the people of:

A. Jharkhand B. Mizoram
C. Manipur D. Meghalaya

70. Neighbouring states of Tamil Nadu are:

A. Andhra Pradesh, Odisha, Karnataka
B. Kerala, Andhra Pradesh, Maharashtra
C. Karnataka, Chhattisgarh, Kerala
D. Andhra Pradesh, Kerala, Karnataka

71. Which one of the following should NOT be the objective of teaching EVS at primary level as per NCF-2005?

A. To nurture the curiosity and creativity of the child particularly in relation to the natural environment.
B. To engage the child in exploratory and hands on activities to acquire basic cognitive and psycho-motor skills through observation, classification, inference, etc.

C. To train children to locate and comprehend relationships between the natural, social and cultural environment.
D. To develop precise quantitative skills among children through understanding of environmental issues.

72. EVS for classes-III to V is a subject area which integrates:
A. the concepts and issues of Science.
B. the concepts and issues of Science, Social studies and Environmental education.
C. the concepts and issues of Social science and Science.
D. the concepts and issues of Science and Environmental education.

73. Which of the following is true w.r.t. EVS?
A. EVS is a subject taught from classes I to V.
B. For classes I and II, EVS is taught through language and Mathematics.
C. For classes II, III and IV, issues and concerns of EVS are taught through language and Mathematics.
D. For classes I and II, concerns and issues of EVS are taught through Science and Social science.

74. Children get lot of space to learn EVS through exploration. This indicates that:
A. EVS is learnt through rote.
B. EVS is learnt through information.
C. EVS is child centred.
D. EVS is teacher centred.

75. Which of the following is a subtheme under the theme suggested in the EVS syllabus?
A. Family and Friends
B. Food
C. Animals
D. Things we make and do

76. Which of the following is a desirable practice for an EVS teacher?
A. Addressing multicultural dimensions of diverse classrooms.
B. Encouraging children to provide important information related to the concepts of EVS.
C. Linear arrangement of six themes of EVS.
D. Relying only in textbooks.

77. Which of the following is/are important in constructing knowledge in EVS by the children?
(*a*) Active participation of children.
(*b*) Community members of children
(*c*) Text-books of EVS
(*d*) Description and definition given in the textbook of EVS
A. (*a*), (*b*) and (*c*) B. (*a*) and (*c*) only
C. (*a*), (*c*) and (*d*) D. (*c*) only

78. Children can be effectively engaged in EVS learning through:
(*a*) Narratives
(*b*) Stories
(*c*) Effective explanation of concepts by the teacher
(*d*) Effective demonstration and explanation of concepts by the teacher
A. (*a*), (*c*), (*d*) B. (*a*) and (*b*) only
C. (*c*) and (*d*) only D. (*a*), (*b*) and (*c*)

79. Objective/s of EVS teacher who encourages his/her children to observe animals and make pictures on their own is/are to:
(*a*) Develop creativity of children
(*b*) Develop observation and design skills of children
(*c*) Develop aesthetic sense of children
A. (*a*) only B. (*a*) and (*c*) only
C. (*b*) only D. (*a*), (*b*) and (*c*)

80. In EVS learning of crafts and arts while working in groups, is encouraged because:
(*a*) Group learning is easier and very effective strategy for teachers to tackle the problem of indiscipline of the class.
(*b*) Group learning promotes peer learning.
(*c*) Group learning improves social interactions.
(*d*) Group learning help in completing the syllabus of EVS in time.
A. (*a*) and (*d*) only B. (*b*) and (*d*) only
C. (*b*) and (*c*) only D. (*c*) and (*d*) only

81. Which of the following is/are the most effective resource for EVS learning?
(*a*) Family members
(*b*) Members of the community
(*c*) Newspapers
(*d*) Classroom
A. (*d*) only B. (*c*) and (*d*) only
C. (*a*), (*b*) and (*c*) D. (*a*) and (*b*) only

82. Which of the following principle of learning is followed in EVS?
A. Global to local B. Abstract to concrete
C. Unknown to known D. Known to unknown

83. Which of the following is NOT a tool for Formative Assessment of learning in EVS?
A. Portfolio
B. Rating scale
C. Anecdotal records
D. Annual achievement test

84. Which of the following should be avoided while assessing children in EVS?
A. Judging the answers given by children in terms of right or wrong.
B. Discuss "What we have learnt" given at the end of each chapter of EVS textbook of class V
C. Use indicators for assessment
D. Qualitative assessment of children's learning

85. A teacher of class V conducts an activity in which she asks her children to drop some sugar on the ground and asks them to wait until the ants come there. Children can be given meaningful learning from this activity if teacher ______ .

A. encourages her/his children to observe the activity
B. encourages his/her children to share their experiences
C. encourages her/his children to observe, share their experiences followed by discussion on the activity.
D. encourages her/his children to answer the questions at their home related to the activity.

86. Consider the following list:

Tortoise, Crocodile, Crow, Duck, Fish

In this list which one of the following is different from the others?

A. Fish B. Crow
C. Crocodile D. Tortoise

87.

Column-I (City/State)	Column-II (Most liked food)
(*a*) Hongkong	I. Boiled tapioca with any cury
(*b*) Kerala	II. Fish cooked in mustard oil
(*c*) Kashmir	III. Sea fish cooked in coconut oil
(*d*) Goa	IV. Chholay Bhature
	V. Cooked Snakes

The correct match of term of Column-I with that of Column-II is:

	(*a*)	(*b*)	(*c*)	(*d*)
A.	V	II	III	IV
B.	V	I	II	III
C.	V	III	II	I
D.	III	II	IV	I

88. Which one of the following bird's species moves its neck back and forth with a jerk.

A. Owl B. Crow
C. Barbet D. Mynah

89. Consider the following description of houses:

(*a*) In Rajasthan the villagers live in mud houses with roofs of thorny bushes.
(*b*) In Manali (Himachal Pradesh) houses are made on bamboo pillars.
(*c*) In Leh two floor houses are made of stones. The ground floor is for animals and for storing necessary things.

The correct statement(s) is/are:

A. (*a*) and (*b*) B. (*b*) and (*c*)
C. (*a*) and (*c*) D. Only (*c*)

90. Consider the following statements about elephants:

(*a*) Elephants do not rest very much, they sleep 2 to 4 hours only in a day.
(*b*) An adult elephant can eat more than 200 kg or leaves and twigs in a day.
(*c*) They love to play with mud and water, the mud keeps their skin cool.
(*d*) In elephant herd the oldest female elephant decides everything.

The correct statements are:

A. (*a*), (*b*) and (*c*) B. (*b*), (*c*) and (*d*)
C. (*c*), (*d*) and (*a*) D. (*a*), (*b*) and (*d*)

PART- IV

Language-I : English

Directions (Qs. 91-99) : *Read the passage given below and answer the questions that follow by selecting the correct/most appropriate options:*

1. Kangri Karchok, the Kailash Purana of the Tibetans describes the sacred elephant-mouthed river or Langchen Khambab as a long and extensive river that rises from the 'lake unconquerable', the Tso Maphan or Manasarovar that flows from the mountainous regions of Tibet. According to this holy book, this cold river with its sands of gold, circles the holy Manasarovar seven times before taking its course to the west.

2. The Langchen Khambab flows down from the red coloured mountains of the Kanglung Kangri Glacier in the Trans-Himalayan region of Tibet, channelling its way through the earth forests of Tholing and Tsparang of the Gugi Kingdom. These earth forests are full of pillars formed by rocks that collectively appear like a forest from a far—an 'out of the world' landscape that was formed by geological movements of the earth and erosion by wind and water. The Khyunglung ruins also lies on the northern bank of the Sutlej river in this valley which was once known as the 'Garuda Valley'.

3. This mighty river then flows north-west for about 260 km before entering Himachal Pradesh through Shipki La cutting across the formidable Himalayan ranges of Zanskar, the Greater Himalaya and the Dhauladhar. Subsequently, the waters meander through the gigantic Kinnaur Kailash-Jorkanden Range at Reckong Peo creating the terrifying Sutlej gorge. Then it streams into Shimla, Kullu, Mandi and Bilaspur and is responsible for the rich cultivation of grapes, apples and apricots all along its banks. After its confluence with the River Spiti at Khab it is known as Sutlej.

4. It is I ,448 km in length, making it the longest among the five rivers of Punjab. Extensively used for irrigation, it is topographically divided into the Upper Sutlej Basin and Lower Sutlej Basin. It leaves the Himachal boundary to enter the plains of the Punjab at the Bhakra Dam, the second highest gravity dam and a major point of water supply and electricity generation for the North of India.

91. What makes the earth forests of Tholing and Tsparang look amazing?
A. The ruins on the banks of the Sutlej.
B. Abundance of flora and fauna.
C. Cool breeze that makes people feel drowsy.
D. Pillars formed by rocks resembling a forest.

92. Langchen Khambab is a boon for the North of India because:
A. it is a major source of water supply and power generation.
B. it brings along with it mountain soil and minerals.
C. the prosperity of the whole of India depends on it.
D. it abounds in aquatic animals.

93. Read the following sentences:
(*a*) Kangri Karchok is a holy book of the Tibetans.
(*b*) Langchen Khambab is responsible for rich cultivation of various types of fruits in the Himachal Pradesh.
A. (*a*) is true, (*b*) is false
B. (*b*) is true, (*a*) is false
C Both (*a*) and (*b*) are true
D. Both (*a*) and (*b*) are false

94. Which one of the following words is most similar in meaning to the word 'gigantic' as used in the passage (Para 4)?
A. terrifying B. high
C. formidable D. huge

95. Which one of the following words is the most opposite in meaning to the word 'sacred' as used in the passage (Para 1)?
A. pure B. noble
C. unholy D. moral

96. Which part of the following sentence contains an error?
I am not (*a*)/ in best position (*b*)/ to advise you (*c*)/ in this matter (*d*).
A. (*a*) B. (*b*)
C. (*d*) D. (*c*)

97. Which part of speech is the underlined word in the following sentence:
I don't know why he is so hostile to me.
A. Adjective B. Adverb
C. Preposition D. Pronoun

98. 'Lake unconquerable' refers to:
A. Langchen Khambab river
B. Lake Manasarovar
C. Lake Rakshatal
D. The Sutlej river

99. According to Kangri Karchok, Langchen Khambab does not/is not:
A. have sands of gold.
B. circle the Manasarovar seven times.
C. flow very gently through the hills.
D. a cold river.

Directions (Qs. No. 100-105): *Read the extract given below and answer the questions that follow by selecting the correct/most appropriate options:*

Light Brigade

By Alfred Tennyson

Half a league, half a league,
Half a league onward,
All in the valley of Death
Rode the six hundred.
"Forward the Light Brigade!
Charge for the guns!" he said.
Into the valley of Death
Rode the six hundred.
Forward, the Light Brigade!"
Was there a man dismay'd?
Not tho' the soldier knew
Some one had blunder'd.
Theirs not to make reply,
Theirs not to reason why,
Theirs but to do and die.
Into the valley of Death
Rode the six hundred.

100. The expression 'the valley of death' refers to:
A. the place where the dead soldiers are lying buried.
B. the impending death of soldiers.
C. the house of death.
D. a nightmarish place.

101. Which of the following statements is ***not*** true?
The military discipline teaches the soldiers:
A. to do and die.
B. to obey their commander's order.
C. to act tactfully in the battlefield.
D. not to ask any question.

102. Which of the following adjectives does not apply to the soldiers?
A. courageous B. disciplined
C. patriotic D. impractical

103. Name the figure of speech used in 'the Valley of Death'.
A. Metaphor B. Simile
C. Synecdoche D. Metonymy

104. Which literary device is used in the expression, 'to do and die'?
A. Assonance B. Alliteration
C. Simile D. Personification

105. In the first stanza of the extract, the soldiers are:
A. talking to each other about their personal problems.
B. waiting for their commander's order.
C. thinking about the result of the war.
D. seen riding fast to the enemy territory.

106. In the multilingual classroom learners can interact ______ .
A. in the medium of instruction followed by the school.
B. in their own language and can be a mix of words from more than one language.
C. only in the language prescribed in three-language formula.
D. in the language with which the teacher is familiar.

107. Diagnostic tests are administered to ______ .
A. find out deficiencies of the students with a view to planning remedies.
B. assess the suitability of a candidate for a specific programme.
C. test the language proficiency of students for providing them jobs.
D. judge the students' capabilities.

108. Structural approach gives more importance to ______.
A. speech and reading B. reading only
C. speech only D. reading and writing

109. Which among the following does not come under meaning based activities?
A. Interacting with the text.
B. Using previous knowledge.
C. Reading the text and then narrating the same to peers.
D. Reading out every word aloud and translating it.

110. ______ comprehension is the skill of reading a piece of text closely or intensely for the purpose of extracting specific information from the text.
A. Inferential B. Global
C. Local D. Transactional

111. It is a type of writing in which the teacher provides the situation and helps the class to prepare it. The teacher continuously provides feedback, direction and expansion of ideas to the learners.
A. Controlled writing B. Guided writing
C. Free writing D. Product writing

112. A teacher asked the students of class V to read the text thoroughly. Then she asked them to answer the questions with reference to the context (RTC). In this process she is encouraging students for ______ .
A. skimming B. scanning
C. intensive reading D. extensive reading

113. The term 'Comprehensible input' is associated with ______ .
A. Lev Vygotsky B. Stephen Krashan
C. Noam Chomsky D. James Asher

114. Which one of the following is not a sub skill of reading?
A. Connecting B. Predicting
C. Synthesizing D. Transcripting

115. Which one of the following is least important in enhancing speaking skill of children?
A. Listening patiently to children's talk.
B. Giving them an opportunity to express their feelings and ideas.
C. Asking closed ended questions.
D. Organizing discussions on a given topic.

116. At primary level literature is helpful in developing language of learners as:
A. it encourages the learners to complete the worksheets based on it.
B. it is an authentic material covering various genres.
C. it develops teachers' interpretative, creative and critical abilities.
D. it is a good basis for the only expansion of vocabulary.

117. A teacher prepares a worksheet and removes every seventh word from the text. Then she asks the learners to read the text after that they were asked to complete the worksheet with missing word. The task given on the worksheet is a:
A. speaking task B. writing task
C. cloze test D. open test

118. 'Language is arbitrary' means that ______.
A. something is determined by judgement and for a specific reason.
B. it is based on a valid reason and not on chance.
C. there is a strong relation between the words of a language and their meaning.
D. there is no inherent relation between the words of a language and their meaning.

119. The teacher observed that Pravin could not write a paragraph on her own even after brainstorming the topic. However, she was able to write it under adult or peer guidance. This guidance is called ______ .
A. Team teaching
B. Counselling
C. Scaffolding
D. Socialization

120. The purpose of textual exercise is not to:
A. develop creativity among learners.
B. provide opportunity to express themselves.
C. memorise the answers to the questions.
D. give exposure to language learning.

PART-V

Language-II : Hindi

निर्देश (प्र.सं. 121 से 128) : *निम्नलिखित गद्यांश को पढ़कर पूछे गए प्रश्नों के सबसे उपयुक्त उत्तर वाले विकल्प को चुनिए :*

पाठ्यक्रम को कक्षाक्रम से बहुत कड़ाई के साथ बाँध देने के परिणामस्वरूप बच्चे का विकास एक अनवरत प्रक्रिया नहीं बन पाता, अपितु कृत्रिम खंडों में बँट जाता है। एक स्थिर पाठ्यक्रम बच्चे की व्यक्तिगत रुचियों और क्षमताओं के विकास में सहयोग न देकर एक मजबूरी बन जाता है, जिसे बच्चा और उसका अध्यापक दोनों बेबस होकर स्वीकार करते हैं। यदि एक बच्चा किसी विषय में अपने सहपाठियों से अधिक दिलचस्पी रखता है, तो पाठ्यक्रम की बदौलत उसे पूरे एक वर्ष या इससे भी अधिक प्रतीक्षा करनी होती है, जब वह उस विषय में कुछ अधिक विस्तृत जानकारी अध्यापक और नई पुस्तक से प्राप्त कर सकेगा। श्री अरविंद आश्रम के शिक्षा केंद्र में, जहाँ पाठ्यक्रम पूर्वनिधारित और स्थिर नहीं रहता, बच्चों को अपनी व्यक्तिगत रुचि और सामर्थ्य के अनुसार किसी विषय की जानकारी की प्रगति जारी रखने की छूट रहती है। सामान्य स्कूलों में, जहाँ यह छूट नहीं दी जाती। होता प्रायः यह है कि नई कक्षा में आने पर उसे वही विषय बिल्कुल नया और अपरिचित लगता है, जिसके बारे में काफी-कुछ वह पिछली कक्षा में जान चुका था। विशेष तौर पर ऐसा तब होता है, जब पाठ्यक्रम पाठ्यपुस्तकों का पर्याय हो, जैसा भारत में है।

121. पाठ्यक्रम का निर्माण करते समय बच्चों की _______ का ध्यान रखा जाना चाहिए।
A. क्षमताओं और आर्थिक पृष्ठभूमि
B. क्षमताओं और पारिवारिक स्तर
C. क्षमताओं और रुचियों
D. रुचियों और आर्थिक पृष्ठभूमि

122. यह संभव है कि अलग-अलग बच्चे अलग-अलग विषयों में _______ रखते हों।
A. समान रुचियाँ B. समान क्षमताएँ
C. भिन्न रुचियाँ D. भिन्न पूर्वाग्रह

123. पाठ्यक्रम को पाठ्यपुस्तकों का पर्याय _______
A. होना चाहिए। B. नहीं होना चाहिए।
C. कहा जा सकता है। D. माना जाता है।

124. 'बच्चों को यह छूट दी जानी चाहिए कि वे अपनी रुचि व क्षमता के अनुसार किसी विषय की विस्तृत जानकारी प्राप्त कर सकें।' यह स्थिति :
A. सराहनीय है। B. निंदनीय है।
C. असंभव है। D. अव्यावहारिक है।

125. 'बे' उपसर्ग का प्रयोग किस शब्द में **नहीं** किया जा सकता?
A. बस B. अदब
C. ईमान D. फिजूल

126. 'प्रतीक्षा' शब्द से एक नया शब्द बन सकता है :
A. प्रतीक्षाशाली B. प्रतीक्षारत
C. प्रतीक्षावान D. प्रतीक्षाहीन

127. 'वर्ष' में 'इक' प्रत्यय लगाने पर नया शब्द बनेगा :
A. वर्षिकी B. वर्षिक
C. वार्षिकी D. वार्षिक

128. अनुच्छेद के आधार पर कहा जा सकता है :
A. पाठ्यक्रम स्थिर होना चाहिए।
B. पाठ्यक्रम में लचीलापन होना चाहिए।
C. पाठ्यक्रम पूर्णतः अस्थिर होना चाहिए।
D. पाठ्यक्रम जानकारीपरक होना चाहिए।

निर्देश (प्र.सं. 129 से 135) : *निम्नलिखित गद्यांश को पढ़कर पूछे गए प्रश्नों के सबसे उपयुक्त उत्तर वाले विकल्प को चुनिए :*

आज जब भी कोई गाँव का नाम लेता है तो एक अलग ही छवि उभरती है। वह छवि कहती है कि वहाँ गरीबी है। वहाँ अशिक्षा और अज्ञान है। वहाँ अंधविश्वास है, गंदगी है, बीमारी है। हमें विचार करना है कि सच क्या है? क्या हमारे गाँव ऐसे ही थे जैसे आज हैं? आज जो गाँवों की दुर्दशा हुई है उसके लिए जिम्मेदार कौन है? इन सवालों की पड़ताल करते हुए हमें नई समझ बनानी है तथा गाँवों के सही स्वरूप की पहचान करनी है। वैसे यह खुदा का शुक्र है कि गाँवों पर कई तरह के आक्रामक दुष्प्रभावों के बावजूद उनका मूल स्वरूप नहीं बदला है। जो दूरस्थ गाँव हैं–शहर के पड़ोस से दूर उनकी निजता तो खासी बची हुई है। ऐसी स्थिति में हमारा दायित्व, एक शिक्षित समाज का दायित्व क्या बनता है? हमें विचार करना है। मगर ऐसा कोई भी विचार गाँवों को आँखों से देखे बिना, स्वयं देखकर समझे बिना नहीं किया जा सकता। तो हमें अपनी फर्स्ट हैंड समझ बनाने के लिए गाँव चलना है।

अपने मूल स्वरूप में गाँव एक वेधशाला है। एक विद्याशाला है। गाँव वेधशाला या प्रयोगशाला इसलिए है कि ज्ञान को रोज वहाँ कर्म की कसौटी पर कसा जाता है। आजमाया जाता है। जो ज्ञान कर्म की कसौटी पर खरा न उतरे तो उसे खारिज कर दिया जाता है। हर ज्ञान के होने की शर्त यह है वह सृजन और उत्पादन की शान पर तराशा जाए।

129. ज्ञान के होने की अनिवार्य शर्त है :
A. सृजन और धन B. सृजन और उत्पादन
C. धन और उत्पादन D. उत्पादन और ज्योति

130. अनुच्छेद के आधार पर कहा जा सकता है कि :
A. गाँव में नकारात्मक परिवर्तन भी हुए हैं।
B. गाँव में समस्त परिवर्तन सकारात्मक हैं।
C. गाँव में बीमारी और अज्ञान ही है।
D. गाँव में लोग अशिक्षित और अज्ञानी हैं।

131. गाँव को ठीक से समझने के लिए जरूरी है :
A. गाँव के किस्से सुनना B. गाँव को टी.वी. पर देखना
C. गाँव के बारे में पढ़ना D. स्वयं गाँव में जाना

132. गाँव को प्रयोगशाला क्यों कहा गया है?
A. ज्ञान को जानकारी की कसौटी पर कसा जाता है।
B. ज्ञान को कर्म की कसौटी पर कसा जाता है।
C. ज्ञान को निरंतर बढ़ाया जाता रहता है।
D. ज्ञानवान व्यक्ति ज्ञान का प्रयोग करते हैं।

133. 'फर्स्ट हैंड समझ' से तात्पर्य है :
A. ज्ञानवान व्यक्तियों से जानकारी लेना।
B. दूसरों के अनुभव से समझ बनाना।
C. स्वयं के अनुभव से समझ बनाना।
D. स्वयं के पूर्वज्ञान, पूर्वाग्रहों से समझ बनाना।

134. 'शिक्षित' शब्द में प्रत्यय है :
A. क्षित B. त
C. इत D. क्षत

135. गाँव की छवि में क्या शामिल **नहीं** है?
A. गंदगी B. अशिक्षा
C. अज्ञान D. कर्म

136. प्राथमिक स्तर पर कौन-सी गतिविधि बच्चों की मौखिक अभिव्यक्ति के विकास में सबसे कम प्रभावी है?
A. घटना वर्णन करना।
B. कहानी को शब्दशः दोहराना।
C. कहानी को अपनी भाषा में कहना।
D. चित्र दिखाकर कहानी कहलवाना।

137. मुहावरे और लोकोक्तियों के प्रयोग के संदर्भ में कौन-सा कथन उचित है?
A. ये भाषा का अनिवार्य हिस्सा है।
B. ये भाषा-प्रयोग को प्रभावी बनाते हैं।
C. ये भाषा को नियंत्रित करते हैं।
D. भाषा का अलंकरण इनका कार्य है।

138. मीता ने सभी बच्चों को एक अनुच्छेद दिया जिसमें हर पाँचवें शब्द की जगह रिक्त स्थान था, जिसे बच्चों को भरना था। मीता ने किसका प्रयोग किया?
A. पठन परीक्षण B. लेखन परीक्षण
C. व्याकरण परीक्षण D. क्लोज परीक्षण

139. बच्चों में _______ और ______ के माध्यम से लेखन कौशल का विकास किया जा सकता है।
A. रेखांकन, चित्रांकन B. चित्रांकन, लिपि-चिह्नों
C. रेखांकन, लिपि-चिह्नों D. लिपि-चिह्नों, अक्षर बनावट

140. मुदिता अक्सर 'श' को 'स' बोलती है। मुदिता की भाषा-शिक्षिका के रूप में आप इस स्थिति के बारे में क्या कहेंगे?
A. भाषागत त्रुटि का होना B. क्षेत्रीय भाषा का प्रभाव
C. भाषागत ज्ञान का अभाव D. भाषा-प्रयोग में लापरवाही

141. निम्नलिखित में से कौन-सा प्रश्न बच्चों की भाषा-क्षमता के विकास में सर्वाधिक सहायक है?
A. डाल-डाल का इस्तेमाल करते हुए वाक्य बनाओ।
B. तितली कली के पास कब गई होगी और क्यों?
C. तितली और कली ने क्या खेल खेला?
D. तुम्हारी मनपसंद किताब कौन-सी है?

142. 'सामाजिक अंतःक्रिया' की अवधारणा _______ से संबंधित है।
A. स्किनर B. पियाजे
C. चॉम्स्की D. वाइगोत्स्की

143. स्किनर ने भाषा सीखने की प्रक्रिया में _______ पर सर्वाधिक बल दिया।
A. अंतःक्रिया B. अनुकरण
C. भाषा अर्जन क्षमता D. सृजनात्मकता

144. बच्चों की भाषाई-क्षमताओं के आकलन के लिए ______ सर्वाधिक सहायक है।
A. बच्चों की परस्पर अनौपचारिक बातचीत
B. बच्चों की कक्षा में औपचारिक बातचीत
C. बच्चों और शिक्षक की परस्पर औपचारिक बातचीत
D. बच्चों का शिक्षक द्वारा प्रदत्त अभ्यास कार्य करना

145. कौन-सा प्रश्न कक्षा में बहु-भाषिकता को पोषित करता है?
A. अच्छी लगने वाली महक को क्या कहेंगे?
B. बुरी लगने वाली महक को क्या कहेंगे?
C. तुम्हारे घर में किस-किसकी महक आती है?
D. फूलों के नाम अपनी भाषा में लिखो।

146. 'इस कहानी में पहाड़ी, घाटी शब्दों का इस्तेमाल हुआ है। पहाड़ी इलाके से जुड़े हुए और शब्द सोचकर लिखो।'—यह अभ्यास प्रश्न _______ का उदाहरण है।
A. संदर्भ में व्याकरण B. शब्द-भंडार में विकास
C. शब्द-कोश का विकास D. पर्यायवाची शब्दों से परिचय

147. शिक्षण-प्रक्रिया को रुचिकर बनाने में _______ शिक्षण-सामग्री सहायक होती है।
A. ऑडियो-वीडियो B. वैविध्यपूर्ण
C. वीडियोपरक D. पत्र-पत्रिकाएँ

148. प्राथमिक स्तर पर भाषाई क्षमताओं का विकास ______ है और साहित्य ______ है।
A. साधन, साध्य B. साध्य, उद्देश्य
C. साध्य, साधन D. उद्देश्य, साध्य

149. प्राथमिक स्तर पर कौन-सा भाषा शिक्षण का उद्देश्य नहीं है?
A. अपने द्वारा कही गई बात की तार्किक पुष्टि करना।
B. भाषा का सृजनशील एवं कल्पनाशील प्रयोग करना।
C. रचनाओं के माध्यम से विभिन्न विषयों से जुड़ना।
D. भाषा संबंधी व्याकरण को पूर्णतः कंठस्थ करना।

150. कक्षा में भाषा की ______ के प्रति ______ बनकर उसका उपयोग भाषा शिक्षण में करना चाहिए।
A. विविधता, विद्वान B. विविधता, संवेदनशील
C. संवेदनशीलता, कठोर D. एकरूपता, संवेदनशील

Answers

1	2	3	4	5	6	7	8	9	10
B	B	A	A	B	A	D	B	A	B
11	12	13	14	15	16	17	18	19	20
D	A	D	C	C	C	D	D	B	C
21	22	23	24	25	26	27	28	29	30
D	A	D	B	D	D	A	D	D	C
31	32	33	34	35	36	37	38	39	40
D	A	A	D	A	B	B	D	D	B
41	42	43	44	45	46	47	48	49	50
B	C	D	B	B	B	C	C	D	A
51	52	53	54	55	56	57	58	59	60
A	A	C	C	B	B	A	B	C	D
61	62	63	64	65	66	67	68	69	70
C	D	D	B	A	D	B	B	B	D
71	72	73	74	75	76	77	78	79	80
D	B	B	C	C	A	A	B	D	C
81	82	83	84	85	86	87	88	89	90
C	D	D	A	C	B	B	D	C	C
91	92	93	94	95	96	97	98	99	100
D	A	C	D	C	B	B	B	C	B
101	102	103	104	105	106	107	108	109	110
C	D	A	B	D	B	A	D	D	C
111	112	113	114	115	116	117	118	119	120
B	C	B	D	C	B	C	D	C	C
121	122	123	124	125	126	127	128	129	130
C	C	B	A	D	B	D	B	B	A
131	132	133	134	135	136	137	138	139	140
D	B	C	C	D	B	B	D	A	B
141	142	143	144	145	146	147	148	149	150
B	D	B	A	D	A	B	C	D	B

Explanatory Answers

1. In developmental psychology and developmental biology, a critical period is a maturational stage in the lifespan of an organism during which the nervous system is especially sensitive to certain environmental stimuli. If, for some reason, the organism does not receive the appropriate stimulus during this "critical period" to learn a given skill or trait, it may be difficult, ultimately less successful, or even impossible, to develop certain associated functions later in life. Functions that are indispensable to an organism's survival, such as vision, are particularly likely to develop during critical periods. "Critical period" also relates to the ability to acquire one's first language. Researchers found that people who passed the "critical period" would not acquire their first language fluently.

2. Kohlberg's Six Stages of Cognitive Moral Reasoning:

Stage 1: Obedience and punishment orientation

- Egocentric deference to superior power or prestige, or a trouble-avoiding set.
- Objective responsibility.

Stage 2: Naively egoistic orientation

- Right action is that which is instrumental in satisfying the self's needs and occasionally others'.
- Relativism of values to each actor's needs and perspectives.
- Naive egalitarianism, orientation to exchange and reciprocity.

Stage 3: Good-boy/good-girl orientation

- Orientation to approval, to pleasing and helping others.

- Conformity to stereotypical images of majority or natural role behaviour.
- Action is evaluated in terms of intentions.

Stage 4: Authority and social-order-maintaining orientation

- Orientation to "doing duty" and to showing respect for authority and maintaining the given social order or its own sake.
- Regard for earned expectations of others.
- Differentiates actions out of a sense of obligation to rules from actions for generally "nice" or natural motives.

Stage 5: Contractual/legalistic orientation

- Norms of right and wrong are defined in terms of laws or institutionalized rules which seem to have a rational basis.
- When conflict arises between individual needs and law or contract, though sympathetic to the former, the individual believes the latter must prevail because of its greater functional rationality for society, the majority will and welfare.

Stage 6: The morality of individual principles of conscience

- Orientation not only toward existing social rules, but also toward the conscience as a directing agent, mutual trust and respect, and principles of moral choice involving logical universalities and consistency.
- Action is controlled by internalized ideals that exert a pressure to act accordingly regardless of the reactions of others in the immediate environment.
- If one acts otherwise, self-condemnation and guilt result.

5. One of the first important challenges to Piaget's theory came from Russian developmentalist Lev Vygotsky. Vygotsky's socio-cultural theory focused on how culture—the beliefs, values, traditions, and skills of a social group—is transmitted from generation to generation. Rather than depicting children as independent explorers who make critical discoveries on their own, Vygotsky viewed cognitive growth as a socially mediated activity—one in which children gradually acquire new ways of thinking and behaving through cooperative dialogues with more knowledgeable members of society. Vygotsky also rejected the notion that all children progress through the same stages of cognitive growth. He argued that the new skills children master through their interactions with more competent people are often specific to their culture rather than universal cognitive structures. So from Vygotsky's perspective, Piaget largely ignored important social and cultural influences on human development.

6. **Private speech** is speech spoken to oneself for communication, self-guidance, and self-regulation of behaviour. Children from two to about seven years old can be observed engaging in private speech. Although it is audible, it is neither intended for nor directed at others. Private speech was first studied by Lev Vygotsky and Jean Piaget; in the past 30 years private speech has received renewed attention from researchers. Researchers have noted a positive correlation between children's use of private speech and their task performance and achievement, a fact also noted previously by Vygotsky. It is when children begin school that their use of private speech decreases and "goes underground".

7. The term 'scaffolding' comes from the works of Wood, Bruner and Ross (1976). The term 'scaffolding' was developed as a metaphor to describe the type of assistance offered by a teacher or peer to support learning. In the process of scaffolding, the teacher helps the student master a task or concept that the student is initially unable to grasp independently. The teacher offers assistance with only those skills that are beyond the student's capability.

   Of great importance is allowing the student to complete as much of the task as possible, unassisted. The teacher only attempts to help the student with tasks that are just beyond his current capability. Student errors are expected, but, with teacher feedback and prompting, the student is able to achieve the task or goal. When the student takes responsibility for or masters the task, the teacher begins the process of "fading", or the gradual removal of the scaffolding, which allows the student to work independently.

   "Scaffolding is actually a bridge used to build upon what students already know to arrive at something they do not know. If scaffolding is properly administered, it will act as an enabler, not as a disabler" (Benson, 1997).

8. **The Concrete-Operational Stage (7 to 11 years):** During Piaget's concrete-operational period, children rapidly acquire cognitive operations and apply these important new skills when thinking about objects and events that they have experienced. A cognitive operation is an internal mental activity that enables children to modify and reorganize their images and symbols to reach a logical conclusion. With these powerful new operations in their cognitive arsenal, grade-school children progress far beyond the static and centered thinking of the preoperational stage. For every limitation of the preoperational child, we can see a corresponding strength in the concrete operator. Below we provide a couple of examples of operational thought: *conservation* and *relational logic*.

9. Schemas: Schemas are the basic building blocks of such cognitive models, and enable us to form a mental representation of the world. Piaget defined a schema as: "a cohesive, repeatable action sequence possessing component actions that are tightly interconnected and governed by a core meaning."

In more simple terms Piaget called the schema the basic building block of intelligent behaviour—a way of organizing knowledge. Indeed, it is useful to think of schemas as "units" of knowledge, each relating to one aspect of the world, including objects, actions, and abstract (*i.e.,* theoretical) concepts.

11. Howard Gardner proposed the theory of multiple intelligences. According to him, intelligence is not a single entity; rather distinct types of intelligences exist. Each of these intelligences are independent of each other. This means that, if a person exhibits one type of intelligence, it does not necessarily indicate being high or low on other types of intelligences. Gardner also put forth that different types of intelligences interact and work together to find a solution to a problem. Gardner studied extremely talented persons, who had shown exceptional abilities in their respective areas, and described eight types of intelligence.

15. Dyslexia, also known as reading disorder, is characterized by trouble with reading despite normal intelligence. Different people are affected to varying degrees. Problems may include difficulties in spelling words, reading quickly, writing words, "sounding out" words in the head, pronouncing words when reading aloud and understanding what one reads. Often these difficulties are first noticed at school. When someone who previously could read loses their ability, it is known as "alexia". The difficulties are involuntary and people with this disorder have a normal desire to learn. People with dyslexia have higher rates of attention deficit hyperactivity disorder (ADHD), developmental language disorders, and difficulties with numbers.

16. Inclusive Education is that type of education which supports equal education to each and every child without any sort of discrimination with respect to their gender, caste, creed, race, colour, ability or disability. The Right to Education Act, 2009 also stands for such type of education. It clearly indicates free and compulsory elementary education to all children of the age group 6-14 years. The present paper highlights the provision of inclusive education in context of the Right to Education Act. It also throws light on the present scenario of inclusive education in India and suggests some useful recommendations for making it more beneficial and effective for both the abled and disabled children equally. It calls for the joint support of the teachers, parents, authorities and children themselves to accomplish the goal of total literacy and education in India.

17. Constructivist teaching is based on constructivist learning theory. This theoretical framework holds that learning always builds upon knowledge that a student already knows; this prior knowledge is called a schema. Because all learning is filtered through pre-existing schemata, constructivists suggest that learning is more effective when a student is actively engaged in the learning process rather than attempting to receive knowledge passively. A wide variety of methods claim to be based on constructivist learning theory. Most of these methods rely on some form of guided discovery where the teacher avoids most direct instruction and attempts to lead the student through questions and activities to discover, discuss, appreciate and verbalize the new knowledge.

According to Audrey Gray, the characteristics of a constructivist classroom are as follows:

- the learners are actively involved.
- the environment is democratic.
- the activities are interactive and student-centered.
- the teacher facilitates a process of learning in which students are encouraged to be responsible and autonomous.

19. In the NCF 2005 conceptualisation of child-centred pedagogy, teachers were to consider theories of psychological development as well as students' 'interests', 'characteristics', and 'needs'.

Child-centred' pedagogy means giving primacy to children's experiences, their voices and their active participation. This kind of pedagogy requires us to plan learning in keeping with children's psychological development and interests. The learning plans therefore must respond to physical, cultural and social preferences within the wide diversity of characteristics and needs.

20. The distinction between the 'emotional' and the 'cognitive' brain is fuzzy and context-dependent. Indeed, there is compelling evidence that brain territories and psychological processes commonly associated with cognition, such as the dorsolateral prefrontal cortex and working memory, play a central role in emotion. Furthermore, putatively emotional and cognitive regions influence one another via a complex web of connections in ways that jointly contribute to adaptive and maladaptive behaviour.

This work demonstrates that emotion and cognition are deeply inter-woven in the fabric of the brain, suggesting that widely held beliefs about the key constituents of 'the emotional brain' and 'the cognitive brain' are fundamentally flawed. We conclude by outlining several strategies for enhancing future research. Developing a deeper understanding of the emotional-cognitive brain is important, not just for understanding the mind but also for elucidating the root causes of its disorders.

21. Active learning is a situation where children construct their knowledge by their active engagement in learning process. It is in contrast to objectivist, where knowledge was supplied by teacher or more learned person to a young learner or less knowledgeable person. Learning does not mean only passive receiving or acquiring of information or only listening. You should understand that knowledge transmission is not knowledge creation. You should provide a learning environment where learners actively create their meaning and develop their understanding through their active engagement in various contexts. A learning environment promoting participation, cooperation, collaboration for construction of knowledge is basically an active learning environment. There are strategies like simulations, role-playing, multimedia supported learning environments, games, intentional learning environments, storytelling, case studies, dialogues, scaffolding, learning by design, group cooperation, collaborative learning, etc., which promotes active learning.

22. Students learn by connecting new knowledge with knowledge and concepts that they already know, thereby constructing new meanings (NRC, 2000). Research suggests that students connect knowledge most effectively in active social classrooms, where they negotiate understanding through interaction and varied approaches. Instructors should be aware that students, as novice learners, often possess less developed or incomplete conceptual frameworks (Kober, 2015). As a result, it may take time to learn how to "chunk" knowledge into similar, retrievable categories, grow larger conceptual ideas, and inter-connect ideas. They may also harbor misconceptions or erroneous ways of thinking, which can limit or weaken connections with new knowledge (Ambrose, et. al, 2010).

Instructors can build approaches that help students develop and learn pathways to becoming expert learners whose conceptual frameworks are deeply inter-connected, transferable, rooted in a solid memory and skills foundation, and easily retrieved (Ambrose, et. al, 2010). Students build strong conceptual frameworks when instructors: help them assess and clarify prior knowledge; facilitate social environments through active learning activities that interconnect ideas and vary approaches to knowledge; and invite students to reflect, co-build course road maps, and pursue other forms of metacognition.

27. In infancy, toddlerhood, and early childhood, the body's physical development is rapid. On average, newborns weigh between 5 and 10 pounds, and a newborn's weight typically doubles in six months and triples in one year. By 2 years old the weight will have quadrupled, so we can expect that a 2 year old should weigh between 20 and 40 pounds. The average length of a newborn is 19.5 inches, increasing to 29.5 inches by 12 months and 34.4 inches by 2 years old.

During infancy and childhood, growth does not occur at a steady rate. Growth slows between 4 and 6 years old: During this time children gain 5-7 pounds and grow about 2-3 inches per year. Once girls reach 8-9 years old, their growth rate outpaces that of boys due to a pubertal growth spurt. This growth spurt continues until around 12 years old, coinciding with the start of the menstrual cycle. By 10 years old, the average girl weighs 88 pounds, and the average boy weighs 85 pounds.

We are born with all of the brain cells that we will ever have—about 100-200 billion neurons (nerve cells) whose function is to store and transmit information. However, the nervous system continues to grow and develop. Each neural pathway forms thousands of new connections during infancy and toddlerhood.

28. Principles of Human Growth and Development

1. Development is Continuous
2. Development is Gradual
3. Development is Sequential
4. Rate of Development Varies Person to Person
5. Development Proceeds from General to Specific
6. Most Traits are Correlated in Development
7. Growth and Development is a Product of Both Heredity and Environment
8. Development is Predictable
9. Development brings about both structural and functional changes.
10. There is a Constant Interaction Between All Factors of Development

29. Main Causes of Individual Differences:

1. **Heredity:** One of the most significant and chief causes of individual differences is heredity. Individuals inherit various physical traits like face with its features, colour of eyes and hair, type of skin, shape of skull and size of hands, colour blindness, baldness, stub-finger and tendency to certain diseases like cancer and tuberculosis, mental traits like intelligence, abstract thinking, aptitudes and prejudices. Now it is an admitted fact that heredity differences result in the quantity and rate of physical as well as mental development being different and different individuals.
2. **Environment:** Environment significantly influences individual differences. Changes in child's environment are reflected in the changes in his personality. Psychologically speaking, a person's environment consists of sum total of stimulation which he receives from conception until his death.

Environment consists of physical, intellectual, social, moral, political, economic and cultural forces. All these forces cause individual differences. Modern psychologists believe that individual differences are caused by both heredity and environment. Personality is the outcome of mutual interaction between heredity and environment.

30. Primary and secondary socialization

Primary socialization refers to socialization during the early years of childhood, and is carried out by the family or close community. It is during primary socialization that children first begin to learn about the basic values and norms and other features of the culture making up the way of life of their society. They also begin to acquire their sense of who they are as individuals—their individual identities—and significant elements of their social identities such as their gender, ethnicity and sexuality. In most cases, these identities formed during childhood will remain throughout people's lives and are much more difficult to change in adulthood than other identities.

Secondary socialization refers to socialization which takes place beyond the family and close community. It is carried out through agencies of secondary socialization such as the education system, the peer group (a group of people of similar age and status), the workplace, the mass media and religious institutions. While life-long socialization plays a very important part in forming our identities, individuals also have the free will to enables them to carve out their own personal identities also have the free will to enable them to carve out their own personal identities and influence how others see them, rather than simply being influenced by them. Individuals are not simply the passive victims of the socialization process.

For example, while the mass media might influence our lifestyles, attitudes and values, and how we see ourselves and how others see us, individuals may also react to what they read, see or hear in the media in different ways. A woman from a minority ethnic background may define herself as black or Asian, but she may also see herself mainly as a woman, a mother, a teacher or a Muslim. Similarly, we have some choices in the consumer goods we buy, the clothes we wear, and the leisure activities we choose to follow. Through these choices, we can influence how others see us, and the image of ourselves we project to them.

32. The side of a square = 4 cm

$\therefore$ Area = (side)^2

$= 4^2 = 16 \text{ cm}^2$

it is cut into 4 equal squares

$\therefore$ The area of each small square $= \frac{16}{4} = 4 \text{ cm}^2$.

34. A number that is divisible by all the numbers from 1 to 10 (both inclusive)

= LCM of 1, 2, 3, 4, 5, 6, 7, 8, 9, 10

2	1, 2, 3, 4, 5, 6, 7, 8, 9, 10
2	1, 3, 2, 5, 3, 7, 4, 9, 5
3	3, 1, 5, 3, 7, 2, 9, 5
5	1, 5, 1, 7, 2, 3, 5
	1, 7, 2, 3, 1

$= 2 \times 2 \times 3 \times 5 \times 1 \times 7 \times 2 \times 3 \times 1$

$= 60 \times 42$

$= 2520.$

35. Given, the total number of coins = 25

Let the number of ₹ 5 coins = x

Then, the number of ₹ 10 coins = $(25 - x)$

Therefore,

$5x + 10(25 - x) = ₹\ 160$

$\Rightarrow \quad 5x + 250 - 10x = 160$

$\Rightarrow \quad 250 - 5x = 160$

$\Rightarrow \quad 5x = 250 - 160$

$\Rightarrow \quad 5x = 90 \Rightarrow x = 18$

$\therefore$ The number of ₹ 5 coins = x = 18

and the number of ₹ 10 coins

$= (25 - x)$

$= 25 - 18 = 7.$

36. $17.5 \times 3 - 21 \div 7 - 3 \times 12.5$

$= 17.5 \times 3 - 3 - 3 \times 12.5$

$= 52.5 - 3 - 37.5$

$= 52.5 - 40.5$

$= 12.$

37. Let the number of trees in the garden is x

Then, the number of neem trees $= \frac{1}{6}x$

$5 = \frac{1}{6}x$

i.e., $x = 30$

$\therefore$ The number of trees = x = 30

and the number of Ashoka trees $= \frac{1}{2}x$

$\therefore$ the number of eucalyptus trees

$= x - \left(\frac{x}{6} + \frac{x}{2}\right)$

$= x - \left(\frac{x + 3x}{6}\right)$

$= x - \frac{2}{3}x = \frac{1}{3}x = \frac{30}{3} = 10.$

38. Total travel time of the journey as the train leaves 16:30 pm
Total time taken on 29 august
= 24 hours – 16:30 hours
= 7:30 hours
Total time taken on 30 august
= 24 hours
Total time taken on 31st august
= 8:45 hours
Total travel time of the journey
= 7:30 hours + 24 hours + 8:45 hours
= 40 hours 15 minutes.

39. Convert each length in smallest unit to arrange in decreasing order.
1 meter = 1000 mm
1 decimeter = 100 mm
1 centimeter = 10 mm
A. 8500 mm, 8008 mm, 8080 mm, 8000 mm
B. 8080 mm, 8500 mm, 8000 mm, 8008 mm
C. 8000 mm, 8080 mm, 8500 mm, 8008 mm
D. 8500 mm, 8080 mm, 8008 mm, 8000 mm
Therefore, Option (D) is in decreasing order.

40. Let the length of rectangle form wire = l cm
then, perimeter = $2(l + b)$ [given, width = b = 30 cm]
$$180 \text{ cm} = 2(l + 30)$$
$$\Rightarrow \quad l + 30 = 90 \text{ cm}$$
$$\Rightarrow \quad l = 90 - 30 = 60 \text{ cm.}$$

56. Cost of item [$\frac{1}{2}$ kg tomotoes + 1 kg potatoes + $\frac{1}{2}$ kg carrot + 250 g chillies + 6 lemons]
= ₹ (20 + 12.50 + 40 + 25 + 15)
= ₹ 112.50
∴ money will be get back
= ₹ 200 – ₹ 112.50 = ₹ 87.50.

57. Since the digits of the number are prime numbers, the possible options for the digits are 1,2,3,5,7.
As the sum of the digits of the number is divisible by both 3 and 4, the sum of the digits of the number will also be divisible by 12.
Since the digits are consecutive prime numbers the maximum sum of digits that can be obtained is 12 by using 5 and 7 as the two digits.
So, it is clearly evident from the above arguments that the number must be 57.

58. From 7 am to 4:30 pm
= 5 + 4:30 = 9:30 hours
and parking rate
(*d*) more than 8 hours and up to 12 hours = ₹ 150.

59. Arranged in ascending order
as, .77, 7.007, 7.07, 7.70, 7.707
Here, number of third place = 7.07.

60. Given, five digit number,
The digit at ten's place = 8
$$\therefore \quad \text{unit's place} = \frac{1}{4} \times 8 = 2$$
thousand place = 0
hundreds place = 4
and ten thousands place = 2 × 3 = 6
Therefore, the number = 60482.

62. Malleswari won the world title in the 54 kg division in 1994 and 1995 and placed third in 1993 and 1996. In 1994, she won silver at the World Championships in Istanbul and in 1995 she won the Asian Weightlifting Championships in Korea in the 54 kg category. She won the title in China that year with a record lift of 113 kg at the World Championships. Even before her Olympic win, Malleswari was a two-time weightlifting world champion with 29 international medals, which includes 11 gold medals. Along with the national and international medals, Malleswari was also awarded with the Rajiv Gandhi Khel Ratna in 1999, Arjuna Award in 1994, and Padma Shri in 1999. At the 2000 Sydney Olympics, Malleswari lifted 110 kg in the "snatch" and 130 kg in the "clean and jerk" categories for a total of 240 kg. She won the bronze medal and became the first Indian woman to win an Olympic medal. She is also the first and only Indian woman weightlifter to win an Olympic medal.

63. Based on the method of planting
(*a*) **Directly sown plants:** Okra, leafy vegetables, carrot, radish, peas and beans
(*b*) **Transplanting:** Tomato, brinjal, chilli, cauliflower, cabbage, onion, potato, sweet potato, cassava, pointed gourd, etc.
(*c*) **Crops grown from underground parts:**
- **Root vegetables:** Radish, carrot, turnip, beetroot
- **Rhizome:** Colocasia, ginger
- **Bulb:** Onion, garlic
- **Tuber:** Potato, sweet potato, cassava and yam.

64. *Allocasuarina decaisneana* or desert oak is a medium-sized, slow-growing tree found in the dry desert regions of the Northern Territory, South Australia and Western Australia. The Anangu peoples know the tree as kurkara. The dioecious tree typically grows to a height of 10 to 16 metres and as high as 20 m and a width of 3 to 8 m. They mature to an adult form with spreading limbs and bushy foliage. It is the only member of its family in Central Australia and its large cylindrical cones are the biggest in its family. The trees have a cork-like bark that is deeply furrowed and is known to protect the trees from fire.

65. *Nepenthes* is a genus of carnivorous plants, also known as tropical pitcher plants, or monkey cups, in the monotypic family Nepenthaceae. The genus comprises about 170 species, and numerous natural and many cultivated hybrids. They are mostly liana-forming plants of the Old World tropics, ranging from South China, Indonesia, Malaysia, and the Philippines; westward to Madagascar (two species) and the Seychelles (one); southward to Australia (three) and New Caledonia (one); and northward to India (one) and Sri Lanka (one). The greatest diversity occurs on Borneo, Sumatra, and the Philippines, with many endemic species. Many are plants of hot, humid, lowland areas, but the majority are tropical montane plants, receiving warm days but cool to cold, humid nights year round. A few are considered tropical alpine, with cool days and nights near freezing. The name "monkey cups" refers to the fact that monkeys have been observed drinking rainwater from these plants.

66. The Civil Disobedience Movement (The First Phase) and the Dandi March—March 12, 1930-March 5, 1931—Gandhi, on March 12, 1930 started march from the Sabarmati Ashram with 72 people and reached Dandi (coastal Gujarat) in April 6, 1930, and broke the salt law by picking up a handful of salt at Dandi and announced the commencement of Civil Disobedience Movement.

67. The first sign of malaria is high fever with shivering. The shivering is felt when the parasites are released in the blood in large numbers. The other symptoms are headache, nausea and muscular pain. Each malarial attack lasts for 6 to 10 hours duration. The patient on treatment and recovery becomes weak, exhausted and anaemic. It also causes enlargement of spleen and liver. Malaria can be conclusively diagnosed by microscopic examination of the blood for *Plasmodium* parasite.

Earlier a drug Quinine obtained from the back of *Cinchona* tree was used to treat malaria. Nowadays new, better drugs have come up which should be taken on the advice of doctors. Efforts are underway to produce anti-malarial vaccine.

69. Cheraw Dance is also known as Bamboo Dance. It is a folk dance of Mizoram, in which the dancers move by stepping alternately in and out of the pairs of horizontal bamboos. Thus, a grid of bamboo poles is an integral part of this dance. The performers tap the bamboos open and closed in. They tap the bamboos open and closed in rhythmic beats. The dancers step in and out of the squares formed by the bamboos with ease and grace. The pattern and stepping of the dance resemble the movements of birds, swaying of trees.

70. Tamil Nadu is the Eleventh largest state in India and covers an area of 130,058 square kilometres. It is bordered by Kerala to the west, Karnataka to the northwest, Andhra Pradesh to the north, the Bay of Bengal to the east and the Indian Ocean to the south. Cape Comorin (Kanyakumari), the southernmost tip of the Indian Peninsula which is the meeting point of the Arabian Sea, the Bay of Bengal, and the Indian Ocean.

71. NCF 2005 and Objectives of Environmental Studies: The present syllabus is designed to forge an integrated perspective for the primary stage of schooling that draws upon insights from Sciences, Social Sciences and Environmental Education. The National Curriculum Framework 2005 indicates some of the objectives of teaching science and Social Sciences at the primary stage as follows:

- to train children to locate and comprehend relationships between the natural, social and cultural environment;
- to develop an understanding based on observation and illustration, drawn from lived experiences and physical, biological, social and cultural aspects of life, rather than abstractions;
- to create cognitive capacity and resourcefulness to make the child curious about social phenomena, starting with the family and moving on to wider spaces;
- to nurture the curiosity and creativity of the child particularly in relation to the natural environment (including artifacts and people);
- to develop an awareness about environmental issues;
- to engage the child in exploratory and hands-on activities to acquire basic cognitive and psychomotor skills through observation, classification, inference, etc.;
- to emphasise design and fabrication, estimation and measurement as a prelude to the development of technological and quantitative skills at later stages;
- to be able to critically address gender concerns and issues of marginalisation and oppression with values of equality and justice, and respect for human dignity and rights.

72. Environment education is already an integral part of school curriculum. The National Curriculum Framework (NCF)-2005 infuses the components of environmental education as part of different disciplines in the treatment of content in Physics, Mathematics, Chemistry, Biology, Geography, History, Political Science, Health and Physical Education, Art, Music, etc. As a follow-up of NCF-2005, syllabi and textbooks for all the stages of school education have been developed by the National

Council of Educational Research and Training (NCERT). For Classes I and II, Environmental Studies (EVS) components are integrated with language and mathematics. For classes III to V, the NCERT has developed EVS syllabus and the textbooks integrating Science and Social Science components. For classes VI onwards, essential EVS components are integrated across subject areas. Central Board of Secondary Education (CBSE) has also issued directives to schools to impart environmental education to students.

74. Child-centred approach: The curriculum gives primacy to children's experiences and their active participation. The identified concepts, skills, issues/ concerns included in the EVS curriculum are developmentally age-appropriate with the understanding of the child progressing gradually from self to the immediate surrounding and further to the wider environment.

In order to follow a child centred approach in EVS, the learning process followed under each theme moves from simple to complex, concrete to abstract, informal to formal in a logical and phased manner. (*e.g.* food in the family → sources of food → conservation of food).

75. Themes in EVS: The syllabus for Classes III-V is woven around six common themes given below; the predominant theme on 'Family and Friends' encompasses four sub-themes:

1. Family and Friends:

(*i*) Relationships;

(*ii*) Work and Play;

(*iii*) Animals;

(*iv*) Plants;

2. Food;
3. Shelter;
4. Water;
5. Travel;
6. Things We Make and Do.

81. Significance of Learning Resources in EVS: Use of educational resources for teaching learning of EVS is critical because:

- EVS is the process of recognising values and clarifying concepts in order to develop skills and attitudes necessary to understand and appreciate inter-relationship between the humans, culture and biophysical surroundings.
- Outdoor-based learning processes are effective in EVS.
- Real-life based experience, in physical, biological, social and cultural aspects of life are appropriate for EVS. Use of local resources and material facilitate real-life based learning.
- EVS aims to enhance cognitive ability, capacity and resourcefulness in child and to make her curious about social phenomena—starting with the family and moving on to the wider space. Using learning resources creatively one can achieve this.
- By using local resources, teachers can help students to construct their own knowledge, develop skills and values providing them direct learning experiences.

Besides these educational benefits there are several social advantages too.

- With the help of local resources you can build strong relationship with society and neighbouring communities.
- Students can connect to the world around them through their studies and vice-versa, which is an important part of learning.
- Students will become aware of their immediate environment.
- Students will be sensitised towards the conservation of their immediate environment.

In order to gain these advantages, a teacher must have the knowledge and skills to identify, develop, and use local learning resources.

82. Facilitate Exploration from 'Known to Unknown' and 'Coincrete to Abstract' : In the earlier years, it is said to be more effective to ensure that new concepts and information is explained 'in relation to' a known one. It is so because during this period the ability to learn abstract concepts is rather limited. Thus new information is recognised and understood by the child 'in relation' to an existing one. When appropriate connections and linkages are made in the child's mind about his/her own immediate experiences, he/she is enabled to understand more abstract or sophisticated concepts and arguments later.

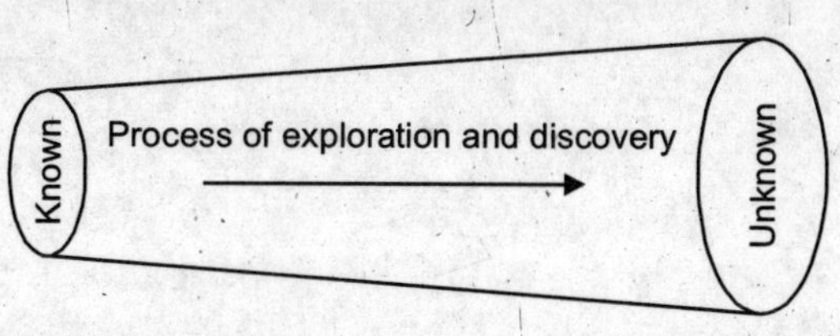

An example of this from the current EVS syllabus is the theme on 'Plants'. Traditionally in many textbooks, the concept of 'Plants' is introduced to young children by providing explanations on 'typical parts of a plant'. However, in the current syllabus, keeping in mind the development and progression of concepts from concrete to abstract, the concept of 'plants' is first introduced through the theme of 'Food' which is familiar, starting with what plants do children eat; and what parts of a plant do they eat, etc.

The advantages of such an instructional design for EVS are that:

- Children learn about their environment through their environment.
- Locate new learnings on a tested and well developed ground.

84. An achievement test is a test of developed skill or knowledge. The most common type of achievement test is a standardized test developed to measure skills and knowledge learned in a given grade level, usually through planned instruction, such as training or classroom instruction. Achievement tests are often contrasted with tests that measure aptitude, a more general and stable cognitive trait.

Achievement test scores are often used in an educational system to determine the level of instruction for which a student is prepared. High achievement scores usually indicate a mastery of grade-level material, and the readiness for advanced instruction. Low achievement scores can indicate the need for remediation or repeating a course grade.

88. Mynah can move its neck back and forth with a jerk while Owl has the maximum capacity to rotate its neck up to 360°.

89. The rural setting in Rajasthan displays rich cultural heritage. The villages in Rajasthan displays varied lifestyle depending upon the topography, history, caste system etc. prevalent in the region. Each village is made special by its bazaars and fairs and festivals which give each village a distinct aura. The village dwelling is mostly comprised of hutment mostly circular in appearance. These simple hamlets are most basic and earliest form of civilization which is present in its most unadulterated form in the villages of Rajasthan.

These huts have thatched roofs; their walls have layers of clay, cow dung and hay serving as plaster for the wall which make them termite free and blend with the sand of countryside around it. The walls are also thatched with grass and hay sticks. Occasionally clay moulded Kelu are also used for the purpose. The outer boundary of houses and landholdings are called baras which are comprised of dry branches of nettle like shrub whose long, sharp thorns serves as a deterrent for straying cattle.

These commodities not only make the huts hygienic but also make them refreshingly cold and comfortable despite being set in oppressively hot setting of the desert. In winters the same setting offers comfortable and warm environment making for a comfortable stay.

The houses in Leh and Ladakh are made of stones. The walls of the houses are coated with mud and Lime. Most of the houses are found with two floors. The ground and the first floor. The wooden floor and the wooden ceiling, protected them from the cold.

90. Elephants do not rest very much. They sleep for only two to four hours in a day. Elephants love to play with mud and water. The mud keeps their skin cool. Their big ears also work like fans. The elephants flap these to keep themselves cool.

An elephant herd has mainly females and baby elephants. The oldest female is the leader of the herd. A herd may have 10 to 12 female elephants and young ones. Male elephants live in the herd till they are 14-15 years old. Then they leave their herd and move around alone.

Previous Paper (Solved)

CTET—PAPER-I, JULY 2019*

PART- I

Child Development and Pedagogy

Directions: *Answer the following questions by selecting the correct/most appropriate options.*

1. Which of the following constructs does Right to Education Act, 2009 advocate?
A. Inclusive education B. Segregation
C. Mainstreaming D. Integrated education

2. .... is the philosophy that all children have a right to get equal education in a regular school system.
A. Mainstreaming
B. Special education
C. Multi-cultural education
D. Inclusion

3. A teacher should:
A. promote students belonging to certain cultures.
B. ignore cultural differences and diversity amongst students.
C. communicate that she respects and values all cultures in the classroom.
D. maximize comparisons amongst students.

4. Children learn effectively when:
A. they memorise facts given in the textbook.
B. they copy answers written by the teacher on the blackboard.
C. they actively participate in different activities and tasks.
D. the teacher fully controls everything that happens in the class including the children.

5. Children should .... questions in the class.
A. be discouraged to ask B. not be allowed to ask
C. be stopped from asking D. be encouraged to ask

6. Which of the following is **NOT** a key process through which meaningful learning occurs?
A. Repetition and practice
B. Instruction and direction
C. Exploration and interaction
D. Memorization and recall

7. Which of the following represents the correct matching of children in column-A with their primary characteristic in column-B?

	Column-A		Column-B
(*a*)	Gifted	(*i*)	Lacks reading fluency
(*b*)	Learning disabled	(*ii*)	Can think of original solutions
(*c*)	Creative	(*iii*)	Tendency to get distracted easily
(*d*)	Attention Deficit Hyperactivity Disorder (ADHD)	(*iv*)	Ability to learn quickly and independency

	(*a*)	(*b*)	(*c*)	(*d*)
A.	(*iv*)	(*i*)	(*ii*)	(*iii*)
B.	(*iv*)	(*iii*)	(*i*)	(*ii*)
C.	(*i*)	(*ii*)	(*iv*)	(*iii*)
D.	(*iv*)	(*iii*)	(*ii*)	(*i*)

8. Children's errors:
A. should be immediately corrected by asking them to do repeated practice
B. are a part of learning and give an insight into their thinking.
C. are insignificant in the teaching-learning process.
D. reflect how careless children are.

9. Assessment:
A. should be a part of the teaching-learning process.
B. should be done only in terms of marks.
C. should be based on objective type written tasks.
D. should be undertaken as a separate activity.

10. In a constructivist frame, learning is:
A. passive and individualistic.
B. the process of acquisition of knowledge.
C. a change in behaviour as a result of experience.
D. active and social in its character.

11. When teachers have positive beliefs about students and their abilities, the students?
A. become relaxed and stop putting in any efforts to learn.
B. become demotivated and stressed.
C. are not affected in any way.
D. are eager and motivated to learn.

12. A teacher can encourage children to become effective problem solvers by:
A. giving them plenty of opportunities to answer similar kinds of questions from the textbook.
B. emphasizing on rote memorisation of the information given in the textbook.
C. encouraging children to make intuitive guesses and to look at multiple solutions to the problem.
D. writing step-by-step solution to all the questions in the textbook.

*Exam was held on 07-07-2019.

13. Use of methods where learner's own initiative and efforts are involved is an example of:
A. Deductive method
B. Learner-centred method
C. Traditional method
D. Inter-personal intelligence

14. What principle does the following highlight?
"Students who do not perform well, feel that they are not 'good enough' and feel demotivated. They are then likely to give up easily without trying or persisting in doing tasks."
A. Cognition and emotions are not related.
B. Heredity and environment are not separable.
C. Heredity and environment are not related.
D. Cognition and emotions are not separable.

15. Which of the following is the primary socialising agency?
A. School B. Government
C. Media D. Family

16. The major proposition of Jean Piaget's theory is that:
A. Children's thinking is superior to adults.
B. Children's thinking is quantitatively different from adults.
C. Children's thinking is qualitatively different from adults.
D. Children's thinking is inferior to adults.

17. Gender is a/an:
A. psychological entity B. social construct
C. economic concept D. biological determinant

18. Which of the following correctly identifies the broad domains of development?
A. Emotional; intellectual; spiritual and self
B. Physical; personality; spiritual and emotional
C. Social; physical; personality; self
D. Physical; cognitive; social and emotional

19. Which of the following statements about intelligence is correct?
A. Intelligence is a relatively permanent change in behaviour as a result of experience.
B. Intelligence is hereditary trait that involves mental activities such as memory and reasoning.
C. Intelligence is multi-dimensional involving several abilities not entirely measureable by intelligence tests.
D. Intelligence is the ability to think convergently.

20. In progressive-education children are seen as:
A. passive imitators B. active explorers
C. blank slates D. miniature adults

21. According to Lev Vygotsky, learning is:
A. an individual activity B. a passive activity
C. a conditioned activity D. a social activity

22. Which of the following characterizes a child in the preoperational stage?
A. Goal-directed behaviour
B. Deferred Imitation
C. Irreversibility of thought
D. Circular reactions

23. Which of the following statements regarding children and their learning is correct?
A. Children's motivation to learn and their capability to learn is predetermined by heredity only.
B. Children's socio-economic background determines and limits their motivation and learning capability.
C. Children have to be rewarded and punished to make them motivated for learning.
D. All children are naturally motivated to learn and are capable of learning.

24. There are individual variations in the rate of motor development, yet the sequence of motor development is from .... to ....
A. proximodistal, cephalocaudal
B. gross motor development; fine motor development
C. fine motor development; gross motor development
D. cephalocaudal; proximodistal

25. The period that initiates the transition to adulthood is:
A. Middle childhood B. Pre-operational period
C. End childhood D. Adolescence

26. According to Jean Piaget, children:
A. learn by observing others following a process of observational learning.
B. can be conditioned to behave in particular ways by carefully controlled stimulus–response associations.
C. can be taught to behave and learn in specific manner using principles of rewards and punishment.
D. actively construct knowledge as they manipulate and explore the world.

27. Lev Vygotsky refers to the verbal dialogues that children have with themselves as:
A. private speech B. distorted speech
C. problematic speech D. egocentric speech

28. Associating toys, articles of clothing, household items, occupations and colours with specific sex, is a demonstration of:
A. gender stereotyping B. gender theory
C. gender relevance D. evolved gender identity

29. In an elementary classroom it is important to _____ the experiences that a child brings with her.
A. neglect B. ignore
C. build on D. deny

30. A child argues that Heinz shouldn't steal the drug (medicine that can save his wife) because he will be caught and sent to jail if he does so. According to Kohlberg, which stage of moral understanding does the child fall under?
A. The social-order maintaining orientation
B. The punishment and obedience orientation
C. The universal ethical principle orientation
D. The instrumental purpose orientation

PART- II

Mathematics

Directions: *Answer the following questions by selecting the* ***correct/most appropriate*** *options.*

31. How will you cater to the needs of visually challenged students of your classroom in an inclusive school?
A. Use alternate teaching-learning methods and resources.
B. Send them to special educator.
C. Provide them extra time for practise.
D. Make them sit with high achievers.

32. A Class-III student perform multiplication of 16 × 25 as follows:

$$16 \times 25 = 8 \times 2 \times 5 \times 5$$
$$= 8 \times 5 \times 2 \times 5$$
$$= 40 \times 10$$
$$= 400$$

Which property of multiplication has the student used in this question?
A. Associative law
B. Repeated addition
C. Inverse multiplication law
D. Distributive law

33. Which of the following is **not** related to early number concept?
A. Class inclusion B. Conservation
C. Measurement D. Classification

34. Which of the following statements is true regarding 'Numeral' and 'Number'?
(*a*) A numeral is a symbol used to represent number.
(*b*) Same number can be represented by different numerals.
A. (*a*) is correct and (*b*) is incorrect.
B. (*b*) is correct and (*a*) is incorrect.
C. Both (*a*) and (*b*) are correct.
D. Both (*a*) and (*b*) are incorrect.

35. Which of the following is ***not*** a mathematical process?
A. Visualisation B. Memorisation
C. Estimation D. Transposition

36. Read the following word problems on addition:
I. There are 15 oranges in one basket and 17 oranges in another basket. How many oranges are there altogether?
II. The price of a mobile phone which is for ₹ 9,950 is increased by ₹ 375 after budget. What is the new price?

Which of the following statements is correct?
A. 'I' represents 'aggregation' structure of addition whereas 'II' represents 'augmentation' structure of addition.
B. Both represents aggregation structure of addition.
C. Both represents augmentation structure of addition.
D. 'I' represents augmentation structure of addition whereas 'II' represents aggregation structure of addition.

37. Identify the correct statement about the ability to conserve different physical quantities in 'measurement' as proposed by Piaget.
A. Conservation of volume is grasped before conservation of mass.
B. Conservation of weight is grasped before conservation of number.
C. Conservation of length is grasped before conservation of number.
D. Conservation of weight is grasped before conservation of volume.

38. A teacher gives the following task to the students of class-IV:
"Arrange 25 tiles in all possible rectangular arrays."
Which of the following mathematical concepts can be addressed through this task?
A. Area, factors, perimeter B. Area, perimeter, volume
C. Area, volume, length D. Volume, area, length

39. Which one of the following sets are Problem Solving Strategies in Mathematics?
A. Drawing, working back, rote learning
B. Reasoning, using variable, look for a pattern
C. Memorisation, Guess & test, drawing
D. Trial-error, drawing, memorisation

40. Van Hiele's levels refers to stages in the development of:
A. Place value B. Geometrical thinking
C. Fractions D. Number concept

41. As per the recommendation of NCF 2005, Primary School mathematics curriculum should:
A. focus on procedural knowledge
B. provide rigour in mathematical concepts
C. prepare children for advanced mathematics.
D. relate to children's everyday experiences.

42. Which of the following teaching-learning resources is best suited to explain the concept of multiplication of two decimal numbers say 0.3 × 0.2 = 0.06?
A. Taylor's abacus B. Number chart
C. Graph paper D. Dienes blocks

43. Which of the following is ***not*** an effective strategy to assess primary level students' learning in mathematics?
A. Analysing children's errors to understand their reasoning.

B. Designing tasks which elicit more than one level of response.
C. Using primarily group administered tasks.
D. Designing tasks to differentiate between rote memorisation and conceptual understanding.

44. Which of the following is ***not*** a characteristic of effective mathematics pedagogy?
A. Following strict time rules when introducing a new concept.
B. Focussing patterns of students errors.
C. Making connections with everyday experiences.
D. Using various teaching-learning strategies for a single concept.

45. In a school, half of students play badminton, one-fourth (1/4th) play volleyball, one-eighth (1/8th) play tennis, one-sixteenth (1/16th) play chess and remaining go for swimming. If the number of students playing volleyball is 160, how many students play chess?

A. 120	B. 80
C. 20	D. 40

46. How many quarters are there in $18\frac{3}{4}$?

A. 75	B. 72
C. 35	D. 68

47. Digits 2, 3, 4, 6, 7, 8 are arranged in the following blanks:

....

\+ ....

The largest possible number after addition is:

A. 1605	B. 1560
C. 1308	D. 808

48. Deepa goes to a post-office to post/mail letters and parcels. The postal rates depicted are as below:

Letter Weighing:	
(i) 20 g or less	– ₹ 5.00
(ii) Per every addition 20 g	– ₹ 2.00
Parcel Weighing:	
(i) 50 g or less	– ₹ 5.00
(ii) For every additional 50 g	– ₹ 3.00

Deepa wants to send two parcels weighing 250 g and 300 g respectively and two letters each to 20 g and 35 g respectively. How much postal charge does she have to pay?

A. ₹ 48	B. ₹ 39
C. ₹ 49	D. ₹ 41

49. A whole number is added to 50 and the same number is subtracted from 50. The sum of the resulting numbers is

A. 50	B. 0
C. 100	D. 25

50. Read the following Railway timings of New Delhi-Chennai Rajdhani express and answer the question:

Station	**Arrival**	**Departure**
New Delhi	–	15:55
Bhopal	23:55	00:05
Nagpur	05:25	05:35
Vijaywada	14:15	14:30
Chennai	20:45	end

Which of the following statements is true?
A. The duration of Journey from Nagpur to Chennai is 15 hr. 10 min.
B. The duration of Journey from New Delhi to Nagpur is 11 hr. 30 min.
C. The duration of Journey from Bhopal to Chennai is 21 hr. 40 min.
D. The duration of Journey from Bhopal to Vijaywada is 13 hr. 10 min.

51. Which of the following represents descending order of numbers?
A. 30.5, 3.50, 3.055, 3.05, 3.005, 0.355
B. 30.5, 3.50, 3.05, 3.055, 3.005, 0.355
C. 30.5, 3.05, 3.055, 3.50, 3.005, 0.355
D. 3.05, 3.005, 3.50, 3.055, 30.5, 0.355

52. A shopkeeper mixed 5.3 kg of almonds, 2100 g of raisin, 2.2 kg of cashews and packed the mixture equally into two dozen packets. What is the weight to each packet?

A. 400 g	B. 450 g
C. 500 g	D. 300 g

53. A beaker is 3/7th filled with water. Another 16 L of water is needed to fill the beaker to its brim. What is the capacity of the beaker?

A. 50 L	B. 100 L
C. 28 L	D. 14 L

54. Asha plans to save some money from household expenditure to buy a mobile phone. Every week she saves ₹ 50 on Monday, ₹ 100 on Wednesday and ₹ 80 on Friday and spends ₹ 60 from this on Sunday. How many weeks would she take to save enough to buy a mobile phone of ₹ 5,950?

A. 35	B. 30
C. 40	D. 25

55. What number am I?
I am a 2 digit even number.
I am common multiple of 3, 4, 6.
I have total 9 factors.

A. 56	B. 24
C. 36	D. 48

56. The side of a square is 10 cm. How many times will the new perimeter become if the side of the square is doubled?

A. 4 times	B. 3 times
C. 2 times	D. Remains same

57. Which of the following letters have both horizontal and vertical lines of symmetry?
A. X B. C
C. Y D. A

58. If $(11011)_2$ = (______)$_{10}$, then number in the blank space is:
A. 27 B. 30
C. 33 D. 22

59. What is the correct sequence a teacher of Class-III needs to follow to explain the concept of 'Quarter' (1/4) to the students?
(*a*) Write symbol of Quarter on black board.
(*b*) Provide concrete material and divides into Quarters.
(*c*) Show pictures representing 'Quarter'.
A. (*a*), (*c*), (*b*) B. (*b*), (*c*), (*a*)
C. (*c*), (*a*), (*b*) D. (*a*), (*b*), (*c*)

60. 72 × 28 = 36 × 4 × ....
The number in the blank is:
(*a*) multiple of 7 (*b*) a prime number
(*c*) less than 10 (*d*) an even number
(*e*) factor of 56
Which of the following is correct?
A. (*a*), (*d*), (*b*) B. (*c*), (*d*), (*e*)
C. (*a*), (*d*), (*e*) D. (*a*), (*b*), (*c*)

PART- III

Environmental Studies

Directions : *Answer the following questions by selecting the* ***correct/most appropriate*** *options.*

61. We all observe old wells which have dried up. Our elders say that about 25-30 years ago there was sufficient water in the wells, but now these have completely dried up. Select from the following the possible correct reasons for drying up of water in the wells.
(*a*) The lakes (ponds) in which rain water used to collect are no longer there.
(*b*) The soil around the trees, well and nearby area is now covered with coaltar/cement.
(*c*) No one uses wells as there are taps in every house.
(*d*) A number of electric motor driven pumps have come up to draw underground water.
A. (*b*), (*c*) and (*d*) B. (*c*), (*d*) and (*a*)
C. (*a*), (*b*) and (*d*) D. (*a*), (*b*) and (*c*)

62. In EVS concepts and issues have not been compartmentalized into science and social science. Why?
A. The child looks at her/his environment in holistic manner.
B. It is a good teaching-learning strategy.
C. It is for decreasing the syllabus load.
D. Syllabus of EVS has been prescribed as such by CBSE.

63. In which one of the following cities the mountains of sand called "Sand Dunes" are found?
A. Abu Dhabi B. Berlin
C. Thimpu D. Kabul

64. In EVS themes have been proposed instead of topics in the syllabus. Why?
A. To enhance the environmental comprehension of the learners.
B. For developing connected and interrelated understanding of issues of the learners' local environment.
C. Theme based EVS transaction is easy as compared to the topics.
D. For reducing chapters in EVS.

65. Which one of the following is **not** one of the six broad themes of EVS in the present syllabus?
A. Shelter B. Things we make and do
C. Work and play D. Food

66. Which of the following is true w.r.t. EVS subject for classes I and II?
A. Issues and concerns related to EVS are transacted through language and mathematics.
B. EVS is a new subject introduced at the classes I to II.
C. EVS as subject is not easy to understand at classes I and II.
D. Issues and concerns related to EVS are transacted through language.

67. Which one of the following is very important in constructing knowledge in EVS?
(*a*) Active participation of the learner.
(*b*) Relating child's knowledge with the teachers knowledge.
(*c*) Learning EVS outside the four walls of the classroom.
(*d*) Relating child's local knowledge to the school knowledge.
A. (*d*) only B. (*a*) only
C. (*a*) and (*d*) only D. (*a*), (*c*) and (*d*)

68. The most effective strategy to engage learners in EVS is ....
A. Reading of textbook
B. Explanations by teacher
C. Classroom Demonstration
D. Narratives

69. Which one of the following is **not** true w.r.t. EVS?
A. EVS is based on child centred learning.
B. EVS provides opportunities to the learners to explore their environment.

C. EVS emphasizes descriptions and definitions.
D. Nature of EVS is integrated.

70. A teacher always begins by conducting activities followed by questions and discussions. The objective of conducting activities, questions and discussion is to ....

(*a*) Assess the children's process skills
(*b*) Provide an opportunity to the children to explore
(*c*) Provide an opportunity to the children to express themselves
(*d*) Discriminate between the children bases on their pace of learning

A. (*c*) only B. (*b*), (*c*) and (*d*)
C. (*a*), (*b*) and (*c*) D. (*d*) only

71. Children should be encouraged to tap sources other than textbooks and teachers in EVS. Why?

(*a*) Textbook and teacher are not the only sources of EVS learning.
(*b*) It will promote the involvement of parents and communities.
(*c*) It will provide opportunity to teachers to know the child's background.
(*d*) It will develop psychomotor skills and aesthetic sense of the children.

A. (*a*), (*b*) and (*c*) B. (*b*), (*c*) and (*d*)
C. (*c*) and (*d*) only D. (*b*) and (*c*) only

72. Which of the following should ***not*** be the indicator for assessment in EVS?

A. Co-operation
B. Remembering
C. Questioning
D. Concern for justice and equality

73. In EVS, teachers should provide opportunities to the children to assess themselves. Self-assessment is ....

A. Assessment as learning
B. Assessment of learning
C. Assessment for learning
D. CCE

74. A teacher conducts an experiment on "How does food get spoilt?"

Teacher makes groups of learners and provides them material related to the experiment. Why does teacher form groups of learners?

(*a*) It promotes peer learning.
(*b*) It improves social interaction.
(*c*) Group learning is effective way of learning EVS without burden.
(*d*) Group learning is an essential strategy to maintain discipline in the class.

A. (*c*) and (*d*) only B. (*a*) and (*c*) only
C. (*b*) and (*d*) only D. (*a*) and (*b*) only

75. Which of the following is **not** the objective of teaching EVS?

A. To develop an awareness about environmental issues.
B. To engage the child in exploratory and hands on activities.
C. To encourage children to provide textbook definitions.
D. To nurture the curiosity and creativity of the child.

76. Picture reading is an important activity in EVS. Which of the following indicator/indicators of learners can be assessed through picture reading?

(*a*) Observation and recording
(*b*) Expression
(*c*) Analysis
(*d*) Experimentation

A. (*a*), (*b*) and (*c*) B. (*a*) and (*c*) only
C. (*a*) and (*b*) only D. (*d*) only

77. Which technique is used in the rating scale?

A. Observation B. Checklist
C. Assignments D. Written question

78. Consider the following statements about the practices followed under "Jhoom farming":

(*a*) After obtaining one set of crops the land is left as it is for some years.
(*b*) The bamboo or weeds which grow on the land are pulled out and burnt.
(*c*) The ash obtained on burning the weeds etc. is used as fertilizer.
(*d*) When the land is ready for farming it is deeply ploughed before dropping the seeds.

The correct statement(s) is/are:

A. only (*d*) B. (*b*) and (*c*)
C. (*a*) and (*d*) D. only (*a*)

79. In a hilly area it was observed that the people have built their houses using stones, mud, lime and wood. These houses have two floors. On the ground floor they provide space for animals to live and also store necessary things, on the first floor they stay. The roofs of the houses are flat and made of thick tree trunks. This hilly area is a part of:

A. Meghalaya B. Himachal Pradesh
C. Jammu and Kashmir D. Arunachal Pradesh

80. It is believed that the animals that are awake at night can see objects only in:

A. green and yellow B. orange and red
C. black and white D. violet and blue

81. Earthworms are considered friends of the farmers. Select from the following the correct reasons for the same:

(*a*) Earthworms eat the dead leaves and plants and their droppings fertilise the soil.
(*b*) Earthworms eat the weeds and save the main crop.
(*c*) Earthworms soften the soil by digging underneath.
(*d*) The tunnels made by the earthworms provide easy passage to air and water into the soil.

A. (*b*), (*c*) and (*d*) B. (*c*), (*d*) and (*a*)
C. (*a*) and (*c*) only D. (*a*), (*b*) and (*c*)

82. Tribal people have been using bronze to make many things since thousand of years. Bronze is still used in our houses. Select from the following the most correct statement about bronze.
A. It is a mixture of copper and brass.
B. It is a mixture of copper, zinc and aluminium.
C. It is a mixture of copper and tin.
D. It is an element like aluminium and copper.

83. Boiled tapioca with any curry made using coconut is a preferred food of the people of:
A. West Bengal B. Bihar
C. Tamil Nadu D. Kerala

84. Select from the following a set of festivals celebrated on the full-moon day.
A. Holi, Mahashivratri, Buddhajayanti
B. Holi, Rakshabandhan, Guru Nanak's Birthday
C. Diwali, Mahashivratri, Guru Nanak's Birthday
D. Diwali, Guru Nanak's Birthday, Rakshabandhan

85. Which one of the following groups of states has a coast on Arabian sea?
A. Andhra Pradesh, Telangana, Odisha
B. Kerala, Karnataka, West Bengal
C. Tamil Nadu, Andhra Pradesh, Karnataka
D. Karnataka, Kerala, Gujarat

86. Where is Jharkhand located on the map of our country?
A. East of West Bengal
B. North of Odisha
C. South-East of Chhattisgarh
D. West of Uttar Pradesh

87. Which of the following is ***not*** obtained from petroleum?
A. Wax B. Grease
C. Coal D. Diesel

88. A boy boarded a train on 30th June, 2019 at Madgaon for Nagarcoil. The train departed at 09:45 hours from Madgaon and reached Nagarcoil at 07:15 hours on the next day. If the distance covered by the train during this time interval is 1140 km, the average speed of the train was:
A. 53 km/h B. 54.5 km/h
C. 57 km/h D. 51.5 km/h

89. In one of the forests of our country the village council (Panchayat) allots the land to the forest people (Adivasis) for farming in a special unit called 'tin'. What is tin?
A. A land on which a farmer grows one tin of seeds
B. A land from which a farmer produces one tin of seeds
C. A unit of land specially designed for the farmers of the forests.
D. A land with dimensions 100 m × 100 m

90. You are located at X and your school is located at Y. There is no straight path from your house to school. So, you first go to A which is 30 m due north of X, then go to B which is 40 m due west of A, then go to C which is 30 m due north of B and finally you reach your school at Y which is 40 m due west of C. With respect to your school the correct direction of your house is:
A. Due South B. Due East
C. South-East D. North-West

PART- IV

Language-I : English

Directions (Qs. 91-99) : *Read the passage given below and answer the questions that follow.*

The future of water will be a gamble-resting entirely on the way we decide to play the game here. Either we continue to use water irresponsibly, threatening the very existence of this planet, or we adopt sustainable and smart water management practices to build a water secure future.

By 2050, India's total water demand will increase by 32 percent from now. Industrial and domestic sectors will account for 85 percent of the additional demand. Over-exploitation of ground-water, failure to recharge acquifers and reduction in catchment capacities due to uncontrolled urbanisation are all causes of the precarious tilt in the water balance.

If the present rate of groundwater persists, India will have only 22 percent of the present daily per capita water available in 2050, possibly forcing the country to import its water. Optimists believe that India's people some 1.7 billion by 2050, will have integrated water efficient practices into their daily lives. If the ambitious water sustainability goals set by global industries and governments are testament we dare say that the world has begun to recognize water as a resource after all.

While beverages giants are focussed on returning water to the communities where they manufacture their drinks, food processing players are engaging with farmers and upstream actors to minimise water usage across the supply claim and textile houses are evangelising the concept of sustainable fashion. Companies have realised the risks emanating from the possibility of a water-scarce future. This has triggered companies to re-engineer processes, implement water optimizing, technologies, establish water audit standards, and use a collaborative approach to deal with the water crisis.

91. The problem of acute water scarcity in future cannot be dealt with by companies through:
A. implementing water optimizing technologies
B. discovering a viable substitute for water.
C. re-engineering processes
D. establishing water audit standards.

92. Which one of the following words is most similar in meaning to the word 'threatening' as used in the passage?

A. menacing B. coercing
C. persisting D. frightening

93. Which one of the following words is most opposite to the meaning of the word 'increase' as used in the passage?

A. perceive B. achieve
C. relieve D. decrease

94. Identify the clause in the **bold** part of the following sentence:

He breathed his last in the village **where he was born.**

A. Adjective clause
B. Adverb clause
C. Principal clause
D. Noun clause

95. What part of speech is the **bold** word in the following sentence?

I do not know **why** he is so curious about it.

A. Noun clause
B. Principal clause
C. Adverb clause
D. Adjective clause

96. We will face a severe water-scarcity problem in future mostly because:

A. water is not a renewable source.
B. by 2050, demand for water will increase considerably.
C. we do not use water responsibly.
D. ground-water level water is steadily decreasing.

97. Which of the following will ***not*** lead to a severe water imbalance?

A. over-exploitation of water.
B. failure to recharge acquifers.
C. uncontrolled urbanisation.
D. flawless water infrastructure.

98. Persistent ground water depletion will ***not*** necessitate :

A. shutting down of industries
B. adoption of smart water management technologies
C. using water judiciously
D. import of water

99. Optimists cannot pin their hope for better water management on:

A. reducing demand for water by using new technologies.
B. discovering new ways of augmenting water supply.
C. treating sea water for domestic and industrial sectors.
D. integrating water efficient practices into daily use.

Directions (Qs. 100-105) : *Read the extract given below and answer the questions that follow by selecting the correct/most appropriate options.*

All creation drinks with pleasure,
Drinks at Mother Nature's breast;
All the just, and all the evil,
Follow down her rosy path.
Kisses she bestowed, and grape wine,
Friendship true, proved e'en in death;
Every worm knows nature's pleasure,
Every cherub meets his God.
Gladly, like the planets flying
True to heaven's mighty plan,
Brothers, run your course now,
Happy as a knight in victory.

100. What is the hallmark of a true friend?

A. He helps you to enjoy the fruits of nature.
B. He proves true even in death.
C. He can take on all the evils for you.
D. He saves you from troubles.

101. Rosy path is followed ....

A. the evil
B. both just and evil
C. neither the just nor the evil
D. the just

102. Identify and name the figure of speech used in "All creation 'Drinks at Mother Nature's breast"

A. Simile B. Personification
C. Alliteration D. Metonymy

103. What does the expression, "Brothers, run your course now" mean?

A. Don't let failures upset you.
B. Seek god's help when you are in difficulty.
C. Cultivate a positive attitude to life.
D. Keep on moving towards your goal.

104. How can we say that God's creatures are most fortunate and happy?

A. They have no friends to share their joys and sorrows.
B. They do not have enough pleasures at their disposal.
C. They have a benevolent Mother Nature to look after them.
D. The world they live in lacks romance and beauty.

105. Which of the following **does not** support the idea that Mother Nature's love embraces all?

A. She bestows kisses on all her children.
B. She loves all the just but not all the evil.
C. She also blesses us with true friendship.
D. All creation drinks at Mother Nature's heart.

Directions (Qs. 106-120) : *Answer the following questions by selecting the most appropriate option out of the given options.*

106. Which of the following classroom practices helps a teacher to develop oral language among the students?
A. Chorus recitation/individual recitation of the poem after memorising it.
B. Participating in role-plays on any one of their favourite scenes.
C. Practising the correct pronunciation of new or unfamiliar words.
D. Chorus reading of the text with the teacher.

107. In a constructivist classroom language learning would most importantly be based on:
A. minute observation and record of each child's handwriting development.
B. correction of spelling errors and making sure that they are not repeated.
C. carefully completing the language syllabus.
D. group discussion and peer interaction.

108. As a language teacher which one of the following is most important for you regarding teaching of grammar?
A. Avoiding grammar rules.
B. Using functional approach.
C. Using grammar translation method.
D. Memorising grammar rules.

109. Which one of the following is a correct statement about a textbook?
A. A textbook is the final thing for the teacher.
B. It helps to achieve the objectives laid down in the curriculum.
C. The textbooks are the only source to read.
D. It is planning of educational activities for the session.

110. The purpose of diagnostic test in language learning is to:
A. fill the progress report of students.
B. plan and prepare question paper for summative assessment.
C. know the gaps in learners understanding.
D. give feedback to the parents in the PTMs.

111. The purpose of Continuous Comprehensive Evaluation (CCE) in language is:
A. to assess their learning gaps.
B. to give regular tests *i.e.* weekly tests.
C. fo assess the level of competencies achieved by the children.
D. to assess the students' understanding of the textbook.

112. Under which act did English get the status of the associate official language?
A. Associate Official Language Act, Article-343
B. Three Language Formula
C. National Curriculum Framework
D. Official Language Act, Article-343

113. A teacher is appreciating a child for his 'overall language use', though some of the words were misspelt by him. The teacher is using .... approach in her class.
A. Communicative B. Constructivist
C. Whole language D. Structural

114. Which approach lays a lot of emphasis on habit formation?
A. Communicative approach
B. Behaviouristic approach
C. Eclectic approach
D. Cognitive approach

115. In the context of 'theory of multiple intelligence' which one of the following intelligences is related to language?
A. Fluency-Accuracy Intelligence
B. Linguistic-Verbal Intelligence
C. Vocabulary Grammar Intelligence
D. Visual-Spatial Intelligence

116. Banishing mother tongue in the classroom is the characteristic feature of .... method.
A. Bi-lingual B. Grammar translation
C. Natural D. Direct

117. .... deals with the level of meaning in language.
A. Semantics B. Collocation
C. Colloquial D. Syntax

118. A Hindi speaking teacher gets posted in a primary school which is in the area of Punjab. Since he doesn't know the local language of that area. He should:
A. motivate the community to learn Hindi, as it's a national/official language.
B. communicate in English as it is difficult for him to understand their local dialect.
C. use the child's language as a resource and start teaching.
D. apply for the transfer to a Hindi speaking area.

119. While designing a working activity for a language class a teacher should most importantly focus on:
A. giving clear instructions for the task.
B. providing all the necessary vocabulary required for the task.
C. assigning an authentic piece of writing task.
D. choosing a topic from their surroundings.

120. Some children do not have exposure to English outside the classroom. So, the teacher's proficiency in spoken English is essential because:
A. the teacher can edit the errors in student's learning process.
B. the students may listen to and process the new language before they actually communicate in it.
C. students can imitate, practise and drill the statements or sentences used by the teacher.
D. the teacher can give more time to grammar drills.

PART- V

Language-II : Hindi

निर्देश (प्र.सं. 121 से 128) : *निम्नलिखित गद्यांश को पढ़कर पूछे गए प्रश्नों के सबसे उपयुक्त उत्तर वाले विकल्प को चुनिए :*

सुप्रसिद्ध गीतकार गोपालदास 'नीरज' ने अपनी एक रचना में कहा है:

जैसा हो आघात रे वैसा बजे सितार
तेरी ही आवाज की प्रतिध्वनि है संसार।

हम वाद्ययंत्रों पर जैसा आघात करते हैं वैसी ही ध्वनि उनसे निकलती है। यदि कठोरता से आघात करते हैं तो कठोर ध्वनि उत्पन्न होती है, लेकिन यदि कोमलता से आघात करते हैं तो कर्णप्रिय कोमल ध्वनि उत्पन्न होती है। यदि हम किसी वाद्ययंत्र को नियमपूर्वक ठीक से बजाते हैं तो सही राग उत्पन्न होता है, अन्यथा सही राग उत्पन्न होने का प्रश्न ही नहीं उठता। सही राग उत्पन्न न होने की स्थिति में गुणीजन हमारे गायन अथवा वादन की ओर आकर्षित ही नहीं होंगे। हमारे जीवन रूपी सितार की भी यही स्थिति होती है। यदि हम अनुशासन में रहते हुए प्रत्येक कार्य नियमानुसार करते हैं तो जीवन रूपी सितार से उत्पन्न होने वाला प्रत्येक राग रूपी कार्य हमें सार्थकता और आनंद ही प्रदान करेगा।

इस संसार में हम जो कुछ सोचते, कहते अथवा करते हैं वही हमारे पास लौटकर आता है। न कम, न अधिक। जब हम किसी खंडहर अथवा वादी में कोई अच्छा शब्द या वाक्य बोलते हैं तो कुछ देर बाद वही अच्छा शब्द या वाक्य गूँजता हुआ हमें सुनाई पड़ता है और यदि हम सुरीली आवाज निकालते हैं तो वैसी ही सुरीली आवाज लौटकर हमारे पास आती है, लेकिन यदि हम डरावनी आवाज निकालते हैं तो वैसी ही डरावनी आवाज लौटकर आती है। हम जैसा एक बार बोलते हैं वैसा ही कई बार सुनने को अभिशप्त होते हैं। पर यह बात अनुभव करते हुए भी इसका आशय हम समझते नहीं। चूँकि आवाज के लौटकर आने में थोड़ा वक्त लगता है, इसलिए हम उसे स्वतंत्र घटना मान लेते हैं। यह अहसास नहीं कर पाते कि हमारे ही किए हुए काज, हमारे ही सोचे हुए भाव अलग दिशा से हमारे पास आते दिख रहे हैं।

121. जीवन के साथ सितार की तुलना किसलिए की गई है?
A. सितार बजाने की भाँति जीने का भी एक सलीका होता है।
B. जीवन तो सुरीला ही होता है।
C. तुलना ही असंगत है।
D. जीवन सितार की भाँति संगीतमय होना चाहिए।

122. 'हम जैसा करते हैं वैसा पाते हैं'—यह समझाने के लिए लेखक ने किसका उदाहरण दिया है?
A. आघात का B. गूँज का
C. अनुशासन का D. सितार का

123. प्रत्यय की दृष्टि से उस शब्द को पहचानिए जो शेष शब्दों से भिन्नहो।
A. निकलता B. सार्थकता
C. कठोरता D. कोमलता

124. 'यदि कोई अच्छा शब्द या वाक्य बोलते हैं तो...' की कर्मवाच्य में रचना होगी :
A. यदि कोई अच्छा शब्द या वाक्य बोला जाए तो...
B. यदि कोई अच्छा शब्द या वाक्य बोलेंगे तो...
C. यदि कोई अच्छा शब्द या वाक्य बोलते रहेंगे तो....
D. यदि कोई अच्छा शब्द या वाक्य बोलें तो....

125. 'घृणास्पद' का संधि-विच्छेद होगा :
A. घृणा + स्पद B. घृणा + आस्पद
C. घृणाः + पद D. घृणाः + पद

126. कौन-सा विशेषण गोपालदास 'नीरज' के लिए उपयुक्त नहीं है?
A. रचनाकार B. कवि
C. गीतकार D. संगीतकार

127. एक ही वाद्ययंत्र से कोमल और कठोर ध्वनि निकलना किस पर निर्भर होता है?
A. श्रोता की रुचि पर B. हलके या तेज आघात पर
C. वाद्ययंत्र पर D. बजाने वाले की कला पर

128. 'कर्णप्रिय' ध्वनि का आशय है:
A. कानों को प्रिय B. कानों से प्रिय
C. कानों पर प्रिय D. कानों में प्रिय

निर्देश (प्र.सं. 129 से 135) : *निम्नलिखित गद्यांश को पढ़कर पूछे गए प्रश्नों के सबसे उपयुक्त उत्तर वाले विकल्प चुनिए:*

हमारा जीवन जिन मानवीय सिद्धांतों, अनुभवों और सांस्कृतिक संस्कारों के संबल से समस्त सृष्टि के लिए महत्वपूर्ण बना है, परोपकार की भावना उन्हीं में एक है। मानव को दूसरे मानव के प्रति वैसा ही संवेदनात्मक उत्तरदायित्व निभाना चाहिए, जैसे वह स्वयं के प्रति निभाता है। जीवन को केवल परोपकार, पर सेवा और निःस्वार्थ प्रेम के लिए ही वास्तविक समझना चाहिए क्योंकि नश्वर शरीर जब नष्ट हो जाएगा तो उसके बाद हमारा कुछ भी इस दुनिया के जीवों की स्मृति में नहीं रहेगा। हम जग जीवों की स्मृति में सदा-सदा के लिए तभी बने रह सकते हैं, जब हम अपने नश्वर शरीर को वैचारिक, बौद्धिक और आत्मिक चेतना से पूर्ण कर निःस्वार्थ भाव से स्वयं को जीव सेवा में समर्पित करेंगे।

हमें स्थिरता से और शांतिपूर्वक यह विचार करते रहना चाहिए कि हमारे जीवन का सर्वश्रेष्ठ उद्देश्य और एकमात्र लक्ष्य हमारे द्वारा किया जाने वाला त्याग है। त्याग योग्य व्यक्तित्व प्राप्त करने के लिए गहन तप की आवश्यकता है। त्याग का भाव किसी मनुष्य में साधारण होते हुए नहीं जन्म लेता। इसके लिए मनुष्य को जीवन-जगत और इसके जीवों के संबंध में असाधारण वैचारिक रचनात्मकता अपनाकर निरंतर योग, ध्यान, तप व साधना करनी होगी। उसे इस स्थिति से विचरते हुए विशिष्ट आध्यात्मिक अनुभवों से लैस होना होगा। आवश्यकता होने पर उसे जीवों की वास्तविक सेवा करनी होगी। जब ऐसी विशेष मानवीय परिस्थितियाँ उत्पन्न होंगी, तब ही मानव में त्याग भाव आकार ग्रहण करेगा।

129. त्याग के योग्य व्यक्तित्व प्राप्त करने के लिए आवश्यक है:
A. साधारण पात्रता B. सर्वोच्च मानवीयता
C. सद्गुणों की प्राप्ति D. असाधारण रचनात्मकता

130. 'आध्यात्मिक अनुभवों से लैस' होना होगा। रेखांकित शब्द का अर्थ है :

A. पूर्ण B. रिक्त
C. सतर्क D. सज्जित

131. 'आध्यात्मिक' शब्द का निर्माण किस उपसर्ग की सहायता से हुआ है?

A. अधि B. आधि
C. आध्य D. अ

132. रचना की दृष्टि से शेष से भिन्न शब्द को अलग कीजिए :

A. वैचारिक B. बौद्धिक
C. वास्तविक D. मालिक

133. शरीर को 'नश्वर' कहा जाता है, क्योंकि वह :

A. अल्पायु होता है। B. नाशवान होता है।
C. छोटा होता है। D. अत्यल्प होता है।

134. लोग हमें तभी याद रखेंगे जब हम :

A. वास्तविक ज्ञान अर्जित करेंगे।
B. निःस्वार्थ भाव से सेवा करेंगे।
C. वैचारिक उन्नति करेंगे।
D. नश्वर शरीर को त्याग देंगे।

135. जीवन का श्रेष्ठ उद्देश्य किसे बताया गया है?

A. तप B. त्याग
C. रचनात्मकता D. शिक्षा

136. भाषा में आकलन का अर्थ है :

A. भाषा-प्रयोग की क्षमता का आकलन
B. आलंकारिक भाषा के प्रयोग का आकलन
C. साहित्यिक विधाओं की जानकारी का आकलन
D. भाषा-व्याकरण का आकलन

137. बच्चों की लेखन क्षमता का आकलन करते समय आप सर्वाधिक महत्वपूर्ण किसे मानते हैं?

A. शुद्ध वर्तनी B. विचार तत्त्व
C. सुंदर लेखन D. व्याकरणिक ज्ञान

138. 'बच्चे अपनी जन्मजात भाषा अर्जन क्षमता के सहारे परिवेश में मौजूद भाषा अर्जित करते हैं।' यह कथन किसे महत्व नहीं देता?

A. समृद्ध भाषा परिवेश को
B. भाषा-नियमों में परिवर्तन को
C. भाषा-नियमों में विस्तार को
D. भाषा-अनुकरण करने को

139. प्राथमिक स्तर पर भाषा कौशलों का विकास ....।

A. साध्य है B. संभव नहीं है
C. कठिन है D. साधन है

140. प्राथमिक स्तर पर बच्चों की मौखिक अभिव्यक्ति का विकास करने की दृष्टि से सर्वाधिक महत्वपूर्ण गतिविधि है :

A. कहानी को ज्यों का त्यों दोहराना।
B. कहानी सुनकर चित्र बनाना।
C. कहानी सुनकर शब्दशः लिखना।
D. कहानी सुनकर उसे अपनी भाषा में कहना।

141. पहली कक्षा में पढ़ने वाली रोशनी लिखते समय अपनी मातृभाषा के शब्दों का प्रयोग करती है। भाषा शिक्षक के रूप में आप क्या करेंगे?

A. मातृभाषा वाले शब्दों पर लाल घेरा लगाएँगे।
B. मातृभाषा वाले शब्दों का हिंदी अनुवाद लिख देंगे।
C. मातृभाषा वाले शब्दों को स्वीकार करेंगे।
D. रोशनी को समझाएँगे कि यह गलत है।

142. प्राथमिक स्तर पर बच्चों की सहज और स्वाभाविक मौखिक अभिव्यक्ति में सबसे कम महत्वपूर्ण है :

A. शुद्ध उच्चारण B. बोलने में आत्मविश्वास
C. मौलिक विचार D. स्पष्टता

143. प्राथमिक स्तर पर बच्चों का भाषा-विकास सर्वाधिक रूप से निर्भर करता है :

A. भाषा के कठोर आकलन पर
B. भाषा की पाठ्य-पुस्तक पर
C. समृद्ध भाषिक परिवेश पर
D. भाषा की व्याकरणिक जानकारी पर

144. .... वाले बच्चों को मुख्यतः लिखने में कठिनाई का सामना करना पड़ता है।

A. डिस्ग्राफिया B. डिस्केलकुलिया
C. अफेजिया D. डिस्लेक्सिया

145. प्राथमिक स्तर पर भाषा शिक्षण का उद्देश्य है :

A. विषय सामग्री के माध्यम से केवल कठिन शब्दों के अर्थ जानना।
B. दूसरे के विचारों को शब्दशः दोहराने मात्र की कुशलता का विकास।
C. पठन के द्वारा ज्ञानार्जन एवं आनंद प्राप्ति में समर्थ बनाना।
D. विभिन्न साहित्यिक विधाओं की रचनाओं और रचनाकारों के नाम याद करना।

146. प्राथमिक स्तर की पाठ्य-पुस्तकों में विषय-वस्तु का फलक .... हो जिसमें .... के सरोकार झलकते हों।

A. विस्तृत, समाज B. उच्च, समाज
C. उच्च, विद्यालय D. विस्तृत, अभिभावकों

147. भाषा वैज्ञानिक दृष्टि से भाषा और बोली में :

A. अंतर होता है। B. आंशिक संबंध होता है।
C. आंशिक संबंध नहीं होता। D. अंतर नहीं होता।

148. बहु-भाषिकता हमारी .... भी है और हमारी सभ्यता व .... का अभिन्न अंग भी।

A. चुनौती, संस्कृति B. पहचान, संस्कृति
C. समस्या, पहचान D. विडम्बना, संस्कृति

149. एक तीन साल के बच्चे से किसी भी ऐसे विषय पर अच्छी तरह से बातचीत की जा सकती है जो उसके .... दायरे के अंदर आता हो।

A. संज्ञानात्मक B. भौगोलिक
C. विद्यालयी D. भावनात्मक

150. 'विश्व की सभी भाषाएँ थोड़े से फेरबदल से एक ही लिपि में लिखी जा सकती है।' यह कथन :

A. आंशिक रूप से सत्य है। B. पूर्णतः सत्य नहीं है।
C. पूर्णतः सत्य है। D. भ्रामक है।

Answers

1	2	3	4	5	6	7	8	9	10
A	D	C	C	D	D	A	B	A	D
11	12	13	14	15	16	17	18	19	20
D	C	B	D	D	C	B	D	C	B
21	22	23	24	25	26	27	28	29	30
D	C	D	B	D	D	A	A	C	B
31	32	33	34	35	36	37	38	39	40
A	A	C	C	B	A	D	A	B	B
41	42	43	44	45	46	47	48	49	50
D	C	C	A	D	A	A	C	C	A
51	52	53	54	55	56	57	58	59	60
A	A	C	A	C	C	A	A	B	C
61	62	63	64	65	66	67	68	69	70
C	A	A	B	C	A	D	D	C	C
71	72	73	74	75	76	77	78	79	80
A	B	A	D	C	A	A	D	C	C
81	82	83	84	85	86	87	88	89	90
B	C	D	B	D	B	C	A	A	C
91	92	93	94	95	96	97	98	99	100
B	A	D	A	A	A	D	A	C	B
101	102	103	104	105	106	107	108	109	110
B	B	D	C	B	B	D	B	B	C
111	112	113	114	115	116	117	118	119	120
C	D	C	B	B	D	A	C	D	B
121	122	123	124	125	126	127	128	129	130
A	A	A	A	B	D	B	A	D	D
131	132	133	134	135	136	137	138	139	140
A	D	B	B	B	A	B	D	A	D
141	142	143	144	145	146	147	148	149	150
C	A	C	A	C	A	D	B	A	C

Explanatory Answers

1. Right to Education Act, 2009 advocates inclusive education. The 86th Constitutional Amendment Act, 2002 inserted Article 21A in the Constitution of India to provide free and compulsory education of all children in the age group of 6 to 14 years as a Fundamental Right in such a manner as the state may, by law, determine. The Right of Children to Free and Compulsory Education (RTE) Act, 2009, which represents the consequential legislation envisaged under Article 21A, means that every child has a right to full time elementary education of satisfactory and equitable quality in a formal school which satisfies certain essential norms and standards.

2. Inclusion is the philosophy that all children have a right to get equal education in a regular school system. The Right to Education Act provides for universal elementary education but ironically limits private education providers who can make this possible.

3. A teacher should communicate that he/she respects and values all cultures in the classroom. Appreciate and accommodate the similarities and differences among the students' cultures. Effective teachers of culturally diverse students acknowledge both individual and cultural differences enthusiastically and identify these differences in a positive manner. This positive identification creates a basis for the development of effective communication and instructional strategies. Social skills such as respect and cross-cultural understanding can be modelled, taught, prompted and reinforced by the teacher.

4. Children learn effectively when they actively participate in different activities and tasks. Another important part of students learning is their ability to revise what they have learnt in class in their own free time. Students can understand the concepts taught from their own point of view and at their comfortable pace since lessons are taught at an average speed in classrooms.

5. Children should be encouraged to ask questions in the class. It isn't only important to ask questions of others, but also to get into the practice of questioning our own actions and work.

8. Children's errors are a part of learning and give an insight into their thinking. Most people have heard the sayings "you learn from your mistakes" or "Adversity is the school of wisdom". Meanwhile, it is a general consensus that making mistakes is an important part of the learning process. This is because if, instead of giving up in frustration after making a mistake, we work constructively to understand the mistake, the strategy to solve the problem stays with us better than if we just memorize the solution.

9. Assessment should be a part of the teaching-learning process. Assessment for learning is an approach to teaching and learning that creates feedback which is then used to improve students' performance. Students become more involved in the learning process and from this gain confidence in what they are expected to learn and to what standard.

10. In a constructive frame, learning is active and social in its character. In this frame knowledge is constructed by the learner as they reconcile new information with past experiences, analyze various source materials, and work collaboratively with others.

11. When teachers have positive beliefs about students and their abilities, the students are eager and motivated to learn. Teacher's belief that every student has the ability to learn and make progress is essential. Students become more confident about their own abilities through beholding their teachers' beliefs. Thus new opportunities for students to learn are created.

12. A teacher can encourage children to become effective problem solvers by encouraging children to make intuitive guesses and to look at multiple solutions to the problem. As a teacher, it is helpful to observe those moments when children have problems and help them think about ways to solve their own problems. Anticipate problems before they escalate and help children indentify possible solutions.

13. Use of methods where learner's own initiative and efforts are involved is an example of learner-centred method. A learner-centred approach/method starts from the belief that the learner is at the centre of the learning process.

15. In general, it may be said that the total society is the agency for socialisation and that each person with whom one comes into contact and interact is in some way an agent of socialisation. Socialisation is found in all interactions but the most influential interaction occurs in particular groups which are referred to as agencies of socialisation.

The oblivious beginning of the process for the new-born child is his immediate family group, but this is soon extend to many other groups. Other than the family, the most important are the schools, the peer groups (friends circle) and the mass media.

16. Before Piaget's work, the common assumption in psychology was that children are merely less competent thinkers than adults. Piaget showed that young children thin in strikingly different ways compared to adults. It proposes discrete stages of development, marked by qualitative differences, rather than a gradual increase in number and complexity of behaviours, concepts, ideas, etc.

17. Gender refers to the socially constructed characteristic of women and men, such as norms, roles and relationships of and between groups of women and men. It varies from society to society and can be changed.

19. Intelligence is multi-dimensional involving several abilities not entirely measurable by intelligence tests. Intelligence is defined as mental capability that involves the ability to reason, to plan, to solve problems, to think abstractly, to comprehend complex ideas, to learn quickly and to learn from experience. It is not merely book learning, a narrow academic skill or test-taking smartness.

20. In progressive-education children are seen as active explorers. The progressive education philosophy says that educators should teach children how to think rather than relying on role memorization. Advocates argue that the process of learning by doing is at the heart of this style of teaching. The concept, known as experiential learning, uses hands-on projects that allow students to learn by actively engaging in activities that put their knowledge to use.

21. According to Lev Vygotsky, learning is a social activity. According to Lev, learning cannot be separated from its social context. Social interaction plays a fundamental role in the process of cognitive development.

22. Irreversibility of thought characterizes a child in the preoperational stage. The preoperational stage is the second stage in Piaget's theory of cognitive development. This stage begins around age 2 and last until approximately age 7. During this period, children are thinking at a symbolic level but are not yet using cognitive operations.

25. The period that initiates the transition to adulthood is adolescent. Adolescent is the phase in the life of a human which accelerates from being a child to an adult. It is the phase of transition and change. Adolescent brings a lot of change in the life of any person. From hormonal changes to physical, there are a lot of changes which occurs during this phase. The emotional and hormonal changes helps the bringing a lot of changes in the person.

26. According to Jean Piaget, children construct their own knowledge in response to their experiences. Piaget believed that children take an active role in the learning process, acting much like little scientists as they perform experiments, make observations and learn about the world. As kids interact with the world around them, they continually add new knowledge, build upon existing knowledge, and adapt previously held ideas to accommodate new information.

27. Lev Vygotsky refers to the verbal dialogues that children have with themselves as private speech. According to him, private speech if used effectively can help in development of a child. It can be used to control oneself. He was a psychologist from the 'Soviet Union' who wrote extensively on psychology dealing with culture and history. He is also known for introducing a new theory and development of Vygotsky circle along with students Alexander Luria.

30. A child argues that Heinz shouldn't steal the drug (medicine that can save his wife) because he will be caught and sent to Jail if he does so. According to Kohlberg, the stage of moral understanding the child fall under the punishment and orientation.

Lawrence Kohlberg's stages of moral development are as follows:

(*i*) Obedience and punishment orientation.
(*ii*) Individualism and exchange.
(*iii*) Good interpersonal relationships.
(*iv*) Maintaining the social order.
(*v*) Social contract and individual rights, and
(*vi*) Universal principles.

45. Let total students in the school = x

No. of students who play Badminton = $\frac{x}{2}$

No. of students who play Volleyball = $\frac{x}{4}$

No. of students who play Tennis = $\frac{x}{8}$

No. of students who play Chess = $\frac{x}{16}$

No. of students who go for swimming

$$= x - \left(\frac{x}{2} + \frac{x}{4} + \frac{x}{8} + \frac{x}{16}\right)$$

$$= x - \left(\frac{8x + 4x + 2x + x}{16}\right) = x - \frac{15x}{16} = \frac{x}{16}$$

Given that,

No. of students who play volleyball = 160

$$\frac{x}{4} = 160$$

$$x = 640$$

No. of students who play Chess = $\frac{x}{16} = \frac{640}{16} = 40$

46. $18\frac{3}{4} = \frac{75}{4} = 75 \times \frac{1}{4}$

$\because$ quarter = $\frac{1}{4}$

$\therefore$ 75 quarters are there in $18\frac{3}{4}$.

47.

$$\begin{array}{r} 8 \quad 6 \quad 3 \\ +\ 7 \quad 4 \quad 2 \\ \hline 16 \quad 0 \quad 5 \\ \hline \end{array}$$

← largest possible No. After addition

48. Total charge of two letters = $\underbrace{(20\text{ g})}_{\text{I}} + \underbrace{(35\text{ g})}_{\text{II}}$

$$= \underbrace{(20\text{ g})}_{\text{I}} + \underbrace{(20\text{ g} + 15\text{ g})}_{\text{II}}$$

= ₹ 5 + (₹ 5 + ₹ 2) = ₹ 12

Total charge of two parcel

$$= \underbrace{(250\text{ g})}_{\text{I}} + \underbrace{(300\text{ g})}_{\text{II}}$$

$$= \underbrace{(50\text{ g} + 50\text{ g} + 50\text{ g} + 50\text{ g} + 50\text{ g})}_{\text{I}}$$

$$+ \underbrace{(50\text{ g} + 50\text{ g} + 50\text{ g} + 50\text{ g} + 50\text{ g} + 50\text{ g})}_{\text{II}}$$

= (₹ 5 + ₹ 3 + ₹ 3 + ₹ 3 + ₹ 3)
+ (₹ 5 + ₹ 3 + ₹ 3 + ₹ 3 + ₹ 3 + ₹ 3)
= ₹ 17 + ₹ 20 = ₹ 37

Total postal charge that Deepa had to pay
= ₹ 12 + ₹ 37 = ₹ 49

49. Let the numbers are

$a = 50 + x$
$b = 50 - x$

The sum of the resulting numbers = $a + b$
$= 50 + x + 50 - x = 100$

50. (A) Duration of Journey from Nagpur to Chennai
= 20 : 45 – 5 : 35   Departure Time (Nagpur) – Arrival Time (Chennai)
= 15 hr. 10 min.

Hence option (A) statement is true.

51. Descending order

30.5 > 3.50 > 3.055 > 3.05 > 3.005 > 0.355

52. Total weight of the mixture

$= 5.3 \times 1000\text{ g} + 2100\text{ g} + 2.2 \times 1000\text{ g}$
$= 5300 + 2100 + 2200 = 9600\text{ g}$

Required weight of each packet

$= \frac{9600}{24}$ [$\because$ Two dozen = 2 × 12 = 24)
$= 400\text{ g}$

53. Let the capacity of the beaker is x L.

The beaker part which is filled with water = $\frac{3}{7}x$

Rest part = $x - \frac{3}{7}x = \frac{4}{7}x$

According to question,

$$\frac{4}{7}x = 16$$

$$x = \frac{16 \times 7}{4}$$

$$x = 28 \text{ L}$$

$\therefore$ The capacity of beaker is 28 L.

54. Asha saves money in a week = 50 + 100 + 80
= ₹ 230

Asha, spends money in a week = ₹ 60

$\therefore$ Net saving in a week = ₹ 230 – ₹ 60
= ₹ 170

$\therefore$ Required week to save enough money to buy a mobile phone

$$= \frac{₹\ 5950}{₹\ 170}$$

= 35 weeks

55. Cheek the options.

(A) 56

(*i*) 2-digit even no.

(*ii*)

2	56
2	28
2	14
7	7
	1

$56 = 2^3 \times 7$

This is common multiple of 2, 4, 8, 7, 14, 28, 56.

(*iii*) Total factors = (3 + 1) (1 + 1) = 8

(B) 24

(*i*) 2-digit even no.

(*ii*)

2	24
2	12
2	6
3	3
	1

$24 = 2^3 \times 3^1$

This is common multiple of 2, 3, 4, 8, 6, 12, 24.

(*iii*) Total factors = (3 + 1) (1 + 1) = 4 × 2 = 8

(C) 36

(*i*) 2-digit even no.

(*ii*)

2	36
2	18
3	9
3	3
	1

$36 = 2^2 \times 3^2$

This is common multiple of 2, 3, 4, 6, 9, 12, 18, 36.

(*iii*) Total factors = (2 + 1) (2 + 1) = 3 × 3 = 9.

$\therefore$ 36 fullfill the all given condition, hence 36 is the required number.

56. Given, Side of a square = 10 cm

Perimeter of the square = 4 × *a* = 4 × 10
= 40 cm

New side of the square = 2 × 10 = 20 cm

New perimeter of the square = 4 × 20 = 80 cm
= 2 × 40 cm
= 2 × perimeter of initial square

Hence, new perimeter becomes 2 times.

57. (A) X has both horizontal and vertical lines of symmetry ···X··· X

(B) C has only horizontal line of symmetry ···C···

(C) Y has only vertical line of symmetry

Y

(D) A has only vertical line of symmetry

A

58. $(11011)_2 = 1 \times 2^4 + 1 \times 2^3 + 0 \times 2^2 + 1 \times 2^1 + 1 \times 2^0$
$= 16 + 8 + 0 + 2 + 1 = 27$

60. $72 \times 28 = 36 \times 4 \times ?$

$$? = \frac{72 \times 28}{36 \times 4} = 14$$

(*a*) Multiple of 7

(*d*) An even number

(*e*) Factor of 56

Hence, option (C) is the correct.

62. In EVS concepts and issues have not been compartmentalized into science and social science because the child looks at her/his environment in holistic manner. The word 'environment' is derived from the French word 'environner' which means to 'encircle or surround'. Thus our environment can be defined as the physical, chemical and biological world that surrounds us as well as the complex of social and cultural conditions affecting an individual or community.

63. In Abu Dhabi the mountains of sand called "Sand Dunes" are found. Sand dunes form some of the most spectacular and dynamic landforms on the planet. Individual sand granules accumulate through both water and wind (eolian) transportation, a process known as saltation. Individuals saltating granules form transversely to the wind's direction forming small ripples. As more granules collect, dunes form. Sand dunes conform in any landscape on Earth, not just deserts.

68. The most effective strategy to engage learners in EVS is narratives. Narrative-based learning is a learning model grounded in the theory that humans define their experiences within the context of narratives—which serve as cognitive structures and a means of communication, as well as aiding people in framing and understanding their perceptions of the world.

72. The EVS learning is around 10 processes as mentioned below. Thus the nature of learning indicators in EVS is process based. For classes III-V these learning indicators are same, however, the progression of learning from classes III-V can be seen through the complexity in the indicator.

(*i*) Observation and Reporting
(*ii*) Discussion
(*iii*) Expression
(*iv*) Explanation
(*v*) Classification
(*vi*) Questioning
(*vii*) Analysis
(*viii*) Experimentation
(*ix*) Concern for justice and equality
(*x*) Co-operation

73. In EVS, teachers should provide opportunities to the children to assess themselves. Self-assessment is assessment as learning. There are different modes of assessing what a child has learned. Occasionally the child himself/herself and his/her peers need to assess the learning, and the teacher should make it an important part of the learning process. Teacher asked every child to describe an animal or bird that they actually observed, during a class presentation. After that he asked each child to list two good things and one aspect that needed improvement in their own presentation. This was a form of self-assessment.

75. The major objectives of EVS teaching-learning is to enable children to:

(*i*) learn about the environment.
(*ii*) learn through the environment.
(*iii*) learn for the environment.
(*iv*) enhance/promote curiosity and creativity in relation to the surroundings.
(*v*) develop an appreciation for diversity (language, family, habits, variations in plants, animals, culture, etc.) in the surroundings.
(*vi*) Develop sensitivity towards senior citizens, people with disability and disadvantaged groups of society, focusing on their strengths as well as the areas of concern.

81. Earthworm (Eiseniafetida) is the earthworm species which is found in soil. It decomposes the residue which are on earth surface. Earthworm are known as best decomposer. They form a by-product after decomposing the plants/animals wastes which is called vermicompost. This is rich in nutrients and several enzymes which are really beneficial for maintaining the soil and plant health. They make the small holes in soil which provides oxygen/aeration to roots of the plants. During decomposition earthworm released some amino acids which are helpful to fight the disease in crops. They improve the physical and chemical properties of soil. All above statements support that earthworms are farmers friend.

82. Tribal people have been using bronze to make many things since thousand of years. Bronze is still used in our houses. It is one of the earliest metals known to man. It is defined as an alloy made of copper and another metal, usually tin. Compositions vary, but most modern bronze is 88% copper and 12% tin. Bronze may also contain manganese, aluminium, nickel, phosphorus, silicon, arsenic or zinc.

85. Karnataka, Kerala and Gujarat states have a coast on Arabian Sea. Arabean Sea, north-western part of the Indian Ocean forming part of the principal sea route between Europe and India. It is bounded to the west by the Horn of Africa and the Arabian Peninsula, to the north by Iran and Pakistan, to the east by India, and to the south by the remainder of the Indian Ocean.

87. Coal is not obtained from Petroleum. Coal is a hard rock which can be burned as a solid fossil fuel. It is mostly carbon but also contains hydrogen, sulphur, oxygen and nitrogen. It is a sedimentary rock formed from peat, by the pressure of rocks laid down later on top.

88. Distance covered by train from Madgaon to Nagarcoil = 1140 km

Time taken by train to cover this distance = $21\frac{1}{2}$ hrs

Then average speed of the train

$$= \frac{\text{Distance covered}}{\text{Time taken}} = \frac{1140}{\frac{43}{2}} = \frac{1140 \times 2}{43}$$

$$= 26.5 \times 2 = 53 \text{ km/h}$$

90.

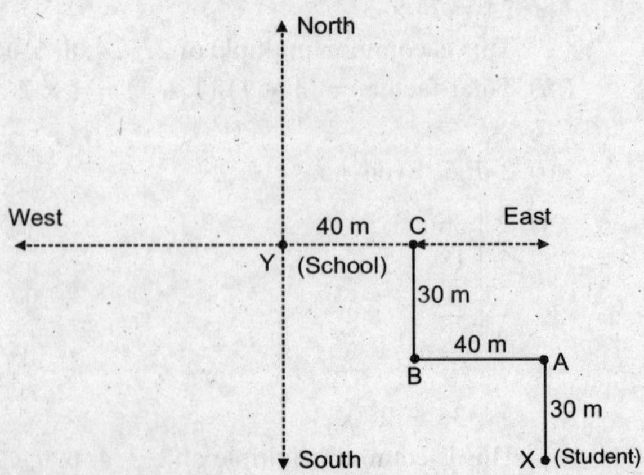

With respect to school the correct direction of house is South-East.

Previous Paper (Solved)

CTET—PAPER-I, DECEMBER 2018*

PART- I

Child Development and Pedagogy

Directions: *Answer the following questions by selecting the* ***correct/most appropriate*** *options.*

1. Which one of the following best describes a teacher's role?
 A. Creating a relaxed space where children learn through dialogue and inquiry
 B. Teacher's most important role in the classroom is to maintain discipline
 C. A teacher should adhere to the prescribed textbook
 D. Completing the syllabus on time leaving enough time for revision is important

2. Which one of the following classrooms encourages rich learning?
 A. A classroom with structured and planned learning driven by textbook content
 B. A classroom with a variety of material displayed in the class beyond the reach of children so that the material lasts longer
 C. A classroom with open activity corners and a variety of children's lilerature in open shelves accessible any time of the day
 D. A classroom with neatly organized material in cupboards brought out once a week for free play

3. Which one of the following best describes the role of textbooks in the classroom?
 A. They form the most essential learning resource in a resource-starved context.
 B. They are one of the resource and reference materials available in the class.
 C. They maintain homogeneity in learning across a State or the Nation.
 D. They provide guidance to teachers and parents about the course of study.

4. The National Curriculum Framework-2005 derives its understanding from:
 A. cognitive theories B. humanism
 C. behaviourism D. constructivism

5. The children in a class can be considered to be motivated if:
 A. they ask questions seeking clarification from the teacher
 B. they come to school neatly dressed in uniform
 C. they maintain discipline in the class
 D. all are regular in attendance

6. Which one of the following is the most suitable to improve children's learning?
 A. Teacher should facilitate children to interact with each other on real-life situations.
 B. Regular assessment test should be conducted.
 C. Teacher should explain the content using different examples and illustrations.
 D. All types of learning material should be there in the class.

7. The discipline which has a significant role in a learning environment is of the kind which helps:
 A. children rote memorize their lessons
 B. children to regulate and monitor their own learning
 C. to create silence
 D. teachers to give instructions

8. Which one of the following statements is true about the role of heredity and environment?
 A. Environment plays a significant role only in the child's language development.
 B. Certain aspects of development are influenced more by heredity and others more by environment.
 C. A child's ability to learn and perform is completely decided by the genes.
 D. Good care and a nutritious diet can fight off any disorder a child is born with.

9. Which one of the following statements **cannot** be attributed to Piaget's theory?
 A. Children act on their environment.
 B. Development occurs in qualitative stages.
 C. Children construct and use knowledge about their world.
 D. Learning takes place through constant practice.

10. Which one of the following is **not** a limitation of the preoperational thought?

*Exam was held on 09-12-2018.

A. Irreversibility
B. Tendency to concentrate
C. Development of the symbolic thought
D. Egocentrism

11. Play has a significant role in development of young children for the following reasons, **except**:
A. they acquire new skills and learn when to use them
B. they gain mastery over their body
C. it stimulates their senses
D. it is just a pleasant way to spend time

12. Which one of the following questions invites children to think critically?
A. What are the different ways in which we can solve this?
B. Do you know the answer to this?
C. What is the right answer?
D. Can you think of a similar situation?

13. Which one of the following options best describes progressive education?
A. Project method, ability grouping, ranking
B. Learning by doing, project method, cooperative learning
C. Thematic units, regular unit tests, ranking
D. Personalized learning, ability grouping, labelling students

14. Which one of the following statements about progressive education explains—Education is life itself?
A. Life is the true educator.
B. School education should continue as long as possible.
C. Schools are not required, children can learn from their life experiences.
D. Education in schools should reflect the social and natural world.

15. Which one of the following can be considered as a contribution of Kohlberg's theory?
A. His belief is that children are moral philosophers.
B. His theory has supported an association between cognitive maturity and moral maturity.
C. The theory has elaborate testing procedures.
D. It establishes a clear relationship between moral reasoning and action.

16. The Zone of Proximal Development refers to:
A. the point in learning when support can be withdrawn
B. the phase when maximum development is possible
C. the developmental phase when child takes complete responsibility for learning
D. a context in which children can almost perform a task on their own with the right level of support

17. An androgynous personality:
A. adheres to stereotypical gender roles prevalent in the society
B. refers to men with feminine traits
C. has a balance of what are generally considered masculine and feminine traits
D. tends to be assertive and arrogant

18. Children acquire gender roles through all of the following, **except**:
A. tutoring
B. media
C. socialization
D. culture

19. One of the critiques of standardized tests has been that:
A. they do not give a clear picture of a child's ability
B. they represent largely the mainstream culture and are therefore biased
C. their language is difficult to understand
D. the tests cannot be administered on large populations

20. The theory of multiple intelligence says that:
A. intelligence can be multiplied with effective pedagogy
B. intelligence can be rapidly accelerated
C. intelligence can be of several kinds
D. paper-pencil tests are not helpful

21. Teacher can utilize both assessment for learning and assessment of learning to:
A. monitor children's progress and set appropriate goals to fill their learning gaps
B. know children's progress and achievement level
C. know learning needs of child and select teaching strategy accordingly
D. assess child's performance at periodic intervals and certify his/her performance

22. Which one of the following is **not** related to Continuous and Comprehensive Evaluation?
A. It is useful to label children as slow, poor or intelligent.
B. It has been mandated by the Right to Education Act of India.
C. It is an integral part of teaching-learning process.
D. It focuses on child's achievement in different learning areas.

23. Giftedness in children can be attributed to:
A. a disciplined routine
B. an interplay between heredity and environment
C. a resource-rich environment
D. successful parents

24. Children coming from socio-economically disadvantaged backgrounds need a classroom environment which:

A. categorizes children based on their abilities
B. teaches them good behaviour
C. values and uses their cultural and linguistic knowledge
D. discourages the use of their language so that they learn the mainstream language

25. The intervention needed for creative and talented children in the classroom rests on:
A. giving them the responsibility of teaching other children
B. use of customized and stimulating instructional methods by the teacher
C. giving extra time to them
D. being affectionate towards them

26. Which one of the following ways is **not** a suitable way to help hyperactive children learn?
A. Reprimanding them often for being restless
B. Breaking up a task into small, manageable segments
C. Offering alternative ways of learning
D. Including physical activity in their daily schedule

27. Patterns of divergent thinking identify children, who are:
A. resilient B. disabled
C. dyslexic D. creative

28. Which one of the following does **not** describe the ways in which a teacher can model problem solving for children in the classroom?
A. Ask questions with convergent answers
B. Discuss your thought processes about solving a particular problem
C. Be honest about making mistakes while solving something
D. Use vocabulary like think, ideas, trial and different answers

29. Which one of the following is an emotion?
A. Stimulus B. Memory
C. Fear D. Attention

30. A three-year-old child explains that milk is produced by a machine at the milk booth.
Which one of the following offers the best explanation of the child's understanding?
A. The child's family does not offer a stimulating environment to the child.
B. The child has very limited exposure of the world.
C. The child's answer is based on his/her experience of buying milk from the milk booth.
D. The child has never seen cows.

PART- II

Mathematics

Directions: *Answer the following questions by selecting the **correct/most appropriate** options.*

31. Harish started his journey at 18 : 40 and finished at 22 : 20. The time taken in completing the journey is:
A. 3 hours 20 minutes
B. 3 hours 40 minutes
C. 3 hours 80 minutes
D. 4 hours 40 minutes

32. A bucket of capacity 2000 mL is to be filled by using containers measuring 200 mL and 300 mL. Which one of the following combinations of containers is not correct for fllling the bucket completely by the containers of 200 mL and 300 mL respectively?
A. 6, 3 B. 1, 6
C. 4, 4 D. 7, 2

33. Which one of the following is the best approximation of $\frac{7.1 \times 3.85}{9.09}$?
A. $\frac{7 \times 3}{10}$ B. $\frac{7 \times 3}{9}$
C. $\frac{7 \times 4}{9}$ D. $\frac{7 \times 4}{10}$

34. If one small square in the grid is of area 4 sq. units, what is the perimeter of the rectangle drawn on the grid?

A. 12 units B. 32 units
C. 8 units D. 24 units

35. A child scored 75 marks in each of five subjects. What is the median marks obtained by the child?
A. 70 B. 75
C. 375 D. 15

36. Which one of the following can be folded to form the given solid?

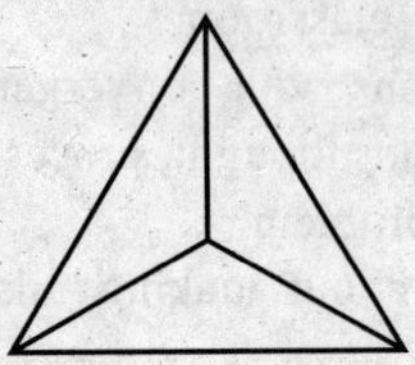

A. 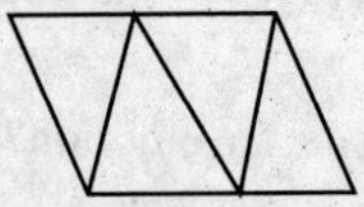 B. 

C.  D. 

37. If Red part in the following pie chart is 40, what is White part?

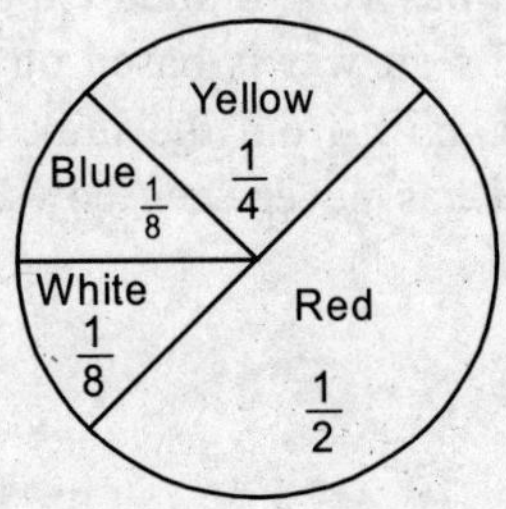

A. 20 B. 5
C. 10 D. 12

38. Observe the following solid shape:

Which one of the following is the top view of the given solid?

A. 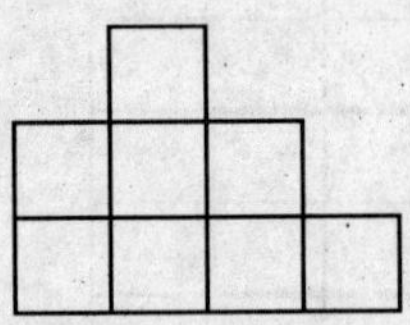 B. 

C. 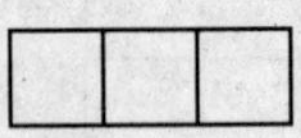 D. 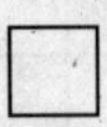

39. Which one of the following costs more?

I. 200 packets of ₹ 250 each
II. 20 dozens of ₹ 250 each item

A. Cannot be calculated
B. I
C. II
D. Both I and II are equal

40. The sum of 1 – 1 + 1 – 1 + 1 – 1 .... to even number of terms is:

A. 2 B. zero
C. –1 D. +1

41. The assessment of what children learn in mathematics in primary classes should **not** focus on:

A. development of reasoning skills
B. understanding of the mathematical concepts
C. development of mathematical language
D. preciseness in answering mathematics problems

42. What sequence of the following instructions should be followed in development of a mathematical concept in elementary classes?

I. Drawing pictures
II. Using symbolic representation
III. Providing experiences
IV. Explaining through language

A. III, I, II, IV B. IV, III, I, II
C. III, IV, I, II D. IV, III, II, I

43. A child subtracted two numbers as shown below :

$$\begin{array}{r} 83 \\ -\,27 \\ \hline 64 \end{array}$$

Which one of the following statements gives idea about the child's learning of subtraction?

A. It is a mistake and it can be rectified by repeated practice.
B. The child has misconceptions about place value in the process of subtraction.
C. The child does not know how to subtract.
D. The child knows the process of subtraction of two-digit numbers.

44. Arrange the following steps of cycle of learning and assessment in order :

I. Teaching-learning integrated with assessment.
II. Planning and organization of teaching-learning and assessment.
III. Developing progress reports.
IV. Reporting and communicating feedback of children's learning and progress.

A. II, IV, I, III B. II, I, III, IV
C. I, II, IV, III D. IV, I, II, III

45. Why are Roman numerals **not** commonly used in writing numbers like the Hindu-Arabic numerals?

A. Children get confused with the English alphabet and Roman numerals.
B. The Roman numerals do not employ place value, so calculations are difficult to perform using these numerals.
C. Roman numerals are difficult to remember.
D. The formation of numbers using Roman numerals is a complicated task.

46. A teacher encourages the children in her class to explain the physical properties of the objects around them in their own words.

What is the most appropriate objective of the teacher to do such an activity with her students?

A. It is a useful activity which introduces a child to the shapes.

B. It is a very interesting activity which can be performed in the free time for revisiting the concept of shapes.

C. Children enjoy explaining the objects in their own language like they enjoy playing dumb charades.

D. It makes the children observe the physical properties of an object informally which deepens their understanding about shapes.

47. The mathematics used by illiterate shopkeeper:

A. should be discussed by the teachers in classrooms as an alternate strategy in solving related problems

B. is not useful in the mathematics classroom

C. is very useful in solving all mathematical problems

D. has ambiguity and very low level of correctness in it

48. How should a teacher handle a heterogeneous group of children in a mathematics classroom?

A. By doing questions according to low ability children in the class and giving the complex questions as home assignments to higher ability children

B. By grouping the children of same ability together and giving them questions according to their ability

C. By grouping all children together in the same classroom

D. By grouping the children of different abilities together so that they can learn from each other

49. The learning outcomes in mathematics are developed:

A. to prepare children for year-end examinations

B. such that children may be told small steps for calculations

C. to increase the achievement of children in various educational surveys

D. to define classwise competencies and skills to be achieved by children

50. Which one of the following happenings in the classroom is an activity?

A. Children engaged in exploration

B. Teacher explaining how to do sums

C. Children reciting counting in form of rhymes

D. Children copying from blackboard

51. To develop skill of counting among children, which one of the following is **not** required to be learned as pre-number concept?

A. Creating groups

B. One to one correspondence

C. Seriation

D. Reciting number names randomly

52. On asking a child 'What is area?" he/she answered length × breadth. What can you say about the child's understanding about the concept of area?

A. The child is confused between, the concept of area and perimeter.

B. The child has no idea about the concept of area.

C. The child used the area of rectangle as general idea of area of any closed shape.

D. The child is right in saying area is length × breadth.

53. Which one of the following statements is true with respect to mathematics learning?

A. Mathematics can only be learnt by rigorous practice.

B. Mathematics is a difficult subject to learn.

C. Generally girls are weaker in mathematics.

D. Everybody can learn mathematics.

54. To teach the Pythagoras theorem, a teacher has distributed a sheet on which four right-angled triangles were drawn and asks the child to find the relationship between the sides of a triangle.

In the above situation, the teacher used:

A. laboratory method

B. inductive method

C. deductive method

D. lecture method

55. Which one of the following statements is **not** true about 'concept maps'?

A. Concept maps help in linking prior knowledge to new instruction.

B. Concept maps represent a collection of interconnected concepts and links connecting them.

C. Concept maps should be constructed by teachers only.

D. Concept maps are hierarchical in nature.

56. $\frac{2}{3}+\frac{4}{5}$ is:

A. $\frac{8}{15}$ B. $\frac{6}{8}$

C. $1\frac{6}{15}$ D. $1\frac{7}{15}$

57. For the given shapes, which one of the following statements is **not** correct?

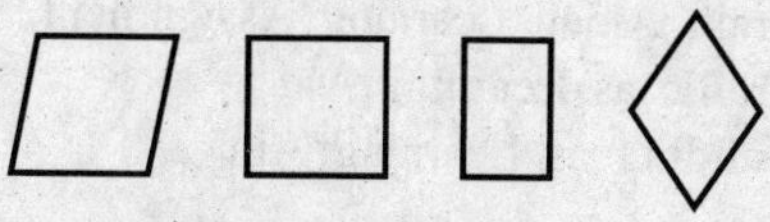

A. Two of them are rectangles.

B. All are parallelograms.

C. One of them is not a parallelogram.

D. Two of them are rhombuses.

58. Which one of the following represents the number 'eleven thousand eleven hundred eleven'?

A. XIXIXI
B. 111111
C. 12111
D. 11000110011

59. The points A and B represent numbers on a number line as shown below :

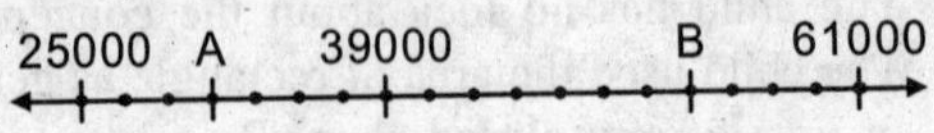

The distance between the points A and B is:

A. 22000 units
B. 29000 units
C. 84000 units
D. 22 units

60. How many packets of $\frac{1}{16}$ kg sugar can be made from $3\frac{1}{4}$ kg of sugar?

A. 64
B. 52
C. 48
D. 12

PART- III

Environmental Studies

*Directions : Answer the following questions by selecting the **correct/most appropriate** options.*

61. Which is most relevant to the mid-day meal time in school?

A. It wastes a lot of precious time of teaching-learning.
B. It has nothing to do with teaching-learning.
C. It is a good teaching-learning opportunity for EVS teaching-learning.
D. It is for children who come empty stomach to school.

62. What does 'learning without burden' in the context of Environmental Studies imply?

A. The EVS curriculum needs to be reduced to half
B. Less weight of school-bag
C. Less number of chapters in EVS textbooks
D. Load of incomprehension needs to be reduced

63. What purpose does group learning serve in an EVS classroom?

A. To manage students easily and reduce workload
B. Boys and girls can learn separately
C. To segregate high performers and low achieving students and to do remedial teaching
D. To inculcate values of cooperation and working together to enable each child participate actively and learn

64. What is the full form of 'BALA'?

A. Braille Aided Learning Assessment
B. Brain Aided Learning Assignment
C. Braille as Learning Aid
D. Building as Learning Aid

65. What do 'alternative frameworks' mean?

A. All ideas that are firmly held by children
B. Textbook explanations of various physical phenomena
C. Ideas that differ from the formally accepted explanations of the concepts
D. Ideas presently held by scientists and social scientists

66. Women are weaker than men. It is a:

A. superstition
B. myth
C. scientific fact
D. stereotype

67. What is the location of Jammu & Kashmir and Goa with respect to Bihar in India?

A. South-west and North-east
B. East and West
C. West and East
D. North-west and South-west

68. Under which of the following conditions will the process of evaporation be slowest?

A. Both surface area and temperature decrease
B. Both surface area and temperature increase
C. Surface area increases but temperature decreases
D. Surface area decreases but temperature increases.

69. The ability to understand relative position of places, distances and directions is:

A. graphic skill
B. directional skill
C. mapping skill
D. positional skill

70. Which National Curriculum Framework (NCF) recommended Environmental Studies to be taught as an integrated curricular area at the primary level?

A. NCF-1975
B. NCF-2005
C. NCF-1988
D. NCF-2000

71. Which region has the practice of shifting cultivation in India?
A. South-eastern region
B. North-eastern region
C. Southern region
D. North-western region

72. Which one of the following statements is **not** true for hydropower generated from river dams?
A. Dams displace indigenous people from their river lifelines.
B. Dams encourage sustainable growth.
C. It does not pollute water or air.
D. Hydropower facilities can have large environmental impacts.

73. Which of the following is/are greenhouse gas/gases?
A. Water vapour
B. Carbon dioxide
C. Methane
D. All of the above

74. Why are cold deserts in India **not** affected by the monsoon?
A. Cold deserts are at a very high altitude.
B. Cold deserts have hot summers and extremely cold winters.
C. Cold deserts lie in the rain shadow of the Himalayas.
D. Air is very thin in cold deserts.

75. Which one of the following is responsible for turning Taj Mahal yellow?
A. Chlorine
B. Nitrogen dioxide
C. Sulphur dioxide
D. Sulphur

76. Who built the Golconda Fort?
A. Pallava Dynasty
B. Chola Dynasty
C. Chalukya Dynasty
D. Kakatiya Dynasty

77. What is the mass of an object with a density of 15 g/mL and a volume of 3 mL?
A. 12 g B. 18 g
C. 45 g D. 5 g

78. Which one of the following is a scalar quantity?
A. Weight B. Mass
C. Gravity D. Momentum

79. An object in which no light rays can pass through is called:
A. convex B. opaque
C. translucent D. transparent

80. What will be the weight of an object on the surface of the earth whose mass is 10 kg on the moon's surface?
A. 10 N B. 60 kg
C. 10 kg D. 60 N

81. The rate of dissolution of a solute depends on:
A. weight B. pressure
C. temperature D. surface area

82. Sushma wants her students to be sensitized for 'conservation of trees'. Which one of the following is the most suitable strategy to do so?
A. Helping children to adopt and nurture a plant
B. Conducting a debate in classroom
C. Group discussion
D. Poster making

83. Abhay asked his students to do a survey in groups on diseases that people in their neighbourhood suffered from. The survey is not mentioned in the textbook. Which option is **not** relevant for this teaching-learning strategy?
A. It helped the community understand the diseases that they suffered from.
B. It provided opportunity to interact with community.
C. It helped children connect learning with real life.
D. It enabled children understand data handling and work together.

84. To talk about emergency situations, Priya asked children's experiences when they faced any emergencies. Children narrated their experiences with fire, electric shock and road accidents. She asked questions, assessed their existing understandings and discussed safety aspects using resources such as road safety advertisements from newspapers and also used LPG and electric bill to discuss safety guidelines on fire and electric shock respectively. Which is the most appropriate approach that Priya employed?
A. Humanistic approach
B. Cognitive approach
C. Experiential learning approach
D. Enquiry approach

85. 'Community' is an important teaching and learning resource, because:
A. one can accept all knowledge available in the community uncritically
B. it is inexpensive and accessible
C. elderly people are wise and have time
D. it provides learning opportunity in real setting

86. In EVS teaching-learning, linking classroom learning to life outside school and enriching it implies:
A. going beyond curriculum
B. going beyond the textbooks
C. linking textbooks to global environmental issues and concerns
D. whole school approach

87. To class III students, Rama taught that a father, mother and their children constitute nuclear family and if grandparents and other relatives stay along, then it is an extended family. What do you think of this?
A. The concept of family has to be taught like this.
B. The definition of a family is incorrect.
C. Rama is insensitive towards her students.
D. The teaching-learning approach is not inclusive.

88. Which of the following is/are activity/activities in EVS classroom?
A. Use of blackboard
B. Picture reading
C. Field visit
D. All of the above

89. Environmental Studies curriculum may lead to holistic learning of children if it is:
A. thematic B. integrated
C. inclusive D. All of the above

90. The EVS textbook has a chapter on snake charmer. It is intended to make children aware and be sensitize
A. that animal keeping is good source of livelihood
B. that it is an illegal act
C. for snake charmers as children do not see them often these days
D. that snake charmers may not harm snakes and they need to be provided with alternatives before depriving them of their livelihoods

PART- IV

Language-I : English

Directions (Qs. 91-105) : *Answer the following questions by selecting the* ***correct/most appropriate*** *options.*

91. Iconic mode of learning is based on the system of using:
A. different types of graph
B. a variety of activities
C. symbols
D. images and diagrams

92. While reading for comprehension, we understand that some pairs are examples of homograph. Which one of the following is a homograph?
A. mail [post]/male [gender]
B. warm/tepid [being neither too hot nor too cold]
C. lead [metal]/lead [give direction]
D. lead [give direction]/ dead [mortal]

93. A 'sight word' is a vocabulary item:
A. that helps in judging the effectiveness of the author's style
B. that needs proper visual understanding of the context
C. that is to be learnt by heart
D. that the reader recognizes and finds meaningful on sight without a complicated analysis

94. Which one of the following methods is suggested for teaching grammar at primary level?
A. Translation method
B. Deductive method
C. Textbook method
D. Inductive method

95. Flower and Hayes regarded which one of the following skills as 'problem-creating and solving skill'?
A. Writing B. Listening
C. Speaking D. Reading

96. Find out the function word from the following:
A. Seizing B. And
C. Champion D. Handsome

97. What do you mean by 'review'?
A. Assessment
B. Guess
C. Evaluation
D. Critical evaluation

98. Content words are called:
A. empty words
B. functors
C. grammatical words
D. lexical words

99. 'Cloze' means:
A. assessing B. finishing
C. missing part D. close

100. The last stage of writing is:
A. advanced writing
B. controlled writing
C. guided writing
D. free writing

101. The procedure of alphabetic method is:
A. letters—words—phrases— paragraph
B. letters—words—phrases— sentences
C. words—phrases—sentences— paragraph
D. letters—words—sentences— paragraph

102. "You ask, what has my government done for you? I can answer in two words a lot!"

The question put up here is:

A. explanatory
B. rhetorical
C. stylized
D. a prompt

103. According to the observation in the National Curriculum Framework (NCF)-2005, English is a .... language in India.

A. global
B. second
C. foreign
D. first

104. Read the exchange:

Teacher : Shall we go out to the garden and find out the names of those flowers near the corridor?

Student : Yes, yes, yeah.

Teacher : Yes, Ma'am, please.

Here, the teacher:

A. offers an alternative language activity
B. relates language function with politeness
C. makes a polite suggestion to start reading
D. confirms the student's request

105. Which one of the following helps in learning the second language without using the printed text?

A. Situational approach
B. Natural approach
C. Language immersion
D. Grammar-translation method

Directions (Qs. 106-114) : *Read the passage carefully and answer the questions that follow by selecting the* ***correct/ most appropriate*** *options.*

When it comes to structures that are both majestic and well-fortified, the classic European castle is the pinnacle of design. Across the ages castles changed, developed, and eventually fell out of use but they still command the fascination of our culture.

Castles were originally built in England by Norman invaders in 1066. As William the Conqueror advanced through England, he fortified key positions to secure the land he had taken. Castles also served as bases of operation for offensive attacks. Troops were summoned to, organized around, and deployed from castles. In this way castles served both offensive and defensive roles in military operations.

Not limited to military purposes, castles also served as offices from which the lord would administer control over his fiefdom. They would address disputes, handle business, feast, and enjoy festivities. In this way castles served as important social centres in medieval England. Castles also served as symbols of power.

The first castles constructed in England were made from earth and timber. Those who constructed them took advantage of natural features, such as hills and rivers, to increase defenses. Since these castles were constructed from wood, they were highly susceptible to attacks by fire. Wooden castles were gradually replaced by stone, which greatly increased the strength of these fortifications; however, being made from stone did not make these castles entirely fireproof. Attackers could hurl flaming objects into the castle through the windows or ignite the wooden doors.

The demise of castles can ultimately be attributed to gunpowder. During the 15th century, artillery became powerful enough to break through stone walls. This greatly undermined the military role of castles. Castles were then replaced by artillery forts that had no role in civil administration, and country houses that were indefensible. Though castles no longer serve their original purposes, remaining castles receive millions of visitors each year from those who wish to experience these majestic vestiges of a time long passed.

106. Which one of the following is **not** a function of castles as expressed in the passage?

A. Castles were the places where knights would keep their best horses.
B. Castles served both offensive and defensive purposes militarily.
C. Castles served as symbols of power.
D. Castles were important social centres in medieval England.

107. Which one of the following best describes the main idea in Paragraph 2?

A. It details all of the purposes that English castles served.
B. It describes how and why William the Conqueror took control of England.
C. It explains why castles were first built in England and the military purposes they served.
D. It shows how Norman lords were often scared and frequently retreated.

108. The original castles were first made from earth and timber because:

A. wooden castles were prettier than dirty stone castles
B. it takes a lot more time and energy to build a stone castle
C. it did not occur to people to build castles out of stone
D. people did not realize how weak wooden castles would be against fire

109. Wooden castles were converted to stone castles as:
A. stone castles stay cooler in the summer
B. wooden castles take a long time to build
C. wooden castles are uncomfortable
D. stone castles offer better defense

110. Which one of the following best explains how gunpowder was the nemesis of traditional castles?
A. Cannons were able to knock down stone walls, so castles offered little protection.
B. Wars were fought with guns and hiding in castles was no longer necessary.
C. Artillery forts with large cannons became more stylish than traditional castles.
D. Defending castles grew difficult, since attackers could just shoot castle defenders.

111. Which one of the following titles would best describe the content of this passage?
A. Fancy Living : Learning about Castles, Palaces and Fortresses
B. William the Conqueror : Bringing Castles to England
C. Defending the Castle : Technologies Used to Defend Medieval Castles
D. A Short History of Castles : The Rise and Fall of Castles in England

112. Which one of the following is an opinion?
A. Castles were used as offices of administration during the Middle Ages.
B. Stone is more resistant to fire than wood.
C. William the Conqueror built the first castles in England.
D. It is unfortunate that castles no longer serve their original purposes.

113. Choose a word from the given options which means almost the same as the word 'vestiges' used in the passage.
A. Creation
B. Reminder
C. Outskirts
D. Farrago

114. Choose a word which serves as the antonym of the word 'pinnacle'.
A. Steeple
B. Nadir
C. Crest
D. Apex

Directions (Qs. 115-120) : *Read the extract given below and answer the questions that follow by selecting the* ***correct/most appropriate*** *options.*

My mother bore me in the southern wild,
And I am black, but O ! my soul is white;
White as an angel is the English child :
But I am black as if bereav'd of light.

My mother taught me underneath a tree
And sitting down before the heat of day,
She took me on her lap and kissed me,
And pointing to the east began to say.

Look on the rising sun : there God does live
And gives his light, and gives his heat away.
And flowers and trees and beasts and men receive
Comfort in morning joy in the noonday.

And we are put on earth a little space,
That we may learn to bear the beams of love,
And these black bodies and this sun-burnt face
Is but a cloud, and like a shady grove.

115. 'The Little Black Boy' was born in:
A. the east coast
B. the desert wastes
C. the servants' house
D. the southern wild

116. 'The Little Black Boy' wished that he could be:
A. white
B. educated
C. older
D. free

117. The mother of 'the Little Black Boy' says God put people on earth:
A. to learn how to treat one another as equals
B. to learn to endure his love
C. to work off their sins
D. to prepare them for future trials

118. The mother of 'the Little Black Boy' says his dark skin and face are:
A. a cloud
B. a blessing
C. a veil
D. a curse

119. The phrase 'like a shady grove' is:
A. a personification
B. a metaphor
C. a simile
D. an example of alliteration

120. Through the phrase 'as if bereav'd of light', the poet hints at:
A. colour of the boy
B. low self-esteem of the child
C. lack of hope for the future
D. All of the above

PART- V

Language-II : Hindi

निर्देश (प्र.सं. 121 से 127) : *नीचे दिए गए अनुच्छेद को पढ़कर पूछे गए प्रश्नों के **सही/सबसे उपयुक्त** उत्तर वाले विकल्प को चुनिए।*

हेंवल घाटी के गाँववासियों ने चीड़ के पेड़ों के हो रहे विनाश के विरुद्ध जुलूस निकाले। घास-चारा लेने जा रही महिलाओं ने इन पेड़ों से लीसा टपकाने के लिए लगाए गए लोहे निकाल दिए व उनके स्थान पर मिट्टी की मरहम-पट्टी कर दी। महिलाओं ने पेड़ों का रक्षा-बंधन भी किया। आरंभ से ही लगा कि वृक्ष बचाने में महिलाएँ आगे आएँगी। वन कटने का सबसे अधिक कष्ट उन्हीं को उठाना पड़ता है, क्योंकि घास-चारा लाने के लिए उन्हें और दूर जाना पड़ता है। कठिन स्थानों से घास-चारा एकत्र करने में कई बार उन्हें बहुत चोट लग जाती है। वैसे भी पहाड़ी रास्तों पर घास-चारे का बोझ लेकर पाँच-दस कि.मी. या उससे भी ज्यादा चलना बहुत कठिन हो जाता है। इस आंदोलन की बात ऊँचे अधिकारियों तक पहुँची तो उन्हें लीसा प्राप्त करने के तौर-तरीकों की जाँच करवानी पड़ी। जाँच से स्पष्ट हो गया कि बहुत अधिक लीसा निकालने के लालच में चीड़ के पेड़ों को बहुत नुकसान हुआ है। इन अनुचित तरीकों पर रोक लगी। चीड़ के घायल पेड़ों को आराम मिला, एक नया जीवन मिला। पर तभी खबर मिली कि इस इलाके के बहुत से पेड़ों को कटाई के लिए नीलाम किया जा रहा है। लोगों ने पहले तो अधिकारियों को ज्ञापन दिया कि जहाँ पहले से ही घास-चारे का संकट है, वहाँ और व्यापारिक कटान न किया जाए। जब अधिकारियों ने गाँववासियों की माँग पर ध्यान न देते हुए नरेंद्रनगर में नीलामी की घोषणा कर दी, तो गाँववासी जुलूस बनाकर वहाँ नीलामी का विरोध करते हुए पहुँच गए। वहाँ एकत्र ठेकेदारों से हेंवल घाटी की महिलाओं ने कहा, "आप इन पेड़ों को काटकर हमारी रोजी-रोटी मत छीनो। पेड़ कटने से यहाँ बाढ़ व भू-स्खलन का खतरा भी बढ़ जाएगा।" कुछ ठेकेदारों ने तो वास्तव में वह बात मानी पर कुछ अन्य ठेकेदारों ने अद्वानी और सलेत के जंगल खरीद लिए।

121. हेंवल घाटी में किन पेड़ों के होने वाले विनाश के विरुद्ध जुलूस निकाले गए?
A. आम
B. देवदार
C. चीड़
D. पीपल

122. महिलाओं ने पेड़ों का रक्षा-बंधन क्यों किया?
A. पेड़ों को बचाने के लिए
B. यह उस घाटी की रस्म थी
C. पेड़ों को सुंदर बनाने के लिए
D. उनकी मरहम-पट्टी करने के लिए

123. वन काटने का सबसे अधिक कष्ट महिलाओं को क्यों उठाना पड़ता है?
A. उन्हें वनों से लीसा नहीं मिलता
B. केवल उन्हें ही वन से प्रेम था
C. उन्हें चारा लाने के लिए दूर जाना पड़ता है
D. उन्हें वनों की घनी छाया नहीं मिलती

124. चीड़ के पेड़ों को किससे बहुत नुकसान हो रहा था?
A. कुछ ठेकेदारों से
B. बहुत ऊँचे अधिकारियों से
C. अधिक घास-चारा लाने से
D. बहुत अधिक लीसा निकालने से

125. पेड़ काटने से किसका खतरा बढ़ जाएगा?
A. लकड़ी और चारे का
B. बाढ़ और लकड़ी का
C. भू-स्खलन और बाढ़ का
D. भू-स्खलन और लकड़ी का

126. 'रोजी-रोटी' शब्द है :
A. शब्द-युग्म
B. संज्ञा
C. सर्वनाम
D. विशेषण

127. "कुछ ठेकेदारों ने तो वास्तव में वह बात मानी"—वाक्य में निपात है :
A. वह
B. कुछ
C. ने
D. तो

निर्देश (प्र.सं. 128 से 142) : *नीचे दिए गए प्रश्नों के **सही/सबसे उपयुक्त** उत्तर वाले विकल्प को चुनिए।*

128. प्राथमिक स्तर पर बच्चों में लिखने का कौशल इस सीमा तक हो कि वे :
A. मानक वर्तनी में लिख सकें
B. सुंदर अक्षरों में लिख सकें
C. छोटी कहानी लिख सकें
D. विभिन्न उद्देश्यों के लिए लिख सकें

129. हिंदी भाषा के संदर्भ में एक महत्वपूर्ण उद्देश्य है कि बच्चे :
A. कही या लिखी गई बात को शब्दशः कह और लिख सकें
B. अपना शब्द-भंडार विकसित कर सकें

C. व्याकरण के नियमों को याद कर सकें

D. कही या लिखी गई बात आलोचनात्मक दृष्टि से परख सकें

130. प्राथमिक स्तर पर हिंदी भाषा का शिक्षण करते समय आप किस बिंदु पर सर्वाधिक बल देंगे?

A. हिंदी भाषा की मानक वर्तनी

B. हिंदी भाषा के मुहावरे और लोकोक्तियाँ

C. हिंदी भाषा की विभिन्न वाक्य-संरचनाएँ

D. हिंदी भाषा का सौंदर्य और आंचलिकता

131. पहली कक्षा की हिंदी भाषा की पाठ्य-पुस्तक में आप किस विधा को सबसे अधिक महत्व देंगे?

A. निबंध

B. कहानी

C. नाटक

D. डायरी

132. पढ़ने का प्रारंभ .... से ही हो और किसी उद्देश्य के लिए हो।

A. अर्थ

B. अक्षर

C. शब्द

D. वाक्य

133. भाषा अर्जित करने के संदर्भ में कौन-सा कथन उचित नहीं है?

A. बच्चों को नियम बनाना सिखाया जाता है।

B. यह एक सहज प्रक्रिया है।

C. यह एक स्वाभाविक प्रक्रिया है।

D. बच्चे भाषा के नियमों को आत्मसात् करते हैं।

134. लिखना सीखने में सबसे अधिक महत्वपूर्ण है :

A. अर्थ की अभिव्यक्ति

B. अक्षर-ज्ञान

C. शब्द-ज्ञान

D. वाक्य-संरचना

135. वाइगोत्स्की ने भाषा-विकास का .... परिप्रेक्ष्य प्रस्तुत किया।

A. संज्ञानवादी

B. व्यवहारवादी

C. समाज-सांस्कृतिक

D. व्यवहार-सांस्कृतिक

136. बहुभाषिक कक्षाओं में बच्चों की घर की भाषा को स्थान देने की दृष्टि से कौन-सा कार्य सर्वाधिक प्रभावी है?

A. अपनी भाषा में अपनी पसंद का कोई गीत सुनाओ

B. हिंदी भाषा के शब्दों को अपनी भाषा में कहो

C. हिंदी भाषा के शब्दों को अपनी भाषा में लिखो

D. हिंदी भाषा में सुनी कहानी को अपनी भाषा में कहो

137. कक्षा पाँच के बच्चों की हिंदी भाषा का आकलन करने में कौन-सा प्रश्न सर्वाधिक उपयोगी है?

A. हीरा समझदार था या मोती? क्यों?

B. झूरी के कितने बैल थे?

C. झूरी के बैलों के नाम बताइए।

D. गया कैसा व्यक्ति था?

138. हिंदी भाषा में आकलन का मुख्य उद्देश्य है :

A. भाषा-प्रयोग संबंधी त्रुटियों का आकलन करना

B. बच्चों के व्याकरण-ज्ञान को जानना

C. बच्चों के शब्द-भंडार का आकलन करना

D. प्रभावी भाषा-प्रयोग में बच्चों की मदद करना

139. तीसरी कक्षा का मोहित अकसर पढ़ते समय शब्दों की पुनरावृत्ति करता है। आप उसके पठन के बारे में क्या कहेंगे?

A. उसे शब्द पढ़ने में कठिनाई होती है

B. उसे पढ़ना नहीं आता

C. उसे पढ़ने में बहुत कठिनाई होती है

D. वह अर्थ की खोज में पुनरावृत्ति करता है

140. भाषा सीखने-सिखाने की प्रक्रिया में सबसे कम महत्वपूर्ण है :

A. भाषा का परिवेश

B. भाषा की पाठ्य-पुस्तक

C. भाषा का आकलन

D. भाषा-शिक्षण की पद्धति

141. भाषा शिक्षक के लिए जरूरी है कि वे भारतीय भाषाओं की .... को स्वीकार करें और समृद्ध साहित्य को .... की दृष्टि से देखें।

A. सराहना, विविधता

B. जटिलताओं, साहित्यिक

C. विषमताओं, सराहना

D. विविधता, सराहना

142. पहली कक्षा के बच्चों के साथ कविता गायन के बाद आप क्या करेंगे?

A. बच्चों से कहेंगे कि वे अपनी भाषा में अपनी पसंद की कोई कविता सुनाएँ

B. बच्चों से कहेंगे कि वे सुनी हुई कविता को शब्दशः सुनाएँ

C. बच्चों से कविता पर आधारित प्रश्न पूछेंगे

D. बच्चों को कविता में आए पाँच शब्द बताने के लिए कहेंगे

निर्देश (प्र.सं. 143 से 150) : *नीचे दिए गए अनुच्छेद को पढ़कर पूछे गए प्रश्नों के **सही/सबसे उपयुक्त** उत्तर वाले विकल्प को चुनिए।*

बच्चों की दुनिया में कोई लड़ाई नहीं होती। उनके लिए दुनिया है और वे इस दुनिया में आना चाहते हैं। बच्चों को यह सुनना अच्छा नहीं लगता कि यह दुनिया इतनी बेकार है, यहाँ करने के काबिल कुछ भी नहीं है और इससे बचकर कितना दूर भागा जा सकता है। संभवतः

सबसे महत्वपूर्ण बात यह है कि न्यू लिटिल स्कूल के शिक्षक खुले और सच्चे हैं अर्थात्, ये लोग उन सभी विषयों पर बात करने के लिए तत्पर रहते हैं जिन पर बच्चे बात करना चाहते हैं। वे अपने सच्चे विचार प्रकट करते हैं और कोई बात अगर वे नहीं जानते तो स्वीकार कर लेते हैं। ज्यादातर शिक्षकों के साथ ऐसा नहीं है। सर्वेक्षण से यह स्पष्ट होता है कि 90 प्रतिशत अमेरिकी शिक्षक विवादास्पद विषयों के बारे में स्कूल में बात करने में विश्वास नहीं करते तथा बच्चों को भी इन विषयों के बारे में बात नहीं करने देते। हालाँकि वे अच्छी तरह जानते हैं कि बच्चों की इन विषयों में सबसे अधिक रुचि होती है। इसलिए पारंपरिक स्कूलों में बच्चे ज्यादा बात नहीं कर सकते और जब करते भी हैं तब वे जो चाहते हैं वह बात नहीं कर सकते और ईमानदारी से नहीं कर सकते। इसके अलावा शिक्षकों को प्रशिक्षण में बार-बार सिखाया जाता है कि अपनी अज्ञानता, अनिश्चय और उलझन को कभी स्वीकार नहीं करें। सबसे अहम बात यह है कि उनमें कूट-कूट कर यह भरा जाता है कि छात्रों से एक पेशेवर दूरी रखें और अपनी व्यक्तिगत जिंदगी और भावनाओं के बारे में कभी खुलकर बात नहीं करें। लेकिन यही वे बातें हैं जिनमें बच्चों की सबसे ज्यादा जिज्ञासा होती है, क्योंकि इसी से वे महसूस कर सकते हैं कि बड़ा होना क्या होता है।

143. 'न्यू लिटिल स्कूल के शिक्षक खुले और सच्चे हैं' में 'खुले' का अर्थ है :
A. बहुत खुले स्थान में रहना
B. बिना दुराव-छिपाव के बात करना
C. व्यापक रूप से सोचने वाले
D. खुले तौर पर काम करने वाले

144. अमेरिकी शिक्षकों के बारे में कौन-सी बात सही है?
A. वे बच्चों के साथ सभी तरह की बात करते हैं।
B. वे बच्चों को सभी तरह की बात करने देते हैं।
C. वे बच्चों के साथ सभी तरह की बात नहीं करते।
D. वे बच्चों के साथ रोचक विषयों के बारे में बात करते हैं।

145. शिक्षकों को प्रशिक्षण में यह सिखाया जाता है कि :
A. वे यह स्वीकार करें कि वे अज्ञानी हैं
B. वे यह स्वीकार करें कि वे उलझे हुए हैं
C. वे यह स्वीकार न करें कि उन्हें ज्ञान नहीं है
D. वे यह स्वीकार न करें कि वे शिक्षक हैं

146. बच्चों की सबसे ज्यादा जिज्ञासा किस बात में है?
A. शिक्षकों के निजी जीवन में
B. शिक्षकों की अज्ञानता में
C. शिक्षकों के प्रशिक्षण में
D. शिक्षकों की उलझनों में

147. पारंपरिक स्कूलों के बारे में कौन-सा कथन सही **नहीं** है?
A. पारंपरिक स्कूलों में बच्चे ज्यादा बात नहीं कर सकते।
B. पारंपरिक स्कूलों में बच्चे ज्यादा बात कर सकते हैं।
C. पारंपरिक स्कूलों में बच्चे मनपसंद बात नहीं कर सकते।
D. पारंपरिक स्कूलों में बच्चे ईमानदारी से बात नहीं कर सकते।

148. "बच्चों की दुनिया में कोई लड़ाई नहीं होती"—वाक्य से तात्पर्य है :
A. बच्चों की दुनिया में कोई लड़ता नहीं है।
B. बच्चों को दुनिया से प्रेम है।
C. बच्चों को लड़ाई पसंद नहीं है।
D. बच्चे लड़ाई नहीं करते।

149. 'विचार' शब्द में 'इक' प्रत्यय लगने से .... शब्द बनेगा।
A. वैचारिक
B. विचारिक
C. वैचारीक
D. विचारइक

150. 'ईमानदारी' शब्द है :
A. भाववाचक संज्ञा
B. व्यक्तिवाचक संज्ञा
C. समूहवाचक संज्ञा
D. जातिवाचक संज्ञा

Answers

1	2	3	4	5	6	7	8	9	10
A	C	B	D	A	A	B	B	D	C
11	**12**	**13**	**14**	**15**	**16**	**17**	**18**	**19**	**20**
D	A	B	D	B	D	C	A	B	C
21	**22**	**23**	**24**	**25**	**26**	**27**	**28**	**29**	**30**
B	A	B	C	B	A	D	A	C	C
31	**32**	**33**	**34**	**35**	**36**	**37**	**38**	**39**	**40**
B	A	C	D	B	C	C	B	C	B
41	**42**	**43**	**44**	**45**	**46**	**47**	**48**	**49**	**50**
D	C	B	B	B	D	A	D	D	A

51	52	53	54	55	56	57	58	59	60
D	C	D	B	C	D	C	C	A	B
61	62	63	64	65	66	67	68	69	70
C	D	D	D	C	B	D	A	C	A
71	72	73	74	75	76	77	78	79	80
B	B	D	C	C	D	C	B	B	*
81	82	83	84	85	86	87	88	89	90
D	A	A	D	D	B	D	D	D	D
91	92	93	94	95	96	97	98	99	100
D	C	D	D	A	B	D	D	C	A
101	102	103	104	105	106	107	108	109	110
B	B	B	B	C	A	C	B	D	A
111	112	113	114	115	116	117	118	119	120
D	D	B	B	D	A	B	A	C	D
121	122	123	124	125	126	127	128	129	130
C	A	C	D	C	A	D	D	D	D
131	132	133	134	135	136	137	138	139	140
B	A	A	A	C	A	A	D	D	B
141	142	143	144	145	146	147	148	149	150
D	A	C	C	C	A	B	B	A	A

Some Selected Explanatory Answers

31. Time taken to complete the journey

= 22 : 20 − 18 : 40

= 3 hours 40 minutes

32. We have,

Bucket capacity = 2000 mL

(*i*) 6 × 200 mL + 3 × 300 mL = 1200 + 900 = 2100 mL ≠ 2000 mL

(*ii*) 4 × 200 mL + 6 × 300 mL = 200 + 1800 = 2000 mL

(*iii*) 4 × 200 mL + 4 × 300 mL = 800 + 1200 = 2000 mL

(*iv*) 7 × 200 mL + 2 × 300 mL = 1400 + 600 = 2000 mL

Hence option (A) 6, 3 combination of container is not correct for filling the bucket.

33. $\frac{7.1 \times 3.85}{9.09}$

The best approximation is $\frac{7 \times 4}{9}$

34. Side of small square $= \sqrt{\text{Area of square}}$

$= \sqrt{4} = 2$ units

∴ Length of rectangle = 4 × 2 = 8 units

and breadth of rectangle = 2 × 2 = 4 units

∵ Perimeter of rectangle = $2(l + b)$

= 2(8 + 4)

= 24 units

35. Marks scored in each of five subject = 75

$n = 5$ (odd)

∴ Median $= \left(\frac{n+1}{2}\right)$ th term

$= \left(\frac{5+1}{2}\right)$ th term

= 3rd term = 75

37. Red part, $\frac{1}{2}$ part = 40

∴ White part, $\frac{1}{8}$ part $= 80 \times \frac{1}{8} = 10$

39. (I) Total cost = 200 packets × ₹250

= ₹50000

(II) Total cost = (20 × 12) × ₹250

= ₹60000

∴ II. cost is more than I.

40. 1 – 1 + 1 – 1 + 1 .... even number of term

∵ The sum of two consecutive term is zero, and the total number of term is even.

∴ Sum = 0

56. $\frac{2}{3}+\frac{4}{5} = \frac{2\times5+4\times3}{15} = \frac{10+12}{15}$

$= \frac{22}{15} = 1\frac{7}{15}$

58. "Eleven Throusand eleven hundred eleven"

$$\begin{array}{r} = 11000 \\ 1100 \\ +\ 11 \\ \hline 12111 \end{array}$$

59. Length of one part = $\frac{3900-25000}{7}$

$= \frac{14000}{7} = 2000$ units

Total part between A and B = 11

∴ Distance between A and B = 11 × 2000

= 22000 units

60. No. of Packets = $\frac{\left(\frac{13}{4}\right)}{\left(\frac{1}{16}\right)} = \frac{13\times16}{4\times1} = 52$

Previous Paper (Solved)

CTET PAPER-I, SEPTEMBER 2016*

PART- I

Child Development and Pedagogy

Directions: *Answer the following questions by selecting the **correct/most appropriate** options.*

1. As a teacher, who firmly believes in social constructivist theory of Lev Vygotsky, which of the following methods would you prefer for assessing your students?
A. Collaborative projects
B. Standardized tests
C. Fact-based recall questions
D. Objective multiple-choice type questions

2. To cater to individual differences in his classroom, a teacher should:
A. have uniform and standard ways of teaching and assessment
B. segregate and label children based on their marks
C. engage in a dialogue with students and value their perspectives
D. impose strict rules upon his students

3. Assessment is purposeful if:
A. it induces fear and stress among the students
B. it serves as a feedback for the students as well as the teachers
C. it is done only once at the end of the year
D. comparative evaluations are made to differentiate between the students' achievements

4. According to NCF, 2005, the role of a teacher has to be:
A. authoritative
B. dictatorial
C. permissive
D. facilitative

5. Research suggests that in a diverse classroom, a teacher's expectations from her students _____ their learning.
A. have a significant impact on
B. are the sole determinant of
C. should not be correlated with
D. do not have any effect on

6. Inclusion of children with special needs:
A. is an unrealistic goal
B. is detrimental to children without disabilities
C. will increase the burden on schools
D. requires a change in attitude, content and approach to teaching

7. "Having a diverse classroom with children from varied social, economic and cultural backgrounds enriches the learning experiences of all students." This statement is:
A. incorrect, because it can confuse the children and they may feel lost
B. correct, because children learn many skills from their peers
C. correct, because it makes the classroom more hierarchical
D. incorrect, because it leads to unnecessary competition

8. A child with hearing impairment:
A. should be sent only to a school for the hearing impaired and not to a regular school
B. will not benefit from academic education only and should be given vocational training instead
C. can do very well in a regular school if suitable facilitation and resources are provided
D. will never be able to perform on a par with classmates in a regular school

9. Which of the following is a characteristic of a gifted learner?
A. He gets aggressive and frustrated.
B. He can feel understimulated and bored if the class activities are not challenging enough.
C. He is highly temperamental.
D. He engages in ritualistic behaviour like hand flapping, rocking, etc.

10. A teacher can enhance effective learning in her elementary classroom by:
A. offering rewards for small steps in learning
B. drill and practice
C. encouraging competition amongst her students
D. connecting the content to the lives of the students

11. Which of the following statements about children are **correct**?
1. Children are passive recipients of knowledge.
2. Children are problem solvers.
3. Children are scientific investigators.
4. Children are active explorers of the environment.

*Exam was held on 18-09-2016.

A. 1, 2 and 4 B. 2, 3 and 4
C. 1, 2, 3 and 4 D. 1, 2 and 3

12. Which of the following is the most effective method to encourage conceptual development in students?
A. New concepts need to be understood on their own without any reference to the old ones.
B. Replace the students' incorrect ideas with correct ones by asking them to memorize.
C. Give students multiple examples and encourage them to use reasoning.
D. Use punishment till students have made the required conceptual changes.

13. Primary schoolchildren will learn most effectively in an atmosphere:
A. where their emotional needs are met and they feel that they are valued.
B. where the teacher is authoritative and clearly dictates what should be done.
C. where the focus and stress are only on mastering primarily cognitive skills of reading, writing and mathematics.
D. where the teacher leads all the learning and expects students to play a passive role.

14. A child sees a crow flying past the window and says, "A bird." What does this suggest about the child's thinking?
1. The child has previously stored memories.
2. The child has developed the concept of a 'bird'.
3. The child has developed some tools of language to communicate her experience.

A. 1 and 2 B. 2 and 3
C. 1, 2 and 3 D. only 2

15. What should a teacher tell her students to encourage them to do tasks with intrinsic motivation?
A. "Come on, finish it before she does."
B. "Why can't you be like him? See, he has done it perfectly."
C. "Complete the task fast and get a toffee."
D. "Try to do it, you will learn."

16. How can a teacher encourage her students to be intrinsically motivated towards learning for the sake of learning?
A. By inducing anxiety and fear
B. By giving competitive tests
C. By supporting them in setting individual goals and their mastery
D. By offering tangible rewards such as toffees

17. In an elementary classroom, an effective teacher should aim at the students to be motivated:
A. to learn so that they become curious and love learning for its own sake
B. to rote memorize so that they become good at recall
C. by using punitive measures so that they respect the teacher
D. to perform so that they get good marks in the end of the year examination

18. Which of the following is an example of effective school practice?
A. Constant comparative evaluation
B. Corporal punishment
C. Individualized learning
D. Competitive classroom

19. The cephalocaudal principle of development explains how development proceeds from:
A. general to specific functions
B. differentiated to integrated functions
C. head to toe
D. rural to ruban areas

20. Which of the following is a sensitive period pertaining to language development?
A. Prenatal period
B. Middle childhood period
C. Adulthood
D. Early childhood period

21. A 6-year-old girl shows exceptional sporting ability. Both of her parents are sportspersons, send her for coaching everyday and train her on weekends. Her capabilities are most likely to be the result of an interaction between:
A. heredity and environment
B. growth and development
C. health and training
D. discipline and nutrition

22. Which of the following are secondary agents of socialization?
A. Family and neighbourhood
B. School and neighbourhood
C. School and immediate family members
D. Family and relatives

23. According to Lev Vygotsky, the primary cause of cognitive development is:
A. equilibration
B. social interaction
C. adjustment of mental schemas
D. stimulus-response pairing

24. In the context of Kohlberg's stages of moral reasoning, under which stage would the given typical response of a child fall?
"Your parents will be proud of you if you are honest. So you should be honest."
A. Punishment-obedience orientation
B. Social contract orientation
C. Good girl-good boy orientation
D. Law and order orientation

25. According to Jean Piaget, which of the following is necessary for learning?
A. Active exploration of the environment by the learner
B. Observing the behaviour of adults
C. Belief in immanent justice
D. Reinforcement by teachers and parents

26. According to Jean Piaget, schema building occurs as a result of modifying new information to fit existing schemes and by modifying old schemes as per new information. These two processes are known as:
A. accommodation and adaptation
B. assimilation and adaptation
C. equilibration and modification
D. assimilation and accommodation

27. In a progressive classroom setup, the teacher facilitates learning by providing an environment that:
A. promotes discovery B. is restrictive
C. discourages inclusion D. encourages repetition

28. Howard Gardner's theory of Multiple Intelligence (MI) suggests that:
A. every child should be taught every subject in eight different ways in order to develop all of the intelligences
B. intelligence is solely determined by IQ tests
C. teachers should use MI as a framework for devising alternative ways to teach the subject matter
D. ability is destiny and does not change over a period of time

29. A 5-year-old girl talks to herself while trying to fold a T-shirt. Which of the following statements is **correct** in the context of the behaviour displayed by the girl?
A. Jean Piaget and Lev Vygotsky would explain this as egocentric nature of the child's thoughts.
B. Jean Piaget would explain this as egocentric speech, while Lev Vygotsky would explain this as the child's attempt to regulate her actions through private speech.
C. Jean Piaget would explain this as social interaction, while Lev Vygotsky would explain this as an exploration.
D. Jean Piaget and Lev Vygotsky would explain this as the child's attemp to imitate her mother.

30. 'Gender' is a/an:
A. biological entity
B. physiological construct
C. innate quality
D. social construct

PART- II

Mathematics

Directions: *Answer the following questions by selecting the correct/most appropriate options.*

31. The prices of fruits per kg are given below:

Watermelon : ₹ 18.50
Cherry : ₹ 72
Grape : ₹ 120.60
Apple : ₹ 78.40

Reshma bought 4½ kg watermelon, 1 kg 200 g cherries, 250 g grapes and 1¾ kg apples. She gave a ₹ 500 note to the shopkeeper. How much did she get back?
A. ₹ 163 B. ₹ 172
C. ₹ 173 D. ₹ 162

32. The size of a soap cake is 7 cm × 5 cm × 2.5 cm. The maximum number of soap cakes which can be packed into two boxes each having internal measurements as 56 cm × 0.4 m × 0.25 m is:
A. 960 B. 1280
C. 2560 D. 640

33. The length of a rectangle is three times its breadth. The breadth is half the side of a square whose perimeter is 72 cm. Then:
A. the area of the rectangle is more than the area of the square
B. the perimeters of both rectangle and square are equal
C. the perimeter of the rectangle is less than the perimeter of the square
D. the areas of the square and rectangle are equal

34. Which one of the following is **not** correct?
A. 55 litres 55 millilitres = 55.55 litres
B. 2005 grams = 2.005 kg
C. The volume of a cuboid of length 45 cm, breadth 15 cm and height 40 cm is equal to the volume of a cube whose side is 0.3 m
D. One hundredth of 10 is equal to 0.1

35. Which of the following is an essential prerequisite to understand multiplication of a two-digit number by a one-digit or a two-digit number?
A. Multiplication as inverse of division
B. Commutative property of addition
C. Commutative property of multiplication
D. Multiplication as distribution over addition

36. Which of the following **cannot** be considered as a reason for fear and failure in mathematics?
A. Gender differences
B. Classroom experiences
C. Symbolic notations
D. Structure of mathematics

37. Which of the following teaching-learning resources would be the most appropriate to teach the concept of addition of two decimal numbers?
A. Abacus
B. Geoboard
C. Beads and string
D. Graph paper

38. The majority of Class IV learners think that multiplication of two numbers always results in a number which is bigger than both the numbers. How will you show that it is always **not** the case?
A. By showing on a grid paper the multiplication of two decimal numbers
B. By showing the multiplication algorithm of one whole number and a fraction on a number line
C. By showing it through repeated addition of numbers
D. By showing the multiplication algorithm of two decimal numbers

39. Which of the following statements is **true** in the context of teaching 'measurement' to primary class students?
A. Non-standard measures should not be used.
B. Standard measures should be followed by non-standard measures.
C. Non-standard measures should be followed by standard measures.
D. Only non-standard measures should be used.

40. Which of the following assessment strategies can be used to make connections of mathematics with real life and promote interdisciplinarity?
A. Field trip, survey, project
B. Field trip, oral test, drill worksheet
C. Survey, project, checklist
D. Field trip, oral test, checklist

41. Which of the following can be used as learning resources for visually challenged in a mathematics classroom?
A. Computer, number chart, geoboard
B. Taylor's abacus, fraction kit, number chart
C. Number chart, computer, geoboard
D. Taylor's abacus, computer, geoboard

42. In the context of 'numbers', primary class children, *i.e.*, the children in age group 8-9 years, are able to accomplish which one of the following sets?
A. Seriation, classification, reversibility
B. Classification, reversibility, proportional reasoning
C. Seriation, reversibility, proportional reasoning
D. Seriation, classification, proportional reasoning

43. A teacher of Class I asks a student to count the total number of objects in a collection of pens, erasers and sharpners. The student puts all the objects in a line and starts counting. He says that there are 2 pens, 5 erasers and 3 sharpners instead of 10 objects. In which principle/principles of counting do you think that the student is facing difficulty?
A. Abstraction principle
B. Abstraction and order irrelevance principles
C. Stable order and abstraction principles
D. One-to-one correspondence principle

44. A teacher of Class II asks her students to write 4 ones and 3 tens. Some students write as 43 instead of 34. As a teacher, how will you help the students in understanding the concept?
A. Tell them it is wrong and ask them to write the correct answer 5 times.
B. Always teach by column method of tens and ones the avoid confusion.
C. Give a lot of questions to practise in column method.
D. Ask the students to represent on abacus and then write.

45. Which of the following statements is **not** true about 'mapping' in mathematics?
A. Mapping can be integrated in many topics of mathematics.
B. Mapping strengthens spatial thinking.
C. Mapping promotes proportional reasoning
D. Mapping is not part of mathematics curriculum.

46. Which of the following aspects of 'shapes' is **not** dealt with at primary level?
A. Tessellation B. Pattern
C. Angle D. Symmetry

47. The mathematical games and puzzles help in:
1. developing a positive attitude towards mathematics
2. making connection between mathematics and everyday thinking
3. making mathematics enjoyable
4. promoting problem-solving skills
Select the correct option:
A. 1 and 4 B. 1, 2 and 3
C. 1, 2, 3 and 4 D. 1 and 2

48. A given rectangle and a parallelogram have the same area. However, many Class IV students respond that the parallelogram has a larger area. How can a teacher help the students to understand that their areas are the same?
A. Using a graph paper B. Using paper folding
C. Using scale D. Using a geoboard

49. Which of the following is **not** an objective of teaching mathematics at primary level according to NCF, 2005?
A. Promoting logical thinking

B. Preparing for learning higher and abstract mathematics
C. Making mathematics part of child's life experiences
D. Promoting problem-solving and problem-posing skills

50. The difference between the place value of 5 in 29503 and the face value of 7 in 32071 is:
A. 43 B. 430
C. 493 D. 2

51. If 30028 = 28 ones + 28 thousands + ______ tens, then the number in the blank space is:
A. 128 B. 200
C. 280 D. 28

52. When the remainder obtained on dividing 80808 by 108 is divided by the remainder obtained on dividing 90909 by 109, then the quotient is:
A. 6 B. 8
C. 12 D. 3

53. If $603 \times 28 = 63 \times 4 \times$ ______, then the number in the blank space is:
A. 28 B. 63
C. 67 D. 21

54. (The smallest common multiple of 30, 45 and 60 between 200 and 400) ÷ (The largest common factor of 15, 24 and 45) is equal to:
A. 90 B. 120
C. 180 D. 60

55. A number is smaller than half of one hundred and lies between 4 tens and 5 tens. Ones digit is one less than tens digit. If the sum of digits is 7, then the product of the digits in the number is:
A. 16 B. 20
C. 24 D. 12

56. In a school, there are 360 students out of which two-thirds are girls and the rest are boys. Three-fourths of the number of boys are players. The number of boys who are not players is:
A. 30 B. 60
C. 75 D. 25

57. Harish bought a scooter for ₹ 49,553. He paid ₹ 8,076 in cash and agreed to pay the remaining amount in 37 equal instalments. What is the amount of each instalment?
A. ₹ 1,121 B. ₹ 1,201
C. ₹ 1,339 D. ₹ 1,021

58. A train left Hyderabad at 13 : 15 on Friday and reached Bengaluru at 07 : 30 on Saturday. The duration of the journey was:
A. 12 hours 45 minutes B. 18 hours 15 minutes
C. 19 hours 45 minutes D. 5 hours 35 minutes

59. The number of minutes in 15 days is equal to the number of seconds in:
A. 5 hours B. 6 hours
C. 8 hours D. 4 hours

60. 15 litres 286 millilitres of orange juice is mixed with 19 litres 714 millilitres of carrot juice. 12 litres 750 millilitres of the mixture is used and the rest is filled in bottles each containing 250 millilitres. The number of bottles is:
A. 85 B. 81
C. 77 D. 89

PART- III

Environmental Studies

***Directions :** Answer the following questions by selecting the **correct/most appropriate** options.*

61. Which of the following groups of animals has excellent sight and can see things four times more than humans?
A. Bees, Mosquitoes, Butterflies
B. Tigers, Leopards, Bulls
C. Snakes, Silkworms, Lizards
D. Kites, Eagles, Vultures

62. Read the given description of farming and identify its type:
"After cutting one crop, the land is left as it is for some years. Nothing is grown there. The bamboos or weeds which grow on that land are not pulled out. They are cut and burnt. The ash makes the land fertile. When the land is ready for farming it is lightly dug up, not ploughed. Seeds are dropped on it."
A. Irrigation farming
B. Cooperative farming
C. Jhoom farming
D. Step farming

63. When a snake charmer plays on his musical instrument *Been*, the snake swings its head to and fro to its sound. How do you think the snake responds to the musical instrument?
A. By seeing the movement of the instrument
B. By responding to the vibrations produced by the instrument
C. By smelling the instrument
D. By hearing the sound produced by the instrument

64. "A family is a unit consisting of mother, father and their two children." This statement is:
A. correct, because this is what all Indian families are like
B. incorrect, because the statement should specify that the children are biological

C. incorrect, because there are many kinds of families and one cannot classify family as being of only one kind
D. correct, since this is an ideal family size

65. The gastric juice in the stomach of human beings is ______ and aids in the digestion of food.
A. alkaline B. amphoteric
C. neutral D. acidic

66. A teacher of Class III had asked children to classify the leaves of the following trees/plants into different groups—lemon, mango, basil, mint, neem, banana, etc. Some students classified leaves as (*a*) leaves with medicinal values and leaves without medicinal values, (*b*) big leaves and small leaves. The teacher marked group (*a*) as right and group (*b*) as wrong.

Which of the following statements reflects the teacher's view of learning and assessment?
A. Classification task is very specific and structured and there is one right answer.
B. The activity is focussed to seek information from leaves which can be interpreted differently.
C. Children bring multiple perspectives in classroom which is to be appreciated.
D. Children can use multiple ways of classification depending upon their experiences.

67. Which among the following considerations would you keep in mind while designing a group activity in your EVS class?
1. Engage the interests of the children.
2. Appeal equally to boys and girls.
3. Use expensive material.
4. Appeal to children of all religious and cultural backgrounds.

A. 2 and 4 B. 2 and 3
C. 1, 2 and 4 D. 1, 3 and 4

68. All of the following statements provide arguments in favour of teachers and students to collectively engage in group activities in EVS, *except one*. Which is that statement?
A. Adult support can help children construct knowledge beyond their ability.
B. Children learn to collaborate and cooperate.
C. Children learn more by talking and discussing with other children.
D. Children show marked improvement in scores because of group activities.

69. Which of the following tools will be appropriate for assessing social-personal qualities of children engaged in learning EVS through group work?
A. Rating scales B. Assignments
C. Paper-pencil tests D. Oral questions

70. Following are some intuitive ideas of children about plants. Which of them is scientifically **correct**?
A. Grass is not a plant.
B. Some vegetables are fruits.
C. Seeds are not parts of a plant.
D. Carrot and cabbage are not plants.

71. A teacher of Class IV told her students—"Ask some old people if there were plants they had seen when they were young but are not seen these days."

Which of the following skills is **not** likely to be assessed by asking this question?
A. Experimentation B. Discussion
C. Questioning D. Expression

72. A teacher asks every child to use some waste material from their homes and make something useful out of it.

The pedagogical intention of the teacher is **not** to:
A. make children understand the concept of recycle, reuse and reduce
B. organize an exhibition of best articles made out of waste
C. judge the best student of the class
D. develop creativity among children

73. Read the following questions:
A. How well did I plan for the activity?
B. How well did I follow the plan?
C. What were my strengths?
D. What exactly did I find difficult?

Answers to the above four types of questions will comprise:
A. teachers' self-assessment
B. self-assessment of children and teachers both
C. summative assessment by the teacher
D. children's self-assessment

74. The language used in an EVS textbook:
A. should be terse and difficult for children to comprehend
B. should be formalized with emphasis on definitions
C. should be technical and formal
D. should be related to everyday language of the child

75. A teacher gives pictures of different animals to his students and asks them to colour the animals that do not live in their houses. The objective of this activity is to develop:
1. creativity 2. observation
3. classification skill 4. data collection

Which of the above are **correct**?
A. 1, 2 and 4 B. 2, 3 and 4
C. 1, 3 and 4 D. 1, 2 and 3

76. In the EVS syllabus, structured around six themes, 'plants' and 'animals' have consciously been included in the theme : 'Family and Friends'. All of the following could be cited as reasons for this inclusion, **except one**. Which one is that?
A. To highlight how lives and livelihoods of some

communities are closely connected with specific animals or plants

B. To enable students to understand plants and animals from a science perspective

C. To help students to locate plants and animals in a social and cultural context

D. To highlight how humans share a close relationship with each other

77. The purpose of 'survey' in teaching-learning of EVS is:

1. to provide an opportunity to interact with community.
2. to make children sensitive to different people.
3. to provide an opportunity to collect information first-hand.
4. to use it as an opportunity for assessment.

Which of the above are **correct**?

A. 1, 2 and 4 B. 1, 3 and 4
C. 1, 2, 3 and 4 D. 1, 2 and 3

Directions (Q. Nos. 78 to 80) *are based on the following paragraph.*

Given are responses of 7-8 years old children after they have observed an experiment done by the teacher, in which water in a bowl is heated and it has evaporated:

"Water has disappeared."
"The bowl has absorbed the water."
"The fire drank the water."
"God drank the water."

78. What do these responses tell us about children and their thinking?

A. Children cannot make a good observation.
B. Children have alternate ideas about evaporation.
C. Children's responses are illogical.
D. Children's thinking is incorrect.

79. How should the teacher deal with these responses?

A. Initiate a discussion to revisit their ideas.
B. Tell the children that they are wrong.
C. Show the standard water cycle chart.
D. Give the definition of evaporation and ask the children to memorize it.

80. Which of the following is an example of a question assessing divergent thinking of children on the topic, 'evaporation'?

A. Draw and label water cycle.
B. Write five advantages of water cycle.
C. What will happen if there is no water cycle?
D. List the steps in sequence of water cycle.

81. Which of the following are the neighbouring states of Jammu & Kashmir?

A. Uttarakhand, Rajasthan
B. Himachal Pradesh, Uttarakhand
C. Himachal Pradesh, Punjab
D. Himachal Pradesh, Uttar Pradesh

82. Match each of the locations with correct description of common houses built in that area:

Locations	*Houses*
(*a*) Manali	1. Elevated houses made on bamboo pillars
(*b*) Rajasthan	2. Houses made of stones/ wood with slanting roofs
(*c*) Assam	3. Houseboats
(*d*) Ladakh	4. Mud houses having roofs made of thorny bushes
	5. Houses made of stones with wooden floor and wooden ceiling

Codes:

	(*a*)	(*b*)	(*c*)	(*d*)
A.	3	4	1	5
B.	4	1	2	3
C.	2	5	1	4
D.	2	4	1	5

83. The different patterns on the skin of animals are:

A. due to the hair on their skin
B. due to the weather conditions they live in
C. an indication of their physical strength
D. due to the reflected light

84. "People who have been living in the forest for at least 25 years have a right to the forestland and what is grown on it." This is mandated by:

A. the Land Acquisition Act, 1894
B. the Constitution (Scheduled Castes) Orders (Amendment) Bill, 2012
C. the Indian Forest Act, 1927
D. the Right to Forest Act, 2007

85. Which of the following is a set of diseases spread by mosquitoes?

A. Dengue, Malaria, Chikungunya
B. Typhoid, Cholera, Chikungunya
C. Malaria, HIV-AIDS, Dengue
D. HIV-AIDS, Cholera, Dengue

86. Pitcher plant (*Nepenthes*):

A. emits sounds of high pitch to attract insects
B. has mouth covered with tiny hooks
C. is not found in India
D. cleverly traps and eats frogs, insects and mice

87. Which of the following sets of eatables is rich in iron?

A. Cabbage, Okra, Jaggery
B. Amla, Spinach, Jaggery
C. Amla, Spinach, Potato
D. Amla, Potato, Tomato

88. Almost in every part of our country, chillies are added while cooking food. Chillies were brought to our country by the traders who came from:

A. Australia B. Uzbekistan
C. South America D. Afghanistan

89. Which of the following birds makes its nest among the thorns of a cactus plant?
A. Dove
B. Sunbird
C. Weaverbird
D. Robin bird

90. Read the following description of an animal and identify it:
"It looks like a bear but it is not. It spends almost 17 hours a day sleeping while hanging upside down on a tree branch. It eats the leaves of the same tree on which it lives. It lives for about 40 years."
A. Sloth
B. Langur
C. Chimpanzee
D. Panda

PART- IV

Language-I : Hindi

निर्देश (प्र.सं. 91 से 99) : *नीचे दिए गए गद्यांश को पढ़कर पूछे गए प्रश्नों के **सही/सबसे उपयुक्त** उत्तर वाले विकल्प को चुनिए।*

लघु उद्योग उन उद्योगों को कहा जाता है जिनके समारम्भ एवं आयोजन के लिए भारी-भरकम साधनों की आवश्यकता नहीं पड़ती। वे थोड़े-से स्थान पर, थोड़ी पूँजी और अल्प साधनों से ही आरम्भ किए जा सकते हैं। फिर भी उनसे सुनियोजित ढंग से अधिकाधिक लाभ प्राप्त करके देश की निर्धनता, गरीबी और विषमताओं से एक सीमा तक लड़ा जा सकता है। अपने आकार-प्रकार तथा साधनों की लघुता व अल्पता के कारण ही इस प्रकार के उद्योग-धंधों को कुटीर-उद्योग भी कहा जाता है। इस प्रकार के उद्योग-धंधे अपने घर में भी आरंभ किए जा सकते हैं और अपने सीमित साधनों का सदुपयोग करके आर्थिक लाभ कमाया जा सकता है और सुखी-समृद्ध बना जा सकता है। भारत जैसे देश के लिए तो इस प्रकार के लघु उद्योगों का महत्व और भी बढ़ जाता है क्योंकि यहाँ युवाओं की एक बहुत बड़ी संख्या बेरोजगार है। इसी कारण महात्मा गांधी ने मशीनीकरण का विरोध किया था। उनकी यह स्पष्ट धारणा थी कि लघु उद्योगों को प्रश्रय देने से लोग स्वावलम्बी बनेंगे, मजदूर-किसान फसलों की बुआई-कटाई से फुर्सत पाकर अपने खाली समय का सदुपयोग भी करेंगे। इस प्रकार आर्थिक समृद्धि तो बढ़ेगी ही, साथ ही लोगों को अपने घर के पास रोजगार मिल सकेगा।

91. उन उद्योगों को लघु उद्योग कहा जाता है :
A. जो कम साधनों से शुरू किए जा सकते हैं
B. जिन्हें निर्धन व्यक्ति आयोजित करते हैं
C. जिन्हें अल्प लाभ मिलता है
D. जो अल्प अवधि तक चलते हैं

92. 'मशीनीकरण' से तात्पर्य है :
A. मशीनों की अधिकाधिक खरीद
B. मशीनों का अधिकाधिक उपयोग
C. मशीनों का अधिकाधिक निर्माण
D. मशीनों की अधिकाधिक उपलब्धता

93. लघु उद्योगों को प्रश्रय देने के संदर्भ में गांधीजी की क्या धारणा थी?
A. समय का सदुपयोग किया जा सके
B. किसानों को बुआई-कटाई से फुर्सत मिल सके
C. मशीनीकरण का विरोध किया जा सके
D. लोगों को आर्थिक रूप से आत्मनिर्भर बनाया जा सके

94. भारत जैसे देश के लिए लघु उद्योग-धंधों का महत्त्व क्यों बढ़ जाता है?
A. क्योंकि यहाँ बहुत-से लोगों को काम की जरूरत है
B. क्योंकि यहाँ मशीनों की उपलब्धता बहुत कम है
C. क्योंकि यहाँ युवा वर्ग को मशीनों पर काम करना नहीं आता
D. क्योंकि यहाँ कम पूंजी वाले लोग अधिक संख्या में हैं

95. 'विषमता' का विपरीतार्थी है:
A. प्रतिकूलता
B. सामान्यतः
C. समानता
D. असमानता

96. 'समृद्ध' शब्द में भाव है:
A. धनी होने का
B. समर्थ होने का
C. रोजगार पाने का
D. खुशहाल होने का

97. 'अल्पता' शब्द है:
A. तद्भव
B. तत्सम
C. देशज
D. विदेशी

98. कौन-सा शब्द-युग्म शेष से भिन्न है?
A. दिन-रात
B. भारी-भरकम
C. पशु-पक्षी
D. माता-पिता

99. गद्यांश के अनुसार 'प्रश्रय' शब्द का भाव है:
A. संरक्षण देना
B. नियुक्ति करना
C. अनुमोदन करना
D. स्वीकृति देना

निर्देश (प्र.सं. 100 से 114) : *नीचे दिए गए प्रश्नों के **सही/सबसे उपयुक्त** उत्तर वाले विकल्प को चुनिए।*

100. पूरी पाठ्यचर्या में .... में भाषा की भूमिका को अनदेखा नहीं किया जा सकता।
A. आकलन-निर्माण
B. मूल्य-निर्धारण
C. ज्ञान-निर्माण
D. व्याकरण-निर्माण

101. प्राथमिक कक्षाओं के भाषा-शिक्षक होने के नाते आपकी सर्वाधिक महत्वपूर्ण भूमिका है:
A. कक्षा में पाठ्य-पुस्तक का सही तरह से निर्वाह करना

B. बच्चों की भाषाई क्षमता के विकास के लिए तरह-तरह के अवसर जुटाना
C. बच्चों को वाद-विवाद के लिए तैयार करना
D. विद्यार्थियों को सर्वाधिक अंक प्राप्त करने के लिए तैयार करना

102. दूसरी कक्षा में पढ़ने वाला रोहित हिन्दी की कक्षा में अपनी मातृभाषा में बात करता है। आप क्या करेंगे?
A. उसे बिल्कुल अनदेखा कर पढ़ाते रहेंगे
B. उसकी भाषा को समझने की कोशिश करेंगे
C. बाकी बच्चों से उसकी भाषा सीखने के लिए कहेंगे
D. उसे डाँटेंगे कि वह कक्षा में मातृभाषा का प्रयोग न करे।

103. 'पढ़ना सीखने के लिए कौन-सा उपकौशल अनिवार्य नहीं है?
A. भाषा की संरचना की समझ
B. भावनात्मक संबंध
C. वर्णमाला याद करने का कौशल
D. अनुमान लगाने का कौशल

104. द्विभाषिक बच्चे .... विकास, सामाजिक सहिष्णुता और .... चिंतन में अपेक्षाकृत बेहतर होते हैं।
A. संक्रियात्मक, केंद्रित B. संज्ञानात्मक, सीमित
C. संज्ञानात्मक, विस्तृत D. संक्रियात्मक, सीमित

105. निम्नलिखित में से किसके अभाव में हम पढ़ नहीं सकते?
A. संयुक्ताक्षरों की पहचान
B. लिपि से परिचय
C. बारहखड़ी से परिचय
D. वर्णमाला की क्रमबद्धता का ज्ञान

106. भाषा और विचार के संबंधों की चर्चा में अग्रणी हैं:
A. वाइगोत्स्की B. पियाजे
C. स्किनर D. चॉम्स्की

107. सिद्धार्थ की माँ ने अपने परिवार के सदस्यों से अनुरोध किया है कि वे घर में एक ही भाषा का प्रयोग करें जिससे कि सिद्धार्थ का भाषाई विकास ठीक से हो सके। उनके बारे में आप क्या कहेंगे?
A. वह भाषा-अर्जन के सिद्धांतों की गहरी समझ रखती हैं।
B. वह सिद्धार्थ को समृद्ध भाषिक परिवेश से वंचित कर रही हैं।
C. वह सिद्धार्थ के भाषिक परिवेश में किसी प्रकार का अवरोध नहीं चाहती।
D. वह सिद्धार्थ के भाषाई विकास के लिए विशेष प्रयत्न कर रही हैं।

108. प्राथमिक स्तर पर भाषा-शिक्षण के संदर्भ में सर्वाधिक महत्वपूर्ण है कि बच्चे:
A. शब्दों को जोड़-जोड़कर वाक्य पढ़ सकें
B. लिखी/छपी सामग्री का अर्थ समझ सकें
C. लिखी/छपी सामग्री को बोल-बोलकर पढ़ सकें
D. अक्षरों को जोड़-जोड़कर पढ़ सकें

109. प्राथमिक स्तर पर लेखन क्षमता के संदर्भ में सर्वाधिक महत्त्वपूर्ण है:
A. सुलेख B. वर्तनी
C. मौलिक विचार D. श्रुतलेख

110. निम्नलिखित में से कौन-सी गतिविधि श्रवण एवं वाचन कौशलों के विकास के लिए सर्वाधिक उपयुक्त होगी?
A. प्रश्नोत्तर सत्र आयोजित करना
B. रेडियो समाचार सुनना
C. कहानी सुनाकर उस पर बच्चों की प्रतिक्रिया जानना
D. हावभाव के साथ कविता बुलवाना

111. वाणी .... होती है और लिखित भाषा की तुलना में काफी तेजी से बदलती रहती है।
A. स्थायी B. गौण
C. स्थिर D. अस्थायी

112. 'बहुभाषी-कक्षा' से तात्पर्य है :
A. जिस कक्षा के शिक्षक/शिक्षिका दो या दो से अधिक भाषाएँ पढ़-लिख सकते हों
B. जिस कक्षा में कम-से-कम दो भाषाओं में पाठ्य-पुस्तक उपलब्ध हो
C. जिस कक्षा में प्रत्येक बच्चे के घर की बोली को सम्मान दिया जाता हो
D. जहाँ बहुत-सी भाषाओं का अध्यापन किया जाता है

113. संज्ञान के स्तर पर विकसित .... अन्य भाषाओं में आसानी से अनूदित होती रहती है।
A. भाषा क्षमता B. ज्ञान क्षमता
C. व्याकरण क्षमता D. तर्क क्षमता

114. भाषा-शिक्षण को .... संदर्भ में रखकर देखने की आवश्यकता है।
A. बहुभाषी B. आर्थिक
C. सांस्कृतिक D. नैतिक

निर्देश (प्र.सं. 115 से 120) : *नीचे दिए गए पद्यांश को पढ़कर प्रश्नों के **सही/सबसे उपयुक्त** उत्तर वाले विकल्प को चुनिए।*

हवा चले अनुकूल तो नावें नौसिखिए भी खे लेते हैं,
सहज डगर पर लँगड़े भी चल बैसाखी से लेते हैं।
मिट जाते जो दीप स्वयं रोशन कर लाख चिरागों को
नमन उन्हें है, जो लौटा लाते हैं गई बहारों को।

फैलाकर के हाथ किसी के सम्मुख झुकना आसाँ है,
बहती नदिया से पानी पी प्यास बुझाना आसाँ है,
नित्य खोदकर नए कुएँ जो सबकी प्यास बुझाते हैं,
वही लोग हैं जो सदियों तक जग में पूजे जाते हैं।

115. कवि उन्हें नमन कर रहा है जो:
A. सरल मार्गों पर चलते हैं
B. दूसरों को प्रेरणा देकर मरते हैं

C. लाखों दीपक जलाते हैं
D. लहरों पर नाव चला लेते हैं

116. कविता में 'बैसाखी' का भावार्थ है:
A. एक फसल B. एक महीना
C. सहारा D. सीढ़ी

117. 'पानी पी प्यास बुझाना आसाँ है'—में अलंकार है:
A. रूपक B. अनुप्रास
C. मानवीकरण D. उपमा

118. समाज उन्हें सदा सम्मानित करता है, जो:
A. नित्य नए कुएँ खोदते हैं
B. प्यासे को पानी पिलाते हैं
C. अपने कामों से सबका हित करते हैं
D. सदियों तक पूजे जाते हैं

119. कवि के अनुसार उनका जीवन आसान नहीं है, जो:
A. स्वयं अपने ही लिए साधन जुटाते हैं
B. लोगों के सामने हाथ फैलाते हैं
C. बैसाखी के सहारे चलते हैं
D. परिश्रम से बीती बहारों को लौटा लाते हैं

120. 'नौसिखिया' है:
A. नया सीखने वाला B. नौ विषय जानने वाला
C. नए विषय पढ़ने वाला D. नया सिखाने वाला

PART- V

Language-II : English

Directions (Qs. 121-128) : *Answer the following questions by selecting the* ***correct/most appropriate*** *options.*

The art of Madhubani painting is the traditional style developed in the Mithila region, in the villages around Madhubani, Bihar. Madhubani literally means a forest of honey. This style of painting has been traditionally used by the women of the region, though today men are also involved to meet the demand. The work is done on freshly plastered mud walls. For commercial purposes, it is now being done on paper, cloth, etc.

The paintings are basically of religious nature. They are done in the special rooms of their homes (in the Pooja room, ritual. area, bridal room), on the main village walls, etc., for ceremonial or ritualistic purposes. The women offer prayers to the deity before starting the work. Figures from nature and mythology are adapted to suit their style. The themes and designs widely painted are the worship of Hindu deities such as Krishna, Rama, Shiva, Durga, Lakshmi, Saraswati, Sun and Moon, Tulsi plant, court scenes, wedding scenes and other social events taking place around them.

Floral, animal and bird motifs, geometrical designs are used to fill up all the gaps. There is hardly any empty space in this style. Cotton wrapped around a bamboo stick forms the brush. The colours applied are prepared by the artists. The skill is handed down the generations, and hence the traditional designs and patterns are widely maintained. It is believed that the genesis of Madhubani paintings came about when King Janaka asked for paintings to be developed for his daughter Sita's wedding.

121. Madhubani paintings are no longer done exclusively by women on walls:
A. as men are better painters
B. as paper is cheaper
C. because cloth is more durable
D. to meet their widespread demand

122. Madhubani paintings are essentially of religious nature when they are done:
A. on the village walls
B. using figures from nature
C. in the Pooja room
D. in the bridal room

123. These paintings become secular when they depict:
A. Tulsi plant
B. wedding scenes
C. court scenes
D. worship of Saraswati

124. A Madhubani painting shows only:
A. flowers and plants
B. geometrical designs
C. a balanced portrayal of all of them
D. Hindu deities

125. The art of Madhubani painting is learnt in the:
A. families at home
B. homes of renowned artists
C. Ashrams of Madhubani
D. schools of art

126. 'Floral' is an adjective derived from the noun, 'flower'. Aural is derived from the noun :
A. ear B. eye
C. mouth D. morning

127. ".... on freshly plastered mud walls."
The word '<u>plastered</u>' is a/an:

A. infinitive B. participle
C. particle D. gerund

128. The word 'genesis' means the same as:
A. original B. spirit
C. growth D. birth

Directions (Qs. 129-143) : *Answer the following questions by selecting the* ***correct/most appropriate*** *options.*

129. Language is not:
A. symbolic B. instinctive
C. social D. arbitrary

130. When language development is a deliberate and conscious effort, language is:
A. acquired B. honed
C. brushed up D. learned

131. What is a 'task' in task-based language learning?
A. A piece of work which exposes learners to language
B. A piece of work which enables learners to do an activity
C. A piece of work for the parents to do their children's homework
D. A piece of activity for teachers to do in the classroom

132. Travelogue is a genre of:
A. poetry B. criticism
C. bibliography D. literature

133. The most important aspect of an effective language classroom is to provide learners with an opportunity to:
A. imitate B. interact
C. interfere D. assess

134. A teacher of Class V is practising 'interactive listening' in the class. She should focus on:
A. listening and responding
B. listening and observing speakers' attitude
C. listening to word stress and intonation
D. listening to the pronunciation

135. A word with same spelling and same pronunciation as another, but with a different meaning is a/an:
A. synonym B. homonym
C. homophone D. antonym

136. A shorter form of a group of words, which usually occurs in an auxiliary verb, is:
A. conjunction
B. connotation
C. connector
D. contraction

137. Aditi, a visually challenged child in Class IV, does not have any text in braille. How can a teacher facilitate her in reading the English textbook?
A. She may ask the principal to arrange a special teacher for her.
B. She may arrange and give the audio CD of the textbook to the child.
C. Instead of focussing on this single child, she may use her energy in teaching the remaining class.
D. She may ask her parents to look after their child.

138. Poetry teaching is generally meant for:
A. language learning
B. learning grammar
C. learning punctuation
D. enjoyment and appreciation

139. Reading English as a second language means:
A. decoding of letters and words
B. reading aloud
C. reading for grammar
D. meaning making

140. When learners give feedback on each other's language, work, learning strategies, performance, etc., it is called:
A. peer assessment
B. formal assessment
C. group assessment
D. self-assessment

141. A teacher after completing a chapter asks the students some questions to review their learning and check their understanding. The questions she is asking will be based on:
A. middle-order thinking skills
B. lower-order thinking skills
C. hyper-order thinking skills
D. higher-order thinking skills

142. A good teaching-learning material (TLM) can best:
A. facilitate the teaching-learning process
B. be a source of entertainment
C. help the teacher to transact material without any modification
D. help the learners acquire a language

143. While providing feedback to the parents, a teacher should **not**:
A. compare the current performance of the child with her previous performance
B. give qualitative feedback about the child
C. share the incidents recorded in the anecdotes
D. compare their child with other children

Directions (Qs. 144-150) : *Answer the following questions by selecting the* ***correct/most appropriate*** *options.*

A remarkable feature of Edison's inventions was their basic simplicity. There were innumerable scientists possessing deep knowledge of electricity, chemistry, etc., but it was this unschooled genius who succeeded where they failed. What were his unique qualities? Firstly, he had an uncanny ability to judge the practical use of any scientific fact. Secondly, he was blessed with patience and perseverance. He would try out countless ideas till he found the right one. Third was his business acumen, which enabled him to earn the large sums of money necessary to conduct experimental work.

Edison's enthusiasm for work and optimistic attitude ensured a long and productive life. Only after crossing the age of seventy-five did he start slowing down. During his final illness, his curiosity about his condition, medicines, and treatment, made the doctors think that possibly he was taking this too as one of his scientific investigations! He passed away on 18 October, 1931, at the ripe old age of eighty-four.

During his lifetime itself Edison became one of the most famous men in the world. Honours were showered on him. Among them was the congressional gold medal in 1928 for his contributions to human welfare. In 1960, he was posthumously elected to the Hall of Fame for Great Americans at New York University. But the tribute that was most eloquent was quite unintended. The authorities contemplated switching off the power supply in New York, the scene of his triumph in 1882, for two minutes as a mark of respect on his death. But 1931 was not 1882. Since normal life would have come to a standstill by the two-minute power cutoff, the idea was given up. There could be no greater tribute to the man than this negative tribute!

144. The most remarkable feature of Edison's inventions was their:
A. multiple usefulness
B. low cost
C. aesthetic aspect
D. fundamental simplicity

145. According to the author, Edison became prosperous because he:
A. made the best use of his time
B. had great business sense
C. had luck on his side
D. worked very hard

146. To conduct experimental work, Edison needed:
A. huge amounts of money
B. calm and quiet atmosphere
C. sophisticated gadgets
D. support of generous patrons

147. Edison's long and productive life can be attributed to:
A. his involvement in charitable work
B. his positive attitude
C. his immensely good health
D. a large circle of friends

148. The word 'uncanny' as used in the passage means:
A. terrific
B. astonishing
C. weird
D. great

149. The opposite of 'famous' is:
A. unknown
B. negligible
C. unnoticeable
D. unpopular

150. Which part of speech is the underlined word?
"... any scientific fact."
A. Adjective B. Adverb
C. Preposition D. Noun

Answers

1	2	3	4	5	6	7	8	9	10
A	C	B	D	A	D	B	C	A	D
11	**12**	**13**	**14**	**15**	**16**	**17**	**18**	**19**	**20**
B	C	A	C	D	C	A	C	C	D
21	**22**	**23**	**24**	**25**	**26**	**27**	**28**	**29**	**30**
A	B	B	C	A	D	A	C	B	D
31	**32**	**33**	**34**	**35**	**36**	**37**	**38**	**39**	**40**
A	B	B	A	D	A	D	A	C	A
41	**42**	**43**	**44**	**45**	**46**	**47**	**48**	**49**	**50**
D	A	B	D	D	A	C	A	B	C
51	**52**	**53**	**54**	**55**	**56**	**57**	**58**	**59**	**60**
B	B	C	B	D	A	A	B	B	D
61	**62**	**63**	**64**	**65**	**66**	**67**	**68**	**69**	**70**
D	C	B	C	D	A	C	A	A	B
71	**72**	**73**	**74**	**75**	**76**	**77**	**78**	**79**	**80**
A	C	B	D	D	B	C	B	A	C

81	82	83	84	85	86	87	88	89	90
C	D	A	D	A	D	B	C	A	A
91	92	93	94	95	96	97	98	99	100
A	B	D	A	C	A	B	B	A	B
101	102	103	104	105	106	107	108	109	110
B	B	C	C	D	A	C	B	C	C
111	112	113	114	115	116	117	118	119	120
C	C	A	A	B	C	B	C	D	A
121	122	123	124	125	126	127	128	129	130
D	C	C	C	A	A	B	D	B	D
131	132	133	134	135	136	137	138	139	140
A	D	B	A	B	D	B	D	D	A
141	142	143	144	145	146	147	148	149	150
B	A	D	D	B	A	B	C	A	A

Explanatory Answers

3. Assessment is an integral part of teaching and learning. Purposeful assessment practices help teachers and students understand where they have been, where they are, and where they might go next. Using different types of assessments as part of instruction results in useful information about student understanding and progress. Educators should use this information to guide their own practice and in partnership with students and their families to reflect on learning and set future goals.

4. National Curriculum Framework for School Education 2000, confidently proclaims that, "As opposed to the epistemic model of the children which does not provide a great scope for their social experiences, the constructivist movement has re-emphasised the active role children play in acquiring knowledge. .... In the constructivist setting, the learners have autonomy for their own learning, opportunities for peer collaboration and support, occasions for learner generated problems that drive the curriculum, time for self-observation and evaluation and outlets for reflection. .... This perspective recognizes the teacher as primarily a facilitator of learning. Rather than dictating what should be done, the facilitative teacher tends to act as a guide, providing resources for learners and enabling them to decide how to learn and why to learn. The constructivist teacher follows no rigid prescriptions for successful teaching, acts as a facilitator of meaning-making rather than leader of all learning. "This knowledge acquisition is a constructive or generative process and each student's knowledge is personal and unique."

6. Inclusion in education is an approach to educating students with special educational needs. Under the inclusion model, students with special needs spend most or all of their time with non-special needs students. Inclusion rejects the use of special schools or classrooms to separate students with disabilities from students without disabilities.

Inclusion is about the child's right to participate and the school's duty to accept the child returning. Inclusion rejects the use of special schools or classrooms, which remain popular among large multi-service providers, to separate students with disabilities from students without disabilities. A premium is placed upon full participation by students with disabilities, in contrast to earlier concept of partial participation in the mainstream, and upon respect for their social, civil, and educational rights. Inclusion gives students with disabilities skills they can use in and out of the classroom.

8. Most hearing-impaired students can lip-read to some extent, but try to determine how well. To help your hearing-impaired students lip-read, make sure to face them when you talk, talk slowly and clearly, and do not yell. As long as they have their amplifiers on, you can speak in a normal tone. Consider arranging chairs in your classroom in a circle so your hearing-impaired students can interact with classmates.

9. The intellectual, emotional, and physical development of gifted and talented students is often uneven. This 'asynchronous' development means that their experiences are measurably different from those of their peers, which may lead to feelings of not fitting in. These feelings can become particularly acute in early adolescence, and gifted and talented students may mask their abilities in order to gain acceptance. He can feel understimulated and bored if the class activities are not challenging enough.

10. A teacher can enhance effective learning in the elementary classroom by connecting the content to the lives of the students.

13. Primary school children will learn most effectively in an atmosphere where their emotional needs are met and they feel that they are valued.

15. Educational psychology has identified two basic classifications of motivation - intrinsic and extrinsic. Intrinsic motivation arises from a desire to learn a topic due to its inherent interests, for self-fulfillment, enjoyment and to achieve a mastery of the subject. On the other hand, extrinsic motivation is motivation to perform and succeed for the sake of accomplishing a specific result or outcome. Students who are very grade-oriented are extrinsically motivated, whereas students who seem to truly embrace their work and take a genuine interest in it are intrinsically motivated.

16. Students who read for the sheer enjoyment of reading are intrinsically motivated. They are not reading for the external rewards sometimes offered by teachers, such as toys, food, candy, or grades. These students also choose to read during their free time both in and out of school, initiating reading without promises of either reward or punishment. Teachers can implement practices in the classroom that either support or undermine student intrinsic motivation.

A teacher can encourage her students to be intrinsically motivated towards learning for the sake of learning by supporting them in setting individual goals and their mastery.

17. Intrinsic Motivation has a number of definitions. Kohn defined intrinsic motivation as "enjoying what one does for its own sake". Intrinsically motivated people tend to "pursue optimal challenges, display greater innovativeness, and ... perform better under challenging conditions". When people are intrinsically motivated they feel interest and enjoyment in what they are doing. They also feel a sense of capability and determination. What they don't feel is tension, stress, and anxiety

18. Individualized learning means instruction is paced to the learning needs of different learners. Learning goals are the same for all students, but students can progress through the material at different speeds according to their learning needs. Individualized learning is an example of effective school practice.

19. The cephalocaudal principle states that growth follows a direction and pattern that begins with the head and upper body parts and then proceeds to the rest of the body. The word *cephalocaudal* is derived from Greek and Latin roots meaning "head-to-tail". The cephalocaudal growth principle means that we develop visual abilities well before we master the ability to walk. The cephalocaudal principle operates both presentally and after birth.

20. A sensitive period is a time that is best for certain capacities to develop because the individual is especially responsive to environmental influences. However, its boundaries are less well defined than those of a critical period.

Research indicates the existence of critical periods or sensitive periods in the various areas of development. The concept of sensitive period is more applicable to language development and social and emotional development. Earlier, it was thought that the early years were a critical period for language development *i.e* the child was biologically ready at this time to acquire language skills. It was essential to give language exposure to a child if language was to be developed properly.

22. Secondary socialization involves learning what is considered as fitting behaviour as a member of a particular group within society. In schools, apart from acquiring knowledge and skills, children learn how to follow instructions and obey those in authority. Individuals also learn about social skills from their peers. Mass media, such as Internet, television and radio, expose people to information that shape their behaviour.

23. The work of Lev Vygotsky has become the foundation of much research and theory in cognitive development over the past several decades, particularly of what has become known as Social Development Theory.

Vygotsky's theories stress the fundamental role of social interaction in the development of cognition as he believed strongly that community plays a central role in the process of "making meaning."

Unlike Piaget's notion that childrens' development must necessarily precede their learning, Vygotsky argued, "learning is a necessary and universal aspect of the process of developing culturally organized, specifically human psychological function". In other words, social learning tends to precede (*i.e* come before) development.

Vygotsky has developed a socio-cultural approach to cognitive development.

25. Piaget's research and theory, is called developmental constructivism, and maintains that children acquire number concepts and operations by construction from the inside and not by internalization. Piaget pointed out that every normal student is capable of good mathematical reasoning if attention is directed to activities of his interest, and if by this method the emotional inhibitions that too often give him a feeling of inferiority in lessons in mathematics are removed.

26. According to Piaget, two major principles guide intellectual growth and biological development: adaptation and organization. For individuals to survive in an environment, they must adapt to physical and mental stimuli. Assimilation and accommodation are both part of the adaptation process. Piaget believed that human beings possess mental structures that assimilate external events, and convert them to fit their mental structures. Moreover, mental structures accommodate themselves to new, unusual, and constantly changing aspects of the external environment.

Piaget's second principle, organization, refers to the nature of these adaptive mental structures. He suggests that the mind is organized in complex and integrated ways. The simplest level is the schema, a mental representation of some physical or mental action that can be performed on an object, event, or phenomenon.

28. Gardner's Multiple Intelligences Theory

Gardner's general recommendation for applying MI theory in the classroom is essentially the same as Sternberg's. He believes that teachers should use MI theory as a framework for devising alternative ways to teach subject matter. Some children learn a subject best when it is presented in a particular format or emphasizes a particular type of ability, whereas other children learn well when the subject is taught under different conditions.

30. Gender and sexuality are not just personal identities; they are social identities. They arise from our relationships to other people, and they depend upon social interaction and social recognition. As such, they influence how we understand ourselves in relation to others.

In sociology, we make a distinction between sex and gender. Sex are the biological traits that societies use to assign people into the category of either male or female, whether it be through a focus on chromosomes, genitalia or some other physical ascription. When people talk about the differences between men and women they are often drawing on sex - on rigid ideas of biology - rather than gender, which is an understanding of how society shapes our understanding of those biological categories.

31. Cost of water melon $= \frac{9}{2} \times 18.50 = ₹\ 83.25$

Cost of cherry $= \frac{6}{5} \times 72 = ₹\ 86.40$

Cost of grapes $= \frac{1}{4} \times 120.60 = ₹\ 30.15$

Cost of apples $= \frac{7}{4} \times 78.40 = ₹\ 137.20$

Total Cost $= ₹\ 83.25 + ₹\ 86.40 + ₹\ 30.15 + ₹\ 137.20$

$= ₹\ 337.00$

She got back $= 500 - 337 = ₹\ 163$

32. The maximum number of soap cakes packed in to two boxes

$$= \frac{2 \times 56 \times 40 \times 25 \times 10}{7 \times 5 \times 25}$$

$$= 2 \times 8 \times 40 \times 2 = 1280$$

33. Let side of square $= x$ cm

Perimeter of square $= 4x$ cm

$4x = 72$

$\Rightarrow$ $x = 18$ cm

$\therefore$ Side of square $= 18$ cm

$\therefore$ Breadth of rectangle $= 9$ cm

Length of rectangle $= 9 \times 3$ cm $= 27$ cm

Perimeter of rectangle $= 2(l + b)$

$= 2(27 + 9) = 2 \times 36 = 72$ cm

Hence, the perimeter of both rectangle and square are equal.

34. 55 ltrs 55 mililitres = 55.055 litres

Hence, 55 litres 55 mililitres $\neq$ 55.55 litres

50. Place value of 5 in 29503 = 500

and face value of 7 in 32071 = 7

Required difference $= 500 - 7 = 493$

51. $30028 - 28028 = 2000 = 200$ tens

52. When 80808 is divided by 108, then remainder = 24

When 90909 is divided by 109, then remainder = 3

Now, $24 \div 3 = 8$

Hence, required quotient = 8

53. $603 \times 28 = 63 \times 4 \times x$

$$\therefore\ x = \frac{603 \times 28}{63 \times 4} = 67$$

Hence, the number in the blank space is 67.

54. L.C.M. of 30, 45, 60 = 180

$180 \times 1 = 180$

$180 \times 2 = 360$

$15 = 3 \times 5$

$24 = 3 \times 2 \times 2 \times 2$

$45 = 3 \times 3 \times 5$

$360 \div 3 = 120$

55. $\because$ The number lies between 40 and 50

sum of digits = 7

$\therefore$ The number = 43

(one's digit 1 less than tens digit)

Hence, the product of the digits = $4 \times 3 = 12$

56. Number of girls = $\frac{2}{3} \times 360 = 240$

$\therefore$ Number of boys = $360 - 240 = 120$

No. of players = $\frac{3}{4} \times 120 = 90$

Hence, no. of boys who are not players = $120 - 90 = 30$

57. Remaining amount = ₹ 49,553 – ₹ 8076 = ₹ 41,477

Amount of each instalment = $\frac{41477}{37}$ = ₹ 1,121

58. The duration of the journey

= 1:15 pm to 1:15 am = 12 hrs

+ 7:30 am – 1:15 am = 6 hrs 15 min

= 12 hrs + 6 hrs 15 minutes

= 18 hrs 15 minutes

59. $24 \times 15 = 360$ hrs $= 360 \times 60$ minutes

6 hrs $= 6 \times 60 \times 60$ seconds

60. 15*l* 286 ml + 19 *l* 714 ml = 35.000 *l*

35.000 *l* – 19 *l* 714 ml = 22.250 *l*

No. of bottles = $\frac{22250}{250} = 89$

Previous Paper (Solved)

CTET PAPER-I, FEBRUARY 2016*

PART- I

Child Development and Pedagogy

Directions: *Answer the following questions by selecting the* ***correct/most appropriate*** *options.*

1. Most classrooms in India are multilingual and this needs to be seen as _______ by the teacher.
A. a problem B. a resource
C. an obstacle D. a bother

2. Mistakes and errors made by students
A. are indicative of the failure of the teacher and the students
B. should be seen as opportunities to understand their thinking
C. should be severely dealt with
D. are a wonderful opportunity to label children as 'weak' or 'outstanding'

3. __________ views children as active builders of knowledge and little scientists who construct their own theories of the world.
A. Pavlov B. Jung
C. Piaget D. Skinner

4. Child-centred pedagogy means
A. asking the children to follow and imitate the teacher
B. giving primacy to children's voices and their active participation
C. letting the children be totally free
D. giving moral education to the children

5. A teacher can help the children to process a complex situation by
A. not offering any help at all so that children learn to help on their own
B. giving a lecture on it
C. breaking the task into smaller parts and writing down instructions
D. encouraging competition and offering a high reward to the child who completes the task first

6. Expecting students to reproduce knowledge in the same way as it is received
A. is an effective assessment strategy
B. is problematic, because individuals interpret experiences and do not reproduce knowledge as it is received
C. is good, since we record everything as it is in our brains
D. is good, since it is easy for the teacher to assess

7. When students are given an opportunity to discuss a problem in groups, their learning curve
A. remains stable B. declines
C. remains the same D. becomes better

8. The pace of development varies from one individual to another, but it follows _______ pattern.
A. a haphazard
B. an unpredictable
C. a sequential and orderly
D. a toe-to-head

9. Which one of the following is correct about development?
A. 'Sociocultural context' plays an important role in development
B. Development is unidimensional
C. Development is discrete
D. Development begins and ends at birth

10. Why do individuals differ from one another?
A. Due to the inborn characteristics
B. Due to the interplay between heredity and environment
C. Because each individual has received a different gene set from his/her parents
D. Because of the impact of the environment

11. Family plays _______ role in socialization of the child.
A. an exciting B. a primary
C. a secondary D. a not-so-important

12. Which one of the following is a correctly matched pair?
A. Formal operational child—Imitation begins, imaginary play
B. Infancy—Applies logic and is able to infer
C. Pre-operational child—Deductive thought
D. Concrete operational child — Is able to conserve and classify

*Exam was held on 21-02-2016.

13. A child says, "Clothes dry faster in the sun." She is showing an understanding of
A. egocentric thinking B. cause and effect
C. reversible thinking D. symbolic thought

14. According to Piaget, children's thinking differs in ________ from adults than in ________.
A. size; correctness
B. kind; amount
C. size; type
D. amount; kind

15. Which one of the following is an example of scaffolding?
A. Giving motivational lectures to students
B. Offering explanations without encouraging questioning
C. Offering both material and non-material rewards
D. Giving prompts and cues, and asking questions at critical junctures

16. According to Vygotsky, children learn
A. by maturation
B. by imitation
C. by interacting with adults and peers
D. when reinforcement is offered

17. Kohlberg has given
A. the stages of physical development
B. the stages of emotional development
C. the stages of moral development
D. the stages of cognitive development

18. Which one of the following situations is illustrative of a child-centred classroom?
A. A class in which the textbook is the only resource the teacher refers to
B. A class in which the students are sitting in groups and the teacher takes turns to go to each group
C. A class in which the behaviour of students is governed by the rewards and punishments the teacher would give them
D. A class in which the teacher dictates and the students are asked to memorize the notes

19. Intelligence is
A. a singular and generic concept
B. the ability to imitate others
C. a specific ability
D. a set of capabilities

20. Early childhood is ________ period for language development.
A. an unimportant B. a sensitive
C. a neutral D. a not-so-significant

21. A teacher remarks in a co-education class to boys, "Be boys and don't behave like girls." This remark
A. is a good example of dealing with boys and girls
B. reflects stereotypical behaviour of discrimination between boys and girls
C. highlights the biological superiority of boys over girls
D. reflects caste discrimination

22. Assessment
A. should actively promote competitive spirit among children
B. should generate tension and stress to ensure learning
C. is a way to improve learning
D. is a good strategy to label and categorize children

23. Which one of the following statements best describes 'Inclusion'?
A. It is the belief that some children cannot learn at all.
B. It is the philosophy that all children have a right to get equal education in a regular school system.
C. It is the philosophy that special children are 'a special gift of God'.
D. It is the belief that children need to be segregated according to their abilities.

24. To cater to the children from 'disadvantaged' background, a teacher should
A. try to find out more about them and involve them in class discussions
B. make them sit separately in the class
C. ignore them as they cannot interact with other students
D. give them a lot of written work

25. Which one of the following behaviours is an identifier of a child with learning disability?
A. Abusive behaviour
B. Writing 'b' as 'd', 'was' as 'saw', '21' as 12'
C. Low attention span and high physical activity
D. Frequent mood swings

26. A child who can see partially
A. should not be given education, since it is not of any use to him
B. needs to be put in a separate institution
C. should be put in a 'regular' school while making special provisions
D. should be put in a 'regular' school with no special provisions

27. Learning
A. has very little connection with emotions
B. is independent of a learner's emotions
C. is influenced by a learner's emotions
D. is not affected by a learner's emotions

28. To enable students to make conceptual changes in their thinking, a teacher should
A. discourage children from thinking on their own and ask them to just listen to her and follow that
B. offer an explanation in a lecture mode
C. make clear and convincing explanations and have discussions with the students
D. offer rewards for children who change their thinking

29. In the context of a primary school classroom, what does active engagement mean?
A. Imitating and Copying the teacher
B. Enquiry, Questioning and Debate
C. Copying answers given by the teacher
D. Memorizing, Recall and Reciting

30. Children are most creative when they participate in an activity
A. under stress to do well in front of others
B. out of interest
C. for rewards
D. to escape their teacher's scolding

PART- II

Mathematics

Directions: *Answer the following questions by selecting the correct/most appropriate options.*

31. According to the NCF, 2005, which one of the following is **not** a major aim of Mathematics education in primary schools?
A. To relate Mathematics to the child's context
B. To enhance problem-solving skills
C. To prepare for higher education in Mathematics
D. To mathematize the child's thought process

32. Which one of the following should be the most important feature of Mathematics textbooks at primary level?
A. Concepts should be presented from complex to simple
B. Concepts should be presented in a strict hierarchical manner
C. Concepts should be presented from concrete to abstract
D. Concepts should be linked to higher classes

33. Which one of the following represents the correct sequence of development of geometrical understanding?
A. Visualization, analysis, informal deduction, formal deduction
B. Formal deduction, informal deduction, visualization, analysis
C. Visualization, analysis, formal deduction, informal deduction
D. Visualization, formal deduction, analysis, informal deduction

34. Which one of the following statements is true?
A. Zero should be introduced at the time of teaching place value.
B. Zero should be the first numeral to be taught.
C. Zero should be introduced after children develop number sense.
D. Zero should be introduced after number 9.

35. A teacher plans the following activities to introduce the concept of 'half' to Class III students:
(*a*) Shows pictures representing 'half'
(*b*) Writes symbol for 'half'
(*c*) Divides many types of concrete materials into 'halves'
(*d*) Uses story or words to represent 'half'

Which one of the following is the correct sequence of the activities that the teacher needs to follow?
A. (*c*), (*d*), (*a*), (*b*)
B. (*a*), (*b*), (*c*), (*d*)
C. (*b*), (*a*), (*c*), (*d*)
D. (*c*), (*a*), (*d*), (*b*)

36. Which one of the following is true about teaching and learning of Mathematics in Class I and II?
A. Only oral Mathematics problems should be done in Class I and II.
B. Mathematics should be integrated with other subjects like language, art, etc.
C. Mathematics should not be taught in Class I and II.
D. Lots of opportunities for practice should be provided.

37. If $1001 \times 111 = 110000 + 11 \times$ ____ , then the number in the blank space is:
A. 211
B. 101
C. 111
D. 121

38. If (the place value of 5 in 15201) + (the place value of 6 in 2659) = 7 × ______, then the number in the blank space is
A. 900
B. 80
C. 800
D. 90

39. If (the product of the common positive factors of 36 and 48) = 999 + 9 ×_______ , then the number which will come in the blank space is
A. 90
B. 9
C. 27
D. 81

40. If the difference of remainders, obtained on dividing 26679 by 39 and 29405 by 34, is divided by 18, then the remainder will be:
A. 9
B. 3
C. 5
D. 8

41. (The smallest common multiple of 36, 54 and 60) ÷ 90 is equal to:
A. 12
B. 5
C. 6
D. 10

42. Sonu has five dozen toffees. He gave 1/3 of these to Amita, 2/5 of these to Anil and 1/12 of these to Hamida. The number of toffees left with Sonu is:

A. 11 B. 5
C. 7 D. 9

43. If 112 ones + 12 thousands = 11012 + _____ tens, then the number in the blank space is

A. 112 B. 101
C. 110 D. 111

44. 51 litre and 750 millilitre of milk is filled in 23 bottles, each of the same size. The quantity of milk in 16 such bottles is

A. 37 litre and 600 millilitre
B. 34 litre and 400 millilitre
C. 35 litre
D. 36 litre

45. A distance of 1/2 centimetre on a map represents 200 kilometre on the ground. If two cities are 1800 kilometre apart on the ground, then their distance on the map will be

A. nine centimetre
B. three and a half centimetre
C. four and a half centimetre
D. six centimetre

46. Which one of the following is **not** correct?

A. One millilitre is one-hundredth of one litre.
B. One lakh is equal to one hundred thousand.
C. One crore is equal to one hundred lakh.
D. One centimetre is one-hundredth of one metre.

47. A cuboidal box is 13 cm long, 11 cm broad and 9 cm high. A cubical box has side 12 cm. Tanu wants to pack 3060 cubes of side 1 cm in these boxes. The number of the cubes left unpacked in these boxes is

A. 45 B. 15
C. 28 D. 30

48. The length and breadth of a rectangle are 48 cm and 21 cm respectively. The side of a square is two-thirds the length of the rectangle. The sum of their areas (in square cm) is

A. 2123 B. 2028
C. 2030 D. 2032

49. The product 672 × 36 × 25 equals

A. the number of seconds in 1 week
B. the number of minutes in 7 weeks
C. the number of hours in 60 days
D. the number of seconds in 5 days

50. When fresh fish is dried, it becomes one-third its weight. Savi bought 2709 kg of fresh fish at the rate of ₹ 27 per kg and, when dried, she sold them at ₹ 97.5 per kg. She earned in all

A. ₹ 15874.5 B. ₹ 14709.5
C. ₹ 14789.5 D. ₹ 14899.5

51. Juhi travelled a distance of 16 km by bicycle at the speed of 15 km per hour, 20 km by scooter at the speed of 50 km per hour and 50 km by car at the speed of 60 km per hour. The total time (in minutes) to travel these distances was:

A. 138 B. 88
C. 114 D. 144

52. Which one of the following is prerequisite to understand decimal representation of a number?

A. Subtraction B. Place value
C. Multiplication D. Addition

53. The four fundamental operations in arithmetic are:

A. calculation, computation, construction and forming equation
B. addition, multiplication, converting fractions into decimals and construction of regular shapes
C. addition, subtraction, multiplication and division
D. addition, division, finding perimeter and area

54. A teacher is teaching 'addition' to Class II students. Which one of the following is the most suitable strategy to follow?

A. Word problems should be used only for the purpose of assessment.
B. Addition should be introduced through word problems.
C. Word problems should be done at the end of the chapter.
D. Word problems should not be done in Class II.

55. A teacher of Class II gives the following word problem on 'addition' to students to solve:

"A basket contains 5 apples and 7 more apples are added to it. How many apples are now there in the basket?"

This type of word problem belongs to which of the following models/categories?

A. Segregation B. Repeated addition
C. Aggregation D. Augmentation

56. "Errors play an important role in Mathematics." This statement is:

A. false, as errors indicate carelessness
B. true, as they give ideas about how children construct Mathematics concepts
C. true, as they give feedback to students about their marks
D. false, as there is no scope of errors in Mathematics

57. Which one of the following teaching-learning materials (TLM) is best suited to explain '1/10 is greater than 1/100' to Class IV students?

A. Number chart B. Abacus
C. 10 × 10 Square grid D. Dienes block

58. Which one of the following is best suited for comparison of sizes (areas) of two or more two-dimensional objects?

A. Estimation
B. Observation
C. Superposition
D. Using non-standard units

59. 'Mathematics puzzles' at primary level help in:
A. providing fun to students
B. testing problem-solving skills
C. promoting problem-solving skills
D. identifying brilliant students of the class

60. Mathematical communication refers to:
A. ability to solve problems
B. skills to participate in Mathematics quiz
C. ability to speak in Mathematics classroom
D. ability to consolidate and organize mathematical thinking

PART- III

Environmental Studies

***Directions :** Answer the following questions by selecting the **correct/most appropriate** options.*

61. A Class V teacher takes an aluminium foil and puts it in water and shows that it floats. She then crumples and squeezes the foil tightly and puts it in water again and shows to the students that it sinks. She then asks the students to think and give reasons why they think this has happened. Which one of the following process skills will be used in answering this question?
A. Classifying B. Observing
C. Measuring D. Hypothesizing

62. In the context of EVS pedagogy, all of the following are desirable practices, **except**
A. nurturing the identity of the child
B. acknowledging the superiority of textbook knowledge over actual observation
C. promoting plurality of texts and contexts
D. building capacity for critical thinking and problem-solving

63. Mahesh, a Class IV teacher, plans to sensitize the students to the concept of 'conservation of trees'. Which one of the following activities is most suited for this purpose?
A. Motivating each student to adopt and nurture one tree
B. Encouraging students to participate in poster competition
C. Making teams of students for group discussion
D. Conducting a debate competition

64. In EVS, children particularly enjoy learning crafts and arts in groups, because
1. it promotes peer learning.
2. it improves social learning.
3. children become happy and respond with enthusiasm when their creative works are appreciated.
4. it promotes discipline in the class.

Select the correct option:
A. 1, 2 and 4 B. 1, 2 and 3
C. 2 and 3 D. 1 and 4

65. 'Experimentation' is one of the indicators of assessment. Which one of the following is the most appropriate way of assessing experimentation indicator?
A. Creative writing B. Demonstration
C. Hands-on activity D. Picture reading

66. Students in primary classes have a lot of alternate conceptions in many topics like living-nonliving, water cycle, plants, etc. The sources of these alternate conceptions can be:
1. family and community
2. textbooks and other books
3. teachers
4. stories and poems

Select the correct option.
A. 1, 2, 3 and 4 B. Only 1
C. 1 and 2 D. 1, 2 and 4

67. Glass jars and bottles are dried well in the sun before filling them with pickles. Why is it so?
A. To remove the dust from them
B. To remove the moisture completely
C. To make pickles tasty
D. To increase their temperature

68. Renu's grandmother shows her a dried-up well and tells her that 15-20 years ago there was water in the well, but now it has completely dried up. What could be the reason(s) for drying up of water in the well?
1. The soil around the trees, well and nearby area is now covered with cement.
2. A lot of boring pumps have come up in the nearby area.
3. Nobody uses the well as there are taps in everybody's house now.

A. Only 3 B. Only 1
C. Only 2 D. 1 and 2

69. An egret sits on a buffalo, because
A. the egret sits on the buffalo for fun
B. the buffalo helps in the transportation of the egret from one place to another

C. the egret wants to scare the buffalo
D. the egret and the buffalo have symbiotic relationship

70. Which one of the following is not a function of roots for the plant?
A. To provide humus
B. To give support to the plant
C. To absorb water and minerals
D. To store food

71. Consider the following statements about Karnam Malleswari:
1. She is a weight lifter of international fame.
2. She is from Karnataka.
3. She has many records to her credit. She could lift weights up to 130 kg.
4. She started lifting weights when she was 12 years old.

The correct statement(s) is/are:
A. 1, 3 and 4 B. Only 1
C. Only 1 and 4 D. 1, 2 and 3

72. The following are some statements regarding step wells or *Baolis*:
1. They are a traditional system of water storage and conservation.
2. They were used as a community resource.
3. They are found /constructed mainly in rain-parched States.
4. They contain only contaminated water.

Which of the above statement(s) is/are correct?
A. 1, 2 and 3 B. Only 1
C. Only 4 D. 1 and 2

73. 'Worli' is a traditional art form. The place 'Worli' is in the State of:
A. Odisha B. Rajasthan
C. Bihar D. Maharashtra

74. The neighbouring States of Tamil Nadu are:
A. Kerala, Gujarat and Karnataka
B. Andhra Pradesh, Goa and Karnataka
C. Goa, Karnataka and Kerala
D. Kerala, Karnataka and Andhra Pradesh

75. Which one of the following has the sense of hearing so sharp that it can make out the difference between the rustling of leaves and the sound of an animal moving on the grass?
A. Vulture B. Silkworm
C. Dog D. Tiger

76. When one is travelling from Ahmedabad to Kerala by a train, one comes across many tunnels. These tunnels are in the hills of:
A. Aravallis B. Western Ghats
C. Eastern Ghats D. Vindhyachal

77. The earth is round. There is actually no 'up' and 'down' on the earth and it is Just relative. We, the people of India, actually stand upside down in relation to the people of:
A. Libya B. Algeria
C. Argentina D. Alaska (USA)

78. It is advised to put oil on stagnant water to prevent breeding of mosquitoes. This is because:
A. mosquitoes are repelled by oil
B. mosquitoes are killed by oil
C. mosquitoes get stuck in the layer of oil
D. oil cuts off oxygen supply, thereby stops the breeding of mosquitoes

79. Which one of the following insects **does not** live together in a colony like honeybees?
A. Ant B. Termite
C. Spider D. Wasp

80. The structure of houses in rural area is linked to the climatic conditions in which they are built. There is a village where houses have following features:
- Houses are made on strong bamboo pillars.
- Inside of houses is also made of wood.
- Houses are made almost 3 m to 3.5 m above the ground.
- Roofs are made with a slope.

If in this village it rains heavily, the village should be part of:
A. Uttar Pradesh B. Rajasthan
C. Bihar D. Assam

81. 'Kudukh' is a language of the people of:
A. Manipur B. Arunachal Pradesh
C. Jharkhand D. Mizoram

82. As per the NCF, 2005, which one among the following is the theme of EVS?
A. Solar system B. Weather
C. Energy D. Food

83. Which one among the following is the strongest argument in favour of adopting a theme-based approach in EVS?
A. It helps in making teaching more interesting and activity-based.
B. It helps in covering a wide range of concepts, issues and skills.
C. It helps in softening subject boundaries and accessing knowledge holistically.
D. It helps in giving a structure to lesson plans and makes teaching more effective.

84. Stories are an important aspect of teaching-learning EVS in primary classes. Which one of the following is **least** appropriate reason for including storytelling as pedagogy in EVS classroom?
A. Stories cut across various subject areas.
B. Stories help in class management

C. Stories provide contexts to relate EVS concepts.
D. Stories include experiences of the people.

85. The content in an EVS textbook should:
1. avoid descriptions and definitions.
2. discourage rote learning.
3. provide opportunities to the child to question and explore.
4. give only written information to the child.

Select the correct option.

A. 2 and 3 B. Only 3
C. 1, 2 and 3 D. 1 and 4

86. Which one of the following statements about assessment procedures is least appropriate?

A. Preparing a list of learning indicators and sub-indicators makes the reporting more detailed.
B. Remarks like 'fair', 'good' and 'very good' give an understanding about a child's learning.
C. Portfolios of children should not contain only their best work but all kinds of work.
D. Giving personal details and individual feedback to a child is a desirable practice.

87. Read the following question carefully:

"Have you ever seen animals around your house or school that have small babies? Write their names in the notebook."

Which process skill is assessed through this question?

A. Hypothesis and experimentation
B. Concern for justice
C. Observation and recording
D. Classification and discussion

88. Interdisciplinary nature of EVS addresses environmental issues by using the contents and methods of:

A. social science and environmental education
B. science
C. science, social science and environmental education
D. science and social science

89. The teacher of Class V-A gave the question:

1. Write five advantages of trees.

While the teacher of Class V-B gave the question:

2. What would happen if there were no trees on the earth?

What is the nature of these questions?

A. 1 is open-ended, convergent and 2 is close-ended, divergent
B. 1 is open-ended, divergent and 2 is close-ended, convergent
C. 1 is close-ended, divergent and 2 is open-ended, convergent
D. 1 is close-ended, convergent and 2 is open-ended, divergent

90. Which of the following is/are true about assessing learners in EVS in Class 1?

1. Oral tests, as children may not be able to write
2. Drawing, as children enjoy it
3. 'Teachers' observation and recording
4. There is no need of assessment in view of 'no detention policy'

A. Only 4 B. 1 and 2
C. 3 and 4 D. 1, 2 and 3

PART- IV

Language-I : Hindi

निर्देश (प्र.सं. 91 से 105) : *नीचे दिए गए प्रश्नों के सही/सबसे उपयुक्त उत्तर वाले विकल्प चुनिए।*

91. भाषा सीखने का उद्देश्य है

A. आदेश-निर्देश दे पाना और सुन पाना
B. दूसरों की बातों को समझ पाना
C. अपने मन की बात कह पाना
D. प्रत्येक स्थिति में भाषा का प्रयोग कर पाना

92. "बच्चों के भाषाई विकास में समाज की महत्वपूर्ण भूमिका होती है।" यह विचार किसका है?

A. स्किनर B. चॉम्स्की
C. वाइगोत्स्की D. पियाजे

93. विद्यार्थियों का भाषाई विकास समग्रता से हो सके, इसके लिए सबसे उपयुक्त अनुशंसा होगी

A. भाषा प्रयोग के विविध अवसरों की
B. सतत एवं व्यापक आकलन की
C. सर्वोत्कृष्ठ पाठ्य-पुस्तकों की
D. शब्दकोश एवं विश्वकोश के प्रयोग की

94. लिखित भाषा का प्रयोग

A. कार्यालयी कार्यों के लिए ही किया जाता है
B. अपनी अभिव्यक्ति के लिए किया जाता है
C. केवल साहित्य सृजन के लिए किया जाता है
D. केवल प्रतिवेदन-लेखन के लिए किया जाता है

95. भाषा की कक्षा में भाषाई खेलों का आयोजन मुख्यतः

A. आकलन का काम करता है
B. रोचकता और जोश लाता है
C. अध्यापक के काम को सरल बनाता है
D. भाषा सीखने की प्रक्रिया में स्वाभाविकता लाता है

96. कविता-कहानियों पर चर्चा करने एवं प्रश्न पूछने का उद्देश्य

A. कल्पनाशीलता का पोषण करना मात्र है

B. भाषा सीखने का आकलन करना मात्र है
C. साहित्य के प्रति बच्चों की रुचि जाग्रत करना है
D. भाषा की विभिन्न छटाओं का अनुभव कराना है

97. भाषा का अस्तित्व एवं विकास .... के बाहर नहीं हो सकता।
A. साहित्य B. समाज
C. विद्यालय D. परिवार

98. किसी समावेशी कक्षा में कौन-सा कथन भाषा-शिक्षण के सिद्धांतों के अनुकूल है?
A. बच्चे अपने अनुभवों के आधार पर भाषा के नियम नहीं बना पाते
B. भाषा विद्यालय में रहकर अर्जित की जाती है
C. व्याकरण के नियमों का ज्ञान भाषा-विकास की गति त्वरित करता है
D. प्रिंट-समृद्ध माहौल भाषा सीखने में मदद करता है।

99. प्राथमिक स्तर पर विद्यार्थियों के भाषा-शिक्षण के संदर्भ में कौन-सा कथन सही है?
A. बच्चे समृद्ध भाषिक परिवेश में सहज रूप से स्वतः भाषा में सुधार कर सकते हैं
B. बच्चों की भाषाई संकल्पनाओं और विद्यालय के भाषाई परिवेश में विरोधाभासी भाषा सीखने में मदद करता है
C. बच्चे भाषा की जटिल और समृद्ध संरचनाओं का ज्ञान विद्यालय में ही अर्जित करते हैं
D. सतत रूप से की जाने वाली टिप्पणियाँ एवं अनवरत अभ्यास भाषा सीखने में रुचि उत्पन्न करते हैं

100. प्राथमिक स्तर की कक्षा में भिन्न-भिन्न प्रांतों के अलग-अलग भाषा बोलने वाले बच्चों का नामांकन हुआ है। ऐसी स्थिति में भाषा की कक्षा बच्चों के भाषाई विकास के संदर्भ में
A. अवरोध ही प्रस्तुत करती है
B. बहुत बड़ी समस्या बन जाती है
C. अनमोल संसाधन के रूप में कार्य करती है
D. जटिल चुनौती के रूप में सामने आती है

101. पहली कक्षा की भाषा अध्यापिका अपने एक विद्यार्थी के भाषाई विकास के संबंध में चिंतित हैं, क्योंकि
A. विद्यार्थी को घर पर बात करने के बहुत कम अवसर मिलते हैं
B. विद्यार्थी के माता और पिता की मातृभाषा अलग-अलग है
C. विद्यार्थी अपने साथियों से बहुत झगड़ता है
D. विद्यार्थी पठन-पाठन में रुचि प्रदर्शित नहीं करता है

102. बच्चों के बोलना सीखने के संदर्भ में कौन-सा कथन सही है?
A. बड़े परिवार में बच्चों की 'बोलना' सीखने की गति तेज होती है
B. निर्धन परिवारों से आए बच्चों की 'बोलना' सीखने की गति धीमी होती है
C. कहने-सुनने के अधिक से अधिक अवसर मिलने पर बच्चे बोलना सरलता से सीखते हैं
D. सभी बच्चों की 'बोलना' सीखने की गति एकसमान होती है

103. विद्यालय/कक्षा में समृद्ध भाषाई परिवेश से तात्पर्य है
A. बोलने-सुनने, पढ़ने-लिखने के अधिक से अधिक अवसर
B. एक से अधिक भाषाओं के शब्दकोश की उपलब्धता
C. अध्यापक को एक से अधिक भाषाओं की जानकारी
D. मुख्य धारा की भाषा सुनने के अधिक से अधिक अवसर

104. अपने विद्यार्थियों के भाषा संबंधी क्रमिक विकास का आकलन करने के लिए आपकी निर्भरता मुख्य रूप से किस पर है?
A. मौखिक कार्य करवाने पर
B. गृहकार्य की उत्तर-पुस्तिकाओं के अवलोकन पर
C. कक्षाकार्य के अवलोकन पर
D. पोर्टफोलियो के अवलोकन पर

105. आपके विद्यार्थी पाठ में आए नवीन/अपरिचित शब्दों के अर्थ जान सकें, इसके लिए आप
A. शब्दकोश देखना सिखाएँगी
B. शब्द का अर्थ लिखकर बताएँगी
C. पाठ के संदर्भ में अर्थ समझने की स्थिति पैदा करेंगी
D. पाठ के अंत में दिए गए 'शब्दार्थ' देखने के लिए कहेंगी

निर्देश (प्र.सं. 106 से 114) : *नीचे दिए गद्यांश को पढ़कर पूछे गए प्रश्नों के **सही/सबसे उपयुक्त** उत्तर वाले विकल्प चुनिए।*

माँ : रमेश, मीना क्यों रो रही है?

रमेश : मैंने चाटा मारा था। मुझे पढ़ने नहीं दे रही थी।

माँ : लेकिन तुम इस समय क्यों पढ़ रहे हो? यह भी कोई पढ़ने का समय है? क्या आजकल पढ़ाई चौबीसों घंटे की हो गई? दिमाग है या मशीन? और क्या पढ़ने के लिए बहन को पीटना जरूरी है?

रमेश : माँ, पढूँगा नहीं तो कक्षा में अव्वल कैसे आऊँगा? मुझे तो फर्स्ट आना है तुम भी तो यही कहती थी।

माँ : हाँ कहती थी, पर तुम? हर वक्त खेल-खेल-खेल। फर्स्ट आना था तो शुरू से पढ़ा होता। अब जब परीक्षाएँ सर पर आ गईं तो रटने बैठे हो! तुम क्या समझते हो कि ऐसे रटने से अव्वल आ जाओगे? अरे! पढ़ना थोड़ी देर का ही काफी होता है, अगर नियम से मन लगाकर पढ़ा जाए।

रमेश : अब रहने दो माँ। मैं आज खेलने भी नहीं जाऊँगा। कोई आए तो मना कर देना। अब मुझे पढ़ने दो—"अकबर का जन्म... अकबर का जन्म... अमरकोट में हुआ था... अमरकोट में..."

माँ : अकबर का जन्म जहाँ भी हुआ हो, तुम्हारा जन्म यहीं हुआ है और मैं तुम्हें रट्टू तोता नहीं बनने दूँगी। पढ़ने के समय पढ़ना और खेलने के समय खेलना अच्छा होता है।

106. मीना और रमेश हैं, परस्पर
A. भाई-बहन B. सहपाठी
C. रिश्तेदार D. मित्र

107. रमेश ने मीना की पिटाई की, क्योंकि वह
A. अक्सर शैतानियाँ करती थी
B. पढ़ नहीं रही थी

C. पढ़ने नहीं दे रही थी
D. कक्षा में अव्वल आ सकती थी

108. कक्षा में प्रथम आने के लिए आवश्कय है
A. खेलकूद छोड़ देना
B. रात-दिन पढ़ाई करना
C. पढ़ाई के दिनों परिश्रम करना
D. शुरू से नियमित पढ़ाई करना

109. "यह भी कोई पढ़ने का समय है?" प्रश्न का आशय है
A. यह समय पढ़ने का नहीं है
B. यह भी पढ़ने का एक समय है
C. यह पढ़ने का ही कोई समय है
D. पढ़ने को कोई समय नहीं होता

110. जो शब्द शेष से भिन्न हो, उसे छाँटिए।
A. प्रथम B. अव्वल
C. फर्स्ट D. परीक्षा

111. कौन-सा विशेषण रमेश के लिए उपयुक्त है?
A. लापरवाह B. पढ़ाकू
C. परिश्रमी D. रट्टू तोता

112. 'पर तुम?' का भाव है
A. पर तुम पढ़ते ही रहे
B. पर तुमने ध्यान नहीं दिया
C. पर तुमने रटना ही सीखा
D. पर तुमने पढ़ना छोड़ दिया

113. अकबर का जन्म कहाँ हुआ था?
A. अमरकोट B. दिल्ली
C. फतहपुरी D. आगरा

114. 'बहुत निकट आना' के लिए मुहावरा है
A. तोता रटंत B. पास आना
C. सर पर आना D. अव्वल आना

निर्देश (प्र.सं. 115 से 120): *निम्नलिखित काव्यांश को पढ़कर दिए गए प्रश्नों के **सही/सबसे उपयुक्त** उत्तर वाले विकल्प को चुनकर लिखिए।*

जीवन के इस मोड़ पर
कुछ भी कहा जाता नहीं।
अधरों की ड्योढ़ी पर
शब्दों के पहरे हैं।
हँसने को हँसते हैं
जीने को जीते हैं
साधन-सुभीतों में
ज्यादा ही रीते हैं।
बाहर से हरे-भरे
भीतर घाव मगर गहरे
सबके लिए गूँगे हैं—
अपने लिए बहरे हैं।

115. "कुछ भी कहा जाता नहीं"—ऐसा क्यों?
A. बंधन और बेबसी के कारण
B. गूँगा होने के कारण
C. भीतर के घावों के कारण
D. साधन सुविधओं के अभाव के कारण

116. कविता की पंक्तियों में मुख्यतः बात की गई है
A. घावों के हरे-भरे होने का
B. गूँगा-बहरा होने की
C. साधन-सुभीतों की
D. कुछ भी न कह पाने की विवशता की

117. 'रीते' शब्द में भाव है
A. परायेपन का B. खालीपन का
C. खोखलेपन का D. अपनेपन का

118. कविता की पंक्तियों के आधार पर कहा जा सकता है कि
A. कवि घावों के गहरे होने से दुखी है
B. कवि के जीवन में बहुत अभाव है
C. कवि कुछ भी करने की स्थिति में नहीं है
D. कवि कुछ भी कहने या सुन पाने की स्थिति में नहीं है

119. 'ड्योढ़ी' का अर्थ है
A. देहरी B. दरवाजा
C. चौखट D. घर

120. 'भीतर के घाव' से तात्पर्य है
A. घर के भीतर की अशांति B. हृदय की पीड़ा
C. अंदरूनी चोट D. शारीरिक क्षति

PART- V

Language-II : English

Directions (Qs. 121-135) : *Answer the following questions by selecting the **correct/most appropriate** options.*

121. Stephen Krashen's theory of second language acquisition **does not** consist of
A. the Input Hypothesis
B. the Acquisition Learning Hypothesis
C. the Learnability Hypothesis
D. the Natural Order Hypothesis

122. The use of dictionary **does not** help learners to
A. be proficient in oral communication

B. find the meaning of words
C. check the part of speech of a word
D. find out how to say a word

123. Constructivism in language learning focuses on
A. engaging learners in exploring new knowledge
B. the role of imitation
C. memorizing grammar rules
D. the dominant role of the teacher in the classroom

124. The major objective of teaching English at primary level is
A. speaking English in British accent
B. scoring good marks in the exams
C. knowing the grammar of English
D. using English in different situations of life

125. In learning a language, students' talking time should be increased because
A. teachers feel relaxed while students are talking
B. they enjoy spending time talking with their friends
C. they can learn the correct pronunciation from each other
D. they use the target language for various purposes

126. A teacher of Class V is planning to teach grammar. Which one of the following might be a good strategy for teaching grammar?
A. Asking students to carefully note down the rules from the blackboard
B. Giving clear explanations of the rules with examples
C. Asking students to do drill work only to learn rules
D. Giving the practice of grammar in context as a strategy

127. Which one of the following is **not** true in relation to the use of children literature?
A. Their reading proficiency deteriorates and gets worse.
B. It helps in developing learners' imagination.
C. It broadens their mental horizon.
D. It makes them understand and respect diverse cultures.

128. While assessing a group work, a teacher **should not** focus on
A. cooperative learning process
B. assessing each child's work
C. taking initiatives in work
D. showing concern for others

129. A diagnostic test in English will help the language teacher to identify.
A. slow learners in her class
B. learning difficulties the learner faces in English
C. the topic which the learner has not learnt by heart
D. intelligent learners in her class

130. While teaching English, a teacher is not able to draw attention of some students sitting at the back. She should
A. stop explaining the concept and start dictating the notes to students
B. scold them for not paying attention
C. ignore them and carry on
D. engage them by asking questions and evaluating her teaching method

131. When a child learns a language naturally, without much practice, it is called
A. language adaptation
B. language learning
C. language acquisition
D. language generalization

132. The communicative approach to teach English focuses on
A. correct pronunciation of words
B. linguistic competence plus an ability to use the language appropriately
C. the practice of selected and graded structure patterns
D. the structural accuracy of the sentences

133. Which one of the following is most important in developing reading skill at primary level?
A. Ability to comprehend the text already read
B. Only knowing the correct Order of alphabet
C. Ability to read words correctly
D. Ability to read phrases correctly

134. While reading, a learner needs to
A. translate the written symbols into corresponding sounds, to grasp their meaning
B. perceive end decode letters in order to read words
C. understand every word to grasp the meaning of the text
D. guess the contextual meaning of new words to understand the text

135. Diphthongs are
A. double consonant sounds
B. vowel sounds
C. double vowel sounds
D. consonant sounds

Directions (Qs. 136 to 143): *Read the passage given below and answer the questions that follow by selecting the* ***correct/most appropriate*** *options.*

Raja Ram Mohan Roy is considered the pioneer of modern Indian Renaissance for the remarkable reforms he brought about in the 18th century India. Among his efforts, the abolition of the Sati-pratha—a practice in which the widow was compelled to sacrifice herself on the funeral pyre of her husband—was prominent. His efforts were also instrumental in eradicating the Purdah system and child marriage. In 1828, Ram Mohan Roy formed the Brahmo Samaj, a group of people, who had no faith in idol-worship and were against the caste restrictions.

Raja Ram Mohan Roy's father was a wealthy Brahmin and strictly performed the duties set by the religion. Ram Mohan himself was also devoted to Lord Vishnu and in his 14th year, he wanted to become a monk but his mother. Tarini Devi objected to his desire.

Ram Mohan viewed education as a medium to implement the social reforms. So in 1815, Ram Mohan came to Calcutta and the very next year, started an English College by putting in his own savings. He was well aware that the students should learn the English language and scientific subjects and that's why he criticized the government's policy of opening only Sanskrit schools. According to him, Indians would lag behind if they do not get to study modern subjects like Mathematics, Geography and Latin. The government accepted this idea of Ram Mohan and also implemented it but not before his death. Ram Mohan was also the first to give importance to the development of mother tongue. His *Gaudiya Byakaran* in Bengali is the best of his prose works. Rabindranath Tagore and Bankimchandra also followed in the footsteps of Ram Mohan Roy.

Ram Mohan Roy was a staunch supporter of free speech and expression and fought for the rights of Vernacular Press. He also brought out a newspaper in Persian called *Miratul Akhbar* (the Mirror of News) and a Bengali weekly called *Sambad Kaumudi* (the Moon of Intelligence). In those days, items of news and articles had to be approved by the government before being published. Ram Mohan protested against this control by arguing that newspapers should be free and that the truth should not be suppressed simply because the government did not like it.

136. Raja Ram Mohan Roy is known for his
A. literary reforms B. political reforms
C. social reforms D. economic reforms

137. When he was a teenager, Raja Ram Mohan Roy expressed his desire to become a
A. monk B. teacher
C. businessman D. journalist

138. Raja Ram Mohan Roy believed that Indians would lag behind if they
A. did not learn traditional skills
B. gave up study of Sanskrit
C. did not study modern subjects
D. forgot their cultural roots

139. Raja Ram Mohan Roy strongly supported
A. physical education
B. freedom of speech and expression
C. moral education
D. rituals and observances

140. The word 'eliminating' most nearly means
A. eradicating B. banning
C. dismissing D. banishing

141. The word which is opposite in meaning to 'encouraged' is
A. misled B. disheartened
C. suppressed D. crushed

142. Which 'part of speech' is the underlined word in the sentence given below?
"He was a staunch supporter of <u>free</u> speech and expression."
A. Conjunction B. Noun
C. Adverb D. Adjective

143. 'Raja Ram Mohan Roy viewed education ...."
The 'voice' in the above sentence has been correctly changed in
A. Education is viewed ....
B. Education has been viewed ....
C. Education had been viewed ....
D. Education was viewed ....

Directions(Qs. 144 to 150): *Read the passage given below and answer the questions that follow by selecting the* ***correct/most appropriate*** *options.*

Your body is made up of sixty per cent water and you lose the essential fluid every minute of every day as you breathe, digest, and hopefully work up a sweat. It is important that you put back every drop. Starting now, drink eight 230 ml glasses of water every single day—that's the minimum your body needs daily. That is the non-negotiable sugar savvy hydration Mantra. Many times when you think you're hungry, sleepy, depressed, and/or irritated, you're actually just dehydrated. Drinking enough water actually helps you combat water retention. Sounds counterintuitive, but think about it. If you are running around in n semi dehydrated state all the time, Your body is going lo hang on to every single drop, giving you that puffy, unhealthy appearance. When you are properly hydrating, your body gets the message that all systems are operating smoothly and it continues its work of flushing out your system and ridding itself of the excess fluids.

If your goal is to lose weight: water is a must. When you're dehydrated, your body sends out signals that you need assistance. Many people mistake those thirsty SOS signals for hunger and take in hundreds of extra calories. They also don't solve the real problem—thirst! Drinking water can be a powerful appetite suppressant and allows you to cue into your real hunger. Your body also needs plenty of water for proper digestion. som you can get the most from the foods you eat. You are less susceptible to food cravings when your stomach is full and you're getting all the nutrients you need. Drink two glasses of water before every meal—you'll eat less! Your body uses water for fat.

144. _______ helps fight water retention.
A. Drinking enough water
B. Exercising regularly
C. A regular morning walk
D. Having a balanced diet

145. Our systems operate satisfactorily
A. when we enjoy a sound sleep
B. when we are properly hydrated
C. if we consume lots of fruits and vegetables
D. if excess fat is reduced

146. The best way to lose weight is to
A. take weight-reducing pills

B. exercise at least twice a day
C. drink plenty of water
D. eat less starchy food

147. When we arc dehydrated, we think we
A. want to vomit
B. are tired
C. need food
D. are about to collapse

148. The word 'irritated' most nearly means
A. troubled B. uneasy
C. frustrated D. annoyed

149. The word which is opposite in meaning to assistance' is
A. resistance B. persistence
C. existence D. fragrance

150. "Your body uses water for fat."
The 'voice' in the above sentence has been correctly changed in
A. Water could be used for fat by our body.
B. Water is being used by our body for fat.
C. Water is used for fat by your body.
D. Water was used for fat by our body.

Answers

1	2	3	4	5	6	7	8	9	10
B	B	C	B	C	B	D	C	A	B
11	12	13	14	15	16	17	18	19	20
B	D	B	B	D	C	C	B	D	B
21	22	23	24	25	26	27	28	29	30
B	C	B	A	B	C	C	C	B	B
31	32	33	34	35	36	37	38	39	40
C	C	A	A	D	D	B	C	D	D
41	42	43	44	45	46	47	48	49	50
C	A	C	D	C	A	C	D	A	D
51	52	53	54	55	56	57	58	59	60
A	B	C	B	C	B	D	B	C	D
61	62	63	64	65	66	67	68	69	70
B	B	A	B	C	A	B	D	D	A
71	72	73	74	75	76	77	78	79	80
A	A	D	D	A	B	D	D	C	D
81	82	83	84	85	86	87	88	89	90
C	D	C	B	B	D	C	C	A	D
91	92	93	94	95	96	97	98	99	100
D	C	A	B	D	D	B	D	A	C
101	102	103	104	105	106	107	108	109	110
A	C	A	D	C	A	C	D	A	D
111	112	113	114	115	116	117	118	119	120
D	B	A	C	B	D	B	B	C	B
121	122	123	124	125	126	127	128	129	130
A	A	A	D	C	B	C	B	B	D
131	132	133	134	135	136	137	138	139	140
C	A	A	B	C	C	A	C	B	D
141	142	143	144	145	146	147	148	149	150
C	D	D	A	B	C	B	B	A	C

Some Selected Explanatory Answers

1. The unmarked classroom in India is essentially multilingual and multicultural. These features can be used as a resource rather than regarding it as an obstacle. A similar approach should inform the teaching of English. Children do need to learn English but not at the cost of their own languages. In the paradigm of multilinguality, it is eminently possible to organise methods, material, teacher training and classroom transaction in a way that the languages of children are not ignored while English still gets acquired, with levels of proficiency not commonly witnessed hitherto among children.

2. The common saying, "Failure is a ladder to success" is practically interpreted in human life. Sometimes a student prepares for an exam and yet he fails; it becomes necessary for him to find out where he had lagged behind. This failure becomes an eye-opener for him so that he can realise his weak portion/mistake and work hard on that particular subject, matter or discipline (in which he finds himself weak) to ultimately emerge successful. Similarly, mistakes and errors teach students to rectify the same area of their weakness or where they lagged their concentration so that they can concentrate and strengthen that portion/area to get through the exam. Thus, it is proved that the mistakes and errors made by students should be seen as opportunity to understand their thinking.

3. Swiss philosopher and psychologist Jean Piaget remarks that children do not think like grown-ups. Of course, it does not take a theory or a genius to find children's utterances cutely surprising or exasperatingly illogical. It took both to understand, as Piaget began to suspect after thousands of conversations with children, that their thinking has its own kind of order and its own kind of logic. He championed a new way of thinking about children that provided the theoretical foundation for today's educational reform movement. It was a shift comparable to the displacement by modern anthropology of stories of "noble savages." One might say that Piaget was the first to take children's thinking seriously. So it is truly observed that Piaget views children as active builders of knowledge and little scientists who construct their own theories of the world.

4. In child-centred pedagogy, teacher tries to create an atmosphere that motivates the children to explore new skills and knowledge. Teachers are not supposed to transfer facts into passive children's minds; rather facilitate their discovery of relevant information. Thus, child-centred pedagogy means giving primacy to children's voices and their active participation so that they can use their in-born intellect and show their creativities.

5. Dividing work into smaller units or breaking the task into smaller parts makes the task less arduous for children. When the children are burdened with lots of assignments, it perturbs them. Therefore, to ease them, it is required that the teacher should help them break down the assignments into smaller, less complex tasks. For example, if the children are doing math assignments that may consist of five, ten or fifteen sums/problems. In such condition, allow them to complete five math problems before presenting them with the remaining five or ten problems. Moreover, it is also required that the teacher guides them writing down the instructions.

6. If the students are made to reproduce knowledge in the same way as it is received, it will be problematic to do so, because individuals interpret experiences and do not reproduce knowledge as it is received. Such learning of anything will be just rote learning as parrots learn to utter something by copying the voice of human beings or others without understanding what is actually said or explained. Therefore, it is viably better to let the students express the received knowledge the way they have understood and the way they interpret the same. It will help the teacher assess the quantity and quality of knowledge the students have received.

7. It is undeniably correct, when students are given an opportunity to discuss a problem in groups, their learning curve becomes better. On the contrary, if students go for individual study in isolation to solve a problem, it will be a one-way study; rather it can be called as flat study without any criticism. The students may not have a refined solution or answer to any problem unless it is sifted by the sieve of criticism in the form of different views cropping therein. It is group discussion where the students express their acquired knowledge and argue with others on the topic/subject broached for discussion. It helps them find out where they are right and where they are wrong, and that finally brings the refined answer, making their learning curve better.

8. Children develop at different rates and paces, therefore, the notion of inter-individual differences exists; a single individual can show more rapid change in some developmental areas than in others; thus, intra-individual differences also exist. Regardless of the perspective, there are certain principles of development that apply to all children. Thus, the pace of development varies from one individual to another, but it follows a sequential and orderly pattern. However, there appears to be a specific time during development in which a developing structure is most sensitive to external conditions.

9. Socio-cultural contexts share the conviction that children's learning and development take place in historically situated activities that are mediated by their culture through inter-subjective experiences in which they participate with other members of their communities. These approaches emphasise that each culture presents its children with activities that are deemed valuable for their education and appropriate for their participation. Often these opportunities are tailored in some way to the developmental and individual capabilities of children in tacit or explicit ways.

10. Of course, individuals differ from one another due to the interplay between heredity and environment, which helps us in distinguishing an individual from others in phonotypical perspective. An important contributor to the differences between individuals derives from their plasticity. Such plasticity is widespread in organisms from the simple to the most complex. Adaptability plasticity enables the organism to cope with a novel challenge not previously encountered by its ancestors. Conditional plasticity appears to have evolved from repeated challenges from the environment so that the organism responds in a particular manner to the environment in which it finds itself. The resulting phenotypic variation can be triggered during development in a variety of ways, some mediated through the parent's phenotype. Climatic and geographical condition *i.e.* environment make human appearance, habits and way of living different from one another.

11. Family is usually considered to be the most important agent of socialisation. As infants, we fully depend on others to survive. Our parents guide us to function and care for ourselves. They, along with other family elders, also teach us about close relationships, group life, and how to share resources. Additionally, they provide us with our first system of values, norms, and beliefs – a system that is usually a reflection of their own social status, religion, ethnic group, and more. Family is our life's first school where we learn the most basic things, which are practically evident in our society. So the family plays a primary role in socialisation of the child.

12. Concrete operational thought involves operations (mental actions that allow children to do mentally what they had done physically before) and reversible thought. Children in this stage are able to conserve and classify. The ability to reverse mental actions on real-concrete objects and the ability to focus on more than one dimension of an object facilitate conservation.

13. Causes and effects – understood by children make them learn the significance of a particular object. If the wind blows well, they would fly the kites because they have observed and experienced that kites fly well if the wind blows well. Similarly, if a child says, "Clothes dry faster in the sun", she is showing an understanding of cause and effect in the light of her previous experience, as she has observed and found that clothes get dry faster in the heat of sun vis-à-vis under the shade.

14. Answer of the question raised here, lies in Jean Piaget's systematic study of cognitive development. According to Piaget, children's thinking differs in kind from adults than in amount. Before Piaget's work, the common assumption in psychology was that children are merely less competent thinkers than adults. He showed that young children think in strikingly different ways compared to adults. According to Piaget, children are born with a very basic mental structure (genetically inherited and evolved) on which all subsequent learning and knowledge is based.

15. One of the main benefits of scaffolded instruction is that it provides for a supportive learning ambiance. In a scaffolded learning ambiance, students are at their liberty to ask questions, provide feedback and support their peers in learning new material. When you incorporate scaffolding in the classroom, you become more of a mentor and facilitator of knowledge rather than the dominant content expert. This teaching style provides the incentive for students to take a more active role in their own learning. Students share the responsibility of teaching and learning through scaffolds that require them to move beyond their current skill and knowledge levels.

16. Vygotsky's theory views human development as a socio-genetic process by which children gain mastery over cultural tools and signs in the course of interacting with others, especially with their adults and peers in their environments. This process of interaction between the child and a more competent adult is said to effect development if the interaction occurs within the child's zone of proximal development. Initially, the adult interacting with child assumes most of the responsibilities or guiding the problem solving, but gradually this responsibility transfers to the child. Language is a primary form of interaction through which adults transmit to the child the rich body of knowledge that exists in the culture. As learning progresses, the child's own language comes to use as his or her main means of intellectual adaptation. Eventually, children can use internal language to direct their own behaviour and this transition is known as internalisation.

17. The stages of moral development introduced by Lawrence Kohlberg constitute an adaptation of a psychological theory originally conceived by the Swiss psychologist Jean Piaget. Kohlberg began work on this topic in 1958 when he was a psychology graduate student at the University of Chicago. He expanded and developed this theory throughout his life. The theory holds that moral reasoning, the basis for ethical behaviour. has six identifiable developmental stages, each more adequate at responding to moral dilemmas than its predecessor.

18. A child-centred classroom is a class in which the students sit in groups and the teacher takes turns to go to each group to teach them. To achieve this goal, schools, teachers, guidance counsellors, and other educational specialists may employ a wide variety of educational methods, from modifying assignments and instructional strategies in the classroom to entirely redesigning the ways in which students are grouped and taught in a school.

19. Intelligence is a set of capabilities to perceive information, and retain it as knowledge to be applied towards adaptive behaviours within an environment.

20. A sensitive period refers to a period of development when a child is sensitive to a particular stimuli or type of interaction. During this period, a child remains sensitive to catch and understand the clues of the adult and the words delivered by them. And thus, once the language a child grasps, he/she tries to use it while interacting with his/her parents or elders. Generally, the language learnt during this period, scarcely slips out from the memory screen of the children.

21. A teacher's emphasis upon the male students of his class to behave like boys rather than like girls, smacks of stereotypical behaviour of discrimination between boys and girls. By saying, "Be boys and don't behave like girls", the teacher means to say that boys are superior to girls in mannerism or intelligence and that's why they are instructed not to follow girls in mannerism or application of intelligence, which is obviously a sex discrimination.

22. The assessments best suited to guide improvements in student learning are the quizzes, tests, writing assignments and other assessments — that teachers administer on a regular basis in their classrooms. Teachers trust the results from these assessments because of their direct relation to classroom instructional goals. Moreover, results are immediate and easy to analyse at the individual student level. To use classroom assessments to make improvements, however, teachers must change both their view of assessments and their interpretation of results. Specifically, they need to see their assessments as an integral part of the instruction process and as crucial for helping students learn. Thus, assessment is a way to improve learning.

23. Inclusion or anything inclusive indicates covering all, *e.g.* inclusive development of education system. Thus the statement, "It is the philosophy that all children have a right to get equal education in a regular school system" best describes 'Inclusion', because here the emphasis is put on the right of **all** children (as mentioned above).

24. The children having disadvantaged background have either no access or less access to privileges utilised by the children of advantaged background. Hence, many of such unprivileged children remain deprived of the education they deserve. They need to attend a school and be educated. Therefore, to cater to the children from disadvantaged background, a teacher should try to find out more about them and involve them in class discussions so that they can also attain education like others by attending the class and participating in class discussions conducted by teachers.

25. Learning disabilities are an umbrella term for a wide variety of learning problems. A learning disability is not a problem with intelligence or motivation. Children with learning disabilities aren't lazy or dumb. In fact, most are just as smart as others. Their brains are simply wired differently. This difference affects how they receive and process information. Children writing 'b' as 'd', 'was' as 'saw', '21' as '12' indicates their learning disability as they are unable to distinguish figures and words that appear similar with a twist of difference.

26. Teachers' negative attitudes, lack of provision and short of supporting materials in regular school are reasons that parents prefer sending even partially sighted children to special education schools instead of regular schools. However, a child who can see partially should be put in a regular school while making special provisions. These provision comprise some special facilities and care, which the teachers are supposed to provide and take care of. For example, if a partially sighted student needs to be addressed, he/she should be called with his/her name instead of calling like "Hey" or "You" etc. A teacher can find out as to which colour contrast suits the affected child. Black writing on a white matt surface makes effective contrast without glare, although black on yellow sometimes better. There is a need to use a multi-sensory approach – allowing children to handle, smell and look closely at objects. Involve a visually impaired learner with practical demonstrations such as science experiments. Besides, there are more provisions, which the partially sighted children need in a regular school.

28. To enable students to make conceptual changes in their thinking, a teacher should make clear and convincing explanations and have discussions with the students, as clear and convincing explanations leave least doubts in students' minds. Moreover, discussion on any subject makes the matter more comprehensive, because every student is given chance to speak and ask questions for clarification.

29. In the context of a primary school classroom, active engagement means enquiry, questioning and debate, as the students are in action (active) – almost their all senses are involved there. They are using eye to look at the addressee (teacher or classmates), they are using brain and tongue to ask question or debate, they even sometimes move their body parts also while speaking. In the contrary, the passive engagement involves such activities as looking, listening etc. Here, the students are not in movement; rather they are passively receiving what is being taught to them.

30. Children are most creative when they participate in an activity out of interest, because they are keen to participate in that particular activity, and therefore, they concentrate well on that task/work, which ultimately paves the way for creativity. Reluctance for anything hardly brings any positive result. Therefore, to have a desired result of one's participation, it is vitally important that the child must have interest, as that will not only let him/her enjoy doing the activity but also bring the desired and sometimes unexpected result of his/her endeavour done out of interest.

37. $1001 \times 111 = 111111$

$= 110000 + 11(100 + 1)$

$= 110000 + 1100 + 11$

$= 111111$

Hence, the number in the blank space = 101.

38. Place value of 5 in 15201 = 5000

The place value of 6 in 2659 = 600

$\therefore$ 5000 + 600 = 5600 = 7 × (800)

Hence, the number in the blank space = 800.

39. Product of common factors of 36 and 48

$= 1 \times 2 \times 3 \times 4 \times 6 \times 12 = 1728$

$999 + 9 \times x = 1728$

$9x = 1728 - 999 = 729$

$\Rightarrow \quad x = \frac{729}{9} = 81$

Hence, the number in the blank space = 81.

40.

```
     684              864
39)26679(         34)29405(
   234               272
   ---               ---
    327               220
    312               204
    ---               ---
     159               165
     156               136
     ---               ---
       3                29
```

29 – 3 = 26

26 ÷ 18 then we get remainder = 8.

41. $36 = 2 \times 2 \times 3 \times 3$

$54 = 2 \times 3 \times 3 \times 3$

$60 = 2 \times 2 \times 3 \times 5$

$= \frac{2 \times 2 \times 3 \times 3 \times 3 \times 5}{2 \times 3 \times 5 \times 3} = 6.$

42. 5 dozen = 5 × 12 = 60

$\frac{1}{3} \times 60 = 20$

$\frac{2}{5} \times 60 = 24$

$\frac{1}{12} \times 60 = 5$

Hence, number of toffees left with Sonu = 60 – (20 + 24 + 5) = 60 – 49 = 11.

43. $112 + 12000 = 12112$

$\Rightarrow \quad 11012 + 10x = 12112$

$\Rightarrow \quad 10x = 12112 - 11012 = 1100$

$\Rightarrow \quad x = \frac{1100}{10} = 110$

Hence, the number in the blank space = 110.

44. $\because$ 23 bottles of milk = 51750 ml

$\therefore$ 16 bottles of milk $= \frac{51750}{23} \times 16$

$= \frac{828000}{23}$ ml = 36000 ml

$\therefore$ Quantity of milk in 16 bottles = 36 litre.

45. $200 \text{ km} = \frac{1}{2}$ cm

$1800 \text{ km} = \frac{\frac{1}{2}}{200} \times 1800$

$= \frac{1}{2 \times 200} \times 1800 = \frac{9}{2}$ cm

$= 4\frac{1}{2}$ cm

Hence, required distance is four and a half centimetre.

46. One millilitre is one hundredth of one litre is not correct.

47. Volume of cuboidical box = $13 \times 11 \times 9 \text{ cm}^3$

$= 1287 \text{ cm}^3$

Volume of cube = $(12)^3 = 1728 \text{ cm}^3$

Total volume of the box = $1287 + 1728 = 3015 \text{ cm}^3$

No. of unpacked cubes = 3060 – 3015 = 45.

48.

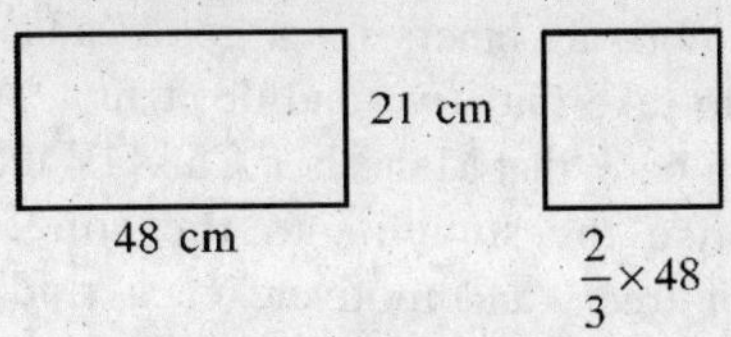

Area of rectagle = $48 \times 21 = 1008 \text{ cm}^2$

Side of square = $\frac{2}{3} \times 48 = 32$ cm

Area of square = $32 \times 32 = 1024 \text{ cm}^2$

Sum of the areas = $1008 + 1024 = 2032 \text{ cm}^2$.

49. The product of 672 × 36 × 25 = 604800

The number of seconds in 1 week

= 24 × 7 × 60 × 60 = 604800

Hence, option (A) is correct.

50. Cost price of fish = 2709 × 27 = ₹ 73143

$$\text{Selling price of fish} = \frac{1}{3} \times 2709 \times 97.5$$
$$= 903 \times 97.5 = ₹\ 88042.5$$
$$\text{Profit} = 88042.5 - 73143$$
$$= ₹\ 14899.5$$

51.
$$t_1 = \frac{16}{15} \text{ hrs}$$
$$t_2 = \frac{20}{50} \text{ hrs} = \frac{2}{5} \text{ hrs}$$
$$t_3 = \frac{50}{60} \text{ hrs} = \frac{5}{6} \text{ hrs}$$
$$t_1 + t_2 + t_3 = \frac{16}{15} + \frac{2}{5} + \frac{5}{6} = \frac{32+12+25}{30}$$
$$= \frac{69}{30} \text{ hrs} = \frac{69}{30} \times 60 \text{ minutes}$$
$$= 69 \times 2 = 138 \text{ minutes}$$

Hence, total distance covered by Juhi in 138 minutes.

61. In this case study, the students do not go through a book about what is demonstrated by their Class V teacher practically and what results in that experiment. However, the students carry on observing whatever is displayed to them. This observation makes them understand that activity much better than understanding by reading about it. Thus, by watching or observing, they may come to know about the reason as to why that aluminium foil sinks in water.

62. Acknowledging the superiority of textbook knowledge over actual observation is not a desirable practice in the context of EVS pedagogy, because having observation of anything in Environmental Studies pedagogy is as good as having concrete experience of anything. Thus, students of EVS learn more by observing than studying the textbook.

63. If you want to motivate others for a good cause, it is you who have to take initiative and do it first. As the example is given here, that Mahesh, a Class IV teacher, plans to sensitise the students to the concept of 'conservation of trees' and motivate each student to adopt and nurture one tree. For this, Mahesh needs to create an ambiance of motivation by explaining the students the benefits of planting and conserving the trees to save the environment we live in and that can be done by planting trees and forbidding others from felling them. This will be a right example of motivation and virtue as well.

64. There is a huge difference between if children learn something in groups and learn all alone. While learning crafts and arts in groups, they enjoy the activity, because it promotes peer learning, improves social learning and they become happy and respond with enthusiasm when their creative works are appreciated. In groups, children can share their knowledge and experience with each other, as at that time the group becomes like a small society for them that improves social learning. Moreover, when someone is appreciated before his/her classmates or fellow children for his/her good work, he/she feels pride as his/her reputation is made among those children who spend quality time with him/her and also witness his/her accomplishment.

65. Students learn in a variety of ways. Studies show that students learn best when learning is active, when they are engaged in hands-on classroom games and activities, and involved themselves in what they are learning. Scientists believe that when children use all of their senses it helps the brain create pathways that make it easier and quicker to retain information. In fact, students of all ages can benefit from adding hands-on classroom games and activities to their learning. No matter which subject you are learning, hands-on classroom games and activities can be added and adapted to any curriculum.

67. Glass jars and bottles are dried well in the sun before filling them with pickles to remove the moisture completely. Water in any form greatly affects the shelf life of food. Excessive moisture can result in product deterioration and spoiling the edibility of food. That's the reason why the glass jars or bottles are dried well.

68. The reason behind drying up the well that Renu's grandmother shows to her, is due to blocking up the emanating point of water, which has been covered with cement. The natural soil, through which the water moves, has been blocked by cement. Apart from it, installation of several boring pumps that take out humongous amount of water from the water reserve beneath the layer of our earth is another reason that made the well dry and deprived of water.

69. An egret sits on a buffalo, because the egret and the buffalo have symbiotic relationship. Their symbiosis lies on mutual help. There are several tiny insects, which sit mostly on buffalo's upper parts of body. They irritate buffalo by biting or some of them even sucking blood as well, whereas egrets eat such insects, thereby reducing their number on buffalo's body. Egrets fulfil their hunger by eating them and thus, buffalo gets relieved from the pinching insects. That is why there is a symbiotic relationship between egret and buffalo.

70. Humus is a dark organic material in the soil that makes the soil fertile. Roots cannot provide humus because it is formed by decomposition of vegetables and animal matter.

71. Karnam Malleswari (born 1 June 1975) is a retired Indian weightlifter from Andhra Pradesh state of India. She won the world title in the 54 kg division in 1994 and 1995 and was placed third in 1993 and 1996. She won another bronze medal at the 2000 Olympics, becoming the first Indian woman to win an Olympic medal. In 1995, she received the Rajiv Gandhi Khel Ratna, India's highest sporting honour, and in 1999 the civilian Padma Shri award.

73. Maharashtra is known for its Warli (Worli) folk paintings, which was first discovered in the early seventies. The Warli is the largest tribe found on the northern outskirts of Mumbai, in Western India. Despite being so close to this metropolis, Warli tribesmen shun all modern urbanisation. Worli is also the name of a location in Mumbai city.

74. Kerala, Karnataka and Andhra Pradesh are neighbouring states of Tamil Nadu, which was earlier Madras state. At the time of its formation in 1950, Madras state included the whole of present-day Tamil Nadu, Coastal Andhra, Rayalaseema and Telangana, the Malabar region of North Kerala, and Bellary, South Canara and Udupi districts of Karnataka. Coastal Andhra and Rayalaseema were separated to form Andhra State in 1953, while South Canara and Bellary districts were merged with Mysore State, and Malabar District with the State of Travancore-Cochin to form Kerala in 1956. In 1969, Madras State was renamed to Tamil Nadu, meaning "Tamil country".

75. Though vultures are basically carrion (flesh of dead animals) eaters, they also prey on some other animals like rabbits, squirrels etc. Due to their exemplary eyesight, they are able to spot and pounce upon their prey easily. Vulture is an endangered animals and the alarming decrease in its number predicts its imminent extinct in near future. Therefore, initiatives have been taken by the government of India for preservation of vultures. Survival of vultures is a matter of grave concern for human life, as they eat carrion and thus, they clean the environment from rotting and stench of the dead flesh that causes several diseases.

77. Geographically, Alaska is situated at such a place on the earth as it is just opposite to our India in location. Thus, when earth is viewed like a sample globe presenting human presence in India, people of both the places would look like standing upside down at both the places.

78. Generally, mosquitoes breed on dirty stagnant water while dengue mosquitoes breed on clean stagnant water. In both the cases, if oil is splattered well on the surface of water, it cuts off the oxygen supply to larva of the mosquitoes, thereby stemming their breeding.

80. There are some reasons behind why the houses in rural Assam are made of woods and bamboos. Due to poverty, most of the villagers remain unable to construct the cemented pukka house. Even if they construct the houses using earthen soil, they are washed away by concurrent floods as Assam is India's worst flood affected state. However, most often than not, the wooden houses made on strong bamboo pillars survive the heavy rain. Houses are made almost 3 m to 3.5 m above the ground so that water may not get inside the houses. Roofs are made with slope so that the rainwater does not get choked at the roof. If the currents of flood water are extremely strong, they may extirpate the wooden houses, but such houses continue to float on the water rather than getting sunk. So in such case, the chances of survival for them remain there from being drowned.

81. Kurukh (also Kurux and Oraon or Uranw) is a Dravidian language spoken by nearly two million Oraon and Kisan tribal peoples of Odisha and surrounding areas of India (Bihar, Jharkhand, Madhya Pradesh, Chhattisgarh, and West Bengal), as well as by 50,000 in northern Bangladesh, 28,600 a dialect called Dhangar in Nepal, and about 5,000 in Bhutan. It is most closely related to Brahui and Malto (Paharia). The language is marked as being in a "vulnerable" state in UNESCO's list of endangered languages. In Jharkhand, some tribes near its Capital city Ranchi speak Kurukh.

84. Of course, stories are an important aspect of teaching-learning EVS in primary classes, and if found to be didactic and full of guidance. However, telling stories will be the least appropriate reason behind helping in class management, as it has no relevance with management classes.

86. Giving personal details and individual feedback to a child is a desirable practice, but it is least appropriate about the assessment procedure, because it will not serve the purpose. Assessment process must cover preparation of a list of learning indicators and sub-indicators, remarks like 'fair', 'good' and very good'; portfolios of children's all kinds of work and so forth.

87. If you have watched any activity of the animals and their babies, and observed it deeply, the entire episode of their names and activities is automatically recorded in your mind, because you have observed it. However, recording here means keeping the record of what has been observed by you. In such case, you may illustrate the whole episode on being asked. Here the process skill of observation and recording is assessed that helped you do this task well.

89. **Close-ended** questions are those which can be answered by a simple "yes" or "no," while open-ended questions are those which require more thought and more than a simple one-word answer. However, Close-ended questions can also be very complicated. For example, "Is 1 in binary equal to 1 in counting numbers?" is a close-ended question that not everyone would be able to answer instantly.

Convergent questions are usually within a very finite range of acceptable accuracy, which may be at several levels of cognition – comprehension, application, analysis, or the ones where the answerer makes inferences or conjectures based on personal awareness, or on material read, presented or known.

Open-ended questions are the ones that require more than one word answers. The answers could come in the form of a list, a few sentences or something longer such as a speech, paragrapn or essay. For example — What were the most important wars fought in the history of India? What are you planning to buy today at the supermarket? How exactly did the grudge between the two of you come to an end?

Divergent questions allow students to explore different avenues and create many different variations and alternative answers or scenarios. Correctness may be based on logical projections, may be contextual, or arrived at through basic knowledge, conjecture, inference, projection, creation, intuition, or imagination. These types of questions often require students to analyse, evaluate, or synthesise a knowledge base and then project or predict different outcomes.

90. Children's minds are mild and compliant that can be moulded easily during childhood but if uninteresting and lengthy questions are asked to them, they would get perplexed and respond with wrong answers sometimes despite knowing the right ones. Therefore, while assessing the learners of Class-I in EVS, it must be kept in mind that they are asked for oral test. They should be asked to make drawing, as they enjoy drawing. The teachers must be observing and keeping the record of what they have observed in the children. This process of assessment will definitely help the teachers gauge the ability and mentality of the children.

Previous Paper (Solved)

CTET PAPER-I, SEPTEMBER 2015*

PART- I

Child Development and Pedagogy

Directions: *Answer the following questions by selecting the* ***most appropriate*** *options.*

1. Children have the potential to create knowledge and make meaning. From this perspective the role of a teacher is that of a:
A. Communicator and Lecturer
B. Facilitator
C. Director
D. Negotiator

2. Which one of the following is ***not*** a characteristic of gifted children?
A. High self efficacy
B. Below average mental processes
C. Solving problems insightfully
D. Higher order mental processes

3. According to the pre-conventional level of Kohlberg's theory, to which of the following would an individual turn when making a moral decision?
A. Personal needs and desires
B. Individual values
C. Family expectations
D. Potential punishment involved

4. Regarding learners' individual differences, the teacher should:
A. solve the problems based on deductive method
B. most of the time use algorithms
C. provide facts to students to memorize them
D. provide a variety of learning situations

5. Which one of the following is ***not*** the principle of child development?
A. All areas of development are important
B. All development results from an interaction of maturation and experience
C. All development and learning proceed at an equal rate
D. All development follows a sequence

6. Which one of the following would be the most effective way of conducting assessment?
A. Assessment is an inbuilt process in teaching learning
B. Assessment should be done twice in an academic session – at the beginning and at the end
C. Assessment should be done by an external agency and not by the teacher
D. Assessment should be at the end of the session

7. Which one of the following is related to creativity?
A. Convergent thinking
B. Emotional thinking
C. Egoistic thinking
D. Divergent thinking

8. Which one of the following statements about children would Vygotsky agree with?
A. Children learn when they are offered lucrative rewards
B. Children's thinking can be understood by conducting laboratory experiments on animals
C. Children are born 'evil' and need to be controlled through punishment
D. Children learn through social interaction with peers and adults

9. Children are:
A. adult-like in their thinking and there is a quantitative increase in their thinking as they grow up
B. like empty vessels in which knowledge given by the adults is filled
C. passive beings who can produce exact copies of the information transmitted to them
D. curious beings who use their own logic and abilities to explore the world around them

10. Which of the following statements about children's errors is correct?
A. Children's errors are part of the learning process
B. Children commit errors when the teacher is lenient and does not punish them for mistakes
C. Children's errors are insignificant for the teacher and she should just strike out of the mistakes and not pay any attention to them
D. Children commit errors because they are careless

*Exam was held on 20-09-2015.

11. A teacher needs to ensure that all learners in her class feel accepted and valued. To do this, the teacher should:
   A. look down upon children from 'disadvantaged' background so that they feel they have to work harder
   B. find out students who speak 'good' English and are from 'rich' backgrounds and present them as role models
   C. get to know the social and cultural background of her students and encourage diverse opinions in the class
   D. make strict rules and punish children who do not follow them

12. Suresh generally likes to study alone in a quiet room whereas Madan likes to study in a group with his friends. This is because of difference in their:
   A. Aptitudes B. Learning styles
   C. Levels of reflectivity D. Values

13. India has a lot of linguistic diversity. In this context, what is the most appropriate statement about multilingual classrooms at primary level especially class I and II?
   A. The schools should admit only those students whose mother tongue is the same as the language of instruction
   B. The teacher should respect all languages and encourage children to communicate in all of them
   C. The teacher should ignore children who use their mother tongue in the class
   D. Students should be penalized for using their mother tongue or local language

14. What is meant by 'nature' in 'nature-nurture' controversy?
   A. Biological givens or the hereditary information
   B. Temperament of an individual
   C. Complex forces of the physical and social world
   D. The environment around us

15. Mass Media is becoming a very important agency of socialization. Which one of the following is the most appropriate statement?
   A. Socialization is done by the parents and the family only
   B. Access to mass media is growing and mass media influences attitudes, values and beliefs
   C. Children cannot directly interact with media
   D. Media is a very good way to advertise and sell products

16. How children learn? Which one of the following is ***not*** true with respect to this statement?
   A. Children learn when they are cognitively ready
   B. Children learn in a number of ways
   C. Children learn as they are naturally motivated
   D. Children learn in class only

17. Which one of the following strategies should a primary school teacher adopt to motivate her students?
   A. Use incentives, rewards and punishment as motivating factors for each activity
   B. Help children set goals as per their interests and support them in working towards the same
   C. Set standard goals for the entire class and have rigid parameters to assess achievement of those goals
   D. Encourage competition for marks amongst individual student

18. Which one of the following is the primary agent of socialization?
   A. Computer B. Heredity
   C. Political parties D. Family

19. Giving children group work is an effective pedagogic strategy since:
   A. it allows some children to dominate the others in small groups
   B. children learn from each other and support each other in the learning process
   C. children will be able to do their work quickly
   D. it helps to reduce the teacher's work

20. A child with normal intelligence shows difficulty in reading and comprehending language. It indicates that the child is showing symptoms of:
   A. Dysgraphia B. Dyscalculia
   C. Dyspraxia D. Dyslexia

21. The period of infancy is from:
   A. birth to 2 years B. birth to 3 years
   C. 2 to 3 years D. birth to 1 year

22. According to Piaget, a child between 2 to 7 years is in the .... stage of cognitive development.
   A. Formal operational B. Concrete operational
   C. Sensorimotor D. Preoperational

23. Development proceeds from .... to ....
   A. complex → hard
   B. specific → general
   C. simple → easy
   D. general → specific

24. When adults adjust to the assistance they provide to facilitate progression of the child from current level of performance to potential level of performance, it is called:
   A. Scaffolding
   B. Participatory learning
   C. Collaborative learning
   D. Proximal development

25. The process of changing the existing schemas to include new information is called:
   A. Assimilation B. Accommodation
   C. Egocentrism D. Adaptation

26. In middle childhood, speech is more .... rather than ....

A. socialised, egocentric
B. animistic, socialised
C. mature, immature
D. egocentric, socialised

27. The child centred education involves:

A. children sitting in a corner
B. learning in restricted environment
C. activities that do not include play
D. hands on activities for kids

28. The class teacher observed Raghav in her class playing melodious self-composed music on his keyboard. The class teacher thought that Raghav seemed to be high in .... intelligence.

A. bodily-kinesthetic
B. musical
C. linguistic
D. spatial

29. When a teacher considers boys as naturally better at mathematics than girls, it shows that the teacher is:

A. gender biased
B. moralistic
C. right-minded
D. ethical

30. Inclusive education assumes that we should change the .... to fit the ....

A. System / child
B. Environment / family
C. Child / environment
D. Child / system

PART- II

Mathematics

Directions: *Answer the following questions by selecting the **most appropriate** options.*

31. 10290 books are to be packed in wooden boxes. If 98 books can be packed in one box and the cost of one box is ₹ 518, then the total cost of boxes needed for this purpose is:

A. ₹ 54,390 B. ₹ 54,292
C. ₹ 54,908 D. ₹ 53,872

32. Which of the following is the best sequence to teach the topic, 'Measurement of Length' at primary stage?

A. Comparison → using non-standard measures → developing standard unit → using standard measures
B. Comparison → using non-standard measures → using standard measures → developing standard unit
C. Developing standard unit → using standard measure → using non-standard measures → comparison
D. Using standard measures → using non-standard measures → developing standard unit → comparison

33. Learning objective for fourth grade students is given as:
"Students are able to order and compare two decimal numbers upto two decimal places".
This learning objective refers to:

A. Process goal B. Disposition goal
C. Social goal D. Content goal

34. Which one of the following manipulative tools is required to develop geometrical concepts of 'symmetry' and 'reflection' in Class IV?

A. Beads string B. Dot paper
C. Abacus D. Two sided counter

35. A debate was conducted in mathematics period of Class V on "Zero is the most powerful number".

This activity encourages the child to:

A. analyse and communicate
B. write numbers containing zero(s)
C. solve problems containing numbers ending with zero(s)
D. collaborate with friends

36. If a learner is having problem with numbers and calculations she/he may be having disability known as:

A. dysgraphia
B. dyscalculia
C. visual-spatial organization disability
D. dyslexia

37. Manipulative tools are important for learners at primary level as they help them most to:

A. speed up mental and oral calculations
B. perform better in examination
C. understand basic mathematical concepts
D. solve word problems

38. Which one of the following questions is open ended?
A. How will you multiply 15 by 3?
B. Write any two numbers whose product is 45
C. Use number line to find 3 times 15
D. Find 15 × 3

39. Some students of Class II, face difficulty in the addition of two digit numbers involving 'carrying over'. Reason behind this problem is lack of:
A. interest in mathematics
B. understanding of difference between face value and place value
C. understanding the importance of zero
D. understanding of regrouping process

40. Which one of the following is an important characteristic of a good mathematics textbook at primary level?
A. Concepts should be introduced through contexts
B. It should only contain numerous exercises to give rigorous practice
C. It should be attractive and colourful
D. It must be thick and large

41. According to 'Van Hiele level of Geometry' students who can describe and sort out shapes on the basis of appearance are at:
A. level 1 – Analysis
B. level 2 – Informal Deduction
C. level 3 – Formal Deduction
D. level 0 – Visualization

42. Communication in mathematics class refers to developing ability to:
A. interpret data by looking at bargraphs
B. give prompt response to questions asked in the class
C. contradict the views of others on problems of mathematics
D. organise, consolidate and express mathematical thinking

43. If a learner is able to perform the four basic operations on whole numbers, fractions and decimal numbers, the learner is at:
A. Partitioning phase B. Factoring phase
C. Operating phase D. Quantifying phase

44. National Curriculum Framework, 2005 recommends that teaching of mathematics at primary level should focus on:
A. preparation for higher mathematics
B. abstract concepts of mathematics
C. helping students to connect classroom learning with everyday life
D. helping students to acquire international standards in learning of mathematics

45. Which one of the following is ***not*** an important aspect of Number-sense?
A. Seriation B. Counting
C. Writing Numbers D. Conservation

46. A teacher gives 36 tiles to students of class IV and asks them to arrange them in all possible rectangles. Which one of the following concepts ***cannot*** be addressed by using this activity?
A. Multiplication B. Area
C. Volume D. Factors

47. Ten thousands + Ten hundreds + Ten tens is equal to:
A. 11110 B. 11100
C. 11010 D. 101010

48. The sum of remainders obtained on dividing 12112 by 11 and 13223 by 13 is:
A. 3 B. 4
C. 5 D. 2

49. The difference between the place value of 6 and the face value of 4 in 56431 is:
A. 999 B. 5600
C. 5996 D. 2

50. The product of the smallest common multiple and the biggest common factor of 30, 36 and 42 is:
A. 7460 B. 7660
C. 7650 D. 7560

51. The sum of all the positive factors of 84 which are multiples of 7, is:
A. 113 B. 189
C. 196 D. 112

52. When it is 8:49 p.m. in Delhi, it is 1:19 a.m. on the next day in Sydney. What time will be in Sydney when it is 11:19 a.m. in Delhi?
A. 3:19 a.m. B. 3:49 p.m.
C. 6:29 p.m. D. 6:49 a.m.

53. On a map, half centimetre shows 125 kilometres on the ground. If two cities are actually 2000 kms apart on the ground, then the distance between them on the map is:
A. 6 cm B. 8 cm
C. 10 cm D. 4 cm

54. Which one of the following is ***not*** correct?
A. 25 hundredths = $\frac{25}{100}$
B. 0.57 is the same as 0.5700

C. Area of a square of side 30 cm is the same as the area of a rectangle 4.5 m × 0.2 m

D. 2009 millilitres = 2 litres 9 millilitres

55. There are 660 students in a school. Two-thirds of them are boys. Three-fourths of the number of boys are players and one-fourth of the girls are players. Total number of players in the school is:

A. 370 B. 385

C. 395 D. 330

56. Renu wants to lay tiles on the floor of her house which is 9 m long and 7 m wide. Among the following sizes of tiles, which one should she buy so that the floor is tiled without cutting any tile?

A. 40 cm × 65 cm B. 55 cm × 40 cm

C. 35 cm × 45 cm D. 35 cm × 35 cm

57. Number of seconds in 6 hours is equal to the number of minutes in:

A. 12 days B. 15 days

C. 16 days D. 10 days

58. There are four cuboidal boxes with dimensions (in cm) as given below:

	Length	Breadth	Height
(*i*)	20	25	18
(*ii*)	23	20	20
(*iii*)	20	22	21
(*iv*)	24	20	19

Using which boxes can 18440 wooden centimetre cubes be packed?

A. (*i*) & (*iii*) B. (*ii*) & (*iii*)

C. (*ii*) & (*iv*) D. (*i*) & (*ii*)

59. The length of a rectangle is two times that of a square whose perimeter is 80 cm. If breadth of the rectangle is 20 cm, then the area (in cm^2) of the rectangle exceeds the area of the square by:

A. 150 cm^2 B. 300 cm^2

C. 400 cm^2 D. 100 cm^2

60. Haroon went to a fruit shop. He bought one and a half dozen bananas at the rate of ₹ 2.50 per banana, three and a half kilogram apples at ₹ 57.60 per kg, one and a half kg of mangoes at ₹ 75.40 per kg and 750 grams of grapes at ₹ 120 per kg. If he gave a note of ₹ 500 to the fruitseller, he will get back:

A. ₹ 24.85 B. ₹ 14.95

C. ₹ 50.30 D. ₹ 28.10

PART- III

Environmental Studies

***Directions :** Answer the following questions by selecting the most appropriate options.*

61. The nature of environment studies does ***not*** advocate that:

A. children make fewer mistakes

B. children get space to learn by doing

C. children ask a lot of questions

D. children get a lot of space to explore

62. A teacher took up plants as the theme to teach class IV students. She provided the following learning opportunities:

(*a*) Collection of leaves in groups.

(*b*) Discussions about shapes, sizes and other features of leaves.

(*c*) Making a herbarium

For such activities, what should the teacher ***not*** encourage the most?

A. Children's initiative to memorise as many names of leaves as possible

B. Children's detailing of the work

C. Children's continuous engagement with the activity

D. Children's interaction with each other, observation and cooperation

63. Which one of the following should ***not*** be done by the EVS teacher while assessing students?

A. Compare with previous assessment record of students

B. Record information in the light of the students learning potential

C. Focus only on a few aspects of students work

D. Write qualitative statements about students work

64. 'Community' is an important teaching-learning resource in EVS at primary level because:

A. it is a very inexpensive resource

B. it is an easily available resource

C. it comprises wise and elderly people

D. it provides learning opportunity in real setting

65. A person boarded an express train on 30th August, 2015 at Ahmedabad for Trivandrum. The train departed from Ahmedabad at 13.30 hours and reached Trivandrum at 7.30 hours on 1st September, 2015. If the distance between Ahmedabad and Trivandrum is 2268 km, the average speed of the train between the two stations was:

A. 42 m/s B. 15 m/s
C. 9 m/s D. 54 m/s

66. Gurpreet travels for the first time from New Delhi to Cheenai in a train. Which one of the following rivers is he ***not*** likely to cross during his train journey?

A. Godavari B. Ganga
C. Krishna D. Narmada

67. Which one of the following places in our country is a "Cold Desert"?

A. Jaisalmer B. Ladakh
C. Meghalaya D. Darjeeling

68. In Class V Environmental Studies Textbook one lesson, "Blow Hot Blow Cold" is a story written by Dr. Zakir Hussain. He has written many such stories for children. At the time of his death, he was the:

A. Chief Justice of India
B. Vice-President of India
C. President of India
D. Prime Minister of India

69. Which one of the following matches is ***not*** a correct way of food preservation?

A. Potato – Chips B. Milk – Paneer
C. Apple – Jam D. Raw Mango – Pickle

70. Consider the following characteristics of the houses:

1. Ground floor without windows
2. Slanting wooden roofs made of tree trunks
3. House made almost 10-12 feet above the ground on stone pillars
4. Thick walls made of stone, mud and lime
5. Wooden floors

Which of the above characteristics can be found in the houses of Leh and Ladakh?

A. 2, 3, 4 B. 3, 4, 5
C. 1, 4, 5 D. 1, 2, 3

71. Study the following:

Crows make their nests high up on a tree using all kinds of things, even pieces of wood and wires. A clever bird who does not make its own nest lays eggs in a crow's nest. The poor crow hatches them along with its own eggs.

Which bird is this?

A. Indian Robin B. Barbet
C. Koel D. Sunbird

72. Which one of the following is ***not*** a seed?

A. Wheat B. Black Pepper
C. Sago (Sabudana) D. Aniseed

73. Rehana goes to Kerala along with her family. There she sees tall trees which are very different from those in her hometown, Shimla. Which trees could she have seen in Kerala?

A. Coconut B. Apple
C. Hitchi D. Pine

74. From the following materials collected from a vegetable market by children, identify those with seeds inside:

Potato, Tomato, Pear, Chikoo, Lady finger, Bitter-gourd, Onion, Cucumber

A. Tomato, Pear and Chikoo
B. Tomato, Pear, Chikoo, Lady finger, Cucumber
C. Tomato, Pear, Chikoo, Lady finger, Bitter-gourd, Cucumber
D. Pear and Chikoo

75. Neeta goes to Andhra Pradesh and she purchases two sarees, which are exclusively made there. What are they called?

A. Pochampally and Kalamkari
B. Pochampally and Kanjivaram
C. Kalamkari and Chanderi
D. Kalamkari and Kantha

76. Which one of the following diseases may be caused by stagnant water?

A. Malaria B. Polio
C. Pneumonia D. Chicken pox

77. Which of the following makes a correct pair?

A. Assam – Bihu
B. Orissa – Bharatnatyam
C. Tamil Nadu – Lavani
D. Karnataka – Kathak

78. The Eskimo makes his house i.e. 'igloo' from ice. What is the reason for this?

A. Ice does not allow cold air and water to come inside
B. The air between the ice walls prevents the inside heat from escaping
C. Ice is available free of cost, other material will cost a lot
D. Only ice is available in polar regions

79. Which one of the following is ***not*** a characteristic feature of the roots of a Banyan tree?

A. Roots hang down from the branches
B. There are underground roots
C. Roots store food
D. Roots provide support to trees like pillars

80. As a newly appointed EVS teacher in a school, your foremost priority before beginning to teach would be to:

A. indentify the slow learners in the class
B. prepare detailed chapterwise notes for learners
C. prepare socio-cultural profiles of the learners
D. prepare lesson plans in advance

81. Poems and stories are effective in transacting the themes of EVS. This is because poems and stories:

1. can be rich depictions of the child's environment
2. can provide contextual learning environment
3. can explain various abstract concepts effectively
4. can nurture creativity and aesthetic sense

A. 1, 2 and 4 B. Only 3
C. Only 2 D. 1 and 2

82. As a teacher of Class V, which of the following resources would you find best to use while dealing with a topic on 'conservation of fuels'?

A. Reference books
B. Posters
C. Newspapers
D. Textbooks

83. A teacher of Class IV asks students to put their worksheet, observation reports and material collected during a term in a folder. These folders can be called:

A. Portfolios
B. Assignments
C. Projects
D. Anecdotal records

84. The chapter in Class V NCERT EVS textbook titled, 'Sunita in Space' describes astronaut Sunita Williams' experiences in spaceship. What could be the reason/ reasons for including this?

1. This incident gives a peep into the life of an astronaut.
2. This incident describes physical conditions in a spaceship.
3. This incident challenges gender stereotypes.
4. This incident helps in explaining the concept of gravity.

A. 4 only
B. 1, 2 and 3
C. 1, 2, 3 and 4
D. 1 only

85. An EVS teacher, usually begins her class by posing a few key questions. Of the following reasons, select which one is the ***least*** preferred?

A. Learner's thinking can be stimulated
B. The questions arouse curiosity in learners
C. Questions help in contextualising topics
D. Learner's thinking can be restricted

86. While making groups for an activity, an EVS teacher should:

A. ensure separate groups for boys and girls
B. make groups according to their marks
C. make two groups only, each with a lot of students
D. ensure cooperation and participation of all members

87. Which one of the following characteristics an EVS textbook at primary level should ***not*** have?

A. It caters to diverse backgrounds of the students
B. It includes true stories and incidents
C. It focuses on definitions and explanations of abstract concepts
D. It presents natural and socio-cultural environment in an integrated manner

88. Which one of the following the National Curriculum Framework (NCF, 2005) ***does not*** propose in the context of EVS teaching?

A. Linkages with children's experience and context
B. Hands on activities
C. Familiarity with technical terms
D. Thematic Approach

89. To draw and understand maps, which of the following abilities is/are required to be developed in primary level students?

1. Understanding of relative position of places.
2. Understanding of relative distances and directions of places.
3. Understanding of symbols and scale.
4. Drawing precisely according to scale.

A. only 3 B. 1, 2 and 3
C. Only 4 D. 1 and 2

90. Which of the following objectives is ***not*** related to EVS teaching in primary classes?

A. To memorise basic scientific concepts and principles
B. To provide opportunities to explore the environment
C. To develop skills like observation, measurement, prediction and classification
D. To develop sensitivity towards the physical and social environment

PART- IV

भाषा-I : हिन्दी

निर्देश (प्र.सं. 91 से 120): *नीचे दिए गए गद्यांश को पढ़कर **पूछे गए प्रश्नों के सबसे उचित उत्तर वाले विकल्प को चुनिए।***

स्थूल एवं बाह्य पदार्थ सूक्ष्म एवं मानसिक पदार्थों एवं भावों की अपेक्षा अधिक महत्व के विषय नहीं हैं। जो व्यक्ति रचनात्मक कार्य करने में समर्थ है, उसे भौतिक स्थूल लाभ अथवा प्रलोभन न तो लुभाते हैं और न ही प्रोत्साहित करते हैं।

विश्व में विचारक दस में से एक ही व्यक्ति होता है। उसमें भौतिक महत्वाकांक्षाएँ अत्यल्प होती हैं। 'पूँजी' का रचयिता कार्ल मार्क्स जीवनभर निर्धनता से जूझता रहा। राज्याधिकारियों ने सुकरात को मरवा डाला, पर वह जीवन के अंतिम क्षणों में भी शांत था, क्योंकि वह अपने जीवन के लक्ष्य का भली-भांति निर्वाह कर चुका था। यदि उसे पुरस्कृत किया जाता, प्रतिष्ठा के अंबारों से लाद दिया जाता, परन्तु अपना काम न करने दिया जाता तो निश्चय ही वह अनुभव करता कि उसे कठोर रूप से दंडित किया गया है। ऐसे अनेक अवसर आते हैं जब हमें बाहरी सुख-सुविधाएँ आकर्षित करती हैं, वे अच्छे जीवन के लिए अनिवार्य लगने लगती हैं किंतु महत्वपूर्ण यह है कि क्या हमने जीवन का उद्देश्य प्राप्त कर लिया? यदि इसका उत्तर 'हाँ' है तो बाह्य वस्तुओं का अभाव नहीं खलेगा और यदि 'नहीं' है तो हमें अपने को भटकने से बचाना होगा और लक्ष्य की ओर बढ़ना होगा।

91. मनुष्य को बाहरी सुख क्यों लुभाते हैं?

A. सम्पन्नता के लिए

B. भरे-पूरे जीवन के लिए

C. अच्छे जीवन के लिए

D. आराम के लिए

92. "जो व्यक्ति रचनात्मक कार्य करने में <u>समर्थ</u> हैं..."
वाक्य में रेखांकित शब्द के स्थान पर कौन-सा शब्द प्रयुक्त ***नहीं*** किया जा सकता है?

A. क्षमतावान B. सक्षम

C. शक्तिशाली D. सामर्थ्यवान

93. 'प्रतिष्ठा के <u>अंबारों से</u> लाद दिया जाता'–रेखांकित का तात्पर्य है :

A. ढेर से B. आभार से

C. कृतज्ञता से D. भार से

94. "भली भाँति निर्वाह कर चुका था।"
उपर्युक्त वाक्यांश में क्रिया-विशेषण है :

A. भली भांति B. निर्वाह

C. कर चुका D. भली

95. 'महत्त्वाकांक्षा' किन शब्दों से मिलकर बना है?

A. महत्त्व + आकांक्षा B. महत्व + आकांक्षा

C. महत्त्वा + कांक्षा D. महत् + आकांक्षा

96. भौतिक लाभ किन्हें नहीं लुभाते?

A. सामर्थ्यवान लोगों को

B. जीवन का लक्ष्य पूरा करने वालों को

C. रचनात्मक कार्य करने वालों को

D. धन-संपन्न लोगों को

97. 'पूँजी' का रचयिता कार्ल मार्क्स कथन से संकेत मिलता है कि 'पूँजी' का अर्थ है :

A. एक विचार B. एक ग्रंथ

C. विरासत D. धन-संपत्ति

98. विचारकों की एक विशेषता यह है कि उनमें :

A. भौतिक महत्त्वाकांक्षाएँ कम होती हैं।

B. पद-प्रतिष्ठा प्राप्त करने की इच्छा होती है।

C. रचनात्मक कार्य करने की क्षमता होती है।

D. महत्त्वाकांक्षाएँ नहीं होतीं।

99. सुकरात को अपना काम न करने देने की स्थिति कठोर दंड जैसी प्रतीत होती है क्योंकि :

A. वह जीवन के कार्य समाप्त कर चुका था।

B. वह स्थूल प्रलोभनों की अपेक्षा नहीं करता था।

C. उसे जीवन का उद्देश्य प्राप्त करने से रोक दिया गया होता।

D. वह अन्तिम क्षणों में भी शान्त था।

निर्देश (प्र.सं. 100 से 105): *निम्नलिखित काव्यांश को पढ़कर दिए गए प्रश्नों के **सबसे उचित** उत्तर वाले विकल्प चुनकर लिखिए।*

रोना और मचल जाना भी क्या आनंद दिखाते थे।
बड़े-बड़े मोती-से आँसू, जयमाला पहनाते थे।
मैं रोई, माँ काम छोड़कर आई, मुझको उठा लिया।
झाड़-पोंछकर चूम-चूम गीले गालों को सुखा दिया।
आ जा बचपन। एक बार फिर दे-दे अपनी निर्मल शांति।
व्याकुल व्यथा मिटाने वाली, वह अपनी प्राकृत विश्रांति।
वह भोली-सी मधुर सरलता, वह प्यारा जीवन निष्पाप।
क्या फिर आकर मिटा सकेगा तू मेरे मन का संताप?
मैं बचपन को बुला रही थी, बोल उठी बिटिया मेरी।
नंदन-वन-सी फूल उठी, यह छोटी-सी कुटिया मेरी।

100. 'बचपन' शब्द है :

A. विशेषण B. क्रिया-विशेषण
C. सर्वनाम D. संज्ञा

101. 'नंदन-वन-सी फूल उठी, यह छोटी-सी कुटिया मेरी' का भाव है :

A. कुटिया सुंदर हो गई
B. कुटिया में आनंद उमड़ उठा
C. कुटिया में शांति छा गई
D. छोटी कुटिया बड़ी हो गई

102. 'मिटा सकेगा **तू** मेरे मन का संताप?'
उक्त पंक्ति में 'तू' किसे कहा गया है?

A. बचपन को B. कवि को
C. पाठक को D. बच्चे को

103. कवयित्री अपने बचपन को क्यों बुलाना चाहती हैं?

A. अपनी बिटिया की याद में
B. बचपन के आनंद की याद में
C. बचपन के खेलों की याद में
D. अपनी माँ की याद में

104. बच्चे की आँखों से निकलते आँसुओं को देखकर क्या अनुभूति होती है?

A. सुख की B. विजय की
C. प्यार की D. कष्ट की

105. 'व्याकुल व्यथा मिटाने वाली' में प्रयुक्त अलंकार है :

A. रूपक अलंकार B. उपमा अलंकार
C. अनुप्रास अलंकार D. यमक अलंकार

निर्देश : *नीचे दिए गए प्रश्नों के **सबसे उचित** उत्तर वाले विकल्प को चुनिए।*

106. किसी भी भाषा पर अधिकार प्राप्त करने के लिए सबसे महत्त्वपूर्ण है :

A. शब्दों के अर्थ जानना
B. उस भाषा की वाक्य-संरचना जानना
C. उस भाषा का अधिकाधिक प्रयोग करना
D. उस भाषा का व्याकरण जानना

107. समावेशी कक्षा में बच्चों की आवश्यकताओं को पूरा करने में भाषा-शिक्षक के रूप में आपकी मुख्य जिम्मेदारी ***नहीं*** है :

A. बच्चों की भाषा संबंधी क्षमताओं की पहचान करना
B. बच्चों को विभिन्न प्रकार की दृश्य-श्रव्य सामग्री उपलब्ध कराना
C. बच्चों का आकलन करते समय अति उदार बनना
D. विभिन्न आवश्यकताओं वाले बच्चों के लिए उपलब्ध संसाधनों की खोज करना

108. पढ़ने की संस्कृति के विकास के क्रम में .... पठन को प्रोत्साहित किए जाने की आवश्यकता है।

A. वैयक्तिक B. सस्वर
C. मौन D. सामूहिक

109. भाषा की पाठ्य-पुस्तक में सबसे महत्वपूर्ण पक्ष है :

A. आकर्षक चित्र
B. पाठों का उद्देश्यपूर्ण चयन
C. अभ्यासों की बहुलता
D. कागज की गुणवत्ता

110. समग्र भाषा पद्धति पर आधारित कक्षा :

A. गतिविधियों के आयोजन पर बल देती है
B. बच्चों के भाषायी विकास की स्पष्ट समझ पर बल देती है
C. बाल साहित्य को पढ़कर सुनाने पर बल देती है
D. सभी भाषाओं को सीखने पर बल देती है

111. विद्यालय के बाहर का जीवन और वहाँ प्राप्त ज्ञान एवं अनुभव भाषा सीखने के लिए आवश्यक प्रेरणा देते हैं, क्योंकि :

A. मानक वर्तनी का सम्यक् ज्ञान मिलता है
B. लेखन की विभिन्न शैलियों का परिचय मिलता है
C. समृद्ध भाषिक परिवेश मिलता है
D. इससे व्याकरणिक नियमों की जानकारी प्राप्त होती है

112. पहली कक्षा में प्रवेश लेने से पहले आमतौर पर बच्चे :

A. पठन-लेखन में दक्ष होते हैं
B. स्व-अभिव्यक्ति जानते हैं
C. भाषा के व्याकरणिक नियम जानते हैं
D. तुतलाकर बोलते हैं

113. सुरभि अकसर 'ड़' वाले शब्दों को गलत तरीके से उच्चारित करती है। आप क्या करेंगे?

A. उसे 'ड़' वाले शब्दों की सूची पढ़ने एवं लिखकर अभ्यास करने के लिए देंगे
B. उसे 'ड़' वाले शब्दों को अपने पीछे-पीछे दोहराने के लिए कहेंगे
C. उसे सहजता के साथ अपनी बात कहने के लिए प्रोत्साहित करेंगे।
D. उसे 'ड़' वाले शब्दों की सूची पढ़ने एवं बोलकर अभ्यास करने के लिए देंगे।

114. प्राथमिक स्तर पर पढ़ने की क्षमता का आकलन करने की दृष्टि से सबसे **अधिक** महत्वपूर्ण है :

A. विराम-चिह्नों का ज्ञान
B. पढ़ने में प्रवाह
C. अर्थ का निर्माण
D. वर्णों की पहचान

115. भाषा की कक्षा में कहानी सुनाने का मूल उद्देश्य है :

A. बच्चों की कल्पनाशक्ति का विकास

B. बच्चों में 'सुनकर दोहराने' की आदत का विकास

C. बच्चों को अनुशासन में रखना

D. बच्चों का मनोरंजन करना

116. प्राथमिक कक्षाओं में बच्चे बहुत कुछ लेकर विद्यालय आते हैं, जैसे–अपनी ...., अपने अनुभव, दुनिया को देखने का अपना दृष्टिकोण आदि।

A. समस्याएँ B. भाषा

C. पाठ्य-पुस्तकें D. कमियाँ

117. बच्चों की मौखिक अभिव्यक्ति के विकास का अर्थ यह **नहीं** है :

A. वाद-विवाद में बेझिझक होकर बोलना

B. कहानी सुनकर शब्दशः दोहराना

C. अपनी कल्पनाओं की मौखिक अभिव्यक्ति

D. बातचीत में सक्रिय भागीदारिता का निर्वाह करना

118. भाषा की कक्षा में यह जरूरी है कि :

A. भाषा-शिक्षक भाषा का पूर्ण ज्ञाता हो

B. भाषा-शिक्षक बच्चोंकी उच्चारणगत शुद्धता पर विशेष ध्यान दे

C. भाषा-शिक्षक बच्चों की वर्तनी को बहुत कठोरता से ले

D. स्वयं भाषा-शिक्षक की भाषा प्रभावी हो

119. प्राथमिक स्तर पर बच्चों की भाषायी क्षमताओं का विकास करने का अर्थ है :

A. भाषिक संरचनाओं पर अधिकार

B. भाषा-प्रयोग की कुशलता पर अधिकार

C. भाषा-अनुकरण की कुशलता पर अधिकार

D. भाषिक नियमों पर अधिकार

120. व्याकरण-शिक्षण की आगमन विधि की विशेषता है :

A. पहले नियम बताना

B. पहले नियम का विश्लेषण करना

C. पहले मनोरंजक गतिविधियाँ करना

D. पहले उदाहरण प्रस्तुत करना

PART- V

Language-II : English

Directions (Q. Nos. 121 to 129): *Read the passage given below and answer the questions that follow by selecting the* ***most appropriate*** *options:*

One Sunday morning, I was travelling on a subway in Mumbai. People were sitting quietly–some reading newspapers, some lost in thought. It was a calm, peaceful scene.

Then suddenly, a man and his children entered the subway car. The children were so loud and rambunctious that instantly the whole climate changed.

The man sat next to me and closed his eyes, apparently oblivious to the situation. The children were yelling back and forth, throwing things, even grabbing people's papers. It was very disturbing. And yet, the man sitting next to me did nothing.

It was difficult not to feel irritated. I could not believe that he could be so insensitive as to let his children run wild and do nothing about it. It was easy to see that everyone else on the subway felt irritated, too. So finally, I turned to him and said, "Sir, your children are really disturbing a lot of people. I wonder if you couldn't control them a little more?"

The man lifted his gaze as if to come to a consciousness of the situation for the first time and said softly, "Oh, you're right. I guess I should do something about it. We just came from the hospital where their mother died an hour ago. I don't know what to think and I guess they don't know how to handle it either".

Can you imagine what I felt at that moment. My paradigm shifted. Suddenly I saw things differently, and because I saw things differently, I thought, felt and behaved differently. My irritation vanished; my heart was filled with the man's pain. Feelings of sympathy and compassion flowed freely. "Your wife just died? Oh, I am sorry! Can you tell me about it? What can I do to help?" Everything changed in an instant.

121. The primary purpose of the author is to:

A. narrate an amusing incident

B. show how indulgent parents spoil their children

C. show a radical shift in attitude

D. highlight the problems of subway travellers

122. The word 'oblivious' (Para 3) means:

A. unaware B. neglectful

C. inconsiderate D. insensitive

123. The word which is opposite in meaning to 'compassion' (para 6) is:

A. coarseness B. dislike

C. wildness D. cruelty

124. 'I *felt* differently.'
Tense of the above sentence has been correctly changed into present continuous in:
A. I am feeling differently
B. I had been feeling differently
C. I was feeling differently
D. I have been feeling differently

125. 'My irritation vanished.'
The sentence given above has been correctly changed into interrogative form in:
A. Couldn't my irritation vanish?
B. Hadn't my irritation vanished?
C. Didn't my irritation vanish?
D. Did my irritation vanish?

126. The children's behaviour on the subway was:
A. irritating B. disgusting
C. shocking D. amusing

127. How did the man (children's father) react to the unruly behaviour of his children?
A. He rebuked them
B. He tried to control them
C. He did nothing
D. He enjoyed their antics

128. It can be inferred from the man's behaviour that he was:
A. an indulgent parent
B. mentally distrubed
C. unsocial
D. insensitive

129. When the writer learnt the truth:
A. his heart was filled with the man's suffering
B. he was angry with himself for being judgemental
C. he decided to help the man out
D. he felt apologetic

Directions (Q. Nos. 130 to 135) : *Read the passage given below and answer the questions that follow by selecting the most appropriate options:*

Your attitudes are the perspectives from which you view life. Some people seem to have a good attitude towards most things. Some people seem to have a bad attitude towards everything. But when you look closer, you will find that most of us have a combination of attitudes, some good, some not so good.

Whatever attitude we have towards anything will affect how we feel about it, which in turn determines whether or not we will do well. So our right attitudes play a very important part in helping us become successful.

In fact, as we can see, a good attitude is essential for achievement of any kind ! We so often hear of someone who is said to have a "bad attitude". The term is often applied to young people, especially to teenagers who frequently get into trouble, but we often hear it about adults, too. The implication is always that the individual in question is not going to make it if he doesn't change his attitude.

I would agree, without a good attitude it is not possible to see the opportunities ahead and set one's sights to reach them. But even more important is the fact that in order to possess the kind of feelings which work for us, we've got to have the right attitude to start with.

But where do we get our attitudes from? Are we born with them or do they just appear out of nowhere? Our attitudes are no accident. They don't just happen. Our attitudes are created and influenced entirely by our beliefs.

130. Which one of the following statements is correct?
A. Our attitudes are influenced by our parents only
B. Our attitudes are created and controlled by our beliefs
C. Our attitudes are the results of our personal experience
D. We are born with our attitudes

131. The word 'determine' most nearly means:
A. influence B. overcome
C. engage D. govern

132. Which part of speech is the **bold** word in the sentence given below?
'Some people seem to have a good attitude **towards** most things.'
A. Preposition B. Adjective
C. Conjunction D. Adverb

133. A/An .... attitude is absolutely necessary for attainment of any kind.
A. cheerful B. optimistic
C. good D. virtuous

134. The term "bad attitude" is used for young people because they:
A. behave irresponsibly
B. often get into difficulty
C. are unpredictable
D. defy all kinds of authority

135. Right attitudes are absolutely essential to:
A. win the goodwill of our peers and superiors
B. have harmonious relations with others
C. promote our mental well-being
D. succeed in life

Directions : *Answer the following questions by selecting the **most appropriate** options.*

136. Which of the following is the highest level of cognitive ability?

A. Knowing B. Understanding
C. Evaluating D. Analysing

137. Why is story telling most important in an English language class at primary level?

A. It is useful for developing integrated language skills
B. It develops moral values among the students
C. It improves students' vocabulary
D. It creates fun in the class

138. A good teacher is one who:

A. gives them ample opportunities to learn
B. gives them useful information
C. explains concepts and principles
D. gives printed notes to students

139. Which of the following helps in learning the second language without using the printed text?

A. Situational approach
B. Natural approach
C. Language immersion
D. Grammar-translation method

140. A person, who is a fluent speaker, is likely to possess:

A. Logico-mathematical ability
B. Bodily-kinesthetic ability
C. Musical ability
D. Verbal-linguistic ability

141. Which approach emphasizes interaction as the means and the goal of learning a language?

A. Communicative B. Oral-aural
C. Immersion D. Silent way

142. Maximum participation of students during teaching in a language class-room is possible through:

A. Lecture method
B. Translation method
C. Inductive method
D. Discussion and demonstration methods

143. Dyslexia is an intellectual disability that negatively affects the understanding abilities in terms of:

A. Oral language B. Sign language
C. Dialect D. Reading

144. The Linguist, Noam Chomsky maintains that every child has an innate Language Acquisition Device (LAD) that he/she uses for:

A. Phonemes B. Universal Grammar
C. Complex words D. Semantics

145. The structural approach advocates:

A. resorting to fluency
B. selection and gradation of material
C. assessing learners' performance
D. using mother tongue

146. According to socio-cultural theory of Vygotsky:

A. Self-directed speech is the lowest stage of the scaffolding
B. Children can think in abstract terms if abstract material is provided at a lower age
C. Children think in different domain and do not take a complete perspective
D. Culture helps in language development

147. What is the main purpose of poetry recitation in a language classroom?

A. To appreciate and enjoy the poem
B. To give their opinions about the poem
C. To become aware of the poet and her works
D. To know the historical background of the poem

148. Who strongly maintains that language is learnt by imitation of stimuli and reinforcement of correct responses?

A. Albert Bandura B. Kurt Lewin
C. Tolman D. B.F. Skinner

149. Under which activity do recognising sounds and deducing meanings from them come?

A. Speaking B. Listening
C. Reading D. Writing

150. During the process of language learning, students lack confidençe in their pronunciation. How can one overcome this?

A. Providing scope for special activities with the help of language experts for removing speaking defects
B. Correcting mistakes immediately
C. Reading aloud in the classroom
D. Organizing play like tasks in which children can talk to one another

Answers

1	2	3	4	5	6	7	8	9	10
B	B	D	D	C	A	D	D	D	A
11	12	13	14	15	16	17	18	19	20
C	B	B	A	B	D	B	D	B	D
21	22	23	24	25	26	27	28	29	30
A	D	D	A	B	A	D	B	A	A
31	32	33	34	35	36	37	38	39	40
A	B	D	B	A	B	C	B	D	A
41	42	43	44	45	46	47	48	49	50
D	D	C	C	C	C	B	A	C	D
51	52	53	54	55	56	57	58	59	60
C	B	B	C	B	C	B	B	C	C
61	62	63	64	65	66	67	68	69	70
A	A	C	D	B	B	B	C	B	C
71	72	73	74	75	76	77	78	79	80
C	C	A	C	A	A	A	B	C	C
81	82	83	84	85	86	87	88	89	90
A	C	A	B	D	D	C	C	B	A
91	92	93	94	95	96	97	98	99	100
C	C	A	A	A	C	B	A	C	D
101	102	103	104	105	106	107	108	109	110
B	A	B	C	C	C	C	A	B	B
111	112	113	114	115	116	117	118	119	120
C	B	C	C	A	B	B	D	B	D
121	122	123	124	125	126	127	128	129	130
C	A	D	A	C	A	C	B	A	B
131	132	133	134	135	136	137	138	139	140
D	A	C	B	D	C	A	A	B	D
141	142	143	144	145	146	147	148	149	150
A	D	D	B	B	D	A	D	B	C

Some Selected Explanatory Answers

1. Though a traditional pedagogical teaching approach gives emphasis on the teacher's role as the holder of the wisdom, the teacher as facilitator, puts the onus on the students to become involved in their own learning, which is by virtue of their potential to create knowledge and make meaning by their own efforts and application of I.Q. The facilitator's is supposed to introduce subjects of discussion, encourage sharing of perspectives, and integrate students' share experiences. A good facilitator stimulates his/her students' thinking, encourage exploration, make associations and be a connector.

2. A gifted child is identified by his/her educational performance in school as to how talented or laudable he/she is in his/her studies. As far as the characteristics of gifted children are concerned, below average mental processes cannot be a characteristic of such children because it pertains to their mental ability to perceive the things taught to them or what appears to them. Mental process or mental functions are terms often used interchangeably for all the things that children can do with their minds. Of course, the event of perceiving something is different from the entire process, or capacity of perception, i.e., one's ability to perceive things.

4. Students come to learning situations with already formulated knowledge, ideas and understandings they have. Such previous knowledge works as the raw materials for the new knowledge they create. However, if they are provided with the situations that prompt them to learn, it helps them a lot in solving the problems put before them. For example, a teacher presents a class problem to measure the length of the "Mayflower". Rather than starting the problem by introducing the ruler, the teacher allows students to reflect and to construct their own methods of measurement. It is a sort of providing a learning situation to students. Thus, the teacher should provide a variety of learning situations.

5. It will be incorrect to say that all development and learning in a child proceed at an equal rate; rather development proceeds at varying rates from child to child as well as unevenly within different areas of each child's functioning. Each child is a unique person with an individual pattern and timing of growth, as well as individual personality, temperament, learning style, and experiential and family backgrounds. They have their own individual strengths, needs, and interests; for some children, special learning and developmental needs or abilities are identified.

6. Assessment is essential to allow the students to get the educational support they need to succeed, to see the effectiveness of different educational methods, and to ensure that education budgets are being spent effectively. Inevitably, assessment also risks marking teachers, learners and institutions as successes or failures. In today's world, we have very good multimedia (Computer based) resources which have inbuilt assessment tasks in the concept presentation and teachers should try to use these resources.

7. Divergent thinking is a thought process or method used to generate creative ideas by exploring many possible solutions. It is often used in conjunction with its cognitive opposite, convergent thinking, which follows a particular set of logical steps to arrive at one solution, which in some cases is a 'correct' solution. By contrast, divergent thinking typically occurs in a spontaneous, free-flowing, 'non-linear' manner, such that many ideas are generated in an emergent cognitive fashion.

8. According to Lev Vygotsky (1962), a Russian teacher and psychologist, man learns through his interactions and communications with others. He examined how people's social environments influence the learning process. He suggested that learning takes place through the interactions students have with their peers, teachers, elders and other experts. Consequently, teachers can create a learning environment that maximizes the learner's ability to interact with each other through discussion, collaboration, and feedback.

9. Children are curious beings who use their own logic and abilities to explore the world around them, as they use their sense, their minds and their bodies to find out about and make sense of what they feel and experience in the world around them. They demonstrate their ability to reason, negotiate and think logically. They make decisions and take increasing responsibility for their own learning.

10. Errors made by children are a part of the learning process, as errors are the basis of application and they allow for experimentation. If children are afraid of making errors or mistakes, then they will also be afraid of trying anything new, of being creative, of thinking in a different way to know and explore something. By committing mistakes, they come to know as to where they need to avoid what and where they need to adopt what, as that would enable them to succeed in their efforts to reach the desired goal.

12. Learning styles are just a subset of a much wider range of individual differences affecting the process of language learning. Age, aptitude, motivation, general intelligence, sensory preferences and sociocultural conditions are all examples of other important factors influencing the way learners react to classroom instruction.

    Individual-vs group-oriented: The former learners are likely to be independent also in terms of self-esteem and personal identity; they tend to work on the basis of intrinsic motivation, and may like to establish their own working plan; on the other hand, group-oriented people may be more dependent on a group or an external authority to define their personal identity and social role; they tend to be motivated by extrinsic motivations; they may benefit by being provided with a clearly described working plan.

14. In describing age old nature-nurture controversy, by nature, we mean inborn biological givens—the hereditary information we receive from our parents at the moment of conception. By nurture, we mean the complex forces of the physical and social world that influence our biological makeup and psychological experiences before and after birth.

15. Since the advent of television, mass media have become prominent socialization agents. The use of more personalized forms of media, such as text messaging and participation in social networking sites, has expanded exponentially in recent years. Media are rich sources of information about government, politics, and current affairs. Media also establish linkages between leaders, institutions, and citizens. In contrast to typing and mailing a letter, it is easier than ever for people to contact leaders directly using e-mail and Facebook.

17. A primary school teacher should adopt a Instructional Behaviours That Motivate Students by helping them to set achievable goals for themselves. Failure to atain unrealistic goals can disappoint and frustrate students. Encourage students to focus on their continued improvement, not just on their grade on any one test or assignment. Help students evaluate their progress by encouraging them to critique their own work, analyze their strengths, and work on their weaknesses. For example, consider asking students to submit self-evaluation forms with one or two assignments.

18. Socialization is the process by which human infants begin to acquire the skills necessary to perform as a

functioning member of their society, and is the most influential learning process one can experience. The family is the primary agency of socialisation. It is here that the child develops an initial sense of self and habit-training—eating, sleeping etc. To a very large extent, the indoctrination of the child, whether in primitive or modem complex society, occurs within the circle of the primary family group. The child's first human relationships are with the immediate members of his family—mother or nurse, siblings, father and other close relatives.

20. Dyslexia, also known as reading disorder, is characterized by trouble with reading despite normal intelligence. Different people are affected to varying degrees. Problems may include difficulties in spelling words, reading quickly, writing words, "sounding out" words in the head, pronouncing words when reading aloud and understanding what one reads.

21. The period from birth to two years of age is a critical time for an infant's health, growth and development. New parents and parents-to-be will find information here to help their children with the best possible start in life.

23. Growth and development is one of the important subject of psychology. Development implies changes in shape, form or structure resulting in improved working. It implies qualitative changes.

Development proceeds from general to specific responses: It moves from a generalized to localized behaviour. The newborn infant moves its whole body at one time instead of moving only one part of it. It makes random kicking with its legs before it can coordinate the leg muscles well enough to crawl or to walk.

25. Accommodation: A part of adaptation involves changing or altering our existing schemas in light of new information, a process known as accommodation. Accommodation involves altering existing schemas, or ideas, as a result of new information or new experiences.

31. $\text{Number of boxes} = \frac{10290}{98} = 105$

$\because$ Cost of 1 box = ₹ 518

$\therefore$ Cost of 105 boxes = ₹ 518 × 105 = ₹ 54390

47. Ten thousands + Ten hundreds + Ten tens

= 10000 + 1000 + 100

= 11100

48. 12112 ÷ 11 gives remainder = 1

13223 ÷ 13 gives remainder = 2

$\therefore$ Sum of remainders = 1 + 2 = 3

49. Place value of 6 in 56431 = 6000

Face value of 4 in 56431 = 4

Required difference = 6000 – 4 = 5996

50. L.C.M. of 30, 36 and 42 = 1260

H.C.F. of 30, 36 and 42 = 6

Required number = 1260 × 6 = 7560

51. All the positive factors of 84 which are multiple of 7 = 7, 14, 21, 28, 42, 84

Required Sum = 7 + 14 + 21 + 28 + 42 + 84

= 196

52. In Delhi 8 : 49 p.m.

In Sydney 1 : 19 a.m.

Difference = 13 : 19 – 8.49 = 4 : 30

In Delhi 11 : 19 a.m.

In Sydney 11 : 19 a.m. + 4 : 30

= 15 : 49

= 3 : 49 p.m.

53. $\because \quad 125 \text{ km} = \frac{1}{2} \text{ cm}$

$$2000 \text{ km} = \frac{1}{2 \times 125} \times 2000$$

$$= \frac{2000}{250} = 8 \text{ cm}$$

54. $\text{Area of Square} = \left(\frac{30}{100}\right)^2 = \left(\frac{3}{10}\right)^2$

$$= \frac{9}{100} \text{m}^2 = 0.09 \text{m}^2$$

Area of rectangle = 4.5 × 0.2

$$= \frac{45}{10} \times \frac{2}{10} = \frac{90}{100}$$

$$= \frac{9}{10} \text{m}^2 = 0.9 \text{m}^2$$

$\because$ Area of square ≠ area of rectangle.

Hence, it is not correct.

55. $\text{No. of boys} = \frac{2}{3} \times 660$

= 2 × 220 = 440

No. of girls = 660 – 440 = 220

$\text{No. of boys players} = \frac{3}{4} \times 440$

= 3 × 110 = 330

No. of girls players $= \frac{1}{4} \times 220$

$= 55$

Total number of players in the school

$= 330 + 55 = 385$

56. Area of the floor $= 900 \times 700 \text{ cm}^2$

Area of each tile $= 35 \times 45 \text{ cm}^2$

$\therefore$ No. of tiles $= \frac{9 \times 7 \times 100 \times 100}{35 \times 45}$

$= 20 \times 20 = 400$

57. $6 \times 60 \times 60$ seconds $= x \times 24 \times 60$ days.

$\therefore \quad x = \frac{6 \times 60 \times 60}{24 \times 60} = 15$ days

58. (*i*) $20 \times 25 \times 18 = 9000 \text{ cm}^3$

(*ii*) $23 \times 20 \times 20 = 9200 \text{ cm}^3$

(*iii*) $20 \times 22 \times 21 = 9240 \text{ cm}^3$

(*iv*) $24 \times 20 \times 19 = 9120 \text{ cm}^3$

Clearly (*ii*) + (*iii*) = 9200 + 9240 = 18440

Hence, using (*ii*) and (*iii*) boxes can 18440 wooden centimetre cubes be packed.

59. Side of the square $= \frac{\text{Perimeter}}{4}$

$= \frac{80}{4} = 20$ cm

Area of the square $= (20)^2 = 400 \text{ cm}^2$

$\therefore$ Length of the rectangle $= 2 \times 20 = 40$ cm

Area of the rectangle $= 40 \times 20 = 800 \text{ cm}^2$

Difference $= 800 - 400 = 400 \text{ cm}^2$

Hence, area of the rectangle exceeds the area of the square by 400 cm^2

60. Cost of bananas = ₹ 2.50 × ₹ 18 = ₹ 45

Cost of apples $= 3 \times 57.60 + \frac{1}{2} \times 57.60$

$= 172.80 + 28.80$

= ₹ 201.60

Cost of mangoes $= \frac{3}{2} \times 75.40$

$= 3 \times 37.70 =$ ₹ 113.10

Cost of grapes = ₹ $\frac{3}{4} \times 120 =$ ₹ 90

Total cost = 45 + 201.60 + 113.10 + 90 = ₹ 449.70

He will get back = 500 − 449.70 = ₹ 50.30

Previous Paper (Solved)

CTET PAPER-I, FEBRUARY 2015*

PART- I

Child Development and Pedagogy

Directions: *Answer the following questions by selecting the* ***most appropriate*** *option.*

1. Which one of the following is best suited for emotional development of children?
A. Democratic classroom environment
B. No involvement of the teachers as it is the task of the parents
C. Controlled classroom environment
D. Authoritarian classroom environment

2. Which one of the following is ***not*** a suitable formative assessment task?
A. Open-ended questions
B. Project
C. Observation
D. Ranking the students

3. To be an effective teacher it is important to
A. emphasize dictating answer from the book.
B. focus on individual learning rather than group activity.
C. avoid disruption caused due to questioning by students
D. be in touch with each and every child

4. Teachers need to create a good classroom environment to facilitate children's learning. To create such a learning environment, which one of the given statements is ***not*** true?
A. Approval of the child's efforts
B. Compliance with teachers
C. Acceptance of the child
D. Positive tone of the teacher

5. Given below are some statements about boys and girls. According to you, which one of these is true?
A. Boys should help in activities outside the home.
B. Boys should help in household chores.
C. All boys should be taught Science and girls, Home Science.
D. Girls should help in household chores.

6. A child's notebook shows errors in writing like reverse images, mirror imaging, etc. Such a child is showing signs of
A. Learning disadvantage
B. Learning disability
C. Learning difficulty
D. Learning problem

7. Teachers, in order to help learners construct knowledge, need to focus on
A. making sure the learner memories everything.
B. scores/marks obtained by the learner.
C. involving the learner for active Participation
D. mastering learning of concepts by the learner.

8. Giftedness from teacher's point of view is a combination of
A. High Ability – High Creativity – High Commitment
B. High Motivation – High Commitment – High Talent
C. High Ability – High Talent – High Commitment
D. High Talent – High Creativity – High Memory

9. According to NCF 2005, errors are important because they
A. are an important tool in classifying students into groups of 'passed' and 'failed'.
B. provide a way to the teachers to scold the children.
C. provide an insight into the child's thinking and help to identify solutions.
D. provide space for removing some children from the class

10. 'Out-of-the-box' thinking is related to
A. Consistent Thinking
B. Memory-based Thinking
C. Divergent Thinking
D. Convergent Thinking

11. The assessment of students can be used by teachers in teaching to develop insight into
A. identifying the students who need to be promoted to the higher class.
B. not promoting those students who do not meet school standards.
C. changing the teaching approach according to the learners' need.

*Exam was held on 22-02-2015.

D. creating groups of 'bright' and 'weak' students in the class.

12. Learning experiences should be planned in a manner so as to make learning meaningful. Which of the given learning experiences does not facilitate meaningful learning for the children?
A. Repetition based on mere recall of content
B. Formulating questions on content
C. Discussion and debate on the topic
D. Presentation on the topic

13. Giving punishment, verbal or non-verbal, to the children results in
A. motivating them to work
B. protecting the child's image
C. improving their scores
D. damaging their self-concept

14. Which one out of the following provides information about the roles and behaviours which are acceptable in a group, during early childhood period?
A. Siblings and Teachers
B. Teachers and Peers
C. Peers and Parents
D. Parents and Siblings

15. Making students members of a cleanliness community to motivate them for the same, reflects
A. Socio-cultural conceptions of motivation
B. Behaviouristic approach to motivation
C. Humanistic approach to motivation
D. Cognitive approach to motivation

16. Which of the following age groups falls under later childhood category?
A. 11 to 18 years
B. 18 to 24 years
C. Birth to 6 years
D. 6 to 11 years

17. Aarjav says that language development is influenced by one's innate predisposition while Sonali feels that it is because of the environment. This discussion between Aarjav and Sonali is about
A. Critical and Sensitive feeling
B. Stability and Instability argument
C. Continuous and Discontinuous learning
D. Nature and Nurture debate

18. The teacher noticed that Pushpa cannot solve a problem on her own. However, she does so in the presence of adult or peer guidance. This guidance is called
A. Lateralization
B. Pre-operational thinking
C. Zone of proximal development
D. Scaffolding

19. A teacher, labelled the head of a committee, as 'chairperson' instead of 'chairman'. It indicates that the teacher
A. follows a more acceptable term
B. has a good command of language
C. is using a gender-free language
D. has gender bias

20. Continuous and Comprehensive Evaluation is essential for
A. fine tuning of test with the teaching
B. diluting the accountability of the Board of Education
C. correcting less-frequent errors more than more-frequent errors
D. understanding how learning can be observed, recorded and improved upon

21. In Lawrence Kohlberg's theory, which level signifies the absence of morality in the true sense?
A. Level III B. Level IV
C. Level I D. Level II

22. Which one of the following is not correct for the progressive model of socialization of children?
A. Active participation in the group work and learning social skills.
B. Children accept what they are offered by the school irrespective of their social backgrounds.
C. There should be a place for democracy in the classroom.
D. Socialization is an adoption of social norms.

23. In learning, assessment is essential for
A. Grades and Marks
B. Screening test
C. Motivation
D. Fostering of the purpose of segregation and ranking

24. Fitting new information into existing schemes is known as
A. Accommodation B. Equilibration
C. Assimilation D. Organisation

25. We all differ in terms of our intelligence, motivation, interest, etc. This principle refers to
A. Individual difference
B. Theories of Intelligence
C. Heredity
D. Environment

26. Students of disadvantaged groups should be taught along with the normal students. It implies
A. Inclusive Education
B. Special Education
C. Integrated Education
D. Exclusive Education

27. "Anyone can become angry—that is easy, but to be angry with the right person, to the right degree, at the right time, for the right purposse, and in the right way—that is not easy." This is related to
A. Emotional development
B. Social development
C. Cognitive development
D. Physical development

28. Deficiency in the ability to write, associated with impaired handwriting, is a symptom of
A. Dysgraphia B. Dyspraxia
C. Dyscalculia D. Dyslexia

29. According to Piaget theory, which one out of the following will not influence one's cognitive development?
A. Language B. Social experiences
C. Maturation D. Activity

30. Which of these does not imply practical intelligence in the Triarchic theory?
A. Reshaping the environment
B. Thinking practically about oneself only
C. Choosing an invironment in which you can succeed
D. Adapting to the environment

PART- II

Mathematics

Directions : *Answer the following questions by selecting the most* ***appropriate*** *option.*

31. Which of the following is ***not*** correct?
A. 3 hours 14 minutes = 194 minutes
B. 2 kg 30 g is the same as 2030 g
C. 3 litres 80 millilitres = 38 millilitres
D. Area of a square of side 10 cm = Area of the rectangle of length 100 cm and breadth 0.01 m

32. On dividing 110111 by 11, the sum of the quotient and the remainder is
A. 11011 B. 11001
C. 10101 D. 10011

33. What should be subtracted from the product 102×201 to get 19999?
A. 503 B. 602
C. 103 D. 401

34. Number of degrees in two and two-third of a right-angle is
A. 240 B. 270
C. 180 D. 210

35. A one-litre carton of juice is in the shape of a cuboid and has a square base of size 8 cm by 8 cm. The depth of juice in the carton, in centimeters, is closest to
A. 20 B. 22
C. 16 D. 18

36. Which one of the following statements is true?
A. The product of three odd numbers is an even number.
B. The difference of an even number and an odd number can be an even number.
C. The sum of two odd numbers and one even number is an even number.
D. The sum of three odd numbers is an even number.

37. The sum of place values of 5 in 6251, 6521 and 5621 is
A. 550 B. 15
C. 5550 D. 5050

38. At primary level use of tangram, dot games, patterns, etc. helps the students to
A. understand basic operations
B. enhance spatial understanding ability
C. develop sense of comparing numbers
D. strengthen calculation skills

39. Which one of the following does not match curricular expectations of teaching mathematics at the primary level?
A. Represent part of whole as a fraction and order simple fractions
B. Analyse and infer from representation of grouped data
C. Develop a connection between the logical functioning of daily life and that of mathematical thinking
D. Develop language and symbolic notations with standard algorithms of performing number operations.

40. The main goal of Mathematics education is
A. to formulate theorems of Geometry and their proofs independently.
B. to help the students to understand mathematics.
C. to develop useful capabilities.
D. to develop children's abilities for mathematization.

41. A teacher uses the exploratory approach, use of manipulatives and involvement of students in discussion while giving the concepts of mathematics.

She uses this strategy to
A. achieve the higher aim of teaching mathematics.
B. develop manipulative skills among the students.
C. create a certain way of thinking and reasoning.
D. achieve the narrow aim of teaching mathematics.

42. A teacher asks Shailja of class V about the perimeter of a figure.
She also asked Shailja to explain the solution in her words. Shailja was able to solve the problem correctly but was not able to explain it. This reflects that Shailja is having
A. poor confidence level and poor mathematical skills
B. poor understanding of concept of perimeter but good verbal ability
C. lower language proficiency and lower order mathematical proficiency
D. lower language proficiency and higher order mathematical proficiency

43. The section, 'Practice Time' included in different topics in Mathematics textbook aims at
A. providing fun and enjoyment to students having a change in daily routine
B. having a change in daily routine
C. ensuring better utilization of time
D. providing extended learning opportunities

44. Formative Assessment in Mathematics at primary stage includes
A. identification of learning gaps and deficiencies in teaching.
B. identification of common errors.
C. testing of procedural knowledge and analytical abilities.
D. grading and ranking of students.

45. It is important to conduct mathematical recreational activities and challenging geometrical puzzles in the class as
A. they can create interest in low achievers and slow learners in mathematics.
B. they bring students out of the monotonous and boring routines of mathematics classroom.
C. they give space to gifted learners.
D. they are helpful to enhance spatial and analytical ability of every learner.

46. 'Vedic Mathematics' is becoming popular nowadays especially amongst primary school children and is used to enhance
A. the algorithmic understanding of students in mathematics
B. the problem solving skills of students in mathematics
C. the concentration of students in mathematics
D. the calculation skills and speed in mathematics

47. Akanksha wants to become a good mathematics teacher. To be a good mathematics teacher she must have
A. good communicative skills and the knowledge of close-ended questions.
B. conceptual knowledge, understanding and ability to relate content of mathematics with real life.
C. good knowledge of Number System, Algebra and Geometry.
D. Ability to solve the problems in no time.

48. A teacher introduced multiplication in her class as repeated addition and then by grouping of same number of objects taken multiple times she introduced the 'x' symbol and further conducted a small activity of finding product using criss-cross lines or matchsticks. Here the teacher is
A. providing remedial strategies for low achievers in mathematics.
B. using multiple representations to make the class interesting.
C. developing a lesson and taking students 'from concrete to abstract concept'.
D. catering to learners with different learning styles.

49. 13 students of class V A and 15 of class V B participated in a writing competition. They scored marks as follows:

Class V A 14, 6, 15, 12, 11, 11, 7, 9, 17, 13, 3, 10, 18

Class V B 13, 9, 0, 7, 14, 6, 0, 9, 16, 9, 13, 16, 5, 18, 11

What inference can you draw from the given data?
A. Both the sections performed equally well because the highest score of both the sections is 18.
B. Class V A performed better because the average score of VA is more.
C. Both the sections performed equally well because the total marks scored by both the sections are the same.
D. Both the sections performed equally well because the average marks of both the sections are the same.

50. How many $\frac{1}{10}$ are in $\frac{6}{5}$?

A. 8 B. 5
C. 12 D. 10

51. A train leaves a station at 6 : 14 a.m. and reaches its destination after 13 hours 48 minutes. The time at the destination is

A. 8 ; 02 p.m. B. 8 : 12 p.m.
C. 7 : 02 p.m. D. 7 : 12 p.m.

52. (Sum of multiples of 7 between 21 and 49) ÷ (Biggest common factor of 25 and 30) is equal to
A. 35 B. 37
C. 14 D. 21

53. The sum of all the positive factors of 96 is
A. 251 B. 252
C. 155 D. 156

54. As per the NCF 2005, the narrow aim of teaching Mathematics at schools is
A. to teach daily life problems related to linear algebra
B. to develop numeracy related skills
C. to teach algebra
D. to teach calculation and measurements

55. Ravi has three dozen chocolates. He gave one-third of them to his neighbour, one-sixth to Rehana and one-fouth to his sister. How many chocolates are left with him?
A. 9 B. 10
C. 6 D. 8

56. Perimeter of a square is 44 cm. The perimeter of a rectangle is equal to the perimeter of this square. The length of the rectangle is 5 cm more than the side of the square. The sum of areas (in cm^2) of the square and the rectangle is
A. 217 B. 229
C. 169 D. 140

57. A child who is able to perform all number operations and is able to explain the concept of fractions is at
A. partition phase B. operational phase
C. emergent phase D. quantifying phase

58. What is the value of
$-1 + 2 - 3 + 4 - 5 + 6 - 7 + ... + 1000$?
A. 500 B. 2000
C. 0 D. 1

59. From the unit of 'Shapes' the teacher asked the students to "make/draw any picture by using shapes". The objective that can be achieved through this activity is
A. Application B. Knowledge
C. Comprehension D. Creating

60. Arjun, a student of class IV, is able to answer all questions related to Number System orally, but commits mistakes while writing the solutions of problems based on Number System. The best remedial strategy to remove errors in his writing is
A. to give him 10 practice tests.
B. to relate real life experiences with mathematical concepts.
C. to provide him a worksheet with partially solved problems to complete the missing gaps.
D. to teach more than one way of solving problems of Number System.

PART- III

Environmental Studies

Directions : Answer the following questions by selecting the most appropriate option.

61. Which of the following is/are tools and techniques of assessment in EVS at primary level?
1. Project work 2. Field trip
3. Journal writing 4. Concept mapping
A. Only 2 and 3
B. Only 4
C. 1, 2, 3 and 4
D. Only 1 and 2

62. Study the following statements about the jhoom farming practised in Mizoram :
1. After cutting one crop, the land is left as it is for some years.
2. The bamboo or weeds which grow on that land are cut and burnt.
3. The land is deeply ploughed before sowing the seeds.
4. In one farms three or four different types of crops are grown.
5. Chemical fertilizers and pesticides are also used as per need.

The correct statements are
A. 3, 4 and 5 B. 1, 2 and 4
C. Only 1 and 2 D. Only 2 and 4

63. Teaching of EVS should encourage process skills, which are the core of inquiry-based, hands-on learning. Which one of the following is not such a skill?
A. Predicting B. Determination
C. Inferring D. Observation

64. Radha uses travel tickets of different types. Which of the following concepts could be effectively discussed by using such tickets?
1. The cost of travel by different means is different.
2. The cost of travel depends upon the fuel used by the vehicle.
3. We need tickets to travel by public transport from one place to another.
4. Understanding the reservation process.

Choose the most appropriate option :

A. 3 and 4 B. 1 and 4

C. 1 and 3 D. 2 and 4

65. Which one of the following strategies seems most appropriate for teaching maps to primary graders?

A. Drawing of the map by the teacher on the black-board and asking learners to locate different places

B. Instructing learners to bring the map of India from their home

C. Showing an atlas to learners and asking them to locate different places

D. Facilitating learners to construct maps of their immediate surroundings by using their own symbols and focusing on relative position and direction of things

66. Mahika, a teacher of class V, wants her students to observe the plants in the surroundings. For meaningful learning, what should she encourage the children to do?

A. Understanding that plants are living beings

B. Appreciating that plants are useful for us

C. Writing the names of maximum number of plants

D. Observing the difference in their heights, leaves, smell and place of growing

67. Which one of the following should be a most important aspect of EVS teaching at primary level?

A. Conducting activities and developing skills

B. Achieving success in assessment

C. Understanding the basic concepts of science

D. Connecting learners to the natural and socio-cultural environment

68. 'Mapping' at primary level promotes which of the following skills in learners?

A. Neat drawing

B. Calculations and Estimations

C. Drawing according to scale

D. Idea about relative positions and orientations

69. Study the following table :

	June 2007	*December 2014*
Price of petrol in ₹/litre	47.74	61.33
Price of diesel in ₹/litre	35.21	50.51

After studying the above table, Devmeet a class V student, wrote the following in his notebook :

1. Petrol is a more expensive fuel than diesel.
2. The percentage increase in price of diesel is more than that of petrol.
3. Diesel is cheaper and that is why public transport runs on it.
4. Diesel is a cheaper fuel than petrol. People should buy diesel vehicle.

Which one of the following is correct?

A. 2 and 3 are inferences

B. 3 and 4 are inferences

C. 1 and 4 are observations

D. 1 and 3 are observations

70. All of the following are indicative of the general approach to be followed for EVS in primary classes except from

1. concrete to abstract
2. simple to complex
3. local to global
4. abstract to concrete

A. Only 2 B. Only 4

C. Only 1 and 2 D. Only 2 and 3

71. NCF 2005 has not recommended any prescribed curriculum and text-books for EVS for classes I and II. The most appropriate reason for this;

A. To reduce the load of curriculum

B. EVS is only for class III onwards

C. Learners in class I and II cannot read and write

D. To provide contextual learning environment

72. A teacher has to teach about cultural diversity in food in our country to class IV students. Which of the following is the best way to teach this topic?

A. Show flash cards having pictures of various food items.

B. Give a project to students about different kinds of food taken by the people of various states in our country.

C. Ask students what they have eaten followed by a discussion.

D. Ask students to collect information about the kind of food taken in their family.

73. If we observe birds, we find that most of the birds often move their neck. It is because

A. in most of the birds, the eyes are fixed and cannot move.

B. their ears are covered and they can fly.

C. the birds have two eyes.

D. their eyes can focus on two different objects at a time.

74. Reena loves mangoes. She wants to preserve these for winters. Which one of the following is a good way of preserving them?

A. Make 'aam papad' and pickle.

B. Prepare juice and store in an airtight container.

C. Put in a plastic bag.

D. Store in a refrigerator.

75. The neighbouring states of Kerala are

A. Tamil Nadu and Andhra Pradesh

B. Karnataka and Maharashtra
C. Andhra Pradesh and Karnataka
D. Karnataka and Tamil Nadu

76. In which one of the following states of our country do most people like to eat sea fish cooked in coconut oil?
A. Mizoram B. Goa
C. Jammu and Kashmir D. Bihar

77. Which one of the following animals' front teeth keep on growing throughout its life? It has to keep gnawing on things to keep its teeth from becoming too long.
A. Termite B. Squirrel
C. Lizard D. Rat

78. A farmer is growing paddy crop over and over again using excess of fertilizers and pesticides in his fields. This practice will make the soil of his fields
A. useful for the paddy crops only
B. fit for ploughing
C. barren
D. fertile for other crops also

79. Study the following statements about "Desert Oak" :
1. Desert Oak is a tree that grows almost as tall as our classrooms, i.e., about 4 meters.
2. The roots of this tree go down nearly 30 times its height till they reach water.
3. Water is stored in the trunk of this tree.
4. This tree is found in Abu Dhabi

The correct statements are
A. 1, 2 and 4 B. 2, 3 and 4
C. Only 1 and 2 D. 1, 2 and 3

80. A person boarded a train on 02.01.2015 at madgaon for Nagercoil. The train departed from Madgaon at 07 : 45 hours and reached Nagercoil at 04 : 45 hours on the next day i.e., 03.01.2015. If the distance between these two stations is 1140 km, the average speed of the train was approximately
A. 54 km/h B. 51 km/h
C. 59 km/h D. 57 km/h

81. A person living in New Delhi wants to visit first Bhopal (Madhya Pradesh) and then Ranchi (Jharkhand). The directions of his journey will be first towards
A. east and then towards south
B. west and then towards south
C. south and then towards east
D. south and then towards west

82. Which one of the following characteristics is shared by all the animals given below?

Lizard, Sparrow, Turtle, Snake
A. They lay eggs.
B. They are poisonous.
C. They can live on land as well as in water.
D. Their bodies are covered with scales.

83. Stories and poems can be effectively used in teaching of EVS at primary level. The main purpose of using them in EVS is to
A. cater to diversity in classroom
B. providing contextual learning environment
C. make lessons enjoyable
D. promote linguistic skills

84. How would a primary teacher effectively assess her students of class IV on the topic of "Scarcity of water"?
A. Asking children to write slogans on saving water
B. Conducting a written test on the above topic
C. By finding out how they have started saving water in their day-to-day life
D. Organising a poster making activity on water conservation

85. Your principal asks you to take class V students on an educational visit. What would you include while planning for such a visit to make it meaningful?
A. Preparing structured activity sheet about the place to be visited and sharing the same with the students before the visit for an authentic and meaningful learning
B. Asking students to find and read the information about the place to be visited
C. Taking enough food and games to enjoy
D. Ensuring that students should be disciplined and should visit the place quietly

86. Which of the following should ***not*** be an appropriate indicator for assessment in EVS at primary level?
A. Remembering
B. Questioning
C. Concern for justice and equality
D. Cooperation

87. This plant has leaves which are used as vegetables. Its seeds are used to produce oil. The plant is
A. Spinach B. Coconut
C. Cabbage D. Mustard

88. Study the following statements about bronze :
1. It is an element like aluminium, iron and copper.
2. It is made by melting copper and tin in a furnace.
3. Tribal people have been using bronze since thousands of years.
4. The objects made of bronze are lighter but much stronger than those made of aluminium.

The correct statements are
A. Only 1 and 4 B. Only 2 and 3
C. 1, 2 and 3 D. 2, 3 and 4

89. Which one of the following is a set of diseases caused/spread by mosquitoes?
A. Chikungunya, Malaria, Typhoid
B. Cholera,, Dengue, Malaria
C. Chikungunya, Dengue, Malaria
D. Chikungunya, Cholera, Typhoid

90. On a state map, at its one corner it is mentioned "Scale 1 cm = 110 meters". If on the map the measured distance between any two cities is 9.7 cm, the actual distance between the two cities is approximately.
A. 1.067 km B. 2.01 km
C. 11 km D. 10 km

PART- IV

Language-I : English

Directions (Qs. No. 91 to 96): *Read the given passage and answer the questions that follow by selecting the* ***most appropriate*** *option.*

INVICTUS

Out of the night that covers me,
Black as the pit from pole to pole,
I thank whatever goods may be
For my unconquerable soul.

In the fell clutch of circumstance
I have not winced nor cried aloud.
Under the bludgeoning of chance
My head is bloody, but unbowed.

Beyond this place of wrath and tears
Looms but the Horror of the shade,
And yet the menace of the years
Finds, and shall find, me unafraid.

– William Ernest Henley

91. The phrase 'unconquerable soul' means a person who is
A. invincible B. compassionate
C. noble D. sensitive

92. Lines 5 and 6 show that the speaker
A. refuses to surrender
B. remains undaunted even under the worst circumstances.
C. is overwhelmed by adverse circumstances.
D. accepts life's challenges

93. 'Wrath and tears' means
A. unbearable suffering
B. anger causing havoc
C. anger and sorrow
D. unfavourable circumstances

94. The phrase 'menace of the years' suggests
A. threats of the times.
B. danger to life.
C. cruel fate.
D. evils of life

95. The word 'winced' in the second stanza means
A. recoiled B. ruffled
C. frightened D. worried

96. The poetic device used in 'Black as the pit from pole to pole' is
A. metaphor B. irony
C. simile D. parallelism

Directions (Q. No. 97 to 105) : *Read the passage given below and answer the questions that follow by selecting the* ***most appropriate*** *option.*

Adversity provides us with an opportunity to develop our character in a natural, recurring and powerful way that only the challenges of adversity offer. According to Solomon, adversity refines and reveals the gold and silver of our character.

A lot of times adversity comes our way as a direct or indirect result of our own actions. We make a bad choice or a bad decision, or we simply fail to do something we should have done. When I made bad investment decisions, I had to accept responsibility for my greed and naive choices. Yes, several men had misrepresented the opportunities to me, but the fact is, I am the one who made the decisions. And I experienced the very consequences, that Solomon had cautioned us about. Any time you make a contribution to your own adversity, you need to accept responsibility for it. Don't simply blame someone or something else.

Nonetheless, throughout our lives we will experience a great deal of adversity that is not a result of our own actions. It is critically important that we do not assign fault to ourselves or to those who had nothing to do with it. When a friend of mine lost his daughter to leukemia, he confided to me that he felt God was punishing him for his past sins. In other words, he was blaming himself. It is believed that adversity sometimes has a purpose that we cannot know or understand. As tempting as it may be, to try to figure out such a mystery is not only an exercise in futility, it is foolish also.

97. Adversity provides us with an opportunity to
A. introspect
B. develop our character
C. test our friends
D. evaluate our own character

98. The author quotes Solomon to
A. lend force to his argument
B. show his veneration for him
C. emphasize that adversity is part of life
D. embellish his prose

99. Most often our misfortunes are the result of our own
A. idleness B. haste
C. follies D. actions

100. The synonym for 'cautioned' is
A. warned B. threatened
C. suggested D. persuaded

101. The phrase 'exercise in futility' means
A. a foolish approach
B. something that is pointless
C. hopes of future
D. an irrational act

102. Identify the correct statement
A. Adversity is purposeless
B. Adversity is a curse
C. The mystery of adversity can be easily understood
D. Adversity helps us improve our character

103. Which of the following statements is ***not*** true?
A. Adversity is a test of our character
B. The bravest are bogged down by misfortunes
C. Adversity refines our character
D. Adversity sometimes has a purpose

104. The antonym for the word 'adversity' is
A. prosperity B. luxury
C. luck D. emptiness

105. When adversity strikes us we blame
A. supernatural powers and evil spirits
B. providence
C. our stars
D. everything and everyone except ourselves

Directions : *Answer the following questions by selecting the **most appropriate** option.*

106. In the primary classes, it is recommended that children should be taught in their mother tongue because
A. it enables children to comprehend
B. it creates a natural environment
C. children develop self-confidence
D. it promotes regional languages

107. A common developmental reading disorder is
A. Impairment B. Dyslexia
C. Aphasia D. Autism

108. The most important purpose of formative assessment is
A. to judge the performance of teachers and schools
B. to form an opinion about the best student in the class
C. to score and rank students on the basis of their performance
D. to provide qualitative feedback on students' learning

109. Role Play should be an integral part of every language classroom because
A. it enables girls and boys to interact freely.
B. it is an effective classroom management technique.
C. it enables students to engage in meaningful talk.
D. it enables students to memorize the story.

110. A student of class V has just read a text about the water problems of a community living on the outskirts of a city. After reading the chapter, the student remarks how difficult it must be to struggle for water every day. Which comprehension strategy does this remark reveal?
A. Read aloud
B. Summarizing
C. Metacognition
D. Inferential reading

111. Which one of the following is an example of Basic Interpersonal Communication Skills (BICS)?
A. Explaining a procedure to a peer during an experiment
B. Discussing response to a story in a small group in the classroom
C. Taking notes during a lecture or a talk
D. Negotiating turn taking with a peer during free play

112. B.F. Skinner claimed that language is learnt through
A. repetition and approximation
B. reinforcement and engagement
C. drill and practice
D. immersion and employment

113. A language teacher wants her students to write for an authentic audience and purpose. What would be the best writing task to achieve this?
A. Students write a letter to the principal expressing their opinion on a school-related issue.
B. Students write answers to questions given at the end of the chapter after discussing them with each other.
C. Students write a movie review of a movie they watched recently.
D. Students write on the topic, 'My School'.

114. Writing is a _______ and not a _______.
A. product; process
B. product; formation
C. process; product
D. process; formation

115. Rani is from Delhi. She has taken admission in a school in Assam. In the final exams, she faces difficulty in writing a composition on 'Bihu'. The most probable reason for Rani's problem is that
A. there is a discontinuity between her home environment and the school curriculum.
B. her parents are unable to help her in understanding the school culture.
C. she is not a hardworking girl and is not trying to adapt to the school curriculum.
D. her background is deficient and is not on a par with standard school culture.

116. A child reads 'She bought three apples' as 'She bought tree apples' and explains it as 'applies from trees'. How would you rate this child's reading skills?
A. She reads without comprehension
B. She reads with spelling errors.
C. She reads carelessly.
D. She reads with comprehension.

117. Which of the following is not true about sentences in the passive voice?
A. Any declarative sentence can be passivized.
B. The verb in passive sentences is always in perfect participle form.
C. It is generally used where the subject is hidden, not clear or not significant.
D. Sentences with intransitive verbs cannot be passivized.

118. Storytelling should be used frequently in classrooms because
A. it provides space for teachers to engage in other academic tasks
B. it lays the foundation of logical understanding and imagination
C. it lays the foundation for other academic engagements
D. it allows students to imagine and relax

119. Which one of the following principles is not appropriate for vocabulary development?
A. Passive vocabulary should be learnt by heart
B. Provide opportunities to consult a dictionary
C. Integrate new words with old
D. Make a new word 'real' by connecting it to the learners' world

120. A language textbook for class 1 starts with poems and stories (complete text) and ends with the alphabet. Which approach does this kind of arrangement reflect in language pedagogy?
A. Eclectic approach
B. Top-down approach
C. Aesthetic approach
D. Bottom-up approach

PART- V

भाषा-II : हिन्दी

निर्देश (प्र.सं. 121 से 126): *नीचे दिए गए गद्यांश को पढ़कर निम्नलिखित प्रश्नों में सबसे उचित विकल्प चुनिए।*

यह तो आप जानते हैं कि पृथ्वी प्रारम्भ में आग का गोला थी। मुझे ठीक-ठीक नहीं पता कि ऐसी आग में मुझ पानी का जन्म हुआ। लगता यह है कि हमारी पृथ्वी ज्यों-ज्यों ठंडी होती गई तो उसमें मौजूद गैसों में क्रियाएँ हुईं। हाइड्रोजन और ऑक्सीजन की रासायनिक क्रियाओं से मेरा जन्म हुआ है। इन दोनों ने अपना अस्तित्व मिटाकर मुझे बनाया। पहले मैं पृथ्वी के ऊपर भाप रूप में ही था। फिर जाने क्या हुआ कि मैं ठोस बर्फ बन गया। कल्पना करो चारों ओर बर्फ ही बर्फ। जब सूर्य की किरणें हम पर पड़तीं तो चारों ओर सौन्दर्य बिखर पड़ता। लाखों बर्फ के ही दबाव से निचली परत पिघलने लगी थी। फिसलकर हम पहुँचे सागर में। वहाँ की तो बात ही निराली थी। वहाँ अब तक हमसे पहले पहुँचे पानी में छोटे-छोटे जीव तैरने लगे थे। घोंघे, मछलियाँ और कछुवे भी। धीरे-धीरे सृष्टि का विस्तार हुआ। जल के बाद स्थल में जीव बनने लगे और आज आप उसी शृंखला के अंग हैं और अपने को मनुष्य कहते हैं।

121. यह आत्मकथा किसकी है?
A. बर्फ की
B. पानी की
C. मनुष्य की
D. पृथ्वी की

122. सबसे पहले जीवधारी कहाँ पैदा हुए?
A. बर्फ में
B. भाप में
C. जल में
D. स्थल में

123. बर्फ क्यों फिसलने लगी थी?
A. अपनी गर्मी से पिघल रही थी
B. बर्फ के बोझ और दबाव से निचली परत पिघल रही थी
C. सूर्य ने पिघला दिया था
D. समुद्र की लहरें आ गई थीं

124. मनुष्य किस शृंखला का अंग है?
A. जीवधारियों की शृंखला का
B. जलजीवों की शृंखला का
C. प्राकृतिक शृंखला का
D. प्राकृतिक परिवर्तन शृंखला का

125. चारों ओर सौंदर्य .... पड़ता।
रिक्त स्थान के लिए शब्द होगा।
A. चमक B. दमक
C. बिफर D. बिखर

126. कौन-सी संज्ञा बहुवचन में नहीं है?
A. घर बनने लगे हैं। B. जीव जल में तैर रहे हैं।
C. घोंघे चल रहे हैं। D. कछुवे की चाल देखें।

निर्देश (प्र.सं. 127 से 135): *नीचे दिए गए गद्यांश को पढ़कर निम्नलिखित प्रश्नों में सबसे उचित विकल्प चुनिए।*

आसमान में मुक्का मारना कोई बुद्धिमानी का काम नहीं समझा जाता। बिना लक्ष्य के तर्क करना भी बुद्धिमानी नहीं है। हमें भली-भाँति समझ लेने की आवश्यकता है, कि हमारा लक्ष्य क्या है? हम जो कुछ प्रयत्न करने जा रहे हैं वह किसके लिए है? साहित्य हम किसके लिए रचते हैं, इतिहास और दर्शन क्यों लिखते और पढ़ते हैं? राजनीतिक आन्दोलन किस महान् उद्देश्य की सिद्धि के लिए करते हैं? मनुष्य ही वह बड़ी चीज है जिसके लिए सब यह किया करते हैं। हमारे सब प्रयत्नों का एक लक्ष्य है, मनुष्य वर्तमान दुर्गति के पंक से उद्धार पाए और भविष्य में सुख और शांति से रह सके। वह शास्त्र, वह ग्रंथ, वह कला, वह नृत्य, वह राजनीति, वह समाज-सुधार जंजाल-मात्र है जिससे मनुष्य का भला न होता हो। मनुष्य आज हाहाकार के भीतर त्राहि-त्राहि पुकार रहा है। हमारे राजनीतिक और सामाजिक सुधार से अन्न-वस्त्र की समस्या सुलझ सकती है फिर भी मनुष्य सुखी नहीं बनेगा। उसे सिर्फ अन्न-वस्त्र से ही संतोष नहीं होगा। इसके बाद भी उसका मनुष्य बनना बाकी रह जाता है। साहित्य वही काम करता है। मनुष्य नामक प्राणी तो पशुओं में ही एक विकसित प्रजाति है और यदि मनुष्यता के गुण और मूल्य उसमें नहीं हैं तो वह मनुष्य नामक पशु ही है, मनुष्य नहीं। भोजन करना, सोना और वंश-वृद्धि जैसे काम प्रकृति के द्वारा तय हैं, सच्चा मानव बनने के लिए उसे जो दृष्टि चाहिए उसे पाने में साहित्य सहायक हो सकता है।

127. आसमान में मुक्का मारने से आशय है
A. लोगों का ध्यान आकर्षित करना
B. अपनी श्रेष्ठता सिद्ध करना
C. वीरतापूर्ण कार्य करना
D. निरर्थक कार्य करना

128. बुद्धिमानी नहीं है
A. निरुद्देश्य तर्क करना
B. राजनीतिक आंदोलन करना
C. आसमान में मुक्का मारना
D. निष्फल कार्य करना

129. साहित्य, कला, नृत्य आदि व्यर्थ हैं यदि उनसे
A. मनुष्य का हित न हो सके
B. लक्ष्य न पाया जा सके
C. धन न कमाया जा सके
D. यश प्राप्त न हो सके

130. अन्न-वस्त्र आदि की समस्याएँ हल हो सकती हैं
A. अच्छे साहित्य से B. आवश्यकताओं की पूर्ति से
C. सामाजिक सुधारों से D. राजनीतिक आन्दोलनों से

131. मनुष्य के लिए प्रकृति द्वारा तय कामों में नहीं हैं
A. अन्न-वस्त्र की पूर्ति B. वंश-वृद्धि
C. सोना D. भोजन करना

132. मनुष्य एक पशु ही है यदि उसमें
A. साहित्य के प्रति रुचि न हो
B. मानवीय मूल्य न हों
C. सम्पन्नता न हो
D. सामाजिकता न हो

133. दिए गए शब्दों में से अर्थ की दृष्टि से भिन्न शब्द छाँटिए
A. निशाना B. लक्ष्य
C. उद्देश्य D. उद्धार

134. अनुच्छेद में 'जंजाल' शब्द किस अर्थ में प्रयुक्त हुआ है?
A. त्राहि-त्राहि B. झंझट
C. समस्या D. प्रयत्न

135. 'बुद्धिमानी' शब्द है
A. विशेषण B. क्रिया
C. संज्ञा D. सर्वनाम

निर्देशः *निम्नलिखित प्रश्नों के उत्तर देने के लिए* ***सबसे उचित*** *विकल्प चुनिए।*

136. प्राथमिक स्तर पर आधारभूत कौशल हैं
A. लिखना और बोलना B. पढ़ना और लिखना
C. सुनना और बोलना D. पढ़ना और सुनना

137. इनमें से .... अक्षर-बोध की विधि ***नहीं*** है।
A. वाक्य विधि B. प्रत्यक्ष विधि
C. वर्ण विधि D. शब्द विधि

138. 'किसी कण में चित्रात्मक तथा रंग-बिरंगे चार्ट होने चाहिए।' कौन-सा विकल्प इसके उद्देश्य की पूर्ति ***नहीं*** करता?
A. बच्चों के कल्पनालोक के रंगों तथा आकृतियों को पहचान नहीं मिलती
B. बच्चों को सीखने-सिखाने का वातावरण प्रदान करते हैं
C. उससे शैक्षिक वातावरण को बनाने में मदद मिलती है
D. बच्चे उसकी सामग्री से सीखने का प्रयास करते हैं

139. बच्चों की श्रवण-योग्यता का विकास करने में सर्वाधिक सहायक है
A. भाषा-प्रयोगशाला B. ऑडियो टेप
C. शब्दों का श्रुतलेख D. परस्पर बातचीत

140. प्राथमिक स्तर पर भाषा शिक्षण के अन्तर्गत बातचीत एक महत्त्वपूर्ण उपकरण है, क्योंकि
A. यह सीखने और सीखी हुई बातों को सुदृढ़ बनाने का एक आधारभूत माध्यम है
B. बच्चों को बातचीत करना अच्छा लगता है
C. बातचीत शिक्षण का अनिवार्य अंग है
D. हमारी पाठ-योजना में पहले से ही प्रस्तावित है

141. प्राथमिक स्तर पर बच्चों की भाषा प्रयोग की क्षमता सम्बन्धी रिकॉर्ड तैयार करने के उपरांत कौन-सा कार्य सर्वाधिक महत्वपूर्ण है?
A. रिकॉर्ड की वैधता की जाँच करना
B. रिकॉर्ड की विश्वसनीयता की जाँच करना
C. रिकॉर्ड को सुरक्षित करना
D. रिपोर्टिंग करना

142. प्राथमिक स्तर पर पढ़ने की क्षमता के आकलन में सबसे कम महत्वपूर्ण है
A. पढ़ने में प्रवाह
B. चित्रों से अनुमान लगाकर पढ़ना
C. समझकर पढ़ना
D. अक्षर जोड़कर पढ़ना

143. प्राथमिक स्तर पर भाषा-शिक्षण में बाल साहित्य का प्रयोग किए जाने के पक्ष में सर्वाधिक ठोस तर्क है
A. इन्हें पढ़ाने में शिक्षक को मजा आता है
B. इनका प्रयोग बच्चों के भाषा-अनुभवों को विस्तृत करता है
C. यह पाठ्य-पुस्तक से बेहतर होता है
D. इन्हें पढ़ाना अपेक्षाकृत सरल होता है

144. तीसरी कक्षा में पढ़ने वाली सुनयना अकसर 'स' को 'श' कहती है। भाषा शिक्षक होने के नाते आप क्या करेंगे?
A. वह जब भी 'स' को 'श' कहेगी, उसे टोकेंगे ताकि उसमें सुधार हो सके
B. उसके इस तरह के प्रयोग पर बिल्कुल ध्यान नहीं देंगे
C. यह क्षेत्रीय प्रभाव हो सकता है इसलिए उसे स्वयं ही सुधार करने के लिए पर्याप्त समय देंगे
D. उसे 'स' और 'श' के उच्चारण-स्थान की पूर्ण जानकारी देंगे

145. अमित पढ़ते समय कठिनाई का अनुभव करता है। वह .... से ग्रस्त है।
A. डिस्कैल्कुलिया B. अफेजिया
C. डिस्लेक्सिया D. डिस्ग्राफिया

146. दी गई सहायक सामग्री में से शेष से भिन्न सहायक सामग्री चुनिए
A. समाचार-पत्र B. टेलीविजन
C. पत्र-पत्रिकाएँ D. बाल साहित्य

147. प्राथमिक स्तर पर एक अध्यापिका 'संज्ञा' पढ़ाते समय पहले 'संज्ञा' की परिभाषा बताती है। उसके बाद उससे सम्बन्धित उदाहरण समझाती है। अध्यापिका व्याकरण शिक्षण की कौन-सी विधि अपनाती है?
A. प्रत्यक्ष विधि B. सूत्र विधि
C. आगमन विधि D. निगमन विधि

148. प्राथमिक स्तर पर अधिकांशतः बच्चे .... कविताएँ पसन्द करते हैं।
A. लयपूर्ण कविताएँ
B. छोटी कविताएँ
C. वीर रस की कविताएँ
D. नैतिक मूल्यों से ओत-प्रोत कविताएँ

149. प्राथमिक स्तर पर हिंदी भाषा सिखाने का सर्वोपरि उद्देश्य है
A. भाषा के विभिन्न प्रयोगों की क्षमता का विकास करना
B. भाषा की कठिन बातों को सरलता से समझना
C. भाषा के मानक स्वरूप को पूर्णतः आत्मसात् करना
D. भाषा के व्याकरणिक नियमों को पूर्णतः आत्मसात् करना

150. बच्चों की लेखन क्षमता के आकलन में सबसे कम महत्त्वपूर्ण है
A. मानक-वर्तनी B. विचारों की स्पष्टता
C. मौलिकता D. कल्पनाशीलता

Answers

1	2	3	4	5	6	7	8	9	10
A	D	D	B	B	B	C	A	C	C
11	12	13	14	15	16	17	18	19	20
C	A	D	D	A	D	D	D	C	D
21	22	23	24	25	26	27	28	29	30
C	B	C	C	A	A	A	A	B	B
31	32	33	34	35	36	37	38	39	40
C	D	A	A	C	C	C	B	B	D
41	42	43	44	45	46	47	48	49	50
C	D	D	A	D	D	B	C	B	C

51	52	53	54	55	56	57	58	59	60
A	D	B	B	A	A	B	A	D	C
61	62	63	64	65	66	67	68	69	70
C	B	B	C	D	D	D	D	B	B
71	72	73	74	75	76	77	78	79	80
D	B	A	A	D	B	B	C	D	A
81	82	83	84	85	86	87	88	89	90
C	A	B	C	A	A	D	B	C	A
91	92	93	94	95	96	97	98	99	100
A	B	C	A	A	C	B	A	D	A
101	102	103	104	105	106	107	108	109	110
B	D	B	A	D	A	B	D	C	D
111	112	113	114	115	116	117	118	119	120
D	C	A	C	A	A	A	B	A	B
121	122	123	124	125	126	127	128	129	130
B	C	B	A	D	D	D	C	A	C
131	132	133	134	135	136	137	138	139	140
A	B	D	B	C	C	B	A	D	A
141	142	143	144	145	146	147	148	149	150
D	D	B	C	C	B	D	A	A	A

Some Selected Explanatory Answers

1. Classroom environment encompasses a broad range of educational concepts, including the physical setting, the psychological environment created through social contexts, and numerous instructional components related to teacher characteristics and behaviors. In theory, providing the space and time for democratically driven class meetings is a good way for young students to comprehend the differences between positive and negative social behavior.

3. An effective teacher can relate to his or her students. The best teachers work hard to figure out how to relate to each of their students. Common interest can be hard to find, but exceptional teachers will find a way to connect with their students even if they have to fake it. For instance, you may have a student who is a Lego fanatic. You can relate to that student if you do something as simple as ordering a Lego catalog and then going through it and discussing it with that student. Even if you have no actual interest in Lego's, the student will think you do and thus naturally create a connection.

4. Compliance with teacher is not needed to create a good classroom environment for child learning.

7. Learning is an active process in which the learner uses sensory input and constructs meaning out of it. The more traditional formulation of this idea involves the terminology of the active learner (Dewey's term) stressing that the learner needs to do something; that learning is not the passive acceptance of knowledge which exists "out there" but that learning involves the learners engaging with the world.

8. "Gifted and talented children are those identified by professionally qualified persons who by virtue of outstanding abilities are capable of high performance. These are children who require differentiated educational programs and/or services beyond those normally provided by the regular school program in order to realize their contribution to self and society".

   Children capable of high performance include those with demonstrated achievement and/or potential ability in any of the following areas, singly or in combination:
   - general intellectual ability
   - specific academic aptitude
   - creative or productive thinking
   - leadership ability
   - visual or performing arts
   - psychomotor ability."

9. Error are important because they provide an insight into child's thinking and help to solve it. Errors they make, and the changing patterns of procedure use provides insights into important and help to aspects of how children represent and process information in the domain.

10. Divergent Thinking, namely Openness and Extraversion, were found to facilitate divergent thinking production. Openness assesses intellectual curiosity, imagination, artistic interests, liberal attitudes, and originality. The

high correlation between Openness and divergent thinking is indicative of two different ways of measuring the same aspects of creativity. Openness is a self-report of one's preference for thinking "outside the box". Divergent thinking tests represent a performance-based measure of such.

11. Assessment can be one of the most difficult aspects of teaching. The educational, emotional, and formative ramifications of judging a young person's work can weigh heavily on the mind of a teacher. But in spite of the anxiety it poses, knowing how to assess students in order to improve instruction is a core principle of effective teaching. Assessment to the students can be used by teachers in teaching to develop insight into changing the teaching approach according to the student.

13. Verbal aggressiveness in communication has been studied to examine the underlying message of aggressive behavior and to gain control over occurrences.Infante and Wigley (1986) defined verbal aggressiveness as "a personality trait that predisposes persons to attack the self-concepts of other people instead of, or in addition to, their Positions on topics of communication.Punishment result into damaging self-concept.

16. The Centers for Disease Control and Prevention (CDC) and National Center of Birth Defects and Developmental Disabilities (NCBDD) defined the following age categories associated with developmental milestones: infants and toddlers (0-2 years), preschoolers (3-5 years), middle childhood (6-8 years), late childhood (9-11 years) and early to middle adolescence (12-17 years).

18. Instructional scaffolding is a learning process designed to promote a deeper level of learning. Scaffolding is the support given during the learning process which is tailored to the needs of the student with the intention of helping the student achieve his/her learning goals.

Instructional scaffolding is the provision of sufficient support to promote learning when concepts and skills are being first introduced to students.

Use of instructional scaffolding in various contexts:

- modeling a task
- giving advice
- providing coaching

19. Gender-neutral language is a form of linguistic prescriptivism that aims to minimize assumptions about the gender or biological sex of people referred to in speech or writing. Gender-neutral job titles do not specify the gender of the person referred to, particularly when the gender is not in fact known, or is not yet specified (as in job advertisements). Examples include firefighter instead of fireman; flight attendant instead of steward or stewardess; bartender instead of barman or barmaid; and chairperson or chair instead of chairman or chairwoman.

20. The continuous and comprehensive evaluation was initiated based on the recommendations to reform evaluation practices in school education by National curriculum for elementary and secondary education .. It is essential for understanding how learning can be observed, recorded and improved upon.

24. **Assimilation:** The process of taking in new information into our previously existing schemas is known as assimilation. The process is somewhat subjective, because we tend to modify experiences and information somewhat to fit in with our pre-existing beliefs. In the example above, seeing a dog and labeling it "dog" is an example of assimilating the animal into the child's dog schema.

26. **Inclusive Education**

Inclusive education is concerned with removing all barriers to learning, and with participation of all learners vulnerable to exclusion and marginalization. It is a strategic approach designed to facilitate learning success for all children. It addresses the common goals of decreasing and overcoming all exclusion from the human right to education, at least at the elementary level, and enhancing access, participation and learning, success in quality basic education for all.

28. Dysgraphia is a deficiency in the ability to write, primarily in terms of handwriting, but also in terms of coherence. Dysgraphia is a transcription disability, meaning that it is a writing disorder associated with impaired handwriting, orthographic coding (orthography, the storing process of written words and processing the letters in those words), and finger sequencing.

30. Webster (1996) defines intelligence as the "capacity for learning, reasoning, understanding, and similar forms of mental activity" and reflective of differences in capacity, ability, and aptitude among individuals.. The overarching assumption of these systemic theories is that intelligence is not a single entity but a multifaceted structure and that traditional definitions of intelligence have been excessively narrow. Thinking practically about oneself does not imply practical intelligence in the Triarchic theory.

31. (A) 3 hours 14 minutes = 194 minutes

$= (3 \times 60 + 14)$ minutes = 194 minutes

(B) 2 kg 30 gm = 2030 gm

$= (2000 + 30)$ gm = 2030 gm

(C) 3 litres 80 millilitres = 380 ml

= 3000 ml + 80 ml = 3080 ml

(D) Area of square = $(10)^2 = 100$ cm^2

Area of rectangle $= 100 \times \frac{1}{100} \times 100$

$= 100$ cm^2

Clearly option (C) is not correct.

32. When 110111 is divided by 11,

then we get quotient = 10010

and remainder = 1

Hence, required sum = 10010 + 1

= 10011

33. The product of $102 \times 201 = 20502$

$\therefore$ Required number = 20502 – 19999 = 503

34. $2\frac{2}{3} \times 90° = \frac{8}{3} \times 90° = 8 \times 30 = 240°$

35. $\because$ 1 litre = 1000 cm^3

$\therefore$ Depth of Juice in the carton

$= \frac{1000}{8 \times 8} = \frac{125}{8}$

= 15.625 cm which is closest 16 cm (closest)

36. The sum of two odd numbers and one even number is an even number.

(5 + 7 + 8) = 20

(7 + 9 + 10) = 26

37. The place value of 5 in 6251 = 50

The place value of 5 in 6521 = 500

The place value of 5 in 5621 = 5000

$\therefore$ Required sum = 50 + 500 + 5000 = 5550

43. Practice time included in different topics in mathematics textbook provides extended learning opportunities.

44. Formative assessment including diagnostic testing is a range of formal and informal assessment procedures employed by teachers during the learning process in order to modify teaching and learning activities to improve student attainment.

45. Vedic Mathematics is a book written by the high-ranking Hindu cleric Bharati Krishna Tirthaji and first published in 1965. It contains a list of mental calculation techniques claimed to be based on the Vedas. The mental calculation system mentioned in the book is also known by the same name or as "Vedic Maths". Its characterization as "Vedic" mathematics has been criticized by academics, who have also opposed its inclusion in the Indian school curriculum. Vedic Mathematics is becoming popular nowadays among student it enhance the calculation skills and speed in mathematics.

50. $\frac{6}{5} \div \frac{1}{10} = \frac{6}{5} \times \frac{10}{1} = 12$

There are 12 times $\frac{1}{10}$ in $\frac{6}{5}$

51. 6 : 14 a.m. + 13 hrs 48 minutes

= 20 : 02

= 8 : 02 pm

The time at the destination is 8:02 pm

52. Multiples of 7 between 21 and 49 are 28, 35 and 42

Sum of 28, 35 and 42 = 105

Factors of 25 are 1, 5 and 25

Factors of 30 are 1, 2, 3, 5, 6, 10, 15 and 30

Biggest Common factor of 25 and 30 = 5

$105 \div 5 = 21$

53. $96 = 1 \times 96$

$= 2 \times 48$

$= 3 \times 32$

$= 4 \times 24$

$= 6 \times 16$

$= 8 \times 12$

All factors of 96 are 1, 2, 3, 4, 6, 8, 12, 16, 24, 32, 48 and 96

Sum of factors = 252

55. Total number of chocolates = $12 \times 3 = 36$

Remaining number of chocolates

$= 36 - \left[\frac{1}{3} \times 36 + \frac{1}{6} \times 36 + \frac{1}{4} \times 36\right]$

= 36 – [12 + 6 + 9]

= 36 – 27 = 9

56.

Square	Rectangle
P = 44	P = 44
11 cm	(11 + 5) cm

Perimeter of Square = 44 cm

$\therefore$ Side of Square $= \frac{44}{4} = 11$ cm

Area of Square = $11 \times 11 = 121$ cm^2

Length of rectangle = 11 + 5 = 16 cm

Perimeter of rectangle = 44 cm

$\Rightarrow 2(l + b) = 44$

$l + b = 22$

$\therefore$ $b = 22 - 16 = 6$ cm

Area of rectangle = $16 \times 6 = 96$ cm^2

Area of Square + area of rectangle

$= 121 + 96 = 217$ cm^2

58. – 1 + 2 – 3 + 4 – 5 + 6 – 7 + ... + 1000

= (2 + 4 + 6 + 8 + ...+ 1000) – (1 + 3 + 5 + ... + 999)

= Sum of even numbers of n terms – sum of odd numbers of n terms

$n(n + 1) - (n)^2$

$= (500) \times (500 + 1) - 500 \times 500$
$= 250000 + 500 - 250000 = 500$

68. Position and Orientation

- Give and follow instructions for movement that involves distances, directions, and half or quarter turns.
- Describe their position relative to a person or object.

73. Motions of the head and neck are intended to maintain a motionless visual field (the steadicam-like ability you reference) but also to obtain a new visual field very rapidly, with minimal time wasted in transit. Chickens don't actually keep their head in one position while walking -- they seem to bob back-and-forth, but this actually maximizes the amount of time spent at one point while moving. Each jerk of the neck is accompanied by a blink of the nictitating membrane to eliminate the image of a moving background.

75. Kerala is a state located in southwestern India. Neighbouring states include Karnataka to the north and Tamil Nadu to the south and east; to the west is the Arabian Sea. Besides the state capital Thiruvananthapuram (Trivandrum), the other major cities in Kerala are Kochi (Cochin), Kozhikode (Calicut), Thrissur and Kollam. The principal spoken language is Malayalam.

76. Goan cuisine consists of regional foods popular in Goa, located along India's west coast along the Arabian Sea.Chicken, lamb, seafood, coconut milk, rice, and local spices are some of the main ingredients in Goan cuisine. The area is located in a tropical climate, which means that spices and flavors are intense. The cuisine is mostly seafood-based; the staple foods are rice and fish. Kingfish (vison or visvan) is the most common delicacy.

82. Reptiles are vertebrates that have scales on at least some part of their body, leathery or hard-shelled eggs, and share a number of other features. Snakes, lizards, turtles, crocodilians, and birds are reptiles. Like all vertebrates, reptiles have bony skeletons that support their bodies.

87. Peppery, crispy mustard greens, also known as leaf mustard, is indeed one of the most nutritious green-leafy vegetables available around. Its lovely top greens have actually more vitamin A, carotenes, vitamin K, and flavonoid anti-oxidants than some of commonly consumed fruits and vegetables.

89. Mosquito-borne diseases or mosquito-borne illness are disease caused by bacterial, viruses or parasite-stransmitted by mosquitoes. They can transmit disease without being affected themselves.

Diseases transmitted by mosquitoes include: malaria, dengue, filariasis, West Nile virus, chikungunya, yellow fever, Japanese encephalitis, Saint Louis encephalitis, Western equine encephalitis, Eastern equine encephalitis,Venezuelan equine encephalitis, La Crosse encephalitis and Zika fever.

107. Developmental reading disorder (DRD), more commonly called dyslexia, occurs when your brain has a hard time processing language. You might misread the letters in a word and/or have difficulty reading irregular or unfamiliar words. Dyslexia is the most common type of reading disorder, affecting two to eight percent of young children.

108. Formative assessment including diagnostic testing is a range of formal and informal assessment procedures employed by teachers during the learning process in order to modify teaching and learning activities to improve student attainment. It typically involves qualitative feedback (rather than scores) for both student and teacher that focuses on the details of content and performance. It is commonly contrasted with summative assessment, which seeks to monitor educational outcomes, often for purposes of external accountability.

111. Interpersonal communication is an exchange of information between two or more people. It is also an area of study. Basic interpersonal communicative skills(BICS) : the language skills required for face-to-face communication, where interactions are context-embedded takes 2 to 3 yrs to develop to native like level .

112. In most of the literature concerning the topic of SLA, discussions of the behaviouristic approach are only brief because most of its content is not incorporated in today's teaching methods. Skinner stated that learning needs to be trained in the same way as muscles are trained, i.e. all learning behaviour has to be trained frequently through repetition, drill and rote learning to reach positive effects. As all the other approaches named before, Skinner's theory should bring a change into the classrooms to improve learning. He constituted the importance of learning by doing, and wants students to be an active part in the lesson.

118. Stories from the psychological and educational points of view represent essential parts in the child's development and the development of the child's language.

Stories have their magic function as through reading the plot the reader may feel to have become someone else for a while and imagine someone else's thoughts and feelings. They offer similar potential for development of personality in mother tongue as well as in foreign language learning. Stories bear a great deal of significancy within acquiring language skills.

Previous Paper (Solved)

CTET PAPER-I, SEPTEMBER 2014*

PART- I

Child Development and Pedagogy

Directions: *Answer the following questions by selecting the **most appropriate** option.*

1. Cognitive development is supported by
   A. conducting relevant and well-designed tests as frequently as possible
   B. presenting activities that reinforce traditional methods
   C. providing a rich and varied environment
   D. focussing more on individual activities in comparison to collaboration

2. Human developments is
   A. quantitative
   B. qualitative
   C. unmeasurable to a certain extent
   D. both quantitative and qualitative

3. The nature-nurture debate refers to
   A. genetics and environment
   B. behaviour and environment
   C. environment and biology
   D. environment and upbringing

4. Which of the following is a passive agency of socialization?
   A. Health club
   B. Family
   C. Eco club
   D. Public library

5. In Vygotsky's theory, which aspect of development gets neglected?
   A. Social
   B. Cultural
   C. Biological
   D. Linguistic

6. Which of the following stages are involved when infants "THINK" with their eyes, ears and hands?
   A. Concrete operational stage
   B. Pre-operational stage
   C. Sensory motor stage
   D. Formal operational stage

7. Ria does not agree with Rishabh about setting up a class picnic. She thinks that the rules can be revised to suit the majority. This kind of peer disagreement, according to Piaget, refers to
   A. Heteronomous morality
   B. Cognitive immaturity
   C. Reaction
   D. Morality of cooperation

8. Which one of the following is a form of Sternberg's Triarchic Theory of Intelligence?
   A. Practical Intelligence
   B. Experimental Intelligence
   C. Resourceful Intelligence
   D. Mathematical Intelligence

9. Who developed the first intelligence test?
   A. David Wechsler
   B. Alfred Binet
   C. Charles Edward Spearman
   D. Robert Sternberg

10. Phonological awareness refers to the ability to
    A. reflect and manipulate the sound structure
    B. speak fluently and accurately
    C. know, understand and write
    D. master the rules of grammar

11. Gender discrimination in a classroom
    A. does not affect the performance of the students
    B. may lead to diminished effort or performance of the students
    C. may lead to enhanced effort or performance of the male students
    D. is done more by the male teachers than their female counterparts

12. Which one of the following is an example of learning style?
    A. Visual B. Accrual
    C. Factual D. Tactual

*Exam was held on 21-09-2014.

13. A teacher collects and reads the work of the class, then plans and adjusts the next lesson to meet student needs. He/She is doing
A. Assessment of learning
B. Assessment as learning
C. Assessment for learning
D. Assessment at learning

14. Teachers who work under School Based Assessment
A. are overburdened as they need to take frequent tests in addition to Monday tests
B. need to assign project work in each subject to individual students
C. observe students minutely on a daily basis to assess their values and attitudes
D. feel a sense of ownership for the system

15. "How do grades differ from marks?" This question belongs to which of the following classes of questions?
A. Divergent
B. Analytic
C. Open-ended
D. Problem-solving

16. Girl students
A. learn questions on Mathematics well but face difficulty only when they are asked to reason them out
B. are as good in Mathematics as boys of their age
C. perform less competently in spatial concepts than boys of their age
D. possess more linguistic and musical abilities

17. Difficulty in recalling sequence of letters in words and frequent loss of visual memory is associated with
A. Dyslexia
B. Dyscalculia
C. Dysgraphia
D. Dyspraxia

18. 'Education-of-all-in-schools-for-all' could be a tagline for which of the following?
A. Cohesive education
B. Inclusive education
C. Cooperative education
D. Exclusive education

19. Fluency, elaboration, originality and flexibility are the factors associated with
A. giftendness
B. talent
C. divergent thinking
D. acceleration

20. Gifted students may be asked to spend more time on questions dealing with
A. remembering
B. understanding
C. creating
D. analysing

21. Leaning disabilities in Mathematics can be assessed most appropriately by which of the following tests?
A. Aptitude test
B. Diagnostic test
C. Screening test
D. Achievement test

22. Concept maps are most likely to increase understanding of new concepts by
A. transferring knowledge between content areas
B. focussing attention on specific detail
C. prioritizing academic content for study
D. increasing ability to organize information logically

23. According to the theory of social learning of Albert Bandura, which one of the following is true?
A. Play is essential and should be given priority in school
B. Modelling is a principal way for children to learn
C. An unresolved crisis can harm a child
D. Cognitive development is independent of social development

24. Deductive reasoning involves
A. reasoning from general to particular
B. reasoning from particular to general
C. active construction and reconstruction of knowledge
D. methods including inquiry learning and heuristics

25. When children learn a concept and use it, practice helps in reducing the errors committed by them. This idea was given by
A. E.L. Thorndike
B. Jean Piaget
C. J.B. Watson
D. Lev Vygotsky

26. Which of the following skills is associated with emotional intelligence?
A. Memorising
B. Motor processing
C. Envisaging
D. Empathising

27. The inner force that stimulates and compels a behavioural response and provides specific direction to that response is
A. Motive
B. Perseverance
C. Emotion
D. Commitment

28. Which term is often used interchangeably with the term "motivation"?
A. Incentive
B. Emotion
C. Need
D. Inspiration

29. _________ motives deal with the need to reach satisfying feeling states and to obtain personal goals.
A. Effective
B. Affective
C. Preservation-oriented
D. Safety-oriented

30. Which one of the following is a factor that affects learning positively?
A. Fear of failure
B. Competition with peers
C. Meaningful association
D. Pressure from parents

PART- II

Mathematics

31. The difference of the place value and the face value of 5 in 35362 is
A. 0 B. 495
C. 4995 D. 5005

32. 10 ones + 10 tens + 10 thousands equal
A. 11100 B. 101010
C. 10110 D. 11011

33. The sum of the positive factors of 210 is
A. 576 B. 575
C. 573 D. 366

34. Gorang worked $4\frac{1}{2}$ hours on Monday, 190 minutes on Tuesday, from 5 : 20 a.m. to 9 : 10 a.m. on Wednesday, and 220 minutes on Friday. He is paid ₹ 42 per hour. How much did he earn from Monday to Friday?
A. ₹ 560 B. ₹ 580
C. ₹ 540 D. ₹ 637

35. The sum of the greatest 4-digit number and the smallest 3-digit number is
A. 7000 B. 9899
C. 10099 D. 10999

36. Twenty-six and twenty-six hundredths is written as
A. 2626 B. 26.26
C. 262.6 D. 2.626

37. The product of remainders of 19009 ÷ 11 and 9090 ÷ 11 is
A. 4 B. 5
C. 8 D. 12

38. How many $\frac{1}{6}$ are there in $3\frac{1}{3}$?
A. 12 B. 15
C. 18 D. 20

39. What number should be subtracted from the product 1109 × 505 so as to get 505050?
A. 49495 B. 55005
C. 54995 D. 59495

40. Which of the following is not correct?
A. 1 mm is one-tenth of 1 cm
B. 1 kg 12 grams = 1.012 kg
C. 10 metre 10 cm = 1010 cm
D. $\frac{23}{100} = 2.30$

41. A tank contains 240 litres (L) 128 millilitres (mL) of milk, which can be filled completely in 16 jars of the same size. How much milk will be their in 22 such jars?
A. 330 L 176 mL B. 331 L 760 mL
C. 331 L 176 mL D. 332 L 650 mL

42. Number of degrees in four and two-third right-angles is
A. 310 B. 420
C. 330 D. 400

43. A water tank is 11 m long, 10 m wide and 9 m high. It is filled with water to a level of 6 m. What part of the tank is empty?

A. $\frac{1}{4}$ B. $\frac{1}{3}$

C. $\frac{1}{6}$ D. $\frac{2}{3}$

44. Perimeters of a rectangle and a square are equal. Perimeter of the square is 96 cm and breadth of the rectangle is 4 cm less than the side of the square. Then two times the area (in square cm) of the rectangle is

A. 560 B. 960

C. 1040 D. 1120

45. Difference of (smallest common multiple of 4, 5 and 6) and (smallest common multiple of 5, 6 and 9) is

A. 30 B. 45

C. 48 D. 60

46. As per NCF 2005, teaching of numbers and operations on them, measurement of quantities, etc. at primary level caters to the

A. narrow aim of teaching mathematics

B. higher aim of teaching mathematics

C. aim to mathematise the child's thought process

D. aim of teaching important mathematics

47. In Class 3, a teacher asked the students to add 4562 and 728. A student responded to the question as follows :

$$\begin{array}{r} 4562 \\ +\ 728 \\ \hline 11842 \\ \hline \end{array}$$

The response reflects that the child lacks the

A. Skill of addition

B. Concept of place value

C. Skill of addition by regrouping

D. Concept of order property of addition

48. Which of the following problems from the textbook of Class IV refers to 'multidisciplinary problem'?

A. Draw the flag of India and identify the number of lines of symmetry in the flag

B. Draw the mirror image of a given figure

C. How many lines of symmetry are there in a given figure?

D. To draw a line of symmetry in a given geometrical figure

49. The following grid is drawn on a square paper :

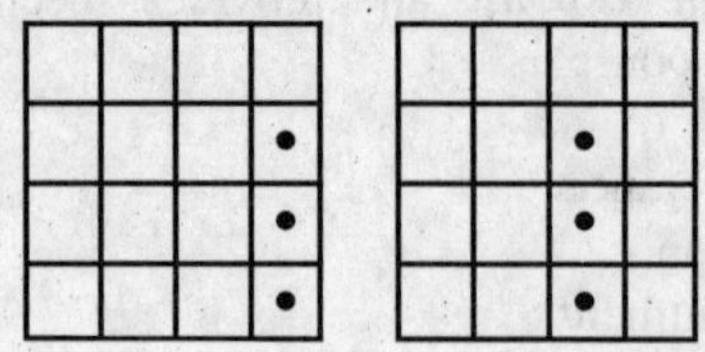

Th H T O Th H T O

This representation reflects

A. position of numbers on abacus

B. concept of place value

C. equivalence of tens and ones

D. mathematical game

50. Children at primary stage are able to classify the given shapes based on their appearance. According to Van Hiele levels of geometry, they are at

A. Visualization stage

B. Analytic stage

C. Informal deduction stage

D. Formal deduction stage

51. Manipulative models, static pictures, written symbols, spoken and written language, real world situations or contexts are five ways to represent

A. Mathematical thinking and ideas

B. Geometrical proof

C. Mathematics curriculum

D. Mathematical vocabulary

52. After teaching the concept of division, a teacher created a 'Mathematical Wall' in the classroom and asked the students to write any two division facts in the assigned columns within 48 hours :

MATH WALL			
Ankit 25÷5=5	Ankur 0÷6=0	Babita	Bobby
Pragya	Dhruv	Sohan	Harsh
Rahul	Smita	Sunil	Tushar

This activity can help the teacher to

A. make the classroom environment noise free

B. engage the students for next two days in some mathematical work

C. give opportunity of expression to every child and to learn from each other

D. keep the record of number of facts learnt by the students

53. Possible indicator pertaining to visual memory barrier hampering with learner's mathematical performance is

A. difficulty in retaining mathematical facts and difficulty in telling time

B. difficulty in using a number line

C. difficulty to count on within a sequence

D. difficulty in handling small manipulations

54. A teacher in class III distributed the following cards and asked the children to match the same shapes.

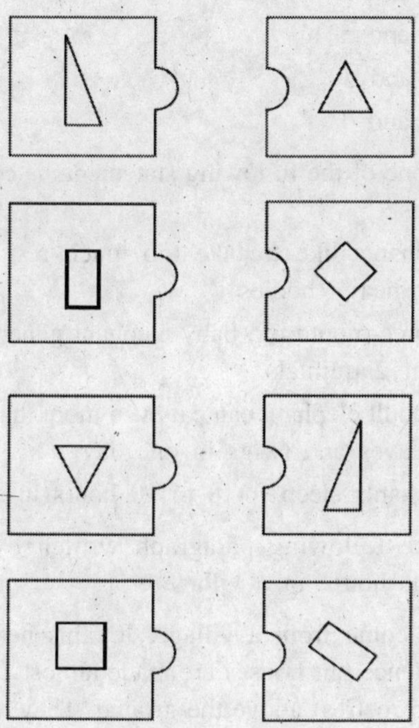

Objective of this game is to

A. make the classroom environment engaging and joyful

B. help children to recognize same shapes in different orientations

C. enhance eye-hand coordination

D. develop the concept of similarity and congruency

55. Geo-Board is an effective tool to teach

A. basic geometrical concepts like rays, lines and angles

B. geometrical shapes and their properties

C. difference between 2D and 3D shapes

D. concepts of symmetry

56. Proficiency in Mathematical language in classroom can be enhanced by presenting the problems in the following sequence:

A. Everyday language → Mathematized situation language → Language of Mathematical problem solving → Symbolic language

B. Symbolic language → Language of Mathematical problem solving → Mathematized situation language → Everyday language

C. Everyday language → Language of Mathematical problem solving → Mathematized situation language → Symbolic language

D. Language of Mathematical problem solving → Mathematized situation language → Symbolic language → Everyday language

57. Procedural fluency in Mathematics implies knowledge of rules, formulae or algorithms and implementing them with accuracy and flexibility and efficiency. Flexibility in Mathematics refers to

A. ability to solve different types of problems from the same topic

B. ability to solve problems from arithmetic and geometry with same efficiency

C. ability to solve a particular kind of problem using more than one approach

D. ability to solve problems with accuracy, writing all steps

58. A child mentally calculated (27 + 38) as 65. When he was asked to explain his method of addition, he responded that 38 is near to 40 so (27 + 40) is 67, then I removed 2 to get 65.

This strategy of addition is

A. Direct modelling

B. Regrouping

C. Compensating

D. Incrementing

59. Mental Math activities are important because they provide a chance to

A. develop mental computation procedures as the students try to identify the relationship between numbers for fast calculations

B. master procedures learnt in class using paper-pencil

C. master algorithms learnt and practice more number of problems in less time

D. develop their speed with accuracy for calculations and help to improve performance in examinations

60. A child of primary class is not able to differentiate between number, operation symbols, coins and clock hands. This indicates that the child has problem regarding

A. Auditory memory

B. Working memory

C. Visual processing

D. Language processing

PART- III

Environmental Studies

***Directions** : Answer the following questions by selecting the most appropriate option.*

61. Bronze is a mixture of two metals. These two metals are

A. Copper and Zinc B. Copper and Tin
C. Copper and Iron D. Aluminium and Tin

62. Select from the following a group that comprises of methods of cooking food:

A. Boiling, Kneading, Roasting
B. Baking, Boiling, Rolling
C. Frying, Soaking, Roasting
D. Baking, Frying, Roasting

63. Select the correct statement about Mount Everest:

A. It is a part of Jammu and Kashmir and the height of its peak is 8900 m.
B. It is a part of Nepal and the height of its peak is 8900 m.
C. It is a part of India and the height of its peak is 9850 m.
D. It is a part of Tibet and the height of its peak is 9850 m.

64. "Desert Oak" is a tree whose roots go deep into the ground till they reach water. The depth of these roots is nearly 30 times the height of the tree. This tree is found in

A. Rajasthan B. Abu Dhabi
C. Australia D. Russia

65. A train started from Gandhidham on 16th July, 2014 at 05:15 hours and reached Nagercoil on 18th July, 2014 at 04:45 hours. The distance covered by the train is 2649 km. The average speed of the train, in km/hr, is nearly

A. 57 B. 56
C. 55 D. 54

66. Which is the best period for the people of Bihar state to start bee-keeping?

A. January to March
B. April to June
C. July to September
D. October to December

67. Select the correct statements about the 'Khejadi' tree:

a. This tree is mainly found in desert areas.
b. It grows without much water.
c. It is a shady tree and children like to play in its shade.
d. It stores water in its trunk and people use thin pipes to drink this water

A. a, b and c
B. b, c and d
C. a, c and d
D. a, b and d

68. Which one of the following statements is correct about elephants?

A. Elephants like to take too much rest because of their heavy bodies
B. A three-month-old baby elephant generally weighs about 2 quintals
C. An adult elephant can eat even more than 2 quintals of leaves and twigs in one day
D. Elephants sleep for 8 to 10 hours in a day.

69. Read the following paragraph written by a student about his house in a village :

"I have come from a village. It rains heavily at our place. Hence our houses are made almost 10 to 12 feet (3 to 3.5 metres) above the ground. They are made on bamboo pillars. The inner sides of our houses are also made of wood."

This village must be in

A. Andhra Pradesh B. Assam
C. Tamil Nadu D. Uttarakhand

70. In Braille script, rows of raised dots are made on a thick paper. This script is based on

A. 4 points B. 6 points
C. 8 points D. 10 points

71. Which one of the following birds can rotate its neck backwards to a large extent?

A. Mynah B. Owl
C. Crow D. Koel

72. In which of the following parts of our country do people grow eatables such as tapioca and coconut in their courtyards and they find food prepared using these to be very tasty?

A. Andhra Pradesh B. Assam
C. Goa D. Kerala

73. A doctor prescribed some medicines to a patient and also suggested him to eat jaggery, amla and more green leafy vegetables. This patient must be suffering from

A. Fever B. Typhoid
C. Malaria D. Anaemia

74. Some birds can see four times as far as we can see. These birds are

A. Crows, Kites, Nightingales
B. Eagles, Pigeons, Parrots
C. Kites, Eagles, Vultures
D. Doves, Crows, Peacocks

75. With respect to the location of Delhi on the map of India, the capital of Himachal Pradesh (Shimla) and the capital of Madhya Pradesh (Bhopal) are located respectively in its

A. North-East and North-West
B. South-West and South-East
C. North and South
D. South-East and North-West

76. The abbreviation EVS stands for

A. Environmental Skills
B. Environmental Science
C. Environmental Sources
D. Environmental Studies

77. Which one of the following is not an objective of teaching of EVS at primary stage?

A. Learning in the classroom must be linked to the life outside the school
B. Teachers must ensure perfect discipline in the classroom
C. Children must be encouraged to ask questions
D. Children must be encouraged to explore their immediate environment

78. Aanchal frequently asks probing and imaginative questions in her Class V EVS class. By doing so, she aims at improving

A. observation skills
B. emotional skills
C. thinking skills
D. speaking skills

79. While teaching the topic on 'Our friend – Birds' to Class III students, Nalini followed the following methodologies :

a. Showing a documentary film on birds
b. Using a chart having pictures of different birds and explaining briefly
c. Taking the students to the nearby park and asking them to observe the birds carefully

Nalini is using different approaches of learning in order to

A. follow her lesson plan
B. meet different requirements of learners having multiple intelligences
C. impress other teachers and parents
D. promote reasoning skills in the students

80. Which one of the following teaching strategies will be more effective for maximum involvement of students in teaching the topic of 'Games we play'?

A. Take the students to the play-field and make them play different games on different days
B. Make play-cards of different games and show it to students
C. Ask the students to learn the names of different indoor and outdoor games
D. Ask the students to watch sports programmes on television and prepare a simple project on the same

81. Which one of the following is not a suitable Formative Assessment task in EVS?

A. Explain the definitions of important terms given in the lesson
B. Perform the given practical activity and record your observations
C. Draw labelled diagram of given experimental set-up
D. Discuss disadvantages of water

82. After teaching the lesson on animals, Sheetal arranged a visit of her Class IV students to the zoo. This would help the students to

A. develop skills of animal protection
B. have a change in the daily time table routine
C. co-relate classroom learning to real-life situations
D. develop sensitisation about how to domesticate animals

83. Shalini wants to introduce the topic on 'Nutrition' to her Class V students. She should

A. draw the diagram of the digestive system on the blackboard
B. give examples of different foods rich in nutrients
C. use chart showing different kinds of foods
D. ask the students to open their tiffin boxes, see the contents, followed by her explanation

84. Rashmi was taught the followed steps (not in sequence) to be followed while preparing a question paper :

i. Writing the questions
ii. Preparing the design
iii. Editing the question paper
iv. Preparing the blueprint

The correct sequence of steps to be followed is

A. iv, ii, i, iii B. ii, iv, i, iii
C. iv, i, ii, iii D. i, ii, iv, iii

85. Harpreet wants to suggest to her students as to how an individual can contribute in the best possible way towards environmental protection. Her best suggestion would be

A. use public transport system for travelling
B. do not keep a personal vehicle like car, scooter, etc
C. avoid frequent travel outside the home
D. get the engine of personal vehicle checked regularly

86. Out of the following, the most effective way to arouse curiosity in Class V students is to

A. provide more hands-on experiences
B. give them more practice in written work
C. conduct frequent unit tests
D. ask probing and imaginative questions

87. Asking the question "How will our life get affected if there were no electricity for a month?" aims at

A. sensitizing the students on using electricity judiciously
B. assessing the students on sources of electricity
C. promoting imaginative and thinking skills of students
D. assessing the students on their general awareness

88. The section on 'Survey and Write' in some chapters of EVS textbook for Class V primarily aims at

A. assessing the students on their general awareness
B. providing opportunity to students to explore and learn
C. helping the students to learn basic concepts of the subject
D. improving practical skills of students

89. Gunjan organises the following activities on different days to sensitise students to the concept of conservation of trees :

a. Encouraging every student to adopt a tree and look after it
b. Organizing a debate on forest conservation
c. Organizing a poster-making competition on trees
d. Showing children storage of logs of wood

Which one of the above activities will be least effective in achieving the desired objective?

A. a B. b
C. c D. d

90. After having taught the lesson 'What if it finishes' to Class V students, Sheela administered a test to know the level of understanding of students about the topic. To her surprise, she observed that large number of students had not understood the related concepts. This could be mainly due to the reason that

A. she did not use the correct methodology to teach the topic
B. the cognitive level of students was not good
C. the topic was not suitable for inclusion in the textbook
D. students did not find the topic interesting

PART- IV

Language-I : English

Directions (Qs. No. 91 to 99): *Read the given passage and answer the questions that follow by selecting the **most appropriate option:***

In this floating village in Brazil, there is only one way to travel. Students go to school by boat. Locals go to worship by boat. Taxis arrive by boat. Even the soccer field is often a boat. There are three homemade fields on land, but they are submerged now in the annual flooding of the Black River. If the wooden goal posts had nets, they would be useful this time of year only for catching fish. So young players and adults improvise. They play soccer at a community centre that has a roof but no walls. They play on the dock of a restaurant. And they play on a parked ferry, a few wearing life jackets to cushion their fall. The high-water mark in the Rio Negro this year was the fifth highest in more than a century of measurements.

As scientists study the impact of deforestation on the Amazon basin, and the cooling and warming of the Pacific

Ocean, extreme patterns observed over the last 25 or 30 years raise an important unanswered question : "Are these trends human-induced climate change, or can we explain this with natural variability?"

Villagers said that passing boats sometimes knocked down power lines during periods of exceptionally high water. And while the soccer fields are usually available for about half the year, the land has recently been dry enough for only four or five months of play. "We don't have a place for the children to play," said de Sousa, a shop owner. "They are stuck in the houses, bored." The most adventurous, though, will find a game somewhere.

91. The floating village is famous for its

A. Black River

B. Craze for sports

C. annual flooding

D. suffering of the locals

92. The wooden goal posts had nets that are ________ during floods.

A. floating around

B. used as nets

C. useless

D. misused

93. "The passing boats sometimes knocked down power lines" suggests that the

A. rescue boats are careless

B. water was charged

C. the flood levels were high

D. electric poles had fallen

94. A word that can best replace the word 'improvise' is

A. contrive B. share

C. plan D. devise

95. In this paragraph, 'to cushion' means to

A. separate B. protect

C. pad D. abate

96. Identify the correct statement

Flooding has _______ over a period of time.

A. remained the same

B. been increasing

C. been unpredictable

D. been decreasing

97. Pick out the false statement

A. The lines remain in place during the floods

B. The residents enjoy football the most

C. The goal posts and nets are useless during the floods

D. The community centre is the only space for playing

98. The antonym of the word 'exceptionally' is

A. extraordinary B. generally

C. markedly D. easily

99. "... will find a game somewhere" suggests that

A. people will play football in the water

B. football is lost during the floods

C. the Black River is no threat to a game of football

D. high grounds are reserved for the popular game

Directions (Q. Nos. 100 to 105) : *Read the given poem and answer the questions that follow by selecting the* ***most appropriate option.***

THE LAST CONQUEROR

Victorious men of earth, no more
Proclaim how wide your empires are;
Though you bind-in every shore
And your triumphs reach as far
As night or day,
Yet you, proud monarchs, must obey
And mingle with forgotten ashes, when
Death calls ye to the crowd of common men.
Devouring Famine, Plague, and War,
Each able to undo mankind,
Death's servile emissaries are;
Nor to these alone confined,
He hath at will
More quaint and subtle ways to kill;
A smile or kiss, as he will use the art,
Shall have the cunning skill to break a heart.

100. "...servile emissaries" means

A. risky behaviour

B. humble messengers

C. those who protect

D. messengers of peace

101. "More quaint and subtle ways to kill;
A smile or kiss, as he will use the art,"
– tells the reader that the speaker

A. believes in human goodness

B. is afraid of his enemies

C. hates wars

D. distrusts human nature

102. "... the cunning skill" – refers to

A. a weapon of war

B. skilful soldier

C. a manipulative king

D. hidden threat

103. "... mingle with forgotten ashes" means
A. dead persons
B. fires on the battlefield
C. threats to life
D. hidden dangers

104. Here, 'subtle' means
A. stupid B. hidden
C. suggestive D. sullen

105. "And your triumphs reach as far As night or day,"
– The poetic device found in these words is a
A. pathetic fallacy B. metaphor
C. simile D. formula

Directions (Q. No. 106 to 120) : *Answer the following questions by selecting the* ***most appropriate option.***

106. The teaching of reading by associating characters or groups of characters with sounds is the ______ method.
A. morphemic B. direct
C. phonic D. whole-language

107. Teachers can remediate for the student with language learning difficulty by
A. focusing on individual progress with individualized instruction
B. providing notes that are summarized and simplified
C. initially, giving information as reading only, no writing
D. conduct extra classes for the student to 'catch up' with others

108. Teachers can demystify abstract grammatical terminology so that students can write through the
A. explicit teaching of certain structures
B. separating of spoken and written forms of language
C. linking of spoken language with writing
D. frequent feedback on only grammatical errors

109. Language is taught by beginning with simple sentences instead of the initial sounds and blends. This implies that
A. communication is based on complete sentences
B. pronunciation has no place in language acquisition
C. grammar and pronunciation have equal place in language teaching
D. grammar is an important basis of communication

110. Which activity best supports the practice of speaking skills?
A. Students independently research a topic and present a formal report
B. Teacher's giving purposeful dictation by integrating it with a spoken activity
C. Individually, students read a case-study and draft a response
D. Students tell their version of a story based on some hints, and apply it to a problem-solving situation

111. Develop a resource box for Class I. Teacher gives 3 instructions to each student regarding which items are to be put in it. [e.g. : puppets, pieces of coloured fabric, brushes, stencils, colour pencils, small toys, etc.] Student follows instructions. The activity is
A. listening with concentration for specific information needed for a task
B. stage in a listening session when a listener completes a task
C. listening to natural conversation between teacher and student
D. listening to a speech which is semiscripted

112. Vocabulary in the target language should be kept under control, i.e., graded. This can be done by
A. teachers providing a short list of words that are commonly used
B. students learning and practising in the context of real situations
C. students write/speak using a graded list of new words
D. students read a prescribed book and take a vocabulary quiz

113. To achieve communicative competence, learners need to be competent in four aspects : linguistic, sociolinguistic, discourse, and strategic competences. Here, 'linguistic competence' concerns students.'
A. use of syntax lexis and structures
B. expression of meaning of what they communicate
C. use of formats and stylistic devices
D. content organization and use of vocabulary

114. Examples of "Creative Reading" projects for assessment are
A. reference work done in the library for more information on the theme
B. surfing the internet for related information
C. dramatization, role-play and re-writing from a different point of view
D. reading for meaning

115. The teacher's cues for activities are given in the first language, in a second language class. This ______ exploits the communicative potential of a given structure.
A. sandwich approach
B. communicative approach
C. bilingual technique
D. structural technique

116. The second language classroom is a confluence of varied languages. Teachers should give their students
A. adequate self-explanatory notes
B. summaries and simplified versions of texts
C. worksheets with a variety of tasks while covering the syllabus
D. comfortable environments to develop requisite skills

117. "... supply 'comprehensible input' in low anxiety situations" is the basis of language acquisition. An example would be
A. teacher-directed learning in the classroom
B. collaboration of students in learning situations
C. home work designed to use parents' support
D. students receive feedback for error correction regularly

118. How can teachers respond to or 'correct' students' writing in ways that are effective?
A. Correcting every error in the essay
B. Writing detailed comments in the margin
C. Offering encouraging and summary remarks
D. Locating patterns of error and suggesting improvement

119. Some parents of students with learning difficulties may have unrealistic expectations from their children. The teacher can support such students by
A. persuading them to liaise with other such students
B. explaining to the parents about the child's characteristics and abilities
C. providing instructions for dealing with the students at home
D. making a clear reference to the learning objectives

120. Educators use YouTube to teach visual learners with videos, podcasts for auditory learners and interactive games for tactile learners in a language class. Here, multi-media caters to individual
A. linguistic differences
B. learning styles
C. authentic second language
D. learning disabilities

PART- V

भाषा-II : हिन्दी

निर्देश (प्र.सं. 121 से 128): *नीचे दिए गए गद्यांश को पढ़कर* ***सबसे उचित विकल्प*** *का चयन कीजिए*

मैं दिखाना चाहती हूँ कि हम आलोचनात्मक शिक्षाशास्त्र के जरिए चीजों पर पर्दा डालने की कोशिश नहीं करते, क्योंकि अब तो यही चलन बन गया है। हम आमतौर पर कहते हैं अरे, सीखने का कितना खुशनुमा माहौल है और देखो, बच्चे कैसे-कैसे प्रयोग कर रहे हैं, वगैरह। मगर अब ये खुशनुमा ढंग से सीखना भी एक ढर्रा बन गया है, इसको बहुत बेजान बना दिया गया है। हम अकसर सोचते हैं कि बस कोई गतिविधि करना ही काफी है, भले ही वो बिल्कुल निरर्थक हो, भले ही बच्चे उसके जरिए कुछ न सीख रहे हों। बस गतिविधियाँ करवाने की मारामारी मची हुई है। आज हमारे यहाँ यही हालात हैं। इसलिए मुझे लगता है कि हमें इस बारे में एक नए सिरे से सोचना चाहिए। बेशक, गतिविधि का महत्व है मगर बच्चों को वो चीजें मत सिखाइए जो बाद में आनी है। मसलन, उन्हें नंबर लाइन सिखाकर उसके आधार पर टाइम लाइन की बात मत कीजिए। हर चीज को एक सन्दर्भ में कीजिए। इसकी वजह यह है कि बच्चे इसी तरह सीखते हैं। संख्याएँ संदर्भ से ही आती हैं। संख्या एक बहुत अमूर्त धारणा है। एक बच्चे के लिए 'दो' समझना अमूर्त बात है। वह कैसे समझेगा कि किसी चीज के 'दो' होने का क्या मतलब है?

121. बच्चों के सीखने के तरीके में सबसे अधिक क्या महत्वपूर्ण है?
A. संख्या B. संदर्भ
C. गतिविधि D. उपर्युक्त सभी

122. गद्यांश में किसके ढर्रा बन जाने की बात की गई है?
A. प्रयोग करने के
B. खुशनुमा माहौल के
C. खुशनुमा ढंग से सीखने के
D. गतिविधि करने के

123. गद्यांश के अनुसार
A. गतिविधि कराना उचित नहीं है
B. गतिविधियों का निरंतर प्रयोग करते रहना चाहिए
C. गतिविधि के जरिए बच्चे कुछ नहीं सीखते
D. गतिविधियाँ सार्थक होनी चाहिए

124. बच्चों के लिए क्या मुश्किल है?
A. संख्या जैसी अमूर्त अवधारणा को समझना
B. गतिविधियों का महत्व समझना
C. संख्याओं के महत्व को समझना
D. गतिविधियों के माध्यम से सीखना

125. अकसर लोग क्या सोचते हैं?

A. गतिविधि कराना ही काफी है

B. किसी भी गतिविधि से बच्चे सीखते हैं

C. गतिविधि से समय की बचत होती है

D. गतिविधियाँ बहुत बेजान होती हैं

126. 'गतिविधियाँ करवाने की मारामारी मची हुई है' का आशय है

A. गतिविधियाँ कराते समय मार-पीट हो रही है

B. गतिविधियाँ कराना बहुत महँगा पड़ता है

C. सभी लोग देखादेखी निरर्थक गतिविधियाँ भी करवाने में लगे हुए हैं

D. सभी लोग देखादेखी सार्थक गतिविधियाँ करवाने में लगे हुए हैं

127. 'अमूर्त' का विलोम है

A. मूर्त B. साकार

C. प्रत्यक्ष D. मूर्तिवान

128. ''हालात'' का समानार्थी है

A. हालत B. स्थिति

C. समस्या D. परिप्रेक्ष्य

निर्देश (प्र.सं. 129 से 135): *नीचे दिए गए गद्यांश को पढ़कर **सबसे उचित विकल्प** का चयन कीजिए*

देखिए, यह सिर्फ सिद्धांत की बात नहीं है, यह तो हमारे अनुभवों और व्यवहार से भी दिखाई दे रही है। आज क्या स्थिति है? शिक्षा में हमने बहुत प्रगति की है। पहले बहुत कम स्कूल थे, अब हर गाँव में और हर मोहल्ले में स्कूल है। बहुत दूरस्थ इलाके में भी स्कूल खुल चुके हैं लेकिन उन स्कूलों में जो शिक्षा मिल रही है वह नाममात्र की शिक्षा मिल रही है। पाँचवी पास हो जाएँगे, छठी, आठवीं में बच्चा पहुँच जाएगा लेकिन उनकी लिखने, पढ़ने और हिसाब करने की योग्यता बहुत कमजोर है। यह क्यों हो रहा है? इसलिए हो रहा है कि इस देश में जितने पैसे वाले लोग हैं उन्होंने अपनी व्यवस्था अलग बना ली है और उनको अब इस बात की परवाह नहीं है कि सरकारी स्कूलों में पढ़ाई हो रही है या नहीं। कितने शिक्षक हैं, क्या व्यवस्था है, शिक्षक आता है या नहीं, ये सारी चीजें हैं जिनसे उनको कोई मतलब नहीं है।

129. शिक्षा में प्रगति हुई है, गद्यांश के अनुसार इसका प्रमाण है

A. बच्चे अच्छा सीख रहे हैं

B. दूर-दराज के गाँवों में भी स्कूल खुल गए हैं

C. दूर-दराज के गाँवों में सभी बच्चे पढ़ने जाते हैं

D. बच्चे हिसाब में पक्के हो गए हैं

130. दूरस्थ इलाकों में

A. अच्छी शिक्षा मिल रही है

B. अच्छे शिक्षक पढ़ाते हैं

C. अच्छी शिक्षा नहीं मिल रही हैं

D. शिक्षक रोज समय पर आते हैं

131. बच्चे पढ़ाई में कमजोर हैं, इसका कारण है

A. पैसे वाले लोगों ने अपने अलग स्कूल खोल लिए हैं

B. पैसे वाले लोगों को इस बात से कोई सरोकार नहीं है

C. पैसे वाले लोग गाँव में कम जाते हैं

D. पैसे वाले लोगों की व्यवस्था खराब है

132. गद्यांश के अनुसार बच्चों की बेहतर शिक्षा के लिए

A. अधिक स्कूल खोले जाने चाहिए

B. शिक्षा-व्यवस्था में से पैसे वाले लोगों को निकाल देना चाहिए

C. बच्चों, शिक्षकों और पूरी शिक्षा-व्यवस्था पर ध्यान दिया जाना चाहिए

D. बच्चों को अधिक समय तक पढ़ाना चाहिए

133. 'शिक्षा' में 'इक' प्रत्यय लगने पर शब्द बनेगा

A. शैक्षिक B. शिक्षिक

C. शैक्षीक D. शिक्षित

134. 'प्रगति' में कौन-सा प्रत्यय लगेगा?

A. वान B. वाला

C. शील D. दार

135. गद्यांश में किस शब्द के एक से अधिक अर्थ हैं?

A. शिक्षा B. प्रगति

C. योग्यता D. पास

निर्देश (प्र.सं. 136 से 150): *निम्नलिखित प्रश्नों के उत्तर देने के लिए **सबसे उचित विकल्प** का चयन कीजिए*

136. विद्यालय आने से पूर्व बच्चों के पास

A. व्याकरण की समझ बिल्कुल नहीं होती

B. व्याकरण की पूर्ण समझ होती है

C. व्याकरण की सचेत समझ नहीं होती

D. व्याकरण की सचेत समझ होती है

137. 'प्राथमिक स्तर की शिक्षा मुख्यतः भाषा-शिक्षा है।' इस कथन का निहितार्थ यह है कि

A. बच्चों को केवल भाषा की ही शिक्षा दी जाए

B. बच्चों के भाषा-विकास पर ध्यान दिया जाए

C. बच्चों को अनेक भाषाएँ सिखाना अनिवार्य है

D. बच्चों को मानक भाषाएँ सिखाई जाएँ

138. जो शिक्षक बच्चों का भाषा से अर्थपूर्ण परिचय कराना चाहते हैं

A. वे पाठ्य-पुस्तक में रोजमर्रा की भाषा को स्थान देते हैं

B. वे साहित्य के शिक्षण पर बल देते हैं

C. वे भाषागत शुद्धता पर अत्यधिक बल देते हैं

D. वे बच्चों की भाषा का आकलन नहीं करते

139. पढ़ने की प्रक्रिया में सर्वाधिक महत्वपूर्ण है

A. वर्णमाला का क्रमिक ज्ञान

B. शब्दों को पढ़ने की कुशलता

C. वाक्यों को पढ़ने की कुशलता

D. पढ़ी गई पाठ्य-वस्तु का अर्थ ग्रहण करना

140. एक भाषा-शिक्षक के रूप में आप अपनी क्या जिम्मेदारी महसूस करते हैं?

A. समय-सीमा के भीतर भाषा का पाठ्यक्रम पूर्ण करना

B. समय-सीमा के भीतर पाठ्य-पुस्तक पूर्ण करना

C. बच्चों को भाषा के विविध स्वरूपों और प्रयोगों से परिचय

D. बच्चों द्वारा भाषा परीक्षाओं में अच्छे अंक लाना

141. मातृभाषा में शिक्षा से

A. कक्षा में पढ़ाई करने में सुविधा होगी

B. शिक्षार्थियों की अधिकाधिक प्रतिभागिता होगी

C. बेहतर परिणाम निकलेंगे

D. उपर्युक्त सभी

142. भाषा सीखने-सिखाने के सम्बन्ध में कौन-सा कथन सही नहीं है?

A. भाषा परिवेश से सीखी जाती है।

B. भाषा अर्जित करना सहज होता है।

C. संचार-माध्यम भाषा सीखने में मदद करते हैं।

D. भाषा विद्यालय में ही अर्जित की जाती है।

143. लिखना

A. एक तरह की बातचीत है

B. एक यांत्रिक कौशल है

C. अत्यंत जटिल कौशल है

D. पढ़ना के बाद सीखा जाता है

144. भाषा-कौशलों के सम्बन्ध में कौन-सा कथन सही है?

A. भाषा-कौशल परस्पर अंतःसंबंधित होते हैं।

B. भाषा-कौशल परस्पर अंतःसंबंधित नहीं होते।

C. भाषा-कौशल एक-दूसरे पर प्रभाव नहीं डालते हैं।

D. भाषा-कौशल स्तरानुसार सीखे जाते हैं।

145. भाषा सीखने में बातचीत का इस रूप में सर्वाधिक महत्व है कि

A. इससे बच्चों का अच्छा समय व्यतीत हो जाता है

B. शिक्षक और बच्चे दोनों ही बातचीत में रस लेते हैं

C. बच्चे विभिन्न उद्देश्यों के लिए भाषा का प्रयोग करना सीखते हैं

D. बच्चे दूसरों के शुद्ध उच्चारण का अनुकरण कर सकते हैं

146. प्राथमिक स्तर पर बच्चों की भाषा का आकलन करने में क्या सबसे कम उपयोगी है?

A. चित्र देखकर कहानी, कविता लिखना

B. पाठ के अंत में दिए सवालों का जवाब लिखना

C. किसी घटना का वर्णन करना

D. नानी को चिट्ठी लिखते हुए अपनी नई दोस्त के बारे में बताना

147. पहली कक्षा की नादिरा पढ़ते हुए बार-बार अटकती है। ऐसे में आप क्या करेंगे?

A. नादिरा को डाँटेंगे कि वह सही से क्यों नहीं पढ़ती

B. उसे पढ़ने के लिए मना कर देंगे

C. उससे कहेंगे कि पहले पढ़ना सीख लो फिर कक्षा में पढ़ना

D. धैर्य से काम लेते हुए पढ़ना सीखने में उसकी मदद करेंगे

148. भाषा सीखने और भाषा अर्जित करने में अंतर का सर्वप्रमुख कारण है

A. भाषा की पाठ्य-पुस्तकें

B. भाषा में आकलन

C. भाषायी परिवेश

D. भाषा का व्याकरण

149. आपके विचार से भाषा-शिक्षण के संदर्भ में सबसे कम महत्वपूर्ण है

A. भाषा-शिक्षण के प्रति शिक्षक का नजरिया

B. भाषागत विविधता के प्रति संवेदनशीलता

C. भाषा के आकलन की प्रक्रियाएँ

D. किसी भाषा विशेष का साहित्य

150. हिन्दी भाषा की कक्षा में मोना लिखते समय कठिनाई का अनुभव करती है। यह समस्या किससे सम्बन्धित है?

A. डिस्लेक्सिया B. डिस्ग्राफिया

C. डिस्केलकेलिया D. डिस्लेखिया

Answers

1	2	3	4	5	6	7	8	9	10
C	D	A	D	C	C	D	A	B	A
11	12	13	14	15	16	17	18	19	20
B	A	C	D	B	B	A	B	A	C
21	22	23	24	25	26	27	28	29	30
B	D	B	A	A	D	A	C	B	C
31	32	33	34	35	36	37	38	39	40
C	C	A	D	C	B	A	D	C	D
41	42	43	44	45	46	47	48	49	50
A	B	B	D	A	A	B	A	B	A
51	52	53	54	55	56	57	58	59	60
A	C	A	B	B	A	C	C	A	C
61	62	63	64	65	66	67	68	69	70
B	D	B	C	B	D	A	B	B	B
71	72	73	74	75	76	77	78	79	80
B	D	D	C	C	D	B	C	B	A
81	82	83	84	85	86	87	88	89	90
D	C	D	B	A	D	C	B	D	A
91	92	93	94	95	96	97	98	99	100
B	C	C	A	C	D	D	B	C	B
101	102	103	104	105	106	107	108	109	110
D	D	A	C	C	C	A	C	D	D
111	112	113	114	115	116	117	118	119	120
A	B	A	C	C	D	B	D	B	B
121	122	123	124	125	126	127	128	129	130
B	C	D	A	A	C	A	B	B	C
131	132	133	134	135	136	137	138	139	140
B	C	A	C	D	C	B	A	D	C
141	142	143	144	145	146	147	148	149	150
D	B	D	A	C	B	D	C	D	B

Some Selected Explanatory Answers

31. Given number = 35362

Place value of 5 = 5000

Face value of 5 = 5

Difference = 5000 − 5 = 4995.

32. 10 ones = 10 × 1 = 10

10 tens = 10 × 10 = 100

10 thousands = 10 × 1000 = 10000

Sum of above = 10 + 100 + 10000 = 10110.

33. Factors of 210 are

1 × 210
2 × 105
3 × 70
5 × 42
6 × 35
7 × 30
10 × 21
14 × 15

∴ All factors of 210 are

1, 2, 3, 5, 6, 7, 10, 14, 15, 21, 30, 35, 42, 70, 105 and 210

Sum = 1 + 2 + 3 + 5 + 6 + 7 + 10 + 14 + 15 + 21 + 30 + 35 + 42 + 70 + 105 + 210
= 576.

34. Total time worked

$$= 4\frac{1}{2}\text{hrs} + 3\frac{1}{6}\text{hrs} + \frac{23}{6}\text{hrs} + \frac{11}{3}\text{hrs}$$

$$= \left(\frac{9}{2} + \frac{19}{6} + \frac{23}{6} + \frac{11}{3}\right)\text{hrs}$$

$$= \left(\frac{27+19+23+22}{6}\right)\text{hrs}$$

$$= \left(\frac{91}{6}\right)\text{hrs}$$

Total amount earned = $\frac{91}{6} \times 42 = 91 \times 7 = ₹\,637.$

35. Greatest 4 digit number = 9999

Smallest 3 digit number = 100

Required sum = 9999 + 100 = 10099.

36. $26 + \frac{26}{100} = 26.00 + 0.26 = 26.26$

37.

```
11) 19009 (1728
    11
    ---
     80
     77
     ---
      30
      22
      ---
       89
       88
       ---
        1
```

∴ Remainder = 1

```
11) 9090 (826
    88
    ---
     29
     22
     ---
      70
      66
      ---
       4
```

∴ Remainder = 4

Required product = 1 × 4 = 4.

38. $3\frac{1}{3} \div \frac{1}{6} = \frac{10}{3} \times \frac{6}{1} = 10 \times 2 = 20$

∴ Required number = 20

39. Product of 1109 × 505 = 560045

According to the question,

505050 = 560045 − x

⇒ x = 560045 − 505050

= 54995.

40. $\frac{23}{100} = 2.30$ is not correct because $\frac{23}{100} = 0.23.$

41. 16 jars contain 240.128 litres

1 jar contains = $\frac{240.128}{16}$ = 15.008 litres

22 jar contain = 15.008 × 22

= 330.176 litres

= 330 L 176 mL.

42. ∵ 1 right angle = 90°

∴ $4\frac{2}{3} \times 90° = \frac{14}{3} \times 90 = 14 \times 30 = 420°.$

43. 9 m high − 6 m high = 3 m high

Empty part = $\frac{3}{9} = \frac{1}{3}$

44. Perimeter of square = perimeter of rectangle = 96 cm

∵ Side of square = $\frac{96}{4}$ = 24 cm

∴ Breadth of rectangle = 24 − 4 = 20 cm

$2(l + b) = 96$

$l + b = 48$

$l = 48 - 20$

= 28 cm

Area of rectangle = $l \times b$ = 28 × 20 = 560 cm^2

2 times area of rectangle = 560 × 2 = 1120 cm^2.

45. L.C.M. of 4, 5 and 6 = 60

L.C.M. of 5, 6 and 9 = 90

Required difference = 90 − 60 = 30.

Previous Paper (Solved)

CTET PAPER-I, FEBRUARY 2014*

PART- I

Child Development and Pedagogy

Directions: *Answer the following questions by selecting the **most appropriate** option.*

1. In the progressive model of education as implemented by CBSE, socialization of children is done in such a way so as to expect them to
   A. give up time-consuming social habits and learn how to score good grades
   B. be an active participant in the group work and learn social skills
   C. prepare themselves to conform to the rules and regulations of society without questioning
   D. accept what they are offered by the school irrespective of their social background

2. Which of the following is based on Vygotsky's sociocultural theory?
   A. Operant conditioning
   B. Reciprocal teaching
   C. Culture-neutral cognitive development
   D. Insight learning

3. A teacher says to her class, "As individual assignments are designed to help individual students learn more effectively, all students should complete assignments prescribed without any assistance". She is referring to which of the following stages of Kohlberg's moral development?
   A. Conventional stage 4 —*law and order*
   B. Post-conventional stage 5 —*social contract*
   C. Pre-conventional stage 1 —*punishment avoidance*
   D. Pre-conventional stage 2 —*individualism and exchange*

4. Fourteen-year-old Devika is attempting to develop a sense of herself as a separate, self-governing individual. She is developing
   A. hatred for rules
   B. autonomy
   C. teenage arrogance
   D. maturity

5. In context of progressive education, which of the following statements is true according to John Dewey?
   A. There should not be a place for democracy in a classroom
   B. Students should be able to solve social problems themselves
   C. Curiosity does not belong to the inherent nature of students rather it is to be cultivated
   D. Students should be observed and not heard in the classroom

6. A disorder related to language comprehension is
   A. apraxia B. dyslexia
   C. aspeechxia D. aphasia

7. Following are the critical views about the "Theory of Multiple Intelligences", ***except***
   A. it is not research-based
   B. different intelligences demand different methods for different students
   C. gifted students usually excel in a single domain
   D. it lacks of empirical support

8. 'Theory of Multiple Intelligences' cannot be legitimized as it
   A. is not possible to measure different intelligences as there are no specific tests
   B. does not place equal importance on all seven intelligences
   C. is based only on sound empirical studies done by Abraham Maslow throughout his life
   D. is not compatible with general intelligence 'g', which is most important

9. The individual differences of students in a classroom are
   A. disadvantageous as teachers need to control a diverse classroom
   B. detrimental as they lead to student-student conflicts
   C. inexpedient as they reduce the speed of the curriculum transaction to the level of the slowest student
   D. advantageous as they lead teacher to explore a wider pool of cognitive structures

*Exam was held on 16-02-2014.

10. School-based assessment was introduced to
A. decentralize the power of Boards of school education in the country
B. ensure the holistic development of all the students
C. motivate teachers to punctiliously record all the activities of students for better interpretation of their progress
D. encourage schools to excel by competing with the other schools in their area

11. Which one of the following is ***not*** related to other options?
A. Organizing question-answer sessions
B. Taking feedback from students on a topic
C. Conducting quiz
D. Modeling the skills of self-assessment

12. Which one of the following questions is correctly matched with its specified domain?
A. Could you group your students on the basis of their achievement in Mathematics? : Evaluating
B. What was the turning point in the cricket match telecasted last night? : Creating
C. Write down a new recipe to cook chicken by using herbs. : Application
D. Determine which of the given measures would most likely lead to achieve best results. : Analyzing

13. Which of the following is the most effective way to convey students from disadvantaged sections that you expect them to participate and succeed?
A. Articulate your confidence in their ability to succeed
B. Develop your own interest in the topics to be taught
C. Compare them with other children as frequently as possible to make them realize their goal
D. Emphasize the point that you have high expectation of them

14. Following are the examples of developmental disorder, ***except***
A. autism
B. cerebral palsy
C. post-traumatic stress
D. attention deficit hyperactivity disorder

15. Multiple pedagogical techniques, assorted learning material, multiple assessment techniques and varying the complexity and nature of the content are associated with which of the following?
A. Universal design for learning
B. Remedial teaching
C. Differentiated instruction
D. Reciprocal teaching

16. Which of the following is true about gifted learners?
A. They make everyone else smarter and are essential for collaborative learning
B. They always lead others and assume extra responsibility in the classroom
C. They may achieve lower grades due to their heightened sensitivity
D. Their importance is primarily due to their brainpower

17. Inclusion in schools primarily focuses on
A. making subtle provisions for special category children
B. fulfilling the needs of children with disabilities only
C. meeting the need of the disabled child at the expense of entire class
D. including the educational needs of illiterate parents in schools

18. The cause of learned helplessness in children is their
A. acquired behaviour that they will not succeed
B. callous attitude towards classroom activities
C. non-compliance with expectations of their parents
D. moral decision for not taking up studies seriously

19. If a student is consistently getting lower grades in school, her parents can be advised to help her by
A. working in close association with teachers
B. withholding mobile phones, movies, comics and extra time for play
C. narrating her the hardships of life for those who do not possess proper education
D. forcing her to work harder at home

20. Which of the following does ***not*** deter problem solving?
A. Insight
B. Mental sets
C. Entrenchment
D. Fixation

21. A teacher is connecting a text to the previously learnt text and showing children how to summarize it. She is
A. helping children to develop their own strategy to comprehend it
B. insinuating that there is no need to go through the entire text
C. reinforcing the importance of text from the assessment point of view
D. encouraging children to mug it up as effectively as possible

22. What kind of errors is common between a learner who is learning his mother tongue and the learner who learns the same language as a second language?
   A. Overgeneralization
   B. Simplification
   C. Developmental
   D. Hypercorrection

23. The stress affects performance in examinations. This fact reflects which of the following relationships?
   A. Cognition-Emotion
   B. Stress-Omission
   C. Performance-Anxiety
   D. Cognition-Competition

24. A teacher is trying to counsel a child who is not performing well after an accident. Which one of the following is most appropriate about counseling in schools?
   A. It is about the palliative measures for making people comfortable
   B. It builds self-confidence of people by letting them explore their own thoughts
   C. It is about giving the best possible advice to students about their future career options
   D. It can be done only by the professional experts

25. Which of the following would encourage the least a student who wants to become a highly creative theater artist?
   A. Try to win the State level competition that will ensure you scholarship
   B. Develop empathetic, amicable and supportive relationships with your peer theater artists
   C. Devote your time to those theatrical skills that you find most enjoyable
   D. Read about the performances of the world's best theater artists and try to learn

26. Which of the following theorists would be of the opinion that students study hard for their personal growth and development?
   A. Bandura B. Maslow
   C. Skinner D. Piaget

27. Which of the following factors supports learning in a classroom?
   A. Increasing the number of tests to motivate children to learn
   B. Supporting the autonomy of children by the teachers
   C. Sticking to one particular method of instruction to maintain uniformity
   D. Increasing the time interval of periods from 40 minutes to 50 minutes

28. Mature students
   A. believe that emotion has no place in their studies
   B. resolve easily all their conflicts with their intellect
   C. sometimes need emotional support in their studies
   D. do not get upset by studies in difficult situations

29. A child coming to pre-school for the first time cries profusely. After two years when the same child goes to the primary school for the first time, he does not express his tension by crying rather his shoulder and neck muscles become tense. This change in his behaviour can be explained on the basis of which of the following principles?
   A. Development proceeds in a sequential manner
   B. Development is gradual
   C. Development is different in different people
   D. Development is characterized by differentiation and integration

30. Which of the following statements is true?
   A. Genetic makeup impacts responsiveness of an individual to qualities of the environment
   B. Adoptive children possess same IQs as their adoptive siblings
   C. Experience does not influence brain development
   D. Intelligence remains unaffected by the schooling

PART- II

Mathematics

Directions : Answer the following questions by selecting the ***most appropriate option.***

31. The Perimeter of a square is 20 cm. A rectangle has the same width as the square. The length of the rectangle is double its width. The area, in square cm, of the rectangle is
   A. 30 B. 50
   C. 100 D. 25

32. The internal length, breadth and height of a rectangular box A are 20 cm, 18 cm and 5 cm respectively and that of box B are 18 cm, 12 cm and 5 cm respectively. The volume of box A is how many times that of box B?
   A. 4
   B. 5
   C. 6
   D. 3

33. Which of the following is ***not*** correct?
A. Area of a square of side 10 cm = Area of a rectangle of length 10 cm and breadth 0.1 m
B. 1 metre 5 centimetre $\neq$ 1.5 metre
C. 0.40 is same as 0.4
D. Rupee $\frac{3}{4}$ = Rupee 0.75

34. One orange costs five and half rupees and one kg apple costs ₹ 80. Then the total cost of one and half dozen of oranges and one and three-fourth kg of apples is
A. ₹ 219
B. ₹ 229
C. ₹ 239
D. ₹ 209

35. NCF, 2005 states that Mathematics teaching should be ambitious, coherent and important. Here, 'ambitious' refers to achievement of
A. narrow goals of Mathematics
B. linking of Mathematics with other subjects
C. application of Mathematics
D. higher goals of Mathematics

36. In Class II, concept of even number and odd number was introduced by activity of pairing the given number with concrete objects. Then teacher asked the students to check
(*i*) whether the total number of crayons in their colour boxes is even in number or odd in number
(*ii*) whether the number of pages in their Maths notebook is odd or even.
This task of finding even or odd number of crayons/pages is
A. assessment for learning
B. assessment as learning
C. assessment at the end of learning
D. assessment of learning

37. After explaining the operation of subtraction in Class II, teacher drew the following diagram on the board and asked the students to fill in the circles :

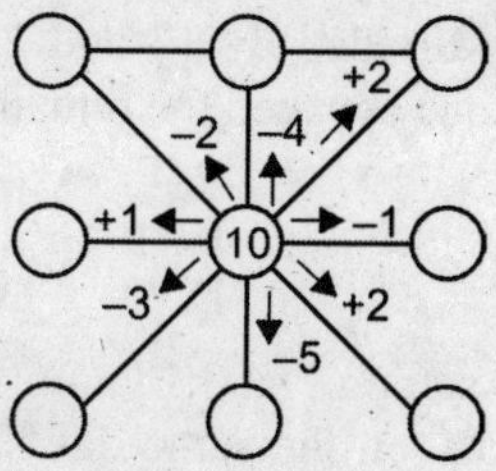

The purpose of the exercise is
A. strengthening skill of addition and subtraction
B. summative assessment
C. arranging fun activity for the students
D. mathematization of mind

38. How many rectangles are there in the following figure?

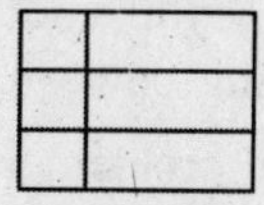

The above question is testing
A. knowledge of learner
B. understanding of learner
C. creativity of learner
D. memory of learner

39. Which of the following activities is meant to enhance problem-solving abilities of students of Class III?
A. A crossword puzzle containing clues for all key terms learnt like even number, odd number, composite number, prime number, etc.
B. A group project : How the students of primary wing shall be distributed equally in four houses (house system of school) so that every house has talented students from sports, arts, cultural and academic activities?
C. Conduct an interclass quiz in the class on 'numbers and operations'
D. A worksheet containing problems on four basic operations like—Find 25 × 34, 451 ÷ 11, etc.

40. The recommended key concept in the unit of 'multiplication' in Class III is
A. multiplication of 2-digit number with 2-digit number
B. properties of multiplication–order property and group property
C. word problem based on multiplication
D. multiplication of 3-digit numbers by 10

41. From the unit of 'fraction', teacher asked the students to list any five fractions.
This question refers to
A. higher level of thinking
B. analytical thinking
C. spatial thinking
D. lower level of thinking

42. In an exercise, the question was—Measure the lengths of the line segments P •——• Q and R •——• S.
The child answered—
length of AB = 5 cm, length of AB = 3 cm
This refers to
A. conceptual error
B. procedural error
C. error due to habit of naming line segment as AB
D. reading error

43. A teacher distributed newspaper in Class V and asked the students to read the cricket scores of Indian team in latest match. Then she asked them to draw bar graph of the scores. The teacher is trying to
A. help the students to make connections between mathematical concepts and real life

B. teach them through project approach
C. make the class joyful and communicating
D. enhance reasoning power of the students

44. The following word problem was given to a child of Class IV :
Mumbai has 336 bus stops. Delhi has 127 more bus stops than Mumbai. How many bus stops are there in all, in Delhi?
The child's response to the above problem is recorded as-

336	Mumbai	
336	127	Delhi

Total bus stops in Delhi are 336 + 127 = 463.
The teacher shall report about his performance as
A. the child can find the answer correctly but his expression is poor
B. the child is good at visualizing and analyzing, and his problem-solving ability is appreciable
C. the child has not adopted the right procedure. He needs to practice more
D. the child is not able to write all steps required properly

45. A student was asked to read the following numbers :
306, 408, 4008, 4010
He read as follows :
Thirty six, forty eight, four hundred eight, forty ten
The reason for error in reading is that
A. the student does not like Maths class and finds the class boring
B. the student has understood the concept of place value but does not know how to use it
C. the student is not fit for study of Maths
D. the student is not able to understand the concept of place value and feels comfortable using two-digit numbers only

46. The parameter(s) of assessment for 'time' for Class IV shall be
A. reading time on analogous clock only
B. reading time on digital and analogous clock, concept of half past, quarter past, quarter to, a.m., p.m., relation between minutes and seconds
C. reading time on digital clock, concept of a.m. and p.m. only
D. reading time on digital clock only

47. 'Tall shape of Mathematics' mentioned in NCF, 2005 refers to
A. solving challenging problems
B. creating Maths game
C. providing hands-on experience
D. building of one concept on other

48. Consider the following :
5 + 3 = ?
The open-ended question corresponding to the above close-ended question is
A. Find the sum of 5 and 3.
B. What shall be added to 5 to get 8?
C. Give any two numbers whose sum is 8.
D. What is the sum of 5 and 3?

49. Farhan went to school library and found that 100 books kept in story section are spoiled. 20 books are missing. 219 are kept in shelf and 132 were issued to students. How many story- books were there in the library?
Teacher can teach the following value through this question
A. Helping others
B. Sharing books with others
C. Taking good care of books
D. Sense of cooperation

50. The product of the place values of 5 and 6 in 70560 is
A. 300 B. 3000
C. 30000 D. 30

51. When 3010301 is divided by 43, the quotient is
A. 70707 B. 70007
C. 7077 D. 7007

52. What should be subtracted from the product 3001 × 101 to get 300311?
A. 2790 B. 2090
C. 2970 D. 270

53. (Smallest common multiple of 36 and 60) + (Biggest common factor of 18 and 45) is equal to
A. 20 B. 30
C. 40 D. 10

54. (10 tens + 11 hundreds + 12 ones) equals
A. 1213 B. 111012
C. 101112 D. 1212

55. The number of factors of 42 is
A. 7 B. 8
C. 9 D. 6

56. When 3488 is divided by 12 and 2478 is divided by 11, the difference between the remainders in both cases is
A. 5 B. 6
C. 7 D. 3

57. A train leaves station P at 8:18 a.m. and reaches station Q at 10:28 p.m. on the same day. The time taken by the train to reach Q is
A. 14 hours 10 minutes
B. 14 hours 46 minutes
C. 18 hours 46 minutes
D. 13 hours 10 minutes

58. 14 L 280 mL of orange juice and 18 L 830 mL of carrot juice were mixed together. This mixture was filled in 15 bottles each containing 1.5 L. How much mixture was left?

A. 11 L 105 mL B. 9 L 610 mL
C. 11 L 605 mL D. 10 L 610 mL

59. One-fourth of a pizza was eaten by Renu. The rest was equally distributed among 12 children. What part of the pizza did each of these children get?

A. $\frac{1}{16}$ B. $\frac{1}{32}$
C. $\frac{3}{16}$ D. $\frac{1}{8}$

60. The number of seconds in 6 hours equals the number of minutes in

A. 4 days B. 10 days
C. 15 days D. 2 days

PART- III

Environmental Studies

Directions : Answer the following questions by selecting the most appropriate option.

61. Select the true statements from the following :

I. Elephants love to play with muddy water as it keeps their skin cool.
II. Most elephants like to take rest and sleep nearly 10 hours a day.
III. A three-month-old elephant weighs about 200 kg.
IV. Most adult elephants eat about 100 kg of leaves/twigs in one day.

A. II and IV only
B. I and IV only
C. I, III and IV
D. I and II only

62. Select the correct statements about Madhubani paintings:

1. To make these paintings, indigo, turmeric, colours from flowers and trees, etc., are used.
2. The paintings show human beings, animals, trees, flowers, birds, fish, etc.
3. It is a very old form of folk art and is named after the place Madhubani.
4. Madhubani is a well-known district of Rajasthan.

A. 1, 3 and 4
B. 1, 2 and 4
C. 2, 3 and 4
D. 1, 2 and 3

63. A bird makes its nest high up on a tree. This bird could be

A. Sunbird B. Indian Robin
C. Crow D. Dove

64. Pochampally is a village which is famous for the special cloth which is also called Pochampally. This village is a part of

A. Kerala
B. Karnataka
C. Andhra Pradesh
D. Tamil Nadu

65. Select the correct statements about 'Desert Oak':

1. It is a tree found in Australia.
2. This is a special kind of tree which has its roots growing from its branches.
3. The roots of this tree go deep into the ground till they reach water.
4. This tree stores water in its trunk. Local people use thin pipe to drink this water.

A. 1, 2 and 4 B. 1, 3 and 4
C. 2, 3 and 4 D. 1, 2 and 3

66. Select the correct statements about Abu Dhabi:

1. It is located in desert area.
2. Water is costlier than petrol in Abu Dhabi.
3. Arabic is the local language here.
4. Money used in Abu Dhabi is called Dinar.

A. 1, 2 and 4 B. 1, 3 and 4
C. 2, 3 and 4 D. 1, 2 and 3

67. There are animals that awake at night. These animals can see things only in

A. violet and blue colours
B. green and yellow colours
C. black and white colours
D. red and orange colours

68. Here in Fig. I, a 24-hour clock is shown and in Fig. II and Fig. III, sleeping times of two animals X and Y are shown by shaded portions. Select the correct statement about the sleeping times of X and Y :

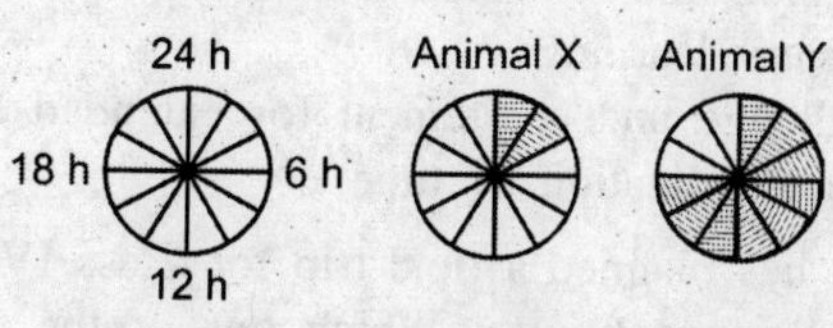

Fig. I Fig. II Fig. III

A. X sleeps for 20 hours while Y sleeps for 18 hours
B. X sleeps for 18 hours while Y sleeps for 4 hours
C. X sleeps for 4 hours while Y sleeps for 18 hours
D. X sleeps for 4 hours while Y sleeps for 20 hours

69. What is the Dead Sea?
A. A sea whose water is poisonous
B. A sea which is saltiest of all oceans and seas
C. A sea in which high and low tides are very frequent
D. A sea in which it is dangerous to sail ships

70. Anjali desires to emphasize on cultural/regional diversity in food habits, while teaching the topic on 'Food' to Class III students. Which one of the following learning experiences given to students can bring about the desired result?
A. Use a chart showing foods of different cultures/ regions and explain
B. Ask students from different cultures/regions to bring food from home, display it and share the information with classmates
C. Explain the information given in the text-book about different foods in greater detail
D. Request an external professional cooking agency to display food of different regions/cultures

71. Preeti wants to lay greater emphasis on 'Pollution' while teaching environmental concerns to Class V students. Which one of the following activities is likely to be most effective in achieving the desired objective?
A. Asking students to prepare charts on different kinds of pollution
B. Taking students on a field visit to a polluted river
C. Asking students to take up group projects related to different kinds of pollution
D. Inviting experts to talk on air, water and noise pollution

72. Neha uses the following assessment techniques in the subject of EVS for Class V :
I. Hands-on activities assessment
II. Home assignment assessment
III. Project work assessment
IV. Oral testing
Which one of the following pairs of techniques is likely to be more objective assessment?
A. II and III B. I and IV
C. II and IV D. I and II

73. A good home assignment in EVS should primarily focus on
A. revision and reinforcement
B. mastery learning
C. challenge and excitement for extended learning
D. better utilization of time

74. Shalini has planned a field trip for Class IV students to the Science Centre. Which one of the following general instructions given to the students is irrelevant for the trip?
A. Ask questions for your doubts on displays
B. Carry your full schoolbag for the day
C. Do not go anywhere without informing me
D. Take a notepad and pen with you

75. Good EVS curriculum at primary stage should
A. include more practice questions in end exercises
B. provide opportunities to explore surroundings
C. focus more on detailed explanation of concepts
D. emphasize more on exact definition of terms

76. Poems and stories have been included in EVS textbooks for primacy stage in order to
A. develop literary skills in students
B. provide fun and enjoyment in learning of the subject
C. enhance understanding of fundamental concepts
D. have a change in routine and monotony of presentation of content

77. Four perspective teachers were asked to make a presentation on the theme 'Travel' to Class V students. Each of them mainly focussed on one of the following strategies
A. Using charts to show different modes of travel along with explanation
B. Using textbook content to explain different modes of travel
C. Asking students to collect pictures of different modes of travel and prepare a scrapbook
D. Asking students to narrate their own travel experiences using various modes of travel

78. 'Think and Discuss' section in one chapter of EVS textbook in Class V includes the following statement: "What would happen if you don't get petrol or diesel for a week in your village or town?"
The statement primarily aims at
A. sensitizing students on using oil judiciously
B. assessing students on sources of petrol and diesel
C. promoting imaginative and thinking skills to understand real life concerns
D. creating awareness about scarcity of petrol and diesel

79. The technique of 'Classroom questioning' in teaching of EVS can be used best for
A. drawing attention of students
B. arousing curiosity in the learners
C. promoting practical skills
D. maintaining discipline in the class

80. One of the major objectives of teaching of EVS at primary stage is to
A. develop in depth understanding of basic concepts of the subject
B. prepare students for studies at the next stage
C. help the learners link classroom learning to life outside the school
D. acquire skills to carry out hands-on activities independently

81. Which one of the following is ***not*** a suitable activity at primary stage to sensitize students to the concept of conservation of trees?
A. Orgánizing a slogan-writing competition on trees
B. Encouraging every student to adopt a tree and look after it
C. Showing children storage of logs of wood
D. Organizing a poster-making competition on trees

82. While teaching the topic on 'Water' in her EVS classroom, Anjali organizes role-play on different sources of water and individual actions to conserve water. The activity is primarily aimed at
A. improving social skills of students
B. breaking monotony in the process of learning
C. ensuring active participation of students in the process of learning
D. enhancing students' knowledge on sources of water

83. EVS curriculum at primary stage has been developed to include pure Science as well as Social Science concepts. This has been done primarily to
A. enable a learner look at environment in a holistic manner
B. reduce the number of subjects to be studied
C. reduce the load of schoolbag
D. reduce the requirement of subject teachers

84. Which one of the following will be more effective learning experience to emphasize more on social inequalities in an EVS class?
A. Showing video films on related issue
B. Organizing special lectures on related issue
C. Conducting a quiz contest on the issue
D. Asking the students to undertake group projects

85. While discussing liking and disliking a student says, "I and my mother both love to eat snakes. Whenever we feel like eating snakes, we go to a nearby hotel and eat Ling-hu-fen." This student must belong to
A. Assam
B. Hong Kong
C. Odisha
D. Arunachal Pradesh

86. Study the following statements about Braille script :
I. Braille is written on a thick paper by making dots (raised points).
II. This script is based on eight points.
III. Rows of dots are made with a pointed tool.
IV. It is read by running the fingers on the raised dots.
The correct statements are
A. I, Ill and IV B. I, II and IV
C. II, III and IV D. I, II and III

87. Select the correct statements from the following:
1. Animals that have outside ears and hair on their body give birth to the young ones.
2. Animals that do not have outside ears and hair on their body lay eggs.
3. Animals that do not have outside ears and hair on their body give birth to the young ones.
4. Animals that have outside ears and hair on their body lay eggs.
A. 1 and 3 only B. 2 and 4 only
C. 2 and 3 only D. 1 and 2 only

88. Select the correct statements about beekeeping:
I. January to March is the best time to start beekeeping.
II. Honeybees are attracted to the Lichi flowers.
III. Boxes are needed for keeping bees and storing honey produced by them.
IV. Sugar is purchased to make syrup for honeybees.
A. II and III only
B. I and IV only
C. II, III and IV
D. I and II only

89. A student noted down the following information in her diary about her journey from Ahmedabad to Nagarcoil:

Date	Station	Arrival Time	Departure Time	Distance from Gandhidham (in kilometres)
10.2.2014	Ahmedabad	11:30 a.m.	11:50 a.m.	301
12.2.2014	Nagarcoil	04:45 a.m.	00:00	2649

From the above information, the following conclusions were drawn :
1. The distance between Ahmedabad and Nagarcoil is 2348 km.
2. The train covers this distance in 40 hours 55 minutes.
3. The train covers this distance in 28 hours 55 minutes.
4. The average speed of the train is about 80 km per hour.
The correct conclusions are
A. 1, 3 and 4 B. 1, 2 and 4
C. 1 and 2 only D. 1 and 3 only

90. Which of the following information may be obtained from a reserved rail ticket?
1. Date and time of booking, date and time of start of journey
2. Coach number, berth number and fare
3. Name, age and sex of the passengers
4. Train number with name, boarding station and last station
5. Date and time of arrival at the destination
A. 1, 2 and 4 only
B. 1, 2, 3 and 4
C. 1, 2, 4 and 5
D. 1, 3 and 5 only

PART- IV

Language-I : English

Directions (Qs. No. 91 to 99): *Read the given passage and answer the questions that follow by selecting the **most appropriate option:***

He has reservations on the treatment of dance in Indian films, but, given a chance to work on his own terms, legendary Kathak Dancer Pandit Birju Maharaj would like to work more in Bollywood. The 75-year-old tells us, "In my opinion, dance is adulterated in Bollywood. To make it more dramatic, the dancers are asked to perform in an exaggerated manner. That makes any kind of dance impure, especially classical dance. I'd like to work more in Hindi films, provided my dance is not tampered with."

The Kathak maestro tells us that over the years he's been highly impressed with how some female actors have showcased classical dance on screen. On being asked on how he sees the passion for dance among youngsters in the country, Birju Maharaj says, "I see that the young generation is divided in their response to classical dance. But in all my interactions with the younger lot, I have been impressed. These children have such amazing presence of mind, listening and learning while I talk and teach them." It is often said that classical dance doesn't receive due credit, but the man who is an authority on the subject thinks Delhi receives the art well. "I feel that classical dance might not be on a rise, in popularity, but I have always been overwhelmed by the response that I have received in Delhi. My performances have always been applauded by packed houses in the Capital," he opines.

91. The information presented here about Birju Maharaj can be found in a/an
A. newspaper article
B. diary
C. encyclopedia
D. autobiography

92. The observation that 'dance is adulterated' means that the dance form is
A. not practiced according to tradition
B. found in adult entertainment
C. performed only in films
D. suitable to be performed by adults

93. Here, "to perform in an exaggerated manner" suggests that performers
A. are not professionally trained
B. deliberately distort the dance form
C. only dance for a selected audience
D. cannot dance

94. A 'packed house' during his performance suggests that it was
A. jammed in tightly
B. filled into
C. exceeding allotted time
D. well-attended

95. The younger dancers have 'presence of mind' means that they
A. are open to learning the pure form of the dance
B. prefer traditional styles of dancing
C. can combine to perform in the traditional and modern styles
D. are calm while they prepare to perform

96. Birju Maharaj's assessment of his popularity lies in
A. the large numbers of practitioners and admirers of his style in Delhi
B. the influence of traditional styles in modern dance
C. his migrating to Mumbai on popular demand by producers
D. the number of dances he has choreographed in films

97. A word that can replace the phrase 'tampered with' in the passage is
A. falsified
B. misrepresented
C. disturbed
D. misused

98. An antonym for the word 'showcased' is
A. advertised
B. published
C. abridged
D. withheld

99. A synonym for the word 'inspired' from the text is
A. adulterated
B. impressed
C. received
D. divided

Directions (Q. No. 100 to 114) : *Answer the following questions by selecting the **most appropriate option.***

100. To evaluate reading comprehension at Class III level, students may be asked to
A. retell a story in their own words or to summarize the main idea or the moral of the story
B. take a short dictation of what they have read
C. write a diary based on one of the characters
D. use a set of identified vocabulary on their own

101. An exercise, where words are left out of a shorter passage, and the pupil must fill in the blanks with suitable words based on her reading, assesses her ability to
A. comprehend
B. use new words
C. summarize
D. spell words

102. Creating or retrieving what the student wants to say and then generating a suitable text to say it, are stages of the .... process.
A. listening
B. writing
C. speaking
D. creative

103. Use of grammar, punctuation and spelling pertains to
A. text production while writing
B. formal speech
C. listening to a lecture
D. informal conversation

104. Read the following exchange:
Speaker 1 : Have you been to Indore?
Speaker 2 : Who?
Speaker 1 : To Indore, in Madhya Pradesh.
Speaker 2 : Umm....I am not sure, ...
During the assessment of student's speaking skills marks(s) would be deducted during this exchange for
A. none of them
B. the second speaker
C. both of them
D. the first speaker

105. "A student recommends the reading of the latest best seller, saying that it is very interesting. You listen, trying to make out whether the student's observation is sincere or not." This type of listening can be described as
A. critical
B. comprehension
C. sympathetic
D. active

106. "Children deserve most of the credit for the language that they acquire." This observation implies that in modern classrooms
A. students pursue their own lines of enquiry
B. students need not attend L2 classes
C. students may choose L2 on their own
D. the teacher establishes the task and supports or facilitates learning

107. Types of 'text media' are
A. audio discs and tapes
B. illustrations and diagrams
C. motion pictures and documentaries
D. digital e-books, e-journals

108. Which of the following resources will help to break down communication barriers and enable children to study and learn in both Ll and L2?
A. Multilingual
B. Multimedia
C. More textual
D. Communicative

109. Students learning a language often lack confidence when speaking due to the language's unique pronunciation rules. One way to overcome this problem is
A. children reading aloud in class
B. using game-like activities which require verbal interactions in the classroom
C. conducting special speech therapy with a counsellor
D. correcting errors whenever they happen

110. The contemporary target language classroom is a confluence of varied languages and language abilities. Teachers should restructure their practices by exposing students to
A. summaries and simplified versions of the learning materials, e.g., stories, grammar notes, etc.
B. worksheets with a variety of tasks which cover the syllabus, and students give their responses in class under teacher's guidance
C. appropriate challenges based on the syllabus; in a secure environment, opportunities for all students to explore ideas and gain mastery
D. adequate self-explanatory notes, either prepared by teacher or from material writers

111. For students to gain language skills from textbooks, the textbook learning should
A. correlate with assessment and achievement
B. lead to using the textbook sparingly
C. expose them to more literary reading
D. become more cost-effective compared to technologically supported courses

112. While teaching hearing impaired students in an inclusive class, it is necessary for teachers to
A. make sure that they are including signs and nonverbal signals to strengthen any communication
B. conduct regular a special class for such students
C. be in constant touch with the parents of such students
D. use cue cards to signal the teaching content

113. While translating a subject and using the translation in the mainstream curriculum, the benefit is
A. promoting national identity
B. enriching linguistic capability and appreciation
C. enabling teachers who are not competent in the mainstream language to take classes
D. standardizing cultural identity

114. Some criteria for the selection of language items should involve
A. enough worksheets for practice
B. everyday vocabulary and sentences
C. their learnability, coverage and teachability
D. a focus on language rules

Directions (Q. Nos. 115 to 120) : *Read the given poem and answer the questions that follow by selecting the* ***most appropriate*** *option.*

Sprinkle, squish between my toes,
The smell of ocean to my nose.
I can feel each grain of sand,
It falls from air into my hand.
The shells I find along the shore,
Picked up by birds that fly and soar.
They sparkle like the ocean's waves,
And carry sand from all the lakes.
I walk,
That's where my feet leave prints to be.
I walk all the way to the end of the land,
The land that holds this beautiful sand.

—Morgan Swain

115. The poem's central theme is
A. a factual description of nature
B. sharing experiences with nature
C. a recollection of a visit
D. an introspection by the writer

116. Here, "to the end of the land" refers to the
A. sealine
B. land
C. sky
D. horizon

117. Here, "That's where my feet leave prints to be" means that the writer
A. knows that everything is temporary
B. relives past visits
C. expects to forget the experience
D. hopes to remember his visit

118. The phrase in the poem that conveys the same meaning as "along the tip of the sea" is
A. "each grain of sand"
B. "end of the land"
C. "air into my hand"
D. "like the ocean's waves"

119. The poetic device used in the line "They sparkle like the ocean's waves" is a/an
A. hyperbole
B. exaggeration
C. simile
D. allegory

120. A word that can replace 'squish' is
A. crush
B. hold
C. scrunch
D. trample

PART- V

भाषा-II : हिन्दी

निर्देश (प्र.सं. 121 से 128): *नीचे दिए गए गद्यांश को पढ़कर* ***सबसे उचित*** *विकल्प का चयन कीजिए–*

जीवन में बहुत अंधकार है और अंधकार की ही भाँति अशुभ और अनीति है। कुछ लोग इस अंधकार को स्वीकार कर लेते हैं और तब उनके भीतर जो प्रकाश तक पहुँचने और पाने की आकांक्षा थी, वह क्रमशः क्षीण होती जाती है। मैं अंधकार की इस स्वीकृति को मनुष्य का सबसे बड़ा पाप कहता हूँ। यह मनुष्य का स्वयं अपने प्रति किया गया अपराध है। उसके दूसरों के प्रति किए गए अपराधों का जन्म इस मूल पाप से ही होता है। यह स्मरण रहे कि जो व्यक्ति अपने ही प्रति इस पाप को नहीं करता है, वह किसी के भी प्रति कोई पाप नहीं कर सकता है। किन्तु कुछ लोग अंधकार के स्वीकार से बचने के लिए उसके अस्वीकार में लग जाते हैं। उनका जीवन अंधकार के निषेध का ही सतत उपक्रम बन जाता है।

121. गद्यांश में 'अंधकार' शब्द किस ओर संकेत करता है?
A. पाप की ओर
B. बुराइयों और कठिनाइयों की ओर
C. अपराधों की ओर
D. गरीबी की ओर

122. लेखक ने किसे सबसे बड़ा पाप कहा है?
A. प्रकाश पाने की क्षीण आकांक्षा
B. मनुष्य का अपने प्रति पाप न करना
C. अंधकार को स्वीकार न करना
D. अंधकार को स्वीकार कर लेना

123. जब व्यक्ति स्वयं के प्रति किए गए अन्याय, शोषण के विरुद्ध आवाज नहीं उठाता तो
A. इससे दूसरों के प्रति अन्याय, शोषण को बढ़ावा मिलता है
B. वह केवल अपने प्रति अन्याय करता है
C. इससे शांति का माहौल बना रहता है
D. वह दंड का अधिकारी बन जाता है

124. 'अंधकार का निषेध' किस ओर संकेत करता है?
A. अन्याय, शोषण, बुराइयों को सदा के लिए समाप्त करना
B. समाज में फैले अंधकार को प्रकाश में बदल देना
C. समाज को अंधकार से मुक्त कराने के लिए प्रयत्नशील रहना
D. यह मानना कि समाज में अन्याय, शोषण, बुराइयाँ नहीं हैं

125. इस गद्यांश का मुख्य उद्देश्य है
A. अंधकार और प्रकाश की व्याख्या करना
B. अन्याय और बुराइयों को दूर करने के लिए प्रेरित करना
C. तरह-तरह के लोगों की विशेषताएँ बनाना
D. पाप और पुण्य की व्याख्या करना

126. इस गद्यांश में 'उपक्रम' का अर्थ है
A. आरंभ, शुरुआत
B. तैयारी, योजना
C. आयोजन, समारोह
D. व्यवसाय, कार्य

127. जीवन में बहुत अंधकार है। रेखांकित अंश में कौन-सा कारक है?
A. अपादान कारक
B. अधिकरण कारक
C. करण कारक
D. सम्प्रदान कारक

128. "....और अंधकार की ही भाँति अशुभ और अनीति है।" वाक्य में निपात है
A. ही
B. की
C. है
D. और

निर्देश (प्र.सं. 129 से 143): *सबसे सही विकल्प का चयन कीजिए।*

129. प्राथमिक स्तर की शिक्षा में सम्प्रेषण का माध्यम .....ही होनी चाहिए, क्योंकि इसी भाषा में ही बच्चे का मस्तिष्क सबसे पहले क्रियाशील होता है।
A. अंग्रेजी
B. मातृभाषा
C. प्रदेश की भाषा
D. हिन्दी

130. भाषा की पाठ्य-पुस्तकों में दिए गए अभ्यास
A. बच्चों को चीजों को परखने, गहराई से जुड़ने और व्यापक अनुभव-स्तर से तादात्म्य का अवसर देते हैं
B. बच्चों की भाषायी और सांस्कृतिक विविधता को सीमित करते हैं
C. बच्चों को विस्तृत अभ्यास करने और शिक्षकों को बच्चों की भाषा में सुधार करने के तरीके बताते हैं
D. बच्चों का सही-सही आकलन करने में सदैव मदद करते हैं कि वे क्या नहीं जानते

131. हिन्दी भाषा में सतत आकलन का सर्वाधिक उचित तरीका है
A. हर पन्द्रह दिन में सरल परीक्षा लेना
B. बच्चों को अपने अनुभवों को कहने-लिखने के पर्याप्त अवसर देना
C. बच्चों से समूह में परियोजना-कार्य करवाना
D. बच्चों से अनौपचारिक बातचीत करना

132. भाषा-कक्षाओं में प्रदर्शित सामग्री केवल तब सजावटी हो जाती है जब
A. बच्चों को पढ़ना-लिखना सिखाने में उसका उपयोग नहीं होता
B. वह बच्चों को अनिवार्यतः कोई मूल्य न सिखाए
C. वह सामग्री पाठ्य-पुस्तक की न हो
D. बच्चे उसे आते-जाते देखते हैं

133. चॉम्स्की के अनुसार बच्चों के पास भाषा सीखने की क्षमता जन्मजात होती है। अतः हिन्दी भाषा की कक्षा में बच्चों को
A. विविध भाषा-प्रयोगों से परिचय प्राप्त करने के अवसर दिए जाने चाहिए
B. व्याकरण के नियम समझा दिए जाएँ ताकि वे अपनी इस क्षमता के माध्यम से जल्दी भाषा सीख सकें
C. सतत और व्यापक आकलन की प्रक्रिया से मुक्त रखें, उन पर अनावश्यक बोझ न डालें
D. कुछ भी न पढ़ाने की आवश्यकता नहीं है

134. निम्नलिखित में से कौन-सा नियम पढ़ना सीखने में मुश्किल पैदा नहीं करता?
A. यह सुनिश्चित करना कि ध्वनि के नियम सीखकर उन पर अमल किया जाए
B. बच्चों पर सावधानीपूर्वक पढ़ने के लिए जोर डालना
C. शब्द-प्रति-शब्द पढ़ते हुए गति को बढ़ाने का आग्रह करना
D. चित्र, संदर्भ और पूर्व अनुभवों के आधार पर अनुमान लगाते हुए पढ़ने के अवसर देना

135. प्राथमिक स्तर पर भाषा-शिक्षण का मुख्य उद्देश्य है
A. चार अक्षर वाले शब्द पढ़-लिख लेना
B. पाठ्य-पुस्तक के अंत में दिए गए सभी अभ्यासों को पूरा करना
C. दूसरों की बातों को धैर्य से सुनना और सुनी गई बात पर अपनी टिप्पणी देना
D. वर्णमाला को क्रम से याद करना

136. "तुम्हारे आस-पास ऐसे कौन-कौन से फूल हैं, जिनकी बहुत तेज महक है? फूलों के नाम अपनी भाषा में लिखो।" हिन्दी भाषा के इन अभ्यासों का क्या उद्देश्य है?
A. पाठ को अपने अनुभव-संसार से जोड़ने के अवसर देना और बहुभाषिकता को पोषित करना
B. बच्चों की भाषा को कक्षा में स्थान देते हुए यह जानना कि क्या वे अपनी भाषा में लिख सकते हैं

C. बच्चों को फूलों और उनकी महक के बारे में विस्तृत जानकारी देना
D. बच्चों से यह जानना कि कितने फूलों के नाम जानते हैं

137. संगीता अक्सर शब्दों को उलटा लिखती है और लिखते समय कुछ अक्षरों को छोड़ देती है। उसे लिखने में कठिनाई होती है। उसकी समस्या .... से सम्बन्धित है।
A. डिस्ग्राफिया
B. डिस्केलकुलिया
C. दृष्टिबाधिता
D. डिस्लेक्सिया

138. प्राथमिक स्तर पर बच्चों के शुरुआती भाषा-विकास में सर्वाधिक योगदान दे सकते/सकती है/हैं
A. टी.वी. पर देखे जाने वाले पंद्रह मिनट के कार्टून कार्यक्रम
B. गृहकार्य पर व्यय किए जाने वाले तीस मिनट
C. एफ.एम. पर पन्द्रह मिनट सुने जाने वाले समाचार
D. परिवार में होने वाली परस्पर गुणवत्तापूर्ण बातचीत

139. यदि सुलेखा 'रेलगाड़ी' को 'रेलगाडि' लिखती है तो एक भाषा-शिक्षक के रूप में आप क्या करेंगे?
A. सुलेखा से 'रेलगाड़ी' शब्द तीस बार लिखवाएँगे ताकि दुबारा गलती न हो
B. उसकी कॉपी पर 'रेलगाड़ी' शब्द लिखेंगे और सुलेखा से पूछेंगे कि लिखे हुए दोनों शब्दों में क्या अन्तर है। उसे अपना शब्द स्वयं ठीक करने के लिए कहेंगे
C. 'रेलगाडि' शब्द पर घेरा लगाकर सही शब्द लिखकर सुलेखा की कॉपी वापस कर देंगे
D. 'रेलगाडि' शब्द पर घेरा लगाएँगे और सुलेखा को डाँटेंगे ताकि वह आगे से शब्दों को सही-सही लिखे

140. एक समावेशी कक्षा में कविता पढ़ाने के लिए आप क्या करेंगे?
A. कविता को चार्ट पेपर पर लिखकर बच्चों की पहुँच से दूर दीवार पर लगा देंगे और उसकी ओर संकेत करके कविता जोर-जोर से पढ़ेंगे
B. कविता को टेपरिकॉर्डर से सुनाएँगे ताकि सभी बच्चों पर ध्यान दिया जा सके
C. कविता को पढ़ाने के लिए एक से अधिक विधियों का प्रयोग करेंगे ताकि बच्चों को विभिन्न इंद्रियों से अनुभव करने का अवसर मिल सके
D. एक ही कविता को पाँच बार सुनाएँगे, पाठ करवाएँगे ताकि सभी बच्चों की समझ में आ जाए

141. विद्यालय आने से पूर्व बच्चों के पास
A. पाँच हजार वाक्य होते हैं
B. अपनी भाषा की जटिल और समृद्ध संरचनाएँ होती हैं
C. अपनी भाषा का सम्पूर्ण बाल साहित्य होता है
D. पाँच हजार शब्द होते हैं

142. हिन्दी भाषा-शिक्षक को यह स्वीकार करना चाहिए कि
A. गलतियाँ सीखने-सिखाने की प्रक्रिया का अभिन्न हिस्सा है
B. गलतियों पर बिल्कुल ध्यान न देने से वे सुधर जाती हैं
C. बच्चों को उनकी गलतियाँ समझाना उनके भाषा-विकास में महान बाधा है
D. बच्चों को भाषा सिखाना जरूरी नहीं है

143. जब बच्चे कहानियाँ पढ़ते हैं, तो
A. वे बिना किसी उद्देश्य के पढ़ते हैं
B. वे घटनाओं, पात्रों में उलझ जाते हैं
C. वे अन्य लोगों के अनुभवों में प्रवेश करते हैं
D. उनका नैतिक विकास अनिवार्यतः होता है

निर्देश (प्र.सं. 144 से 150): *नीचे दिए गए गद्यांश को पढ़कर **सबसे उचित विकल्प** का चयन कीजिए–*

शिक्षा केवल तभी बच्चों के आत्मिक जीवन का एक अंश बनती है, जबकि ज्ञान सक्रिय कार्यों के साथ अभिन्न रूप से जुड़ा हो। बच्चों से यह आशा नहीं की जा सकती कि पहाड़े या समकोण चतुर्भुज का क्षेत्रफल निकालने के नियम आप से आप उन्हें आकर्षित करेंगे। जब बच्चा यह देखता है कि ज्ञान सृजन के या श्रम के लक्ष्यों की प्राप्ति का साधन है, तभी वह ज्ञान पाने की इच्छा उनके मन में जागती है। मैं यह चेष्टा करता था कि छोटी उम्र में ही शारीरिक श्रम में बच्चों को अपनी होशियारी और कुशाग्र बुद्धि का परिचय देने का अवसर मिले। स्कूल का एक सर्वाधिक महत्त्वपूर्ण कार्यभार है–बच्चों को ज्ञान का प्रयोग करना सिखाना। छोटी कक्षाओं में यह खतरा सबसे ज्यादा होता है कि ज्ञान निरर्थक बोझ बनकर रह जाएगा, क्योंकि इस उम्र में बौद्धिक श्रम नई-नई बातें सीखने से ही संबंधित होता है।

144. लेखक के अनुसार शिक्षा का अर्थ है
A. ज्ञान का प्रयोग करना
B. श्रम करना
C. विषय पर अधिकार प्राप्त करना
D. ज्ञान प्राप्त करना

145. ज्ञान-प्राप्ति की इच्छा कब जगती है?
A. जब हम यह देखें कि ज्ञान हमारे भौतिक जीवन के लक्ष्यों की प्राप्ति का साधन है
B. जब हम यह देखें कि ज्ञानवान मनुष्य ही श्रम का अधिकारी है
C. जब हम यह देखें कि ज्ञान के द्वारा हम समस्त सुखों का लाभ उठा सकते हैं
D. जब हम यह देखें कि ज्ञान के द्वारा सृजनात्मक कार्य किए जा सकते हैं

146. लेखक के अनुसार–
A. शारीरिक श्रम में तेज बुद्धि की आवश्यकता नहीं होती
B. शारीरिक श्रम में समझदारी और तेज बुद्धि की भी आवश्यकता होती है
C. शारीरिक श्रम बच्चों को होशियार बनाता है
D. शारीरिक श्रम ही एकमात्र महत्त्वपूर्ण तत्व है

147. गद्यांश के अनुसार ज्ञान कब निरर्थक बोझ बन जाता है?
A. जब उसे कक्षाओं तक सीमित कर दिया जाए
B. जब उसे शारीरिक श्रम से न जोड़ा जाए
C. जब उसका सक्रिय प्रयोग न किया जाए
D. जब उस पर पूर्णतः अधिकार न किया जाए

148. 'इच्छा' शब्द में 'इक' प्रत्यय जोड़ने से बनने वाला नया शब्द है
A. ऐच्छिक
B. इच्छिक
C. ईच्छिक
D. एच्छिक

149. 'कार्य' का बहुवचन रूप है
A. कार्यें
B. कार्य
C. कार्यक्रमों
D. कार्यों

150. 'बौद्धिक' शब्द में मूल शब्द है
A. बुद्ध
B. बौद्ध
C. बौद्धि
D. बुद्धि

Answers

1	2	3	4	5	6	7	8	9	10
B	B	A	B	B	D	C	A	D	B
11	12	13	14	15	16	17	18	19	20
D	D	A	C	C	C	A	A	A	A
21	22	23	24	25	26	27	28	29	30
A	C	A	B	A	B	B	C	D	A
31	32	33	34	35	36	37	38	39	40
B	B	B	C	D	A	A	B	B	B
41	42	43	44	45	46	47	48	49	50
D	C	A	B	D	B	D	C	C	C
51	52	53	54	55	56	57	58	59	60
B	A	A	D	B	A	A	D	A	C
61	62	63	64	65	66	67	68	69	70
C	D	C	C	B	D	C	C	B	B
71	72	73	74	75	76	77	78	79	80
C	B	C	B	B	B	D	C	B	C
81	82	83	84	85	86	87	88	89	90
C	C	A	D	B	A	D	C	C	A
91	92	93	94	95	96	97	98	99	100
A	A	B	D	A	A	B	D	B	A
101	102	103	104	105	106	107	108	109	110
A	B	A	B	A	A	D	A	B	C
111	112	113	114	115	116	117	118	119	120
A	A	B	C	B	A	D	B	C	D
121	122	123	124	125	126	127	128	129	130
B	D	A	D	B	D	B	A	B	A
131	132	133	134	135	136	137	138	139	140
B	A	A	D	C	A	A	D	B	C
141	142	143	144	145	146	147	148	149	150
B	A	C	A	D	B	C	A	B	D

Some Selected Explanatory Answers

31. Perimeter of square = 20 cm

$\therefore$ Side of square = $\frac{20}{4} = 5\text{cm}$

Breadth of rectangle = 5 cm

Length of rectangle = 5 × 2 = 10 cm

Area of rectangle = $l \times b$ = 10 × 5

= 50 cm^2.

32. Volume of box A = 20 × 18 × 15 cm^3

= 5400 cm^3

Volume of box B = 18 × 12 × 5 cm^3

= 1080 cm^3

Clearly, 1080 × 5 = 5400

$\therefore$ Volume of box A is 5 times the volume of box B.

33. A. Area of square = 10 × 10 = 100 cm^2

Area of rectangle = $10 \times \frac{1}{10} \times 100 = 100\text{cm}^2$

B. 1 m 5 cm = 105 cm

1.5 m = 150 cm

C. $0.40 = \frac{40}{100} = \frac{4}{10}$

$0.4 = \frac{4}{10}$

D. ₹ $\frac{3}{4} = \frac{300}{4}$ paise = 75 paise

₹ $0.75 = \frac{75}{100} \times 100 = 75$ paise

Clearly, 1 m 5 cm ≠ 1.5 m.

34. Cost of 1 orange = ₹ $5\frac{1}{2}$ = ₹ $\frac{11}{2}$

$\therefore$ Cost of 18 oranges = ₹ $\frac{11}{2} \times 18$

= ₹ 99

Again cost of 1 kg of apple

= ₹ 80

Cost of $\frac{7}{4}$ kg of apples = ₹ $80 \times \frac{7}{4}$

= ₹ 140

Total cost = 140 + 99 = 239.

50. Given number = 70560

The place value of 5 = 500

The place value of 6 = 60

The product of 500 × 60 = 30,000.

51. 43) 3010301 (70007

301

301

301

×

$\therefore$ Quotient = 70007.

52. The product of 3001 × 101 = 303101

303101

−300311

2790

$\therefore$ Required number = 2790

53. LCM of 36 and 60 = 180

HCF of 18 and 45 = 9

According to the question

$\frac{180}{9} = 20.$

54. 10 tens + 11 hundreds + 12 ones

= 10 × 10 + 11 × 100 + 12 × 1

= 100 + 1100 + 12

= 1212.

55. 1 × 42 = 2 × 3 × 7

2 × 21

3 × 14

6 × 7

$\therefore$ factors of 42 are 1, 2, 3, 6, 7, 14, 21 & 42

Hence, number of factors of 42 is 8.

56. 12) 3488 (290

24

108

108

8

11) 2478 (225

22

27

22

58

55

3

Difference between the remainders in both cases = (8 – 3) = 5.

57. 8 : 18 a.m. P ——— Q 10 : 28 p.m.

Time taken by the train to reach Q

= 12 hrs + 2 hrs 10 minutes

= 14 hrs 10 minutes.

58.

14 L	280 mL
18 L	830 mL
33 L	110 mL

$$15\times\frac{3}{2}L = \frac{45}{2}L = 22.5 \text{ L}$$

33 L + 110 mL − 22.5 L = 10.5 L + 110 mL

∴ Mixture left = 10 L 610 mL

59. $\text{Rest} = 1-\frac{1}{4} = \frac{3}{4}$

$$\frac{3}{4}\div\frac{12}{1} = \frac{3}{4}\times\frac{1}{12}=\frac{1}{16}$$

∴ $\text{Required part} = \frac{1}{16}$.

60. The number of seconds in 6 hrs

= 6 × 60 × 60

= 21600

$$\text{Required days} = \frac{21600}{60\times24}$$

= 15 days.

Previous Paper (Solved)

CTET PAPER-I, JULY 2013*

PART- I

Child Development and Pedagogy

Directions: *Answer the following questions by selecting the* ***most appropriate*** *option.*

1. The following three aspects of intelligence are dealt by Sternberg's triarchic theory except
A. componential B. social
C. experiential D. contextual

2. Howard Gardner's theory of multiple intelligences emphasizes
A. general intelligence
B. common abilities required in school
C. the unique abilities of each individual
D. conditioning skills in students

3. The sounds *th*, *ph*, *ch* are:
A. Morphemes B. Graphemes
C. Lexemes D. Phonemes

4. In order to avoid gender stereotyping in class, a teacher should
A. try to put both boys and girls in non-traditional roles
B. appreciate student's good work by saying 'good girl' or 'good boy'
C. discourage girls from taking part in wrestling
D. encourage boys to take risk and be bold

5. Schools should cater to Individual differences to
A. narrow the gap between individual students
B. even out abilities and performance of students
C. understand why students are able or unable to learn
D. make individual students feel exclusive

6. What kind of support can a school provide to address the individual differences in students?
A. Follow a child-centred curriculum and provide multiple learning opportunities to students
B. Apply every possible measure to remove the individual differences in students
C. Refer slow learners to special schools
D. Follow same level of curriculum for all students

7. Continuous and Comprehensive Evaluation emphasizes
A. continuous testing on a comprehensive scale to ensure learning
B. how learning can be observed, recorded and improved upon
C. fine-tuning of tests with the teaching
D. redundancy of the Board examination

8. School Based Assessment
A. Dilutes the accountability of Boards of Education
B. Hinders achieving Universal National Standards
C. Helps all students learn more through diagnosis
D. Makes students and teachers non-serious and casual

9. "Readiness for learning" refers to
A. general ability level of students
B. present cognitive level of students in the learning continuum
C. satisfying nature of the act of learning
D. Thorndike's law of Readiness

10. A teacher has some physically challenged children in her class. Which of the following would be appropriate for her to say?
A. Wheel-chaired bound children may take help of their peers in going to hall.
B. Physically inconvenienced children may do an alternative activity in the classroom.
C. Mohan why don't you use your crutches to go to the playground.
D. Polio afflicted children will not present a song.

11. Learning disabilities may occur due to all of the following except
A. Cerebral dysfunction B. Emotional disturbance
C. Behavioural disturbance D. Cultural factors

12. An inclusive school
A. Is committed to improve the learning outcomes of all students irrespective of their capabilities
B. Differentiate between students and sets less challenging achievement targets for specially abled children
C. Committed particularly to improve the learning outcomes of specially abled students
D. Decides learning needs of students according to their disability

13. Gifted students
A. Need support not ordinarily provided be the school
B. Can manage their studies without a teacher
C. Can be good models for other students
D. Cannot be learning disabled

*Exam was held on 28-07-2013.

14. Giftedness is due to
A. Genetic makeup
B. Environmental motivation
C. Combination of (A) and (B)
D. Psychosocial factors

15. Which of the following is appropriate for environment conducive to thinking and learning in children?
A. Passive listening for long periods of time
B. Home assignments given frequently
C. Individual tasks done by the learners
D. Allowing students to take some decisions about what to learn and how to learn

16. Learning Disability in motor skills is called
A. Dyspraxia B. Dyscalculia
C. Dyslexia D. Dysphasia

17. Learning Disability
A. is a stable state
B. is a variable state
C. need not impair functioning
D. does not improve with appropriate input

18. The following are the steps in the process of problem solving except
A. Identification of a problem
B. Breaking down the problem into smaller parts
C. Explore possible strategies
D. Anticipate outcomes

19. A teacher should
A. treat errors committed by students as blunders and take serious note of each error
B. measure success as the number of times students avoid making mistakes
C. not correct students while they're trying to communicate ideas
D. focus more on lecturing and provide a foundation for knowledge

20. Seema is desperate to score A$^+$ grade in an examination. As she enters the examination hall and the examination begins, she becomes extremely nervous. Her feet go cold, her heart starts pounding and she is unable to answer properly. The primary reason for this is that
A. she may not be very confident about her preparation
B. she may be thinking excessively about the result of this examination
C. invigilator teacher on duty may be her class teacher and she is of very strict nature
D. she may not be able to deal with sudden emotional outburst

21. Which of the following congnitive verbs are used to analyse the information given?
A. Identify B. Differentiate
C. Classify D. Describe

22. Rajesh is a voracious reader. Apart from studying his course books, he often goes to library and reads books on diverse topics. Rajesh does his project even in the lunch break. He does not need prompting by his teachers or parents to study for tests and seems to truly enjoy learning. He can be best described as a(n)
A. fact-centred learner
B. teacher motivated learner
C. assessment-centred learner
D. intrinsically motivated learner

23. Children in pre-primary get satisfaction from being allowed to discover. They become distressed, when they are discouraged. They do so due to their motivation to
A. reduce their ignorance
B. affiliate with the class
C. create disorder in the class
D. exercise their power

24. Understanding Human Growth and Development enables a teacher to
A. gain control of learners' emotions while teaching.
B. be clear about teaching diverse learners.
C. tell students how they can improve their lives.
D. practice her teaching in an unbiased way.

25. Which one of the following is true?
A. Development and learning are unaffected by socio-cultural contexts
B. Students learn only in a certain way
C. Play is significant for cognition and social competence
D. Questioning by teacher constrains cognitive development

26. Which one of the following is true about the role of heredity and environment in the development of a child?
A. The relative contributions of peers and genes are not additive
B. Heredity and environment do not operate together
C. Propensity is related to environment while actual development requires heredity
D. Both heredity and environment contribute 50% each in the development of a child

27. Socialization is
A. Rapport between teacher and taught
B. Process of modernization of society
C. Adaptation of social norms
D. Change in social norms

28. A PT teacher wants here her students to improve fielding in the game of cricket. Which one of the following strategies will best help his students achieve that goal?
A. Tell students how important it is for them to learn to field

B. Explain the logic behind good fielding and rate of success
C. Demonstate fielding while students observe
D. Given students a lot of practice in fielding

29. A teacher wishes to help her students to appreciate multiple views of a situation. She provides her students multiple opportunities to debate on this situation in different groups. According to Vygotsky's perspective, her students will ________ various views and develop multiple perspectives of the situation on their own.
A. internalize B. construct
C. operationalize D. rationalize

30. Sita has learned to eat rice and dal with her hand. When she is given dal and rice, she mixes rice and dal and starts eating. She has ______ eating rice and dal into her schema for doing things.
A. Accommodated B. Assimilated
C. Appropriated D. Initiated

PART- II

Mathematics

31. Perimeter of a square is 24 cm and length of a rectangle is 8 cm. If the perimeters of the square and the rectangle are equal, then the area (in square cm) of the rectangle is
A. 16 B. 24
C. 32 D. 64

32. The difference of the place value and the face value of the number 3 in 12345 is
A. 0 B. 295
C. 297 D. 305

33. Which one of the following is *not* correct?
A. 56.7 kilogram = 5670 grams
B. A cube has six faces
C. One millimetre = 0.1 cm
D. 0.10 is same as 0.1

34. The speed of a boat in a river is 20 km per hour and the speed of another boat is 23 km per hour. They travel in the same direction from the same place at the same time. The distance between the boats after three and half hours is
A. 10 km B. 10.5 km
C. 11 km D. 11.5 km

35. When 90707 is divided by 9, the remainder is
A. 3 B. 5
C. 6 D. 7

36. When a fresh fish is dried it becomes 1/3 of its weight. Sunita buys 1500 kg fresh fish for ₹ 25 per kg and sell them, when dried, for ₹ 80 per kg. How much does she earn?
A. ₹ 2,500 B. ₹ 2,700
C. ₹ 3,000 D. ₹ 3,500

37. Look at the following pattern:

$(9 - 1) \div 8 = 1$
$(98 - 2) \div 8 = 12$
$(987 - 3) \div 8 = 123$
$(9876 - 4) \div 8 = 1234$

According to this pattern
$(987654 - 6) \div 8 = ?$

A. 12345 B. 123456
C. 123465 D. 123467

38. 750 ml juice is filled in one bottle and six such bottles are packed in one carton. The number of cartons needed for 450 litres of juice is
A. 75 B. 80
C. 90 D. 100

39. Internal length, breadth and depth of a (rectangular) box are 4 cm, 3 cm and 2 cm respectively. How many such boxes are needed to pack 8664 centimetre cubes?
A. 351 B. 361
C. 391 D. 722

40. "Write the equivalent fraction $\frac{1}{3}$." The above question asked to students of Class IV refers to
A. lower-level demand task as it requires procedural skills only
B. lower-level demand task as it is based on memorization only
C. higher-level demand task as it is based on procedure with connection
D. higher-level demand task as it is based on procedure without connection

41. Students often make a mistake in comparing the decimal numbers. For example, 0.50 is larger than 0.5. The most probable reason for this error is
A. lack of practice of these types of questions in the class
B. lack of concrete experience of representation of decimal number on number line
C. careless attempt by the students
D. misconception regarding the significance of zero in ordering decimal

42. A teacher prompts the students to prepare Mathematical journal with the theme "Application of Mathematics in Daily life". This activity is
A. to test the students understanding of Mathematical concepts

B. to provide opportunity to students share their ideas and knowledge
C. to help students to sense of Mathematics
D. to help students to connect Mathematical concepts and its applications and to share their knowledge and ideas

43. According to Van Hiele level of geometric thought, the five levels are—visualization, analysis, informal deducation, formal deducation and rigour. Some polygons are given to a child of Class III for sorting.

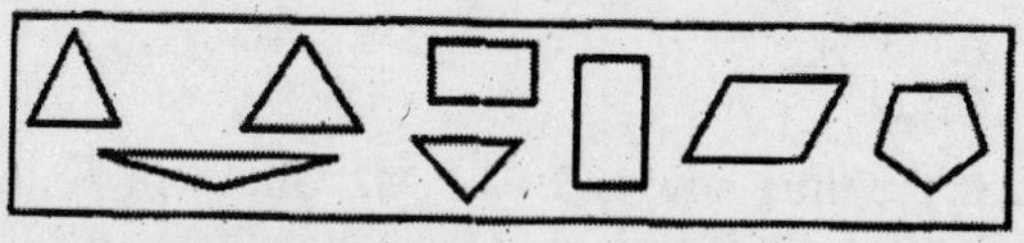

He classified the polygons on the basis of the number of sides. This child is at ______ level of Van-Hiele Geometrical thought
A. Visualization B. Analysis
C. Informal deducation D. Formal deduction

44. A child displays difficulty in differentiating between numbers, operations and symbols, two clock hands, different coins etc. This implies that the specific barrier affecting his learning is
A. poor verbal, visual, auditory and working memory
B. poor visual processing ability *i.e.* visual discrimination, spatial organization and visual coordination
C. poor language processing ability *i.e.,* expression, vocabulary and auditory processing
D. poor motor skills, reading and writing skills

45. NCF 2005 emphasises on Constructivist Approach of learning as it focuses on
A. memorization of definitions and formulae
B. submission of regular homework.
C. active participation of learner through engaging activities.
D. effective lecture and instructions by teacher

46. Following are array diagram using bindis to represent 15.

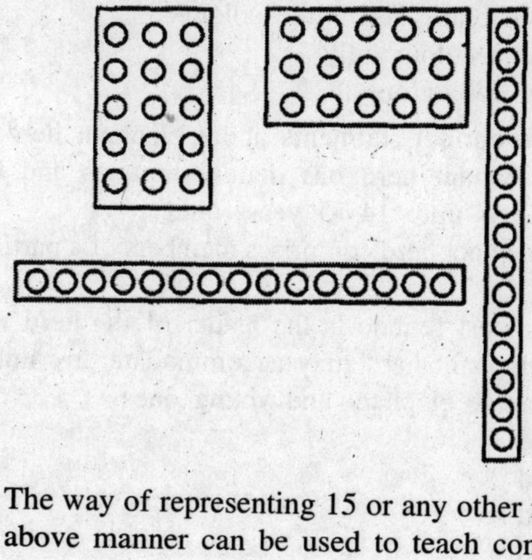

The way of representing 15 or any other number in the above manner can be used to teach concept of
A. area and commutative property
B. commutative property of multiplication, identification of prime and composite numbers, area of rectangle
C. representation of a number as product of two numbers, commutative property of multiplication, multiplicative identity, identification of prime and composite numbers, area of rectangle using units quantity
D. representation of a number as product of two numbers, commutative property of multiplication, multiplication identity, identification of prime and composite numbers

47. Which of the following questions is open-ended?
A. Write the numbers 25, 71, 19, 9, 8, 17, 85 in ascending order.
B. Which is more? $\frac{1}{3}$ or $\frac{7}{5}$
C. Write any four numbers greater than 2.7.
D. What is 7 more than $\frac{2}{7}$?

48. The most appropriate tool to expose the students of class II to plane figures, its vertices and edges is
A. Geo-board B. Nets of 3D solids
C. Cubes D. Black-board surface

49. Following is a problem from text-book of class V: "There are 4 poles of measure 105 cm, 215 cm, 150 cm and 235 cm respectively. If they have to be cut into pieces of equal length, what is the maximum length of each piece?"
This question is asked to
A. test knowledge of factors and multiples
B. check the skill of finding HCF
C. enhance problem solving skills using learnt concepts
D. give practice of word problems based on HCF and LCM

50. Following is a problem from text book of class III: "Which mathematical operation will be used to solve the following problem?
A milkman sold 1410 litres of milk in 10 days. How many litres of milk did he sell in a day?"
Which competence of Bloom's cognitive domain is referred in the above question?
A. Knowledge B. Comprehension
C. Analysis D. Synthesis

51. Rashid is studying in class V. He can classify various types of triangles in different categories but has difficulty in understanding the abstract proof for the sum of three angles in a triangle to be always 180°. According to Piaget Cognitive Theory Rashid is at
A. Concrete operational stage

B. Formal operational stage
C. Sensorimotor stage
D. Pre-operational stage

52. According to NCF 2005
"Developing children's abilities for mathematization is the main goal of mathematics education. The narrow aim of school mathematics is to develop 'useful' capabilities."
Here, mathematization refers to develop child's abilities.
A. In performing all number operations efficiently including of finding square root and cube root.
B. To formulate Theorems of Geometry and their proofs independently
C. To translate word problems into linear equations.
D. To develop the child's resources to think and reason mathematically, to pursue assumptions to their logical conclusion and to handle abstraction.

53. The highlights of a good textbook are that
1. They contain numerous exercises to give rigorous practice.
2. All concepts can be introduced through situations.
3. Only solved examples are included.
4. They must be thick and heavy.

A. 1 and 2 B. 3 and 4
C. 1 and 3 D. 2 and 4

54. NCF 2005 emphasises that
A. Succeeding in Mathematics should be mandatory for every child
B. Students should be tested first for their logico-mathematical ability
C. Maths curriculum shall be separate for low achievers
D. Maths shall be taught to selective students

55. The difference between the smallest common multiple and biggest common factor of 5, 10 and 35 is
A. 30 B. 35
C. 65 D. 75

56. The number of factors of 105 is
A. 3 B. 4
C. 6 D. 8

57. If the time now is 2.17 P.M., what will be the time 11 hours and 59 minutes from now?
A. 11.57 A.M. B. 9.59 A.M.
C. 2.16 A.M. D. 2.17 A.M.

58. Number of degrees in three and one-half right angles is
A. 285 B. 295
C. 305 D. 315

59. 11 ones + 11 tens + 11 hundreds equals
A. 144 B. 1221
C. 12321 D. 111111

60. The sum of five hundred nine and three thousand twenty-eight is
A. 3537 B. 3087
C. 837 D. 387

PART- III

Environmental Studies

61. The name of the scientist who first peeped into a mosquito stomach and proved that mosquitoes spread malaria and for his research was awarded Nobel Prize in medicine in December 1902 is
A. Charles Darwin B. Gregor Mendel
C. George Mistral D. Ronald Ross

62. Rajat said to his friend, "I cannot play because I am down with fever. I pass through a cycle of shivering, fever and headache and finally sweating. After my blood test doctor prescribed me a bitter medicine." Rajat might be suffering from
A. Typhoid B. Diarrhoea
C. Cholera D. Malaria

63. Who was Al-Biruni?
A. A Qutabshahi Sultan who ruled our country for about 40 years
B. A trader from Afghanistan who came to study the dryfruit markets of our country
C. A traveller from Uzbekistan who wrote a book which is helpful to know the past of our country
D. A traveller who travelled from Kashmir to Kanyakumari to study the culture of Indian people

64. The animals that are awake at night can see objects
A. in all colours
B. only in black and white colours
C. in green colour only
D. in red colour only

65. Select the correct statments about elephant herd:
1. An elephant herd has mainly females and baby elephants upto 14-15 years old.
2. An elephant herd comprises members of a particular family.
3. The oldest female is the leader of the herd.
4. An elephant herd may accommodate any number of female elephant and young ones.

A. 1 and 2
B. 1 and 3
C. 2 and 4
D. 3 and 4

66. Inside the petals, in the middle of a flower we find a thin powdery structure, called
A. Anther
B. Pollen
C. Radicle
D. Stigma

67. If you go to Ahmedabad (Gujarat) by train, then at Ahmedabad railway station, you will find that most of the vendors are selling
A. Dhokla-chutney and lemon rice
B. Chholay-bhature and lassi
C. Idli-chutney and vada-chutney
D. Puri-shaak and thanda doodh

68. The birds move their neck very often because
A. they can fly
B. the birds eyes are fixed
C. the birds have small eyes
D. their ears are covered with feathers

69. After diagnosis, a doctor says to a patient that there is less haemoglobin in his blood. Which of the following should he eat to make up the deficiency of iron?
A. Rice, sugar, amla
B. Green-leafy vegetables, wheat, orange.
C. Jaggery, lemon, pea
D. Amla, green-leafy vegetables, jaggery

70. National Curriculum Framework, 2005 strongly recommends that teaching of EVS at primary stage should primarily aim at
A. developing understanding of basic concepts of the subject
B. memorizing basic principles of the subject
C. linking classroom learning to life outside the school
D. acquiring skills to carry out experiments independently

71. Which one of the following is *not* consistent with the requirements of EVS curriculum at primary stage?
A. It should equip the learners with knowledge and skills to enter the world of work
B. It should inculcate in learners a concern for environment
C. It should engage learners in acquiring methods and processes leading to generation of new knowledge
D. It should suit cognitive level of the learners

72. Higher priority and space has been given in NCERT textbooks on EVS to
A. explain basic concepts of the subject
B. provide opportunities to learners for contemplation and wondering
C. provide exact definitions of technical terms
D. include large number of practice questions

73. Which one of the following is *not* an objective of including poems and stories in EVS textbooks?
A. To develop interest in the subject
B. To have a change in routine and monotonous content
C. To provide fun and enjoyment for learners
D. To promote imaginative and creative ability in the learners

74. Good EVS curriculum should be 'true to the child, true to life and true to the subject'. Which of the following characteristics of a curriculum *does not* meet the above requirements?
A. It promotes the value of freedom from feat and prejudice
B. It requires the learner to view the subject as a social enterprise
C. It emphasises more on processes of teaching and learning
D. It emphasizes more on terms and definitions

75. Nalini wants to introduce the topic on 'Animals—our friends' to Class III students. In order to introduce the topic more interestingly, the best teaching strategy would be to
A. use a chart showing pictures of different animals
B. draw pictures of different animals on the blackboard
C. show a video film on animals and their usefulness
D. ask the students to see pictures of animals given in the textbook

76. Class V NCERT EVS textbooks include a section 'what we have learnt' in the end of every chapter. It is suggested that answer to questions included in this section should not be assessed in terms of right or wrong. This shift has been done because
A. children cannot write correct answers at this stage
B. it enhances convenience to teachers in assessment
C. it helps the teacher to know how children are learning
D. it reduces subjectivity in assessment

77. Experimenting, Exploring, Investigating and Questioning constitute essential elements of active learning of EVS. A teacher arranges the following activities related to the concept of 'Food we should eat'.
A. Draws the diagrams of all such foods on the blackboard
B. Gives examples of different foods each in essential components of food
C. Asks students to collect related information from all possible sources
D. Shows a video on the topic
Which one of the above four activities satisfy the condition for active learning?

78. While teaching the topic on 'Air is everywhere' to Class IV students, Gitika plans to perform the following activities:
A. Take the students to a field trip
B. Explain the concept through specific examples
C. Use multimedia capsule to explain the concept
D. Ask probing questions related to the topic
Which one of the above proposed activities is *not* relevant for teaching of the topic effectively?

79. The section on 'Do this and find out' included in different topics in EVS textbooks aim at
A. providing direct hands-on experiences
B. improving performance in examination
C. learning definitions of scientific terms
D. keeping the students engaged at home

80. A good assignment in EVS should primarily aim at
A. revise the lesson for effective learning
B. ensure better utilization of time
C. keep the students engaged and disciplined
D. provide extended learning opportunities

81. As an EVS teacher, the major objective of organizing a field trip to a zoo should be
A. to provide fun and enjoyment to students
B. to have a change in monotony of routine teaching schedule
C. to provide active learning experience to students
D. to satisfy parents on quality of education

82. Which one of the following is *not* an objective of study of EVS in relation to Social Sciences?
A. It should enable children to question the existing ideas and practices
B. It should enable children to grow up as responsible member of society
C. It should enable children to respect differences of cultural practices
D. It should enable children to learn correct definition of key terms

83. Kavita wants to emphasise more on social issues like poverty, illiteracy and class inequalities in an EVS class. Which one of the following learning experiences will be more effective to achieve this objective?
A. Organising special lectures on related issues
B. Asking the students to prepare charts on related social issues
C. Asking the students to undertake group projects to collect and analyse related information
D. Asking the students to write slogans on related issues

84. Formative Assessment in EVS at primary stage *does not* include
A. identification of learning gaps of students
B. identification of deficiencies in teaching
C. enhancement of students' learning
D. grading and ranking of students

85. Given below are some human activities:
1. Digging of mines
2. Constructing dams
3. Collection of leaves and herbs to sell them in the market
4. Weaving baskets from bamboo
5. Making leaf plates out of fallen leaves
The activities responsible for the disappearance of forest is/are
A. only 1 B. 1 and 2 both
C. 1, 2 and 3 D. 2, 3, 4 and 5

86. Select correct statements about Bronze:
1. Bronze is an element like iron, silver and gold.
2. Bronze is made on melting copper and tin.
3. Bronze is very strong and is used in making cannons and statues.
4. The utensils made of Bronze are lighter and stronger than that of aluminium.
A. 2 and 3 B. 3 and 4
C. 4 and 1 D. 1 and 3

87. A person living in Gandhidham (Gujarat) wants to visit first Bhopal (Madhya Pradesh) and then Hyderabad (Andhra Pradesh). The directions of his journey will be
A. First towards East and then towards South
B. First towards West and then towards South
C. First towards South and then towards West
D. First towards South and then towards East

88. On a city map it was mentioned "Scale 1 cm = 110 metres". If the distance between two localities on the map is 15 cm, then the actual distance between the two localities is
A. 1165 centimetres
B. 1100 metres
C. 1500 metres
D. 1.65 kilometres

89. Mount Everest is a part of
A. India B. Tibet
C. Nepal D. Myanmar

90. Study the following duties/responsibilities:
1. Help others in carrying their bags.
2. Let the group follow you and keep at the front.
3. Ask those to stay back who cannot climb properly.
4. Look after those who are not well and arrange food for the group.
5. Find a good place to stop and rest.
Which of the above are the responsibilities of a group leader in mountaineering?
A. 1, 2 and 3 B. 2, 3 and 4
C. 3, 4 and 5 D. 1, 4 and 5

PART- IV

Language-I : English

Directions (for Qs. No. 91 to 99): *Read the given passage and answer the questions that follow by selecting the most appropriate option:*

Why do poets use poems to tell about social injustices? The answer is simple. This way a poet can catch and hold the reader's attention, his/her emotions. Usually, poets in their works present facts in order to capture attention of many people. These are not new facts that are presented to an audience. Poems are always aimed at reaching feelings of people and, thus, pulling strings. Literature of every state shows all the complexity of every epoch. When the situation is the same at several countries, it has a worldwide significance. Before talking about poetry, we should answer the queston: What is poetry? Poetry is a special way of describing stituations, things, ideas, feelings. Poets present their ideas in short phrases.

A poem can be compared to a photograph as it reflects real life, real situations and feelings. In a poem, a poet captures the exact moment and represents it the way he/she has seen it. When you read a poem you see the poet's subjective evaluation of facts, situations and the epoch in general. Poets of the Romantic Movement wrote their poems to share their feelings. They wrote to help people understand their time from the poet's point of view.

91. A poem reflects the culture of the
A. period it belongs to B. historical past
C. imaginary life D. present only

92. Here, the expression 'pulling strings' means
A. challenging beliefs
B. promoting popular notions
C. secretly controlling thoughts
D. exerting strength

93. A word in the passage which means a quality of being intricate is
A. general B. photograph
C. complexity D. evaluation

94. Romantic Movement is a literary period when the poetry mostly
A. is religious and philosophical
B. dealt with the supernatural and violence
C. focused on self-reliance and independence
D. emphasised on emotion and imagination

95. The structure of poetry is usually characterized by
A. sequences of two or more words without an 'action word'
B. long winded sentences
C. lengthy descriptive stanzas
D. short, factual stanzas

96. An example of 'subjective evaluation' is
A. Everybody likes dishes prepared with potatoes
B. The potato is a staple in some countries
C. There are over 25 types of potatoes around the world
D. The potato has a large percentage of starch content

97. The meaning of the word 'epoch' is a
A. lengthy, complex poem
B. type of literary work in England
C. distinctive point of time
D. being great and impressive

98. The purpose of poetry is to ______ the reader.
A. distract B. appeal to
C. disturb D. confuse

99. The themes of poems are usually about
A. everyday happenings
B. heroism and death
C. romance
D. important life events

Directions (for Qs. Nos. 100 to 105): *Read the given poem and answer the questions that follow by selecting the most appropriate option.*

Between the Miles

Because existence can become severe
in one day,
just sense me and I'll be there.
In the mind's eye,
I'm not so far away.
If you hold out your hand,
in the whispers,
I'll become the zephyr...
and besiege you.
If your eye's upon the stars,
in the crystalline darkness,
I'll become the moon.
And the light shall guide you.
If you rest upon the ground,
in the warmth,
I'll become the grass.
And embrace you.
If you turn outside,
in the wetness,
I'll become the rain.
And upon your forehead, kiss you.
If you free the air,
in the light of day,
I'll become the sun.
And smile for you.

Between the miles-
if you need me.
If you need a friend.
Let me be the friend, I want to be.

—Heather Stoop

100. 'The zephyr' is a
A. fine quality of cloth B. scent of odour
C. strong stream of air D. gentle, mild breeze

101. An example of a metaphor is
A. 'I'll become the grass.'
B. 'Between the miles'
C. 'I want to be'
D. 'If you rest upon the ground'

102. A synonym of the word 'besiege' is
A. surround B. attack
C. befriend D. trap

103. The theme of the poem is about
A. separation B. relationship
C. travel D. nature

104. The 'crystalline darkness' suggests that surrounding is
A. black and sombre
B. in the moonlight
C. lit up by the stars only
D. pitch dark and quiet

105. In the poem, the poet suggests that friendship is unaffected by
A. individual independence
B. changing feelings
C. time and distance
D. differences in attitude

Directions: *Answer the following questions by selecting the most appropriate option:*

106. A learner's competence in English will improve when she/he receives ______ of learning experience that is appropriate.
A. an equal level
B. a slightly higher level
C. a range of levels
D. a slightly easier, lower level

107. A 'mental block' associated with English language learning is
A. interest in Sports and Arts
B. disinterest in studies in general
C. lack of opportunities to use English
D. dyslexia–a disability

108. A company labels its frozen snacks 75% fat free rather than contains 25% fat so that people will view them more positively. This is an example of a
A. prototype
B. phoneme
C. subjective utility
D. semantic slanting

109. When children first start to speak in sentences, their speech may be described as
A. babbling B. exceptionally soft
C. telegraphic D. multilingual

110. Which observation supports Noam Chomsky's ideas about language acquisition?
A. Children's language development follows a similar pattern across cultures
B. The stages of language development occur at about the same ages in most children
C. Children acquire language quickly and effortlessly
D. All of these

111. What is the system of rules that governs how words can be meaningfully arranged to form phrases and sentences?
A. Language B. Syntax
C. Morpheme D. Phoneme

112. A twelve-year-old child enjoys using *puns*. This enjoyment indicates that she has
A. semantic slanting
B. deductive reasoning
C. mental blocks
D. metalinguistic awareness

113. Did you really ______ the money yesterday?
A. knead B. kneed
C. need D. needed

114. You don't smoke, ______ ? [tag question]
A. have you B. are you
C. do you D. don't you

115. A 'critical period' during language learning is
A. the period during which language can be acquired with greater ease than any other time
B. the length of time before a comprehensive assessment takes place in class
C. best preparatory period for any language project
D. special time set aside for students to intensively practice language use

116. The two skills required to take notes effectively are
A. using symbols and abbreviations instead of words
B. re-writing a text, using your own words
C. writing legibly with correct punctuation
D. writing fluently, using conjunctions

117. Remediation, when students find difficulty in the use of different 'modals' would be for them to
A. be given ample practice in using modals in a set of sentences
B. frame sentences on their own and teacher corrects them
C. learn about the structures outside the classroom through suitable activities
D. practice by collaboratively completing tasks where structures are used integratively, in a variety of real life situations

118. What is wrong with the following multiple choice question?

Tick (✔) the most appropriate:

The Metro theatre is located _____ Lodhi Road.

1. over 2. at
3. beside 4. behind

A. All answers are wrong
B. Two are wrong
C. The statement is not correctly framed
D. 'Over' is the correct answer

119. Receptive Language skills are

A. using grammatical structures accurately
B. writing in a range of styles
C. listening and reading for information
D. being able to self-correct while using language

120. The 'Natural Order' in the process of learning English suggests that, children

A. are slow at learning to speak when not in school
B. learn to read and write simultaneously
C. are able to speak first and then listen
D. acquire some language structures earlier than others

PART- V

भाषा-II : हिन्दी

निर्देश : *नीचे दिए गए गद्यांश को पढ़कर, सबसे उचित विकल्प का चयन कीजिए–*

हमारे देश में आधुनिक शिक्षा नामक एक चीज प्रकट हुई है। इसके नाम पर यत्रतत्र स्कूल और कॉलेज कुकुरमुत्तों की तरह सिर उठाकर खड़े हो गए हैं। इनका गठन इस तरह किया गया है कि इनका प्रकाश कॉलेज व्यवस्था के बाहर मुश्किल से पहुँचता है। सूरज की रोशनीए चाँद से टकराकर जितनी निकलती है, इनसे उससे भी कम रोशनी निकलती है। एक परदेशी भाषा की मोटी दीवार इसे चारों ओर से घेरे हुए है। जब मैं अपनी मातृभाषा के जरिए शिक्षा के प्रसार के बारे में सोचता हूँ तो उस विचार से साहस क्षीण होता है। घर की चारदीवारी में बंद दुल्हन की तरह यह भयभीत रहती है। बरामदे तक ही इसकी स्वतंत्रता का साम्राज्य है : एक इंच आगे बढ़ी कि घूँघट निकल आता है। हमारी मातृभाषा का राज प्राथमिक शिक्षा तक सीमित है : दूसरे शब्दों में, यह केवल बच्चों की शिक्षा के लिए उपयुक्त है, मानी यह कि जिसे कोई दूसरी भाषा सीखने का अवसर नहीं मिला, हमारी जनता की उस विशाल भीड़ को शिक्षा के उनके अधिकार के प्रसंग में बच्चा ही समझा जाएगा। उन्हें कभी पूर्ण विकसित मनुष्य नहीं बनना है और तब भी हम प्रेमपूर्वक सोचते हैं कि स्वराज मिलने पर उन्हें संपूर्ण मुनष्य के अधिकार हासिल होंगे।

121. इन स्कूल-कॉलेजों में किस भाषा में पढ़ाई होती है?

A. देशी भाषा में B. मानक भाषा में
C. विदेशी भाषा में D. गृहभाषा में

122. लेखक किस विचार से सहमत नहीं है?

A. मातृभाषा में ही पढ़ाया जाए।
B. मातृभाषा का प्रयोग केवल प्राथमिक स्तर तक ही उपयुक्त है।
C. मातृभाषा का प्रयोग बहुत सीमित है।
D. अन्य भाषाएँ भी सीखना बुरा नहीं है।

123. लेखक ने मातृभाषा की तुलना किससे की है?

A. दुल्हन से B. चारदीवारी से
C. बरामदे से D. घूँघट से

124. आधुनिक शिक्षा के नाम पर ऐसा क्या हुआ जो लेखक को अप्रिय है?

A. सूर्य की रोशनी का चाँद से टकराना
B. स्कूल-कॉलेजों का अनियोजित तरीके से खुलना
C. मातृभाषा के जरिए शिक्षा देना
D. लोगों को शिक्षा का अधिकार प्राप्त न होना

125. 'विचार' शब्द में 'इक' प्रत्यय लगने पर जो शब्द बनेगा, वह है–

A. विचारिक B. वैचारिक
C. वैचारीक D. वेचारिक

126. 'साहस' शब्द है–

A. विशेषण B. क्रियाविशेषण
C. भाववाचक संज्ञा D. क्रिया

127. 'घर की चारदीवारी में बंद दुल्हन की तरह यह भयभीत रहती है।' वाक्य में रेखांकित अंश है

A. क्रिया-विशेषण B. निश्चयवाचक सर्वनाम
C. अनिश्चयवाचक सर्वनाम D. संबंधवाचक सर्वनाम

128. स्कूल और कॉलेजों का कुकुरमुत्तों की तरह सिर उठाने से तात्पर्य है कि स्कूल और कॉलेज

A. नियम के तहत खोले गए हैं।
B. अवांछनीय रूप से खोले गए हैं।
C. योजना के तहत खोले गए हैं।
D. वांछित रूप से खुलवाए गए हैं।

निर्देश: *नीचे दिए गए गद्यांश को पढ़कर सबसे सही विकल्प का चयन कीजिए।*

राजनीतिक बहसों की गरमी में हम जो भी कहें, अपने राष्ट्रीय अभिमान की अभिव्यक्ति में हम जितना भी जोर से चीखें, सक्रिय राष्ट्रीय सेवा के प्रति हम अत्यंत उदासीन रहते हैं, क्योंकि हमारा देश प्रकाश से हीन है। मानव स्वभाव में निहित कंजूसी के कारण जिन्हें हमने नीचा रख छोड़ा है, उनके प्रति अन्याय से हम बच भी नहीं सकते। समय-समय पर उनके नाम पर हम पैसा इकट्ठा करते हैं, लेकिन उनके हिस्से में शब्द ही आते हैं, पैसा तो अंततः हमारी पार्टी के ही लोगों के पास पहुँचता है। संक्षेप में, जिनके पास बुद्धि, शिक्षा, समृद्धि और सम्मान है, हमारे देश के उस अत्यंत छोटे हिस्से, पाँच प्रतिशत और आबादी के अन्य पंचानवे प्रतिशत के बीच की दूरी समुंदर से भी अधिक चौड़ी है।

129. लेखक के अनुसार, हम किनके प्रति अन्याय करते हैं?
A. जो कंजूस हैं। B. जो निम्न वर्ग के हैं।
C. जो जोर से चीखते हैं। D. जो राष्ट्र की सेवा नहीं करते।

130. लेखक के अनुसार, हम किनके नाम पर पैसा इकट्ठा करते हैं?
A. सभी मानवों के नाम पर
B. कंजूस लोगों के नाम पर
C. निम्न वर्ग के लोगों की भलाई के नाम पर
D. पार्टी के नाम पर

131. 'लेकिन उनके हिस्से में शब्द ही आते हैं......' वाक्य में रेखांकित शब्द किस अर्थ की ओर संकेत करता है?
A. बड़बोलेपन की तरफ
B. कभी न पूरे होने वाले वादों की तरफ
C. अपमानजनक भाषा की तरफ
D. भाषिक सामग्री की तरफ

132. किस शब्द में स्वर रहित पंचम वर्ण के स्थान पर अनुस्वार (.) का प्रयोग किया जा सकता है?
A. सम्मान B. अत्यन्त
C. अन्याय D. अक्षुण्ण

133. 'राष्ट्रीय' शब्द में कौन-सा प्रत्यय है?
A. इय B. य
C. ईय D. रीय

134. 'जितना भी जोर से चीखें' वाक्य में क्रिया है
A. अकर्मक B. सकर्मक
C. प्रेरणार्थक D. द्विकर्मक

135. गद्यांश के आधार पर कहा जा सकता है कि
A. संसाधनों का बँटवारा समान रूप से है।
B. संसाधनों का असंतुलित बँटवारा वर्ग-भेद की खाई को बढ़ाता है।
C. केवल पाँच प्रतिशत आबादी के साथ ही बुद्धि है।
D. पंचानवे प्रतिशत आबादी समुंदर के किनारे रहती है।

निर्देश : *सबसे उचित विकल्प चुनिए :*

136. भाषा की पाठ्य-पुस्तक में सबसे महत्वपूर्ण पक्ष है
A. वस्तुनिष्ठ अभ्यास
B. व्याकरणिक नियमों की सैद्धांतिक व्याख्या
C. पाठों का उद्देश्यपूर्ण चयन
D. कागज की गुणवत्ता और छपाई

137. मौखिक कुशलता में शामिल है
A. तत्सम शब्दों के प्रयोग की कुशलता
B. तीव्र गति से बोलने की कुशलता
C. बोलते समय दृष्टांतों का प्रयोग करने की कुशलता
D. विभिन्न प्रकार की औपचारिक-अनौपचारिक चर्चाओं में बेझिझक बोलने की कुशलता

138. भाषा के कौशल हैं
A. सुनना, बोलना, पढ़ना, लिखना
B. बोलना, पढ़ना, लिखना, समझना
C. पढ़ना, लिखना, सुनना, समझना
D. लिखना, समझना, पढ़ना, स्मरण

139. बच्चे विद्यालय आने से पहले
A. कोई भी भाषा बोल नहीं सकते।
B. सभी भाषाएँ पढ़ सकते हैं।
C. सब कुछ लिख सकते हैं।
D. अपनी बोलचाल की भाषा के अनुभवों से लैस होते हैं।

140. किस तरह के परिवेश में बच्चों का भाषा-विकास अपेक्षाकृत बेहतर होगा?
A. एकल परिवार जहाँ माता-पिता मानक भाषा का प्रयोग करते हैं।
B. संयुक्त परिवार जहाँ परिवार के सभी सदस्य बच्चों के साथ निरंतर अंतःक्रिया करते हैं।
C. आधुनिक तकनीक से लैस कक्षा जहाँ भाषा-प्रयोगशाला का निरंतर प्रयोग होता है।
D. शिक्षक द्वारा मानक भाषा का प्रयोग करना

141. सुनना कौशल में शामिल है
A. दूसरों की बात सुनने में रुचि, धैर्य और प्रतिक्रिया
B. प्रश्नों को ध्यानपूर्वक सुनने की क्षमता का विकास
C. शांतिपूर्वक सुनना
D. सुने हुए शब्दों की केवल पुनरावृत्ति

142. किस प्रकार का प्रश्न प्राथमिक बच्चों की भाषायी क्षमता का आकलन करने में सर्वाधिक सक्षम है?
A. कहानी को दोहराइए।
B. याद की गई कविता सुनाइए।
C. किसी दृश्य का वर्णन कीजिए।
D. पाठ में से चार संज्ञा शब्द छाँटिए।

143. बच्चों में पठन-संस्कृति का विकास करने के लिए अनिवार्य है
A. कक्षा में मुखर वाचन करने का अभ्यास।
B. बाल साहित्य पठन हेतु प्रेरणा।
C. वर्तनी विन्यास का अभ्यास।
D. पठित सामग्री का लेखन-अभ्यास।

144. प्राथमिक स्तर पर भाषिक रेखांकन और चित्रांकन
A. एक सह-शैक्षणिक गतिविधि मात्र है।
B. बच्चों की अनुकरण प्रवृत्ति को पोषित करता है।
C. काव्य-व्याख्या का एकमात्र मार्ग है।
D. लेखन-अभ्यास का एक महत्वपूर्ण चरण है।

145. सुहास पढ़ते समय कठिनाई का अनुभव करता है। वह .... से ग्रसित है।
A. डिस्ग्राफिया B. डिस्लेक्सिया
C. डिस्केलकुलिया D. डिस्थीमिया

146. भाषा-शिक्षक को स्वयं अपनी भाषा-प्रयोग की क्षमता को बढ़ाना चाहिए क्योंकि
A. वह भाषा का शिक्षक है।

B. विद्यालय का निर्देश है।

C. इससे वह दूसरों पर प्रभाव डाल सकता है।

D. उसका भाषा-प्रयोग कक्षा में भाषा-वातावरण का निर्माण करता है।

147. भाषा-अर्जन और भाषा-अधिगम में मुख्य अंतर है–

A. पाठ्य-पुस्तक के अभ्यासों का अभ्यास करने का।

B. स्वाभाविकता का।

C. भाषा के नियमों को स्मरण करने का।

D. भाषा लेखन के अभ्यास का।

148. एक बहुभाषिक कक्षा में बच्चों की गृहभाषा के प्रयोग को

A. सम्मान देना चाहिए।

B. प्रोत्साहन नहीं देना चाहिए।

C. अत्यंत सीमित कर देना चाहिए।

D. कदापि प्रोत्साहन नहीं करना चाहिए।

149. प्राथमिक स्तर पर भाषा-शिक्षण का उद्देश्य है–

A. साहित्य की विधाओं से परिचित कराना

B. हिंदी के विविध रूपों से परिचय कराना

C. कुशल लेखक बनाना

D. कुशल वक्ता बनाना

150. भाषा एक औजार है जिसका उपयोग करते हैं–

A. जिंदगी को समझने के लिए

B. जिंदगी से जुड़ने के लिए

C. जीवन-जगत को प्रस्तुत करने के लिए

D. ये सभी

Answers

1	**2**	**3**	**4**	**5**	**6**	**7**	**8**	**9**	**10**
B	C	D	A	C	A	B	C	B	C
11	**12**	**13**	**14**	**15**	**16**	**17**	**18**	**19**	**20**
D	A	A	C	D	A	B	B	C	D
21	**22**	**23**	**24**	**25**	**26**	**27**	**28**	**29**	**30**
B	D	A	B	C	A	C	D	A	B
31	**32**	**33**	**34**	**35**	**36**	**37**	**38**	**39**	**40**
C	C	A	B	B	A	B	D	B	A
41	**42**	**43**	**44**	**45**	**46**	**47**	**48**	**49**	**50**
D	D	A	B	C	D	C	A	C	C
51	**52**	**53**	**54**	**55**	**56**	**57**	**58**	**59**	**60**
A	D	A	A	C	D	C	D	B	A
61	**62**	**63**	**64**	**65**	**66**	**67**	**68**	**69**	**70**
D	D	C	B	B	B	A	B	D	C
71	**72**	**73**	**74**	**75**	**76**	**77**	**78**	**79**	**80**
A	B	B	D	C	C	C	A	A	D
81	**82**	**83**	**84**	**85**	**86**	**87**	**88**	**89**	**90**
C	D	C	D	B	A	A	D	C	D
91	**92**	**93**	**94**	**95**	**96**	**97**	**98**	**99**	**100**
A	C	C	D	A	A	C	B	A	D
101	**102**	**103**	**104**	**105**	**106**	**107**	**108**	**109**	**110**
A	A	B	C	C	B	C	D	A	D
111	**112**	**113**	**114**	**115**	**116**	**117**	**118**	**119**	**120**
B	D	C	C	A	A	D	A	C	D
121	**122**	**123**	**124**	**125**	**126**	**127**	**128**	**129**	**130**
C	B	A	B	B	C	B	B	B	C
131	**132**	**133**	**134**	**135**	**136**	**137**	**138**	**139**	**140**
B	B	C	A	B	C	D	A	D	B
141	**142**	**143**	**144**	**145**	**146**	**147**	**148**	**149**	**150**
A	C	B	D	B	D	B	A	B	D

Some Selected Explanatory Answers

1. Sternberg's Triarchic Theory of Intelligence: Sternberg (1997) defines *intelligence* as a group of mental abilities necessary for children or adults to adapt to any environmental context, and also to select and shape the contexts in which they live and act. By limiting his definition of intelligence to universally necessary mental abilities, Sternberg would exclude some of Gardner's "intelligences," such as musical and bodily-kinesthetic abilities. Sternberg's (1985a) triarchic theory of intelligence embraces three elements, or aspects, of intelligence: *componential, experiential* and *contextual.*

- The componential element is the *analytic* aspect of intelligence; it determines how efficiently people process information. It tells people how to solve problems, how to monitor solutions and how to, evaluate the results.
- The experiential element is *insightful* or *creative;* it determines how people approach novel or familiar tasks. It allows people to compare new information with what they already know and to come up with new ways of putting facts together—in other words, to think originally.
- The contextual element is *practical;* it determines how people deal with their environment. It is the ability to size up a situation and decide what to do: adapt to it, change it, or get out of it.

2. Theory of Multiple Intelligences: Harvard psychologist Howard Gardner, author of *Frames of Mined: The Theory of Multiple Intelligences,* has revolutionized theoretical views about intelligence and creativity. He challenged the more traditional view of intelligence as a one-dimensional measurement of mental capacity with his theory of multiple intelligences, identifying nine distinct forms of intelligence possessed by all numan beings to varying degrees. Each individual, he contends, has a unique intellectual profile comprising the following:

1. *Verbal-Linguistic Intelligence:* The strength of an individual's verbal skills and his or her sensitivity to the sounds and rhythms of words and their meanings.
2. *Mathematical-Logical Intelligence:* The capacity for abstract and conceptual thinking, and for recognizing orderly patterns of numbers.
3. *Musical Intelligence:* Developed skills in identifying and creating sound properties.
4. *Visual-Spatial Intelligence:* The ability to understand the relationship of space and to visualize abstractly in images.
5. *Bodily-Kinesthetic Intelligence:* Developed sense of body motion and controlling the movement of physical objects.
6. *Interpersonal Intelligence:* Developed sensitivity of temperament and what drives the desires of others.
7. *Intrapersonal Intelligence:* The ability to be self-reflective with one's own values, perceptions, opinions and thought processes.
8. *Naturalist Intelligence:* The capacity to indentify and classify living organisms in nature.
9. *Existential Intelligence:* Sensitivity to complex issues surrounding our existence and developed skills in pondering deep questions.

Gardner's theory has been primarily applied to the process of independent learning, examining how diverse individuals learn best, based on the composition of their intelligence profile.

3. Language has a hierarchical structure. This means that language is a system that brings together parts to make more complex wholes. For example, sounds are the parts that come together to make whole words. Words are the parts that come together to make whole phrases. Phrases are the parts that come together to make whole sentences. *Phonemes* are basic sounds that are the smallest speech units in language. A letter in the alphabet can have several different basic sounds. For example, *i.e.,* sounds different in the words ill, like and listen. Each of these sounds represents a different phoneme. Letters are also joined together to represent different phonemes, like ph, ch, th. These basic sounds do not have any meaning when they stand alone. *Morphemes* include root words, prefixes and suffixes. Many words, such as cat, play and hide, are single morphemes. Other words have several morphemes. For example, the word impatiently has three morphemes: im- is a prefix, patient is the root word, and -ly is a suffix. Morphemes are the smallest units of language that have meaning. The meaning of a word refers to its denotation and connotation. *Syntax* is the system of rules that tells us how we can put words together to make meaningful sentences. A simple rule of syntax is that a sentence must have a verb phrase and a noun phrase. Figure below analyses a simple sentence to show the hierarchical structure of language.

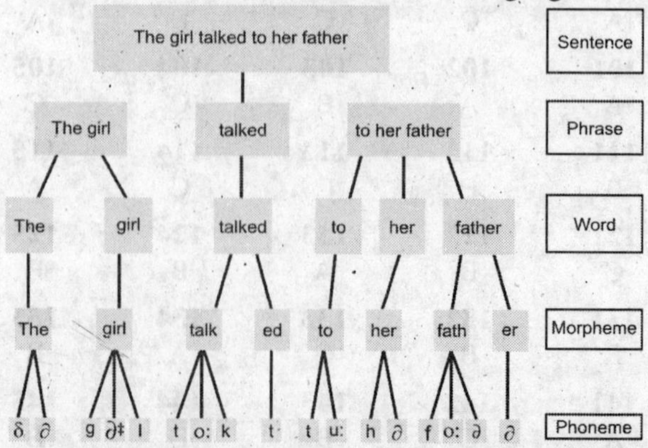

Fig. *An analysis of a simple sentence*

7. The concept of Continuous and Comprehensive Evaluation has two aspects:
(i) It should be continuous.
(ii) It should be comprehensive.
For comprehensive evaluation of student's growth different techniques such as observation of behaviour in various situations, records of interest, initiative and creativity may be used for evaluation in non-scholastic areas. Cumulative record cards will also show growth of learners in non-scholastic areas.
These information relating to the growth of the learner in non-scholastic areas and scholastic areas should be made available to learners, teachers and parents.
Continuous and Comprehensive Evaluation should not be an end in itself. It should provide direction to students, parents and teachers in their efforts.

8. School based Evaluation is held at school level unlike external examination conducted by the Boards of School Education. This is done by the teachers according to the schedule developed by the school and guidelines given by the Board. Though this evaluation has been done at school level all along, certain shortcomings have crept into this system. These shortcomings can be attributed to various factors. The basic factor is the misconception of teachers regarding the place of evaluation and its importance in the educational process. The other factor has been the imitation of the practice of external examination which is generally held at the end of the session.
In the School Based System of evaluation, the focus on the purpose of assessment has changed. Now, it includes readiness testing, screening of development, evaluation of performance in cognitive, affective and psychomotor domains more frequently, systematically and effectively.
School Based Evaluation has following characteristics:
- It is broader, more comprehensive and continous than traditional system.
- Aims primarily to help learners for systematic learning and development.
- Takes care of the needs of the learner as responsible citizens of the future.
- Is more transparent, futuristic and provides more for association among learners, teachers and parents.

In other words, School Based Evaluation is child-centred, school-centred and multidimensional evaluation. Hence, in its true spirit, it triggers an all round development of the learner. It encourages all kinds of learning in life both inside the school as well as outside it. It is child-centred as it attempts to consider the learner as a unique entity for its individual pattern of development. It builds on individual child's abilities, progress and development in achieving already set goals and objectives of education as an individual and not just his/her position in relation to other learners.
It also provides opportunities to teachers to know the following about their learners:
- What they learn?
- How they learn?
- What type of difficulties limitations they face in realising together?
- What do the children think?
- What do the children feel?
- What are their interests and dispositions?

Further, this evaluation helps a learner to use his/her potential in a better manner and also provides insight to the teachers to discover the methods which may be helpful to the individual learner in resolving his/her problems and difficulties.
Besides being *child-centred*, this evaluation is *school-centred* as well. It means that no outside agency interferes in this evaluation process. It is entirely school based and done by the teacher. The teacher is trusted and given full responsibility of evaluating students with the brief that the teacher knows best about his/her students.
School Based Evaluation is *multidimensional*. Its multidimensional nature is reflected in recognizing and taking care of learners' social, emotional, physical, intellectual and other areas of development which are interrelated and cannot be considered in isolation. It also calls for the use of multiple techniques and tools of evaluation.

9. Readiness refers to a student's knowledge, understanding, and skill related to a particular sequence of learning. It is influenced by a student's cognitive proficiency as well as prior learning, life experiences, and attitudes about school. Readiness can vary widely over time, and according to topic and circumstance. Tiered activities are one way to address readiness effectively; for example, all students study the same concept but complete activities appropriate to their readiness levels. Readiness also can be addressed through small group sessions or the provision of one-to-one teacher and peer support or coaching.

11. Learning disability has been defined in different ways. The definition depends on culture, socio-economic condition and the attitude of the researcher. Here, we give some of the importance definitions of learning disability.
Kirk (1962) defined learning disability as, "A learning disability refers to a retardation, disorder or delayed development in one or more of the processes of speech, language, reading, spelling, writing or Arithmetic resulting from a possible cerebral dysfunction and/or emotional or behavioural disturbance and not from

mental retardation, sensory deprivation or cultural or instructional factors".

Alan O. Ross has defined a learning disabled child as, "A child of at least average intelligence whose academic performance is impaired by a developmental lag in the ability to sustain selective attention. Such a child requires specialized instruction in order to permit the use of his or her full intellectual potential."

12. Inclusive schools recognise and respond to the diverse needs of their students, accommodating both different styles and rates of learning and ensuring quality education to all through appropriate curricula, organisational arrangements, teaching strategies, resource use and partnerships with their communities. Whilst inclusive beliefs, policies and practices specifically address the needs of students with disabilities and additional learning needs, they are equally beneficial for the full range of students. Schools that are inclusive adopt the belief that wherever possible all children should learn together regardless of differences; that all children can learn and achieve their potential; and that the continuum of students' needs should be matched by a continuum of programs, support and services. All students regardless of their ability or disability benefit from schools adopting inclusive practices.

Definitions of Inclusiveness : Inclusiveness is evident when:

- a school's enrolment practices do not discriminate between students with disabilities and those without disabilities;
- school services and facilities are equally accessible to students with disabilities and those without disabilities;
- curriculum programs are designed in such a way that the learning needs of all students are catered for;
- assessment and certification procedures are responsive to the learning outcomes targets and goals of students with and without disabilities;
- specialist services and equipment that students need to be able to experience success with their learning are supplied; and
- the school environment is friendly and teachers and students respond positively to student diversity.
- Features of an Inclusive School.

An inclusive education is characterised by a blurring of the boundaries between children with and those without additional learning needs, so that the focus is on:

- the level of capacity each individual child possesses to learn and progress;
- the learning and well-being outcomes sought; and
- the environment and support which the school undertakes to provide.

13. Gifted students are those who perform or who have demonstrated the potential to perform at high levels in academic or creative fields when compared to others of their age, experience or environment. These students require services not ordinarily provided by the general education program. Students possessing these abilities may be found in all populations, across all economic strata, and in all areas of human endeavour. Gifted students may demonstrate the following characteristics:

- takes initiative
- shows leadership
- is curious
- takes creative risks
- uses ideas and learning in new situations
- shows persistence
- becomes passionately interested in a topic or idea
- chooses difficult tasks
- has a keen sense of humour
- expresses thoughts with ease, often at great length
- has many different and unusual ideas
- is resourceful in solving problems

14. Giftedness is generally considered to come from both nature (heredity), and nurture (the environment). Research has shown that giftedness often runs in families. However, as with all children, gifted children need to be raised in an interactive and stimulating environment. The environment begins to influence a child's development before birth and during the birth. The first five years of a child's life are especially important in determining his or her later development, as it is during this period that the brain is undergoing very rapid growth and development. An enriched environment offers gifted children additional stimulation, experience, and interaction to meet their particular needs.

16. Dyspraxia (Developmental Coordination Disorder): Dyspraxia, sometimes known as Developmental Coordination Disorder (DCD), is chiefly a difficulty with organising movement. Gross and fine movements will be affected. Problems with gross motor skills will be revealed in a lack of balance and rhythm, poor posture, weak muscle tone, a clumsy, awkward gait and a tendency to bump into people and objects, or even to trip and fall easily. There may be poor integration of the two sides of the body and poor hand-eye coordination. Difficulties with fine motor skills will show up in poor manipulative skills, such as dressing, eating with a knife and fork, doing jigsaws and holding a pencil in the correct grip to produce neat writing. Hand dominance may be late in becoming established.

In some cases, there is difficulty in coordinating the muscles involved in speaking (sometimes called oral or verbal dyspraxia), leading to exaggerated movements of the mouth or poorly articulated speech.

17. Learning disability refers to a group of disorders that affect a broad range of academic and functional skills (not due to hearing or vision disorder) including the child's ability to:

- Read
- Write
- Spell
- Mathematical abilities
- A learning disability is not indicative of low intelligence.
- Children with learning disabilities have difficulty in achieving their expected intellectual level because of deficient brain functioning.
- About 2% to 10% of children suffer from these disabilities.

Probable Causes:

- Genetic (hereditary predisposition)
- Mother's intake of alcohol during pregnancy
- Abnormal development of brain in the womb
- Low birth weight of the child
- Premature delivery
- Head injuries
- Lead poisoning

21. Table: Action Verbs Corresponding to Bloom's Taxonomy

Domain	*Levels*	*Appropriate Verbs*
Cognitive	1. Knowledge	Arrange, Define, Describe, Identity, Label, List, Name, Identify, Match, Memorize, Order, Recognize, Recall, Recite, Repeat.
	2. Comprehension	Classify, Discuss, Distinguish, Explain, Identify, Indicate, Locate, Review, Rewrite, Summarize, Tell, Translate.
	3. Application	Apply, Choose, Compute, Demonstrate, Operate, Practice, Prepare, Solve.
	4. Analysis	Analyze, Calculate, Compare, Contrast, Criticize, Diagram, Differentiate, Distinguish, Examine, Experiment, Evaluate, Relate, Separate, Select.
	5. Synthesis	Assemble, Compose, Construct, Create, Combine, Design, Formulate, Organize, Prepare, Set up, Summarize, Tell, Write.
	6. Evaluate	Appraise, Evaluate, Judge, Score.
Affective	1. Receiving	Accept, Attempt, Willing
	2. Responding	Challenge, Select, Support, Visit
	3. Valuing	Defend, Display, Offer, Choose
	4. Organization	Judge, Volunteer, Share, Dispute
	5. Characterization	Consistently, Join, Participate
Psychomotor	1. Imitation	Repeat, Mimic, Follow
	2. Manipulation	Practice with minimal assistance, Create, Modify
	3. Precision	Perform without error, Perform without assistance
	4. Articulation	Demonstrate proficiency, Perform with confidence, perform with style or flair
	5. Naturalization	Perform automatically.

22. Extrinsic and Intrinsic Motivation

Two main categories of motivation are recognised—*extrinsic* and *intrinsic* motivation. Intrinsic motivation is seen when learners willingly engage in an activity purely for the personal satisfaction it brings. It is the kind of motivation displayed by young children in the preschool years and students of any age when they study for the pure joy and satisfaction of learning. Intrinsic motivation is almost entirely absent in students with a history of learning difficult in school. Extrinsic motivation, on the other hand, is seen at work when an individual tries hard to learn in order to gain some reward or to avoid negative consequences of not learning. Both forms of motivation are extremely important. The motivation available in any given learning situation is the sum total of intrinsic plus extrinsic influences.

31. Let area of rectangle = A cm^2

From formula,

$$\text{Area of rectangle} = \text{Length} \times \text{Breadth}$$

$$A = 8 \times \text{Breadth}$$

$$\text{Breadth} = \frac{A}{8} \text{ cm}$$

According to the question,

$$\text{Perimeter of square} = \text{Perimeter of rectangle}$$

$$24 = 2\ (\text{length} + \text{breadth})$$

$$24 = 2\left(8+\frac{A}{8}\right)$$

or, $$12 = 8+\frac{A}{8}$$

or, $$\frac{A}{8} = 12 - 8$$

$$A = 4 \times 8 = 32 \text{ cm}^2$$

32. ∴ Place value and face value of 3:

1 2 3 4 5

300 (Place value)

3 (Face value)

∴ Difference = 300 – 3 = 297.

33. 1 kilogram = 1000 grams
∴ 56.7 kilogram = 56.7 × 1000
= 56700 gms.

34. Here, two boats are travelling in same frame, hence speed of current in the river is not accountable.
Distance travelled = Speed × time
Distance travelled by boat with speed 20 km/hr in 3.5 hrs. = 20 × 3.5
= 70 kms
Similarly, distance travelled by boat with speed 23 km/h in same time 3.5 hrs
= 23 × 3.5 = 80.5 km
Distance between two boats
= 80.5 – 70 = 10.5 km.

35. From Divisibility test by 9,
Sum of all digits given in the number is divided by 9.
9 + 0 + 7 + 0 + 7 = 23

Now, $\frac{23}{9} = 2\frac{5}{9}$

Hence, remainder = 5.

36. Cost price of 1500 kg of fresh fish
= 1500 × 25 = ₹ 37,500
When dried,
Weight of dried fish = $\frac{1500}{3}$ = 500 kg
Selling price of 500 kg dried fish
= 500 × 80 = ₹ 40,000
∴ Earning = Selling price – cost price
= ₹ 40,000 – ₹ 37,500
= ₹ 2,500.

37. On following the same pattern, we get
(9 – 1) ÷ 8 = 1
(98 – 2) ÷ 8 = 12
(987 – 3) ÷ 8 = 123
(9876 – 4) ÷ 8 = 1234
(98765 – 5) ÷ 8 = 12345
(987654 – 6) ÷ 8 = 123456.

38. 450 litres = 4,50,000 ml

Number of bottles = $\frac{4,50,000}{750}$

Number of cartons = $\frac{4,50,000}{750 \times 6}$

= $\frac{4,50,000}{4500}$ = 100.

39. Volume of 1 rectangular box
= 4 × 3 × 2 = 24 cm^3
Number of rectangular box required to pack the given volume = $\frac{8664}{24}$ = 361.

41. We know that, there is no significance of zero at the right most position after any digit (other than zero) on the right side of decimal.

42. It will help the students to understand the real life application of mathematics and enhance their concepts, knowledge & ideas.

43. On first sight, the child will differentiate two or more geometrical figures by counting their number of sides used in the figure.

44. Difficulty in differentiating between numbers, operations and symbols arises due to poor visual processing ability.

46. In this manner, child understands multiplication and its properties. Number 15 can be represented as product of two numbers.
15 ⇒ 3 × 5 = 5 × 3 (commutative property).

47. Number of numbers greater than 2.7 is infinity. And infinity represents open end. Hence, correct option is (C).

52. Main goal of mathematics education is to develop children's abilities to think and analyse their logical assumption mathematicaly.

53. A good textbook should contain all clear points about concept of topics and based on that numerous exercises to give rigorous practice.

54. Mathematics is a subject which we use in every moment of our life. It is a mandatory topic for all children.

55. Smallest common multiple is LCM of 5, 10 and 35.
= 70
Biggest common factor is HCF of 5, 10 and 35
= 5
Difference of two = 70 – 5 = 65.

56. Number of factors, we get by LCM
105 = 1 × 105
= 3 × 35
= 5 × 21
= 7 × 15
∴ All factors of 105 are :
1, 3, 5, 7, 15, 21, 35 and 105
Hence, number of factors of 105 = 8.

57. 2.17 P.M. + 11 hours + 59 minutes = 2.16 A.M.

58. 1 right angle = 90°
3.5 right angles = 3.5 × 90° = 315°.

59. 1100 + 110 + 11 = 1221.

60.
$$\begin{array}{r} 509 \\ +\ 3028 \\ \hline 3537 \end{array}$$

61. Malaria is one of the most widespread diseases caused by mosquitoes. But about a hundred years ago people thought that malaria is caused due to bad air. In fact, the word malaria has been taken from the old Italian words mala: which means bad; and aria which means air. People also called it marsh fever because it occurred more in the areas where, there were marshy ponds or puddles with stagnant water, giving a foul smell.

Causes of Malaria: Malaria is actually caused by a tiny germ which lives in the body of mosquitoes. This germ is called plasmodium. Plasmodium does not harm the mosquito. But when the mosquito bites a human being, the germs pass into the human body along with its saliva and cause fever.

Sir Ronald Ross, a doctor who worked in India, discovered in 1897 that it is the female anopheles mosquito which spreads malaria. The female anopheles feeds on the blood of human beings. It has special mouthparts which can pierce the skin of human beings. The male anopheles, on the other hand, feeds on juices of fruits and flowers and so, cannot spread malaria.

62. **Symptoms of Malaria:** A person suffering from malaria suffers from fever, severe headache and chills that can last up to several hours. This can occur in regular intervals for three to four days, often accompanied by vomiting and convulsions. Without treatment the liver and spleen become swollen and it is followed by anaemia (bloodlessness) and jaundice.

    Diagnosis: The presence of absence of malaria can be confirmed by blood test only. A drop of blood is made into a smear on a glass slide. The slide is then observed under a microscope to look for the cause of fever.

63. **Al-Biruni:** A foreign traveller from Uzbekistan, he visited India in the 11th century. He left behind an account of his travels in his book Kitab-ul Hind which was written in Arabic.

64. The organs of sight are the eyes. Some animals like jumping spider have simple eyes that detect light, dark and movement. Most insects have compound eyes.

Spider

Mosquito

Kite

Vulture

Some birds like kites, eagles, vultures can see the things clearly from a distance of eight metres, what we can see from a distance of two metres. It is because their eyes are faced forward. This arrangement increases the amount of overlap between the two eyes. This overlap makes the animal a better judge of distance because the brain is able to compare the overlapping views of the same picture. This is called binocular vision. Most of the birds have their eyes on either side of the head. Their eyes can able to compare the overlapping views of the same picture. This is called binocular vision. Most of the birds have their eyes on either side of the head. Their eyes can focus on two different things at a time. When they look straight, both their eyes focus on the same object.

66. **Parts of A Flower**

    Each flower has a stalk called the pedicel. Some flowers are without pedicel; such flowers are called sessile flowers. The basal swollen portion of a flower is called thalamus. the parts of a flower arranged in a ring form are called whorls. Most flowers have four whorls.

    1. **Calyx:** The outermost whorl is the calyx. Calyx consists of green leaf like structure called sepals. The sepals protect the flower in its bud stage.
    2. **Corolla:** Corolla consists of petals. The petals vary in size and shape. The petals of most of the flowers are colourful. Being brightly coloured, they attract insects for pollination.
    3. **Stamen:** The third whorl is that of stamen. Each stamen consists of a filament and an anther. The anther is a sac-like structure, present at the tip of the filament. It produces powdery mass called pollen or pollen grains. Pollen grains produce male cells or the sperm. Stamen is the male part of a flower.
    4. The central part of the flower is female part. It consists of a carpel or pistil. It has three parts. Basal swollen portion is called ovary. It contains ovules. The ovary continues in a long neck-like style. The style ends in a knob like part called stigma. Stigma serves a landing place for pollens during pollination. Female sex cells are present inside the ovules. Ovary develops into a fruit and ovules develop into seeds.

    A flower which consists of all the four whorls calyx, corolla, stamen and carpel is called a complete flower. Some flowers with both male and female reproductive parts are called bisexual or hermaphrodite flowers. Others may have either male or female parts, such flowers are called unisexual flowers.

68. Most of the birds have their eyes on either side of the head. Their eyes can focus on two different things at a time. When they look straight ahead, both their eyes focus on the same object. You must have seen birds moving their neck very often. Do you know why? In most of the birds, eyes are fixed and cannot move. So birds have to turn their heads to see around.

69. Iron is a very important mineral. It is needed for the formation of a compound, called haemoglobin in our blood which helps in carrying oxygen to all parts of the body. Do you know in adolescence (10-19 years)

iron requirement of the body increases? The need for iron increases specifically for girls. We must include iron rich foods in our daily diet.

Sources of Iron

- Green leafy vegetables like spinach, mustard leaves, fenugreek, mint, etc.
- Whole cereals and legumes
- Liver, heart, kidney and egg yolk.
- Gur/jaggery
- Dates and pomegranate.

70. NCF 2005 emphasizes the following five guiding principles:

- Connecting knowledge to life outside the school
- Ensuring that learning is shifted away from rote methods.
- Enriching the curriculum to provide for overall development of children rather than remain textbook centric.
- Making examinations more flexible and integrated into classroom life.
- Nurturing an over-riding identity informed by caring concerns within the democratic polity of the country.

86. Bronze is an alloy of copper and Tin.

87.

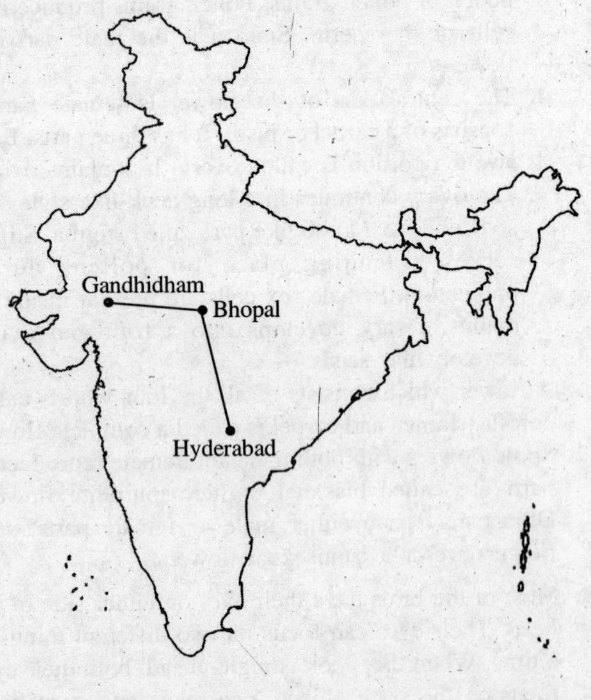

89. Mount Everest, the highest peak in the world, is situated in Nepal.

107. English Language, the language of news, business, information, opportunity, employment, power and prestige in India, has become the synonym of all progress in the recent years. Notwithstanding, the fact that today it enjoys the status of a big business in the wake of globalization, teaching and learning of it in educational institutions in our country is rather inadequate and unproductive. The situation is worse in small towns and rural areas where most of the students observe English as a terrifying subject as they register failure therein and thereof. Today, a majority of students enter the college and receive education with the notion that they are learning, not for knowledge but for employment. Moreover, the first requirement for any kind of job is to be well versed in English. While the urban students get conducive environment both at home and at college, the rural students remain bereft of the same. The result is that they lack in even the basic functional knowledge of English. Poor souls, who otherwise are considered quite intelligent in other subjects, develop inferiority complex in English classes due to their inadequate knowledge and poor command over the language. Unable to use English as the students in big cities do, the students in rural areas develop an aversion and build an antagonistic attitude towards the language. This preconceived notion results into a mental block before the child ventures into learning English language. This fact brings countless problems for the child throughout his education.

108. 2. Key properties of language

(*a*) **Phonemes**—the base of the language hierarchy. The smallest speech units in a language that can distinguish perceptually. (English language consists of 40 phonemes) ex- çh and th.

(*b*) **Morphemes**—smallest units of meaning in a language. Ex- un-friendly-ly contains 3 morphemes.

(*c*) **Semantics**—area of language concerned with understanding the meaning of words and word combinations. May consists of denotation (dictionary meaning) or connotation (secondary implications)

(*d*) **Syntax**—system of rules that specify how words can be arranged into sentences.

109. Language is a system of symbols and rules that is used for meaningful communication. A system of communication has to meet certain criteria in order to be considered a language:

- A language uses symbols, which are sounds, gestures, or written characters that represent objects, actions, events, and ideas. Symbols enable people to refer to objects that are in another place or events that occurred at a different time.
- A language is meaningful and therefore can be understood by other users of that language.
- A language is generative, which means that the symbols of a language can be combined to produce an infinite number of messages.

- A language has rules that govern how symbols can be arranged. These rules allow people to understand messages in that language even, if they have never encountered those messages before.

The Building Blocks of Language: Language is organized hierarchically, from phonemes to morphemes to phrases and sentences that communicate meaning.

Phonemes: Phonemes are the smallest distinguishable units in a language. In the English language, many consonants, such as t, p, and m, correspond to single phonemes, while other consonants, such as c and g, can correspond to more than one phoneme. Vowels typically correspond to more than one phoneme. For example, corresponds to different phonemes depending on whether it is pronounced as in bone or woman. Some phonemes correspond to combinations of consonants, such as ch, sh, and th.

Morphemes: Morphemes are the smallest meaningful units in a language. In the English language, only a few single letters, such as I and a, are morphemes. Morphemes are usually whole words or meaningful parts of words, such as prefixes, suffixes, and word stems.

Example:

The word "disliked" has three morphemes: "dis," "lik," and "ed."

Syntax: Syntax is a system of rules that governs how words can be meaningfully arranged to form phrases and sentences.

Example:

One rule of syntax is that an article such as "the" must come before a noun, not after: "Read the book," not "Read book the."

Language Development in Children: Children develop language in a set sequence of stages, although sometimes particular skills develop at slightly different ages:

- Three-months-old infants can distinguish between the phonemes from any language.
- At around six months, infants begin babbling, or producing sounds that resemble many different languages. As time goes on, these sounds begin to resemble more closely the words of the languages the infant hears.
- At about thirteen months, children begin to produce simple single words.
- By about twenty-four months, children begin to combine two or three words to make short sentences. At this stage, their speech is usually telegraphic. Telegraphic speech, like telegrams, contains no articles or prepositions.
- By about age three years, children can usually use tenses and plurals.
- Children's language abilities continue to grow throughout the school-age years. They become able to recognize ambiguity and sarcasm in language and to use metaphors and puns. These abilities arise from metalinguistic awareness, or the capacity to think about how language is used.

110. Biological Influences on Language Acquisition: The main proponent of the view that biological influences bring about language development is the well-known linguist Noam Chomsky. Chomsky argues that human brains have a language acquisition device (LAD), an innate mechanism or process that allows children to develop language skills. According to this view, all children are born with a universal grammar, which makes them receptive to the common features of all languages. Because of this hard-wired background in grammar, children easily pick up a language when they are exposed to its particular grammar.

Evidence for an innate human capacity to acquire language skills comes from the following observations:

- The stages of language development occur at about the same ages in most children, even though different children experience very different environments.
- Children's language development follows a similar pattern across cultures.
- Children generally acquire language skills quickly and effortlessly.
- Deaf children who have not been exposed to a language may make up their own language. These new languages resemble each other in sentence structure, even when they are created in different cultures.

119. Receptive skills: The receptive skills are listening and reading, because learners do not need to produce language to do these, they receive and understand it. These skills are sometimes known as passive skills. They can be contrasted with the productive or active skills of speaking and writing.

Example:

Often in the process of learning new language, learners begin with receptive understanding of the new items, then later move on to productive use.

In the classroom: The relationship between receptive and productive skills is a complex one, with one set of skills naturally supporting another. For example, building reading skills can contribute to the development of writing.

Previous Paper (Solved)

CTET PAPER-I, NOVEMBER 2012*

PART- I

Child Development and Pedagogy

Directions: *Answer the following questions by selecting the* ***most appropriate*** *option.*

1. Theory of multiple intelligences implies the following *except*

A. intelligence is a distinct set of processing operations used by an individual to solve problems

B. disciplines should be presented in a numbers of ways

C. learning could be assessed through a variety of means

D. emotional intelligence is not related to IQ

2. A child of 16 years scores 75 in an IQ test; his mental age will be ________ years.

A. 12 B. 8

C. 14 D. 15

3. Which one of the following optimizes motivation to learn?

A. Personal satisfaction in meeting targets

B. Extrinsic factor

C. Motivation to avoid failure

D. Tendency to choose very easy or difficult goals

4. Smallest unit of meaning in a language is

A. pragmatics B. syntax

C. morpheme D. phoneme

5. IQ scores are generally ________ correlated with academic performance.

A. least B. perfectly

C. highly D. moderately

6. Successful inclusion requires the following *except*

A. Involvement of parents

B. Capacity building

C. Sensitization

D. Segregation

7. Which of the following would be the most appropriate way to encourage disadvantaged children to attend school regularly?

A. A child collector employed by the school, must bring children from homes everyday

B. Paying ₹ 5 per day to attract children

C. Opening residential schools

D. Not allowing children to attend school may be made a legally punishable offence

8. The best way to avoid gender discrimination in a school may be

A. formation of a rule to shun gender discrimination in the school and enforce it strictly

B. selection of more boys than girls for a music competition

C. metacognition of their gender-biased behaviours by teachers

D. recruitment of equal number of male and female teachers

9. Gifted students are

A. non-assertive of their needs

B. independent in their judgements

C. independent of teachers

D. introvert in nature

10. The up-scaling of performance in the scholastic areas on the basis of performance in co-scholastic areas can be justified as

A. it follows the policy of compensatory discrimination for the marginalized students

B. it ensures universal retention

C. it develops respect for manual labour

D. it caters to individual differences

11. In the Information Processing Model of thinking, the following steps are said to take place :

1. Response execution 2. Response selection

3. Pre-Processing 4. Categorisation

The correct sequence of these steps is

A. 3, 1, 4, 2 B. 4, 3, 2, 1

C. 3, 4, 2, 1 D. 2, 4, 3, 1

12. A child cannot distinguish between 'saw' and 'was', 'nuclear' and 'unclear'. He/She is suffering from

A. dyslexemia

B. dysmorphemia

C. dyslexia

D. word jumbling disorder

13. Learning disabilities are generally found

A. more often in children belonging to rural areas as compared to urban areas

B. in specially those children whose paternal relatives have such problems

C. in children with average to superior IQ

D. more often in boys as compared to girls

*Exam was held on 18-11-2012.

14. An empowering school will promote which of the following qualities the most in its teachers?
A. Tendency to experiment
B. Memory
C. Disciplined nature
D. Competitive aptitude

15. Adolescents may experience
A. feeling of self-actualization
B. feeling of satiation about life
C. anxiety and concern about themselves
D. feeling of fear about sins committed in childhood

16. Orthopedically impaired children are likely to have
A. dyslexia
B. dysgraphia
C. dysthymia
D. dyscalculia

17. Partial reinforcement
A. works best in training animals
B. is more effective than continuous reinforcement
C. is less effective than continuous reinforcement
D. cannot be applied in actual classrooms

18. Vygotsky theory implies
A. child will learn best in the company of children having IQ lesser than his/her own
B. collaborative problem solving
C. individual assignments to each student
D. after initial explanation, do not support a child in solving difficult questions

19. Monika, a Maths teacher, asks Radhika a question. On not getting any answer from Radhika, she quickly moves on and asks Mohan another question. She rewords her question after realizing that Mohan is struggling to find the answer. This tendency of Monika reflects that she is
A. supporting gender stereotyping of roles by favouring Mohan
B. trying not to put Radhika in an embarrassing situation
C. well aware of the fact that Radhika is not capable of answering questions
D. slightly nervous about her question

20. Assessment for learning takes into account the following *except*
A. mistakes of students
B. learning styles of students
C. strengths of students
D. needs of students

21. One of the identical twin brothers is adopted by a socio-economically rich family and the other by a poor family. After one year, which one of the following may be most likely observed about their IQ scores?
A. Socio-economic level does not affect the IQ score
B. The boy with rich socio-economic family will score greater than the boy with poor family
C. Both of them will score equally
D. The boy with poor family will score greater than the boy with rich socio-economic family

22. Which one of the following is an example of a fine motor skill?
A. Climbing
B. Hopping
C. Running
D. Writing

23. Which of the following characteristics is the hallmark of the problem-solving approach?
A. The problem is based on only one principle/topic
B. There is an implicit hint given in the problem statement
C. The problem is original
D. There is usually one approach for getting the right answer

24. Which of the following is true in relation to errors made by children?
A. Correcting every error would take too much time and be tiresome for a teacher
B. Errors can be corrected by children themselves, therefore a teacher should not immediately correct them
C. If a teacher is not able to correct all errors in the classroom it indicates that the system of teacher education has failed
D. A teacher should not notice every error otherwise syllabus will not be covered

25. In order to instil a positive environment in a primary class, a teacher should
A. narrate stories with positive endings
B. wish each child in the morning
C. not discriminate and set the same goal for every child
D. allow them to make groups on their own on the basis of sociometry during group activities

26. While selecting material for the portfolio of students ________ of ________ should be there.
A. inclusion; parents
B. exclusion; students
C. inclusion; other teachers
D. inclusion; students

27. Which would be the best first theme to start with in a nursery class?
A. My best friend
B. My neighbourhood
C. My school
D. My family

28. Learners who demonstrate an earnest desire for increased knowledge and academic competence are said to have a
A. Work-avoidance orientation
B. Mastery orientation
C. Performance-approach orientation
D. Performance-avoidance orientation

29. A teacher can make problem-solving fun for students by doing all the following *except*
A. providing open ended material
B. giving time for free play
C. providing endless opportunities for creative thinking
D. expecting perfection from the students while they are trying to do things by themselves

30. Of the following, the greatest advantage of interdisciplinary instruction is that
A. teachers are less likely to feel overwhelmed by the multiplicity of topics needed to be addressed in a traditional curriculum
B. students are less likely to develop a dislike for particular topics of different subject areas
C. teachers are permitted greater flexibility in planning lessons and activities
D. students are given opportunities to generalize and apply newly learned knowledge in multiple contexts

PART- II

Mathematics

Directions : ***Answer the following questions by selecting the most appropriate option.***

31. A child of Class III reads 482 as four hundred eighty two but writes it as 40082. What does this indicate for a teacher?
A. Teacher should teach the concept of place value when the children are able to write numbers correctly
B. Child is not attentive in the class and is a careless listener
C. Child is a careful listener but has not established sense of place value
D. Child is confusing the expression of number in expanded form and in short form

32. Shailja can express a number in different ways. For example 4 = 2 + 2 or 4 = 1 + 3 etc. In which developmental phase of numbers is she?
A. Operating phase
B. Quantifying phase
C. Partitioning phase
D. Factoring phase

33. Floor of a square room of side 10 metres is to be completely covered with square tiles, each having length 50 centimetres. The smallest number of tiles needed is
A. 500 B. 200
C. 300 D. 400

34. One orange costs two and a half rupees. How much will three and a half dozen oranges cost?
A. ₹ 120 B. ₹ 90
C. ₹ 105 D. ₹ 112

35. A chocolate has 12 equal pieces. Manju gave one-fourth of it to Anju, one-third of it to Sujatha and one-sixth of it to Fiza. The number of pieces of chocolate left with Manju is
A. 4 B. 1
C. 2 D. 3

36. What should be added to the product 140×101 to get 14414?
A. 364 B. 264
C. 274 D. 278

37. The perimeter of two squares is 12 cm and 24 cm. The area of the bigger square is how many times that of the smaller?
A. 5 times B. 2 times
C. 3 times D. 4 times

38. The sum of all the factors of 100 is
A. 223 B. 115
C. 216 D. 217

39. (Smallest common multiple of 12 and 16) × (Smallest common multiple of 10 and 15) is equal to
A. 480 B. 960
C. 720 D. 1440

40. The sum of place values of 2 in 2424 is
A. 2020 B. 4
C. 220 D. 2002

41. To introduce subtraction of two-digit numbers in Class III, a teacher proceeded in the following steps:
Step I : Revision of two-digit numbers with understanding of place value system.
Step II : Use of tally marks to show that smaller number can be subtracted from larger number.
Step III : Application of subtraction on numbers under each column of place value.
In this case teacher is developing the lesson
A. from system concept → algorithm → operation
B. from system concept → operation → algorithm
C. from operation → system concept → algorithm
D. from algorithm → system concept → operation

42. Students are asked to establish a relation between vertically opposite angles. They draw various figures, measure the angles and observe that vertically opposite angles are equal.

In this case, students according to Van Hiele thought are at

A. Deduction level
B. Visualization level
C. Analytic level
D. Informal Deduction level

43. Rubrics of assessment for the geometry lesson on points and lines in Class IV shall be

A. can differentiate between line, ray and line segment and can define them
B. can differentiate between line and line segment, can mark a point, can draw a line segment of given length accurately
C. can measure the line in cms and inches accurately, can name the line
D. can measure the line segment in cms and inches accurately and can mark end points of line segment

44. "Which two numbers when multiplied give the product 24?"
This question

A. helps the child to think metacognitively
B. is an open ended question as it has more than one answer
C. is a closed-ended question as it has definite number of answers
D. suggests general problem-solving strategy to the child so that he/she can answer correctly

45. In a class, a teacher asked the students to define a quadrilateral in different ways
– using sides, using angles, using diagonals etc.
The teacher's objective is to

A. help the students to solve all problems of quadrilateral based on definitions
B. help the students to explore various definitions
C. help the students to understand quadrilateral from different perspectives
D. help the students to memorize all definitions by heart

46. Uma was not able to understand the concept of odd and even numbers. In order to improve her understanding, the teacher took some 20 pebbles of different colours and asked her to pair them up and sort out the numbers from 1 to 20 for which pebbles get paired up or do not get paired up. Uma

A. needs personal attention
B. is a visual learner
C. is a kinesthetic learner
D. is an auditory learner

47.

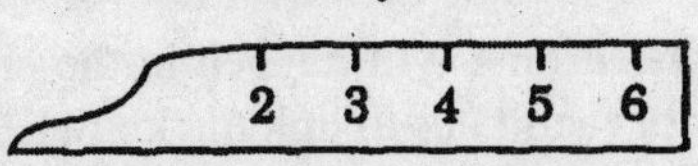

Pradeep was shown a broken ruler and asked, where is 5 cm on the ruler. He picked up the ruler and pointed at the mark of 5 cm on the ruler. His answer

A. is reflecting that he has the misconception that 5 cm refers to a point and not a length
B. is correct as he rightly pointed out the mark of 5 cm on the ruler
C. is incorrect as he is showing a point only and not the distance between two points marked as 0 and 5
D. is incorrect as the ruler is broken and he must start with 2 and should point at 7 as the desired mark

48. Higher Order Thinking Skills (HOTS) based questions demand the

A. knowledge and some degree of cognitive efforts
B. knowledge of facts, rules, formulae
C. knowledge of algorithm
D. knowledge of symbols and diagrams

49. Classroom discussion was initiated in Class V on 'Sale' in festival season, during topic of 'Percentage'. This type of discussion in classroom

A. starts heated arguments in class and spoils the atmosphere of the class
B. helps the students to listen to each other's opinion and encourages them to present their argument
C. must be avoided as it raises the noise level of class and disturbs others
D. helps the students to enhance their debating skills

50. Most appropriate formative task to assess the students' understanding of data analysis is

A. Survey-based Project
B. Quiz
C. Role play
D. Crossword

51. Piaget believed that learning results from social instruction and a mathematics teacher believing in Piaget's theory shall use

A. chalk and talk method
B. lots of manipulatives and lab activities in the class
C. group project and group discussion
D. differentiated instruction

52. In the figure, side of each square is 1 cm. The area, in square cm of the shaded part is

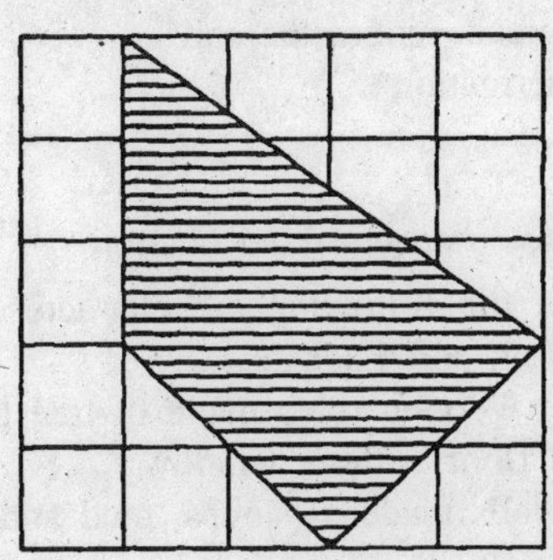

A. 11
B. 8
C. 9
D. 10

53. Internal length, breadth and height of a rectangular box are 10 cm, 8 cm and 6 cm respectively. How many boxes are needed to pack 6240 centimetre cubes?
A. 17 B. 12
C. 13 D. 15

54. When 121012 is divided by 12, the remainder is
A. 4 B. 0
C. 2 D. 3

55. Number of hours and minutes from 6 : 14 a.m. to 8 : 02 p.m. on the same day is
A. 14 hours and 16 minutes
B. 2 hours and 12 minutes
C. 12 hours and 16 minutes
D. 13 hours and 48 minutes

56. Which one of the following is ***not*** correct?
A. 3 litres 30 millilitres = 330 millilitres
B. 1 paisa = ₹ 0.01
C. one and a half dozen = 18
D. 1 millimetre = 0.1 centimetre

57. How many $\frac{1}{6}$ are there in $\frac{2}{3}$?
A. 6 B. 2
C. 3 D. 4

58. The number of degrees in four and one-third right angles is
A. 405 B. 390
C. 395 D. 400

59. Hamida always allow her students to observe the number pattern and to form conjectures on their own in order to enhance their mathematical abilities. She wrote the following problems on board and asked the students to write the answers:
21 ÷ 7 =
2.1 ÷ 0.7 =
0.21 ÷ 0.07 =
0.021 ÷ 0.007 =
Through the set of questions, she wants the students to observe that
A. if both the divisor and the dividend are decreased by power of 10, the quotient is also decreased by the power of 10
B. as one factor is divided by 10 and the other is multiplied by 10, the product remains same
C. as one divisor is decreased by 10 and the other is increased by power of 10, the product remains same
D. if both the divisor and the dividend are increased or decreased by power of 10, the quotient remains the same

60. The students of Class V were able to attempt the problem $\frac{1}{2} \div \frac{1}{3}$ correctly, but not able to solve the problem. "How many $\frac{1}{3}$ cake pieces are there in half a cake?". The reason is
A. students are not able to understand the mathematical equivalence of the two problems
B. students' language development is poor
C. problem is of higher difficulty level for Class V
D. operations on fractions are taught without contextualisation and language support

PART- III

Environmental Studies

Directions: *Answer the following questions by selecting the* ***most appropriate*** *option.*

61. Growing the same crop over and over and using so many chemicals makes the soil
A. fit for irrigation
B. fertile
C. barren
D. useful for a special kind of crop

62. Select from the following the characteristics of the houses of Leh and Ladakh:
1. Slanting wooden roofs made of tree trunks
2. Ground floor without window
3. Thick walls made of stones, mud and lime
4. Wooden floors

A. 1, 2, 4 B. 1, 2, 3
C. 2, 3, 4 D. 3, 4, 1

63. The group called Tarun Bharat Sangh is associated with
A. running free coaching classes for the children belonging to EWS
B. rebuilding old lakes
C. helping specially abled children in learning
D. providing cooked mid-day meal in schools

64. Environmental factors that shape the development of a child include all of the following *except*
A. quality of nutrition B. physique
C. culture D. quality of education

65. An effective teaching-learning will happen in the class when a teacher helps or facilitates to link the knowledge a student has with the new concept to be taught. The objective behind this is to promote
A. reinforcement

B. correlation and transfer of knowledge
C. individual differences
D. learner autonomy

66. A Science Exhibition was organised in Rohan's school. It was organised with an objective. Which in your view is the most appropriate objective?
A. Satisfy the parents
B. Train students for various professions
C. Provide a creative channel for learners
D. Establish a name for the school

67. Select the correct statement about bronze which was used in making big guns (cannons) found in the fort of Golconda.
A. Bronze is an alloy of copper and platinum
B. Bronze is an element
C. Bronze is an alloy of copper and zinc
D. Bronze is an alloy of copper and tin

68. A portion of railway time-table for the route of an express train is given below :

S. No.	Station Name	Arrival Time	Departure Time	Distance (km)	Day
4	Surat	16.15	16.20	530	1
5	Valsad	17.23	17.25	598	1
6	Bhiwandi Road	21.10	21.20	772	1
7	Madgaon	7.35	7.45	1509	2

As per above information the distance between Surat and Madgaon and the time taken to cover this distance by the train, respectively are
A. 1509 km; 15 hours 30 minutes
B. 979 km; 15 hours 15 minutes
C. 979 km; 15 hours 20 minutes
D. 1509 km; 15 hours 25 minutes

69. While doing experiments and practical work, Shyama's performance is the best in her class. She is considered a very creative person. So, she is learning a concept by
A. modelling
B. imitation
C. convergent thinking
D. divergent thinking

70. Al-Biruni came from a country now called
A. Oman B. Afghanistan
C. Bangladesh D. Uzbekistan

71. 'Nepenthes' is a plant which traps and eats frogs, insects and even mice. In our country this plant is found in
A. Odisha B. Arunachal Pradesh
C. Meghalaya D. Assam

72. Select the one which is different from the others
A. Coal B. Petrol
C. Paraffin wax D. Grease

73. In the villages of Bihar-many farmers do bee-keeping and collect honey to earn extra money. The best time to start bee-keeping is
A. October to December B. January to March
C. April to June D. July to September

74. Sarita's teacher engages her in a number of group activities such as group discussions, group projects, etc. Which learning dimension is her teacher following?
A. Learning as a social activity
B. Learning through recreation
C. Language guided learning
D. Competition based learning

75. A public school has about two to three children with special needs in every class. Some children are physically or mentally challenged. These children study with other children while sitting in the same class. The public school mentioned above follows which of the following?
A. Compensatory learning
B. CCE
C. Inclusive education
D. Peer education

76. One Pashmina shawl is as warm as ________ normal sweaters and ________ hours are taken to weave a plain Pashmina shawl.
A. 10; 250 B. 10; 200
C. 06; 250 D. 06; 200

77. While discussing about friction, a teacher gave a number of examples to explain the concept. Some of the examples where friction is useful in our day-to-day life as quoted by the teacher are given below:
1. We are able to write because of friction between the tip of the pen and the paper.
2. We are able to walk because of friction between our feet and the ground.
3. A ball thrown vertically upwards comes back to us due to friction.
4. We are able to stop a moving vehicle by applying brakes because of friction.
The correct examples were
A. 4, 1 and 2 B. 1, 2 and 3
C. 2, 3 and 4 D. 3, 4 and 1

78. Exercises and activities in an EVS textbook should be provided
A. at different places in the book
B. at the end of the unit
C. at the end of the chapter
D. inbuilt in the topics

79. EVS teacher should
A. accept and respect views of parents
B. focus exclusively on experiments
C. focus exclusively on books and tests
D. accept and respect perception of children

80. The best way to assess a child at primary level is to use
A. Summative assignments
B. Portfolios
C. Periodic tests
D. Home assignments

81. A teacher uses audio-visual aids and physical activities in her teaching because they
A. provide relief to the teacher
B. facilitate effective assessment
C. provide a diversion to learners
D. utilize maximum number of senses to enhance learning

82. The use of poems and story-telling to explain concepts in an EVS class helps to
A. promote the ability to imagine and explore the nature of the world at the local and global level
B. take care of the language and cultural diversity among learners
C. channelize the energies of the students in the right direction
D. make the lesson enjoyable and interesting

83. In co-operative learning, older and more proficient students assist younger and lesser skilled students. This leads to
A. intense competition
B. higher achievement and self-esteem
C. higher moral development
D. conflict between the groups

84. Seema learns every lesson quickly by rote method, whereas Leena understands each lesson after discussion and brainstorming. It denotes the developmental principle of
A. continuity
B. inter-relationships
C. individual differences
D. general to specific

85. The following are the methods to teach EVS *except*
A. Guided enquiry
B. Explaining through lectures
C. Problem-solving
D. Cooperative learning

86. Dyslexia is associated mainly with difficulties in
A. reading B. hearing
C. speaking D. speaking and hearing

87. Select the correct statements about snakes:
1. Only four types of poisonous snakes are found in our country.
2. Cobra is a poisonous variety of snakes.
3. A poisonous snake has four hollow teeth (fangs) through which the poison enters the body of a person when the snake bites.
4. Medicine for snake bites is made from the snake's poison.

A. 2, 1 and 3 B. 1, 2 and 4
C. 2, 3 and 4 D. 3, 4 and 1

88. Select the correct characteristics of petroleum from the following:
A. dense and dark fluid without smell
B. smelly, thick, dark coloured oil
C. smelly, thin, pale liquid
D. pleasant smelling, thin, blue coloured liquid

89. Select from the following a group of diseases caused by mosquitoes:
A. Malaria, Cholera, Typhoid
B. Malaria, Dengue, Cholera
C. Malaria, Chikungunya, Typhoid
D. Dengue, Malaria, Chikungunya

90. For making Madhubani paintings the artists use
A. coloured paste of powdered rice
B. specially made poster colours
C. fibre paints of very good quality
D. paints made by dissolving silver and gold

PART- IV

Language-I : English

Directions : *Answer the following questions by selecting the **most appropriate** option.*

91. Which is a function word?
A. someone B. however
C. booking D. principal

92. *Strut, stride* and *trudge* are words that describe a manner of
A. walking B. galloping
C. running D. riding

93. Decorum in spoken language pertains to
A. appropriate gestures
B. correct grammatical usage
C. voice quality or loudness
D. clarity and purity of style

94. "You ask, what is our aim? I can answer in one word : Victory". Churchill asks a question and then goes on to answer it. Such a question is
A. stylised B. a prompt
C. explanatory D. rhetorical

95. A fellow traveller at the airport has just finished reading the newspaper and you want him/her to pass it to you. Choose how you will make the request.
A. Could you possibly pass me the newspaper?
B. Pass me the paper.
C. Pass me the paper, please.
D. Can you pass me the paper?

96. Read this exchange.
Teacher : Do you like to read a storybook instead?
Student : Yes.
Teacher : Yes, please.
Here the teacher
A. makes a polite suggestion to start reading
B. confirms the student's request
C. offers an alternative language activity
D. relates language function with politeness

97. *Speaker 1:* Where are you from?
Speaker 2 : Kashmir.
During the assessment of students' speaking-listening skills, mark/s would be deducted during this exchange for
A. the first speaker
B. the second speaker
C. both
D. neither

98. While writing, one of the cohesive devices used is
A. preposition B. phrase
C. ellipsis D. adjective

99. If the piece of writing is brief, complete, in the third person, without digressions and emotional overtones and logically arranged, it is a
A. newspaper article
B. classified advertisement
C. memorandum
D. report

100. Use of the medium of motion pictures offers a/an ________ experience for the student.
A. vicarious B. abstract
C. indirect D. concrete

101. According to the recommendations of NCF 2005, technology could be integrated
A. used only judiciously subject to the economic and social goals of a community
B. with the larger goals and processes of educational programmes
C. with revisions to meet current development policies of the Central Government
D. as an add-on to the main educational goals

102. *The documents have been downloaded by the students. The students have downloaded the documents.*
The two given statements can be differentiated by drawing students' attention to the
A. change in the verb forms
B. use of 'by' in the passive form
C. differences in the arrangement of words
D. roles of the subject and object in both sentences

103. Which pair constitutes types of 'cognitive style'?
A. Field dependence/field independence
B. Individual/team work
C. Project oriented/paper-pencil activity
D. Grammatical accuracy/fluency

104. The process of word formation consists of
A. using synonyms or euphemisms
B. compounding and conversion
C. conversion and meaning
D. spelling and compounding

105. When reading, to 'decode' means to
A. replace long words with symbols
B. make notes
C. read superficially for the general meaning
D. recognize words to understand their meanings

Directions: *Read the given poem and answer the questions that follow (Q. No. 106 to 111) by selecting the* ***most appropriate*** *option.*

Human Nature

Is it human nature
to desire forbidden fruit
to hunger for a blossom
so obsessed with passion
that we forget the pain,
which inevitably arises
once we tease ourselves
with the thought of it
or taste a tiny part of it,
and it becomes the predator
eating at us like a carnivore
that saves the head for last
savouring the brain to feed its own
and we, still craving illicit nectar
enjoying the fact that it is devouring us?

—***C.J. Grant***

106. Another word in the poem that suggests '*forbidden*' is
A. illicit B. obsess
C. crave D. savour

107. "It becomes the predator" means
A. being strong and positive against any threat
B. strong emotions influence one negatively
C. pursuit of happiness
D. being cautious against outside influences

108. An example of personification in the poem is
A. like a carnivore
B. saves the head
C. tease ourselves
D. illicit nectar

109. "Eating at us like a carnivore" refers to
A. exerting a strong influence
B. being attacked by a wild beast
C. being attacked by a human enemy
D. being eaten up by an unknown entity

110. "We, still craving illicit nectar" can be explained by focusing on the word
A. nectar B. we
C. craving D. illicit

111. A synonym for the word 'savouring' is
A. avoiding B. smelling
C. flavouring D. experiencing

Directions: *Read the given passage and answer the questions that follow (Q. No. 112 to 120) by selecting the* ***most appropriate*** *option.*

The day the cat was killed, Maddy watched her mother wind that old clock with her same little smile, cranking the gold key into its funny little hole, as grandma wandered around the dining table in her dressing gown while her nurse read a pulp fiction on the front step, while her brothers scraped their forks against the table and dripped the last bits of potatoes and corn from their open, awful mouths, that clock sat heavy on the white carpet, at the end of the hall, mom humming along to that terrible ticking. It made Maddy's teeth clench. Truly, there was no point to these silly, endless family dinners. Always being six o'clock sharp and never over until that clock was wound, thirteen years of her life wasted for this nonsense so far, burnt up in boredom, when all the while she had some very important matters to attend to back in her bedroom.

The long-case clock had been left by the previous owner, or maybe the one before that, no one was sure. Cloaked in pine wood and always counting, no birds printed around the clock face, no farm scenes or flowers, just black numbers and wiry hands and that was that. Then near the bottom, a long silver pendulum behind a square of smokey glass. It was too heavy to tip, too tall to place anything on top, old and faded and always suspect. Her brothers avoided it at night and the cat avoided it entirely (or used to). The clock face glowing round and white, over the wooden suit, like a pale faced ghost or a porcelain reaper, feetless and shadows for arms. And mom would sing along with the pendulum while the boys knocked over the kitchen chairs wrestling and playing tag, and grandmother would nap by the television and the nurse would paint her nails. All the time, her mom would smile and hum.

112. The use of the word 'cranking' conveys the meaning that
A. gold was not a suitable metal for a clock key
B. the key did not fit the lock properly
C. the clock doesn't work
D. the key was used with irritation on the mother's part

113. The siblings were 'awful mouths' is the following figure of speech :
A. Epigram
B. Comparison
C. Oxymoron
D. Transferred epithet

114. "Truly, there was no point to these silly, endless family dinners." The correct transformation would be
A. The subject was pre-occupied with some personal work and was impatient with others at the dinner table.
B. The subject found her siblings mentally unstable and took long to finish dinner.
C. Her mother forced her to sit through a lengthy dinner ritual.
D. The food could only appeal to the youngsters, not a teenager.

115. The tone of the story is
A. autobiographical
B. biographical
C. narrative
D. reflective

116. The clock was 'always suspect'. The subject thought
A. it had one hand missing
B. that it wasn't working at all
C. it tended to move slowly
D. it broke down periodically

117. "The clock face was glowing round and white." This observation is further enhanced by the observation that it was like
A. ceramic B. gold
C. radium D. silver

118. "It made Maddy's teeth clench." The idiom 'to clench one's teeth' can be introduced in an EBL class by
A. giving a worksheet where students use the idiom in a number of situations
B. giving a detailed meaning of the expression
C. giving other similar idioms and asking children to guess the meanings in context
D. guiding students to find other 'teeth' idioms on their own by looking up the word 'idioms'

119. The word ________ in the story means 'incline'. [para 2]
A. drip B. hum
C. sharp D. tip

120. "All the time, her mom would smile and hum." This suggests that Maddy
A. thought that her mother didn't care about her family
B. admired her mother's calm
C. thought her mother was indifferent to time
D. was convinced her mother was more attuned to the mechanical working of the clock — not the time

PART- V

भाषा-II : हिन्दी

निर्देश : *निम्नलिखित प्रश्नों के उत्तर देने के लिए **सबसे उचित** विकल्प चुनिए।*

121. भाषा का प्राथमिक रूप है

A. सांकेतिक B. व्याकरणिक
C. लिखित D. मौखिक

122. 'गणित, विज्ञान, सामाजिक विज्ञान की कक्षाएँ एक तरह से भाषा की ही कक्षाएँ हैं।' इस कथन के समर्थन में कौन-सा तर्क सबसे कमजोर है?

A. विभिन्न विषयों के शिक्षण में भाषा-शिक्षण एक मुख्य उद्देश्य होता है
B. विभिन्न विषयों की अवधारणात्मक समझ की अभिव्यक्ति भी भाषा-विशेष में होती है
C. विभिन्न विषयों की अवधारणाएँ किसी भाषा-विशेष में बनती हैं
D. विभिन्न विषयों के अध्ययन-अध्यापन में भाषा साधन का कार्य करती है

123. तमिल भाषी सुहेल प्रायः 'भजन', को 'बजन' कहता है। भाषा के शिक्षक के रूप में आप क्या करेंगे?

A. सुहेल को उसकी त्रुटि के लिए डाँटेंगे
B. तमिल और हिन्दी भाषा का तुलनात्मक अध्ययन करते हुए महाप्राण ध्वनियों से युक्त भाषिक सामग्री का प्रयोग करेंगे
C. सुहेल को बताएँगे कि सही शब्द 'भजन' है
D. 'भजन' शब्द का बार-बार उच्चारण करवाएँगे

124. कहानियाँ बच्चों के भाषा-विकास में किस प्रकार सहायक हैं?

A. ये भाषिक नियम ही सिखाती हैं
B. बच्चों के खाली समय का सदुपयोग करने में मदद करती हैं
C. ये पाठ्य-पुस्तक का सबसे महत्वपूर्ण हिस्सा है
D. ये बच्चों की कल्पनाशक्ति, सृजनात्मकता और चिंतन को बढ़ावा देती हैं

125. हिन्दी भाषा की पाठ्य-पुस्तक में लोकगीतों को शामिल करने का कौन-सा उद्देश्य सबसे कम महत्वपूर्ण है?

A. लोकगीतों से संबद्ध राज्यों की जानकारी देना
B. लोकगीतों की रसानुभूति
C. लोकगीतों के माध्यम से भारत की सांस्कृतिक विशेषताओं से परिचित कराना
D. लोकगीतों की भाषिक विशेषताओं से परिचित होने का अवसर मुहैया कराना

126. भाषा की कक्षा में कौन-सी शिक्षण-युक्ति सबसे कम प्रभावी है?

A. उचित गति एवं प्रवाह के साथ पढ़ने पर बल देना
B. शुद्ध उच्चारण पर अत्यधिक बल देना
C. बच्चों की रुचि के अनुसार परिचित विषय या प्रसंग पर चर्चा
D. दूसरों की हस्तलिखित सामग्री, पत्र आदि पढ़वाना

127. लेखन-कुशलता का विकास करने में सबसे कम महत्वपूर्ण है

A. प्रतिलिपि
B. अधूरी कहानी को पूरा करना
C. कहानी-कविता आदि का सृजनात्मक लेखन
D. आँखों-देखी घटनाओं को लिखना

128. निम्नलिखित में से किस उद्देश्य के लिए प्राथमिक स्तर पर भाषा **नहीं** सीखी जाती?

A. जीवन की विभिन्न स्थितियों को साधना
B. भाषा का व्याकरण सीखना
C. मन की बात कहना-सुनना
D. अपनी अनेक जरूरतों को पूरा करना

129. भाषा की प्रकृति के सम्बन्ध में कौन-सा कथन उचित ***नहीं*** है?

A. भाषा कठोरता से व्याकरणिक नियमों का अनुसरण करती है
B. भाषाएँ एक-दूसरे के सान्निध्य में फलती-फूलती हैं
C. भाषा एक नियमबद्ध व्यवस्था है
D. भाषा का जितना अधिक प्रयोग किया जाएगा, उतना ही भाषा पर पकड़ मजबूत होती जाएगी

130. प्राथमिक स्तर पर आप कहानियों, कविताओं में किस पक्ष को सबसे ज्यादा महत्वपूर्ण मानते हैं?

A. प्रत्यक्ष उपदेशात्मकता
B. कहानियों, कविताओं का व्याकरणिक नियमों की जानकारी की दृष्टि से समृद्ध होना
C. घटनाओं, शहरों, पदों में दोहराव
D. प्रतिष्ठित लेखकों की कहानियाँ, कविताएँ बच्चों को पढ़ाई जाएँ

131. बहुभाषिक कक्षा के संदर्भ में आप इनमें से किस गतिविधि को सर्वाधिक उचित समझते हैं?

A. 'स्वतंत्र' शब्द को दस बार बोलिए।
B. 'सूर्य अस्त हो गया।' वाक्य को 10 बार लिखिए।
C. हिन्दी पाठों में आए 'चिड़िया', 'पुस्तक', 'कुआँ' को आपकी भाषा में क्या कहते हैं? बताइए।
D. 'लड्डू', 'खत' शब्दों के हिन्दी रूप कंठस्थ कीजिए।

132. हिन्दी भाषा के सतत और व्यापक मूल्यांकन के संदर्भ में कौन-सा कथन उचित ***नहीं*** है?

A. यह बच्चे के संदर्भ में ही मूल्यांकन करता है
B. यह बच्चों को उत्तीर्ण-अनुत्तीर्ण श्रेणियों में विभाजित करने में विश्वास रखता है
C. सतत और व्यापक मूल्यांकन बच्चों की सीखने की क्षमता और तरीके के बारे में जानकारी देता है
D. यह बताता है कि बच्चों को किस तरह की मदद की जरूरत है

133. कलिका हिन्दी भाषा में बोलते समय कई बार अटकती है। आप क्या करेंगे?
A. उसे प्रवाहपूर्ण अभिव्यक्ति के नमूने सुनाएँगे और कहेंगे कि उसे भी हू-ब-हू ऐसे ही बोलना है
B. कक्षा के बाकी बच्चों से कहेंगे कि कलिका के समक्ष प्रवाहपूर्ण अभिव्यक्ति के नमूने प्रस्तुत करें
C. कक्षा में केवल कलिका को ही बार-बार बोलने के लिए कहेंगे
D. धैर्य रखते हुए उसे सहज अभिव्यक्ति के लिए प्रोत्साहित करेंगे

134. बच्चों की पठन-कुशलता का विकास करने में सर्वाधिक महत्वपूर्ण है
A. भाषिक संरचनाओं का अभ्यास
B. अर्थ की अपेक्षा उच्चारणगत शुद्धता पर विशेष ध्यान देना
C. विभिन्न संदर्भों से जुड़ी सामग्री
D. पाठ्य-पुस्तक में दिए गए अभ्यास

135. भाषा-अर्जन के संबंध में कौन-सा कथन उचित ***नहीं*** है?
A. भाषा के नियम सीखे जाते हैं
B. परिवेश से प्राप्त भाषिक आँकड़ों के आधार पर सहज रूप से भाषिक नियम बनाए जाते हैं
C. भाषा-अर्जन में भाषिक परिवेश महत्वपूर्ण होता है
D. इसमें समाज-सांस्कृतिक विशेषताओं को सहज रूप से आत्मसात् किया जाता है

निर्देशः *गद्यांश को पढ़कर निम्नलिखित प्रश्नों (प्र. सं. 136 से 142)* ***में सबसे उचित*** *विकल्प चुनिए।*

कुछ कहा जा रहा हो उससे कहीं महत्वपूर्ण होता है अपनी बात कहने का तरीका। आप कितनी ही जरूरी बात क्यों न कहें, अगर आपकी बात कोई सुने नहीं, महसूस ही न करे, तो उसे कहने का फायदा ही क्या? किसी के कहे को सुनने के लिए, उसे महसूस करने के लिए, पूरा ध्यान केंद्रित करने की जरूरत होती है और वही मिलता था मुझे उस महान संगीतज्ञ बीथोवन के स्वरों द्वारा—पूरा ध्यान। आप पूछ सकते हैं कि "आवाजाही और बातचीत के शोर से भरे किसी कमरे के दूसरे छोर पर बैठा कोई बच्चा उन आठ कोमल स्वरों को भला कैसे सुनता होगा?" इस सवाल का जवाब तो कोई भी शिक्षक दे सकता है। ये स्वर तो वे बच्चे ही सुन पाते थे जो पियानो के बिलकुल पास खड़े हों, और तब उनका स्पर्श दूसरों को आगाह करता था। पर कुछ ही क्षणों में तेजी से फैलती वह खामोशी ही बोलने लगती थी और जब तक आखिरी स्वर की गूंज खत्म होती, सभी बच्चे शांत हो चुके होते थे। वे खामोशियाँ, वे सन्नाटे याद रहेंगे मुझे... सात क्या उसके भी कई-कई सालों बाद भी।

136. लेखिका के अनुसार अपनी बात कहने के संदर्भ में सबसे महत्वपूर्ण क्या है?
A. ध्यान केंद्रित करने के लिए आवाजों का प्रयोग करना
B. सवाल का जवाब देना
C. जो कुछ कहा जा रहा है
D. बात कहने का तरीका

137. संवाद तभी सार्थक होता है जब
A. मधुर आवाज
B. शांत माहौल
C. जरूरी बात कहना
D. कहने-सुनने वाले सक्रिय हों

138. 'खामोशी ही बोलने लगती है', से अभिप्राय है
A. खामोशी तेज आवाज में बोलती है
B. खामोश बच्चे बोलने लगते हैं
C. जब कुछ बच्चे धीरे-धीरे बोलना बंद कर देते हैं तो बाकी बच्चों को पता चल जाता है कि उन्हें भी शांत होना है
D. खामोशी बच्चों से कहती है कि चुप हो जाओ

139. लेखिका के अनुसार
A. एक शिक्षक अपने बच्चों को बहुत अच्छी तरह जानता है
B. बच्चों को शांत करने के लिए संगीत का ही प्रयोग करना चाहिए
C. बच्चे बहुत शोर करते हैं
D. बच्चे बहुत बोलते हैं

140. 'महत्वपूर्ण' शब्द है
A. विकारी
B. यौगिक
C. रूढ़
D. योगरूढ़

141. निम्नलिखित में से कौन-सा शब्द स्त्रीलिंग है?
A. जवाब
B. सवाल
C. पियानो
D. बातचीत

142. 'इस सवाल का जवाब तो कोई भी शिक्षक दे सकता है।'
A. निपात
B. संबंधबोधक
C. क्रिया-विशेषण
D. सर्वनाम

निर्देशः *गद्यांश को पढ़कर निम्नलिखित प्रश्नों (प्र.सं. 143 से 150)* ***में सबसे उचित*** *विकल्प चुनिए।*

जहाँ तक मैं समझता हूँ, मेरी आत्मिक शक्तियों के विकास में बार्सीलोना और उसके निवासियों का सबसे सुंदर चित्रण भी सहायक नहीं हो सकता था। स्योम्का और फेद्का को पीटर्सबर्ग के जलमार्गों को जानने की क्या जरूरत है, अगर जैसी कि संभावना है, वे वहाँ कभी नहीं जा पाएँगे? अगर स्योम्का का वहाँ कभी जाना होगा भी, तो उसे इससे कोई फर्क नहीं पड़ेगा कि उसने यह स्कूल में पढ़ा था या नहीं, क्योंकि तब इन जलमार्गों को वह व्यवहार में जान ही जाएगा और अच्छी तरह जान जाएगा। मैं नहीं समझ सकता कि उसकी आत्मिक शक्तियों के विकास में इस बात की जानकारी से कोई मदद मिल सकती है कि वोल्गा में सन से लदे जहाज नीचे की ओर जाते हैं और अलकतरे से लदे जहाज ऊपर की ओर; कि दुबोव्का नाम का एक बंदरगाह है; कि फलाँ भूमिगत परत फलाँ जगह तक जाती है; कि सामोयेद लोग बारहसिंगा गाड़ियों पर सफर करते हैं, वगैरह-वगैरह।

143. स्योम्का और फेद्का हैं
A. विद्यार्थियों के नाम
B. कर्मचारियों के नाम
C. शहरों के नाम
D. शिक्षकों के नाम

144. लेखक के अनुसार वह पढ़ाई निरर्थक है
A. जो बंदरगाहों के बारे में न बताए
B. जिसका उपयोग बच्चे अपने रोजमर्रा के जीवन में न करते हों
C. जिसमें जलमार्गों के बारे में नहीं पढ़ाया जाता
D. जानकारी नहीं दी जाती

145. बच्चे ढेर सारी जानकारी हासिल करके
A. आत्मिक विकास नहीं कर सकते
B. कक्षा में अव्वल आ सकते हैं
C. बहुत कुछ सीख सकते हैं
D. विद्वान् बन सकते हैं

146. बच्चे बहुत कुछ स्वतः ही तभी सीख जाते हैं जब
A. माता-पिता बताते हैं
B. वे किताब में पढ़ते-देखते हैं
C. शिक्षक उन्हें सिखाते हैं
D. वे चीजों को व्यवहार में लाते हैं

147. व्यावहारिक जीवन में उपयोग में न आने वाली बातों को जानने या न जानने से फर्क नहीं पड़ता, क्योंकि
A. बाद में शिक्षक बता ही देंगे
B. बच्चे कुशाग्रबुद्धि होते हैं
C. ये बातें व्यावहारिक जीवन को प्रभावित नहीं करतीं
D. बच्चे अभी इन बातों का उपयोग करने योग्य नहीं हैं

148. 'निवासी' का बहुवचन रूप है
A. निवासिएँ B. निवासों
C. निवासियों D. निवासी

149. निम्नलिखित में से कौन-सा 'चित्रण' के लिए उपयुक्त विशेष ***नहीं*** है?
A. मनोहारी B. सौंदर्य
C. कलात्मक D. सुंदर

150. 'फर्क' का समानार्थी है
A. अंतर B. हानि
C. प्रभावकारी D. असरदार

Answers

1	2	3	4	5	6	7	8	9	10
A	A	A	D	D	D	C	C	B	D
11	**12**	**13**	**14**	**15**	**16**	**17**	**18**	**19**	**20**
C	C	B	D	C	B	B	B	A	D
21	**22**	**23**	**24**	**25**	**26**	**27**	**28**	**29**	**30**
A	D	B	C	C	D	D	C	D	D
31	**32**	**33**	**34**	**35**	**36**	**37**	**38**	**39**	**40**
C	C	D	C	D	C	D	D	D	A
41	**42**	**43**	**44**	**45**	**46**	**47**	**48**	**49**	**50**
A	C	B	B	C	A	B	A	B	A
51	**52**	**53**	**54**	**55**	**56**	**57**	**58**	**59**	**60**
C	C	C	A	D	A	D	B	D	D
61	**62**	**63**	**64**	**65**	**66**	**67**	**68**	**69**	**70**
C	C	B	B	B	C	C	B	D	D
71	**72**	**73**	**74**	**75**	**76**	**77**	**78**	**79**	**80**
C	A	A	A	C	C	A	D	B	B
81	**82**	**83**	**84**	**85**	**86**	**87**	**88**	**89**	**90**
D	A	B	C	B	A	A	B	D	A
91	**92**	**93**	**94**	**95**	**96**	**97**	**98**	**99**	**100**
B	A	A	D	A	D	B	C	D	D
101	**102**	**103**	**104**	**105**	**106**	**107**	**108**	**109**	**110**
B	D	A	B	C	A	B	D	C	D
111	**112**	**113**	**114**	**115**	**116**	**117**	**118**	**119**	**120**
C	C	C	A	C	B	D	A	B	D
121	**122**	**123**	**124**	**125**	**126**	**127**	**128**	**129**	**130**
A	A	B	D	A	D	A	B	A	C
131	**132**	**133**	**134**	**135**	**136**	**137**	**138**	**139**	**140**
C	B	D	C	A	D	D	C	A	B
141	**142**	**143**	**144**	**145**	**146**	**147**	**148**	**149**	**150**
D	A	A	B	A	D	C	C	B	A

Some Selected Explanatory Answers

1. The theory of multiple intelligences (MI) was developed by Howard Gardner, a professor of cognition and education at Harvard University. Introduced in his 1983 book, *Frames of Mind,* and refined in subsequent writings, the theory contends that human intelligence is not a single complex entity or a unified set of processes (the dominant view in the field of psychology). Instead, Gardner posits that there are several relatively autonomous intelligences, and that an individual's intellectual profile reflects a unique configuration of these intelligences.

Definition of Multiple Intelligence: In his 1999 formulation of MI theory, *Intelligence Reframed,* Gardner defines intelligence as "a biopsychological potential to process information that can be activated in a cultural setting to solve problems or create products that are of value in a culture." By considering intelligence a potential, Gardner asserts its emergent and responsive nature, thereby differentiating his theory from traditional ones in which human intelligence is fixed and innate. Whether a potential will be activated is dependent in large part on the values of the culture in which an individual grows up and the opportunities available in that culture, although Gardner also acknowledges the role of personal decisions made by individuals, their families, and others. These activating forces result in the development and expression of a range of abilities (or intelligences) from culture to culture and also from individual to individual.

Gardner's definition of intelligence is unique as well in that it considers the creation of products such as sculptures and computers to be as important an expression of intelligence as abstract problem solving. Traditional theories do not recognize created artifacts as a manifestation of intelligence, and therefore are limited in how they conceptualize and measure it.

Identified intelligences: As of 2001, Gardner has identified eight intelligences:

1. Linguistic intelligence, exemplified by writers and poets, describes the ability to perceive and generate spoken or written language.
2. Logical-mathematical intelligence, exemplified by mathematicians and computer programmers, involves the ability to appreciate and utilize numerical, abstract, and logical reasoning to solve problems.
3. Musical intelligence, exemplified by musicians and composers, entails the ability to create, communicate, and understand meanings made out of sound.
4. Spatial intelligence, exemplified by graphic designers and architects, refers to the ability to perceive, modify, transform, and create visual or spatial images.
5. Bodily-kinesthetic intelligence, exemplified by dancers and athletes, deals with the ability to use all or part of one's body to solve problems or to fashion products.
6. Naturalistic intelligence, exemplified by archaeologists and botanists, concerns the ability to distinguish, classify, and use features of the environment.
7. Interpersonal intelligence, exemplified by leaders and teachers, describes the ability to recognize, appreciate, and contend with the feelings, beliefs, and intentions of other people.
8. Intrapersonal intelligence, apparent when individuals pursue a particular interest, choose a field of study or work, or portray their life through different media, involves the ability to understand oneself including emotions, desires, strengths, and vulnerabilities and to use such information effectively in regulating one's own life.

Gardner does not claim this roster of intelligences to be exhaustive; MI theory is based wholly on empirical evidence, and the roster can therefore be revised with new empirical findings. In the MI framework, all intelligences are equally valid and important, and though significantly independent of one another, they do not operate in isolation. Human activity normally reflects the integrated functioning of several intelligences. An effective teacher, for example, relies on linguistic and interpersonal intelligences, and possesses knowledge of particular subject areas as well.

2. $\text{IQ} = \dfrac{\text{Mental Age}}{\text{Real Age}} \times 100 \Rightarrow 75 = \dfrac{\text{Mental Age}}{16} \times 100$

$\Rightarrow \text{Mental Age} = \dfrac{75 \times 16}{100} = 12$.

3. Motivation is "hypothetical construct used to explain the initiation, direction, intensity, and persistence of goal-directed behaviour." It is a force that energizes and directs behaviour toward a goal." It is a "directive, sustaining quality that energizes and maintains learning activities." Motivation is related to Learning Theory, and shares much common ground. But they are distinct emphases. *Learning Theory* focuses on the establishment and strengthening of new behaviours, attitudes and concepts. *Motivation* focuses on the energy, vitality, and intensity of learning, on the learner's own *intention* to learn. Learning Theory emphases the learning *what*, motivation the learning *why*. Where there is proper motivation for learning, there is better achievement, better student attitudes and fewer classroom problems.

The Nature of Motivation: Motivation can be general or specific. General motivation toward learning is an enduring and broad disposition to master variety of learning situations. It is the kind of motivation found, for example in the "industry" pole of Erikson's "Industry-Inferiority" stage of personality development. General motivation is stable over time and situation, and resides in the learner rather than the teacher or class.

Specific motivation energizes a student toward a particular learning situation. It is unstable, changing from class and even from topic to topic within a given class. Specific motivation resides primarily in the teacher and the particular content to be learned.

The Locus of Motivation: Motivation can be extrinsic or intrinsic. Extrinsic motivation is impersonal and is based on rewards that originate from outside the learner. Students achieve in order to win parents' approval, or to gain the praise of their teacher, or to earn high grades. Under an extrinsic system of motivation, learners are passive players. They engage in appropriate behaviour only when offered attractive incentives or to avoid aversive consequences. Excessive use of extrinsic motivation can make learners dependent on the rewards. When the rewards stop, so does the behaviour.

Intrinsic motivation is based on the personal satisfaction derived from achieving learning goals. Students achieve because of their own personal desire to learn. They enjoy the subject, or they are personally interested in mastering it. Intrinsic motivation depends on the learner being an active player in learning process. Such students engage in appropriate behaviour because they want to grow, and learn, and master their subjects. Both are important. Extrinsic motivation may be required to get students started in a new subject and to initially direct them down the right path. Students who do not enjoy learning for learning's sake, who are not interested in a given subject, or are disadvantaged in some tangible way may need the motivational boost of external rewards to initiate their learning. If successfully tied to the quality of students' performance, these rewards can actually raise the level of their intrinsic motivation.

Learning is complex—and *motivating* students to learn is complex as well, requiring a variety of motivational approaches. We will present motivation as a matter of reinforcing desired behaviour (traditional behaviourism), providing appropriate models for behaviour (social learning theory), creating a sense of curiosity (cognitive learning theory), making material meaningful (information processing theory), meeting personal needs (humanism), and encouraging achievement through successful experience (aspiration and achievement theories).

4. Phonemes are the smallest distinguishable units in a language. In the English language, many consonants, such as t, p, and m, correspond to single phonemes, while other consonants, such as c and g, can correspond to more than one phoneme. Vowels typically correspond to more than one phoneme. For example, o corresponds to different phonemes depending on whether it is pronounced as in bone or woman. Some phonemes correspond to combinations of consonants, such as ch, sh, and th.

5. IQ scores are moderately good at predicting academic performance. But on its basis alone it will be difficult to predict a specific persons academic performance because performance is an academic field also depends on personal characters such as one's sillingness to study.

6. Inclusive education is a pedagogical model which is based on the basic curriculum of psycho-social support to the disabled child, based on the ideas of an Italian doctor and pedagogue, Maria Montessori, and, even more, the Swiss pedagogue Adolpfe Ferriere and Edouard Claparede. According to them, schools should be completely adopted to the needs of the students, and not adopt students to schools. The main difference between the integrative and the inclusive pedagogical approach in educating developmentally disabled children is in the fact that, in the first case, the child is integrated into the existing, unchanged educational environment, while the inclusive model demands transformation, adoption of the environment to the educational possibilities and needs of each particular developmentally disabled child. This means that the inclusive approach starts from the opinion that schools are necessary to transform (curriculum, methods, teachers' education) so that the child with certain disabilities could successfully learn accompanied by their schoolmates.

9. A typical child in a classroom can either be a normal child with average capabilities or an exceptional or differently-abled one requiring more attention from the teacher.

An exceptional child is the one whose performance deviates from the norm, either below or above, to such an extent that special educational programmes and intervention strategies had to be planned to fulfil their academic needs.

Types of Exceptional Children: Students can be broadly classified to the following three categories:

(*a*) Cognitively Exceptional Children

(*b*) Physically Exceptional Children

(*c*) Socio-Culturally Exceptional Children

COGNITIVELY EXCEPTIONAL CHILDREN

The children belonging to this category can be further subdivided into the following types:

(*i*) The Gifted

(*ii*) The Mentally Retarded

(*iii*) Children With Learning Disabilities

Gifted Children: Children possessing high intellectual level and special abilities and talents are regarded as gifted.

According to Guilford, the gifted are those students whose potential intellectual powers are at such a high ideational level in both productive and evaluative thinking that it can be reasonably assumed, that they could be the future problem solvers, innovators of the culture if adequate educational experiences are provided.

Characteristics of Gifted Children:

- **Physical Characteristics:**

By and large, these children have superior physical abilities like

1. Greater birth weight,
2. Early walk and talk,
3. Early puberty,
4. Superior motor ability, etc.

- **Intellectual Characteristics:**

1. High IQ,
2. Precocious,
3. Varied interests,
4. Higher scholastic performance,
5. Rich cognitive processes of abstract thinking, reasoning, generalizing, critical & reflective thinking and creativity.

- **Personality Characteristics:**

1. Ambitious,
2. Higher levels of motivation and enthusiasm,
3. Impulsive,
4. Confident.

Identification of the Gifted:

- Parents, teachers and social workers can help in identifying in identifying gifted children at a very early date. Careful observation of the child in different setting and for considerable amount of time has to be worked out for early detection of giftedness.
- General intelligence tests, creativity test, word association test, Achievement tests serve as useful tools.
- School records, report cards also provide valuable information on giftedness.

Education of the Gifted:

The two major approaches to teaching gifted are acceleration and enrichment.

- **Acceleration:** These programmes allow gifted students to move ahead at their own pace, even if this means jumping to higher grade levels.
- **Enrichment:** These programmes allow the students to remain in the same grade but provide special programmes and special activities to cover the topics in greater detail and depth.

It is generally agreed that the education of the gifted pupils should emphasize the following objectives to cater to their giftedness.

1. Analytical perception
2. Methods of problem solving
3. Employing Analysis & Synthesis
4. Conceptual Thinking
5. Scientific Objectivity
6. Originality and creativity
7. Independent study habits
8. Encouragement of special interests

12. Dyslexia is a language-based learning disability. Dyslexia refers to a cluster of symptoms, which result in people having difficulties with specific language skills, particularly reading. Students with dyslexia usually experience difficulties with other language skills such as spelling, writing, and pronouncing words. Dyslexia affects individuals throughout their lives; however, its impact can change at different stages in a person's life. It is referred to as a learning disability because dyslexia can make it very difficult for a student to succeed academically in the typical instructional environment, and in its more severe forms, will qualify a student for special education, special accommodations, or extra support services.

13. Learning disability (LD) is a term used to denote a neurological handicap that interferes with a person's ability to receive, process, store, and retrieve information. LD creates a gap between a person's ability and performance caused by an alternation in the way information is processed. Repetition and drilling does not alter this processing, but presenting materials in a different way helps. Individuals with LD are generally of average or above average intelligence.

- LD can affect one's ability to read, write, speak or compute math, and can impede socialization skills.

- Early diagnosis and appropriate intervention and support are critical for the individual with LD.
- Because it is often a 'hidden handicap,' LD is not easily recognized, accepted or considered serious.
- It is believed that LD never goes away, but can be compensated for.
- Attention deficits and hyperactivity are sometimes coupled with LD, but not always.
- LD is not the same as the following handicaps: mental retardation, autism, deafness, blindness, and behavioral disorders.

LD is a neurological condition that is beyond the control of the individual. Such a student is more normal than different. There are degrees of LD–mild, moderate, and severe. It might go undiagnosed as late as secondary school, university, or even never at all. They younger the child when diagnosed, greater is the possibility of remediation. When a student is older, it is coping strategies that need to be strengthened.

Environmental Causes: These could be poverty, inadequate housing, family dysfunction, and parental psychopathology or substance abuse, dysfunctional peers, too much of television viewing, inadequate or improper schooling.

The three major types of LD are :

1. **Dyslexia:** A person has trouble understanding written words, sentences or paragraphs.
2. **Dysgraphia:** A person finds it hard to form letters or writes within a defined space.
3. **Dyscalculia:** A person has difficulty solving arithmetic problems and grasping math concepts.

1. DYSLEXIA

Dyslexia is a disorder manifested by difficulty in learning to read, despite conventional instruction, adequate intelligence and socio-cultural opportunity. It is dependent upon fundamental cognitive disabilities, which are frequently of constitutional origin.

Characteristics of Dyslexia

- Speech difficulties are common in children with dyslexia. Stuttering and lisping are quite common. Delayed spoken language is often an indicator of dyslexia.
- Spatial difficulties leading to reversal of letters (B-d), words (saw, was) and sometimes even sentences and difficulty in scanning from left to right.
- Visual memory difficulties in recalling sequence of letters in words (spelling).
- Difficulties in visual and motor figure ground resulting in illegible handwriting, difficulties in scanning lines and discrimination of letters.
- These characteristics appear more often in combination.

Apart from difficulties with phonological processing, dyslexia is also associated with differences in cognition and learning.

2. DYSGRAPHIA

A neurological-based writing disability in which a person has difficulty expressing thoughts on paper and with writing associated with unreadable penmanship and problems in gripping and manipulating a pencil.

The written form of language is the highest the most complex form of communication. In the hierarchy of language skill, writing is the last to be learned. Prerequisite to writing is a foundation of previous learning and experiences in listening, speaking, and reading. Even though dysgraphia is difficulty with handwriting, the other components of written expression spelling and written expression which are impaired in children with learning disabilities need to be considered.

Common Signs of Dysgraphia:

- Bad or illegible handwriting
- Awkward or cramped pencil grip.
- Avoidance of tasks involving writing.
- Inconsistent in the way letters and words look.
- Difficulty in expressing ideas on paper.
- Inability to properly form letter.
- Writing may be slow and laboured.
- Difficulty keeping letters on the line.
- Inability to understand the relative sizes of letters.
- Crowding of letters within words.
- Poor spacing between words.
- Difficulty in reading written work even when the spelling is correct.

3. DYSCALCULIA

Dyscalculia is the type of learning disability resulting in difficulty in learning numerical and mathematical ideas and concepts.

Clinical Signs of Dyscalculia

- Difficulty with common math processes such as addition, subtraction, multiplication.
- Difficulty with math concepts such as sequencing of numbers, and sequencing of rules required in mathematical problems.
- Poor retention and retrieval of math concepts.

- Inability to work with numbers or symbols.
- Inconsistency in understanding and application of math rules.
- Poor sense of direction and time, e.g., difficulty with reading maps, telling time, etc.
- Difficulty in applying rules in sports.
- Trouble keeping track of scores and players during card and board games.
- Inability to handle money transactions in day-to-day living.

14.

Traditional Schooling	*Enriching Schooling*	*Empowering Schooling*
Teacher centred	Student centred	Experience centred
Subjects and classes	Self Directed	Virtual authenticity
Sorting and ranking individuals	Continuous assessment	Multi-literacies
Competency:	***Competency:***	***Competency:***
Memory	Critical thinking	Risk taking
Competitive	Collaborative	Ethical
	Creative	Interactive

15. The word Adolescence is derived from the Latin word Adolescere, which means Growing Up or Growing Towards. It is a significant Transitional Period between Childhood and Adulthood in Human Development.

Definition of Adolescence

Adolescence is generally defined with reference to a period of years. The World Health Organisation (WHO) defines Adolescence as the period of life between 10 to 19 years, and youth as between 15 to 24 years. WHO clearly recognises that Adolescence is a phase rather than a fixed period in an individual's life. However, Adolescents do not constitutes a Homogeneous Group. Their needs vary with their Sex, Stage of Development, Life Circumstances, and the Socio-Economic conditions of their environment.

Adolescence may not be seen only in reference to the precise number of years in an individual's life, as its periodicity varies from person to person. It can start as early as 9 years and as late as 14 years. Moreover, defining the age of Adolescence varies from one Socio-cultural setting to another. A young person attending school may be considered an Adolescent in one place, while another person of the same age in another place may be married and considered an adult.

Adolescence is the transition period of Physical, Psychological, and Social Maturation from Childhood to Adulthood, the period extending from Puberty to the attainment of Adulthood.

Emotional Changes and Social Development

All periods of an individual's life tend to be characterised by developments that are physical, emotional, psychological, and social in origin. But the period of adolescence more than any other is characterised by an upsurge of these changes and behavioural contradictions.

It should be noted that these changes are normal and universal. The following developmental tasks during adolescence make this phase of life distinct from all other phases.

Traditionally, Adolescence has been thought of as a period of Storm and Stress, a Time of Heightened Emotional Tension resulting from the Physical and Hormonal Changes taking place.

These Physical Changes are accompanied by marked Psychological Changes. Though Bodily Changes Occur Rapidly, Emotional Development takes time to stabilise, i.e. though Adolescents are Physically Capable of Fulfilling Adult Roles, their Emotions may not be completely free from the patterns and reactions Set of Childhood.

Adolescent Emotionality can also be attributed to the fact that boys and girls come under considerable Social Pressure at this age, and face New Conditions and Challenges for which they receive little, if any, preparation during Childhood. By no means do all Adolescents go through a period of such intense storm and stress. True, most Teenagers do experience emotional instability from time to time, which is a logical consequence of having to make adjustments to new patterns of behaviour and to new social roles and expectations. For example, problems related to romance are very real at this time. As long as the romance is moving along smoothly, Adolescents are happy, but they become despondent when things go wrong. Similarly, with the end of their schooling in sight, Adolescents begin to worry about their future. Adolescents want to be treated as adults, and become upset and rebellious if authority figures such as parents and teachers do not treat them so. Instead of having temper tantrums, however, they may express their anger by sulking, refusing to speak, or loudly criticising those who have angered them. Adolescence is also marked by the development of abstract thinking, which enables Teenagers to think critically, to evaluate situations rationally and systematically, and to detect and question inconsistencies between rules and behaviour. Parents as well as service providers often overlook this development, which is one of the basic reasons for the so-called Generation Gap. Socially, Adolescence is marked by shifts from dependency to autonomy. It also involves learning social responses to physical maturity, the management of sexuality, the acquisition of skills, and changes in peer groups. The desire to be part of a gang or a large group is replaced by a preference for maintaining fewer, steadier, long lasting, and more meaningful relationships. Society generally does not define a distinct role for Adolescents. Hence Adolescents are caught in the ambiguous overlap between the categorically defined roles of childhood and those of adulthood. Society and parents do not understand the different psychological needs and normal developmental behaviour of early , middle and late adolescence and this often leads to understanding of normal adolescent behaviour as deviant/problematic/abnormal.

At times, this generates among them aggressive and reactionary behaviour, which often evokes social disapproval. Adolescents often experience anxiety and emotional stress to an unusual degree compared with people belonging to other age groups.

The following are some of the Psychological Changes that take place during Adolescence:

- Increased Risk-Taking Behaviour
- Search for Identity
- Increased Influence of the Peer-Group
- New Social Groupings

CHANGES IN INTERESTS

- Concern about their Bodies (Body Image Concerns)
- Interest in Sexuality
- Changes in Family Relationships

16. Orthopedically impaired children include those with a severe orthopedic impairment which adversely affects their educational performance (Federal Register, 1977). Some conditions or diseases which have crippling results include spina bifida, polimyelitis, multiple sclerosis, paralysis, amputation, muscular dystrophy, juvenile rheumatoid arthritis, bone diseases and congenital malformation.

A child who is orthopedically handicapped is usually not mentally handicapped. This child's deficiencies are most evident in the areas of mobility, motor coordination and social interaction. The child's physical limitations are as varied as the condition causing the impairment. Emotional problems may develop in children who have been rejected or isolated by their peers as a result of an orthopedic handicap.

A child with a physical problem has difficulty moving either part, or all, of his body. Sometimes only a small part of his body, like fingers or toes, are affected. Other times a child can't walk or sit up alone.

Children with physical disabilities might:

- Walk or move in an unusual way
- Be very clumsy
- Fall or stumble very easily, especially on uneven ground
- Have trouble controlling certain parts of their body
- Need special equipment like crutches, braces or a wheel-chair.

17. Continuous vs Partial Reinforcement: In experiments on learning the experimenter can arrange to deliver reinforcement according to a specific schedule. In the context of learning, two kinds of schedules namely continuous and partial have been found very important. In continuous reinforcement the participant is given reinforcement after each target response. This kind of schedule of reinforcement produces a high rate of responding. However, once the reinforcement is withheld, response rates decrease very quickly, and the responses acquired under this schedule tend to extinguish. Since organism is getting reinforcement on each trial, the effectiveness of that reinforcer is reduced. In such schedules where reinforcement is not continuous, some responses are not reinforced. Hence, they are called partial or intermittent reinforcement. There are several ways in which one might reinforce responses according to an intermittent schedule. It has been found that partial reinforcement schedules often produce very high rates of responding, particularly when responses are reinforced according to ratio. In this kind of schedule, an organism often makes several responses that are not reinforced. Therefore, it becomes difficult to tell when a reinforcement has been discontinued completely and when it has merely been delayed. When reinforcement is continuous it is easier to tell when it has been discontinued. This kind of difference has been found crucial for extinction. It has been found that extinction of a response is more difficult following partial reinforcement than following continuous reinforcement. The fact that the responses acquired under partial reinforcement are highly resistant to extinction is called partial reinforcement effect.

18. Vygotsky's theory of social development

A fundamental principle of Vygotsky's theory of social development is that full cognitive development requires social interaction. Vygotsky emphasised the importance of culture for learning. At a broad level, culture teaches children both *what* to think and *how* to think. At the individual level, children learn through problem solving that is shared with someone else (e.g. adult, peer). Compared with Piaget, Vygotsky gave greater emphasis to the importance of language in learning. Vygotsky argued that language is crucial for collaborative problem solving and that such collaborative problem solving is important for children's cognitive development.

Vygotsky also argued that learning occurs in the 'zone of proximal development', which is the gap between what a child can do without help and what they could do with appropriate guidance or collaboration. With such help from adults or peers, children can perform tasks they would be incapable of completing on their own. Furthermore, teaching and learning will be more effective if there is a continual adjustment of the level of help given so that children becomee more independent at solving problem.

20. The assessment for learning involves increased levels of student autonomy, but not without teacher guidance and collaboration. The assessment for learning is sometimes seen as being akin to 'formative assessment' and can be seen as informing teaching. There is more emphasis towards giving of useful advice to the student and less emphasis on the giving of marks and the grading function:

- Teacher designs learning
- Teacher designs assessment with feedback to student
- Teacher assesses what has been learnt (student develops insight into what has not)

22. Control and coordination of body parts in their movements is covered under motor skills. These are essential skills helps in body balance and movements and by these we can perform the desired muscle movement to perform a desired task. It is necessary to develop these skills for better writing skills and handwriting.

It mainly covers Fine and Gross Motor Skills. Gross motor skills are those which are responsible for movements of main joints of the body like in shoulder, elbow, knew etc. These movements help the children to develop control and coordination while running, jumping, skipping and other similar activities. Fine motor movements basically controls and coordinate of smaller joints movements like of fingers, toe etc. and are essential for writing skills and handwriting.

As a result of under developed motor skills students may complain for pain in hands while writing, Poor handwriting, slow writing speed, incomplete classroom work etc. are some of the other problems which may arise due to poor fine motor skills.

Children with better motor skills may perform well in sports, may develop good handwriting and will write faster than other children and have good drawing abilities.

23. What is Problem Solving Method?

- Problem solving is a process to choose and use the effective and benefical tool and behaviours among the different potentialities to reach the target.
- It contains scientific method, critical thinking, taking decision, examining and reflective thinking.
- This method is used in the process of solving a problem to generalize or to make synthesis.

Steps of Problem Solving Process

1. Choosing the topic and emergence of problem.
2. Delimitation of the problem.
3. Planning the application.
4. Preparing the working guide.
5. Providing the sources.
6. Examining the problem.
7. Getting a conclusion.
8. Disputating the topics, views and findings.

Advantages of Problem Solving Method

- It provides the active participation of the students in teaching-learning activity.
- It habituates student to study regularly and organized.
- It provides students to gain scientific view and thinking.
- It makes students to be interested in learning.
- It helps to improve the sense of responsibility of students.
- It provides students to face the problems boldly and to deal with it in a scientific approach.
- It helps students to adopt the view of benefit from others ideas and to help each other.
- It predicates the learning to a more logical and doughty foundation.
- It improves the ability of making proposes and putting forward the hypothesis.
- It helps students to adopt the idea of not to be hurry to make a decision.

Disadvantages of Problem Solving Method

- It takes too much time.
- It is not possible to apply this method to all disciplines.
- It can load some worldly burdensomes to students.
- It can be difficult for students to provide the materials and sources which is required for solving the problem.
- Evaluating the learning can be difficult.

Techniques Used in Problem Solving Method

A. Induction: It is like teaching with discovering method. Cases are observed carefully. The similarities and dissimilarities are found. Then you can reach the general rule or law with the techniques "generalization" or "making abstract" from the similarities.

B. Deduction: It is reverse of induction technique. Some general laws and rules which are reached before are given to the students and want them to apply this method to different singular case. The convenience of it to the one of the case is controlled mentally.

26. Portfolio Assessment: A portfolio is a collection of materials which are representative of the skills, ideas, thoughts and values of an individual as reflected in their work. The portfolio needs to be maintained through the year.

The gradual collection of material created by the learner over the year will reflect growth in thinking, an evolution in skills and also a change in attitude. A portfolio is a purposeful collection of selective significant samples of student work accompanied by clear criteria for performance which evidence student effort, progress or achievement. A portfolio is different from a folder in that it includes:

- Explicit guidelines for selection
- Comprehensible criteria
- Clear objectives
- Selective and significant pieces
- Students' self-reflection pieces
- Evidence of student participation in selection of content

A portfolio can exhibit the student's, progress and achievement in several areas.

28. Goal theorists viewed motivation as an integrated pattern of *beliefs* that lead to different ways of approaching, engaging in and responding to achievement situations. Initially, two major kinds of motivationally relevant goal patterns or goal orientations emerged, namely *ego-* and *task-involved goals* (Nicholls, 1984). Later theorists re-named these perceived purposes or orentations to achievement situations as mastery and performance goals. A performance goal orientation refers to engagement in a learning task with the purpose of demonstrating one's ability.

A mastery goal orientation denotes engagement with the purpose to increase one's competence, knowledge and skill. Roughly speaking, performance orientation derived from the expectancy-value perspective and mastery orientation was mainly based on the intrinsic motivation perspective. The idea that performance goals have to be divided into performance approach (wanting to demonstrate high ability) and performance avoidance goals (wanting to hide incompetence) is a development.

30. Teaching in interdisciplinary approach is another way of involving the learners in the learning process. It prepares the learners for the real world where things are not found in isolation. Here the learners can find new applications and uses of the things taught. They discover new possibilities for the learning and hence become more dedicated in the learning process.

33. Side of square $= 10$ m $= 1000$ cm

Area of square $= 1000 \times 1000$ cm^2

$\therefore$ Number of tiles $= \dfrac{1000 \times 1000}{50 \times 50}$

$= 400.$

34. 1 orange cost $= ₹\,2\frac{1}{2} = ₹\,\frac{5}{2}$

$\therefore$ Cost of 42 oranges $= ₹\,\frac{5}{2} \times 42$

$= ₹5 \times 21 = ₹105.$

35. Number of pieces of chocolate left

$= 12 - \left(\frac{1}{4} \times 12 + \frac{1}{3} \times 12 + \frac{1}{6} \times 12\right)$

$= 12 - (3 + 4 + 2)$

$= 12 - 9 = 3.$

36. Let x will be added.

$140 \times 101 + x = 14414$

$x = 14414 - 14140$

$= 274$

If 274 added to the product of 140×101 then we get 14414.

37. Side of small square $= \frac{12}{4} = 3$ cm

Area of small square $= (3)^2 = 9$ cm^2

$\therefore$ Side of big square $= \frac{24}{4} = 6$ cm

Area of big square $= (6)^2 = 36$ cm^2

Clearly, area of big square = 4 times area of small square.

38. All factors of 100 are

1, 2, 4, 5, 10, 20, 25, 50 and 100

Sum of all the factors of 100

$= 1 + 2 + 4 + 5 + 10 + 20 + 25 + 50 + 100$

$= 217.$

39. LCM of (12 and 16) × LCM of (10 and 15)

$= 48 \times 30 = 1440.$

40. Sum of place value of 2 in 2424

$= 2000 + 20 = 2020.$

42. Van Hiele's Geometric Thinking Level and Phase-based Learning

In the field of geometry, the best and most well-defined model for student levels of thinking is based Van Hiele's model. The levels are visualisation, analysis, informal deduction, formal deduction, and rigor. The first Van Hiele's level of thinking is known as visualisation level. At this level, students are able to recognise geometric shapes. The second level in the model is known as analysis level where students are able to identify the properties of certain shapes. The third level in the model is informal deduction where students are able to comprehend the relation between shapes and create the relationships. The fourth level in the model is formal deduction. At this level, students can appreciate the meaning and importance of deduction and the role of postulates, theorems, and proofs. Finally, the fifth level in Van Hiele's model is rigor. At this level, students come to understand how to work in an axiomatic system. They are able to make more abstract deductions. However, lower secondary school students can usually only achieve up to the third level in Van Hiele's model, which is informal deduction.

46. Learning Styles

Learning Style	*Description*
1. Visual	Seeing and reading
2. Auditory	Listening and Speaking
3. Kinesthetic	Touching and doing

48. Higher Order Thinking Skills (HOTS) is a intellectually disciplined process of actively and skillfully conceptualizing, applying, analyzing, synthesizing, and/ or evaluating information gathered from, or generated by observation, experience, reflection, reasoning, or communication as a rubric to belief and action.

Higher Order Thinking are also called "critical" or "strategic" thinking, it can be described as the ability to use information to solve problems, analyze arguments, negotiate issues or make predictions. It involves examining assumptions and values, evaluating evidence, and assessing conclusions.

Therefore, HOTS are intellectual processes where students have to activate their minds in order to understand the hidden meaning from the information introduced to them, realize the relations among ideas, draw principles and rules, analyze and classify, generate and combine new ideas, evaluate and judge.

51. Both Piaget and Lev Vygotsky argue that learning results from social interaction. They believe that learning is a social process and that language plays a significant role in instruction and cognitive growth. Vygotsky argues that "learning awakens a variety of internal developmental processes that are able to operate only when the child is interacting with people in his environment and in cooperation with his peers." This social interaction is necessary to create the zone of proximal development, but once the process is internalized, the child can use the process independently.

To develop intellectual and moral autonomy, Piaget argues that it is necessary for children to exchange points of view and learn to defend and justify answers.

52. Area of shaded part = 25 – 16 = 9 cm^2.

53. Number of boxes = $\frac{6240}{10\times8\times6} = \frac{624}{6\times8} = 13$.

54. $121012 \div 12 = 10084\frac{4}{12}$

$\therefore$ remainder = 4.

55.

	hrs		min
	20	:	02
–	6	:	14
	13 hrs		48 min.

56. 3 litres 30 millilitres = 3030 millilitres.

57. $\frac{2}{3}\div\frac{1}{6}=\frac{2}{3}\times\frac{6}{1}=4.$

58. $4\frac{1}{3}\times90^\circ = \frac{13}{3}\times90^\circ$

$= 13 \times 30 = 390^\circ$.

64. Health is a multi-dimensional concept because it is shaped by biological, social, economic and cultural factors. Health is not merely the absence of disease but is influenced and shaped by the access to basic needs like food security; safe water supply, housing, sanitation and health services. Within this broader definition of health, individual health is intrinsically interrelated with social factors. Therefore while individual health is important it is necessary to delineate its linkages with the physical, social and economic environment in which people live.

Children's health is an important concern for all societies since it contributes to their overall development. Health, nutrition and education are important for the overall development of the child and these three inputs need to be addressed in a comprehensive manner. While the relationship between health and education is seen more in terms of the role that the latter plays in creating health awareness and health status improvements, what is not adequately represented in the debates is the reciprocal relationship between health and education, especially when it comes to children. Studies have shown that poor health and nutritional status of children is a barrier to attendance and educational attainment and therefore plays a crucial role in enrollment, retention, and completion of school education. The concerns related to health, nutrition and other inputs that contribute to the overall development of the child, therefore need to be part of the curriculum on 'Health and Physical Education' at the primary, secondary and senior secondary schools.

67. Bronze is an alloy of copper and tin. Bronze contains not only tin, and it contains a variety of alloys of arsenic, phosphorus, aluminium, manganese, and silicon with copper are commonly termed bronze.

69.

Convergent Thinking (CT)	*Divergent Thinking (DT)*
Non creative people have convergent thinking.	Creative people have divergent thinking.
Produces single correct answer.	Produces variety of responses.
It is stimulus bound.	It is stimulus free.
In CT, problem is solved by known or common method.	In DT, problem is solved in different innovative methods.
CT is rigid, stereotyped & mechanically operated.	DT is novel, exploratory & venturesome.
CT is measured by Intelligence test which includes remembering, recognition & manipulation of some concrete material.	DT is measured by creativity tests in which novelty, flexibility & originality are given more weightage.
It is known as Reasoning or Rational Thinking.	It is known as Creative Thinking, Imaginative or Original Thinking.

70. More than a thousand years ago, a traveller came to India. His name was Al-Biruni. The place that he came from is now called Uzbekistan. Al-Biruni carefully observed and noted down the details of all that he saw. He wrote especially about those things that he found very different from his own country.

71. Nepenthes khasiana is endemic to Meghalaya in India and it is considered as an endangered plant in the wild. It is one of the Carnivorous plants (also known as insectivorous plant), which derive some or most of their nutrients from trapping and consuming insects. It grows in the soil which is poor in nutrients, especially nitrogen. It is popularly known as Pitcher plant.

73. Bee-keeping is the maintenance of honey bee colonies, commonly in hives, by humans. A bee keeper keeps bees in order to collect honey and other products of the hive, to pollinate crops, or to produce bees for sale to other bee-keepers. A location where bees are kept is called an apiary or "bee yard".

75. Inclusive Education is a term used to describe a system of education that seeks to welcome children with special needs and include them in the main stream. The philosophy of the Inclusive Education highlights the principle that all children, regardless of their abilities have the right to be educated and be a part of the integrated school system.

76. It is believed that a pashmina shawl is as warm as six sweaters! It is very thin yet very warm. The goats from which the soft pashmina wool is collected, are found on very high altitudes of 5000 metres. In winter, the temperature here drops below 0°C (–40°C). A coat of warm hair grows on the goat's body which protects it from extreme cold. The goats shed some of their hair (fur) in summer. This hair is so fine that six of these would be as thick as one hair of yours! The fine hair cannot be woven on machines and so weavers of Kashmir make these shawls by hand. This is a long and difficult process. After almost 250 hours of weaving, one plain pashmina shawl is made. Imagine how long it would take to make a shawl with embroidery.

80. Portfolio Evaluation: Portfolios used for assessment purposes are most commonly characterized by collections of student work that exhibit to the faculty and the student the student's progress and achievement in given areas. Included in the portfolio may be research papers and other process reports, multiple choice or essay examinations, self-evaluations, personal essays, journals, computational exercises and problems, case studies, audiotapes, videotapes, and short-answer quizzes. This information may be gathered from in-class or out-of-class assignments.

Portfolio evaluation is a useful assessment tool because it allows faculty to analyze an entire scope of student work in a timely fashion. Collecting student work overtime gives schools a unique opportunity to assess a students' progression in acquiring a variety of learning objectives. Using student portfolios also gives faculty the ability to determine the content and control the quality of the assessed materials.

81. Different types of Learning experiences are needed to retain the learning concepts. Teaching materials become essential for the expansion of learning. Our senses are the gateways of acquiring knowledge about the surroundings. As people are different in their appearances, thoughts and in actions, the five senses are also different from one another in its activities. Learning through senses create a clear and quality learning. The functions of brain is to select all the sensual experiences, classify, inter change and interlink these experiences into general concepts. The sensual experiences stimulate the various concepts about the world. Many senses are involved while performing an activity or gaining experiences.

Example: During teaching, the learners listen to the teacher and also observe the facial expressions by their eyes. Learning takes place at different levels among the learners. Some learn by visual sense and others by learning skill and few others by tactile, and listening skills. So, the teacher tries to teach through multi-sensory approach to the students. It is essential to use more additional Teaching and Learning Materials in multi-sensory approach. Use of the best result oriented equipments is known as 'Educational Technology'. In short, Educational technology involves in the best use of techniques, preparation and uses of methods and evaluation.

The instruments which enhance the learning experiences come under Technology of Education. The ultimate aim of educational technology is to attain the learning objectives in a short period in its designing, application and evaluation.

The equipments in educational technology help the learners in effective learning.

It should develop knowledge, retention, capacity, motivation, comprehension, interest in learning and widen the acquired knowledge. The use of technology in education enables to improve all types of teaching methods and enhances students learning outcome.

83. Co-operative learning methods is one of the examples of Group Activities involving team work. This method can be used/organized regularly for various subjects like Maths, Science, Social science & Languages.

In order to develop in students the skills of cooperation, belongingness & team spirit & to reduce individual competition amongst them, the teacher should adopt the cooperative learning method.

Co-operative Learning is not individual learning but group learning or peer learning. In co-operative learning, students work together to achieve a common goal. There is greater participation & involvement of the students in a Co-operative Learning.

Co-operative Learning generates more intrinsic motivation than does individualized learning. The feeling of belongingness produces positive attitudes & team spirit in the students.

Co-operative Learning is specifically useful for learning various skills & knowledge. The teacher should therefore be familiar with the process of organizing co-operative learning in her class or school.

84. Rote Learning: Rote learning is a learning technique which focuses on memorization. The major practice involved in rote learning is learning by repetition by which students commit information to memory in a highly structured way. The idea is that one will be able to quickly recall the meaning of the material the more one repeats it. Rote methods are routinely used when quick memorization is required, such as learning one's lines in a play or memorizing a telephone number. Rote learning is widely used in the mastery of foundational knowledge.

Educational theorists suggest a distinction between meaningful learning and rote learning. Rote learning is often emphasized in primary and secondary educational settings, and consists of simple memorization of information, without concern for relationships among concepts, to merely regurgitate in the exams. In contrast, in a higher educational scenario, meaningful learning results from linking new information to relevant, preexisting concepts in the cognitive structure of an individual. The most important factor for learning is what the learners already know.

Brain-storming: Brain-storming is a creative problem solving technique very widely used in the industries. It is now frequently used in the classrooms. Osborn (1953) developed this technique following the principle of deferred judgement because he believed that judgement and imagination cannot go together in creative thinking. They help each other only if kept apart. Evaluation is not ruled out, it is only postponed. This provides psychological safety to the children while thinking for solutions. It can be used individually as well as in a group.

- It is a technique conducted in the classroom.
- The basis of brain storming is generating ideas in a group situation based on the principle of suspending judgement.
- A principle which is scientifically researched, has proved to be highly productive in group efforts.
- The generation phase is separate from the judgement phase of thinking.

Brain-storming is useful for attacking specific (rather than general) problems and where a collection of good, fresh, new ideas are needed.

86. Dyslexia: Dyslexia is a disorder manifested by difficulty in learning to read, despite conventional instruction, adequate intelligence and socio-cultural opportunity. It is dependent upon fundamental cognitive disabilities, which are frequently of constitutional origin.

Characteristics of Dyslexia

- Speech difficulties are common in children with dyslexia. Stuttering and lisping are quite common. Delayed spoken language is often an indicator of dyslexia.
- Spatial difficulties—leading to reversal of letters (B-d), words (saw, was) and sometimes even sentences and difficulty in scanning from left to right.
- Visual memory difficulties in recalling sequence of letters in words (spelling).

- Difficulties in visual and motor figure ground-resulting in illegible handwriting, difficulties in scanning lines and discrimination of letters.

These characteristics appear more often in combination. Apart from difficulties with phonological processing, dyslexia is also associated with differences in cognition and learning.

Language Problems: Dyslexic children have problems with reading, a lack of awareness of phonemes that make up words, difficulties with spelling, sequencing of letters in words, and difficulty with pronouncing words (may reverse sounds).

- Early warning signs are delay in speech, delay in learning the alphabet, numbers, days of the week, month, colours, shapes, and other basic information. They also have difficulties understanding subtleties of language such as jokes or slang, concept words (forward/backward, near/far) etc. there may be mispronunciations, omission of sounds and immature vocabulary.
- Auditory and visual processing difficulties may also be present. Here children have difficulty distinguishing between words that sound alike (pig/big). There is trouble rhyming words, and in blending sounds into words. Visual processing difficulties may include inability to recognize letters, words, or other printed symbols quickly and accurately. For example, there may be confusion with *b* and *d*, or read for saw and on for no.

Motor Coordination: Motor coordination problems are common. These children may be clumsy or awkward. It may be difficult for them to write, draw, or copy with neatness and accuracy. There may be problems with fine motor skills such as tying shoes, buttoning, using scissors or learning to sew.

88. It is not easy to find out where oil is, deep down below the earth. Scientists use special techniques and machines to find this out. Then through pipes and machines petroleum is pumped up. This oil is a smelly, thick, dark coloured liquid. It contains many things mixed in it. To clean and separate these, it is sent to a refinery.

It is from this 'petroleum' or oil that we get kerosene, diesel, petrol, engine oil and fuel for aircrafts. L.P.G. (cooking gas), wax, coaltar and grease are also obtained from this. It is also used in making several other things like plastics and paints.

89. Malaria, Dengue, Chikungunya and Filaria are diseases spread by mosquitoes.

Medicine for Malaria: From early times, the dried and powdered bark of the Cinchona tree was used to make a medicine for malaria. Earlier people used to boil the bark powder and strain the water which was given to patients. Now tablets are made from this.

90. Mithila paintings also known as Madhubani folk art is the traditional art of the Mithila region of Bihar. They are produced by village women who make three dimensional images using vegetable colour with few earthen colours and finished in black lines on cow dung treated paper. Madhubani paintings are made from the paste of powdered rice. These pictures tell tales especially about Sita's exile, Ram-Laxman's forest life, or depict the images of Lakshmi, Ganesha, Hanuman and others from Hindu mythology.

91. Content Words: Content words, or lexical words (including nouns, verbs, adjectives, and most adverbs), are words that carry the content or the meaning of a sentence. They are open-class words. Open classes accept the addition of new morphemes (words), through such processes as compounding, derivation, inflection, coining, and borrowing.

Examples:

- **Nouns:** John, room, answer
- **Adjectives:** happy, new, large, gray
- **Verbs:** search, grow, hold, have
- **Adverbs:** really, completely, very, also, enough

Function Words: In contrast to content words, function words (also called grammatical words) are words that have little lexical meaning or have ambiguous meaning, but instead serve to express grammatical relationships with other words within a sentence. Function words are closed-class words. Languages do not easily add new words to this set. They are always relatively few and resistant to change. They are lexically unproductive and are generally invariable in form.

Examples:

- **Prepositions:** of, at, in, without, between
- **Pronouns:** he, they, anybody, it, one
- **Determiners:** the, a, that, my, more, much, either, neither
- **Conjunctions:** and, that, when, while, although, or
- **Auxiliary:** verbs be (is, am, are), have, got, do
- **Particles:** no, not, nor, as

94. Rhetorical questions are those questions that do not expect an answer. These are used simply as a way of drawing attention to something.

Study the following sentences:

- Do you know what time it is?
  (Meaning: You are late.)
- 'I can't find my glasses.' 'What is this, then?'
  (Meaning: Here it is, stupid.)

A rhetorical question is sometimes used to draw attention to a negative situation.

- What is the use of asking her? (Meaning: It is no use asking her.)
- 'I can sing better than you.' 'Who cares?' (= Nobody cares.)
- 'Have you lost your tongue?' (= Why don't you say anything?)
- 'Who do you think you are?' (= You are not as important as you think.)

98. Cohesive devices are used to tie pieces of text together in specific ways. Halliday and Hasan (1976) proposed five major types of grammatical cohesive ties: reference, substitution, ellipsis, conjunction and lexical ties.

101. The National Curriculum Framework (NCF 2005) is one of four National Curriculum Frameworks published in 1975, 1988, 2000 and 2005 by the National Council of Educational Research and Training NCERT in India. The document provides the framework for making syllabii, textbooks and teaching practices within the school education programmes in India.

The approach and recommendations of NCF-2005 are for the entire educational system. A number of its recommendations, for example, focus on rural schools. The syllabus and textbooks based on it are being used by all the CBSE schools, but NCF-based material is also being used in many State schools.

103. Learning Styles (Cognitive Styles)

Individuals differ in their learning styles (also termed cognitive styles). An outline of the main categories of learning styles is given below.

Field dependence and field independence: These terms refer to ways in which individuals perceive and order the world around them; some people tend to see patterns as wholes, whereas others focus on particular parts. Witkin and his colleagues carried out extensive research into this phenomenon using tests that involve the separation of figure from background or context. Individuals who are higher on one dimension that another are not better or worse because of it, since field dependence or field independence are not value-laden. Following Table shows the main differences between the two types of cognitive style.

Field dependent	*Field independent*
Need structured materials	Impose own structure on material
May have difficulty recoganizaing material already organized in another way	Can break down material and recognize it
May need clear instructions on how to solve problems	Likely to solve problems without specific guidance
May need to learn to use mnemonics	
Are better at learning and remembering social information	May need assistance with materials containing social information
Are likely to work in social careers such as psychiatric nursing or social work	Are likely to work in science or practical things like mechanics surgical nursing.

Reflective and impulsive styles: These styles refer to an individual's tendency to either produce an answer to a problem very quickly, or to spend some time in reflection before giving an answer. The kind of test used in this situation is called the 'matching familiar figures test' and consists of a number of pictures of familiar objects that the individual has to match with another picture. There are two styles of answering the problem; some people answer very quickly and others take time to answer. Kagan considers the former to be impulsive and the latter reflective, taking only the speed variable into account. Thus, whether or not a person in accurate is not relevant to the test. Students can be taught to become more reflective by the use of self-instruction and scanning strategies.

Kolb's learning style inventory: Another approach to cognitive style is Kolb's learning style inventory.

104. Word-formation is a process of creating new words by means of existing elements and according to the patterns and rules of a given language.

Word Formation Process consists of

1. Derivation
2. Compounding
3. Conversion
4. Quantitative changes

Derivation: Derivation is a kind of word-formation when a new word is formed by adding a derivational morpheme (usually suffix or prefix) to the root.

1. Suffixation is a kind of word-formation when a new word is formed by adding a suffix to the root.
2. Prefixation is a kind of word-formation when a new word is formed by adding a prefix to the root.

Compounds:

1. *Endocentric compounds*–the two constituent elements are clearly the determinant and determinatum (*ashtray, mousetrap, stepladder*)
2. *Exocentric compounds*–the determinatum is not expressed (*hangover, killjoy, ladybird, forget-me-not*)

Conversion or zero derivation: The process of converting words from one part of speech to another without adding any derivative element is called conversion or *zero derivation*.

Quantitative Changes (shortening)

- *Clipping*
- *Blending*
- *Graphical Abbreviations*
- *Back-formation*

Clipping (shortening) : The shortening of words consists of the reduction of a word to one of its parts, as a result of which the new form is used as an independent lexical unit. This type of word-formation is in English highly productive.

Blending

- Blending is a word-formation process of forming a new lexeme from **parts of two or more other words**. E.g., *smog* < smoke + fog, *brunch* < breakfast + lunch, *tranceiver* < transmitter + receiver, *bit* < binary digit, *chunnel* < channel + tunnel...

Graphical abbreviations

- New lexical units formed from the *initial letters* of the words and pronounced as one word – *acronyms*. E.g., *UNESCO, AIDS, NATO, laser, radar.*
- New lexical units formed from the *initial letters* of the words with *alphabetic reading*. E.g., *BC, SOS, TV, VIP, VAT.*
- Initial abbreviation in which the first element is a letter and the second a complete word. E.g., *A-bomb, E-mail, U-pronunciation* (U < upper class).
- Latin abbreviations. E.g., *AD, BC, i.e., e.g., pa.*
- Shortenings formed by a part of a word and the remaining part expressed by a capital letter or a figure. E.g., 2*-nite, 4 you, par-T.*

Previous Paper (Solved)

CTET PAPER-I, JANUARY 2012*

PART- I

Child Development and Pedagogy

Directions: *Answer the following questions by selecting the* ***most appropriate*** *option.*

1. A teacher, after preparing a question paper, checks whether the questions test specific testing objectives. He is concerned primarily about the question paper's
A. validity
B. content coverage
C. typology of questions
D. reliability

2. Critical pedagogy firmly believes that
A. the teacher should always lead the classroom instruction
B. the learners need not reason independently
C. what children learn out of school is irrelevant
D. the experiences and perceptions of learners are important

3. School-based assessment is primarily based on the principle that
A. assessment should be very economical
B. teachers know their learners' capabilities better than external examiners
C. students should at all costs get high grades
D. schools are more efficient than external bodies of examination

4. Learners display individual differences. So a teacher should
A. insist on uniform pace of learning
B. provide a variety of learning experiences
C. enforce strict discipline
D. increase number of tests

5. Vygotsky emphasized the significance of the role played by which of the following factors in the learning of children?
A. Social B. Hereditary
C. Moral D. Physical

6. A teacher makes use of a variety of tasks to cater to the different learning styles of her learners. She is influenced by
A. Piaget's cognitive development theory
B. Kohlberg's moral development theory
C. Gardner's multiple intelligence theory
D. Vygotsky's socio-cultural theory

7. A teacher never gives answers to questions herself. She encourages her students to suggest answers, have group discussions and adopt collaborative learning. This approach is based on the principle of
A. active participation
B. proper organization of instructional material
C. setting a good example and being a role-model
D. readiness to learn

8. Which of the following is a teacher-related factor affecting learning?
A. Mastery over the subject-matter
B. Proper seating arrangement
C. Availability of teaching-learning resources
D. Nature of the content or learning experiences

9. A school gives preference to girls while preparing students for a State level solo-songs competition. This reflects
A. Gender bias B. Global trends
C. Pragmatic approach D. Progressive thinking

10. The most effective method to teach the concept of germination of seeds is
A. to give detailed explanations
B. to make the students plant seeds and observe stages of germination
C. to draw pictures on the black-board and give descriptions
D. to show pictures of seed growth

11. When a child 'fails', it means
A. the child is not fit for studies
B. the child has not memorized the answers properly
C. the child should have taken private tuition
D. the system has failed

12. The emphasis from teaching to learning can be shifted by
A. focusing on examination results
B. adopting child-centered pedagogy
C. encouraging rote learning
D. adopting frontal teaching

13. Inclusive Education
A. includes teachers from marginalized groups
B. celebrates diversity in the classroom
C. encourages strict admission procedures
D. includes indoctrination of facts

*Exam was held on 29-01-2012.

14. Which of the following is an objective question?
A. Essay type question
B. Short answer question
C. Open ended question
D. True or False

15. Which of the following is a feature of progressive education?
A. Flexible time-table and seating
B. Instruction based solely on prescribed text books
C. Emphasis on scoring good marks in examinations
D. Frequent tests and examinations

16. According to Piaget's stages of Cognitive Development, the sensory-motor stage is associated with
A. concerns about social issues
B. imitation, memory and mental representation
C. ability to solve problems in logical fashion
D. ability to interpret and analyze options

17. According to Kohlberg, a teacher can instill moral values in children by
A. giving strict instructions on 'how to behave'
B. giving importance to religious teachings
C. laying clear rules of behaviour
D. involving them in discussions on moral issues

18. Young learners should be encouraged to interact with peers in the classroom so that
A. the teacher can control the classroom better
B. they can learn answers to questions from each other
C. the syllabus can be covered quickly
D. they learn social skills in the course of study

19. When a child with a disability first comes to school, the teacher should
A. conduct an admission test
B. refer the child to a special school according to the disability
C. seclude him from other students
D. discuss with the child's parents to evolve collaborative plans

20. Errors of learners often indicate
A. socio-economic status of the learners
B. how they learn
C. the need for mechanical drill
D. absence of learning

21. Which of the following is the first step in the scientific method of problem-solving?
A. Formation of hypothesis
B. Verification of hypothesis
C. Problem awareness
D. Collection of relevant information

22. Human personality is the result of
A. only heredity
B. upbringing and education
C. interaction between heredity and environment
D. only environment

23. Individual attention is important in the teaching—learning process because
A. children develop at different rates and learn differently
B. learners always learn better in groups
C. teacher training programmes prescribe it
D. it offers better opportunities to teachers to discipline each learner

24. Which of the following is a domain of learning?
A. Professional
B. Experiential
C. Affective
D. Spiritual

25. When a child gets bored while doing a task, it is a sign that
A. the child needs to be disciplined
B. the task may have become mechanically repetitive
C. the child is not intelligent
D. the child is not capable of learning

26. In the context of education, socialization means
A. always following social norms
B. creating one's own social norms
C. respecting elders in society
D. adapting and adjusting to social environment

27. Which of the following is a principle of development?
A. All processes of development are not interconnected
B. It does not proceed at the same pace for all
C. Development is always linear
D. It is a discontinuous process

28. Human development is divided into domains such as
A. physical, spiritual, cognitive and social
B. physical, cognitive, emotional and social
C. emotional, cognitive, spiritual and social-psychological
D. psychological, cognitive, emotional and physical

29. A teacher uses a text and some pictures of fruits and vegetables and holds a discussion with her students. The students link the details with their previous knowledge and learn the concept of nutrition. This approach is based on
A. Construction of knowledge
B. Classical conditioning of learning
C. Theory of reinforcement
D. Operant conditioning of learning

30. A child starts to cry when his grandmother takes him from his mother's lap. The child cries due to
A. Separation anxiety
B. Social anxiety
C. Emotional anxiety
D. Stranger anxiety

PART- II

Mathematics

Directions: *Answer the following questions by selecting the* ***most appropriate*** *option.*

31. Rizul is a kinesthetic learner. His teacher Ms. Neha understood his style of learning. Which of the following strategies should she choose to clear his concept of multiplication?

A. Counting the points of intersection on criss-cross lines

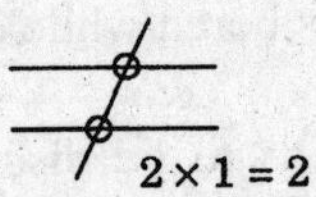

B. Forcing him to memorize all tables

C. Use strings and beads of two different colours to get the multiples of 2, 3, etc.

D. Skip counting

32. Use of Abacus in Class II does *not* help the students to

A. understand the significance of place value

B. read the numbers without error

C. write the numeral equivalent of numbers given in words

D. attain perfection in counting

33. In which of the following divisions, will the remainder be more than the remainder you get when you divide 176 by 3?

A. 174 ÷ 4 B. 175 ÷ 3

C. 176 ÷ 2 D. 173 ÷ 5

34. 500 cm + 50 m + 5 km =

A. 500 m B. 555 m

C. 5055 m D. 55 m

35. Sum of place values of 6 in 63606

A. 60606 B. 6606

C. 6066 D. 18

36. The difference of 5671 and the number obtained on reversing its digits is

A. 4906 B. 3916

C. 7436 D. 3906

37. Study the following pattern:

1 × 1 =	1
11 × 11 =	121
111 × 111 =	12321
....	
....	

What is 11111 × 11111?

A. 123454321 B. 12345421

C. 123453421 D. 1234321

38. 'Recognition of patterns and their completion' is an essential part of Mathematics curriculum at primary stage as it

A. develops creativity and artistic attributes in students

B. prepares students to take up competitive examinations

C. helps the students in solving 'Sudoku' puzzles

D. promotes creativity amongst students and helps them to understand properties of numbers and operations

39. Which of the following is correct?

A. Predecessor of successor of 1000 is 1000

B. Predecessor of predecessor of 1000 is 999

C. Successor of predecessor of 1000 is 1001

D. Successor of predecessor of 1000 is 1002

40. A shop has 239 toys. Seventy more toys were brought in. Then 152 of them were sold. The number of toys left was

A. 239 + 70 + 152 B. 239 − 70 + 152

C. 239 + 70 − 152 D. 239 − 70 − 152

41. A pencil costs two and a half rupees. Amit buys one and a half dozen pencils and gives a 100 rupee note to the shopkeeper. The money he will get back is

A. ₹ 45 B. ₹ 65

C. ₹ 30 D. ₹ 55

42. In the product 3759 × 9573, the sum of tens' digit and units' digit is

A. 7 B. 9

C. 16 D. 0

43. What time is 4 hours 59 minutes before 2:58 P.M.?

A. 9:59 A.M. B. 10:01 A.M.

C. 9:59 P.M. D. 9:57 A.M.

44. If 567567567 is divided by 567, the quotient is

A. 111 B. 10101

C. 1001001 D. 3

45. 19 thousands + 19 hundreds + 19 ones is equal to

A. 21090 B. 20919

C. 19919 D. 191919

46. How many $\frac{1}{8}$ are in $\frac{1}{2}$?

A. 8 B. 4

C. 2 D. 16

47. Most appropriate strategy that can be used to internalize the skill of addition of money is

A. Use of models
B. Role play
C. Solving lots of problems
D. Use of ICT

48. A teacher uses the following riddle in a class while developing the concept of base 10 and place value: 'I am less than 8 tens and 4 ones.'
The objective of this activity is

A. to have some fun in the class and to break monotony
B. to reinforce the concept of base 10 and place value
C. to do summative assessment
D. to introduce the concept of tens and ones to the students

49. The objective of teaching number system to Class III students is to enable the students

A. to see the numbers as groups of hundreds, tens and ones and to understand the significance of place values
B. to master the skill of addition and subtraction of four-digit numbers
C. to master the skill of reading large
D. to count up to 6 digits

50. To teach various units of length to the students of Class III, a teacher shall take the following materials to the class

A. Centimeter ruler and measuring tape
B. Rulers of different lengths and different units, measuring rod, measuring strip used by architects
C. Measuring tape with centimeter on one side and meter on the other side
D. Relation chart of various units

51. The concept of areas of plane figures can be introduced to the students of Class V by

A. measuring the area of any figure with the help of different objects like palm, leaf, pencil, etc.
B. calculating the area of rectangle by finding length and breadth of a rectangle and using the formula for area of a rectangle
C. stating the formula for area of rectangle and square
D. calculating the area of figures with the help of counting unit squares

52. Computational skills in Mathematics can be enhanced by

A. describing algorithm only
B. conducting hands-on activities in class
C. clarifying concepts and procedures followed by lots of practice
D. giving conceptual knowledge alone

53. Ms. Reena uses a grid activity to teach the concept of multiplication of decimals. A sample is illustrated below:

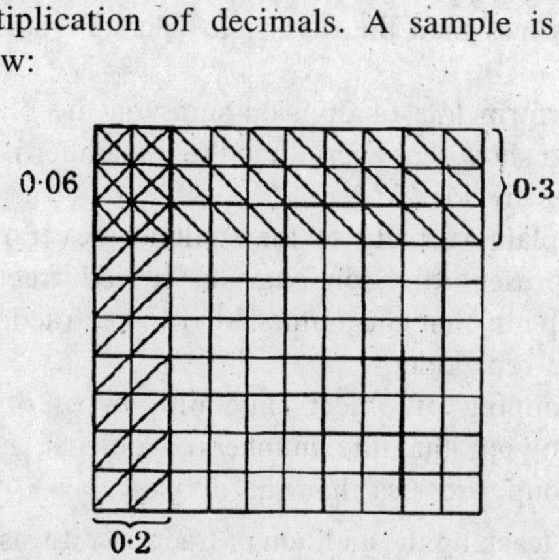

$$0.2 \times 0.3 = 0.06$$

Through this method, Ms. Reena is

A. focusing more on conceptual knowledge and problem-solving and less on procedural knowledge
B. using traditional approach of learning
C. focusing on developing problem-solving skill
D. focusing more on procedural knowledge and less on conceptual knowledge

54. To assess the students' competency on solving of word problems based on addition and subtraction, rubrics of assessment are

A. comprehension of problem, identification of operation to be performed representation of problem mathematically, solution of problem and presentation of problem
B. understanding of problem and writing of correct solution
C. identification of problem, performing correct operation
D. incorrect, partially correct, completely correct

55. While planning a lesson on the concept of fraction addition, a teacher is using the activity of strip folding:

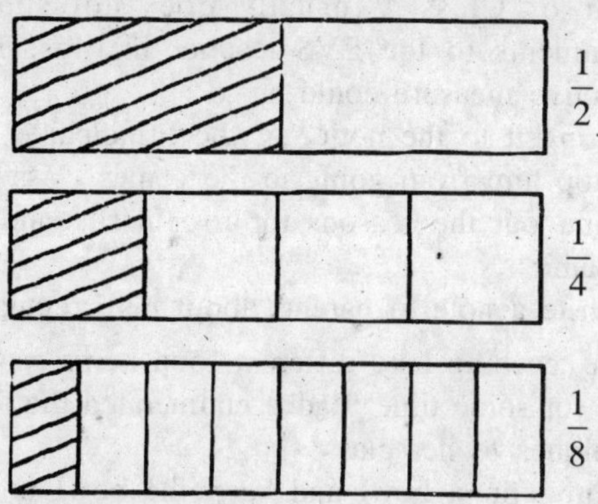

The above activity is a

A. content activity
B. post-content activity
C. wastage of time
D. pre-content activity

56. A suitable approach for explaining that a remainder is always less than the divisor to Class IV students can be

A. perform lots of division sums on the black-board and show that every time the remainder is less than the divisor
B. explain verbally to the students, several times
C. represent division sums as mixed fractions and explain that the numerator of the fraction part is the remainder
D. grouping of objects in multiples of divisor and showing that the number of objects, not in the group, are less than the divisor

57. While teaching the addition of fractions, it was observed by Mr. Singh that the following type of error is very common: $\frac{2}{3}+\frac{2}{5}=\frac{4}{10}$

Mr. Singh should take the following remedial action

A. Give more practice of same type of problems
B. Give pictorial representation to clear the concept of addition of unlike fractions, followed by drill of same type of problems
C. Advise the students to work hard and practise the problems of fraction addtion
D. Explain the concept of LCM of denominator

58. The figure consists of five squares of the same size. The area of the figure is 180 square centimeters. The perimeter (in cm) of the figure will be

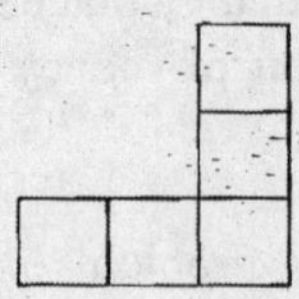

A. 45 B. 48
C. 72 D. 36

59. The NCF (2005) considers that Mathematics involves a certain way of thinking and reasoning. The vision can be realized by

A. giving special coaching to students
B. adopting exploratory approach, use of manipulatives, connecting concepts to real life, involving students in discussions
C. rewriting all text-books of Mathematics
D. giving lots of problem worksheets to students

60. The solid as shown in the figure is made up of cubical blocks each of side 1 cm. The number of blocks is

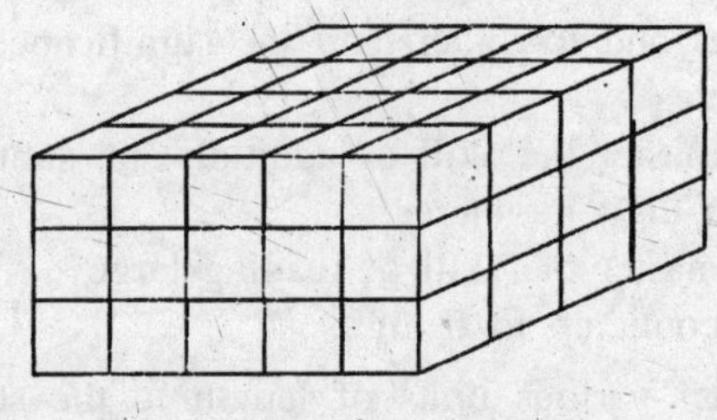

A. 52 B. 60
C. 72 D. 48

PART- III

Environmental Studies

Directions: *Answer the following questions by selecting the **most appropriate** option.*

61. Samir of Class V usually does not submit his assignments to the EVS teacher in time. The best corrective measure could be to

A. bring it to the notice of the Principal
B. stop him from going to the games class
C. find out the reasons for irregularity and counsel Samir
D. write a note to parents about his irregularity

62. While teaching how different food items can be kept fresh for some time, Radha enumerated the following techniques to her class

(a) Put it in a bowl and keep the bowl in an open container having cold water
(b) Wrap it in a damp cloth
(c) Spread it open in sunshine
(d) Cut it into small pieces and keep it in the dark

Which one of the following food items is she referring to, corresponding to technique 'b' above?

A. Cooked rice B. Onion, garlic
C. Green coriander D. Kaju Burfi

63. While teaching the topic 'Friction' to Class V students, a teacher gave a number of examples to explain that friction is also useful to us in many ways. Which one of the following examples was quoted by her incorrectly?

A. We are able to write due to friction between the tip of the pen and the paper
B. We are able to walk because of friction between our shoes and the ground
C. An object thrown vertically upwards always comes back to us due to friction
D. A vehicle stops on application of brakes

64. While performing experiments with water, Jyoti observed that an empty steel bowl floats but a small iron nail sinks in water. This can be explained by the fact that

A. iron is lighter than water and steel is heavier than water
B. force on a steel bowl is more than its weight whereas force on an iron nail is lesser than its weight
C. force on an iron nail is more than its weight whereas force on a steel bowl is lesser than its weight
D. iron is heavier than water and steel is lighter than water

65. Which one of the following four teaching methodologies followed by four different Science teachers for teaching the topic 'Air Pollution' is most appropriate?
A. Dictating the answers to all the questions in the exercise after completing the topic
B. Showing a documentary film on 'Air pollution' to the students
C. Asking the students to collect air samples before and after Diwali, study their quality and tabulate the findings
D. Asking the students to read the topic from the textbook loudly and explaining the meaning of concepts/terms

66. A teacher can identify a stressed child when the child shows the following behaviour:
A. Aggressive behaviour
B. Full concentration in studies
C. Excessive talking
D. Hyperactivity

67. The major purpose of periodic parent-teacher interactions is to
A. share the information about ongoing events in the school
B. discuss the child's strengths and weaknesses for reinforcement and improvement
C. develop a social relationship with each other
D. highlight each other's shortcomings

68. All big cities are facing the problem of environmental pollution as a result of a large number of vehicles on the roads. The best way an individual in the city can contribute towards environmental protection is by
A. getting the engine of personal vehicle checked regularly for environmental safe limits
B. using a public transport system for travelling
C. avoiding frequent travel outside the home
D. not keeping a personal vehicle like scooter, car etc.

69. While teaching the topic on 'Air is everywhere,' a teacher asks the following questions from the students:
1. Is there air in the soil?
2. Is there air inside water?
3. Is there air inside our body
4. Is there air inside our bones?

Which one of the following skills is the teacher trying to develop in the learners?
A. Classification skills B. Thinking skills
C. Emotional skills D. Observation skills

70. Which one of the following is a good cooking practice?
A. Washing the vegetables nicely and then cutting
B. Cutting the vegetables and then washing these in running water
C. Keeping the vegetables in sunshine for some time before cutting and cooking
D. Cooking the vegetables by deep frying to kill bacteria

71. While teaching the topic on 'Air' an EVS teacher wanted to demonstrate that air has weight and occupies space. Her colleague suggested the following four different activities for this purpose to her
(*a*) Place an empty inverted beaker on the surface of the water and start pressing it down
(*b*) Suck the juice through a straw
(*c*) Blow air in a balloon
(*d*) Tie two inflated balloons to a rod and establish equilibrium. Then puncture one of the balloons.

Which of the above activities will lead to demonstrating the desired result?
A. (*a*) and (*b*) B. (*a*) and (*d*)
C. (*b*) and (*d*) D. (*a*) and (*c*)

72. A Science teacher administered a test after teaching the topic on 'Respiration' and observed that majority of the students did not understand the difference between respiration and breathing. This could be due to the reason that
A. she could not explain the related concept effectively in the class
B. she was not their class teacher
C. the students could not understand the question correctly
D. there was usually lot of indiscipline in her class

73. In order to separate a mixture of sand and salt, which one of the following four sequences of processes has to be used?
A. Filtration, decantation, evaporation, sedimentation
B. Evaporation, sedimentation, decantation, filtration
C. Decantation, sedimentation, evaporation, filtration
D. Sedimentation, decantation, filtration, evaporation

74. Rekha's mother adds Phitkari (Alum) to water collected from the pond every day in order to
A. decolourize water
B. sediment light suspended impurities
C. change hard water into soft water
D. kill germs in water

75. Weight-lifters are generally required to make more muscles and body mass. For this purpose, they need to take a diet which is rich in
A. Proteins B. Carbohydrates
C. Fats D. Vitamins

76. Which one of the following teaching strategies will be most effective for maximum involvement of students in teaching the concept of food chain?

A. Ask students to collect related information from internet
B. Ask students to copy all examples of different food chains written on the black-board
C. Make play-cards of organisms and ask student groups to arrange them to depict different food chains
D. Ask students to explore possible food chains operating in different habitats

77. An air-pump is kept in an aquarium in order to

A. make water cleaner
B. provide more carbon dioxide to water plants
C. allow more oxygen to dissolve in water
D. enhance the beauty of the aquarium

78. Anjali's friend suggested the following four ways to avoid tooth decay

1. Brush your teeth twice a day
2. Wear braces to avoid enamel decay
3. Avoid sweets, chocolates and carbonated drinks
4. Rinse mouth after every meal

Which of the above ways should Anjali follow?

A. 2, 3 and 4 B. 3, 4 and 1
C. 4, 1 and 2 D. 1 and 3

79. Study the Venn diagram given below:

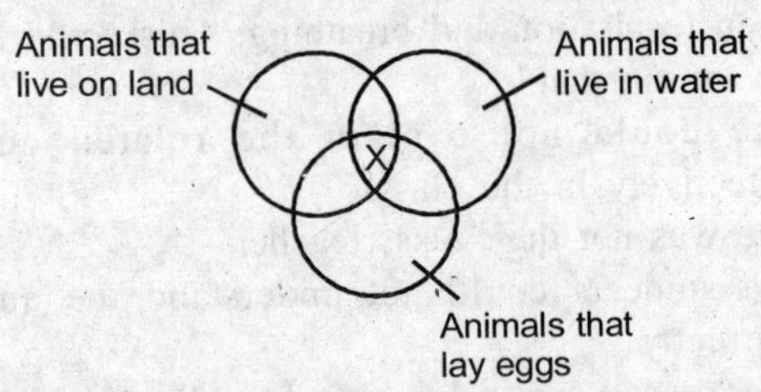

Which of the following animals can be placed at 'X'?

A. Crocodile B. Eel
C. Shark D. Fish

80. Which one of the following pairs of life processes occurs both in plants and animals?

A. Growth and food making
B. Reproduction and food making
C. Reproduction and germination
D. Growth and reproduction

81. In which one of the following groups are the words intimately related?

A. Mosquito, Malaria, Anaemia, Iron
B. Iron, Malaria, Anaemia, Blood
C. Iron, Haemoglobin, Anaemia, Amla
D. Mosquito, Dengue, Iron, Jaggery

82. A fish dies when it is put in an aquarium filled with previously boiled water but cooled to room temperature. This happens because the water in the aquarium is

A. unfit for swimming by fish
B. depleted in oxygen
C. unfit for drinking by fish
D. depleted in minerals

83. Which one of the following best describes the features on the surface of the Moon?

A. No air, no gravity, smooth surface
B. No water, enough air, high mountains
C. No water, deep craters, high mountains
D. No air, no gravity, no water

84. Arti noticed the following precautions related to prevention of spread of a disease on a poster:

1. Do not let water collect around you
2. Keep water pots, coolers and tanks clean
3. Spray oil if water has collected at some place
4. Use nets to protect yourself

The poster is aimed at creating awareness about the spread of

A. Dengue and Japanese Encephalitis
B. Small pox and Malaria
C. Dengue and Eye flu
D. Typhoid and Cholera

85. After having been taught about the rich flora and fauna in India, the students of primary classes were taken to Ranthambhore National Park by the school. This would help the students to

A. develop respect for nature
B. co-relate classroom learning to real-life situations
C. develop skills for environmental protection
D. have fun and enjoy with friends on an outdoor trip

86. In order to introduce the topic on 'Nutrition' in class more effectively, a teacher should

A. show the model of human denture
B. ask the students to open their tiffin boxes, see the contents, followed by teacher's explanation
C. give examples of different foods rich in nutrients
D. draw the diagram of digestive system on the black-board

87. Engage, Explore, Explain, Elaborate and Evaluate are five important 'Es' in relation to effective teaching of Science.

To provide practical experiences to the students related to the concept of 'Necessary conditions for germination', a Science teacher asks them to do the following activities:

1. Soak seeds overnight and keep these is a wet cotton cloth.
2. Observe the seeds after two days and record the changes.
3. Read the book and attempt the given worksheet.

Which of the five 'Es' given above are *not* being covered in the above activities given by the teacher?

A. Engage and Evaluate B. Explain and Elaborate
C. Explore and Evaluate D. Engage and Explore

88. The topic 'Depletion of Petroleum and Coal' was taught to Section A of a class by using multimedia capsule while the other Section B was taught through diagrams drawn on the Green Board. It was found later that students of Section A understood the topic to a better extent. This could be due to the reason that

A. Green Board is not a good visual aid
B. Multiple approach is closer to everyday life situations
C. Use of multimedia aids is comparatively more economical
D. Audio-visual aids engage all the senses for better retention

89. There are four below average students in a class. Which one of the following strategies will be most effective to bring them at par with the other students?

A. Make them sit in the front row and supervise their work constantly
B. Identify their weak areas of learning and provide remedial measures accordingly
C. Ensure that they attend the school regularly
D. Give them additional assignments to do at home

90. Which one of the following sequences of steps is the correct way of preparing a balanced question paper?

A. Preparing a design, preparing a blueprint, writing and editing the questions, writing the marking scheme
B. Preparing the design, writing the questions, preparing the marking scheme, matching with the blueprint
C. Writing and editing the questions, matching with the design preparing the blueprint, writing the marking scheme
D. Writing the questions, preparing the blueprint, matching with the design, writing the marking scheme

PART- IV

Language-I : English

Directions : *Answer the following questions by selecting the **most appropriate** option.*

91. Telling interesting stories to young learners is primarily meant for improving their

A. Writing skills
B. Speaking skills
C. Listening skills
D. Reading skills

92. The best way to sensitize young learners to rhythm and intonation is

A. by reading out poems in different metres and explaining them
B. by making the learners listen to nursery rhymes and recite them effectively
C. by making the learners copy out simple poems in neat handwriting
D. by explaining the rules of phonetics in simple words

93. An effective language teacher

A. will make children learn all the answers to the questions given in the textbook
B. will use the textbook as well as other material as resources for teaching
C. will prepare question papers using only the questions given in the textbook
D. will rely entirely on the prescribed textbook

94. The most effective tool to assess values and attitude of learners is

A. Anecdotal Record
B. Portfolio
C. Unit Test
D. Summative Test

95. A teacher engages her learners in a fun activity before beginning a new lesson. The purpose of this activity is to

A. discipline the learners before the lesson
B. divert the attention of the learners
C. reduce the workload of the teacher
D. motivate and energise the learners

96. The main purpose of using oral drill is

A. to assess the comprehension skills of learners
B. to improve pronunciation and accuracy
C. to enhance the speaking skills of learners
D. to improve the retention capacity of learners

97. Continuous and Comprehensive Evaluation should be adopted by all schools because

A. it is the latest development in the field of education
B. traditional pen-paper tests do not assess and enhance all the attributes and abilities of learners
C. it frees the learners from studies and hard work
D. it affords teachers opportunities to test learners frequently

98. Knowledge of more than one language

A. becomes a burden to the teacher in the language classroom
B. confuses the learners while learning a new language
C. is very helpful in teaching and learning a new language
D. causes interference in learning a new language

99. Seating arrangement should be flexible so that
A. many group, pair and whole-class activities can be conducted easily
B. children do not form permanent friendship groups
C. the teacher ensures equality prevails in her classroom
D. children have the freedom to move their seats wherever they want

100. Curriculum is an educational programme which does *not* state
A. the number of lessons to be taught in a term
B. the means of evaluating whether the educational objectives have been achieved or not
C. the content (material etc.), teaching strategies and learning experiences which will be necessary to achieve this purpose
D. the educational purpose of a programme

101. Which of the following is an important stage in the writing process?
A. Editing
B. Memorisation
C. Calligraphy
D. Comprehension

102. A 'sight word' is a vocabulary item
A. that needs proper visual understanding of the context
B. that is to be learned by heart
C. that helps in judging the effectiveness of the author's style
D. that the reader recognizes and finds meaningful on sight without a complicated analysis

103. Scanning means darting over much of a text to search for
A. the opinion of the author
B. difficult words
C. a specific item or piece of information that we wish to discover
D. the central idea

104. We use real objects to teach young learners new words because
A. it helps in teaching the correct spelling of words
B. we can teach vocabulary only through objects
C. young learners are not capable of abstract thinking
D. it helps learners associate words with objects they see in real life

105. A good introduction to a text should be
A. telling the students anything that they can find out for themselves by reading the text
B. a detailed explanation of the meaning of the text
C. blocking the student's active involvement by means of questioning
D. short and to the point

Directions (Q. No. 106 to 111) : *Read the poem given below and answer the questions that follow by selecting the* ***most appropriate*** *option.*

Night

The sun descending in the west,
The evening star does shine;
The birds are silent in their nest,
And I must seek for mine.
The moon, like a flower,
In heaven's high bower,
With silent delight
Sits and smiles on the night.
Farewell, green fields and happy groves,
Where flocks have took delight.
Where lambs have nibbled, silent moves
The feet of angels bright;
Unseen they pour blessing,
And joy without ceasing,
On each bud and blossom,
And each sleeping bosom.
They look in every thoughtless nest,
Where birds are covered warm;
They visit caves of every beast,
To keep them all from harm.
If they see any weeping
That should have been sleeping,
They pour sleep on their head,
And sit down by their bed.

106. The evening star rises when
A. the sun descends in the west
B. the birds leave their nests
C. it is midnight
D. it is dawn

107. Here, 'bower' represents
A. a flower vase
B. a potted plant
C. a framework that supports climbing plants
D. a bouquet of flowers

108. The poet compares moon to
A. an angel
B. a flower
C. a bird in the nest
D. an evening star

109. The angels come down on earth to
A. take blessing and joy
B. spread moonlight
C. give blessing and joy
D. make people dance and have fun

110. Birds' nest is described as 'thoughtless' because
A. the occupants are asleep without any care
B. the angels are blessing the birds to be happy
C. the birds are covered in the warmth of their nest
D. it is made without any thought

111. The figure of speech used in the line 'In heaven's high bower' is
A. Simile
B. Metaphor
C. Personification
D. Alliteration

Directions (Q. No. 112 to 120) : *Read the passage given below and answer the questions that follow by selecting the **most appropriate** option.*

Our body is a wondrous mechanism and when subjected to unusual stress over a period of time, it adapts itself to deal more effectively with that stress. Therefore, when you exert you muscles against resistance, they are forced to adapt and deal with this extraordinary workload. This is the principle of weight training. Strands of muscle fibres become thicker and stronger in response to the demands placed on them.

One of the great merits of weight training is the strength of your heart. During weight training, your heart is forced to beat faster and stronger in order to pump sufficient blood to the muscles being worked. In time, your heart, like your body, will adapt to this extra-work had by becoming stronger and more efficient. Since your body needs a given amount of blood to perform its daily tasks, your heart will now need fewer beats to pump the same quantity of blood. Sounds good? There's more. Your entire circulatory system is given a thorough workout every time you exercise, which increases its overall efficiency. Even the neural paths from your brain's command centres to each individual muscle become more effective, enabling easier recruitment of muscle fibres for carrying out physical tasks. In essence, your body becomes a well-oiled and finely-tuned piece of machinery, whirring along without any breakdown. In today's stress-filled world, you need all the help you can get.

112. The principle of weight training is
A. training muscles to exert more pressure
B. disposing extra workload
C. thickening of body through extra consumption
D. helping the body adapt to increased stress

113. Weight training makes the muscles
A. resist workload B. thicker and stronger
C. become stranded D. become intense

114. During weight training, the heart pumps
A. more blood
B. required blood
C. an extraordinary amount of blood
D. less blood

115. A stronger and more efficient heart
A. needs fewer beats to pump the same amount of blood
B. can rest longer, reducing its workload
C. is assisted by muscles of the body
D. beats faster and more often to pump blood

116. When neural paths become more effective
A. the brain opens new pathways for communication
B. the brain employs various muscles easily for physical tasks
C. the muscles function effectively and independently
D. the brain functions at extraordinary speed

117. What does the term 'well-oiled' in the passage denote?
A. Serviced B. Massaged
C. Greased D. Healthy

118. Which one of the following is the most appropriate title for the passage?
A. Stress-busting
B. The Mechanics of Weight Training
C. How to retain your health?
D. Health is Wealth

119. What does the above passage suggest?
A. Physical exercise is necessary occasionally
B. We should ignore physical exercise
C. We should subject our body to as much exercise as it can withstand
D. We should carry out physical exercise as a routine

120. The word 'wondrous' (first line) is
A. a noun B. an adverb
C. an adjective D. a verb

PART- V

भाषा-II : हिन्दी

निर्देश: *निम्नलिखित प्रश्नों के उत्तर देने के लिए **सबसे उचित** विकल्प चुनिए।*

121. बहुभाषिक कक्षा के संदर्भ में आप इनमें से किस गतिविधि को सर्वाधिक उचित समझते हैं?
A. 'लड्डू', 'खत' शब्दों के हिन्दी रूप कंठस्थ कीजिए।
B. 'स्वतंत्र' शब्द को दस बार बोलिए।
C. 'सूर्य अस्त हो गया।' वाक्य को 10 बार लिखिए।
D. हिन्दी पाठों में आए 'चिड़िया', 'पुस्तक', 'कुआँ' को आपकी भाषा में क्या कहते हैं? बताइए।

122. हिन्दी भाषा के सतत और व्यापक मूल्यांकन के संदर्भ में कौन-सा कथन उचित ***नहीं*** है?
A. यह बताता है कि बच्चों को किस तरह की मदद की जरूरत है
B. यह बच्चे के संदर्भ में ही मूल्यांकन करता है
C. यह बच्चों को उत्तीर्ण-अनुत्तीर्ण श्रेणियों में विभाजित करने में विश्वास रखता है
D. सतत और व्यापक मूल्यांकन बच्चों की सीखने की क्षमता और तरीके के बारे में जानकारी देता है

123. प्राथमिक स्तर पर आप कहानियों, कविताओं में किस पक्ष को ज्यादा महत्वपूर्ण मानते हैं?

A. प्रतिष्ठित लेखकों की कहानियाँ, कविताएँ बच्चों को पढ़ाई जाएँ
B. प्रत्यक्ष उपदेशात्मकता
C. कहानियों, कविताओं का व्याकरणिक नियमों की जानकारी की दृष्टि से समृद्ध होना
D. घटनाओं, शहरों, पदों में दोहराव

124. भाषा की प्रकृति के सम्बन्ध में कौन-सा कथन उचित ***नहीं*** है?

A. भाषा का जितना अधिक प्रयोग किया जाएगा, उतना ही भाषा पर पकड़ मजबूत होती जाएगी
B. भाषा कठोरता से व्याकरणिक नियमों का अनुसरण करती है
C. भाषाएँ एक-दूसरे के सान्निध्य में फलती-फूलती हैं
D. भाषा एक नियमबद्ध व्यवस्था है

125. निम्नलिखित में से किस उद्देश्य के लिए प्राथमिक स्तर पर भाषा ***नहीं*** सीखी जाती?

A. अपनी अनेक जरूरतों को पूरा करना
B. जीवन की विभिन्न स्थितियों को साधना
C. भाषा का व्याकरण सीखना
D. मन की बात कहना-सुनना

126. कलिका हिन्दी भाषा में बोलते समय कई बार अटकती है। आप क्या करेंगे?

A. धैर्य रखते हुए उसे सहज अभिव्यक्ति के लिए प्रोत्साहित करेंगे
B. उसे प्रवाहपूर्ण अभिव्यक्ति के नमूने सुनाएँगे और कहेंगे कि उसे भी हू-ब-हू ऐसे ही बोलना है
C. कक्षा के बाकी बच्चों से कहेंगे कि कलिका के समक्ष प्रवाहपूर्ण अभिव्यक्ति के नमूने प्रस्तुत करें
D. कक्षा में केवल कलिका को ही बार-बार बोलने के लिए कहेंगे

127. तमिल भाषी सुहेल प्रायः 'भजन', को 'बजन' कहता है। भाषा के शिक्षक के रूप में आप क्या करेंगे?

A. 'भजन' शब्द का बार-बार उच्चारण करवाएँगे
B. सुहेल को उसकी त्रुटि के लिए डाँटेंगे
C. तमिल और हिन्दी भाषा का तुलनात्मक अध्ययन करते हुए महाप्राण ध्वनियों से युक्त भाषिक सामग्री का प्रयोग करेंगे
D. सुहेल को बताएँगे कि सही शब्द 'भजन' है

128. 'गणित, विज्ञान, सामाजिक विज्ञान की कक्षाएँ एक तरह से भाषा की ही कक्षाएँ हैं।' इस कथन के समर्थन में कौन-सा तर्क सबसे कमजोर है?

A. विभिन्न विषयों के अध्ययन-अध्यापन में भाषा साधन का कार्य करती है
B. विभिन्न विषयों के शिक्षण में भाषा-शिक्षण एक मुख्य उद्देश्य होता है
C. विभिन्न विषयों की अवधारणात्मक समझ की अभिव्यक्ति भी भाषा-विशेष में होती है
D. विभिन्न विषयों की अवधारणाएँ किसी भाषा-विशेष में बनती हैं

129. भाषा का प्राथमिक रूप है–

A. मौखिक B. सांकेतिक
C. व्याकरणिक D. लिखित

130. हिन्दी भाषा की पाठ्य-पुस्तक में लोकगीतों को शामिल करने का कौन-सा उद्देश्य सबसे कम महत्वपूर्ण है?

A. लोकगीतों की भाषिक विशेषताओं से परिचित होने का अवसर मुहैया कराना
B. लोकगीतों से संबद्ध राज्यों की जानकारी देना
C. लोकगीतों की रसानुभूति
D. लोकगीतों के माध्यम से भारत की सांस्कृतिक विशेषताओं से परिचित कराना

131. कहानियाँ बच्चों के भाषा-विकास में किस प्रकार सहायक हैं?

A. ये बच्चों की कल्पनाशक्ति, सृजनात्मकता और चिंतन को बढ़ावा देती हैं
B. ये भाषिक नियम ही सिखाती हैं
C. बच्चों के खाली समय का सदुपयोग करने में मदद करती हैं
D. ये पाठ्य-पुस्तक का सबसे महत्वपूर्ण हिस्सा है

132. लेखन-कुशलता का विकास करने में सबसे कम महत्वपूर्ण है–

A. आँखों-देखी घटनाओं को लिखना
B. प्रतिलिपि
C. अधूरी-कहानी को पूरा करना
D. कहानी-कविता आदि का सृजनात्मक लेखन

133. भाषा की कक्षा में कौन-सी शिक्षण-युक्ति सबसे कम प्रभावी है?

A. दूसरों की हस्तलिखित सामग्री, पत्र आदि पढ़वाना
B. उचित गति एवं प्रवाह के साथ पढ़ने पर बल देना
C. शुद्ध उच्चारण पर अत्यधिक बल देना
D. बच्चों की रुचि के अनुसार परिचित विषय या प्रसंग पर चर्चा

134. भाषा-अर्जन के संबंध में कौन-सा कथन उचित ***नहीं*** है?

A. इसमें समाज-सांस्कृतिक विशेषताओं को सहज रूप से आत्मसात् किया जाता है
B. भाषा के नियम सीखे जाते हैं
C. परिवेश से प्राप्त भाषिक आँकड़ों के आधार पर सहज रूप से भाषिक नियम बनाए जाते हैं
D. भाषा-अर्जन में भाषिक परिवेश महत्वपूर्ण होता है

135. बच्चों की पठन-कुशलता का विकास करने में सर्वाधिक महत्वपूर्ण है–

A. पाठ्य-पुस्तक में दिए गए अभ्यास
B. भाषिक संरचनाओं का अभ्यास
C. अर्थ की अपेक्षा उच्चारणगत शुद्धता पर विशेष ध्यान देना
D. विभिन्न संदर्भों से जुड़ी सामग्री

निर्देश (प्र. सं. 136 से 143): *गद्यांश को पढ़कर निम्नलिखित प्रश्नों में* ***सबसे उचित*** *विकल्प चुनिए।*

जहाँ तक मैं समझता हूँ, मेरी आत्मिक शक्तियों के विकास में बार्सीलोना और उसके निवासियों का सबसे सुंदर चित्रण भी सहायक नहीं हो सकता था। स्योम्का और फेद्का को पीटर्सबर्ग के जलमार्गों को जानने की क्या जरूरत है, अगर जैसी कि संभावना है, वे वहाँ कभी नहीं जा पाएँगे? अगर स्योम्का

का वहाँ कभी जाना होगा भी, तो उसे इससे कोई फर्क नहीं पड़ेगा कि उसने इस स्कूल में पढ़ा था या नहीं, क्योंकि तब इन जलमार्गों को वह व्यवहार में जान ही जाएगा और अच्छी तरह जान जाएगा। मैं नहीं समझ सकता कि उसकी आत्मिक शक्तियों के विकास में इस बात की जानकारी से कोई मदद मिल सकती है कि वोल्गा में सन से लदे जहाज नीचे की ओर जाते हैं और अलकतरे से लदे जहाज ऊपर की ओर; कि दुबोव्का नाम का एक बंदरगाह है; कि फलाँ भूमिगत परत फलाँ जगह तक जाती है; कि सामोयेद लोग बारहसिंगा गाड़ियों पर सफर करते हैं, वगैरह-वगैरह।

136. स्योम्का और फेद्का हैं–

A. शिक्षकों के नाम B. विद्यार्थियों के नाम
C. कर्मचारियों के नाम D. शहरों के नाम

137. लेखक के अनुसार वह पढ़ाई निरर्थक है–

A. जानकारी नहीं दी जाती
B. जो बंदरगाहों के बारे में न बताए
C. जिसका उपयोग बच्चे अपने रोजमर्रा के जीवन में न करते हों
D. जिसमें जलमार्गों के बारे में नहीं पढ़ाया जाता

138. बच्चे ढेर सारी जानकारी हासिल करके–

A. विद्वान् बन सकते हैं
B. आत्मिक विकास नहीं कर सकते
C. कक्षा में अव्वल आ सकते हैं
D. बहुत कुछ सीख सकते हैं

139. बच्चे बहुत कुछ स्वतः ही तभी सीख जाते हैं जब–

A. वे चीजों को व्यवहार में लाते हैं
B. माता-पिता बताते हैं
C. वे किताब में पढ़ते-देखते हैं
D. शिक्षक उन्हें सिखाते हैं

140. व्यावहारिक जीवन में उपयोग में न आने वाली बातों को जानने या न जानने में फर्क नहीं पड़ता, क्योंकि–

A. बच्चे अभी इन बातों का उपयोग करने योग्य नहीं हैं
B. बाद में शिक्षक बता ही देंगे
C. बच्चे कुशाग्रबुद्धि होते हैं
D. ये बातें व्यावहारिक जीवन को प्रभावित नहीं करतीं

141. 'निवासी' का बहुवचन रूप है–

A. निवासी B. निवासिएँ
C. निवासों D. निवासियों

142. निम्नलिखित में से कौन-सा 'चित्रण' के लिए उपयुक्त विशेषण ***नहीं*** है?

A. सुंदर B. मनोहारी
C. सौंदर्य D. कलात्मक

143. 'फर्क' का समानार्थी है–

A. असरदार B. अंतर
C. हानि D. प्रभावकारी

निर्देश (प्र. सं. 144 से 150 तक): *गद्यांश को पढ़कर निम्नलिखित प्रश्नों में से* ***सबसे उचित*** *विकल्प चुनिए।*

कुछ कहा जा रहा हो उससे कहीं महत्वपूर्ण होता है अपनी बात कहने का तरीका। आप कितनी ही जरूरी बात क्यों न कहें, अगर आपकी बात कोई सुने नहीं, महसूस ही न करे, तो उसे कहने का फायदा ही क्या? किसी के कहे को सुनने के लिए, उसे महसूस करने के लिए, पूरा ध्यान केंद्रित करने की जरूरत होती है। और वही मिलता था मुझे उस महान संगीतज्ञ बीथोवन के स्वरों द्वारा–पूरा ध्यान। आप पूछ सकते हैं कि "आवाजाही और बातचीत के शोर से भरे किसी कमरे के दूसरे छोर पर बैठा कोई बच्चा उन आठ कोमल स्वरों को भला कैसे सुनता होगा?" इस सवाल का जवाब तो कोई भी शिक्षक दे सकता है। ये स्वर तो वे बच्चे सुन ही पाते थे जो पियानो के बिल्कुल पास खड़े हों, और तब उनका स्पर्श दूसरों को आगाह करता था। पर कुछ ही क्षणों में तेजी से फैलती वह खामोशी ही बोलने लगती थी। और जब तक आखिरी स्वर की गूंज खत्म होती, सभी बच्चे शांत हो चुके थे। वे खामोशियाँ, वे सन्नाटे याद रहेंगे मुझे .... सात क्या उसके भी कई-कई सालों बाद भी।

144. लेखिका के अनुसार अपनी बात कहने के संदर्भ में सबसे महत्वपूर्ण क्या है?

A. जो कुछ कहा जा रहा है
B. बात कहने का तरीका
C. ध्यान केंद्रित करने के लिए आवाजों का प्रयोग करना
D. सवाल का जवाब देना

145. संवाद तभी सार्थक होता है जब–

A. कहने-सुनने वाले सक्रिय हों
B. मधुर आवाज
C. शांत माहौल
D. जरूरी बात कहना

146. 'खामोशी ही बोलने लगती है।' ये अभिप्राय है–

A. खामोशी बच्चों से कहती है कि चुप हो जाओ
B. खामोशी तेज आवाज में बोलती है
C. खामोश बच्चे बोलने लगते हैं
D. जब कुछ बच्चे धीरे-धीरे बोलना बंद कर देते हैं तो बाकी बच्चों को पता चल जाता है कि उन्हें भी शांत होना है

147. लेखिका के अनुसार–

A. बच्चे बहुत बोलते हैं
B. एक शिक्षक अपने बच्चों को बहुत अच्छी तरह जानता है
C. बच्चों को शांत करने के लिए संगीत का ही प्रयोग करना चाहिए
D. बच्चे बहुत शोर करते हैं

148. 'महत्वपूर्ण' शब्द है–

A. योगरूढ़ B. विकारी
C. यौगिक D. रूढ़

149. निम्नलिखित में से कौन-सा शब्द स्त्रीलिंग है?

A. बातचीत B. जवाब
C. सवाल D. पियानो

150. 'इस सवाल का जवाब तो कोई भी शिक्षक दे सकता है।' वाक्य में आए 'भी', 'तो' शब्द हैं–

A. सर्वनाम B. निपात
C. संबंधबोधक D. क्रिया-विशेषण

Answers

1	2	3	4	5	6	7	8	9	10
B	D	B	B	A	C	A	A	A	B
11	12	13	14	15	16	17	18	19	20
D	B	B	D	A	B	D	D	D	C
21	22	23	24	25	26	27	28	29	30
C	C	A	C	B	D	B	D	A	A
31	32	33	34	35	36	37	38	39	40
A	C	D	C	A	D	A	D	A	C
41	42	43	44	45	46	47	48	49	50
D	A	A	C	B	B	B	B	A	B
51	52	53	54	55	56	57	58	59	60
A	B	A	A	D	D	B	C	B	B
61	62	63	64	65	66	67	68	69	70
C	A	C	B	C	A	B	B	D	A
71	72	73	74	75	76	77	78	79	80
B	A	D	B	A	C	C	B	A	D
81	82	83	84	85	86	87	88	89	90
C	B	C	A	B	B	D	D	B	A
91	92	93	94	95	96	97	98	99	100
C	B	B	B	D	B	B	C	A	A
101	102	103	104	105	106	107	108	109	110
D	D	C	D	D	A	A	B	C	A
111	112	113	114	115	116	117	118	119	120
B	A	B	B	A	B	D	B	D	C
121	122	123	124	125	126	127	128	129	130
D	C	D	B	C	A	C	B	B	B
131	132	133	134	135	136	137	138	139	140
A	B	A	B	D	B	C	B	A	D
141	142	143	144	145	146	147	148	149	150
D	C	B	A	A	D	B	C	A	B

Some Selected Explanatory Answers

3. Table: Advantages of SBA (School Based Assessment) compared with external examinations

Point	Characteristics of SBA	Characteristics of External Exams
Scope	Extends the range and diversity of assessment collection opportunities, task types and assessors	Much narrower range of assessment opportunities: less diverse assessment; one exam per year
Authenticity	Assessment done by students' own teacher; less possibility of cheating as teacher knows student capabilities; assessments more likely to be realistic	Removes assessment entirely from teaching and learning; stressful conditions may lead to students not demonstrating real capacities
Validity	Improves validity through assessing factors that cannot be included in public exam settings	Limits validity by limiting scope of assessment, e.g. difficult to assess interaction skills in exam environment

Reliability	Improves reliability by having more than one assessment by a teacher who is familiar with the student; allows for multiple opportunities for assessor reflection/standardisation	Even with double marking, examiners' judgments can be affected by various factors (task difficulty, topic, interest level, tiredness, etc); little opportunity for assessor reflection / review
Fairness	Fairness is achieved by following commonly-agreed processes, outcomes and standards; teacher assumptions about students and their oral language levels is made explicit through collaborative sharing and discussion with other teachers	Fairness can only be achieved by treating everyone the same, *i.e.* setting the same task at the same time for all students.
Feedback	Students can receive constructive feedback immediately after the assessment has finished, hence improving learning	The only feedback is usually a grade at the end of the course; no opportunities for interaction with assessor; no chance to ask how to improve
Positive washback (*beneficial influence on teaching and learning*)	Ongoing assessment encourages students to work consistently; provides important data for evaluation of teaching and assessment practices in general	Examination is purely summative, and does not serve any teaching-related purpose; effects on teaching and learning may even be negative; may encourage teaching to the test and a focus on exam technique, rather than outcomes.
Teacher and student empowerment	Teachers and students become part of the assessment process; collaboration and sharing of expertise take place within and across schools	Teachers play little to no role in assessment of their students and have no opportunity to share their expertise or knowledge of their students; students treated as numbers
Professional development	Builds teacher assessment skills, which can be transferred to other areas of the curriculum	Teachers have no opportunity to build their assessment skills; get little or no feedback on how to improve as teachers

5. Lev Vygotsky (1896-1934) a Russian psychologist and philosopher in the 1930's, is most often associated with the social constructivist theory. He emphasizes the influences of cultural and social contexts in learning and supports a discovery model of learning. This type of model places the teacher in an active role while the students' mental abilities develop naturally through various paths of discovery. Vygotsky's theory is one of the foundations of constructivism. It emphasizes three major themes:

Major themes:

- Social interaction plays a fundamental role in the process of cognitive development. In contrast to Jean Piaget's understanding of child development (in which development necessarily precedes learning), Vygotsky felt social learning precedes development. He states: "Every function in the child's cultural development appears twice: first, on the social level, and later, on the individual level; first, between people (inter-psychological) and then inside the child (intra-psychological)."
- The More Knowledgeable Other (MKO). The MKO refers to anyone who has a better understanding or a higher ability level than the learner, with respect to a particular task, process, or concept.
- The Zone of Proximal Development (ZPD). The ZPD is the distance between a student's ability to perform a task under adult facilitation and/or with peer collaboration and the student's ability solving the problem independently. For learners there is zone of proximal development for each task they are expected to master. Learning occurred in this zone.

Vygotsky focused on the connections between people and the socio-cultural context in which they act and interact in shared experiences. According to Vygotsky, humans use tools that develop from a culture, such as speech and writing, to mediate their social environments. Initially children develop these tools to serve solely as social functions, ways to communicate needs. Vygotsky believed that the internalization of these tools led to higher thinking skills.

6. American psychologist, Howard Gardner developed a theory of Multiple Intelligences (1983) which can go some way towards explaining different learner styles. According to Gardner there are eight different types of intelligences.

The eight intelligences are:

- **Linguistic–**The word player
- **Logical/Mathematical**–The questioner
- **Visual/Spatial**–The visualiser
- **Musical**–The music lover
- **Bodily/Kinaesthetic–**The mover
- **Interpersonal**–The socialiser
- **Intrapersonal–**The loner
- **Naturalistic**–The nature lover (added by Gardner at a later date)

7. Active Learning Approach: It is an approach of learning in which a learner learns through audio, visual, and audio-visual mode, role play, collaborative learning, project based learning, project based learning, here the teacher is a facilitator only. He/she can only help the students to learn the way they want. The teacher prepares a number of activities such as critical reading, questioning, quiz, puzzle, memory games review where in the students actively participate in the activities. The students have the freedom to participate in the activity. The job of the teacher is to create a conducive environment that enthuse/motivate the students for independent learning and participation.

12. The UNESCO Information and Communication Technologies in Teacher Education (2002) notes that in contrast to the traditional teaching-learning paradigm, a new paradigm of the teaching-learning process is emerging based on three decades of research in human learning that encompasses the following views of the human learning process:

- Learning is a natural process.
- Learning is a social process.
- Learning is an active and not a passive process.
- Learning may either be linear or non-linear.
- Learning is integrative and contextualized.
- Learning is based on a strength model of student abilities, interest, and culture.
- Learning is assessed through task completion, products, and real problem solving of both individual and group efforts.

A Paradigm Shift: From Teaching to Learning

A shift from teacher-centred instruction to learner-centred instruction is needed to enable students to acquire the new 21st century knowledge and skills. The following table identifies the shift that will take place in changing from a focus on teaching to a focus on learning.

Table: Teacher-Centred and Learner-Centred Learning Environments

Classroom activity	Teacher-centred, Didactic	Learner-centred, Interactive
Teacher role	Fact teller, Always expert	Collaborator, Sometimes learner
Instructional emphasis	Facts memorization	Relationships, Inquiry and invention
Concepts of knowledge	Accumulation of facts, Quantity	Transformation of facts
Demonstration of success	Norm referenced	Quality of understanding
Assessment	Multiple choice items	Criterion referenced, Portfolios and performances
Technology use	Drill and practice	Communication, access, collaboration, expression

Shifting the emphasis from teaching to learning can create a more interactive and engaging learning environment for teachers and learners. This new environment also involves a change in the roles of both teachers and students. As shown in above Table (adapted from Newby et al., 2000), the role of the teacher will change from knowledge transmitter to that of learning facilitator, knowledge guide, knowledge navigator and co-learner with the student. The new role does not diminish the importance of the teacher but requires new knowledge and skills. Students will have greater responsibility for their own learning in this environment as they seek out, find, synthesize, and share their knowledge with others. ICTs provide powerful tools to support the shift to learning centred education and the new roles of teachers and students.

Table: Changes in Student and Teacher Roles in Learner-Centred Environments

Changes in Teacher Role	
A shift from:	***A shift to:***
Knowledge transmitter, primary source of information, content expert, and source of all answers	Learning facilitator, collaborator, coach, mentor, knowledge navigator, and colearner
Teacher controls and directs all aspects of learning	Teacher gives students more options and responsibilities for their own learning
Changes in Student Role	
A shift from:	***A shift to:***
Passive recipient of information	Active participant in the learning process
Reproducing knowledge	Producing and sharing knowledge, participating at times as expert
Learning as a solitary activity	Learning collaboratively with others

13. Inclusive Education: In inclusive education, the children with disabilities are educated in the "least restrictive environment" appropriate to meet their "unique needs." In inclusion the children learn together and learn to live together.

15. Progressive education was a revolt against the traditional schools of the United States those existed at the beginning of 19th century. It grew from the belief that schools had failed to keep pace with rapid changes in American life. The traditional school says Dewey, "Stressed specific subjects-reading, writing, arithmetic, geography, history, and grammar. The teacher lectured or dictated a lesson, and the students copied it in their notebooks.

The students then learned by heart what was in their note-books and recited what they learned from their textbooks. The teacher en-forced order and quiet except for recitation periods. Students sat at rows of desks fastened to the floor, and they could not move or talk without permission."

The term "progressive education" has been used to describe ideas and practices that aim to make schools more effective agencies of a democratic society. Although there are numerous differences of style and emphasis among progressive educators, they share the conviction that democracy means active participation by all citizens in social, political and economic decisions that will affect their lives.

Progressive educators tried to reform elementary school methods in several ways. They thought teachers should pay more attention to the individual child and not treat all children alike.

Progressive educators believed that children learn best when they are genuinely interested in the material, and not when they are forced to memorize facts that seem useless to them. Children should learn by direct contact with things, places, and people, as well as by reading and hearing about them. Thus, elementary schools should include science laboratories, workshops, art studios, kitchens, gymnasiums, and gardens. Progressive educators believed that this would develop the child's physical, social, and emotional nature as well as its mind.

In addition, progressive educators stressed greater freedom, activity, and informality in the classroom. They believed that children learn better when they can move about and work at their own pace. They thought children should gather materials from many sources rather than from just one textbook, and should work in groups with other students. Discussion, dramatics, music, and art activities became a larger part of classroom procedures.

16. Piaget's Stages of Cognitive Development

Stage	*Approximate Age*	*Characteristics*
Sensorimotor	0-2 years	Begins to make use of imitation, memory, and thought. Begins to recognize that objects do not cease to exist when they are hidden *i.e.* they develop **object permanence.** Moves from reflex actions to **goal-directed** activity. The child gradually develops the ability to act with an objective in mind such as reaching out for a toy.
Preoperational	2-7 years	Gradually develops use of language and ability to think in symbolic form Able to think operations through logically in one direction. Has difficulties seeing another person's point of view.
Concrete operational	7-11 years	Able to solve concrete (hands-on) problems in logical fashion, *e.g.* can understand fractions in mathematics better if explained with the help of a pizza cut into 4 or 6 or 8 slices. Understands laws of conservation which means the amount or quantity of an object remains the same even if their arrangement is changed. eg. A tall and narrow glass and a short and wide bottomed glass will have the same amount of water if say 50 ml water have been poured into them. The tall glass won't have more water even if it appears to have more. Able to classify and seriate ie. Able to put things into various categories and in a sequence based on any one aspect such as size, weight, height and so on. Understands reversibility, *e.g.* can assemble pieces of building blocks to make an object, dismantle them and join them again to make the objects.
Formal operational	11- adult	Able to solve abstract problems in logical fashion, *e.g.*, can think of an imaginary problem and can offer logical solutions to it. Becomes more scientific in thinking. Develops concerns about social issues, identity.

17. Kohlberg's Theory

Lawrence Kohlberg (1976, 1986) stressed that moral development primarily involves moral reasoning and occurs in stages. Kohlberg arrived at his theory after interviewing children, adolescents, and adults (primarily males) about their views on a series of moral dilemmas.

Kohlberg's Levels and Stages of Moral Development

Kohlberg constructed a theory of moral development that has three main levels with two stages at each of the levels. A key concept in understanding Kohlberg's theory is *internalization,* which refers to the developmental change from externally controlled behaviour to internally controlled behaviour.

Preconventional reasoning is the lowest level of moral development in Kohlberg's theory. At this level, the child shows no internalization of moral values. Moral reasoning is controlled by external rewards and punishment.

Conventional reasoning is the second, or intermediate, level in Kohlberg's theory. At this level, the child's internatlization is intermediate. The child abides internally by certain standards, but they are essentially the standards imposed by other people, such as parents, or by society's laws.

Postconventional reasoning is the highest level in Kohlberg's theory. At this level, morality is completely internalized and not based on external standards. The student recognizes alternative moral courses, explores options, and then decides on the moral code that is best for him or her.

In studies of Kohlberg's theory, longitudinal data show a relation of the stages to age, although few people ever attain the two highest stages, especially stage 6 (Colby & others, 1983). Before are 9, most children reason about moral dilemmas at a preconventional level. By early adolescence, they are more likely to reason at the conventional level.

Kohlberg stressed that underlying changes in cognitive development promote more advanced moral thinking. He also said that children construct their moral thoughts as they pass through the stages — that they do not just passively accept a cultural norm for morality. Kohlberg argued that a child's moral thinking can be advanced through discussions with others who reason at the next higher stage. Kohlberg thought that the mutual give-and-take of peer relations promotes more advanced moral thinking because of the role-taking opportunities they provide children.

20. A drill is "A type of highly controlled oral practice in which the students respond to a given cue. The response varies according to the type of drill." Drills are used usually at the controlled practice stage of language learning so that students have the opportunity to accurately try out what they have learned. Drills help students to develop quick, automatic responses using a specific formulaic expression or structure, such as a tag ending, verb form, or transformation.

Drills can be useful teaching-learning material because they provide practice of small, manageable chunks of language. This helps to build confidence and automatic use of structures and expressions that have been drilled. Also, they can be part of a teaching or learning sequence that progresses from more towards less controlled practice.

Mary Spratt (1991) notes that drills can be either mechanical or meaningful. Mechanical drills are controlled by the teacher who provides drill cues to which students respond. These drills can give beginning students a chance to articulate the new language fluently. Meaningful drills are controlled by the teacher as well as by the students who must understand the drill cues in order to respond. Meaningful drills are more desirable than mechanical drills because they provide a reason for speaking and are thus more engaging and motivating.

21. Problem solving refers to a deliberate and purposeful act on the part of an individual aiming to realize some set goals or objectives by making use of some novel methods, higher thinking and systematic steps. The systematic steps followed in a scientific method of problem-solving may be identified as problem awareness, problem understanding, collection of relevant information, formulation of hypotheses, selection of a proper solution and verification of the arrived solution.

Strategies of effective problems solving refer to those special strategies and tactics that can help a lot in finding the ways of solving the problem in quite an economic and effective way. Usually these may include algorithms, (strategy to generate a solution by exhausting every possible answer for ending up with the correct solution) and heuristics, the rule of thumb for arriving at a quick solution like sub goal analysis, means—end analysis, working backward and using an analogy etc.

Problem solving behaviour of an individual depends upon a number of factors broadly classified in two categories–factors lying in the nature of the problem (like its simplicity or complexity, its similarity or dissimilarity with the problem solved in the past etc.) and factors associated with the problem solver like his level of previous learning, interest and motivation, way of solving the problem, his mind set, functional fixedness, mental and physical status and the time spent by him on solving the problem and the situation and facilities available for him in his environment at the time of problem solving etc.

22. Determinants of Personality

Personality is the result of both heredity and environment and also the situation.

Heredity: Heredity refers to those factors that were determined at conception. Physical appearance, temperament, energy level and biological rhythms are the characteristics which are generally influenced by one's Parents' i.e., One's Biological, Physiological and Inherent Psychological Make up. The Heredity approach feels that personality of an individual is the Molecular Structure of the genes, located in the chromosomes.

Environment: Culture plays an important role in the formation of personality, *i.e.,* early conditioning, the norms among the family, friends and social groups. With the socialisation process in the group, personalities are altered over time.

Situation: Though an individual personality is constant, it does change depending on the situation. Different demands in different situations call forth different aspect of one's personality.

The relationship of these three factors affects the formation and development of Personality. Psychological inheritance is entirely an internal contribution. Group and culture are the early environmental factors that form later behaviour. Family and social setting during the early stages of education are the important factors which influences the initial formation of personality. Whatever the child learns here lasts for life time. Later in life, it is the Peer groups or Primary affiliations at work, social activities which shape the Personality.

24. According to Benjamin Bloom, the development of the learners can be classified under three domains. They are:

1. Cognitive Domain
2. Affective Domain
3. Psycho motor Domain

Cognitive Domain

In general, cognitive domain develops the cognitive level of the students in various areas. It consists of the following objectives.

1. Knowledge
2. Understanding
3. Application
4. Analysis
5. Synthesis
6. Evaluation

Learning in the cognitive domain refers to the Knowledge stage. From Knowledge, it moves to the level of Understanding. In a new environment, the Application of the new Knowledge is Analysed, Synthesized and Evaluated. All these objectives are incorporated in teaching. But in the Primary level, the first three levels of objectives only can be achieved. But in the present situation, the teachers thrust information upon the learners. It has been found in a research study that nearly 80% of the memorized information are forgotten by the learners because it is not applied in life situations. So, instead of stressing the students for memorization of concepts or information, opportunities must be provided for application of the Knowledge in real life situations. In the higher level, the learners must be involved in Analyzing, Synthesizing and Evaluating the content related gathered information.

Affective Domain

It states the stimulation of students' feelings and emotions.

Objectives:

1. Appreciation
2. Interest
3. Attitudes
4. Value System
5. Character Formation

The above mentioned Affective Domain qualities must reach the learners through Teaching Learning Activities.

Stages of affective domain:

1. Students readiness for stimuiation or willingness to gain information
   (*a*) Awareness of stimulation
   (*b*) Interest
   (*c*) Selected concept
2. Expression of Emotion (Stimulation based action)
3. Understanding the value of received information
4. Integrating our values with the other values and establish relationship
5. Behavioural changes are based on the understanding of values

Learning environment in Affective Domain:

1. Learning environment provides protection, broad mind and confidence
2. Learner centered Teaching Approach
3. Individual differences are expressed by problem solving and analysis approach

Psycho Motor Domain

Psycho motor deals with the nervous system of the learners. Developing the activity skills of the learners is the basic aim of Psycho motor domain. In this,

1. Motivation
2. Response

3. Self restraint
4. Synchronization
5. Rhythm

The psycho motor activities are considered important because of its relevance in subjects like Maths and Science to develop manipulative skills.

1. Developing the experimental skill
2. Developing the constructional skill
3. Developing the problem solving skill
4. Developing the observation skill
5. Developing the Drawing skill

The objective of manipulative skills includes all the above mentioned skills which take place generally during examinations.

27. Principles of Development

Although all individuals grow and develop in their own unique way and in their own contexts, there are some basic principles which underlie the process of development and can be observed in all human beings. These are called the principles of development.

1. Development follows a pattern
2. Development proceeds from general to specific (global to analytical)
3. Development leads to integration
4. Development is continuous
5. Individuals differ with respect to the rate of development
6. Development occurs at different rates for different parts of the body
7. Development proceeds from ego-centricism to allocentricism
8. Development proceeds from heteronomy to autonomy
9. Development is Predictable

28. Domains of Development

Development is an inclusive term that incorporates changes in several areas. These areas or domains deal with 3 broad categories:

1. **Physical and motor development:** It refers to changes in body-size and structure, functioning of various body systems, brain development, perceptual and motor development.
2. **Cognitive development:** It refers to the development of cognitive and intellectual processes, including memory, attention, intelligence, academic knowledge, problem solving, imagination and creativity. It also includes development of language.
3. **Socio-emotional development:** It refers to how we develop relationships with other people, and how our emotions emerge and change as we grow older. It includes emotional communication and self-control, understanding of self and others, inter-personal skills, personality, and emergence of friendship and moral reasoning.

These domains or areas are inter-related and combine in a holistic manner to make a person's developmental pattern unique. Each domain influences and is influenced by others. As a baby develops physically, several motor skills are acquired. As the baby becomes capable of grasping, reaching, sitting, crawling, standing and walking, he/she is able to better explore the environment, resulting in further cognitive development. Improved thinking and understanding helps formation of better social relations as well as emotional expression and comprehension. On the whole, each domain helps the child move towards enriched experiences, learning and overall development.

32. An abacus has beads that slide on rods. It can be used to count, add, subtract, multiply and more.

33. 176 ÷ 3 then we get remainder = 2

But 173 ÷ 5 then remainder = 3

3 is greater than 2

∴ D is correct answer.

34. 5 km = 5000 m

50 m = 50 m

500 cm = 05 m

5055 m

35. Sum of place values of 6 in 63606

= 60000
600
6
60606

36. 5671
−1765
3906

37. 1 × 1 = 1

11 × 11 = 121

111 × 111 = 12321

— — — — — — —

∴ 11111 × 11111 = 123454321.

39. Successor of 1000 = 1001

Predecessor of 1001 = 1000

∴ Predecessor of successor of 1000 is 1000.

40. A shop has 239 toys.

increased = 70 toys

sold = 152 toys

∴ The number of toys left = 239 + 70 − 152.

41. Cost of 1 pencil = ₹ 2½

Cost of 18 pencils = ₹ $\frac{5}{2}\times18=$ ₹ 45

100 – 45 = ₹ 55

The money he will get back = ₹ 55.

42. Product of 3759 × 9573 = 35984907

The sum of 0 + 7 = 7.

43. 2:58 P.M. = 14:58

Hrs	min.		
14	: 58		60 + 58 = 118
–4	: 59		– 59
9	: 59 A.M.		59

44. 567567567 ÷ 567 = 1001001.

45.
$$\begin{array}{r} 19000 \\ 1900 \\ 19 \\ \hline 20919 \end{array}$$

∴ Sum = 20919.

46. $\frac{1}{2}\div\frac{1}{8}$

$=\frac{1}{2}\times\frac{8}{1}=4.$

58. Area of 5 squares = 180 cm^2

Area of 1 square = 36 cm^2

Side of 1 square = 6 cm

Perimeters of figure = Side × 6

= 12 × 6

= 72 cm.

60. l = 5 cm

b = 4 cm

h = 3 cm

∴ No. of blocks = 5 × 4 × 3

= 60.

63. Friction is a force that opposes the relative motion between two surfaces of objects in contact. The force of friction always acts in a direction opposite to that of the applied force. Friction is due to irregularities on the surfaces of the objects in contact. Friction depends on the smoothness of the surfaces in contact. The force of friction depends on the nature of the surfaces in contact. Since friction is a type of force, it is measured in Newton (N).

Examples of friction:

- We are able to walk because of frictional forces between ground and our feet.
- We are able to write because of friction between ball point and the paper surface.
- Nails and screws stick to wall surfaces because of friction.
- Lighting a match stick is because of friction between match stick and the side surface of match box.
- Wear and tear of soles of our shoes is due to friction.
- When a tyre deflates, it is difficult to move the vehicle because of increased friction between the tyre and road surface.
- Machines gets heated up and produce noise because of friction.

72. Respiration and energy: Respiration and breathing are not the same. The purpose of breathing is to provide out cells with oxygen for use in respiration. Respiration is the process of using oxygen to release the energy in the food that we eat. Each of our cells contains tiny structures called mitochondria. This is where respiration takes place. There are many mitochondria in cells that carry out a lot of respiration, such as leg muscle cells, and few mitochondria in less active parts of the body, such as skin cells.

73. To the mixture of sand and salt in a beaker add water. The salt will dissolve in water and sand will remain undissolved. Now keep this beaker for some time. The sand will settle down at the bottom of the container (sedimentation). The sand can be separated by gently pouring the liquid without disturbing the sand (decantation) and filtration. Decantation is the process of transferring a liquid from one container to another without disturbing the sediments that are present at its bottom while filtration is the process of separating a mixture by passing the it through a material containing fine holes that will allow only one component of the mixture to pass through.

This decanted liquid contains salt dissolved in it. Take the solution in a kettle and heat the kettle. Water will be converted into steam. When a metal plate with ice over it is placed above the spout of the kettle, the steam coming out of the kettle comes in contact with the plate and is condensed to water.

Hence a mixture of sand and salt can be separated by sedimentation, decantation, filtration, evaporation and condensation.

74. Alum is added in water to settle sand and clay particles. Alum dissolves in water and load or weigh down clay and dust particles making them heavier and increasing the rate of sedimentation.

75. Protein is needed to build muscle tissue and also helps the body repair muscle tissue that has been damaged. Bodybuilders and regular exercisers benefit from increasing protein consumption through their regular diet and by taking protein supplements.

77. The most important purpose of an air pump is to aerate the water, increasing dissolved oxygen so fish can breathe. The pump does not force oxygen directly into the water, but rather agitates the surface so oxygen is dissolved more quickly.

81. Amla is used to treat the anemia. Anemia is a condition which is caused due to luck of blood in the body. It is a common disorder these days. The amount of red blood cells (RBC) reduces in the body. RBCs contain haemoglobin. Iron is essential in the formation of haemoglobin. The skin turns pale due to deficiency of Iron. Hence, intake of amla helps to treat anemia.

83. The Moon is made up of solid rock. The surface consists of mountains, peaks and craters, deep valleys and plains. The plains of the Moon are also called *maria*.

The Moon does not have water or atmosphere, and is not suitable for existence of life. Although seen at night, the moon may also be present in the sky during the daytime, but the Sun is generally bright enough to hide it.

The Moon takes about 27 days to rotate once on its axis, and about the same time to revolve around the Earth. As a result, *the same side of the Moon always faces the Earth.*

The Moon is the only celestial body ever visited by humans. In *July 1969*, the American Astronauts *Neil Armstrong* and *Edwin Aldrin* became the first men to land on the surface of a celestial body. As their spacecraft *Apollo 11* descended onto the Moon's surface, they saw the beautiful sight of the Earth rising above the horizon of the moon. Neil Armstrong became the first man to step onto the surface of the Moon.

84. Japanese encephalitis is a viral disease that infects animals and humans. It is transmitted by mosquitoes and in humans causes inflammation of the membranes around the brain.

And Dengue fever is a disease caused by a family of viruses that are transmitted by mosquitoes.

87. The 5 E Model of Constructivism

The 5 E's is an instructional model based on the Constructivist approach to learning, which says that learners build or construct new ideas on top of their old ideas. The 5 E's can be used with students of all ages, including adults.

Each of the 5 E's describes a phase of learning, and each phase begins with the letter "E". Engage, Explore, Explain, Elaborate, and Evaluate. The 5 E's allows students and teachers to experience common activities, to use and build on prior knowledge and experience, to construct meaning, and to continually assess their understanding of a concept.

Engage: This phase of the 5 E's starts the process. Students encounter the material, define their questions, lay the groundwork for their tasks, make connections from new to unknown and identify relevance. An "engage" activity should do the following:

1. Make connections between past and present learning experiences.
2. Anticipate activities and focus students thinking on the learning outcomes of current activities. Students should become mentally engaged in the concept, process, or skill to be learned.

Explore: This phase of the 5 E's provides students with a common base of experiences. Students directly involved with material, inquiry drives the process, teamwork is used to share and build knowledge base. They identify and develop concepts, processes, and skills. During this phase, students actively explore their environment or manipulate materials.

Explain: This phase of the 5 E's helps students explain the discoveries, processes and concepts they have been exploring. They have opportunities to verbalize their conceptual understanding or to demonstrate new skills or behaviors. This phase also provides opportunities for teachers to introduce formal terms, definitions, and explanations for concepts, processes, skills, or behaviours.

Elaborate: This phase of the 5 E's extends students' conceptual understanding and allows them to practice skills and behaviours. Through new experiences, the learners develop deeper and broader understanding of major concepts, obtain more information about areas of interest, and refine their skills. They apply learning to other situations sometimes leading to a new inquiry.

Evaluate: This phase of the 5 E's encourages learners to assess their understanding and abilities and lets teachers evaluate students' understanding of key concepts and skill development. Rubrics, checklists, teacher interviews, portfolios, problem-based learning outputs, and embedded assessments are made use of. Results are used to evaluate and modify further instructional needs.

92. It has been found that children who know nursery rhymes have an advantage over those who do not. Nursery rhymes appear to help children: (*a*) learn the intonation patterns of a language (*b*) learn new words and concepts, (*c*) understand the basis of learning to read and write, and (*d*) gain appreciation of poetry.

Rhythm: Rhythm is musical aspect of language. It makes pronunciation more appealing than it would otherwise be. When person plays upon a harmonium, his fingers on hands move from one note to the other at regular interval. This is rhythm in music. English has stress timed rhythm. It means equal time elapses between one stressed syllable and the next. It does not matter how many or how few stresses syllables may came in between for instance.

Intonation: Intonation refers to the rise and fall of pitch in voice or it is the variation in pitch. The variation in pitch is done by slacking or tightening our vocal cards and the sound. In pronunciation intonation is quite important. The meaning can be changed just by change of pitch.

94. Portfolio assessment is nothing but assessing the learners' overall performance in a course over a period of time. It is like preparing a progress report of each learner. Portfolios, in fact, are purposefully collected examples of the learners' work that portray their achievements, progress and endeavour. Both processes and products of learning are included in it. Portfolios may focus on one or more academic achievement. The learners' self-evaluation is an important component of portfolio development. Portfolios exhibit children's authentic work samples. They enable teachers and parents to understand the learners' activities and their gradual development.

96. Language is a mirror which reflects the personality of a speaker. Personality involves behaviour, communication skills, interpersonal relationships, attitude towards life and ethics. Communication plays pivotal role in the development of personality. Sound, one of the significant elements in oral communication leads the speaker to proper pronunciation. Pronunciation has gained prominence in teaching learning process of English language.

Pronunciation is definitely of highest importance that people notice when one speaks English. It reveals one's knowledge of English. One, having good knowledge of grammar, can't be understood because of improper pronunciation. Certain factors, such as the native language, the age, phonetic ability, attitude and motivation affect the pronunciation of learner. Flexibility, clarity, fluency, accuracy proper listening, proper articulation including stress and accent helps to improve one's pronunciation.

Different drilling techniques are useful for purifying and teaching the correct and accurate pronunciation of the utterances and words.

There are many useful drills for purifying and teaching the correct and accurate pronunciation of the utterances and words.

(*a*) Word Association Drill
(*b*) Oral Drill
(*c*) Drill for Illustrating a Learned sound
(*d*) Mobility Drill
(*e*) Comparative Drill
(*f*) Tongue Twisters

97. Continuous and Comprehensive Evaluation (CCE) refers to a system of school-based assessment of students that covers all aspects of students' development.

It is a developmental process of assessment which emphasizes on two fold objectives. Continuity in evaluation and assessment of broad based learning and behavioural outcomes.

The objectives of the CCE scheme are:

⇒ To help develop cognitive, psychomotor and affective skills.

⇒ To lay emphasis on thought process and de-emphasise memorization.

⇒ To make evaluation an integral part of teaching-learning process.

⇒ To use evaluation for improvement of student's achievement and teaching learning strategies on the basis of regular diagnosis followed by remedial measures.

⇒ To use evaluation as a quality control devise to raise standards of performance.

⇒ To determine social utility, desirability or effectiveness of a programme and take appropriate decisions about the learner, the process of learning and the learning environment.

⇒ To make the process of teaching and learning a learner-centered activity.

100. Curriculum is an important element of education. Aims of education are reflected in the curriculum. In other words, the curriculum is determined by the aims of life and society. Aims of life and society are subject to constant change.

Hence, the aims of education are also subject to change and dynamic. The aims of education are attained by the school programmes, concerning knowledge, experiences, activities, skills and values. The different school programmes are jointly known as curriculum.

Meaning of Curriculum

The term curriculum has been derived from a Latin word 'Currere' which means a 'race course' or a runway on which one runs to reach a goal. Accordingly, a curriculum is the instructional and the educative programme by following which the pupils achieve their goals, ideals and aspirations of life. It is curriculum through which the general aims of a school education receive concrete expression.

Traditional concept: The traditional curriculum was subject-centered while the modern curriculum is child and life-centered.

Modern Concept of Curriculum

Modern education is the combination of two dynamic processes. The one is the process of individual development and the other is the process of socialization, which is commonly known as adjustment with the social environment.

Definition of Curriculum

The term curriculum has been defined by different writers in different ways:

1. **Cunningham:** "Curriculum is a tool in the hands of the artist (teacher) to mould his material (pupils) according to his ideas (aims and objectives) in his studio (school)".
2. **Morroe:** "Curriculum includes all those activities which are utilized by the school to attain the aims of education".
3. **Froebel:** "Curriculum should be conceived as an epitome of the rounded whole of the knowledge and experience of the human race."
4. **Crow and Crow:** The curriculum includes all the learners' experience in or outside school that are included in a programme which has been devised to help him developmentally, emotionally, socially, spiritually and morally".
5. **T.P. Nunn:** "The curriculum should be viewed as various forms of activities that are grand expressions of human sprit and that are of the greatest and most permanent significance to the wide world".

102. Learning to read is essential in life. When children begin to learn to read they will encounter high frequency words or sight words. A sight word is a word known by sight and the word's identity is triggered in memory very rapidly.

105. The introduction explains the background to the text, its purpose and the points covered. A good introduction will be short and will help to guide the reader.

Previous Paper (Solved)

CTET PAPER-I, JUNE 2011*

PART- I

Child Development and Pedagogy

Directions: *Answer the following questions by selecting the **most appropriate** option.*

1. Which of the following should be considered the most important quality of a teacher at primary level?
A. Patience and perseverance
B. Competence in methods of teaching and knowledge of subjects
C. Competence to teach in highly standardised language
D. Eagerness to teach

2. A teacher, because of his/her democratic nature, allows students to sit all over the class. Some sit together and discuss or do group reading. Some sit quietly and read themselves. A parent does not like it. Which of the following may be the best way to handle the situation?
A. Parents should request the principal to change the section of their ward
B. Parents should show trust in the teacher and discuss the problem with the teacher
C. Parents should take away the child from that school
D. Parents should complain against the teacher to the principal

3. The stage in which a child begins to think logically about objects and events is known as
A. Formal operational stage
B. Pre-operational stage
C. Concrete operational stage
D. Sensori-motor stage

4. 'Mind mapping' refers to
A. a plan of action for an adventure
B. drawing the picture of a mind
C. researching the functioning of the mind
D. a technique to enhance comprehension

5. The best way, specially at primary level, to address the learning difficulties of students is to use
A. expensive and glossy support material
B. easy and interesting textbooks
C. story-telling method
D. a variety of teaching methods suited to the disability

6. Which of the following will foster creativity among learners?
A. Providing opportunities to question and to nurture the innate talents of every learner
B. Emphasizing achievement goals from the beginning of school life
C. Coaching students for good marks in examination
D. Teaching the students the practical value of good education

7. According to Piaget, at which of the following stages does a child begin to think logically about abstract propositions?
A. Formal operational stage (11 years and up)
B. Sensori-motor stage (Birth–02 years)
C. Pre-operational stage (02–07 years)
D. Concrete operational stage (07–11 years)

8. Learning can be enriched if
A. more and more teaching aids are used in the class
B. teachers use different types of lectures and explanation
C. due attention is paid to periodic tests in the class
D. situations from the real world are brought into the class in which students interact with each other and the teahcer facilitates

9. Which of the following statements ***cannot*** be considered as a feature of the process of learning?
A. Learning is a comprehensive process
B. Learning is goal-oriented
C. Unlearning is also a learning process
D. Educational institutions are the only place where learning takes place

10. A student of V-grade with 'visual deficiency' should be
A. helped with his/her routine-work by parents and friends
B. treated normally in the classroom and provided support through Audio CDs
C. given special treatment in the classroom
D. excused to do a lower level of work

11. Which of the following is ***not*** related to the socio-psychological needs of the child?
A. Need for emotional security

*Exam was held on 26-06-2011.

B. Regular elimination of waste products from the body
C. Need for company
D. Need for appreciation or social approval

12. Which is the place where the child's 'cognitive' development is defined in the best way?
A. School and classroom environment
B. Auditorium
C. Home
D. Playground

13. .... is considered a sign of motivated teaching.
A. Remedial work given by the teacher
B. Questioning by students
C. Pin drop silence in the class
D. Maximum attendance in the class

14. Which of the following is ***not*** a sign of an intelligent young child?
A. One who has the ability to communicate fluently and appropriately
B. One who carries on thinking in an abstract manner
C. One who can adjust oneself in a new environment
D. One who has the ability to cram long essays very quickly

15. "Children actively construct their understanding of the world" is a statement attributed to
A. Pavlov B. Kohlberg
C. Skinner D. Piaget

16. Kritika who does ***not*** talk much at home, talks a lot at school. It shows that
A. teachers demand that children should talk a lot at school
B. she does not like her home at all
C. her thoughts get acknowledged at school
D. the school provides opportunities to children to talk a lot

17. A teacher should make an attempt to understand the potentialities of her/his students. Which of the following fields is related to this objective?
A. Social Philosophy
B. Media Psychology
C. Educational Psychology
D. Educational Sociology

18. Motivation, in the process of learning,
A. differentiates new learning from old learning
B. makes learners think unidirectionally
C. creates interest for learning among young learners
D. sharpens the memory of learners

19. The term 'curriculum' in the field of education refers to
A. overall programme of the school which students experience on a day-to-day basis
B. evaluation process
C. text-material to be used in the class
D. methods of teaching and the content to be taught

20. At lower classes, play-way method of teaching is based on
A. principles of methods of teaching
B. psychological principles of development and growth
C. sociological principles of teaching
D. theory of physical education programmes

21. "A young child responds to a new situation on the basis of the response made by him/her in a similar situation as in the past." This is related to
A. 'Law of Effect' of learning
B. 'Law of Attitude' of learning process
C. 'Law of Readiness' of learning
D. 'Law of Analogy' of learning

22. .... is ***not*** considered a sign of 'being gifted'.
A. Fighting with others
B. Novelty in expression
C. Curiosity
D. Creative ideas

23. Education of children with special needs should be provided
A. by methods developed for special children in special schools
B. in special schools
C. by special teachers in special schools
D. along with other normal children

24. To make assessment a 'useful and interesting' process, one should be careful about
A. labelling students as intelligent or average learners
B. using a variety of ways to collect information about the student's learning across the scholastic and co-scholastic boundaries
C. using technical language to give feedback
D. making comparisons between different students

25. 'Dyslexia' is associated with
A. Mathematical disorder
B. Reading disorder
C. Behavioural disorder
D. Mental disorder

26. Parents should play a .... role in the learning process of young children.
A. proactive B. sympathetic
C. neutral D. negative

27. "Development is a never ending process." This idea is associated with
A. Principle of continuity
B. Principle of integration
C. Principle of interaction
D. Principle of interrelation

28. The 'insight theory of learning' is promoted by
A. Pavlov B. Jean Piaget
C. Vygotsky D. 'Gestalt' theorists

29. In which of the following stages do children become active members of their peer group?
A. Adulthood B. Early childhood
C. Childhood D. Adolescence

30. Four distinct stages of children's intellectual development are identified by
A. Erikson B. Skinner
C. Piaget D. Kohlberg

PART- II

Mathematics

Directions: *Answer the following questions by selecting the* ***most appropriate*** *option.*

31. In a dice, the numbers on the opposite faces add up to 7. Which amongst the following will fold into a dice?

A.
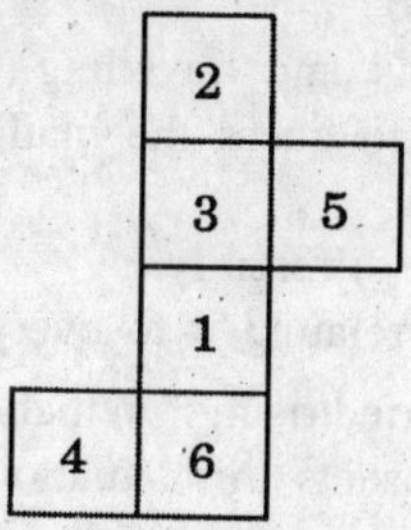

B.
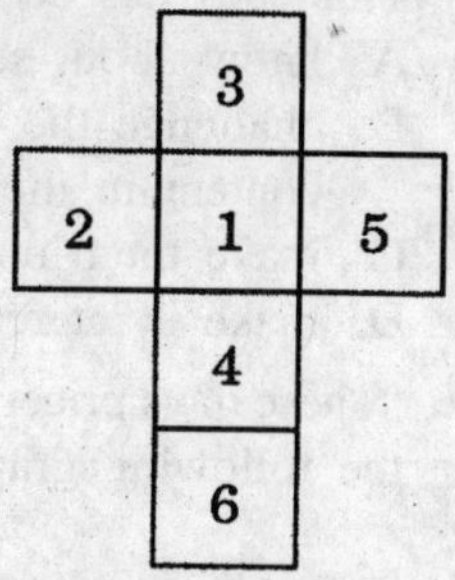

C.
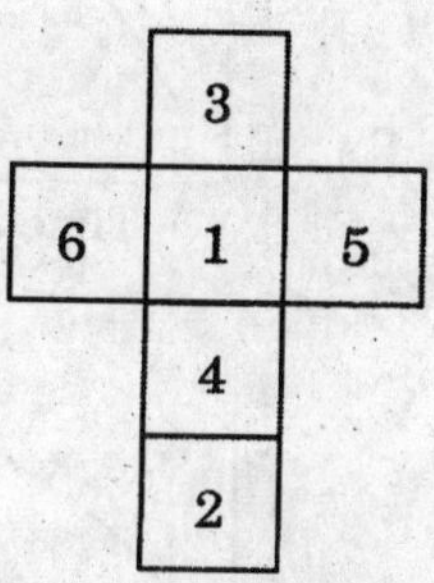

D.
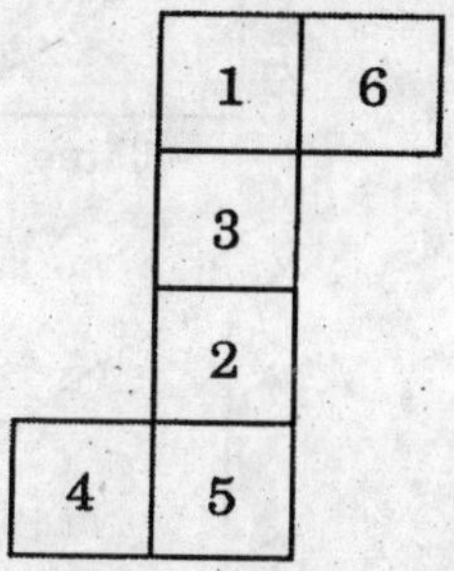

32. "Problem solving" as a strategy of doing mathematics involves
A. estimation
B. extensive practice
C. using clues to arrive at a solution
D. activity based approach

33. Sequence the following tasks as they would be taken up while developing the understanding of shapes and space across primary classes:
1. Matches the properties of 2-D shapes by observing their sides and corners
2. Describes intuitively the properties of 2-D shapes
3. Sorts 2-D shapes
4. Describes the various 2-D shapes by counting their sides, corners and diagonals

A. 3, 1, 4, 2 B. 4, 2, 1, 3
C. 3, 2, 4, 1 D. 1, 4, 2, 3

34. The purpose of a diagnostic test in mathematics is
A. to plan the question paper for the end-term examination
B. to know the gaps in children's understanding
C. to give feedback to the parents
D. to fill the progress report

35. When faced with word problems, Rajan usually asks "Should I add or subtract?"
"Should I multiply or divide?". Such questions suggest
A. Rajan cannot add and multiply
B. Rajan seeks opportunities to disturb the class
C. Rajan has problems in comprehending language
D. Rajan lacks understanding of number operations

36. A rhombus has diagonals of length 8 cm and 6 cm. Find its perimeter.
A. 28 cm
B. 18 cm
C. 20 cm
D. 24 cm

37. To introduce the concept of area, a teacher can start with
A. explaining of formulae for finding area of figures of different shapes
B. comparing area of any figure with the help of different objects like palm, leaf, pencil, notebook, etc.
C. calculating area of a rectangle by finding length and breadth of a rectangle and using the formula for area of a rectangle (*i.e.* length × breadth)
D. calculating area of figures with the help of counting unit square

38. The NCF (2005) considers that Mathematics involves 'a certain way of thinking and reasoning'.
From the statements given below, pick out on which does ***not*** reflect the above principle:
A. Giving students set formulae to solve the numerical questions
B. The way the material presented in the textbooks is written
C. The activities and excerises chosen for the class
D. The method by which it is taught

39. A teacher asked in a class to represent 1/8 of . Which amongst the following is an incorrect representation?

A. 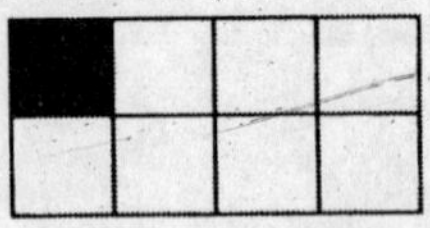

B. 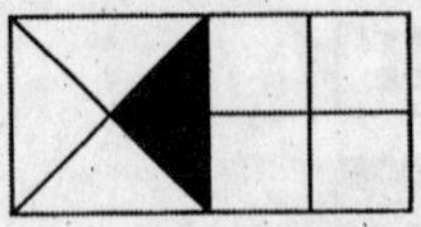

C. 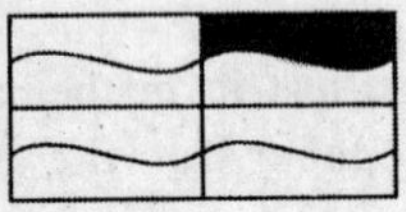

D. 

40. 407928 is read as
A. Four lakh seven thousand nine hundred twenty eight
B. Four lakh seventy nine thousand twenty eight
C. Forty seven thousand nine hundred twenty eight
D. Forty thousand nine hundred twenty eight

41. Sequence the following tasks as they are taken up while developing the concept of measurement:
1. Learners use standard units to measure length.
2. Learners use non-standard units to measure length.
3. Learners verify objects using simple observation.
4. Learners understand the relationship between metric units.

A. 4, 1, 3, 2   B. 1, 2, 4, 3
C. 2, 1, 3, 4   D. 3, 2, 1, 4

42. If an operator Å is defined as

$4 \oplus 3 = 4 + 5 + 6$

$5 \oplus 4 = 5 + 6 + 7 + 8$

$6 \oplus 4 = 6 + 7 + 8 + 9$

what will $n \oplus 8$ be equal to?
A. n + 36   B. n + 28
C. 8n + 28   D. 8n + 36

43. "Start a discussion in the class on things in the child's environment which roll and slide. Help children to look at their shapes and see how some things roll and others slide."

Source: Math Magic II, NCERT

Suggestions like this have been given in the NCERT textbook of Class-II to help a teacher understand that
A. discussions bring multiple perspectives into the classroom
B. discussion is the best strategy for the mathematics classroom
C. it is imperative for the teachers to draw the children's attention to the things around them
D. discussions supplemented with demonstration help students to understand concepts better

44. To be a "good" mathematician one must be able to
A. master the techniques of answering questions
B. memorise most of the formulae
C. solve the problem in no time
D. understand, apply and make connections across the concepts

45. The weight of some mangoes is 2 kg 600 g and that of some apples is 1 kg 450 g. The weight of the mangoes is greater than that of the apples by
A. 150 g   B. 4 kg 50 g
C. 1 kg 150 g   D. 1 kg 200 g

46. The chapters in the NCERT textbook of mathematics of Class-IV have titles like "The Junk Seller", "Trip to Bhopal", "The Way the World Looks".
This shift has been done to
A. know about selling junk and travelling
B. challenge the students to guess the mathematical content in the chapters
C. make them understand differently
D. make it interesting by relating it to everyday life

47. "These days prices have started rising." Which amongst the following graphs represents this situation?

A. 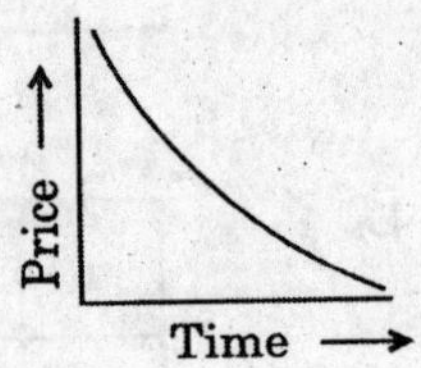

B. 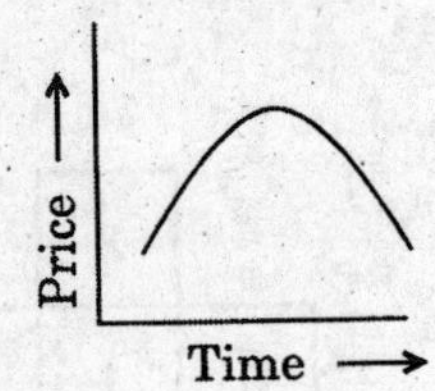

C. 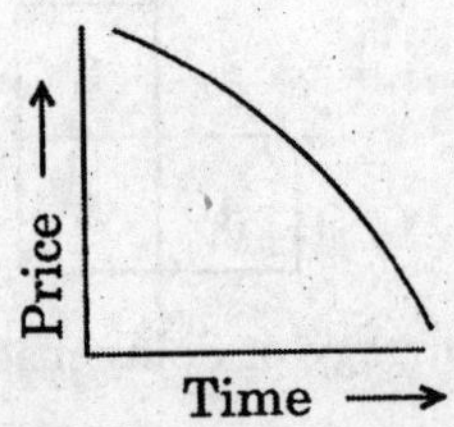

D. 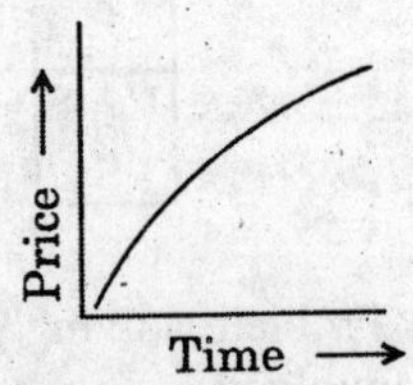

48. While teaching comparison of fractions in which the numerators are same *e.g.* $\frac{3}{5}$ and $\frac{3}{7}$. Rohit's response was "since the numerators are same and since 7 is larger than 5, therefore $\frac{3}{7}$ is bigger than $\frac{3}{5}$."
This suggests that
A. Rohit has not practised well
B. Rohit does not understand the magnitude of fractions
C. Rohit does not know the concept of numerator and denominator
D. Rohit does not know the concept of equivalent fractions

49. To introduce the concept of fractions, a teacher can begin with
A. identifying fractional parts of things around them
B. identifying numerators and denominators of different fractions
C. finding fractions on a number line
D. writing fractions in the form of $\frac{a}{b}$ where $b \neq 0$

50. Examine the following matchstick patterns:

1st stage **2nd stage** **3rd stage**

If the pattern continues, how many matchsticks are needed in the 15th stage?
A. 62 B. 105
C. 65 D. 61

51. The length of a rectangle is 'l' and its width is half of its length. What will be the perimeter of the rectangle if the length is doubled keeping the width same?
A. $3l$ B. $4l$
C. $5l$ D. $6l$

52. Which is true for a hexagonal pyramid?
A. It has six hexagonal faces joined by six rectangular faces
B. It has six faces and each face is a hexagon
C. It has a hexagonal base with six triangular faces meeting at a point
D. It has two hexagonal faces and six rectangular faces

53. How many 4-digit numbers are there in the Hindu-Arabic Numeration System?
A. 9000 B. 99
C. 8999 D. 9999

54.  is $\frac{3}{4}$ of a 'unit'. What will be $1\frac{1}{2}$?

A. 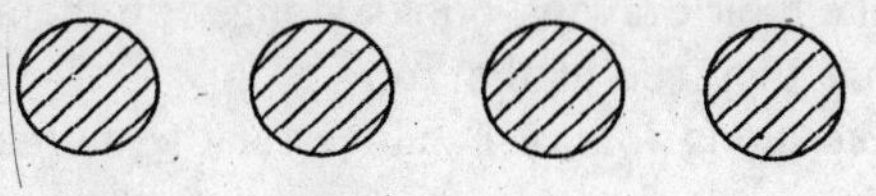

B. 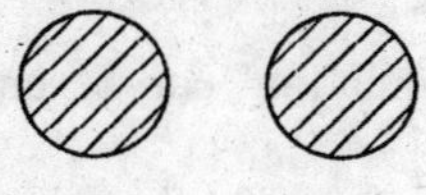

C. 

D. 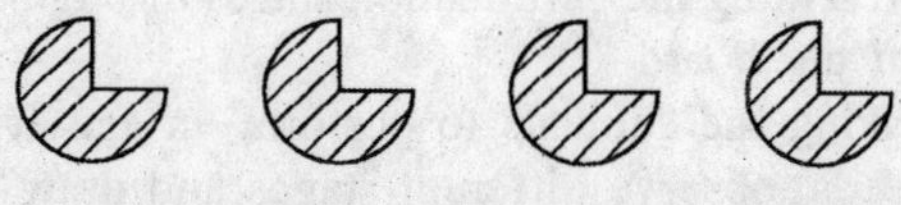

55. The number 49532 rounded off to the nearest thousand is
A. 50000 B. 49000
C. 49500 D. 41000

56. In the following, which is the greatest number?
A. $(2 + 2 + 2)^2$ B. $(4)^2$
C. $(2 \times 2 \times 2)^2$ D. $[(2 + 2)^2]^2$

57. Look at the following table:

Station		Bus 1	Bus 2	Bus 3
New Delhi	Departure	19:15	12:30	16:45
Faridabad	Arrival	20:22	13:25	19:10
	Departure	20:37	13:35	19:22
Mathura	Arrival	00:40	18:10	21:55

Which bus takes the least time to reach Mathura from New Delhi?
A. Both Bus 2 and Bus 3 take equal time
B. Bus 1
C. Bus 2
D. Bus 3

58. When teaching addition of fractions, a teacher came across the following error:

$$\frac{1}{2}+\frac{1}{3}=\frac{2}{5}$$

What remedial action can the teacher take in such a situation?
A. Help the child to understand the concept of LCM
B. Ask the child to practise as much as she can
C. No intervention is needed because she will understand as she grows
D. Help the child to understand the magnitude of each fraction

59. Vikas teaches mathematics to a class of 56 students. He believes that conducting a test is effective if the feedback is given immediately. He conducted a short class test of 10 marks. What is the *best possible way* of giving the feedback effectively?
A. Pick out any copy at random and discuss the method followed in the copy on the board
B. He can let the students check each other's answer
C. He can explain the solution of each problem on the board and ask the students to check their answer on their own
D. He can have a whole class discussion on ways in which they have got their solutions and which is the effective strategy to arrive at the correct answer

60. When teaching 'shapes', a teacher can plan a trip of historical places as
A. shapes are an integral part of any architecture and such trips encourage connections across disciplines
B. she has completed most of the syllabus well in time and needs to provide leisure
C. it would be a good break from the routine mathematics class and an opportunity to improve communicative skills
D. field trips have been recommended by CBSE, so they are a must

PART- III

Environmental Studies

Directions: *Answer the following questions by selecting the **most appropriate** option.*

61. Which of the following statements about assignments is correct?

A. Assignments can be done by parents, brothers or sisters depending on the talent that they possess

B. Assignments need to be given as classwork followed by homework every day to provide variety and practice

C. Assignments should be the only method of assessment

D. Assignments provide learners an opportunity to search for information, construct their own ideas and articulate them

62. Simple experiments and demonstrations can be performed in the EVS class

A. to control the students to ensure discipline in the class

B. to enable children to learn on their own and sharpen their observation skills

C. to follow what is being done in the senior classes

D. to discuss ideas, record and analyse observations on the basis of questions raised by students

63. Durga lives in a village and cooks food on a chulha (earthen stove) using wood or cow dung cakes as fuel. She has been suffering from severe cough for the last three months. This may be due to the

A. old age and pollution inside and outside her hut

B. carbon monoxide produced by burning fuel which may have been deposited in her respiratory tract

C. soot produced by burning the fuels which may have been deposited in her respiratory tract

D. smoke produced by burning fuels which may have caused her allergy

64. A school planned an educational trip for Class-V students to Rajasthan. What would be your expectation from the children during the visit?

A. They should observe everything without asking questions about it

B. They should enjoy themselves

C. They should observe keenly, make notes and share their observations with other students and the teacher

D. They should note down their questions, if any, and ask the parents after reaching home

65. Rina separated the garbage from the house into two piles as shown below:

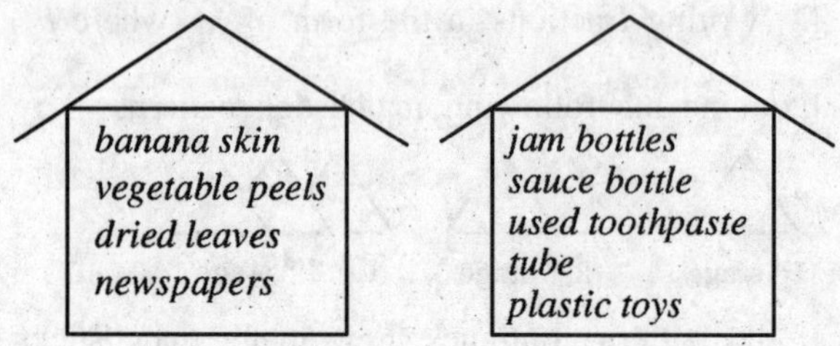

Rina has separated the garbage waste into two piles depending on the criteria

A. have odour/are odourless

B. can be decomposed/cannot be decomposed

C. can be recycled/cannot be recycled

D. are household/industrial waste

66. After the lunch break, while teaching EVS, you find that students are not taking interest in the lesson. What would you do?

A. Ask them to put their heads down on the desk and relax

B. Use audio-visual aids based on multiple intelligences to make the lesson interesting

C. Change the topic immediately

D. Take the children out to play in the ground

67. As an EVS teacher, you plan to take the students to the zoo. Which of the following activities would you ***not*** allow the students to undertake?

A. Try to find out the food taken up by different animals at the zoo

B. Collect photographs of the animals they expect to see at the zoo

C. Take their drawing books along with them to draw what they see at the zoo

D. Take along lots of eatables for the animals at the zoo

68. The concept of 'seed germination' can be taught best by

A. showing photographs of seed germination

B. showing germinated seeds to the class and explaining the process of germination

C. presenting the germination stages through drawings on the board

D. asking the students to perform an activity to sow seeds, observe different stages and draw them

69. Mira and Divya are young girls. Mira likes to eat samosas, cutlets and bread. Divya, on the other hand, takes an iron deficient diet. Which of the following disorders are Mira and Divya likely to suffer from, respectively?

A. Scurvy and anaemia
B. Anaemia and night blindness
C. Obesity and anaemia
D. Obesity and scurvy

70. A lemon sinks in normal water but floats in salty water because the density of

A. lemon decreases in salt water
B. salt water is more than normal water
C. normal water is more than salt water
D. lemon increases in salt water

71. Cooked rice can be preserved for a longer time in a refrigerator because

A. refrigerators contain certain chemicals which kill the microbes
B. microbes become inactive at low temperature
C. microbes are destroyed and killed at low temperature
D. moisture content in the food is reduced at low temperature

72. Malaria can be detected by testing the blood for the presence of

A. Plasmodium in red blood cells
B. ruptured liver cells in blood
C. larvae of mosquito in blood
D. eggs of mosquito in red blood cells

73. The use of poems and story telling to explain concepts in an EVS class helps to

A. channelize the energies of the students in the right direction
B. make the lesson enjoyable and interesting
C. promote the ability to imagine and explore the nature of the world at the local and global level
D. take care of the language and cultural diversity among learners

74. Chipko Movement was strengthened under the leadership of

A. Sunder Lal Bahuguna B. Amrita Devi Bishnoi
C. Medha Patkar D. A.K. Banerjee

75. Vitamines are substances

A. that increase our metabolic rate leading to loss of weight
B. required as medicines to make us healthy
C. that build muscles to keep us strong
D. required in small quantities to prevent deficiency diseases

76. In rural areas, cow dung is used to coat the floor and walls of huts to

A. keep the insects away
B. make them smooth and clean
C. make them rough to increase friction
D. give a natural colour to the floor

77. A farmer wanted to separate the grains from the chaff. This can be achieved by the process called

A. Handpicking B. Threshing
C. Winnowing D. Harvesting

78. Which one of the following is ***not*** an objective of including riddles and puzzles in the EVS textbook?

A. To develop curiosity and ability to think creatively
B. To develop critical thinking ability in students
C. To develop reasoning ability in students
D. To confuse the mind of the students and let them enjoy the confusion

79. Giving importance to individual experiences of children in an EVS class will benefit the teacher

A. to save her energy as children enjoy talking
B. to know the unique experiences of children
C. to help and improve the language and communication skills of the children
D. to connect the subject to the learners' experiential world and promote reflection and learning

80. To make children aware of different kinds of fuel, a teacher can

A. discuss with children about possible kinds of fuel that can be used for cooking, along with a short film
B. show pictures of fuels on a chart
C. ask children to list different fuels
D. show some samples of fuels in the class

81. The skills required to read a map include

A. ability to understand relative position of places, distances and directions
B. excellent drawing and painting skills
C. ability to use calculations and sketch positions on a globe
D. excellent communication skills to draw out the expressive ability

82. It has been observed that the process of digestion is faster inside the stomach than outside because

A. the food is churned in the stomach thereby increasing the surface area for quicker enzyme action
B. the digestive juices inside the stomach are acidic, while outside they are alkaline
C. the amount of digestive juices produced in the stomach in the presence of food is much more
D. the digestive juices when kept outside the stomach become inactive

83. The idea of showing a sample of a railway ticket in the EVS textbook is to

A. give them an opportunity to interact with real information and develop the skill of observation
B. give the students an idea of the rail fare
C. provide them the knowledge of various abbreviations used in the ticket
D. enhance the skills of students to arrive at conclusions

84. Which of the following statements is ***not*** an objective of teaching EVS at the primary level?
A. To internalise the values of concern for life and environment
B. Arouse curiosity about the natural and social environment
C. Engage in exploratory and hands-on activities that lead to the development
D. To load learners with terms and definitions for assessment

85. An egret bird is often seen on a buffalo's back. This is because the egret
A. feeds on insects present in the grass
B. loves to sing while sitting on the buffalo's back
C. rests after flying for a while
D. feeds on parasites on the buffalo's back

86. Which of the following represents one of the objectives of teaching EVS at Primary School?
A. To connect the experiences of the learners in school with the outside world
B. To make learners aware of technical terms and definitions
C. To assess technical terms related to EVS
D. To inform the learners about the books they should read to expand their knowledge

87. The difference between boiling and evaporation is that
A. changing of boiling liquid into vapour can be seen but evaporation cannot be seen
B. boiling causes a change of state of water while evaporation does not
C. evaporation can take place at any temperature while boiling cannot
D. boiling causes reduction in volume of liquid while evaporation does not

88. A man blood group 'O' marries a woman with blood group 'A'. The chance of their first child having blood group 'O' is
A. 75% B. 50%
C. 100% D. 25%

89. A Shooting Star is a
A. star which moves with a constant speed
B. shining object which moves with a constant speed in the atmosphere
C. star with a tail at the end
D. meteoroid which catches fire as it enters the Earth's atmosphere

90. At the primary stage, assessments should consist of
A. home assignments and class assignments every week to rate young/learners under the categories of pass or fail
B. continuous and unstructured teacher observations to be shared with learners and parents
C. formal tests and games done every week and recorded in the Report Card
D. half-yearly and annual examinations at the end of the year

PART- IV

Language-I : English

Directions: *Answer the following questions by selecting the **most appropriate** option.*

91. Mary, a young teacher, believes in personalised learning because she thinks that
A. children must enjoy their learning
B. every person must be exposed to learning
C. every learner is unique and needs to be given a chance to develop to the best of their ability
D. all learners must learn on their own

92. Read the two sentences given below:
The lizard ate the fly.
The fly ate the lizard.
A teacher can use this example to explain that
A. they are a collection of words
B. there is no difference in the two sentences because both have the same words
C. when subject and object change positions, the meaning of the sentence changes
D. they are examples of reported speech

93. Leena uses Big Reading Books in her language classes to
A. use them for big students of different ages
B. allow students to read at home
C. ensure books carry a lot of information
D. use these illustrated colourful books for reading together

94. The Right of Children to Free and Compulsory Education Act, 2009 stipulates that learning should be
A. supported by extra coaching
B. restricted to co-scholastic subjects
C. carefully monitored by frequent testing
D. through activities in a child-friendly manner

95. A teacher can cater to the learning styles of all the children by
A. employing a variety of teaching methods and modes of assessment which cater to diversity among learners

B. teaching every lesson thoroughly and revising the lessons
C. testing the children frequently
D. advising the children to join drawing/dance/music classes

96. Grammar should be taught by
A. enabling practice in context
B. asking students to learn rules
C. making learners do written assignments
D. giving clear explanations

97. As part of a class project, a teacher planned a salad fruit celebration day in which all learners needed to participate. The boys protested as they felt that boys do not cook. The teacher should
A. respect the sentiments of the boys and allow them not to participate in the class project
B. ignore such protests and tell the boys what she thinks of their bias
C. complain to the head of the school seeking action against the boys
D. make an attempt to counsel the boys, impressing upon them that gender stereotyping is not healthy

98. Children who are differently abled join a new school. Teachers give different reactions. Which one reflects the concept of inclusive education?
A. "Such children should go to special schools where they will learn better."
B. "Oh! How can I teach children who cannot even read?"
C. "I'm worried that my class may not accept these children and some of the mischievous children may even harm the poor kids."
D. "Good, it will provide a good opportunity for the children to learn to help each other and be supportive."

99. A child studying in Class-III says : "I dranked the water." It indicates that the child
A. is careless and needs to be told that she should be conscious of such errors
B. has not learnt grammar rules properly
C. should memorise the correct sentence
D. has over-generalized the rule for making past tense verbs, showing that learning is taking place

100. How will a teacher best teach 'writing' skills to a class?
A. By asking students to learn articles and rewrite them
B. By brainstorming ideas and asking students to write in their own words
C. By asking students to write neatly
D. Through dictation

101. Ritu often makes errors in Subject-Verb concord. The teacher can help her by
A. asking Ritu to write the rules ten times in her notebook
B. taking up many examples for the entire class and paying special attention to Ritu
C. explaining to her the rules of grammar
D. asking Ritu to learn the rules and scolding her

102. Lalita, a teacher of young learners, provides them with opportunities to play with clay, water and sand so as to
A. dirty their hands so that they may learn to wash them
B. build fine motor skills, especially of the fingers and thumb
C. encourage play with no other objective
D. please them and make them happy

103. Ria is unable to pronounce the words 'smile' and 'school' clearly. As her teacher, what will you do?
A. Asking the entire class to repeat the words and appreciating Ria when she repeats them correctly
B. Make Ria repeat the 'words' many times
C. Make Ria understand the meaning and sound pattern and get the class as a whole to listen to these words through an audio-visual medium
D. Humiliate Ria by isolating her and asking her to repeat the words

104. In a diverse classroom, learners find it difficult to speak and write good English and often lapse into their mother-tongue because
A. they are slow learners
B. they are not motivated to learn
C. they lack enough competence and the structures of the two languages are different
D. they do not have the ability to learn English

105. The spoken skills in a language teaching classroom can be developed through
A. group activities where learners can talk in whichever language they would like to
B. engaging in small talk as confident agressive learners
C. emotionally connecting with learners
D. enabling activities with a focus on conversation skills leading to communicative competence

Directions: *Read the poem given below and answer the questions that follow (Q. No. 106 to 111) by selecting the* ***most appropriate*** *option.*

On A Tired Housewife

Here lies a poor woman who was always tired,
She lived in a house where help wasn't hired:
Her last words on earth were: 'Dear friends,
I am going

To where there's no cooking, or washing, or sewing,
For everything there is exact to my wishes,
For where they don't eat there's no washing of dishes.

I'll be where loud anthems will always be ringing, But having no voice I'll be quit of the singing.
Don't mourn for me now, don't mourn for me never,
I am going to do nothing for ever and ever.'

Anonymous

106. The woman described in the poem
A. worked in the house of a rich man
B. was very busy doing chores
C. was no more
D. lived in her own house

107. The woman was always tired because
A. she had hardly anything to eat
B. she was physically very weak
C. she was suffering from a serious ailment
D. she did all the household work without any help

108. The woman wanted to go to a place where
A. people would sincerely mourn for her
B. people didn't sing or dance
C. people didn't cook, wash or sew
D. people would take good care of her

109. The woman's account in the poem shows
A. how we should help each other
B. how overworked a housewife is
C. that there is no work in heaven
D. how a woman can escape from work

110. 'For everything there is exact to my wishes,' In this line, the word 'exact' can be interpreted to mean
A. leading B. contrary
C. contributing D. according

111. The rhyme pattern in the poem is
A. aa, ab, bc, cd, de B. ab, ab, ab, ab, ab
C. aa, ab, cd, cd, ee D. aa, bb, cc, dd, ee

Directions: *Read the passage given below and answer the questions that follow (Q. No. 112 to 120) by selecting the* ***most appropriate*** *option.*

1. Max Weber laid the foundation for my belief that decent and hard-working people with high aspirations make great nations, no matter what the odds are. This was the first piece of the development puzzle for me. Mahatma Gandhi opened my eyes to the importance of good leadership in raising the aspirations of people, making them accept sacrifices to achieve a grand vision, and most importantly, in converting that vision into reality. He unleashed the most powerful instrument for gaining trust—leadership by example. He ate, dressed, travelled and lived like the poor. Walking the talk was extremely important to the Mahatma who understood the pulse of our poeple like no other Indian leader. The biggest lesson for me from Gandhi's book and life is the importance of leading by example. I realized fairly early that this was the second piece of the development puzzle.

2. Frantz Fanon's book on the colonizer mindset of elites in a post-colonial society opened my eyes to the role of the bureaucracy and the elite in decelerating the progress of the poor and the disenfranchised. The colonial mindset of the 'dark elite in white masks' in a post-colonial society—the mindset that the ruled and the rulers have different sets of rights and responsibilities with a huge asymmetry in favour of the rulers—was indeed the third piece of the development puzzle. I see this attitude of the Indian elite every day in how they send their children to English medium schools while forcing the children of the poor into vernacular schools, extol the virtues of poverty while living in luxury, and glorify the rural life while they sit comfortably in cities.

Source: 'A Better India, A Better World'
—N.R. Narayana Murthy (Adapted)

112. The main purpose of the author in the above passage is to
A. prioritise goals for only economic development of India
B. discuss the different writers he has read
C. argue why India should not be considered a developed country
D. delineate the lessons he has learnt for the development of a nation

113. The first piece of the development puzzle, according to the author, is
A. the need for making people understand the importance of leading an idealistic and simple life
B. creating a team of industrious people for a national cause
C. the importance of decent, inspired and industrious people for a nation's development
D. imbuing the citizens of the country with decency and aspirations

114. Mahatma Gandhi proved that only leadership by example can
A. inspire people to eat, dress, travel and live like the poor
B. mobilise the people of a country against colonial rule
C. fully and properly understand the pulse of the people of a country
D. gain the trust of the people so that they are willing to make sacrifices for a larger cause

115. The expression 'walking the talk' means
A. practising what one preaches
B. addressing public gatherings in an election campaign
C. talking to the common people by mingling with them
D. being diplomatic in one's behaviour and words

116. The colonial mindset of 'dark elite in white masks' with reference to the passage is
A. the bureaucratic practice of according topmost priority to confidentiality in official dealings
B. discriminating people on the basis of the colour of their skin
C. an assumption that the administrators and politicians have more rights and privileges than the common people
D. looking down upon the poor and the disenfranchised

117. Extolling 'the virtues of poverty while living in luxury' is an instance of
A. the need to make people adopt a simple life
B. the hypocrisy of the people of our country
C. practising what you preach
D. the ideal of a good government

118. 'I realized fairly early that this was the second piece of the development puzzle.'
The underlined part of this sentence is a/an
A. Verb clause
B. Adjective clause
C. Adverbial phrase
D. Noun clause

119. Pick out a word or phrase from the second paragraph of the passage that means the same as 'to make (something) go slower'.
A. vernacular
B. disenfranchised
C. dark elite
D. decelerating

120. 'Development' is a noun with '-ment' as a suffix. Which of the following will become a noun if we add the suffix '-ment' to it?
A. Endure B. Extort
C. Enter D. Enchant

PART- V

भाषा-II : हिन्दी

निर्देशः *निम्नलिखित प्रश्नों के उत्तर देने के लिए **सबसे उचित** विकल्प चुनिए।*

121. भाषा की कक्षा का माहौल कैसा होना चाहिए?
A. जहाँ शिक्षक बोले और बच्चे ध्यान से सुनें
B. जहाँ भाषागत शुद्धता पर अत्यधिक बल हो
C. दीवारों पर सूक्तियाँ लिखी हों
D. जहाँ बच्चों को उनकी बात कहने और सुनने के अधिकाधिक अवसर मिलें

122. पहली कक्षा में पढ़ने वाली अंकिता अक्सर 'ड़' वाले शब्दों को गलत तरीके से बोलती है। आप क्या करेंगे?
A. अंकिता को 'ड़' वाले शब्दों की सूची देंगे।
B. अंकिता को 'ड़' वाले शब्दों को अपने पीछे-पीछे दोहराने के लिए कहेंगे।
C. स्वयं 'ड़' वाले शब्दों को सहज भाव से उसके समक्ष प्रस्तुत कर उससे धैर्यपूर्वक बोलने का अभ्यास कराएँगे।
D. उसे 'ड़' वाले शब्दों की सी.डी. सुनने के लिए देंगे।

123. पाठ पढ़ने-पढ़ाने के बाद किस तरह के सवाल बच्चों की समझ का मूल्यांकन करने में सहायक ***नहीं*** होते?
A. पढ़े गए पाठ से जोड़ते हुए अपने निजी अनुभवों को व्यक्त करने वाले प्रश्न
B. 'क्यों', 'कैसे' वाले प्रश्न
C. 'क्या शिक्षा मिलती है?' वाला प्रश्न
D. 'यदि-तो' वाले प्रश्न

124. लगभग दो साल के बच्चे तार वाली भाषा (टेलीग्राफिक स्पीच) का प्रयोग करते हैं। तार वाली भाषा का अर्थ है
A. अंग्रेजी शब्दों का उपयोग
B. संक्षिप्त वाक्यों का प्रयोग करना
C. मुख्य अर्थ को व्यक्त करने वाले संज्ञा, क्रिया, विशेषण आदि दो शब्दों वाली अभिव्यक्ति
D. तार में प्रयुक्त होने वाले शब्दों का प्रयोग

125. प्राथमिक स्तर पर आप किस तरह का बाल-साहित्य उचित समझते हैं?
A. ऐसा साहित्य जो प्रसिद्ध साहित्यकारों द्वारा लिखा गया हो
B. ऐसा साहित्य जिसमें शब्दों और घटनाओं का दोहराव हो
C. केवल कविताएँ
D. केवल कहानियाँ

126. एक समावेशी कक्षा में 'भाषा-शिक्षण' की समस्या है
A. उपयुक्त पाठ्य-सामग्री का अभाव
B. विद्यार्थियों की योग्यताओं में भिन्नता होना
C. विद्यार्थियों में असमान रुचि का होना
D. उपयुक्त भाषा-परिवेश का निर्माण न हो पाना

127. प्राथमिक स्तर पर बहु-सांस्कृतिक पृष्ठभूमि वाली कक्षा में बच्चे लक्ष्य भाषा के परिवेश से भाषा अर्जित करते हुए

A. धीमे-धीमे भाषा के रचनात्मक प्रयोग का अभ्यास करने लगते हैं

B. उसे शुद्ध-अशुद्ध रूप में पहचानते हैं

C. व्याकरणिक नियमों की शुद्धता को परखते हैं

D. लक्ष्य भाषा की अपनी भाषा से तुलना करते हैं

128. प्राथमिक स्तर पर बच्चे किस प्रकार की कविताएँ पसंद करते हैं?

A. जो कोई सीख देती हों

B. जिनमें लयात्मकता हो

C. जो अनिवार्य रूप से राजा-रानी से जुड़ी हों

D. जो तुकांत न हों

129. राधिका अक्सर 'लड़का' को 'लका', 'कमाई होने लगी' को 'कमाई होगी' लिखना जैसी गलतियाँ कर बैठती है। यह इस ओर संकेत करता है कि

A. उसके लेखन के स्तर में सुधार की आवश्यकता है

B. राधिका को मात्राओं का ज्ञान नहीं है

C. राधिका के विचारों की तेज गति के साथ उसकी लेखनी नहीं चल पाती

D. राधिका ध्यान से नहीं लिखती

130. राहुल को जब भी कक्षा में उत्तर देने के लिए कहा जाता है वह हकलाने लगता है। इसका क्या कारण हो सकता है?

A. राहुल को सही उत्तर नहीं पता होता

B. यह राहुल की आदत है

C. राहुल बड़े समूह के सामने अपनी बात कहने में मनोवैज्ञानिक दबाव महसूस करता है

D. राहुल जानबूझकर ऐसा करता है ताकि उसे जवाब न देना पड़े

131. ग्राह्यात्मक कौशलों में शामिल हैं

A. बोलना, लिखना

B. सुनना, पढ़ना

C. पढ़ना, लिखना

D. सुनना, बोलना

132. इनमें से प्राथमिक स्तर पर भाषा-शिक्षण का कौन-सा उद्देश्य अनिवार्यतः *नहीं* है?

A. विभिन्न संदर्भों और स्थितियों में अपनी बात व्यक्त करने की कुशलता का विकास

B. भाषा के आलंकारिक प्रयोग की क्षमता का विकास

C. मानवीय मूल्यों का विकास

D. विभिन्न संदर्भों में प्रयुक्त शब्दों के सही अर्थ ग्रहण करना

133. प्राथमिक स्तर पर 'सुनना-बोलना' कौशल के विकास में कौन-सी विधियाँ अधिक सहायक हैं?

A. कविता-पाठ और भाषा-प्रयोगशाला

B. भूमिका-निर्वाह (रोल-प्ले) और समाचार-वाचन

C. भूमिका-निर्वाह और बातचीत करना

D. कहानी-कथन और श्रुतलेख

134. बच्चों के भाषा-विकास की क्रमिक प्रगति का रिकॉर्ड रखने में कौन-सा सर्वाधिक सहायक है?

A. पोर्टफोलियो

B. लिखित परीक्षा की उत्तर-पुस्तिकाएँ

C. नोट-बुक

D. शिक्षक-डायरी

135. कक्षा में कुछ बच्चे गलत वर्तनी का प्रयोग करते हुए लिखते हैं। आप क्या करेंगे?

A. शब्दों को दस-दस बार सही तरीके से लिखने के लिए कहेंगे

B. बच्चों को उनकी त्रुटियों का अहसास कराएँगे

C. गलत वर्तनी वाले शब्दों पर लाल स्याही से घेरा या क्रॉस लगाएँगे

D. इसे एक सहज और स्वाभाविक प्रक्रिया मानते हुए कक्षा में 'प्रिंट'-समृद्ध माहौल का निर्माण करेंगे

निर्देश : गद्यांश को पढ़कर निम्नलिखित प्रश्नों (प्र.-सं. 136 से 144) में ***सबसे उचित*** *विकल्प चुनिए।*

गाँधीजी मानते थे कि सामाजिक या सामूहिक जीवन की ओर बढ़ने से पहले कौटुम्बिक जीवन का अनुभव प्राप्त करना आवश्यक है। इसलिए वे आश्रम-जीवन बिताते थे। वहाँ सभी एक भोजनालय में भोजन करते थे। इससे समय और धन तो बचता ही था, सामूहिक जीवन का अभ्यास भी होता था। लेकिन यह सब होना चाहिए, समय-पालन, सुव्यवस्था और शुचिता के साथ।

इस ओर लोगों को प्रोत्साहित करने के लिए गाँधीजी स्वयं भी सामूहिक रसोईघर में भोजन करते थे। भोजन के समय दो बार घंटी बजती थी। जो दूसरी घंटी बजने तक भोजनालय में नहीं पहुँच पाता था, उसे दूसरी पंक्ति के लिए बरामदे में इंतजार करना पड़ता था। दूसरी घंटे बजते ही रसोईघर का द्वार बंद कर दिया जाता था, जिससे बाद में आने वाले व्यक्ति अंदर न आने पाएँ।

एक दिन गाँधीजी पिछड़ गए। संयोग से उस दिन आश्रमवासी श्री हरिभाऊ उपाध्याय भी पिछड़ गए। जब वे वहाँ पहुँचे तो देखा कि बापू बरामदे में खड़े हैं। बैठने के लिए न बैंच है, न कुर्सी। हरिभाऊ ने विनोद करते हुए कहा, ''बापूजी आज तो आप भी गुनहगारों के कठघरे में आ गए हैं।''

गाँधीजी खिलखिलाकर हँस पड़े। बोले, ''कानून के सामने तो सब बराबर होते हैं न?''

हरिभाऊ जी ने कहा, ''बैठने के लिए कुर्सी लाऊँ, बापू?'' गाँधीजी बोले, ''नहीं, उसकी जरूरत नहीं है। सजा पूरी भुगतनी चाहिए। उसी में सच्चा आनंद है।''

(स्रोतः गाँधीजी के रोचक संस्मरण —डॉ. कृष्णवीर सिंह)

136. गाँधीजी ने किस बात की पूरी सजा भुगतने की बात की?

A. देर से रसोईघर में पहुँचने की

B. सामूहिक जीवन की

C. आश्रम-जीवन बिताने की

D. गलत नियम बनाने की

137. सामूहिक जीवन बिताने के लिए सबसे महत्वपूर्ण है
A. समूह के लिए बनाए गए नियमों का पालन
B. सब समान स्तर के हों
C. समान विचारधारा होना
D. समूह के सदस्यों की आपसी प्रतिस्पर्धा

138. "कानून के सामने तो सब बराबर होते हैं न?" गाँधीजी का यह कथन इस ओर संकेत करता है कि
A. गाँधीजी झेंप गए थे
B. कानून किसी तरह का भेदभाव नहीं करता
C. गाँधीजी पूरी ईमानदारी से नियमों का पालन करने में विश्वास रखते थे
D. कानून के हाथ लंबे होते हैं

139. दूसरी घंटी के बाद रसोईघर का दरवाजा क्यों बंद कर दिया जाता होगा?
A. ताकि लोग समय से भोजन करें और नियम का पालन भी
B. ताकि लोग अंदर न आ सकें
C. ताकि लोग एकाध दिन उपवास कर सकें
D. ऐसा गाँधीजी का निर्देश था

140. सभी भोजनालय में एक साथ भोजन करते थे। इससे
A. सुव्यवस्था रहती थी
B. गाँधीजी और हरिभाऊ जी को बहुत असुविधा हुई
C. सामूहिक जीवन का महत्व पता चलता था
D. केवल धन की बचत होती थी

141. 'शुचिता' शब्द का क्या अर्थ है?
A. सरलता B. निष्पक्षता
C. पवित्रता D. निर्मलता

142. इनमें कौन-सा 'इक' प्रत्यय का उदाहरण है?
A. कौटुम्बिक B. आधिक्य
C. माणिक्य D. अत्यधिक

143. 'भोजनालय' का संधि-विच्छेद है
A. भोजन + आलय B. भोजन + लय
C. भोज + नालय D. भोजन + अलय

144. 'रसोईघर' शब्द है
A. तत्सम B. रूढ़
C. योगरूढ़ D. यौगिक

निर्देश : *गद्यांश को पढ़कर निम्नलिखित प्रश्नों (प्र. सं. 145 से 150) में सबसे उचित विकल्प चुनिए।*

लोक कथाएँ हमारे आम जीवन में सदियों से रची-बसी हैं। इन्हें हम अपने बड़े-बूढ़ों से बचपन से ही सुनते आ रहे हैं। लोक कथाओं के बारे में यह भी कहा जाता है कि बचपन के शुरुआती वर्षों में बच्चों को अपने परिवेश की महक, सोच व कल्पना की उड़ान देने के लिए इनका उपयोग जरूरी है। हम यह भी सुनते हैं कि बच्चों के भाषा के विकास के संदर्भ में भी इन कथाओं की उपयोगिता महत्वपूर्ण है। ऐसा इसलिए कहा जाता है क्योंकि इन लोक कथाओं के विभिन्न रूपों में हमें लोक जीवन के तत्व मिलते हैं जो बच्चों के भाषा-विकास में उल्लेखनीय भूमिका निभाते हैं। अगर हम अपनी पढ़ी हुई लोक कथाओं को याद करें तो सहजता से हमें इनके कई उदाहरण मिल जाते हैं। जब हम कहानी सुना रहे होते हैं तो बच्चों से हमारी यह अपेक्षा रहती है कि वे पहली घटी घटनाओं को जरूर दोहराएँ। बच्चे भी घटना को याद रखते हुए साथ-साथ मजे से दोहराते हैं। इस तरह कथा सुनाने की इस प्रक्रिया में बच्चे इन घटनाओं को एक क्रम में रखकर देखते हैं। इन क्रमिक घटनाओं में एक तर्क होता है जो बच्चों के मनोभावों से मिलता-जुलता है।

(क्या बताती हैं लोक कथाएँ—कमलेश चंद्र जोशी)

145. लोक कथाओं में शामिल है
A. लोक की उड़ान
B. घटनाएँ
C. लोक कल्पना
D. लोक जीवन के रंग

146. लोक कथाओं में किस परिवेश की महक की बात की गई है?
A. विद्यालयी परिवेश की
B. ग्रामीण परिवेश की
C. बच्चों के आस-पास मौजूद परिवेश की
D. शहरी परिवेश की

147. बच्चों से हमारी क्या अपेक्षा रहती है?
A. घटनाओं की भाषा को समझना
B. वे कहानी में मजे लें
C. वे कहानी की घटनाओं को याद रखें ताकि आगे की कहानी से जुड़ा जा सके
D. कहानी सुनना

148. अनुच्छेद के आधार पर कहा जा सकता है कि इसका मुख्य बिन्दु है
A. कहानी में याद रखना जरूरी है
B. लोक कथाएँ हमारे जीवन का हिस्सा हैं
C. लोक कथाओं में लोक तत्व होता है
D. लोक कथाओं के माध्यम से कल्पना, तर्क और भाषा का विकास किया जा सकता है

149. 'परिवेश की महक' पद का अर्थ है
A. परिवेश की कहानियाँ
B. परिवेश की खुशबू
C. परिवेश की गंध
D. परिवेश की विशिष्टताएँ, सीमाएँ

150. 'कहानी की क्रमिक घटनाओं में एक तर्क होता है जो बच्चों के मनोभावों से मिलता-जुलता है।' वाक्य किस ओर संकेत करता है?
A. बच्चे भी कहानी के क्रम में ही सोचते हैं
B. कहानियाँ बच्चों की मानसिक दशा को दर्शाती हैं
C. बच्चे भी कहानी के बारे में लगभग उसी तरह सोचते हैं जिस तरह कहानी में घटनाएँ घटती हैं
D. कहानियों में एक क्रम होता है

Answers

1	2	3	4	5	6	7	8	9	10
A	B	C	C	D	A	A	D	D	B
11	12	13	14	15	16	17	18	19	20
B	A	B	D	D	C	C	C	A	B
21	22	23	24	25	26	27	28	29	30
D	A	D	B	B	A	A	D	D	C
31	32	33	34	35	36	37	38	39	40
B	D	A	B	D	C	B	A	D	A
41	42	43	44	45	46	47	48	49	50
D	C	D	D	C	D	D	D	A	A
51	52	53	54	55	56	57	58	59	60
C	C	A	D	A	D	D	A	D	A
61	62	63	64	65	66	67	68	69	70
D	B	C	C	B	B	D	D	C	B
71	72	73	74	75	76	77	78	79	80
B	A	C	A	D	A	C	D	D	A
81	82	83	84	85	86	87	88	89	90
A	A	A	D	D	A	C	B	D	B
91	92	93	94	95	96	97	98	99	100
C	C	D	D	A	B	D	D	D	B
101	102	103	104	105	106	107	108	109	110
B	B	C	C	D	C	D	C	B	D
111	112	113	114	115	116	117	118	119	120
D	D	C	D	A	C	B	D	C	D
121	122	123	124	125	126	127	128	129	130
D	C	A	C	B	D	A	B	C	C
131	132	133	134	135	136	137	138	139	140
B	B	C	A	D	A	A	C	A	C
141	142	143	144	145	146	147	148	149	150
C	A	A	D	D	C	C	D	D	C

Some Selected Explanatory Answers

3. Piaget's Stages of Development and Their Application to Patient Teaching and Learning

The best known psychologist who promoted the cognitive development theory was Jean Piaget. He observed children and their process of making sense of the world around them. Piaget developed a four-stage model of how the mind processes new information. He established four stages of learning:

1. The sensorimotor stage from birth to 2 years old
2. The preoperational stage from 2 to 4 years old
3. The concrete operational stage from 7 to 11 years old
4. The formal operational stage from 11 to 15 years old

In the sensorimotor stage, the infant builds an understanding of him or herself and reality by interacting with the environment. At this stage the child is only able to differentiate between itself and other objects. The child's outlook is essentially egocentric in the sense that he or she is unable to take into account others' point of view. The learning process takes place through assimilation and accommodation. Assimilation represents organization of information and absorbing it into the existing schema; accommodation happens when an object cannot be assimilated and the schema has to be modified to include the object. The child also recognizes self as an agent of action and begins to act intentionally, such as shaking a rattle to make a noise. In the sensorimotor stage, the child achieves object permanence, realizing that things continue to exist even when they no longer are present to the senses.

In Piaget's preoperational stage, the child is not able to conceptualize abstract ideas, instead requiring concrete physical situations. Objects are classified in simple ways considering their important features. For example, a child can classify objects by a single feature such as grouping together all the red blocks regardless of shape or all the square blocks regardless of colour. The child learns to use language and to represent objects by images and words. Thinking is still egocentric, meaning the child has difficulty taking the viewpoint of others. However, the child learns to classify items using different criteria and to manipulate numbers. Linguistic skills increase and open the way for greater socialization of action and communication with others.

In Piaget's concrete operational stage, the child begins to think in the abstract and is able to conceptualize by creating logical interpretations of various physical experiences. The child can think logically about objects and events attaining conservation of number (at age 6), mass (at age 7), and weight (at age 9). The child classifies objects according to several features and can order them in series along a single dimension such as size. From the ages of 7 to 11 years, children begin to develop logic, although they can only perform logical operations on concrete objects and events. In the concrete operational stage of development and learning, the physical experience accumulates and the accommodation process is increased.

In the last stage of Piaget's formal operations, cognition reaches its final form of development. The child is an adolescent now entering the formal operational stage that continues throughout the rest of his or her life. The child can think logically about abstract propositions and test hypotheses systematically. He or she becomes concerned with the hypothetical, the future, and ideological problems.

The child no longer requires concrete objects to make rational judgements, but is able to use deductive and hypothetical reasoning in his or her thinking process. In the formal operational stage, children develop the ability to perform abstract intellectual operations and reach affective and intellectual maturity. Most importantly, children build up their capacity to appreciate others' points of view as well as their own. Their ability to use abstract thinking is very similar to that of an adult.

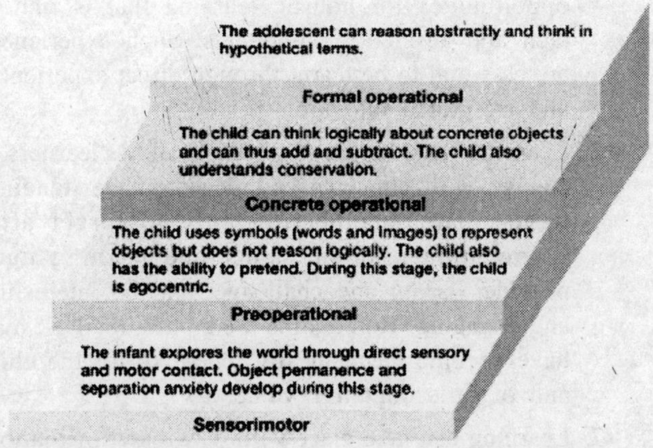

4. Mind mapping is a technique for graphically representing ideas and concepts that is based on association and emphasis, key elements involved in memorizing and retrieving information. The concept of mind mapping is a product of the research of Tony Buzan (1993), who is credited with the invention of mind mapping. In 1990 he registered the term, which is trademarked under the Buzan Organization. Haber's (1970) research on visual memory also contributed significantly to the development of mind mapping. Mind mapping is an effort to simulate a brain map or network of how information is processed. Like brain cells that branch out to form neural pathways and thereby form associations and links, the mind map starts with a subject and related ideas branch from it.

9. Characteristics of learning

1. All children are naturally motivated to learn and are capable of learning.
2. Making meaning and developing the capacity for abstract thinking, reflection and work are the most important aspects of learning.
3. Children learn in a variety of ways-through experience, making and doing things, experimentation, reading, discussion, asking, listening, thinking and reflecting, and expressing oneself in speech, movement or writing–both individually and with others. They require opportunities of all these kinds in the course of their development.
4. Teaching something before the child is cognitively ready takes away from real learning. Children may 'remember' many facts but they may not understand them or be able to relate them to the world around them.
5. Learning takes place both within school and outside school. Learning is enriched if the two aren as

interact with each other. Art and work provide opportunities for holistic learning that is rich in tacit and aesthetic components. Such experiences are essential to be learnt through direct experience, and integrated into life.

6. Learning must be paced so that it allows learners to engage with concepts and deepen understanding, rather than remembering only to forget after examinations. At the same time learning must provide variety and challenge, and be interesting and engaging. Boredom is a sign that the task may have become mechanically repetitive for the child and of little cognitive value.
7. Learning can take place with or without mediation. In the case of the latter, the social context and interactions, especially with those who are capable, provide avenues for learners to work at cognitive levels above their own.

12. Cognitive Development: Cognitive development, also known as mental on intellectual development is the development of the mental abilities and capacities which help an individual to adjust his behaviour to the even changing environmental conditions or to enable him to accomplish a task that needs complex cognitive abilities. Various aspects of cognitive development are—development of concepts, perception, language, memory, reasoning, thinking, imagination and intelligence.

Piaget's theory on cognitive development: According to Piaget, a child goes through the following series of developmental stages:

- Sensori-motor stage
- Pre-conceptual stage
- Intuitive stage
- Concrete operation stage
- Formal operation stage

13. Motivation is generally considered to be of two types, extrinsic and intrinsic. Extrinsic classroom motivation refers to the external factors teachers being to bear upon the learning process such as marks, rewards, punishments, prizes, and social approval. As the child progresses through school, many short-sighted and ineffectual teachers resort more and more to this type of motivation. Thus, the high school or college student interested only in a mark and who couldn't care less about what he is learning in the course is not an uncommon phenomenon. He is, however, a sharp contrast to the first-grade youngster who is so eager to read, so interested to learn, and so ready to ask questions and seek answers. This youngster is motivated by *intrinsic* motivation which, simply defined, is an inner search for meaning. Furthermore, this type of motivation is not peculiar to primary grade children nor does it automatically disappear as individuals mature. On the contrary, it can be stimulated in most individuals on any age level by a creative and perceptive teacher.

Intrinsic motivation is initiated through an active, learner-centric, self-recognized goal. The individual is confronted with a problem, with a situation he doesn't understand, or with a condition that upsets his mental complacency. As he consciously organizes his resources to meet this situation, a purpose emerges that guides his actions until satisfaction is realized.

The implications of this type of motivation upon the teacher's planning are twofold. First, if the teacher has considerable freedom in determining the content of his program, he may simply capitalize upon the genuine, spontaneously voiced interests and questions of the pupils. A class, for instance, may become so interested, so concerned, so excited, and so voluble about last week's tornado scare that they may raise in class such questions as, "What is a tornado?" "What causes tornadoes?" "What does wind velocity mean?" "Why are tornados more frequently found in some parts of our country than in others?" A clever teacher may then use these questions as a guide to a very worthwhile learning experience for the class. This type of intrinsic motivation, when used in the classroom, is usually referred to as *natural* motivation. It can motivate, when used correctly, a very desirable learning experience.

15. Piaget's Cognitive Developmental Theory: Piaget's theory states that children actively construct their understanding of the world and go through four stages of cognitive development. Two processes underlie this cognitive construction of the world: organization and adaptation. To make sense of our world, we organize our experiences. For example, we separate important ideas from less important ideas. We connect one idea to another. In addition to organizing our observations and experiences, we *adapt* out thinking to include new ideas.

Piaget (1954) believed that we adapt in two ways: assimilation and accommodation. Assimilation occurs when children incorporate new information into their existing knowledge. Accommodation occurs when children adjust their knowledge to fit new information adn experiences. Consider an 8-year-old girl who is given a hammer and nails to hang a picture on the wall. She has never used a hammer, but from experience and observation she realizes that a hammer is an object to be held, that it is swung by the handle to hit the nail, and that it is usually swung a number of times.

Recognizing each of these things, she fits the current task into her existing knowledge (assimilation). However, the hammer is heavy, so she holds it near the top. She swings too hard and the nail bends, so she adjusts the pressure of her strikes. These adjustments reveal her ability to alter her knowledge (accommodation).

17. Psychology is the scientific study of human behaviour and mental processes. Educational psychology is the science of human behaviour applied to the teaching and learning processes. Like general psychology, educational psychology is a science; therefore, its findings are generated through research that relies heavily on the scientific method. However, its purpose in study is to produce practical knowledge about educational settings and behaviours.

Educational psychology helps teachers understand issues such as how students learn, what motivates students to learn, how to design instruction that maximizes learning, and how to assess student learning and curricular effectiveness. It also can assist teachers to becŏme more aware of their thoughts and actions and understand the effects these thoughts and actions have on others.

18. Motivation : It comes from the Latin word 'movers' which means 'to move' or to 'initiate'. Thus motivation can be represented by a cycle consisting of (i) a need or a drive which (ii) arouses instrumental behaviour & in turn (iii) results in achieving a goal.

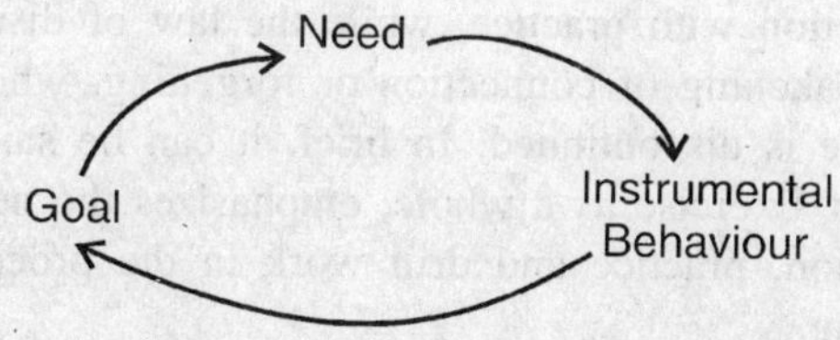

According to Goods: "Motivation is the process of arousing, sustaining & regulating activity".

Crow & Crow: "Motivation is considered with the arousal of interest in learning & to a great extent is basic to learning".

Locke: Proposed that "will" always initiates action in man which is determined by some pressing uneasiness (Desire).

"Motivation is the outcome of motives".

Gates & others: "Motives are conditions either physiological or psychological within the organism that disposes it to act in certain ways".

Maslow: Motivation is constant, never ending, fluctuating & complex & is an almost universal characteristic of particularly every organism state of affairs".

19. A curriculum is what constitutes a total teaching-learning program composed of overall aims, syllabus, materials, methods and assessment. In short it provides a framework of knowledge and capabilities, seen as appropriate to a particular level.

20. Play-way method: Play is the spontaneous and joyous activity of the child. He learns many things through play. It is the chief source of learning. In the beginning the child's informal education starts with play. In the classroom the play-way atmosphere should pervade. The teacher should teach in a play way spirit. It is a psychological method and according to naturalists it is the principal method of learning. Froebel and Montessori adopted this method for educating the children. In Kindergarten and Activity schools play way has been very useful.

Underlying Principles of Play-Way

The following are the underlying principles of play-way method:

Learning by Doing: Learning through some activity is more in line with the fundamental urges of the child. This not only leads to a desirable sensory training but also provides opportunity for the gratification of urges like self-expression, self-assertion and construction.

Related to Life: If we relate the activities in the classroom with the life of the child, the child does not feel that he is living in an artificial atmosphere at school and therefore the tendency to avoid attendance in the school does not arise.

Methods of Teaching: Rigid, formal and bookish methods should be replaced by activities natural to the child. These should be based on the needs and interests of the child.

Sympathetic Attitude: Sympathetic attitude is conducive to efficient learning and the child also does not live under the strain of the artificial atmosphere. Report is established easily and children accept the suggestions of the teacher without much hesitation.

Free Expression: Opportunities should be provided for free expression in any form which may be of interest to the child.

Individual's Importance: The teaher should realize that interests and needs of children are seldom alike. Therefore, while planning education through play-way he should cater to the needs of each child individually.

Advantages of Play-Way

The play-way method has a number of advantages which are given below:

Natural Motivation: Play-way being the natural urge of the child, he takes keen interest in it. Play gives him happiness and satisfaction and education is a by-product of the activities.

Whole-hearted Response: In play-way there is wholehearted response of the child and he becomes serious about his work.

Balanced Development of Personality: Play-way provides means for the social, emotional and moral development of the child besides giving intellectual training.

Self-discipline: When the child is engaged in an activity of an interest, he does not need any external control. He lives according to the self-imposed regulations. It becomes self-disciplined.

Self-advancement: Play-way ensures self-advancement through self-education.

Training of the Sensory Organs: Training of the sensory organs is not ignored.

Methods of Teaching Based on the Play-Way Principle

(1) **Kindergarten :** In this method children are taught through sound movement. Play-spirit permeates the learning process. Activity centres round gifts which were evolved by Froebel, who was the originator of this method. (2) Montessori Method. (3) Project Method. (4) Dalton Plan. (5) Heuristic Method. (6) Basic Education. (7) Self-government. (8) Extra Curricular activities like scouting, girl guiding, N.C.C., excursions and school functions.

21. **Trial and Error Theory of Learning:** The Pioneer of this theory was Edward L. Thorndike (1874-1949). He had conducted experiments on chickens, cats and rats. Thorndike propounded the following three Laws of Learning on the basis of his experiments:

1. The Law of Readiness
2. The Law of Effect
3. The Law of Exercise

1. **The Law of Readiness:** This law is indicative to learner's state to participate in the learning process. Readiness according to Thorndike is preparation for action. It is very essential for learning. If the child is ready to learn he learns more quickly, effectively and with greater satisfaction than if he is not ready to learn. It warns us not to make the child learn till he is ready to learn and also not to miss any opportunity of providing learning experience if the child is, already, prepared to learn. The right movements concerning the learning situation and the learner's state of mind should be very well-recognized and maximum use of this knowledge should be made by the teacher. He should also attempt to motivate the students by arousing their attention, interest and curiosity.

2. **The Law of Effect:** According to this law learning takes place properly when it results in satisfaction and the learner derives pleasure out of it. In the situation when the child meets a failure or gets dissatisfaction, the progress on the path of learning is blocked. All the pleasant experiences have a lasting influence and are remembered for a long time, while the unpleasant ones are soon forgotten. Therefore, the satisfaction and dissatisfaction, pleasure or displeasure obtained as a result of some learning ensure the degree of effectiveness of that learning.

   In the words, this law emphasizes the role of rewards and punishment in the process of learning. Getting reward as a result of some learning motivates and encourages the child to proceed on the same path with more intensity and enthusiasm while the punishment of any sort discourages him and creates distaste and repulsion towards that learning.

3. **The Law of Exercise:** This law has two sub-parts-law of use and law of disuse. The statements regarding these sub-parts run as under:

Law of Use: "When a modifiable connection is made between a situation and response that connection's strength is, other things being equal, increased."

Law of Disuse: "When a modifiable connection is not made between a situation and response, dufing a length of time, that connection's strength is decreased."

In this way, Law of use refers to the strengthening of connection with practice, while the law of disuse to the weakening of connection or forgetting, when the practice is discontinued. In brief, it can be said that Law of Exercise as a whole, emphasizes the need of repetition, practice and drill work in the process of learning.

In addition to the laws of readiness, exercise and effect, Thorndike's idea of connectionism provided some of the following important laws:

1. Law of Multiple response or varied reactions.
2. Las of Attitude.
3. Las of Analogy.
4. Law of Associative shifting.

The above laws of learning can be discussed as following:

1. **Law of Multiple Response:** This law implies that when an individual is confronted with a new situation, he responds in a variety of ways trying first one response and then another before arriving at the correct one.
2. **Law of Attitude:** Learning is guided by a total attitude or 'set' of the organism. The learner performs the task properly if he has developed a healthy attitude towards the task.

3. **Law of Analogy:** An individual responds to a new situation on the basis of the responses mady by him in a similar situation in the past *i.e.* he makes responses by comparison or analogy.
4. **Law of Associative Shifting:** This law states that "Any response may be elicited from the learner, of which he is capable, in association with any situation to which he is sensitive."

23. **Inclusive Education:** Inclusion describes much more than the acceptance of children with disabilities/exceptionalities in the mainstream. Inclusive education programmes do not focus on the accommodation of these children into a general education setting, but are focused on the restructuring of schools to accept and provide for the needs of all students. In inclusive education, mainstreaming and integration are viewed as intermediary steps to the ultimate goal of teaching all students together. In inclusive program specialized instruction and support are provided to any student who is in need of support without labelling him as disabled or exceptional. In other words, no discrimination is made among the exceptional or non-exceptional children. All the children in all shades of their exceptionality/disability are welcome by making necessary arrangements and accommodations for their education in the same school and classes along with their non disabled peers.

25. Dyslexia is a disorder manifested by difficulty in learning to read, despite conventional instruction, adequate intelligence and socio-cultural opportunity. It is dependent upon fundamental cognitive disabilities, which are frequently of constitutional origin.

27. **The Principles of Development**

(*i*) **Development follows a pattern or a sequence:** Development tends to proceed from the head downward. This is called the **cephalocaudal principle.** According to this principle, the child first gains control of the head, then the arms, then the legs. Infants gain control of head and face movements within the first two months after birth. In the next few months, they are able to lift themselves up using their arms. By 6 to 12 months of age, infants start to gain leg control and may be able to crawl, stand, or walk.

Development also proceeds from the center of the body outward according to the **proximodistal principle**. Accordingly, the spinal cord develops before other parts of the body. The child's arms develop before the hands, and the hands and feet develop before the fingers and toes. Fingers and toes are the last to develop.

(*ii*) **Development proceeds from general to specific responses:** It moves from a generalized to localized behaviour. The newborn infant moves its whole body at one time instead of moving only one part of it. It makes random kicking with its legs before it can coordinate the leg muscles well enough to crawl or to walk.

(*iii*) **Development is a continuous process:** Development does not occur in spurts. Growth continues from the moments of conception until the individual reaches maturity. It takes place at slow regular pace rather than by 'leaps and bounds'. Although development is a continuous process, yet the tempo of growth is not even, during infancy and early years growth moves swiftly and later it slacken.

(*iv*) **Different aspects of growth develop at different rates:** Neither all parts of the body grow at the same rate nor do all aspects of mental growth proceed equally. They reach maturity at different times. Development also depends on maturation. **Maturation** refers to the sequence of biological changes in children. These orderly changes give children new abilities. Much of the maturation depends on changes in the brain and the nervous system. These changes assist children to improve their thinking abilities and motor skills. A rich learning environment helps children develop to their potential.

(*v*) **Most traits are correlated in development:** Generally, it is seen that the child whose intellectual development is above average is so in health size, sociability and special aptitudes.

(*vi*) **Growth is complex:** All of its aspects are closely interrelated. The child's mental development is intimately related to his physical growth and its needs.

(*vii*) **Growth is a product of the interaction of the organism and environment:** Among the environmental factors one can mention nutrition, climate the conditions in the home, the type of social organization in which individual moves and lives.

(*viii*) **There are wide individual differences in growth:** Individual differences in growth are caused by differences in heredity and environment.

(*ix*) **Growth is both quantitative and qualitative:** These two aspects are inseparable. The child not only grows in 'size'; he grows up or matures in structure and function too.

(*x*) **Development is predictable:** It is possible for us to predict at an early age the range within which the mature development of the child is likely to fall. However, mental development cannot be predicted with the same degree of accuracy.

28. Kohler's Gestalt or insightful Learning

The learning theory named as "Learning by Insight" is the contribution of Gestalt Psychologists. Gestalt Psychology began with the work of German psychologists who were studying the nature of perception. Wertheimer is, generally, considered to be the Gestalt Psychology founding father. Wertheimer, Kohler, Koffka and Lewin all four of these men, originally German, eventually settled in America, are the leaders of what is historically known as Gestalt Psychology.

"Gestalt" is a German noun for which there is no English word equivalent, so the term was carried over into English psychological literature. The nearest English translation of Gestalt is 'configuration' or more simply an organised whole in contrast to a collection of parts. Gestalt psychologist consider the process of learning as a Gestaltan organised whole. A thing cannot be understood by study of its constituent parts but only by study of it as a totality, is a basic idea behind this theory.

Educational Implicationing of the Theory of Insightful Learning

This theory brings the following important facts into lime-light:

1. The whole is greater than the parts and, therefore, the situation should be viewed as a whole.
2. The use of blind fumbling and mechanical trial and error should be minimised. The learner should try to see relevant relationships and act intelligently.
3. The purpose or motive plays the central role in the learning process.

29. In an effort to assert their identity and independence, Adolescents tend to pull away from the close emotional ties that they share with their parents and prefer the company of their friends.

Wherever the sociocultural milieu does not permit interaction between boys and girls, Adolescents of each gender group develop a 'homo-social' orientation and form gender-specific peer groups. While at home, Adolescents often prefer being alone and demand their privacy. This desire to be left alone by family members promotes their dependence on the peer group, from which they derive approval and support for their changed behavioural patterns.

Some Adolescents may spend most of their time outside the home with members of their peer group. It is understandable that peers would have a greater influence on Adolescent Attitudes, Speech, Interests, Appearance, and Behaviour than Family Members. Most Adolescents, for example, discover that if they wear the same types of clothes as favoured by popular members of the Peer-Group, their chances of acceptance are enhanced.

31. Clearly (B) is the correct answer.

As 7 is the sum of opposite faces

$2 + 5 = 7$

$3 + 4 = 7$

$6 + 1 = 7.$

32. Traditionally the approach to teaching and learning mathematics has been teacher centred, instruction based and behaviourist-learning and mastering a method/ algorithm and then applying them in 'word problems'. In the new approach the role of the teacher is that of a facilitator, who creates meaningful contexts, poses appropriate questions, introduces games and puzzles to help children evolve strategies for problem solving.

The Activity Based Approach is unique and effective to attract school children. The teachers who are involved in implementing this method have developed activities for each learning unit which facilitated readiness for learning. The aim of activity-based approach is for learners to construct process of self-learning and problem solving and transfer of information and skills. This method has brought out the potential of the learners in classroom situations.

Need of Activity Based Approach :

- Encourages independence and team learning.
- Provides a wide variety of manipulative open-ended and creative activities.
- Provides students experience and active participation in the exploration of their environment.
- Make students advance at their own rate–the rate that is with their abilities, interest and motivations.
- Encourages self-reliance and development of initiative in an atmosphere of trust.
- Encourages children to follow many of their own interests and desires to learn.
- Problem-solving, critical and creative thinking and deep understanding are emphasized.
- Learners are encouraged to explore the new knowledge independently.

34. Diagnostic Tests

The tests which have been devised to provide information about the specific nature of pupil's difficulties in given subject areas are called diagnostic tests. The term diagnosis has been borrowed from the medical profession where it implies "Identification of disease by means of patient's symptoms."

The word diagnosis is used more or less in the same sense in education. We may say that educational diagnosis is "The determination of the nature of learning difficulties and deficiencies."

According to **Atkinson Mark M. (1969)** "Educational diagnosis is required for pupils to enable education to discover individual strengths and weaknesses as a basis for planning their educational guidance." **Surgen Pau, V.** laid down the following essential steps in educational diagnosis:

- Identifying the pupils who are having difficulties.
- The errors or learning difficulties of pupils.
- Discovering the casual factors.

Educational diagnosis implies all activities in measurement and interpretation that helps to identify growth at large and their casual factors for individuals or for class groups.

Purpose of Diagnostic Tests

Diagnostic tests measure some what narrower aspects of achievement than survey tests.

Diagnostic tests yield measures of highly related abilities underlying achievement in a subject. They are designed to identify particular strengths and weaknesses on the part of the individual child and within reasonable limits to reveal the underlying causes.

The immediate aim is to locate areas in which additional instruction or remedial education is required or in which teaching methods have to be improved. No rigid time limit need be specified in the case of diagnostic tests. Diagnosis should be individualized as much as possible and every student should be allowed as much time as he needs reasonably.

It may be noted that the preparation of blue print may altogether be avoided in a diagnostic test.

Edward and Stanley have stressed that the factors such as teaching methods and the teaching-learning process, social and emotional problem, physical factors, intellectual and mental factors. Factors associated with learning difficulties will have significant influence on learning. To determine the degree and nature of their influence educational diagnosis is often necessary.

36. From right angled triangle AOB

$AB = \sqrt{4^2+3^2} = 5$

$\therefore$ Perimeter $= 5 \times 4$

$= 20$ cm.

42. From given pattern

$n \oplus 8 = n + n + 1 + n + 2 + n + 3 + n + 4 + n + 5 + n + 6 + n + 7$

$= 8n + 28.$

45. Weight of Mangoes = 2 kg 600 g

Weight of Apples = 1 kg 450 g

$\therefore$ Difference = 1 kg 150 g

50. Number of matchsticks in the stages 1st, 2nd, 3rd, ... are 6, 10, 14, 18, ... respectively.

$\therefore$ In 15th stage no. of matchsticks required

$= a + 14d$

$= 6 + 14 \times 4$

$= 6 + 56$

$= 62.$

51. Since, length $= l$ and breadth $= \frac{l}{2}$

$\therefore$ Perimeter $= 2\left(l+\frac{l}{2}\right) = 3l$

Again, length $= 2l$ and breadth $\frac{l}{2}$

$\therefore$ Perimeter $= 2\left(2l+\frac{l}{2}\right) = 5l.$

53. The total number of four digit numbers

$= (9999 - 1000) + 1$

$= 8999 + 1 = 9000.$

54. Clearly answer (D) is correct because

$\frac{3}{4}+\frac{3}{4}=\frac{6}{4}=1\frac{1}{2}.$

55. Since last three digits are 532

$\therefore$ Cleraly nearest thousand is = 50000

56.
$(2 + 2 + 2)^2 = 6^2 = 36$

$4^2 = 4 \times 4 = 16$

$(2 \times 2 \times 2)^2 = (8)^2 = 64$

$[(2 + 2)^2]^2 = [(4)^2]^2 = 16^2 = 256$

Clearly (D) is greatest.

57. Bus 1 —

24 : 40
19 : 15
5 : 25

Bus 2 —

18 : 10
12 : 30
5 : 40

Bus 3 —

21 : 55
16 : 45
5 : 10

69. Anaemia, also known as Iron Deficiency Anaemia (also called IDA) is a condition in which a lack of iron causes a drop in haemoglobin in the blood and red blood cells in the body. These red blood cells (RBCs) are responsible for carrying oxygen to the tissues. The main causes of the anaemia are inadequate iron in the diet and too much of blood loss from the body.

70. The hypothesis of floating lemon in salt water is that salt water and fresh water have different densities. Since an lemon will sink within regular water, adding salt to the water will increase the density of the water and allow the lemon to float. A lemon floats in salt water because salt water is more dense than water straight from the tap. The greater buoyancy allows the lemon to float in the salt water, provided it is salty enough. In order for something to float, the buoyant force has to greater than or equal to the weight of the object. The buoyant force is equal to the weight of the liquid that is displaced by the object. To figure out the weight of the water that is displaced, you multiply the density of the water by the volume and then multiply that by gravity. The density of fresh water is less than salt water; therefore the weight of the water displaced will be greater in the case of the salt water, resulting in a greater buoyant force. The more salt that is present in the water the more buoyant an object becomes. Salt water has more particles with which to hold up the lemon. This is because rather than floating and taking up space, the salt dissolves into ions which are attracted to the water molecules and bind very tightly to them, packing more matter into the space. The mass of the ordinary water consists of the mass of the hydrogen and oxygen that it contains. Salt water has the additional mass of the sodium and chlorine atoms that dissolve into the water. To test this in an experiment, fill up two glasses with fresh water. Add six tablespoons to one of the glasses and place an lemon in each cup.

71. Growth of micro-organisms in nature is dependent on various factors. The factors influencing the growth of micro-organisms are physical, chemical and biological in nature. The important factors which contribute to the growth of micro-organisms in food are temperature, pH, moisture content, redox potential, nutrient content, inhibiting substances and other micro-organisms present in food.

Growth of micro-organisms is influenced by the temperature which has effect on biocatalytic activity of enzymes present in them. Every organisms has its minimum, optimum and maximum limits of temperature for its survival, growth and biocatalytic activity. Micro-organisms present in food are influenced by the temperature at which they are processed and preserved. Temperature also influences food for their chemical composition and oxidation status. Food at room temperature are influenced by the growth of mesophilic micro-organisms. Most of the food spoilage is caused by microbial growth at mesophilic temperature. Therefore, the practice of preserving food at low temperature in refrigerators is to prevent spoilage by mesophilic micro-organisms. However, continuous practice of storing food at low temperature may result in natural enrichment of psychrophilic and psychrotrophic microorganisms which become cause of food spoilage in refrigerators or cold storages.

72. Malaria is a protozoan disease, which are a group of eukaryotic single-celled organisms that infect humans and inhabit the body as parasites. Malaria is caused by four species of the protozoan genus *Plasmodium, P. falciparum, P. vivax, P. malariae*, and *P. ovale*. Plasmodium enter the human body when bit by the infected female mosquito called Anopheles. Plasmodium travel through small vessels to the liver where they multiply and then invade red blood cells.

74. Chipko Movement, started in 1970's, was a non violent movement aimed at protection and conservation of trees and forests from being destroyed. The name of the Chipko moment originated from the word 'embrace' as the villagers used to hug the trees and protect them from wood cutters from cutting them. Chipko movement was based on the Gandhian philosophy of peaceful resistance to achieve the goals.

The Chipko Movement gained momentum under Sunderlal Bahuguna, an eco activist, who spent his whole life persuading and educating the villagers, to protest against the destruction of the forests and the Himalayan mountains by the government. It was he, who made appeal to the Prime Minister of India Mrs Indira Gandhi to ban the cutting of tress. He shouted the slogan 'ecology is the permanent economy'. Another main leader of the movement was Mr. Chandi Prasad Bhatt, who advocated the development of small scale local industries, which were based on the sustainable use of the forests resources, for the local benefits.

75. Vitamins are a class of organic compounds categorized as essential nutrients for life and maintenance of normal health. These are required in small quantity in body, thus falling in the category of micronutrients, because body uses them without breaking down, as happens to carbohydrate and other macronutrients.

Vitamins are mainly classified into two broad categories, *viz:*

Fat soluble vitamins

- Vitamin-A
- Vitamin-E
- Vitamin-D
- Vitamin-K

Water soluble vitamins

- Vitamin-B complex
- Vitamin-C (Ascorbic acid)

77. Winnowing is the process of separating lighter components of a mixture from the heavier ones by using wind or moving air is known as winnowing.

82. Stomach churns the food to mix digestive juices. The food in the stomach is churned into semi solid. The churned semi-solid food is called chime. Gastric juice is secreted from the wall of stomach and mixed with food. Gastric juice contains some enzymes and hydrochloric acid. The enzymes present in the gastric juices break down protein from food. The hydrochloric acid kills the harmful bacteria present if any in the food and helps the gastric enzymes to work.

87.

S.No.	Boiling	Evaporation
1.	It occurs at specific temperature.	It occurs at all temperatures.
2.	It requires heat energy to be supplied by external sources.	In general liquid absorbs heat energy from its surroundings.
3.	It takes place throughout the liquid.	It is a surface phenomenon and occurs only at the surface of the liquid.
4.	It is not accompanied by cooling. Temperature of liquid has increased.	In this process the region surrounding the evaporating liquid gets cooler.
5.	It is rapid and noisy process.	It is slow and quiet process.
6.	Temperature of the liquid remains constant at the boiling point.	Usually the temperature of liquid drops.

89. Meteor: A small chunk of rock, no larger than a few feet in diameter, that is travelling through space and enters the Earth's atmosphere; commonly known as a shooting star.

94. The Constitution (Eighty-sixth Amendment) Act, 2002 inserted Article 21-A in the Constitution of India to provide free and compulsory education of all children in the age group of six to fourteen years as a Fundamental Right in such a manner as the State may, by law, determine. The Right of Children to Free and Compulsory Education (RTE) Act, 2009, which represents the consequential legislation envisaged under Article 21-A, means that every child has a right to full time elementary education of satisfactory and equitable quality in a formal school which satisfies certain essential norms and standards.

Article 21-A and the RTE Act came into effect on 1 April 2010. The title of the RTE Act incorporates the words 'free and compulsory'. 'Free education' means that no child, other than a child who has been admitted by his or her parents to a school which is not supported by the appropriate Government, shall be liable to pay any kind of fee or charges or expenses which may prevent him or her from pursuing and completing elementary education. 'Compulsory education' casts an obligation on the appropriate Government and local authorities to provide and ensure admission, attendance and completion of elementary education by all children in the 6-14 age group. With this, India has moved forward to a rights based framework that casts a legal obligation on the Central and State Governments to implement this fundamental child right as enshrined in the Article 21A of the Constitution, in accordance with the provisions of the RTE Act.

The RTE Act provides for the:

(*i*) Right of children to free and compulsory education till completion of elementary education in a neighbourhood school.

(*ii*) It clarifies that 'compulsory education' means obligation of the appropriate government to provide free elementary education and ensure compulsory admission, attendance and completion of elementary education to every child in the six to fourteen age group. 'Free' means that no child shall be liable to pay any kind of fee or charges or expenses which may prevent him or her from pursuing and completing elementary education.

(*iii*) It makes provisions for a non-admitted child to be admitted to an age appropriate class.

(*iv*) It specifies the duties and responsibilities of appropriate Governments, local authority and parents in providing free and compulsory education, and sharing of financial and other responsibilities between the Central and State Governments.

(*v*) It lays down the norms and standards relating inter alia to Pupil Teacher Ratios (PTRs), buildings and infrastructure, school-working days, teacher-working hours.

(*vi*) It provides for rational deployment of teachers by ensuring that the specified pupil teacher ratio is maintained for each school, rather than just as an average for the State or District or Block, thus ensuring that there is no urban-rural imbalance in teacher postings. It also provides for prohibition of deployment of teachers for non-educational work, other than decennial census, elections to local authority, state legislatures and parliament, and disaster relief.

(*vii*) It provides for appointment of appropriately trained teachers, i.e. teachers with the requisite entry and academic qualifications.

(*viii*) It prohibits

(*a*) physical punishment and mental harassment;
(*b*) screening procedures for admission of children;
(*c*) capitation fee;
(*d*) private tuition by teachers and
(*e*) running of schools without recognition,

(*ix*) It provides for development of curriculum in consonance with the values enshrined in the Constitution, and which would ensure the all-round development of the child, building on the child's knowledge, potentiality and talent and making the child free of fear, trauma and anxiety through a system of child friendly and child centred learning.

100. Brainstorming is a superior technique for generating ideas. This technique is used for generating any and all possible solutions to a problem, encouraging students to come up with creative, exciting and radical ideas without fear of criticism, generating spontaneous reactions to an issue(s) and/or finding solutions to specific problems.

YOUR SPACE

YOUR SPACE

CTET/STETs

PRACTICE TEST PAPER (SOLVED)

(WITH EXPLANATORY ANSWERS)

TEST PAPER–1

PART- I

Child Development and Pedagogy

1. Observe the picture given below:

What type of development it denotes?

A. Mental Development
B. Physical Development
C. Emotional Development
D. Psychomotor Development

2. When Anu was in 4th standard, she used to participate very actively in all classroom works. But after entering 5th standard, she appeared quite gloomy and in attentive. Which method do you adopt to solve the problem?

A. Observation B. Action Research
C. Case Study D. Testing

3. The developmental stage in which logical thinking and abstract thinking are at the best:

A. Infancy B. Childhood
C. Adolescence D. Old age

4. Which of the following is not a characteristic of a five year old child?

A. Imitates
B. Acquires body balance
C. Shows interest in play
D. Has abstract thinking ability

5. A child's first means of communication is through:

A. Cooing B. Crying
C. Smiling D. Through simple words

6. A child who used to play with white rabbits became fearful of seing even white coloured objects later. This is due to :

A. Conditioning B. Mental disturbances
C. Adjustment Problem D. Dislike Play

7. Observe the dots, see whether there forms a figure? Which characteristic of mind explains this perception?

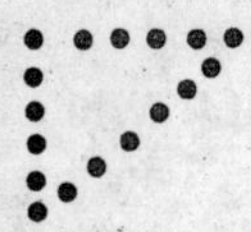

A. Similarity B. Proximity
C. Continuity D. All of the above

8. According to Gestalt theory, learning is most effective by :

A. Repetition B. Problem solving
C. Trial and error D. Conditioning

9. As per the Piaget's theory on Cognitive development, the following figures are developed to measure a particular ability of the children :

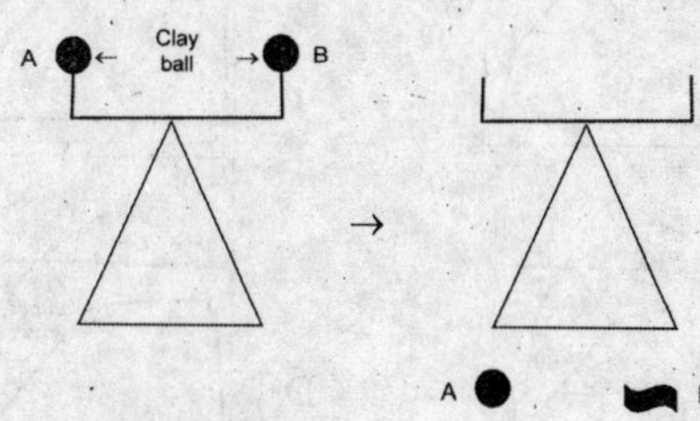

Here, it used to identify :

A. Reversibility B. Ability in classification
C. Logical thinking D. Ability to infer

10. Minitha had learned type writing. When she reached high school, she has to learn computer where she could able to operate computer keyboard very easily. This can be attributed to :

A. Transfer of training
B. Practice on keyboard
C. Interest in using computer
D. Simplicity of the keyboard

11. "We only thinking when we confronted with problem". Who proposed it?

A. Pestalozzi B. Maria Montissori
C. John Dewey D. Rousseaue

12. When the teacher asked Prathibha to count 50 note books from the school storeroom, she had counted ten books at first. Then she had four bunches of notebooks of the same hight. This way she counted 50 books easily.
Here, Prathibha manifests :
A. Visio-spatial intelligence
B. Logico-mathematical intelligence
C. Intra personal intelligence
D. Naturalistic intelligence

13. Teacher asked the students to rearrange the letters in the word 'CTA' to make a meaningful name of an animal. Most of them could make it easily. What ability is measured in this context?
A. Concepts on animals
B. Language ability of children
C. Interest in activity
D. Interest in play

14. While assessing the physical efficiency of the children in her class, the teacher Deepa directly graded them with A, B, C. What kind of grading is this?
A. Absolute Grading B. Direct Grading
C. Point Grading D. Relative Grading

15. Observe the figures given below and choose the right one representing Freud's idea of human mind.

A.
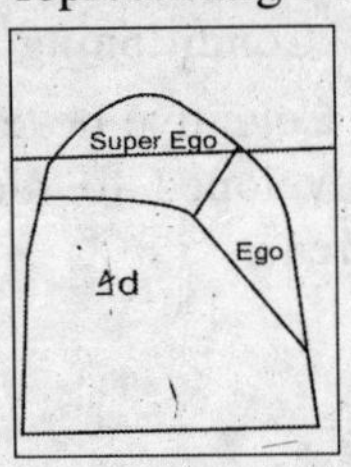

B.
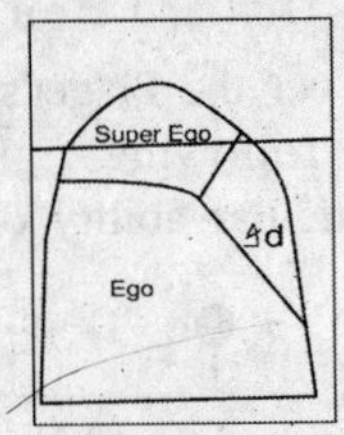

C.
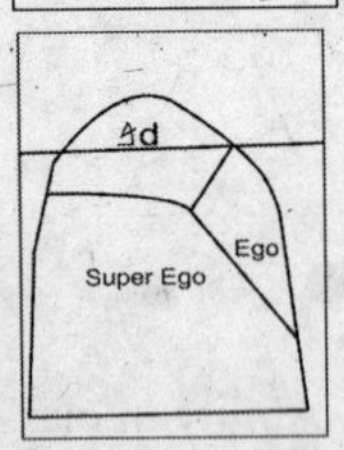

D.
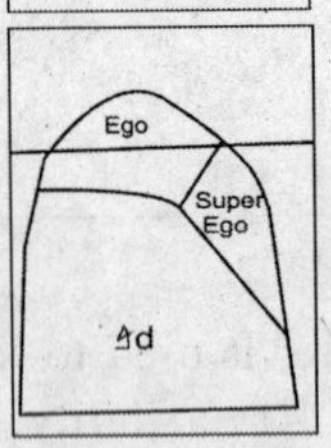

16. 'Jithitha has a treasure of knowledge on local plants and flowers, but her teacher used to ignore it in the classroom'. Here, the teacher :
A. Doesn't consider the local knowledge
B. Doesn't consider the girl child
C. Doesn't consider the nature of child
D. All of the above

17. Read the following characteristics of a child.
(*i*) He is not lazy
(*ii*) He has many abilities
(*iii*) While doing arithmatics in the classroom, he used to reverse numbers and constantly makes mistakes.
What problem does he face?
A. Learning Backwardness B. Learning Disability
C. Physical Disability D. Mental Disability

18. Have you heard of Thathagath? He passed his M.Sc. in physics at the age of 12. He could do this because :
A. He is brilliant
B. Got immediate acceleration
C. Got continuous support from parents and teachers
D. All of the above

19. 'Adapted teaching manual' is now used in the classroom for :
A. For effective classroom transactions
B. To promote learning of (CWSN) Children with Special Needs
C. To catch attention of children
D. To make classroom participatory

20. 'Adarsh a nine year old child, who is very restless. He couldn't concentrate on a task and complete it'. What problem does he face?
A. ADHD B. Autism
C. Aphasia D. Disphraxia

21. 'A teacher used to encourage her children to ask questions. She also used to promote those children asking good evaluatory questions'. This process helps the children to :
A. Learn subject well
B. Develop critical thinking ability
C. Utilize the knowledge of the teacher well
D. Ensure their participation

22. What instructional method is the best to ensure development of creativity among students?
A. Problem solving
B. Project
C. Brain storming
D. Enquiry

23. Suppose children possess certain misconcepts in their subject of study, what is the best method to be adopted in the classroom to solve it?
A. Indicate the error and correct it at once
B. Let it to solve by children themselves
C. Organise appropriate learning experience and help them to solve it
D. Let them ask somebody to solve it

24. For formulating the curriculum which factor is most important?
A. Teachers ability
B. Children's capabilities and needs
C. National ideologies
D. Social and cultural ideals

25. When does an activity become collaborative?
A. Group members do have a common goal but not well organised
B. Well organised, but do not have a common goal
C. Well organised group, working on a common goal
D. None of the above

26. Read the definition given below.
"It is our ability to know what we know and what we don't know".
What does it represent?
A. Cognition B. Intelligence
C. Meta Cognition D. Knowledge

27. According to Katherene Bridges, a new born child does possess only one emotional state at the time of birth. Then, What it is?
A. Distress B. Delight
C. Diffuse excitement D. Disgust.

28. How does Piaget relate the cognitive structure of a person to his environment?
A. Cognitive structure develop freely without having environmental influence
B. Cognitive structure develops through the interaction with the environment
C. Cognitive development is purely a biological process
D. None of the above

29. 'In Maslow's need hierarchy', which is the highest need that does a person aspire?
A. Safety Needs
B. Physiological Needs
C. Self Actualisation Needs
D. Self Esteem Needs

30. Which one is not useful to adopt in Primary classroom as a scaffolder?
A. Make use of the acquired knowledge
B. Let students share experiences related to the issue
C. Repeating and mastering idea
D. Let students to share their incomplete ideas

PART- II

Mathematics

31. In the natural number [7]7 7(7)7 how many times the place value of 7 in the circle is the place value of 7 in the square?
A. 10 B. 100
C. 1000 D. 10000

32. 5.10 m cloth is required for stitching shirts for Arun, Ajith and Abijith. Arun requires 20 cm of cloth more than that for Ajith. Abijith requires 10 cm cloth less than that for Arun. How much centimetres of cloth is required for Ajith?
A. 150 B. 160
C. 170 D. 180

33. When a five digit number is added to a four digit number which of the following cannot come as the answer?
A. 109988 B. 109989
C. 109998 D. 109999

34. How many $\frac{1}{100}$ are there in 2.16?
A. 6 B. 16
C. 21 D. 216

35. When 100 rupee note was changed Ravi got coins of 50 paise, 1 Rupee, 2 Rupee and all notes of denomination of Rupees 5 and more. What is the total number of coins and notes he got?
A. 10 B. 9
C. 8 D. 7

36. What is the maximum area in square centimetres for a rectangle of perimeter 80 cm?
A. 80 B. 400
C. 1600 D. 6400

37. Which of the following is a possible sum of four consecutive counting numbers?
A. 17 B. 18
C. 19 D. 20

38. If $1\frac{1}{2}$ kg of tomato costs rupees 30, what is the price of $2\frac{3}{4}$ kg of tomatos?
A. 45 B. 50
C. 55 D. 60

39. If 500 sheets of paper costs Rupees 140, What is the cost of one sheet of paper?
A. ₹ 0.14 B. ₹ 0.70
C. ₹ 0.28 D. ₹ 1.40

40. Which of the following is equal to 77 × 555?
A. 55 × 777 B. 755 × 75
C. 75 × 557 D. 775 × 55

41. In the following Tangram figure, how much part of the square is the shaded region?

A. $\frac{1}{7}$ B. $\frac{1}{9}$
C. $\frac{1}{14}$ D. $\frac{1}{16}$

42. The area of a square is 100 cm^2. A new square is obtained by increasing the sides by 1 cm. How much more is the area of the new square than the area of the first one?
A. 1 B. 10
C. 11 D. 21

43. The perimeter of a square is 28 cm. A square of side 1 cm is cut off from each of the four corners. What is the perimeter of the remaining part?
A. 28 B. 24
C. 20 D. 16

44. Which of the following model can be constructed using 18 match sticks completely?
A. Rectangular prism B. Square prism
C. Pentagonal prism D. Hexagonal prism

45. Which is the next number in the pattern 1, 3, 7, 13, 21, ...?
A. 29 B. 31
C. 33 D. 34

46. A train starts from Ernakulam at 13.30 on 30-06-2012 and reaches Delhi at 11.40 on 02-07-2012. What is the time taken for the journey?
A. 70 hours 10 minutes B. 44 hours 40 minutes
C. 46 hours 10 minutes D. 47 hours 40 minutes

47. Given below is the figure of a stair of bricks. How many bricks are needed to build a stair of 10 steps like this?

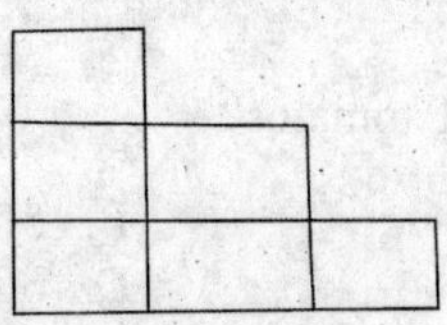

A. 55 B. 50
C. 45 D. 10

48. Given below is a grid for constructing a dice. Which of the following is the figure of a dice constructed from this grid?

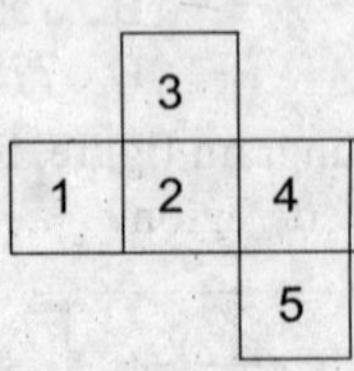

A. 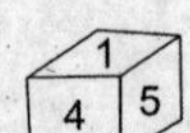

B. 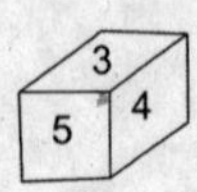

C. 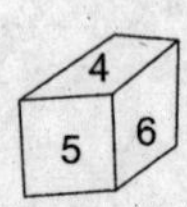

D. 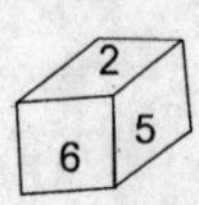

49. How much millimetre is 0.1 km?
A. 1000000 B. 100000
C. 10000 D. 1000

50. 78 × 96 × 54 = 404352 Then what is 39 × 48 × 27?
A. 25274 B. 50544
C. 101088 D. 202176

51. Which of the following is not a concept related to division?
A. equal distribution
B. repeated subtraction
C. repeated addition
D. opposite of multiplication

52. Which of the following is not a goal of Mathematics learning as per NCF 2005?
A. Mathematication of thought process
B. Visualisation of Mathematics
C. Including more Mathematical concepts at primary level
D. Giving importance to the method of problem solving

53. Whose birthday is related to the celebration of National year of Mathematics 2012?
A. Bhaskaracharyar B. Aryabhatan
C. Bhrahma Guptha D. Sreenivasa Ramanujan

54. Given below are the various stages of concept building in Mathematics learning
(*a*) Relating to figures
(*b*) Using concrete objects
(*c*) Expressing in appropriate language
(*d*) Relating with symbols
Arrange these in the order of concept formation.
A. [*b, c, a, d*] B. [*b, a, c, d*]
C. [*c, b, a, d*] D. [*c, a, b, d*]

55. Which of the following is not a practice to be followed by teacher in a Mathematics class?
A. raising thought provoking questions
B. working out all the problems
C. making opportunity for self evaluation
D. encourage thinking through simple examples

56. Which of the following is the characteristic of induction method?
A. From a general principle to a particular problem
B. From many examples to general principle
C. Analysis of a principle
D. Establish a fact through experiments

57. Which of the following is not a stage in problem analysis?
A. Identify the problem exactly
B. Identifies various ways
C. Workingout the steps
D. Choosing appropriate method

58. Different stages of finding the area of a rectangle are given below. Arrange them in the order of introducing the concept of area
a : By multiplying length and breadth
b : Spreading unit squares

c : By drawing unit squares
d : By counting, using stamps, postcards etc.
A. [d, b, c, a] B. [d, c, b, a]
C. [c, a, b, d] D. [a, b, c, d]

59. Which of the following activity can lead to developing creativity among children?
A. Preparation of multiplication facts
B. Finding perimetre of various rectangles
C. Analysing tables relating to time and distance
D. Constructing and colouring various geometrical shapes

60. Various stages of a construction in mathematics are given below. Arrange them in order.
a : Formation of approximate model
b : Identifying appropriate method / tools
c : Self evaluation of the product
d : Completing the construction with precession and accuracy
A. [a, b, d, c]
B. [c, d, b, a]
C. [b, a, d, c]
D. [a, d, b, c]

PART- III

Environmental Studies

61. The part of the eye which is taken out during eye donation is __________
A. Lense B. Cornea
C. Retina D. Iris

62. The importance of moon mineralogy maper is Chandrayan-I is __________.
A. Taken the photographs of moon craters
B. Collecting information about lunar gases
C. Confirm the presence of water in the moon
D. Identify the minerals in the moon

63. The most suitable statement for the word 'Science'—
A. The cumulative knowledge acquired by human race and its effectiveness
B. The cumulative knowledge acquired by human race and the process of enquiry involved in it.
C. The process involved in the enquiry and its effectiveness
D. The knowledge acquired by scientist

64. One of the causes Alzheimers disease is the excess presence of ________.
A. Aluminium B. Sodium
C. Potassium D. Iron

65. Which one of the statement is not related to Carbon dioxide?
A. Greenhouse gas
B. Essential for photosynthesise
C. Involve in carbon cycle
D. Cause depletion of ozone

66. Which one of the following is not the controlled variable in an experiment that find out the influence of water in plant growth?
A. Sunlight B. Manure
C. Water D. Soil

67. The primary consumer in a food chain is ________.
A. Green plants B. Grass hoper
C. Frog D. Snake

68. Which one of the following is the wrong statement about might?
A. Light passes through straight line
B. Earth is opaque
C. Shadow of the earth
D. The revolution of the earth

69. Observes an object in various directions and find out the change in shape. Examine what happen when various objects having different weight dropped from various hights. Observe the changes occures in shadows according to time. The most appropriate process skill acquired by children through the above learning experience.
A. Classification
B. Using number relations
C. Using space-time relations
D. Communicating

70. The maintenance of atmospheric temperature suitable for the existance of species in earth is ______.
A. The sun rays are absorbed by the earth surface
B. The sun rays are reflected by the earth surface
C. The reflection and rereflection of sun rays by the earth surface
D. Presence of ozone layer

71. The phenomenon which occurs when moon comes between sun and earth is _______.
A. Lunar eclips B. Solar eclips
C. Full moon D. Dark moon

72. "90% of homes in a village is using convensional energy source for cooking. While 10% are adopting LPG as their energy source". Which is the most suitable chart form to illustrate the above data?
A. Tree chart B. Table chart
C. Pie chart D. Flow chart

73. 'Oryza Sativa' - is the scientific name of _________.
A. Rabi B. Wheat
C. Paddy D. Maize

74. Find out the odd one?
A. Wind mill
B. Solar pannel
C. Hydro electric power station
D. Nuclear power station

75.

Traits	Students									
	1	2	3	4	5	6	7	8	9	10
1. Punctuality										
2. Responds to the questions										
3. Shows interesting in scientific hobbies										
4. Active in cocurricular activities										

In which category, the tool mentioned above is included?
A. Rating scale B. Check list
C. Anecdotal record D. Cumulative record

76. Which one of the following is not a mammal?
A. Dolphin B. Bat
C. Whale D. Shark

77. The theme of the 'silent spring' written by Rachelcarson is ______.
A. Origin of Cosmos
B. Repercussion of pesticides in the environment
C. Richness of the beauty of the nature
D. Climate change

78. Which one of the following statement is not relevant to the planning page of teaching manual?
A. Planning in modular pattern
B. Detailed the microprocess of activities
C. Include the activities from Textbook, Hand book and Self developed activities.
D. Mention achievement status of students

79. What is LED?
A. Light emitting device B. Light emitting diode
C. Light energy device D. Light energy diode

80. What is the reason for celebration of the National Science day on Feb. 28?
A. Birthday of C.V. Raman
B. Death of C.V. Raman
C. The day in which C.V. Raman awarded Nobel Prize
D. The day in which Raman effect is invented

81.
A: Integrated Learning → B: Environmental Study → C: Science → D: Basic Science

Which one of the following is the most appropriate sequence?
A. A → B → D → C B. C → B → D → A
C. B → A → C → D D. A → C → D → B

82. The soil suitable for agriculture is ______.
A. Soil having high water storage capacity, humus, presence of air
B. Soil having low water storage capacity, high humus and presence of air
C. Soil having high water storage capacity, humus and low air presence
D. Soil having low water storage capacity, air presence and high humus

83. Labourers lifted a heavy log on a lorry. They arranged five pulleys in a 2nd order system. Calculate the actual weight of the log, if the effort applied is 1000 kg.
A. 50 kg B. 500 kg
C. 5000 kg D. 15000 kg

84. Find out the statement which is not suitable with the assumption of assessment.
A. Assessment for learning
B. Learning for assessment
C. Assessment as learning
D. Assessment of learning

85.
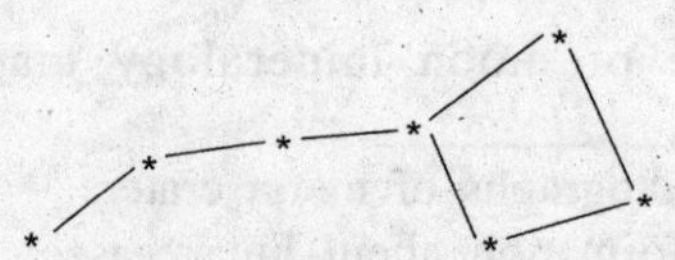

Name the stellar group illustrated above.
A. Leo B. Great Bear
C. Orion D. Herculis

86. The phenomenon which do not occure in plants is ______.
A. Respiration B. Transpiration
C. Diffusion D. Sublimation

87. Find out the statement which is not suitable to the concept of environmental study.
A. Learning about the environment
B. Various studies occure in the environment
C. Learning through the interaction with environment
D. Learning for the environment

88. Which one of the following is related to the high yield of milk?
A. Green revolution
B. White revolution
C. Blue revolution
D. Industrial revolution

89. Which one of the following is not related to the concept of 'Live Corner'?
A. Aquarium B. Vivarium
C. Planetarium D. Terrarium

90. The reason behind the contraversory about the prohibition of BT Brinjal is ______.
A. Causes genetic disorders
B. Causes the distruction of other plants
C. Demand excess use of pesticides
D. Lack of adequate nutrients

PART- IV

Language-I : English

Directions : (Q. 91-97) : *Read the following passage and answer the questions that follow.*

Trees are the best friends of man, for they provide him protection from harshness of nature, be it rains, or sunlight. Trees have their historic, scientific, medical and religious uses. When an apple fell on Isaac Newton's head, it lead to the discovery of gravitation, helping the invention of aircraft. Over two millennia ago, Buddha attained enlightenment under the Bodhi tree at Bodhgaya. A descendant of the same tree at the same spot attracts millions of pilgrims and tourists every year. The Forest Research Institute at Dehradun, which has a unique museum of trees, was an instrumental in preserving the Bodhi tree at Bodhgaya. Similarly, the Botanical Garden in Kolkata has one of the oldest and largest banyan tree in India. It also has a unique palm tree that gives its first crop only at the age of 120. Such trees are part of the environmental heritage of the country and need to be protected form hazards, natural or otherwise. The Indian National Trust for Art and Cultural Heritage's (INTACH) plan to catalogue and preserve all heritage trees needs to be welcomed. The programme will give a boost to environmental tourism and increase our understanding of the role, trees have played in the evolution of civilization.

91. The main focus of the passage is :
A. Trees protect man from the harshness from nature
B. Trees have historic, medical and religious uses
C. Trees led to the discovery of the theory of gravitation
D. Need to protect heritage trees

92. One of the unique palm trees that gives its first crop only at the age of 120 is in :
A. The Forest Research Institute at Dehradun
B. The Botanical Garden in Kolkata
C. Bodhgaya
D. The Botanical Garden in Ootty

93. Which among the following make the Forest Research Institute at Dehradun famous?
A. Unique museum of Trees
B. Oldest and largest Banyan trees
C. Unique palm trees
D. Helped the invention of aircraft

94. The word used as synonym for the word "Peril" in the passage :
A. Harshness B. Hazards
C. Heritage D. Historic

95. A pilgrim centre mentioned in the passage is at :
A. Kolkata B. Bodhi
C. Dehradun D. Bodhgaya

96. While dealing with the above passage in the class, one among the following activity is NOT helpful for language generation.
A. Students are asked to write this passage five times
B. Essay competition on protecting trees
C. Debate on cutting trees
D. Listen to world famous speeches on environment

97. A branch of study that deals with plants and trees.
A. Archeology B. Botany
C. Geography D. Environmental Science

Directions (Qs. 98 - 120) : *Choose the right answer out of the options given :*

98. He scarcely ate anything, ... ?
A. did he ? B. doesn't he ?
C. didn't he ? D. does he ?

99. 'Bullocks are useful animals' .- Singular form of this sentence is :
A. A bullock is a useful animal
B. A bull is a useful
C. Bullocks are useful animal
D. Any bullocks is useful animal

100. Pick out the correct sentence :
A. I had been writing letters since all the morning
B. I wrote letters all the morning
C. I have written letters all the morning
D. I have been writing letters all the morning

101. A little boy was walking ______ her.
A. together B. across
C. beside D. besides

102. Each men and each woman has a vote.
A. The above sentence is wrong
B. The above sentence is right
C. The above sentence is partially right
D. The above sentence is partially wrong

103. Only a few members ________ for the examination.
A. turned down B. turned up
C. turned out D. turned in

104. Futurity is expressed in the following sentence.
A. The former president had visited our state
B. The former president has arrived
C. The former president arrives
D. The former president arrived

105. Pinky always writes 'dad' instead of 'bad'. The teacher identified this problem as :
A. Dislexia B. Disgraphia
C. Discalculia D. Anomia

106. One of the best teaching learning strategies for the standard I and II English class is :
A. Long lectures B. Seminar presentation
C. Narration D. Symposium

107. What strategy will you adopt if you want your learners to produce a good notice?
A. Supply a variety of notices in groups for analysis
B. Dictate them the notice intended to get
C. Ask them to copy from the leader
D. Ask them to learn byheart the sentences for the notice

108. Which type of continuous assessment is inculcating interpersonal intelligence among co-learners?
A. Self assessment B. Peer assessment
C. Teacher assessment D. Parent assessment

109. Pick out the wrong statement on the basis of theory of learning :
A. Remedial teaching increases the slow learners
B. Over crowded classrooms create slow learners
C. Social and economic backwardness of the parents produce slow learners
D. Ill health makes one a slow learner

110. One among the following DOES NOT express suggestion :
A. Let's drink a cup of tea?
B. Shall we go to the beach?
C. How about going for a drive?
D. May I take your note book?

111. The one which is a feature of 'learning' when compared with 'acquisition' is ______.
A. Conscious B. Flexible
C. Informal D. Whole learning

112. "English is a library language" which among the following explains the meaning of this statement :
A. Voluminous reference books are in English language
B. Stock register in libraries are in English language
C. Librarians speak English
D. Labels on books in libraries are in English language

113. 'Need based vocabulary development' believes in .....
A. Pre-teaching of vocabulary
B. Post-teaching of vocabulary
C. On-demand supply of vocabulary
D. No teaching of vocabulary at all

114. Which one is NOT an objective of "teacher version" in a constructivist class room?
A. Comparision of own attempt with that of teachers
B. Refinement of own attempt
C. Showing next higher level of performance
D. Substitute for learner attempt

115. What is expansion of ZPD as stated in Vygotsky's theory on construction of knowledge?
A. Zone of Proximal Design
B. Zone of Proximal Department
C. Zone of Proximal Development
D. Zone of Proximal Derivative

116. 'The mental universe of an English speaker may be completely different from that of a chinese speaker, because they happened to speak different language's. What hypothesis of language is discussed in this statement?
A. External stimulus - response
B. Thought - text
C. Filling - in process - construction process
D. Input - output

117. The feature that is NOT related to spontaneous response in face to face communication.
A. Prompt response B. Sudden response
C. Speedy response D. Structured response

118. 'Mr. Raman have a dictionary'. What category of error is underlined?
A. Synthetic B. Morphological
C. Related to punctuation D. Phonological

119. We don't go to school ____ Sundays.
A. in B. on
C. under D. at

120. 'Yesterday, I was late to bed; but I got a sound sleep'. What does sound means in the sentence?
A. I got a complete sleep
B. I produced sound during sleep
C. I heard a sound during the sleep
D. Someone produced sound to distract my sleep

PART- V

भाषा-II : हिन्दी

निर्देश : नीचे दिए गए गद्यांश को पढ़कर सबसे उचित विकल्प का चयन कीजिए :

किसे कहूँ मैं शिक्षा? क्या है शिक्षा का सच? कैसा होता है शिक्षित व्यक्ति और कैसा होता है पढ़ा-लिखा समाज? मेरे गुरु श्री दयालचन्द्र जी सोनी तो पूरी एक काव्यात्मक पुस्तक लिख गए। इस पुस्तक का नाम है 'हूं अणभणियों शिक्षित हूँ'। उनका आशय स्पष्ट है कि हर पढ़ा-लिखा आदमी अनपढ़ है। उन्होंने जब यह पुस्तक लिखी तो साफ कहा कि यह किताब उनके पूरे जीवन की शिक्षा का सार है। तब फिर हमें यह भी मान लेना चाहिए कि हमारा पूरा पढ़ा-लिखा समाज खासा अनपढ़ है। अशिक्षित है। तब फिर बताइए कि शिक्षा को कहाँ खोजें।

कहते हैं कि शिक्षा बालक के जन्म के साथ बालक को मिली प्रतिभा का विकास है। उसकी सोयी हुई शक्तियों को जगाने का नाम शिक्षा है। मगर ऐसा तो तब सम्भव है जब हम यह जान लें कि कौन-कौन सा बालक कौन-कौन सी प्रतिभा के साथ पैदा हुआ है? उसके शरीर में एवं उसके मन-मस्तिष्क में कौन-कौन सी शक्तियाँ सोयी हुई हैं? इसका अर्थ यह हुआ कि जो-जो बालक शाला में आया है उसको हम पहले पढ़ें। हर बालक को पढ़-पढ़ कर पहचानें कि वह क्या है? उसकी प्रदत्त प्रतिभा क्या है? और कौन-कौन सी सुषुप्त शक्तियों को लिए हुए वह हमारे सामने उपस्थित हुआ है।

121. 'उसकी प्रदत्त प्रतिभा क्या है?' वाक्य है–
A. संदेहवाचक B. विधानवाचक
C. नकारात्मक D. प्रश्नवाचक

122. 'शरीर' में 'इक' प्रत्यय लगने पर शब्द बनेगा–
A. शारिरिक B. शरीरिक
C. शारीरीक D. शारीरिक

123. लेखक के अनुसार शिक्षित होना और साक्षर होना–
A. दोनों में थोड़ा-बहुत अंतर है
B. दोनों समान हैं
C. दोनों में मूलभूत अंतर होता है
D. दोनों पर्यायवाची हैं

124. यहाँ 'पढ़ा-लिखा' होने से तात्पर्य है–
A. निरक्षर होना B. शिक्षित होना
C. अशिक्षित होना D. साक्षर होना

125. 'शिक्षा' का अर्थ है–
A. बच्चों में विद्यमान शक्तियों को प्रस्फुटित करना
B. बच्चों को जानकारी देना
C. बच्चों को केवल अक्षर ज्ञान देना
D. बच्चों को शक्तिशाली बनाना

126. लेखक के अनुसार–
A. सभी बच्चों की शक्तियाँ सुषुप्त अवस्था में ही रहती हैं
B. सभी बच्चे समान रूप से प्रतिभाशाली होते हैं
C. बच्चों में अलग-अलग प्रतिभा होती है
D. सभी बच्चे शाला जाकर प्रतिभाशाली बन जाते हैं

127. बच्चों को शिक्षा देने के लिए सबसे पहले क्या जरूरी है?
A. बच्चों को पढ़ाना
B. प्रतिभाओं के विभिन्न रूप जानना
C. बच्चों को प्रतिभाओं के अनुसार वर्गीकृत करना
D. बच्चों की समस्त क्षमताओं, प्रतिभाओं को जानने के लिए उन्हें पढ़ना

128. इस गद्यांश में शिक्षा का कौन-सा सिद्धांत निहित है?
A. पढ़े-लिखे लोग अनपढ़ होते हैं
B. सभी बच्चे समान रूप से प्रतिभाशाली होते हैं
C. सभी बच्चों में वैयक्तिक भिन्नता होती है
D. शक्तियाँ सदैव सुषुप्त अवस्था में ही रहती हैं

129. 'हर बालक को पढ़-पढ़ कर पहचानें कि वह क्या है?' वाक्य में 'पहचानें' क्रिया का कर्त्ता हो सकता है
A. वह B. मैं
C. हम D. तुम

निर्देश : *नीचे दी गई पंक्तियों को पढ़कर सबसे उचित विकल्प का चयन कीजिए :*

दम्भ का जहाँ-जहाँ पड़ाव था,
सत्य से जहाँ-जहाँ दुराव था,
वह चला कि अग्नि-बाण मारता,
पाप की अहा-अहा उजाड़ता,
वज्र बन गिरा गिरे विचार पर।

130. 'जहाँ-जहाँ' शब्द है–
A. भिन्नार्थी शब्द-युग्म B. एकार्थी शब्द-युग्म
C. पुनरुक्त शब्द-युग्म D. विपरीतार्थक शब्द-युग्म

131. 'पाप' का विलोम शब्द है–
A. निरपराध B. प्रायश्चित
C. अपाप D. पुण्य

132. नौजवान शहीद ने किसे नष्ट किया?
A. अहंकार और असत्य को B. अहंकार को
C. असत्य को D. अहंकार और सत्य को

133. 'गिरे विचार' से तात्पर्य है–
A. उलझे विचार B. सभी प्रकार के विचार
C. मिथ्या विचार D. सत्य और हित से परे विचार

134. नौजवान शहीद ने अग्नि-बाण इसलिए चलाए क्योंकि वह–
A. अपनी शक्ति की गरिमा बनाए रखना चाहता था
B. अपना साम्राज्य स्थापित करना चाहता था
C. सुराज स्थापित करना चाहता था
D. वज्र गिराना चाहता था

135. 'दुराव' शब्द से तात्पर्य है–
A. बैर B. दुर्गम स्थल
C. आवरण D. काठिन्य

निर्देश : *सबसे उचित विकल्प चुनिए :*

136. भाषा में रचनात्मक आकलन का सर्वाधिक बेहतर उदाहरण है–
A. इकाई-परीक्षा लेना
B. बच्चों को अपने खट्टे-मीठे अनुभव लिखने के लिए कहना
C. श्रुतलेख
D. प्रश्नों के उत्तर लिखवाना

137. हिंदी भाषा के प्रश्न-पत्र में आप किस प्रश्न को सर्वाधिक उचित मानते हैं?
A. लेखक ने पहाड़ों पर होने वाली बारिश का वर्णन एक अलग तरीके से किया है। आप बारिश संबंधी अपना अनुभव लिखिए।
B. विशेषणों के कितने और कौन से भेद होते हैं
C. प्रत्ययों की परिभाषा लिखिए
D. सर्वनाम के भेदों को उदाहरण सहित स्पष्ट कीजिए

138. चॉम्स्की के अनुसार .... के कारण बच्चे भाषा सीखते हैं।
A. व्याकरणिक नियमों की जानकारी से ही
B. भाषायी समाज
C. भाषा-अर्जन क्षमता
D. भाषा-आकलन क्षमता

139. भाषा-शिक्षण में अनिवार्य है–
A. वर्तनी संबंधी गृहकार्य
B. मानक भाषा पर बल
C. समग्रतावादी दृष्टिकोण
D. विशेष आवश्यकता वाले बच्चों के साथ भिन्न व्यवहार

140. विशेष आवश्यकता वाले बच्चों की भाषा का आकलन करते समय–
A. उनके प्रति दया भाव रखना चाहिए
B. उन्हें प्रश्न-संख्या में विशेष छूट मिलनी चाहिए
C. उन्हें अधिक अंक देने का प्रयास करना चाहिए
D. उनकी क्षमता और सीमाओं का ध्यान रखना चाहिए

141. उच्च प्राथमिक स्तर पर कहानी, कविता पढ़ने के बाद यह जरूरी है कि बच्चे–
A. उन्हें अपने अनुभव संसार से जोड़ सकें
B. प्रश्नों के लिखित उत्तर दे सकें
C. उसे अपने शब्दों में दोहरा सकें
D. विपरीत भाव की कहानी या कविता लिख सकें

142. प्लेटो का यह कथन कि 'बच्चा बड़ों के बीच एक विदेशी की तरह होता है' किस भाषिक सच्चाई की ओर संकेत करता है?
A. बच्चों की भाषा के प्रति बड़ों का दृष्टिकोण संकीर्णता से परिपूर्ण होता है।
B. बच्चे अपनी भाषा में बोलते हैं जिसे बड़े सही-सही नहीं समझ पाते
C. बच्चा बड़ों से उम्र में छोटा होने के कारण अजनबी बना रहता है
D. बच्चों की भाषा अपरिपक्व होती है

143. 'भाषा की कक्षा' में कहानियाँ–
A. भाषा-कौशल के विकास का एकमात्र साधन है
B. मनोरंजन का साधन है
C. पाठ्य-पुस्तक का एक पाठ है
D. विभिन्न प्रकार की भाषायी संरचनाएँ और चिंतन-विकास की संभावनाएँ लिए होती हैं

144. राष्ट्रीय पाठ्यचर्या की रूपरेखा 2005 के अनुसार कौन-सा कथन सही है?
A. प्राथमिक स्तर पर भाषा सीखने-सिखाने में केवल पढ़ने पर बल देना चाहिए
B. भाषा केवल भाषा की कक्षा तक सीमित होनी चाहिए
C. भाषा-शिक्षण एक प्रकार से अन्य विषयों की कक्षाओं में भी मौजूद रहता है
D. बच्चे विद्यालय आकर ही भाषा सीखते हैं

145. भाषा-कौशलों के संदर्भ में कौन-सा कथन सही है?
A. सभी कौशल एक-दूसरे के साथ अंतःसंबंधित होते हैं
B. सुनना, बोलना, पढ़ना और लिखना एक क्रम से सीख जाते हैं
C. सुनना और पढ़ना निष्क्रिय कौशल है
D. पढ़ना और लिखना कौशल में कोई संबंध नहीं है

146. उच्च प्राथमिक स्तर पर भाषा की पाठ्य-पुस्तक में विविध प्रकार की साहित्यिक रचनाओं के समावेश का मुख्य उद्देश्य यह है
A. पाठ्य-पुस्तक निर्माण की परंपरा का निर्वाह करना
B. बच्चों को सभी प्रकार की साहित्यिक विधाओं में पारंगत करना
C. विभिन्न प्रकार की साहित्यिक विधाओं की भाषायी संरचनाओं से परिचित होने का अवसर देना
D. विभिन्न साहित्यिक विधाओं के प्रसिद्ध रचनाकारों से परिचित कराना

147. रश्मि अपनी कक्षा को बाहर मैदान में ले जाती है और पर्यावरण पर आधारित कविता-पाठ का कार्य करती है। रश्मि का उद्देश्य है–
A. अपने शिक्षक-प्रशिक्षण में सीखी बातों का निर्वाह करना
B. बच्चों को रोजमर्रा की चर्चा से कुछ अलग माहौल देना
C. बच्चों को मैदान में घूमने का अवसर देना
D. मैदान के प्राकृतिक वातावरण के साथ संबंध जोड़ते हुए कविता को समझने का अवसर देना

148. भाषा में आकलन करने के बाद महत्वपूर्ण सोपान होना चाहिए–
A. आँकड़ों का पुनः पुनः परीक्षण करना
B. आकलन से प्राप्त आँकड़ों के आधार पर बच्चों के अभिभावकों से विचार-विमर्श करना
C. आँकड़ों को सहेज कर रखना
D. आँकड़ों को तत्काल नष्ट करना

149. विद्यालय में एक से अधिक भाषाओं का शिक्षण–
A. व्यावहारिक नहीं है
B. जटिल समस्याएँ उत्पन्न करता है
C. अनेक भाषाओं के शिक्षकों के रोजगार को बढ़ावा देता है
D. बहुभाषिकता और राष्ट्रीय सद्भाव का प्रसार करता है

150. भाषा-शिक्षण की 'प्रत्यक्ष-विधि' में
A. भाषा की विविध संरचनाओं के लेखन हेतु अभ्यास पर बल दिया जाता है
B. मातृभाषा का निरर्थक हस्तक्षेप होता है
C. 'भाषा-अर्जन' की स्वाभाविक स्थिति का निर्माण होता है
D. अतिरिक्त शिक्षण सामग्री की कोई आवश्यकता नहीं

Answers

1	2	3	4	5	6	7	8	9	10
B	C	C	D	B	A	D	B	A	A
11	**12**	**13**	**14**	**15**	**16**	**17**	**18**	**19**	**20**
C	A	B	B	D	D	B	D	B	A
21	**22**	**23**	**24**	**25**	**26**	**27**	**28**	**29**	**30**
B	A	C	B	C	C	C	B	C	C
31	**32**	**33**	**34**	**35**	**36**	**37**	**38**	**39**	**40**
B	B	D	D	A	B	B	C	C	A
41	**42**	**43**	**44**	**45**	**46**	**47**	**48**	**49**	**50**
D	D	A	D	B	C	A	C	B	B
51	**52**	**53**	**54**	**55**	**56**	**57**	**58**	**59**	**60**
C	C	D	A	B	B	C	A	D	A
61	**62**	**63**	**64**	**65**	**66**	**67**	**68**	**69**	**70**
B	C	B	A	D	C	B	D	C	C
71	**72**	**73**	**74**	**75**	**76**	**77**	**78**	**79**	**80**
B	C	C	D	B	D	B	D	B	D
81	**82**	**83**	**84**	**85**	**86**	**87**	**88**	**89**	**90**
A	B	C	B	B	D	B	B	C	A
91	**92**	**93**	**94**	**95**	**96**	**97**	**98**	**99**	**100**
D	B	A	B	D	A	B	A	A	D
101	**102**	**103**	**104**	**105**	**106**	**107**	**108**	**109**	**110**
C	B	B	C	B	C	A	B	A	D
111	**112**	**113**	**114**	**115**	**116**	**117**	**118**	**119**	**120**
A	A	C	D	C	B	D	B	B	A
121	**122**	**123**	**124**	**125**	**126**	**127**	**128**	**129**	**130**
D	D	C	D	A	C	D	C	C	C
131	**132**	**133**	**134**	**135**	**136**	**137**	**138**	**139**	**140**
D	A	D	C	A	B	A	C	C	D
141	**142**	**143**	**144**	**145**	**146**	**147**	**148**	**149**	**150**
A	B	D	C	A	C	D	B	D	C

Some Selected Explanatory Answers

31. Place value of 7 in square and circle

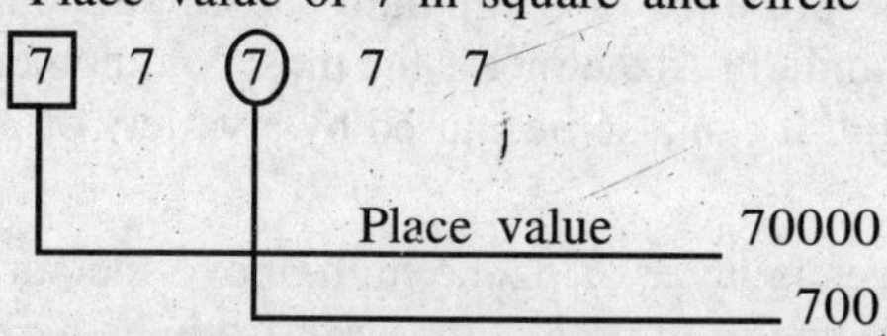

i.e., 700 × 100 = 70,000

Hence, the place value of 7 in the circle is 100 times is the place value of 7 in the square.

32. Let cloth required for Ajith be x cm.

According to question,

For Arun, = $(x + 20)$ cm

and cloth required for Abhijith

$$= (x + 20) - 10 \text{ cm}$$
$$= x + 10 \text{ cm}$$

$\because$ 5.10 m = 510 cm

$\therefore$ $x + x + 20 + x + 10 = 510$

$\Rightarrow$ $3x = 510 - 30$

$$x = \frac{480}{3} = 160 \text{ cm}$$

$\therefore$ Cloth required for Ajith is 160 cm.

34. Let no. be x.

$\therefore$ $x \times \frac{1}{100} = 2.16$

$\Rightarrow$ $x = 2.16 \times 100 = 216.$

35. Given perimeter of rectangle = 80 cm.
Here, rectangle will be also square

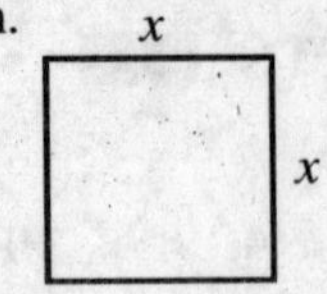

∴ Perimeter of sq. rectangle/square

⇒ $2(x + x) = 80$

⇒ $2x = 40$

⇒ $x = 20$ cm

∴ Maximum area of rectangle/square

= $x^2 = (20)^2 = 400$ sq. cm.

36. First we have, sum of four consecutive numbers
= 1 + 2 + 3 + 4 = 10
then, again other sum of four consecutive numbers
= 2 + 3 + 4 + 5 = 14
and again next sum of four consecutive no.
= 3 + 4 + 5 + 6 = 18
Hence, four consecutive numbers are 3, 4, 5 and 6 and their sum is 18.

38. Given, $1\frac{1}{2}$ kg = $\frac{3}{2}$ kg and $2\frac{3}{4} = \frac{11}{4}$ kg.

∴ $\frac{3}{2}$ kg of tomato costs = ₹ 30

∴ 1 kg of tomato costs = ₹ $\frac{30}{3/2}$ = ₹ 20

∴ $\frac{11}{4}$ kg of tomato costs = ₹ $20 \times \frac{11}{4}$ = ₹ 55.

39. 500 sheets of paper cost ₹ 140.

∴ 1 sheet of paper costs = ₹ $\frac{140}{500}$ = ₹ 0.28.

40. Since, 77 × 555 = 42,735
Then, 55 × 777 = 42,735
Multiplication 77 × 555 = 42,735
only option (A) is correct.

42. Here, Area of square = 100 cm^2
∴ Side = 10 cm

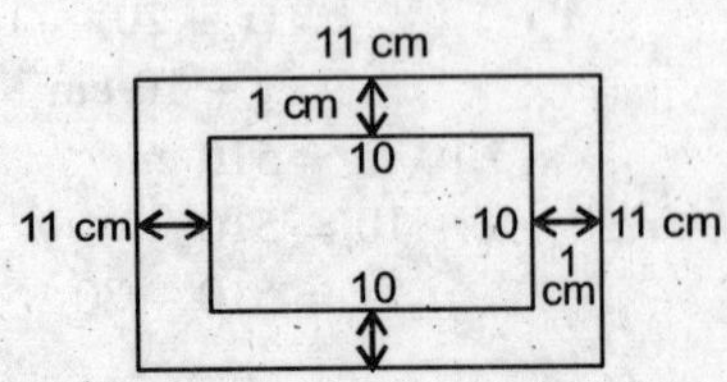

According to question,
Now side of new square = 11 cm.
∴ Area of new square = 121
∴ More area = 121 – 100 = 21 sq. cm.

45.

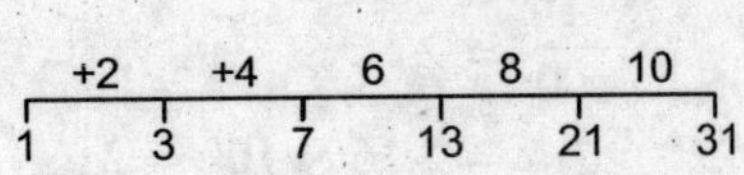

46. Train starts from Ernakulam at 13:30 on 30-06-12
∴ After 24 hours it will 13:30 on 01-07-12
or, 1:30 PM on 01-07-12
Now 1:30 + 30 = 2:0 PM on 01-07-12
∴ 2:00 PM + 10:00 PM = 12;00 PM
∴ 12;00 PM —11:40→ 11 : 40 on 02-07-12
∴ Total time taken for journey
= 46 hrs. 10 minutes

hrs.	*mins*
24	00
.	30
10	00
11	40
45	70

or 46 hrs 10 minutes.

47. Total no. of bricks require after 10 steps:
1 + 2 + 3 + 4 + 5 + 6 + 7 + 8 + 9 + 10 = 55 bricks.

49. 1 km = 1000 m
1 m = 100 cm
1 cm = 10 ml
∴ 1 km = 10,00,000 millimetre
Now, 0.1 km = 100000 millimetre.

50. 39 × 48 × 27 = 50544.

51. Repeated addition is not a concept related to division.

61. Carnea is a part of eye, it is transparent layer which covers and protects the outer part of eye. It is taken out during eye donation.

62. Chandrayan-I, confirms the presence of water in the moon. It was India's first unmanned lunar probe. Chandrayan-I was launched by ISRO in October 2008.

63. Science, is the knowledge about the structure and behaviour of the natural and physical word, base on facts that we can prove. The cumulative knowledge acquired by human race and process of enquiry involved in it.

64. The excess-presence of aluminium causes Alzheimers disease. Similarly Alzheimer is the most common cause of dementia. It can also be caused by a variety of other facture.

65. Ozone layer is layer of ozone high above the surface of earth that helps to protect the earth from the harmful radiation from the sun. Hence, cause deplection of ozone is not related to carbon dioxide (O_2).

66. Water is a liquid without colour, smell or taste that falls on rain, is in lakes, rivers etc. It is used for drinking and washing. It is not controlled variable in an experiment that find out the influence of water in the growth of plants.

67. An animal that eats grass and other green plants in a food-chain is called primary consumer. Grosshopper is primary consumer.

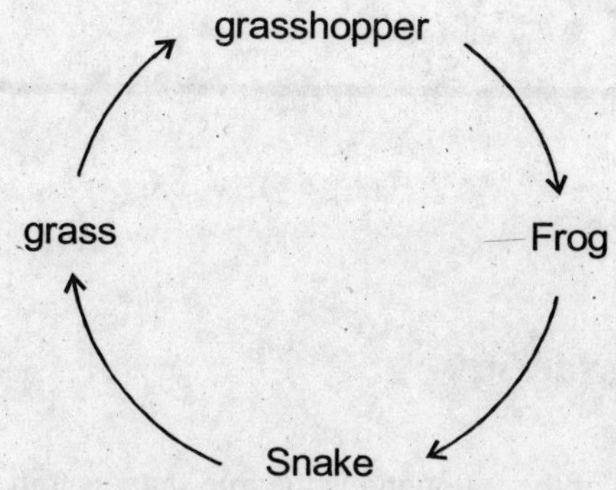

71. Solar Eclipse : When moon comes between the sun and the earth is called solar eclipse.

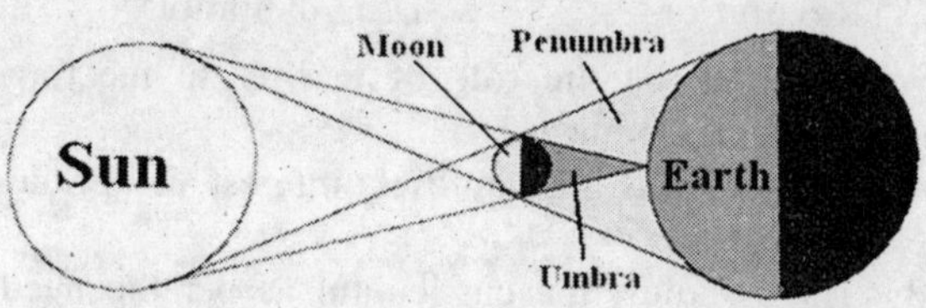

72. The most suitable data is pie-chart.

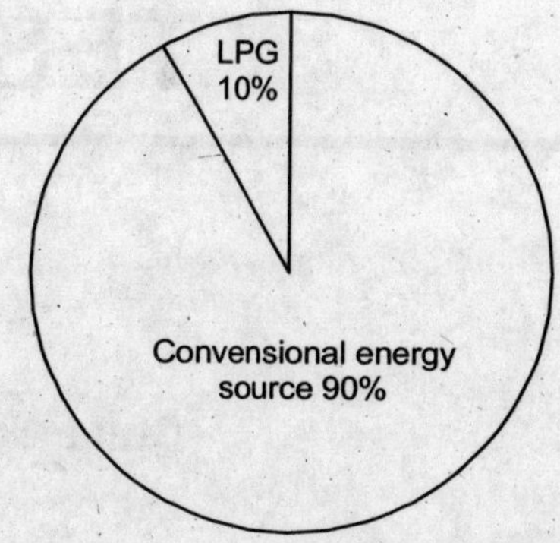

73. The scientific name of paddy (rice) is Oryza Sativa'

74. Nuclear power station is man-made resource, other are natural resources.

76. Shark is not a mammal except dolphin, bat and whale.

77. Silent spring is a book written by Rachelearson and published by Houghton. The book is widely credified with helping launch the contemporary American environmental movement, under repercussion of pesticides in the environment.

79. LED is abbreviated as Light Emitting Diode.

81. Integrated learning → Environment study → Basic science → Science

Hence, Option (A) is correct.

82. The soil having low water storage capacity, human and lower air presence is suitable for agriculture.

83. The actual weight of log = 5 × 1000 kg.

= 5000 kg.

TEST PAPER–2

PART- I

Child Development and Pedagogy

1. The best method to study growth and development of the child is:
A. Psychoanalytic Method
B. Comparative Method
C. Developmental Method
D. Statistical Method

2. Socialization is a process by which children & adults learn from:
A. Family B. School
C. Peers D. All of these

3. Which one of the following is the true statement corresponding to Cephalocaudal Principle of Child's Development?
A. Development is from head to foot
B. Development is from foot to head
C. Development is from middle to periphery
D. None of these

4. Determinants of Individual differences in human beings relate to:
A. Differences in Environment
B. Differences in Heredity
C. Interaction between Heredity & Environment
D. Both Heredity & Environment interacting separately

5. Term PSRN in development implies:
A. Problem solving, reasoning & numeracy
B. Problem solving relationship & numeracy
C. Perceptual skill, reasoning & numeracy
D. Perceptual skill, relationship & numbers

6. Vygotsky proposed that Child Development is:
A. Due to genetic components of a culture
B. A product of social interaction
C. A product of formal education
D. A product of assimilation & accommodation

7. Gardner formulated a list of seven Intelligencies, Which among the following is not one of them?
A. Spatial Intelligence
B. Emotional Intelligence
C. Interpersonal Intelligence
D. Linguistic Intelligence

8. Which of the following is the true statement in reference to intelligence?
A. Intelligence is the ability to adjust
B. Intelligence is the ability to learn
C. Intelligence is the ability of Abstract Reasoning
D. All of these

9. 'A Child can think logically about objects & events' This is the characteristic given by Piaget of stage:
A. Sensory Motor B. Pre Operational
C. Concrete Operational D. Formal Operation

10. Which of the following does not belong to the categories of Coping strategies that women commonly engaged in?
A. Acceptance B. Resistance
C. Revolution D. Adaptation

11. What should be the role of teacher in meeting the individual differences?
A. Try to know the abilities, interest & aptitude of individuals
B. Try to adjust the curriculum as per the needs of individuals
C. Both (A) & (B)
D. None of these

12. If a child has mental age of 5 years & chronological age of 4 years then what will be the IQ of child?
A. 125 B. 80
C. 120 D. 100

13. Which of the following is not the tool for Formative Assessment in scholastic domain?
A. Conversation Skill
B. Multiple Choice Question
C. Projects
D. Oral Questions

14. A few students in your class are exceptionally bright, You will teach them:
A. Along with the class
B. Along with higher classes
C. By using Enriched programmes
D. Only when they want

15. The major purpose of diagnostic test is that of Identifying:
A. The General area of weakness in class performance
B. Specific nature of remedial programme needed
C. The causes underlying academic difficulties
D. The specific nature of pupil difficulties

16. Special education is related to
A. Educational for talented students
B. Educational programmes for disabled
C. Training programmes for teachers
D. Training programme for retarded

17. In CCE, Formative & Summative Assessment totals to:
A. 40% & 60% respectively
B. 60% & 40% respectively
C. 50% & 50% respectively
D. None of the above

18. Frobel's most important contribution to education was his development of the:
A. Vocational school B. Kindergarten
C. Public school D. Latin school

19. Which article enjoins that 'All minorities whether based on religion or language shall have the right to establish & administer education institutions of their choice'?
A. Article 29(1) B. Article 29(2)
C. Article 30(1) D. Article 30(2)

20. If a child writes 16 as 61 & gets confused between *b* & *d*, this is case of:
A. Visual Impairment B. Learning Disability
C. Mental Impairment D. Mental Retardation

21. As a teacher what techniques you would follow to motivate students of your class:
1. By setting induction
2. Use of blackboard
3. By illustration
4. By active participation of students
A. 1, 2 & 3 B. 1 & 4
C. 2 & 4 D. All of these

22. What are the factors related to learner that effects the learning?
A. Physical & Mental health of the learner
B. Level of aspiration & achievement motivation
C. Readiness & Willpower
D. All of these

23. Cognitive Development means:
A. Development of intelligence
B. Development of child
C. Development of Physical Skills
D. Development of individual

24. Creative writing should be an activity planned for:
A. Only those children reading on grade level
B. Only those children spell & write cohesive sentences
C. Only those children who want to write for newspaper
D. All children

25. Which of the following are the External Factors affecting the interest of students in classroom?
A. Emotions & Sentiments
B. Culture & Training
C. Attitudes of students
D. Goals & motives

26. An intelligent student is not doing well in studies. What is the best course of the action for the teacher?
A. Wait till he performs better
B. Find out reason for his under achievement
C. Give him grace marks in the examination
D. Ask his parents to withdraw from school

27. The term Identical Elements is closely associated with:
A. Similar test questions B. Jealousy between peers
C. Transfer of learning D. Group Instructions

28. Who was the pioneer of Classical Conditioning?
A. Skinner B. Pavlov
C. Watson D. Thorndike

29. It is said that teacher should be resourceful, This means that:
A. He should have enough money & property so that he may not have to take up tuitions
B. He should have contacts with high authorities so that he may not be harmed
C. He should have adequate knowledge so that he may be able to solve the problems of students
D. He should have good reputation among students so that authorities may not be able to take any punitive measure against him

30. Which of the following Motives are considered as primary motives?
A. Physiological Motives B. Psychological Motives
C. Social Motives D. Educational Motives

PART- II

Mathematics

31. The graph of the equation $y = -4$ is a line
A. parallel to x-axis
B. parallel to y-axis
C. passing through origin
D. none of these

32. The angle of elevation of the sun when the length of a shadow of a vertical pole is equal to its length is
A. 60° B. 45°
C. 90° D. 180°

33. Sum of a number of two digits and the number obtained by reversing the digits of the first number is 110. If the difference of the digits is 4, then the number is

A. 62 B. 73
C. 84 D. 51

34. A and B can do a piece of work in 4 days and A alone can do it in 12 days. In how many days B alone can do this work?

A. 5 B. 6
C. 7 D. 8

35. A man travels some distance at a speed of 12 km/hr and returns at 9 km/hr. If the total time taken by him is 2 hrs 20 minutes, then the distance is

A. 18 km B. 14 km
C. 13 km D. 12 km

36. In a two digit number, the digit in ten's place exceeds the digit in unit's place by 4. The sum of the digits is 1/7 of the number, then the digit at the unit's place is

A. 5 B. 4
C. 3 D. 1

37. The area of a square is 64 cm^2. Then its perimeter is

A. 64 cm B. 32 cm
C. 46 cm D. 48 cm

38. The HCF of two numbers is 11 and their LCM is 693. If one of the numbers is 77, then the other number is

A. 88 B. 33
C. 99 D. None of these

39. Find the smallest number of five digits exactly divisible by 16, 24, 36 and 54.

A. 10368
B. 10432
C. 10560
D. None of these

40. The average of seven consecutive numbers is 20. The largest of these numbers is

A. 20 B. 22
C. 23 D. 24

41. The volume of the greatest sphere cut off from a cylindrical wood of base radius 1 cm and height 5 cm is

A. $\frac{4}{3}(5\pi)\,cm^3$ B. $\frac{4}{3}\pi\,cm^3$
C. $5\pi\,cm^3$ D. None of these

42. Rational expression $\frac{x^3-1}{x^2-1}$ in the lowest form is

A. $\frac{x^2-x+1}{x+1}$ B. $\frac{x^2-x+1}{x-1}$
C. $\frac{x^2+x+1}{x-1}$ D. $\frac{x^2+x+1}{x+1}$

Directions (Qs. 43-45) : *The circle graph given here shows the spending (in degrees) of a country on various sports during the particular year. Study the graph carefully and answer the next three questions.*

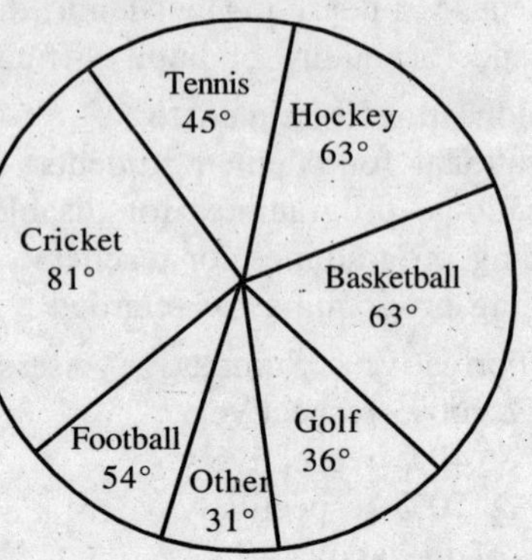

43. What percentage of the total spending is spent on tennis?

A. $12\frac{1}{2}\%$ B. $22\frac{1}{2}\%$
C. 25% D. 45%

44. If the total amount spent on sports during the year was ₹ 2 crores, the amount spent on cricket and hockey together was

A. ₹ 8,00,000 B. ₹ 80,00,000
C. ₹ 1,20,00,000 D. ₹ 1,60,00,000

45. If the total amount spent on sports during the year be ₹ 180,00,000, the amount spent on basketball exceeds that of tennis approximately by

A. ₹ 2,50,000 B. ₹ 3,60,000
C. ₹ 3,75,000 D. ₹ 4,10,000

46. The radius of a sphere whose volume and surface area have same value, is

A. 1 unit B. 2 units
C. 3 units D. 4 units

47. In the number 3.4625, the place value of the digit 2 is

A. 1000 B. 100
C. 1/1000 D. 1/100

48. Divide 50 by half and add 20. From the same, subtract 35. What do you get?

A. 10 B. 85
C. 15 D. None of these

49. What number should be put in the blank box?

7	5	9	18
6	3	7	21
4	3	9	
7	4	8	24

A. 9 B. 27
C. 36 D. None of these

50. What is the next number after the following? 4, 9, 25, 49, ?

A. 64 B. 81
C. 100 D. 121

51. When the numerator of a fraction is increased by 4, the fraction increases by 2/3. What is the denominator of the fraction?

A. 6 B. 7
C. 8 D. None of these

52. The HCF of $(x - 1)$, $(x^2 - 1)$ and $(x^3 - 1)$ is

A. $(x - 1)$ B. $(x^2 - 1)$
C. $(x^3 - 1)$ D. $(x + 1)$

53. The mean of five numbers is 26. If one number is excluded, their mean is 25, then the excluded number is

A. 20 B. 15
C. 30 D. 34

54. How many carats are there in one gram?

A. 3 B. 4
C. 5 D. None of these

55. A plot has width of 44 feet and length of 90 feet. What is the size of the plot?

A. 500 square yards B. 450 square yards
C. 440 sq. yards D. None of these

56. One of, the students of a class hardly talks in the class. How would you encourage him to express himself?

A. By organizing discussions
B. By organizing educational games/ programmes in which children feel like speaking
C. By giving good marks to those who express themselves well
D. By encouraging children to take part in classroom activities

57. Success in developing values is mainly dependent upon:

A. government B. society
C. family D. teacher

58. Each digit 1, 2, 3, 4, 5, 6, 7, 8 and 9 is represented by a different letter A, B, C, D, E, F, G, H and I but not necessarily in that order. Further each of A + B + C, C + D + E, E + F + G and G + H + I is equal to 13. What is the sum of C, E and G?

A. 7 B. 9
C. 11 D. Cannot be determined

59. Which of the skills do you consider most essential for a teacher?

A. encourage children to search for knowledge
B. have all the information for the children
C. ability to make children memorize materials
D. enable children to do well in tests

60. Absenteeism can be stopped by:

A. Teaching B. Punishing the students
C. Giving the sweets D. Contacting the parents

PART- III

Environmental Studies

61. Which of the following is a biodegradable waste?

A. Plastics B. Polythene
C. Glass D. None of these

62. Dachigam National Park is in which state?

A. Himachal Pradesh B. J&K
C. Tamilnadu D. Sikkim

63. Who started the Chipko Movement?

A. Kiran Bedi B. S. L Bahuguna
C. Medha Patkar D. None of these

64. When was PROJECT TIGER launched?

A. 2011 B. 1970
C. 1973 D. 2007

65. How much percentage of water in the oceans is drinkable?

A. 97.2% B. 2.15%
C. 0.65% D. 0.0%

66. What is BOD_5?

A. Biochemical Oxygen Demand in 5 hrs
B. Biochemical Oxygen Demand in 5 days
C. Biochemical Oxygen Demand in 5 months
D. Biochemical Oxygen Demand in 5 minutes

67. What type of radiation is trapped on the earth's surface by the greenhouse effect?

A. UV rays B. γ -rays
C. X-rays D. IR rays

68. London smog is found in ....

A. Summer during day time
B. Summer during morning time
C. Winter during day time
D. Winter during morning time

69. A tight whirlpool of wind formed in the stratosphere which surrounds Antarctica is called ....

A. Polar stratospheric cloud
B. Polar Vortex
C. Both A & B
D. None of these

70. Bhopal gas tragedy occurred due to ....

A. Methane B. Phosgene
C. Methyl-isocyanate D. Methyl amine

71. White lung cancer is caused by ....

A. Asbestos B. Paper
C. Textiles D. Silica

72. Which of the following has greatest affinity for haemoglobin?

A. CO B. NO
C. O_2 D. CO_2

73. The first nuclear disaster occurred in the history of world on

A. 16th August, 1945 B. 26th August, 1945
C. 06th August, 1945 D. 08th August, 1945

74. When did Supreme Court of India ordered Ministry of Environment & Forests to establish a special division to develop a green belt around Taj Mahal?

A. 2004 B. 1994
C. 1984 D. None of these

75. Silent Valley, which has been raised to the status of National park, is situated in ....

A. J&K B. Tamilnadu
C. West Bengal D. Kerala

76. Which of the following device(s) is used to control particulate pollutants?

A. Gravity settling chamber
B. Cyclone collector
C. Fabric filter
D. All of the above

77. Noise pollution (Regulation & Control) Rules 2001 deals with ....

A. Noise pollution due to fire crackers
B. Noise pollution due to loudspeakers
C. Noise pollution due to public address system
D. Both B & C

78. Which book has been prepared by International Union for Conservation of Nature and Natural Resources (IUCN) concerning endangered species of plants and animals?

A. White Data Book B. Red Data Book
C. Blue Data Book D. None of these

79. The BISHNOI Sect was founded by

A. B. R. Ambedkar B. Bhajan Lal
C. Guru Jambheshwar D. King of Jodhpur

80. High concentration of which of the following causes leaf curling, leaf drop and reduced leaf size in plants?

A. SO_2 B. CO
C. NO_2 D. None of these

81. Traces of radioactive waste present in water can cause ....

A. Cancer B. Eye cataract
C. DNA breakage D. All of these

82. How much area is covered under forest in India?

A. 33.47 % B. 29.47 %
C. 22.47 % D. 19.47 %

83. The Greenhouse effect was first recognized by ....

A. Jean-Baptiste Greenwood
B. Jean-Baptiste Fourier
C. Jean-Baptiste Greenhouse
D. None of the above

84. Which of the following is responsible for global warming?

A. Chloroflouro carbons
B. Methane
C. Carbon dioxide
D. All of these

85. Which of the following acid is present in Acid rain?

A. HNO_3 B. H_2SO_4
C. CH_3COOH D. Both A & B

86. The situation of depletion of Ozone layer is referred as OZONE HOLE, if the ozone level decreases below

A. 800 DU B. 400 DU
C. 200 DU D. None of these

87. Which of the following is a non-governmental organization dedicated to wildlife conservation?

A. World Wildlife Fund for Nature, INDIA
B. Indian Board for Wildlife
C. National Wildlife Action Plan
D. All of these

88. Everyone has the right to a Nationality is covered in .... of Universal Declaration of Human Rights.

A. Article 10 B. Article 15
C. Article 20 D. Article 25

89. Ten per cent law is given by

A. Lindmann B. Goldmann
C. Beckmann D. None of these

90. Environment Impact Assessment(EIA) was formally established in USA in year

A. 1967 B. 1969
C. 1971 D. 1973

PART- IV

Language-I : English

Directions (Q. 91-97) : *Read the passage carefully and answer that follow by choosing the best alternative:*

In these times of worldwide, skyrocketing energy costs, experts are turning to perhaps the only energy source that is still immune to price fluctuations: the Sun. Economic necessity appears to be largely responsible for the rapidly growing acceptance of solar heat as an alternative source. Electricity has been a clean and versatile form of energy that continues to grow in importance for lighting, heating and cooking, and for powering our increasingly automated and computerized society. The demand for electricity is expected to grow more in future than the average trend in the past. A mix of energy sources is required as hedge against shortages in any one area, and the electricity supply companies are taking a second look at renewable generating technologies, particularly those based in the sun. Every 15 minutes, the sun delivers to earth radiant energy to meet all mankind's power needs for a full year. But harnessing this energy is complicated by two properties of sunlight: its diffuseness and its variability with time of day, season and weather conditions. These factors pose formidable technical challenges for the efficient conversion of solar radiation into bulk, utility grade electric power. Nevertheless, solar technologies are attractive to utilities because they are environment-friendly and offer a low regulatory risk, limited capital risk, and less lead time.

91. Why are experts, according to the passage, looking at the sun as an energy source?
A. due to depletion of other sources of energy
B. as other energy forms pollute the environment
C. increasing costs of other sources
D. all of the above

92. Experts are impressed with the solar energy technologies because...
A. of them being good for the environment
B. they require less investment
C. they can be employed in quick time
D. all of these

93. Why is sun such an important source of alternative energy?
A. it is available free of cost
B. it is available everywhere in the world
C. it can satisfy human energy requirements alone if tapped properly
D. all of these

94. What is the major difficulty in employing solar energy?
A. fluctuations in weather
B. by nature sunlight is diffuse
C. sunlight varies from time to time
D. all of these

95. Why are power generating companies looking at mix energy options?
A. the sources of energy are getting scarce but demand is increasing
B. government is controlling prices of electricity
C. alternative sources of energy are available free and without regulations
D. all of these

96. Identify the word closest in meaning to the word: "VERSATILE"
A. limited
B. resourceful
C. permanent
D. invariable

97. Identify the word opposite in meaning to the word: "FORMIDABLE"
A. alarming
B. frightening
C. terrible
D. insignificant

Directions (Qs. 98-105) : *Read the passage carefully and answer the questions that follow by choosing the best alternative:*

The political system always dominates the entire social scene; and hence those who wield political power are generally able to control all the different social sub-systems and manipulate them to their own advantage. The social groups in power therefore have always manipulated the education systems, especially when these happen to depend upon the state for their very existence to strengthen and perpetuate their own privileged position. But herein lies a contradiction. For the very realization of their selfish ends, the social groups in power are compelled to extend the benefits of these educational systems to the under-privileged groups also. The inevitable task is generally performed with three precautions abundantly taken care of: One, the privileged groups continue to be the principal beneficiaries of the educational system, dominate the higher stages of education or the hard core of prestigious and quality institutions or the most useful of courses, so as to safeguard their dominant position of leadership in all walks of life; Second, the system is so operated that under-privileged groups can utilize it only marginally in real terms and the bulk of them become either dropouts or pushouts and get reconciled to their own interior status in society; Third, the few from the weaker section that survive and succeed in spite of all the handicaps are generally co-opted within the system to prevent dissatisfaction.

98. Who, according to the passage, can manipulate the systems to their advantage?
A. social activists
B. popular people
C. political powerful people
D. all of the above

99. How do socially powerful people try to maintain their privileged position?
A. by maintaining control over political systems
B. by maintaining control over social systems
C. by maintaining control over education systems
D. all of these

100. Why underprivileged sections have to reconcile to their inferior status?
A. they are unable to effectively utilize the education system
B. they have no interest in the system
C. they are illiterate
D. all of these

101. Which is the best explanation as to why the few from the weaker section that survive and succeed in spite of all the handicaps are generally co-opted within the system?
A. to prevent the revolt in the society
B. to satisfy their instinct
C. to augument the position of the privileged class
D. all of these

102. Which system, according to the passage, dominates the social system?
A. political system
B. education system
C. caste system
D. monetary system

103. Identify the word closest in meaning to the word: "PERPETUATE".
A. abort B. ruin
C. continue D. omit

104. Identify the word opposite in meaning to the word: "PRESTIGIOUS".
A. obscure
B. influential
C. esteemed
D. impressive

105. What is the major idea reflected in the passage?
A. powerful people are unable to fully control the system
B. major benefits have been snatched by the underprivileged
C. both of these
D. none of these

106. While writing a notice, the writer should prefer...
A. active voice
B. passive voice
C. any voice
D. none of these

107. Where will you add disclosures in a letter?
A. below the signature and the right side margin
B. below the signature and the left side margin
C. above the signature and the right side margin
D. any of these

108. 'Phonetics' is basically associated with...
A. sounds
B. sentences
C. grammar
D. all of these

109. Remedial teaching...
A. fills the gap that creeps into a pupil's learning
B. rectifies the concepts which have been misunderstood
C. helps in retaining homogeneity in the class
D. all of these

110. Learning a language is a...
A. gradual process B. fast process
C. instant process D. all inclusive process

111. Study of meaning in a language is known as...
A. syntax B. semantics
C. morphology D. linguistics

112. "REGISTER" is...
A. variety of language according to region in a particular country
B. variety of language according to countries
C. any of these
D. none of these

113. /m/ sound in the word 'make' is....
A. labio-dental B. dental
C. bilabial D. alveolar

114. Which of the following organs of speech is also known as 'VELUM'?
A. hard palate B. voice box
C. alveolar ridge D. soft palate

115. The major difference between an 'ARTICLE' and 'SPEECH' is....
A. speech is more formal
B. speech is more informal
C. speech is more descriptive
D. all of these

116. Communicative Language Teaching replaced basically...
A. Natural Language Processing
B. Structural Teaching
C. Situational Language Teaching
D. Motivational Teaching

117. Find the word nearest in meaning to : REMORSE
A. obdurate
B. hard
C. penitent
D. none of these

118. Find the word opposite in meaning to : INSIPID
A. impalatable
B. bland
C. tame
D. savoury

119. Identify the correct passive voice of the sentence: Obey me.
A. I should be obeyed
B. Let I be obeyed
C. both, a and b
D. none of these

120. Find the appropriate preposition to fill in the sentence: She lives .... Mumbai.
A. at B. in
C. into D. on

PART- V

भाषा-II : हिन्दी

निर्देश (प्र.सं. 121 से 126): *कविता की पंक्तियाँ पढ़कर निम्नलिखित प्रश्नों में* **सबसे उचित** *विकल्प चुनिए।*

मेघ आए, बड़े बन-ठन के सँवर के
आगे-आगे नाचती-गाती बयार चली
दरवाजे-खिड़कियाँ खुलने लगीं गली-गली
पाहुन ज्यों आए हों गाँव में शहर के।
मेघ आए बड़े बन-ठन के सँवर के
पेड़ झुक झाँकने लगे गरदन उचकाए
आँधी चली, धूल भागी घाघरा उठाए,
बाँकी चितवन उठा नदी ठिठकी घूँघट सरके।
मेघ आए बड़े बन-ठन के सँवर के।
बूढ़े पीपल ने आगे बढ़कर घर की
बरस बापद सुधि लीन्ही
बोली अकुलाई लता ओट हो किवार की
हरसाया ताल लाया पानी परात भर के
मेघ आए बड़े बन-ठन के सँवर के।
क्षितिज-अटारी गहराई दामिनी दमकी,
क्षमा करो गाँठ खुल गई अब भरम की
बाँध टूटा झर-झर मिलन के अश्रु ढरके,
मेघ आए बड़े बन-ठन के सँवर के।

121. 'मेघ आए बड़े बन-ठन के सँवर के' पंक्ति का भाव किसमें है?
A. बादलों ने सूरज को ढक लिया है
B. बादलों ने बिजली से शृंगार किया है
C. बादल सज-धज कर आए हैं
D. भूरे-काले बादल आकाश में घिर आए हैं

122. मेघों के आने से लगता है
A. बादल आसमान में छा गए हैं
B. मानों कहीं उत्सव मनाया जा रहा है
C. मानों गाँव में शहर से मेहमान आए हों
D. इनमें से कोई नहीं

123. 'बरस बाद सुधि लीन्ही' — इस पंक्ति का भाव किसमें है?
A. बादल एक बरस के बाद आए हैं
B. बादलों ने याद किया है
C. बादल बन सँवर कर आए हैं
D. बादल मेहमान बन कर आए हैं

124. पूरी कविता में कौन-सा अलंकार है?
A. श्लेष अलंकार B. रूपक अलंकार
C. मानवीकरण अलंकार D. उत्प्रेक्षा अलंकार

125. बूढे पीपल ने किस प्रकार मेघों का स्वागत किया?
A. झुककर प्रणाम करके B. प्रसन्न होकर
C. गले लगाकर D. उलाहना देकर

126. 'पाहुन' शब्द का क्या अर्थ है?
A. आना B. पालना
C. मेहमान D. पैर

निर्देश (प्र.सं. 127 से 135): *गद्यांश को पढ़कर निम्नलिखित प्रश्नों में* **सबसे उचित** *विकल्प चुनिए।*

गिजुभाई न केवल बच्चों की क्षमताओं, बौद्धिकता में विश्वास व्यक्त करते हैं अपितु वे उनकी सर्जनात्मकता में भी अगाध आस्था रखते हैं। उनके अनुसार कुछ हत्याएँ पीनल कोड की धारा के अधीन नहीं आती। उनमें कानूनवेत्ताओं को अपराध जैसी कोई चीजें नजर नहीं आतीं। कानूनवेत्ताओं की न्याय नीति-सम्बन्धी मर्यादाएँ सिर्फ पीनल कोड से बँधी होती हैं। शिक्षाशास्त्रियों के पास राज्य, रूढ़ि अथवा धर्म की कोई सत्ता नहीं है इसलिए जीवन के प्रति जो अपराध होते हैं उनके लिए न कोई पीनल कोड, न कोई उन्हें निंदनीय मानता, न कोई धार्मिक भय है। जीवन के प्रति होने वाला एक ऐसा ही अपराध है — बालक की सृजन-शक्ति की हत्या। ईश्वर ने मनुष्य का सृजन किया और उसे अपनी सृजन-शक्ति प्रदान की। मनुष्य के सृजन की अनंत शक्ति के समान ही अगणित है। साहित्य एक सृजन है, चित्रकला दूसरा सृजन है, संगीत तीसरा सृजन है और स्थापत्य चौथा सृजन है। इस तरह गिनने बैठा जाए तो मनुष्य के द्वारा बनाई गई अनेकानेक कृतियों को गिनाया जा सकता है। जब शिक्षक या अभिभावक यह तय करते हैं कि बच्चे को क्या करना चाहिए, क्या नहीं करना चाहिए — वस्तुतः इन निर्णयों में ही वे बालक की सृजन-शक्ति का दमन कर देते हैं।

127. गिजुभाई का किसमें विश्वास **नहीं** है?
A. उनकी रचनात्मकता में
B. उनके भविष्य का निर्णय शिक्षकों एवं अभिभावकों द्वारा तय करने में
C. बच्चों की बौद्धिकता में
D. उनकी क्षमताओं में

128. कौन-सा अपराध पीनल कोड की धारा के अधीन **नहीं** आता है?
A. बालक की सृजन-शक्ति का दमन
B. रिश्वत लेना
C. धोखाधड़ी करना
D. चोरी करना

129. 'बच्चे क्या करें और क्या न करें' जब शिक्षक और अभिभावक यह तय करते हैं तब
A. बच्चे में रचनात्मकता भर जाती है
B. अभिभावक व बच्चों के सम्बन्धों में प्रगाढ़ता आती है
C. बच्चे में पढ़ने-लिखने के प्रति रुचि जाग्रत हो जाती है
D. बच्चे में सृजन-शक्ति का दमन होता है

130. निम्नलिखित में से 'सृजन' के अंतर्गत **नहीं** आता है:
A. किसी विषय पर अपने विचार लिखना
B. प्रश्नों के उत्तर रटना
C. कहानी-लेखन
D. मिट्टी से खिलौने बनाना

131. 'साहित्य' शब्द में 'इक' प्रत्यय लगाने पर शब्द बनेगा
A. साहित्यीक
B. सहित्यिक
C. साहित्यिक
D. साहित्यइक

132. बौद्धिक, ऐतिहासिक शब्दों में मूल शब्द तथा प्रत्यय हैं
A. बौद्ध (मूल शब्द) + 'इक' प्रत्यय, ऐतिहास (मूल शब्द) + 'इक' प्रत्यय
B. बुद्ध (मूल शब्द) + 'इक' प्रत्यय, इतिहास (मूल शब्द) + 'इक' प्रत्यय
C. बौद्धि (मूल शब्द) + 'क' प्रत्यय, ऐतिहास (मूल शब्द) + 'इक' प्रत्यय
D. बुद्धि (मूल शब्द) + 'इक' प्रत्यय, इतिहास (मूल शब्द) + 'इक' प्रत्यय

133. न्याय-नीति में __________ समास है।
A. कर्मधारय B. द्वंद्व समास
C. अव्ययीभाव D. तत्पुरुष

134. 'ईश्वर' का पर्यायवाची **नहीं** है
A. जगदीश B. परमेश्वर
C. परमात्मा D. ब्रह्मा

135. 'समान' का विलोम शब्द है
A. सामना B. असमानता
C. सामान D. असमान

निर्देश (प्र.सं. 136 से 150) : *निम्नलिखित प्रश्नों के उत्तर देने के लिए सबसे उचित विकल्प चुनिए।*

136. भाषा
A. जानने का अर्थ उसका व्याकरण जानना है
B. सीखने-सिखाने में पाठ्य-पुस्तकों का विशेष महत्त्व होता है
C. जीवन की विभिन्न स्थितियों को साधती है
D. व्याकरण पर ही आधारित होती है

137. भाषा की कक्षा में समाचार-पत्र-पत्रिकाओं का उपयोग यह सुनिश्चित करता है कि
A. शिक्षण-सामग्री का उपयोग हो रहा है
B. बच्चों की भाषा पर समाचार-पत्र-पत्रिकाओं का प्रभाव पड़े
C. बच्चों को मुख्य शीर्ष याद है
D. बच्चे प्रमाणित लेख, समाचार आदि पर अपनी प्रतिक्रिया देने की क्षमता रखते हैं

138. सुलेखा जब-तब बच्चों के साथ बातचीत करती रहती है। वह
A. बच्चों को वाचाल बनाना चाहती है
B. सदैव बच्चों की परीक्षा ले रही है
C. समय नष्ट कर रही है
D. बच्चों को भाषा अर्जित करने के लिए परिवेश दे रही है

139. सुमन बचपन से ही गुजराती बोल-समझ लेती है। वह कभी विद्यालय नहीं जाती। यह उदाहरण है
A. भाषा-अर्जन का B. सुमन की प्रतिभा का
C. भाषा सीखने का D. भाषा में पिछड़ेपन का

140. भाषा में सतत और व्यापक मूल्यांकन का उद्देश्य है
A. केवल बच्चों की कमियाँ जानना
B. केवल यह जानना कि बच्चों ने कितना सीखा
C. बच्चों को उत्तीर्ण-अनुत्तीर्ण श्रेणी में रखना
D. बच्चों द्वारा भाषा सीखने की प्रक्रिया को जान्ना, समझना

141. सस्वर पठन का मुख्य उद्देश्य है
A. मौन पठन करना
B. बच्चों की पढ़ने-सम्बन्धी झिझक को समाप्त करना
C. बोल-बोलकर पढ़ना
D. द्रुत गति से पठन करना

142. भाषा-शिक्षण में कौन-सा बिन्दु सबसे कम महत्त्वपूर्ण है?
A. भाषायी अभ्यास B. भाषिक परिवेश
C. पाठ्य-सामग्री D. परीक्षाएँ

143. सतत मूल्यांकन का एक निहितार्थ है
A. बच्चों के भाषा-प्रयोग का निरंतर अवलोकन करना
B. बच्चों के परीक्षा-सम्बन्धी भय को समाप्त करना
C. प्रतिदिन परीक्षाएँ लेना
D. हर महीने परीक्षाएँ लेना

144. भाषा के आधारभूत कौशल
A. क्रमबद्ध रूप से चलते हैं
B. हमेशा अर्जित किए जाते हैं
C. सर्वथा पृथक् हैं
D. अंतःसंबंधित होते हैं

145. शिक्षक की स्वयं की भाषा-प्रयोग की कुशलता
A. बच्चों के भाषा-प्रयोग के लिए आदर्श रूप प्रस्तुत करती है
B. बच्चों के भाषा-प्रयोग पर कोई प्रभाव नहीं डालती है
C. बच्चों को आलंकारिक भाषा-प्रयोग के लिए प्रेरित करती है
D. बच्चों को भाषा का अनुकरण करने के लिए बाध्य करती है

146. भाषा-अर्जन और भाषा-अधिगम में महत्त्वपूर्ण अंतर है
A. भाषा का कठिनाई-स्तर
B. भाषा की पाठ्य-पुस्तक
C. भाषा सीखने-सिखाने की पद्धति
D. भाषिक परिवेश की उपलब्धता

147. भाषा की पाठ्य-पुस्तक में __________ से सम्बन्धित पाठ होने चाहिए।
A. संस्कृति B. साहित्य
C. विज्ञान D. उपर्युक्त सभी

148. आकलन

A. मूलतः शिक्षक-केंद्रित ही होता है

B. केवल यह बताता है कि बच्चे ने क्या नहीं सीखा

C. भाषा सीखने-सिखाने की प्रक्रिया का अभिन्न अंग है

D. पाठ-समाप्ति पर ही किया जाता है

149. मौखिक भाषा के आकलन का सर्वोत्तम तरीका है

A. किताब पढ़ना

B. अन्त्याक्षरी

C. प्रश्नों के तयशुदा उत्तर देना

D. अनुभव बाँटना व बातचीत

150. स्वाभाविक अभिव्यक्ति, कल्पनाशीलता, कौशल और सोच को विकसित करना

A. भाषा-शिक्षण को किसी प्रकार की दिशा नहीं देता

B. भाषा-शिक्षण का एकमात्र उद्देश्य है

C. भाष-शिक्षण का उद्देश्य नहीं है

D. भाषा-शिक्षण का एक महत्त्वपूर्ण उद्देश्य है

Answers

1	2	3	4	5	6	7	8	9	10
C	D	A	C	A	B	B	D	C	C
11	**12**	**13**	**14**	**15**	**16**	**17**	**18**	**19**	**20**
C	A	B	C	C	B	A	B	C	B
21	**22**	**23**	**24**	**25**	**26**	**27**	**28**	**29**	**30**
D	D	A	D	B	B	C	B	C	A
31	**32**	**33**	**34**	**35**	**36**	**37**	**38**	**39**	**40**
A	B	B	B	D	B	B	C	A	C
41	**42**	**43**	**44**	**45**	**46**	**47**	**48**	**49**	**50**
B	D	A	B	A	C	C	B	A	D
51	**52**	**53**	**54**	**55**	**56**	**57**	**58**	**59**	**60**
A	A	C	C	C	B	D	A	A	D
61	**62**	**63**	**64**	**65**	**66**	**67**	**68**	**69**	**70**
D	B	B	C	C	B	D	D	B	C
71	**72**	**73**	**74**	**75**	**76**	**77**	**78**	**79**	**80**
C	B	C	B	D	D	D	B	C	B
81	**82**	**83**	**84**	**85**	**86**	**87**	**88**	**89**	**90**
D	D	B	D	D	C	A	B	A	B
91	**92**	**93**	**94**	**95**	**96**	**97**	**98**	**99**	**100**
C	D	C	D	A	B	D	C	C	A
101	**102**	**103**	**104**	**105**	**106**	**107**	**108**	**109**	**110**
A	A	C	A	D	B	B	A	D	D
111	**112**	**113**	**114**	**115**	**116**	**117**	**118**	**119**	**120**
B	D	B	D	A	C	C	D	C	B
121	**122**	**123**	**124**	**125**	**126**	**127**	**128**	**129**	**130**
D	C	A	C	D	C	B	A	D	B
131	**132**	**133**	**134**	**135**	**136**	**137**	**138**	**139**	**140**
C	D	D	D	D	C	D	D	A	D
141	**142**	**143**	**144**	**145**	**146**	**147**	**148**	**149**	**150**
B	D	A	D	A	C	D	C	D	D

Some Selected Explanatory Answers

31. It is parellel to x-axis.

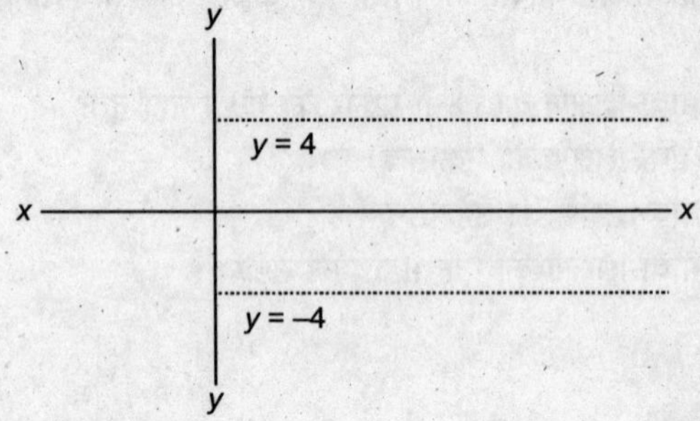

32. $\Delta ABC, \dfrac{AC}{AB} = \sin\theta$

$\Rightarrow \dfrac{x}{x\sqrt{2}} = \sin\theta \Rightarrow \sin\theta = \dfrac{1}{\sqrt{2}} = 45°.$

The angle of elevation is 45°.

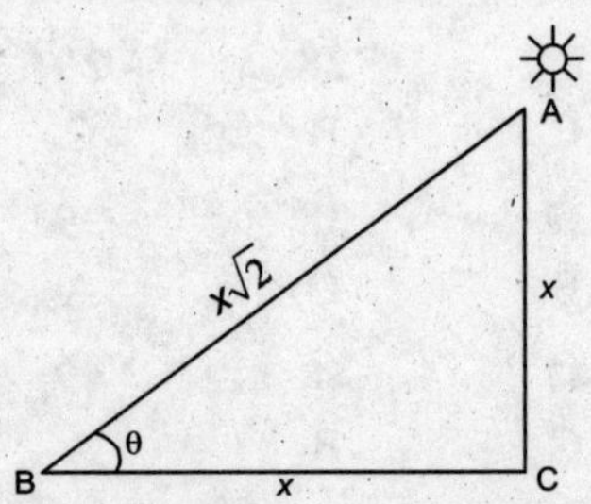

33. Let no. of ten's digit = x and unit digit = y

∴ two digit number = $10x + y$

According to question,

After reversing the number = $10y + x$

∴ Their sum,

$$10x + y + 10y + x = 110$$

$$\Rightarrow 11x + 11y = 110$$

$$\Rightarrow x + y = 10 \quad ....(i)$$

Now, their difference,

$$x - y = 4 \quad ....(ii)$$

From equation (*i*) and (*ii*), we get

$$x + y = 10$$
$$x - y = 4$$
$$2x = 14$$
$$\Rightarrow x = 7 \quad \text{and } y = 3$$

∴ Number = 10 × 7 + 3 = 73.

34. (A + B)'s 1 day work = $\dfrac{1}{4}$

A's 1 day work = $\dfrac{1}{12}$

∴ B's 1 day work = $\dfrac{1}{4} - \dfrac{1}{12} = \dfrac{3-1}{12} = \dfrac{2}{12} = \dfrac{1}{6}$

∴ B alone can do this work in

$$= \frac{1}{1/6} = 6 \text{ days}$$

35. We have, D = $T\left(\dfrac{s_1 s_2}{s_1 + s_2}\right)$

$s_1 = 12 \text{ kmh}^{-1}$, $s_2 = 9 \text{ kmh}^{-1}$

T = 2 hrs 20 min. = $2\frac{1}{3}$ hrs = $\frac{7}{3}$ hrs

∴ Distance, $D = \dfrac{7}{3} \times \left(\dfrac{12 \times 9}{12 + 9}\right)$

$$= \frac{7}{3} \times \frac{12 \times 9}{21} = 12 \text{ km.}$$

37. Area = 64 cm^2

∴ side = 8 cm

Perimeter of square = $4s$ = 4 × 8 = 32 m.

38. One number × Other number = HCF × LCM

∴ Other number = $\dfrac{\text{HCF} \times \text{LCM}}{\text{One number}}$

$$= \frac{11 \times 693}{77} = 99.$$

39. LCM of 16, 24, 36 and 54

2	16,	24,	36,	54
2	8,	12,	18,	27
2	4,	6,	9,	27
3	2,	3,	9,	27
3	2,	1,	3,	9
	2,	1,	1,	3

∴ LCM = 2 × 2 × 2 × 3 × 3 × 2 × 3 = 432

The smallest 5-digit number = 10,000

∴ Smallest 5-digit number which is exactly on dividing 10,000 by 432 remainder is 64.

∴ Required number = 10,000 + 432 – 64 = 10,368.

40. Seven consecutive numbers are x, $x + 1$, $x + 2$, $x + 3$, $x + 4$, $x + 5$, $x + 6$.

According to question,

$$\frac{x+x+1+x+2+x+3+x+4+x+5+x+6}{7} = 20$$

$$\Rightarrow \frac{7x+21}{7} = 20$$

$$\Rightarrow 7x + 21 = 20 \times 7 = 140$$

$$\Rightarrow 7x = 140 - 21 = 119$$

$$\therefore x = \frac{119}{7} = 17$$

∴ largest number = x + 6 = 17 + 6 = 23.

41. Volume sphere = $\frac{4}{3}\pi r^3$

Since, radius of cylinder is equal to sphere i.e., 1 cm.

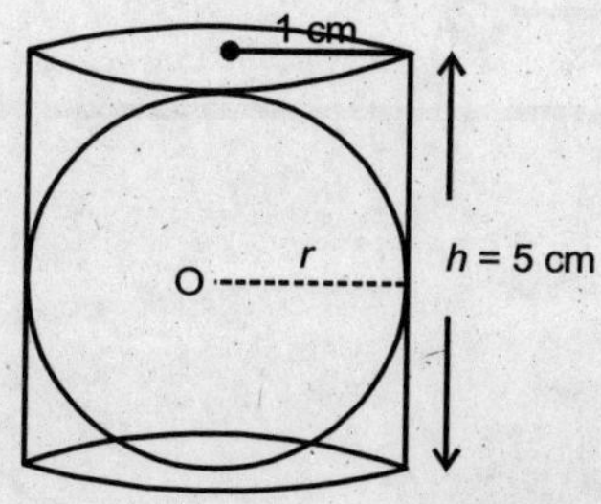

$\therefore$ volume of sphere = $\frac{4}{3}\pi(1)^3$ cm^3 = $\frac{4}{3}\pi$ cm^3.

42. We have, $\frac{x^3-1}{x^2-1}$

[$\because$ $A^3 - B^3 = (A - B)^3 + 3AB(A - B)$ and $A^2 - B^2 = (A - B)(A + B)$]

$$= \frac{(x-1)^3 + 3x(x-1)}{(x+1)(x-1)}$$

$$= \frac{(x-1)^3}{(x+1)(x-1)} + \frac{3x(x-1)}{(x+1)(x-1)} = \frac{(x-1)^2}{x+1} + \frac{3x}{x+1}$$

$$= \frac{x^2+1-2x+3x}{x+1} = \frac{x^2+x+1}{x+1}.$$

43. Percentage spending is spent on tennis

$$= \frac{45\times100}{360} = \frac{5\times5}{2} = \frac{25}{2}\% = 12\frac{1}{2}\%.$$

44. Percentage spending is spent on cricket

$$= \frac{81\times100}{360} = \frac{45}{2}\% = 22\frac{1}{2}\%$$

Percentage spending is spent on hockey

$$= \frac{63\times100}{360} = \frac{35}{2}\% = 17\frac{1}{2}\%$$

$\therefore$ Total amount spend on sports = ₹ 2 crore = ₹ 2,00,00,000

Money spent on cricket = ₹ 2,00,00,000 $\times \frac{45}{2} \times \frac{1}{100}$ = ₹ 45,00,000

Money spent on hockey = ₹ 2,00,00,000 $\times \frac{35}{2} \times \frac{1}{100}$ = ₹ 35,00,000

Total amount spent on cricket and hockey together = ₹ 45,00,000 + ₹ 35,00,000 = ₹ 80,00,000.

46. Volume of sphere = $\frac{4}{3}\pi r^3$

Surface area of sphere = $4\pi r^2$

According to question, volume of sphere = surface area of sphere $\frac{4}{3}\pi r^3 = 4\pi r^2$

$\Rightarrow$ $r = 3$ units

47. Number = 3.4625

Place value of the numbers

$\therefore$ Place value of 2 in 3.4625 is $\frac{1}{100}$.

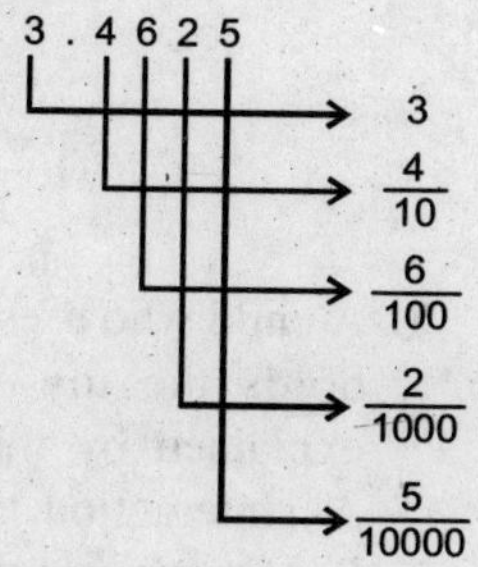

48. $50 \div \frac{1}{2} + 20 - 35$

$= 50 \times 2 + 20 - 35$

$= 100 + 20 - 35 = 120 - 35 = 85.$

52. HCF of $(x - 1)$, $(x^2 - 1)$ and $(x^3 - 1)$

$x - 1 = (x - 1)$

$x^2 - 1 = (x - 1)(x + 1)$

and $x^3 - 1 = (x - 1)[(x - 1)^2 + 3]$

$\therefore$ HCF = $(x - 1)$.

54. 1 gram = 5 carats.

55. Area = 90 × 44 = 3960 sq. feet

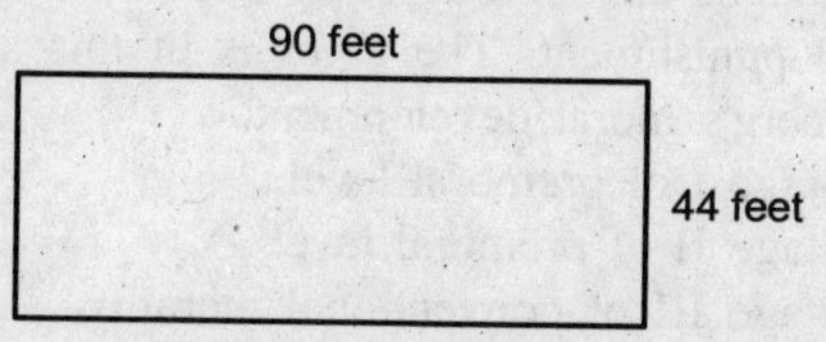

$\because$ 1 yard = 3 feet

$\therefore$ 1 sq. yard = 9 sq. feet

$\because$ 9 sq. feet = 1 sq. yard

$\therefore$ 1 sq. feet = $\frac{1}{9}$ sq. yard

$\therefore$ 3960 sq. feet = $\frac{3960}{9}$ sq. yard = 440 sq. yard

61. The domestic sewage can be readily decomposed by natural processes which enhances capacity of the nature to decompose and recycle.

62. Jammu & Kashmir.

63. Sir Sundarlal Bahuguna started Chipko Movement. Uttarakhand Chipko Movement is related to conservation of forest.

64. Project tiger launched in India. in 1973. It is related to protection of tigers in India.

TEST PAPER–3

PART- I

Child Development and Pedagogy

1. A child who uses both its hands to hold a toy, gradually holds the toy with its fingers. This can be best explained by this developmental principle.
A. Interaction
B. Development is predictable
C. Individual differences
D. Development proceeds from general to specific

2. Comparatively, emotions shift easily in ....
A. childhood B. infancy
C. adolescence D. puberty

3. The modification of existing knowledge structures as a result of exposure to new information or experiences is ....
A. accommadation B. assimilation
C. schema D. equilibration

4. A child of class I obeys the orders of the elders to avoid punishment. The child is in this stage of the Kohlberg's moral development.
A. Stage I of premoral level
B. Stage II of premoral level
C. Stage III of conventional morality
D. Stage IV of conventional morality

5. One of the following perspectives proposes that all children have an innate language acquisition device which is responsible for language acquisition called the ....
A. nativist perspective
B. humanistic perspective
C. behavioristic perspective
D. socio-cultural perspective

6. One of the following speaks about the social expectations for every stage of development.
A. developmental tasks
B. developmental hazards
C. conflicts
D. congnitive abilities

7. Pick the correct statement from the following.
A. Physical health is important than mental health
B. Mental health is important than physical health
C. Physical and mental health are interrelated and both are important
D. Mental health is important for intellectuals and physical health is important for labourers.

8. The performance of a student is less than his aptitude in Mathematics. He requires ....
A. extra coaching
B. training in memory techniques
C. best teaching
D. guidance

9. 'Prediction' is the characteristic of the following psychological concept.
A. Interest B. Attitude
C. Creativity D. Aptitude

10. A classroom teacher would like to know the opinion of class X students on certain issues. The appropriate method to know the opinion is ....
A. case study
B. observation
C. interview
D. attitude

11. Relation between intelligence and creativity is ....
A. positive
B. negative
C. no specific relation
D. positive in students having an above average I.Q.

12. Learning outcome depends upon the following.
A. learner, learning material, learning process and teacher
B. learning material, learning process and teacher
C. learner, learning material and teacher
D. learning process and teacher

13. One of the following methods is more suitable to teach the heterogenous group of students for self-paced learning.
A. lecture method
B. historical method
C. programmed instruction method
D. loud reading method

14. A child is not able to learn a task properly because of nonattainment of age. The learning factor involved is ....

A. cognitive B. personal
C. environmental D. social

15. "Law of exercise" is the contribution of this school.

A. Behaviorism B. Constructivism
C. Gestalt school D. Psychoanalysts

16. Three students of class IX stand in 1st, 2nd and 3rd positions interchangeably in all their achievement tests. All the time they feel jealous of one another.

In this case, the teacher needs to concentrate on this domain for their healthy development.

A. conative B. affective
C. psychomotor D. cognitive

17. Involvement of the learner ....

A. is active in R–S conditioning than in S–R conditioning
B. is active in S–R conditioning than in R–S conditioning
C. is active in both S–R and R–S conditionings
D. is passive in both S–R and R–S conditionings

18. Essential component of learning is

A. experience B. teaching
C. objectives D. guidance

19. According to Vygotsky, children's self-directed speech is called ....

A. private speech
B. egocentric speech
C. culture-oriented speech
D. social speech

20. A teacher and two to four students form a collaborative group and take turns in leading dialogues on the content of a text. It is called ....

A. reciprocal teaching
B. remedial teaching
C. extended teaching
D. cooperative learning

21. A student of class V has learnt many things when the class teacher appreciated the behavior of his classmates. The learning theory involved is ....

A. insight learning
B. social learning
C. instrumental conditioning
D. classical conditioning

22. Change in the neurological system of a person due to the process of memory is known as ....

A. engram
B. genetical memory
C. biogenetical memory
D. linguistic memory

23. A class VIII rural student learns the periodic table in a similar fashion to learning 'VIBGYOR', the colours of the rainbow. The technique involved in this learning is ....

A. mnemonics
B. paired association
C. ideas association
D. word association

24. To carry out the provisions of the RTE Act, 2009, 'funding' is the responsibility of ....

A. the central government
B. the state government
C. SSA and RMSA
D. both central and state governments

25. As per the NCF–2005, assessment at Class I and II is ....

A. no test in any form
B. oral test
C. a simple written or oral test
D. based on the syllabus

26. One of the following indicates the learner's higher cognitive ability.

A. Retention
B. Reasoning
C. Imitation
D. Observation

27. One of the following is the reason for learning disability.

A. Possessing I.Q. less than 70
B. In appropriate teaching
C. Comitting errors in solving the problems
D. Defect in the perceptual process

28. Innovative way of problem solving is mostly observed in this learning.

A. S-R conditioning
B. R-S conditioning
C. Insight learning
D. Social learning

29. One of the following actions of a teacher indicates that he is a good leader.

A. doing things right
B. doing the right things
C. setting the things right
D. asking to do right things

30. A child comforts another child who is crying by offering her toy. The behavior of the child who tried to comfort the other child represents ....

A. social development
B. social and emotional development
C. emotional development
D. cognitive development

PART- II

Mathematics

31. There are three sectors in a pie-diagram. If the angles of two sectors are 80° and 140°, then the angle of the third sector is ....

A. 220° B. 60°
C. 140° D. 80°

32. A cricket ball's cost is ₹ 36 and the cost of a cricket bat is 12½ times that of the cost of the cricket ball. The cost of the cricket bat (in rupees) is ....

A. 450 B. 350
C. 550 D. 650

33. The value of $\left(1^2-\frac{1}{3^2}\right)\left(1^2-\frac{1}{4^2}\right)\left(1^2-\frac{1}{5^2}\right)........\left(1^2-\frac{1}{100^2}\right)$ is ....

A. $\frac{101}{150}$ B. $\frac{7}{150}$
C. $\frac{9}{200}$ D. $\frac{3}{100}$

34. In a ΔABC, if ∠A = 90° and ∠B = 2∠C, then ∠C is ....

A. 15° B. 30°
C. 45° D. 90°

35. The present age of a father is 42 years and of his son is 12 years. The ratio of age of the father to his son 2 years ago was ....

A. 7 : 2 B. 4 : 1
C. 2 : 7 D. 1 : 4

36. If 2 m 60 cm cloth is required for one shirt, then the cloth required for 7 shirts is ....

A. 14 m 80 cms B. 18 m 20 cms
C. 15 m 20 cms D. 16 m 80 cms

37. The value of $\sqrt{1.44\times6.25}$ is ....

A. 2 B. 1
C. 4 D. 3

38. If x, y, z are any three rational numbers and if $x > y$, $y > z$, then $x > z$. This property is known as ....

A. Law of Tricotomy B. Transitive Property
C. Associative Property D. Closure Property

39. A school has 560 students. If the number of girls is $14\frac{2}{7}$ % of the number of boys, then the number of girls in the school is ....

A. 320 B. 80
C. 70 D. 490

40. If a clock shows 8 o'clock, then the angle between the two hands is ....

A. 240° B. 120°
C. 145° D. 125°

41. To represent equal numerical values, same type of diagrams are used in ....

A. bar diagrams B. pie diagrams
C. sectors D. pictographs

42. There are some bags, where 21 bags are kept in each room. If the bags are kept in 16's and 20's per room, 4 bags are left out. The total number of bags that are there in all is ....

A. 48 B. 80
C. 84 D. 76

43. The value of $\frac{9}{-17}\times\left(\frac{3}{7}-\frac{4}{5}\right)$ is

A. $\frac{-117}{595}$ B. $\frac{117}{595}$
C. $\frac{595}{117}$ D. $\frac{-595}{117}$

44. The ratio between ₹ 2 and 60 paise is ....

A. 1 : 30 B. 30 : 1
C. 10 : 3 D. 3 : 10

45. If one angle is the average of the other two angles and the difference between the greatest and least angles is 60°, then the formed triangle is called ....

A. an isosceles triangle
B. an equilateral triangle
C. a right angled triangle
D. a right angled isosceles triangle

46. The difference between the largest 6-digit number and the smallest 5-digit number is ....

A. 999998 B. 888888
C. 988888 D. 989999

47. The summer vacation was declared for all the schools from April 24th. If the vacation is for 49 days, then the schools reopen on ....

A. June 11th B. June 12th
C. June 10th D. June 13th

48. If two-thirds, half and one-seventh of a number is added to itself, the result is 37. Then the number is ....

A. $14\frac{2}{97}$ B. $16\frac{2}{97}$
C. $18\frac{2}{97}$ D. $15\frac{1}{97}$

49. The value of a vehicle depreciates every year by 5%. If the present value of the vehicle is ₹ 50,000, then its value after two years (in rupees) is ....

A. 45,125 B. 47,500
C. 52,500 D. 54,875

50. The centre and end points of an arc of a circle are collinear. The arc is called as ....

A. diameter B. chord
C. major arc D. semicircle

51. If $\frac{b}{a}=2$ and $\frac{c}{b}=3$, then the value of $\frac{a+b}{b+c}$ is ....

A. $\frac{3}{4}$ B. $\frac{2}{3}$
C. $\frac{3}{8}$ D. $\frac{3}{2}$

52. The cost of 4 dozen papers is ₹ 24. The cost of 1 score of papers (in rupees) is ....

A. 40 B. 20
C. 10 D. 42

53. The perimeter of a semicircle is 36 cms. Its diameter (in centimetres) is ....

A. 7 B. 14
C. 22 D. 35

54. The value of 0.2727 .... + 0.7373 .... is ....

A. 1.001 B. 1.01
C. 1.0202....... D. 1.0101......

55. The author of 'Pancha Siddhantika' is ....

A. Aryabhatta B. Varahamihira
C. Bhaskaracharya D. Brahmagupta

56. The terminal competency to be achieved in Geometry at the primary stage is ....

A. to understand the types of triangles
B. to draw a circle when radius is given
C. to draw an angle equal to the given angle
D. to express the concept of a circle and technical words associated with it

57. Students are asked to find the various characteristics of a rectangle by using a geometric box. The teaching method adopted is the...........

A. playway method
B. problem solving method
C. heuristic method
D. project method

58. In the lesson plan presently being prepared in schools, the aspect to be indicated after content analysis is ....

A. teaching learning activities
B. competencies to be achieved
C. teaching learning material
D. evaluation

59. "Student verifies the outcome when two fractions are multiplied". This specification belongs to the objective of ....

A. understanding
B. knowledge
C. application
D. skill

60. To evaluate a text book as per the Hunter's score card, the content is to be assessed for .... points.

A. 50 B. 250
C. 100 D. 300

PART- III

Environmental Studies

61. Examine the following :

1. The tip of the tongue – sweet taste
2. The back of the tongue – sour taste
3. The edges of the tongue – bitter taste
4. The middle of the tongue – salty taste

Identify the correct pairs :

A. 1, 3 B. 2, 4
C. 2, 3 D. 1, 4

62. The first-aid kit in a classroom contains tartaric acid, iodine, antiseptic lotion and potassium permanganate. The item/items you use to give first-aid to the victim of scorpion bite is/are ....

A. iodine
B. potassium permanganate or tartaric acid
C. antiseptic lotion
D. antiseptic lotion and iodine

63. The number of players and extra players present in a kabaddi team respectively are...........

A. 5, 2 B. 6, 4
C. 7, 5 D. 8, 2

64. Examples for pollination by water and pollination by wind respectively are ....

A. hydrilla, maize B. wheat, vallisneria
C. drosera, paddy D. eichornia, pistia

65. Skeleton of a man : bones : : skeleton of leaf : ....

A. chlorophyll B. veins
C. xylem D. stomata

66. A farmer collected 'sword suckers' to grow in his field. The crop is ....

A. potato B. turmeric
C. plantain D. sweet potato

67. The skin disease caused due to vitamin deficiency is ....

A. Pellagra B. Eczema
C. Acne D. Measles

68. A farmer has a field with sand soil in coastal region. Suggest a suitable crop which can be grown in his field.

A. Turmeric B. Sugarcane
C. Chillies D. Casuarina

69. A person wishes to stay in a forest and study the life of wild animals. The type of the house he has to live in is ....

A. a tent house B. a mud house
C. a stilt house D. a hut

70. The abundant presence of these plants decreases the nitrogen percentage in the air.

A. leguminous plants B. plantains
C. water hyacinth D. coconut

71. The gas that destroys chlorophyll in plant leaves is ....

A. CO_2 B. SO_3
C. H_2S D. SO_2

72. Pick up the wrong statement with reference to water.

A. It is not an element
B. It is a good conductor of electricity.
C. $2H_2 + O_2 \rightarrow 2H_2O$
D. It has a constant ratio of hydrogen and oxygen

73. Examine the following statements

1. Need not clean toilet daily.
2. White washing of a house to be taken up periodically.
3. Store the garbage in the dustbin only forever.
4. Water and food vessels must be covered with lids.

Identify the correct responses from the following options.

A. 1, 3 B. 1, 4
C. 2, 4 D. 3, 4

74. Latitudes and longitudes on a globe are........

A. latitudes are horizontal imaginary lines and longitudes are vertical imaginary lines
B. latitudes are vertical imaginary lines and longitudes are horizontal imaginary lines
C. both latitudes and longitudes are horizontal imaginary lines
D. both latitudes and longitudes are vertical imaginary lines

75. 'Gramasabha' means ....

A. it is meeting in which the sarpanch and all ward members participate
B. it is a meeting headed by the sarpanch in which all the people of a village attend
C. it is a meeting of sarpanch and the upasarpanch with village secretary and other empoloyees of the grama panchayat
D. it is a meeting headed by the sarpanch in which all ward members, youth associations and caste heads attend

76. 'Shravanbelagola' and 'Mahabalipuram', the historical places are located respectively in these states.

A. Andhra Pradesh, Tamil Nadu
B. Kerala, Karnataka
C. Tamil Nadu, Karnataka
D. Karnataka, Tamil Nadu

77. The area of India is ....

A. 3.28 million sq. kms B. 32.8 million sq. kms
C. 3.28 billion sq. kms D. 32.8 billion sq. kms

78. Read the following and identify the correct pair :

1. Kuchipudi – Tamil Nadu
2. Bhangra – Punjab
3. Bharatanatyam – Andhra Pradesh

A. 2, 3 B. 1, 3
C. 1, 2 D. 2 only

79. Eastern and western ghats of peninsular plateau meet here.

A. Seshachala hills B. Nallamala mountains
C. Nilgiri mountains D. Papi hills

80. The hot deserts are situated between these latitudes on either side of the equator.

A. 15° – 30° B. 30° – 45°
C. 5° – 15° D. 0° – 5°

81. Health, revenue, fire services and education belong to this category.

A. All are ordinary services
B. All are emergency services
C. Health and fire services are emergency services, revenue and education services are ordinary services
D. Health and fire services are ordinary services; revenue and education services are emergency services.

82. The popular names of Gopal Krishna Gokhale and Dadabhai Naoroji respectively are ....

A. Iron man, Punjab Kesari
B. Grand old man of India; Iron man
C. Punjab Kesari; Socrates of Maharashtra
D. Socrates of Maharashtra; Grand old man of India

83. This is not an organ of the United Nations Organization

A. The Secretariat
B. The General Assembly
C. The World Health Organization
D. The International Court of Justice

84. Examine the following and identify the mismatch:

1. Mud house – Rajasthan
2. Igloo – Lake
3. Skyscraper – Big city

A. 3 only B. 2 only
C. 1 only D. 3 and 1

85. The product of science is indicated by ....
A. the scientific method of inquiry
B. accumulated and systematized body of knowledge
C. the scientific attitude
D. gathering of data

86. Most important initial step towards achievement of an aim is ....
A. skill
B. ability
C. objective
D. goal

87. The method that helps in developing manipulative skills among the students is ....
A. lecture method
B. historical method
C. laboratory method
D. lecture cum demonstration method

88. The arrangements that shows the creatures living on the land is ....
A. aquarium
B. terrarium
C. herbarium
D. vivarium

89. The plan meant for evaluating the learning outcomes of the students in the classroom is called ....
A. unit plan
B. subject plan
C. lesson plan
D. year plan

90. The evaluation that is used for grading purpose is called ....
A. formative evaluation
B. summative evaluation
C. diagnostic evaluation
D. grading evaluation

PART- IV

Language-I : English

91. Choose the correct word to fill in the blank in the sentences.
Copper is .... useful metal.
A. a
B. an
C. the
D. any

92. I forget his name
In the above sentence, the underlined word is a.........
A. noun
B. verb
C. conjunction
D. pronoun

93. Identify the correct sentence.
A. How far your house it is from here?
B. You are doing that why?
C. How far is it from here to your house?
D. Where you are going now?

94. Choose the correct word to fill in the blank in the sentence
Rama can speak ....
A. fast
B. wonderful
C. fastly
D. severely

95. If you combine the following two sentences,
1. He is strong
2. He can work hard
You will get :
A. He can work hard because he is strong.
B. He is strong when he can work hard.
C. Though he is strong, he can work hard.
D. Although he can work hard, he is strong.

96. To make the past perfect tense, we use this helping verb
A. have
B. had
C. has
D. having

97. The opposite of 'equality' is ....
A. unequality
B. disequality
C. nonequality
D. inequality

98. Identify the correctly spelt word.
A. accomodation
B. accommodation
C. acommodation
D. accommodetion

99. Choose the correct word to fill in the blank in the sentences.
We went .... the market last Sunday.
A. up
B. onto
C. to
D. off

100. Choose the correct phrase to fill in the blank in the sentence.
They .... living here since 1999.
A. have been
B. has been
C. are being
D. have being

101. Identify the 'positive degree' of the sentence.
Raju is taller than Amar.
A. Amar is not tall as Raju.
B. Amar is not so tall as Raju.
C. Amar can be tall like Raju.
D. Amar is as tall as Raju.

102. Identify the correct 'question tag' for the statement.
Your brother is a teacher, ...
A. is he
B. isn't it?
C. isnt he
D. isn't he?

103. What is the meaning of the word underlined in the sentence?
The water glittered in the sunlight.
A. shone
B. shine
C. shown
D. shining

104. If you combine the following two sentences,
1. She likes English.
2. She likes Mathematics.

You will get :
A. She not only likes English, but also Mathematics.
B. She likes not only English, but also Mathematics.
C. Not only English but also she likes Mathematics.
D. She likes English and not only Mathematics.

105. The 'reported' form of the sentence, The teacher said to the pupils, "Listen." is ....
A. The teacher said the pupils to listen
B. The teacher told the pupils listen
C. The teacher asked the pupils to listen.
D. The teacher suggested the pupils to listen.

106. Identify the questioin to get the answer.
Yes. We go there every year.
A. Did you been to Ooty?
B. Have been to Ooty ever?
C. Did you go to Ooty never?
D. Have you ever been to Ooty?

107. In a letter to an officer, the 'subscription' is ....
A. Yours sincerely, B. Your faithfully,
C. Yours faithfully, D. Yours' faithfully,

108. Identify the correct sentence that contains all the words in the box.
Sun, clouds, makes, the, the, us, for
A. The sun makes us for the clouds
B. The sun makes the clouds for us
C. The clouds makes the sun for us
D. The sun clouds makes for us

109. Read the four parts of a sentence
They are marked 1, 2, 3 and 4.
1. because it was interesting
2. interested in the book
3. that he could not put it down
4. he was so
The correct sequence of the parts is
A. 4, 2, 3, 1 B. 2, 3, 1, 4
C. 1, 3, 2, 4 D. 4, 3, 1, 2

Directions (Qs. 110 to 114) : *Read the following and answer the questions given below.*

John Ruskin says, "All books are divisible into two classes, the books of the hour and the books of all time."

Similarly, some books are read by 95% of people for some years and then they are virtually forgotten. Take for example, 'detective' novels. We may not have heard about the authors of detective novels like Erle Stanley Gardner. Although the taste of readers is changing, 5% of people continue to read 'classics'. Mark Twain said, "A classic is a book which people praise but don't read."

Books are good companions and good counsellors. They are like good friends. As a good friend walks in when others walk out, books also walk in to console you. They offer the best solace you think of.

110. According to Ruskin, books can be divided into ....
A. some categories B. three categories
C. four categories D. two categories

111. According to this passage, ...
A. some books are read and forgotten
B. very few books are read but forgotten
C. most of the books are read but forgotten
D. no book is read and forgotten

112. According to this passage, ...
A. a majority of people read classics
B. every reader reads classics
C. more than half of the readers read classics
D. a small percentage of people read classics

113. The writer of this passage compares books to ....
A. friends B. classics
C. time D. detectives

114. The writer of this passage says that books can make us...........
A. feel sad B. feel better
C. feel dejected D. feel serious

115. Language games can consolidate the pupils skills of ....
A. listening and speaking only
B. speaking and reading only
C. reading and writing only
D. listening, speaking, reading and writing

116. We teach a supplementary reader for ....
A. learning pronunciation B. learning syntax
C. extensive reading D. intensive reading

117. Read the question in the box given below :
Choose the correct word to fill in the blank
Ravi goes to school .... bicycle.
1. by 2. on
3. with 4. over
The above test item tests the ....
A. lexical item B. knowledge
C. skill D. speech

118. At schools, teachers conduct unit tests, terminal exams and annual exams to ensure ....
A. continuous and comprehensive evaluation
B. summative evaluation
C. diagnostic evaluation
D. formation evaluation

119. In microteaching, the sequence of events is:
A. Teacher trainees improve their spoken English
B. They prepare a microlesson plan, teach, get the feedback, replan and reteach
C. They teach, get the feedback, prepare a microlesson and reteach
D. They prepare a microlesson plan and improve their teaching

120. One of the basic elements of spoken English is fluency. Fluency is the ability of a speaker ....
A. to pause at the right place while speaking
B. to speak fast
C. to speak as fast as he can
D. to speak as slowly as he can

PART- V

भाषा-II : हिन्दी

निर्देशः *निम्नलिखित प्रश्नों के उत्तर देने के लिए* **सबसे उचित** *विकल्प चुनिए।*

121. निम्नलिखित में से कौन-सा उच्च प्राथमिक स्तर पर भाषा शिक्षण का उद्देश्य ***नहीं*** है?
A. दूसरों के अनुभवों से जुड़ पाना और संदर्भों में चीजों को समझना
B. सही रूप में समझना
C. व्याकरण के नियमों को रटना
D. निजी अनुभवों के आधार पर भाषा का सृजनशील प्रयोग

122. भाषा की पाठ्य-पुस्तक में ऐसे पाठ रखे जाएँ जो–
A. बच्चों के परिवेश से जुड़े हों
B. केवल व्याकरणिक नियमों का ही अभ्यास कराते हों
C. अत्यंत छोटे हों
D. सरल भाषा से युक्त हों

123. द्वितीय भाषा के रूप में हिंदी सीखने का मुख्य उद्देश्य है–
A. दैनिक जीवन में हिंदी में समझने तथा बोलने की क्षमता का विकास करना
B. मानक हिंदी लिखने में निपुणता प्राप्त करना
C. हिंदी और अपनी मातृभाषा के अंतर को कंठस्थ करना
D. हिंदी के व्याकरण पर अधिकार प्राप्त करना

124. माधुरी पढ़ते समय कभी-कभी वाक्यों, शब्दों की पुनरावृत्ति करती है। इसका यह भाषायी व्यवहार दर्शाता है कि–
A. वह पढ़ने में ज्यादा समय लेती है
B. वह समझ के साथ पढ़ने की कोशिश कर रही है
C. वह अटक-अटक कर ही पढ़ सकती है
D. उसे पढ़ना बिलकुल नहीं आता

125. 'उसने पढ़ा।', 'उसने खाया।' और 'उसने चीखा'। जैसे भाषा-प्रयोग दर्शाते हैं–
A. नियमों का अति सामान्यीकरण
B. नियम का उल्लंघन
C. संदर्भ की समझ न होना
D. नियम कंठस्थ न होना

126. व्याकरण-शिक्षण के संदर्भ में कौन-सा कथन सही है?
A. व्याकरण-शिक्षण अत्यंत आवश्यक है
B. व्याकरण-शिक्षण के लिए समय-सारणी में अलग से काव्यांशों की व्यवस्था होनी चाहिए
C. भाषा-प्रयोग की अपेक्षा भाषा-नियमों को ही महत्त्व देना चाहिए
D. बच्चे परिवेश में उपलब्ध भाषिक प्रयोगों के आधार पर स्वयं भाषा के नियम बनाने की क्षमता रखते हैं

127. सुहेल एक साल पहले असम से पंजाब आया है। वह हिंदी भाषा का प्रयोग करते समय त्रुटियाँ करता है। एक शिक्षक के रूप में आप किस कथन को सही मानेंगे?
A. सुहेल की मातृभाषा का प्रभाव लक्ष्य भाषा पर नहीं पड़ने देना चाहिए
B. उसे रोज एक घंटा हिंदी भाषा के शब्द बोलने का अभ्यास करना चाहिए
C. सुहेल को भाषा प्रयोग के अधिकाधिक अवसर व प्रोत्साहन देना चाहिए
D. सुहेल को बार-बार उसकी त्रुटियों के बारे में बताना चाहिए

128. सपना अपनी कक्षा के बच्चों को मौखिक अभिव्यक्ति के अवसर देने के लिए अनेक क्रियाकलाप करती हैं। आप निम्नलिखित में से सबसे ज्यादा प्रभावी किसे मानते हैं?
A. समाचार-पत्र का वाचन करना
B. विभिन्न परिस्थितियों में संवाद-अदायगी करना
C. शब्दों को जोर-जोर से बोलना
D. कहानी को बोल-बोलकर पढ़ना

129. कक्षा में मौजूद बहुभाषिकता–
A. भाषा-शिक्षण में एक संसाधन के रूप मे प्रयुक्त हो सकती है
B. बच्चों को 'लक्ष्य भाषा' सीखने के लिए हतोत्साहित करती है
C. शिक्षक के लिए एक जटिल और कठोर चुनौती है
D. भाषा-शिक्षण में बाधक है

130. भाषा के संदर्भ में निदानात्मक परीक्षण का उद्देश्य है–
A. बच्चों की भाषा-प्रयोग संबंधी कठिनाइयों के संभावित कारणों की पहचान करना
B. बच्चों हेतु भाषा-प्रयोग के अवसर जुटाना
C. बच्चों को अगली कक्षा में प्रोन्नत करना
D. बच्चों को विभिन्न श्रेणियों में विभक्त करना

131. उच्च कक्षाओं में–
A. भाषा की पाठ्य-पुस्तक अत्यंत महत्वपूर्ण है
B. साहित्य साध्य है और भाषा-कौशल साधन
C. केवल छन्द-अलंकारों को समझने के प्रयास करना ही भाषा-शिक्षण का उद्देश्य है
D. भाषा-कौशल साध्य हैं और साधन है–साहित्य

132. भाषा के सतत और व्यापक मूल्यांकन का उद्देश्य है–
A. मूल्यांकन की परंपरा का निर्वाह करना
B. बच्चों की सीखने की प्रक्रिया को समझ कर उपयुक्त शिक्षण-अधिगम प्रक्रिया अपनाना
C. अगली कक्षा में प्रोन्नत करने हेतु साक्ष्य जुटाना
D. बच्चों की त्रुटियों की पहचान करना

133. उच्च प्राथमिक स्तर पर भाषा-शिक्षण की प्रक्रिया में सबसे अधिक महत्वपूर्ण है–
A. समाचार-पत्र, पत्रिकाओं या अन्य भाषिक सामग्री में कही गई बात के निहितार्थ, सोच, सरोकार की पहचान करना
B. पाठ्य-पुस्तक में दिए गए साहित्यिक अंशों की विस्तृत व्याख्या
C. पठन-कौशल पर अधिक बल देना
D. पाठों के शब्दों का अर्थ जानने के लिए शब्दकोश का प्रयोग करना

134. उपचारात्मक शिक्षण की सफलता मुख्यतः निर्भर करती है–
A. समस्याओं के कारणों की सही पहचान पर
B. बच्चों की समाज-सांस्कृतिक पृष्ठभूमि पर
C. बच्चों की भाषागत त्रुटियों की सूची बनाने पर
D. समस्याओं की पहचान पर

135. भाषा-अर्जन–
A. प्रयासपूर्ण होता है
B. शिक्षक की आवश्यक उपस्थिति की माँग करता है
C. भाषा की कक्षा में ही संभव है
D. सहज, स्वाभाविक होता है

निर्देश (प्रसं. 136 से 141 तक): *कविता की पंक्तियाँ पढ़कर निम्नलिखित प्रश्नों में* **सबसे उचित** *विकल्प चुनिए।*

नदी के उस पार जाने को
मेरा बहुत मन करता है माँ;
वहाँ कतार में
बँधीं है नावें बाँस की खूँटियों से।
उसी रास्ते दूर-दूर जाते हैं
हल जोतने किसान
कंधों पर हल रखे,
रँभाते हुए गाय-बैल
तैरकर जाते हैं उस पार
घास चरने
शाम को जब वे
लौटते हैं घर
ऊँची-ऊँची घास में छिपकर
हुक्के–हो करते हैं सियार।
माँ तू बुरा न माने तो
बड़ा होकर मैं नाव खेने वाला
एक नाविक बनूँगा।

136. इस कविता में कौन किसे संबोधित कर रहा है?
A. लेखक के रूप में एक बच्चा माँ को
B. लेखक नाविक की माँ को
C. कोई किसी को नहीं
D. लेखक अपनी माँ को

137. लेखक नाविक क्यों बनना चाहता है?
A. वह हल चलाना चाहता है
B. वह नदी की यात्रा का मजा लेना चाहता है
C. वह नाव चलाने संबंधी अपने शौक को पूरा करना चाहता है
D. वह नदी पार के सौंदर्य का आनंद उठाना चाहता है

138. नावों को बाँसों की खूँटियों से क्यों बाँधा गया होगा?
A. नाविक ऐसा ही करते हैं
B. कहीं लहरें नाव को बहाकर न ले जाएँ
C. बाँसों की खूटियाँ पानी में तैरती रहती हैं
D. ताकि कोई दूसरा व्यक्ति नाव न ले जाए

139. 'माँ तू बुरा न माने तो' पंक्ति किस ओर संकेत नहीं करती?
A. लेखक जानता है कि माँ उसे नाविक नहीं बनने देगी
B. लेखक माँ की इच्छा के अनुसार कार्य करना चाहता है
C. माँ को बुरा लग गया है
D. लेखक माँ के संवेगों का ध्यान रखता है

140. कविता में पुनरुक्त शब्द-युग्म आए हैं–
A. ऊँची-ऊँची
B. दूर-दूर, ऊँची-ऊँची
C. गाय-बैल
D. दूर-दूर

141. 'तैरकर जाते हैं उस पार' पंक्ति में 'तैरकर' शब्द को पहले रखा गया है क्योंकि–
A. कविता में क्रिया शब्द पहले आते हैं
B. लेखक तैरने पर बल देना चाहता है
C. लेखक तुक मिला रहा है
D. वह क्रिया शब्द है

निर्देश (प्र.सं. 142 से 150): *गद्यांश की पढ़कर निम्नलिखित प्रश्नों में* **सबसे उचित** *विकल्प चुनिए।*

क्या आपने कभी महसूस किया है कि किसी सवाल का सही उत्तर मिल जाने के बाद सिर्फ उकताहट के सिवा कुछ बाकी नहीं बचता। इसके बाद सारे रास्ते बंद से लगने लगते हैं। दूसरी ओर एक गलत जवाब उतना ही रोचक होता है जितना कोई रहस्यमय कत्ल!

मुझे इस बात पर आश्चर्य होता है कि अपने अट्ठाईस वर्षों के अध्यापन के अनुभव में मैंने गलत उत्तरों से कितना कुछ सीखा है। अपनी खुद की और अपने विद्यार्थियों, दोनों द्वारा की गई गलतियों से। अब जब भी कोई विद्यार्थी किसी प्रश्न का गलत उत्तर देता है तो मैं उससे सबसे पहले यह पूछता हूँ कि उसने ऐसा उत्तर क्या सोचकर दिया?

कला-संकाय के छात्र अक्सर यह शिकायत करते हैं कि विज्ञान-संबंधी परीक्षाएँ उतनी रोमांचक नहीं होतीं–क्योंकि उनके प्रश्नों और उत्तरों का सही-सही अनुमान लगाया जा सकता है। यदि व्यक्ति को किसी प्रश्न को हल करने का तरीका पहले से ही मालूम है तो उसके लिए कोई चुनौती नहीं बचती। यह सही है, भौतिक विज्ञान के शिक्षक बहुत कड़ी मेहनत करते हैं और सुनिश्चित करना चाहते हैं कि उनके विद्यार्थी सही उत्तर तक पहुँच पाएँ।

हालाँकि यह भी अपनी जगह सच है कि भौतिक विज्ञान के शिक्षक के लिए सबसे मजेदार स्थिति तब पैदा होती है जब विद्यार्थी एक ऐसा गलत जवाब दे जिसमें गलती होते हुए भी कुछ सोचने के लिए मजबूर कर देने की क्षमता हो। यही वह स्थिति होती है जब भौतिकी के किसी पहलू पर पकड़ बनाने की कोशिश कर रहे विद्यार्थी के दिमाग की कशमकश को समझा जा सकता है।

बहुत-से गलत जवाबों की तह में कुछ सही तथ्य और सोचने की शक्ति छुपी होती है। हो सकता है कि उत्तर देने वाला अपना तर्क सही न दे पाया हो, या शिक्षक द्वारा दी गई व्याख्या को सही प्रकार से न समझ पाया हो,

या फिर ऐसा भी हो सकता है कि जिस रूप में उसके समक्ष तथ्य प्रस्तुत किए गए उन्हीं में कोई कमी रह गई हो। हो सकता है कि भौतिक विज्ञान के सहज नियमों को समझने में ही कोई भूल हुई हो।

142. गलत जवाब को रोचक क्यों कहा गया है?
A. गलत जवाब में बेतुकी बातें होती हैं
B. गलत जवाब पर हँसने को मिलता है
C. गलत जवाब प्रश्नकर्त्ता को सोचने के लिए प्रेरित कर सकते हैं
D. गलत जवाब रोचक ही होते हैं

143. लेखक ने अपने और अपने विद्यार्थियों के गलत जवाब से क्या सीखा?
A. लोगों के सोचने के तरीके अलग-अलग होते हैं
B. गलत जवाब देने से रोमांच समाप्त हो जाता है
C. लोग गलत जवाब देकर रोमांच महसूस करते हैं
D. सवालों के सही जवाब

144. कला-संकाय के छात्रों को विज्ञान की परीक्षाएँ उतनी रोमांचक नहीं लगती थीं, क्योंकि–
A. विज्ञान की परीक्षाओं में अच्छे सवाल नहीं होते थे
B. विज्ञान की परीक्षाएँ अनुमान लगाने का अवसर नहीं देतीं क्योंकि उसके जवाब तयशुदा हैं
C. विज्ञान की परीक्षाओं में चुनौतीपूर्ण प्रश्न होते हैं
D. विज्ञान के सभी सवालों के जवाब सुनिश्चित हैं

145. अनुच्छेद के आधार पर इनमें से कौन-सा कथन **गलत** है?
A. भौतिक विज्ञान के शिक्षक सही उत्तर के लिए बहुत मेहनत करते थे
B. गलत जवाब बच्चों के दिमाग में चल रही चिंतन प्रक्रिया को उजागर करने की कोशिश करते हैं
C. गलत उत्तर से दिमाग में कशमकश होने लगती है
D. भौतिक विज्ञान के शिक्षक बच्चों से सही जवाब चाहते थे

146. गलत जवाब का क्या कारण नहीं हो सकता?
A. समझ न आना
B. व्याख्या को सही रूप में प्रस्तुत न करना
C. नियमों में कमियाँ
D. तर्क का अभाव, तथ्यों की सही उपलब्धि

147. पाठ में मुख्य रूप से यह कहा गया है कि–
A. गलत जवाब शिक्षकों को अच्छे लगते हैं
B. गलत जवाब यह बताता है कि बच्चे के दिमाग में क्या चल रहा है
C. गलत जवाब की मुख्य जिम्मेदारी बच्चे की है
D. गलत जवाब बच्चों की चिंतन-प्रक्रिया को कुंद कर देते हैं

148. 'विज्ञान' में 'इक' प्रत्यय लगाने से शब्द बनेगा–
A. वैज्ञानिक B. वेज्ञानिक
C. विज्ञानीक D. विज्ञानिक

149. परीक्षा, प्रश्न, गलती शब्द के बहुवचन रूप हैं–
A. परीक्षाओं, प्रश्नों, गलतियों B. परीक्षायें, प्रश्न, गलतियों
C. परीक्षाएँ, प्रश्न, गलतियाँ D. परीक्षाएँ, प्रश्नों, गलतियाँ

150. अपनी खुद की और अपने विद्यार्थियों .... वाक्य में रेखांकित सर्वनाम है–
A. संबंधवाचक सर्वनाम
B. निजवाचक सर्वनाम
C. पुरुषवाचक सर्वनाम
D. अनिश्चयवाचक सर्वनाम

Answers

1	2	3	4	5	6	7	8	9	10
D	C	C	A	D	D	C	D	D	D
11	**12**	**13**	**14**	**15**	**16**	**17**	**18**	**19**	**20**
C	A	C	B	A	B	A	A	D	D
21	**22**	**23**	**24**	**25**	**26**	**27**	**28**	**29**	**30**
B	A	A	D	A	B	D	C	B	B
31	**32**	**33**	**34**	**35**	**36**	**37**	**38**	**39**	**40**
C	A	A	B	B	B	D	B	C	B
41	**42**	**43**	**44**	**45**	**46**	**47**	**48**	**49**	**50**
D	C	B	C	C	D	B	B	A	D
51	**52**	**53**	**54**	**55**	**56**	**57**	**58**	**59**	**60**
C	C	B	D	B	D	C	B	A	B
61	**62**	**63**	**64**	**65**	**66**	**67**	**68**	**69**	**70**
D	B	C	A	B	C	A	D	C	A
71	**72**	**73**	**74**	**75**	**76**	**77**	**78**	**79**	**80**
D	B	C	A	B	D	A	D	C	A
81	**82**	**83**	**84**	**85**	**86**	**87**	**88**	**89**	**90**
C	D	C	B	B	C	D	B	C	B

91	92	93	94	95	96	97	98	99	100
A	B	C	A	A	B	D	B	C	A
101	102	103	104	105	106	107	108	109	110
B	D	A	B	C	D	C	B	A	D
111	112	113	114	115	116	117	118	119	120
A	D	A	B	D	C	A	B	B	A
121	122	123	124	125	126	127	128	129	130
C	A	A	B	D	C	C	B	A	A
131	132	133	134	135	136	137	138	139	140
D	B	D	A	D	A	B	B	D	B
141	142	143	144	145	146	147	148	149	150
C	C	A	B	C	C	B	A	D	B

Some Selected Explanatory Answers

31. Sum of angles of two sectors = 80 + 140 = 220°

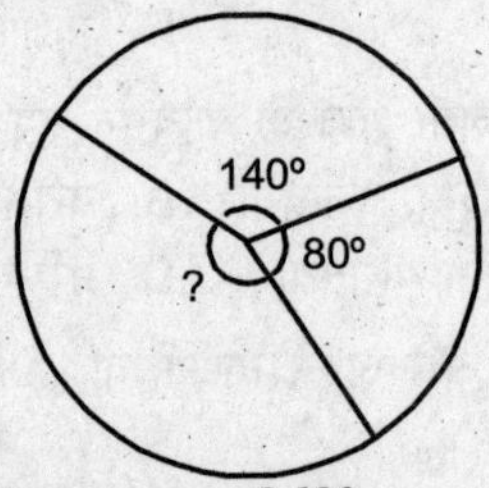

Angles of all sectors = 360°

∴ Angle of third sector = 360° – 220° = 140°.

32. Let cost of cricket bat = ₹ x

Cost of cricket ball = ₹ 36

According to question,

$$₹\ 36 \times 12\frac{1}{2} = ₹\ x$$

$$\Rightarrow \quad x = 36 \times \frac{25}{2} = ₹\ 18 \times 25$$

$$x = ₹\ 450.$$

34. In ΔABC, $\angle A + \angle B + \angle C = 180°$

$\angle 90° + 2\angle C + \angle C = 180°$

$\because \angle B = 2\angle C$

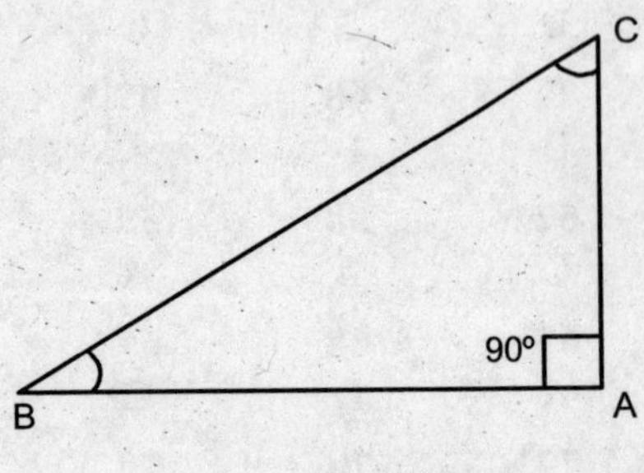

$\Rightarrow \quad 90° + 3C = 180$

$\Rightarrow \quad 3C = 180 - 90$

$= 90$

$\therefore \quad C = 30°.$

35. Age of father = 42 yrs.

Age of son = 12 years

Before 2 years ago,

Age of father = 42 – 2 = 40 years

and Age of son = 12 – 2 = 10

∴ Their ratio = 40 : 10 = 4 : 1.

36. Cloth required for 1 shirt = 2m 60 cm

∴ Cloth required for 7 shirts = 2m 60 cm × 7

= 18 m 20 cm.

37. $\sqrt{1.44 \times 6.25} = 1.2 \times 2.5 = 3.$

40.

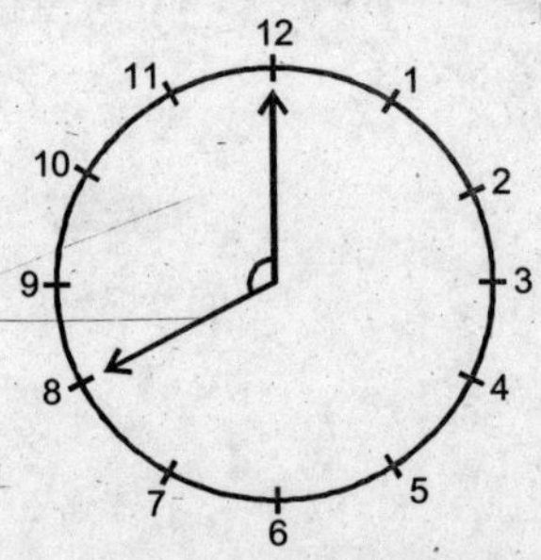

Total angle = 360°, No. of division = 12

∴ Angle of one division = $\frac{360}{12}$ = 30°

∴ Angle between two hands, when clock shows 9 O'

= 90°

∴ Angle between 8 to 9 O' clock = 30°

∴ Angle between two clocks

= 90° + 30° = 120°.

41. In a pictograph, same types of diagrams are used.

42. LCM of 16 and 20

4	16, 20
	4, 5

∴ LCM = 4 × 4 × 5 = 80

∴ Required no. of bags = 80 + 4 = 84.

43. $-\frac{9}{17}\times\left(\frac{3}{7}-\frac{4}{5}\right)$

$= -\frac{9}{17}\times\left(\frac{15-28}{35}\right)$

$= -\frac{9}{17}\times\frac{-13}{35} = \frac{117}{595}.$

44. 2 = 2 × 100 = 200 paise
∴ 200 paise : 60 paise
= 10 : 3.

45. 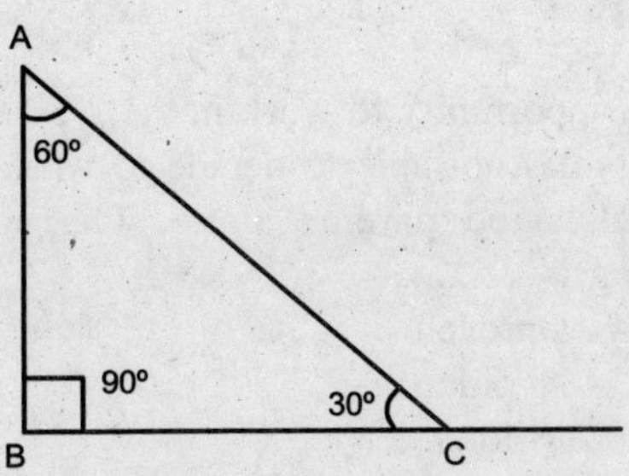

46. Largest 6-digit number = 999999
smallest 5-digit number = 10000
∴ Their difference = 999999 – 10000 = 98,9999.

47. Declared summer vocation = 24th April
No. of vocation = 49 days
∴ 24th April + 6 = 30 April
∴ May = 31 days
In June no. of days = 12 days
∴ School reopened on 12th June.

48. Let no. be x.
According to question,

$\frac{2}{3}x+\frac{1}{2}x+\frac{1}{7}x+x = 37$

$\Rightarrow \frac{28x+21x+6x+42x}{42} = 37$

$\Rightarrow \frac{97x}{42} = 37$

$\Rightarrow 97x = 1554$

$\therefore x = \frac{1554}{97} = 16\frac{2}{97}.$

49. Depreciation after 2 years

$= ₹\,50,000\times\left(1-\frac{5}{100}\right)^2$

$= ₹\,50,000\times\left(\frac{19}{20}\right)^2$

$= ₹\,50,000\times\frac{19}{20}\times\frac{19}{20}$

$= ₹\,45,125.$

50. ADB is a semicircle, 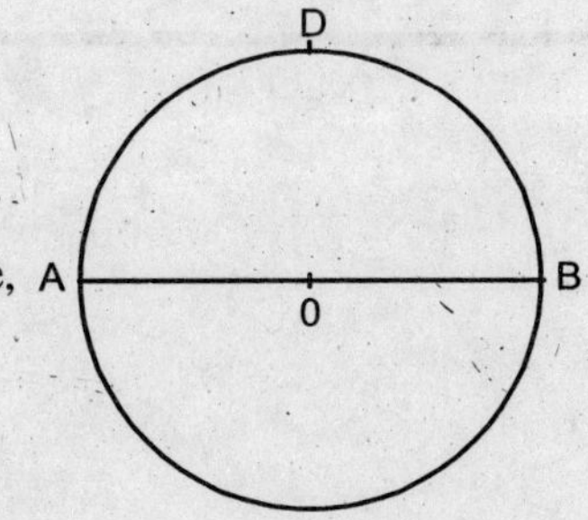

51. Given, $\frac{b}{a} = 2$ and $\frac{c}{b} = 3 \Rightarrow c = 3b,\ b = 2a.$

The value of $\frac{a+b}{b+c}$

$\Rightarrow \frac{a}{b+c} + \frac{b}{b+c} = \frac{a}{b+3b}+\frac{b}{b+3b}$

$= \frac{a}{4b}+\frac{1}{4}$

$= \frac{a}{4\times 2a}+\frac{1}{4}$

$= \frac{1}{8}+\frac{1}{4} = \frac{1+2}{8}$

$= \frac{3}{8}.$

53. $\pi r + d = 36$ [$d = 2r$]

$\frac{22}{7}r+2r = 36$

36r = 36 × 7

$r = 7$

$\therefore d = 2r = 7 \times 2 = 14$ cm.

54. We have, $0.2727 = \frac{27}{99}$

and $0.7373 = \frac{73}{99}$

$\therefore$ The value of $\frac{27}{99}+\frac{73}{99} = \frac{27+73}{99} = \frac{100}{99}$ ...

= 1.0101...

TEST PAPER–4

PART- I

Child Development and Pedagogy

1. Concept of 'developmental tasks' was first introduced by ....
A. Elizabeth Hurlock B. Sigmund Freud
C. Piaget D. Robert Havighurst

2. An educationist conducted a study on the 'influence of the leadership styles of the head of the institutions on the adjustment of their students'. The 'adjustment of students' in this study means ....
A. dependence B. independence
C. interference D. intervention

3. Modifications in the existing schema in response to new information and experience is called ....
A. assimilation B. accommadation
C. metacognition D. megaschema

4. A student of class V asked his classmate not to copy in the examination as he will be punished if caught by the invigilator. This demonstrates the following level of moral judgement of Kohlberg.
A. Preconventional
B. Conventional
C. Postconventional
D. Unconventional

5. One of the following tests assesses the intelligence accurately.
A. Culture free test
B. Culture fair test
C. Culturally oriented test
D. Culture lag test

6. Ambiguous stimuli are present in one of the following tests.
A. Projective B. Rating scales
C. Inventories D. Nonprojective

7. Development of a three-year old child is delayed due to lack of nutritious food. The factor responsible for this developmental delay is ....
A. environment
B. heredity
C. genetical
D. heredity and environment

8. Laxman got an opportunity to work in the USA which he likes most, but is not able to decide to work as he has to leave his aged parents alone. The conflict Laxman if facing is ....
A. Approach – Approach
B. Avoidance – Avoidance
C. Approach – Avoidance
D. Double approach

9. Ramu's handwriting is good. His performance is average in Mathematics. Overall, his performance is good when compared to his classmates. This example talks about this type of individual difference.
A. intra-individual difference
B. inter-individual difference
C. both intra and inter-individual difference
D. interfering individual difference

10. Daniel Goleman popularized this concept.
A. multiple intelligence
B. intelligence quotient
C. emotional intelligence
D. intelligence classification

11. Choose the most effective motivation from the following.
A. Sustained intrinsic motivation
B. Sustained extrinsic motivation
C. Sustained or unsustained intrinsic motivation
D. Sustained or unsustained extrinsic motivation

12. Following the traffic signals such as red, green and orange are related to this type of learning theory.
A. Insight
B. Discovery
C. Conditioning
D. Programmed conditioning

13. One of the following approaches is suitable for solving a problem innovatively.
A. Classical conditioning
B. Operant conditioning
C. Trial and error
D. Gestalt

14. A child learns more if he is
A. taught through textbook
B. taught through computer
C. taught through lecture method
D. taught through activity method

15. The teacher in the classroom makes effort
A. to provide experiences to students
B. to provide supportive learning environment
C. to provide opportunity to reflect
D. all of the above

16. Most children learn their native language
A. at the age of one year B. at the age of four years
C. at the age of six years D. at the age of two years

17. A child who learned to pronounce 'but' has later on pronounced 'put' in the same way. The type of transfer of learning here is ....
A. bilateral B. positive
C. negative D. zero

18. Overlearning leads to ....
A. enhancement of memory B. confusion
C. less retention D. loss of memory

19. According to Vygotsky, children speak to themselves ....
A. as they fear adults
B. for self-guidance
C. to gain self-confidence
D. as a practice before speaking to others

20. Organizing effective learning in the following schools is a challenging task.
A. Sainik schools
B. Inclusive schools
C. Play schools
D. Special schools for hearing impaired

21. In a group of boys and girls who are equal in all other aspects except gender, the learning of girls was more. Here, the learning factor is ....
A. personal B. environmental
C. material D. interest

22. One of the following leadership styles of a teacher is appropriate for creating a nonthreatening learning environment.
A. Laisez faire B. Participative
C. Charismatic D. Autocratic

23. One of the following enhances learning.
A. Learning for earning
B. Learning for rewards
C. Learning for examinations
D. Learning to learn

24. Teaching should be a planned activity for ....
A. untrained teachers B. trained teachers
C. newly recruited teachers D. all teachers

25. The objective of 'inclusive education' is ....
A. to protect the orthopaedically disabled children
B. to fulfil the needs of the mentally retarded children
C. to fulfil the needs of all special children
D. to fulfil the needs of all children

26. Formulating the specific instructional objectives and writing them properly in behavioral terms is part of this teaching phase.
A. Implementation phase B. Preactive phase
C. Interactive phase D. Postactive phase

27. Conducting of annual examinations is a/an ....
A. assessment for learning
B. comprehensive evaluation
C. assessment of learning
D. criterion referenced evaluation

28. According to the RTE Act, 2009, no child admitted in a school shall be held back in any class or expelled from school till the completion of ....
A. primary education
B. upper primary education
C. secondary education
D. elementary education

29. A teacher tried to inculcate the habit of appreciation towards nature among the students. The learning domain related here is ....
A. affective B. cognitive
C. psychomotor D. conative

30. According to NCF-2005, the association of learning with fear, discipline and stress rather than enjoyment and satisfaction ....
A. leads to disciplined learning
B. is detrimental to learning
C. keeps students alert during the process of learning
D. makes them face any stressful situation

PART- II

Mathematics

31. The value of $4 - (7 - 6 \div 2)$ is ....
A. 8 B. 2
C. $\frac{7}{2}$ D. 0

32. Two pipes can fill a water tub in 5 minutes and 7 minutes respectively. A third pipe can empty it in 3 minutes. If all three pipes are kept open simultaneously, then the part of the tub that can be filled in one minute is ....

A. $\frac{12}{35}$ B. $\frac{10}{21}$

C. $\frac{41}{105}$ D. $\frac{1}{105}$

33. 80 apples are distributed among A, B and C in the ratio 2 : x : 4. If both A and C together got 60 apples, then the value of x is ....

A. 4 B. 1
C. 2 D. 3

34. The average of the first 5 consecutive even numbers and the first 3 consecutive prime numbers is ....

A. 4 B. 4.75
C. 3.7 D. 5

35. The number of axes of symmetry of an equilateral triangle are ....

A. 4 B. 2
C. 3 D. 1

36. In a pie-diagram, different values are represented by ....

A. rectangles B. squares
C. circles D. sectors

37. One of the following pairs is a co-prime.

A. 14, 9 B. 9, 12
C. 27, 21 D. 14, 16

38. If $\left(\frac{5}{2}\right)^2 \times \left(\frac{5}{2}\right)^{a+5} = \left(\frac{2}{5}\right)^{-8}$; then the value of 'a' is ....

A. 8 B. −15
C. −1 D. 1

39. A vehicle travels 14 kms in 25 minutes. If its speed remains the same, then the distance travelled in 5 hours is (in kms.) ....

A. 160 B. 168
C. 537 D. 540

40. The length, breadth and height of a room is 8 m; 6 m and 5 m respectively. Then the total area of four walls is (in sq.m.) ....

A. 120 B. 240
C. 140 D. 280

41. If the angles of a triangle are in the ratio 1 : 2 : 7; then the triangle is ....

A. an acute angled triangle
B. an obtuse angled triangle
C. a right angled triangle
D. an equilateral triangle

42. If a bargraph is drawn to 1 cm = 10 units, then the length of the bar representing a quantity of 52 units is (in cms) ....

A. 5.2 B. 0.25
C. 2.5 D. 0.52

43. The least number that leaves the remainders 5, 7 and 18 when divided by 8, 10 and 21 respectively is ....

A. 840 B. 837
C. 873 D. 804

44. If $1-\frac{4}{x}+\frac{4}{x^2}=0$, then the value of $\frac{2}{x}$ is ....

A. −1 B. 0
C. 1 D. $\frac{1}{2}$

45. The car parking charges are given as :

1. ₹ 60 for 4 hours 2. ₹ 100 for 8 hours
3. ₹ 260 for 24 hours 4. ₹ 180 for 12 hours

Which one of the following pairs is in proportion?

A. 1 and 2 B. 1 and 3
C. 2 and 3 D. 1 and 4

46. Bangalore Express started at 19.00 hours from Kachiguda and reached Bangalore at 07.15 hours on the next day. Then the time taken for the journey is ....

A. 12 hours and 15 minutes
B. 11 hours and 15 minutes
C. 10 hours and 15 minutes
D. 13 hours and 15 minutes

47. The base of a cylinder is ....

A. parabolic B. elliptical
C. circular D. semicircular

48. If $(4x)^3 = 4^{3^3}$, then the value of 'x' is ....

A. 4^6 B. 4^8
C. 4^3 D. 4^{24}

49. If $\frac{100}{99}$ is written as a repeating and non-terminating decimal fraction, then its periodicity is ....

A. 3 B. 2
C. 10 D. 1

50. A man buys a scooter for ₹ 4,700 and spends ₹ 800 on its repairs. If he sells the scooter for ₹ 5,800, then his gain percent is ....

A. $4\frac{4}{7}$ B. $5\frac{5}{11}$
C. 10 D. 12

51. If the volume of a cube is 1,728 cu.cms., then its side (in cms) is ....

A. 14 B. 12
C. 13 D. 16

52. The value of $3.\bar{6}-0.\bar{8}$ is ....

A. $2.\bar{8}$ B. $2.\bar{6}$
C. $2.\bar{5}$ D. $2.\bar{7}$

53. The value of $\frac{39}{26} \div \frac{13}{52} + \frac{9}{5}$ is ....

A. $\frac{29}{25}$ B. $\frac{39}{5}$

C. $\frac{54}{5}$ D. $\frac{5}{54}$

54. If two sides of a triangle are 8 cm and 11 cm, then its possible third side is (in cms) ....

A. 4 B. –2

C. 3 D. 1

55. The mathematician who first declared that the approximate value of the constant ratio between the circumference and diameter of a circle is 3.1416 is ....

A. Varahamihir

B. Bhaskaracharya

C. Aryabhatta

D. Srinivasa Ramanujan

56. "Student shows fractions on a number line". This specification relates to the objective of ....

A. knowledge B. understanding

C. application D. skill

57. A person takes a loan of ₹ 10,000 from a bank at 12% rate of interest to purchase a motorcycle. If he wants to repay the loan after 3 years. how much amount has he to pay? The method to be adopted to teach this problem is the ....

A. deductive method

B. analysis–synthesis method

C. problem solving method

D. inductive method

58. The use of domino cards in the Mathematics kit is that students can ....

A. write numbers

B. do multiplication

C. draw parallel lines

D. do addition and subtraction

59. The type of questions suitable to test definitions and properties in Mathematics is...........

A. objective type B. short answer type

C. essay type D. very short answer type

60. The school Mathematics club facilitates more for........

A. the teacher to improve his professional competency

B. the preparation of various school records

C. the teacher to complete the syllabus in extra hours

D. the students to clarify their doubts in Mathematics

PART- III

Environmental Studies

61. Locate the true statements with respect to a 'hinge joint'.

1. It allows the forearm to bend forward only
2. It allows the forearm to bend backward only
3. It allows the knee to bend backward only
4. It allows the knee to bend forward only

A. 2, 3 B. 1, 3

C. 4, 3 D. 2, 4

62. Identify the mismatch

A. Incisors – biting and cutting

B. Canines – grinding

C. Premolars – chewing

D. Molars – tearing

A. 1, 3 B. 3, 4

C. 2, 3 D. 2, 4

63. Number of umpiring officers in a Kabaddi game is ....

A. 2 B. 4

C. 6 D. 8

64. Identify the correct statements related to 'cross-pollination'.

1. Occurs only in unisexual flowers
2. The pollen grains of the flower can reach the ovule of the same flower
3. Needs the help of pollinating agents
4. Seeds produced are often more healthy than the seeds produced by self-pollination

A. 1, 4 B. 2, 3

C. 1, 2 D. 3, 4

65. In the life history of a frog, the hormone that initiates the process of metamorphosis is, ...

A. Adrenaline

B. Aldosterone

C. Cortisol

D. Thyroxin

66. While running, the heartbeat speeds up. The nervous system responsible for this is the ....

A. central nervous system

B. sympathetic nervous system

C. peripheral nervous system

D. parasympathetic nervous system

67. To control rats, one should add this chemical to their bait.

A. Zinc phosphide

B. 2, 4-dichlorophenoxy acetic acid

C. Naphthalene acetic acid

D. Indole butyric acid

68. A doctor advised a patient to take citrus fruits regularly because the patient is suffering from ....
A. red rashes on the body
B. crooked legs
C. swelling and bleeding of gums
D. cough with sputum

69. In the process of preparation of cement, the products formed when pulverized limestone and clay are heated are ....
A. calcium silicates and calcium aluminates
B. calcium silicates and calcium bicarbonate
C. ferrous silicates and ferrous aluminates
D. ferrous carbonates and ferrous bicarbonates

70. It is found that in a particular area, the proportion of atmospheric nitrogen is found less. Identify the reason.
A. More animals are present
B. Ground water is more
C. Plants bearing root nodules are present abundantly
D. Decomposers are less

71. The diseases communicable by air are ....
A. diphtheria, typhoid B. rubella, flu
C. filaria, tuberculosis D. conjunctivitis, malaria

72. Hard water does not give a lather with soap because ....
A. it is highly coloured
B. it contains suspended impurities
C. it contains sodium chloride
D. it contains carbonates of calcium and magnesium

73. The minimum age limit for election to the post of a sarpanch, grama panchayat member, mandal parishad territorial constituency (MPTC), and member of zilla parishad territorial constituency (ZPTC) is ....
A. 18 years for grama sarpanch and MPTC member and 21 years for ZPTC member
B. 18 years for all grama sarpanch, MPTC and ZPTC members
C. 18 years for grama sarpanch, 21 years for MPTC and ZPTC members
D. 21 years for all grama sarpanch, MPTC and ZPTC members

74. Ramaiah has a son and a daughter. The daughter has a daughter. The relationship between Ramaiah's son and daughter's daughter is ....
A. uncle – niece
B. grandfather – granddaughter
C. brother-in-law – sister-in-law
D. brother – sister

75. The area of Andhra Pradesh is ....
A. 2,57,045 sq. kms.
B. 2,77,504 sq. kms.
C. 2,75,045 sq. kms.
D. 2,70,455 sq. kms.

76. In the Braille script, the English letter, "I" can be identified with which of these raised round marks?
A. Left middle and right top raised round marks
B. Left top and right middle raised round marks
C. Left top and right top raised round marks
D. Raised round marks on the left top and left bottom

77. The shortest and longest days in a year are ....
A. 21st March and 22nd December
B. 21st June and 23rd September
C. 23rd September and 21st June
D. 22nd December and 21st June

78. For the reason, the Krishna river flows towards the East.
A. Malwa plateau is slightly slanted towards the East.
B. Malwa plateau is slightly slanted towards the South.
C. Deccan plateau is slightly slanted towards the East.
D. Deccan plateau is slightly slanted towards the West.

79. In this year, our national anthem, 'Jana Gana Mana' was first sung.
A. 1905 B. 1911
C. 1947 D. 1950

80. The statement that relates to migration is ....
A. Naresh went to Dubai in 2005 for employment and settled there.
B. Ramaiah's family goes to district headquarters for labour work in the winter season and returns to his village at the outbreak of the monsoon.
C. Raheem went to America to study higher education and returned to India after 2 years.
D. Budege Jangam caste people of Cherlapalli leave the village before Sankranti festival and return to their village in the month of June.

81. Read the following statements:
1. Ghat roads are laid on hills.
2. Metal roads save fuel.
3. Journey is comfortable on tar roads.
4. Laying cement roads is inexpensive.
Identify the incorrect statements.
A. 1, 3 B. 2, 4
C. 2, 3 D. 1, 4

82. Dhaka, the capital of Bangladesh, is located on 90° East longitude. When the time is 6.00 am in Dhaka, the Indian standard time and Greenwich mean time are respectively ....
A. 6.30 am; 3.00 am
B. 6.00 am; 2.00 am
C. 5.00 am; 1.00 am
D. 5.30 am; 12.00 midnight

83. These are fundamental duties and fundamental rights respectively.
A. Protect the environment; a citizen can live in any part of the country
B. Seeking justice through courts of law; a citizen can receive education

C. Protecting national integration; paying the taxes on time
D. A citizen can follow any religion; paying the taxes on time

84. The earliest Europeans who came to India for spices were ....
A. Britishers only
B. Portuguese and Romans
C. Portuguese only
D. Britishers and Greeks

85. The concept of environmental studies is ....
A. direction oriented
B. action oriented
C. knowledge oriented
D. thought oriented

86. The teaching of environmental studies at the primary level aims at making a student to become a prudent consumer. The principle involved in it is the ....
A. principle of child centeredness
B. principle of conservation
C. principle of elasticity
D. principle of activity centeredness

87. The topics like 'changes in the seasons and climates,measurement of temperature and pressure of the atmosphere' are best examples for correlating between these subjects.
A. Geography and the atmosphere
B. Humidity and the atmosphere
C. Science and Geography
D. Geography and the environment

88. The main purpose of learning experiences is to...........
A. build a rapport between the student and the content
B. build a rapport between the student and the teacher
C. build a rapport between the student and the classroom
D. build a rapport between the student and the local environment

89. The preparation of a standardized test is based on.........
A. objective based teaching
B. content based teaching
C. type of the teaching-learning material used
D. method of teaching adopted

90. Suspended judgement is a characteristic of a person who possesses.............
A. future vision
B. reflexive thinking
C. scientific attitude
D. reasoning and judging ability

PART- IV

Language-I : English

91. Raghu, a friendly and lovely boy, plays piano very well. Identify the adjectives in the above sentence.
A. lovely, well
B. friendly, lovely, well
C. friendly, lovely
D. friendly, very, well

92. Match the phrases given on the left with the 'sea' words given on the right. Then choose the correct answer.

1. the land at the bottom of the sea	(*a*) seaweed
2. land along the edge of the sea	(*b*) seafood
3. plants growing in the sea	(*c*) seabed
4. fish and fish-like animals from	(*d*) seashore

A. 1 – (*d*); 2 – (*a*); 3 – (*c*); 4 – (*b*).
B. 1 – (*c*); 2 – (*a*); 3 – (*b*); 4 – (*d*).
C. 1 – (*b*); 2 – (*c*); 3 – (*a*); 4 – (*d*).
D. 1 – (*c*); 2 – (*d*); 3 – (*a*); 4 – (*b*).

93. Identify the word that occurs only in the plural.
A. glasses
B. clothes
C. potatoes
D. tools

94. What would you say in a hotel when you have to wake up early for an important meeting?
A. Could I have a call at 6 a.m., please?
B. Can I ask you to call me at 6 a.m., please?
C. May I have a call at 6 a.m.?
D. Shall I have a call at 6 a.m.?

95. Identify the part of the sentence that has an error. The parts are labelled as (*a*), (*b*), (*c*) and (*d*).
Would you (*a*)/follow me (*b*)/ wherever (*c*)/ I would go?(*d*).
A. (*a*)
B. (*b*)
C. (*c*)
D. (*d*)

96. Identify the set of words containing only insects.
A. bee, ant, hare, fly
B. ant, bee, moped, butterfly
C. ant, bee, ladybird, butterfly
D. bee, butterfly, owl, ant

97. There is a word in the sentence whose letters, when rearranged, will give you the name of a part of your body. Identify that word.
'I think all this rough play on the hockey field will mar the image of the game!'
A. image
B. mar
C. game
D. rough

98. I don't like those bangles; ...., they are too expensive. Identify the correct option to fill in the blank.
A. besides
B. beside
C. apart from
D. in addition

99. He is arriving .... the 3.15 train.
Choose the correct preposition to fill in the blank.
A. in B. on
C. with D. to

100. A : I don't like cucumbers.
B : ....
Identify the grammatically correct response of 'B'.
A. Neither I do B. I don't either
C. I do too D. I nor do

101. 'How do people learn languages?' The passive form of the above sentence is ....
A. How are languages learnt by people?
B. How were languages learnt?
C. Languages are learnt by people how?
D. How are languages learnt?

102. Tomorrow, there is a meeting in our school. Come early, ...?
Choose the question tag to complete the sentence
A. do you B. don't you
C. will you D. won't you

103. Salim said, "Prem is ill."
The reported form of the above sentence is ....
A. Salim said that Prem was ill
B. Salim told that Prem was ill
C. Salim said me that Prem was ill
D. Salim said me Prem was ill

104. Two people were injured in an accident and they were taken to ....
Identify the correct option to complete the sentence.
A. a hospital B. an hospital
C. the hospital D. hospital

105. I go out less than I used to.
The above sentence can also be written without changing the meaning as ....
A. I go out as many times as I used to
B. I don't go out as much as I used to
C. I used to go out as much as I do now
D. I go out at least as much as I used to

106. Tom and Bill are .... friends.
Choose the correct option to fill in the blank.
A. not longer B. no more
C. no longer D. not any much

107. Identify the correct order of the parts of the sentences (1, 2, 3, 4 and 5) given below.
1. children living in villages
2. in inner city areas
3. than do their counterparts
4. research shows that
5. watch more television
A. 1, 5, 2, 4, 3 B. 1, 5, 3, 4, 2
C. 4, 1, 5, 3, 2 D. 4, 1, 3, 5, 2

108. The letter 'o' in comic is pronounced as the 'o' in ....
A. college B. computer
C. cork D. cold

109. The horse is limping. It must have hurt its ....
Choose the correct option to complete the sentence.
A. mane B. hoof
C. paw D. claws

110. I .... him for his bravery and honesty.
Identify the appropriate word to fill in the blank.
A. condemn B. admire
C. content D. plead

Directions (Qs. 111 to 114) : *Read the following passage and answer the questions given below:*

The proverb, 'Cowards die many times before their death' is extracted from Shakespeare's 'Julius Caesar'. The complete form of this proverb is 'Cowards die many times before their death; the valiant never taste of death but once.'

Caesar utters this maxim when his wife Calpurnia pleads with him not to go to the Senate on that day as she fears that he may die. Caesar declares that only cowards give in to fear. One should not lose heart when one encounters difficult situations in life. In such situations, one should gather all the forces at one's command and try to overcome them. If a person gives up in the face of adverse conditions, he cannot progress in life, as life is not a bed of roses. He or she should face the problems squarely and find ways to overcome them, as that is the only way to become successful in life.

111. The proverb, 'cowards die many times before their death' is uttered by ....
A. Shakespeare B. Julius Caesar
C. Calpurnia D. The valiant person

112. Caesar's wife requests him ....
A. not to go to the Senate
B. go to the Senate
C. not to die
D. not to lose heart

113. Caesar says, when one encounters difficult situations, ...
Identify the latter part of the above sentence.
A. he should give up hope
B. he should leave it to God
C. he should seek someone's help
D. he should not give up hope

114. One should face problems squarely.
Here 'squarely' means ....
A. surely B. bravely
C. cleverly D. patiently

115. A student passes your test on spoken English but cannot speak English outside the school. Then your test is not ....
A. valid B. reliable
C. practicable D. scorable

116. The discourse-oriented pedagogy is more effective than the other methods because ....

A. it encourages a learner's autonomy
B. it discourages a learner's inquiry
C. it follows the behaviorist theory of learning
D. it emphasizes teaching rather than learning

117. The number of syllables in the word, 'inter-nationalization' is ....

A. six B. nine
C. seven D. eight

118. The function-based and task-centred approach is the ....

A. structural approach
B. S-O-S approach
C. communicative approach
D. situational approach

119. The activity of 'learners giving directions to each other's home as if they were going to visit each other's is an example of ....

A. dramatization B. role-play
C. simulation D. situation drill

120. Identify the set of capital letters that have similar strokes/patterns.

A. IMH B. EFH
C. AEM D. THV

PART- V

भाषा-II : हिन्दी

निर्देशः *निम्नलिखित प्रश्नों के उत्तर देने के लिए **सबसे उचित** विकल्प चुनिए।*

121. भाषा-शिक्षण का संप्रेषणपरक उपागम

A. संदर्भ में भाषा-प्रयोग की कुशलता पर बल देता है
B. मातृभाषा-प्रयोग का निषेध करता है
C. 'बोलना' कौशल पर बल देता है
D. भाषिक संरचनाओं की जानकारी पर बल देता है

122. भाषा-शिक्षण के संदर्भ में कौन-सा कथन सही ***नहीं*** है?

A. भाषा-शिक्षण में केवल भाषायी शुद्धता पर ही अधिक बल रहता है
B. भाषा सीखने में अन्य विषयों का अध्ययन-अध्यापन सहायक होता है
C. समृद्ध भाषा-परिवेश भाषा अर्जित करने में सहायक होता है
D. भाषा-अर्जन और भाषा-अधिगम में अंतर होता है

123. एल.एस. वाइगोत्स्की के अनुसार

A. चिंतन भाषा को निर्धारित करता है
B. भाषा एवं चिंतन एक-दूसरे से स्वतंत्र रूप से विकसित होते हैं
C. भाषा एक अर्जित योग्यता है
D. भाषा चिंतन को निर्धारित करती है

124. लोकगीतों को भाषा की कक्षाओं में स्थान दिया जाना चाहिए, क्योंकि

A. लोकगीत गाए जा सकते हैं
B. केवल लोकगीतों के माध्यम से पारंपरिक मूल्यों की शिक्षा दी जा सकती है
C. इससे बच्चे संस्कृतिगत विशेषताओं से परिचित होते हैं
D. लोकगीतों को बढ़ावा देना भाषा-शिक्षण का मुख्य उद्देश्य है

125. एक बहुसांस्कृतिक पृष्ठभूमि वाली कक्षा में भाषा सीखने के बारे में कौन-सा विचार उचित है?

A. भाषा सिखाने के लिए व्याकरणिक नियमों का और अधिकाधिक प्रयोग होना चाहिए
B. भाषा परिवेश का निर्माण किया जाए ताकि भाषा-अर्जन की सहज स्थिति बन सके
C. बच्चों में भाषा सीखने की क्षमता बलपूर्वक विकसित करनी होती है
D. अधिकाधिक पुस्तकों का निर्माण किया जाए

126. 'मैंने चाट खाई और फिर मैंने हँसी।' शर्मिला का यह भाषा-प्रयोग मुख्यतः किस ओर संकेत करता है?

A. नियमों का अति सामान्यीकरण
B. भाषा-प्रयोग में असावधानी
C. भाषा की समझ न होना
D. व्याकरणिक नियमों की जानकारी न होना

127. लिखित कार्य की जाँच में बच्चों की सहायता लेने से

A. बच्चे ज्यादा गलतियाँ ढूँढना सीख जाते हैं
B. बच्चों को दूसरों की हस्तलिखित सामग्री को पढ़ने का अवसर और अवलोकन-क्षमता के विकास का अवसर मिलता है
C. बच्चे दूसरों के विचारों से परिचित होते हैं
D. केवल पठन-कौशल का अभ्यास होता है

128. सुलेखा ने पाठ को पढ़ते हुए 'जीवन' को 'जिंदगी' पढ़ा। यह इस ओर संकेत करता है कि

A. उसे केवल पठन-अभ्यास की बहुत आवश्यकता है
B. सुलेखा ध्यान से नहीं पढ़ती
C. वह अक्षर-पहचान की बजाय अर्थ को समझते हुए पढ़ रही है
D. उसे अक्षरों की पहचान में भ्रम हो जाता है

129. पाठ पढ़कर बच्चों से प्रश्न बनवाने से

A. शिक्षक को यह जानने का अवसर मिलता है कि बच्चों ने पाठ को कितनी गहराई से समझा है
B. कक्षा-कार्य की अच्छी युक्ति पूरी होती है
C. प्रश्न बनाने की आदत का विकास होता है
D. इस बात का पता चलता है कि बच्चे प्रश्नवाचक शब्दों से परिचित हैं या नहीं

130. भाषा सीखने में जो त्रुटियाँ होती हैं
A. उन्हें जल्दी से दूर किया जाना चाहिए
B. वे बच्चों की त्रुटियों की ओर संकेत करती हैं
C. वे सीखने की प्रक्रिया का स्वाभाविक हिस्सा होती हैं जो समय के साथ दूर होने लगती हैं
D. उन्हें कठोरता से लेना चाहिए

131. 'पढ़ना' कौशल में सबसे ज्यादा महत्त्वपूर्ण है
A. केवल अक्षर पहचान
B. तेज गति से पढ़ना
C. संदर्भानुसार अर्थ ग्रहण करना
D. शब्दों-वाक्यों को शुद्ध रूप से उच्चरित करना

132. किसी भाषा कक्षा में कहानी-कथन की आवश्यकता के संदर्भ में कौन-सा तर्क उचित ***नहीं*** है?
A. सभी बच्चों की क्षमता को ध्यान में रखते हुए यह उचित नहीं है।
B. बच्चों को शब्द-भंडार के विकास के अवसर प्राप्त होते हैं।
C. सभी बच्चों की क्षमता-अनुसार कल्पना-शक्ति का विकास होता है।
D. सभी बच्चों को भाषा सुनने का परिवेश मिलता है।

133. 'बच्चे भाषा सीखने की क्षमता के साथ पैदा होते हैं।' मुख्यतः यह किसका विचार है?
A. ईवान पैवलोव B. नॉओम चॉम्स्की
C. जीन पियाजे D. एल.एस. वाइगोत्स्की

134. स्वलीन विकार (ऑटिस्टिक डिस्ऑर्डर) में बच्चा
A. सामाजिक अंतःक्रिया और संप्रेषण में कठिनाई का अनुभव करता है
B. अक्सर खाने से मना कर देता है
C. अपने ही कार्यों में लीन रहता है
D. अपने हाथ-पैर हिलाने में कठिनाई का अनुभव करता है

135. भाषा-शिक्षण की कौन-सी विधि मातृभाषा को मध्यस्थ बनाए बिना दूसरी भाषा को सिखाने पर बल देती है?
A. अनुवाद विधि
B. व्याकरण एवं अनुवाद विधि
C. प्रत्यक्ष विधि
D. द्विभाषीय विधि

निर्देशः *गद्यांश को पढ़कर निम्नलिखित प्रश्नों (प्र.सं. 136 से 144) में सबसे उचित विकल्प चुनिए।*

मैं जिस घर में रहती थी, वहाँ मेरी आदत बहुत सवेरे उठने की थी। एक दिन उतने सवेरे एक छोटा बच्चा, जो शायद डेढ़ साल से कम का होगा, मेरे कमरे में आया। मैंने सोचा कि वह शायद भूखा होगा और उससे पूछा कि वह कुछ खाना चाहता है? उसने उत्तर दिया, "कीड़े।" मैंने आश्चर्य से कहा, "कीड़े?" जब उसने देखा कि मेरी समझ में उसकी बात नहीं आ रही है तो मेरी सहायता के लिए उसने एक शब्द और जोड़ा, "अंडा।" मैंने अपने मन में सोचा कि इतने सवेरे कुछ पीना चाहता है क्या? यह आखिर कहना क्या चाह रहा है? उसने फिर कहा, 'नीना, अंडे, कीड़े।' अब मुझे पूरी बात समझ में आ गई। एक दिन पहले, उसकी बहन नीना कागज पर अंडे की शक्ल बनाकर उसमें रंग भर रही थी। इस बच्चे की इच्छा थी कि वह भी रंग भरे, पर नीना ने उसे गुस्से में आकर भगा दिया। उसने नीना का विरोध नहीं किया और बड़े धैर्य और लगन के साथ मौके का इंतजार करता रहा। मैंने उसे क्रेयॉन का रंग दे दिया और उसका चेहरा खुशी से दमक उठा। उससे अंडे के आकार की रेखा नहीं खींची गई, तो मैंने उसके लिए चित्र बना दिया। फिर उसने अपनी टेढ़ी-मेढ़ी लकीरों से उसमें रंग भरना शुरू कर दिया। उसकी बहन सीधी रेखाओं में रंग भरती थी, और उसने कीड़े की तरह लहदार रेखाओं में रंग भरा।

—मारिया मांटेसरी

136. बच्चे ने 'कीड़े' के बाद 'अंडा', 'नीना अंडे कीड़े' शब्दों का प्रयोग किया, क्योंकि
A. वह अंडा बनाना चाहता था
B. वह कागज और क्रेयॉन चाहता था
C. वह जान गया था कि लेखिका उसकी बात समझ नहीं पाई है
D. वह रंग भरने की बात बताना चाहता था

137. अनुच्छेद से पता चलता है कि डेढ़ साल के बच्चे
A. संप्रेषण के लिए कथ्य के मुख्य शब्दों का प्रयोग करते हैं
B. रंग चाहते हैं
C. तसवीरें चाहते हैं
D. कागज चाहते हैं

138. टेढ़ी-मेढ़ी लकीरों को 'कीड़े' कहना इस ओर संकेत करता है कि बच्चा
A. लकीरों को कीड़ा मानता है
B. टेढ़ी-मेढ़ी लकीरें ही बना सकता है
C. दो अलग चीजों में आकृति के आधार पर समानता खोज लेता है
D. हर हालत में अपनी बात कह देता है

139. डेढ़ साल का बच्चा 'अंडा' नहीं बना पाया। यह बात किस ओर संकेत करती है?
A. बच्चे ने अंडा देखा नहीं इसलिए वह अंडा नहीं बना पाया
B. उसका अभी अपने हस्त संचालन की गति और दिशा पर नियंत्रण नहीं हो पाया है
C. बच्चा अंडा नहीं बना सकता
D. बच्चा चित्र बनाने में सक्षम नहीं है

140. रेखाओं को बच्चे ने 'कीड़े' कहा। बच्चा वृत्त को क्या कह सकता है?
A. पेड़ B. छतरी
C. चम्मच D. चूड़ी

141. 'उतने सवेरे' पद में 'उतने' शब्द किस ओर संकेत करता है?
A. सवेरे का वह समय जितने बजे लेखिका को उठने की आदत है
B. बहुत जल्दी
C. सवेरे की ओर
D. बहुत सवेरे की ओर

142. अनुच्छेद में से मिश्रित वाक्य का उदाहरण है
A. अब मुझे पूरी बात समझ में आ गई।
B. मैंने आश्चर्य से कहा, "कीड़े?"
C. उसने नीना का विरोध नहीं किया और बड़े धैर्य और लगन के साथ मौके का इंतजार करता रहा।
D. यह आखिर कहना क्या चाह रहा है?

143. 'उसका चेहरा खुशी से दमक उठा।' वाक्य में रेखांकित अंश के स्थान पर कौन-सा मुहावरा आएगा?
A. खुशी से फूला न समाया
B. गद्-गद् हो गया
C. खिल उठा
D. खुश हो गया

144. 'इतने सवेरे कुछ पीना चाहता है क्या?' वाक्य में 'कुछ' शब्द है
A. अनिश्चयवाचक सर्वनाम
B. निश्चयवाचक सर्वनाम
C. अनिश्चय संख्यावाचक विशेषण
D. प्रश्नवाचक सर्वनाम

निर्देशः *कविता की पंक्तियाँ पढ़कर निम्नलिखित प्रश्नों (प्र.सं. 145 से 150) में* ***सबसे उचित*** विकल्प चुनिए।

जग-जीवन में जो चिर महान,
सौंदर्य पूर्ण औ सत्यप्राण,
मैं उसका प्रेमी बनूँ नाथ!
जिससे मानव-हित हो समान!
जिससे जीवन में मिले शक्ति
छूटे भय-संशय, अंध-भक्ति,
मैं वह प्रकाश बन सकूँ नाथ!
मिल जावे जिसमें अखिल व्यक्ति!

—सुमित्रानंदन पंत

145. कवि ने 'चिर महान' किसे कहा है?
A. जो सत्य और सुंदर से संपूर्ण हो
B. शक्ति को
C. मानव को
D. ईश्वर को

146. कवि कैसा प्रकाश बनना चाहता है?
A. जो जीने की शक्ति देता है
B. जिसमें मनुष्य सभी भेदभाव भुलाकर एक हो जाते हैं
C. जिससे सब तरफ उजाला हो जाए
D. अंधकार दूर हो जाए

147. कवि ने 'अखिल व्यक्ति' का प्रयोग क्यों किया है?
A. कवि भारत के व्यक्तियों की ओर संकेत करना चाहता है
B. कवि सांसारिक बात करना चाहता है
C. कवि समस्त विश्व के व्यक्तियों की बात करना चाहता है
D. कवि अमीर लोगों की बात करना चाहता है

148. कविता के किस अंश में तर्कहीन आस्था का उल्लेख हुआ है?
A. मैं वह प्रकाश बन सकूँ, नाथ!
B. जिससे मानव-हित हो समान!
C. छूटे भय-संशय, अंध-भक्ति,
D. मिल जावें जिसमें अखिल व्यक्ति!

149. कवि ने कविता की पंक्तियों के अंत में विस्मयादिबोधक चिह्न का प्रयोग क्यों किया है?
A. इससे कविता का सौंदर्य बढ़ता है
B. पूर्ण विराम की लीक से हटने के लिए
C. कविता को तुकांत बनाने के लिए
D. कवि अपनी इच्छा प्रकट कर रहा है

150. कविता का मूल भाव क्या है?
A. विश्व-परिवार की भावना
B. सत्य की प्राप्ति
C. कल्याण
D. अमर दान की प्राप्ति

Answers

1	2	3	4	5	6	7	8	9	10
D	A	B	A OR B	A	A	A	C	C	C
11	**12**	**13**	**14**	**15**	**16**	**17**	**18**	**19**	**20**
A	C	D	D	D	B	C	A	B	B
21	**22**	**23**	**24**	**25**	**26**	**27**	**28**	**29**	**30**
A	B	D	D	D	B	C	D	A	B
31	**32**	**33**	**34**	**35**	**36**	**37**	**38**	**39**	**40**
D	D	C	D	C	D	A	D	B	C
41	**42**	**43**	**44**	**45**	**46**	**47**	**48**	**49**	**50**
B	A	B	C	D	A	C	B	B	B
51	**52**	**53**	**54**	**55**	**56**	**57**	**58**	**59**	**60**
B	D	B	A	C	D	B	A OR D	B	D
61	**62**	**63**	**64**	**65**	**66**	**67**	**68**	**69**	**70**
B	D	C	A	D	B	A	C	A	C

71	**72**	**73**	**74**	**75**	**76**	**77**	**78**	**79**	**80**
B	D	D	A	C	A	D	C	B	A
81	**82**	**83**	**84**	**85**	**86**	**87**	**88**	**89**	**90**
B	D	A	C	B	B	C	A	A	C
91	**92**	**93**	**94**	**95**	**96**	**97**	**98**	**99**	**100**
C	D	B	A	D	C	B	A	B	B
101	**102**	**103**	**104**	**105**	**106**	**107**	**108**	**109**	**110**
D	C	A	D	B	C	C	A	B	B
111	**112**	**113**	**114**	**115**	**116**	**117**	**118**	**119**	**120**
B	A	D	B	A	A	D	C	C	B
121	**122**	**123**	**124**	**125**	**126**	**127**	**128**	**129**	**130**
A	A	B	C	B	D	B	C	A	C
131	**132**	**133**	**134**	**135**	**136**	**137**	**138**	**139**	**140**
C	C	C	A	C	B	A	C	B	D
141	**142**	**143**	**144**	**145**	**146**	**147**	**148**	**149**	**150**
A	C	C	A	A	B	C	C	D	C

Some Selected Explanatory Answers

31. The value of $4 - (7 - 6 \div 2)$
$= 4 - (7 - 3)$
$= 4 - (4) = 0.$

32. In 5 minutes, first pipe can fill the complete tub

$\therefore$ In 1 minute, first tub can fill $\frac{1}{5}$th part of the tub

Similarly, in 1 minute 2nd tub can fill $\frac{1}{7}$th part of the tub and in 1 minute 3rd pipe can empty $\frac{1}{3}$rd part of the tub

sign for : + for filling the tub – for emptying of the tub

$\therefore$ Net effect in 1 minute, when all the three pipes are open,

$$= \frac{1}{5}+\frac{1}{7}-\frac{1}{3} = \frac{21+15-35}{105} = \frac{36-35}{105} = \frac{1}{105}.$$

$\therefore$ The part of tub that can be filled in one minute is $\frac{1}{105}$.

35. The lines of symmetry of an equilateral triangle is 3.

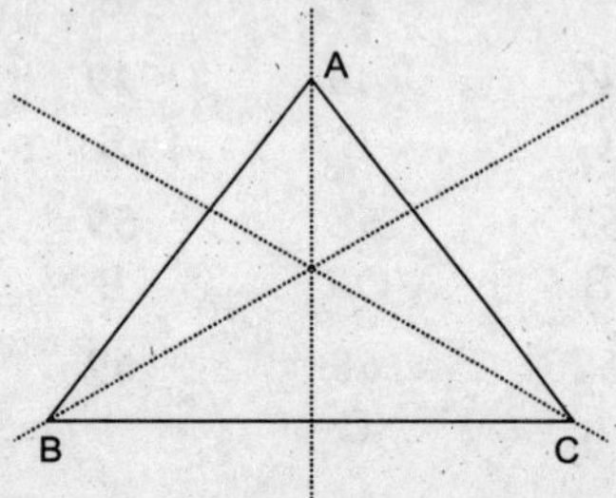

36. Pie-diagram represented by sectors.

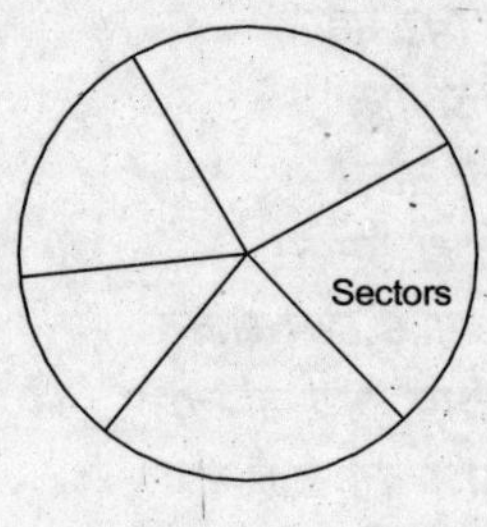

38. We have, $\left(\frac{5}{2}\right)^2 \times \left(\frac{5}{2}\right)^{a+5} = \left(\frac{5}{2}\right)^8$

$\Rightarrow \quad \left(\frac{5}{2}\right)^{2+a+5} = \left(\frac{5}{2}\right)^8$

$\Rightarrow \quad 2 + a + 5 = 8$

$\Rightarrow \quad 7 + a = 8 \Rightarrow a = 1.$

39. Distance = 14 kms

Time = 25 minutes $= \frac{25}{60} = \frac{5}{12}$ hrs.

Speed $= \frac{\text{distance}}{\text{time}} = \frac{14}{5/12} = \frac{14 \times 12}{5} = 33.6$ km/h.

$\therefore$ Distance = Speed × Time = 33.6 × 5 = 168 kms.

41. One angle of triangle be $x°$.
According to question, angles of Δs are x, $2x$ and $7x$.

$\therefore \quad x + 2x + 7x = 180$

[$\because$ Sum of all angle of triangle is 180°]

$\Rightarrow \quad 10x = 180$

$\Rightarrow \quad x = 18$

angles on, $x = 18°$, $2x = 2 \times 18 = 36°$

and $7x = 7 \times 18 = 126°$

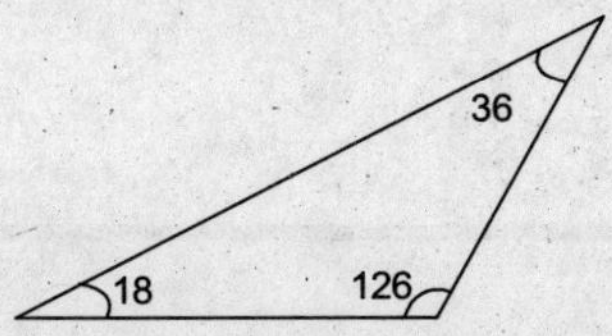

Hence, angle is an obtuse angled-triangle.

43. LCM 8, 10 and 21.

2	8, 10, 21
	4, 5, 21

$\therefore$ LCM of 8, 10 and 21 = 2 × 4 × 5 × 21 = 840.

44. $$1-\frac{4}{x}+\frac{4}{x^2} = 0$$

$$\left(1-\frac{2}{x}\right)^2 = 0$$

$$1-\frac{2}{x} = 0 \Rightarrow \frac{2}{x} = 1.$$

45. (*a*) ₹ 60 for 4 hours

$$\text{Ratio} = \frac{60}{4} = \frac{15}{1}$$

(*d*) $\frac{180}{12} = \frac{15}{1}$

(*a*), (*d*) are in proportion.

46. Here, 19:00 hours = 7:00 PM

Since Banglore express stated at 7 PM and reached at 07:15 AM

Time between 7:00 PM to 7:00 AM = 12 hours and 15 minutes more time after 12 hours

$\therefore$ Time taken for journey 12 hours 15 minutes.

47. The base of cylinder

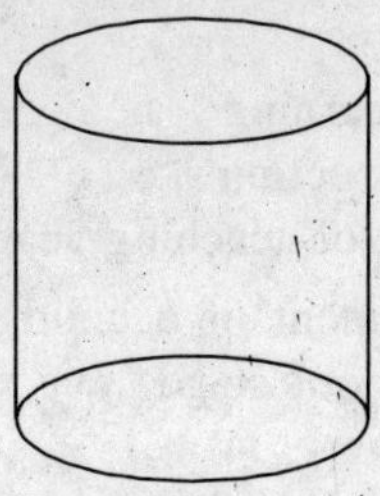

50. CP of scooter = ₹ 4,700

Money spends on repairs = ₹ 4,700 + ₹ 800 = ₹ 5,500

$\therefore$ Total CP of scooter = ₹ 5,500

SP of scooter = ₹ 5,800

$\therefore$ SP > CP

$\therefore$ gain = ₹ 5,800 – ₹ 5,500 = ₹ 300

$$\text{gain\%} = \frac{\text{gain}}{\text{CP}} \times 100$$

$$= \frac{300}{5500} \times 100 = \frac{300}{55}$$

$$= 5\frac{5}{11}\%.$$

51. Let side of cube be x.

$\therefore$ volume of cube $= x^3$

$1728 = x^3$

$\Rightarrow x = (1728)^{1/3}$

$= 12$ cm.

52. We write in vulgar fractions,

$$3.\bar{6} = 3+\frac{6}{9} \text{ and } 0.\bar{8} = \frac{8}{9}$$

$$\therefore \quad 3.\bar{6} - 0.\bar{8} = 3+\frac{6}{9}-\frac{8}{9}$$

$$= \frac{27+6-8}{9}$$

$$= \frac{25}{9} = 2.7777$$

$$= 2.\bar{7}.$$

53. $$\frac{39}{26} \div \frac{13}{52} + \frac{9}{5}$$

$$= \frac{39}{26} \times \frac{52}{13} + \frac{9}{5}$$

$$= 3 \times 2 + \frac{9}{5}$$

$$= 6 + \frac{9}{5}$$

$$= \frac{30+9}{5} = \frac{39}{5}.$$

TEST PAPER–5

PART- I

Child Development and Pedagogy

Directions :** Answer the following questions by selecting the* ***most appropriate *option:*

1. A child learns more if he is
A. taught through textbook
B. taught through computer
C. taught through lecture method
D. taught through activity method

2. The teacher in the classroom makes effort
A. To provide experiences to students
B. To provide supportive learning environment
C. To provide opportunity to reflect
D. All of the above

3. There are two main objectives of education
A. To instill subject knowledge in the children and to cause mental development of the children
B. To provide subject knowledge and prepare for examination
C. To provide subject knowledge and help in memorization
D. To provide subject knowledge and develop vocational skill

4. Most children learn their native language
A. at the age of one year
B. at the age of four years
C. at the age of six years
D. at the age of two years

5. Children of 6-11 years age group need
A. Democratic environment in the classroom
B. Autonomy in learning
C. Activity based interactive learning
D. All of the above

6. A child shows jealousy at the age of
A. 6 months
B. 12 months
C. 18 months
D. 24 months

7. Students learn in variety of ways
A. From the lecture of the teacher
B. Through experiment, discussion, asking questions, doing activities and through reflection
C. Teacher directed and controlled textbook based teaching
D. None of the above

8. Children of 6-11 years age group have following characteristics
A. Children are natural and active learners
B. Depend on teachers for learning
C. Children receive knowledge from teachers
D. Children are not interested in learning

9. Which statement about a creative child is **not** true?
A. A creative child is curious
B. A creative child is not adventurous
C. A creative child is extrovert
D. A creative child is ambitious

10. New knowledge is acquired through
A. transmission of knowledge
B. memorization
C. experience and searching new meanings
D. None of the above

11. Teaching is a process of
A. Transmitting knowledge by the teacher to the learners
B. Directing learning
C. Giving instruction
D. Facilitating of teaching learning

12. Social development of a child actually begins
A. in early school stage
B. in infancy
C. in early childhood
D. in later childhood

13. A suitable method of teaching primary class children is
A. Trial and error method
B. Imitation method
C. Lecture method
D. Play-way method

14. In India, primary education system is laying emphasis on
A. Developing understanding
B. Strengthening spiritual aspects
C. Developing critical thinking
D. Encouraging rote learning

15. Teaching becomes much more effective provided
A. Students are given autonomy and control to work on their own
B. Students learning is directed and controlled by the teacher
C. Teacher plays a central role in explaining the facts
D. Teacher directs learning

16. Learning is a process of
A. Memorizing facts
B. Memorizing the text material
C. Meaning making through experience
D. Preparing for examination

17. I.Q. of a talented child is
A. 130 B. 140
C. 125 D. 120

18. A student's development depends on
A. Heredity
B. Environment
C. Heredity and Environment
D. None of the above

19. A good teacher is one who
A. Causes desired behavioural change in the learner
B. Transmits knowledge verbally
C. Narrates information
D. Transmits curriculum

20. Instruction at the primary stage needs to be
A. Teacher centred
B. Textbook centred
C. Student centred
D. Teacher and Textbook centred

21. What is essential for learning?
A. Self experience B. Self thinking
C. Self activity D. All of the above

22. A child of 6 or 7 years old is not able to accept other's view point
A. because he is too young
B. because he is ego centric
C. because he is not intelligent
D. because he is imaginative

23. Children of 6-11 years age group need the following for learning
A. Availability of concrete activities or experiences
B. Transfer of knowledge by the teacher
C. Provision of opportunities for memorization
D. Motivation to attain high rank in the class

24. Which among the following plays the most important role for emotional development of a child in early childhood?
A. Teachers B. Peer-groups
C. Neighbours D. Parents

25. Education psychology is
A. pure science B. an applied science
C. a normative science D. None of the above

26. Ink blot test of personality is
A. a subjective test
B. an objective test
C. a projective test
D. None of the above

27. For the 6-11 years age group learning is
A. an active process of knowledge construction
B. a process of passive memorization
C. a process of hearing attentively in the classroom
D. a process of studying a textbook

28. Learning in children occurs through
A. Memorizing the knowledge
B. Reading the textbook
C. Transmission of knowledge by the teacher
D. Doing activity

29. Learning takes place effectively, if a child
A. is made ready to learn
B. repeats what he learns
C. feels satisfied
D. does all the above

30. What is ***not*** true about growth?
A. Growth is physical
B. Growth is quantitative
C. Growth is measurable
D. Growth is a life long process

PART- II

Mathematics

31. Simplify
$8.5-\left(4.07-\overline{1.2-0.9}\right)$ of 1.6
A. 2.468 B. 24.68
C. 68.24 D. 6.824

32. Find the median of the following data :
24, 36, 46, 17, 18, 25, 35
A. 36 B. 18
C. 25 D. 35

33. Find the value :

$$\frac{1-\tan^2 45}{1+\tan^2 45}$$

A. ∞ B. 1
C. –1 D. 0

34. HCF of 315, 441, 357 is
A. 17 B. 19
C. 21 D. 16

35. Find the value of $\angle x$ in the given triangle.

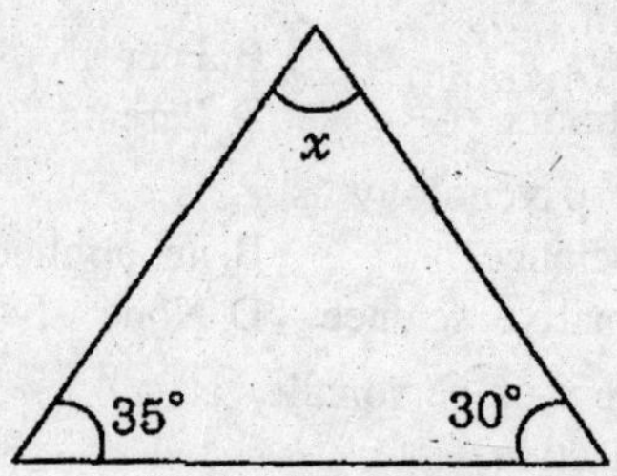

A. 65° B. 60°
C. 115° D. 145°

36. A train is moving at a uniform speed of 75 km/hour. How far will it travel in 20 minutes?
A. 25 km B. 20 km
C. 15 km D. 7.5 km

37. The place value of '0' in 273045 is
A. 1000 B. 0
C. 100 D. 10

38. Find the sum of the AP : –37, –33, –29, ... of first 12 terms.
A. –180 B. 180
C. 810 D. –108

39. Simplify : $\frac{2\times3^4\times2^5}{9\times4}$
A. 108 B. 72
C. 18 D. 144

40. Find the smallest number by which the number 81 must be divided to obtain a perfect cube.
A. 27 B. 81
C. 9 D. 3

41. Hindu-Arabic numeral of LXXXVI is
A. 95 B. 56
C. 86 D. 126

42. If the simple interest for 5 years is ₹ 77.50, find the simple interest for 4 years for the same principal and rate.
A. ₹ 124 B. ₹ 15.5
C. ₹ 387.5 D. ₹ 62

43. Find the volume of the right circular cone with radius 3.5 cm & height 12 cm.
A. 308 cm^3 B. 154 cm^3
C. 77 cm^3 D. 231 cm^3

44. Write a Pythagorean triplet whose two members are 16 & 63.
A. 79 B. 32
C. 65 D. 126

45. Diameter of a circular garden is 9.8 m. Find its area.
A. 75.46 m^2 B. 80.46 m^2
C. 47.49 m^2 D. 75.86 m^2

46. Find the roots of the equation.
$2x^2 - 5x + 3 = 0$
A. $-1, \frac{3}{2}$ B. $1, \frac{3}{2}$
C. $1, -\frac{3}{2}$ D. –1, 1

47. The angle subtended by an arc at the centre is ....the angle subtended by it at any point on the remaining part of the circle.
A. double B. three times
C. same D. four times

48. Cube root of 4096 is
A. 24 B. 14
C. 16 D. 12

49. Simplify : 25 × 8358 × 4
A. 837900 B. 835100
C. 835800 D. None of these

50. Find the surface area of a sphere of diameter 21 cm.
A. 1386 cm^2 B. 693 cm^2
C. 66 cm^2 D. 462 cm^2

51. One card is drawn from a well shuffled deck of 52 cards. Find the probability of getting a king of red colour.
A. $\frac{3}{13}$ B. $\frac{1}{26}$
C. $\frac{3}{26}$ D. $\frac{2}{13}$

52. If $a = 2$, $b = 3$, $c = 4$, then find the value of $a^3 + b^3 + c^3 - 3abc$.
A. 64 B. 27
C. 99 D. 72

53. The population of a city decreased from 25000 to 24500. The percentage of decrease is

A. 5% B. 2%
C. 4% D. 3%

54. Milk was bought for ₹ 150. For what price should it be sold to gain 20% profit?

A. ₹ 170 B. ₹ 180
C. ₹ 130 D. ₹ 120

55. Divide the polynomial $3x^4 - 4x^3 - 3x - 1$ by $x - 1$ the remainder is

A. –5 B. 5
C. 2 D. –2

56. Solve : 501 × 502

A. 152502 B. 125502
C. 251502 D. 551202

57. What could be the possible one's digits of the square root of the number 9801?

A. 1, 9 B. 3, 9
C. 3, 3 D. 0, 1

58. Find the distance between the pairs of points : (–5, 7); (–1, 3).

A. $2\sqrt{2}$ B. $-2\sqrt{2}$
C. $4\sqrt{2}$ D. $-4\sqrt{2}$

59. Find the angle which is equal to its supplementary angle.

A. 45° B. 180°
C. 90° D. 360°

60. 1500 families with 2 children were selected randomly and following data were recorded :

Number of girls in a family	2	1	0
Number of families	475	814	211

Compute the probability of a family choosen at random having 1 girl

A. $\frac{407}{750}$ B. $\frac{207}{250}$
C. $\frac{40}{500}$ D. $\frac{307}{350}$

PART- III

Environmental Studies

61. The Palas, Pratiharas and Rashtrakutas fought for control of ....the symbol of power after Harsha's reign.

A. Punjab B. Kannauj
C. Ujjain D. Kanchi

62. An amalgam of metal has which other element

A. Carbon B. Sodium
C. Gold D. Mercury

63. If pH of any solution is 2, means it is

A. Weak acid B. Weak base
C. Strong acid D. Strong base

64. Which of the following is the oldest Vedas?

A. Rigveda B. Yajurveda
C. Samaveda D. Atharvaveda

65. Where in India horned Rhinoceros are found?

A. Gujarat B. Assam
C. Karnataka D. Kerala

66. A neutral body has

A. only positive charge, no negative charge
B. only negative charge, no positive charge
C. equal amount of both positive and negative charge
D. no charge at all

67. The western coastal strip, south of Goa is referred as

A. Malabar B. Konkan
C. Kannad D. Northern Circar

68. DDT is

A. An antibiotic
B. Non-degradable pollutant
C. Degradable fertilizer
D. Dichlorodifluro Titanium

69. Who founded the Lodhi Dynasty?

A. Bahlol Lodhi B. Ibrahim Lodhi
C. Sikander Lodhi D. None of the above

70. Which of the following bacteria is used as an indicator of water pollution?

A. Staphylococcus B. Streptococcus
C. Diplococcus D. Coliform

71. A student of class VIII performs an experiment to separate, constituents of a mixture, the chart of the process is shown here. What are A and B respectively?

Magnet Filter
Mixture → Water is added → Salt solution
↓ ↓
(A) (B)

A. Iron nail and sand
B. Iron nail and sugar
C. Wooden pieces and sand
D. Stainless steel and sugar

72. The birth place of Buddha is
A. Ayodhya
B. Sarnath
C. Lumbini
D. Bodh Gaya

73. Konark Temple is located in
A. Rajasthan
B. Madhya Pradesh
C. Orissa
D. Tamil Nadu

74. In the balanced equation $\underline{a}\ Al + \underline{b}\ NaOH + \underline{c}\ H_2O \rightarrow \underline{d}\ NaAlO_2 + 3\ H_2(g) \uparrow$ the value of $\underline{a}\ \underline{b}\ \underline{c}\ d$ are respectively
A. 3, 2, 1, 3
B. 2, 2, 2, 2
C. 3, 3, 3, 3
D. 2, 3, 2, 2

75. Which of the following is **not** an instance of an exercise of a fundamental right?
A. Seeking employment of Bihari labourers in Punjab
B. Establishing mission school by Christian missionaries
C. Getting the same salary by men and women working on same position
D. Inheriting parental property by the children

76. Which of the following statement is correct for chemical reaction?
A. Chemical reactions are reversible
B. Energy is absorbed during all chemical reactions
C. Chemical reaction involves breaking and making of chemical bonds
D. All of the above

77. In reflex action, reflex arch is formed by
A. Brain → Muscle → Spinal cord
B. Receptor → Spinal cord → Muscle
C. Muscle → Brain → Spinal cord
D. Muscle → Receptor → Spinal cord

78. Who is considered the Mastermind behind German unification?
A. Frederic William B. Garibaldi
C. Bismark D. Hitler

79. According to 2011 census, the density of population in India is
A. 382 B. 324
C. 421 D. 518

80. If a bar magnet cut lengthwise into four parts, the total number of poles will be
A. Two B. Four
C. Eight D. Six

81. In Human Development Report, 2010 India's position is
A. 116 B. 119
C. 123 D. 132

82. 'Dantewada' which recently came into news for Maoist attack, is located in
A. Assam B. Chhattisgarh
C. West Bengal D. Andhra Pradesh

83. Population becomes human capital when there is investment made in the form of
A. Education
B. Training
C. Medical care
D. All of the above

84. Sometimes during cooking the bottom of vessel, becomes black from out side. This means that
A. Food is over cooked
B. Vessel is made up of steel
C. Fuel is not burning completely
D. The used fuel is non-conventional

85. Pancreas has
A. only endocrine cells
B. only exocrine cells
C. two types of cells exocrine and endocrine
D. only one type of cell function both in endocrine as well as exocrine manner

86. Chief Election Commissioner of India is
A. S.Y. Quraishi
B. N. Gopalaswami
C. Navin Chawla
D. None of the above

87. A fresh egg sinks in pure water whereas it floats in saturated salty water, this is due to
A. the fluid matter inside the egg shell
B. higher density of the pure water
C. higher density of the salty water
D. egg shell is made up of calcium which is lighter than pure water

88. Which of the following method is used to produce Oxygen gas in laboratory ?
A. Heating of $KClO_3$ with MnO_2
B. Electrolysis of H_2O
C. Photosynthesis
D. Both (A) and (C)

89. Who amongest following was the Member of Constituent Assembly?
A. Pt. Neki Ram Sharma
B. Sir Chhotu Ram
C. Shri Ranbir Singh Hooda
D. Shri Sher Singh

90. A ball is thrown up with a certain velocity, it attains 50 m and come back to the thrower, then the
A. Total distance covered by it is 50 m
B. Total displacement covered by it is 100 m
C. Total displacement is zero
D. Total distance covered by it is 120 m

PART- IV

Language-I : English

91. Choose the correct **preposition** for the blank:
John, do you remember Mary ? She is an old friend .... school times.
A. from B. to
C. of D. in

92. Choose the right answer:
'I visited the parliament' means
A. I always live there
B. I came there for a short time
C. I was born there
D. None of these

93. Complete the sentence by choosing the correct option:
Potato chips are ....
A. crispy B. crunchy
C. salty D. All of the above

94. Choose one word for the following group of words:
'a sweet dish served after the main meal'
A. Desert B. Dessert
C. Deseert D. Deserte

95. Choose the correct form of **verb** given in bracket for the blank:
They .... in the river yesterday (swim).
A. swimming B. swam
C. swum D. swims

96. Choose the correct meaning of the phrase *'idled away'*:
A. wasted
B. admired
C. rested
D. None of the above

97. Choose the correct **pronoun** for the blank:
She has an apple in .... hand.
A. his B. hers
C. her D. him

98. Choose correct article for the blank:
This wine is ...... expensive.
A. an B. the
C. a D. Zero article

99. Choose the correct word for the blank:
My Mother is at home. Where is ....?
A. yours
B. yours'
C. your
D. None of the above

100. Choose the correct word for the blank:
There is hardly .... time left for the train to depart.
A. much B. more
C. any D. most

Directions : Read the passage given below and answer the questions that follow ***(Q. No. 101 to 110)*** *by selecting the* **most appropriate** *option:*

The Ghost in the Forest

Many people who live near the Theme Park are afraid to go into the forest area. There is a legend, that a woman who once lived in the forest as an outlaw hundreds & hundreds of years ago, still walks there as a ghost at night.

The legend says, she was a great warrior from a rich family, but the wicked king, who ruled the country, killed her family and burned her castle, that is quite close to the Theme Park.

Her name was Maureen. Maureen escaped being killed, by running into the forest. Because of this, the king made an announcement to reward the person who reported anything about Maureen by giving a handsome amount of 500 gold coins.

Many of the poor people, who knew Maureen liked her very much and they told her what the king was going to do. Maureen decided to fight the king. She did this by helping the poor, robbing the rich and giving their money to the poor. Every time someone rich come through the forest, she would rob him. Maureen was a heroine for the poor, but in the end, one of the poor betrayed her.

She was caught by the king's soldiers and hung in the forest by the king from one of the old oak trees.

The legend says, that her ghost still walks there by night. So Beware!!!

101. 'One of the poor <u>betrayed</u> Maureen.'
The underlined word means
A. Be supportive to
B. Be disloyal to
C. Be or give sign of
D. None of the above

102. What reward would the king give for anyone who found Maureen?
A. He would give 500 silver coins
B. He would give 50 gold coins
C. He would give 500 gold coins
D. He would give 50 silver coins

103. Who betrayed Maureen?
A. One of the rich betrayed Maureen
B. One of the poor betrayed Maureen
C. One of the king's soldiers betrayed Maureen
D. One of her family members

104. Find the word from the passage which is the **antonym** of 'Punish'.
A. Price B. Reward
C. Penalty D. Blame

105. Who made an announcement to reward the person?
A. Ghost B. King
C. Queen D. Woman

106. What was the king like?
A. He was good B. He was nice
C. He was wicked D. He was generous

107. Who killed Maureen's family & burned her castle?
A. The king killed her family
B. The queen killed her family
C. The witch killed her family
D. No one

108. Why are some people afraid of the forest area in the Theme Park?
A. Because there is darkness
B. Because the ghost of a man lives there
C. Because the ghost of a woman walks at night
D. Because there is a lion

109. Where did Maureen go after her family was killed and her castle was burnt?
She went ....
A. to the Theme Park for the day
B. to the forest
C. to the poor people
D. None of the above

110. How did Maureen help the poor?
A. By fighting the king
B. By robbing the king
C. By robbing the rich who came into the forest
D. By killing the rich

111. Choose the correct meaning of 'Look before you leap'.
A. Think carefully before taking an action
B. See before you jump
C. See carefully and then jump
D. Act carefully

112. Choose the correct **opposite** word for the underlined word :
Tho teacher isn't <u>kind.</u> He's ....
A. nice B. ugly
C. funny D. harsh

113. Which is the correct order of the words?
art / study / do / ? / you
A. You study art do?
B. You do art study?
C. Do you study art?
D. None of the above

114. Choose the **plural form** of the words given in the brackets :
.... (ox) and .... (goose) are animals.
A. Oxess, geese B. Oxen, geese
C. Oxen, goose D. Oxes, goose

115. Which words can fill the blanks correctly?
He .... already .... when you arrived.
A. has, start B. had, started
C. had, starts D. None

116. Choose the correct word for the blank:
In meetings, she often says what she thinks
She is quite ....
A. outgoing B. outspoken
C. shy D. decisive

117. Choose the **odd** one out:
A. Left B. Milkshake
C. Right D. Forward

118. Which sentence is correctly **punctuated?**
A. Ms. Jones went to dinner with mr and mrs brown.
B. Ms Jones went to dinner with Mr. and Mrs. Brown.
C. ms. jones went to dinner with Mr. and Mrs. brown.
D. Ms. Jones went to dinner with Mr. and Mrs. Brown.

119. Choose ***one word*** for the underlined words:
It was foggy and I watched my friend <u>move out of sight</u> into the distance as he walked away.
A. toss B. throw
C. pour D. disappear

120. Choose the most appropriate word for the blank:
She entered the room .... since the baby was sleeping.
A. quiet B. quitely
C. quite D. quietly

PART- V

भाषा-II : हिन्दी

121. पथ–पथ्य युग्म का अर्थ है
A. रास्ता–रोगी का भोजन B. रोगी का भोजन–रास्ता
C. मत–भोजन D. कोई नहीं

122. 'गायक' का संधि-विच्छेद है
A. गा + यक B. गाय + इक
C. गै + अक D. ग + आयक

123. प्रत्यय के योग से बना शब्द कौन-सा है?
A. सुगंध B. अपमान
C. मालिन D. अनुकूल

124. समुद्रगुप्त 'भारत का नेपोलियन' था। यहाँ 'नेपोलियन' किस प्रकार की संज्ञा का उदाहरण है?
A. व्यक्तिवाचक B. जातिवाचक

C. भाववाचक D. समूहवाचक

125. निम्नलिखित में से अशुद्ध शब्द छाँटिए

A. क्षत्रिय B. धोखा

C. श्रेष्ठ D. अविष्कार

निर्देश : निम्नलिखित गद्यांश को पढ़कर दिये गये प्रश्नों (प्रश्न सं. 126-135) के उत्तर सबसे उचित विकल्प चुनकर दीजिए:

बुद्धिजीवी वह है, जो विचार के माध्यम से सत्य का अन्वेषण करता है। सत्य की अवधारणा सुन्दर है, किन्तु बहुत अमूर्त और द्वैधात्मक भी है....शायद समस्त सार्वभौमिक अवधारणाओं की तरह वह थोड़ा अस्पष्ट होती है। बुद्धिजीवी यदि अन्य दार्शनिकों और तत्त्ववेत्ताओं से थोड़ा अलग होता है, तो मेरे विचार में इसलिए कि वह सार्वभौमिक और विशिष्ट के बीच नाजुक और मूल्यवान सन्तुलन बनाने का प्रयास करता है....समाज की हर विशिष्ट समस्या पर विचार करते समय उसके सामने कुछ ऐसे 'मूल्य' होते हैं, जो 'परम और शाश्वत' होते हैं...जरूरी नहीं, वह उन्हें परिभाषित करे—किन्तु उनके आलोक में वह अच्छे और बुरे, नैतिक और अनैतिक, सही और गलत का विवेक अर्जित करता है। वह जो है, उसके यथार्थ का तटस्थ ढंग से यथावत विश्लेषण करता है....पूर्ण रूप से वस्तुपरक होना उसकी प्राथमिक शर्त है...किन्तु वह ही काफी नहीं है। वस्तुपरक तो वैज्ञानिक, समाजशास्त्री, गणितज्ञ भी होते हैं....यदि बुद्धिजीवी उनसे अलग हैं, तो इसलिए कि वह जो है, उसका अवलोकन करते समय, जो 'होना चाहिए' उसके बारे में विचार करता है...और इस तरह एक नैतिक आयाम स्वतः ही उसके बौद्धिक कार्य-कलाप के साथ जुड़ जाता है। बुद्धि के माध्यम से वह आलोचनात्मक चेतना, का संवाहक बन जाता है।

चेतना का यह तत्व ही है, जो भारतीय परम्परा में बुद्धिजीवी को एक मनीषी का गौरव प्रदान करता है। एक ऐसा व्यक्ति ही मनीषी की मर्यादा को प्राप्त करता है—जिसका विचार तन्त्र मनुष्य का समूचा अस्तित्व हो...और यह तभी सम्भव हो सकता है, जब वह अपनी बुद्धि को प्रज्ञा में परिलक्षित कर सकने के योग्य हो—प्रज्ञा वह समझदारी है, जहाँ मनुष्य अपने आत्म में रहकर भी समूची सृष्टि से...जिसमें चराचर सब शामिल है, एकात्म स्थापित कर लेता है।

126. सत्य की अवधारणा होती है

A. सार्वभौमिक और स्पष्ट

B. मूर्त और अस्पष्ट

C. सार्वभौमिक, अमूर्त और द्वैधात्मक

D. उपर्युक्त सभी

127. बुद्धिजीवी के कार्य-कलापों में नैतिक आयाम कब जुड़ता है?

A. आलोचनात्मक चेतना आ जाने से

B. जब वह 'क्या होना चाहिए' इसकी परिकल्पना करता है

C. जब वह तटस्थ हो जाता है

D. जब वह वस्तुपरक हो जाता है

128. वस्तुपरक ज्ञान होता है

A. कल्पना पर आधारित ज्ञान

B. वस्तु पर आधारित ज्ञान

C. वस्तु को परखने वाला ज्ञान

D. वास्तविक तथ्यों पर आधारित ज्ञान

129. भारतीय परंपरा में 'मनीषी' कहलाता है ....

A. ज्ञानवान व्यक्ति

B. प्रज्ञावान व्यक्ति

C. तीक्ष्ण बुद्धि वाला व्यक्ति

D. सचेतन व्यक्ति

130. 'शाश्वत' का विलोम है

A. नश्वर B. मर्त्य

C. अमर D. अक्षर

131. बुद्धिजीवी अन्य तत्ववेत्ताओं से किस प्रकार अलग है?

A. वह वस्तुपरकता पर जोर देता है

B. वह तटस्थता पर जोर देता है

C. वह शाश्वत मूल्यों पर जोर देता है

D. वह बौद्धिक होता है

132. बुद्धि 'प्रज्ञा' में कब रूपान्तरित होती है?

A. जब आलोचनात्मक चेतना का आविर्भाव होता है

B. जब ज्ञान का आलोक प्राप्त होता है

C. जब मनुष्य का चिन्तन व्यापक होता है और समस्त चराचर जगत उसकी दृष्टि बिन्दु में सम्मिलित हो जाता हो

D. उपर्युक्त में से कोई नहीं

133. 'संवाहक' शब्द का अर्थ है

A. लाने वाला B. ले जाने वाला

C. बहने वाला D. उपर्युक्त में से कोई नहीं

134. 'चराचर' का आशय है

A. चरने वाला और नहीं चरने वाला

B. चलने वाला और नहीं चलने वाला

C. सजीव और निर्जीव

D. उपर्युक्त सभी

135. अवतरण के आधार पर 'प्रज्ञा' का पर्याय चुनिए

A. बुद्धि B. ज्ञान

C. सत्य D. समझदारी

136. 'वनवासी' शब्द में समास है

A. द्विगु B. द्वन्द्व

C. तत्पुरुष D. कर्मधारय

137. निम्न में से दंतव्य वर्ण है

A. ट् B. च्

C. त् D. उ

138. शब्दकोश में पहले आने वाला शब्द है

A. वक्त B. वरक

C. वक्र D. वर्ग

139. निम्नलिखित में से तत्सम शब्द है

A. कोयल B. कपाट

C. ऊँट D. काठ

140. 'अकिंचन' का अर्थ है
A. जिसके पास कुछ न हो
B. जो निर्धन हो
C. जो कुछ न करता हो
D. उपर्युक्त सभी

141. 'निजत्व' संज्ञा शब्द है
A. व्यक्तिवाचक B. भाववाचक
C. द्रव्यवाचक D. जातिवाचक

142. संयुक्त व्यंजन 'क्ष' की ध्वनियाँ हैं
A. क् + अ + ष B. क् + अ + श
C. क् + अ + छ् D. क् + अ + स्

143. 'निर्भय' का संधि-विच्छेद है
A. नि + भय B. नि + रभय
C. निः + भय D. नृ + भय

144. निम्नलिखित में से शुद्ध शब्द छाँटिए
A. अगामी B. केन्द्रिय
C. अधीन D. दिक्षा

145. 'केर-बेर का संग होना' का अर्थ है
A. दोनों अलग-अलग
B. विपरीत स्वभाव वालों का साथ-साथ रहना
C. भाग्य की बात
D. दयावान व निष्ठुर का साथ

146. निम्न में कौन-सी सकर्मक क्रिया है?
A. आना B. जाना
C. लेना D. मरना

147. निम्न में से कौन-सा 'कामदेव' का पर्यायवाची शब्द **नहीं** है?
A. मन्मथ B. मनोज
C. अनंग D. मरीचि

148. निम्न में से भाववाचक संज्ञा है
A. पराया B. अपना
C. जागरण D. सभ्य

149. भाषा सम्बन्धी भूल को कहते हैं
A. पाप B. त्रुटि
C. अपराध D. द्रोह

150. निम्नलिखित में से तद्भव शब्द है
A. सायं B. गृह
C. चंचु D. सुर

Answers

1	2	3	4	5	6	7	8	9	10
D	D	A	B	D	C	B	A	B	C
11	**12**	**13**	**14**	**15**	**16**	**17**	**18**	**19**	**20**
D	C	D	D	A	C	C	C	A	C
21	**22**	**23**	**24**	**25**	**26**	**27**	**28**	**29**	**30**
D	B	A	D	B	C	A	D	D	D
31	**32**	**33**	**34**	**35**	**36**	**37**	**38**	**39**	**40**
A	C	D	C	C	A	B	A	D	D
41	**42**	**43**	**44**	**45**	**46**	**47**	**48**	**49**	**50**
C	D	B	C	A	B	A	C	C	A
51	**52**	**53**	**54**	**55**	**56**	**57**	**58**	**59**	**60**
B	B	B	B	A	C	A	C	C	A
61	**62**	**63**	**64**	**65**	**66**	**67**	**68**	**69**	**70**
B	D	C	A	B	C	A	B	A	D
71	**72**	**73**	**74**	**75**	**76**	**77**	**78**	**79**	**80**
A	C	C	B	D	C	B	C	A	C
81	**82**	**83**	**84**	**85**	**86**	**87**	**88**	**89**	**90**
B	B	D	C	C	A	C	A	C	C
91	**92**	**93**	**94**	**95**	**96**	**97**	**98**	**99**	**100**
C	B	D	B	B	A	C	D	A	C
101	**102**	**103**	**104**	**105**	**106**	**107**	**108**	**109**	**110**
B	C	B	B	B	C	A	C	B	C
111	**112**	**113**	**114**	**115**	**116**	**117**	**118**	**119**	**120**
A	D	C	B	B	B	B	D	D	D

121	122	123	124	125	126	127	128	129	130
A	C	C	C	D	C	B	D	B	A
131	**132**	**133**	**134**	**135**	**136**	**137**	**138**	**139**	**140**
C	C	B	C	D	C	C	A	B	A
141	**142**	**143**	**144**	**145**	**146**	**147**	**148**	**149**	**150**
B	A	C	C	B	C	D	C	B	D

Some Selected Explanatory Answers

31. Simplify :

$8.5-\left(4.07-\overline{1.2-0.9}\right)$ of 1.6

$= 8.5 - (4.07 - 0.3) \times 1.6$

$= 8.5 - (3.77) \times 1.6$

$= 8.5 - 6.032$

$= 2.468$

32. First write in increasing order

17, 18, 24, 25 , 35, 36, 46

Here, $n = 7$ which is odd number

$\therefore$ median $= \left(\dfrac{n+1}{2}\right)^{th}$ term $= \left(\dfrac{7+1}{2}\right)^{th}$ term

$= 4^{th}$ term $= 25$

33. $\dfrac{1-\tan^2 45°}{1+\tan^2 45°} = \dfrac{1-(1)^2}{1+(1)^2} = \dfrac{1-1}{1+1} = \dfrac{0}{2} = 0$

34. HCF of 315, 441, 357

```
357)441(1
    357
    ---
     84)357(4
        336
        ---
         21)84(4
            84
            --
            xx

21)315(15
   21
   ---
   105
   105
   ---
    x
```

$\therefore$ HCF of 315, 441 and 357 = 21

35.

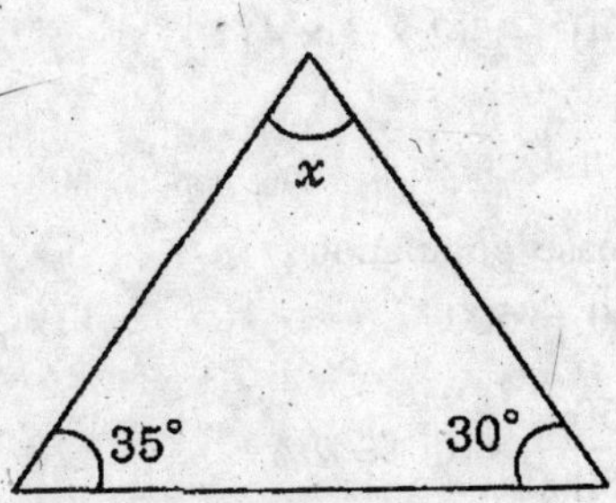

We have,

$x + 35 + 30 = 180°$

$\Rightarrow x + 65 = 180°$

$\Rightarrow x = 180 - 65$

$\therefore x = 115°.$

36. In 60 minutes, the train travelled 75 km.

In 20 minutes, the train travelled

$= \dfrac{75}{60} \times 20 = 25$ km

37. The place value of 0 in 273045 is 0.

38. $a = -37$, $d = 4$, $n = 12$

$$S_{12} = \frac{n}{2}\{2a+(n-1)d\}$$

$$= \frac{12}{2}\{2\times(-)37+(12-1)4\}$$

$$= \frac{12}{2}\{-74+44\}$$

$$= 6(-30) = -180$$

39. $\dfrac{2\times 3^4\times 2^5}{9\times 4} = \dfrac{2\times 3^4\times 2^5}{3^2\times 2^2} = \dfrac{2^6\times 3^4}{3^2\times 2^2}$

$= 2^{6-2} \times 3^{4-2}$

$= 2^4 \times 3^2$

$= 16 \times 9 = 144$

40.

3	81
3	27
3	9
3	3
	1

if $81 = 3 \times 3 \times 3 \times 3$

if 81 is divided by 3,

it becomes a perfect cube.

41. LXXXVI = L + XXX + VI = 50 + 30 + 6 = 86

42. S.I. of 5 years = ₹ 77.50

S.I. of 4 years = $\frac{77.50}{5} \times 4$

= ₹ 15.50 × 4 = ₹ 62

43. Volume of cone = $\frac{1}{3}\pi r^2 h$

$= \frac{1}{3} \times \frac{22}{7} \times \frac{7}{2} \times \frac{7}{2} \times 12$

= 154 cm^3

44. Two members are 16 and 63

$2m = 16$

$m = 8$

$m^2 - 1 = 64 - 1 = 63$

$m^2 + 1 = 64 + 1 = 65$

∴ third side = 65

$(65)^2 = (63)^2 + (16)^2$

$4225 = 3969 + 256$

$= 4225.$

45. Diameter of circle = 9.8 m

∴ radius of circle = 4.9 m

Area of circle = πr^2

$= \frac{22}{7} \times 4.9 \times 4.9$

= 22 × .7 × 4.9

= 75.46 m^2

46. $2x^2 - 5x + 3 = 0$

$a = 2, b = -5, c = 3$

∴ $D = b^2 - 4ac$

$= (-5)^2 - 4(2)(3)$

$= 25 - 24 = 1$

$x = \frac{-b \pm \sqrt{D}}{2a}$

$= \frac{5 \pm 1}{2(2)} = \frac{5 \pm 1}{4}$

$\alpha = \frac{5 \pm 1}{4} = \frac{6}{4} = \frac{3}{2}$

$\beta = \frac{5-1}{4} = \frac{4}{4} = 1$

∴ Roots are 1, $\frac{3}{2}$.

47. Angle of the centre is double the angle of circumstances.

Because ∠AOB = 2∠ACB.

48.

2	4096
2	2048
2	1024
2	512
2	256
2	128
2	64
2	32
2	16
2	8
2	4
2	2
	1

∴ $\sqrt[3]{4096}$

= 2 × 2 × 2 × 2 = 16

Hence, cube root of 4096 = 16.

49. 25 × 8358 × 4

= 100 × 8358 = 835800.

50. Diameter of sphere = 21 cm

∴ radius of sphere = $\frac{21}{2}$ cm

Surface area of sphere = $4\pi r^2$

$= 4 \times \frac{22}{7} \times \frac{21}{2} \times \frac{21}{2}$

= 63 × 22

= 1386 cm^2.

51. Required probability = $\frac{2}{52} = \frac{1}{26}$.

52. $a = 2, b = 3, c = 4$

∴ $a^3 + b^3 + c^3 - 3abc$

$= (2)^3 + (3)^3 + (4)^3 - 3(2 \times 3 \times 4)$

= 8 + 27 + 64 – 72

= 99 – 72 = 27.

53. Number of decrease population

= 25000 – 24500 = 500

% decrease = $\frac{500}{25000} \times 100 = 2\%$.

54. $100 + 20 = 120$

when CP ₹ 100 then SP = ₹ 120

when CP ₹ 150, then SP = ₹ $\frac{120}{100} \times 150$

$\therefore$ SP = ₹ 180

55. $3x^4 - 4x^3 - 3x - 1$ is divided by $x - 1$

$\therefore x - 1 = 0 \Rightarrow x = 1$

$= 3(1)^4 - 4(1)^3 - 3(1) - 1$

$= 3 - 4 - 3 - 1$

$= -5$

$\therefore$ remainder = -5

56. 501×502

$(500 + 1) \times (500 + 2)$

$= (500)^2 + (1 + 2)500 + (1 \times 2)$

$= 250000 + 1500 + 2 = 2{,}51{,}502.$

57. Possible one's digit of $\sqrt{9801}$ is 1, 9

because square of 1 = 1

square of 9 = 81

58. (–5, 7) A ———— B (–1, 3)

$AB = \sqrt{(-1+5)^2 + (3-7)^2}$

$= \sqrt{16+16} = \sqrt{32}$

$= 4\sqrt{2}$

59. Supplement of 90 is 90°
because (180° – 90°) = 90°

60. Required probability $= \frac{814}{1500}$

$= \frac{407}{750}$.

YOUR SPACE